THE OXFORD HANDBOOK OF

FEMINIST THEORY

THE OXFORD HANDBOOK OF

FEMINIST THEORY

LISA DISCH
and
MARY HAWKESWORTH

Oxford University Press is a department of the University of Oxford. It furthers the University's objective of excellence in research, scholarship, and education by publishing worldwide. Oxford is a registered trademark of Oxford University Press in the UK and certain other countries.

Published in the United States of America by Oxford University Press
198 Madison Avenue, New York, NY 10016, United States of America

© Oxford University Press 2016

First issued as an Oxford University Press paperback, 2018

All rights reserved. No part of this publication may be reproduced, stored in a retrieval system, or transmitted, in any form or by any means, without the prior permission in writing of Oxford University Press, or as expressly permitted by law, by license, or under terms agreed with the appropriate reproduction rights organization. Inquiries concerning reproduction outside the scope of the above should be sent to the Rights Department, Oxford University Press, at the address above.

You must not circulate this work in any other form
and you must impose this same condition on any acquirer.

Library of Congress Cataloging-in-Publication Data
The Oxford handbook of feminist theory / Lisa Disch and Mary Hawkesworth.
pages cm. — (Oxford books)
Includes index.
ISBN 978–0–19–932858–1 (hardcover : alk. paper) 978–0–19–087282–3 (paperback : alk. paper)
1. Feminist theory.   I. Disch, Lisa Jane, editor.   II. Hawkesworth, M. E., 1952– editor.
HQ1190.O975 2016
305.4201—dc23
2015025262

Contents

List of Contributors ... ix

Introduction. Feminist Theory: Transforming the Known World ... 1
MARY HAWKESWORTH AND LISA DISCH

1. Affect ... 16
MARIANNE LILJESTRÖM

2. Agency ... 39
LOIS MCNAY

3. Biopolitics ... 61
RUTH A. MILLER

4. Civilization ... 79
ANN TOWNS

5. Coloniality of Gender and Power: From Postcoloniality to Decoloniality ... 100
BRENY MENDOZA

6. Cyborgs and Virtual Bodies ... 122
KRISTA GENEVIÈVE LYNES AND KATERINA SYMES

7. Development ... 143
ELORA HALIM CHOWDHURY

8. Diaspora ... 164
ANITA MANNUR AND JANA EVANS BRAZIEL

9. Formal, Informal, and Care Economies ... 179
SUZANNE BERGERON

10. Embodiment ... 207
SHATEMA THREADCRAFT

11. Experience — 227
    JUDITH GRANT

12. Feminist Jurisprudence — 247
    JULIET A. WILLIAMS

13. Feminist Standpoint — 261
    KRISTEN INTEMANN

14. Gendered Divisions of Labor — 283
    MARY BETH MILLS

15. Governance — 304
    KI-YOUNG SHIN

16. Health — 326
    AMANDA J. GRIGG AND ANNA KIRKLAND

17. Identities — 346
    NADINE EHLERS

18. Institutions — 367
    CELESTE MONTOYA

19. Intersectionality — 385
    BRITTNEY COOPER

20. Intersexuality, Transgender, and Transsexuality — 407
    TALIA MAE BETTCHER

21. Markets/Marketization — 428
    MARIANNE H. MARCHAND AND ROCÍO DEL CARMEN OSORNO VELÁZQUEZ

22. Materialisms — 454
    ELIZABETH WINGROVE

23. Microphysics of Power — 472
    JOHANNA OKSALA

24. Migration — 490
    RHACEL SALAZAR PARREÑAS AND CAROLYN CHOI

25. Militarization and War — 508
    Kathy E. Ferguson and Sharain Sasheir Naylor

26. Nature — 530
    Stacy Alaimo

27. Norms and Normalization — 551
    Dean Spade and Craig Willse

28. Performativity and Performance — 572
    Moya Lloyd

29. The Personal is Political — 593
    Renee Heberle

30. Policy — 610
    Emanuela Lombardo and Petra Meier

31. Politics — 632
    Linda M. G. Zerilli

32. Pop Culture/Visual Culture — 651
    Rebecca Wanzo

33. Posthuman Feminist Theory — 673
    Rosi Braidotti

34. Pregnancy, Personhood, and the Making of the Fetus — 699
    Silja Samerski

35. Prison — 721
    Sarah X Pemberton

36. Race and Racialization — 741
    Zenzele Isoke

37. Religion — 761
    Lisbeth Mikaelsson

38. Representation — 781
    Lisa Disch

39. Reproduction: From Rights to Justice? — 803
CAROLE H. BROWNER

40. Science Studies — 832
DEBOLEENA ROY

41. Sex/Gender — 852
MARA VIVEROS VIGOYA

42. Sexual Difference — 874
ALISON STONE

43. Sexualities — 894
LEILA J. RUPP AND CARLY THOMSEN

44. State/Nation — 915
JOHANNA KANTOLA

45. Storytelling/Narrative — 934
SHARI STONE-MEDIATORE

46. Subjectivity and Subjectivation — 955
ANNA MARIE SMITH

47. Temporality — 973
BONNIE G. SMITH

48. Transnational — 991
LAURA BRIGGS

49. Violence — 1010
JINEE LOKANEETA

Index — 1031

List of Contributors

Stacy Alaimo is Professor and Distinguished Teaching Professor in the Department of English at the University of Texas, Arlington.

Suzanne Bergeron is Professor and Director of Women's and Gender Studies at the University of Michigan, Dearborn.

Talia Mae Bettcher is Professor and Chair of Philosophy at California State University, Los Angeles.

Rosi Braidotti is Distinguished University Professor and Founding Director of the Centre for the Humanities at Utrecht University.

Jana Evans Braziel is Professor and Chair of Global & Intercultural Studies at Miami University.

Laura Briggs is Professor and Chair of Women, Gender, Sexuality Studies at the University of Massachusetts, Amherst.

Carole H. Browner is Professor in the Department of Anthropology, the Department of Women's Studies, and in the Center for Culture and Health at the University of California, Los Angeles.

Carolyn Choi is a PhD candidate in the Department of Sociology at the University of Southern California.

Elora Halim Chowdhury is Associate Professor and Chair of Women's and Gender Studies at the University of Massachusetts, Boston.

Brittney Cooper is Assistant Professor of Women's and Gender Studies and Africana Studies at Rutgers University.

Lisa Disch is Professor of Political Science and Women's Studies at the University of Michigan, Ann Arbor.

Nadine Ehlers is Senior Lecturer in Cultural Studies at the University of Wollongong.

Kathy E. Ferguson is Professor of Political Science and Women's Studies at the University of Hawai'i at Mānoa.

Judith Grant is Professor and Chair of Political Science at Ohio University.

Amanda J. Grigg is a PhD candidate in the Department of Political Science at the University of North Carolina.

Mary Hawkesworth is Distinguished Professor of Political Science and Women's and Gender Studies at Rutgers University.

Renee Heberle is Professor of Political Science, Co-Director of the Program in Law and Social Thought, and Interim Director of the School for Interdisciplinary Studies at the University of Toledo.

Kristen Intemann is Associate Professor of Philosophy at Montana State University.

Zenzele Isoke is Associate Professor of Gender, Women, and Sexuality Studies at the University of Minnesota.

Johanna Kantola is Academy Research Fellow in the Department of Philosophy, History, Culture, and Art Studies at the University of Helsinki.

Anna Kirkland is Associate Professor of Women's Studies at the University of Michigan, Ann Arbor.

Marianne Liljeström is Professor of Gender Studies at the University of Turku.

Moya Lloyd is Professor of Political Theory at Loughborough University.

Jinee Lokaneeta is Associate Professor of Political Science at Drew University.

Emanuela Lombardo is Lecturer in Political Science in the Department of Political Science and Administration at the Universidad Complutense de Madrid.

Krista Geneviève Lynes is Associate Professor of Communication Studies at Concordia University and Canada Research Chair in Feminist Media Studies.

Anita Mannur is Associate Professor of English and Global and Intercultural Studies Studies and Director of Women's, Gender and Sexuality Studies at Miami University.

Marianne H. Marchand is Professor of International Relations and Political Science at Universidad de las Américas, Puebla.

Lois McNay is Fellow and Professor of the Theory of Politics at Somerville College, University of Oxford.

Petra Meier is Professor of Political Science at the University of Antwerp.

Breny Mendoza is Professor of Gender and Women's Studies at California State University, Northridge.

Lisbeth Mikaelsson is Professor of the Study of Religion at the University of Bergen.

Ruth A. Miller is Professor of History at the University of Massachusetts, Boston.

Mary Beth Mills is Professor of Anthropology at Colby College.

Celeste Montoya is Associate Professor of Women and Gender Studies at the University of Colorado, Boulder.

Sharain Sasheir Naylor is a PhD candidate in the Department of Political Science at the University of Hawai'i at Mānoa.

Johanna Oksala is Academy of Finland Research Professor in the Department of Philosophy, History, Culture, and Art Studies at the University of Helsinki, and a Visiting Professor in the Department of Philosophy at the New School for Social Research.

Rhacel Salazar Parreñas is Professor of Sociology and Gender Studies at the University of Southern California.

Sarah X Pemberton is Assistant Professor of Political Theory at the University of South Florida.

Deboleena Roy is Associate Professor of Women's, Gender, and Sexuality Studies and Neuroscience and Behavioral Biology at Emory University.

Leila J. Rupp is Professor of Feminist Studies at the University of California, Santa Barbara.

Silja Samerski is a Postdoctoral Fellow at the Carl von Ossietzky University of Oldenburg.

Ki-young Shin is Associate Professor in the School of Interdisciplinary Gender Studies at Ochanomizu University.

Anna Marie Smith is Professor of Government at Cornell University.

Bonnie G. Smith is Distinguished Professor of History at Rutgers University.

Dean Spade is Associate Professor of Law at the Seattle University School of Law.

Alison Stone is Professor in the Department of Politics, Philosophy, and Religion at Lancaster University.

Shari Stone-Mediatore is Trumbull G. Duvall Professor of Philosophy at Ohio Wesleyan University.

Katerina Symes is PhD candidate in the Communication program at Concordia University.

Carly Thomsen is a Postdoctoral Fellow at the Center for the Study of Women, Gender, and Sexuality at Rice University.

Shatema Threadcraft is Assistant Professor of Political Science at Rutgers University.

Ann Towns is Associate Professor of Political Science at the University of Gothenburg.

Rocío del Carmen Osorno Velázquez is an independent researcher and has worked as an adviser and consultant at Fundación Universidad de las Américas, Puebla;

Universidad Iberoamericana, Puebla; and Benemérita Universidad Autónoma de Puebla.

Mara Viveros Vigoya is Associate Professor in the School of Gender Studies and the Department of Anthropology at Universidad Nacional de Colombia.

Rebecca Wanzo is Associate Professor of Women, Gender, and Sexuality Studies, and Associate Director of the Center for Humanities at Washington University, St. Louis.

Juliet A. Williams is Professor of Gender Studies and Associate Dean of Social Sciences at University of California, Los Angeles.

Craig Willse is Assistant Professor in the Cultural Studies program at George Mason University.

Elizabeth Wingrove is Professor of Political Science and Women's Studies at the University of Michigan, Ann Arbor.

Linda M. G. Zerilli is the Charles E. Merriam Distinguished Service Professor of Political Science and Director of the Center for the Study of Gender and Sexuality at the University of Chicago.

THE OXFORD HANDBOOK OF

FEMINIST THEORY

INTRODUCTION

FEMINIST THEORY
Transforming the Known World

MARY HAWKESWORTH AND LISA DISCH

Introduction

FEMINIST theory is a vibrant intellectual practice that raises new questions, brings new evidence, and poses significant challenges to academic disciplines spanning the humanities, social sciences, and natural sciences. Some feminist scholars trace the earliest manifestations of feminist argument to the ancient world, recovering the works of women philosophers such as Pythagorean Aesara of Lucania, who included dimensions of women's experiences in her analysis of human existence (Waithe 1987; Lopez McAlister 1996), and Su Ruolan, a female prodigy of China's Former Qin period (AD 350–394), whose masterpiece *Armillary Sphere (Xuanji) Diagram* defies Chinese logocentrism (Da 2015).[1] Others locate the origin of feminist theory in the democratic revolutions of the eighteenth century—in the demand that the natural rights of "Man" ought to liberate women and men alike from traditional naturalized forms of domination and the relations of servitude and deference that they authorized (Offen 2000). Within this frame, Olympe de Gouges ([1791] 1989) and Mary Wollstonecraft ([1792] 1975) are celebrated as the first feminist theorists, as they were the first to systematically elaborate this demand for equal rights as a theoretical argument. Yet, as Kumari Jayawardena (1986) has pointed out, debates on women's rights and education also surfaced in China in the eighteenth century, and there were movements for women's social emancipation in India in the early nineteenth century. The reasoning central to these diverse mobilizations, traces of which persist in feminist projects today, was that sexual difference is no more a legitimate ground for political exclusion than are ancestry and wealth.

The architectural principle of this volume is that feminist theory is more fruitfully conceived as a multifaceted, multisited project than as a bounded field (Ferguson 2015). Feminism would not exist as a theoretical endeavor without the political struggles for women's empowerment that have emerged in all regions of the world. Grounded in the investigation of women's and men's lives and convinced of the arbitrariness of exclusion based on sexual difference, feminist theory has flourished as a mode of critical theory that illuminates the limitations of popular assumptions about sex, race, sexuality, and gender and offers insights into the social production of complex hierarchies of difference.

Feminist theory began to be institutionalized academically in the early 1970s with the founding of the first women's studies programs in the United States and the establishment of the first scholarly journals to feature or focus on feminist theory: *Feminist Studies* (1972), *Signs* (1975), *Frontiers* (1975), *Camera Obscura* (1976), and *Feminist Review* (1979). Even within the academy, feminist theory resists conceptualization as a field because it is resolutely interdisciplinary. Growing exponentially over the past four decades and cutting across the divisions of knowledge that structure contemporary universities, feminist theory has been characterized as "oppositional research" because it challenges the right of the powerful across these diverse disciplines to define realities (Devault 1999, 1). Although feminist theory takes many forms, and lively methodological and substantive debates characterize the endeavor, feminist research shares several defining features, including the convictions that widely held presumptions about the naturalness of sexed embodiment, gender identity, and heterosexuality are mistaken, and that sex, gender, and normative sexuality are political constructs, rather than natural givens, and vary cross-culturally and from one historical era to another. In contrast to the consignment of sex, gender, and sexuality to the private sphere, feminist theorists concur that interlocking processes of racialization, gendering, and heterosexualization structure public institutions as well as manifold dimensions of social and political life.

Contesting "Feminist Theory"

Feminist theories arise in conjunction with feminist activism and academic practices, seeking to illuminate the barriers and constraints that circumscribe women's lives, explain their dynamics and persistence, and identify mechanisms for change. From the outset, feminist theories have been diverse and contentious, reflecting the specific conditions of their emergence. Early efforts by Western feminist theorists in the academy to analyze the proliferation of rich and diverse feminist theories gave rise to a classification system commonly referred to as the *hyphenation model*. Within this framework, approaches to feminist theorizing were analyzed in the context of the larger Western philosophical traditions to which they had affinities, such as liberal feminism, socialist/Marxist feminism, psychoanalytic feminism (Elshtain 1981; Jaggar 1983). Radical feminism alone emerged within this schema as a freestanding critique of the "mindcuffs of phallogocentrism," an attempt to achieve a thorough repudiation of "malestream thought," and to diagnose the "l'homm(o)sexualité" characteristic of Western philosophy (Daly 1973, 1978; O'Brien 1981; Ruth 1981; Irigaray 1985a, 1985b).

As a guide to feminist theories, the hyphenation model was useful in showing the continuities and shared assumptions underlying certain approaches to feminist theorizing and particular traditions in Western thought. At the same time, the hyphenation model tended to make feminist theory seem derivative of mainstream schools of thought, and its emphasis on divisions obscured what feminist theories had in common. According to Judith Grant's (1993) analysis, "second wave" feminist theories—liberal, socialist, radical, psychoanalytic, and postmodern—all shared certain fundamental (and problematic) core thematics, including the notion that women were/are oppressed as women, that experience is an appropriate analytical tool for understanding women's oppression, and that the personal is political; that is, the system of gender oppression, which is political, is manifested in interpersonal relations (on "the personal is political," see Heberle, chapter 30, this volume).[2]

Concerns over the subjectivism and empiricism of the appeal to "experience" and over the essentialism in the appeal to a universal "women's" oppression sparked vibrant debates and fueled an outpouring of feminist anthologies featuring feminist self-critique (e.g., Butler and Scott 1992; de Lauretis 1986; Eisenstein and Jardine 1980; Nicholson 1990; Schor and Weed 1994; Weed 1989). These debates, in turn, prompted new ways of conceptualizing and classifying feminist intellectual production. What became known in the United States as the "equality-difference" debate—the question of whether feminist arguments should claim women's rights in the abstract (perhaps at the risk of validating norms grounded exclusively in men's lives) or emphasize women's distinctive contributions to politics based on their purportedly unique capacities for caring, empathy, pacifism, and so on—was especially pivotal. In its aftermath, some feminist scholars distinguished approaches to feminist theory that (1) problematize women's exclusion from the major institutions of the public world (social, political, economic, religious, academic) from approaches that (2) focus on difference as a primary category of analysis (women's differences from men, as well as systemic differences among women based on race, class, nationality, sexuality, historicity), and approaches that (3) embrace the postmodern refusal of categorization. While some analysts treat the shift from "equality feminism" to "difference feminism" to "postmodern" or "poststructuralist feminism" as a chronological development from the 1970s to the 1990s (Zalewski 2000), other feminist scholars resist the teleological narrative and instead link these various approaches to feminist theorizing to particular geographic and institutional sites, organizing them spatially and with reference to intellectual traditions rather than temporally (Friedman 1998). Clare Hemmings (2005, 2011), however, has analyzed these Western feminist representations of Western feminist theory, interrogating the "political grammar" of the stories feminists tell about the trajectories of feminist theory—as trajectories of progress (from essentialism to multiplicity), of loss (unity to fragmentation), and of return (to politics via materiality).

Several feminist theorists have pointed out that a taxonomy of feminist theory that organizes the field in terms of equality feminism, difference feminism, and postmodern feminism, whether positing a chronology or acknowledging simultaneous coexistence, has an implicit ideological agenda, for it occludes the vibrant tradition of socialist/Marxist feminist theorizing (Ebert 1996; Hawkesworth 1988; Squires 1999). The point is not simply that the theoretical premises and transformative strategies of liberal feminism, difference feminism, and poststructuralist feminism are at odds with those of socialist feminism, although they are. Poststructuralism, for example, challenges the basic assumptions of Marxist thought, including its philosophical materialism, historical materialism, and referential theory of language as well as its faith in the power of rational analysis and collective action for achieving emancipatory ends. The larger issue is that a taxonomy that depicts feminist theory solely in terms of equality, difference, and postmodern approaches literally erases socialist/Marxist feminist theorizing, along with anarchist feminism, indigenous feminism, and ecological feminism, from the history and current practices of feminism. Such an erasure forecloses a range of transformative strategies of particular import in this period of globalization—strategies central to feminist theorizing in the global South. For this reason, some socialist feminist theorists have suggested that the "equality feminism, difference feminism, and postmodern feminism" typology should be understood in relation to the increasing neoliberal hegemony on the global scene and its project of depoliticization (Ebert 1996; Squires 1999).

We do not propose a new taxonomic scheme in this introduction. Any such effort is bound to be incomplete or worse—pernicious—in privileging some feminist approaches as more theoretically sophisticated, more radical, or more critical than others. Instead, we identify three common characteristics of feminist theory in the late twentieth and twenty-first centuries: (1) efforts to denaturalize that which passes for difference, (2) efforts to challenge the aspiration to produce universal and impartial knowledge, and (3) efforts to engage the complexity of power relations through intersectional analysis.

Denaturalizing Difference

Race and sex are typically construed as individual attributes or demographic characteristics. Both are understood as biological or physical traits. In contrast to this "primordial view," feminist theorists conceptualize race and sex as political constructs, the product of particular ways of thinking that privilege some while disadvantaging others. Building on insights from critical race theory and postcolonial theory, feminists conceptualize racialization and gendering as political processes that create and sustain divisions, stratifications, and modes of domination within and across intellectual and national borders. In contrast to the presumption that race and sex are part of the "given" aspects of human existence and, as such, apolitical and ahistorical, feminist scholarship (Jordanova 1989; Laqueur 1990; Poovey 1988) traces the mobilization of biology for markedly political purposes from the seventeenth century to the nineteenth century. Indeed, biology was used to create an allegedly empirical justification for racial and sexual hierarchies at the very moment when the language of political equality was deployed against the feudal order.

Thomas Laqueur (1990) has carefully documented how sexual dimorphism is intimately tied to the politics of modernity. As natural science displaced theology in Enlightenment metaphysics, the "one sex" model of embodiment that had dominated European political thought and practice for nearly two millennia gave way to a "two sex" model that posited men and women as incommensurate opposites, rather than as embodied "souls" ordered along a continuum based on proximity to the divine. Laqueur's work helps to explain how the purportedly universal rights of the Enlightenment could stop short at women. Although corporeal differences carried political and social consequence in earlier eras, in the eighteenth century the relevant markers of difference were newly lodged in the genitalia or reproductive organs. In the eighteenth century, proponents of "natural philosophy" proposed that human biology should be understood in terms of sexual dimorphism, "a fixed oppositeness, that was somehow foundational and beyond culture," providing a "natural foundation" for differentiated social roles and responsibilities and legal status, as well as divisions of power and opportunity (Laqueur 2012, 806).

In the midst of Enlightenment proclamations of universal rights derived from the "self-evident truth" that all men are created equal, political theorists and republican revolutionaries in both the United States and France extrapolated from the new biological dimorphism grounds for excluding women from membership in the political community. Asserting that reproductive physiology determines individual character and political capacity, political theorists and republican revolutionaries on both sides of the Atlantic adopted the notion that sexual difference dictates proper political status and behavior, insisting that any transgression of the gendered political order threatened the very basis of society and civilization. To shore up women's supposed biological incapacity for politics, theorists recommended and lawmakers passed legislation barring women from participation in political clubs, political organizations, and political parties and from political office (Landes 1988, 1998; Cody 2001, 2005). Over the course of the nineteenth century, women's exclusion became part of the colonial project. As Ann Towns (2009, 2010) has demonstrated, it was embraced in Europe as an indication of "more advanced civilization," and then imposed as a "civilizing" measure on colonies in Africa and Asia as European nations expanded their colonial empires. These colonial impositions displaced earlier indigenous forms of women's political authority (Okonjo 1994; Oyewumi 1997; Chatterjee 2013).

Feminist theorists took from the analysis of sex an important insight that they generalized to other social markers: the insistence that "difference" is not a fact of nature but a vector of power. To resist the replication of proliferating hierarchies of difference, feminist scholars have sought ways to analyze social phenomena through categories that do not posit inherent difference. For example, with respect to sex and sexualities, feminist theory focuses on pleasure and desire, identities, practices, and domination and subordination—all of which cut across man/woman, heterosexual/homosexual, and sex/gender binaries. Feminist science scholars have also challenged the biological ground of sexual dimorphism (Fausto-Sterling 1986, 1993). They have shown that there are more than two naturally occurring sexes. Whether defined in terms of chromosomes (XY/XX), hormones (androgens/estrogens), gonads (reproductive organs, such as testes and ovaries), internal morphology (seminal vesicles and a prostate gland as opposed to vagina, uterus, and fallopian tubes), external genitalia (penis and scrotum / clitoris and labia), or secondary sex characteristics (body hair, facial hair, breasts), none of the typical correlates of biological sex conform to the demands of dichotomous classification. Chromosomes, hormones, sperm production, and egg production all fail to differentiate all men from all women or to provide a common core within each sex. "No matter how detailed an investigation science has thus far made, it is still not possible to draw a clear dividing line even between male and female" (Devor 1989, 1). Rather than being given in nature, sexual dimorphism is imposed by human beings who are trying to make sense of the natural world. As Suzanne Kessler and Wendy McKenna noted, this imposition is as characteristic of scientific inquiry as it is of everyday observation:

> Scientists construct dimorphism where there is continuity. Hormones, behavior, physical characteristics, developmental processes, chromosomes, and psychological qualities have all been fitted into dichotomous categories. Scientific knowledge does not inform the answer to the question, "What makes a person a man or a woman?" Rather it justifies (and appears to give grounds for) the already existing conviction that a person is either a man or a woman and that there is no problem differentiating between the two. Biological, psychological, and social differences do not lead to our seeing two genders. Our seeing two genders leads to the "discovery" of biological, psychological, and social differences.
>
> (Kessler and McKenna 1978, 163)

By denaturalizing difference, feminist theorists open new research questions concerning the demarcation and regulation of bodies. They also contextualize "difference" within the dynamics of diaspora and decolonization; potent contradictions of globalization, war making, and militarization; and manifold resistances against oppressive forces structuring and constraining life prospects in very different regions of the world.

Situating Knowledge

Feminist theory has famously challenged the epistemic privilege of philosophy, science, literature, and other "authoritative" accounts of the world written exclusively from the perspective of socially privileged men. In the words of historian Susan Geiger (1990, 169), "What constitutes feminist work is a framework that challenges existing androcentric or partial constructions of women's lives." Dozens of feminist works have documented "noxious representations" of women in canonical texts, representations that "violate universal maxims about respect for persons" (O'Neil 1989, 70). Both ancient and modern philosophers have advanced universal claims about human nature and contradicted them by reifying gender difference in ways that suggest that women are not fully human (Hawkesworth 1990, 17–46). Many contemporary philosophers and political theorists have distanced themselves from the blatant sexism that riddles canonical texts, but they have not abandoned the conviction that sex is morally and epistemically irrelevant to theory. On the contrary, interlocking notions of universality and the fungibility of knowers exclude concerns about physical, temporal, and geopolitical specificity in ways that enable, rationalize, and sustain exclusions grounded in race and gender. For this reason, feminist theorists have attempted to specify when and under what conditions the "sex of the knower is epistemically significant" (Code 1981, 1991; Alcoff 2000).

Feminist scholarship offers a critique of dominant, disciplinary conceptions of objectivity that posit a "view from nowhere" (Nagel 1986), illuminating the role of social values in cognition, which has important implications beyond investigations in which women are the objects of inquiry. They have pointed out that the continuing invocation of conceptions of objectivity rooted in erroneous notions of value neutrality can have pernicious consequences (Longino 1990). Rather than capturing things as they are, appeals to objectivity "bolster the epistemic authority of the currently dominant groups, composed largely of white men, and discredit the observations and claims of the currently subordinate groups, including, of course, the observations and claims of many people of color and women" (Jaggar 1989, 158). On this view, dominant conceptions of objectivity serve "as a potent agent for maintaining current power relationships and women's subordination" (Berman 1989, 224) precisely because they accord authority to androcentric claims not merely by masking their bias, but by certifying their "neutrality."

Conceptions of objectivity premised upon self-purging of bias, value, or emotion and conceptions of objectivity dependent on the intersubjective correction of the same sources of error imply that the fundamental threat to objectivity is idiosyncrasy. The feminist discovery of persistent patterns of sexist error in "objective" inquiry suggests that the target of the various corrective strategies has been mislocated. If social values incorporated within individual consciousness present an important obstacle to objective knowledge, then norms of objectivity that blind the individual to the formative role of social values or assure the individual that intersubjective consensus is sufficient to counteract shared social biases will fail to produce objective accounts of the world. For if certain social values structure conceptions of self and perceptions of the social and natural worlds, then neither isolated acts of pure intellect nor intersubjective testing will suffice to identify them. Instead, objective inquiry requires the systematic probing of precisely that which appears unproblematic. Indeed, who does the probing may be a matter of central concern to those committed to objective inquiry. For what is taken as given, what appears to be natural, what seems to fall outside the legitimate field of investigation may be related to the gender, race, class, and historical situatedness of the investigator.

As Linda Martin Alcoff (2007, 42) has pointed out, feminist theory rejects the notion that all knowers are fungible or interchangeable, arguing instead that the situatedness of a particular knower can be relevant to judgment calls about "issues of coherence, consistency, relevance, plausibility, and credibility." Recognizing that specific experiences, social locations, modes of perceptual practices and habits, styles of reasoning, and sets of interests may affect empirical and normative claims, feminist theorists conclude that "all knowers are not "epistemically equal" (Code 1993, 1995; Alcoff 2007). Feminists' "critical orientation may be different and richer in regard to certain kinds of gender-related issues, richer in the sense of being based on more direct and comprehensive knowledge and experience" (Alcoff 2007, 46).

As the chapters in the *Oxford Handbook of Feminist Theory* make clear, feminist theorizing from women's and men's lives has profound effects on how central categories are conceptualized, whether the field of analysis is aesthetics, biology, cultural studies, development, economics, film studies, health, history, literature, politics, religion, science studies, sexualities, violence, or war.

Intersectionality and the Politics of Embodiment

Much contemporary feminist theoretical work is "intersectional" (Crenshaw 1989, 1991; see Cooper, chapter 20 in this volume). That is, it takes from black feminism a fundamental insight about power: that the various systems of oppression—such as racism, patriarchy, capitalism, and heterosexuality—are interacting and co-constituting (Combahee River Collective [1977] 1995). In black feminist theory, intersectionality has afforded a means to analyze the dynamics of marginalization and to call attention to the inequities of power and privilege within the (purportedly general) category "women." Intersectional analysis draws attention to the complex means by which power is encoded within particular bodies, exploring how specific gender norms are racialized, reserving the category "men" or "women" to those in dominant classes, while denying gendered inclusion to those deemed "inferior," "subhuman," or "deviant." Conventions regarding masculinity and femininity are not just "sex roles" (to use a term from an earlier discourse) but are shot through with specific norms constitutive of class, race, and sexuality.

Bodies, then, do not exist outside politics and culture, beyond the reach of the state. Sex and race are political categories that have often accorded legal status (which determines citizenship rights), educational and employment opportunities, levels of income and wealth, and access to prestige and power. In most parts of the world, babies "are assigned" a sex and a race before they are given a name and those designations carry legal weight that haunts the individual from the cradle to the grave (Matambanadzo 2005, 214). Affixed to birth certificates, passports, driver's licenses, draft cards, credit applications, marriage licenses, and death certificates, raced-sexed legal status sculpts the contours of individual freedom and belonging in ways that ensure that domination and subordination are thoroughly corporeal.

Demonstrating that embodiment is profoundly political is one of the most distinctive contributions of feminist scholarship. Indeed, feminist theory has shown not only that embodiment itself is political, but also that embodied power permeates politics at the national and international levels. State policies have excluded certain kinds of bodies from political rights and citizenship. National and international population policies have constructed women of color as "targets" of development in ways that make childbearing a political issue, affecting who is born and altering the complexion of nations. Feminist studies of laws, norms, and organizational practices that enforce racial segregation and maintain separate spheres for men and women emphasize that states use laws and policy as mechanisms of racialization and gendering—*constructing* relations of power and forms of inequality that shape the identities and aptitudes of individuals. Far from being natural givens, politics *produces* race and gender, not only by creating and maintaining raced and gendered divisions within the population, but also by defining race and gender characteristics and according differential rights on the basis of those definitions.

Racialization and gendering create forms of inequality written on the body, which shape how individuals understand themselves and what they can make of themselves. Feminist theory seeks to denaturalize the production of such social and political hierarchies by illuminating *racing-gendering*—the political process through which particular identities are sculpted in ways that simultaneously create the dominant and the subordinate and naturalize those social relations of domination. The dynamics of racing-gendering are so pervasive that feminist and critical race theorists have generated a *theory of raced-gendered institutions* to account for them (Acker 1992; Kenney 1996; Hawkesworth 2003). In recent years, some of the most exciting innovations in feminist theory have come from theorists in the global South, who challenge naturalizations of other modes of embodiment, investigating how stratifications of race, ethnicity, class, nationality, and sexuality are written on particular bodies to create and sustain complex hierarchies of difference. This work examines embodied differences in relation to complex mechanisms of social inclusion and exclusion, including the organization of domestic activity; divisions of paid and unpaid labor; structures of the formal, informal, and subsistence economies; segregation of labor markets; production, distribution, and consumption; and terms and conditions of labor exchange as well as skewed access to rights, opportunities, and offices.

This Handbook: Aim, Organization, and Audience

The *Handbook* captures a plurality of approaches to feminist theory across a diverse array of topics and disciplines at the present moment. We do not present a chronological history of feminist thought. Nor can we claim to come close to being comprehensive. And we scrupulously avoid an attempt to create or accredit a canon.

We hope instead to present the complexity of feminist challenges to established knowledge, while also engaging areas of contestation within feminist theory. To those ends, we have taken a unique approach to the content of the *Handbook*. Rather than replicate discussions of the current themes and debates in feminist theory that are widely available in scholarly books and journal articles, we have commissioned original essays by noted feminist scholars, asking each to provide a critical genealogy of a topic, which situates key concepts in relation to mainstream and feminist approaches, thereby illuminating the transformations that feminist theorists have wrought. The *Handbook* features systematic analyses of signature subjects that span multiple academic disciplines, demonstrating the ways in which critical gender and intersectional analysis engages pressing contemporary issues as well as perennial concerns.

We present these concepts alphabetically, as part of an effort to challenge both chronological and disciplinary orderings of knowledge and received views about the "natural order of things." For example, we might have organized the material to begin with agency and embodiment, moving from there to performativity and normativity, and then on to institutions and politics. We have not done so because to impose such a conceptual organization would replicate entrenched liberal presuppositions that posit the individual as preceding the social—a frame that feminist theorists have demonstrated to be markedly androcentric. Alternatively, if we were to open the volume with nature, we would be harking back to a form of biological determinism that has become the uninterrogated ground of modernity—but that is thoroughly misguided from a feminist theoretical perspective. Alphabetical ordering is attractive not just for what it avoids but also for what it makes possible. Following the precedents set in dictionaries, lexical ordering presumes the equal weight of each entry and the openness of the set of entries. Thus it provides an implicit invitation to add new items as the project of feminist theory grows and changes over time.

We imagine the *Handbook* making an impact on three distinct groups of readers. The first cohort comprises readers who are new to feminist theory. Such readers will find an assemblage of accessibly written chapters that demonstrate how feminist scholars frame the topic under investigation and generate new research questions, concepts, and analytical tools to contribute to transformative theory and practices. The second audience is feminist scholars. Whether these readers are preparing a new syllabus, updating an old one, starting a new research venture, or just curious about theoretical developments in areas outside their expertise, they will find chapters laying out cutting-edge arguments by the leading scholars in the field. The third audience is aspirational. We hope it will include scholars who are unfamiliar with feminist theory and who want to confront feminist thinkers and make themselves accountable to feminist arguments in their areas of expertise.

For this audience, the *Handbook* will serve not only as a ready reference but also as a transformative one. The chapters challenge the mistaken notion that feminist theory pertains only to questions related to women, gender, or sexuality, offering nothing that mainstream scholars might wish to take into account. The chapters illuminate dimensions of social, cultural, political, economic, scientific, national, and transnational life that go undetected in mainstream discourses. They create ways of comprehending the politics of difference, which refuses essentialism, while also resisting the temptation to reduce processes of racialization and gendering to questions of embodiment. They document the manifold ways in which hierarchies of difference are produced, sustained, challenged, and transformed through knowledge production and regimes of visuality and through economic restructuring, the practices of international governmental and financial institutions, and the laws, norms, and policies of nation-states, communities, workplaces, and households.

The fifty chapters encompass topics that bridge academic terrains that are often treated in isolation from one another, covering:

1. Standard topics of social and political science (e.g., civilization, development, divisions of labor, economies, institutions, markets, migration, militarization, prisons, policy, politics, representation, state/nation, the transnational, violence)
2. Terms of art in cultural studies and humanities (e.g., affect, agency, experience, identities, intersectionality, jurisprudence, narrative, performativity, popular culture, posthumanism, religion, representation, standpoint, temporality, visual culture)
3. Discourses associated with medicine and science (e.g., cyborgs, health, intersexuality, nature, pregnancy, reproduction, science studies, sex/gender, sexuality, transsexuality)
4. Topics of contemporary critical theory that have been transformed through feminist theorization (e.g., biopolitics, coloniality, diaspora, microphysics of power, norms/normalization, postcoloniality, race/racialization, subjectivity/subjectivation)

We took care to assemble feminist theoretic work on this range of topics in order to show that feminist theory is (or ought to be) what Latour (1988, 43–49) calls an "obligatory point of passage," a body of knowledge that must be taken into account by scholars, regardless whether they have a particular interest in women, gender, or sexuality.

Our contributors come from a range of academic specializations that include Africana studies, anthropology, biology, communication studies, cultural studies, English, history, international relations, law, philosophy, political science, sociology and women's/gender studies. Our contributors are not representative of the presence of feminism worldwide, as they are drawn in large measure from the global North. Nonetheless, over one-third are based outside the United States, in Australia, Belgium, Canada, Colombia, Finland, Germany, Mexico, the Netherlands, Norway, Spain, Sweden, and the United Kingdom. Feminist theory is, without question, a global project.

The *Handbook* would look different had it been produced in the 1980s, a time when feminist literary critics, who took their critical paradigms from deconstruction and psychoanalysis, exercised considerable influence in defining what counted as feminist theory (Moses 1998). At that time, any Feminist Theory Handbook would likely have devoted chapters to the very terms *deconstruction* and *psychoanalysis* and would have expected the latter to address the conflict between object relations and Lacanian psychoanalysis (which figured so centrally in so many feminist theory debates). It would undoubtedly have given a chapter to *difference*, which would have addressed *différance* as well, and one to *identification* as well as other psychoanalytic terms of art. It would also have included chapters on "gynocriticism," a feminist interpretive strategy focused on the work of women writers as a distinct literary tradition characterized by genres that differed in significant ways from those associated with canonical male writers (Showalter 1987), and "gynesis," an exploration of the feminine as a particular kind of discursive effect, or as that which is radically repressed by phallogocentrism (Jardine 1982, 1985). We mention this not to suggest that today those terms are unimportant or to dismiss those debates, and certainly not to imply that the terms and topics we have selected will stand the test of time. We intend only to note that in the 1980s, feminist theorists across disciplines were more likely to share a common critical vocabulary rooted in interpretive strategies that are characteristic of the humanities. Today, feminist theory takes inspiration from multiple critical paradigms, and feminist projects are diffused throughout the academy. The *Handbook* aims to be both a celebration of and a guide to that state of affairs.

Notes

1. Mary Ellen Waithe (1987) notes that Aesara of Lucania, who lived in the fourth or the third century BCE, used the Pythagorean conception of *harmonia* to conceptualize law and justice in the home as well as in the polis, advancing an ethical theory, a psychology of moral development, and a theory of obligation grounded in women's, men's, and children's lives. Su Ruolan's *Xuanji Diagram (Armillary Sphere Diagram)* is an embroidery of palindromic poems. Within this 29 x 29 character grid, poems can be read backward and forward in any number of line combinations, yielding 7,958 three-, four-, five-, six- and seven-character poems. The name, *Armillary Sphere Diagram*, "refers to the resemblance between the rows and columns of reversible writing and the astronomical instrument that features spinning, concentric, and metal circles." (Da 2015, 678–679).
2. Recent scholarship by feminist historians has called the "wave" metaphor into question, suggesting that there has been far more continuity in feminist activism since the late eighteenth century than was previously imagined. See, for example, Rupp (1997); Henry (2004); Offen (2000); Springer (2002); Hewitt (2010). Some feminists, however, defend the wave metaphor. See Aikau, Erickson, and Pierce (2007).

References

Acker, Joan. 1992. "Gendered Institutions: From Sex Roles to Gendered Institutions." *Contemporary Sociology* 21 (5): 565–569.
Aikau, Hokulani K., Karla A. Erickson, and Jennifer L. Pierce. 2007. *Feminist Waves, Feminist Generations: Life Stories from the Academy*. Minneapolis: University of Minnesota Press.
Alcoff, Linda. 2000. "On Judging Epistemic Credibility: Is Social Identity Relevant." In *Women of Color and Philosophy*, edited by Naomi Zack, 235–262. Oxford: Blackwell.
Alcoff, Linda Martin. 2007. "Epistemologies of Ignorance: Three Types." In *Race and Epistemologies of Ignorance*, edited by Shannon Sullivan and Nancy Tuana, 39–57. Albany: State University of New York Press.
Berman, Ruth. 1989. "From Aristotle's Dualism to Materialist Dialectics: Feminist Transformation of Science and Society." In *Gender/Body/Knowledge*, edited by A. Jaggar and S. Bordo, 224–255. New Brunswick, NJ: Rutgers University Press.

Butler, Judith, and Joan W. Scott. 1992. *Feminists Theorize the Political*. New York and London: Routledge.

Chatterjee, Indrani. 2013. "Monastic Governmentality, Colonial Misogyny, and Postcolonial Amnesia in South Asia." *History of the Present: A Journal of Critical History* 3 (1): 57–98.

Code, Lorraine. 1981. "Is the Sex of the Knower Epistemologically Significant?" *Metaphilosophy* 12: 267–276.

Code, Lorraine. 1991. *What Can She Know? Feminist Theory and the Construction of Knowledge*. Ithaca, NY: Cornell University Press.

Code, Lorraine. 1993. "Taking Subjectivity into Account." In *Feminist Epistemologies*, edited by Linda Alcoff and Elizabeth Potter, 15–48. New York: Routledge.

Code, Lorraine. 1995. *Rhetorical Spaces: Essays on Gendered Locations*. New York: Routledge.

Cody, Lisa Forman. 2001. "Sex, Civility, and the Self: Du Coudray, D'Eon, and Eighteenth-Century Conceptions of Gendered, National and Psychological Identity." *French Historical Studies* 24 (3): 379–407.

Cody, Lisa Forman. 2005. *Birthing the Nation: Sex, Science, and the Conception of Eighteenth Century Britons*. Oxford: Oxford University Press.

Combahee River Collective. (1977) 1995. "A Black Feminist Statement." In *Words of Fire: An Anthology of African American Feminist Thought*, edited by Beverly Guy Sheftall, 232–240. New York: New Press.

Crenshaw, Kimberlé. 1989. "Demarginalizing the Intersection of Race and Sex: A Black Feminist Critique of Antidiscrimination Doctrine, Feminist Theory and Antiracist Politics." *University of Chicago Legal Forum* 4: 139–167.

Crenshaw, Kimberlé. 1991. "Mapping the Margins: Intersectionality, Identity Politics, and Violence against Women of Color." *Stanford Law Review* 43: 1241–1299.

Da, Nan Z. 2015. "On the Decipherment of Modern China and Spurned Lovers: Zhai Yongming's *Most Tactful Phrases*." *Signs: Journal of Women in Culture and Society* 40 (3): 667–693.

Daly, Mary. 1973. *Beyond God the Father*. Boston: Beacon Press.

Daly, Mary. 1978. *Gyn/Ecology: The Metaethics of Radical Feminism*. Boston: Beacon Press.

De Gouges, Olympe. (1791) 1989. *Rights of Woman*. Translated by V. Stevenson. London: Pythia Press.

de Lauretis, Teresa. 1986. *Feminist Studies/Critical Studies*. Bloomington: Indiana University Press.

Devault, Marjorie. 1999. *Liberating Method: Feminism and Social Research*. Philadelphia, PA: Temple University Press.

Devor, Holly. 1989. *Gender Blending: Confronting the Limits of Duality*. Bloomington: Indiana University Press.

Ebert, Teresa. 1996. *Ludic Feminism and After*. Ann Arbor: University of Michigan Press.

Eisenstein, Hester, and Alice Jardine. 1980. *The Future of Difference*. New Brunswick and London: Rutgers University Press.

Elshtain, Jean Bethke. 1981. *Public Man, Private Woman*. Princeton, NJ: Princeton University Press.

Fausto-Sterling, Anne. 1986. *Myths of Gender*. New York: Basic Books.

Fausto-Sterling. 1993. "The Five Sexes: Why Male and Female Are Not Enough." *The Sciences* (March/April): 20–24.

Ferguson, Kathy. 2015. "The Future of Feminist Political Theory." Remarks at a Roundtable at the Annual Meetings of the Western Political Science Association. Las Vegas, Nevada.

Friedman, Susan Stanford. 1998. *Mappings: Feminism and the Cultural Geographies of Encounter.* Princeton, NJ: Princeton University Press.

Geiger, Susan. 1990. "What's So Feminist about Women's Oral History?" *Journal of Women's History* 2 (1): 169–182.

Grant, Judith. 1993. *Fundamental Feminism: Contesting the Core Concepts of Feminist Theory.* New York: Routledge.

Hawkesworth, Mary. 1988. "Feminist Rhetoric: Models of Politicization." *Political Theory* 16 (3): 444–467.

Hawkesworth, Mary. 1990. *Beyond Oppression: Feminist Theory and Political Strategy.* New York: Continuum.

Hawkesworth, Mary. 2003. "Congressional Enactments of Race-Gender: Toward a Theory of Raced-Gendered Institutions." *American Political Science Review* 97 (4): 529–550.

Hemmings, Clare. 2005. "Telling Feminist Stories." *Feminist Theory* 6 (2): 115–139.

Hemmings, Clare. 2011. *Why Stories Matter: The Political Grammar of Feminist Theory.* Durham and London: Duke University Press.

Henry, Astrid. 2004. *Not My Mother's Sister.* Bloomington: Indiana University Press.

Hewitt, Nancy. 2010. *No Permanent Waves: Recasting Histories of U.S. Feminism.* New Brunswick, NJ: Rutgers University Press.

Irigaray, Luce. 1985a. *Speculum of the Other Woman.* Translated by Gillian Gill. Ithaca, NY: Cornell University Press.

Irigaray, Luce. 1985b. *This Sex Which Is Not One.* Translated by Catherine Porter. Ithaca, NY: Cornell University Press.

Jaggar, Alison. 1983. *Feminist Politics and Human Nature.* Totowa, NJ: Rowman and Allenheld.

Jaggar, Alison. 1989. "Love and Knowledge: Emotion in Feminist Epistemology." In *Gender/Body/Knowledge*, edited by Alison Jaggar and Susuan Bordo, 145–171. New Brunswick, NJ: Rutgers University Press.

Jardine, Alice. 1982. "Gynesis." *Diacritics* 12: 54–65.

Jardine, Alice. 1985. *Gynesis: Configurations of Woman and Modernity.* Ithaca, NY: Cornell University Press.

Jayawardena, Kumari. 1986. *Feminism and Nationalism in the Third World.* London: Zed Books.

Jordanova, Ludmilla. 1989. *Sexual Visions: Images of Gender in Science and Medicine between the 18th and 20th Centuries.* Madison: University of Wisconsin Press.

Kenney, Sally. 1996. "New Research on Gendered Political Institutions." *Political Research Quarterly* 49 (June): 445–466.

Kessler, Suzanne, and Wendy McKenna. 1978. *Gender: An Ethnomethodological Approach.* New York: John Wiley.

Landes, Joan. 1988. *Women and the Public Sphere in the Age of the French Revolution.* Ithaca, NY: Cornell University Press.

Landes, Joan. 1998. *Feminism, the Public and the Private.* New York: Oxford University Press.

Laqueur, Thomas. 1990. *Making Sex: Body and Gender from the Greeks to Freud.* Cambridge, MA: Harvard University Press.

Laqueur, Thomas. 2012. "The Rise of Sex in the Eighteenth Century: Historical Context and Historiographical Implications." *Signs: Journal of Women in Culture and Society* 37 (4): 802–813.

Latour, Bruno. 1988. *The Pasteurization of France.* Translated by Alan Sheridan and John Law. Cambridge, MA: Harvard University Press.

Longino, Helen. 1990. *Science as Social Knowledge.* Princeton, NJ: Princeton University Press.

Lopez McAlister, Linda. 1996. *Hypatia's Daughters: Fifteen Hundred Years of Women Philosophers*. Bloomington: Indiana University Press.
Matambanadzo, Saru. 2005. "Engendering Sex: Birth Certificates, Biology, and the Body in Anglo-American Law." *Cardozo Women's Law Journal* 11: 213–246.
Moses, Claire Goldberg. 1998. "Made in America: 'French Feminism' in Academia." *Feminist Studies* 24 (2): 241–274.
Nagel, Thomas. 1986. *The View from Nowhere*. New York: Oxford University Press.
Nicholson, Linda J. 1990. *Feminism/Postmodernism*. New York and London: Routledge.
O'Brien, Mary. 1981. *The Politics of Reproduction*. Boston: Routledge and Kegan Paul.
Offen, Karen. 2000. *European Feminisms, 1700-1950*. Redwood City, CA: Stanford University Press.
Okonjo, Kamene. 1994. "Women and the Evolution of a Ghanian Political Synthesis." In *Women and Politics Worldwide*, edited by Barbara Nelson and Najma Chowdhury, 285–297. New Haven, CT: Yale University Press.
O'Neil, Eileen. 1989. "(Re)Presentations of Eros: Exploring Female Sexual Agency." In *Gender/Body/Knowledge*, edited by Alison Jaggar and Susan Bordo, 68–91. New Brunswick, NJ: Rutgers University Press.
Oyewumi, Oyeronke. 1997. *The Invention of Women: Making an African Sense of Western Gender Discourses*. Minneapolis: University of Minnesota Press.
Poovey, Mary. 1988. *Uneven Developments*. Chicago: University of Chicago Press.
Rupp, Leila. 1997. *Worlds of Women: The Making of an International Women's Movement*. Princeton, NJ: Princeton University Press.
Ruth, Sheila. 1981. "Methodocracy, Misogyny, and Bad Faith: The Response of Philosophy." In *Men's Studies Modified*, edited by Dale Spender, 43–53. Oxford: Pergamon.
Showalter, Elaine. 1987. "Women's Time, Women's Space: Writing the History of Feminist Criticism." In *Feminist Issues in Literary Scholarship*, edited by Shari Benstock, 30–44. Bloomington: Indiana University Press.
Springer, Kimberly. 2002. "'Third Wave' Black Feminism?" *Signs: Journal of Women in Culture and Society* 27 (4): 1059–1082.
Squires, Judith. 1999. *Gender in Political Theory*. Cambridge, UK: Polity Press.
Schor, Naomi, and Elizabeth Weed. 1994. *The Essential Difference*. Bloomington: Indiana University Press.
Towns, Ann. 2009. "The Status of Women as a Standard of 'Civilization.'" *European Journal of International Relations* 15 (4): 681–706.
Towns, Ann. 2010. *Women and States: Norms and Hierarchies in International Society*. Cambridge, UK and New York: Cambridge University Press.
Waithe, Mary Ellen. 1987. *A History of Women Philosophers, 600 BC-500 AD*. Vol. 1. Dordrecht: Martinus Nijhoff/Kluwer.
Weed, Elizabeth. 1989. *Coming to Terms: Feminism, Theory, Politics*. New York and London: Routledge.
Wollstonecraft, Mary. (1792) 1975. *Vindication of the Rights of Woman*. Edited by Carol H. Poston. New York: W. W. Norton.
Zalewski, Marysia. 2000. *Feminism after Postmodernism: Theorizing through Practice*. New York and London: Routledge.

CHAPTER 1

AFFECT

MARIANNE LILJESTRÖM

INTRODUCTION

During the last few decades, affect studies within feminist research have given expression to challenging epistemological and ontological questions. The bases for these challenges are the numerous discussions and readings of affect as emotive intensities, emotional affections, intuitive reactions, and life forces. Affect has created a space for the rethinking of and new thinking about theoretical issues that range from the dualism between body and mind to critique of identity politics and critical reading. This theorizing has underlined the sensual qualities of being, the capacity to experience and understand the world in ways that are profoundly relational and productive.

Feminist scholarship has, since the 1990s, taken a broad interest in the question of affect. In the fields of philosophy, history, literature, cinema studies, art history, media and cultural studies as well as in sociology, anthropology, politics, and natural sciences, feminist scholars have turned to questions of affect and topics of affectivity in search of a new critical vocabulary for investigating and conceptualizing the subject of feminism as embodied, located, worldly, contextualized, and relational. This search has been highly visible in the abundance of publications, conferences, and course syllabi that, across the humanities and social sciences, have established affects, emotions, feelings, and passions as a lively and productive research area. Many scholars prefer to characterize this lively research field as the *affective turn* in critical theory and research.

For many, this so-called affective turn forms a reaction to the alleged limitations of poststructuralist theories, the structuralist legacy, and commitments to linguistic models. Especially, new materialist critique has pointed to shortcomings of textual analyses that have on occasion diminished and even belittled the sensorial and material in descriptions of culture and society. In contrast, the critique strives in its attention to affects to highlight questions of material, biology, and energetic forces. The debate between poststructuralists and new materialists has rekindled questions of ontology linked to considerations about differences between various identity categories, that is, the intersectional approach to feminist knowledge production, as it is currently and regularly called.

In this chapter, I begin with a presentation of different examples of the wide spectrum of contemporary feminist affect studies. Subsequently, I discuss the notion of the affective turn, examining its characteristics and, above all, concentrating on how it has been described as a reaction and a challenge to alleged limitations of poststructuralism and deconstruction. Then, I take a closer look at various—and often conflicting—definitions of affect, emphasizing demarcations from such notions as emotion, feeling, and sentiment. Further, I deal with diverse understandings of the linkages between epistemology and ontology when considered through the lens of affects. After exploring these links to methodological questions regarding how to engage affects, I end with some reflections on feminist politics of affects, underlining the importance of the contextualization and historicization of affects.

FEMINIST AFFECT STUDIES

Feminist research on affects has specifically aimed at exploring the connections among affect, gender, sexuality, class, and race in terms of power, regulation, and control. Special attention has been given to the politics of the personal as connected to affects, and research on affects has been through the prism of power widely linked to thinking about personal and collective memory and trauma. This is of particular concern to scholars who situate themselves within feminist cultural studies of emotion and affect, but also to those situated within other disciplinary fields in the social and natural sciences (such as Ahmed 2004, 2010a; Berlant 1997, 2000; Brennan 2004; Brown 1995; Butler 1997, 2004; Cvetkovich 1992 2003; Love 2007; Munt 2007; Ngai 2005; Probyn 2005; Sedgwick 2003; Skeggs 2005; Woodward 2009). While focusing on the body, many feminist scholars have studied the negotiation of affect and emotions in the public sphere and, thus, engaged with political, economic, and cultural effects of affects and the "emotionalization" of life. As Lauren Berlant (2000, 1) has observed, intimacy contains an aspiration for something shared, where "the inwardness of the intimate is met by a corresponding publicness." These works examine how power is manifested through feeling and how politically proper ways of life and knowledge production are circulated through discourses and affectivity. Many of these works are linked to re-visiting the well-known feminist slogan "the personal is political," the exploration of which resulted in many important feminist studies on emotion. In her article reviewing affect studies, Kristyn Gorton (2007, 337) notes that scholars' interest in the affective responses of the public underline the need to clarify the use of the feminist slogan "the personal is political" so that individual stories do not replace social struggle.

Film and media researchers have in turn examined synesthetic sensations, bodily experiences, and powerful impressions (Marks 2002; Sobchack 2004), while scholars who studied crossings between private and public spheres and affective dimensions of feminism have theorized the role of affects in marking individual and collective bodies (Ahmed 2004; Berlant 2000; Cvetkovich 2003; Probyn 2005; Ngai 2005). Furthermore, the affective turn within queer studies has dealt partly with a historicization of affects resulting in a parade of interesting and influential work, especially on negative emotions: studies in trauma cultures (Cvetkovich 2003), on bereavement, suffering, and melancholy (Brown 1999; Butler 2004), and shame (Ahmed 2004; Munt 2007; Probyn 2005; Sedgwick 2003).

This positioning of affects in relation to norms and power understands them as formative for subjects, social relations, politics, and political mobilization. Lauren Berlant's skilled and inspiring research can be considered as significant for this historicizing of affects. Referring to the statement by Gilles Deleuze and Felix Guattari that affects act in the nervous systems of worlds, not persons, Berlant asks how and on what terms a specific affective response becomes exemplary for a collective historical time. Berlant (2008, 1–2) defines affects as the active presence of the body in connection to the intensities of the present: affects entrench subjects within historical fields; hence, the study of affects concerns communication about the terms for production of historical instances as deeply embedded moments.

Especially, new materialists have criticized feminist cultural studies for overemphasizing deconstructive readings of representations. Certainly, one can argue that since the 1990s, there has been a limitless use of textual metaphor within cultural research (as in deconstructive readings of bodies, landscapes, or artifacts as texts without considering their materiality): a whole range of intellectual questions can be thought as bypassed or lost if the focus is solely on the semantic and symbolic. In spite of this, such a critique risks promoting a rather limited or perhaps even flat understanding of reading as a critical activity. Perhaps more important is that this critique can foreclose reading, interpretation, experience, and ethics as important intellectual issues within feminist research. Feminist literary researchers have, however, noticed how affect and interpretation are inseparable, how interpretation is always a question of contagious affects and dynamic meetings between texts and readers (Armstrong 2000; Ngai 2005; Pearce 1997; Sedgwick 2003).

Feminist affect studies have certainly also been inspired by new materialism and its critique, especially concerning the stitching up and elimination of boundaries between organisms and environments, between human affect and affect of matter. However, in some cases quite arbitrary contradictions are constructed between "earlier" feminist work and feminist new materialism. For example, in contrast to earlier feminist work on bodies and affects, Jessica Ringrose and Rebecca Coleman (2013) want to move away from what they call "simply a one-way (male) gaze" (129) and "a simple feminist pronouncement of objectification" (132) to elaborate Deleuze's transcendental empiricism in order to map out how bodies' capacities to affect and be affected are extended or fixed via gendered relations. Their material consists of young people's relations to bodily images in their everyday lives, and they ask how the (self-)objectification of girls' and boys' bodies works through relations of looking at and through images. Using extensively a new materialist and Deleuzian terminology, they, firstly, construct previous feminist research in a highly unsatisfactory way as both poor, and inadequate. Secondly, as a matter of fact, it is hard to see where their scarcely surprising results differ, for example, from what a critical deconstructive reading and a discourse analysis could have made possible in connection to the same material. For instance, they state that they "show *how* extensive gender norms create fixity through gender and sexual dualisms when *looking* captures girls, reducing them to their body parts or the 'wrong' sexuality, as 'skets'" (128). Manifestations presenting a different vocabulary and terminology and declaring previous feminist research as "old-fashioned" and unsatisfactory do not guarantee new and inspiring research results on affects and affective bodily relations.

Striving to re-evaluate ontology and materiality gives the notion of affect an exceptional status within the critical thinking that places itself within the realm of the "ontological turn" and new materialism's critique of poststructuralism and its focus on language, discourse, and ideology (Ahmed 2008; Hemmings 2005; Hird 2004). According to Anu Koivunen, this critique, however, neglects a considerable amount of critical work within especially feminist poststructuralism, which argues for the cultural—and historical—coincidental and contingent character of affects and emotions; additionally, this critical work studies emotions and emotion cultures as uncertain technologies of the subject (2010, 8–28; see also Hemmings 2005; Riley 2000; Terada 2001). In contrast to what currently has become a quite commonly accepted view that especially the revitalizing of new materialist approaches has brought about an "affective turn" within critical thinking, it is important not to lose sight of the specific feminist history of research and thinking on affects.

THE AFFECTIVE TURN

Affective turn is currently a broadly adopted term describing the revived interest, increased discussion and research concerning affects and affect theories. The most common, already well-established way of describing the *affective turn* defines it as a striving to eliminate an important set of dichotomies that allegedly characterizes the research done from a poststructuralist deconstructive approach. The "turn" to affect is described as having the potential to overcome important dichotomies characteristic of constructivist research: that between mind and body and between passions and actions. Patricia Tiniceto Clough (2007)—who has established an influential position as distributor of general summaries and characteristics of the "affective turn"—gives in the introduction to the anthology *The Affective Turn. Theorizing the Social*, a broad description of this development and shift in critical theory. She portrays it as various movements *from* a set of previous understandings *to* more complex and challenging considerations. Many of her remarks are today generally adapted ways of describing the shift to studies in affects. According to Clough, the shifts involve the following: from psychoanalytic criticism of subject identity, representation, and trauma to an engagement with information and affect; from privileging the organic body to exploring nonorganic life; from the presumption of equilibrium-seeking closed systems to engaging the complexity of open systems under conditions of metastability; from focusing on an economy of production and consumption to focusing on the economic circulation of pre-individual bodily capacities or affects in the domain of biopolitical control (2007, 2).

This description gives affect wide-ranging explanatory strength and the role of linkage between different understandings: Clough describes the shift in thought as an intensification of self-reflexivity in information and communication systems, including the human body (defined as processes turning back on themselves to act on themselves); in archiving machines, including all forms of media technologies and human memory; in capital flows, including the circulation of value through human labor and technology; and in bio-political networks of disciplining, surveillance, and control (2007, 3). Thus, she leaves hardly "anything" outside affect, which comes to encompass all levels of life and being. Her definition is hence in concert with Felix Guattari's, according to whom there is no position outside of affect forces, but "affect is all there is" (see Bertelsen and Murphie 2010, 140). This is in sharp contrast to Sara Ahmed's view, according to which the "affective turn" is a question of how we can theorize positive affect and the politics of good feeling because so much cultural research has been done on bad feelings.

Clough's characterization of the affective turn as a movement from a previously atemporal—often insufficiently theorized space—to a perhaps more sophisticated development of critical thinking is a quite ordinary and widely accepted way of making differences and drawing lines between both theoretical understandings, constructions, and methodological research tools. In her two other texts on the state of affect studies and the affective turn, Clough notes that the "affective turn" has "returned" critical theory and cultural criticism to bodily matter, where it points to a dynamism immanent to both bodily matter and matter generally—that is, to matter's capacity for self-organization in being informational. She considers this "resumption" to be the most provocative and enduring contribution of the "affective turn" (2010b, 206–207; see also Clough 2010a). Because of Clough's influential position in defining the "affective turn," I will take a closer look at her way of constructing the differences between the mentioned threads of critical thinking in connection to the body.

In dealing with both bodily matter and matter in general, and especially with categorizations and portrayals of the body, Clough operates with a whole range of oppositions, above all between organic matter and nonorganic matter, closed and open systems of matter, and dynamic and equilibrist organisms. As in connection to more general descriptions of the affective turn that are specifically linked to questions of the body, philosophical strands of critical thinking are also here placed in opposition to each other—namely, constructionism and poststructuralism, on the one hand, and a Deleuze and Guattari-inspired thinking about materiality, on the other (Clough 2007, 8, 11, 12). By underlining the differing aspects on the body as a "closed system" and as "dynamic matter," Clough extends these contrasts from placing Deleuzian bio-philosophy in opposition to an understanding of the body as a "closed system seeking equilibrium and homeostasis," to what she names the organism's "autopoiesis." She uses this term to point to the way in which the organism engages with its environment: being closed to information, the organism cannot merely be determined by the environment, but it engages the environment autopoietically; that is, it selects the environment in ways that allow it to construct itself. It seeks—according to Clough (11)—homeostasis and equilibrium because disturbances to these are seen as destructive. However, these views on the relationship of the organism to its environment should not be linked to understandings of context—which I discuss later—as such understandings connect basically to epistemology, a level of scholarly thinking Clough does not explicitly deal with.

In accordance with Clough's (2007, 12) reading of Deleuze, his bio-philosophy offers a new sense of the organism: living systems form machinelike assemblages involving ways of transversal becoming open to information "in far-from-equilibrium conditions of metastability." Without further exemplification, Deleuze-inspired thinking about organisms (bodies among them) is put in direct opposition to those approaches that, in Clough's view, prioritize homeostasis and equilibrium before openness and complexity. Because the view about matter as informational is of decisive importance in Clough's thinking, some clarification about what it means is in order. She stresses that information is basically a matter of contact and connectibility, a modulation of affectivity and attention by reducing the real through the exclusion of possibilities (17). This extremely abstract definition is quite hard to grasp. Seemingly, the main idea is to underline (in contrast to representationalism) complexity, openness, and the secondary role of interpreting meaning. Once more, she highlights that to understand matter as informational is to recognize its inherent capacity for self-organizing out of complexity (18).

Thus, Clough's definition of body and bodily matter is crucial to her sidestepping of questions of the subjectivity, actions, and experiences of subjects. For her, thinking of the body as an open system means to understand "pre-individual bodily capacities or affectivity in relation to the passage from discipline to control" (which describes a shift in biopolitics, from disciplinary societies to what Deleuze describes as "societies of control"; Clough 2007, 17); in this arena, control should not be understood as the production of subjects expressing internalized norms, but control aims at a "never-ending modulation of moods, capacities, affects, and potentialities, assembled . . . in bodies of data and information" (19). Clough understands control as an extension of Foucault's biopolitics, in which the focus is not on the individual body/subject, but on the species body (ibid). She underscores that control societies call into question politics of representation and subject identity, they call into question autobiographical experimental writing, the political effectiveness of self-reflexivity in the production of knowledge (20).

In line with Clough, Lisa Blackman and Couze Venn (2010), in their introductory article on affect in the journal *Body & Society*, produce the same contrasting and oppositional constructions by naming something as contemporary "good theory," referring to one of the journal contributors who says that the "turn to affect" is characterized by making certain assumptions about materiality. It is assumed that "good theory" is one that no longer keeps a distance from biology as a set of explanations and as a knowledge practice. This contradicts social constructionism or discursive approaches to bodily matters that are characterized as being hostile to the biological either as a competing set of explanations or as a disciplinary apparatus (Blackman and Venn 2010, 13).

In their introduction to *The Affect Theory Reader,* Melissa Gregg and Gregory J. Seigworth (2010, 6) map eight main orientations in the study of affect. They call the first approach the "sometimes archaic and often occulted practices of human/nonhuman nature as intimately interlaced." The second is located in the more recent but "often not less occulted (though better-funded) assemblages of the human/machine/inorganic, such as cybernetics, the neurosciences, ongoing research in artificial intelligence, robotics, and bio-informatics/bio-engineering" (ibid). The third is found in some nonhumanist philosophical traditions, especially those that try to move beyond various gendered and other cultural limitations in philosophy (6–7). The fourth occurs in certain lines of psychological and psychoanalytic studies in which a quite shameless biologism remains co-creatively open and this route is more prone to a categorical naming of affects. The fifth is found in a more indirect politically engaged work, which attends to various (hard and fleeting) materialities of everyday life and experience. The sixth appears in different attempts to turn away from the so-called linguistic turn and its associate constructionism in reactivating work that had taken place well before and alongside the turn in question and often focusing ethico-aesthetic spaces influenced by a various range of affective encounters (7–8). The seventh is located in critical discourses on emotions that have left behind subjectivity in order to unfold regimes of expressivity linked, above all, to diffusions of feelings and passions (8). The last, the eighth, is situated in practices of science and in science studies, concerning especially such work that grips multiple approaches to materialism (8).

The approaches mentioned overlap and are mostly quite hard to distinguish from each other: it seems that the mapping is done precisely in order to point to the multiple directions and roots of the "affective turn." The approaches are partly organized along the already frequently noticed lines of distinctions and oppositions: human/nonhuman, sciences/humanities, and materialisms/constructionism/psychoanalysis. Nevertheless, the map presents a multiplicity of research agendas, understandings, and adaptations of the category of affect. It does not—as is so common in generalizing presentations of the affective turn—advocate the concept as something novel in critical thinking, a sort of new and higher stage of thinking complexity. Furthermore, the map demonstrates the multidisciplinary character of affect studies: the debates do not deal only with philosophical matters but also with questions concerning, for example, artificial intelligence, cultural research, and queer studies. The map also challenges rhetorically the narrative of the affective turn, which often simplifies and reduces the multiple approaches and understandings.

Because of its focus on the collective and subjective experiences of oppression and discrimination, feminism has shown an interest in affects and emotions from the beginning of its history. In earlier temporal contexts, feminist scholarship focused on questions concerning the constructed juxtaposition of emotion and reason, of the role of emotions in feminist knowledge production, the importance of psychoanalytic thinking in figuring out practices of subjugation (cf. Frye 1983; Lorde 1984; hooks 1989; Jaggar 1989; Young 1990). Taking this history seriously makes it hard to talk about an affective turn within feminist studies and scholarship. Simultaneously, the relationship between feminism and affects is also a question about a continued difficulty to theorize affect partly because of the dominant historical trajectory of connecting women with emotion in a repressive and dismissive way.

Defining Affect and Emotion

There is a great diversity within the field of feminist affect studies, as well as within the research field of affect studies in its entirety, concerning theoretical approaches and methodological aspects of the notion itself as well as the topics for research. Conceptual divisions have emerged that relate to the different disciplinary preferences of two sets of scholars. Those in the humanities and social sciences often prefer the notion of "emotion" or "feeling" when investigating problems of cognition, social, cultural, and subjective phenomena and their interpretation. In contrast, biologists—among others—who examine bodily questions mostly prefer the notion of affect. However, there is still much disagreement on the definitions and use of the notion of affect. In this section, I concentrate first on definitions of affect—as contrasted to the those of the category of emotion—which have maybe been the most common way for scholars to situate themselves within the field of affect studies. Second, I look at how affect has been defined as materiality.

Lone Bertelsen and Andrew Murphie (2010) mention three different aspects of affect that sum up the approaches that circulate in contemporary feminist scholarly discussions. First, they see affect as transitive, as the movement of the impersonal (or what Guattari calls the "pre-personal") in which we are caught up, for example, global warming. Second, affect is understood as more personal, literally familiar, as emotion or feeling "the folding of broader affective intensities into the nervous system, eventually to become recognizable as the *register*, eventually the representation, of the ongoing folding of self and world, *as* the person" (140). Third, affect is assumed to lie between the former two. Bertelsen and Murphie refer here to Baruch Spinoza's statement of affect as "power to affect and be affected," a definition that many scholars in spite of philosophical strand have adopted. Affect in this understanding is seen, not so much a stage as an ongoing passage from one state to another (140). Within these broad aspects there are, however, several different understandings and definitions of the concept.

After some decades of intensified theoretical discussion within affect studies, *affect* and *emotion* are not used interchangeably in the majority of definitions and interpretations; rather, scholars defend a preference for one or the other. Sometimes scholars see affect and emotion as two aspects of the same phenomenon: for example, Rei Terada (2001, 4) writes that "by emotion we usually mean a psychological, at least minimally interpretive experience whose physiological aspect is affect", and she combines these two notions within the category of feeling, which she thinks is a wide-ranging term that indicates both physiological sensations (affects) and psychological states (emotions). Moreover, Teresa Brennan (2004, 5–6), who links psychological thinking with science, defines *affect* as a physiological move involving a judgment, which makes it essentially equivalent to emotion. Brennan concentrates, however, on transmission of affects, a process she considers social in origin, but physical and biological in effect (3).

Brennan's definition differs from, for example, that of Elspeth Probyn, who clearly separates emotion from affect: for Probyn (2005, 25), emotion refers to the social expression of affect, while "affect is the biological and physiological experience of it." Interestingly, Probyn uses here the notion of experience, which directs affects away from bodily sensations to reasoning. This is perhaps the most significant split between feminist affect studies and critical affect studies in general: are emotions/affects/feelings connected primarily to bodily sensations or to cognition? Lawrence Grossberg (2010, 316) formulated this division clearly when emphasizing emotion as the articulation of affect as ideology: "Emotion is the ideological attempt to make sense of some affective production. So, I don't think that we've yet done the actual work of parsing out everything that is getting collapsed into the general notion of affect. Basically, it's become everything that is non-representational or non-semantic—that's what we now call affect."

When Robert C. Solomon (2004, 76, 80, 88), subscribing to a "cognitive theory of emotions" embodying affect and feeling without rendering these unanalyzable, states that emotions are a kind of judgment "or rather, a complex of interlocking judgments, desires, and intentions," he is seeing emotions as subjective engagements with the world; that is, he is seeing them, at least in part, as experience. Furthermore, Ahmed (2010a, 23) underlines that to be affected by something is to evaluate that thing, but she thinks that instead of referring directly to experience, the evaluations are expressed in how bodies turn toward things, and how affects get "sticky." Ahmed's (2004, 11) use of experience has a somewhat different emphasis compared to Solomon's: in her opinion, the subject does not always know how she feels because it is not self-present—the lack of which has since Freud been articulated as "the unconscious"—and emotions are an effect of this splitting of experience. In a footnote, she declares that emotions involve the materialization of bodies and hence show the instability of "the biological" and "the cultural" as ways of understanding the body. In interpreting these, she does not want to look at them as separated (17).

Critique of the Inside-Out/ Outside-in Model

Another thread of the discussion about how to define the notions of affect and emotion deals with the historically quite long-lived argumentation of emotions as always social and escaping the limits of an individual—that is, the inside-out/outside-in model of thinking affects and emotions. Writing in a phenomenological frame, Sara Ahmed, in her book *The Cultural Politics of Emotions* (2004), questions both the psychological inside-out and the sociological outside-in model. Her alternative is to look at emotions as relational; instead of asking what emotions are, she asks what they do. She asserts that we do not "have" emotions, but our actions and individuality are formed by contacts with others (2004, 4). In her later work, in which she, in contrast to earlier texts, also writes about affect—not only emotions and feelings—Ahmed discusses affect as "contagious," which in her opinion helps to challenge an inside-out model of affect by showing how affects pass between bodies, affecting bodily surfaces. Furthermore, she asserts that the inside-out model tends to underestimate the extent to which affects are contingent. The affect becomes an object only given the contingency of how we are affected (2010b, 36).

In connection to the models mentioned, Ahmed also discusses Teresa Brennan's (2004, 1) notion of "feeling the atmosphere," how the atmosphere gets into the individual. Despite their similar viewpoints, Brennan underlines that "affects do not arise within a particular person but also come from without" (3); however, Ahmed is not content with this outside-in model. According to her, it is of decisive importance how we arrive, how we enter a room "with the atmosphere," and how this affects the impressions we receive (2010b, 36–37). Additionally, Elspeth Probyn (2010, 76), when talking about the effects of the "contagiousness of 'collective affects' " as exposing the breaches in the borders between self and other, notes that affect neither impinges on the body from the outside nor erupts from the inside.

Most scholars agree that the move to an intensified interest in affects, emotions, sentiments, and feelings is parallel to a renewed attention to the body as a challenging problematic for knowledge and experience. However, within feminist thinking and research, the question of embodiment and corporeality has been repeatedly present since the early 1990s, a circumstance that also underlines the renewed interest in emotions (Koivunen 2010, 13; cf. Grosz 1994; Ahmed and Stacey 2001). In their critique of the "routinizing critical project" and "habitual anti-biologism" (which all feminist thinking, above all, is blamed for), Eve Sedgwick and Adam Frank (1995, 1–2) present as their alternative Silvan Tomkins's (1962) theory of affects, according to which affects are inherently linked psychologically and physiologically. Tomkins differs between the thoroughly embodied drive system and the affect system, where drives are quite constrained compared to affects. In their reading of Tomkins, Sedgwick and Frank highlight the much greater freedom of affects with respect to time, aim, and object. "Affects can be, and are, attached to things, people, ideas, sensations, relations, activities, ambitions, institutions, and any number of other things, including other affects . . . This freedom of affects also gives them a structural potential not enjoyed by the drive system," Tomkins writes (quoted in Sedgwick 2003, 18–19). In Sedgwick's opinion, then, Tomkins shows that instead of the commonsensical understanding that the drive system is the primary motivator of human behavior and that affects are secondary to drives, the opposite is true: motivation itself, even the motivation to satisfy biological drives, is the business of the affect system (20).

Together with Brian Massumi's essay on the autonomy of affects, Sedgwick's and Frank's revitalization of Tomkins made 1995—as Melissa Gregg and Gregory Seigworth (2010) have claimed—a "watershed moment for the most recent resurgence of interest and intrigue regarding affect and theories of affect" (5). This watershed moment consists, then, of two rereadings: Tomkins (1962) and Gilles Deleuze's (1988) work on Spinoza's philosophy. These rereadings have been extremely influential in discussions within affect studies, and they are also pivotal in the critique of poststructuralism and representationalism. Sedgwick (2003, 21) makes this explicit: "If texture and affect, touching and feeling, seem to belong together, then, it is not because they share a particular delicacy of scale . . . What they have in common is that at whatever scale they are attended to, both are irreducibly phenomenological. To describe them primarily in terms of structure is always a qualitative misrepresentation." But as noted, there are other feminist timelines to follow in connection with affect studies: the strong body of feminist work on emotion and affect gets easily sidestepped in the robust wave of new materialist critique of poststructuralism and deconstruction.

Affects as Autonomous: Excess and Indeterminacy

Ahmed's approach to affect as stickiness contrasts with much of new materialist feminist work. Within the Deleuze-inspired strand of critical thinking—the "ontological turn"—Brian Massumi's thinking on affects has had a major impact. According to Massumi (2002, 25), affect constitutes a nonlinear complexity out of which the narrations of conscious states, such as emotion, are subtracted, but always with "a never-to-be-conscious autonomic remainder." Massumi underlines the autonomy of affect and its indeterminacy, autonomy from conscious perception and language as well as emotion. He states that if conscious perception is to be understood as the narration of affect (as it is in the case of emotion), there nevertheless always is "a virtual remainder, an excess of affect" (25). He emphasizes that it is precisely from this excess that the narration of emotion is subtracted in order to afterward "fit conscious requirements of continuity and linear causality" (29). He thinks that consciousness is limiting in a "limitless" virtual field, where any actualization becomes the limit of that field. Therefore, in contrast to autonomous affects as intensities and beyond narration, emotions represent for Massumi determinacy, subjective content, and the sociolinguistic fixing of a quality of experience defined as personal (28).

In line with Massumi's understandings, Lone Bertelsen and Andrew Murphie try to determine the moment when consciousness becomes limiting for affect (maybe turning it into something like emotion): they suggest that if affects are intensities, then refrains are affects "cycled back." (Bertelsen and Murphie 2010, 139). Here they refer to the constitutive role of refrains that Felix Guattari (1995) defined as the "logic of affects." Bertelsen and Murphie (2010, 139) understand the beginning of the affective events as a powerful indetermination "on the horizon," where the force of this indetermination calls for refrains to fold the chaos into the beginning of structure, to bring a little order, as Deleuze and Guattari (1987, 311) have also put it. Hence, the refrains can be seen as closures, but, as the authors underline, they are also openings to change. This is made possible because affects as transitions link across senses, events, and temporality, between or within different aspects of refrains. Thus, refrains constitute what will always be fragile territories in time (Bertelsen and Murphie 2010, 138–139). What comes to the temporality of affect in this framework can, therefore, according to Patricia Clough (2010b, 209), be understood in terms of thresholds, bifurcation, and emergence, as the temporality of the virtual.

Kathleen Stewart provides a more accessible version of Clough's quite abstract and intricate statement. Stewart (2007, 2) defines ordinary affects as things that happen "in impulses, sensations, expectations, daydreams, encounters, and habits of relating, in strategies and failures, in forms of persuasion, contagion, and compulsion, in modes of attention, attachment, and agency, and in publics and social worlds of all kinds that catch people up in something that feels like *something*." She thinks that these affects are not rooted in fixed conditions of possibility but in actual lines of potential that a "something" coming together calls to mind and sets in motion (2). Referring to Roland Barthes, she writes that they are immanent, obtuse, and erratic, in contrast to the "obvious meaning" of the semantic message and symbolic signification, and they do not work through "meanings" as such (3). The significance of affects lies in the intensities they build and in the thoughts and feelings they make possible. The question they beg is not what they might mean in an order of representations, but where they might go and what potential modes of knowing, relating, and attending to things are already somehow present in them in a state of potentiality and resonance. Stewart connects affects to the other central notions dealt with in this chapter by writing that "at once abstract and concrete, ordinary affects are more directly compelling than ideologies, as well as more fractious, multiplicitous, and unpredictable than symbolic meanings" (3).

Further Debates about Definitions

In her article "Creating Disturbance: Feminism, Happiness and Affective Differences," Sara Ahmed engages in a short polemic with Massumi's views and argues that the distinction between affect and emotion underdescribes the work of emotions, which involve forms of intensity, bodily orientation, and direction that are not simply about "subjective content" or qualification of intensity. Emotions are not "after-thoughts" but shape how bodies are moved by the worlds they inhabit. Ahmed continues by noting that the intensities that Massumi describes as affects are in her opinion also "directed," a directedness that is not simply about subjects and interior feelings, but about how things cohere in a certain way. Though one can separate an affective response from an emotion (e.g., bodily sensations from the feeling of being afraid), this does not mean that they are separate in practice. In fact, they slide into each other; they cohere, even when they are separated (Ahmed 2010c, 32). Alternatively, Sianne Ngai (2005, 27) has offered a contrasting approach to the difference between affect/emotion as "a modal difference of intensity or degree, rather than a formal difference of quality or kind."

Clough wants to take the affective turn beyond body-as-organism in order to elaborate "the historically specific mode of organization of material forces that the biomediated body is." She wants to do this "encompassingly," in relation to both capital accumulation in the domain of affect and the accompanying relations of power in the shift of governance from discipline to biopolitical control (Clough 2010b, 208). Thus, Clough (2007, 2) underlines that affect is not only theorized in terms of the human body, but also in relation to the technologies that allow us to "see" affect and to produce affective bodily capacities beyond the body's organic-physiological constraints. She defines the biomediated body as "a historically specific mode of organization of material forces, invested by capital into being, as well as elaborated through various discourses of biology and physics, thermodynamics and complexity, metastability and nonlinear relationality, reconfiguring bodies, work, and reproduction" (2010b, 207). As noted, she also puts the biomediated body in opposition to the autopoietic character of body-as-organism, by which she means a body open to energy but informationally closed to environment (207–208). I think that Rosi Braidotti helps to clarify this somewhat abstract and quite cryptic understanding of Clough's biomediated body by pointing to the functions of advanced capitalism, where bodies are reduced to their informational substrate in terms of energy resources—leveling out other categorical differences. What constitutes capital value in our social system is the accumulation of information itself, its immanent vital qualities, and self-organizing capacity (Braidotti 2013, 62). Clough provides a list of procedures, operationalized as surveillance techniques, to test and monitor the capacities of affective or bio-mediated bodies, such as DNA testing, brain fingerprinting, neural imaging, body-heat detection, and iris or hand recognition.

Advocating a new ontology in line with the proponents of new materialism, Braidotti (2006) takes a somewhat original position in the debate on, or the juxtaposition of, affect and emotion. For her, the return of the real, material body is an effect of bio-technologies, and she considers this to be a question of affects and ethics: in *Transpositions: On Nomadic Ethics* (164), she writes that in our connectedness with all living things, we are necessarily immersed in affects, emotions, and passions, the motor of subjectivity (164). Hence, in connecting materiality with affects and subjectivity, Braidotti moves beyond the oppositions between poststructuralism and new materialism. She deals with bodily materialism—similarly to Elizabeth Grosz—through an Irigarayan understanding of sexual difference, and she advocates an ethics of transformation from negativity into positivity. For her, ethics entails overcoming negative structures of our passions. This requires a new, interrelational subjectivity, a new feminist philosophy of joy and positivity in order to enable feminists to account for changes and transformations (201–202).

Thus, there are different points of entrance to understandings of affects within feminist research and within critical thinking in general. These can be clearly linked to distinct philosophical traditions, such as the Spinozian or the phenomenological, but there are also theorists adapting a mixture of outlooks, for example, Sara Ahmed and Eve Sedgwick.

Ontology and Epistemology

In this section, I take a closer look at some of the discussions that have dealt with the usefulness of the notion of affect in connecting (or creating oppositions between) ontological and epistemological questions. This has been a problem of constant attention and reflection within feminist theory, especially in discussions about the links between "externally" directed feminist theoretical critique and "internal," self-reflective epistemological positions. As we have seen, the usage and definitions of affect are highly dependent on the scholars' positioning within particular theoretical-philosophical traditions.

According to Eve Sedgwick, within critical theory there has been a poststructuralist overemphasis on truth and knowledge, and for Massumi, signification characterizes (passive) death. Both think that a turn to ontology—which for Massumi represents (active) life—is the alternative to the overemphasis in question (cf. Hemmings 2005, 557). Lauren Berlant (2011) thinks that an imagined contradiction between an ontological and an epistemological approach has been created, and she argues that Massumi represents the nervous system as being so autonomous that affective acts cannot be intended, in contrast to affective facts that potential entities can manipulate to foreclose future capacities for consciousness. "Positing the subject of history mainly as reactive and recessive, this sensorial construction of the historical field has engendered quite a bit of suspicion," Berlant writes (14). In Ranjana Khanna's interpretation, the efforts of Deleuze and Guattari to exceed the anthropomorphic character of the subject results in a de-materialization and de-territorialization of the subject when affect is moved beyond it, for example, to a manifestation of becoming-animal. Here, affect becomes a way of creating a new ontology as a form of broad group belonging. However, Khanna (2012, 216) criticizes Deleuze's and Guattari's understandings of affect as vague and hollow: the category of affect becomes dull when it is expressed in prosaic statements of care or emotion. Her critique does not concern the existence of affect movements beyond the subject, expressivity, and observation but the circumstance that even the slightest mention of content within the ontological approach is identified as symptomatic and suspicious.

Deleuze's thinking, for that matter, makes both the division between textuality and materiality and the distinction between the outside-in and inside-out models of affect impossible. But in dealing with the movement of bodies through their dynamic interactions with other bodies, Deleuze (1992, 625) does not—contradictory to reductive views—deny or forget about subjectivity: "A body affects other bodies, or is affected by other bodies; it is this capacity for affecting and being affected that also defines a body in its individuality."

In this scenario, psychoanalysis is often described in a banal way, as if it has never been concerned with bodies, technologies, new ontologies, or the convergence between body and mind. As a matter of fact, it has become quite common within contemporary feminist affect studies to supersede psychoanalytic and deconstructive thinking on behalf of Deleuzian understanding of affect. In Khanna's view, psychoanalysis can easily be understood as an open system, a technology, and a questioning of the influence and ethics that Deleuzians ascribed the new ontologies of body technologies. Anu Koivunen takes psychoanalysis as an example of how feminist research has, over several decades, dealt with articulations of subjective and social experiences of injustice. She asks what the long history of feminist engagement with psychoanalysis has been but working with affects. Although feminist knowledge production has perhaps mainly moved "from desire to affect," she also demands on the bases of contemporary understandings of affect a reconceptualization of feminist psychoanalytic work (Koivunen 2010, 22; cf. Gorton 2007, 345; Berlant 2012).

Khanna (2012) sees affect as relationalities, the opening of the singular to the other. Instead of mediating a new ontology, affect points our attention to a materiality shaped by the technological, to confluences between ontology and the experiential or ontic—that is, to an epistemological task that sees affect as a spectral form of this convergence (230–231). In line with Khanna, many feminist theorists have seen the innovative stimulation and transformative meaning of affective politics precisely in the gap between the ontological and the epistemological. For example, in her article on affective solidarity, Clare Hemmings (2012) deals with the problematic opposition between ontological and epistemological standpoints about existence and politics.

In this opposition between the ontological and the epistemological, according to Hemmings (2012, 147), either an overindividualized perception of subjectivity or a deterministic view of the social world and its transformative perspectives is underlined, and in both cases, the significance of affect for gendered change is undermined (147). Feminist epistemologies have emphasized the importance of intersubjectivity and relationality both as critiques of existing fantasies about objective knowledge produced by autonomous subjects, and as ways to evaluate other forms of knowledge that prioritize dialogue and collectivity. This feminist work accentuates the meaning of emotions for others as a way of changing ourselves and the world, and turns affect into a way of moving between ontology and epistemology (on earlier feminist accounts, see among many Jaggar and Bordo 1989; Probyn 1993). In her critique of Eve Sedgwick, Hemmings (2012, 148) thinks that Sedgwick joins those who demand a refocusing of the ontological via a critical understanding of affect as a special key to life beyond or on the side of the social regulation of our existence; these thinkers reason that because we cannot have direct access to the ontological, bodily states give guidelines to how we exist instead of how we describe or understand how we exist.

Moreover, Hemmings (2005, 557) has noted that both Sedgwick and Massumi need to ignore the range of poststructuralist work that does not follow the pattern criticized by them, such work that actually attends to emotional investments, political connectivity, and the possibility of change. Hemmings's example is feminist standpoint epistemology, which she considers an established body of inquiry into the relationship *between* the ontological, epistemological, and transformative. Further, she thinks that its genealogical resonances echo back and forth across the last few decades, countering an affective chronology whose advocates prioritize grand shifts in ways that promote rather than caution against generalizations. Epistemology and ontology are, in her opinion, never separate and opposed.

METHODOLOGY

Thus, it can be noted that the critique of representationalism and the rise of new materialism, with its focus on questions of life and matter, lies in the center of a currently highly influential way of understanding and defining affect. As Ben Highmore (2010, 119) has put it, there is a tension between "a creaturely body," by which he means bones, gristle, mucus, bile, blood, and so on, and a textual body reflected back through metaphor or other figural elements, a dualism that, according to him, has long cast its shadow over philosophy. Highmore shows, however, the entanglement of materiality and textuality by asking if emotions are just metaphorical conventions when they are described by, for example, flavors, if the emotional condition of bitterness, for instance, releases the same gastriatic response as the ingestion of bitter flavors (120). I find his question of how we are to make our way from one modality of thinking to another decisive and highly important for our strivings to locate the meaning, knowledge, and experience of embodiment and bodily matter.

Despite some rapprochement between the views of those scholars who situate themselves within feminist cultural studies and those who underline the importance of asking ontological questions about matter and life, these strands still approach affects quite differently both theoretically and methodologically. While Sara Ahmed (2010b, 30) thinks that affect does not have autonomy and her purpose is to "begin with the messiness of the experiential, the unfolding of bodies into worlds, and the drama of contingency, how we are touched by what we are near." Hemmings (2005, 563), in her turn, endeavors to know how, then, we can engage affect in light of the critical projects in which we are engaged. This question is echoed by Clough (2010a, 228): "How to present affect so that the presentation performs its connection to individuation, near-actualization, virtuality, resonance and more? What now is method? What now is style?"

For Hemmings, the attention to affect is about everyday experience rather than macro abstractions, and affective attachments are unpredictable because they are haphazard. Kathleen Stewart's (2007, 3) methodological "advice" follows the same line of thinking, but on a quite abstract level: "To attend to ordinary affects is to trace how the potency of forces lies in their immanence to things that are both flighty and hardwired, shifty and unsteady but palpable too." Hemmings grasps the problem with the high level of abstraction among many advocates of new materialist and Deleuzian philosophy in approaching and studying affects. According to her, Brian Massumi's definition of affective autonomy, for example, places it outside the reach of critical interpretation. Affect is thus valuable to the extent that it is not vulnerable to the moods of theoretical impulses. In her view, "Massumi is suggesting not that we *look for* something outside culture, but that we *trust that* there is something outside culture" (2005, 562, 563; italics hers). Hemmings thinks that we are here left with a riddle-like description of affect as something scientists can detect the loss of, social scientists and cultural critics cannot interpret, but philosophers imagine. For Hemmings, Massumi is advocating a new academic attitude rather than a new method, an attitude or faith in something other than the social and cultural—a faith in the wonders that might emerge if we were not so attached to pragmatic negativity (559).

Elspeth Probyn (2010), in her turn, makes an important methodological observation when she notes that an abstract way of approaching affect and emotion places writing itself in an uninterested relation to affect. This she finds a contradiction in terms because affects are inherently interested: "How can you represent a sense of emotional and affective intensity if the feeling in question is generalized in the amorphous category of Affect?" (74). According to her, an epistemological point hovers in the background: a precise emotion demands precise description because affects have specific effects. Precise descriptions of the affective can also affect other concepts. Thus, Probyn thinks that some general gesture to affect does not work. Her advice is that if we want to refresh our concepts, we need to follow through on what different affects do at different levels (74).

In answering her question of how to engage affect, Clough refers to Mike Featherstone's thinking about the transformation of "consumer culture" and its deployment of a "body-without-image"—that is, the body of the digitalized image or simulation. In this way, Clough links affect studies to the changed relationship of the market and biopolitics in neoliberalism (2010a, 228–229). For Clough, the importance of a turn to affect is the way it pushes for a reformulation of methodology and presentational style "so that thought can become resonant with the current condition of generativity in a neoliberal political economy" (229). Instead of giving methodological answers, she formulates several significant questions: What is a critical cultural studies to be? How is social, political, and cultural change to be evaluated when measurement is no longer a matter of linear time but one of relationality, and where the frame of the relation also changes with the measurement (229)?

In elaborating the question of how affect studies have challenged the frameworks of critical thinking, many scholars deal with the issue of disciplinary boundaries and the ways of their questioning, crossing, or surpassing. Simultaneously, they formulate the challenging question of how characteristics of "natural phenomena" can be translated into sources of social, cultural, and political change. Clough (2010a), for example, underlines the necessity to rethink relationships between social sciences, humanities, and sciences, which have for a relatively long time directed our thinking about what matter is; what bodily forms of life are; and how we understand technology, sociality, and subjectivity. Interestingly enough, she states that a result of the rethinking of the interdisciplinary relationships might be overturning, from a hegemonic position, those sources of change taken for granted by scholars in the social sciences and the humanities, "such as political-economic power, cultural difference, semiotic chains of signification and identity and linguistic-based structures of meaning making" (223). Hence, Clough clearly wants to give more consideration to processes observed precisely within sciences. Therefore, rethinking change should happen, above all, in the social sciences and the humanities, while the "natural" sciences appear strangely "pure." Nevertheless, the study of sciences should be critical or should proceed with an openness to experimentation of a philosophical kind: we should think about "how we will conceptualize what the sciences are debating about perception, cognition, affect, bodies, matter, evolution, thermodynamic equilibrium, autopoiesis, energy, timespace, cosmic relationality, life and death" (224).

In the wake of these debates, the volume *Working with Affect in Feminist Readings: Disturbing Differences* (Liljeström and Paasonen 2010) explores the place and role of affect in feminist knowledge production in general and in textual methodology in particular. With a focus on practices of reading, the researchers investigate diverse methodological possibilities of working with and through affect in feminist research, asking, what implications does working with affect have for practices of reading and what kinds of considerations of scholarly agency, accountability, and ethics does it entail? Instead of positioning considerations of materiality, affect, and embodiment in opposition to textual analysis, their interrelations as intimate codependence are investigated. Thus, the volume includes texts on issues of embodiment as well as on the power of texts and images to move their viewers in highly bodily ways, and it does not attach itself to any singular theoretical framework, paradigm, or definition concerning the "affective turn."

In an interview, Lawrence Grossberg (2010, 314) emphasized that he disagrees with how Deleuze and Guattari are often used in concrete research, "where there is a leap from a set of ontological concepts to a description of an empirical and affective context." According to him, and it seems hard to disagree, affect is forced to cover too much ground: "There are too many forms, too many effectivities, too many organizations, too many apparatuses," and he thinks that "affect can let you off the hook" because it has too often come to serve as a "magical" term. He continues, "I think there is a lot of theorizing that does not do the harder work of specifying modalities and apparatuses of affect, distinguishing affect from other sorts of non-semantic effects, or . . . analyzing the articulations between . . . the ontological and the 'empirical' " (315).

Feminist Politics of Affect and the Importance of Contextualization

Feminist scholars have employed affect in examining both oppression and political solidarity and change. Simultaneously, just as affects can reproduce practices of hierarchy and control, they can also generate resistance and collectivity. On the one hand,

Sara Ahmed has shown in her book *The Promise of Happiness* (2010) how the structural and the affective are intertwined, how affects are constantly controlled and directed, and in what ways oppression is carried out on affective and emotional levels. On the other hand, Clare Hemmings (2005, 558) has commented that all feminist (standpoint) work shares in its divergence a commitment to political accountability, community, and the pertinence of positive affect for belonging and change. Feminist politics of affect is about collectivity, the relations between affects, emotions, and politics. Referring to Raymond Williams's well-known concept "structures of feeling" in which he offers a crucial link between cognition and affect, Heather Love (2007, 12) reflects on affect as a motivational system, grounds for forging new collectives, and the diagnostic usefulness of affect in relation to individual subjects.

In line with thinking of affects as collective, Lauren Berlant stresses—somewhat along with both Brian Massumi and Teresa Brennan—that affective atmospheres are shared, not solitary, and that bodies are continuously busy judging their environments and responding to the atmospheres in which they find themselves. Moreover, Berlant (2011, 15) refers here to Raymond Williams's notion of "the structure of feeling," and she suggests that affective responses exemplify shared historical time. Furthermore, other feminist scholars state the collective character of affects: Gatens (2004, 115) notes that the body is "always already wholly implicated in its milieu." Ahmed, however, underlines that before we are affected, before something happens that creates an impression on the skin, things are already in place that incline us to be affected in some ways more than others. To read affect from her perspective, we need better understandings of this "in place," and how the "in place" involves psychic and social dimensions, which means that in-place is not always in the same place (Ahmed 2010a, 230).

Berlant (2011, 158) makes a distinction between the context of affect (the structure of affect in a certain historical time) and a personal or subjective affective experience: "What looks like a shamed response in one decade, may look angry in another one," she states. For Berlant, "the evidence" suggests a distinction between the structure of an affect and what we call that affect when we encounter it: "What really matters are the repetition of relation, the buildup, the pressure over time that becomes a habit that seems intuitive. One assesses what affective events are according to one's education in attunement, in tracking repetition, form, and norm." Therefore, affects always have content and form. They are not types of pre-ideological transparency, but quite the opposite: they are learnt, hardly known, and often make more sense than the event (159). Hence, Berlant, in connection with thinking about the content and many-sidedness of affects, does not deny the value and meaning of subjectivity, such a crucial notion for feminist affect studies. She writes: "The multiple tethers of the subject to the world (and of the world's to the subject), expressed in relational activity and the work of intuition, are rarely registered in psychoanalytic and affect theory." Subsequently, she expresses that these theories continue to "tend to see the subject as having one or two clear and dominant channels of experience and which therefore often fail the analytic situation of describing the overdetermining work of ideology, atmosphere, the unconscious, distraction, ambivalence, attention—in short, the many ways the subject takes up a position in any episode and in the world" (287–288, n30).

In scholarly work, political, temporal, national, and so on, contexts are constantly produced. As a methodology, contextualization refers both to social reality described as context and to the contextualization of the context at hand as representation and interpretation. "Context" as a notion refers to both historiographic contexts describing the past and to contemporary temporal contexts. These double contexts influence each other (Liljeström 2004, 169–171). Thus, reflective and affective contextualization requires multiple and explicit contexts: this is necessary in order to show the interactions between research questions, affective readings and those contexts that are crystallized as history. At the same time, just as interpretations and stories about the past form contextualized sources for research, contemporary historical writing functions as an intertextual source for research. Besides the interaction between contexts, we affectively contextualize and historicize our own feminist research rhetoric and, especially, the research genres and academic fields to which we refer and in which we position ourselves. Therefore, it is of the utmost importance to pay attention to how institutionalized discursive practices organize our research and texts and how the politics of affects and historization appear in the positioning of the researcher. Hence, *context* means both those conditions that regulate the production of texts and those frameworks where the references and meanings of the researcher are formed. Thus, the meaning of context and affects is essential in historicizing concepts, thoughts, and theories.

References

Ahmed, S. 2004. *The Cultural Politics of Emotions*. Edinburgh: Edinburgh University Press.
Ahmed, S. 2008. "Imaginary Prohibitions: Some Preliminary Remarks on the Founding Gestures of the New Materialism." *European Journal of Women's Studies* 15: 23–39.
Ahmed, S. 2010a. *The Promise of Happiness*. Durham, NC: Duke University Press.
Ahmed, S. 2010b. "Happy Objects." In *The Affect Theory Reader*, edited by M. Gregg and G. Seigworth, 29–51. Durham, NC: Duke University Press.
Ahmed, S. 2010c. "Creating Disturbance: Feminism, Happiness and Affective Differences." In *Working with Affects in Feminist Readings: Disturbing Differences*, edited by M. Liljeström and S. Paasonen, 31–44. London and New York: Routledge.
Ahmed, S., and J. Stacey, eds. 2001. *Thinking through the Skin*. London: Routledge.
Armstrong, I. 2000. *The Radical Aesthetic*. Oxford: Blackwell.
Berlant, L. 1997. *The Queen of America Goes to Washington City*. Durham, NC: Duke University Press.
Berlant, L. 2000. "Intimacy: A Special Issue." In *Intimacy*, edited by L. Berlant, 1–8. Chicago: University of Chicago Press.
Berlant, L. 2008. *The Female Complaint: The Unfinished Business of Sentimentality in American Culture*. Durham, NC: Duke University Press.
Berlant, L. 2011. *Cruel Optimism*. Durham, NC: Duke University Press.
Berlant, L. 2012. *Desire/Love*. Brooklyn, NY: Punctum Books.

Bertelsen, L., and A. Murphie. 2010. "An Ethics of Everyday Infinities and Powers: Félix Guattari on Affect and the Refrain." In *The Affect Theory Reader*, edited by M. Gregg and G. Seigworth, 138–157. Durham, NC: Duke University Press.
Blackman, L., and V. Couze. 2010. "Affect." *Body & Society* 16 (1): 7–28.
Braidotti, R. 2006. *Transpositions: On Nomadic Ethics*. Cambridge: Polity Press.
Braidotti, R. 2013. *The Posthuman*. Cambridge: Polity Press.
Brennan, T. 2004. *The Transmission of Affect*. Ithaca, NY: Cornell University Press.
Brown, W. 1995. *States of Injury: Power and Freedom in Late Modernity*. Princeton, NJ: Princeton University Press.
Brown, W. 1999. "Resisting Left Melancholia." *boundary 2* 25 (3): 19–27.
Butler, J. 1997. *The Psychic Life of Power: Theories in Subjection*. Redwood City, CA: Stanford University Press.
Butler, J. 2004. *Precarious Life. The Powers of Mourning and Violence*. New York: Verso.
Clough, P. T. 2007. Introduction to *The Affective Turn: Theorizing the Social*, edited by Patricia Ticineto Clough and Jean Halley, 1–33. Durham, NC: Duke University Press.
Clough, P. T. 2010a. "Afterword." *Body & Society* 1 (16): 222–230.
Clough, P. T. 2010b. "The Affective Turn: Political Economy, Biomedia and Bodies." In *The Affect Theory Reader*, edited by M. Gregg and G. Seigworth, 206–225. Durham, NC: Duke University Press.
Cvetkovich, A. 1992. *Mixed Feelings: Feminism, Mass Culture and Victorian Sensationalism*. New Brunswick, NJ: Rutgers University Press.
Cvetkovich, A. 2003. *An Archive of Feelings: Trauma, Sexuality and Lesbian Public Cultures*. Durham, NC: Duke University Press.
Deleuze, G. 1988. *Spinoza: Practical Philosophy*. San Francisco, CA: City Lights.
Deleuze, G. 1992. "Ethology: Spinoza and Us." In *Incorporations*, edited by J. Crary and S. Kwinter, 625–633. Brooklyn, NY: Zone Books.
Deleuze, G., and F. Guattari. 1987. *A Thousand Plateaus*. Minneapolis: University of Minnesota Press.
Frye, M. 1983. *The Politics of Reality: Essays in Feminist Theory*. Berkeley, CA: Crossing Press.
Gatens, M. 2004. "Privacy and the Body: The Publicity of Affect." In *Privacies: Philosophical Evaluations*, edited by B. Rössler, 113–132. Redwood City, CA: Stanford University Press.
Gorton, K. 2007. "Theorizing Emotion and Affect: Feminist Engagements." *Feminist Theory* 8 (3): 333–348.
Gregg, M., and G. J. Seigworth. 2010. "An Inventory of Shimmers." In *The Affect Theory Reader*, edited by Gregg and Seigworth, 1–25. Durham, NC: Duke University Press.
Grossberg, L. 2010. "Affect's Future: Rediscovering the Virtual in the Actual." In *The Affect Theory Reader*, edited by Gregg and Seigworth, 309–338. Durham, NC: Duke University Press.
Grosz, E. 1994. *Volatile Bodies: Toward a Corporeal Feminism*. Bloomington: Indiana University Press.
Guattari, F. 1995. *Chaosmosis: An Ethico-Aesthetic Paradigm*. Bloomington: Indiana University Press.
Hemmings, C. 2005. "Invoking Affect. Cultural Theory and the Ontological Turn." *Cultural Studies* 19 (5): 548–567.
Hemmings, C. 2012. "Affective Solidarity: Feminist Reflexivity and Political Transformation." *Feminist Theory* 13 (2): 147–161.

Highmore, B. 2010. "Bitter after Taste: Affect, Food, and Social Aesthetics." In *The Affect Theory Reader*, edited by Gregg and Seigworth, 118–137. Durham, NC: Duke University Press.

Hird, M. 2004. "Feminist Matters: New Materialist Considerations of Sexual Difference." *Feminist Theory* 5 (2): 223–232.

hooks, b. 1989. *Talking Back: Thinking Feminist, Thinking Black*. Cambridge, MA: South End Press.

Jaggar, A. 1989. "Love and Knowledge: Emotion in Feminist Epistemology." In *Gender/Body/Knowledge. Feminist Reconstructions of Being and Knowing*, edited by A. Jaggar and S. Bordo, 145–171. New Brunswick, NJ: Rutgers University Press.

Jaggar, A. and S. Bordo, eds. 1989. *Gender/Body/Knowledge. Feminist Reconstruction of Being and Knowing*. New Brunswick, NJ: Rutgers University Press.

Koivunen, A. 2010. "An Affective Turn? Reimagining the Subject of Feminist Theory." In *Working with Affect in Feminist Readings: Disturbing Differences*, edited by M. Liljeström and S. Paasonen, 8–28. London and New York: Routledge.

Khanna, R. 2012. "Touching, Unbelonging, and the Absence of Affect." *Feminist Theory* 13 (2): 213–232.

Liljeström, M. 2004. *Useful Selves: Russian Women's Autobiographical Texts from Postwar Period*. Helsinki: Kikimora Publications.

Liljeström, M., and S. Paasonen, eds. 2010. *Working with Affect in Feminist Readings: Disturbing Differences*. London and New York: Routledge.

Lorde, A. 1984. *Sister Outsider: Essays and Speeches*. Berkeley, CA: Crossing Press.

Love, H. 2007. *Feeling Backward: Loss and the Politics of Queer History*. Cambridge, MA: Harvard University Press.

Marks, L. 2002. *Touch: Sensuous Theory And Multisensory Media*. Minneapolis: University of Minnesota Press.

Massumi, B. 2002. *Parables for the Virtual: Movement, Affect, Sensation*. Durham, NC: Duke University Press.

Munt, S. 2007. *Queer Attachments: The Cultural Politics of Shame*. Aldershot, UK: Ashgate.

Ngai, S. 2005. *Ugly Feelings*. Cambridge, MA: Harvard University Press.

Pearce, L. 1997. *Feminism and the Politics of Reading*. London: Arnold.

Probyn, E. 1993. *Sexing the Self: Gendered Positions in Cultural Studies*. London: Routledge.

Probyn, E. 2005. *Blush: Faces of Shame*. Minneapolis: University of Minnesota Press.

Probyn, E. 2010. "Writing Shame." In *The Affect Theory Reader*, edited by M. Gregg and G. Seigworth, 71–90. Durham, NC: Duke University Press.

Riley, D. 2000. *The Words of Selves: Identification, Solidarity, Irony*. Redwood City, CA: Stanford University Press.

Ringrose, J., and R. Coleman. 2013. "Looking and Desiring Machines: A Feminist Deleuzian Mapping of Bodies and Affects." In *Deleuze and Research Methodologies*, edited by J. Ringrose and R. Coleman, 125–144. Edinburgh: Edinburgh University Press.

Sedgwick, E. K. 2003. *Touching Feeling: Affect, Pedagogy, Performativity*. Durham, NC: Duke University Press.

Sedgwick, E. K., and A. Frank. 1995. "Shame in the Cybernetic Fold: Reading Silvan Tomkins." In *Shame and Its Sisters: A Silvan Tomkin Reader*, edited by E. K. Sedgwick and A. Frank, 1–32. Durham, NC: Duke University Press.

Skeggs, B. 2005. "The Making of Class and Gender through Visualizing Moral Subject Formation." *Sociology* 39 (5): 965–982.

Sobchack, V. 2004. *Carnal Thoughts: Embodiment and Moving Image Culture*. Berkeley: University of California Press.

Solomon, R. C. 2004. *Thinking about Feeling: Contemporary Philosophers on Emotions*. New York: Oxford University Press.

Stewart, K. 2007. *Ordinary Affects*. Durham, NC: Duke University Press.

Terada, R. 2001. *Feeling in Theory: Emotion after the "Death of the Subject."* Cambridge, MA: Harvard University Press.

Young, I. M. 1990. *Throwing like a Girl and Other Essays in Feminist Philosophy and Social Theory*. Bloomington: Indiana University Press.

Woodward, K. 2009. *Statistical Panic: Cultural Politics and Poetics of Emotions*. Durham, NC: Duke University Press.

CHAPTER 2

AGENCY

LOIS MCNAY

INTRODUCTION

The idea of agency is a key concept in feminist theory; yet, despite this centrality, its meaning is widely contested. In an immediate sense, agency appears to be a straightforward idea denoting the ability of individuals to have some kind of transforming effect or impact on the world. But this apparent simplicity is belied by the fact that although agency is a universal capacity, it is socially realized in a variable and unequal fashion: it means different things according to the cultural context and some individuals and groups clearly have more agency than others. In other words, agency is inseparable from the analysis of power and, therefore, is not so much a thing in itself as a vehicle for thinking through broader issues, such as the nature of freedom and constraint. Matters of power and emancipation are, of course, paramount for feminists given that throughout history, and in a variety of ways, women have been repeatedly denied the status of autonomous social actors. But it is also precisely these matters that are the source of disagreement among feminists inasmuch as they bring to the fore the twofold significance of agency as both a descriptive and a normative category. Feminist analysis of what women actually do in the world, the recovery and revalorization of unnoticed and invisible forms of women's agency, is inextricably tied to its emancipatory political project of overcoming gender inequality. While most feminists are in broad agreement that gendered agency needs to be re-envisioned beyond the conceptual limitations of the sovereign actor, there is little agreement about the normative entailments of such a project.

In this chapter, I trace key developments in feminist thought on agency through this underlying tension between its descriptive and normative modes. Feminist theories of agency that endorse certain modes of action as inherently emancipatory are often held to be problematic because of the essentialist assumptions about the nature of femininity that underpin them and also because of their explicit prescriptiveness. This adjudicative agenda is somewhat mitigated in feminist theories of agency as resistance that are grounded in a more nuanced understanding of the workings of power in relation to gendered subjectivity and in more inclusive notions of emancipatory action as subversion from within. Ideas of resistance have themselves been subject to extensive criticism, however, partly for their tendency to romanticize mundane practices and partly for their failure to appreciate that agency need not always take an oppositional form. Feminist anthropologists argue that resistance is a peculiarly Western preoccupation, one that leads to the discounting of other types of active agency in which women in nonsecular societies create meaningful identities for themselves within, not against, the dominant cultural norms. In order to retain a sensitivity to other modalities of agency, some theorists maintain that the feminist analytic or descriptive agenda should be separated from its prescriptive one. It is thought that holding the latter in abeyance will permit greater appreciation of the thick texture of agential practice in other cultures. This is an unsatisfactory solution, however, since it rests on a naive understanding of the separability of fact from norm and weakens the inherently political nature of feminist critique. I go on to consider how some theorists have sought to bypass the normative dilemmas of judgment that frequently accompany debates on agency by radically transforming the ontological framework within which to think about the capacity for action. While the work of postidentity and posthuman theorists has provocative implications for thought on agency, its plausibility as the grounds for feminist critique and politics is undermined by its speculative and socially weightless nature. A challenge for feminist theory in the future is to formulate notions of agency in the light of the intensification of gender and other inequalities and growing forms of social and economic vulnerability that have been unleashed by neoliberal modes of governance.

Descriptive and Prescriptive Aspects of Agency

Concepts of agency are mostly situated somewhere along the broad theoretical spectrum bounded by voluntarism, on the one end, and determinism, on the other. Agency is commonly understood as the capacity of a person (or other living and material entities) to intervene in the world in a manner that is deemed, according to some criterion or another, to be independent or relatively autonomous. In virtue of its purposive quality, agency often overlaps with a cluster of adjacent concepts—autonomy, free will, intentionality, choice, reflexivity, and so on, though the substantive meaning of each of these is deeply contested. Differently put, agency denotes a cluster of actions considered to be categorically distinct from the types of unreflective, habitual, and instinctual behaviors which are held to be quasi-automatic responses to external structural forces. If individuals are to be understood to be more than docile subjects or passive bearers of pre-given social roles, then purposive agency must be a fundamental and self-evident property of personhood. After all, women have frequently overcome considerable symbolic and material constraints to make their presence felt in the world in innovative and challenging ways. Yet, while agency is counterposed to determinism, it is not reducible to the voluntarism of the sovereign agent. For many theorists, it does not make sense to think of agency outside a social context, as a purely abstract set of capacities and potentials, because the ability to act is always mediated by the dominant norms and relations of power that shape any situation. It may well be a potentially universal feature of personhood but, given that its substantive content varies according to context and that it is realized unevenly—some individuals have demonstrably "more" agency than others—this means that it is also always a situated conception, inseparable from an analysis of power. It hardly needs restating that feminist theories of agency are particularly attuned to such issues of power and domination, given that, until relatively recently, patriarchy has construed women as being largely incapable of autonomous action and, by implication, of full personhood in virtue of the inherently fragile, volatile, and generally "inferior" condition of female embodiment.

The immediate problem that confronts feminist theorists, then, is how to uncover and revalorize the myriad of neglected forms of female agency without falling back into voluntarist theories of sovereign agency that are, it is widely agreed, unsuited to the purpose. The feminist critique of "sovereign agency" is well established, but its basic underlying claim is that by cleaving to hyperbolic notions of the actor as an autonomous, unencumbered, and fully rational being (Teflon man), a masculinist perspective on the world is tacitly upheld. This perspective fails to sufficiently address the foundational fact of social interdependence and the associated idea that individuals are formed through embodied interaction and social norms, rather than preexist them in any simple sense. In practice, this means that it disregards the concrete circumstances of many women's lives, which, because of the gendered division of labor, have been and continue to be deeply circumscribed by conventional norms of femininity and the demands of others. Ideas of sovereign agency also implicitly reinforce a heroic model of action that, from the classical social contract theorists through Marx and Weber to Arendt and Rawls, is understood in grandiose terms as a public, inaugural type of activity, a break with the world that institutes a new kind of being. This disembodied heroism downgrades mundane and practical types of social agency, many of them associated with the private and domestic spheres and more often than not carried out by women. Care work, domestic labor, childrearing are viewed as secondary, quasi-natural activities of little intrinsic merit or social significance, belonging to what Arendt famously called the "dark background of mere givenness" (1973, 301). Against this background, the mode of agency as transcendence has not only greater social significance but also an enhanced moral status. Relational ties and empathetic bonds associated with the situated, and therefore feminine perspective of the concrete other are relegated to a secondary ethical status in comparison with the detached and impartial morality associated with the masculine perspective of the Generalized Other (e.g., Benhabib 1992).

Following from the critique of the sovereign actor, feminists are in broad agreement that agency needs to be rethought as a situated, embodied, and relational phenomenon. The situatedness of agency denotes the idea, discussed earlier, that while it is a universal potential, the substantive content and form of action is unthinkable outside specific cultural and social contexts. It also has an additional meaning derived from the phenomenological idea of the situation—namely, that agency cannot be fully understood from an exclusively objective perspective but must also be grasped from the subjective perspective of the individual's own experience of the world. Such an interpretative approach does not seek to recover the experiential "truth" of women's social existence but rather a fuller explanation of the ways in which an individual's self-understanding may motivate or disincline her to act in certain ways. Emphasis on the embodied nature of agency draws attention, inter alia, to action as a type of practice that, while it has existential sense and purpose, need not take the form of full, reasoned intentionality. It highlights the emotional and affective dimensions of agency and also, most importantly from a feminist perspective, the ways in which dynamics of social control are internalized as bodily norms. A significant swathe of social action takes the form of habitual, routinized, pre-reflexive types of practice, and it is at this embodied level that the hierarchical social structures of class, gender, and race are often naturalized and secured in an "invisible" fashion. The objective structures and tendencies that shape the world are taken into the body as a set of durable psychological and physical dispositions (e.g., the feminized habitus) and are then endlessly reproduced and also subtly transformed in the flux of daily existence (see Bourdieu 2000, 128–159). As a relational phenomenon, agency displaces the ontological primacy granted to the monological, pre-social agent, replacing it with a twofold emphasis on its constitution through intersubjective relations and structural hierarchies of power. Agency is not a solipsistic assertion of individual will but is inextricably bound up in the web of the interpersonal relations constitutive of social being that give rise to an endless diversity of pragmatic shared projects and goals. Subtending these horizontal intersubjective relations are vertical relations of power—hierarchies of gender, class, and race—that have a profound influence on action and life trajectories in general but often operate at one remove from dynamics of immediate social interaction.

Despite broad agreement about the general theoretical lines along which agency should be theorized, feminists vigorously disagree over the determinate content of any particular conception. These disagreements are indicative of an inescapable feature of thinking about agency in a feminist context—namely, that it is simultaneously a descriptive and normative enterprise. As an emancipatory political project, feminism is closely wedded to the idea of critique, that is, to a type of critical thought that describes the world in such a way as to make visible avenues for progressive social change immanent in the present moment. The disclosure of unnoticed and undervalued forms of women's agency is simultaneously an attempt to reflect on potential forms of action that may, in some way, empower women and contribute to the dismantling of persistent gender inequalities. This intertwinement of descriptive and normative projects is brought into sharp relief in discussions of agency, and while feminists may loosely share a diagnosis of women's secondary social position, they are far from agreed on the best way of changing it.

Famously, for example, ideas of women's moral agency as an ethics of care, formulated by Carole Gilligan (1982), Virginia Held (1993), and others have been criticized for deploying an idealized notion of interpersonal relations—paradigmatically expressed in the mother-child dyad—while disregarding how this intersects with gendered dynamics that associate women with a traditional domestic role. In the face of what they see as the exaggerated stress placed on a "good" relationality by care theorists, other feminists have sought to retrieve a qualified notion of independent agency or "relational autonomy" (Mackenzie and Stoljar 2000). Given feminism's commitment to empowering women, it cannot afford to dispense with ideas of autonomy lest this erode the grounds for emancipatory critique and progressive political intervention. Yet, while these feminists are united in their opposition to autarkic notions of agency, on the one side, and romanticized relationality, on the other, they remain divided over whether relational autonomy should be conceptualized in substantive or procedural terms. In the view of theorists of substantive autonomy, some ways in which women choose to live must be judged to be intrinsically lacking in autonomy, as the product of a false consciousness that unthinkingly reproduces oppressive, stereotypical notions of femininity. Speaking of teenage mothers, for instance, Natalie Stoljar maintains that "women who accept the norm that pregnancy and motherhood increase their worthiness accept something false. And because of the internalisation of the norm they do not have the capacity to conceive it as false" (Stoljar 2000, 109). On the view of proceduralists, however, what matters is not the substantive content of a particular lifestyle as much as whether the choice to live in that way is made in a fully reflexive manner—that is, as part of a self-conscious commitment to realizing a consistent set of ethical values in one's life whatever they may be (e.g., Friedman 2003). Many feminist debates about women's agency turn around these procedural and substantive issues—debates about whether or not women should choose to undergo elective cosmetic surgery, whether sex work/prostitution may be viewed as an empowered life choice or act of desperation, whether the wearing of the veil should be regarded as submission to patriarchy or a political statement, and so on (e.g., Chambers 2008; Frank 2006; Scott 2010).

There are two major problems with feminist attempts to conceptualize agency as relational autonomy. First, they remain narrowly focused on the conventional problem of individual choice—stuck in what Kimberly Hutchings (2013) terms a "loosers/choosers" paradigm—rather than focusing on the underlying power structures that create the possibilities for gendered agency in the first place. Second, both procedural and substantive notions of autonomy may easily become a smokescreen for acts of judgement and prescription, thereby setting up "dynamics of patronage and resentment" in which some feminists seem "to know better than those of (or to) whom they speak" (Hutchings 2013, 22). Ultimately, this adjudicative style of thought on agency undermines a fundamental feminist commitment to difference and forging a pluralist politics open to as yet unrealized paths of action rather than following preordained procedures and goals. The move of feminist theorists to conceptualize agency as resistance goes some way to overcoming these two problems, as we will see in the next section. Ideas of resistance reroute theoretical discussions of agency away from matters of individual choice toward those pertaining to power and the underlying conditions of possibility for different modalities of action. They also shift thought on agency away from a normatively stipulative mode toward ethically open-ended notions of subversion from within.

Agency as Resistance

A decisive moment in theorizing agency comes with third-wave feminism and its application of elements of poststructural theory to address issues of gender and social difference. Agency is no longer thought to be so much on the axis of voluntarism versus determinism—that is, a matter of freedom from constraint. Rather, it is understood as a type of practice that is brought into being and given its determinate content by constraint itself—namely, agency as resistance. Although the norms and practices through which individuals understand themselves are given to them by their social context, the way in which these are realized in daily life are not straightforward. Even the seemingly natural and inevitable norms that shape gender identity are always mediated through multifarious individual practices and thus reproduced in a way that may permit variation, and even innovation. This space of structured indeterminacy or regulated liberty is the space of freedom, the site where acts of resistance to the disciplinary control of individuals may emerge.

It is the influential work of Judith Butler (1990, 1993) on gender performativity that offers the fullest account of what agency as resistance might mean. On her view, gender norms have an essentially reiterative structure that ensures both their deep social entrenchment and the grounds for their potential subversion. The compulsive cultural reiteration of gender norms guarantees their pervasive materialization in the bodies of individuals as the seemingly natural identities of heterosexual masculinity and femininity. Yet, the very fact that cultures need to ceaselessly reiterate these norms is indicative of the latter's fragility, of the extent to which heterosexuality is not natural or inevitable but a set of culturally defined behaviors that have to be laboriously elicited from the bodies of individuals. This foundational precariousness inherent in the reiterative structure of gender yields the possibility of subversion from within. Immanent in the enactment of gender norms is the possibility that they will be performed differently, that something will go awry in the process of reiteration, and individuals will not automatically reproduce the cultural stereotypes imposed on them but will, in fact, displace them. Hence Butler's celebrated analysis of gay drag as a subversion of the apparent givenness of heterosexual identity through its augmented parody of the multiple but suppressed forms of desire and identification (the performed identity, sexuality of the performer, and sex of the performer) that underpin even the most supposedly secure of subject positions. As an imitation without an original, drag draws attention to the performative and contingent nature of all identities. Gay marriage, same-sex parenting, or gay men fathering children with straight women can all be said to enact analogous subversions in their appropriation of conventional forms of heterosexuality to legitimate "excentric" or nonconventional relations of love, care, and commitment. Contra theorists of substantive autonomy, the logic of resistance demonstrates that empowered agency need not involve an outright rejection of oppressive norms but rather operates through displacement from within, receiving its specific form and rationale from the constraint itself.

A normative entailment of conceiving agency as resistance is that there is no blueprint for emancipation. The pathway to freedom cannot be prescribed in advance—by exhorting women to reject patriarchal notions of femininity—but rather emerges in a spontaneous and relatively unpredictable fashion in the multifarious ways in which individuals enact gendered and other cultural norms. Resistance moves feminism beyond the adjudicative mode of some of its formulations of agency as autonomy toward more open-ended and experimental forms of politicized ethics. Freedom is not about stipulating the way individuals "ought" to live but rather encouraging them to interrogate the limits of what appears to be natural and inevitable in present forms of identity and attempting to go beyond them. Resistance is predicated on a subtle understanding of the workings of power and desire in which it is unrealistic to expect individuals to reject wholesale the very symbolic structures through which they understand themselves as active subjects. Norms can be a source of pleasure and meaning as well as subjugation. It may be infeasible therefore to stipulate that women should reject outright certain types of femininity as inherently oppressive because of the deep investments ("passionate attachments") they have in them as desiring subjects. In short, agency as resistance rebuts political prescription and endorses a processual notion of emancipation as a particular way of inhabiting social structures to create oppositional spaces and "pathways" to empowerment.

Despite its tremendous impact, Butler's idea of performative agency has also attracted considerable criticism. One line of criticism is that Butler does not, in fact, give us a theory of agency so much as an account of some of the structural preconditions that are necessary (but not sufficient) to explain its emergence. Her structural focus on the formation of subjectivity in language leads to the misleading construal of resistance as a linguistic process of reiteration and resignification rather than as the situated practices of embodied agents. The emphasis on the reiterative structure of gender is a deliberate theoretical move on Butler's part intended to circumvent voluntarist misreadings of performativity as freely willed performance in which individuals choose to rework embodied norms regardless of social constraints. On her view, intention and will cannot be said to precede action in any simple, causal sense; rather, the potential for action is generated by the reiterative structure of signification itself. However, as a number of critics have pointed out, this rather esoteric and abstract recasting of agency as linguistic dynamics leaves important questions unanswered, especially those that pertain to the political or oppositional impact of any given act of subversion.

It is not the imitative structure of gender itself—its intrinsic repeatability—that gives action its subversive political force; rather, this force is generated by the concrete conditions in which action takes place: the nature of the audience, the intention of the performer, and the site of the performance. In a conventional theatrical context, for instance, drag has little if any disruptive effect. In fact, in many ways, it could be said to obliquely reaffirm dominant heteronormativity. Drag only acquires a destabilizing force when it is played out in specific contexts and interpreted in a particular way by a relatively politicized audience. The structural rendering of agency as resignification has led some feminists to criticize Butler for endorsing a rarefied cultural politics "removed from our everyday ways of talking and thinking about ourselves" (Fraser 1995, 67). Other feminists have rebuked her for seeking to provide a universal guarantee for counterhegemonic action as an ever-present structural possibility, when, in fact, none exists. Agency is always historically singular: "if the ability to effect change in the world and in oneself is historically and culturally specific . . . then the meaning and sense of agency cannot be fixed in advance" (Mahmood 2005, 14–15; Zerilli 2005, 57).

Another set of criticisms focuses on the difficulties inherent to the formulation of counterhegemonic agency as resistance—namely, that it romanticizes mundane social practices, attributing them with a questionable contestatory force. This is not to deny that individuals routinely display active, creative agency in the shaping of their lives; they are not passive bearers of pre-given social roles. It is, however, to insist on a careful understanding of what it is that renders a given action or set of practices "resistant," how it is precisely that they can be deemed to challenge, albeit in an tangential manner, the hegemonic order. Too often, the idea of resistance is used to denote any kind of meaning-giving activity that, given that the latter is a ubiquitous feature of social life, leads potentially to the indiscriminate application of the label of resistance to many types of action. Indeed, in Wendy Brown's view, ideas of resistance form part of a postmodern sensibility that is wary of the authority of any type of normative critique, and takes refuge instead in the "local viewpoint and tendency toward positioning without mapping" (Brown 1995, 49). This deliberately constrained perspectivalism renders ideas of resistance ineffectual as coherent political responses to types of social injustice: "resistance goes nowhere in particular, has no inherent attachments, and hails no particular vision . . . resistance is an effect of and reaction to power, not an arrogation of it" (Brown 1995, 49). From this perspective, some critics maintain that Butler's idea of performativity results in a narrow "lifestyle" politics of identity that overestimates its own subversive impact while failing to address its own implication in the rationale of a commodified individualism (Fraser 2013). In short, the construal of agency as resistance is problematic because it is far from clear what is being "resisted" and what, if any, are the "political" effects of such actions.

Agency, Judgment, and Critique

Skepticism about notions of resistance takes on a significant new dimension in the context of cross-cultural analysis, leading a number of feminists working on women in non-Western contexts to rethink ideas of agency beyond its parameters. Their claim is that although, on the face of it, ideas of resistance appear to disrupt conventional accounts of the sovereign actor, they in fact fail to break fully from a "liberal political imaginary" in their presumption that the individual will always inherently desire her own freedom and liberation (Mahmood 2005, 155). The elevation of resistance to a universal feature of agency is at heart a Western liberal notion that has little analytical relevance to the lives and practices of women and other subordinate groups living in a nonsecular context: "the desire for freedom and liberation is a historically situated desire whose motivational force cannot be assumed a priori" (Mahmood 2001, 223). Lila Abu-Lughod argues, for instance, that the preoccupation with uncovering subversive intent in situations of constraint can easily slide into a romanticization of agency that underestimates the workings of power and reads "all forms of resistance as signs of the resilience and creativity of the human spirit in its refusal to be dominated" (Abu-Lughod 1990, 42). To avoid this, she recommends a change in theoretical emphasis, insofar as everyday practices are not interpreted in terms of their putative resistant qualities but are, instead, understood as symptoms of the complex, often indirect, and conflicting ways in which forms of power intersect to secure subordination. Although Abu-Lughod does not entirely abandon the idea of resistance, the implication of her argument is that it should be used sparingly at best in the analysis of the agential practices of subordinated groups.

Saba Mahmood takes this skepticism a step further arguing, in the *Politics of Piety*, that the category of resistance is analytically irrelevant to understanding many of the agential practices of women in non-Western societies that do not correspond to its subversive logic. Not only is the contestatory force imputed to acts of resistance often not sufficiently justified, but agency is also reified in schematic dualisms of conformity and subversion, domination, and resistance. The search, by Western feminists, for submerged acts of resistance invokes a "teleology of progressive politics," where agency is unfailingly regarded as motivated by the ahistorical desire to be free from subordination: "to analyze people's actions in terms of realized or frustrated attempts at social transformation is to necessarily reduce the heterogeneity of life to the rather flat narrative of succumbing to or resisting relations of domination" (Mahmood 2001, 222). In fact, on Mahmood's view, many societies have flourished with discourses other than those of emancipation and it is therefore crucial to understand agency according to its own immanent logic and cultural specificity. What may appear from a Western perspective to be a case of "deplorable passivity and docility" may in fact turn out to be an active way of inhabiting norms. Drawing on Foucault's work on practices of the self, she examines acts of veiling and the other pietist practices of female participants in the mosque movement in Egypt as a deliberate process of ethical formation oriented not to the refusal of dominant norms but toward the establishment of a meaningful and valued role for themselves within the terms of their culture.

Mahmood's critique of agency as resistance is motivated in part by pressing political concerns. In the aftermath of the attacks of September 11, it is all too easy for feminist cross-cultural critiques of patriarchy to become unwitting instruments of an anti-Muslim Islamaphobia. This troubling misappropriation of feminism is, in Mahmood's view, inadvertently facilitated by its dual character as both an analytical and normative project, as "both a diagnosis of women's status across cultures and a prescription for changing the situation of women who are understood to be marginalized, subordinated or oppressed" (Mahmood 2005, 10). These analytical and normative elements become blurred when the failure of secular feminists to discern a subversive import in, say, the religious practices of non-Western women becomes part of a denunciation of these cultures as oppressive tout court. This is paradigmatically expressed in interpretations of the veil as the "symbol and evidence of the violence Islam has inflicted upon women" regardless of the part it plays in allowing women to actively affirm an esteemed identity through the virtuous inhabitation of traditional norms. It is easy to see how feminist judgments, no matter how well intentioned, may be misleadingly appropriated by those with a more aggressive, right-wing political agenda. To thwart such an unfortunate complicity, Mahmood argues, the feminist analysis of agency should be detached from its normative, political project of women's emancipation. By suspending the goals of a prescriptive political agenda, greater space is created for a thicker understanding of agency in its array of modalities, "we leave open the possibility that the task of thinking may proceed in directions not dictated by the logic and pace of immediate political events" (2005, 196).

Mahmood recognizes that it is naïve to think that the analysis of agency can be detached altogether from normative questions of emancipation; these two forms of inquiry cannot remain deaf to each other. But, despite this acknowledgment, her work is pervaded by a simplified understanding of facts and norms in which objective description seems to be easily detachable from normatively informed critique. The relation between the two is in fact more complicated and ineluctable than Mahmood allows, because even thick ethnocentric description, alive to the variations of agency, is necessarily always a particular interpretation of the social world informed in some way by the prior theoretical and normative commitments of its author. Indeed, Mahmood's own "thick" ethnography is driven by a latent normative agenda (the rebuttal of secular liberalism) that undermines its supposed analytic detachment. This interpretative bias has resulted in criticisms of her study for its narrowness and failure to situate the pious practices of the mosque movement women in a broader social and political context. Mahmood does not take into account, for instance, that the majority of women involved in the movement in Cairo are relatively well-off Egyptians. Their privileged class location may well enable them to find a way of enhancing their own personal autonomy through devotional practices, but their reproduction of patriarchal norms of womanhood "effectively delimited the agential possibilities of Muslim women from other social strata and with affinities to other ideologies" (Bangstad 2011, 32–33). She is also criticized for underplaying the internal complexities of modern Salafism, which is a variegated religious movement embracing a spectrum of tendencies—some more amenable to women's rights than others—and maintaining differing alliances to other political movements, both secular and religious. Because she brackets the wider political and social context, Mahmood's study has been accused of ahistoricism and perpetuating a reverse orientalism, or "mirror-game," that opposes a schematic image of Salafi piety as the radical "other" to an equally monolithically conceived Western secularism (Bangstad 2011, 39). In short, the methodological naivety of Mahmood's proposal that the suspension of normative assumptions somehow ensures a fuller account of agential practices is only underscored by her own failure to adequately consider how her underlying normative agenda may skew her ethnography.

The simplification of the fact-norm relation means that Mahmood frames the feminist analysis of agency in terms of a misleading antithesis between moral prescriptivism, on one side, and value-free description, on the other. An inescapable consequence of feminism's status as a political movement committed to promoting gender equality is that an ineliminable normative thread runs through its key interpretative concepts, such as agency. The point of describing the world from the perspective of women's agency is to facilitate deeper understanding of the various ways in which gender inequalities are secured and to trace out possible pathways to empowerment. Contra Mahmood's depiction, this ineradicable normative thread need not inevitably take the form of ethnocentric denunciation or an uncritical advocacy of liberal norms under the guise of a spurious neutrality. As Seyla Benhabib puts it, "It does not follow that if we respect human beings as culture-creating beings that we must either 'rank or order' their worlds as a *whole* or disrespect them by dismissing their life-worlds altogether. We may disagree with *some* aspect of the moral, ethical or evaluative practices without dismissing or holding in disrespect their life worlds altogether" (Benhabib 2002, 41).

Contrary to Mahmood's exaggerated account, there has never been a simple alliance between Western secular liberalism and feminism, the latter has always had a tangential and critical relation to the former. As a consequence, feminists have long sought sensitive solutions to the issue of critique and judgement in the context of an intrinsic commitment to overcoming the subordination of women and respecting the differences of others. Benhabib, for instance, has tried to reconcile these imperatives by redefining universalism in sufficiently anti-essentialist terms as to provide quasi-transcendental criteria on which to base political judgments. In her view, cultures are not self-enclosed, internally unified totalities that are fundamentally alien to each other, but are hybrid, mutually permeable entities that have features in common as well as deep differences. It is such commonalities that provide the potential grounds for cross-cultural critique that simultaneously endeavors to respect cultural pluralism. Alternatively, Linda Zerilli uses Arendt's notion of enlarged thought to develop an idea of cross-cultural exchange as both the gesture of empathic understanding between self and other and the simultaneous awareness of the impossibility of such a gesture. Judgment on this model does not take a prescriptive form but involves the capacity to bring together the perspectives of identification and estrangement and to hold them in tension rather than reconcile them: to "see from multiple standpoints in order to form a critical opinion and to make a judgement" (Zerilli 2009, 313). Similarly, Judith Butler develops an idea of critique that is not oriented to definitive judgment but toward an exploration of the historical conditions that constitute our "affective and evaluative responses" (Butler 2013, 109). There are no easy solutions to these problems of cross-cultural analysis, but the work of these thinkers demonstrates that a normative commitment need not take the form of an overbearing prescriptivism. Of course, the latter is always a potential danger so, at the very least, feminist theorists must deploy a heightened methodological awareness in their own thought about agency, a commitment to a processual normativity rather than a teleological prescriptivism and an attentiveness to the varying modalities of power through which actors are both enabled and constrained (see McNay 2014).

Postidentity Agency

One way through the Gordian knot of descriptive and normative issues surrounding discussions of agency is to transform the theoretical frame altogether. This has been the approach of recent feminist theorizing from what might be loosely termed a post-identity perspective. On this view, the problem with many established theories of agency is that they are too closely focused on matters of gender identity and that, ultimately, this stymies the feminist political imagination. Ideas of gendered agency are unduly constrained by being thought in relation to the already known dimensions of identity—questions of what women are and what they can do—rather than in the unfettered terms of the unknown—the establishment of new, unanticipated modes of being. This rethinking of agency in a post-identity frame is prompted in part by the social transformations set in train by globalizing capital that seem to render identity concerns marginal, even irrelevant, to the most important political problems of the day. Many apparently emancipatory ways of thinking about agency as, say, performativity, have been deradicalized insofar as they have been absorbed into a neoliberal governance of the self that promotes women's autonomy while simultaneously enmeshing it within new forms of inequality and social vulnerability (Fraser 2013; Schwartz 2009). Identity politics is considerably less radical once it has been turned into a kind of lifestyle consumerism that is complicit with rather than disruptive of this logic of organized self-realization. There is a widespread feeling, then, that a politically effective feminism turns around the extent to which it can reconnect its ideals to a broader critique of neoliberal capitalism and reconfigure notions of collective agency beyond too insular a concern with identity.

In this quest to rethink agency in nonidentarian terms, a number of feminist theorists have drawn productively on the work of Hannah Arendt. It is well known that Arendt was opposed to issues of identity or any other "social" matter being considered the proper focus of political action. In her view, the illegitimate intrusion of social concerns into modern political life ("rise of the social") has meant that democracy has become depoliticized and domesticated, reduced to the mere administration of things. To restore its truly egalitarian and emancipatory core, democratic practice should be liberated from social concerns and oriented to the properly political activity of creating genuinely new collective ways of life. The capacity for inaugural creativity represents the quintessence of human freedom and should be therefore the ultimate goal of democratic action. Far from being considered inimical to feminist interests, Arendt's relegation of identity issues to the pre-political arena of social necessity is for postidentity theorists a source of inspiration. It enables them to put aside what Bonnie

Honig terms the "Woman Question in Arendt" and to focus instead on the "Arendt Question in Feminism" (Honig 1995, 3; see also Dietz 2002). The Arendt Question means the reconfiguration of feminist concerns in political rather than social terms as ideas of action and creation, not of identity and recognition. For Honig (1995, 156), for instance, Arendt's performative notion of democratic action suggests a feminist politics that "presupposes not an already known and unifying identity of 'woman' but agonistic, differentiated, multiple nonidentified beings that are always becoming, always calling out for argumentation and amendment." In a similar vein, Linda Zerilli (2005, 9) argues that the relentless focus on "the subject question" in feminism has hampered its ability to think about the nature of freedom and action beyond the assertion of identity. Real women cannot identify with the one-dimensional figure of the oppressed victim that permeates feminist identity politics because perpetual victimhood is not a livable social position (100). Insofar as it is wedded to a "victim discourse," feminist identity politics remains stuck in the parameters of established patterns of subjectivity and agency, in the assertion of the "I can," rather than considering the future-oriented possibilities of the "I will." The "vicious circle of agency" confines feminist politics to a reiteration of the already known and forecloses consideration of how it could be a truly transformative, world-building practice that might create radically new modes of collective being that are "freedom enabling" (Zerilli 2005, 120). The establishment of the newly thinkable in gender is a risky, uncertain business—poised over the "abyss of freedom"—that cannot be prescribed in advance but only experimentally practiced and enacted by present and future generations of feminists. In a similar fashion, other feminists also conceive of political agency in dynamic, agonistic terms as the "subject-in-process" that transcends ideas of authenticity and recognition and establishes "political friendships" across gender lines (Lloyd 2005, 161–169; Nash 1998; Mouffe 1992).

The rethinking of political agency by Arendtian and other post-identity theorists undoubtedly represents an important challenge to feminism to forge new political alliances and forms of collective action if it is to meet the challenges of our time. It also moves feminist thought on agency beyond the vexed issues of resistance and judgment. Resistance and subversion are limited modes of action because their displacements remain within the parameters of the given, within the existing rules of the game rather than challenging the game itself. Insofar as truly radical action is experimental and future oriented, normative issues of judgment are also suspended in favor of a creative and unconfined engagement with the world. It is precisely the ability of the productive imagination to posit an object outside the "use-economy" of an instrumentalized gender politics that is, in Zerilli's view, crucial to freedom-centered feminism. To speak about women as a political collectivity is not to make a truth claim but rather to posit prospective commonality with others and to raise the possibility of those others either accepting or refusing these claims.

Yet, despite these valuable contributions, it is questionable whether post-identity theorists are right to attribute the limitations in feminist accounts of agency to a narrow preoccupation with the cluster of "social" concerns pertaining to gender identity and subjectivity. It could be argued, for example that the agonistic, freedom-centered approach espoused by Zerilli and others presupposes, rather than dissolves, the subject-centered frame that it regards as so problematic. It is hard to see, for example, how debate about the nature and extent of community and about the social impact, liberating or otherwise, of the "newly thinkable" can be resolved without some detour through the subject paradigm that post-identity feminists so strongly criticize. As Amy Allen (2008, 16) puts it, "Simply claiming that freedom is a world question rather than a subject question does not obviate the need for thinking about the individual subject and its capacities for critical reflection and self-transformation, nor does it establish that such matters are not properly political."

Furthermore, there may be good reason to question the causal chain where strongly felt identity claims are held to limit political agency leading, at best, to an insular politics of recognition and, at worst, more extreme forms of separatism. As Linda Alcoff (2006, 38–40) notes, there is strong evidence to suggest that, on the contrary, for many individuals involvement in identity politics fosters an enlarged perspective that enhances activism and participation in broader types of democratic action. It seems, therefore, that it is not identity concerns per se that limit political agency but only those that are construed as cultural authenticity and other such essentialist notions. When identity is conceived in materialist terms as linked to social location and consequently to hierarchical relations of power, then it can be seen as a resource for mobilizing political action rather than as a brake on it. These distinctions are often not acknowledged in the post-identity critique, which tends to dismiss identity matters per se as a political dead-end.

Ultimately, there is good reason to question whether the free-floating notions of agency as world building proffered by post-identity feminists have much political meaning apart from as a utopian cipher. Indeed, their insistence that the "subject question" and the "social question" form part of the same "instrumental and adjudicative" frame that "minimizes the possibility of freedom as action" leads to a troubling lionization of agency as perpetually mobility and limitless creativity (Zerilli 2005, 10). The problem with delinking agency from social issues of identity, subjectivity, and so forth is that is that it is emptied of determinate content and becomes a "socially weightless" category. For Bourdieu, the idea of social weightlessness denotes ways of thinking that are so far removed from the demands and logic of embodied social existence that their descriptive and normative relevance is called into question (2000, 13–14). What falls out of the picture, for example, in post-identity formulations of agency as unconstrained agonism is a consideration of the social barriers and inequalities that prevent many women becoming political agents in the first place. Too often such theories do not even begin to address the social conditions necessary for effective agency and instead simply assume the existence of ready-made political subjects. While remaining true to a purified political logic, such weightless abstractions have little practical relevance to many enduring issues of gender inequality and say little about the substantive contours of radical political agency other than a vague gesture toward an unanticipated otherness.

Posthuman Agency

While post-identity feminism aims to drive a theoretical wedge between action and social identity, their formulations of agency remain, broadly speaking, within a humanist framework. Another strand of post-identity theory, however, strives to detach ideas of agency from their "traditional humanist orbit" altogether and demonstrate how the potential for action—"agentic capacity"—goes beyond the human to include nonhuman entities (Barad 2008, 144). This posthumanism is associated with the school of thinking known as "vitalist materialisms" and also has connections to actor-network theory in the social sciences (Coole and Frost 2010). While they vary in their intellectual sources, posthuman theories expand understanding of agency by reworking foundational assumptions about the nature of social existence, by adopting, in other words, an "ontology first" approach. Many influential accounts of agency, such as Butler's idea of performativity, are influenced by poststructural theory and premised on "negative" ontologies of lack or indeterminacy that denote the fundamental contingency of social existence, that things could always be otherwise, and that emancipatory political agency may take unanticipated and radically new forms. Posthuman theorists proceed from a similar premise of foundational indeterminacy, but they develop this, not through a negative ontology, but through a positive one of plenitude or a primal material vitalism. The world is viewed as an assemblage of complex, dynamic systems—both social and natural—whose unpredictable interactions give rise to a multiplicity of forms of being and dynamics of change. Social relations are conceptualized as dense networks of embodied practices and material forces, operating on multiple levels, from the everyday to the global, and too protean to be mapped according to conventional ideas of determination, first principles, regularity, or any other one-dimensional causal rationale. This vitalist ontology displaces conventional, anthropocentric accounts of the world as being in some sense passively there for humanity and, in highlighting the complex interactions of human and nonhuman elements ("vibrant matter"), points toward new hybrid forms of agentic capacity (e.g., Bennett 2010). It throws into question the unidirectional constructivism that dominates many feminist theories of agency in which the world and its objects are viewed as inert entities that receive meaning and significance from the symbolic representations we make of them. From the vitalist perspective, material being has its own intricate and unpredictable endogenous logic that exceeds conventional dualisms of mind versus body, reason versus emotion, culture versus nature, subject versus object, symbol versus materiality. In short, agency is regarded not as the exclusive property of humans but rather as an ever-changing set of potentialities immanent within the energetic and uncontainable dynamics of material existence.

A number of thinkers have seen the potential in such vitalist ontologies to creatively rethink feminist theories of agency and emancipatory politics. According to Elizabeth Grosz (2010, 41), for instance, feminist theorists often work with negative, subject-centered theories of agency as freedom from patriarchal constraint, but this traps them in a reactive mode of thought that is unable to articulate a truly substantive and positive vision of what the female subject is capable of doing. Drawing on the work of various "philosophers of life," including Darwin, Nietzsche, and Bergson, Grosz argues that agency should be conceptualized not as the individual's freedom from constraint but as systemically generated capacities for action and becoming in life. These capacities for action are not located in the individual person, nor is freedom the exclusive property of the human agent, rather they are effects of the unpredictable interaction of material life forces that engender "zones of indetermination"—that is, possibilities for free action. Agency, autonomy, freedom should be viewed as part of a general ontological condition of "action in life," as possibilities for acting otherwise immanent within the unpredictability of material existence. Grosz maintains that this reframing of freedom gives feminism new resources and questions to think about, for instance, how it may be possible to expand ways of being and acting beyond the conventional procedures and practices of democratic politics. With regard to the politics of gay identity, for example, freedom is not a question of "choice" or recognition or rights, but rather involves the creative expression of who one is and what one enjoys doing, "It is an expression of freedom without necessarily constraining oneself to options already laid out" (Grosz 2010, 153).

Although on Grosz's view, agency is no longer understood as individual transcendence but as a capacity immanent within material life forces, the political entailments of her theory are still roughly compatible with subject-centered accounts. In certain respects, her idea of agency as a process of creative, open-ended experimentation with modes of being is not so dissimilar to Arendtian, Foucauldian, and other agonistic ideas of action considered earlier. The overriding difference is, of course, that Grosz does not limit creative agency to a specially demarcated realm of the political, as, say, Arendt does, but instead regards it as a potentiality inherent in all spheres of existence. In the work of Karen Barad, however, the decentering of human agency is taken much further. Drawing on a variety of sources including, primarily, the philosophy of physics, she aims to shift understanding of agency beyond narrowly human parameters by alerting us to the "extraordinary liveliness" of matter and the radically heterogeneous forms of existence to which it gives rise. Like Grosz, she maintains that feminist ideas of agency are unduly constrained by an anthropomorphic and linguistic frame that posits a knowing, transcendental subject who reflects on and interacts with an essentially passive and external objective world. Butlerian notions of performativity, for example, may have problematized representational notions of language and associated ideas of sovereign agency but their constructivist orientation still prioritizes a thin linguistic determinism over a thick notion of material becoming. On Barad's account of "agential realism," the material world is neither external to the knowing subject nor passively there to be represented; rather, it is an active participant in the realization of knowledge and reality. The human and nonhuman, subject and object are not independent entities separated by clear-cut boundaries but "entangled" phenomena whose ceaseless "intra-actions" produce an endless series of determinate but local and contingent configurations of reality, in Barad's words, "agential cuts" that enact "local resolution[s] within inherent ontological indeterminacy." Agency, then, is neither an attribute of subject or object but a "'doing/being' in its intra-activity" (Barad 2008, 144). The contingent, nonnecessary nature of any agential cut means that it is also inherently exclusionary—in any particular configuration of the material world, some elements will come to the fore, while others will recede. For Barad, a politics and ethics of agential realism lies in the extent to which we are able to remain alert to and scrutinize the exclusions immanent in any agential enactment of material existence, or "worlding of the world," as she expresses it: "Ethics is not a concern we add to the questions of matter, but rather is the very nature of what it means to matter" (Barad 2012, 70).

By deepening appreciation of human interdependence with a complex, nonhuman materiality, posthuman theories potentially expand feminist ethical sensibility beyond a narrow concern with gender to include broader visions of deep environmentalism and other forms of "trans-human" politics (e.g., Alaimo and Hekman 2008). Yet, despite these interesting implications, it is not easy to see how theories of posthuman agency translate into the type of emancipatory and radical political practice that is claimed for them. No doubt, formulations of agency as complex assemblages of human and material dynamics enrich an understanding of causality and interdependence, but they do not straightforwardly yield a viable account of intervention in the world. By construing ideas of agency in such broad ontological terms and so definitively displacing its human core, posthuman theorists arguably empty the category of determinate meaning and immobilize it with regard to specific political action. Without a discernible social actor and by diffusing associated ideas of responsibility, duty, obligation, and so forth, they remove the social grounds that are arguably crucial for effective political action. Notions of causality are understood as being so wide and complex, that action cannot be localized and it is unclear where and how political change can be brought about. It might even be said that what posthuman theorists chose to term agential capacity or the "quasi agency" of things is, in fact, more aptly described as an intricate theory of causation and interdependence and, indeed, Barad has said as much in a recent interview (Barad 2012, 54–55). At the risk of appearing irredeemably humanist, it may be, then, that agency, especially in its collective, political dimensions, is still best thought of as primarily a property of situated social actors rather than entangled material entities in so far as, effective politics—even those with a transhuman dimension—is still bound up with ideas of intentionality and responsibility even though these need not be construed in the voluntarist sense of the sovereign actor.

The ultimate reason why ontologies of plentitude do not yield the kind of radical politics that posthuman theorists claim for them is because they result in a short-circuited mode of reasoning that leaves out a developed account of power. Ontology is unavoidable inasmuch as all political theories make assumptions, explicitly or implicitly, about the fundamental features of social being. It does not follow, however, that that these ontological features are straightforwardly reflected in the practices and structures of the social world. What is left out in the overhasty move from claims about the protean dynamism of material being to more grandiose assertions about the fluid, ever-changing dynamics of agency is a mediating account of power. In place of a differentiated account of power, they substitute a series of dualisms between sameness versus difference, lack versus plenitude, stasis versus flux, separation versus entanglement, binaries versus complex networks, all of which amount to what Zizek (2012, 948) terms "a rude binary opposition between truth and illusion."

Without such an account, Barad's idea of ethics as a sensitivity to the exclusions inherent in any agential cut is rendered virtually inoperable because of the infinitized terms in which it is presented. Given that, on her view, exclusion is a necessary condition of all determinate forms of being and knowledge, ethics becomes an endless, unfocused and, ultimately, undischargeable task. Not all exclusions are inherently harmful or politically regressive, but it is not clear how to distinguish better from worse forms in the absence of an account of power or other normative criteria on which to base such judgments. Indeed, the quasi-naturalism of Barad's materialism pushes out issues of power entirely by collapsing the symbolic order into an undifferentiated, entangled materiality and locating meaning directly in nature. In Slavoj Zizek's (2012, 936) words, it "ontologises correlation itself."

The lack of an account of power similarly weakens Grosz's work, which defers a consideration of the grounds on which political judgments about "freedom" are to be made. For instance, when thinking about freedom and autonomous agency, Grosz (2010, 154) claims that the issue is not "how to give women more adequate recognition . . . , more rights, or more of a voice but how to enable more action, more making and doing, more difference." The problem is that not all "making and doing" is necessarily progressive with respect to the dismantlement of gender and other inequalities and, absent any notion of power, she comes close to a questionable valorization of plurality (flux, indeterminacy, etc.) as inherently valuable in itself. Rights, recognition, political voice might belong, in Grosz's view, to a "reactive" and limited way of thinking about political agency, but they do at least address a social reality in which women are disproportionately represented, among the poor, the displaced, and the exploited.

In short, posthuman theorists jump too quickly from ontology to politics, when in fact the latter cannot be derived from the former without a more thorough account of intervening power relations. Ideas of generative materiality provide one possible (although contestable) account of the ontological conditions necessary for action, but they do not explain agency itself, which is a social set of properties and capacities, realized unevenly among individuals because of asymmetrical distributions of power. Contra assertions of the "extraordinary liveliness" of existence, there are, for instance, many features of social life that are relatively fixed, predictable, and enduring and that present, inter alia, considerable barriers to the formation of effective agency. Rather than address such issues of disempowerment, posthuman theorists tend to uncritically invoke unconstrained dynamics of flux and becoming to explain agency in a way that displaces from view the entrenched, negative aspects of social life that characterize not just the lived reality of gender inequality but also other types of social oppression and inequity.

Conclusion: Agency in a Neoliberal Era

It is undoubtedly the case that the world is changing, that social existence is more fragile, uncertain, and risky, and that feminist theory needs to reflect these transformations in its concepts of agency and change. Whether these uncertainties are best captured in free-floating, glamorized dynamics of complexity and flux is, however, moot. Indeed, for many thinkers now the challenge is to rethink the nature of agency in the context of globalizing capital and, in particular, the spread of neoliberal modes of governance (see McNay 2014). Operating through strategies of marketized individualization, neoliberal governance has increased social precariousness, deepened inequalities, fragmented collective forms of existence, intensified the depredation of the natural environment and had profoundly depoliticizing effects on state and citizen bonds. Moreover, women are especially vulnerable to these changes given their relatively unprotected and disesteemed social role as primary carers and also their overrepresentation in exploited, low-paid forms of employment. New types of "empowered" agency that have emerged for women over the last thirty years or so are simultaneously bound up with new forms of social precariousness. As Angela McRobbie (2008, 6) puts it, there is a "double entanglement" in which globalizing capital "brings forward women as individualized subjects [and] agents of change" insofar as it creates a new, feminized workforce at the same time as it reworks gender hierarchies in which women remain the most vulnerable and exploited subjects.

It is in relation to the intersection of gendered and other inequalities with developing forms of social precariousness that a number of feminist theorists are now seeking to rethink ideas of agency and, more broadly, the changing nature of freedom and constraint (e.g., Madhok, Phillips, and Wilson 2013). For instance, Judith Butler's work on precarious life initially attempted to rethink ethical responsibility in the light of the existential interdependency of the nonsovereign self with its other. But in her recent work with Athena Athanasiou on dispossession, this ontological focus on precariousness is supplemented with an explicitly social one on precarity, or the "condition of induced inequality" specific to neoliberal governmentality. The emerging forms of abjection, suffering, and "social death" that are reactions to widespread economic and social precarity necessitate a rethinking of agency both in terms of modalities of social control and also possibilities for political opposition (Butler and Athanasiou 2013, 12–15). The principal question of agency becomes, as Butler (2012, 9) puts it, paraphrasing Adorno, "whether it is possible to lead a good life in a bad life." From a materialist perspective Nancy Fraser (2013, 221) argues that there is an urgent need for feminists to reformulate ideas of agency and reconnect them to a critique of neoliberal capitalism given that "the dream of women's emancipation . . ., [has been] harnessed to the engine of capitalist accumulation." From a transnational perspective, Pheng Cheah (2006) criticizes theories of cosmopolitan democracy for ignoring the agency of the poor and marginal—especially women in developing countries, where their practices do not conform to lionized dynamics of hybridized cultural exchange. Or, from a sociological perspective, others, such as Veena Das, examine both the way in which systemic social inequities penetrate everyday existence and are lived as embodied suffering, but also the types of recovery and the transcendence that may arise from the midst of such misery and "ordinary" violence (Das 2007; Das et al. 2001; McNay 2014). It is evident from this growing body of work that there can be no single theory or unified model of agency; rather, agency represents a dense, multivalent transfer point for feminists to think about specific instances of gender oppression and transformation in the context of neoliberal governance. It is in these entangled issues of gender inequalities with emergent forms of social vulnerability and empowerment that one of the principal challenges for future feminist theory on agency lies.

References

Abu-Lughod, Lila. 1990. "The Romance of Resistance: Tracing Transformations of Power through Bedouin Women." *American Ethnologist* 17 (1): 41–55.
Alaimo, Stacy, and Susan Hekman, eds. 2008. *Material Feminisms*. Indianapolis: Indiana University Press.
Alcoff, L. 2006. *Visible Identities: Race, Gender and the Self*. Oxford: Oxford University Press.
Allen, A. 2008. *The Politics of Our Selves: Power, Autonomy, and Gender in Contemporary Critical Theory*. New York: Columbia University Press.
Arendt, Hannah. 1973. *The Origins of Totalitarianism*. London: Harcourt, Brace, and Company.
Bangstad, Sindre. 2011. "Saba Mahmood and Anthropological Feminism after Virtue." *Theory, Culture and Society* 28 (3): 28–54.
Barad, Karen. 2008. "Posthumanist Performativity: Toward an Understanding of How Matter Comes to Matter." In *Material Feminisms*, edited by Stacy Alaimo and Susan Hekman, 120–155. Indianapolis: Indiana University Press.
Barad, Karen. 2012. "Matter Feels, Converses, Suffers, Desires, Yearns and Remembers: Interview with Karen Barad." In *New Materialism: Interviews and Cartography*, edited by Rick Dolphijn and Iris van der Tuin, 48–70. Michigan: Open Humanities Press.
Benhabib, Seyla. 1992. *Situating the Self: Gender, Community and Postmodernism in Contemporary Ethics*. Cambridge: Polity Press.
Benhabib, S. 2002. *The Claims of Culture: Equality and Diversity in the Global Era*. Princeton, NJ: Princeton University Press.
Bennett, Jane. 2010. *Vibrant Matter: A Political Ecology of Things*. Durham, NC: Duke University Press.
Bourdieu, Pierre. 2000. *Pascalian Meditations*. Cambridge: Polity Press.
Brown, Wendy. 1995. *States of Injury: Power and Freedom in Late Modernity*. Princeton, NJ: Princeton University Press.
Butler, Judith. 1990. *Gender Trouble: Feminism and the Subversion of Identity*. London: Routledge.
Butler, Judith. 1993. *Bodies That Matter: On the Discursive Limits of Sex*. London: Routledge.
Butler, Judith. 2012. "Can One Lead a Good Life in a Bad Life?" *Radical Philosophy* 176: 9–18.

Butler, Judith. 2013 "The Sensibility of Critique: Response to Asad and Mahmood." In *Is Critique Secular? Blasphemy, Injury and Free Speech*, edited by A. Asad, W. Brown, J. Butler, and S. Mahmood, 95–130. New York: Fordham University Press.
Butler, Judith, and Athena Athanasiou. 2013. *Dispossession: The Performative in the Political*. Cambridge: Polity Press.
Chambers, Clare. 2008. *Sex, Culture, and Justice: The Limits of Choice*. University Park: Penn State University Press.
Cheah, Pheng. 2006. *Inhuman Conditions: On Cosmopolitanism and Human Rights*. Cambridge, MA: Harvard University Press.
Coole, Diana, and Samantha Frost, eds. 2010. *New Materialisms: Ontology, Agency and Politics*. Durham, NC: Duke University Press.
Das, Veena. 2007. *Life and Words: Violence and the Descent into the Ordinary*. Berkeley: University of California Press.
Das, Veena, Arthur Kleinman, Margaret M. Lock, Mamphela Ramphele, and Pamela Reynolds, eds. 2001. *Remaking a World: Violence, Social Suffering, and Recovery*. Berkeley: University of California Press.
Dietz, Mary. 2002. *Turning Operations: Feminism, Arendt and Politics*. London: Routledge.
Frank, Katherine. 2006. "Agency." *Anthropological Theory* 6 (3): 281–302.
Fraser, Nancy. 1995. "False Antitheses." In *Feminist Contentions: A Philosophical Exchange*, edited by S. Benhabib, J. Butler, D. Cornell, and N. Fraser, 59–74. London: Routledge.
Fraser, Nancy. 2013. *The Fortunes of Feminism: From Women's Liberation, to Identity Politics, to Anti-Capitalism*. London: Verso.
Friedman, Marilyn. 2003. *Autonomy, Gender, Politics*. Oxford: Oxford University Press.
Gilligan, Carole. 1982. *In a Different Voice: Psychological Theory and Women's Development*. Cambridge, MA: Harvard University Press.
Grosz, Elizabeth. 2010. "Feminism, Materialism, Freedom." In *New Materialisms: Ontology, Agency and Politics*, edited by Diana Coole and Samantha Frost, 139–157. Durham, NC: Duke University Press.
Held, Virginia. 1993. *Feminist Morality*. Chicago: Chicago University Press.
Honig, Bonnie. 1995. "Towards an Agonistic Feminism: Hannah Arendt and the Politics of Identity." In *Feminist Interpretations of Hannah Arendt*, edited by B. Honig, 135–166. University Park: Penn State University Press.
Hutchings, Kimberly. 2013. "Chosers or Losers? Feminist Ethical and Political Agency in a Plural and Unequal World." In *Gender, Agency and Coercion*, edited by Sumi Madhok, Anne Phillips, and Kalpana Wilson, 14–28. London: Palgrave Macmillan.
Lloyd, Moya. 2005. *Beyond Identity Politics: Feminism, Power and Politics*. London: Sage.
Mackenzie, Catriona, and Natalie Stoljar, eds. 2000. *Relational Autonomy: Feminist Perspectives on Autonomy, Agency, and the Social Self*. Oxford: Oxford University Press.
Madhok, Sumi, Anne Phillips, and Kalpana Wilson, eds. 2013. *Gender, Agency and Coercion*. London: Palgrave Macmillan.
Mahmood, Saba. 2005. *The Politics of Piety: The Islamic Revival and the Feminist Subject*. Princeton NJ: Princeton University Press.
Mahmood, Saba. 2001. 'Feminist theory, embodiment, and the docile agent: Some reflections on the Eygptian Islamic Revival', *Cultural Anthropology*, 16 (2): 202–236.
McNay, Lois. 2014. *The Misguided Search for the Political: Social Weightlessness in Radical Democratic Theory*. Cambridge: Polity Press.

McRobbie, Angela. 2008. *The Aftermath of Feminism: Gender, Culture and Social Change*. London: Sage.
Mouffe, C. 1992. *The Return of the Political*. London: Verso.
Nash, K. 1998. "Beyond Liberalism? Feminist Theories of Democracy." In *Gender, Politics and the State*, edited by V. Randall and G. Waylen, 45–57. London: Routledge.
Schwartz, Joseph. 2009. *The Future of Democratic Equality: Rebuilding Social Solidarity in a Fragmented America*. London: Routledge.
Scott, Joan Wallach. 2010. *The Politics of the Veil*. Princeton, NJ: Princeton University Press.
Stoljar, Natalie. 2000. "Autonomy and the Feminists Intuition." In *Relational Autonomy: Feminist Perspectives on Autonomy, Agency, and the Social Self*, edited by Catriona Mackenzie and Natalie Stoljar, 94–111. Oxford: Oxford University Press.
Zerilli, Linda. 2005. *Feminism and the Abyss of Freedom*. Chicago: Chicago University Press.
Zerilli, Linda. 2009. "Towards a Feminist Theory of Judgement." *Signs* 34 (2): 295–317.
Zizek, Slavoj. 2012. *Less Than Nothing: Hegel and the Shadow of Dialectical Materialism*. London: Verso.

CHAPTER 3

BIOPOLITICS

RUTH A. MILLER

Introduction

The term *biopolitics* is no longer as reputable as it once was. After enjoying remarkable influence in the 1990s and early 2000s, the concept gradually lost favor over the following decade. Feminist theorists were among the first to question both its ethics and its explanatory value (Braidotti 2006, 40). Soon scholars from a variety of fields were challenging its validity. By 2011, editors who had embraced biopolitics as a foundation for their collections (Sarat and Culbert 2009, 6, 11, 21) were denying any deep investment in the term (Sarat 2011, 3). Graduate students who had begun writing dissertations on the concept had to reconceive their projects. Some scholars even felt obligated, in publications that had little or nothing to do with biopolitics, to celebrate their own early lack of interest in it and to express relief that those who had been duped into writing on it were now justly exposed (Stolzenberg 2012, 7).

But the fate of biopolitics as a framework of inquiry hints at more than the volatility of scholarly trends. The vigor with which scholars embraced biopolitics in the early 2000s was astonishing, as was the haste with which so many abandoned it—and then denied ever having been interested in it—near the end of the decade. The term does not on its own seem to merit such extreme reactions. Its invention represented an effort to explain the historical development of birth, death, population, environment, and statistical apparatus as problems of rights and sovereignty at the end of the eighteenth century. Its invention helped scholars to understand the simultaneity of what seemed like a radical shift in rights rhetoric, on the one hand, and the elaboration of pronatalist population policies, environmental protection, and statistical methods, on the other. Neither of these aspects of biopolitics would seem to provoke the responses that it brought about. And yet *biopolitics* as a scholarly term did incite these responses—and feminist theorists were among the first to recognize that the term implied more than it initially appeared to.

The questions that feminist theorists might best ask of biopolitics now, therefore, include: why did the term became as influential as it did at the moment it did? Why should its discrediting have involved such intellectual violence? Why were feminist theorists among the first to recognize its apparent weaknesses? Was its demolition a triumph for critical feminist theory? And, perhaps most importantly given its inclusion in this collection, is the biopolitical as a framework of inquiry really dead—or might feminist theorists once again recuperate it? The story of biopolitics is more complicated than its sudden scholarly embrace and equally sudden scholarly rejection would suggest. In order to understand its historical—and perhaps ongoing—relevance to the field of feminist theory, we need to grapple with these problems.

Biopolitics: Inventing a Framework of Inquiry

In his 1975–1976 lectures, "Society Must Be Defended," and in the first volume of his *History of Sexuality*, Michel Foucault introduced the term "biopolitics" as it is most frequently understood today. Near the end of the eighteenth century, Foucault argued, the sovereign right over life changed. Whereas prior to this period, the sovereign right over life manifested itself most obviously in legal executions—in the taking of a political subject's life—during and after this period, it appeared most prominently in the management, maintenance, and prolonging of a political collective's biological existence. It was not on the scaffold but through health policies, population policies, and birth policies that the right to life now played out. The classical good life had disappeared as a political goal, to be replaced by the long life—or extended, and sometimes indefinite, *living*. As Foucault influentially put it, the classical or juridical sovereign right "to let live and make die" gave way to a biopolitical sovereign right to "make live and let die" (Foucault 2003, 241).

Alongside this shift in the sovereign right over life, a number of other biopolitical sovereign interests, institutions, and apparatuses appeared. Animated by an interest in making live and letting die, for example, governments introduced policies to regulate healthy populations, increase birth rates, promote clean environments, and collect an ever increasing amount of statistical data on these problems. Birth and death ceased to be politically relevant to the individual citizen and, instead, became politically relevant to the population (Foucault 2003, 243–244). Likewise, the environment gradually became a problem of human life—or of the vitality of the species—while the storage of data or information concerning collective health and vitality became one of the predominant means of expressing the right to life (Foucault 2003, 245).

For Foucault, therefore, *biopolitics* was the set of discourses, institutions, and policies that emerged from the redefinition of political life at the end of the eighteenth century. Biopolitics was, specifically, the coming together of biology and politics—and the resulting elaboration of a rhetoric to manage this newly created biological-political realm. As something of a corollary, Foucault also noted that this shift in focus from legal or linguistic to biological life left classical distinctions between left and right or liberal and authoritarian fuzzy at best (Foucault 2003, 241). Instead of distinguishing between active and passive citizens or between rights and duties, sovereigns began to concern themselves solely with the health of an ideologically undifferentiated population. Foucault's challenge to scholars, then, was to reimagine democracy as a mode of governance in which being a living, organic, and reproductive environment—or one part of a such an environment—was a norm to which all political subjects were supposed to aspire. It was to take seriously the idea that modern politics is and has been an inherently biological affair.

Extending the Reach of Scholarship on Biopolitics

Throughout the 1980s and 1990s, a number of scholars took up Foucault's challenge to reconsider rights and sovereignty from a biopolitical perspective. Not all of the themes that Foucault identified as evidence of a shift from classical or juridical to biopolitical governance received an equal amount of attention, however. In general, and until very recently, three issues have primarily concerned scholars of biopolitics. The first of these issues is death as a biopolitical rather than purely political problem. The second is the biopolitical regulation of sexual behavior in the name of a healthy population. The third and, arguably, the most important to feminist theorists, is the biopolitical regulation of reproduction—the elaboration of often invasive pronatalist policies alongside these new systems of rights and citizenship.

Although it is arguably of least interest to feminist theorists, it is worth mentioning, at least, the extensive work on the biopolitics of death—and especially the biopolitics of death as it appears in the writing of Giorgio Agamben. Agamben's writing on biopolitics has been extraordinarily influential to scholarship in a number of fields, and Agamben himself is frequently cited by those who have enthusiastically accepted—as well as by those who have enthusiastically rejected—the explanatory value of biopolitics as a scholarly term. Agamben is fascinated by mass death. Whereas Foucault noted, as *part* of his broader theorization, that biopolitics both blurs the lines between liberal and totalitarian political structures and transforms death from the termination of the individual to the pathology of the population, Agamben emphasizes, develops, and rigorously connects those two themes.

Arguing, for example, that even the earliest "declarations of rights represent the originary figure of the inscription of natural life into the juridico-political order of the nation state" (Agamben 1998, 127), Agamben makes clear that rights granting is *necessarily* a biopolitical activity—an activity that in and of itself transforms biology into a political concern. He continues by suggesting that the debate dominating democratic political thought has thus never been a debate between left and right, liberal and authoritarian, or parliamentary and totalitarian ideologies. On the contrary, if rights granting has been biopolitical from its inception, "the only real question to be asked and to be decided" by modern (or for that matter, premodern) governments has been "which form of organization would be best suited to the task of the care, control, and use of bare life" (Agamben 1998, 121–122). For Agamben, in other words, biopolitics—manifested in particular in the genocidal institution that was the Nazi death camp—has not been an aberration in the story of democracy or of democratic rights; it has been a logical conclusion to this story. According to Agamben, the concentration camp, rather than the city, has become—and has perhaps always been—the preeminent space of democratic political engagement (Agamben 1998, 134–135).

Agamben's death-oriented interpretation of biopolitics achieved prominence in scholarship throughout the 1990s and into the 2000s. And then it came under widespread scholarly attack. Its initial influence arguably had to do with Agamben's courage in insisting that liberal political rights are not accidentally biological, but are by definition so. He made a convincing case that democratic theory has more than enough room for discourses and institutions whose purpose is either the invasive management or the complete elimination of biologically determined populations. The repeated reappearance of concentration camps throughout the twentieth and twenty-first centuries was not accidental, he argued, but rather a manifestation of a quite functional democracy at work.

The movement *against* Agamben's interpretation of biopolitics is more difficult to explain. In part, it had to do with scholarly trends. In part, it also had to do with the fact that whereas Agamben did compellingly disrupt the existing scholarship on rights, subjectivity, and death, he did not do so sufficiently to dampen the accusatory potential of writing in this vein. Commentators simply accused ideological enemies of biopolitical oppression instead of authoritarian or totalitarian oppression. Likely the most vulnerable aspect of Agamben's writing on biopolitics, however, was his inability or unwillingness to provide an alternative to what he presented as an undesirable—indeed, genocidal—democratic theory. After initially embracing his work, many scholars thus returned to the well-worn conclusion that, in the end, unreliable and dissatisfying as it may be, something like the liberal social contract is the best of a collection of bad alternatives (Passavant 2007, 147).

As we shall see, feminist theorists for the most part did not respond to Agamben's work in these ways. The idea that democratic theory and rights rhetoric are necessarily biological—and necessarily inscribed across bodies—was not surprising to scholars working on gender and sexuality, many of whom found in Agamben's interpretation of biopolitics a recognizable framework of inquiry. While many feminist theorists critiqued and engaged with Agamben's writing, therefore, most did not embrace it wholeheartedly only to reject it later. The feminist treatment of Agamben's interpretation of biopolitics was instead both earlier and more complex than what followed in the late 2000s. Despite the fact that death was for the most part less interesting to feminist theorists concerned with biopolitics than were bodies, sexuality, and reproduction, Agamben's death-inflected interpretation of the concept received an arguably more thoughtful reception in the fields of gender and sexuality studies than it did in other scholarly fields. And in fact, it continues to do so.

Before returning to this reception, however, we need to consider how scholars of biopolitics writing at the same time as Agamben treated sexuality and reproduction—issues of more concern to most feminist theorists. Another influential example of biopolitical scholarship, therefore—here with a focus on sexuality, race, and empire—was Ann Stoler's writing in the mid- to late-1990s. Drawing on Foucault's lectures before they were published and made widely accessible, Stoler read the relationship between biopolitical sexual regulation and the creation of biologically defined racial categories quite differently from Agamben. Although Stoler did concern herself with violence, she was less convinced than Agamben that *death* was the unifying factor in biopolitical institutions and rhetoric.

Indeed, Stoler suggests in her work that Foucault's implicit (and Agamben's explicit) use of the Nazi death camp as an endpoint of modern democracy is precisely what left the Foucauldian theory of biopolitics "incomplete" (Stoler 1995, 40–41). By setting aside biopolitics-as-mass death, and focusing instead on biopolitics-as-sexual-and-reproductive regulation, Stoler made two important, if unexpected, claims about the history of biopower. The first is that "the management of non-conjugal sex was implicated in a discourse on 'the defense of society' much earlier than [Foucault] suggests" (Stoler 1995, 40–41). The second is that the production of gendered, sexed, and raced bodies, or embodied identities, that has been central to biopolitical sovereignty was by no means a European invention. What had been previously identified as a modern European racism linked to modern European science and medicine, in other words, could now be situated across global networks. The gendered and raced body of biopolitical sexual regulation appeared simultaneously, according to Stoler, in the metropole *and* in the colony.

Or, put differently, whereas Agamben insisted that biopower shifted political engagement from the city to the concentration camp, Stoler insisted that biopower shifted political engagement from the city to the colony. Famously describing the colony as "the laboratory of modernity" (Stoler 2002, 146–147), Stoler made clear that emphasizing the "make live" rather than the "let die" side of Foucault's biopolitical equation, *especially in an imperial context*, by no means obscured the violent aspects of this mode of sovereignty. On the contrary, regulating reproduction—rather than facilitating death—was key to the creation of the imperial hierarchies that made the more conventional examples of colonial exploitation and violence possible.

Exploring the implications of sexual and reproductive regulation rather than mass death was, for Stoler, the *only* means of excavating biopolitical discourse at its broadest geographical and temporal reach. The shift from the classical or juridical sovereign interest in an individual's life to the biopolitical sovereign interest in a population's health or vitality could help to explain the production of gendered, sexed, and raced bodies, not just in eighteenth- and nineteenth-century Europe, Stoler argued, but in a variety of places and contexts. As other scholars have pointed out as well, biopolitical life played out not just, say, in pronatalist French "propaganda that focused on the military consequences of a decline of fertility," making "national security completely dependent on high birthrate" (Reggiani 1996, 733), but also, for example, in the implementation of the Contagious Diseases Acts in a colonized Caribbean (Briggs 2002, 27). In both situations, as Stoler put it, "the question of who would be a 'subject' and who a 'citizen' converged on the sexual politics of race" (Stoler 1995, 40–41, 133).

So, Agamben is fascinated with death and Stoler is fascinated with life. At least initially, therefore, they seem to present their readers with very different interpretations of biopower. But despite these differences, their interpretations also overlap in a number of areas. For example, both writers reconfigure in similar ways key questions in political theory that are also key questions in feminist theory. Agamben insists that political rights cannot be responsibly addressed without reference to bodies and biology. Although one would be hard-pressed to describe Agamben as a scholar of gender and sexuality, therefore—and although the bodies that appear in his work are usually dead or dying—his reanimation of writing on rights rhetoric is nonetheless useful for scholars of gender, sexuality, and law or politics. The questions that Agamben raises about the operation of biopolitics in the realm of rights are also questions that have concerned scholars of gender, sexuality, and rights. Agamben in this way remains a relevant figure in work on law, sovereignty, democracy, and gender.

Stoler's work has been more obviously important to feminist theorists. By linking political identity, rather than political rights, to bodies, sexuality, and reproduction—and then by taking the colony as her reference point—Stoler became a central figure in the late twentieth-century development of feminist identity theory. Her work suggested that embodied political subjectivity was a distinctively biopolitical, rather than liberal, product—a product of the pronatalist discourses, sexual regulation, relentless rhetoric of hygiene, and institutionalized maintenance of bodies that Foucault associated with biopolitical sovereignty. Stoler's work has thus become a common starting point for theorists concerned with gender, sexuality, political identity, and empire.

More broadly, Stoler—like Agamben—reinvigorated Foucault's biopolitical challenge to traditional, liberal frameworks of inquiry. She and Agamben, writing at the same time, each in a different way, drew on biopolitics to resolve or to obliterate what had seemed to be the unresolvable paradox of liberal democratic political engagement. Agamben made clear that "letting die"—even on a mass scale—was intrinsic to democratic rights, that bodies could never be an afterthought in studies of democratic engagement. Stoler, meanwhile, demonstrated that empire—and all the raced, sexed, and gendered bodies that went with it—was not an accident of modern, liberal democracy; instead, it was its foundation. She showed that modern political identity, regardless of where it is formulated, has always rested squarely on imperial and biopolitical discourses of race, sex, and gender.

Agamben and Stoler, in other words, both suggested that moments of seeming democratic dysfunction were far from dysfunctional—and feminist theorists began increasingly to work through problems of gender and sexuality under the same assumptions.

Bodies, and bodily or biological regulation or violence, were neither marginal to, nor accidents of, democratic engagement. On the contrary, sexuality and reproduction were part of sovereignty—while democratic engagement began with biology.

Feminist Critiques and Extensions of Biopolitics

Once again, though, many feminist theorists have also criticized "biopolitics" as an explanatory model, while others have interpreted the term in a manner far removed from Foucault's initial articulation of it. In general, the criticisms of biopolitics fall into three categories. Some question the overwhelming emphasis on sexuality and reproduction—at the expense of gender or femininity—that appears in most traditional accounts of biopolitics. Foucault, in particular, seems to have been uninterested in grappling with gender as a factor in biopolitical sovereignty—an example of a more pervasive blind spot in his work that has concerned feminist theorists over the past decades (West 2011, 147).

A second set of criticisms hinges on what seems to be a *fear* of the body animating the work of those who, like Agamben, associate biopolitics with the totalitarian, death-driven, regulation of "bare life" (Braidotti 2006, 40). Finally, a third set of criticisms concerns itself with the self-contained, Cartesian body as the sole place where the regulation of this biological, bare, or simply, material life appears. If matter that is alive but disembodied—say, genetic material or, for that matter, genetic code—is irrelevant to theories of biopolitics, or if all living matter is mapped onto discrete bodies, then these theories of biopolitics seem out of place in some of the more recent, especially posthumanist, work in gender and sexuality studies. As much as these criticisms of biopolitics have challenged the very usefulness of the concept as a framework of inquiry, however, they have also led to productive reimaginings of the term within feminist theoretical frameworks.

Foucault's unwillingness or inability to address gender in his otherwise thoughtful work on sexuality, discourse, embodiment, and sovereignty has troubled feminist theorists for years. From his notorious argument that rape is a physical assault like any other physical assault—and that one should not invest a "sexual organ" with more meaning than "a hand, hair, or nose" (Cahill 2000, 43)—to the absence of any serious consideration of gender identity in his studies of sexuality, Foucault's work has seemed insufficient to the requirements of responsible feminist theory. Indeed, some scholars have encouraged feminists to disregard Foucault's work altogether (Burfoot 2003, 49). Others have argued more moderately that since Foucault's interest was not in gender, it might make more sense to read his work for what it does provide rather than mourn it for what it cannot (Fraser 1989, 56). A third option, however, also exists, and this has been to take up Foucault's silence on gender as a challenge. Especially in theorizing biopolitics—a concept that seems inextricably bound to sexuality *and* gender—it has made sense to ask explicitly why gender was absent from this early articulation of biopower.

Jean Elisabeth Pedersen, for example, makes an important empirical point about the enforcement of biopolitical pronatalist (or anticontraceptive) policies in early twentieth-century France. She writes that "the exhaustive list of prohibited substances included all female methods of contraception but did not include condoms," and that we might therefore conclude that "French legislators' expanded political and medical authority to intervene into family life was extended through the bodies of women" (Pedersen 1996, 676–677). Against Foucault—and, indeed, using Foucault's case study as an example—Pedersen demonstrates easily here that biopolitics rests as solidly on the production of gender categories as it does on the regulation of sexuality. One cannot talk about the "making live" part of the biopolitical equation without also considering gender.

At this point, of course, we could simply stop. We could accept that Foucault's interpretation of biopolitics was incomplete with regard to gender in the same way that, as Stoler notes, it was incomplete with regard to empire. Alternatively, though, we can also push this question further: once again, we can ask *why* Foucault sidelined gender in this initial elaboration of biopolitics. One place that feminist theorists have sought answers to this question is in Foucault's original comparison between biopolitical citizenship, on the one hand, and classical, or juridical, citizenship, on the other. If, for Foucault, the normative biopolitical citizen, as opposed to the normative liberal or juridical citizen, is a person whose intimate, biological life is always minutely and pervasively monitored, then invasive bodily regulation of the sort Pedersen describes would be the defining characteristic of the citizen. The woman citizen, determined by gender, would be the neutral citizen.

Or, put differently, Stoler's conclusion that, given a biopolitical rather than juridical framework of inquiry, colonies rather than metropoles have been the laboratories of modernity, suggests in turn that, given a biopolitical rather than juridical framework of inquiry, women rather than men have always been the political norm. In this alternative biopolitical scenario, men were the second sex. And this is the case precisely because, to borrow from Pedersen once more, condoms were *not* criminalized. A better response to Foucault's silence on gender, therefore, is imagining the alternative theories of citizenship to which biopower seems inevitably to lead, rather than faulting him for his apparent unwillingness to consider gender as a factor in politics. It may be the case that biopolitics is *more*, not less, relevant to gender studies than Foucault imagined. And it may also be the case, therefore, that some of the more recent work on biopolitics—much of which is equally silent on gender—can be similarly reinterpreted from a gender-conscious perspective.

Feminist theorists' responses to, criticisms of, and reconfigurations of Agamben's writing on biopolitics, for instance, have frequently found gender or femininity to be an excellent basis for challenging an emphasis on the "letting die" part of the biopolitical equation. As Rosi Braidotti has written, "Speaking from the position of an embodied and embedded female subject I find the metaphysics of finitude a myopic way of putting the question of the limits of what we call life" (Braidotti 2006, 40). For Braidotti, in other words, it is specifically the act of writing as a female subject that makes possible an embrace, rather than a rejection, of biological vitality—even when this vitality is politicized as Agamben's "bare life." Far from leading inevitably to Agamben's (or Heidegger's) "becoming corpse" (Braidotti 2006, 40), Braidotti argues, a responsible and thoughtful biopolitics, aware of female subjectivity, can open up alternative and useful modes of democratic engagement.

Agamben and those influenced by his work may well be frightened of bare life, Braidotti continues—they may condemn this vitality that has always been politicized yet banned from the juridical realm, this vitality that has always "historically been feminized," and this vitality that has always evoked the "natives, animals and others" traditionally associated with "a generative force . . . deprived of political and ethical relevance" (Braidotti 2006, 270). But this terror of the lurking vitality in political life does not mean that vitality is, objectively, something to fear. Once again, Braidotti carefully and deliberately invokes a vital, living, and *female* subjectivity to theorize biopolitics in a different direction. And in doing so, she not only detaches biopolitics from its derogatory connotations; she also sets the groundwork for a new and affirmative biopolitical democratic engagement.

What, though, might this affirmative theory of biopolitics entail? First, and most importantly, Braidotti's biopolitics re-centers the environment as a political concern. Whereas earlier scholars of biopolitics focused primarily on death, sexuality, and reproduction, Braidotti reminds her readers that an equally important concern of biopolitical sovereignty as Foucault initially deployed it, was the environment. The proper space of biopolitical engagement for Braidotti, then, is not the singular embodied individual who may or may not be politically alive. Instead, she suggests, biopolitics happens most properly across nonunitary environmental fields. She demonstrates that a focus on death, or even on a body's reproductive capacities, inappropriately reifies the individual subject, imagined to be independent of other things, who has always been at odds with biopolitical engagement. She makes clear that recognizing the environmental, dispersed qualities of both embodied and disembodied matter is a prerequisite to an effective biopolitical theory.

Once again, however, key to this shift in focus from the dead singular body, or from the dystopian nightmare of the camp, is an acknowledgment that biopolitics is very much a *feminist* concern. Only by thinking simultaneously of life *and* femininity can we begin to imagine a biopolitical subject—or citizen—who works simultaneously as an environment. Femininity thus plays a role not only in the concrete, empirical history of biopolitical institutions—in the fact that biopolitical regulation has always primarily targeted women's bodies. More so, an awareness of female subjectivity is a prerequisite to divorcing biopolitical subjectivity from the rational, self-contained, individual of classical liberal theory. Challenging the assumption that self-conscious individuals—those whose politics may very well bring their biological existence into question—are the preeminent sites or agents of biopolitical engagement, feminist theory keeps us open to the affirmative qualities of biopolitical subjectivity. As Braidotti writes, maintaining vitality "as the defining trait of the subject displaces the unitary vision of consciousness and the sovereignty of the 'I'. Both liberal individualism and classical humanism are accordingly disrupted at their very foundations" (Braidotti 2006, 265).

In focusing on the affirmative qualities of biopolitics, Braidotti, of course, does not argue that biological living is somehow apolitical or pre-political. She, like Agamben, refuses to acknowledge any clear distinction between something called "natural life" and something called "political life." That is to say, like Agamben, Braidotti also recognizes that denying a "generative force" any "political or ethical relevance" is itself a political act—evidence of the biopolitical, rather than the solely biological or the solely political underpinnings of what Agamben terms "bare life." Unlike Agamben, however, Braidotti, once more, finds in this vitality a source of hope. Biopolitics is a positive rather than a negative set of relations. The fact that its key participants are those to whom classical, juridical, humanist, or liberal theories have traditionally denied human status should by no means leave it vulnerable to denunciation. On the contrary, this quality of biopolitics should help us to recognize its value *in particular* as a feminist mode of engagement.

Once we begin to interpret biopolitics in this direction, in fact, we can also begin to excavate other, potentially positive, variations on the biopolitical theme. A second component of Foucault's original elaboration of biopolitics worth revisiting, for example, is the biopolitical data set or statistical apparatus. Like the environment, the data set did not play a prominent role in much of the earlier work on biopolitics. If the data set did appear, it was presented as a further example of the totalitarian endpoint to biopolitical engagement. After all, redefining life with reference to data and information—or privileging statistics on organic existence over the lived experiences of the individual—seems at best exploitative. What could be more dehumanizing than being reduced to an entry on a spreadsheet?

If we set aside this fear of not being human, or of not being fully human, however, we can once again reconsider the ethics of the biopolitical statistical apparatus. We can remain open to the *value* of a politics not only of bare life, not only of bare life operating across environments, but of the information, data, and computation that, along with bodies, live this life. In the same way that Braidotti's turn to the seemingly dehumanizing environmental qualities of biopolitics set the foundation for a positive feminist interpretation of biopolitical subjectivity, this turn toward the seemingly dehumanizing data set can do the same. Braidotti, in fact, hints at the informational or computational as well as environmental qualities of biopolitics in her work. Emphasizing that the nonunitary biopolitical subject is in no way necessarily organic, she writes that "the technological body is... an ecological unit... marked by interdependence with its environment through a structure of mutual flows and data transfer that is best configured by the notion of viral contamination" (Braidotti 2006, 41).

But the importance of information flow, technology, and computation to feminist theories of biopolitics has also animated the writing of other scholars who are more directly concerned with *computation*, gender, and sexuality. Over the past decade, for example, Luciana Parisi has developed a multifaceted theory of sexuality, biology, politics, and, above all, information that extends earlier work on biopolitics in fascinating ways. Although she does not identify herself as a scholar of biopolitics per se, her early work on "micropolitics" and "information trading" (Parisi 2004) can be usefully read as an intervention into the turn-of-the-millennium writing on the biopolitical. The basis of much of Parisi's work on information and computation over the past decade, for example, has been the insistence that the data set or the algorithm cannot be ignored or marginalized as a derivative of some more real or truer organic or political existence. The statistical apparatus is not simply a handy abstract way to express our true interest—physical reality. On the contrary, Parisi insists, taking information seriously as a micropolitical or biopolitical subject in and of itself is as important as, for Braidotti, taking the environment seriously as a biopolitical subject (Parisi 2013, 12).

More to the point, considering the data set as, on its own, a biopolitical subject radically reconfigures both our understanding of gender and sexuality and some of the most fundamental questions that have motivated feminist theory. Parisi, for example, focuses on two aspects of the data at the heart of biopolitical engagement. The first is the simultaneously material and symbolic quality of data—the extent to which the mathematics underlying information theory is a series of physical as well as numerical operations, or the extent to which code is itself physical work (Parisi 2013, 12). The second is the nonlinear or chaotic, rather than linear or "filial," quality of information transfer—especially when the algorithms working through this data encounter a "glitch" (Parisi 2004, 29; 2013, 114). Focusing on these two aspects of biopolitical data in turn allows Parisi to make a series of claims about femininity, gender, and sexuality in the biopolitical realm.

The first of these claims is that the lines between culture and nature or gender and sex are impossible to maintain. Blurring these lines, it is true, has been the project of a number of feminist theorists, as well as of scholars of science and technology studies, for at least three decades. But by taking the problem of biopolitical information transfer as her jumping off point, Parisi is also able to move this conclusion in an unexpected direction. "Feminine desire," she writes, "no longer corresponds to the realm of possibilities or actualities, in which femininity matches with identity—a given essence, such as a biological sex, or a cultural construction, such as a gendered sex" (Parisi 2004, 25). Rather, feminine desire is dispersed across and operates over the fields of data that underlie biopolitical engagement. Relevant neither to the material, biological body nor the linguistic, political subject, feminine desire corresponds here to material-linguistic, or biological-political, environments.

Scholarly debates over whether gender or sex should be the starting point of feminist theory can thus to some extent be bracketed in this alternative context. They can be bracketed, however, not because the politics underlying these debates is unimportant, but because, given a biopolitical framework focused on *data*, gender and sex are constantly trading places across informational-material fields of relations. Neither manifests itself in language *or* in bodies. As Parisi writes,

> the impact of information sciences and technology implies a new politics (a micropolitics) of the body that involves a materialist construction of sex. This

> construction will enable us to grasp amodal dynamics of transmission that locate femininity onto a vaster process of transmission linking the variations of a body on a nature-culture continuum.
>
> (Parisi 2004, 30)

Parisi's conclusion, then, is relatively familiar to feminist theory: neither language nor matter should be privileged in conversations about gender and sexuality. But the logic leading to this conclusion is unexpected and opens up a series of exciting new conversations. Language and matter, for example, are not mutually constitutive here, as they have been in so much scholarship on these issues. Rather, given the nature of biopolitical information technology, language *is* matter. The dichotomies between sex and gender, nature and culture, matter and language dissolve not for political or affective reasons but for empirical ones.

Moreover, as biopolitical data and information are compiled, created, and transmitted, it becomes clear that dissolving the divide between sex and gender or matter and language is only one of many implications of this alternative take on biopolitics. The second aspect of information technology on which Parisi focuses, for example, is its nonlinear and chaotic quality—its vulnerability to the accident or glitch. According to Parisi, since nonlinear contagion is as valid an explanation for the transfer of information—including genetic information—as is filial or linear transfer, we must reconsider traditional associations between the transmission of biological information and the situation of sexuality in the genital organs. "Nonfiliative processes of transmission," Parisi writes,

> expose new implications for the cybernetic folding of technology, nature, and feminine desire. In particular, genetic engineering, from transgenesis . . . to human cloning, challenges the Darwinian and neo-Darwinian notion of evolution based on the organic model of sex. . . . [S]elective pressures, far from providing the conservation of the fittest traits or units, mark an open-ended communication between the body and its environment: an ecology of mutual modifications in which a body responds to selection in the most unpredictable way.
>
> (Parisi 2004, 28)

Taking the data set—in addition to the environment or the body—as a site of biopolitical subject formation, in other words, not only maps gender and sexuality across *continuums* of nature and culture, matter and language, organic and inorganic, or, for that matter, alive and dead (Parisi 2004, 38). More so, it divorces sexuality, feminine desire, and the transmission of information altogether from bodies and genital organs. If "patterns of transmission" are chaotic rather than linear, and if they occur across "a micropolitical field of contagious relations" (Parisi 2004, 41), then "femininity no longer remains specific to one mode of sex. It is not localized in one body or another, in one form-function or another. It is not an identity, an individual unity" (Parisi 2004, 44). On the contrary, femininity operates, again, across the fields of data and information that Foucault initially linked to biopolitical sovereignty.

But in situating femininity in this way, Parisi clearly goes further than Foucault ever imagined in exploring the implications of the biopolitical statistical apparatus. She is also radically re-conceiving many of the questions that have concerned feminist theorists over the past decades. Consider, for instance, the following broad schematic of feminist political theory: the question motivating feminist theorists working within a liberal or classical juridical framework of inquiry has traditionally been how women—as marginalized figures—might achieve full personhood in the public sphere (Pateman 1989, 11). For those working within a biopolitical framework defined with reference to sexuality, reproduction, and (if less so) death, the question shifted to how women might negotiate their positions as quite central figures in a politics that rests on constant bodily and biological intervention or regulation (Stoler 1995). For those, like Braidotti, who have worked within a biopolitical framework defined with reference to the environment, the question becomes how, as female subjects, we might imagine an affirmative, nonunitary, dispersed, and material mode of democratic engagement—how feminism together with biopolitics might operate as a political and ethical set of relations (Braidotti 2006).

For, Parisi, however, whose biopolitical framework invokes primarily information, algorithms, and data sets, the question has become where to locate gender and sexuality in the simultaneously material and symbolic realm of information theory; or, put differently, her question is what it might mean for feminist theory when the "abstract sex"(Parisi 2004, 39) that operates through the biopolitical data set is, via the operations of information technology, the most material manifestation of sex or gender that we can find. Braidotti questioned the negative connotations of being a biopolitical environment, and in doing so made it possible to ask questions about what an engaged, material, feminist biopolitics might entail. Parisi, by questioning the negative connotations of being data, makes it similarly possible to ask pressing questions about the quality of feminine existence. Each has found an affirmative mode of democratic engagement in what are ordinarily presented as the most negative aspects of Foucauldian biopolitics. And each has set the groundwork for a fascinating and growing conversation among feminist theorists of biopolitics, gender, and sexuality.

One of the most thoughtful recent examples of a feminist theory that brings together all of these interpretations of biopolitical engagement—a study that addresses life, reproduction, sexuality, gender, the environment, *and* information—is Catherine Mills's *Futures of Reproduction: Bioethics and Biopolitics*. Mills's concern seems to be the same as that of liberal bioethicists. She asks what an ethical theory of reproduction might look like given recent technological developments. By acknowledging, exploring, but then also leaving aside traditional categories of liberal analysis, however—problems such as rights, duties, choice, and individual will—and by addressing this question within a biopolitical framework, Mills develops a new framework for exploring the ethical implications of evolving reproductive technologies.

Mills argues, for example, that conventional liberal bioethics are not sufficiently open to the possibility that "new technologies also produce opportunities for new ways of thinking about ourselves and our ethical practices" (Mills 2011, 4). Since liberal approaches to new reproductive technologies consider solely the perspective of the self-contained, rational, individual, she continues, they in fact verge on the irresponsible—ignoring the environmental, material, and informational *as well as* subjective character of life or living (Mills 2011, 3). A feminist biopolitical approach to these technologies, contrarily, would operate from a variety of embodied and material perspectives. Such an approach would invite readers to consider the alternative definitions of life and alternative modes of ethical engagement that liberal bioethics leaves inconceivable. As Mills puts it, a feminist biopolitical take on reproductive technologies can lead to a "richer conception of corporeal life and its role in establishing ethical responsiveness" (Mills 2011, 86).

Like Braidotti's and Parisi's, then, Mills's feminist biopolitics sets the groundwork for a hopeful, or at least potentially hopeful, set of political, social, and affective relations outside the realm of the liberal subject. A biopolitical bioethics, unlike a liberal bioethics, can help us to recognize the *various* ways in which both life and ethics might flourish or operate. Indeed, by taking as her starting point one of the most notorious of biopolitical products—eugenics—Mills demonstrates that even difficult or irresolvable ethical topics can, following this shift in focus, lend themselves to unexpectedly encouraging avenues of inquiry (Mills 2011, 11). Reconceiving eugenics in this way, for example, helps Mills to destabilize further the dichotomies between the material and the linguistic, between "biological and social norms" (Mills 2011, 12, 27), between the statistically normal and the statistically anomalous (Mills 2011, 33), and, broadly, between nature and discourse. Like other feminist theorists of biopolitics, Mills finds in these dismantled dichotomies the potential for a thriving, and—more important for her purposes—ethical life.

Mills also, however, uses this alternative interpretation of eugenics as a framework for addressing one of the most enduring problems in feminist theory, biopolitical or otherwise: the problem of the political or politicized body—the problem of "reproductive behaviour com[ing] to be conceived as a domain of moral experience" (Mills 2011, 53). Mills's response to this problem is both intellectually and ethically challenging. Drawing as it does on the past few decades of feminist work on biopolitics, her response both opens up an exciting new realm of inquiry *and* makes very difficult the simple praise or simple censure of any one mode of reproduction, technological development, or political engagement.

Mills notes, for example, that the fact that reproductive behavior has become a domain of moral experience, and the fact that reproductive technologies have destabilized this domain have traditionally led to one of two reactions. The first of these reactions has been to condemn the politicization of reproduction in the name of rescuing what is assumed to have been a previously autonomous or untainted material or embodied existence. The second response has been to condemn, instead, reproductive technologies in the name of rescuing what is assumed to have been a previously coherent political existence or ethical subjectivity. Writing from a feminist biopolitical standpoint, however, Mills insists that these are not the only two options. On the contrary, the collision between ethics and reproductive technologies creates an opportunity to explore, not an obstacle to overcome. Indeed, we can now, Mills writes, "re-imagine ethical subjectivity and freedom in a way that emphasizes contingency over choice, the unexpected over the autonomous and our shared or common coexistence over the determinations of individual will" (Mills 2011, 99). Finding fault or coming to a satisfying, simple conclusion is difficult given this reimagined biopolitical ethical landscape. But the options for exploring new, unexpected, contingent modes of existence are manifold—and exciting.

And so here, then, we reach at least one conclusion to feminist theorists' criticisms of, and engagement with, biopolitics as a term and concept: a robust theory that can animate conversations addressing some of the most well-established questions in the field. The earliest work on biopolitics, especially to the extent that it ignored gender, presented biopolitical engagement as necessarily horrific. Biopolitics was a dystopian nightmare, even if it was impossible to escape. Even as this interpretation of biopolitics was being elaborated, however, feminist theorists were questioning its underpinnings. And indeed, by shifting focus to the environment and the data set—two biopolitical problems that Foucault initially presented but that the earliest theorists of biopolitics largely ignored—feminist scholars reread biopolitics in a distinctively affirmative mode. Moreover, the tension between these two approaches set the stage for scholars like Mills to consider key ethical questions from a feminist biopolitical perspective—without striking an accusatory *or* a laudatory note.

We could in fact make a case that Foucault's silence on gender has been an unexpected boon to feminist theorists of biopolitics. This silence is a challenge, and it has become a challenge that scholars have taken up with great productivity. Deliberately making femininity their touchstone, feminist theorists have not only been able to criticize, but to reimagine, biopolitics as a scholarly term. Braidotti, as a feminist, can question Agamben's fear of bodies and his obsession with death. And she can then reconceive biopolitics as an affirmative, environmental mode of democratic engagement. Parisi, as a feminist, can allay the terror produced by data sets or algorithms gone out of control. And she can then sketch a computational theory of egalitarian feminine desire. Finally, Mills, as a feminist, can take biopolitics as a healthy foundation for an ethical theory of life and reproduction. Each finds the potential productivity—the hint of a flourishing life—in biopolitics *because* each is writing as a feminist.

It is worth re-emphasizing, indeed, that much of the feminist work on biopolitics has *not* sought to criticize or reject the term, but rather to ask whether the problems plaguing earlier theories of biopolitics are actually problems. Feminist theorists, in other words, have questioned the methodological underpinnings of traditional scholarship on biopolitics and have thereby come to alternative—and usually less morbid—conclusions about what biopolitical engagement entails. More to the point, these scholars have found biopolitics an effective framework for thinking about gender, sexuality, law, and politics from the perspective of nonunitary, environmental, computational, and technological systems. By leaving aside the fear—the fear of death and the fear of being a space, environment, tool, or object—feminist theorists of biopolitics have been able to address long-standing problems in the field without losing sight of the rapidly changing, mutable character of life, matter, and existence.

Is the Biopolitical Dead?

A more prosaic aspect of this engagement with biopolitics in the field of feminist theory, however, is that the term has also to some extent been spared the scholarly beating that it has received in other fields. Neither embracing the concept wholeheartedly nor rejecting it entirely, feminist theorists have provided an arena for intellectual engagement with biopolitics that has to some extent protected it from the vagaries of scholarly trends. This does not mean, though, that biopolitics necessarily has a future in feminist theory. It may be the case that what so many scholars found disreputable about the term in the late-2000s may disqualify feminist theorists from usefully engaging with it as well. To ask what, if any, role biopolitics might play in ongoing feminist scholarship, we might therefore return to the questions with which we started—but answer them more specifically from the perspective of feminist theory:

Why, then, did "biopolitics" become as influential as it did at the moment it did, and why should its discrediting have involved such intellectual violence? In the early 2000s, Agamben's death-driven interpretation of biopolitics seemed to be one of the few theories that could adequately explain what many saw as the return of the concentration camp—or at least of a new centrality or acceptability of the camp within democratic politics (Butler 2004, 58, 64, 73). By insisting that the camp was not an accident of liberalism—or unique to fascist totalitarianism—but, rather, the logical conclusion to rights-based democracy, and *always there*, Agamben presented scholars with a variation on biopolitics that responded to what seemed to be a pressing intellectual need. "Biopolitics," as of the early 2000s, was a way to deal with a series of political events that unsettled many formerly complacent liberal thinkers.

When, however, Agamben was unable or unwilling to provide a satisfying solution to the biopolitical problem that he identified—or, less charitably, when a few years passed and liberal thinkers were able to redefine the global policies of the early 2000s as a momentary anomaly in what was otherwise a healthy liberal democratic system—his scholarship, and along with it "biopolitics" writ large, came under attack. Agamben was simply one more obscurantist anti-liberal thinker who willfully ignored the obvious benefits of rights-based democracy to make his marginal intellectual points. "Biopolitics" became, at best, an absurdity and, at worst, ideologically suspect.

And this narrative of the fate of Agamben's death-focused interpretation of biopolitics makes sense if we accept that the term or concept was nothing more than a victim of scholarly trends. It does not, though, adequately explain the intensity of the celebration or the intensity of the later rejection of the term. Returning to the two other questions that started this chapter—why were feminist theorists among the first to recognize the apparent weaknesses of "biopolitics" as an explanatory concept, and was the demolition of the term a triumph for critical feminist theory?—can help to add nuance to the story. Feminist theorists for the most part have never been convinced that the death camp is the preeminent space of biopolitics. As Braidotti notes, those writing *as* feminists frequently found something suspect about distilling all the biopolitical spaces that Foucault elaborated—up to and including the reproductive body—into a story of Auschwitz.

Recognizing this weakness in the death-driven interpretation of biopolitics, feminist theorists have thus perhaps been in a better position to consider and evaluate, rather than to reject, the term. Or, to put it differently, by focusing on the biopolitical qualities of material fields and systems that have little to do with Auschwitz, feminist scholars have been challenged to respond the term on its own merits. Dismissing the term once the camps—or, at least, the camps that came to our attention—were designated accidents or invisible was not an option in the field of feminist theory. And as a result, feminist theorists are perhaps better able to look carefully at why scholars in other fields were so quick to discard it. Because there is clearly something more going on in the repudiation of "biopolitics" as a whole—even if this biopolitics is manifested only in Agamben's work—than a simple frustration at the lack of Agamben's solution to what is usually presented as a problem.

Indeed, Agamben's very inability to respond to the liberal criticism gets at the underlying challenge that biopolitics broadly defined poses to scholarship—and that feminist theory, nearly uniquely, has been willing to address. Biopolitical theory, quite basically, sketches a mode of political existence that does not lend itself to rational, liberal speech. Agamben's silence, therefore, was arguably not the result of his having no solution to the enduring "what else" question that has shored up three centuries of liberal theory. Rather, it was the result of his having, in fact, no words to express the mode of political existence that he had theorized. For Agamben, this lack of speech was devastating. Having founded his work on the classical Aristotelian fear of *not* speaking—of existing as bare life—Agamben could not then negotiate a situation in which a lack of speech was the only response. The most basic flaw in his work, therefore, if there was one, was not that he did not offer an alternative, but that he was unable to evaluate biopolitics on its own nonlinguistic terms.

Feminist theorists however, have traditionally not been frightened of life lived outside Aristotelian categories—categories which, in any case, have traditionally been denied most women—or of the alternative modes of speech that present themselves when these categories are set to the side. Indeed, as Braidotti, Parisi, Mills, and so many other feminist theorists of biopolitics have suggested, having no words to express a mode of political engagement does not by any means leave that mode of political engagement objectionable or unacceptable. On the contrary, speech and life appear together, in a variety of guises, across a variety of fields and environments, and biopolitics offers an excellent framework for exploring the manifold variations on the two. Value neutral as they have been, feminist theories of biopolitics can thus help scholars to come to complex and open-ended conclusions about life, death, reproduction, gender, sexuality, law, and politics outside the constraints of classical liberal theory—and these conclusions can in turn help to frame ongoing, necessary, and likewise productive conversations.

So, is biopolitics dead? Undoubtedly it is. But we need not mourn it, or even pay much attention to its passing because death is by no means the end. As Braidotti writes, "death is overrated" (Braidotti 2006, 40). And as Parisi and Mills continue, there are so many living things to consider. Dead, alive, or both, biopolitics can help us to confront them—or, more accurately, to engage them.

References

Agamben, Giorgio. 1998. *Homo Sacer: Sovereign Power and Bare Life*. Translated by Daniel Heller-Roazen. Redwood City, CA: Stanford University Press.

Braidotti, Rosi. 2006. *Transpositions: On Nomadic Ethics*. Cambridge: Polity Press.

Briggs, Laura. 2002. *Reproducing Empire: Race, Sex, Science and U.S. Imperialism in Puerto Rico*. Berkeley: University of California Press.

Burfoot, Annette. 2003. "Human Remains: Identity Politics in the Face of Biotechnology." *Cultural Critique* 53 (Winter): 47–71.

Butler, Judith. 2004. *Precarious Life: The Powers of Mourning and Violence*. New York: Verso.

Cahill, A. J. 2000. "Foucault, Rape, and the Construction of the Feminine Body." *Hypatia* 15 (1): 43–64.

Foucault, Michel. 2003. *Society Must Be Defended*. Translated by D. Macey. New York: Picador Press.

Fraser, Nancy. 1989. *Unruly Practices: Power, Discourse and Gender in Contemporary Social Theory*. Minneapolis: University of Minnesota Press.

Mills, Catherine. 2011. *Futures of Reproduction: Bioethics and Biopolitics*. London: Springer.

Parisi, Luciana. 2004. "Information Trading and Symbiotic Micropolitics." *Social Text* 22 (3) (Fall): 24–49.

Parisi, Luciana. 2013. *Contagious Architecture: Computation, Aesthetics, and Space*. Cambridge, MA: Massachusetts Institute of Technology Press.

Passavant, Paul A. 2007. "The Contradictory State of Giorgio Agamben." *Political Theory* 35 (2): 147–174.

Pateman, Carole. 1989. *The Disorder of Women: Democracy, Feminism and Political Theory*. Redwood City, CA: Stanford University Press.

Pedersen, J. E. 1996. "Regulating Abortion and Birth Control: Gender, Medicine, and Republican Politics in France, 1870-1920." *French Historical Studies* 19 (3): 673–698.

Reggiani, A. H. 1996. "Procreating France: The Politics of Demography, 1919-1945." *French Historical Studies* 19 (3): 725–754.

Sarat, Austin, and Jennifer L. Culbert. 2009. "Introduction: Interpreting the Violent State." In *States of Violence: War, Capital Punishment, and Letting Die*, edited by Austin Sarat and Jennifer L. Culbert, 1–24. Cambridge: Cambridge University Press.

Sarat, Austin. 2011. "Introduction: Toward New Conceptions of the Relationship of Law and Sovereignty under Conditions of Emergency." In *Sovereignty, Emergency, Legality*, edited by Austin Sarat, 1–15. Cambridge: Cambridge University Press.

Stoler, Ann L. 1995. *Race and the Education of Desire*. Durham, NC: Duke University Press.

Stoler, Ann L. 2002. *Carnal Knowledge and Imperial Power: Race and the Intimate in Colonial Rule*. Berkeley: University of California Press.

Stolzenberg, Nomi. 2012. "Political Theology with a Difference." *USC Law Legal Studies Paper* (No. 12–23). Available at SSRN: http://ssrn.com/abstract=2152120.

West, Robin. 2011. *Normative Jurisprudence: An Introduction*. Cambridge: Cambridge University Press.

CHAPTER 4

CIVILIZATION

ANN TOWNS

CIVILIZATION evokes and provokes. For some, the term *civilization* calls up notions of reason, advancement and emancipation; whereas for others it represents repression and hypocrisy, serving as the intellectual foundation for Western imperialism or totalitarian Islamic fundamentalism. In contrast with concepts such as *governmentality*, which has remained an analytic term of academics, *civilization* has furthermore permeated the language, identities, and practices of actors ranging from public officials and social activists to religious devotees and housewives across the world. It is thus not surprising that *civilization* has fascinated a large number of scholars since it emerged as a term more than two hundred years ago.

This chapter focuses on feminist civilization scholarship of the last few decades. It will show that feminist scholars have tended to approach the concept of civilization in one of two ways. Some treat civilizations as actually existing and distinguishable sociocultural complexes, asking questions about the condition and accomplishments of women within different civilizations. A larger group of scholars has instead approached civilization as discourse, as unfolding processes of differentiation between, for example, "the West" and "Islam" that can be nothing but ephemeral and contextual. These scholars have primarily asked questions about how representations of the status of women or gender are implicated in what Islam or the West are made to be, and with what effects, in particular contexts. The intersection of discourses of civilization and gender with those of race and nation has furthermore often been highlighted in this work.

Both approaches have provided crucial correctives to otherwise gender-blind lines of study, convincingly showing the centrality of women and/or gender to civilization and disrupting some of the conventional assumptions and narratives, particularly about the West and Islam. And since there is not one shared set of assumptions among feminist scholars about what civilizations are or how to study them, the nature of the interventions as well as their strengths and weaknesses differ, as I will show. However, much of the influential work on civilization still seems to proceed without paying any attention to gender whatsoever, and thus the time seems ripe for gender scholars of any persuasion to directly and forcefully engage and expose gender-blind work on civilization. After a discussion of scholarship using the two main approaches to civilization, I will end with a suggestion that feminists pursue and confront gender-blind work a bit more directly and confrontationally.

PRIMORDIAL VIEW: CIVILIZATIONS AS SOCIOCULTURAL ENTITIES

One common way scholars approach civilization is as actually existing sociocultural complexes. Here, a civilization is conceived as the broadest cultural entity in human life, "defined both by common objective elements, such as language, religion, customs, institutions, and by the subjective self-identification of people" (Huntington 1996, 43). A civilization so conceived is made to be a coherent complex, defined by its distinctive and relatively stable cultural content and identity. Some of the questions that have engaged scholars within this approach include, Which are the main civilizations in the world? What are their core cultural features, differences and associated practices? How have civilizations developed over time?

This approach to civilization was brought into very sharp view by the 1996 publication of Samuel Huntington's book *The Clash of Civilizations*. Huntington identified nine distinctive contemporary civilizations with geographical boundaries: Western, Islamic, Orthodox, African, Latin American, Sinic, Hindu, Buddhist, and Japanese. The book does not provide a complete inventory of the central cultural features of each of these civilizations, but it offers a relatively comprehensive list of the allegedly distinguishing characteristics of Western civilization. These include individualism (putatively the most important and distinctive feature of the West), separation of spiritual and temporal authority, the rule of law, democracy, and social pluralism (Huntington 1996, 69–72). In the book, as in the 1993 *Foreign Affairs* article that preceded it, Huntington emphasized difference between civilizational entities, tying values and practices such as democracy unequivocally to Western civilization as opposed to others. "Western concepts differ fundamentally from those prevalent in other civilizations," he argues, contending that "Western ideas of . . . democracy . . . have little resonance in Islam" (Huntington 1993, 40). Because of such differences, and as civilizational distinctions have allegedly become more relevant in the post–Cold War world, Huntington charged that world politics will be dominated by relations, rifts, and in some cases, conflicts between these cultural complexes. He predicted that "the clash of civilizations will dominate global politics. The fault lines between civilizations will be the battle lines of the future" (1993, 22). His representation of Islam and its alleged borders include what might be the most controversial statement of the entire book: "Islam's borders are bloody and so are its innards. The fundamental problem for the West is not Islamic fundamentalism. It is Islam, a different civilization whose people are convinced of the superiority of their culture and are obsessed with the inferiority of their power" (Huntington 1996, 258).

Huntington's clash of civilizations thesis has generated an enormous, and often enormously intense, debate on issues ranging from the nature of civilizations to the validity of specific hypotheses about Islam. By and large, unfortunately, this is a debate of which feminists have stayed clear. However, a few scholars interested in gender, feminism and/or women have picked up and tested some of Huntington's claims. Ronald Inglehart and Pippa Norris's article "The True Clash of Civilizations" is probably the most widely read of these. Inglehart and Norris's main argument is that gender and sexuality issues—not democracy—are the main source of conflict between the West and Islam. Drawing on data from the World Values Survey, they argue that,

> Samuel Huntington was only half right. The cultural fault line that divides the West and the Muslim world is not about democracy but sex. According to a new survey, Muslims and their Western counterparts want democracy, yet they are worlds apart when it comes to attitudes toward divorce, abortion, gender equality, and gay rights.
> (Inglehart and Norris 2003, 62)

For Inglehart and Norris, then, the West and Islam exist as identifiable civilizations in the way Huntington claims, but their main fault line is gender and sexuality issues. A few other scholars have since lent support to their argument (e.g., Alexander and Welzel 2011). Similar claims about a clash between the West and non-Western cultures have also been aired in the work of feminists, such as Susan Moller Okin, who have expressed concern about the implications for women of bringing non-Western gender traditions into the West (e.g., Okin 1999). Here, the empowerment of women is unequivocally attributed to Western values and traditions, leading to anxieties about the presumed conflict between non-Western cultural traditions and sexual equality in multicultural societies.

The thesis that women's rights are the true clash of civilization has since generated a debate of its own. A number of scholars have objected that, with regard to views on sexuality and gender equality, distinctions within civilizations may be more important than distinctions between them. For instance, taking Inglehart and Norris to task, Rizzo and his colleagues (2007) show that there are significant differences in support for gender equality between Arab and non-Arab Muslim societies, with higher levels of support for women's rights in non-Arab Muslim countries (see also Spierings et al. 2009; Fattore et al. 2010). This follows other studies that have documented the diversity in women's rights and opportunities within the Muslim world (e.g., Kandiyoti 1992 and 2007; Bodman and Nayereh 1998; Charrad 2001, 2007 and 2011; Keddie 2007; Moghissi 2005). Responding to generalizing and stereotypical representations of the role and situation of women in Islam, these scholars have made convincing assertions about the wide legal and political diversity throughout the Islamic world. In other words, these scholars claim, there is no coherent "Islamic" approach to women's rights. Charrad (2011, 420) suggests thinking of "Islam as an 'umbrella identity,' an idiom of cultural unity that goes together with considerable variations according to time and place."

A number of factors other than Islam are also identified as important causes of gender inequality in the Islamic world. In an award-winning essay that has received a lot of media attention, Ross (2008) argues that oil, not Islam, should be faulted for the lack of gender equality in the Middle East. Economies that rely on oil production generate a labor market with fewer women, which in turn reduces the political influence of women.[1] Charrad (2001, 2007) has pointed to kin-based solidarities among men rather than Islam in the Muslim Middle East and North Africa as a main reason why inequalities are perpetuated in law, politics, and the economy. In sum, by underscoring the great diversity among Muslim-majority countries and by identifying other causes of gender inequality than "Islamic culture," these critics have charged that claims about a cultural fault line between the West and Islam over women's rights are simply inaccurate. This is a critical intervention at a time when ideas about a clear cultural abyss between Islam and the West flourish.

The work discussed above is more or less expressly concerned with the contents and boundaries of civilizations-as-entities and whether these relate to gender equality and women's rights. The claims about civilizations and their contents are made quite explicit and are subjected to empirical examination. However, there is a much larger and older body of feminist work that implicitly approaches civilizations as actually existing entities—namely, the history scholarship on women in Western civilization and women in Islam. This is scholarship that responds to the marginalization of women in conventional historical accounts about Western civilization and Islam. Here, the interest is the classical feminist aim of recovering female voices and accomplishments—in part, an interest in generating *herstories* rather than history by asking, "where are the women?" In doing so, as we shall see, feminist writers have launched crucial challenges to conventional historical narratives about the liberating nature and historical progressivism of Western civilization as well as to conventional ideas about the oppression of women in the Islamic world. This groundbreaking work has simultaneously tended to reproduce predominant primordial ideas about what Western civilization, Islam, or other civilizations are.

Women in the History of Western Civilization

Feminist scholars writing on women in Western civilization have targeted the cottage industry that has developed around Western civilization courses required at US high schools and in the undergraduate university degrees of many US universities (on these courses, see Kleinbaum 1979; Allardyce 1982). Noting the lack of discussion about the status of women and the contributions of women to civilization in textbooks and other academic treatments, these scholars have made it a point to focus precisely on that: the role and place of women in Western civilization (e.g., Kleinbaum 1979; Walsh 1981; Cantarella 1987; Stephenson 2012). The omission of women in the history of Western civilization is a serious problem in education, they point out, as it not only distorts history but also perpetuates a belief that what women do is of little importance.

When turning the focus on women, these historians have generally followed a canonical narrative about the history and boundaries of Western civilization, moving from one historical period to the next in the geographical areas of southern and Western Europe and the United States. To be sure, the studies generally begin with some mention of prehistoric time, Mesopotamia and Egypt, but they then quickly move to focus attention on what is allegedly the center of classical Western civilization, Greece and Rome. Discussions of women in the Athenian state, Sparta, and Roman society are followed by the medieval period, the Renaissance, the Enlightenment, and nineteenth- and twentieth-century European and US history.

This journey through the conventional history of Western civilization unearths a wealth of interesting and significant information about the role and status of women, information which is used to question and deflate the progressive story about the development of Western civilization. *Women in Western Civilization* (1981) by Elizabeth Miller Walsh is a good illustration. Walsh briefly points to the elevated standing of women in ancient Egypt, where women were the property owners and men had to transfer their property to the wife on marriage (21). Women, furthermore, had the same legal rights, powers in court, and ability to divorce as men, and they could be priestesses as well as hold positions in government and the military (22). In classical Athens, in contrast, women were not enfranchised, could not own property and could not conduct legal business—they were the ward of their husband or nearest male relative. The Athenian democratic state, an alleged pillar of Western civilization, was a slave state in which women were subordinated and isolated in the home, away from the cherished public life of equal citizens, as Walsh points out. She then moves through Roman society, which was also misogynistic but less so, since Roman women had more freedoms and enjoyed more respect than their Greek sisters, to the medieval period and the European Renaissance, during which class and status were more important than gender (e.g., 94). There was thus great variation in the empowerment and status of European women between the medieval period and the Renaissance. By the eighteenth and nineteenth centuries, the era of industrialization, revolution, and democratic breakthroughs, the status of women declined more uniformly. Walsh (1981, 132) writes that "women became as confined to the home in the eighteenth and nineteenth centuries as they had in Athens in 450 B.C.; through the chains of social taboos and the concept of the ideal woman, a concept which required her presence at home."

This crucial shifting of attention to the situation and activities of women in Western civilization reproduces the idea that civilizations exist as bounded cultural complexes, as stated earlier. The narratives tend to follow conventional primordial signposts about the West's geographical boundaries and historical chronology. However, in shifting attention to women, these accounts simultaneously alter some of the fundamental premises of the conventional narratives, with very important implications for how we are to understand Western civilization. The history of Western civilization has often been told as one of liberation and progress, from the origins of democracy in the Athenian state and the Pax Romana of international justice and rule of law, to the Renaissance and Enlightenment periods, which, after the unfortunate medieval period, brought back reason, the state, and all the good things that presumably followed. By focusing on women, feminist scholars have exposed the fundamental and foundational androcentrism in conventional historical accounts of Western civilization. And in doing so, they have stirred up the basic story of progress. As Abby Kleinbaum has stated, a women's history of Western civilization,

> shows us that classical civilization, the Renaissance, and the Enlightenment may well have been high points in the development of the rights of man, but that they also signaled an increasing subordination of women. It asks that we reconsider Sparta and the medieval period of European history in terms not only of the opportunities they offered to men, but also in terms of the possibilities that women were able to realize in these societies . . . women's history tells us that the Emperor wears no clothes; the epic, the song of Western Civilization, is a tune gone sour.
>
> (Kleinbaum 1979, 505)

Making visible the contributions of women and focusing on the historical conditions productive of their situation has thus helped challenge some of the received wisdom about the progressive nature and development of Western civilization. This is a very important contribution indeed, as it fundamentally rewrites the history and periodization of the West. However, by largely adopting the conventional view of the boundaries of the West from the canon they seek to critique, these feminist interventions have not been able to challenge the notion of Western civilization as a separate and distinctive entity in the world. For instance, the ways in which European imperialism and conquests have shaped the very foundation of Western civilization remain largely out of purview. Questions about the contributions of women (and men) in colonized societies to the formation of Western gender institutions and practices are not asked. In short, the border between the West and the Rest remains intact even in these otherwise groundbreaking accounts about women and Western civilization. This, in turn, has implications for how feminisms are practiced. What Uma Narayan has called "the Package Picture view" of civilizations as distinctive and coherent entities creates additional obstacles for feminist alliances. By giving up such a conceptualization, "liberating possibilities with respect to cross-cultural feminist judgments" may open up (Narayan 2012, 5).

Women in the History of Islam

A range of feminist historians have also explored the role and situation of women within Islam over time, similarly treating the Islamic world as an actually existing and identifiable sociocultural complex. These scholars have also responded to the previous lack of focus on women in accounts of Islamic history. "Most general overviews of Islamic history, and perhaps especially those to which students are first introduced, have little or nothing to say about the lives of women," as Hambly (1998, 3) has noted. As a corrective, a wealth of important herstories about the role and condition of women in the Islamic world has emerged (e.g., Al-Hibri 1982a, b; Ahmed 1992; Hambly 1998). These histories have primarily focused on women and on the seventh-century emergence of Islam in Arabia and its subsequent spread to the rest of the Middle East over the following century, the nineteenth-century era of European encroachment on and colonization of the Middle East and various nationalisms, and the twentieth-century history of upheavals and veiling movements.

Over all, the boundaries of Islamic civilization in these historical accounts are made to be much more permeable than those that appear in representations of the history of Western civilization. There is a great deal of emphasis on the continuities between pre-Islamic societies and post-Islamic developments as well as on the ongoing influences of the values and practices with which Islamic practitioners have come into contact during the expansion of Islam and European growing international dominance and colonialism. Cultural hybridity is thus built into the historical narratives about women's role and condition in Islam.

Leila Ahmed's pathbreaking book *Women and Gender in Islam: Historical Roots of a Modern Debate* (1992) is an excellent example of the strengths of this work (see also e.g., Hambly 1998; Roded 1999; Nashat 2006; Walther 2006). I will focus on her discussion of the emergence and spread of Islamic society in the seventh and eighth centuries. "The continuities of Islamic civilization with past civilizations in the region are well recognized," Ahmed begins (3). She thus starts her story in the societies that preceded and bordered the early Islamic societies, in order to explore how gender ideas and practices there came to influence and shape core Islamic discourse. Islam first emerged in the commercial Arabian city of Mecca, a city characterized by the pastoral lifestyle and relations of Arabia. Here, although women were not equal to men, they had greater social power and more liberties than women in the neighboring Byzantine (East Roman) and Sasanian (Iranian) empires. Ahmed describes pre-Islamic Arabia as a region with a variety of marriage customs and both matrilineal and patrilineal systems. What is more, the predominant religion was polytheist, and there were three important female goddesses. Reflecting the major powers in the area at the time, the Byzantine and Sasanian empires, Islam inherited and affirmed key components of their socioreligious visions (Judaism, Christianity, and Zoroastrianism): the worship of a god referred to by a male pronoun, the patrilineal and patriarchal family and female subordination. Islamic society thus came to adopt gender relations that were already practiced in neighboring empires.

Initially, when Islam was still primarily the religion of the people of the Arabic Peninsula, women continued to have a more active social and public role. Indeed, Ahmed contends, the practices sanctioned by Muhammad in the first Muslim society entailed much more positive attitudes toward women than those found in later periods. As Arabian Muslims conquered much of the Byzantine and all of the Sasanian empires in the decades after the death of Mohammed in 632, the status of women declined and their world became more secluded and restricted to childrearing and household activities. Ahmed argues that,

> within ten years of Muhammad's death Arab conquests had carried Islam to lands far beyond, and fundamentally different from, Arabia—to societies that were urban

and that already had elaborate scriptural and legal traditions and established social mores. These societies were more restrictive toward women and more misogynist; at least their misogyny and their modes of controlling women by law and by custom were more fully articulated administratively and as inscribed code.

(Ahmed 1992, 67)

Such historical accounts underscore the importance of including the contributions of conquered societies to the formation of Islamic gender practices and institutions, even with regard to values and practices such as veiling that have come to be seen as intrinsically Islamic.

The rest of Ahmed's book, like other treatments of the history of Islamic civilization, continues to weave in accounts of the transnational processes, intercultural developments, and hybrids that have shaped the Islamic world. Such treatments of history help underscore the importance of considering Islamic formulations of gender in relation to transnational interactions and the larger context within which Islamic society is situated. As Ahmed (1992, 5) emphasizes, not doing so "would falsely isolate Islamic practices and by implication at least suggest that Islamic handling of these matters was special or even unique." Thus, although Islam is treated as a distinguishable sociocultural complex, it is not conceived of as an entirely distinctive entity with clear-cut borders. The history of Islamic civilization is thus conceived of as interconnected with the history of Western civilization (and other societies), not as two separate and internally driven developments.

Process View: Civilizations as Contextually Unfolding

A great many feminist scholars object to the conceptualization of civilizations as sociocultural complexes. In fact, one of the effects of the second major approach to civilizations in feminist work has been to challenge and deconstruct such ideas. In this second view, civilizations are regarded as unfolding processes, sets of boundary-producing practices and discourses that generate temporary and contextual differentiations between civilizations. One important dimension of this understanding is the focus on civilization as boundary production. As Jackson (1999, 143) has elucidated, scholars in this tradition "would maintain that a civilization consists of those practices which serve to distinguish one civilization from another and from the rest of the world, and that the unfolding of these processes and projects never takes place 'inside' any one civilization, but rather 'between' civilizations. Therefore it is not possible to identify an 'essence' of a civilization or other social entity, since no social entity has an existence separate from its relation to other entities." Attempts to find core or general traits within civilizations are thus abandoned in favor of analyses of Self/Other practices that enable the very conceptualization of distinctive civilizations. I would add that many scholars in this tradition also emphasize the local and temporally specific articulations of civilization, suggesting that civilization is best understood as discourse that is ephemeral rather than enduring and context specific rather than general.

This body of feminist work has shown how intimately implicated gender and the status of women are in drawing up civilizational boundaries and establishing a hierarchy between putatively distinctive civilizations or levels of civilization. It also shows how the status of women is used to contest hierarchies and redraw the boundaries between "Islam" and "the West" and between "civilized" and "savage" societies. Rather than assume that civilizations exist as entities and ask questions about the role and condition of women within them, these scholars thus pose questions about what civilization(s) is(are) made to be, how gender and/or the status of women is implicated, and with what effects. For instance, through what discourses, articulations, and social practices did "the West" or "Islam" become objects of thought and behavior? How have gender and the status of women figured into the production of the West or Islam? With what effects in particular contexts? The ideas, discourses, and meaning-laden practices that invoke and produce civilization, and how these relate to gender and with what effects, are thus central objects of analysis. This body of feminist scholarship on civilization is thus in line with Foucault's (1982, 384) recommendation that we turn "a given into a question." My discussion will treat clusters of work on the themes of eighteenth-century European Enlightenment thought, the nineteenth- and early twentieth-century era of European colonialism, and—briefly in the conclusions—the contemporary resurgence in discourses of civilization.

Eighteenth-Century Enlightenment Thought

The development of the concept of civilization is generally attributed to European—primarily French and Scottish—Enlightenment thinkers of the eighteenth century (e.g., Cannadine 2013, 1). A great deal of feminist scholarship has thus focused on textual representations of civilization in the eighteenth and nineteenth centuries. In this context, the noun *civilization* emerged and came to denote the end stage in an evolutionary process that had moved entire societies away from the presumed givens of "natural" existence. The concept came to center on social relations and interactions, particularly between the strong and the weak. The savage stage, when human life was assumed to lie closer to the brute and often violent reality of animals, was contrasted with the civilized stage, when society was governed through law, and human relations were characterized by civility and refinement. Savagery and civilization were thus understood as the beginning and final stages on a spectrum of moral, intellectual, political and technological development, with barbarity serving as a rough midpoint. The idea of progress was, furthermore, central to how Enlightenment thinkers approached the civilizing process. Sebastini (2006, 75) claims that the very idea of progress was a specific contribution of the Scottish Enlightenment, and that it was fundamentally entwined with the idea of civilization. In contrast with present understandings of civilizations in the plural, eighteenth- to early twentieth-century discourses generally identified civilization in the singular, as one (Western) developmental end point.

Feminist scholars have effectively demonstrated the centrality of ideas about women and civilization in the work of Enlightenment thinkers (e.g., Tomaselli 1985, 2006; Knott and Taylor 2006; Sebastini 2013; Towns 2014). Indeed, from the inception of the concept of civilization, the condition of women was used as a crucial measure of a society's level of advancement. As Mander explains,

> [Women's] behavior and the way in which they were treated by men was an index to how far a society had advanced along the path of civilization. Women thus offered the eighteenth-century thinker a concrete and economical means of characterizing the distinctions between societies in different times and places and they were indeed used in this way in many of the conjectural and universal histories that proliferated in Europe after 1750.
>
> (Mander 2006, 98)

Being interested in relations between the strong and the weak, Enlightenment thinkers came to ask questions about relations between the strong and the weak sexes in savagery and civilization. A number of Scottish Enlightenment scholars, such as civil law professor John Millar (University of Glasgow), influential historian William Robertson (University of Edinburgh), and philosopher and judge Henry Home (Lord Kames), advanced arguments about a shared human history of female subjugation (e.g., Sebastini 2006; Towns 2014). In savagery, they argued, brutality and sheer strength were allowed free reign, as human interactions were governed neither by law nor manners. As a consequence, women suffered exploitation and oppression as the physically weaker sex, ending up enslaved, secluded, and treated as beasts of burden. In civilized societies, on the other hand, the rule of law through government placed restraints on—civilized—relations between the strong and the weak, as did the development of manners and refinement. Women thus enjoyed greater freedoms and were able to develop their femininity and become the complementary companions of men in civilized society.

In these analyses of central Enlightenment texts, feminist scholars have shown how ideas about femininity, masculinity, and, particularly, the status of women helped to differentiate between and to hierarchically order societies around the world—savage, barbarous, and civilized. A range of societies from distinctive geographical regions and with very diverse forms of social organizations were grouped together under these simple rubrics, partly by using the alleged status of women as a measuring rod. This feminist work has thus shown how, as early as the eighteenth century, ideas about superior relations between the sexes in domestic society were implicated in setting up international hierarchies between more "advanced" and "backward" peoples around the world. Such analyses have served as important correctives to narratives that emphasize the liberating nature and effects of Enlightenment thought.

Celebrations of the advancement of women, however, coexisted in Enlightenment texts with a deprecation of femininity as traits that needed to be contained and controlled, creating an ambiguous and often contradictory approach to women. If the status of women was used as an indicator of superiority, femininity was simultaneously negatively represented as inertia, weakness, and emotionality. In a careful and close reading of a number of Scottish Enlightenment scholars, Sebastini (2006, 2013) has shown how the civilizing process was understood as movement away from an existence characterized by masculine traits—physical strength, aggression, courage—to one distinguished by putatively feminine characteristics—pacific interactions, conversation, gentleness, sociability, refinement, and civility. This, in turn, was a source of a great deal of ambivalence and anxiety about civilization among these scholars. If taken too far, civilization could presumably degenerate into "effeminacy," the eradication of distinctions between the sexes and the suppression of the necessary male traits of bravery and assertiveness. Moran (2006) similarly shows how the highly influential Scottish physician Dr. John Gregory was concerned with the feebleness associated with the refined life of civilized society. The advantages of "natural" existence for human vigor and hardiness of constitution were exemplified with the contrast between the resilience of savage mothers, who "recover easily and speedily, after bringing forth their young" with the delicacy of civilized mothers whose pregnancies were accompanied by problems presumably unknown in savage life (19). With a focus on gender, feminist scholars have thus shown that Enlightenment treatments of civilization were also wrought with doubts and the civilizing process, a tenuous development that had to be carefully managed.

The association of femininity with undesirable traits such as weakness, inertia, and lack of reason meant that femininity could be ascribed to societies and peoples as a way to identify and denigrate savage Others and establish the superiority of civilized societies. From the scholarship on Enlightenment thought, one can thus detect a second manner (in addition to women's status functioning as an index) in which gender figured into the establishment of international hierarchies—through feminization/masculinization. Sebastini (2006, 2013) examines the intersection of gender and racial hierarchy, showing how humans were classified into racial categories, some of which were denigrated by being feminized. Native Americans were derided as an "effeminate race," with men whose appearance and character resembled that of women. Their long hair and lack of facial and body hair were coupled with claims about feeble sexuality, lack of virility, and indifference toward women. This, in turn, was represented as reason for the demographical problems of Native Americans and their being unable to fight off Europeans. Being conquered and being feminine were thus closely intertwined. At the same time, as Sebastini demonstrates, pointing to uncontrolled or improper masculinity also functioned as a way to define and denigrate the uncivilized. "Negroes" were classified as a lascivious race of excessive sexuality, aggressiveness, and musculature. While they were not feminine, they were portrayed as lacking the carefully managed and controlled masculinity that civilization supposedly entailed.

By the nineteenth century, some of these Enlightenment ideas were being fiercely contested. In my own work (Towns 2010, 2014), I have shown how socialist writers and activists took issue with the claim that the advancement of civilization corresponded with an elevation of the status of women. In 1884, Friedrich Engels published his highly influential *Origin of the Family, Private Property and the State*, in which he argued,

> One of the most absurd notions ever taken over from eighteenth-century enlightenment is that in the beginning of society woman was the slave of man. Among all savages and all barbarians of the lower and middle stages, and to a certain extent the upper stage also, the position of women is not only free, but honorable.
>
> (Engels 1884, 82)

His point could not be clearer: the situation of women in savage society had been seriously mischaracterized by prior Enlightenment thinkers. In fact, Engels and a number of others claimed, the status of women in savagery and civilization demonstrated the negative effects of capitalist development. Forty years earlier, in *the Holy Family* (1845), Marx and Engels had upheld primitive society as a form of primitive communism, often characterized by matriarchy, wherein women prospered. Similar notions were then developed by a range of other important nineteenth-century writers, such as US anthropologist and social theorist Lewis Morgan (1877) and German social democrat August Bebel (1879). Morgan advanced the thesis that primitive society rested on the institution of the matrilineal clan rather than the patriarchal family. Women were thus believed to hold a central and elevated position in savage society. The relatively egalitarian relations between the sexes were then allegedly destroyed by the dramatic transformations in human relations that were brought about through the invention of private property and the emergence of capitalism. Along with capitalism came the patriarchal family as well as the exploitation of women in the labor market and as prostitutes. These institutions were embedded in the very fabric of the civilized state, these critics charged. "Rather than liberating women, the bourgeois state and its legal framework, the epitome of European civilization, were held to exploit and oppress women in this interpretation" (Towns 2014, 600–601).

In my work, I have thus attempted to show that some of the core assumptions about the status of women and civilization came to be challenged in nineteenth-century Europe. And yet, in these challenges, many fundamental assumptions about civilization were simultaneously reproduced. Human development continued to be represented in terms of the familiar stages of savagery and civilization, and the condition of women continued to be used to gauge the advancement of societies conceived of as sharing a developmental stage. The status of women thus still functioned to help draw boundaries and establish hierarchies. However, the status of women was not only used to establish the superiority of (Western) civilization—it was also used to challenge this hierarchy and to assert the superiority of "savage" non-European traditions (e.g., Towns 2010, 2014).

The Nineteenth and Twentieth Centuries: Colonialism, Resistance and Civilizing Missions

It is well known that representations of civilization came to legitimize nineteenth- and early twentieth-century European domination, providing a foundation of meaning that spurred and made sense of the conquests, enslavements, and reorganizations of societies that colonialism entailed. Discourses of civilization and gender in the context of European colonialism have thus also interested a large number of feminist scholars. These scholars have shown that the status of women continued to serve as a potent marker of difference and hierarchy, often setting out the inferiority of the colonized as uncivilized (e.g., Clancy-Smith and Gouda 1998; Thompson 2000; Boddy 2007). For instance, the allegedly general oppression of women under Islam became central in the European colonial imaginary in the nineteenth century, symbolizing the barbarity of the Islamic world and legitimating intervention in the Middle East and North Africa as liberating (e.g., Ahmed 1992). The colonized were, furthermore, alternately feminized, assigned traits such as weakness and naïvité, and masculinized, imagined as oversexed and aggressive. Edwards (1998) has examined how Cambodia was made out to be a docile, female creature in the writing of early twentieth-century French intellectuals. Clancy-Smith (1998) in turn highlighted French representations of Algeria as "over-sexed," permeated by polygamy and harems that presumably hampered the intellectual advancement of the country.

More than simply inform colonial conquests, discourses of gender and civilization produced in some Europeans a sense of obligation to "elevate" these "backward" peoples. Africans, Middle Easterners, Asians, and Native Americans were not only forcibly controlled but also subjected to various projects of moral, intellectual, and cultural uplift. Because the status of women was an indicator of progress, their situation was of particular interest. French military officer and author Eugène Daumas could thus proclaim in 1835 that his aim in writing *La Femme Arabe* (*The Arab Woman*) was to "tear off the veil that still covers the morals, customs and beliefs" of Arab society as a whole (quoted Clancy-Smith 1998, 164). In these civilizing missions, the situation of women continued to serve a pivotal symbolic function in marking out the boundaries of savagery and civilization. Indeed, female circumcised bodies, female bound feet and veiled female hair and faces have all been interpreted as indicative of savagery and as obstacles of progress, along with a series of other practices (for a fascinating account of British colonial attempts to civilize Sudanese women by managing reproduction and genital cutting, see Boddy 2007).

Feminist scholars have shown how women became some of the central agents of the *missions civilisatrice*, the "civilizing missions," of the nineteenth and early twentieth centuries (e.g., Chaudhuri and Strobel 1992; Burton 1994; Rupp 1997; Bowlan 1998;

Midgley 1998; Curtis 2010). It is perhaps not surprising that the civilizing mission spoke so strongly to women. Education and morality were arenas in which women prevailed. What is more, as Anne McClintock (1995) and others have pointed out, health, hygiene, sexuality, and reproduction were also understood as pivotal to civilizational progress or degeneration. These, too, were largely female realms, and a number of individual women and women's groups took it upon themselves to bring morality and educational and hygienic uplift to the "less civilized." Such undertakings often simultaneously served to help persuade audiences in Europe that European women were central to the march of civilization, indeed, that their political emancipation was crucial for progress (e.g., Burton 1994; Towns 2010). In short, the depictions of degraded women in the less civilized world helped authorize European feminists as agents of the progress of civilization and animated arguments in favor of their political enfranchisement.

Discourses of gender and civilization did more than legitimize colonial conquests and fuel civilizing missions, however. Indeed, the story that emerges from the scholarship on gender and civilization in the nineteenth and early twentieth centuries is not a simple one, as these discourses and how they came together were far from uniform. This was an era in which the women's movements—domestic and international—were emerging with force in Europe and in Anglo settler states, demanding suffrage, a right to nationality, mothers' pensions, and a number of other reforms that entailed fundamental changes in the relations of the sexes. A number of critics feared the emancipation of women as a catalyst of the decline of civilization. For some, colonized areas—imagined as enticing spaces of female submissiveness—emerged as inspiration to rejuvenate the metropole with proper sexual hierarchy. For instance, Edwards (1998) contends that French intellectuals of the early twentieth century used images of a feminized Cambodia to be able to retreat into a fictive world where women's role was to serve and obey. Exoticized and feminized, the less civilized paradoxically emerged as superior in terms of the imagined role of women in these societies. For others, the political role accorded to women in some African, Native American and Asian societies provided fuel to the argument that the political empowerment of women was an "antiquated" and "savage" practice that was inappropriate for civilized states (Towns 2009, 2010).

Discussing the status of women also became a way for people around the world to contest the equation of civilization and the West or Western civilization and the geographic region of Europe. Some did so through a wholesale rejection of what was made to be Western civilization and by advancing a particular interpretation of, for example, Islam as an alternative vision. Thompson (2000), among many others, has shown how the condition of women became a site of resistance and contest over civilizational superiority, with "Islam" set forth as a superior alternative to "Western civilization." Focusing on Lebanon and Syria in the 1920s and 1930s, when these states were under a French mandate, she shows how Islamic populists set up a clear binary between Islam and the West, and advanced Islamic civilization as distinctive and superior to Western civilization by focusing on the status of women. Their rendering of Islamic civilization—which differed from the national women's movements and the Salafi's mission to save Islamic civilization by absorbing change coming from Europe into a reformed Islam—entailed a defense of the seclusion of women and protests against such French measures as girls' schools, in the name of Islam (Thompson 2000, 103–109; see also Göle 1996, Towns 2014).

Others contested the alleged superiority of Western civilization by championing a hybrid of West and East as signaling progress (e.g., Chatterjee 1989, 1993; Göle 1996). An Indian nationalist response to Western colonialism, Chatterjee shows, was to separate the domain of culture into two spheres—the spiritual and the material—and to claim superiority over Western civilization in the spiritual domain. India had to westernize by adopting Western material techniques of economic organization, statecraft, science, and technology, Indian nationalists argued, while simultaneously holding on to the superior Indian spiritual essence. Not surprisingly, the domestication of women was considered central to maintaining the distinction between India and the West amid material westernization (Chatterjee 1989). In a discussion of the nineteenth-century Ottoman Empire, Göle (1996) similarly shows how "traditionalists" contended that the spiritual and moral inheritance of Islam must be maintained (with women the main site of tradition), and that westernization be limited to technical, administrative, and material developments. In short, the boundaries between West and Islam (or India) were redrawn *within* societies between the spiritual and material, the feminine and the masculine, with the effect of tying women and femininity closer to tradition and the domestic sphere.

Yet another response to the onslaught of representations of the elevated status of women in Western civilization was to claim compatibility between Western and non-Western traditions in attempts to claim equality or superiority of non-Western civilizations. Göle (1996) shows how nineteenth-century Ottoman reformists argued that support for female empowerment could be found within the sources of Islam and its early Golden Age. There was thus no contradiction between the West and Islam with regard to the status of women, they claimed. Key intellectuals within the Turkist movement of the early twentieth century similarly pointed to women's equal status with men in pre-Islamic Turkey, thus claiming a non-Western origin of sexual equality. Distinctions were also made between "pure Islam" (whose approach to women was compatible with that of both pre-Islamic Turkey and the West) and "degenerated Islam" (which entailed oppressive gender practices; Göle 1996, 46–47). The status of women was thus a means to synthesize Turkey, Islam, and Western civilization. In my work, I have shown that a number of actors around the world have indeed identified non-Western traditions as the source of equality between men and women, using this to challenge the hierarchies set out in European representations of civilization (2010, 2014). I have also shown that the status of women became a means for Latin Americans to claim Western civilization and demand inclusion in the privileged club of civilized society, thus helping extend the geographic scope of Western civilization (2010).

The feminist scholarship on discourses of civilization makes claims about civilization and gender that challenge the view of civilizations as distinctive sociocultural complexes. These scholars have investigated the production of the very boundaries that the primordial approach takes for granted, showing that what counts as "the West" or

"Islam" has been worked out in a context of messy colonial interactions, with the status of women as a primary site to determine distinctions and similarities. The boundaries of both the West and Islam have been challenged and redrawn in the process, in struggles over how to understand and ascribe gender practices, actors, and spheres. It is important to note that discourses on the status of women, then, have not simply legitimized colonialism and the boundaries and superiority of Western civilization. They have also helped challenge "the West" by setting forth alternative visions about the appropriate relations of the sexes, identifying alternative sources for the elevation of women and/or changing the boundaries of the West and Islam.

Where to from Here?

The last few decades have witnessed intensified globalization, a rise in Islamism, a global war on terrorism, and renewed major European and North American interventions in Iraq and Afghanistan. There has also been a marked increase in Muslim migration to Europe. The practical boundaries between "West" and "Islam" continue to be messy and difficult to maintain, in short. Simultaneously, the language of civilization has re-emerged with a vengeance, after laying dormant for decades. Today, civilization is primarily discussed in the plural rather than as a set of stages with one shared end goal. Feminist scholars have nonetheless drawn attention to some remarkable continuities in the discourses of gender and Western civilization in these developments. Much like the colonial conquests in the nineteenth century, NATO's intervention in Afghanistan in 2001 pointed to the plight of Afghan women in order to legitimize the war. These justifications once again "constructed the West as the beacon of civilization with an obligation to tame the Islamic world and liberate its women" (Stabile and Kumar 2005, 766; see also Cloud 2004; Bahramitash 2005; Klaus and Kassel 2005). It is clear that in such representations, the status of women in Islam continues to serve as a potent negative foil in the construction of a distinctive and enlightened West. But, as I have argued, it seems that the link between Western civilization and the elevation of women is far less disputed now than it was in the nineteenth century, other than in certain academic feminist circles (2014).

Feminist scholars have also highlighted the contested interpretations of the proper status of women within "Islamic civilization" in the contemporary context of the rise of Islamism (e.g., Göle 1996; Saktanber 2002). A number of familiar nineteenth-century themes appear today: the status of women continues to differentiate or to make similar Islam and the West; different interpretations claim or disclaim gender equality as Islamic; the proper position of women is worked out in transnational processes marked by flows of ideas and people; and discourses about the "gender-equal West" may actually serve to restrict the space around women in what is made to be "Islamic society." What seems distinctive in this body of work compared to that on the nineteenth century is the focus on the discursive agency of Muslim women. For instance, there is a large literature on Islamic feminism (itself a contested concept), centering on "activists and scholars, including veiled women, who carry out their work toward women's advancement and gender equality within an Islamic discursive framework" (Moghadam 2002, 1136; for an overview of this work, see also Moghadam 2009, Charrad 2011). These women draw strength from their interpretation of the Islamic tradition, insisting that the ethical vision found in the Quran and in early Islamic society was egalitarian, and only later subverted by patriarchal misinterpretations. In such articulations, practices such as veiling become a way to affirm modernity and feminism within the framework of Islam.

The feminist scholarship on civilization is stunning in breadth and depth. A wealth of interesting studies explore the status of women within what is assumed to be existing civilizations, studies that have challenged mainstream accounts of the progressive character of Western civilization as well as of the alleged oppression of women within Islamic society. Feminists, furthermore, pioneered the explosive interest in discourses of civilization that erupted in the 1990s and that has continued for over two decades. However, relatively few feminist studies have directly engaged work on civilization that is inattentive to the centrality of gender—instead, the feminist literature has largely developed in parallel with other work on civilization. There are thus unrealized opportunities to use the insights developed through feminist analyses to directly and more aggressively address and critique the now rather large and established body of work on civilization that does not include gender. It is remarkable—indeed outrageous—that otherwise excellent books and articles on civilization in premier venues are published with virtually no mention of gender or the status of women (e.g., Hobson 2004; Bowden 2009; Cannadine 2013).

The feminist scholarship on civilization has furthermore generated few "internal" debates. The field, if one may call it that, now also seems ripe for discussions about the advantages and shortcomings of different theoretical approaches to gender and the concept of civilization and their implications for the way civilization is studied. One interesting debate that could emerge among feminists concerns just how ephemeral and contextual discourses of civilization and gender are or should be assumed to be. It is theoretically enticing to assume discourse to be locally manifested and transient. Many feminist scholars have thus designed studies that focus on the temporally and geographically specific, with no comparative or longitudinal aspirations. And yet the survey here of the wealth of these specific analyses identifies remarkable continuities in how civilization and the status of women are articulated and performed, over time as well as across contexts. In one of few studies that traces discourse over time, Kinsella (2011) has shown that both gender and civilization have figured into attempts to distinguish between combatants and civilians from the nineteenth century until the present. With more comparative work, across given national contexts and time periods, feminist scholars could ask questions about how far particular discourses on civilization have extended, their mechanisms of reproduction as well as how these discourses transform and are challenged across time and space (for one limited attempt to do so, see Towns 2014). This, in turn, may lead to more analytical engagements with how articulations of "the West" and "Islam" as distinctive simultaneously rest on shared discursive foundations.

NOTE

1. Ross's article has since generated a debate of its own on the relative importance of oil and Islam for gender equality. See e.g., Norris (2009); Charrad (2009); Groh and Rothschild (2012).

REFERENCES

Ahmed, Leila. 1992. *Women and Gender in Islam. Historical Roots of a Modern Debate.* New Haven, CT: Yale University Press.

Al-Hibri, Azizah, ed. 1982a. *Women and Islam.* Oxford: Pergamon Press.

Al-Hibri, Azizah. 1982b. "A Study of Islamic Herstory: or how did we ever get into this mess?" *Women's Studies International Forum* 5(2): 207–219.

Alexander, Amy, and Christian Welzel. 2011. "Islam and Patriarchy: How Robust Is Muslim Support for Patriarchal Values?" *International Review of Sociology* 21(2): 249–276.

Allardyce, Gilbert. 1982. "The Rise and Fall of the Western Civilization Course" *American Historical Review* 87(3): 695–725.

Bahramitash, Roksana. 2005. "The War on Terror, Feminist Orientalism and Orientalist Feminism." *Middle East Critique* 14 (2): 221–235.

Bebel, August. (1879) 1910. *Woman and Socialism.* New York: Socialist Literature.

Boddy, Janice. 2007. *Civilizing Women: British Crusades in Colonial Sudan.* Princeton, NJ: Princeton University Press.

Bodman, Herbert, and Nayereh Tohidi, eds. 1998. *Women in Muslim Societies: Diversity within Unity.* Boulder, CO: Lynne Rienner Publishers.

Bowden, Brett. 2009. *The Empire of Civilization: The Evolution of an Imperial Idea.* Chicago: University of Chicago Press.

Bowlan, Jeanne. 1998. "Civilizing Gender Relations in Algeria: The Paradoxical Case of Marie Bugéja, 1919–1939." In *Domesticating the Empire: Race, Gender, and Family Life in French and Dutch Colonialism*, edited by Clancy-Smith Julia and Frances Gouda, 175–192. Charlottesville: University of Virginia Press.

Burton, Antoinette. 1994. *Burdens of History. British Feminists, Indian Women and Imperial Culture.* Chapel Hill: University of North Carolina Press.

Cannadine, David. 2013. "Civilization." *Yale Review* 101(1): 1–37.

Cantarella, Eva. 1987. *Pandora's Daughters: The Role and Status of Women in Greek and Roman Antiquity.* Baltimore, MD: Johns Hopkins University Press.

Chaudhuri, Nupur, and Margaret Strobel, eds. 1992. *Western Women and Imperialism: Complicity and Resistance.* Bloomington: Indiana University Press.

Charrad, Mounira. 2001. *States and Women's Rights: The Making of Postcolonial Tunisia, Algeria and Morocco.* Berkeley: University of California Press.

Charrad, Mounira. 2007. "Contexts, Concepts and Contentions: Gender Legislation as Politics in the Middle East." *Hawwa, Journal of Women in the Middle East and the Islamic World* 5: 55–72.

Charrad, Mounira. 2011. "Islam in the Middle East: Islam, State, Agency." *Annual Review of Sociology* 37: 417–437.

Chatterjee, Partha. 1989. "Colonialism, Nationalism, and Colonialized Women: the Contest of India." *American Ethnologist* 16(4): 622–633.

Chatterjee, Partha. 1993. *The Nation and its Fragments: Colonial and Postcolonial Histories.* Princeton, NJ: Princeton University Press.
Clancy-Smith, Julia, and Frances Gouda, eds. 1998. *Domesticating the Empire: Race, Gender, and Family Life in French and Dutch Colonialism.* Charlottesville: University of Virginia Press.
Clancy-Smith, Julia. 1998. "Islam, Gender, and Identities in the Making of French Algeria." In *Domesticating the Empire: Race, Gender, and Family Life in French and Dutch Colonialism,* edited by Clancy-Smith Julia and Frances Gouda, 154–174. Charlottesville: University of Virginia Press.
Cloud, Dana L. 2004. "'To Veil the Threat of Terror': Afghan Women and the 'Clash of Civilizations' in the Imagery of the U.S. War on Terrorism." *Quarterly Journal of Speech* 90 (3): 285–306.
Curtis, Sarah. 2010. *Civilizing Habits: Women Missionaries and the Revival of French Empire.* Oxford: Oxford University Press.
Edwards, Penny. 1998. "Womanizing Indochina: Fiction, Nation, and Cohabitation in Colonial Cambodia, 1890–1930." In *Domesticating the Empire: Race, Gender, and Family Life in French and Dutch Colonialism,* edited by Clancy-Smith Julia and Frances Gouda, 108–130. Charlottesville: University of Virginia Press.
Engels, Friedrich. (1884) 1972. *The Origin of the Family, Private Property and the State in the Light of the Researches of Lewis H. Morgan.* New York: International Publishers.
Fattore, Christina, Thomas Scotto, and Arnita Sitasari. 2010. "Support for Women Officeholders in a Non-Arab Islamic Democracy: The Case of Indonesia." *Australian Journal of Political Science* 45(2): 261–275.
Foucault, Michel. 1982. "Polemics, Politics and Problematizations." Interview reproduced in *The Foucault Reader,* edited by Paul Rabinow. New York: Pantheon, 383–385.
Groh, Matthew, and Case Rothschild. 2012. "Oil, Islam, Women, and Geography: A comment on Ross (2008)." *Quarterly Journal of Political Science* 7: 69–87.
Göle, Nilüfer. 1996. *The Forbidden Modern. Civilization and Veiling.* Ann Arbor: University of Michigan Press.
Hambly, Gavin R. G., ed. 1998. *Women in the Medieval Islamic World.* New York: St. Martin's Press.
Hobson, John. 2004. *The Eastern Origins of Western Civilization.* Cambridge: Cambridge University Press.
Huntington, Samuel. 1993. "The Clash of Civilizations?" *Foreign Affairs* 72 (3): 22–49.
Huntington, Samuel. 1996. *The Clash of Civilizations and the Remaking of World Order.* New York: Simon and Schuster.
Inglehart, Ronald, and Pippa Norris. 2003. "The True Clash of Civilizations." *Foreign Policy* 135 (Mar–Apr): 62–70.
Jackson, Patrick Thaddeus. 1999. "'Civilization' on Trial." *Millennium—Journal of International Studies* 28 (1): 141–153.
Kandiyoti, Deniz, ed. 1992. *Women, Islam & the State.* London: MacMillan.
Kandiyoti, Deniz. 2007. "Between the Hammer and the Anvil: Post-Conflict Reconstruction, Islam and Women's Rights." *Third World Quarterly* 28 (3): 503–517.
Keddie, Nikki. 2007. *Women in the Middle East: Past and Present.* Princeton, NJ: Princeton University Press.
Kinsella, Helen M. 2011. *The Image before the Weapon: A Critical History of the Distinction between Combatant and Civilian.* Ithaca, NY: Cornell University Press.

Klaus, Elisabeth, and Susanne Kassel. 2005. "The Veil as a Means of Legitimization: An Analysis of the Interconnectedness of Gender, Media and War." *Journalism* 6 (3): 335–355.Kleinbaum, Abby Wettan. 1979. "Women's History and the Western Civilization Survey." *History Teacher* 12 (4): 501–506.

Knott, Sarah, and Barbara Taylor, eds. 2006. *Women, Gender and Enlightenment*, Basingstoke: Palgrave.

Mander, Jenny. 2006. "No Woman Is an Island: the Female Figure in French Enlightenment Anthropology." In *Women, Gender and Enlightenment*, edited by Sarah Knott and Barbara Taylor, 97–116. Basingstoke: Palgrave.

Marx, Karl, and Friedrich Engels. (1845) 1956. *The Holy Family: or, Critique of Critical Criticism. Against Bruno Bauer and Company*. New York: International Publishers.

McClintock, Anne. 1995. *Imperial Leather: Race, Gender, and Sexuality in the Colonial Contest*. New York: Routledge.

Midgley, Claire, ed. 1998. *Gender and Imperialism*. Manchester: Manchester University Press.

Moghadam, Valentine M. 2002. "Islamic Feminism and Its Discontents: Toward a Resolution of the Debate." *Signs: Journal of Women in Culture and Society* 27(4): 1135–1171.

Moghadam, Valentine M. 2009. *Globalization and Social Movements: Islamism, feminism and the Global Justice Movement*. Lanham: Rowman & Littlefield.

Moghissi, Haideh, ed. 2005. *Women and Islam*. New York: Routledge.

Moran, Mary Catherine. 2006. "Between the Savage and the Civil: On John Gregory's Natural History of Femininity." In *Women, Gender and Enlightenment*, edited by Sarah Knott and Barbara Taylor, 8–30. Basingstoke: Palgrave.

Morgan, Lewis. 1877. *Ancient Society; or, Researches in the Lines of Human Progress from Savagery, Through Barbarism to Civilization*. New York: Henry Holt and Company.

Narayan, Uma. 2012. "Undoing the 'Package Picture' of Cultures." *Jura Gentium. Rivista di filosofia del diritto internazionale e della politica globale* 2: 1–5.

Nashat, Guity. 2006. Introduction to *Women in Islam. From Medieval to Modern Times*, by Wiebke Walther, 3–12. Princeton, NJ: Marcus Wiener Publishers.

Norris, Pippa. 2009. "Petroleum and Patriarchy: A Response to Ross." *Politics & Gender* 5 (4): 553–560.

Okin, Susan with respondents. 1999. *Is Multiculturalism Bad for Women?* Princeton, NJ: Princeton University Press.

Rizzo, Helen, Abdel-Hamid Abdel-Latif, and Katherine Meyer. 2007. "The Relationship between Gender Equality and Democracy: A Comparison of Arab Versus Non-Arab Muslim Societies." *Sociology* 41 (6): 1151–1170.

Roded, Ruth, ed. 1999. *Women in Islam and the Middle East. A Reader*. London / New York: I.B. Tauris Publishers.

Ross, Michael. 2008. "Oil, Islam and Women." *American Political Science Review* 22 (4): 1–17.

Rupp, Leila. 1997. *Worlds of Women: The Making of an International Women's Movement*. Princeton, NJ: Princeton University Press.

Saktanber, Ayşe. 2002. *Living Islam. Women, Religion & the Politicization of Culture in Turkey*. New York: I.B. Tauris & Co.

Sebastini, Silvia. 2006. "'Race', Women and Progress in the Scottish Enlightenment." In *Women, Gender and Enlightenment*, edited by Sarah Knott and Barbara Taylor, 75–96. Basingstoke: Palgrave.

Sebastini, Silvia. 2013. *The Scottish Enlightenment. Race, Gender and the Limits of Progress*. Basingstoke: Palgrave Macmillan.

Spierings, Niels, Jeroen Smits, and Mieke Verloo. 2009. "On the Compatibility of Islam and Gender Equality." *Social Indicators Research* 90: 503–522.

Stabile, Carol, and Deepa Kumar. 2005. "Unveiling Imperialism: media, gender and the war on Afghanistan." *Media, Culture & Society* 27 (5): 765–782.

Stephenson, June. 2012. *Women's Roots: Status and Accomplishment in Western Civilization*. Amazon Digital Services.

Thompson, Elizabeth. 2000. *Colonial Citizens: Republican Rights, Paternal Privilege, and Gender in French Syria and Lebanon*. New York: Columbia University Press.

Tomaselli, Sylvana. 1985. "The Enlightenment Debate on Women." *History Workshop Journal* 20 (1): 101–124.

Tomaselli, Sylvana. 2006. "Civilization, Patriotism, and Enlightened histories of Woman." In *Women, Gender and Enlightenment*, edited by Sarah Knott and Barbara Taylor, 117–135. Basingstoke: Palgrave.

Towns, Ann E. 2009. "The Status of Women as a Standard of 'Civilization.'" *European Journal of International Relations* 15 (4): 1–25.

Towns, Ann E. 2010. *Women and States: Norms and Hierarchies in International Society*. Cambridge: Cambridge University Press.

Towns, Ann E. 2014. "Carrying the Load of Civilization. The Status of Women and Challenged Hierarchies." *Millennium: Journal of International Studies* 42(3): 595–613.

Walsh, Elizabeth Miller. 1981. *Women in Western Civilization*. Cambridge, MA: Schenkman.

Walther, Wiebke. 2006. *Women in Islam. From Medieval to Modern Times*. Princeton, NJ: Marcus Wiener Publishers.

CHAPTER 5

COLONIALITY OF GENDER AND POWER

From Postcoloniality to Decoloniality

BRENY MENDOZA

INTRODUCTION

ANTICOLONIAL feminism is a theoretical and a political project that challenges imperialist and colonizing practices, past and present. This chapter provides a genealogy of anticolonial feminist theory, tracing its emergence from rich traditions of anticolonial, postcolonial and decolonial theories, situating it in relation to other women of color feminisms, and examining its distinctive critiques of colonialism, modernity, Eurocentrism, capitalism, nationalism, and racism. Examining key themes in the works of Maria Lugones, Silvia Rivera Cusicanqui, and Rita Segato, the chapter concludes with a discussion of their alternative account of modernity as a violent process intricately tied to the construction and imposition of race and gender hierarchies.

ANTECEDENTS

The Anglo academic world has traditionally associated anticolonial struggles with national liberation movements designed to achieve "independence," and social justice movements that arise in the context of nation-building after the colonial power has been overthrown. Anticolonial theories are associated with such figures as US-born, Pan African thinker and civil rights activist W. E. B. DuBois, renowned critics of French colonialism Aimée Césaire (2000) and Frantz Fanon, and Ghanian national independence leader Kwame Nkrumah. In 1978, however, Palestinian-American literary theorist Edward Said published his magisterial work, *Orientalism,* expanding the historical frame, the cartography, and the intellectual purchase of colonialism and moving the field from anticolonial to postcolonial theory. In the 1990s, the South Asian Subaltern Studies Group introduced a new generation of postcolonial theorists, including Ranajit Guha, Homi Bhabha, Partha Chatterjee, and Dipesh Chakravorty, and Gayatri Chakravorty Spivak.

By contrast to those who focus on the colonial practices of nations in northern Europe, Latin American and Caribbean scholars have emphasized that anticolonial thought originated in the context of a much earlier colonial period, as a reaction against the violent history of Western colonialism inaugurated in 1492. The sixteenth-century Quechua author Felipe Guamán Poma de Ayala, and the Peruvian mestizo Inca Garcilazo de la Vega wrote the first critiques of Spanish colonialism from the perspective of the colonized. The contemporary decolonial turn in the academic world has been led by Latin American and Caribbean scholars initially associated with the Modernity/Coloniality Group, who constructed an archive of texts from the sixteenth to the twentieth centuries that offer a radical reinterpretation of the relation between capitalism and race. Rather than argue that colonialism was irrelevant to the development of capitalism, the works of José Carlos Mariátegui (2009), for example, a nonorthodox Marxist from Peru, argued as early as the 1920s that race was central to capitalism and that capitalist accumulation could not be understood without attention to the production of racial hierarchies. In its prime, the modernity/coloniality school of thought argued also that modernity and capitalism were not the result of internal or intra-European historical processes but instead were historical outcomes of colonialism. Decolonial theorists included the Peruvian sociologist Anibal Quijano, who theorized the central decolonial concept, the coloniality of power, as well as Argentinians Enrique Dussel, well known for his philosophy of liberation, and Walter Mignolo, a semiotician who became famous for his book *The Darker Side of the Renaissance* (1995); and Puerto Rican philosopher Nelson Maldonado-Torres, who developed the concept of the coloniality of being.

Emergence and Submergence

Anticolonial feminist theory emerges in this rich intellectual context, yet exists on the margins of these critiques of colonialism and on the margins of feminist theory. The brilliant work of Gayatri Chakravorty Spivak, for example, is emblematic of complex marginalization. More than one postcolonial theorist has attempted to revoke Spivak's membership in the South Asian Subaltern Studies Group. In the words of Vivek Chibber (2013, 8), with her 1985 essay, "Subaltern Studies: Deconstructing Historiography," Spivak "parachuted" herself into the South Asian Subaltern Studies Group debates "much like an uninvited guest." By contrast, the Modernity/Coloniality Group has been more open to feminist scholarship, often making gestures to integrate the writings of US feminists of color in their works. Walter Mignolo, for example, cites Gloria Anzaldúa as the muse for "his concept" of border thinking. Borrowing from Anzaldua but at the same time ignoring the extensiveness of her theorization, Mignolo conceives border thinking as a decolonial epistemology that originates in the ways of knowing of the colonized. According to Mignolo, border thinking transcends binaries and dichotomous thinking in order to recover subjugated knowledges from the grips of Eurocentrism (Mignolo 2000). Traces of US black feminist thought are also apparent in the Modernity/Coloniality Group's discussions of the mutual constitution of race and gender and the co-constitution of multiple systems of power. Yet, decolonial theorists quickly mute intersectionality as a theoretical framework, replacing it with Kontopoulos's notion of "heterarchies" that purportedly addresses multiple and heterogeneous global hierarchies more adequately by considering the entanglements of social processes at different structural levels (Grosfoguel 2010, 71). Several feminist scholars appear in the anthologies published by the modernity/coloniality school and are cited throughout their narratives, yet gender analytics occupy a liminal space in decolonial theory. Treatment of Maria Lugones's concept of the "coloniality of gender" is a case in point. Inspired partially by the writings of the Modernity/Coloniality Group, Lugones sees gender as being as central to the conceptualization of the coloniality of power as race was to Quijano and hence as something to be equally understood as a colonial construct. While included in many of the Group's publications and given public lip service, few decolonial theorists incorporate Lugones's "coloniality of gender" into their central tenets. In short, feminist theory may inspire particular men to their own flights of theory, but it has not achieved full recognition as "serious" theory in its own right.

Anticolonial feminist scholarship experiences similar marginalization by feminist theorists in the US, Anglo-American, and European academies. With the notable exception of postcolonial feminist scholarship, which has gained great prestige among US feminists, other forms of anticolonial feminist theorization do not occupy a stable position within feminist theory. Black feminist theorists have long argued that their most innovative theoretical concepts are not treated as "theory" within academic feminism. Nikol Alexander Floyd (2012) has argued that intersectional analysis has suffered such metamorphosis in the hands of "whitestream feminism" that it no longer serves its fundamental purpose of making visible the oppression of women of color in the United States. As May (2014) has argued, the rich concept of intersectionality is actually reduced to a single-axis approach to gender by scholars who reject the focus of intersectionality on black women or question its empirical validity. Other US black feminist scholars find themselves "speaking into a void" or suffering an epistemic backlash within US and European feminist academy (May 2014).

This epistemic backlash is evidenced when the works of Chicana feminists such as Gloria Anzaldúa and Chela Sandoval are caricatured as identity politics or positioned as a fleeting fad, to be superseded by more sophisticated poststructuralist theories (Ortega 2006), or when decolonial feminist theories are qualified as "women of color" feminisms (as opposed to feminisms proper) and segregated in ethnic studies, Latina, Native American, and African American studies programs, where they have largely been ignored or appropriated. The politics of citation in "whitestream feminism" marks the presence of the scholarship of women of color, even as it contorts the content of their ideas, falsifies their genealogies, overrides their contributions to feminist theory, and resubjugates their knowledge (Alexander-Floyd 2012, 9). Works written by "third world feminists" outside of the United States are often deemed unworthy of translation. As a consequence, their work becomes known only after it has been mediated and redeployed by "first world" scholars.

From an anticolonial feminist perspective, theories advanced by women of color are subjected to recolonization as their central ideas and concepts slowly disappear or reappear whitewashed and devoid of their critical impetus. One objective of recent feminist decolonizing discourse is to counter this epistemic backlash by recuperating theoretical work by previously colonized women of color. Part of this effort involves creating a multidimensional lens that can serve as the foundation of decolonial feminism and as a coalitional politics among women of color (Santa Cruz Feminist of Color Collective 2014). Another dimension involves retrieval of overlapping methods and strategies within distinct theorizations by feminists of color that resist global capitalism and neocolonialism (Roshanravan 2014).

When the critique of capitalism and neocolonialism is understood as central to the decolonial feminist project, it becomes clear that women of color feminism is not coterminous with decolonial feminism, despite being an important part of it. Women of color feminists have provided some foundational elements to decolonial feminism, but they do not exhaust them. Women of color scholarship is not a unified genre and does not share a single intellectual or political project (Roshanravan 2014). Nor do the epistemic and substantive claims of women of color necessarily entail decolonizing effects. Thus, identifying what counts as anticolonial feminist theory within and beyond the scholarship of feminists of color is a complicated matter. As Eve Tuck and K. Wayne Yang (2012, 1) have noted, "decolonial desires articulated by white, non-white, immigrant, postcolonial, and oppressed peoples" often reduce decolonization to a metaphor for vague yearnings for liberation or social transformation. Unclear or inchoate decolonizing discourses run the risk of reinstating colonial norms, strengthening rather than weakening them (Tuck and Yang 2012). Decolonization is *not* a metaphor for antiracist, anticapitalist critiques, nor for critiques of Eurocentrism.

Anticolonial theories are defined by criteria linked to political projects that lead to decolonization. But the questions, which criteria and political projects lead to decolonization? what counts as decolonization? and which practices succeed in challenging colonialism and coloniality? are intensively debated. Some suggest that the goal of anticolonial feminist theory is primarily to analyze and challenge imperialistic and colonizing impulses within dominant feminist theories. Others suggest that anticolonial theory must influence political practices on the ground. Some anticolonial feminist scholars investigate the relations among race, gender, and colonization and among race, gender, and the modern nation-state. Exactly how intersectional analysis is situated in relation to feminist theorizing of the hierarchies created and sustained by colonialism is a subject of intense contestation.

In the rest of this chapter, I develop a provisional framework for understanding the theoretical and political projects of anticolonial feminisms. To situate intersectionality, postcolonial feminism, and decolonial feminism in relation to the project of decolonization, I begin by first analyzing their ties to mainstream postcolonial and decolonial theory, fields that continue to be dominated by male scholars.

INTERSECTIONALITY AND ANTICOLONIAL THEORY

Although many feminist scholars consider intersectionality a revolutionary concept that has redefined theoretical, political, and methodological approaches (McCall 2005; Hancock 2011; Cho, Crenshaw and McCall 2013), the concept of intersectionality developed by black feminist thinkers has come under heavy scrutiny over the past decade. Its epistemic value has been called into question by feminist poststructuralist scholars who accuse it of being "merely descriptive" (Jordan-Zachery 2007, cited in Alexander-Floyd 2012, 5). Far from offering anything new, critics have suggested that intersectionality replicates long-standing problems of identity politics, overemphasizing decontextualized categories of identity, focusing too narrowly on a small subset of structural constraints, or overemphasizing racism within feminism. Other critics suggest that intersectionality undermines feminist philosophical and political coherence by challenging the primacy of gender oppression, stigmatizing the category "woman," or circulating narratives that are unable to address the complexity of the social (Zack 2005; Gunnarson, cited in May 2014, 102).

Some scholars have attempted to "correct" the presumed limitations of intersectional analysis associated with the exclusive focus on the oppression of women of color by redeploying the method for the study of all women or, indeed, all people (Garry 2012). But some black feminist theorists resist the conceptual inflation of intersectionality with any study of multiple vectors of power (e.g., whiteness, class, and religion) because it has the effect of erasing women of color and returning white women to the center of analysis. Other scholars have attempted to correct the "problems" of intersectionality by recuperating single-axis analyses that investigate gender or class dynamics, or by excavating complex socio-historical contexts, localized dynamics, and institutional processes or by eschewing categorical logics and taking up multivalent and multilevel approaches (May 2014, 104).

Some of these "correctives" involve little more than superficial adoption of an additive approach, which renders unintelligible the co-constitution of systems of power—gender, race, ethnicity, class, sexuality, nationality—thereby undermining the fundamental premise of intersectional analysis. Thus it is not surprising that many black feminist theorists experience these cavalier critiques and misrepresentations of intersectionality as epistemic violence and as a recolonization of black feminist knowledge.

In contrast to rejection and distortion of intersectionality, postcolonial and decolonial studies, both inside and outside the United States, have embraced the concept.

An intersectional framework has been central to third world feminisms critical of colonialism—feminisms typically classified as postcolonial (Mohanty, Russo, and Torres 1991). For example, in *Imperial Leather*, Ann McClintock (1995), a white postcolonial feminist born in Zimbabwe and raised in South Africa, argued that colonialism and imperialism could not be understood without considering the invention of race. For McClintock, intersectional analysis recognizes that systems of power grounded in gender, race, class, and sexuality are not distinct and isolated realms of experience but are dangerously interlocking, not only in British colonialism, but also in anticolonial struggles. As the Santa Cruz Feminist of Color Collective (2014, 33) has noted, anticolonial feminist theory moves intersectionality beyond critiques of state-based legal practices to illuminate "glocalizing" dynamics—interpenetrations of global and local that construct gender, race, class, and sexuality, not as separable categories, but as mutually constituting systems of power that exist in and through contradictory and conflicting relations.

The boundaries of postcolonial feminism have been porous and subject to contestation over the past two decades. Several anthologies include the writings of black and Chicana feminism within postcolonial feminist theory, publishing these classic texts along with writings by third-world feminists aligned with the South Asian Subaltern Studies Group, and those advancing critiques of Orientalism (Lewis and Mills 2003). Such inclusive approaches make it clear that intersectional analysis has always been central to postcolonial feminism. But homogenizing different traditions of feminist theorizing by women of color under the rubric of postcolonial feminism also carries risks, most notably, that of losing sight of what is most central to anticolonial feminist theory. Postcolonial theory entails a unique theoretical and political program that should not be confused with other theoretical approaches. Important differences exist among black feminist, Chicana feminist, and postcolonial feminist theory and practice. These theoretical frameworks originate in different colonial experiences and periods and have different research agendas. Occupying various subject positions within national, global, and academic frames, scholars and activists contributing to discourses on intersectionality have diverse investments in and relations to coloniality. Emerging from different theoretical traditions and encompassing different political projects, black feminist, Chicana feminist, and postcolonial feminist theory are far from uniform. Rather than assuming shared views, it is important to investigate whether a critique of coloniality and a particular decolonial project underlies specific intersectional analyses.

As has been well documented, the intellectual roots of intersectional analysis are grounded in black feminist theorists' examination of black women's oppression in the United States, which emphasized the complex interrelations of race, class, gender, and dispossession. The concept has been traced to the early nineteenth-century speeches of abolitionist and political agitator Maria Stewart (1803–1880) and later to the scholarship of Anna Julia Cooper (1858–1964), whose worldviews were shaped by the system of slavery established and condoned by US law, as well as the struggle to abolish that system. In the second half of the twentieth century, the Combahee River Collective theorized the intersections of sexuality, race, gender, and class. Kimberlé Crenshaw (1989) coined the term "intersectionality" in her investigation of the failure of US courts to recognize discrimination based on both race and gender. Patricia Hill Collins (1990, 1993) theorized a black feminist standpoint as a crucial intellectual tool with which to illuminate the complex oppressions of contemporary black women in the United States. In these contexts, intersectionality served not only to make visible dimensions of black women's oppression that had been masked by assumptions about woman as a unitary category within feminist theory, but to challenge paradigmatic conceptions of race advanced by "malestream" critical race theory. Emphasizing the multidimensional vectors of power that structured both lived identities and social reality, intersectionality illuminated ties between epistemic location and knowledge production, and offered analytic strategies that linked the material, the discursive, and the structural. Demonstrating the inadequacies of "either/or" (binary) ways of thinking and the futility of efforts to rank oppressions, intersectionality reflects lessons that US black feminist theorists drew from black women's lived experiences of enslavement, uprootedness and dispossession, economic and reproductive exploitation, and Jim Crow segregation, share-cropping and domestic labor, lynching, rape, and race riots, second-class citizenship, and systemic racism under the guise of formal equality.

When deployed by many contemporary black, US-based feminist scholars, the political project of intersectionality remains tied to the US settler colonial state. Historians have used intersectional analysis to demonstrate how gender and sexual oppression were essential to the constitution of slavery and the plantation system. Political economists have shown how slavery and the plantation system have provided a persistent blueprint for economic and social relations in the United States, which continue to map ghettoization, educational segregation, and the prison-industrial complex. Social theorists have traced the way legacies of slavery and legal racial apartheid have become attached to black bodies, influencing individual life prospects, sexual relations, family formation, economic opportunities, residential and employment possibilities, forging lasting ties between the US colonial and postcolonial contexts. Within this historical and intellectual context, intersectionality often fosters political demands for inclusion and equal rights, demands for complete citizenship that are perceived as crucial to living a life in freedom.

Certain inflections of intersectional politics, then, are amenable to a liberal politics of inclusion, which weaken intersectionality's decolonizing potential. Liberal notions of liberty, equality, and justice drawn from the American Declaration of Independence and US Constitution appear as preconditions for the futurity of US black women and men, precisely because they have been so long denied "the blessings of liberty." Yet, in embracing liberal inclusion as a political project, intersectionality suggests strategies of action and preferred outcomes at great remove from other anticolonial struggles outside the United States. Despite their formative influence on postcolonial theorizing, the political aims of US black feminist theorists often diverge significantly from those of anticolonial struggles in most parts of the world.

When adopted as an analytical strategy by anticolonial feminists outside the United States, however, intersectionality identifies new problems and unexpected political possibilities emerging from the complexity of the intersections of gender, race, class, and sexuality in the colonial condition.

Postcolonial/Decolonial Debates and Feminist Theory

Postcolonialism

In the 1990s, the "colonial" reemerged in social, cultural, and political theory. Following the decline of Marxism, the advent of postmodernism/poststructuralism, and post-Marxist cultural theories, postcolonial theory offered sophisticated critiques of capitalism, modernity, and Western colonialism. Inspired by French philosophers such as Michel Foucault and Jacques Derrida, postcolonial theorists changed the terms with which to think about colonialism, capitalism, and nationalism. Focusing on the history of British colonialism and its collapse in the aftermath of World War II, postcolonial thinkers sought to produce an alternative historiography that challenged dominant theories of historical analysis in the West. Supplanting historical materialism with a "history from below" (Chibber 2013), postcolonial scholars created a new theoretical framework for the study of colonial history, which offered an explanation not only of the distinctiveness of colonial capitalism in India, but of the operations of capitalism in other parts of the colonized world. Yet because the South Asian Subaltern Studies Group focused primarily on the colonization of India and other parts of Asia, their views about the relationship between colonialism and capitalism differed dramatically from those of the Latin American Modernity/Coloniality Group, which drew upon earlier phases of Spanish, Portuguese, and French colonization and decolonization. Key differences in views about coloniality, modernity, and capitalism became a hallmark not only of these two schools—postcolonial and decolonial—of anticolonial scholarship but of their feminist counterparts as well.

"Subalternists," often considered the core group within postcolonial theory, argued that that capitalism assumed markedly different forms in Europe and in the colonial world. In contrast to the "modernizing" role that capitalism played in Europe, transforming agricultural economies to industrial economies and aligning bourgeois and working-class interests in the overthrow of the feudal aristocracy, capitalism's effects in South Asia were bifurcated. According to the subalternists, neither the progressive forces nor the universalizing drive materialized fully in the subcontinent because nationalist elites failed to transform the "backwardness" of the peasantry in the process of decolonization (Chibber 2013). In Gramscian terms, the British colonizers and the Indian nationalist capitalist class were unable or unwilling to generalize their particular interests to the subaltern classes that they exploited. Despite superficial changes in law, the old regime and the caste system remained intact. In contrast to the European experience, where the rhetoric of universal rights recruited the exploited working classes to the political project of liberal democracy, in colonial India, capitalist domination involved rule without the consensus of the governed, that is, without hegemony (Chibber 2013, 13). As a consequence of the long history of British colonial domination, liberal views of equality, political freedom, secularism, and contractualism did not take root in India, profoundly altering the postcolonial context. Even following independence, pre-capitalist forms of exploitation and domination remained in place. This "abnormal" development of capitalism split postcolonial society into two political domains, driven by two different and clashing logics: whereas the capitalist class functioned according to the rational pursuit of individual interest, the subaltern was mired in a premodern form of politics, preoccupied with concerns about religion, caste, ethnicity, and community. This unique configuration of classes, according to subalternists, distinguished colonial modernity and capitalism in India, ensuring that they bore little resemblance to European capitalism and modernity. In the absence of hegemony, anticolonial nationalist elites constructed a fictitious form of postcolonial nation-statehood grounded on a spurious legitimacy (Chibber 2013, 17). Precisely because the model of capitalist development in India differed significantly from Europe's, the subalternists argued that Western categories of analysis, and Marxist theory, in particular, were inappropriate for understanding colonial capitalism in the East.

Informed by poststructural critiques of totalizing theories such as economic determinism, Subaltern Studies advanced an alternative narrative of capitalism that eschewed "grand narratives." Attentive to the power of discourse, they relied upon textual analyses to devise critiques of colonialism and capitalism that supplemented discussions of exploitation and domination with investigations of marginality and subalternity (Chibber 2013, 8). Echoing certain strains of the poststructuralist critique of modernity, the subalternists' critique of Eurocentrism rejected universalizing claims and emphasized difference and the local. They highlighted the cultural specificity of "the East," and used cultural and historical analysis to theorize "the subaltern" and to raise questions concerning the subaltern's voice and agency. According to Vivek Chibber (2013, 8), Gayatri Chakravorty Spivak, perhaps the best known postcolonial feminist theorist, was indirectly responsible for these unique features of postcolonial critique.

Postcolonial Feminism

A founder of, and at times ostracized from, the South Asian Subaltern Studies Group, Spivak is said to characterize herself as a "practical deconstructionist feminist Marxist gadfly" (Leitch et al. 2010, 2110). Chastising the subalternists for failing to examine gender and sexuality in their accounts of the postcolonial condition, Spivak has advanced analyses of gendered divisions of labor within capitalism, critiques of Eurocentrism in Western literature, interrogations of epistemic and political borders constructed by neoliberal global capitalism, along with trenchant critiques of Western liberal and radical feminist scholarship. Using textual analysis and cultural criticism as her primary analytical tools, Spivak is renowned for her sophisticated critiques of poststructural, postcolonial, and feminist theories as well as for her analyses of colonial capitalism and postcolonial politics.

In her pathbreaking essay, "Can the Subaltern Speak?" Spivak ([1985] 1988) set the terms of feminist postcolonial criticism. Conceptualizing "epistemic violence" as integral to Western knowledge production, Spivak demonstrated how the discursive production of the subaltern, particularly the poor "third world woman," silenced women of the global South through a form of ventriloquism. Under the guise of giving voice to the oppressed, Western academic and activist discourses substituted Orientalist views of the third world women for the lived realities of subaltern existence. Spivak suggested that every attempt to represent the subaltern woman was a way of asserting the West's superiority over the non-West. By juxtaposing Western "civilization" against the "barbarism" of "the East," academics and activists colonized subaltern experience, while reinscribing the superiority of Western knowledge. By locating epistemic violence in the dynamics of representation itself, Spivak raised the possibility that the subaltern woman could never be known in her own terms. In taking that step, Spivak also called into question the validity of practices within the South Asian Subaltern Studies Group. Indeed, she suggested that postcolonial theorists, who positioned themselves as knowers of and spokespersons for the subaltern, violated the fundamental premises of postcolonial critique. Indeed, Spivak claimed that postcolonial theorists not only failed to provide an alternative to the Orientalism of Western theories, but they reproduced Orientalist discourses by conceiving the subaltern as supine, inescapably oppressed, and essentially "Other" than Western subjects.

In "Under Western Eyes," Chandra Talpade Mohanty brought the full force of postcolonial feminist criticism to bear on Western feminist scholarship. Taking the Third World Series published by Zed Press as her point of departure, Mohanty (1991, 56) demonstrated how binary constructions of first-world and third-world women homogenized women on both sides of the binary with particularly negative consequences for third-world women, who were imagined to be perennially "ignorant, poor, uneducated, tradition-bound, domesticated, family-oriented, victimized." By contrast, white women were uniformly constructed as "educated, modern, having control over their own bodies and sexualities, and the freedom to make their own decisions." These discursive oppositions were not only Eurocentric, but as Leela Gandhi (1998) noted, they fortified an image of a redemptive ideological and political plenitude of Western feminism. Paraphrasing Spivak's denunciation of white men's accounts of their own colonial acts as benevolent rescue missions in which "white men are saving brown women from brown men," Mohanty castigated Western academic feminists who imagined themselves as "white women saving brown women from brown men." Although some scholars criticized Mohanty for homogenizing Western feminism, her analysis was impressively prescient, anticipating the construction of Muslim women as victims of Muslim men in dire need of rescue in post-9/11 discourses circulated not only by leading US feminists but by the US government, Western media, and human rights organizations (Abu-Lughod 2013).

Mohanty also expanded her conception of third-world women beyond the cartographies established by the Subaltern Studies Group. In her analysis of global capitalism, she drew parallels between Western and non-Western capitalist heteropatriarchies, which operated to maximize the exploitation of "third world" women's labor, whether those women worked in the global South or the global North. In their quest to maximize profits by fostering consumption and providing affluent consumers with cheap consumer goods, Mohanty suggested that multinational corporations increased the precariousness of life, driving down wages of women workers in the South, heightening unemployment in the North, and proliferating sweatshops in global cities North and South. By creating a "common context of political struggles" and fostering "common interests" through brutal exploitation, global capitalism was laying a foundation for transnational solidarity among third world women.

Despite the importance of her contributions to feminist postcolonial theory and to transnational feminism, Mohanty does not resolve the relations of power between first- and third-world women that she so deftly analyzes in "Under Western Eyes" (Mendoza 2002). Although she envisions third-world women as revolutionary subjects, she stops short of explaining how the common interests of third-world women living in the colony and in metropolitan centers can be transformed into common political struggles against the destructiveness of global capitalism. Her emphasis on the potential solidarity between third-world women across borders underestimates the difficulty of transnational feminist mobilizations that attempt to unite first-world and third-world women, or white women and women of color. By suggesting that transformative projects arise from the experience of systemic oppression, Mohanty echoes traditional leftists in the West who imagine that the revolution always begins with the most marginalized, which imposes a huge burden on subaltern women. In focusing on shared oppressions that span national boundaries and the geopolitics of North/South, Mohanty also distances herself from arguments of the Subaltern Studies Group, which position the subaltern as a political actor motivated by a set of concerns that are radically different from those of the West (Chibber 2013, 22). Rather than engaging the alterity of the subaltern, Mohanty's transnational feminist orientation aligns more closely with conventional Marxist calls for transnational worker solidarity as the ground for social transformation.

In their efforts to address Eurocentrism and racism within Western feminism, postcolonial feminist scholars have developed riveting analyses of Eurocentric bias in popular culture, film, and mass media, as well as potent critiques of racism and racialization in the views of US nationalists and exceptionalists, Zionists, and postcolonial nationalist elites (Shohat and Stam 2006; Fernandes 2013). Investigating the intersection of gender, race, class, sexuality, and nationality, they have provided superb studies of the power dynamics operating in distinct colonial contexts (McClintock 1995; Stoler 2002). By studying the racial systems constructed within particular colonial contexts, postcolonial feminist scholars have also opened possibilities for dialogue with other anticolonial theorists whose work examines Spanish and Portuguese colonialism rather than British and French colonialism or US imperialism (Stam and Shohat 2012). The erudition and the richness of postcolonial feminist research cannot be questioned.

Yet postcolonial feminism also suffers some of the limitations associated with mainstream postcolonial theory and poststructuralism. Like its mainstream counterpart, postcolonial feminist theory has been accused of cultural determinism and historicism. The political project of postcolonial feminists is also hard to grasp. Although they have emphasized the role of the subaltern and transnationalism in struggles against global capitalism, holding out little hope for the emancipatory potential of the West, postcolonial feminist theorists have also expressed growing concerns about the subaltern's capacity to overturn its colonial condition, particularly in its current instantiation as neoliberal global capitalism. Indeed, as Spivak (cited in Paudyal 2011) recently noted in a lecture in Katmandu, Nepal, the subaltern has been "hegemonized to accept its wretchedness as normal." But if this is so, what becomes of the postcolonial intellectual's project to "train the imagination" of the subaltern to help him/her recover the moral compass lost to neoliberal global capitalism? Claims concerning the subaltern's resignation to wretchedness reveal the social distance that separates the postcolonial feminist scholar from the subaltern. They also signal a departure from Foucault's dictum that the intellectual is irremediably implicated in power/knowledge constellations. Whether postcolonial feminist theorists accept Foucault's insight that they can never advance a political program that represents the subaltern or embrace a Gramscian notion of the organic intellectual who can speak for the subaltern, neither the position of the subaltern nor the position of the postcolonial intellectual in the anticolonial struggle is apparent. The question for the subaltern could just as well be asked of the postcolonial critic: does s/he occupy a privileged position in the struggle for decolonization or is s/he doomed to silence?

Decolonial Theory

Although decolonial theory might be characterized as the most recent arrival on the anticolonial scene, it takes a much longer view of colonialism than its predecessors. Decolonial theorists ground their analyses in the Spanish and Portuguese colonization of the Americas, which began in the sixteenth century and ended in the nineteenth century. Decolonial thought draws attention to long histories of Spanish and Portuguese colonialism that had been bracketed in postcolonial debates that focused exclusively on British or French colonialism. In the earliest phase of European colonial expansion, the first colonial universities were founded in Santo Domingo, Lima, and Mexico City as early as 1538 and 1551. These intellectual centers became sites of heated debates over Eurocentric epistemology and historiography. In these debates, *criollo* elites, mestizo, and indigenous intellectuals sought to demonstrate that European knowledge was unable to recognize, much less comprehend, the cultural differences and forms of governance of the vanquished Inca (Mendoza 2014). More than four centuries before the emergence of the South Asian Subaltern Studies Group, scholars at Spanish universities, such as the University of Salamanca and the Colegio San Gregorio, questioned the justness of empire and colonization. In the famous Valladolid debates (1550–1551), for example, Bartolomé de las Casas and Ginés de Sepulveda debated the humanity of the Amerindians, challenging the dehumanizing effects of colonization as well as the rhetoric of salvation deployed by Spanish missionaries (Mendoza 2006). Felipe Guamán Poma de Ayala, a Quechua nobleman, wrote one of the first chronicles in defense of the Amerindians, contending that the Spanish had no right to control Andean affairs. The mestizo descendant of Incan nobility Inca Garcilaso de la Vega tried to recover the voices and preserve the historical memory of the Amerindians at the very moment they were being subjected to genocide. In a suggestive article entitled "Si, el subalterno puede hablar: un análisis breve de la 'Nueva corónica y buen gobierno' de Felipe Guamán Poma de Ayala y los 'Comentarios reales'" del Inca Garcilazo de la Vega" ("Yes, the subaltern can speak: a brief analysis of 'The First New Chronicle and Good Governance' by Felipe Guamán Poma de Ayala and the "Royal Commentaries" by Inca Garcilaso de la Vega), Lipi Biswan Sen, a professor of the Nehru University of India, notes that these accounts of the subaltern, theorized in the sixteenth century by Guamán Poma de Ayala and Garcilazo de la Vega, anticipated central arguments of the South Asian Subaltern Studies Group. According to Guamán Poma de Ayala and Garcilazo de la Vega, the Amerindians resisted the binary thinking of Europeans, refusing to accept that colonization was a civilizing process. Indeed, the Amerindians inverted the logic of colonization, identifying the Europeans as barbarians who were destroying the civilizations long established by indigenous peoples. In contrast to South Asian subaltern theory that depicts the subaltern as possessing a political psychology incompatible with Western ways of knowing, Guaman Poma de Ayala and Garcilazo de la Vega insisted that the subaltern developed sophisticated Spanish-language skills and used the tools of the master, such as alphabetic writing, which the Incas had not previously developed, to subvert the colonizing discourses of the Europeans (Biswan Sen 2009).

The certitude that the subaltern can speak is one distinguishing feature of decolonial theory; but decolonial thinkers differ from postcolonial/subaltern theory and postcolonial feminism in several additional ways. The Modernity/Coloniality Group insist that capitalism is concomitant to colonialism; it is not an autonomous system imported to the Americas on its own. Taking issue with those who claim that capitalism existed in Europe prior to colonization, decolonial theorists argue that colonialism is what made capitalism possible. In marked contrast to those who claim that capitalism failed to develop in the colony due to conditions internal to indigeneity, the Modernity/Coloniality Group insist that capitalism requires the internal conditions of the colony to realize itself.

Decolonial theorists conceptualize colonialism as the dark side of modernity. Contesting the association of modernity with emancipatory developments in Europe, such as the Reformation, the Enlightenment, and the French Revolution, the Modernity/Coloniality Group suggest more complicated causal relations between colonialism, the age of reason, and the age of revolutions. Just as Hegel suggested that the full realization of reason and freedom is inseparable from despotism, slavery and conquest, decolonial thinkers suggest that slavery, forced labor, and the rightslessness of colonized peoples exist in dialectical relation to liberal notions of liberty, equality, justice and free labor. The colony is both the condition of possibility and the proving ground of the Western nation-state, and rights-bearing citizenship tethered to men of property. In other words, the freedom of the European and the colonial settler depends on the unfreedom of the colonized. Precisely because the freedom of some presupposes the subordination of others, decolonization is always an unfinished project. Although colonialism has ended in most parts of the world, the "coloniality of power" continues to define relations between the West and the Rest.

Peruvian sociologist, Anibal Quijano, theorized the coloniality of power as a process of racialization integral to colonization (2010, 2008). Beginning in 1492 with the conquest of the Americas, European conquistadors proclaimed themselves the lords of the world, the "natural" rulers of all "inferior" peoples. Using conquest as proof of their superiority, the conquerors reclassified entire populations in accordance with finely honed hierarchies grounded in religious doctrines, physiognomies, myths about blood and divine mandates to spread the message and means of salvation. Those conquered through violence were condemned to a zone of non-Being, stripped of humanity, rights, and self-determination.

According to Quijano, the idea of race imposed on the colonized originated in debates during the Spanish Inquisition and the Reconquista. The principle of the "purity of blood" was introduced to distinguish "real" Christians from converted Jews and Moors. By inventing a specious notion of unchanging biology that privileged Catholics, the Spanish Church afforded the monarchy grounds to expel the Moors and Jews from Spain. Although the principle of the purity of blood was invoked initially to legitimate a religious hierarchy, the precedent of tying notions of superiority to a biological base with profound cultural repercussions, proved particularly useful to the colonizing enterprises that followed conquest of the "New World." Imported to America with colonization, the idea of a naturally superior race, identified through its beliefs and deeds, provided a useful tool to differentiate the colonizers from the Amerindians and the imported slaves from Africa. Once marked as inferiors, conquered and enslaved peoples were subjected not only to edicts issued by the Catholic monarchy of Spain, but to civilizing missions, "salvation" efforts, and brutal labor and sexual exploitation.

The idea of race implicit in debates surrounding "the purity of blood" gave rise to hierarchies that restructured the social organization as well as public and private institutions and practices in the "New World." Linking notions of biological and cultural inferiority, race provided a versatile substratum for the coloniality of power, justifying a hierarchical social system that accorded control over human and material resources to the colonizers. According to Quijano, race reordered all aspects of indigenous life, including sex, labor, collective authority, subjectivity, and intersubjectivity. Race designated who would become a slave, an indentured laborer, or a free wage laborer. Race determined political status during the colonial era, and subsequently dictated who would have access to full citizenship in the nation-state. As the foundation of Eurocentrism, race defined what counted as history and knowledge, and condemned the colonized to live as peoples without history, without the rights of man, and without human rights.

As European knowledge production was accredited as the only valid knowledge, indigenous epistemologies were relegated to the status of primitive superstition or destroyed. Eurocentrism locked intersubjective relations between the European and the non-European in a temporal frame that always positioned the European as more advanced. Whether the opposition pitted the civilized against the barbarians, wage workers against slaves, the modern against the premodern, or the developed against the underdeveloped, the superiority of the European was never questioned (Quijano 2008).

Following Quijano, decolonial thinkers have developed a range of concepts that take the coloniality of power as their point of departure. Like Quijano, decolonial theorists emphasize that coloniality is different from colonialism. In contrast to the historically specific acts of colonialism through which one nation imposes its sovereignty on another, coloniality refers to long-standing patterns of power that emerge in the context of colonialism, which redefine culture, labor, intersubjective relations, aspirations of the self, common sense, and knowledge production in ways that accredit the superiority of the colonizer. Surviving long after colonialism has been overthrown, coloniality permeates consciousness and social relations in contemporary life. Edgardo Lander (2000) has theorized the coloniality of knowledge, examining the diverse practices by which non-Western knowledge has been and continues to be silenced or eradicated. Bearing some resemblance to Spivak's notion of epistemic violence, Lander analyzes the physical extermination of non-Western knowledge producers, as well as diverse technologies of intellectual genocide. Drawing insights from Walter Mignolo, Nelson Maldonado Torres (2008) reinterprets the core concepts of existential phenomenology as a manifestation of the coloniality of being. Indeed, he traces how the consciousness of the colonizer structures the Western *cogito* in ways that ensure that those of European ancestry refuse to recognize the full humanity of people of color. Breny Mendoza (2014) theorizes the coloniality of democracy, tracing how the racialization and gendering of non-European men and women has been essential to the construction of white male citizenship and to the perpetuation of white male privilege despite constitutional guarantees of formal equality.

Decolonial Feminism

Decolonial feminism is sometimes traced to the scholarship of Native-American feminists, Chicana feminists, and African feminist anticolonial theory published in the 1960s and 1970s, but the full flowering of this thought is much more recent. Gloria Anzaldúa's *Borderlands/La Frontera* (1987) is often identified as a foundational text of feminist decolonial theory. Her concepts of mestiza consciousness and *pensamiento fronterizo* theorized the subversive character of subjugated knowledges that fracture colonial languages and epistemology in ways that change the terms of debate. Strongly influenced by postcolonial theory, Emma Perez published *The Decolonial Imaginary* in 1999, seeking to challenge the "colonial imaginary" still structuring Chicano, nationalist and patriarchal historiography. Native feminist scholars, such as Paula Gunn Allen

(1986), and African anticolonial scholars, such as Oyeronke Oyewumi (1997), have also analyzed both the impact of colonization on women and the colonizing discourses of Western feminism.

Decolonial feminism is gaining in popularity in various cultural and national contexts. Catherine Walsh (2010), who publishes both in English and Spanish, has analyzed interculturality, subjugated knowledges and decoloniality in Ecuador. Her concept of interculturality is particularly important to decolonial theory because it strays away from concepts such as multiculturalism and pluraculturalism which were deployed by the World Bank to promote neoliberal capitalism. For Walsh "critical interculturality" is not about inclusion and "getting along," but a political, ethical, and epistemic project of the indigenous population of the Andes that seeks to create a new rationality and humanity that reverses Eurocentrism and the coloniality of knowledge. Outside the United States, Madina Tlostanova, a feminist scholar originally from Kabardino-Balkaria, a republic of the Russian Federation, who is now based in Moscow, uses a decolonial framework to analyze post-Soviet space and subjectivity. Tlostanova borrows Mignolo's concept of imperial difference to elucidate the position of the Soviet Union within Western narratives of empire. Here the Soviet empire not only originates outside of modernity and appears as a subaltern empire, but its exteriority to modernity and to Europe's imaginary allows this imperial difference to mutate into colonial difference. This determines the types of feminism that emerge in the post-Soviet space that, while defined in terms of coloniality, are not easily understood under "feminisms of color." Most of her work on gender and decoloniality, however, has not been translated into English. German cultural critic, Freya Schiwy also uses a decolonial lens to investigate gender in the Andes and to theorize subjectivity and coloniality in the field of cultural studies (Schiwy 2010).

Decolonial theory is very influential in Latin America and the Caribbean, although some feminist scholars have questioned its content, geographical purchase, and its gendered lacunae. Within feminist circles, decolonial theory has entered into dialog with intersectional, poststructuralist, indigenous, Afro-Latin American, and mestizo feminists, who have developed their own theories outside of the decolonial option. Rita Segato (2001, 2011), an Argentinean feminist anthropologist based in Brazil, for example, integrates elements of decolonial theory in her work, but is critical of the notion of the coloniality of gender because she is not persuaded by Lugones's claim that gender hierarchies were unknown in indigenous societies. Silvia Rivera Cusicanqui, an Aymara feminist sociologist and activist from Bolivia famous for her work in the *Taller de Historia Oral Andina*, has decried decolonial theory as a colonizing discourse originating in US universities, one that is not only divorced from local struggles of the indigenous peoples in Latin America, but that also misappropriates and misrecognizes decades of work on colonization and decolonization that has taken place in the region (Rivera Cusicanqui 2010, 58). Decolonial theory in Latin America has also been subjected to a double feminist critique. One dimension focuses on decolonial theory's—particularly, Quijano's and Dussel's—lack of attention to gender or its inadequate conceptualization of gender (Lugones 2007, 2010; Mendoza 2010).

Decolonial theory is also gaining momentum in the US feminist academy, although it has not had the instant success that postcolonial theory experienced in the 1990s. In two recent published works, "Heterosexualism and the Colonial Modern Gender System" (2007) and "Towards a Decolonial Feminism" (2010), Maria Lugones has introduced decolonial theory to feminist audiences in the United States, while expanding its parameters to encompass the coloniality of gender and sexuality. In her 2007 essay, Lugones combines intersectionality and Quijano's coloniality of power to further develop her own conception of the coloniality of gender. She critiques Quijano's conception of gender on multiple grounds: it is still trapped in biological determinism; it presupposes sexual dimorphism where none existed; it naturalizes heteronormativity in cultures that did not deem homosexuality either a sexual or a social transgression; and it presumes a patriarchal distribution of power in societies where more egalitarian social relations between men and women were prevalent. In Lugones's view, Quijano's understanding of gender is still Eurocentric. Drawing insights from Native feminist scholarship and Oyewumi's work on the Yoruba to correct Quijano's misconceived notion of gender, Lugones argues that indigenous societies did not have "gender" before European intrusion. Gender did not exist as an organizing principle of power in indigenous societies before the process of colonization. Other principles, such as seniority, provided a basis for power and authority, but they were quite distinct from the social construction of gender. Rather than considering gender a perennial feature of social organization, Lugones argues that gender should be understood as a colonial construct, just as race was a European imposition. In the process of colonization, women and men in the colony were both racialized and sexualized as gender was deployed as a powerful tool to destroy the social relations of the colonized by dividing men and women from each other and creating antagonisms between them. European constructions of gender introduced internal hierarchies that broke down the solidarity between men and women destroying previous ties based on complementarity and reciprocity. In place of harmonious collaboration, European colonizers positioned men and women as antagonists. Through sexual violence, exploitation, and systems of concubinage, the colonizers used gender to break the will of indigenous men and women, imposing new hierarchies that were institutionalized with colonialism. The bodies of women became the terrain on which indigenous men negotiated survival under new colonial conditions. Sacrificing indigenous women to the lust of the conquerors, perversely, became the only means of cultural survival. Lugones labels this systemic sexual violence the dark side of modern/colonial gender system.

Julieta Paredes (2008) advances a critique of Maria Lugones's concept of the coloniality of gender, suggesting that Lugones's analysis misses the centrality of gender to patriarchal indigenous societies prior to European colonization. Lugones carries her analysis a step further in her 2010 essay, "Toward Decolonial Feminism," claiming that the gender system imposed by European colonizers on the colonized differed significantly from the gender system the conquistadors imposed on European women living in the colony. The multifaceted gender system imposed in the colony subordinated European women but dehumanized indigenous, African slave, and poor mestizo men and women.

Accepting the central tenet of coloniality—that the separation of the human from the non-human was concomitant to colonization, Lugones suggests that the racialization of non-Europeans as beasts of burden had critical consequences for the development of complex sex and gender systems. The hierarchical dichotomies that distinguished the civilized human from the natural primitive and culture from nature structured not only the relations between colonizer and colonized, it also legitimated a hierarchy that elevated European men over European women. The human itself was bifurcated: as creatures closer to nature, emotional rather than rational, bound to the animal function of reproduction, European women were lower than men in the great Chain of Being, yet they were still human, marked by culture. Civilized gender involved a hierarchy that subordinated European women to European men, but still marked a gulf between colonizers and colonized. As savages, the colonized manifested biological difference (sex), but they lacked a gender system. Egalitarian relations between indigenous men and women were taken by the Europeans as evidence of barbarity. According to Lugones, then, gender hierarchy marks the civilized status of European women and men; its absence defines the nonhuman, racialized, naturalized non-Europeans, who are sexed but genderless. Whether cast as hypersexualized animals or beasts of burden, indigenous peoples and enslaved peoples were imagined to be a threat to the European gender order. As subhuman beings, the colonized were fit for breeding, brutal labor, exploitation, and/or massacre (Lugones 2010, 206). The coloniality of gender makes clear that gender grants civilized status only to those men and women who inhabit the domain of the human; those who lack gender are subject to gross exploitation or outright genocide. Thus Lugones's theorization of the coloniality of gender as dehumanizing practice that survives colonization helps make sense of contemporary issues such as feminicide, trafficking, and increased violence against non-European women.

In Latin America and the Caribbean, Lugones's analysis of the coloniality of gender has had a mixed reception. Her work has opened the feminist archive to decolonial thinking and produced a respectable group of followers. Yet, her specific claims about the coloniality of gender are controversial among mainstream feminists, indigenous feminists, and feminist scholars working on colonization and decolonization within other theoretical frameworks (Mendoza 2014). Some critiques question the validity of the ethnographic work that Lugones uses to support her arguments. Argentinean anthropologist Rita Laura Segato (2001), for example, draws upon her own research on the Yoruba in Latin America to question Oyewumi's claim that gender was non-existent among the Yoruba. Although she acknowledges that the gender system of the Yoruba is complex and different from European gender and that their form of patriarchy was in many ways less intensive than the European version, Segato provides ample evidence that gender existed as an oppressive status differentiation among the Yoruba. Segato suggests that low intensity patriarchies became more hierarchical when subjected to the logic of gender imposed under colonization—with devastating consequences for Indigenous women. As public and private spheres were separated and gendered, Indigenous women were domesticated and privatized, losing the power they once held in the community. Although Indigenous men retained some communal authority, they were humiliated and symbolically emasculated by the depredations of colonization. Forced to engage the European logic of gender, indigenous men returned to their communities supplementing the old lexicon of power with new hierarchical codes (Segato 2011).

Silvia Rivera Cusicanqui (2004) provides a similar critique grounded in the experiences of Andean society. Although indigenous gender relations were more egalitarian in the private as well as in the public sphere, the Andean gender system was organized around the normative heterosexual couple within a system of complementarity. Kinship systems were bilateral, which afforded men and women equal inheritance rights. Women and men achieved social personhood once they formed a couple and both accumulated prestige as they gained seniority. Cusicanqui notes that all these practices were weakened or destroyed not at the time of colonization but with the advent of republican systems of governance, modernization, and development. Women's roles in the community were weakened but much more recently than Lugones's account of the coloniality of gender suggests (Cusicanqui 2004). According to Cusicanqui, gender relations based on complementarity survived in indigenous communities much longer than has previously been assumed, destroyed in a gradual process of patriarchalization that accompanied modernization and the encroachment of the modern nation-state upon Andean communities.

In Bolivia, since the election of Evo Morales to the presidency, the first indigenous person to hold that office, and in Mexico within Zapatista revolutionary struggles, the debate over whether or not gender preceded colonization has played an important role, influencing revolutionary theories and feminist proposals for state policies, laws, and practices as well as political imaginaries. Outside these political struggles, the question of whether gender is a colonial construct or an ancestral practice may pose a false dilemma. Lugones's concept of the coloniality of gender, Segato's claim that low-intensity patriarchies prior to conquest were exacerbated by colonization, and Cusicanqui's account of patriarchalization as a consequence of nation-state formation postindependence need not be read as contradictory. All three scholars agree that the imposition of a European gender system had profound effects on relations between men and women in the colony, unleashing lethal forces against Native, enslaved, and poor mestizo women sufficient to be considered genocidal. Lugones' conceptualization of the coloniality of gender is useful precisely because it situates gender in relation to the genocidal logic of the coloniality of power. The racializing logic that Europeans imposed on the colonized robbed non-Europeans not only of their status as human but also of their status as gendered beings. Devoid of humanity and gender, non-Europeans were endlessly exploitable, as well as eliminable. Lugones's insights resemble those of US Native feminist scholars who have long claimed that the settler colonial nation-state operated according to a logic of elimination, which enabled the near complete physical and symbolic disappearance of the Amerindian.

Whether drawn from Lugones, US Native feminist scholars, or Latin American feminist scholars, decolonial thinking has important lessons. The racializing logic introduced into the Americas in 1492 did far more than structure a relation between colonizer and colonized; it established ways of thinking and modes of power that have shaped and continue to shape social and political relations that permeate all aspects of life. Recognizing the profound influence of racialization and gendering is essential to an adequate understanding of the past, to efforts to transform the present, and to strategies to envision and produce a different future.

References

Abu-Lughod, Lila. 2013. *Do Muslim Women Need Saving?* President and Fellows of Harvard College.
Alexander-Floyd, Nikol G. 2012. "Disappearing Acts: Reclaiming Intersectionality in the Social Sciences in a Post-Black Feminist Era." *Feminist Formations* 24(1) (Spring): 1–24.
Césaire, Aimé. 2000. *Discourse on Colonialism*. New York: Monthly Review Press.
Chibber, Vivek. 2013. *Postcolonial Theory and the Specter of Capital*. London: Verso.
Cho, Sumi, Kimberlé Crenshaw, and Leslie McCall. 2013. "Intersectionality: Theorizing Power, Empowering Theory." *Signs: Journal of Women in Culture and Society* 38(4) (Summer): 785–810.
Crenshaw, Kimberlé. 1989. "Demarginalizing the Intersection of Race and Sex: A Black Feminist Critique of Antidiscrimination Doctrine, Feminist Theory and Antiracist Politics". *University of Chicago Legal Forum* 140: 139–167.
Du Bois, W. E. B. 1976. *The Souls of Black Folks: Essays and Sketches*. Cutchogue, New York: Buccaneer Books.
Dussel, Enrique. 1985. *Philosophy of Liberation*. Maryknoll, New York: Orbis Books.
Fanon, Frantz. 2004. *The Wretched of the Earth*. New York: Grove Press.
Fernandes, Leela. 2013. *Transnational Feminism in the United States*. New York: New York University Press.
Gandhi, Leela. 1998. *Postcolonial Theory*. New York: Columbia University Press.
Garcilaso de la Vega, Inca. 2008. *Comentarios Reales*. In Diferencia. Barcelona: Linkgua Ediciones, S. L.
Garry, Ann. 2012. "Who Is included? Intersectionality, Metaphors, and the Multiplicity of Gender" In *Out From the Shadows: Analytical Feminist Contributions to Traditional Philosophy*, edited by Sharon L. Crasnow and Anita M. Superson, 493–530. New York: Oxford University Press.
Grosfoguel, Ramon. 2010. "The Epistemic Decolonial Turn: Beyond Political Economy Paradigms." In *Globalization and the Decolonial Option*, edited by Walter D. Mignolo and Arturo Escobar, 65–77. London and New York: Routledge.
Guamán, Poma de Ayala, Felipe. 1936. *Nueva Corónica y Buen Gobierno*/Paris: Institut d'ethnologie.
Gunn Allen, Paula. 1986. *The Sacred Hoop: Recovering the Feminine in American Indian Traditions*. Boston: Beacon Press.
Gunnarson, Lena. 2011. "A Defense of the category 'women.'" In *Feminist Theory* 12(1): 23–27.
Hancock, Ange Marie. 2011. *Beyond the Oppression Olympics: A Politics of Solidarity for the 21st Century*. New York: Palgrave Macmillan.
Hill Collins, Patricia. 1993. "Toward a New Vision: Race, Class, and Gender as Categories of Analysis and Connection." In *Race, Gender and Class* 1(1) (Fall): 25–45.
Kontopoulos, Kyriakos. 1993. *The Logic of Social Structures*. Cambridge: Cambridge University Press.

Lander, Edgardo. 2000. *La colonialidad del saber: eurocentrismo y ciencias sociales. Perspectivas Latinoamericanas*. Buenos Aires: CLACSO.
Leitch, Vincent B., Cain E. William, Finke Laurie A., Johnson, Barbara E. eds. 2010. *The Norton Anthology of Theory and Criticism*. New York; London: W.W. Norton.
Lewis, Reina, and Mills, Sara. 2003. *Feminist Postcolonial Theory*. New York: Routledge.
Lugones, Maria. 2007. "Heterosexualism and the Colonial Modern Gender System." *Hypatia* 22(1) (Winter): 186–209.
Lugones, Maria. 2010). "Towards a Descolonial Feminism." *Hypatia* 25(4) (Fall): 742–759.
Maldonado-Torres, Nelson. 2008. *Against War: Views from the Underside of Modernity*. Durham: Duke University Press Books.
Mariátegui, José Carlos. 2009. *Siete ensayos de interpretación de la realidad peruana* In Diferencia. Barcelona: Linkgua Ediciones.
May, Vivian M. 2014. "'Speaking into the Void'? Intersectionality Critiques and Epistemic Backlash." *Hypatia* 29(1) (Winter): 94–112.
McCall, Leslie. 2005. "The Complexity of Intersectionality." *Signs: Journal of Women in Culture and Society* 30(3): 1771–1800.
McClintock, Anne. 1995. *Imperial Leather*. New York: Routledge.
Mendoza, Breny. 2002. "Transnational Feminisms in Question." *Feminist Theory* 3(3): 295–314.
Mendoza, Breny. 2006. "The Undemocratic Foundations of Democracy: An Enunciation from Postoccidental Latin America." *Signs: Journal of Women in Culture and Society* 31(4) (Summer): 932–939.
Mendoza, Breny. 2010. "La epistemologia del sur, la colonialidad de genero y el feminismo latinoamericano." In *Aproximaciones críticas a las prácticas teórico-políticas del feminismo latinoamericano*, vol. 1, edited by Yuderkys Espinosa Miñoso, 19–36. Buenos Aires: Enla frontera.
Mendoza, Breny. 2014. *Ensayos de Crítica Feminista en Nuestra América*. Mexico D.F.: Editorial Herder.
Mendoza, Breny. 2014. "La cuestión de la colonialidad de género." In Breny Mendoza *Ensayos de Crítica Feminista en Nuestra América*, 45–71. Mexico D.F.: Editorial Herder.
Mignolo, Walter. 1995. *The Darker Side of the Rennaissance: Literacy, Territoriality, and Colonization*. Ann Arbor: University of Michigan Press.
Mignolo, Walter. 2000. *Local Histories/Global Designs. Coloniality, Subaltern Knowledges, and Border Thinking*. Princeton, NJ: Princeton University Press.
Mohanty, Chandra T. 1991. "Under Western Eyes: Feminist Scholarship and Colonial Discourses." In *Third World Women and the Politics of Feminism*, 51–80. Bloomington: Indiana University Press.
Mohanty, Chandra T., Russo, Ann, and Torres, Lourdes. 1991. *Third World Women and the Politics of Feminism*. Bloomington: Indiana University Press.
Nkrumah, Kwame. 1964. *Consciencism*. New York: Monthly Review Press.
Ortega, Mariana. 2006. "Being Lovingly, Knowingly Ignorant: White Feminism and Women of Color" *Hypatia* 21(3) (Summer): 56–74.
Paredes, Julieta. 2008. *Hilando fino desde el feminism comunitario*. La Paz, Bolivia: Comunidad Mujeres Creando Comunidad. CEDEC. Asociación Centro de Defensa de la Cultura.
Paudyal, Mahesh. 2011. http://www.ekantipur.com/the-kathmandu-post/2011/12/23/related_articles/the-dream-of-a-borderless-world/229620.html.
Quijano, Anibal. 2008. "Coloniality of Power, Eurocentrism, and Social Classification." In *Coloniality at Large*, edited by Marel Moraña et al., 181–224. Durham, NC: Duke University Press.

Quijano, Anibal. 2010. "Coloniality and Modernity/Rationality." In *Globalization and the Decolonial Option*, edited by Walter D. Mignolo and Arturo Escobar, 22–32. London and New York: Routledge.

Rivera Cusicanqui, Silvia. 2004. 'La noción de "derecho" o las paradojas de la modernidad postcolonial: indígenas y mujeres en Bolivia.' October. 1–9. Ecuador: Revista Aportes Andinos.

Rivera Cusicanqui, Silvia. 2010. *Ch'ixinakax Utxiwa. Una reflexión sobre prácticas y discursos descolonizadores* Buenos Aires: Tinta Limón y Retazos.

Roshanravan, Shireen. 2014. "Motivating Coalition: Women of Color and Epistemic Disobedience." *Hypatia* 29(1) (Winter): 41–58.

Santa Cruz Feminist of Color Collective. 2014. "'Building on Edge of Each Other's Battles': A Feminist of Color Multidimensional Lens." *Hypatia* 29(1) (Winter): 23–40.

Schiwy, Freya. 2010. "Decolonization and the Question of Subjectivity: Gender, Race, and Binary Thinking." In *Globalization and the Decolonial Option*, edited by Walter D. Mignolo and Arturo Escobar, 125–148. London and New York: Routledge.

Segato, Rita. 2001. "The Factor of Gender in the Yoruba Transnational Religious World." Brasilia. http://www.scribd.com/doc/47347417/THE-FACTOR-OF-GENDER-IN-THE-YORUBA-TRANSNATIONAL-RELIGIOUS-WORLD. Last retrieved 5/27/2014.

Segato, Rita. 2011. "Género y colonialidad: en busca de claves delectura y de un vocabulario estratégico descolonial." In *Feminismos y poscolonialidad. Descolonizando el feminismo desde y en América Latina*, edited by Karina Bidaseca y Vanesa Vazquez Laba, 17–48. Buenos Aires: Godot.

Sen, Lipi Biswan. 2009. 'Sí, el subalterno puede hablar: un análisis breve de la "Nueva corónica y buen gobierno" de Felipe Guaman Poma de Ayala y los "Comentarios reales" del Inca Garcilaso de la Vega' Alicante: Biblioteca Virtual Miguel de Cervantes, 475–502.

Shohat, Ella, and Stam, Robert. 2006. *Flagging Patriotism*. New York: Routledge.

Spivak, Gayatri Chakravorty. 1988. "Can the Subaltern Speak?" In *Marxism and the Interpretation of Culture*, edited by Cary Nelson and Lawrence Grossber, 271–313. London: Macmillan.

Stam, Rober and Shohat, Ella. 2012. *Race in Translation*. New York: New York University Press.

Stoler, Ann Laura. 2002. *Carnal Knowledge and Imperial Power: Race and the Intimate in Colonial Rule*. Berkeley: University of California Press.

Tuck, Eve, and Yang, K. Wayne. 2012. "Decolonization Is Not a Metaphor." *Decolonization: Indigeneity, Education & Society* 1(1): 1–40.

Walsh, Catherine. 2010. "Shifting the Geopolitics of Critical Knowledge: Decolonial Thought and Cultural Studies 'Others' in the Andes." In *Globalization and the Decolonial Option*, edited by Walter D. Mignolo and Arturo Escobar, 78–93. London and New York: Routledge.

Zack, Naomi. 2005. *Inclusive feminism: a third wave theory of women's commonality*. Lanham, MD: Rowman & Littlefield.

CHAPTER 6

CYBORGS AND VIRTUAL BODIES

KRISTA GENEVIÈVE LYNES AND KATERINA SYMES

INTRODUCTION

> The cyborg is our ontology; it gives us our politics—Donna Haraway

THE melding of flesh and machine evoked by the figure of the cyborg has demanded a proper account in theories of embodiment, subjectivity, and social life. For some in the cultural imaginary of the mid-twentieth century, the "cyborg" signalled the fulfilment of a Cartesian promise: the overcoming of the limitations of the body, the transcendence of consciousness in the machine, and the renewal of the subject through reassembly and replacement. For others, the "cyborg" ushered in a more apocalyptic posthuman future in which machines would ultimately supersede humanity, and in which the subject of humanism would lose agency, coherence, autonomy, and rationality. Neither of these positions, however, could be easily taken up by feminists, for whom the overcoming of the body has largely been of a piece with the most violent projects of modernity (including patriarchal domination, colonization, resource extraction, and exploitation) and for whom also the loss of the liberal subject of humanism (a subject from which so many bodies have been forcefully excluded) cannot so easily be mourned, even as it has been foundational to many feminist political claims.

This chapter seeks to unpack the tension between the cyborg as a figure for twentieth-century ontologies, and the cyborg as a figure for feminist liberatory politics, beginning with Donna Haraway's potent "Manifesto for Cyborgs" and following the engagement with the cyborg within feminist theories in the fields of new media studies, science and technology studies, and cultural studies. It draws out the effects of new technologies on embodiment and subjectivity in the late twentieth century, the intersection of concerns with gender with questions of race and ethnicity, and tensions between the real and virtual, and the material and discursive. The chapter ends by examining new modes of thinking contradictions, hybrids, potent fusions, and dangerous possibilities within feminist theory beyond the figure of the cyborg.

Donna Haraway's "Cyborg Manifesto": A Figure for Doing Feminism

Researchers at the Research Unit of the Rockland State Hospital (a psychiatric facility in Orangeburg, New York) Manfred Clynes and Nathan Kline coined the term "cyborg" in the thick of mid-twentieth-century technoscientific, military-industrial, and mass media worlds. While they conjured the term from *cybernetic organism* to capture the possibility that the body might be "freed" from human constraints in space exploration, the term served also to sum up the thoughts, practices, and fantasies of mechanized bodies and lively machines circulating in the post-WWII American cultural context (Clynes and Kline 1960). Given these hegemonic origins, the cyborg stood as an unlikely figure for recuperation within feminist theory or politics. For Donna Haraway (1991, 151), however, "illegitimate offspring are often exceedingly unfaithful to their origins," and such faithlessness (combined with strategies of irony and blasphemy) characterized Haraway's retooling of the cyborg as a potent figure for thinking feminist theory and politics in the late twentieth century.

Haraway's "A Cyborg Manifesto" first appeared in English in 1985 in the journal *Socialist Review*. In it, Haraway sought to theorize the relation between feminism and technoscience, particularly in the interests of countering feminist accounts of science and technology as purely patriarchal discursive formations. Haraway's (1991, 151–153) political-fictional analysis foregrounded three crucial boundary breakdowns in the contemporary moment: between the human and the animal, the organism and the machine, and the physical and the non-physical. Her appropriation of the figure of the cyborg functioned as a description of the ontological shifts under postmodernism, as an epistemological challenge to modern taxonomies, and as a figure for a postcolonial and postmodern feminist politics.

The examples of cyborgs in Haraway's writing—women from the global south working in new micro-electronics industries, mythological figures, new gendered heads of households, and sweatshop laborers—in many respects displaced the technological and science-fiction discourses that framed the cyborg in popular imaginaries. Theorizing a new "informatics of domination," Haraway (1991, 161) characterized the late twentieth-century movement from industrial to postindustrial society as a transformation that denaturalized the categories of modernity—including those of race, class and gender. Bodies, objects, and spaces were all subject to disassembly and reassembly, to new control strategies, and to new boundary conditions and interface procedures. Sex and reproduction could no longer be naturalized, given the proliferation of forms of replication; racial categories were challenged by changing understandings of genetics and by the disintegration of cohesive social systems. The transformations wrought by globalization—the emergence of multinational corporations, export-processing zones, new service industries—contributed to the "feminization" of the workforce,—that is, to labor conditions premised on vulnerability, the exploitation of a reserve labor force, subject to more "flexible" but pervasive time arrangements, and to an "existence that always borders on being obscure, out of place, and reducible to sex" (166). The privatization of public life had transformed the patriarchal nuclear family into a modern family mediated by the welfare state (a "homework" economy, coupled with new right-wing family ideologies and intensified definitions of corporate and state property as private property; 1991, 168). There was, Haraway concluded, no *place* for women in these new social networks, only "geometries of difference and contradiction crucial to women's cyborg identities" (170).

The examples Haraway mobilized serve to displace the cyborg from the spheres of space exploration, robotics, information technologies, or the military to the everyday processes of the gendered division of labor, exacerbated by the conditions of late capitalism and globalization. Rather than situating feminist struggles outside and against cyborg life, she emphasized how gendered embodiment is always already embroiled in technologies of production, reproduction, and communication. Thus, while cyborg theory emerged within feminism to illuminate the impact of techno cultures on gendered embodiment, Haraway also considerably broadened the field of analysis for theories of the cyborg: not only the emerging encounters in Massively Multiplayer Online Games (MMOs) but also the changing experiences of maquiladora workers; not only the amplification of the body through machinic assemblages, but also the extension of labor in the double shift.

Such an account of cyborg life has two important effects for feminist politics: first, as a rhetorical strategy and political method, it proposes a nonessentialized, and necessarily hybrid and fragmented vision of social and bodily reality, both countering the romantic nostalgia within radical movements for unalienated or natural forms of embodiment, and providing a new subject of and in feminist theory. Rather than questions of representation, the cyborg presents instead what Haraway (in another chapter of *Simians, Cyborgs and Women*) calls *material-semiotics*, "nodes in which bodies and meanings co-shape one another" (1991, 194; 2008, 4). The cyborg asserts that there is no transcendent authorization of interpretation, no *hors texte*, and no ontological grounding of Western epistemology (1991, 153). Gender, then, is both a semiotic system and flesh simultaneously, translated into a code or common language in which "heterogeneity is submitted to disassembly, reassembly, investment, exchange" (1991, 164).[1] Further, the lack of access to an originary wholeness leaves no position of innocence with respect to questions of domination, no privileged place from which to speak truth, particularly to "the other," and thus no innocent category "woman" to organize feminism (1991, 157). Haraway named the alternative to innocence "situated knowledge" (also "feminist objectivity"), a position from which to stake a claim in a social world that acknowledges the "radical historical contingency for all knowledge claims and knowing subjects" and simultaneously commits itself to producing faithful accounts of the "real" world (1991, 187).

Second, cyborg life provides an "imaginative resource" for thinking collectivity, intimacy, and critique. Rather than identity, Haraway proposed "affinity" as the ground for thinking the dangerous possibilities and admixtures figured by cyborg politics. She took cyborg politics to be prefigured by the work of Chela Sandoval, whose notion of "oppositional consciousness" derives from occupying a contradictory position outside the stable social categories of race, sex, or class, and by Audre Lorde whose "sister outsider" grounds the political dimension of the feminist cyborg. Haraway was not calling for relativism or pluralism (not all differences are equal, and difference itself is not *necessarily* liberatory), but rather for a consciousness within feminism about the partiality and openness of personal and collective subject positions. Rather than the end of politics, the undoing of the Western subject could present possibilities for more complex alliances across differences that remain "multiple, pregnant, and complex" (1991, 160).

Beyond the figure's capacity for critique, Haraway envisioned the feminist cyborg as a constructive force, capable of generating accounts of the world that encompass complex and contradictory positions. Haraway drew insights about cyborg writing as oppositional technique from Audre Lorde, Cherrie Moraga, Samuel Delaney, Octavia Butler, and Monique Wittig, among others. To illuminate the significance of social life in technoscientific worlds, cyborg writing must be a tool of oppositional consciousness, a mode of "seizing the tools to mark the world that marked them as other" (1991, 175). In this way, writing could become a method for contesting received meanings, accessing the power to signify, intervening in the processes of textualization under late capitalism, a form of play that is "deadly serious" (175). This play is deconstructive, certainly, but allied also to a transformative potentiality, the possibility of reimagining bodies and kinships. The position of the cyborg allows the feminist scholar and activist to "see from both perspectives at once because each reveals both dominations and possibilities unimaginable from the other vantage point" (154).

Indeed, Haraway's observations about writing, irreverence, irony, and blasphemy provide a coda for reading "The Cyborg Manifesto" itself, and its committed critique—from within socialist feminism—of several of the idols of feminist thinking: women as the subject of feminist praxis, the valorization of women's experience, the search for unalienated social relations, or the mapping of feminist politics onto the movement of history. Under the conditions of postmodernism and late capitalism, Haraway mobilized the figure of the cyborg to think a political standpoint for feminism—influenced by the critiques of women of color and by the potent imaginaries of science fiction—within rather than against technoscientific worlds. Her objective was not to mourn the passing of an episteme that was responsible for the violences of patriarchy, colonialism, positivism, and essentialism, but to find within the transformations of postmodernism a different political subject for feminism.

Material-Discursive Negotiations in Technoscientific Worlds

Historic shifts in information systems and virtual reality certainly influenced the emergence of the figure of the cyborg as a predicament for feminist thinking—both as an account of embodiment in the technopolitics of late twentieth-century life, and as a site for feminist accounts of subjectivity and collectivity. So, too, did the intersections of poststructuralist and feminist thought in this period. The cyborg embodied a complex intersection of the material and the discursive, an intersection not fully resolved by Haraway's hyphenated term "material-semiotic." On the one hand, feminist critiques in the 1990s of science theorists such as Hans Moravec, Ray Kurzweil, Marvin Minsky, and Richard Dawkins (who all focused on the enhancement, augmentation, and advances of the human in a posthuman future world), sought to emphasize the persistence of the material body despite technophilic claims to its obsolescence. On the other, poststructuralist feminist theories of the 1990s, drawing from (among other texts) Judith Butler's publication of *Bodies That Matter: On the Discursive Limits of Sex* (1993), emphasized the power/knowledge formations that operate to shape and form what comes to be recognized as bodily "matter," sex and gender. Feminist accounts of cyborg bodies both emphasized the constructed nature of gender in relations of power, and the materiality of bodies, which persisted as limit, lived experience, or as resistance even within the processes of virtualization through various media and discursive frameworks.

Anne Balsamo's (1996, 160) work, for instance, maintained that the cyborg body's symbolic form—its discursive construction as the bearer of signs and cultural meaning—was always already constituted in relation to "real" material bodies. Bridging material and discursive domains, the cyborg demonstrated how bodies are differently articulated within specific social and historical formations. Culturally constructed as "natural," the body is more than a material entity; yet as a material entity, the body cannot be reduced to a discursive construct, since its so-called nature "is culturally determined even when this nature is said to be discursively constructed" (34). Cyborg bodies may be "unnaturally crafted"—and cyborg bodies may posit new forms of gendered embodiment by challenging the very givenness of physical gender identity—but, Balsamo argued, cyborgs cannot simply leave their "meat" behind, because they are "never outside history and concrete relations of power and domination" (40). Balsamo's cyborg, a discursively constituted *material* body, thus challenged the dematerialization of the body associated with postmodern ideology, which elided the historically situated material body in favor of questions of textuality and subject effects.

Virtual Bodies and Information Systems

Although Balsamo emphasized the importance of the body as a material-discursive hybrid, N. Katherine Hayles (1997) notes that she frequently represented practices such as body building or cosmetic surgery as discursive signifiers rather than material actions in the world. The emphasis on the body as a sign obscured the history of various technologies or their intersection with signifying systems to produce the body as a material-discursive object (755–756). Hayles views this problem as symptomatic of a disciplinary divide between scientific and technological disciplines (which rely on what Hayles calls a "naive realism") and cultural and literary studies (which focus more readily on questions of discourse). In many respects, Hayles's account of virtual bodies in cybernetics sets out to articulate a methodology for fleshing out the material-discursive intersections of the body in the "posthuman era."

Hayles's influential text *How We Became Posthuman* (1999) offers an entry point for re-examining the material-discursive effects of techno-science, and by extension the status of the body within the context of virtuality and information systems. Hayles takes up the fantasy of transcendence present in much cybernetic theory (e.g., Hans Moravec's assertion that it will one day be possible to download human consciousness into a computer). While such speculations appear more science fictional than scientific, Hayles (1999, 1) suggests that this idea reflects a defining characteristic of the present cultural moment—that is, "the belief that information can circulate unchanged among different material substrates." Such speculation reinforces the Cartesian divide between consciousness and embodiment, and accordingly has troubling implications for feminist critiques of modernist ontologies.

For Hayles (1999, 18), the idea that consciousness can be separated from the body can only exist under a condition of virtuality, which is to say the "cultural perception that information and materiality are conceptually distinct and that information is in some sense more essential, more important, and more fundamental than materiality." The condition of virtuality necessitates the abstraction of information from its material base; information can move freely between different material substrates only if it is decontextualized and reified. As a disembodied entity, then, information is perceived to be uninhibited by the limitations of time and space, remaining unaffected by changes in context. Information is assumed to be "more mobile, more important, more *essential* than material forms," and thus more able to directly connect the organic human body to the machinic and the prosthetic (19). This understanding of virtuality creates space for unlimited "play" with identity and embodiment, but only insofar as, paradoxically, virtual bodies replace material bodies, figuring as signs for *disembodied* entities.

Although the uninhibited flow of information between different material substrates may reveal the separation between human and machine as *constructed* rather than pre-given, this boundary work dismantles "the human" only to recuperate a liberal humanist understanding of the subject alongside the cybernetic posthuman (Hayles, 1999, 84). Under the condition of virtuality, human beings can be seamlessly articulated with machines precisely because the body is the "original prosthesis;" it is an entity "the human" learns to manipulate (3). As Hayles writes, "extending or replacing the body with other prostheses becomes a continuation of a process that began before we were born" (3). The condition of virtuality not only privileges the separation between information and materiality, but also maintains the Cartesian dualism between mind and body; consciousness and rational thought are given primacy over questions of materiality.

Hayles argues that rather than view the figure of the cyborg as either *anti*human, or a subject to be recuperated by liberal humanism, it may instead assist in revising our very understanding of what it means to be human by pointing to a new type of subjectivity (one that has been central to feminist accounts of cyborg bodies). For Hayles, this new subject is constituted at the intersection of the materiality of informatics and the immateriality of information: "The body's dematerialization depends in complex and highly specific ways on the *embodied* circumstances that an ideology of dematerialization would obscure" (193). In other words, specific *embodied* histories contribute to the bifurcation of mind and body, information and materiality, under the condition of virtuality. Rather than the idealized or externalized form of "the body," Hayles emphasizes the experiential and contextual aspects of "embodiment," located within and between time, place, physiology, and culture.[2]

Part of Hayles's task is to recover a notion of the cybernetic posthuman that recognizes the importance of embodied processes for both humans and machines. For Hayles, "virtual bodies" resist the historical separation between information and materiality, as "embodiment makes clear that thought is a much broader cognitive function depending for its specificities on the embodied form enacting it" (1999, xiv). Bodily life is subject to both the inscription of systems of power/knowledge as signs on the body, and the incorporation of signs, structures and technologies through bodily performance. Much like Butler's understanding of the *performativity* of gendered identity, Hayles sees systems of signs encoded in the body through repeated performances, becoming both habitual and normalized, and sites of struggle against the normative dimensions of the sex/gender system.

For Hayles (1999, 200), incorporating practices *perform* bodily content, while practices of inscription modulate this very performance. The body's competencies and skills are not necessarily conscious and are distinct from discourse. Because of this, incorporated knowledge is resistant to change, since it is habitual and deeply sedimented in a body. Moreover, since incorporating practices are necessarily performative and instantiated, there is always an element of improvisation that is context specific. Thus embodied knowledges are not entirely formalizable, as there are various permutations that cannot be accounted for completely (202). Although Hayles makes a distinction between inscribing and incorporating practices, neither is "natural" or universal. As Hayles suggests, "the body is encultured through both kinds of practices . . . culture not only flows from the environment into the body but also emanates from the body into the environment" (200). The body produces and is produced by culture. This view of the embodied human subject displaces the centrality of the sovereign human agent as the sole producer of meaning. Conscious agency is no longer "in control" of the embodied posthuman, but rather an epiphenomenon. This understanding of the embodied posthuman—the cyborg—offers an account of subjectivity and agency that challenges both scientific objectivism and the imperialist project of mastering and controlling nonhuman entities (Hayles 1999).

Cyborgs in Cultural Theory and Media Worlds

The intersections of the material and the semiotic in feminist cyborg theory provided an important methodology for thinking the co-constitution of social reality and virtual worlds, and for combining critiques of the representation of subjects in the late twentieth century with material critiques of the political economy of information technologies. Feminist scholars brought together accounts of the gendered effects of new technologies on embodiment, subjectivity, and collectivity—for instance in the spheres of reproductive medicine, assembly lines in Free Trade Zones—with readings of forms of self-fashioning in virtual worlds. In doing so, scholars aimed to assess the possibilities and limitations of the cyborg figure for feminist and critical race politics, given the complicity of so many cyborg figures with capitalism, colonialism and neocolonialism, and militarization and privatization.[3] Feminist scholarship responded more positively to the figure of the cyborg as a site for feminist critique than to its possibilities for feminist politics, and most of the literature in the decade following the publication of "The Cyborg Manifesto" cautioned against an overly hasty celebration of the cyborg as an icon for feminism.

Critiques by feminist scholars were mobilized to account for new popular accounts of bodily transcendence in cyberspace and virtual worlds, and new exclusions of gender in emerging information technologies. Particularly, the manner in which virtual "play" was imagined to transcend the binaries of mind and body as well as markers of gender and race, animated feminist critiques of the cyborg in the late twentieth century. Examinations of new cultural formations focused on the very real experiences of racism and sexism, both online and off, which were obscured by emphases on the virtuality of online identities. The popular turn toward the cyborg as a figure for bodily transcendence was thus "an old Cartesian trick, one that [had] unpleasant consequences for those bodies whose speech is silenced by the act of our forgetting; that is to say, those upon whose labor the act of forgetting the body is founded—usually women and minorities" (Stone 1999, 94). These concerns challenged feminist theorists to examine the ontological and political effects of cyborg bodies, particularly in light of the technological proliferations in the late twentieth century.

Technologies of Gender

Feminist scholars were not only concerned about shifting definitions of subjectivity, but also the very processes through which the body takes shape in and through new technological apparatuses. Although Haraway's use of the genre of the manifesto exhorted feminist theorists and activists to take up and identify with the figure of the cyborg, feminist scholars in the 1990s focused more fully on the ways that new technologies and disciplinary apparatuses form and inform gender ideology, rather than the possibilities such technological shifts produced for a feminist politics. Anne Balsamo and Judy Wajcman both focused on how new gendered technological imaginaries and infrastructures mapped new sites of biopower in and through the body and across multiple spheres of activity, including medicine, popular culture, health and beauty. Balsamo's *Technologies of the Gendered Body* used the cyborg as a framework for examining the constitutive effects of gender in relation to new technologies. While cyborg bodies offered technological possibilities for recrafting the material body (e.g., female body-building, cosmetic surgery, or in vitro pregnancy), thus challenging the "givenness" of physical gender identity, such transformative changes were not guaranteed (Balsamo 1996, 11). As Balsamo argued, "contemporary discourses of technology rely on a logic of binary gender-identity as an underlying organizational framework. This underlying structure both enables and constrains our engagement with new technologies" (9–10). In other words, gender operates as both the determining cultural condition and the social consequence of technological deployment; the engagement between bodies and technologies, and the power relations produced during such encounters, are organized through the "technologies of the gendered body" (9). New technologies (such as in vitro fertilization for instance) are therefore mapped onto and coded within existing logics of maternity, affective labor, and female sexuality.

The relation of gendered embodiment to new technologies is thus structured by ideological and cultural processes that remain profoundly patriarchal. This is true not only of the imbrication of women with new technologies but also of the uneven gendered access to technological development. Thus Judy Wajcman, in *Feminism Confronts Technology*, argued that the identification between men and machines became a sexual stereotype, one that had constitutive and asymmetrical effects on both men and women, including varying degrees of childhood exposure to technology, different role models, different forms of schooling, as well as segregated labor markets—all of which led to the construction of men as "technologically endowed," and women as "technically incompetent" (quoted in Cockburn, 159).

This naturalization of the cultural and ideological affinity between men and machines in turn contributes to the gendering of technological use and design. Addressing the impact of technology on the sexual division of labor, Wajcman (1991, 38) argued that "skilled status . . . has been traditionally identified with masculinity and as work women don't do, while women's skills have been defined as non-technical and undervalued." The masculinity of technology is a social product of the ideological and cultural association between men and machines—an association that is integral to the constitution of male gender identity. For Wajcman, then, technologies come to reflect a "male bias," as "the pace and direction of technological development reflect existing gender relations as much as they affect the sexual division of labor" (52). In other words, the technological possibilities for changing sexual divisions of labor are constrained by pre-existing gendered organizations of work (28). While Wajcman's account of the labor conditions in the late twentieth century coincide with Haraway's account of late capitalism, Wajcman is far less confident than Haraway that such shifts hold open the possibility of denaturalizing the race, class and gender categories of modernity, seeing instead in such processes the exacerbation of exploitation through the perpetuation of disciplinary forms of power. Thus, feminist politics have been more focused on technological training for women, as well as critical accounts of and interventions in the constitutive effects of technologies on the gendered body. According to Balsamo, "The question is how to empower technological agents so that they work on behalf of the right kind of social change" (156).

Racial Inscriptions

Hayles's emphasis on processes of inscription and incorporation, as well as on the impossibility of separating information and materiality, emerged in the context of important scholarship on race and cyborg identity. Although Haraway's manifesto situated the cyborg within a complex matrix of identity, many accounts of how bodies come to "matter" in cyborg worlds focused on the gendered nature of the cyborg, rather than the complex intersections of various cultural hierarchies in articulations of identity and inscriptions of the body. "Just as first- and second-wave feminists often failed to include race and the issue of third world women in their politics, so too have many cyberfeminists elided the topic of race in cyberspace . . . [but] the cyborg is not only a hybrid of machine and organism, it is also a racial hybrid" (Kolko, Nakamura, and Rodman 2000, 8). In *Race in Cyberspace*, Kolko, Nakamura, and Rodman theorized the intersections of race, gender and class in the new virtual bodies emerging in cyberspace. They challenged two key assumptions about virtual bodies: (i) that race (like gender) can be superseded in the virtual spaces of media culture and within technoscientific knowledge; and (ii) that race becomes "a controversial flashpoint for angry debate and overheated rhetoric" (1). Polarized into biological essentialism or social constructivism, binary racial cyber-discourses obscured the material-discursivity of racialized bodies in cyberspace.

As Nakamura (2002) argued in *Cybertypes: Race, Ethnicity, and Identity on the Internet*, the notion of a "democratic" cyberspace is founded upon disembodiment. Cyberspace is "unbounded" precisely because it is uncontaminated by the residue of difference, with its potential to disturb, disrupt, and challenge (88). Yet cyberspace continues to rely on essentialized images of the other, as the effacement of racial and ethnic boundaries is achieved through the repeated invocation of these very dividing lines (Nakamura 2002, 94). The Internet "propagates, disseminates, and commodifies images of race and racism" through the use of "cybertypes." Embedded in "computer/human interfaces, the dynamics and economics of access, and the means by which users are able to express themselves online," cybertypes "interact with the "cultural layer" or ideologies regarding race that [users] bring with them to cyberspace" (Nakamura 2002, 3). Online "identity tourism" provides an example of these complex interactions. Although the very possibility of identity tourism questions the essentialism of race as a category, the creation of an online identity frequently occurs through the appropriation of essentialized notions of gender and race. Moreover, identity tourism and racial cybertyping operate under the assumption that race can be easily separated from the body—a view that not only re-articulates the narrative of transcendence, but also constructs difference as a phenomenon that is only "skin deep." As Nakamura noted, "The choice to enact oneself as a samurai warrior in Lambda MOO constitutes deity tourism without any of the risks associated with being a racial minority in real life" (40–41).

As Kolko, Nakamura, and Rodman (2000, 5) contend, "Race matters in cyberspace precisely because all of us who spend time online are already shaped by the ways in which race matters offline, and we can't help but bring our own knowledge, experiences, and values with us when we log on." The constitutive effects of race offline always already shape cyberspace and our interactions within it. It is in this constitutive sense that racial cybertyping reveals the effects of racism both on- and offline; cyberspace and "real life" cannot be separated into two mutually exclusive spaces. As cybertyping reveals, images of the essentialized other guarantee privilege and mobility for some at the expense of these very "others" (Nakamura 2002, 94).

In addition to questions of representation, Nakamura (2002) also analyzed how naturalization of web interface design reveals assumptions about race and ethnicity. Documenting the politics of design decisions, Nakamura notes that "websites that focus on ethnic and racial identity and community often possess interface design features that force reductive, often archaic means of defining race upon the user" (101–102). Individuals are required to select the "race" or "ethnicity" to which they belong from a set of preconstituted categories of "clickable" identities, with no means to define or modify these terms or categories. This practice produces a new kind of cybertyping, relegating racial identity to the paradigm of the singular "clickable box" (101–102).

Alongside the semiotic critique of racial signifiers in cyberspace, Nakamura has also offered a historical materialist critique of new technologies. She suggests that "rhetorics that claim to remedy and erase gender and racial injustices and imbalances through expensive and difficult-to-learn technologies such as the Internet entirely gloss over this question of access" (Nakamura 2002, 9). Cybertyping becomes an epiphenomenon of new technologies partly because questions of access have been elided. Tara McPherson (2012, 23) has also emphasized the methodological entanglement of histories of the internet and race in the mid-century in the United States, extending questions of race beyond considerations of representation in new media to analyses of form, phenomenology, and computation. Far from being the result of scholars not talking to one another, McPherson argues that these disciplinary distinctions are "part and parcel of the organization of knowledge production that operating systems like UNIX helped to disseminate around the world" (24). From discussions of lenticular technologies to covert racism in notions of colorblindness, McPherson's analyses demonstrate how race is embedded within the material-semiotic data infrastructures of the last century.[4]

Feminist and critical race theories of cyborg embodiment have been especially important in making connections between the visual cultures of posthuman bodies and the political, economic and social effects of new technological infrastructures. The analysis of racialized and gendered virtual bodies emphasize the connections to complex histories of racial (and racist) representation, emphasizing the inscription of the surface of virtual bodies co-extensive with the historical emergence of race as a specific category of the modern episteme. At the same time, as Donna Haraway herself emphasized, by examining women workers in the "integrated circuit," questions of race in cyberspace were not exclusively visually coded in new media platforms, but also closely connected to new information infrastructures and thus to the intersection of bodies with profoundly racialized, gendered, and classed forms of labor in institutions and networks emerging under late capitalism. These analyses of complex processes of racialization challenge overly optimistic promises of mobility and exchange within cyberculture and illuminate connections and continuities between cyberspace and social reality.

An Apt Figure for Feminist Politics?

Although the cyborg has been emblematic of critical feminist work on techno cultures in the late twentieth century, its efficacy as a figure for feminist politics has also been called into question. As a figure, Haraway's cyborg aspired to promote a multiracial, coalitional practice of feminism. Jennifer A. González (2000) has argued, however, that the very notion of "hybridity," the joining of distinct and separate identities, is frequently ahistorical, assuming, by definition, a nonhybrid state—an original and essentializing "purity whether pertaining to race, gender, or even species. Such an understanding of hybridity thus "threatens to reproduce a new "transcendental" subject that floats through cyberspace, supposedly free from social constraints, while nevertheless perpetuating a familiar social hierarchy" (47). Although the cyborg may, in itself, be a disruptive presence, it can unintentionally reproduce the very racial and gender stereotypes it seeks to challenge. Mobilizations of the cyborg, in González's view, must continue to problematize the coming together of two distinct and definable entities. For to replicate this reductionism masks questions concerning the legitimacy and patriarchal lineage of hybridity. "If any progress is to be made in a politics of human or cyborg existence, heterogeneity must be taken as a given" (González 1999, 273).

In addition, although in Haraway's text, the cyborg signified modes of alliance and affinity within feminism, certain critical race theorists have taken issue with Haraway's use of writings by women of color and her treatment of oppositional consciousness as analogous to the hybrid fusion of the cyborg. Malini Johar Schueller (2005) notes that the celebration of the cyborg erases the locatedness of specific bodies in distinct geo-political locations and, that the *analogy* between women of color and cyborgs "not only reifies the very binaries of center and margin, colonizer and colonized [...] but also homogenizes, through a colonial imperative, the margin itself" (79). Schueller calls instead for Haraway's focus on "situated knowledge" to be brought into explicit conversation with cyborg embodiment, to trace the "spatio-political differences" between, for instance,

Asian women workers making microchips and antinuclear demonstrators in Santa Rita jail (81).

Cyborg discussions after Haraway have frequently overlooked the specificity of Chela Sandoval's conception of oppositional consciousness. For Haraway, the cyborg is a "technological embodiment of a particular and specific form of oppositional consciousness" which Sandoval (1995, 408) defined as "U.S. third world feminism." Within academia, appeals to the cyborg have ironically repressed Sandoval's "methodology of the oppressed" on which the metaphor of the cyborg rests. For Sandoval, the cyborg is both an oppositional and a differential position, one that does not emerge from the advent of new technologies alone. As a form of consciousness, Sandoval's cyborg is *produced* through a series of concrete practices that cannot be reduced to a particular type of body (González 2000, 47). Cyborg consciousness thus represents a non-essentialized subject that "becomes identifiable through a map of possible *action*" (González 2000, 47). As a contradictory subject position, then, cyborg consciousness describes not a universal hybridity but an "elaborate specificity," a *methodology* rather than a descriptive category (Sandoval 1995, 413–414).[5] The cyborg, then, can only be liberatory insofar as it does not obscure its debt to the "methodology of the oppressed."

Although Balsamo also remains cautious about mobilizing Haraway's cyborg as a utopian image in the service of feminism, she notes that if Haraway's ironic vision of the cyborg enables feminism to reflect on the ways in which women historically have not only experienced fragmented subjectivities and identities but also overcome "physical proscriptions," then the figure may be a provocative one in the service of feminism. Balsamo (1999) suggests that, if we are able to move beyond valorizing the cyborg as a utopian figure in which technology emancipates women from their corporal bodies, we may transform the "feminine" essentialism of the female cyborg into a non-essential figure for contemporary women—a figure that embraces a diversity of women's identities in the disruption of stable oppositions (150).

As these debates suggest, the unresolvable contradictions instantiated by the figure of the cyborg are not necessarily its undoing; they suggest generative tensions, and contribute to productive re-imaginings within the field of feminist theory. As Wolmark (1999) contends, "the cyborg's propensity to disrupt boundaries and explore differently embodied subjectivities . . . [could] be regarded as its most valuable characteristic, and it is undoubtedly one of the reasons for its continued usefulness in feminist and cultural theory" (6).

New Earthly Metaphors: Feminist Accounts of the Human-Nonhuman Relation

Whatever its usefulness may be for reimagining the posthuman, the cyborg may no longer be the most apt metaphor for theorizing the conditions of subjectivity and sociality in contemporary social life. Quite simply, the metaphoric resonance of the cyborg has frequently pulled against its feminist re-imaginings, representing not the critical oppositional figure of the "sister outsider" so much as the celebratory banner for technological developments in communication and culture. Situated in a space of play or symbolizing new forms of Cartesian transcendence signaled by leaving the body behind, the cyborg morphs into what Haraway (2014) recently called a (post)feminist "blissed out techno-bunny." With the proliferation of networked and programmable media, the cyborg is simply, in N. Katherine Hayles's (2006, 159) view, not *networked* enough. As a singular, hybrid entity, the cyborg does not necessarily offer an account of the ways in which humans and machines (and much else in the world) exist together in co-evolving and interconnected systems (165).

Multiple feminist accounts of the posthuman resist mere celebration of the blurring effects of technoscience on twenty-first-century life. Rosi Braidotti (2013, 97) stresses that the posthuman might very well—particularly under global capitalism—exacerbate uneven power relations and "[bring] them to new necro-political heights.". The new "control society" may lend the cyborg more readily to "techno-transcendence" or "consumer-oriented liberal individualism" than to the undoing of binaries of sexual and racial difference. "Advanced capitalism is a post-gender system capable of accommodating a high degree of androgyny and a significant blurring of the categorical divide between the sexes. It is also a post-racial system that no longer classifies people on the grounds of pigmentation [. . .] but remains nonetheless profoundly racist" (98).

Haraway (2008, 4) stresses that the figures that have populated her writing (cyborgs but also OncoMouse (1997), committed mutts, and others) are not in fact representations but rather "material-semiotic nodes or knots in which diverse bodies and meanings co-shape one another". They should not be hypostatized as amplified posthuman subjects whose bodily boundaries are reaffirmed even as flesh and technology, host and parasite become entangled. The cyborg signified not a new *form* of embodiment for feminist theorists but the muddiness of form given the deep interconnection of subjects and objects in the world, in both affirmative and destructive co-constitutive relations.

It is for this reason that in later feminist writings on technoscientific and virtual bodies Haraway replaces the cyborg with more grounded feminist figures. Haraway (2008, 3) stresses in *When Species Meet* that she is "a creature of the mud, not the sky," and elaborates throughout her introductory chapter a refrain of *ordinariness*. Her subject is "ordinary multispecies living on earth" (3). Her method is a "grappling with the ordinary" (3). Her figures are "ordinary beings-in-encounter" (5). Intra-action is both the "dance of relating" but also "prosaic, relentlessly mundane" (26). Her metaphors are not those of networks or rhizomes, but of the *slime* that "holds things in touch" (3). Her prose resists appropriation into technophilic utopias, binding itself closely to the concerns of living and living together ethically.[6] Attachment, accountability, and caring become the affective terms through which she envisages a feminist politics for the twenty-first century. This later work does not contradict "The Cyborg Manifesto" but rather mobilizes a different set of figures to do the work of thinking interconnection and social justice.

Central, then, to the retooling of the cyborg is a more distributed theoretical model for thinking subjectivity and embodiment. No longer bound by the outlines of the figure of the cyborg, feminist theories of embodiment—theories of the posthuman body—stress the larger environment (comprising technologies, certainly, but also multiple nonhuman actors), which profoundly alters what it means to be human. For Hayles (2002, 319), the human subject is but one small part within a larger "distributed cognitive environment"—an environment that includes other human and nonhuman entities, all of which can "think" and "act". This constitutive relation between humans and other "cognizers" is not so much a usurpation of autonomy and self-will, as it is an acknowledgment of the ways in which the human subject influences and is influenced by a plurality of human and non-human agents within the "cognisphere" (319). Karen Barad (2007) further emphasizes the relational aspects of embodied life by replacing the term interaction with "intra-action," signifying that there are no separate individual agencies that precede their interaction. The posthuman body is thus constituted relationally by specific material configurations of the world, and it is in and through those configurations that such things as boundaries and properties are differentially enacted (139). Bodily boundaries are not evident from the outset, but are the result of biologically, culturally and historically specific performative repetitions (155). Rather than matter, Barad proposes "mattering," "a doing, a congealing of agency" (137, 149).

It is thus only through boundary-making and differentiating practices that something like the human may be defined. Matter is itself agentive rather than a fixed essence, and bodily boundaries have always been unclear. The effect for feminism is that gender, race or class become not attributes or properties of the subject, but (gendered and racialized) practices that build worlds and objects in some manners rather than others (Barad 2007, 159). Matter entails entanglement, and the matter at stake for feminism is extended beyond the sphere of the recognizably social or political, and beyond also more narrowly defined signifying structures. In this respect, cybertechnologies themselves must be viewed as coextensive with other social and ecological systems, and with the effects of neoliberalism on social life in the late twentieth and early twenty-first centuries. Tara McPherson (2012, 30–31), for instance, has argued that the organization of information and capital responds to struggles for racial justice and democracy, and thus computational systems must be viewed as influenced by and influencing cultural systems and social relations.

Braidotti's notion of the posthuman similarly decenters the subject without evoking the figure of the cyborg; hybridity emerges from the outset, rather than in the blurring of boundaries that challenge the narratives of modernity. For Braidotti (2013, 35), matter (including what she calls "the specific slice of matter that is human embodiment") is intelligent and self-organizing. Matter should not be opposed to culture or to technological mediation, but instead should be conceived as continuous with these. Within this frame, the figures that emerge are not oppositional or counter-subjectivities (the cyborg vs. the goddess, for instance), but rather a process-oriented political ontology of *auto-poeisis* or "self-styling" (35). This autopoeisis is not simply liberatory; it involves complex negotiations with dominant norms and values. Her approach counters the fantasy of a "trans-humanism" or a "techno-utopia" with a critical posthuman nomadic figure, a figure embedded in an ecology of multiple belongings, a "relational subject constituted in and by multiplicity" (49). The cyborg is thus the result of a profound already existing interrelationality. According to Braidotti (2006, 201), "In nomadic thought, a radically immanent intensive body is an assemblage of forces, or flows, intensities and passions that solidify in space, and consolidate in time, within the singular configuration commonly known as an 'individual' self."

As with Haraway and Barad, this ontological fact does not necessarily produce a liberatory feminist politics. Braidotti emphasizes that in our current historical conjuncture, cyberspace is a highly contested social space. It evolves in concert with a social reality in which capital trades in bodily fluids (in the "cheap sweat and blood of a third world labor force"), and at times more literally in the capitalization of the body itself. Immersed in war and conflict, social and virtual worlds pursue what Achille Mbembe has called a "necropolitics" (quoted in Braidotti 2013, 9). The destruction of binaries in new rhizomatic structures of power may take the vitality of matter as their main target for new processes of sexualization, racialization and naturalization (Braidotti 2013, 96). For Braidotti, a strong theory of posthuman subjectivity is required to re-appropriate these very processes as alternative grounds for the formation of the self. The intra-active nature of agency—what Braidotti calls "transversal subjectivity"—prioritizes relationships, manifested in the ties that bind us each to one another, as the *a priori*.

Donna Haraway's theorization of "companion species" closely resembles the posthumanism of Barad's and Braidotti's. Although all three scholars intensely engage each other's works, there are important differences in their views. Braidotti advances a non-dialectical understanding of materialism, indebted to a Spinozist worldview. Haraway (2008, 3) holds a series of contradictory standpoints in generative tension, in the interests of a committed ethical practice she calls "becoming worldly." In her early work, the cyborg mobilized irony to engage contradictions without resolving them into totalizing wholes. The figures in *When Species Meet* are both material and semiotic, entangled and in alliance. Haraway retains humanist categories of accountability, responsibility and care, but detaches them from ethical abstractions of Western reason and older spectral figures such as Marxist feminism, and uses them to rethink categories such as labor, woman, and human in relation to inter-species life.

In *When Species Meet*, Haraway invokes "companion species" to foreground ties between different humans and non-humans, engaged in complex practices of "becoming with" (2008, 17). Companion resonates across multiple fields—etymologically it signals those with whom one breaks bread; politically, it envisions the comrade; in literature, it refers to a handbook or guide; in business, it suggests a company; in the domain of sexuality, companions hints at illicit and intimate consorts (17–18). Species refers variously to producing ideas or mental pictures, and to affairs of kin and kind. Haraway stresses that species "reeks of race and sex; and where and when species meet, that heritage must be untied and better knots of companion species attempted within and across differences" (18).

As with the cyborg, intra-action for Haraway is both an ontology and a politics. In contrast to the cyborg's rootedness in the techno-utopic imaginaries of science fiction, companion species evoke "ordinary multispecies living on earth" (2013, 3). Multispecies living involves both the co-constitution of bodies through ingestive or parasitical processes, through feeding and eating, through the knowledge-based practices of the scientific laboratory, the industrial factory, the farm, ocean or forest. These intra-actions happen biologically, but also historically, in "situated naturecultures in which all of the actors become who they are *in the dance of relating*, not from scratch, ex nihilo, but full of the patterns of their sometimes-joined, sometimes-separate heritages both before and lateral to *this* encounter" (Haraway 2008, 25).

Companion species, intra-action, becoming with represent different models for thinking a politically committed interconnection. These involve ecological-political struggles (who should eat whom? who can cohabit in specific contact zones?), and entering into responsive relationships, without judgment. Haraway's prosaic examples include an ethologist who always sets down twenty-three bowls for her twenty-two sheep, producing what Haraway calls an "open," a space for something unexpected to happen, a space to be open to the question of surprise, of sociality in another form (2008, 34).

Accountability, care, affect and responsibility are grounded in *touch* that materializes and complicates the abstract ethical imperatives of the democratic tradition. These involve relations of use (animal testing in scientific laboratories, for instance), thinking the labor of inter-species encounter, rather than premising freedom on "shuffling off" necessity on other bodies who do not accede to the category human (women, colonized peoples, others; Haraway 2008, 73). Such political acts are not postfeminist or postracial, but involve committed work to account for "those who must inhabit the troubled categories of woman and human, properly pluralized, reformulated, and brought into constitutive interaction with other asymmetrical differences" (17).

In a recent lecture, Haraway proposes another figure for thinking/doing the work of politics: compost—a most apt figure for "grappling with the ordinary." Haraway plays with the semiotic slippage from posthuman to com*post*, cognizant that compost is further from the goddess than the cyborg, and thus might introduce a new blasphemy into celebrations of the posthuman. To be compost is both to acknowledge the transformative processes in which we *become with* many over the course of our lives and deaths. It also marks an attitude of being un-self-impressed, a quality she lauds in the many female scientists that populate her last book (2008, 35).

Compost is also a potent mode of intra-action—a "cooking" process with enormous transformational potential. It operates at the intersection of the political, biological, ecological and ethical; it is committed to survival and diversity. Compost, Haraway argues, does not so much shift the terms of the cyborg as acknowledge the limits of its resignification for a feminist politics. Becoming worldly, then, is still committed to the cyborg project of embracing "partial, contradictory, permanently unclosed constructions of personal and collective selves" (1991, 157) in the interests of the imaginative apprehension of different models of community and responsibility.

CONCLUSION

The cyborg elicits a tension within feminist theory as a figure, on the one hand, for the massive scientific and techno-cultural shifts in the contemporary moment, for better or for worse, and on the other, for the liberatory potential of a new feminist subject position. As the proliferation of edited anthologies and monographs in cyborg studies suggests, the cyborg served as a galvanizing metaphor for feminist accounts of technoscience and mediated worlds, which challenged the celebratory technological metaphors of the moment. The cyborg functioned for feminism as a mode of critique that drew attention to technologies' role in the production of ecological instability, environmental precarity, and globalizing dynamics, governed by a shift from biopower to more "molecular" forms of power (Braidotti 2013, 97). Yet the playfulness with which the cyborg was taken up in feminist theory, cultural analysis, and contemporary art, also represents feminism's engagement with the ludic potential of signification. Although the cyborg may no longer hold the blasphemous power it did in its earliest articulations, blasphemy continues to prove a useful strategy for feminist figuration.

In this respect, the tension between the repressive and liberatory aspects of the cyborg has served as an important engine for feminist thinking. Precisely because the cyborg signifies at once the technocentric visions of an invulnerable and inpenetrable subject, and the feminist accounts of more permeable and mutable bodily life in alliance, it presents a compelling method (rather than a devoted icon) for feminist theorizing. The cyborg is, in Haraway's terms "bereft of secure guarantees" (1990, 13). Feminist critiques of the cyborg have demonstrated how technoscientific and mediatized practices shaped gendered, racialized and naturalized forms of embodiment, producing new sites of disciplinary control, new surfaces for the inscriptions of unequal power relations. Wajcman, Balsamo, Nakamura, Haraway, Braidotti, and others are keenly aware that the space of the posthuman (and its alliance with some version of the postfeminist) do not signify a transcendence of racialization, sexualization, gendering, or the potent inequalities proliferating around the globe. Yet cyborg feminism acknowledged a need for a counter-politics that rejects technoscience's and mediated worlds' complicity in a conservative nostalgia for organic wholeness and unalienated experience. Cyborg feminism also embraced the possibility that technoscience might provide resources for contesting inequality and building new forms of alliance. Thus cyborg images provided fitting sites for contestation, rather than "giv[ing] in the game, cash[ing] in our chips and go[ing] home" (Haraway 1990, 13).

The cyborg continues to be useful as a *mode* of feminist theorizing, more than as a substantive position about the body or subjectivity. As a mode of theorizing, it takes pleasure in the confusion of boundaries, the capacity of figures to express imaginative possibilities that may unfix the contingent mechanisms of sex/gender, which have captured the body and inscribed it in ideology. Prying open other "potentialities of the body," cyborg theorizing takes pleasure in perverting "standardized patterns of sexualized, racialized and naturalized interaction" (Braidotti 2013, 99). The laugh of the Medusa, the riddle of the Sphinx, and the irony of the Cyborg have all contributed to a vision of feminist politics capable of deterritorializing gender identity and its institutions. Although the normative pull of its patriarchal precedents continues to disrupt the cyborg's potentiality, its tentative and contestatory method remains suggestive for feminist theory.

Notes

1. This insight becomes especially important in later feminist accounts of the materiality of the body and the specificity of performative practices in specific historical contexts, as will be discussed further below.
2. While Hayles further problematizes the distinction between "the body" and "embodiment" in her later work, the distinction nevertheless creates the conditions of possibility for seeing "embodiment" as individually articulated and as resisting culture—in a word, performative (1999, 197).
3. Chris Hables Gray, Heidi J. Figueroa-Sarriera and Steven Mentor's *The Cyborg Handbook* (1995). was one important attempt to gather together key writings in the field, and to assess the proliferation of cyborgs within the fields of science and engineering, medicine, culture, literature and the arts. There were many other such compendia in the decade following the publication of Haraway's text, including among others J. Jack Halberstam and I. Livingstone's *Posthuman Bodies* (1995) and G. Kirkup, L. Janes, F. Hovenden and K. Woodward's *The Gendered Cyborg* (2000)
4. Anne Everett (2009) cautions against the presumption that cyberspace is largely a Western phenomenon, providing a crucial analysis of the use of the Internet to build upon and develop African diasporic consciousness, for instance.
5. Sandoval's methodology of the oppressed involves five technologies, which she names semiotics, deconstruction, meta-ideologizing, democratics, and differential movement. For a detailed account of this, see her *Methodology of the Oppressed*.
6. It is specifically with respect to "ordinariness" that Haraway (2008) critiques Deleuze and Guattari's notion of "becoming-animal." Their scorn for domestic dogs and the old women who keep them, the opposition they posit between the domesticated dog (the object of bourgeois affectation) and the wolf, involves in Haraway's view a lack of respect for the mundane, the ordinary, or the prosaic, as well as a lack of curiosity for actual animals (28–29).

References

Balsamo, A. 1996. *Technologies of the Gendered Body: Reading Cyborg Women*. Durham, NC: Duke University Press.

Balsamo, A. 1999. "Reading Cyborgs Writing Feminism." In *Cybersexualities: A Reader on Feminist Theory, Cyborgs and Cyberspace*, edited by J. Wolmark, 145–156. Edinburgh: Edinburgh University Press.
Barad, K. 2007. *Meeting the Universe Halfway: Quantum Physics and the Entanglement of Matter and Meaning*. Durham, NC: Duke University Press.
Braidotti, R., and N. Lykke, eds. 2006. "Posthuman, All Too Human: Towards a New Process Ontology." *Theory, Culture & Society* 23(7–8): 197–208.
Braidotti, R., and N. Lykke, eds. 2013. *The Posthuman*. Cambridge: Polity Press.
Everett, A. 2009. *Digital Diaspora: A Race for Cyberspace*. New York: State University of New York Press.
González, J. 1999. "Envisioning Cyborg Bodies: Notes from Current Research." In *Cybersexualities: A Reader on Feminist Theory, Cyborgs and Cyberspace*, edited by J. Wolmark, 264–279. Edinburgh: Edinburgh University Press.
González, J. 2000. "The Appended Subject: Race and Identity as Digital Assemblage." In *Race in Cyberspace*, edited by B. E. Kolko, L. Nakamura, and G. B. Rodman, 27–50. New York and London: Routledge.
Gray, C. et al. 1995. *The Cyborg Handbook*. New York: Routledge.
Halberstam, J., and I. Livingstone, eds. 1995. *Posthuman Bodies*. Bloomington: Indiana University Press.
Haraway, D. J. 1991. *Simians, Cyborgs, and Women: The Reinvention of Nature*. New York: Routledge.
Haraway, D. J. 1997. *Modest_Witness@Second_Millenium.FemaleMan©_Meets_Oncomouse™: Feminism and Technoscience*. New York: Routledge.
Haraway, D. J. 2008. *When Species Meet*. Minneapolis: University of Minnesota Press.
Haraway, D. J. 2014. *SF: String Figures, Multispecies Muddles, Staying with the Trouble*. Public lecture. University of Alberta. March 24, 2014. http://www.youtube.com/watch?v=Z1uTVnhIHS8. Last consulted 29 July, 2014.
Hayles, K. N. 1997. "Interrogating the Posthuman Body." *Contemporary Literature*, 38(4): 755–762.
Hayles, K. N. 1999. *How We Became Posthuman: Virtual Bodies in Cybernetics, Literature, and Informatics*. Chicago: University of Chicago Press.
Hayles, K. N. 2002. "Flesh and Metal: Reconfiguring the Mindbody in Virtual Environments." *Configurations*, 10(2): 297–320.
Hayles, K. N. 2006. "Unfinished Work: From Cyborg to Cognisphere." *Theory, Culture, & Society*, 23(7–8): 159–166.
Kirkup, G., L. Janes, F. Hovenden, and K. Woodward, eds. 2000. *The Gendered Cyborg: A Reader*. New York: Routledge.
Kolko, B. E., L. Nakamura, and G. B. Rodman. 2000. "Race in Cyberspace: An Introduction." In *Race in Cyberspace*, edited by B. E. Kolko, L. Nakamura, and G. B. Rodman, 1–13. New York and London: Routledge.
McPherson, T. 2012. "U.S. Operating Systems at Mid-Century." In *Race after the Internet*, edited by Nakamura and P. Chow-White, 21–37. New York: Routledge.
Nakamura, L. 2002. *Cybertypes: Race, Ethnicity, and Identity on the Internet*. New York: Routledge.
Sandoval, C. 1995. "New Sciences: Cyborg Feminism and the Methodology of the Oppressed." In *The Cyborg Handbook*, edited by C. Gray, 407–423. New York: Routledge.

Stone, A. R. 1999. "Will the Real Body Please Stand Up? Boundary Stories about Virtual Cultures." In *Cybersexualities: A Reader on Feminist Theory, Cyborgs and Cyberspace*, edited by J. Wolmark, 69–98. Edinburgh: Edinburgh University Press.

Wajcman, J. 1991. *Feminism Confronts Technology*. University Park: Pennsylvania State University Press.

Wolmark, J. 1999. *Cybersexualities: A Reader on Feminist Theory, Cyborgs and Cyberspace*. Edinburgh: Edinburgh University Press.

CHAPTER 7

DEVELOPMENT

ELORA HALIM CHOWDHURY

DEVELOPMENT is typically discussed as a strategy to improve "quality of life." National governments, international agencies, and philanthropic foundations have launched various initiatives, short term and long term, to produce measurable improvement in the quality of life of people living in conditions of extreme adversity. A quintessentially modern project informed by a belief in progress through rational planning and policy implementation, development has involved interventions to reorganize and relocate human communities, introduce mechanization of farming or "scientific agriculture," generate hydroelectric power, and foster industrialization and urbanization. It has also involved systemic campaigns to alter land use and property ownership, diversify the economy and the range of occupations, expand literacy, "limit fertility," and provide law reform. Contrasting itself to "backwardness," "ignorance," and the corruption of "old ways," development is future oriented, deploying technocratic expertise, and means-ends calculations to promote human progress. Thus does development tell a story of linear progress, of movement from traditional modes of agricultural life to modern industrial and service economies. Embracing visions of modernization, both capitalist and socialist states have assumed that humans possess the ability to control and improve natural and social environments, and have devised intricate projects to transform "traditional" agrarian subsistence economies to industrial, urbanized modern economies.

Feminist interventions into the theory and practice of development have been complicit with its modernist goals even as they have contested the positioning of women within a modernist narrative. Consequently, development is an especially good site at which to trace the emergence of a feminist critical perspective and to see the difference that such a perspective makes. Initial feminist critics of development insisted on—and largely won—the inclusion of women in development projects. Both women and development (WAD) and women in development (WID) struggled to make women's labor and expertise visible to the architects of development programs, so as to extend the benefits of modernization to women as well as to men. Taking it as their task to ameliorate the lives of women in the "Third World," the WAD and WID left "development" itself largely unproblematized, assuming that women's lives would be improved by their incorporation into wage labor. These initial interventions were succeeded by a second approach, gender and development (GAD) which—while again leaving wage labor largely unproblematized—shifted the focus of feminist critique from women to gendered relations of power both in the household and in waged work. With Mohanty's (1991a,b) classic critique of the construction "Third World Women," in mainstream and feminist development discourse alike, a distinctively feminist critical perspective had finally emerged to call into question not simply the sexism of development projects but their modernist goals and assumptions.

The Role of the Expert

In the decades following World War II, as economic development was transformed from the most neglected to the most popular subfield of economics, development expertise was constructed as apolitical, a new scientific specialization that takes the "national economy" as its object of inquiry (Bergeron 2006). Northern technical expertise counted as knowledge, and transfer of that knowledge from the North to South was at the core of the development process (Parpart 1995, 225). Higher education and professional institutions catered to would-be "experts" by offering degrees and diplomas in development studies and public administration. In turn, development agencies' policies and planning assumed that these experts with degrees from Western institutions would be better able to solve the problems of the "developing" world. Borrowing concepts created within industrial corporations, the discipline of economics and the emerging field of comparative politics construed development as a marriage of science and the state "to secure the basis of social harmony through national development" (Cowen 1995, 445).

As Arturo Escobar (1992, 1995) has pointed out, the discovery of "underdevelopment" as a policy problem ushered in a host of new technologies of governance, which created a partnership between science and the state that profoundly influenced the experience of development across the global South. Models for growth that were developed in Western industrialized nations assumed that the problem of underdevelopment could be traced to lack of investment capital. For this reason, the earliest development models prescribed strategies "to fill the savings gap" by shifting labor from subsistence agriculture to the industrial sector, where higher wages would allow increased savings (Bergeron 2006, 39). Development experts argued that capital investment would increase gross national product (GNP), providing benefits for all members of the national community in the long run. Yet, they also noted that efficient development strategies required skewed distribution of income that benefited the affluent because only "the saving class" could provide funds for investment (Bergeron 2006, 40). Like the classical economists who preceded them and the neoliberals who followed them, development experts in the post–World War II era embraced a model of economic growth that required and legitimated significant income differentials. With the advent of econometrics, development experts devised complex mathematical models to measure the maturity of a nation's economy and to prescribe steps to foster growth. Emphasizing aggregate wealth and average GNP, these models did not make reduction in mass poverty a test of economic development, a point made by Jacob Viner as early as 1953 (Bergeron 2006, 41–42).

In his seminal work *Encountering Development: The Making and Unmaking of the Third World* (1995), Escobar likens development to a chimera. Attaining development is an elusive process for the world's poor, one that is marred by tremendous loss. Situated in the field of "postdevelopment" scholarship, Escobar uses a Foucauldian approach to the study of development, arguing against both the positivist tradition of development thought and the political economy tradition concerning development and its impacts in the Third World. Instead, Escobar conceptualizes development as discourse, representations, and discursive constructions and as a set of relations between the powerful and the powerless. In Foucauldian terminology, development is, for Escobar, a regime of truth production. It comprises the will to know and the exercise of power and knowledge to *create* the Third World as we know it. Escobar's genealogy of "development" begins with the Truman administration in the United States as it attempted to restore economic growth after World War II and maintain the dominance of the United States in the world's economic, political, and ideological arenas. Escobar posits "development" as a derivative discourse of Western colonialism and imperialism. In his theory, the ability of the West to control the world's system of knowledge production and to define what counts as knowledge renders the Third World an object of knowledge, paying little or no attention to specificities of culture and difference. Western scholars and practitioners create "scientific" measures that define the Third World in terms of traditional practices, poverty, hunger, and other socioeconomic deficits—that is, as the very signs of "underdevelopment" in need of scientific intervention. In addition, Western experts position themselves and their scientific methods as essential to remedy Third World underdevelopment.

For Escobar, development is an imposition of the West with the consent of the Third World elites who identify and ally with the Western regime of truth. The hegemony of Western scientific knowledge, together with the control of financial resources and political ideology, help proliferate a developmentalist mentality. According to this mentality, indigenous customs, knowledge about the environment, and natural resources belong to the realm of "tradition" that needs to be changed. Thus postdevelopment theorists suggest that development discourses produce and circulate values that undermine and dismantle traditional features specific to each locale. Devaluing customs and local wisdom results in the disempowerment of people in the Third World, who come to see themselves and their cultural heritage in a negative light. To counter development regimes that debilitate the self-understandings and colonize the self-imaginings of people outside the West, Escobar emphasizes the necessity of integrating cultural specificities into critiques and methods of development. Attending to cultural specificities illuminates the intersections of local and global forces, which aid in co-constructing meanings of development. By making explicit distinctions between development alternatives and alternatives to development, and exposing development's illusory promises, Escobar calls for an abandonment of development.

Many feminist scholars share Escobar's disillusionment with mainstream approaches to development. Over the past four decades, feminist political economists have devised several competing frameworks to illuminate gender bias and gendered consequences of development policies and discourses—WAD, WID, and GAD. By taking the lives of women and men at markedly different sites around the globe into consideration, these feminist frames illuminate power dynamics omitted from dominant development discourses. By contesting the presumption that development benefits everyone, these feminist frames demonstrate dynamics of class, gender, race, indigeneity, and region that differentially distribute the benefits and burdens of development within and across global sites. And they help explain why decades of development have made many women worse off.

Gender and Gendering in Development Policies

The economic indicators used to measure growth were drawn not only from the experiences of industrialized nations in the North, they were also drawn from economic sectors dominated by male workers with profound consequences for women, who comprise 70 percent of the world's poor. Precisely because these aggregate indicators were designed to measure distance from subsistence agriculture, they grossly undervalued the economies of the majority of nations in the South structured on the basis of informal, subsistence, and care economies. Because women's labor fell largely within the informal, subsistence, and care sectors, it was rendered invisible by these quantitative measures. As Lourdes Beneria (1997) demonstrates, national accounting measures devised to track progress in development underestimate women's work in four areas: subsistence production, informal paid work, domestic production and related tasks, and volunteer work in the community. Some of the kinds of labor omitted from econometric computations include production of food via hunting, fishing, gathering and kitchen gardening, pounding, husking, and grinding food stuffs, the slaughter of animals, housecleaning, and child care; production of home crafts such as clothing, baskets, and clay pots, as well as services provided by women, including fuel collection, funerals, haircuts, entertainment, and traditional medicine (Waring 1988). When the indicators used to measure development are drawn from practices in Western industrial economies, informal and subsistence economies—the kind of economies in which 70 percent of the world's population continues to work—the measures are actively distorted. As Irene Tinker points out, in East Africa, for example, where women do the bulk of farm and market work, feeding their families and communities, official economic measures indicate that only 5 percent of them are "in the labor force" (Tinker 1976). Development strategies across the world incorporate these gendered distortions related, in part, to their neglect of subsistence and informal sectors. These distortions shape prescriptions for "women and development."

Having rendered women's waged and unwaged labor invisible by placing it outside standardized econometrics, development experts constructed women variously as backward or lazy, but in either case as a "problem" for development. With impressive unanimity, capitalist, Chinese Marxist, Soviet Marxist, and economic nationalist approaches to modernization converged on a singular solution for "the Woman Question." Women should enter the formal labor force both for the sake of the nation's economic development and for the sake of their own emancipation. According to this development logic, integrating women into the labor force in the formal sector would contribute to economic growth and elevate women's status, while also changing outmoded patriarchal mindsets as modern methods of production generated modernist belief systems. Adoption of modern machine technologies was expected to promote norms of rationality, universalism, and egalitarianism, which in turn would engender mobility and achievement. The norms of "modern" society were expected to negate ascription standards—including gender—as determinants of the individual's socioeconomic status. As technological innovation made production less dependent on physical strength, opportunities for women would expand. Greater employment opportunities would contribute to higher aspirations as women began to recognize their own economic power. Inclusion of women in the modern industrial economy would thereby contribute to greater open-mindedness resulting in the destruction of patriarchal ideologies that had justified women's exclusion from the "socially valued" productive sphere and from participation in all aspects of social and cultural life including the institutions of state.

Feminist scholars working in the fields of international political economy and development studies raised a host of questions about the gendered assumptions that inform development policies. Over the last four decades, they developed innovative approaches—WAD, WID, and GAD—to analyze the gendered dimensions and effects of development policies (Moser 1993; Parpart, Connelly, and Barriteau 2000; Staudt 1991, 2008). From their earliest articulation, feminist scholars have devised policy frames to capture the complexity of women's and men's lives in the context of various development regimes, while also examining the world produced through policies that privilege particular conceptions of modernization. Through their interrogation of neo-Malthusian assumptions about poverty, ahistorical and decontextualized assumptions about male breadwinners, and gender dynamics embedded within national and international development strategies, these feminist approaches afford markedly different insights into the nature and practices of development.

Women and Development: Reproduction and "Welfare"

Carolyn Moser (1993) characterized the first initiatives that international development agencies aimed at women as "welfarist." Incorporating biological reductionist assumptions about women drawn from certain European and North American contexts, Western development experts incorporated the ideology of motherhood within their models. They assumed that women were exclusively mothers; that is, their social roles and contributions were defined solely in terms of reproduction. Modernizing nationalist regimes across the global South reinforced these assumptions by circulating discourses emphasizing that the family was key to the well-being of the nation, and women were the key to the well-being of families. Early development partnerships were forged between national governments and international agencies to provide "welfare," including nutrition projects for women and children and for pregnant and lactating mothers, as well as medical interventions to address the high maternal and infant mortality rates of rural, agricultural workers. The development initiatives of the post–World War II era, however, also contained language drawn from a much older antipoverty discourse, calling for intervention to address "overpopulation" (Briggs 2002), to reduce large families and to reduce the number of "irregular marriages" in rural areas as crucial to improving the economy (Rai 2002). Since the nineteenth century, then, international development initiatives have been integrally involved in the politics of intimacy.

For British political economist, Thomas Robert Mathus (1766–1834), population growth was a key factor in the explanation of poverty. From the mid-nineteenth century, the British Malthusian League helped popularize the idea that excessive reproduction caused poverty, constructing overpopulation as a timeless problem that contributes to hunger, homelessness, lack of educational opportunity, unemployment, and substandard housing. As Laura Briggs has documented, the idea of overpopulation as the primary cause of poverty gained popularity in the 1920s through the work of two groups, "reformers associated with the birth control movement and academic demographers and population experts associated with eugenics movement" (2002, 83). Accepting the Malthusian premise that poverty results when population grows faster than wealth, population experts characterized the problem of overpopulation "as a matter of simple arithmetic." Poverty was construed as statistical relation between rising birth rates and falling death rates as life expectancy increased, which contributed to the growth of the population while natural resources, such as land and agricultural production, remained constant. The racial and class bias of this diagnosis was blatant as neo-Malthusians insisted not only that the "global population was growing alarmingly," but that "the segment that was increasing was of the worst sort" (83).

Within the geopolitical context of the Cold War, as the US and Soviet superpowers carved the world into their respective spheres of influence, development assistance assumed a familiar form, combining foreign aid, industrialization, import substitution, and population control. Whether dispensed by international agencies, philanthropies, or affluent nations, technical development assistance included "international family planning" as key to development. The language of "social hygiene" was deployed in ways that combined sanitation, infant and maternal health, and efforts to "improve the race" by "preventing degradation of the population" (Dore 2000, 48). The Rockefeller Foundation used its Bureau of Social Hygiene to fund contraceptive programs in India, China, the Near East, Latin America, and the Caribbean, constructing the "undeveloped world" as a site in need of eugenic assistance as well as social reform (Briggs 2002).

When expert, scientific, and managerial knowledge were unleashed to solve the problem of overpopulation, "improving the race" was defined as a condition of development. As Kathleen Staudt (2008) has pointed out, no effort was made to mask the racism of early development efforts. Implying movement from a lower to a higher stage, development policies were initially designed to transform "uncivilized countries" into "civilized nations," a project that legitimized both colonial domination and the containment of "inferior" races. This civilizing mission used women's bodies as their proving ground. The global South became a laboratory for experimentation with contraceptive methods (spermicidal foams and jellies, Depo-Provera, intrauterine devices, and various forms of birth control pills). Racist notions about the "dull-wittedness" of indigenous peoples led some development experts to counsel against the use of the diaphragm as a birth control method, encouraging adoption of far less reliable foams and jellies (Briggs 2002, 105–107). Focusing on control of population rather than the reproductive wishes of individual women, development experts manifested greater concern with "acceptance rates" (calculated by numbers willing to try contraception) than failure rates of particular contraceptive methods or harmful side effects of particular products. The zeal to address overpopulation also motivated development experts to launch sterilization campaigns. In some nations, "eugenic sterilization laws" were passed that included poverty as a legitimate reason for sterilization (Briggs 2002, 197). Sterilization abuse, along with experimentation on human subjects, became a hallmark of the "welfarist" approach to women and development. One United Nations Children's Fund (UNICEF) study documented an increase in sterilization rates of women in Brazil from 11 percent in the 1960s to 45 percent in the 1990s. Indeed, in one rural area in northeastern Brazil, Maranhão, 79.8 percent of the women had been sterilized (Purewal 2001, 113). In Puerto Rico more than one-third of women of childbearing years had been sterilized by the 1970s (Briggs 2002).

Concerns about "the population bomb" have remained a staple of development discourse (Goldstone 2010), so it is useful to consider what this account of poverty omits from the explanatory frame. When poverty is blamed on overpopulation, the maldistribution of global resources is conveniently elided from the analytic frame, as are all questions about patterns of ownership of the means of production (Rai 2002, 57). The complex systems of resource extraction associated with colonialism and neocolonialism that have fostered underdevelopment and dependency disappear from the explanatory framework. In the words of Laura Briggs (2002, 85), Malthusian assumptions about overpopulation are like "a bulldozer that leveled all counterevidence in its path . . . although it failed utterly as an explanation of poverty . . . it had sufficient force that it persisted even in the face of evidence that flatly contradicted it."

Claims about overpopulation attribute poverty to the behavior of the poor themselves. "Uncontrolled reproduction" positions women in the global South as in need of a kind of technical assistance that only advanced science can remedy. Thus it legitimates neocolonial projects to rescue poor women from dangers posed by their own bodies. The population-control strand of development discourse disseminates paternalist rhetoric about "protecting" women and children from various evils, including self-induced harms. In undertaking this work, development experts purport to have the best interests of women at heart at same time that they abridge women's reproductive freedom, subject their bodies to dangerous experimentation, and initiate programs that deprive women of their traditional livelihoods.

Women in Development: The Virtues of Waged Labor in the Formal Sector

In the early 1970s, critiques of failed development policies began to surface from several sources. In her classic study *Women's Role in Economic Development*, Ester Boserup (1970) demonstrated that agricultural development projects in Africa were directing resources and training programs toward men, when women had traditionally been and continued to be the majority of farmers. Because Western assumptions about "traditional sex roles" shaped policy, women's agricultural expertise was being ignored with dire consequences for agricultural production and for the environment as well as for women and their families. Westerners implementing development projects were replicating Western patterns of male dominance in their choice of trainees and employees in both industrial and agricultural development projects. Far from improving women's status and condition, Boserup showed that development policies were creating new forms of gender inequality, eroding the bases of women's power within traditional communities while also exacerbating poverty.

Triggered by Boserup's recognition that women's condition was being made worse by development policies that failed to recognize women's agricultural labor, feminist scholars and policymakers began conceptualizing a new approach that emphasized the importance of women's labor to development and that became known in the field as "women in development." Construing women as partners in development who possessed needed expertise, WID endorsed the expansion of opportunities for women on dual grounds. Increasing women's participation in development efforts would heighten efficiency, thereby benefiting women as well as development itself.

Viewing the absence of women from development plans and policies as the major problem, WID sought to promote more efficient development by integrating women fully in the development process. Emphasizing that excluding women effectively wasted half the available development resources, WID proponents endorsed three strategies to solve the problem: create separate women's projects that would capitalize on women's spheres of expertise; add women's components to long-standing projects; and integrate women fully into development projects, particularly those involving the mechanization of agriculture and industrialization (Moser 1993; Kabeer 1994; Rai 2002).

Feminists working in the field of development studies successfully lobbied national governments and international institutions to shift to the WID focus. In 1973, for example, the US Foreign Assistance Act was amended to include incorporation of women in national economies as part of its agenda. The US Agency for International Development (USAID) created the Women in Development Office to implement this goal. Where earlier development efforts had targeted men exclusively, and collected no data on women, the USAID WID program specified that women be funded proportionately to their traditional participation in a particular activity or according to their presence in the population, whichever was greater (Poster and Salime 2002). The US government also introduced changes in its tax codes, which encouraged offshore production, while also pressing US firms to employ a largely female labor force (Bayes 2006). In keeping with these policies women were recruited, in the export processing zones that grew up across the global South, to become the factory workers producing textiles, leather goods, toys, electronic goods, and pharmaceuticals, fast becoming the majority of those workers—70 percent to 90 percent depending on the region (Wichterich 2000).

As a policy frame, WID did not contest the assumptions of modernization theory. Assuming that modernization was inevitable, WID proponents sought to extend the benefits of modernization to women as well as men. Ignoring class differences among women, WID programs placed a high premium on efforts to improve women's education and skills so that they could compete more vigorously with men in the labor market. But they failed to consider the toll on women who tried to combine waged work in the formal sector with their unwaged work in the home. Even when they are employed in the formal sector, women continue to work unwaged second and third shifts devoted to production of subsistence foods in small garden plots, food preparation, child care and elder care, early childhood education, and nursing care for the ill and infirm, as well as household cleaning and maintenance. One study in Mexico, for example, demonstrated that 90.5 percent of the economically active women were working a double shift *in the formal sector* compared with 62 percent of the men (Purewal 2001, 106). The demands of unwaged work in the home had to be met over and above the hours devoted to waged labor in the market. The assumption that women's time is infinitely elastic and could expand indefinitely to absorb added responsibilities failed to consider the limits of human exhaustion (Elson 1995; Bedford 2009). Evidence of the harmful physical effects of overwork has become increasingly clear. Since the early 1980s, infant and child mortality rates have increased, reproductive tract infections have increased, and sterility has increased as women's health is taxed beyond endurance (Purewal 2001). Moreover, across the global South women have turned to their daughters for assistance in unwaged work. As a consequence, the numbers of girls in school have decreased and female illiteracy is rising.

The costs associated with WID strategies have also become increasingly clear. As noted earlier, long hours at work in the formal sector impose strains as women continue to assume primary responsibility for unwaged labor within the family. Divorce rates are climbing and women-headed households are growing. Industrial labor can be hazardous, contributing to long-term health problems, including infertility. As capital has become increasingly mobile, factories have opened and closed with unexpected speed, as owners move in search of cheaper labor forces. All of these factors have resulted in formal-sector employment being far less dependable than WID proponents expected.

By emphasizing mechanisms to increase women's productivity in the formal sector, while also expecting women to contribute to the economic well-being of their households, WID recruited women as "partners in development" on markedly unequal terms. The inequality stems from continuing failure to perceive women's unwaged labor in their homes and communities as "work." The UN Development Program (UNDP) has calculated that 70 percent of the work performed by women globally is unwaged and estimates the economic value of women's unwaged labor at hundreds of billions of dollars annually. Ingrid Palmer (1992, 69) characterizes women's unwaged labor as a "reproductive tax," created as the market "externalizes the costs of reproduction and life sustenance and entrusts it to women." The reproductive tax imposes an exacting toll on women in the global South, who are already working a triple shift in subsistence, productive, and reproductive labor.

By relying on the core assumption of modernization theory—that work in the formal sector is the key to women's liberty and equality—WID ignored structural forces that produce inequality. Although WID called attention to certain gendered problems within development, it ignored gender power within and across cultures. WID accredited formal sector norms grounded in men's employment experiences without attending to how poorly these norms suit women's complex responsibilities in the informal and subsistence sectors and within the household and community. WID also incorporated the unwarranted assumption that employment in the formal sector would generate linear progress for women across multiple gendered terrains. These assumptions of modernization theory have not been born out in development projects across the global South (nor, for that matter, in the industrialized nations). Inclusion of women in industrial production coexists with traditional belief systems and traditional patterns of women's subordination. A modicum of progress in one aspect of social life can be offset by setbacks in other areas of life. Increases in violence against women and divorce are more highly correlated with women's increasing economic independence than is the elimination of patriarchal traditions or male gender privilege.

Gender and Development

Concern that the WID frame was perpetuating development strategies detrimental to women, families, and communities spurred the creation of "gender and development" as an alternative analytic framework. Rather than focus exclusively on women, GAD was designed to focus on the unequal relations between men and women and their naturalization as a problem in and for development. Advocating analysis of the complex hierarchies of power grounded in the intersections of race, class, gender, sexuality, indigeneity, ethnicity, and nationality, GAD sought to investigate socially produced subordination and unequal power relations, which prevent equitable development and women's full participation within it. To envision equitable development, feminist proponents of GAD argued that rather than treat men and women across the global South as "target populations" (Schneider and Ingram 1993), they should be incorporated as full participants in decision-making. Thus GAD identified empowerment of the disadvantaged (including women) as integral to development. GAD emphasized how development strategies, including those purporting to be in women's interests (WAD and WID), served to replicate gender and global inequalities in development planning and implementation. As an alternative, GAD suggested that development needed not merely to take women into account but also to bring democracy to bear on the development process by the creation of strategies to allow the poor to both identify their needs and recommend tactics to improve their condition.

The people-centered development envisioned by feminist GAD proponents drew insights from critiques of development advanced by the International Labor Organization (ILO), which pointed out that economic growth defined in terms of income generation in the formal sector was an inadequate conception of development, for it ignored a host of basic human needs (Rai 2002). As early as the 1970s, the ILO argued that "trickle-down development" had reduced neither poverty nor unemployment, because poverty was not an "end" that could be eliminated by means of higher income alone. To remedy poverty in all its complexity required far more than simply putting able-bodied adults to work. For development to be effective, the needs of children, the elderly, and the disabled would have to be incorporated into the development agenda. According to this "basic needs" or "capacities" approach, poverty eradication required satisfaction of an "absolute level of basic needs" for everyone, which included physical needs (food, nutrition, shelter, and health), as well as "agency achievements" such as participation, empowerment, and involvement in community life (Sen 1987). Successful approaches to poverty eradication also required a shift from a focus on household consumption to an understanding that people need infrastructure and services (sanitation, safe drinking water, public transportation, and health and educational facilities). Within this frame, individual and collective self-determination were as central to development as the satisfaction of physical needs and construction of adequate infrastructure. Thus, successful development required development agencies to shift from technocratic administration to fostering democratic deliberation in which the poor fully participated in setting and achieving development goals.

While advocating a focus on empowerment, capacity building, and need satisfaction, feminist proponents of GAD also advanced a critique of critical omissions from earlier articulations of a needs-based approach. Although basic needs advocates had used collective nouns, referring to families and households rather than individuals as their unit of analysis, they did not disaggregate households by gender. On the contrary, they ignored gender relations and gendered distributions of power and goods within families. As Naila Kabeer (1994) points out, households were imagined to be altruistic, benignly governed, and characterized by equitable distributions across age and gender—an image altogether at odds with empirical evidence. In cultivating methodologies to analyze GAD, feminist scholars sought to illuminate gendered divisions of labor in households and workplaces, gendered access to and control over resources and benefits, and critical differences in the material and social positions of women and men in various contexts. Keenly aware that taking women's empowerment seriously within GAD would challenge gender subordination and inequality, feminist development scholars pointed out that deliberations over needs and capacities would likely be confrontational and pose serious risks for women who serve as agents of social change, risks that range from ostracism and rape to murder (Madhok and Rai 2012).

In efforts to improve development policies on the ground, feminist development scholars pressed international agencies, such as UNDP, United Nations Development Fund for Women (UNIFEM), the World Bank, and the International Monetary Fund (IMF) to adopt a GAD framework. Although they have achieved impressive success in this effort, the outcomes have been far from what they had hoped. As Kathleen Staudt (2008) has demonstrated, contrary to its goals of, the shift to GAD has enabled international institutions to shift scarce resources from women-in-development units to men's programs, while substituting notions of "equal treatment" of men and women in development projects for analyses of gender power and redress of gender inequities.

The adoption of "women's empowerment" by the World Bank (2000) as a core commitment in its development agenda provides a useful example of what is lost in translation when an international institution appropriates a feminist policy frame. The World Bank's decision to include women's empowerment in its development objectives was the result of years of feminist efforts to influence the bank's policies (Bedford 2009). In 2002, the World Bank issued new policy guidelines, "Integrating Gender into the World Bank's Work: A Strategy for Action," which require "gender mainstreaming," including gender impact analyses of all its programs as well as the promotion of women's economic development. To groom women as agents of their own empowerment, the World Bank has turned to microfinance. As noted earlier, microcredit provides individual women with small amounts of investment capital, which they repay from their successful economic ventures. "Empowering women" within this context becomes a means to the expansion of capitalist markets, economic growth, and the protection of capital investments.

Feminist critics have pointed out that the meaning of women's empowerment is distorted when transplanted to a profit-maximizing context. Although microcredit programs can assist some women in meeting their most immediate subsistence needs, this falls far short of eliminating poverty. Unlike the loans made within women's informal financial solidarity groups, microloans from capitalist lenders are restricted to profit-generating business ventures and cannot be used to cover other expenses that burden the poor, such as those for funerals, healthcare, food, and fuel. Within the scope of capitalist institutions, microcredit programs focus on individual women rather than on prevailing gender and class/caste relations. Emphasizing changes in individual attitudes to promote self-confidence and economic achievement, they ignore structural inequalities. In addition, microcredit programs increase the debt of poor women, imposing new levels of stress as well as responsibility on individual women (Ireland 2011; Parthasarathy 2012; Moodie 2013).

World Bank discourses frame women's empowerment through microfinance in terms of individual self-help. But rhetoric about self-help as a means of poverty alleviation can also legitimate the government's abandonment of collective responsibility to meet the most basic needs of the people at the very moment that structural adjustment policies (i.e., policy changes required by the World Bank as a condition for the receipt of loans) require governments to cut back on health, education, and welfare provision. Although World Bank strategies to "engender development" put women at the center of development policy, they do so in decidedly nonfeminist ways. Promoting self-employment through microfinance as the paradigm for poverty alleviation shifts responsibility for household income support from men to women, while also shifting the responsibility for "development" from the nation-state to the market. Neoliberalism—the economic policy associated with efforts to strengthen market competition by cutting government regulation of business enterprises as well as government services—supports privatizing imperatives. Operating squarely within neoliberal parameters, the World Bank deploys the language of GAD to favor private lending associations over public-service agencies without necessarily improving the condition or status of women (Poster and Salime 2002). Because microcredit programs generate profit, a new alliance of private microfinance providers, including Citibank and Deutsche Bank, now seek to "financialize" development, turning the poor into a financial asset. Suggesting that the risk in microfinance accrues to the lender, not the borrower, they have secured support from governments and international financial institutions to subsidize their corporate risk in making microloans (Moodie 2013).

In the current era, GAD has been subsumed within a neoliberal framework. By situating women's empowerment in the context of market efficiency and profit-making, structural constraints that circumscribe the conditions in which women and men live and work become invisible. Similarly, the legacies of colonialism and the continuing harms associated with neocolonialism are also rendered invisible in the neoliberal approach to development, as is the maldistribution of resources and risk fueled by capitalism.

Third World States, Structural Adjustment, and Patriarchy

Whether structural adjustment initiatives rely on and reinforce local and global structures of patriarchal power or contribute to resistance and transformation remains a topic of considerable controversy in feminist scholarship. Although the institutional oppression of women in postcolonial states is complicated by the involvement of structural adjustment programs (SAPs), Catherine Scott (1995, 133) points out that the state is an important force for implementing SAPs: "[I]t works to legitimate liberal definitions of democracy that ensure an order amenable to capitalism." But whether capitalism emancipates women is also a subject of contestation. The World Bank's Safe Motherhood initiative, for example, which claims that improving maternal health helps involve women more effectively in development (Herz and Measham 1987), adheres to and shores up traditional gender roles, relegating women to reproductive roles and ascertaining the primacy of those roles by incorporating women into already existing development practices. Instead of looking at how motherhood is instrumentally used by the state to control women's labor and assign them to gendered spheres in society, SAPs tend to perpetuate the masculinized state construct which then supports the universal patriarchy model. In this frame, sexual politics are constitutive of heteropatriarchal social relations, and development processes are formulated and enacted through the disciplining of Third World women's sexualities (Alexander 1997, 63).

The focus on women as the main recipients of loans has also been a source of debate among scholars of critical development. Some argue that microfinance programs have played an important role in enhancing the lives of impoverished rural women and in changing gender relations in the global South, particularly in Bangladesh. Syed M. Hashemi, Sidney Ruth Schuler, and Ann P. Riley (1996), for instance, conducted a study in six Bangladeshi villages from 1991 to 1994 to measure the impacts of microcredit programs on "women's roles and status and in norms related to reproduction." The goal was to determine whether or not women were "empowered" after receiving loans, particularly through development initiatives of the renowned organizations like the Grameen Bank and BRAC. The researchers concluded:

> Participation in Grameen Bank and BRAC increases women's mobility, their ability to make purchases and major household decisions, their ownership of productive assets, their legal and political awareness and participation in public campaigns and protests. Another analysis suggests the programs also decrease women's vulnerability to family violence. . . .
> In spite of focusing narrowly on credit, Grameen Bank (and to a lesser extent, BRAC) functions as a catalyst in transforming the lives of women.
> (Hashemi, Schuler, and Riley 1996, 650)

The findings, according to the researchers, attest that microcredit programs have been effective in empowering women in rural Bangladesh, especially because female loan recipients become a new source of income in the household, and therefore begin to be respected by other family members. Women are then able "to negotiate gender barriers, increase their control over their own lives, and improve their relative positions in their household" (Hashemi, Schuler, and Riley 1996, 650).

NGO activities are often linked with changes in gender relations in rural Bangladesh. Some scholars argue that these organizations have played an important role in challenging the patriarchal and oppressive social norms often defended by religious and rural elites. As S. M. Shamsul Alam explains,

> Since independence in 1971, a quiet revolution has been taking place in Bangladesh, especially in the rural areas where most Bangladeshis live. Rural women are becoming politically organized and asserting themselves. Various NGOs are placing more importance on girl's education. Women are accepting family planning in greater numbers and lowering the birthrate, and women's contribution to the family income- a sign of independence- has increased. Rural Bangladesh, in particular, is going through a rapid social transformation where the Islam-based interpretation of gender relations is constantly being challenged. The Bangladeshi Islamic fundamentalists are responding violently to these challenges.
>
> (Alam 1996, 262)

According to this study, NGOs challenge the religious discourse of elite male authorities in the Bangladeshi countryside; income-generating women have become economically and socially more independent; and NGOs have pushed for education for girls and for an increase in family planning. But that is not the whole story. The NGOs' challenge to the clergy's stronghold on the lives of rural Bangladeshis also has unintended consequences. Islamist leaders have often used religious discourse to incite violence, especially against women, claiming that NGOs are interested in destroying Islam, and "Westernizing" Bangladeshi society with "Christian seals" (Karim 2004). In contrast to optimistic assessments of advancement, women become the battleground where ideas and meanings of tradition and modernity are contested and manifested.

Some scholars have argued that although NGOs have brought about some social changes to rural Bangladesh, these changes have been minimal in challenging gender relations. "Competition" with the clergy and rural elites has led to further exploitation of poor women by microfinancing NGOs, as patriarchal structures have remained intact. As Lamia Karim (2004) explains,

> The work of development NGOs that targeted women as their beneficiaries challenged the authority of rural patriarchy and changed the dynamics of rural power by introducing the NGO as a new patron into the community, and at the same time, by mainstreaming poor women as labor and consumers into the economy. While these NGO programs have created limited opportunities for women and their families to earn a living, they have also created parallel conditions of violence and domination against poor women who are willed into this process not as informed agents but as clients of these NGOs.
>
> (Karim 2004, 301)

NGO programs, such as microcredit, serve as tools for these organizations to expand their clientele by enlisting poor women in need. The market-focused NGOs create patron-client relationships with poor women, who become the foot soldiers for social change and for the achievement of the goals of those organizations (although women are often uninformed of their new "role"). Instead of being conscious agents in the struggle against patriarchal oppression and domination, women become subordinated as debtors to those organizations. Islamists' opposition to this new "role" of women can result in the victimization of poor rural women—both through systemic discrimination and through physical attacks by men.

As NGOs have become profit-oriented organizations and financial sustainability has become crucial for their existence, loan recipients have had to carry the burden of microfinancing programs' heavy market terms. Often, the membership fees and interest rates on microloans are very high. "Most of the micro-credit institutions follow the flat-rate method in calculating total interest, very few follow the declining method. Under the flat rate method, NGOs charge interest rates typically between 10 percent and 30 percent" (Chowdhury et al. 2005, 299). In the case of Grameen Bank, the largest microlending institution in Bangladesh, interest rates in combination with membership fees and other charges near the 28 percent mark (Hashmi 2000, 161). According to Aminur Rahman (1996), as a recipient of a Grameen loan "[t]he member repays all her installments on a specific loan within fifty weeks of its acceptance (2 percent on the capital amount must be paid every week). Then the interest (20 percent yearly) and the emergency fund (25 percent of the calculated interest amount, which is 12.5 times greater than a member's regular weekly installment) must be paid within the remaining last two weeks in order to qualify for the next new extension of credit" (13). The high interest rates, fees, and charges are all to be paid toward the end of the program, making it impossible for a large number of recipients to repay their debt by themselves without taking up additional loans. As Rahman explains, "In my sample, over 95 percent of all members pay the interest and emergency fund through short-term borrowing from sources other than their own" (14). Those who receive loans from Grameen Bank end up entering a "spiral debt cycle." As Shelley Feldman states,

> The Grameen Bank Project, for instance, places responsibility for loan repayment on groups formed as venues of support and learning for new recipients. The reorganization of the social collectivity to ensure loan repayment serves as a mechanism of social control rather than an arena for building social solidarity and creating relations of social obligation and reciprocal exchange, since repayment by all group members is required before new loans are disbursed.
>
> (Feldman 1997, 60)

Microcredit has been and continues to be responsible for increasing poor women's indebtedness. Women, once again, become susceptible to social victimization: as the recipients of the loans, they are the ones responsible for repayment; if they default on their obligation, they are publicly scolded, and are often victims of violence by husbands or family members (since defaulting would be a source of embarrassment or shame).

Women commonly rely on additional loans to repay interest rates and fees because their initial loans are not usually used or invested in long-term income-generating activities. Grameen Bank and BRAC tend to measure the effectiveness of their microlending programs not by how the money is being invested by women or their families, but by the recovery rate of the money lent. "The credibility of a bank worker lies mainly in his successful collection of installments from members. Bank's pressure and the full collection of installments hardly leaves time for the bank worker to supervise the investment of loans" (Rahman 1996, 15). Instead of investing the money in income-generating projects that could boost their earning capabilities, women tend to use their loans in minimally productive or largely unproductive activities. As Anne Marie Goetz explains,

> Low-income women borrowers in Bangladesh invest cautiously in low-risk, familiar, low-productive enterprises.... By far, the bulk of loans taken by women in special credit programs are invested in traditional activities such as paddy husking, petty trade, and livestock rearing, most of which show a negative return to labor when it is imputed to the male agricultural wage rate.... By and large, none of the larger special credit programs have succeeded in shifting women out of traditional income-generating activities, although most do acknowledge the importance of encouraging more profitable and socially valued nontraditional forms of entrepreneurship for women.
>
> (Goetz 1996, 57)

Some experts emphasize that microcredit programs have had an insignificant role in the reduction of poverty in rural Bangladesh. It is a myth that most microcredit programs have been successful in alleviating poverty in the countryside over the long run. In a 1996 survey of 4,364 households in Matlab, a rural region of Bangladesh, Serajul Hoque (2004), examined the impacts of microfinancing on poverty levels in the region, noting,

> The regression results suggest that BRAC's micro-credit program has had a minimal impact on the reduction of poverty. Taken together, the statistically insignificant effect of micro-credit on household consumption and the higher incident of poverty among BRAC households relative to non-BRAC households leads to the conclusion that micro-credit had negligible impact on the reduction of poverty.
>
> (Hoque 2004, 30)

Because most programs lack long-term solutions for the reduction of poverty, loan recipients tend to see little change in their living standards after the first years of borrowing money. As Taj I. Hashmi states,

> Since "livelihood enterprises" are usually secondary or tertiary rather than the primary source of household income, these "seasonal, intermittent and part-time" (and uncertain) sources of income from subsistence-oriented, livestock-rearing or paddy-husking projects for women, cannot be long-term solutions of poverty.... In the long run, as T. W. Dichter suggests, the outcome of such micro-credit-based projects is stagnation and decline in growth as after the second or third loan cycle "either people stop borrowing, or they stop increasing the amount they borrow."
>
> (Hashmi 2000, 164)

Development NGOs have flourished in Bangladesh and other developing countries in the last decades, often bringing with them new mechanisms of social control of subordinate populations. Although some studies have found Grameen's and BRAC's programs to be beneficial for poor villagers, many other researchers have pointed out the problems with microcredit schemes. In addition, these programs have been associated with increasing violence against women in poor areas at the same time as they have shown little results in alleviating poverty in the long run. Instead, the high interest rates on loans and the main goal of loan recovery suggest these profit-oriented NGOs have been more concerned with financially sustaining themselves than with making women concretely better off. Grassroots NGOs led by women have often done a better job in working toward more long-term changes in rural communities and in empowering women. The success of microcredit programs has been overestimated. Their effectiveness has become more myth rather than reality.

Feminists and "the Standpoint" of Women

Many feminist scholars have suggested that alternatives to development must begin with a "woman's standpoint." As Escobar (1995, 181) noted, "The starting place [of questioning the sex bias in development] should be the standpoint of women, 'where an interested and located investigation of the social world must begin: at the place where the knower herself sits.'" When professionals, academics, and bureaucrats start from a "woman's perspective," center on "women's ways of knowing," they can work "in and against" development. The category "woman" however, appears to be prediscursive and deterministic. Escobar rightly points out that "woman," as an undifferentiated category, could be an invention of development (164). Troubling this category, feminist scholar Oyeronke Oyewumi (1997, 16) has asked, "Women? Feminists? What women? What feminists? Who qualify to be women and feminists in these cultural settings, and on what bases are they to be identified?" Oyewumi emphasizes the importance of addressing the hegemonic construction of the feminist, which implicitly invokes dominant, white, heteronormative, middle-class, Euro-American women's worldview. When the hegemonic construction is left unquestioned, women in the Third World are positioned as recalcitrant subjects who are not actors but always acted upon. For example, it is often asserted that the UN Decade for Women and WID discourse were beneficial for Third World women because "[t]hey promoted research on women, channeled funds to women's projects, and put First World *feminists* in touch with the Third World *women activists*, who, in turn, *disseminated* feminist knowledge among the women groups with which they worked" (Escobar 1995, 184; emphasis mine). Within the problematic First World feminist / Third World woman activist dualism, the production of feminist knowledge is conceived as an exclusively Western phenomenon, while women activists across the South are excluded from feminism. When "the standpoint of women" presupposes such Orientalist stereotypes, it can only reinscribe structural hierarchies.

As Chandra Mohanty (1991b, 55) notes, one of the thorniest intellectual problems in contemporary feminist scholarship is the representation of Third World women as Other. Mohanty specifically addresses the problematic depiction of the "third world woman" in Western feminist discourse. Western feminists have been complicit in maintaining a power/knowledge regime of Third World women and Third World development, aligned with white, Western, heteromasculinist constructions of the Third World as a whole. To escape the gaze of "Western eyes," situated knowledges and local voices must be recognized as legitimate sources of knowledge production. Recognizing women, feminists, and activists in their multiplicity, complicity, and agency can aid in dismantling hierarchical binaries. A more sophisticated analytical frame must acknowledge the discursive construction of women as agents of change and as persons harmed by development discourses and practices. Absent that recognition, hegemonic conceptions maintain power inequalities and mask mobilizations that disrupt the dominant global order.

If feminist approaches to development are to transcend their Orientalist roots, they must engage people's own struggles for self-representation and self-determination, refuse fixity, and accommodate heterogeneity, mobility, and discontinuity. Anchored in an interested politics of history and location, feminist approaches can explore what feminist theorist Gloria Anzaldua characterizes as the border, which "is an open wound where the Third World grates against the First and bleeds" (quoted in Lavie and Swedenburg 1996, 14). Border zones are sites of creative cultural creolization that are riddled with pain, loss, and torment as a result of these processes. Borders, hybridity, cyborgs, and diasporas offer new frames of analysis that resist and transcend boundaries through their creative articulation of practices, demonstrating possible ways to corrode the Eurocenter by actively Third Worlding (16).

References

Alam, S. M. Shamsul. 1998. "Women in the Era of Modernity and Islamic Fundamentalism: The Case of Taslima Nasrin of Bangladesh." *Signs: Journal of Women in Culture and Society* 23 (2): 235–267.

Alexander, M. J. 1997. "Erotic Autonomy as a Politics of Decolonization: An Anatomy of Feminist and State Practice in the Bahamas Tourist Economy." In *Feminist Genealogies, Colonial Legacies, Democratic Futures*, edited by M. J. Alexander and C. T. Mohanty, 63–100. New York: Routledge.

Anzaldúa, Gloria. 2010. "La Conciencia de la Mestiza: Towards a New Consciousness." In *Feminist Theory Reader: Local and Global Perspectives*, edited by C. R. McCann and S. Kim, 254–262.

Bayes, Jane. 2006. "The Gendered Impact of Globalization on the United States." In *Women, Democracy, and Globalization in North America: A Comparative Study*, edited by Jane Bayes et al., 145–172. New York: Palgrave.

Bedford, Kate. 2009. *Developing Partnerships: Gender, Sexuality and the Reformed World Bank* Minneapolis: University of Minnesota Press.

Beneria, Lourdes. 1997. "Accounting for Women's Work: The Progress of Two Decades." In *The Women, Gender and Development Reader*, edited by N. Visvanathan et al., 114–120. London: Zed Books.

Bergeron, Suzanne. 2006. *Fragments of Development: Nation, Gender, and the Space of Modernity*. Ann Arbor: University of Michigan Press.

Boserup, Ester. 1970. *Women's Role in Economic Development.* New York: St. Martin's Press.
Briggs, Laura. 2002. *Reproducing Empire: Race, Sex, Science and U.S. Imperialism in Puerto Rico.* Berkeley: University of California Press.
Chowdhury, M. J. A., Ghosh, D. and Wright, R. 2005. "The Impact of Micro-credit on Poverty: Evidence from Bangladesh." *Progress in Development Studies* 5 (4): 298–309.
Cowen, Michael P., and Robert Shenton. 1995. *Doctrines of Development.* New York: Routledge.
Dore, Elizabeth. 2000. "One Step Forward, Two Steps Back: Gender and the State in the Long Nineteenth Century." In *Hidden Histories of Gender and State in Latin America*, edited by Elizabeth Dore and Maxine Molyneux, 3–32. Durham, NC: Duke University Press.
Elson, Diane. 1995. "Male Bias in Macroeconomics: The Case of Structural Adjustment." In *Male Bias in the Development Process*, 164–190. Manchester: University of Manchester Press.
Escobar, Arturo. 1992. "Entry on Planning." In *The Development Dictionary*, edited by Wolfgang Sachs, 132–145. London: Zed Press.
Escobar, A. 1995. *Encountering Development: The Making and Unmaking of the Third World.* Princeton, NJ: Princeton University Press.
Feldman, Shelley. 1997. "NGOs and Civil Society: (Un)stated Contradictions." *Annals of the American Academy of Political and Social Science* 554: 46–65.
Goetz, A. M. 1996. "Who Takes the Credit? Gender, Power, and Control over Loan Use in Rural Credit Programs." *World Development* 24 (1): 45–63.
Goldstone, Jack A. 2010. "The New Population Bomb: The Four Megatrends That Will Change the World." *Foreign Affairs* 89 (1): 31–43.
Hashemi, S. M., Schuler, S. R., and Riley, A. P. 1996. "Rural Credit Programs and Women's Empowerment in Bangladesh." *World Development* 24 (1): 635–653.
Hashmi, T. 2000. *Women and Islam in Bangladesh: Beyond Subjection and Tyranny.* New York: Palgrave MacMillan.
Herz, Barbara and Anthony Measham. 1987. *Safe Motherhood Initiative: Proposals for Action.* Washington, DC: World Bank Discussion Papers.
Hoque, S. 2004. "Micro-credit and the Reduction of Poverty in Bangladesh." *Journal of Contemporary Asia* 34 (1): 21–32.
Ireland, H. M. 2011. *Transnational Feminism and the Microfinance (R)evolution: Excavating Microlending from Neoliberalism.* Eugene: Oregon State University.
Kabeer, Naila. 1994. *Reversed Realities: Gender Hierarchies in Development Thought.* London: Verso.
Karim, L. 2004. "Democratizing Bangladesh: State, NGOs, and Militant Islam." *Cultural Dynamics* 16 (2/3): 291–318.
Madhok, Sumi, and Shirin Rai. 2012. "Agency, Injury and Transgressive Politics in Neoliberal Times." *Signs: Journal of Women in Culture and Society* 37 (3): 645–669.
Mohanty, C. T. 1991a. "Cartographies of Struggle: Third World Women and the Politics of Feminism." In *Third World Women and the Politics of Feminism*, edited by C. Mohanty, A. Russo, and L. Torres, 1–47. Bloomington: Indiana University Press.
Mohanty, C. T. 1991b. "Under Western Eyes: Feminist Scholarship and Colonial Discourses." In *Third World Women and the Politics of Feminism*, edited by C. Mohanty, A. Russo, and L. Torres, 51–80. Bloomington: Indiana University Press.
Moodie, Megan. 2013. "Microfinance and the Gender of Risk." *Signs: Journal of Women in Culture and Society* 38 (2): 279–302.
Moser, Carolyn. 1993. *Gender Planning and Development: Theory, Practice, Training.* New York: Routledge.

Oyewumi, O. 1997. *The Invention of Women: Making an African Sense of Western Gender Discourses.* Minneapolis: University of Minnesota Press.

Palmer, Ingrid. 1992. "Gender Equity and Economic Efficiency in Adjustment Programmes." In *Women and Adjustment Policies in the Third World*, edited by Haleh Afshar and Carolyn Dennis, 69-83. Basingstoke: Macmillan.

Parpart, J. L. 1995. "Deconstructing the Development 'Expert': Gender Development and the 'Vulnerable Groups.'" In *Feminism/Postmodernism/Development*, edited by M. H. Marchand and J. L. Parpart, 221–243. New York: Routledge.

Parpart, Jane, Patricia Connelly, and Eudine Barriteau. 2000. *Theoretical Perspectives on Gender and Development.* Ottawa: International Development Research Centre.

Parthasarathy, S. K. 2012. "Fact and Fiction: Examining Microcredit/Microfinance from a Feminist Perspective." Toronto, Ontario. Association for Women's Rights in Development (AWID). December 3. Available at: http://www.awid.org/Library/Fact-and-Fiction-Examining-Microcredit-Microfinance-from-a-Feminist-Perspective2

Poster, Winifred and Zakia Salime. 2002. "The Limits of Micro-Credit: Transnational Feminism and USAID Activities in the United States and Morocco." In *Women's Activism and Globalization: Linking Local Struggles to Transnational Politics*, edited by Nancy Naples and Manisha Desai, 189–219. New York: Routledge.

Purewal, Navtej. 2001. "New Roots for Rights: Women's Responses to Population and Development Policies." In *Women Resist Globalization: Mobilizing for Livelihood and Rights*, edited by Sheila Rowbotham and Stephanie Linkogle. 96–117. London: Zed Press.

Rahman, Aminur. 1996. "Micro-Credit for Women in Rural Bangladesh: Retrenchment of Patriarchal Hegemony as a Consequence." *Chicago Anthropology Exchange* 13: 6–22.

Rai, Shirin. 2002. *Gender and the Political Economy of Development.* Cambridge: Polity Press.

Schneider, Ann, and Helen Ingram. 1993. "Social Constructions and Target Populations: Implications for Politics and Policy." *American Political Science Review* 87 (2): 334–447.

Scott, C. 1995. *Gender and Development: Rethinking Modernization and Dependency Theory.* London: Lynne Rienner Publishers.

Sen, Amartya. 1987. *On Ethics and Economics.* Oxford: Basil Blackwell.

Staudt, Kathleen. 2008. "Gendering Development." In *Politics, Gender, and Concepts: Theory and Methodology*, edited by Gary Goetz and Amy Mazur, 136–158. Cambridge: Cambridge University Press.

Staudt, Kathleen. 1991. *Managing Development: State, Society and International Contexts.* Newbury Park, CA: Sage.

Tinker, Irene. 1976. *Women and World Development.* Washington, DC: Overseas Development Council.

Waring, Marilyn. 1988. *If Women Counted: A New Feminist Economics.* San Francisco: Harper and Row.

Wichterich, Christa. 2000. *The Globalized Woman: Reports from a Future of Inequality.* London: Zed Books.

World Bank. 2000. *Advancing Gender Equality: World Bank Action Since Beijing.* Washington, DC: World Bank, Gender and Development Group.

CHAPTER 8

DIASPORA

ANITA MANNUR AND JANA EVANS BRAZIEL

INTRODUCTION

"Diaspora" as we wrote in 2003, "does not transcend difference of race, class, gender and sexuality, nor can diaspora stand alone as an epistemological or historical category of analysis" (Braziel and Mannur 2003, 5). Yet, the term *diaspora* is perhaps one of the most often used and vexing terms in a number of fields that promote the intersectional study of race, class, and gender. With its immense critical purchase in the 1990s, stemming from the highly influential journal *Diaspora: A Journal of Transnational Studies*, it continues to be used both descriptively and as an analytic, though not without significant critique. Prior to the 1990s, the term had been almost exclusively used to describe dispersal and the promise of a return to a "homeland" within the Jewish context. *Diaspora* is a Greek word. Its root verb *-sperein* means to "sow" or "scatter," while the prefix *dia-* refers to movement "through." In about 250 BCE the word was used in the Septuagint, a translation of the Torah by a select group of Jewish scholars that was intended for rulers of Alexandria in Egypt. Only later, during the Hellenic period, did the term begin to circulate among Jewish peoples in the Mediterranean world. Diaspora, as Brent Hayes Edwards argues, has had a vexed history that distinguishes between diaspora and exile. The Greek, Edwards (2007, 82) points out, "never translates the important Hebrew words for exile . . . Instead diaspora, is limited to the translation of terms describing literal or figurative processes of scattering, separation, branching off, departure, banishment, winnowing. Another early referent was the Middle Passage and the forcible enslavement of peoples across what Paul Gilroy has referred to as the "black Atlantic." By the early twentieth century, however, diaspora was being used to describe Armenian refugees and other individuals displaced by World War I. Soon, other scholars of race and migration were integrating the term into their critical repertoire to both describe and critique the conditions of transnational movement brought about by systems of indenture, immigration, and varied forms of displacement. One

Caribbean example is the Second Middle Passage and the Indian and Chinese diasporas in the archipelago, particularly in Trinidad, Guyana, and Cuba, following the abolition of slavery and the beginning of indentured servitude in the region. After World War II, the increased numbers of refugees and displaced persons created new mid-century diasporas—a phenomenon that only escalated during the Cold War.

Although there have been innumerable attempts to theorize diaspora, it is worth noting that the concept of diaspora and the work of defining this keyword have gone through many phases. Rather than reiterate what these numerous scholarly publications have put forward, this chapter seeks to examine the relevance of the term *diaspora* in feminist and gender studies. Most feminist scholars of diaspora agree on some fundamental precepts about its usefulness, yet they note that *diaspora* often situates nations within an implicitly gendered logic of filial ties and patrilineal genealogies. In the inaugural issue of the journal *Diaspora*, William Safran, for example, suggests that diasporic communities share many of the following features:

- They, or their ancestors, have been dispersed from an original "centre" to two or more foreign regions.
- They retain a collective memory, vision, or myth about their original homeland, including its location, history, and achievements.
- They believe they are not—and perhaps can never be—fully accepted in their host societies and so remain partly separate.
- Their ancestral home is idealized and it is thought that, when conditions are favorable, either they or their descendants should return.
- They believe all members of the diaspora should be committed to the maintenance or restoration of the original homeland and to its safety and prosperity.
- They continue in various ways to relate to that homeland and their ethno-communal consciousness and solidarity are in an important way defined by the existence of such a relationship.

Implicit in each of these criteria is the notion that diasporic communities aspire to assimilate, while remaining distinct from their host societies. At the same time, the idea of a monolithic homeland, apart and distinct from the country of migration or settlement is taken for granted as a logical construction. Finally, diasporic communities remain committed to the idea of an eventual return to the original homeland (often figured in the scholarship we outline as the "mythic homeland"). Nowhere in this definition is there a possibility to accommodate how diasporic movement is affected by differences of class, gender, race, or sexuality.

However, by the early 2000s, scholars from a variety of fields had developed diaspora as an analytical term, deployed to investigate the myriad forms of exploitation and uneven relations to capital experienced by various diasporic subjects. Emerging scholars of diasporas, particularly in the fields of feminist, ethnic, and queer studies challenged paradigms that naturalized the settler colonialist and imperialist understandings of home and sovereignty, drawing attention to indigenous peoples erased by colonization.

Feminist and queer scholars have adopted critical diaspora as an analytical framework while simultaneously interrogating gendered and sexual dimensions of the patriarchal and imperialist processes that set diasporas in motion.

This chapter examines factors contributing to the proliferation of diaspora studies in the 1990s, how feminist theorists complicated and clarified the use of the term, and how attention to race and sexuality introduced by scholars in ethnic studies and queer studies shifted diaspora from a descriptive category of movement and idealized return to a critical analytic that conceptualizes a range of migratory movements. Advancing important critiques of essentialist notions of diaspora, feminist, Asian American, black Atlantic, and Caribbean scholarship has refuted nostalgic narratives of return characteristic of the work of early diasporic studies scholars, such as William Safran. Challenging certain types of diaspora studies that are "singularly celebratory" (Bald et al. 2013), critical diaspora studies since the early 2000s have rigorously examined forces of imperialism, racism, sexism, and homophobia in theorizing diaspora. Paul Gilroy's scholarship has been particularly generative of these critical trends. We begin our analysis with an exploration of his critical contributions to the field of diaspora studies.

Setting the Terms/Feminist Possibilities

Paul Gilroy's (1995) *The Black Atlantic: Modernity and Double Consciousness* was a groundbreaking interdisciplinary work. Synthesizing methodological insights from sociology, history, literary criticism, and cultural studies, the book made significant contributions to the fields of black cultural studies, African American studies, Caribbean studies, and black British literature and culture. In his definition of diaspora, Paul Gilroy mapped a transnational geography of black cultural production that he named the "black Atlantic." This framework allowed for a provocative rethinking of African diasporic studies and simultaneously critiqued the nationalist frames of African American and black British cultural studies that did not adequately attend to the fact that a great deal of historical and cultural movement took place among Africa, America, and Britain. Gilroy (1995, 15) suggests that diaspora would be most useful if cultural historians considered the "Atlantic as one single complex unit of analysis in their discussions of the modern world and used it to produce an explicitly transnational and intercultural perspective." In effect, Gilroy's definition mapped the myriad charted spaces of the "black Atlantic" as a fertile transnational site of historical and cultural exchange among individuals from countries on the continents of Africa, Europe, and the Americas. At the same time, this single unit of analysis, Gilroy suggested, would put English historiography and literary history in conversation, thereby challenging the nationally defined cultural histories of African American and black British cultural studies. This definition successfully challenged essentialized identities grounded in race, ethnicity, and nationality. Gilroy's work brought the insights of Caribbean, black British, and African American intellectuals and artists into creative fusion. *The Black Atlantic* thus shifted theorizations of cultural production away from nationalist frames toward transnational ones, and offered resistance to racialized essentialism (or "cultural insiderism") as the ground of fertile possibility for black Atlantic cultures. Above all, Gilroy's *The Black Atlantic* challenged black nationalism as the predominant cultural model within African American studies as the uninterrogated paradigm for understanding black history, thought, art, literature, and other forms of cultural production. Offering the ship as a "chronotope" (a concept borrowed from Mikhail Bakhtin), Gilroy (1995, 17) asserted that scholars must "rethink modernity via the history of the black Atlantic and the African diaspora into the western hemisphere."

Despite its theoretical importance, Gilroy's *The Black Atlantic* did not integrate "the Atlantic as one single, complex unit of analysis," as he suggested it would. On the contrary, as Colin Dayan demonstrated, in its conceptualizations of the black Atlantic Gilroy's study repressed Haiti (except as revolutionary memory). Missing from Gilroy's analysis was the plight of Haiti's refugees crossing the treacherous Atlantic, headed for Florida's shores in small, unstable boats. That omission is staggering, given the massive waves of refugees fleeing Haiti's military regime from 1991 to 1994, a phenomenon that was extensively covered by the international media. And that omission undeniably shaped Gilroy's conception of the black Atlantic.

For all that Gilroy's book promised and proffered to cultural critics, it was not all about the "open boat" and the free movements of ideas and cultural practices; it erected and fortified its own discursive boundaries, hemispheric if not national, but boundaries no less. It establishes its own historical blind spots—with salient material, political, intellectual, and cultural ramifications. "The history of those new migrants, called 'boat people' or the 'Haitian stampede,' [arriving in] . . . rickety boats, are not exactly the ships Gilroy has in mind" (Dayan 1996, 10) writes Haitian American literary and cultural critic Colin Dayan in "Paul Gilroy's Slaves, Ships, and Routes," her trenchant and pointed materialist critique of *The Black Atlantic*. In her review, Dayan (1996, 7) incisively elucidates the material blind spots in Gilroy's metaphorical mapping of the black Atlantic, to disclose it as "a cartography of celebratory journeys—[that] reads like an expurgated epic history." *The Black Atlantic* needs to be reread and rethought from the vantage point of those who cannot make the journey, or those who are compelled to do so by circumstances of profound economic impoverishment and disturbing political violence, or those who do not survive the journey across the "black Atlantic." The plight of Haitian refugees adrift on highly regulated transatlantic waters forms a powerful rejoinder to Paul Gilroy's metaphorical ship as chronotope for transatlantic cultural production and exchange as theorized in *The Black Atlantic*. As Dayan asserts, "missing [in Gilroy's study] is the continuity of the Middle Passage in today's world of less obvious, but no less pernicious enslavement." As Dayan demonstrates, Gilroy's omissions are historical, materialist, and hemispheric. Subsequent generations of diaspora scholars have added to this argument.

As cultural critic Samantha Pinto articulates, these omissions are also gendered and decisively masculinist:

> Coming up in the academy at the turn of the millennium, I was part of a generation of scholars raised on Paul Gilroy's formulation of *The Black Atlantic*, a manifesto to shift the nationalist frame of African American studies in the US academy that became the public site of the field's revitalization, as well as its globalization. Encountering Gilroy's model was an exercise in critical desire and alienation—how could I not appreciate the transnational turn that complicated definitions of blackness beyond America's borders? How, too, could I not notice the near silence on women's writing and cultural expressions that haunts the text's new and sweeping conceptualization of the field?
>
> (Pinto 2013, 6)

Although diasporic studies indubitably anchors itself in models put forward by Paul Gilroy and others in the 1990s, Pinto's argument that reading *The Black Atlantic* is at once alienating and able to fulfill a critical desire, speaks to the complex problem of what feminism is able to say in relation to diaspora studies. Even as diasporas are often presented (again, in implicitly masculine terms) as the "bastard child of the nation—disavowed, inauthentic, illegitimate and impoverished imitation of the original" (Gopinath 1995, 317), the nation is often theorized as a masculinist space. Transnational analytics and feminisms, we suggest, offer valuable modes of inquiry through which to interrogate the implicit masculinist bent in diaspora and diaspora studies, and to analyze how these formulations become hegemonic. But analyses of diaspora may address issues of gender and women without integrating feminist modes of analysis.

As much as the term *diaspora* roots itself in a history of movement, one that owes a debt to establishing genealogies to spatial and temporal movements in the past, feminist scholars suggest that the genealogical or patrilineal mode itself, so central to early modes of diasporic critical thought, needs to be systematically interrogated. A way out of this problematic elision of feminist modes of analysis in diaspora studies emerges in Lisa Lowe's landmark and widely anthologized essay, "Heterogeneity, Hybridity, Multiplicity: Marking Asian American Differences." Lowe's critical triptych of terms offered scholars of diaspora ways to describe forms of difference that result from differential and uneven forms of migration history. In addition, Lowe's article clarified how to describe intersectional differences while attending to problematics of gender and racial formation. With an explicit focus on women's writing, Lowe's work gave Asian American scholars of diaspora what Pinto and other feminist scholars found lacking in Gilroy's work. Providing a feminist conceptual vocabulary for understanding the effects of diasporic movement, Lowe called attention to histories of gendered migration and labor that involved alliances across, and not simply between, generations. Lowe challenged the interpretation of Asian American culture in hierarchical and familial terms as a clash between generations, noting that such a limited frame precludes more productive engagement with "horizontal" relationships among diasporic subjects that emerge through coalitions and affiliations. Emphasizing the lateral and intersectional connections among women and not simply across generations has an implicitly feminist bent in that it does not privilege patriarchal histories of descent and lineage.

The move to thinking laterally in Lowe's work has a strong anchoring in feminist modes of inquiry advanced by women of color feminists, such as Trinh T. Minh Ha, Chela Sandoval, and Angela Davis. Feminist theory's explicit understanding of gender as a political formation and not simply as a disparate group of diffuse interests lends traction to the notion that diasporic femininity and cultural practices are "worked out as much 'horizontally' among communities as it is transmitted 'vertically' in unchanging forms from one generation to the next" (Lowe 1996, 64).

Although Lowe does not explicitly use the term *diaspora*, it is clear from her focus on immigration and questions of transnational subjectivity that her essay has deep consequences for scholars of diaspora, notably feminist scholars, who want to find ways to theorize the nation-state outside the logic of filiation and patrilineality that so often characterized diasporic studies prior to the 1990s. These newer approaches provided a critical vocabulary for thinking through difference without privileging a narrative of redemptive return that had been the mainstay of early diaspora studies.

The work of Saidiya Hartman (2007) provides a final example of the strategic questions that feminist scholars have posed to masculinist assumptions about return. Like Stephanie Smallwood (2008) in her equally compelling *Saltwater Slavery: A Middle Passage from Africa to American Diaspora*, Hartman critiques the limitations of a teleologically oriented definition of diaspora. Yet, Hartman's text also deploys the language of affect and nostalgia (as scholars Ann Cvetkovich, Jack Halberstam, and Gayatri Gopinath have argued) to trouble the idea of returning to an original homeland, an idea that Safran posited as a defining characteristic of a diasporic community. In her memoir, *Lose Your Mother: A Journey along the Atlantic Slave Routes*, Hartman explains that as a woman in search of a past, she traveled to Ghana only to find an absence of survivors of her lineage. An absence of photographs and an archive of what she describes as "half-truths and silence" (15) separated Hartman from the "truths" of a past borne out of and through the Middle Passage. When her search took her to the slave dungeons of Elmina and to a space filled with the sedimented bodily remnants of the past in the form of "blood, shit and dirt" (119), she confronted the abject scene of slavery's absence. Rather than feeling a greater connection with the past, this entry into "slavery's archive" afforded only a sense of "greater historical loss" (Gopinath 2010, 170). In contrast to Safran's conception, there is nothing nostalgic about Hartman's "return" to the past. On the contrary, Hartman's memoir suggests that it is impossible to recover a lost past.

The refusal of nostalgia, and the sustained focus on visceral disgust and loss structure Hartman's "return" to the "homeland." Hartman's feminist perspective on diasporic return insists that desires to connect with an original homeland must be understood as desires. Thus Hartman, and other feminists who refuse the nostalgic backward glance of some strands of diaspora studies, provides an important counternarrative to the myth of return present in some theorizations of diaspora.

In her analysis of other feminist texts that refuse any easy recovery of a violent and colonial past, Brinda Mehta (2009, 11) suggests that "the link between trauma, history and the diasporic process is a crucial one to expose the infamy of coloniality in the form of slavery, neocolonial dictatorship, US-led invasions and occupations, environmental degradation and other 'natural' and 'man-made' disasters. At the same time these links initiate the process of healing through resistance and spiritual catharsis." Mehta's contribution underscores the role of trauma in particular histories of gendered migration. Collectively, these feminist analyses suggest that forms of devastation and violence wrought by state-sanctioned, ecological, and imperialist forces produce differential forms of injury on diasporic individuals and communities. Through such avowedly antinostalgic analyses, feminist diaspora studies make visible the gendered stories of migration omitted from the initial conceptualization of diaspora. Gayatri Gopinath (2010, 167) suggests that this feminist logic illuminates non-blood-based affiliation routed in and rooted through difference, which contributes to an "awareness of the difficulties and traps of identifications, rather than in a fantasy of sameness, wholeness or completeness." Taken together, these feminist works challenge the notion that diasporic communities can be defined by a set of structural similarities grounded in desires to return to a biological past and rooted in an original homeland. For Lowe, Gopinath, Mehta, Pinto, and Hartman, diaspora is most useful as a concept when it grapples with the impossibility for women, queer subjects, or otherwise disenfranchised subjects to fully identify with the projects of the nation-state. At the same time, their critical interventions also critique the implicitly gendered logic through which the language of nationhood, belonging, and migration is constructed.

Asylum, Refugees, and Diaspora in Racialized Settings

An important critical move within feminist analyses in diaspora studies is to account for the role of race. The issue of gender within diaspora cannot be understood without also considering race and the effects of racialization. Race inflects diaspora; diasporic movements, or trans-relocations; and diasporic communities across the world. Race also undeniably operates as an identity category for diasporic individuals, forming a sense of shared cultural heritage and common experience forged historically in response to racism in the host country of adoption. Race also operates as an exclusionary category or an actual barrier to movement, transborder migration, and cross-border mobility: historically, the racial classification or categorization of a group determined one's mobility, one's right to move or relocate, or, conversely, restricted one's right to resettle, based on the prejudicial or racist exclusions of the "receiving" country. In conceptualizing the racialized parameters of diasporas, three salient patterns emerge: the racialization (postimmigration) of economic migrants during periods of recession and competition for jobs; the barring of entry to immigrants, even imperiled refugees, based on racialized (and racist) criteria in the country denying admission; and finally, the expulsion of immigrants, permanent residents, and even naturalized citizens based on racist pogroms of national exclusion and systematized forms of deportation from the citizen body.

Diasporas thus may be provisionally organized around two thematic patterns: (1) *outsiders within*—the postmigratory racialization of economic migrants; and (2) *barred entry*—the racialization of refugees by intended countries of destination that bar entry to communities seeking political asylum. A third category includes racialized diasporic communities that are ultimately *forced out*—that is, those diasporic communities (such as South Asians in East Africa, generally, but also Indian diasporas in Uganda, specifically, who were violently expelled by Idi Amin in 1972) who are forced into new diasporas because they are targeted as ethnically "impure" bodies within the nation-state. These are three vantage points from which diasporas can be approached, each of which makes evident that diasporas are always racialized.

The first pattern isolates racialized economic migrants who resettle in a new national space and who, following the re-emergence of push factors (economic recession, high levels of unemployment, competition with citizens for jobs), find themselves negatively racialized and pejoratively characterized as the unwanted foreigner—*étranger* or *ausländer*. This is evident in second-generation citizens, such as Franco-Maghrebi migrants, second-generation children of immigrant parents, who are in fact, French citizens, and for Turkish *Gästarbeiter*, or guest workers, in Germany, as well as for Mexican and Central American economic migrants in the United States.

The second pattern isolates racialized refugees who suffer the discriminatory immigration practices and repressive asylum policies of the countries in which they actively seek refuge. Despite the fact that these individuals never complete a migratory journey, their status as individuals and communities seeking refuge positions them outside the normative bounds of the state. Their "outsider" status, ambiguously defined, suggests that conceptualizations of diaspora need to be capacious enough to accommodate these subjects as well. Within this paradigm, the refugees are actually barred entry into a country, frequently being intercepted at sea or at the intended port of entry, detained in offshore immigration prisons, and ultimately deported back to their home countries despite real, not merely perceived, threats of political retaliation, violent repression, imprisonment, torture, and even death. Although race is rarely deployed as the state's rationale for barring these refugees, race and racialization are inflected in the administrative language, as well as in the public debates surrounding these refugees. Maghrebi economic migrants in France and Turkish *gästarbeiter* in Germany came to those countries seeking better incomes and educational opportunities. Initially, these economic migrants were actively recruited to contribute to the productive power of the French and German post–WWII economies. In the periods of economic recession beginning in the 1970s and continuing into the 1980s, however, these same economic migrants were regarded by French and German citizens as interlopers and undesirable outsiders who were vying for the best jobs, pressing wages downward, and competing with nationals for economic and educational advancement. As a result, these communities have become the targets of virulent forms of European racism that crystallize around ethnicity, nationality, religion, class, and economic push-pull factors.

Some refugees differ from economic migrants such as *Gästarbeiter* in that they do not actively seek better opportunities but are forced to flee their countries of origin as a direct consequence of imperialism and colonialism. The thousands of Vietnamese refugees who fled their nation in the decades after the fall of Saigon have become paradigmatic. In the Asia-Pacific region, most of these Vietnamese "boat people" were not only denied political asylum but also routinely intercepted at sea and detained in immigrant prisons by the Australian government. Similarly, Haitian refugees—also pejoratively referred to as "boat people" by the US media—fleeing political violence, state despotism, military coup d'états, and poverty in their home country—were intercepted, detained, and eventually deported back to Haiti during the period of late Duvalierism.

During the "refugee crisis" of the mid-1990s, the world witnessed a proliferation of racialized violence, systemic forms of "ethnic cleansing," and racial genocides in the Balkan States and Rwanda. Both civil wars led to genocidal regimes of violence, internally displaced persons, and a flood of international refugees seeking asylum (concomitant with a notable and significant decline in the number of people granted asylum). In the wake of 9/11, Arab and Muslim immigrants across the globe have also suffered racial and religious persecution as the backlash against these immigrant communities escalated during the global war on terror. As scholars of diaspora have pointed out, the "global war on terror" has produced ever more codified notions of gendered citizenship and belonging. In the case of the Pakistani diaspora, for instance, programs like the National Security Entry-Exit Registration System (NSEERS) introduced in the United States, more commonly known as "special registration," led to deportation proceedings for close to 85,000 men (Rana 2013). Largely targeting Muslim men, such modes of imperial coercion and control precipitated forms of "voluntary self-deportation" or "return migration" in which male migrants would "choose" to "return" home, creating "entirely new dynamics within the South Asian diaspora." Yet as Rana points out, this is a racialized, gendered, and imperial take on "return" migration, as it is anchored in a fear of carceral terror and chosen as a strategy to avoid having to undergo the humiliation and distress of lengthy detentions or forcible detentions. Rana's gendered analysis attends to the way that the male Muslim body is differentially located in diaspora, subject to the state's processes of "voluntary" return and removal.

To use Lowe's terms, these diasporic communities are heterogeneous, multiply defined and hybrid—whether they are rooted, mobile, or a combination thereof. Even as the migratory flows follow racialized patterns, there is a strongly gendered inflection to who migrates and how these bodies are subject to regulatory mechanisms. Cases of individuals' such as queer and nonnormative subjects seeking asylum, have prompted new lines of inquiry in diaspora studies that have linked gendered analyses of law, legal studies, and migration. Sexual asylum, and its global impact on national immigration laws, is a new and still largely uncharted legal terrain. Within the national context of the United States, scholars and legal activists have focused their efforts in three areas: immigration law, political asylum cases, and judicial court rulings. Internationally, activists, lawyers, and scholars have sought to unearth the material and legal ramifications of the Universal Declaration of Human Rights (1948) and Convention on Refugees (1951), both ratified by the United Nations and formative in the construction of international law.

Queer Diasporas

Emerging at the complex intellectual interstices and fecund intersections of diasporas, gender, and queer studies, the scholarly contributions of myriad theorists have cultivated queer diasporic studies, an area that has been largely (though not exclusively) defined by historical, cultural, or qualitative methods—rather than quantitative methods and analyses. These theorists have emerged from multiple disciplines and interdisciplinary spaces and have drawn on diverse methodological approaches in forging queer diasporic studies. Some of the most important critical work has come from within the field of Asian American diaspora studies. In this section, we provide an overview of the primary contributions of three key critical scholars whose work has most shaped debates around the critical use of the terms *queer* and *diaspora*. To briefly summarize some of the major issues in the field of queer diasporic studies as it interfaces with gender studies, we discuss the contributions of David L. Eng, Gayatri Gopinath, and Martin Manalansan. Their theorizations of "queer diaspora" complicate the interrelated terrains of nonheteronormative practices and international migrations, raising important critiques of both the heterosexual framings of diasporic studies and the nationalist (i.e., US) framings of queer studies. These queer diasporic theorists have also sought to understand the gendered and sexualized foundations of nations, nationality, and migration, challenging both the heteronormativity of diasporic discourses and the nationalist framing of queer discourses.

David L. Eng argues that "mainstream gay and lesbian scholarship fails to embrace queerness as a critical methodology for the understanding of sexual identity as it is dynamically formed in and through racial epistemologies" (Eng 2001, 218). He also criticizes the paucity of "sustained class-based analyses of racial-formation" in gay and lesbian studies, queer studies, and ethnic studies (218). Similarly, diasporic communities have been challenged by queer individuals for their heteronormativity and patriarchal notions of gender and sexuality. As Eng contends, "the patriarchal complicities" of "cultural nationalist project[s]," including minoritarian counternationalist movements and their "disciplining of the domestic, the[ir] forced repression of feminine and homosexual to masculine, of the home to the nation-state, is a formation in need of queering" (210–211). Eng asks, "How might we invoke a queer and diasporic assumption of the domestic to denaturalize claims on the nation-state and home as inevitable functions of the heterosexual?" (211).

Gayatri Gopinath's (2005) *Impossible Desires: Queer Diasporas and South Asian Public Cultures* is another key text for defining and understanding queer diaspora. Through her individual case studies of South Asian feminist and queer texts, Gopinath dislodges diaspora from the logics of patrilineal nationalism, or what she refers to as the "hegemonic nationalist and diasporic logic"(Gopinath 1997, 266). This alternative account of diaspora renders visible the desires and subjectivities that are deemed impossible and unimaginable within the conventional logic of the heteronormative nation and its hegemonic enforcers in diasporic settings. Taking the idea that the queer is a generative site for cultural and political critique seriously, Gopinath provides a rich context for valuing narratives that would otherwise be deemed "useless" because they are "inauthentic," "impoverished," "impure," or "nonreproductive." The queer, in other words, becomes a critical site through which to reframe diasporic communities as spaces other than places in which the nation-state is simply reproduced anew. This understanding of queer in relation to diaspora has been invaluable to feminist and queer scholars of diaspora in offering alternative maps of belonging and nonbelonging to the nation.

Similarly, Martin Manalansan's (2003) use of the term *diaspora* deprivileges the West as a site of queer liberation while also providing a critical vocabulary for understanding how Filipino gay men in diaspora explain their sexualities. In *Global Divas: Filipino Gay Men in the Diaspora*, Manalansan challenges the idea that the term *gay* describes a universally applicable category. In pointing out the hegemonic nature of white gay culture, which oftentimes aligns categories of gayness with whiteness, Manalansan describes the limitations and biases through which queer studies has positioned a homogeneous, monolithic experience for gay men. In his work, Manalansan suggests that diaspora is often only evoked as an endpoint that would position the West as a site of queer liberation. As he notes, the work of "new queer studies" (informed by perspectives of diaspora and globalization) and what would now be part of a queer-of-color critique owes a large debt to the work of feminist scholars who challenged the universality of the category of "woman." As an anthropologist, Manalansan considers how the term *diaspora* complicates queer studies through grounded ethnographic fieldwork.

Global Divas insists on the relevance of critical lexicons of queerness that account for lived realities structured by citizenship, immigration and localized narratives of sexuality. Manalansan rejects the notion of a universal gay male identity that is structured toward a telos of "coming out." Instead, he argues that the identity of the *bakla* that circulates among Filipino gay men in the diaspora is not simply a phase through which men pass before becoming properly enfranchised gay subjects. Attentive to the heterogeneous definitions of queerness, Manalansan (2003, 186) argues that "*bakla* is not a prior condition before assimilating into a gay identity. Rather, *bakla* is equally a modern sense of self that inhabits or dwells in the queer sites of the global city. Filipino gay men recuperate the *bakla* ideology as a way to survive and even flourish within the racial, ethnic, class, and gendered spaces of America."

All of these works add important dimensions to diaspora studies. But they also challenge queer theory for not fully attending to issues of nation, gender, and race. Early queer scholars, activists, and communities were challenged for racial, national, class-based, and gender normative assumptions by working-class or poor queers, transgender queers, intersexed queers, female-to-male (FTM) and male-to-female (MTF) transsexuals, queers of color, and diasporic queers. These perspectives, informed by diaspora and ethnic studies continue to develop in queer-of-color critique. Yet even as interlocutory fields, particularly in ethnic studies, have helped to articulate questions about sexuality, gender and nation within diaspora studies, they also (as in the case of indigenous studies) have provided important critiques of the term *diaspora* and its apparent reification of the idea of the nation-state. In her essay "Queer Theory and Native Studies: The Heteronormativity of Settler Colonialism," Andie Smith is critical of assertions that a "queer diasporic framework productively exploits the analogous relation between nation and diaspora on the one hand, and between heterosexuality and queerness on the other" (Gopinath 2005, 51). In other words, the nation is seen as the site of heterosexuality as the diaspora and the transnational function as the liberatory space open to queer subjects. In such a framework, Smith suggests the "nation" emerges as a monolithic construction. Smith argues that this framework, in which the diasporic subject is read as the fractured subject depends on the "ideological disappearance" of the native subject. Consequently, this type of queer diasporic critique can potentially contributing to what Smith labels a "problematic juxtaposition of a simple national identity with a complex diasporic identity" (Smith 2010, 54) In other words, queer diasporic identities are seen as layered, mobile, and complex because of an access to transnational movement, whereas the indigenous subject is seemingly located in a point of stasis—the binary opposite of the mobile transnational diasporic queer.

Recent scholarship that seeks to bridge indigenous studies and diaspora studies suggests that there are productive ways for these two interdisciplinary fields to converge in their related critiques of the neoliberal US state and global racial capital. Following Gopinath's engagement with the critiques of her own work, we suggest that theorizations of diaspora can and must find ways to engage the politics of indigenous sovereignty across the globe, providing a counter narrative to celebratory accounts of migration and dispersal. A group of South Asian Americanists, for example, caution against "invocations of 'diaspora' that fail to engage indigenous critique [and] thereby facilitate ongoing imperial projects that efface claims and enact indigenous sovereignty and autonomy" (Bald et al. 2013). Andie Smith's own generative essay gestures toward the work of Renya Ramirez, who offers a way to put indigenous critique in conversation with Gopinath's work on remaking home (Smith 2010, 55). For urban ethnographer Ramirez, the concept of "home," critically redefined, offers a way to think through urban subjectivities among native peoples who travel to and from reservations to maintain relationships and develop coalitions. Ramirez advocates thinking about new spaces in urban sites as "hubs," and as Smith reminds us, the hub does not privilege the diasporic subject in relation to the non diasporic subject who remains home" (55).

Among the most important interventions of queer diaspora studies is the refusal to reify the notion of home, nation, or diaspora (Braziel 2008; Mannur 2010). With feminism's systematic commitment to revisiting ideas of home and domesticity, queer diasporic studies have made more strides in challenging the patriarchal logic of diaspora. It has achieved this by rendering it possible to imagine nonheteronormative subjects and nonpatrilineal logics to define diaspora and migration. The deep investment in home, so central to "diaspora" thus meets its challenge in feminist studies of diaspora. Where earlier scholars implicitly structure homologies between the "homeland" and the "home" based on a logic of patrilineality and filial loyalty, feminist and queer scholars such as the ones discussed earlier, challenged the inherently gendered bias of this logic. The diasporic home is a site riven with anxieties precisely because it is expected to produce gendered citizens of the "home nation" (Gopinath 2005; Mannur 2010). Nonetheless, feminist cultural producers who remain vigilant about challenging the patriarchal logic of diaspora repeatedly deploy their cultural aesthetic and political vision to destabilize the notion that the ideas of "home" and "nation" are stable entities. Indeed, it is through the rigorous queer feminist reworkings of diaspora that this notion has systematically been upended, giving rise to a vision of diaspora studies that equally attends to the issues of privilege wrapped up in mobility, staying in place, and forced mobility.

Conclusion

In this chapter, we have followed critical feminism's lead, foregrounding the disorderly intersections of diaspora, nationalism, transnationalism, race, gender, and sexuality. Although the term *diaspora* has a long and contentious history, it has only been with the rise of gender studies and queer studies that the raced and gendered dimensions of immigration and diasporic movement have come to light. While early thought in diaspora studies implicitly adhered to a masculinist ideal of the nation, subsequent theorizations of nation and diaspora have emphasized the impure origins of the nation itself, demonstrating that the term *diaspora* as well as diasporic movements must be situated in alternative lineages and futures.

Feminist scholars of diaspora have called attention to the ways that the war on terror and the politics of deportation have shaped the debates around diaspora. Feminist and critical ethnic studies scholars have criticized the acritical use of the term *diaspora*, questioning the imperialist foundations of the nation-state itself. Indigenous studies, South Asian and black Atlantic diasporic studies have been vibrant intellectual spaces that rigorously attend to historically situated and critical understandings of diaspora. The call for a more critical diaspora studies that is attentive to the issues and exigencies outlined in this chapter is not new. Theorizations of diaspora are not simply singular and fixed spaces, but in constant flux. The work of critical diaspora studies, and feminist articulations of diaspora studies in particular, is to contest and challenge the meanings of diaspora—not just by mapping the forms of movement, but also by attending to the politics of movement and the politics of staying in place. Understanding how nation-states institutionalize policies and practices of detaining those seeking political refuge, racializing some as undesirables because of their nations of origin—is part of the implicit charge of critical diaspora studies. But so is examining the politics of "staying put." As we have argued elsewhere, diaspora is not equivalent to migration. And as

Braziel notes, "While older models of diaspora are generally configured as deracination and uprooting, newer models need to account for multiple affiliations and points of belonging" (Braziel 2008, 15). It is only with a new form of mapping in critical diaspora studies, one that accounts for the relation of imperial power to statehood and regimes of sexuality and bodily citizenship, that the term will continue to retain theoretical and political efficacy.

REFERENCES

Bald, Vivek, Miabi Chatterji, Sujani Reddy, and Manu Vimalassery. 2013. *The Sun Never Sets: South Asian Migrants in an Age of U.S. Power*, Kindle edition. New York: New York University Press.

Braziel, Jana Evans, and Anita Mannur, eds. 2003. *Theorizing Diaspora*. London: Wiley-Blackwell.

Braziel, Jana Evans. 2008. *Diaspora: An Introduction*. London: Wiley-Blackwell.

Cvetkovich, Ann. 2012. *Depression: A Public Feeling*, Kindle edition. Durham, NC: Duke University Press.

Dayan, Joan. 1996. "Paul Gilroy's Slaves, Ships and Routes: The Middle Passage as Metaphor." *Research in African Literatures* 27 (4): 7–14.

Edwards, Brent Hayes. 2007. "Diaspora" in *Keywords for American Cultural Studies*, edited by Bruce Burgett and Glenn Hendler, 81–84. New York: New York University Press.

Eng, David. 2001. *Racial Castration: Managing Masculinity in Asian America*. Durham, NC: Duke University Press.

Gilroy, Paul. 1995. *The Black Atlantic: Modernity and Double Consciousness*. Cambridge, MA: Harvard University Press.

Gopinath, Gayatri. 1995. "'Bombay, U.K. Yuba City': Bhangra Music and the Engendering of Diaspora." *Diaspora* 4 (3): 303–322.

Gopinath, Gayatri. 1997. "Nostalgia, Desire, Diaspora: South Asian Sexualities in Motion." *Positions* 5 (2): 467–489.

Gopinath, Gayatri. 2005. *Impossible Desires: Queer Diaspora and South Asian Public Cultures*. Durham, NC: Duke University Press.

Gopinath, Gayatri. 2010. "Archive, Affect and the Everyday: Queer Diasporic Re-visions." In *Political Emotions*, edited by Janet Staiger, Ann Cvetkovich, and Ann Reynolds, 165–192. London: Routledge.

Hartman, Saidiya. 2007. *Lose Your Mother: A Journey Along the Atlantic Slave Route*. New York: Farrar, Strauss and Giroux.

Lowe, Lisa. 1996. "Heterogeneity, Hybridity, Multiplicity: Marking Asian American Differences." In *Immigrant Acts: On Asian American Cultural Politics*. Durham, NC: Duke University Press.

Manalansan, Martin. 2003. *Global Divas: Filipino Gay Men in Diaspora*. Durham, NC: Duke University Press.

Mannur, Anita. 2010. *Culinary Fictions: Food in South Asian Diasporic Culture*. Philadelphia, PA: Temple University Press.

Mehta, Brinda. 2009. *Notions of Identity, Diaspora and Gender in Caribbean Women's Writing*. London: Palgrave Macmillan.

Pinto, Samantha. 2013. *Difficult Diasporas: The Transnational Feminist Aesthetic of the Black Atlantic*. New York: New York University Press.

Rana, Junaid. 2013. "Tracing the Muslim Body: Race, US Deportation and Pakistani Return Migration." In *The Sun Never Sets: South Asian Migrants in an Age of U.S Power*, edited by Vivek Bald, Miabi Chatterji, Sujani Reddy, and Manu Vimalassery, Kindle edition. New York: New York University Press.

Safran, William. 1991. "Diasporas in Modern Societies: Myths of Homeland and Return." *Diaspora: A Journal of Transnational Studies* 1 (1): 83–99.

Smallwood, Stephanie. 2008. *Saltwater Slavery: A Middle Passage from Africa to American Diaspora*. Cambridge: Harvard University Press.

Smith, Andie. 2010. "Queer Theory and Native Studies: The Heteronormativity of Settler Colonialism." *GLQ: A Journal of Gay and Lesbian Studies* 16 (1–2): 42–68.

CHAPTER 9

FORMAL, INFORMAL, AND CARE ECONOMIES

SUZANNE BERGERON

Introduction

This chapter outlines key feminist contributions to the understanding of the contested meanings of formal, informal, and care economies, with an emphasis on the interactions among these spheres. The first section examines feminist efforts at making visible unpaid and feminized household labor, and includes discussion about different ways feminists have conceptualized and accounted for this labor. It also explores some of the tensions around viewing care work, in both its unpaid and paid forms, as a distinctive kind of labor. The second section of the chapter provides an overview of feminist writing on the complex articulations of social reproduction and capitalism, moving from the "domestic labor debates" of the 1960s and 1970s to contemporary analyses of social reproduction and capitalism in contexts of global restructuring. Then, the chapter turns to an account of how feminists have theorized the gendered dynamics of paid work, including a discussion of occupational segregation, feminization of labor, and work/life balance. Finally, the chapter examines the gender aspects of the informalization of paid employment. Throughout the chapter the focus is on the connection between the household, formal, and informal sectors to make sense of the relationship among women's subordinate position in paid labor markets, their roles in social reproduction, the transnational feminization of labor, and the marginalization of care work.

Making Care Work Visible

Feminists have put domestic and caring labor on the economic map, highlighting both the value of unpaid care activities and the need for a broadened view of economic behavior that includes caring motivations. Their analyses of how the sexual division of labor devalues forms of domestic and care work associated with women provides an important corrective to theories that emphasize masculinist notions of formal sector employment as the only valuable labor contribution. Feminist theories have challenged naturalized conceptions of domestic labor, shifted the boundaries of what counts as economic activity, identified the ways that caring labor (in both its unpaid and waged forms) might be distinctive from other forms of work, and examined the complex nexus of unpaid care work and market labor. This has had enormous implications for thinking about households as sites of accumulation and struggle; the constitution of subjects and the role of gender socialization in structuring inequalities; the naturalization of particular forms of work in gendered bodies; the intersection of gender with raced, classed, national, and sexualized social relations of production; and the dynamics through which work in certain sectors of the paid labor market are undervalued.

Before feminist scholars and activists began to mobilize around the issue in the late 1960s and 1970s, the contribution of women's unpaid household work was virtually invisible in economic frameworks across the spectrum. For instance, neoclassical theory limited economic activity to only those goods and services exchanged for money in markets. Further, it assumed that households divided up work and consumption either jointly or through altruistic decisions on the part of the household head, impeding any awareness of power differentials and/or economic exploitation within the household. Neoclassical theory also created little space for recognizing caring motivations in economic activities, for it rested on the assumption that all economic decisions are made by rational, self-interested economic agents (Nelson 2006). The Marxian tradition was also hampered by a failure to assign economic value to unpaid household work that lay outside of market-based commodity production, and neglected the exploitation that existed within the gender division of unwaged household work. In short, economic theories across the board treated household labor—particularly the work of caring for others done primarily by women– as a natural activity motivated by affection, rather than a socially organized form of production and exploitation (Folbre 1995, 2009).

Feminist challenges to this male bias regarding unpaid household labor include multiple strategies and sites of contestation. Early work on this topic was undertaken by Marxist and socialist feminists, who focused on how women's reproductive work supported capitalism by producing labor power on the cheap. Rather than viewing the household as a site where no labor or exploitation occurred—as mainstream Marxism had done—these theorists highlighted the enormous amount of value produced by domestic labor in providing subsistence and reproduction of the laboring class at a low cost, thus enhancing capitalist profitability through the exploitation of women. Housework made an essential, albeit neglected contribution to the economy and feminist strategies focused on making this work visible and valued (Oakley 1974). The "wages for housework" movement, for instance, called for expanding existing notions of work to include unwaged household labor, and demanded that women be compensated for these efforts (Dalla Costa and James 1975). By extending Marxian theories to the domestic realm, this stream of research also highlights the subversive potential of domestic labor struggles for disrupting capitalist accumulation (Federici 2004).

Chipping away at male bias from another side of the political-economic spectrum, feminists have challenged the free-market neoclassical theory of the household, which naturalizes women's reproductive labor and discounts its value to the economy (Ferber 1987). Neoclassical theory presents households as providers of market labor and as sites of consumption, with only minor recognition of how the household itself functions as a site of production (Ferber and Nelson 1993). When it does take household production into account, it fails to see the division of labor as an inequitable arrangement. For instance, Gary Becker's (1991) influential theory of the household contends that it is more efficient for women to specialize in care work because of their biological function of reproduction. He further contends that this division of labor is the outcome of harmonious decision-making within the family.

In response to this, feminist research has focused on denaturalizing the organization of production within households, contending that what is presented in economics as a natural and universal household form is in fact produced and contingent. Nancy Folbre has shown, for instance, that the division of labor in the North Atlantic in the late nineteenth and early 20th centuries, in which women specialize in domestic work and are relegated to the private sphere, was not inevitable and universal but rather a socially, historically and politically determined outcome (Folbre 1991). Feminist economists have also criticized neoclassical theory's assumption of household harmony, replacing it with a theory of the household as a potential locus of struggle. For instance, as an alternative to mainstream accounts, many feminists have embraced a bargaining model of the household that can take conflict, cooperation and unequal power dynamics into account (e.g., Sen 1990; Agarwal 1997). Since the 1990s, this model has gained significant traction within economics. While it has not replaced Becker's model entirely, it has increasingly been used to frame policies aimed at shifting women's bargaining power and household divisions of labor. The model has even been taken up by development institutions such as the World Bank in attempts to resolve inequitable gender divisions of labor in the global South (see World Bank 2001, 2012).

Feminist scholarship has also brought attention to the ways the unpaid production undertaken by women figures prominently in household subsistence, resistance and survival strategies in the context of capitalist development (Boserup 1970; Tilly and Scott 1978; Nash and Fernandez-Kelly 1983). For example, Ester Boserup's pioneering research highlights the central role of women in subsistence food and cash crop production in Africa and Southeast Asia. Others have identified women's household production as a form of resistance to the penetration of commodity relations in the developing economies (Nash and Fernandez-Kelly 1983; Deere 1976).

Critiquing the invisibility of unpaid work in official macroeconomic and development statistics such as gross domestic product (GDP) has been yet another strategy to put unpaid domestic work and care on the economic map (Waring 1989; Benería 1992). The failure to count unpaid household and subsistence agricultural labor in GDP and other statistical accounts contributes to gender inequality across the globe. While men do engage in unpaid domestic activities, statistically speaking the disproportionate share of care labor, raising crops for family consumption, and other household tasks is done by women. This is no small issue, for such work amounts to between 10 percent to 50 percent of a nation's economic activity, depending on the country in question (Budlender 2008). Feminist research has drawn attention to the policy implications of failing to acknowledge this unpaid care work. An extensive literature dating back to the 1980s, for instance, has theorized and documented the ways that macroeconomic restructuring programs in global South contexts—by cutting state supports for child care, eldercare, food subsidies, and health services—have increased the unpaid labor burdens of women, making them the "shock absorbers" of economic crisis (Elson 1991; Bakker 1994).

Through these interventions, feminists have achieved some success in getting unpaid domestic labor recognized in official statistics. For instance, in 1993 the United Nations extended the definition of work to include such goods as food and handicrafts produced by unpaid workers in households. While many have applauded these efforts at recuperating and counting unpaid work, others, particularly liberal feminists, have worried that valuing domestic and care work only reinforces women's subordinate status and takes the focus away from moving women into the public sphere of money and power (Bergmann 1986; Hirshman 2006). Still others have expressed concern that these new statistical measures push caring labor to the margins by failing to count unpaid services such as child care, eldercare and other such "intangibles." Because the binaries of productive/unproductive, rationality/care, and market/household have structured meaning in these accounts since they were first developed in the 1940s and 1950s, the reluctance to value unpaid caring services is not surprising. In fact, some have argued that the only way to have care count is to develop an entirely new conceptual framework outside of the hermetically sealed notion of "economy" that equates value with markets. The alternative "total social organization of labor" approach, for instance, eliminates the duality of household/market and care/commerce entirely by emphasizing the interconnections between paid and unpaid economic activities, particularly how care work supports and makes possible other type of economic activity (Glucksmann 1995).

The Affective Component of Unpaid Care Work

In addition to these efforts to make unpaid domestic and care work visible as an economic activity, a rich feminist literature has emerged around the concept of caring labor as distinctive from other forms of work both inside and outside the household.

Early on, feminist economic analyses of unpaid domestic work noted that care is a different sort of activity compared to other forms of household production. For example, while other unpaid activity, such as cleaning and laundry, can be shifted to the market without a dramatic change in their quality, caring for the emotional needs of vulnerable populations such as children and the elderly is qualitatively different (Nelson 2013). Care activities are distinct because they require affective interactions, and the quality of care is at least in part determined by the quality of relationships between the givers and receivers of care (England and Folbre 1999). Work associated with such motivations is, however, devalued in an economic sense, in part because "caring about" is thought to be its own reward, done out of love and obligation. Further, such work is devalued because it is associated with women in a society that values masculine-coded activities over feminine ones (England and Folbre 1999). Through numerous case studies, feminists have shown that assumptions about the affective component of caring labor have resulted in devaluation of both women and men who are involved in such activities in their unpaid and paid forms (England et al. 2002).

The strand of feminist economic theorizing that views care work as distinctive does not assume that women are carers because of any natural or biological disposition toward caring affect and connection. Rather, it argues that women are more likely than men to be involved in care work that is motivated by affection and altruistic (rather than self-interested) feelings because of social hierarchies and socialization processes within the existing sex/gender system (Ferber and Nelson 1993). However, there is less reflection within feminist economics on the dilemma of challenging the "masculine" economic motivations of the market by privileging a notion of "feminized" caring affect as its other (Hewitson 1999). When this work is taken up in policy circles, it is often accompanied by troubling gender essentialisms. Gender and development interventions by institutions such as the World Bank and International Monetary Fund (IMF), for instance, call for investing in specifically gendered "rational economic *women*" who are more caring when compared to their male counterparts, and thus more likely to spend their earnings on their children's education and health (Rankin 2001). Such understandings of women's caring affect rely on an assumption regarding women's socialized roles in presumed nuclear heterosexual households, in which women are as more likely to care for the children than are their male partners. This not only recirculates gender and hetero-normativities, but it draws attention away from the practices and needs of what is actually a diversity of household arrangements. Thus it severely restricts the space for care to broaden its meaning to include transgender, same-sex, single-parent households, extrafamiliar networks and others (Lind 2009; Bergeron 2009a). When used in a global South context, these frameworks also tend to contrast the particularly caring nature of poor brown women with the "profligate," uncaring attitudes of their counterpart men of color, thus reproducing class, race, and colonial hierarchies (Hart 1997).

Paid Care Work: The Commodification of Emotional, Affective, and Intimate Labor

Feminist analyses of the affective component of care work are not limited to the sphere of the household. They also include a focus on gender and the affective nature of paid employment. Key contributions include Arlie Hochschild's concept of "emotional labor," expected of (mostly women) workers in the service industry to make clients feel cared for (Hochschild 1983). Hochschild raises concern about how the performances of affect at work alienate female workers from their own authentic feelings. Michael Hardt, drawing on socialist feminist theory, also offers a concept of "affective labor" as constituting domestic care work that is "outside" capitalist values, and in a vein similar to Hochschild's, signals a warning regarding increased manipulations of affective labor to enhance profitability in neoliberal capitalism (Hardt 1999). Others highlight the specificities of contemporary care work in their analysis of what they term "intimate labor"—including care for loved ones; health and hygiene maintenance, such as nail services and massage; and even bearing children for others—all of which have become increasingly commodified in contemporary neoliberal and globalized contexts (Boris and Parreñas 2010). The concept of intimate labor expands care work to include such activities as forms of sex work that may involve the sale and purchase of not just a sexual release but nonsexual forms of commoditized, bounded intimacy and affective relations.

As all of the forms of work that fall under the various labels of care, emotional, affective and/or intimate labor are increasingly being produced within the market, there is some worry about the effects of commodification. Are markets, caring feelings and caring activities at odds with each other? What is to be lost when mixing love and money? There are some liberal feminists (e.g., Bergmann 1986) who do not view household activities as qualitatively different from goods and services produced in markets, and in fact favor the commodification of tasks traditionally assigned to women. But many feminist economists, sociologists, and philosophers highlight differences in the two spheres, and the negative consequences of relying on care received through a monetized transaction in which market rationality holds sway, rather than care freely and authentically given in the context of personal relationships in the family/household. For example, feminist economist Susan Himmelweit (1995) has argued that care is best produced outside market norms because it is based on and fosters relationships and emotional attachment, while market labor is characterized by detachment. Others, as discussed earlier, have raised concerns about the dissonance that the providers of emotional/affective labor experience when they are obligated to produce a particular sort of affect as a condition of paid employment. Arlie Hochschild and Barbara Ehrenreich (2003) have also drawn attention to another danger regarding care's commodification in a global context. Examining the lives of care workers who migrate to the United States and Europe from places like the Philippines, they foreground the alienation and imperialism that occurs with the transfer of love from the migrant women's own left-behind biological children to their global North charges.

Other feminists, however, have challenged what they view as the essentialism that underwrites the notion of separate spheres in which love and money should not mix. Some note that relations of care have historically revolved around economic considerations (Boris and Parreñas 2010) and that this is not a new phenomenon. Others focus on how the binary framing of love/money and household/market obscures interdependence and the need for connection and care within all realms, including the supposedly rational, detached capitalist sphere (Nelson 2013; Eisler 2008). Still others point to the class, race, and heteronormative commitments that locate care work as something ideally produced outside the market. Feminist work in this vein has examined the historical association of these tasks with lower-status poor, women of color, and/or immigrant populations. Drucilla Barker and Susan Feiner (2009), for example, challenge the separation of the realms of love and money by feminist economists, pointing to the lingering impact of nineteenth-century ideologies of private/public that relegated care to the province of the family, where elite white women became the face of social reproduction. While the nurturing qualities of working class and women of color were certainly acknowledged and drawn upon during that period, the forms of care they provided—usually associated with tasks such as cooking and cleaning—were considered inferior to the standards of piety, purity, and domesticity that were the province of elite women as the ideal carers. Thus, the paid care work undertaken largely by immigrant and working-class women, including women of color, was and continues to be stigmatized. To argue that care work being provided for money is inferior, Barker and Feiner argue, demeans the work and reinforces the low status and wages of those who do it.

Along similar anti-essentialist lines, Martin Manalansan (2008) challenges the heteronormative attachments that have naturalized the link between the "authentic" feelings of women and care work. Specifically, he takes on Hochschild and Ehrenreich's global chain-of-care paradigm and its displacement of migrant women's care labor as a dislocation and colonial reappropriation of normative maternal affection. Manalansan shows this narrative to be reinscribing rather than challenging gender norms and expectations, and raises concern about the variety of forms of care that are pushed to the margins because they do not fit the heteronorm and its attendant naturalized gender ideologies. These forms of care include the child care provided by the fathers of the children left behind by migrant mothers, which is too often assumed away by colonial, heteronormative and gender-normative understandings of these men as profligate nonnurturers. It also includes the paid care services provided by a whole range of what he terms "queer creatures," such as women without maternal instincts, gay men, and transpersons. Further unsettling this link between motherhood and authentic caring, Manalansan draws on the experiences of transgender care workers in Israel to highlight the performative aspects of care and also to draw attention to the contradictory and contested aspects of gender, care work, and affect. Studies such as Denise Brennan's (2004) research on how Dominican sex workers' relationships with their Western clients involve complex negotiations of emotion and money also disrupts binaries of authentic/inauthentic, domestic/market, love/money, and care/not care.

Another anti-essentialist approach to caring labor emphasizes processes of economic subjectification that occur within economic processes, thus unsettling binaries of women as carers and men as more detached. For example, in her case studies of households in Australia, Jenny Cameron (2000) highlights the heterogeneity of domestic labor relations that contribute to the production of a wide variety of gendered divisions of labor, and economic subjectivities, with regard to care work. Stephen Healy, in his analysis of eldercare in the United States, also contends that caring affect is not natural and pre-given, but produced in specific contexts. His research suggests that when care is devalued, workers often revert to languages and practices of self-interest. But when care work is supported and valued, there is a greater possibility for the economic subjectivities of these workers to include an affective dimension of connection and care. Healy points to the radical potential of these emerging subjects of economy, as care and connection are oppositional to capitalist ideals of detachment and self-interest (Healy 2008).

While only a handful of political economy scholars are researching affect and caring labor through such an explicitly poststructural lens, feminist scholarship is increasingly moving away from articulating care work in terms of its producers' genuine affection and nurturance. There are a number of reasons for this. As Barker and Feiner discuss, emphasis on "genuine feelings" has metaphorically restricted the concept of care to the domestic sphere, making it a private issue rather than a public one. It has also reinforced heteronormative gender roles and family forms, and has propped up, rather than exposed, racialized devaluations of care in the marketplace (Barker and Feiner 2009; see also Bergeron 2009b). These concerns, and the economic and household restructuring that has taken place globally over the past few decades, in which care work is increasingly being provided to those in the global North by poor and migrant women and men, has shifted feminist inquiry. Care work, despite its great importance to livelihoods, remains largely excluded from state policies that might support it, and even paid domestic laborers are not afforded the regulatory protections given to other workers in most countries. Key issues include the fact that some bodies on the global stage call forth relations of care while others elicit relations of neglect (Vaittinen 2014), and the paradox that the very persons who create agreeable surroundings that allow others to thrive are themselves increasingly dehumanized (Gutiérrez-Rodríguez 2007).

Feminist Approaches to Articulations between Care and Capitalist Spheres

Feminist analyses of the contributions and distinctiveness of domestic and care work have not simply added unpaid labor to existing economic activities: they have transformed understandings of how the economy as a whole functions. Much of this analysis is focused on the relationship between unpaid reproductive labor and capitalist production. This section of the chapter presents an overview of key feminist insights regarding these articulations. It starts with the socialist-feminist domestic labor debates and then turns to a discussion of the contradictions that exist between liberalization and social reproduction in contemporary contexts of global economic restructuring.

From the late 1960s to the 1980s, Marxist and socialist feminists were teasing out the relationship between capitalist production and social reproduction in structuring women's oppression. In contrast to approaches that viewed women's subordination as outside the market, these theorists viewed capitalism as playing an enormous role. This substantial and wide-ranging body of work is often referred to under the heading of the "domestic labor debates." Two interrelated questions were the subject of these debates. The first of these was whether household work is measurable in ways that are commensurate with paid labor, and particularly whether surplus value was produced by domestic activities. Another key area of disagreement had to do with the relative autonomy of the household economy vis-à-vis capitalism and the interrelated issue of whether patriarchy or capitalism was the primary determinant of women's subjugation.

On one side were those who viewed the household form of labor as largely determined by capitalism. These theorists highlighted the profitability of relying on women's household labor as a lower-cost method to provide the meals, cleaning, childrearing, and emotional support for reproducing the labor power of both the adult male worker and future generations of workers, illuminating the enormous amount of value that unpaid household production generated for the capitalist system. Unlike orthodox Marxism, which imagined patriarchy to be a feudal holdover that would be eliminated by capitalism's drive to find new sources for profit by commodifying the use values formerly produced by women in households, feminists identified a symbiosis between the two systems. In another break with Marxist orthodoxy, feminist theorists viewed the exploitation of women's labor in terms on par with that of the exploitation of the proletariat, contending that household labor produced surplus that benefited capital. Much of the debate within this strand of feminism was whether women's production in households was analogous to capitalist production, and if so, whether one could extend Marxian measures of value and surplus value extraction to it (e.g., Delphy 1980; Seccombe 1974; Gardiner 1975).

Placing domestic labor entirely inside of a capitalist logic, however, fails to answer why women are oppressed specifically as *women*. As Heidi Hartmann notes in her classic essay on the unhappy marriage of Marxism and feminism, it is not only capitalists who benefit from women's household labor but also the men who receive these goods and services in the home (Hartmann 1981). Hartmann and others posit the household as a separate mode of noncapitalist production in which gender, not class, is central, and men, not capitalists, are the chief exploiters. Integrating insights from both the radical feminist analysis of patriarchy and Marxist class analysis, they advocate for a dual systems approach to give weight to both patriarchal and capitalist modes of production. Conceptualizing two separate spheres of economic activity, each with its own logic, led to further debate over whether class notions of value can be applied to household production. Most writing in the dual-spheres tradition contends that women's labor is neither analogous nor reducible to market production and thus not measurable in those terms (e.g., Himmelweit and Mohun 1977).

Positing capitalism as a space of detached relations and class exploitation, and the household as one of connection and patriarchal subjugation, dual systems approaches emphasized the tensions and contradictions between the two spheres. To what extent might the requirements of profitability of capitalists be at odds with the requirements necessary to sustain patriarchal relations in the household? Might the drive to accumulate rend the very relations of sociality in the households on which the reproduction of the labor force, and thus capitalism itself, depends?

Crucially, a number of feminist theorists asked if women's location "outside" capitalism provided critical standpoints and alternative knowledges that created possibilities for women to become oppositional forces to both capitalism and patriarchy. As Nancy Hartsock (1983) argued, women's relegation to the reproductive sphere offered them an opportunity to develop a unique standpoint based on their role as carers undertaking relational work in a world that only values detached exchange. Capitalism, though premised on commodification and alienation, depends for its existence on noncommodified social and economic relations. Being located at the crossroads of the relations of alienation and destruction that govern capitalism, on the one hand, and in systems of connection and reproductive labor that are so essential to capitalism's functioning, on the other, potentially makes the contradictions more apparent. Thus women's unique location in economic spaces outside the logic of capitalism (even if articulated with it) might, under certain conditions, allow for the development of oppositional anticapitalist subjectivities. But the idea that women's oppositional standpoint is grounded in a separate spheres approach has also been criticized for contributing to the dualistic thinking that naturalizes gender difference (Haraway 1988). (See the chapter on Standpoint Theory in this volume).

Further, a question remained as to whether capitalism and patriarchy could be considered separate, albeit articulating, systems when to so many feminists it seemed that gender subordination was foundational to the functioning of capitalism itself (Young 1981). Dual systems theorists such as Hartmann, for instance, represented the capitalist system as in itself "sex-blind" (Hartmann 1981, 8). This is at odds with feminist perspectives on capitalism as dependent in its very existence upon the unpaid care work of women in households (Young 1981; see also Mies et al. 1988; Federici 2004). Others queried dual systems theory's universalizing representations of the patriarchal household as the primary site of women's oppression. For instance, Gloria Joseph called into question the dual system's notion of patriarchy in which women as a monolithic group stand in a similar subordinated position to all men. Because of racism, she argued, all black men in the United States surely did not have power over all white women (Joseph 1981). Along similar lines, others pointed out that some groups—such as white, nonimmigrant men in industrial production—were more likely than others to be paid a family wage on which the male-breadwinner/female dependent theory of household production in dual systems theory rests (Molyneux 1979).

Other interventions into the domestic labor debates extended and reformulated dual systems theories by positing the existence and articulation of a diversity of class forms in the economy. Fraad, Resnick, and Wolff (1994), for example, use class analysis to present a picture of economic difference in which there can be multiple forms of both household and market production in a complexly constituted economic system. While acknowledging that the dominant form of household in the United States may be a traditional patriarchal (what they term "feudal") arrangement, they also identify households characterized by class processes, such as communal (joint) ownership and decision-making, single adults who produce for themselves, and so forth. This focus on a variety of possible class processes, which are relatively autonomous from capitalist class processes, and for which capitalism is not determinant, challenges both singular-logic and dual-logic explanations for the exploitation of women's labor. It also creates further space for examining interactions and contradictions among the mix of class processes that structure women's oppression.

But by the late 1980s, there was waning interest in the domestic labor debates in feminist theory circles. For one thing, the abstractions involved in analyzing necessary and surplus labor, forms of appropriation, circuits of production, and the like, were at odds with the complexities of concrete historical analysis and issues of agency and subjectivity that were increasingly informing feminist theories (Vogel 2000). In addition, the 1980s were characterized by economic restructuring. For example, in the North Atlantic there was a decline of Fordist industrialism and a corresponding expansion of the service sector. This increasingly blurred the distinctions between the production of commodities and the production of people, along with binaries of market/household and capitalism/reproduction on which domestic labor theories rest (Weeks 2007). Further, global restructuring transformed the nature of domestic labor and social reproduction. The declining dominance of the male-breadwinner household and nuclear-family form, rising global women's labor force participation, increased labor migration and global householding, and other factors contributed to the emergence of other ways of thinking through the relationship between capitalism and caring labor.

Specifically, there was a shift away from the framework of the domestic labor debates toward a broader concept of social reproduction to capture the reproduction of the labor force on both a daily basis and across generations, meeting the caring needs for children, adults, and even necessary care of the self (Marchand and Runyan 2000; Bakker and Gill 2003). The meaning of *social reproduction* expanded from the earlier conceptualization of that term by socialist feminists in the 1970s and 1980s—as the unpaid domestic labor undertaken by women that underpins capitalist accumulation—to include its production in a variety of sites including unpaid household contexts and the capitalist marketplace (Nakano Glenn 1992; Bakker 2007). It also breaks with the narrow economism of some earlier socialist feminist theorizing, which typically imagined reproduction as unwaged housework and did not include the creation and sustaining of social relations (Weeks 2007). As Evelyn Nakano Glenn states,

> The term social reproduction has come to be more broadly conceived to refer to the creation and recreation of people as cultural, social and physical beings. Thus it involves mental, emotional and manual labor. This labor can be organized in myriad ways—in and out of the household, as paid or unpaid work, creating exchange value or only use value ... It can be done by a family member as unwaged work in the household, by a servant as waged work in the household, or by a short-order cook in a fast-food restaurant as waged work that generates profit.
>
> (Nakano Glenn 1992, 4)

Contemporary analysis of articulations between capitalism and social reproduction defined in these terms highlights the gender inequities of neoliberal economic restructuring since the 1980s. State supports for social reproduction such as aid for dependent children, healthcare, basic food, education, and the like, have eroded, and tensions associated with relying solely on unpaid care work and marketized means of meeting these needs have become more pronounced (Bakker 2007). Tracing out these effects in a developing-country context, Diane Elson moves beyond the dual spheres approach to examine interactions between three sectors of the economy: public (state), private (market), and domestic (unpaid social reproduction), showing how changes in one sphere affect the others. Elson places particular emphasis on how the logics of both the state and market are based on biased assumptions about gender and the domestic sphere that affect all three sectors. Governments cut support for child care and healthcare, assuming these services will be picked up by women in households. This "exhaustion solution" often results in women working a double or even triple day, thus depleting reproductive labor. The household's ability to supply a productive labor force to the market is threatened by this depletion, and declining health, educational attainment, and nutrition result in an erosion of human capital that can interfere with capitalist efficiency and profitability (Elson 2000). Social-reproductive depletion also occurs when economic restructuring policies emphasize marketization and export promotion. In the cases where formerly nontradable goods (such as food) become exports and women's labor is less available to produce nonmarket commodities, social reproduction diminishes and becomes less available to poor households (Hoskyns and Rai 2007).

V. Spike Peterson (2003) has also expanded beyond the dual spheres approach, utilizing a tripartite reproductive, productive, and virtual (RPV) framing of the economy. RPV weaves together the conceptual and material dimensions of gender and economy, connecting understandings of social reproduction with the changing, increasingly flexibilized productive economy and the virtual economy of financial markets, commodified knowledge, and symbols. One goal of the RPV remapping is to denaturalize global political economy. Rather than take the market economy as a disembedded, gender-neutral, extra-discursive given, Peterson emphasizes how the conceptual, cultural, and material are mutually constituted. She also employs RPV to investigate issues in contemporary neoliberalism through an interpretive lens, one that views gender as a symbolic code as opposed to a set of empirical categories. For instance, commodification may shift tasks such as care for children and the elderly away from households and into markets, but still maintains the devaluation of this work within feminized conceptualizations of reproductive labor.

Peterson's interpretive, post-positivist approach to understanding the dynamics between social reproduction and capitalism connects to what the feminist geographer J. K. Gibson-Graham (2006) refers to as an "ontological project" of feminist political economy. That is, the manner in which we represent the economy discursively constructs its very object. Gibson-Graham critiques what she terms the "capitalocentric" approach of those who represent the economy as a space of invariant capitalist logic that determines all outcomes. Feminist theorizing about social reproduction challenges capitalocentric thinking by highlighting historically devalued forms of caring and domestic labor, thereby opening space in which to imagine the economy as a site of cohabitation among economic forms. But too often, feminist theory is more fixated on adding in reproductive labor to the capitalist system to get a more complete picture of the logical workings of the whole, rather than on viewing capitalist, household production and other economic activities as a diversity of practices empty of any overarching logic. To the extent that feminists engage in such thinking, they are contributing to a practice of naturalizing the economy as something "outside" society rather than something that is produced by, and productive of, subjects (Gibson-Graham 2008). Gibson-Graham explicitly emphasizes economic difference to signify the possibility for enacting post-capitalist alternatives. For example, rather than presenting the superexploitation of women as an inevitability of contemporary crises of capitalism, Gibson-Graham highlights the unevenness of these processes. While it is true that some households may be squeezed in terms of increased production of social-reproductive labor, and others may intensify patriarchal forms of exploitation, other households may also be transformed to more egalitarian structures, while still others may turn away from capitalist and/or patriarchal relations to create alternative paid and unpaid ways of meeting care needs, such as through cooperatives and gift economies. Maliha Safri and Julie Graham's research on global households, for instance, highlights the emergence of communal householding among Mexican men who have migrated to the United States (Safri and Graham 2010). They also point to the erosion of gender hierarchical relations as women participate more in decision-making and the divisions of labor shift when the men return home (see also Kunz 2011).

To sum up this section of the chapter: there is a rich history of lively feminist debate on the nature of the relationship between capitalism and social reproduction, and where (or whether) to draw boundaries between the two spheres. Some have located social-reproductive labor inside capitalism proper, as a way to highlight its centrality to class struggles and to build coalitions across feminist and socialist movements. Others have emphasized social reproduction's space on capitalism's exterior, where—in varying combinations—it is viewed as a space to develop oppositional subjectivities in a location outside of capitalism, and/or evidence of the far reach of capital to manipulate economic and social processes in every corner of society. Recent rounds of economic restructuring, beginning with the decline of industry in the North Atlantic and shift away from state-led development in the global South in the 1970s and 1980s, and more recent restructurings related to the global financial crisis in the early twenty-first century, have shifted the boundaries between these two spheres. There has been a simultaneous privatization of social reproduction due to cuts in state support and a commodification of social-reproductive labor through expanded markets for care and domestic services. These shifts, combined with feminist efforts to foster gender equity, have changed both households and markets dramatically. Feminist attention to the contradictions of social reproduction and capitalism that arise in these contexts continue to yield vital critical insights regarding both the impact of these contradictions on women's and men's lives and the spaces that emerge for challenging and transforming oppressive economic structures.

Gender and Formal Labor Market Participation

In addition to illuminating gendered experiences in the household, feminist analyses of the articulations between capitalist production and social reproduction have been essential to understanding gendered operations and outcomes in formal labor markets. This section of the chapter examines those ideas in the context of the interconnected issues of the rise of women's participation in labor markets and the global feminization of formal employment.

Global labor market restructuring during the past fifty years has been a deeply gendered process. There has been an increased integration of women into the formal labor since 1970, from 45 percent to approximately 60 percent of women participating in the labor force in the OECD countries (OECD 2011) and with varying levels of change in the global South totaling approximately 2 percent on average, with the largest increase of over 10 percent in Latin America and the Caribbean (World Bank 2012). There has also been a feminization of work globally across all sectors of the economy: export processing industries, service sector work, and agricultural production.

There are many different feminist understandings of how women's integration into formal labor markets is implicated in gender and other systems of power and privilege. The assumptions of liberal feminism regarding the general merits of capitalism have led many over the past fifty years to see market work as empowering for women. On this view, the confines of domestic life limit women's freedom, while paid labor provides women income, choice, and individual autonomy to transcend those limits. Indeed, in certain influential strands of North Atlantic feminist thought, women's individual success in the paid labor force has been more of less conflated with feminist liberation (Fraser 2013). Further, the focus on empowering work has been taken up with zeal in the context of gender and development projects emanating from the World Bank, the United Nations Development Program, the Nike Foundation, and elsewhere. In these institutions, pronouncements that connect women's access to income-generating opportunities in the formal economy to feminist empowerment abound (Cornwall 2014). But as many feminists have demonstrated, arguments that link paid labor and women's empowerment have significant flaws due to the precarious nature of much paid work available to nonelite women, the frequent hyperexploitation of women's market labor, and the fact that for many, paid work is a survival rather than liberation strategy (Charusheela 2003). A study of work and women's empowerment in Bangladesh, Egypt, and Ghana, for instance, shows that women are empowered by paid labor only under increasingly rare conditions of full labor rights in which they control a regular, dependable source of income (Kabeer et al. 2013).

An intersectional analysis showcases the differential and contradictory outcomes vis-à-vis the paid labor market based on lived experiences at the crossroads of gender, sexuality, class, race, ethnicity, and citizenship. Women of color and working-class women in many regions of the world have long worked outside of the home and have not, on balance, viewed this as their path to empowerment. As bell hooks notes, for instance, rather than viewing the market as the liberator from the family as a source of oppression, many women of color in the United States experienced the market as the more hostile and disempowering space (hooks 2000). Globalization and neoliberal restructuring, and the widening inequalities that have accompanied them, have intensified these debates within feminism. The idea that empowerment in the labor market is the way forward, and that gender equality can be achieved as individual women "lean in" to achieve success, is gaining traction in the popular imagination in part because their particular framing of liberation contributes to neoliberal agendas of marketization and privatization (Fraser 2013).

The feminization of work across sectors further challenges the empowerment thesis. In the past few decades, the types of employment typically associated with women—insecure, unstable, nonunionized—have been on the rise. This has had a negative impact on both poor women's and men's labor market experiences and earnings. Further, economic and occupational restructuring has intensified gendered processes of work as they have drawn more women into paid labor. The growing service sector of the economy tends to distinguish between masculinized fields of information technology, and the lower-paid work traditionally defined as feminine, such as cleaning and care work, where women are often concentrated. The feminization of migration has resulted in large percentages of female migrants performing service jobs in the receiving countries. And even within the technology field, women's participation is often segregated into pink collar areas associated with emotional labor, such as overseas call centers (Freeman 2000).

Gender segregation in employment, in which women and men are slotted into feminine- and masculine-coded jobs, respectively, is a worldwide phenomenon. The rise of multinational export manufacturing since the 1970s, for example, has been a deeply gendered labor process. Corporations in the global South specifically recruit women workers for their supposedly natural feminine traits such as "nimble fingers" for sewing and light assembly. Firms also make colonial and gender assumptions that Asian, Latin American, and other global South workers will be more docile and easy to control (Elson and Pearson 1981). Discourses that highlight women's supposedly natural capabilities in these fields tend to discount the skill level of the work. Further, the assumption of a male- breadwinner-household model positions women as secondary or temporary wage earners, regardless of women's actual circumstances. These gender codes work together to result in occupational segregation and exploitation of women's labor.

Feminist explanations of patterns of gender segregation in the labor market are sharply at odds with the mainstream neoclassical theory that guides dominant economic thinking and policy on the subject. According to neoclassical theory, occupational segregation and the gender wage gap are due to women's choices regarding investment in human capital (education and training), career choice, and years of labor market experience. Women are paid less than men, it is argued, because they choose to allocate their time to domestic work rather than paid work and thus have less experience; they don't invest as much in human capital as men: and they choose professions for which they have skills and interest, even if these are less lucrative than other fields (Mincer and Polachek 1974; Becker 1991). As long as men and women have different preferences and different choices, the wage gap will remain (Mincer and Polachek 1974). As many feminist critics point out, this model does not explain the gendered power dynamics behind the unequal division of labor in the household or the market segregation that set many of these patterns of difference into motion in the first place (England and Folbre 1999). The dominant model also fails to see gender as constitutive of economic processes, viewing it as something "outside" the market (Hart 1997).

There has been a decline in occupational segregation and the wage gap in the past few decades, but this is largely due to the global feminization of labor that has made jobs at the bottom of the formal labor market precarious for both women and men. Thus the shrinking gender gap reflects the declining position of men rather than a major improvement in women's condition. Globally, occupational segregation still finds women overrepresented in occupations such as service, sales, education and health, and in lower-level positions. Men tend to be clustered in managerial, industry, legislative, and IT professions and are more likely to be on the upper rungs of the ladder (ILO 2012). This horizontal and vertical gender segregation contributes to a gender pay gap by which, comparing full-time workers, women make between 50 percent to 85 percent of male wages on average, depending on the country in question (ILO 2012).

Mainstream neoclassical explanations fail to capture the ways in which these labor market outcomes are themselves shaped by gendered, raced, and classed assumptions that disadvantage poor women and men, and women and men of color, in the labor market. Gender segregation is not simply due to gendered preferences that direct female and male workers into different occupations, but is something produced at work via managerial and other imperatives. Carla Freeman (2000), for example, highlights the fashioning of femininity through dress codes and other practices in the pink-collar informatics and communications sectors in Barbados. Leslie Salzinger's (2003) comparative study of a range of Mexican export manufacturing firms finds gender being differently constructed in workplace organizations: with some firms encouraging polarized gender binaries in their workers' subjectivities on the shop floor, while others make less of the distinction and downplay differences between men and women. Linda McDowell's (2009) research on the embodied nature of service work in the United Kingdom and the United States shows that gender, class, and ethnic identities are key to explaining divisions of labor and social status in these fields. These feminist theorists and others writing in the same vein emphasize the discursive production of gendered, raced, and classed labor market experiences, highlighting the multiple and contested character of female and male workers' gender subjectivities and the ways gendering processes are implicated in exploitation and resistance simultaneously.

One point of agreement between both champions and critics of paid work as a feminist empowerment strategy is a concern over the tensions between paid and unpaid work and work/life balance. Formal labor market work is typically constructed around a male breadwinner model that assumes there is someone at home taking care of domestic tasks. For liberal feminists, shifting those tasks formerly relegated to the home into the marketplace has historically been one answer to resolving these tensions. Commodifying meals, child care, household chores, and other former activities can free up women's time to participate in labor markets. Further, many argue that turning to the market to replace formerly home-cooked meals or home-produced clothing could increase overall efficiency in the economy, as market systems provide incentives for lowering costs that home production does not (World Bank 2001).

But the question of who precisely takes up this market-based care work to resolve those burdens has been a point of great contention. At the 1975 World Conference on Women in Mexico City, for example, there was a general emphasis within the official conference on emancipating women through insertion into paid labor. The question of who would do the care tasks was addressed, and many were calling for "balanced lives" that would allow women with families to pursue employment. While the initial discussions leaned toward having men accept more responsibility in the home, this idea was quickly dropped for being too radical. The final statement of the conference plan of action recommended the lightening of reproductive responsibilities for women through the development of marketized services. Others at the conference, particularly from the parallel NGO Forum, disagreed with this position on class grounds, stating that it amounted to the emancipation of the mistress requiring the exploitation of the servant (Olcott 2011). Today, these same concerns are at the forefront of feminist debates. The solution of commodified care may mean that only those women with greater resources will be able to afford it. Further, given intersecting gender, race, class, and national hierarchies, it is often poor and immigrant women and/or women of color who are employed in these low paying and devalued positions (Romero 2013). The question of how to relieve the care burdens of those who cannot afford to purchase their way out of them still goes largely unanswered in most countries' public policies, relegating many women to a "double day" of paid and unpaid labor.

In addition to commodification of tasks, another approach to resolving the double day for women in the paid labor force is the restructuring of families so that men take on more domestic responsibilities. Despite feminist attempts in various parts of the world, dating back to the 1960s and 1970s, to promote sharing of tasks—for instance, the political organizing of Redstockings around the politics of housework in the United States (Mainardi 1970) and Bolivian women going on strike in their homes until their husbands did a greater share of domestic work (Barrios de Chungara 1978)—inequalities remain. Cross-national empirical studies show that the gap between women's and men's unpaid labor in heterosexual-couple households is, statistically speaking, diminishing in many places, but the reasons for this have more to do with women's increased labor market participation giving them fewer hours to invest in housework, rather than men stepping up to the plate (World Bank 2012).

This has not gone unnoticed by policymakers, who in some cases are attempting to address the lingering gender inequities at home to free up women's time to participate in the paid labor force. Kate Bedford's study of the World Bank's attempts to reduce women's domestic labor burdens by fostering sharing partnerships between working women and their husbands in Latin America highlights some of the pitfalls of this strategy, however. First, the Bank's solution is located within deeply heteronormative assumptions about households and their gendered arrangements. Given the large number of households around the world that do not fit the presumed norm, this solution does not resolve the care burdens of single-parent, extended-family, and nonheterosexual-partner households. Further, the partnership solution, when applied in the context of development in the global South, counterposes a supposedly modern ideal of egalitarian households in the North against pathologized, colonial representations of households in the global South that need fixing. Third, such a solution is a neoliberal one. It privatizes care work into the sphere of the household in an attempt to reduce the demands on the state to provide such support (Bedford 2009). Finally, the intrahousehold bargaining models discussed earlier assume that once women are inserted into paid labor, their ability to bargain with their husbands to pick up more of the chores at home will increase, thus creating more sharing of tasks. However, the notions that women's empowerment at home can be inferred from their insertion into paid labor and that increased income implies increased bargaining power have not been borne out in actual practice.

Of course, women's position in the formal labor market does affect their life at home, just as household structure, division of labor, women's say in decision-making, societal norms of gendered family roles, and the like, affect women's labor market experiences. But unlike mainstream discourse on the topic, feminist analysis has shown that the outcome of women's participation in the formal labor market is complicated and contextual. Empirical studies show that in some instances women's domestic responsibilities limit their upward mobility in the paid labor market more than in others. In some households a woman's income is belittled, and she has little control over it; whereas in other contexts women have more independence. The insertion of women into gender-coded paid labor sometimes reinforces rather than challenges ideas about the sexual division of labor in the home; but in other cases the opposite is true. Household structure, pay scale, control over fertility, gender ideologies, contours of economic change, state support for care tasks, access to other income-generating opportunities such as cash crop production, and the like, are all key factors in determining women's labor market experiences, including the level of exploitation of women workers in their paid labor and/or reproductive roles (Stichter and Parpart 2013).

To sum up, this section on formal sector work has touched upon the idealization of wage work as a way out of patriarchal exploitation, but has focused much more attention on how these claims regarding "empowering work" have been held in a critical light by a wide variety of feminist researchers. Another major feminist contribution has been to understand the ways that gender—as it intersects with race, class, nationality, sexuality and other forms of difference—is enforced, performed, re-created and revised in formal work settings. Thus rather than imagining firms "reading off" existing identities and slotting them into positions and hierarchies, feminist research has shown that formal workplaces are productive of gender. Finally, this section has emphasized the complex articulations that exist between care and formal economies.

The Informal Economy and the Feminization of Work

The previous discussion of the formal economy made mention of the feminization of labor that begin with processes of economic restructuring in the 1970s, when the types of employment typically associated with women—precarious, unstable, nonunionized, and unregulated—were on the rise. This section of the chapter further examines the ways that these trends are implicated in the expansion of an informal economy in which gender functions as a major axis of differentiation between formal/informal work. It also discusses debates around how to conceptualize the informal economy and concludes that there is a blurred distinction between the two spheres.

The informal sector was first named as such by the International Labor Organization (ILO) in the early 1970s to capture income-earning activities that fall outside of the official, regulated labor market (ILO 1972). Early understandings of the concept focused on productive activities undertaken for bare subsistence in the global South, with the assumption that this sector of the economy would shrink as modernization and industrialization drew workers into the formal sector. By the 1980s, however, theorists emphasized the articulations between the formal and informal sectors, showing that capitalism relied on informality to maintain profitability, thus challenging the thesis that informal activities would wither away in the process of development (Benería and Roldan 1987).

Through processes of globalization and neoliberal restructuring, the scope and range of these activities has expanded. It is estimated that the informal economy now constitutes more than one-half of all economic production in the global South—with levels approaching 80 percent in Southeast Asia—and approximately 25 percent of the activity in the North (Chen 2012). Defining informality is difficult given institutional, regulatory, and transnational shifts and the sheer heterogeneity of economic activities that fall under its umbrella. However, informal activities can be divided into two broad categories: self-employed informal (nonregulated) enterprises and wage workers. In the former category are owners of unregulated firms, unpaid family members in these firms, microenterprise account operators, and cooperatives. In the latter we find casual, seasonal and temporary labor, home-based subcontract work, and domestic workers. Thus while informal work is typically marginalized in mainstream economic accounts, it constitutes an enormously important form of economic organization, particularly for those at the bottom of the economic hierarchy (Benería and Roldan 1987).

Research on the informal economy tends to portray it in one of the following ways. The dominant approach of mainstream economists and others who advocate for free markets has been to view informalization as a process that unlocks the potential of the poor for growth and poverty reduction outside of regulatory channels (de Soto 1989). This research is focused primarily on the self-employed side of the informal economy and with the growth of small-scale enterprises. There are implicit gender codes at work in these celebratory framings, as owners are celebrated for their masculinized independent, risk-taking spirit (Peterson 2013). Women owners are represented in ways that intriguingly combine these masculine with feminine ideals. Women are rendered as simultaneously entrepreneurial and cooperative and as profit maximizing and family-centered. For example, development policies promoting small businesses, which women can run out of their homes, present the opportunity in terms of economic growth as well as a gain for families because women are still around to do care tasks. These programs tout informal work at home as a good method of balancing women's paid work and family responsibilities (Chant 2003). In the context of microcredit lending—which is often targeted specifically to women, and has already reached over thirty million female recipients—women's greater individual entrepreneurial drive is hailed, on the one hand, while the essentialist assumption that they will use the income for the well-being of the family and household is emphasized, on the other.

Grounded as it is in liberal thought, the celebratory informal ownership literature equates women's empowerment with having access to resources such as credit. While the World Bank and other development organizations proclaim women's empowerment through income-producing activities in the informal sector, others take a more guarded approach, saying that informalization still has not achieved its stated empowerment goals. Still, even these critics are invested in making informalization work better for women, rather than jettisoning it entirely as an antipoverty and empowerment strategy. Critical political economy and critical feminist approaches, in contrast, stress the structural dimensions of change in the informal economy as they relate to capitalism and/or gender dynamics. The flexibilization, outsourcing, casualization of labor, subcontracting, and declines in state protections for workers that have caused the informal economy to grow so dramatically are projects of capitalist accumulation in a neoliberal era. Gender-sensitive research in this framework has emphasized the labor market side, not the ownership side, of the informal sector. It also emphasizes the ways that informalization is a process of feminization. Historically, feminized occupations have been characterized by the absence of contracts, instability, and the part-time and low-paid employment that are attributes of most work in today's informal economy (Peterson 2003). Further, the growth of the informal sector has included an enormous percentage of jobs in feminized activities such as domestic work and caring for children and elderly populations. There has emerged a sexualized, racialized, and classed "regime of labor intimacy" for informal economy workers—many of whom are poor, migrant women who are assumed to be naturally suited to care work—providing labor in others' households (Chang and Ling 2010).

Examining gender variations in participation in the informal sector, feminist research has demonstrated that women are more likely to be found in informal labor situations such as subcontracting work, home-based piecework, domestic work, and sex work. They are also a substantial percentage of own-account small producers. Critical feminist scholars have highlighted the ways that gender hierarchies of valorization have meant that both women and men now find themselves in low-wage, menial, and economically precarious situations. The expanding feminized informal economy characterizes new modes of capitalist accumulation and crisis (Peterson 2013). As Donna Haraway puts it,

> Work is being redefined as both literally female and feminized, whether performed by men or women. To be feminized means to be made extremely vulnerable; able to be disassembled, reassembled, and exploited as a reserve labor force; seen less as workers than as servers; subjected to arrangements on and off the paid job that make a mockery of the limited workday.
>
> (Haraway 1991, 151)

While the critical framework for understanding informalization has been largely focused on the wage labor side of the informal economy, some feminist researchers have looked at the enterprise side, particularly the impact of microcredit on women's economic fortunes and lives. These scholars take issue with the claims of liberal thought that microcredit empowers women. They point out the ways that microcredit is implicated in broader projects of neoliberal governance, which change women from beneficiaries of development aid into clients who are self-responsible for their families' well-being (Rankin 2001). Further, they argue, the rhetoric of microcredit masks the realities of poverty in the global South. Microcredit is used not for entrepreneurship but survival and is more likely to shift the burden of achieving bare subsistence onto women in addition to all their other responsibilities (Roy 2010). Still other critical feminist approaches to understanding informal enterprises take a different position. Rather than viewing these developments as "bringing women in" to the economy—in the optimists' view, to liberate them, or in the critics' view, to subordinate them—these scholars view the informal economy as a potential (although not inevitable) economic space of resistance to neoliberal capitalism. Using a model of economic difference, these authors contend that informal activities, in some cases, might offer a creative solution for those struggling for subsistence, one that gets around the neocolonial and gendered hierarchies of formal markets (Tripp 2001). For example, microcredit loans are often made to a group of women in a credit circle, and thus can foster gender solidarities and emerging post-capitalist subjectivities related to solidarity economies, rather than simply reproducing capitalist relations of domination and exploitation (Worthen 2012).

These varied conceptual and political frameworks lead to different understandings and recommendations for change. Celebratory approaches tend to advocate for ways to increase involvement of women in informal sector activities and/or reduce the inefficiencies that might make microcredit and other opportunities fail to achieve anti-poverty and empowerment goals. Critics call for expanding access to formal sector work with its benefits and protections, or making informal work "decent work" in which there are rights, protection, and voice for workers, so that it looks more like its formal sector counterpart (ILO 2012). The handful of critical scholars who view informalization as a space of postcapitalist possibility would nurture attempts to create opportunities for solidarity and collective forms of production.

Among feminists, there is general agreement on the blurred distinction between informal and formal economic activities, and between informal and unpaid social reproductive activities in households. The increasingly precarious condition of all work suggests that the distinction between formal and informal work is a false one. Both the movement of workers between unpaid and paid social-reproductive work, and the ways that gender, race, and class structure responsibilities for social reproduction in both spheres, blur the distinction here as well. In addition, the unpaid labor of household members, including women and children, often enables survival of families engaged in street vending, home-based piecework, and similar activities. Thus feminist research has highlighted the dubious gendered binary distinctions between public/private, paid/unpaid, market/household, and productive/reproductive (Peterson 2013).

Conclusion

Feminist theorizing over the past few decades has illuminated how the power of gender operates within and across the spheres of care and formal and informal economies. This work has been attentive to the ways in which activities associated with femininity are devalued. For example, feminist research has demonstrated that the relative invisibility of unpaid household labor in mainstream economic theory and policy is related to gendered hierarchies, including that of public/private; that occupational segregation and pay inequities in formal labor markets are evidence of a higher value accorded to masculine activities than feminine ones; and that the expansion of an increasingly precarious informal sector reflects processes of feminization within labor markets. Feminist research has also expanded beyond the binaries of masculine and feminine to highlight how gender intersects with race, class, nation, sexuality, and other relations of power to structure economic arrangements and outcomes.

Feminist theory has also made key contributions to understanding the dynamic interactions among these three spheres. For instance, feminists have highlighted the ways that care work, in both its paid and unpaid forms, contributes to capitalist accumulation, and have emphasized how imagined care arrangements in households—which adhere to gender and hetero-normativities—are implicated in market structures as well as to shifts in state policy. This work has been crucial to understanding the economy, particularly the contours of contemporary neoliberal restructuring. For example, neoliberal efforts to decrease the costs of care (by both the state and firms that provide insurance) have resulted in both a care crisis in households around the globe and a burgeoning of low-wage positions in paid care work. In Europe, Canada, the United States, and elsewhere, many of these positions are taken by migrant women and men in feminized and informalized, part-time, subcontracted, and otherwise precarious conditions of work.

Tracing out the articulations between the care, formal, and informal sectors of the economy has also resulted in a number of different feminist analytical frameworks for understanding how the system as a whole functions. Many feminists maintain a boundary between the household and the marketplace as separate spheres. While connected, each is assumed to have its own internal logic that sometimes moves in concert with the other, while in other moments contradictions emerge. In this vein some view the household, or even the realm of care work in general, as potentially fostering an alternative set of values in which critical consciousness can arise "outside" capitalism, and anticapitalist subjectivities can be developed. Others contend that maintaining the distinctions between these spheres fails to capture the ways that household and market work together as an "assemblage" that produces gendered, raced, and sexualized social realities, such as the precarities of neoliberal capitalism (e.g., Jakobsen 2014). Still others approach the economy as a singular system that mobilizes class, gender, race, nation, and sexuality in a system of racist, imperialist hetero-capitalist patriarchy (Eisenstein 2004). This can be contrasted with feminist analysis that emphasizes the heterogeneity of economic practices as a way of rethinking the economy (e.g., Gibson-Graham 2008). The implications of these different perspectives for feminist activism include a focus on wholesale change as the primary strategy for achieving gender justice versus a focus on the transformative potential of the partial, building on glimmers of alternatives to achieve liberatory aims.

Finally, feminist thinking across the borders of care and formal and informal economies has led to a rethinking of work and economy themselves. Increased attention to the tensions around work/life balance for women engaged in both market labor and unpaid care work has contributed to a productivist framework that tends to view women as the heroes and saviors of the economy in some quarters (see, for example, World Bank 2012). But it has also led some feminists to advocate for a refusal to work in a time in which capital seeks to tie life beyond work to its purposes. Rather than seeking a liberal work/life balance, the goal of this more radical feminist project is to wrest more life from work (Weeks 2011). Further, feminist analysis of care and formal and informal economic practices has led to a rethinking of the economy, not only in terms of how the economy operates but also its goals, what the economy exists for. While mainstream analysis takes a mechanistic approach that emphasizes the growth of market production as the main goal of the economy, feminist analysis has recast the economy not in mechanistic terms but as a space of ethical negotiation (Gibson-Graham 2008), and one focused not on growth but on provisioning for well-being and sustainability (Nelson 2006).

References

Agarwal, B. 1997. "Bargaining and Gender Relations: Within and beyond the Household." *Feminist Economics* 3 (1): 1–51.

Bakker, I. 1994. *The Strategic Silence: Gender and Economic Policy.* London: Zed Press.

Bakker, I. 2007. "Social Reproduction and the Constitution of a Gendered Political Economy." *New Political Economy* 12 (4): 541–556.

Bakker, I., and S. Gill. 2003. "Global Political Economy and Social Reproduction." In *Power, Production and Social Reproduction*, edited by I. Bakker and S. Gill, 3–16. Basingstoke: Palgrave Macmillan.

Barker, D., and S. Feiner. 2009. "Affect, Race and Class: An Interpretive Reading of Caring Labor." *Frontiers* 30 (1): 41–54.

Barrios de Chungara, D. 1978. *Let Me Speak! Testimony of Domitila, A Woman of the Bolivian Mines.* New York: Monthly Review Press.

Becker, G. 1991. *A Treatise on the Family.* Cambridge, MA: Harvard University Press.

Bedford, K. 2009. *Developing Partnerships: Gender, Sexuality and the Reformed World Bank.* Minneapolis: University of Minnesota Press.

Benería, L. 1992. "Accounting for Women's Work: The Progress of Two Decades." *World Development* 20 (11): 1547–1560.

Benería, L., and M. Roldan. 1987. *The Crossroads of Class and Gender.* Chicago: University of Chicago Press.

Bergeron, S. 2009a. "Querying Economics' Straight Path to Development: Household Models Reconsidered." In *Development, Sexual Rights and Global Governance*, edited by A. Lind, 54–64. New York: Routledge.

Bergeron, S. 2009b. "Interpretive Analytics to Move Economics off the Straight Path." *Frontiers: A Journal of Women's Studies* 30 (1): 55–64.

Bergmann, B. 1986. *The Economic Emergence of Women.* New York: Basic Books.

Boris, E., and Parreñas, R. 2010. *Intimate Labors: Cultures, Technologies and the Politics of Care.* Redwood City, CA: Stanford University Press.

Boserup, E. 1970. *Women's Role in Economic Development.* New York: Allen and Unwin.

Brennan, D. 2004. *What's Love Got to Do with It? Transnational Desires and Sex Tourism in the Dominican Republic.* Durham, NC: Duke University Press.

Budlender, D. 2008. "The Statistical Evidence on Care and Non-Care Work across Six Countries." *UNRISD Gender and Development Programme*, Paper No. 4.

Cameron, J. 2000. "Domesticating Class: Femininity, Heterosexuality, and Household Politics." In *Class and Its Others*, edited by J. K. Gibson-Graham, Stephen A. Resnick, and Richard D. Wolff, 47–68. Minneapolis: University of Minnesota Press.

Chang, K., and L. Ling. 2010. "Globalization and Its Intimate Other: Filipina Domestic Workers in Hong Kong." In *Gender and Global Restructuring: Sightings, Signs, Resistances*, 2nd ed., edited by M. Marchand and A. Runyan, 30–47. New York: Routledge.

Chant, S. 2003. "New Contributions to the Analysis of Poverty." CEPAL Women and Development Unit. New York: United Nations.

Charusheela, S. 2003. "Empowering Work: Bargaining Models Reconsidered." In *Toward a Feminist Philosophy of Economics*, edited by D. Barker and E. Kuiper, 287–303. London: Routledge.

Chen, M. 2012. "The Informal Economy: Definitions, Theories and Policies." Women in Informal Employment: Globalizing and Organizing *WIEGO*. Working Paper No. 1. Cambridge, MA: WIEGO.

Cornwall, A. 2014. "Women's Empowerment: What Works and Why?" World Institute for Development Economics Research. Working paper no. 104.

Dalla Costa, M., and S. James. 1975. *The Power of Women and the Subversion of the Community*. Bristol: Falling Wall Press.

De Soto, H. 1989. *The Other Path: The Invisible Revolution in the Third World*. New York: Harper and Row.

Deere, C. 1976. "Rural Women's Subistence Production and the Capitalist Periphery." *Review of Radical Political Economics* 8 (1): 9–17.

Delphy, C. 1980. "The Main Enemy." *Feminist Issues* 1 (1): 23–40. Originally published in 1970 as "Liberation des Femmes: annee zero" in *Partisans*.

Eisenstein, Z. 2004. *Against Empire: Feminisms, Racism and the West*. London: Zed Books.

Eisler, R. 2008. *The Real Wealth of Nations: Creating a Caring Economics*. San Francisco: Bertt-Koehler.

Elson, D. 1991. *Male Bias in the Development Process*. Manchester: University of Manchester Press.

Elson, D. 2000. "The Social Content of Macroeconomic Policies." *World Development* 28 (7): 1347–1364.

Elson, D., and R. Pearson. 1981. "The Subordination of Women and the Internationalization of Factory Production." In *Of Marriage and Market: Subordination in International Perspective*, edited by K. Young, 144–166. London: CSE Books.

England, P., and N. Folbre. 1999. "The Cost of Caring." *Annals of the American Academy of Political and Social Science* 56 (1): 39–51.

England, P., M. Budig, and N. Folbre. 2002. "Contracting for Care." In *Feminist Economics Today*, edited by M. Ferber and J. Nelson, 61–79. Chicago: University of Chicago Press.

Federici, S. 2004. *Caliban and the Witch: Women, the Body, and Primitive Accumulation*. Brooklyn, NY: Autonomedia Press.

Ferber, M. 1987. *Women and Work, Paid and Unpaid*. New York: Garland Press.

Ferber, M., and J. Nelson. 1993. *Beyond Economic Man*. Chicago: University of Chicago Press.

Folbre, N. 1991. "The Unproductive Housewife: Her Evolution in Nineteenth-Century Economic Thought." *Signs* 16 (3): 463–484.

Folbre, N. 1995. "Holding Hands at Midnight: The Paradox of Caring Labor." *Feminist Economics* 1 (1) 73–92.

Folbre, N. 2009. *Greed, Lust and Gender: A History of Economic Ideas*. New York: Oxford.

Fraad, H., S. Resnick, and R. Wolff. 1994. *Bringing It All Back Home: Class, Gender and Power in the Modern Household*. London: Pluto Press.

Fraser, N. 2013. *Fortunes of Feminism: From State-Managed Capitalism to Neoliberal Crisis*. London: Verso.

Freeman, C. 2000. *High Tech and High Heels in the Global Economy: Women, Work and Pink-Collar Identities in the Caribbean*. Durham, NC: Duke University Press.

Gardiner, J. 1975. "Women's Domestic Labor." *New Left Review* 69: 47–58.
Gibson-Graham, J. K. 2006. *The End of Capitalism As We Knew It: A Feminist Critique of Political Economy*. Minneapolis: University of Minnesota Press.
Gibson-Graham, J. K. 2008. "Diverse Economies: Performative Practices for 'Other' Worlds." *Progress in Human Geography* 32 (5): 613–632.
Glucksmann, M. 1995. "Why Work?: Gender and the Total Social Organization of Labor." *Gender, Work and Organization* 2 (2): 63–75.
Gutiérrez-Rodríguez, E. 2007. "Reading Affect: On the Heterotopian Spaces of Care and Domestic Work in Private Households." *Forum for Qualitative Social Research* 8 (2). http://www.qualitative-research.net/index.php/fqs/article/view/240
Haraway, D. 1988. "Situated Knowledges: The Science Question in Feminism and the Privilege of Partial Perspectives." *Feminist Studies* 14 (3): 575–99.
Haraway, D. 1991. *Simians, Cyborgs and Women: The Reinvention of Nature*. London: Routledge.
Hardt, M. 1999. "Affective Labor." *boundary 2* 26 (2): 89–100.
Hart, G. 1997. "From Rotten Wives to Good Mothers: Household Models and the Limits of Economism." *IDS Bulletin* 28 (3): 14–25.
Hartmann, H. 1981. "The Unhappy Marriage of Marxism and Feminism: Toward a More Perfect Union." In *Women and Revolution: A Discussion of the Unhappy Marriage of Marxism and Feminism*, edited by L. Sargent, 1–41. Boston: South End Press.
Hartsock, Nancy. 1983. *Money, Sex, and Power: Toward a Feminist Historical Materialism*. New York: Longman.
Healy, S. 2008. "Caring for Ethics and the Politics of Health Care Reform." *Gender, Place and Culture* 15 (3): 267–284.
Hewitson, G. 1999. *Feminist Economics: Interrogating the Masculinity of Rational Economic Man*. Northampton, UK: Edward Elgar.
Himmelweit, S. 1995. "The Discovery of Unpaid Work: The Social Consequences of the Expansion of Work." *Feminist Economics* 1 (2): 1–19.
Himmelweit, S., and S. Mohun. 1977. "Domestic Labor and Capital." *Cambridge Journal of Economics* 1 (1): 15–31.
Hirshman, Linda. 2006. *Get to Work: A Manifesto for Women of the World*. New York: Viking.
Hochschild, A. 1983. *The Managed Heart*. Berkeley: University of California Press.
Hochschild, A., and B. Ehrenreich. 2003. *Global Woman*. New York: Henry Holt.
Hoskyns, C., and S. Rai. 2007. "Recasting the Global Political Economy: Counting Women's Unpaid Work." *New Political Economy* 12 (3): 277–317.
hooks, b. 2000. *Where We Stand: Class Matters*. New York: Routledge.
ILO. 1972. *Employment, Incomes and Equality: A Strategy for Increasing Productive Employment in Kenya*. Geneva: International Labor Organization.
ILO. 2012. *World of Work 2012*. Geneva: International Labor Organization.
Jakobsen, J. 2014. "Economic Justice after Legal Equality: The Case for Caring Queerly." In *After Legal Equality: Family, Sex, Kinship*, edited by R. Leckey, 77–96. New York: Routledge.
Joseph, G. 1981. "The Incompatable Menage-a-Trois: Marxism, Feminism and Racism." In *Women and Revolution: A Discussion of the Unhappy Marriage of Marxism and Feminism*, edited by L. Sargent, 91–108. Boston: South End Press.
Kabeer, N., with R. Assaad, A. Darkwah, S. Mahmud, H. Sholkamy, S. Tasneem, and D. Tsikata. 2013. *Paid Work, Women's Empowerment and Inclusive Growth: Transforming the Structures of Constraint*. New York: UN Women.

Kunz, Rahel. 2011. *The Political Economy of Global Remittances: Gender, Governmentality, and Neoliberalism.* London: Routledge Press.
Lind, A. 2009. "Development, Global Governance, and Sexual Subjectivities." In *Development Sexual Rights and Global Governance*, edited by A. Lind 1–20. New York: Routledge.
Mainardi, P. 1970. "The Politics of Housework." In *Sisterhood is Powerful*, edited by R. Morgan, 447–454. New York: Vintage Books.
Manalansan, Martin F. 2008. "Queering the Chain of Care Paradigm." *Scholar and Feminist Online* 16: (3). http://sfonline.barnard.edu/immigration/manalansan_01.htm
Marchand, M., and A. Runyan. 2000. *Gender and Global Restructuring: Sightings, Signs, Resistances.* New York: Routledge.
McDowell, Linda. 2009. *Working Bodies: Interactive Service Employment and Workplace Identities.* Malden, MA: Wiley-Blackwell.
Mies, Maria, Claudia Von Werlhof, and Veronika Bennholdt-Thomsen. 1988. *Women: The Last Colony.* London: Zed Press.
Mincer, J., and S. Polachek. 1974. "Family Investments in Human Capital: Earnings of Women." In *Marriage, Family, Human Capital and Fertility*, edited by T. Schultz, 76–108. Washington DC: NBER Books.
Molyneux, M. 1979. "Beyond the Domestic Labor Debate." *New Left Review* 116: 3–27.
Nakano Glenn, Evelyn. 1992. "From Servitude to Service Work: Historical Continuities in the Racial Divison of Paid Reproductive Labor." *Signs* 18 (1): 1–43.
Nash, J., and M. Fernandez-Kelly. 1983. *Women, Men and the International Division of Labor.* Albany: State University of New York Press.
Nelson, J. 2006. *Economics for Humans.* Chicago: University of Chicago Press.
Nelson, J. 2013. "Gender and Caring." In *The Handbook of Research on Gender and Economic Life*, edited by D. Figart and T Warnecke, Northampton, UK: Edward Elgar.
Oakley, Ann. 1974. *Housewife.* London: Allen Lane.
Olcott, Jocelyn. 2011. "The Battle within the Home: Development Strategies and the Commodification of Caring Labors at the 1975 International Women's Year Conference." In *Workers across the Americas: The Transnational Turn in Labor History*, edited by L. Fink 194–217. New York: Oxford.
Organization for Economic Co-operation and Development (OECD). 2011. *Labour Force Statistics 1989-2009, 2010 Edition.* Paris: OECD Publications.
Peterson, V. S. 2003. *A Critical Re-Writing of Global Political Economy: Integrating Reproductive, Productive and Virtual Economies.* New York: Routledge.
Peterson, V. S. 2013. "Informal Work." In *The Handbook of Research on Gender and Economic Life*, edited by D. Figart and T. Warnecke, 169–182. Northampton, UK: Edward Elgar.
Rankin, K. 2001. "Governing Development: Neoliberalism, Microcredit, and Rational Economic Woman." *Economy and Society* 30 (1): 18–37.
Romero, Mary. 2013. "Nanny Diaries and Other Stories: Immigrant Women's Labor in the Social Reproduction of American Families." *Revista de Estudios Sociales* 45: 186–197.
Roy, A. 2010. *Poverty Capital: Microfinance and the Making of Development.* London: Routledge.
Safri, M., and J. Graham. 2010. "The Global Household: Toward a Feminist Postcapitalist International Political Economy." *Signs* 36 (1): 99–125.
Salzinger, Leslie. 2003. *Genders in Production: Making Workers in Mexico's Global Factories.* Berkeley: University of California Press.
Seccombe, Wally. 1974. "Housework under Capitalism." *New Left Review* 83: 85–96.

Sen, A. 1990. "Gender and Cooperative Conflicts." In *Persistent Inequalities: Women and World Development*, edited by I. Tinker, 123–148. New York: Oxford University Press.

Stichter, Sharon, and Jane L. Parpart. 2013. *Women, Employment and the Family in the International Division of Labour.* Basingstoke: Palgrave Macmillan.

Tilly, J., and L. Scott. 1978. *Women, Work and Family.* New York: Holt, Rinehart and Winston.

Tripp, A. 2001. "Non-Formal Institutions, Informal Economies, and the Politics of Inclusion." UN WIDER Working Paper 108.

Vaittinen, T. 2014. "The Power of the Vulnerable Body." *International Feminist Journal of Politics.* doi: org/10.1080/14616742.2013.876301

Vogel, Lise. 2000. "Domestic Labor Revisited." *Science and Society* 64 (2): 151–170.

Waring, M. 1989. *If Women Counted: A New Feminist Economics.* London: Macmillan.

Weeks, K. 2007. "Life within and against Work: Affective Labor, Feminist Critique, and Post-Fordist Politics." *Ephemera* 7 (1): 233–249.

Weeks, K. 2011. *The Problem with Work: Feminism, Marxism, Anti-work Politics and Postwork Imaginaries.* Durham, NC: Duke University Press.

World Bank. 2001. *Engendering Development.* Washington DC: World Bank.

World Bank. 2012. Gender Equality and Development. Washington DC: World Bank.

Worthen, Holly. 2012. "Women and Microcredit: Alternative Readings of Subjectivity, Agency, and Gender Change in Rural Mexico." *Gender, Place and Culture* 19 (3): 364–381.

Young, I. M. 1981. "Beyond the Unhappy Marriage: A Critique of Dual Systems Theory." In *Women and Revolution: A Discussion of the Unhappy Marriage of Marxism and Feminism*, edited by L. Sargent, 43–70. Boston: South End Press.

CHAPTER 10

EMBODIMENT

SHATEMA THREADCRAFT

EMBODIMENT is a central concern of feminist theory insofar as the body is a site for the symbolic construction of sexual difference, a ground for political exclusion or inclusion, a locus of subjectivity, a prospect for self-realization, and the material focus of many labors that typically fall to women and/or define femininity. Not only have women been primarily responsible for caring for the bodies of men, children, and elders, but ideals of Western feminine subjectivity call on them to fashion their own bodies as ornamental surfaces for the male gaze. In turn, Western political theory is at once symbolically centered on the (male) body—by the metaphor of the "body politic"—and profoundly somatophobic. Feminists have shown how the modern body politic was constructed as a replica of the male body and have drawn attention to the ongoing challenges that attend female embodiment as a consequence. Feminists were also among the first to reverse the metaphor—and thus the locus of concern—from that of the body politic to the politics of the body. In doing so, they anticipated the work of the influential scholar of the relationship between the body and power, Michel Foucault.

That women are identified with the body in a deeply somatophobic tradition of thought has created an ambivalence toward embodiment in feminist theory. Is it a condition to be embraced and revalued, or critiqued and transcended? Either alternative reproduces the symbolic structures of male domination. By celebrating embodiment, feminists have naturalized sexual difference; by calling for its transcendence, they have reproduced somatophobia. This chapter argues for moving beyond the celebration/transcendence binary and with the nature/culture opposition that underlies it to place practices of embodiment and their analysis firmly in the domain of disciplinary power.

The chapter briefly reviews Western conceptions of the body, the complex relation between embodiment and selfhood, and the recurrent tendency to imagine generic bodies that purportedly account for all races and genders. It traces themes that privilege the soul, spirit, or mind over the body in traditional philosophical works, from ancient and modern discourses to contemporary accounts. It explores how feminist analyses of embodiment attempt to break with traditional philosophical stances, yet often replicate problematic binaries. In particular, I examine feminist ambivalence toward the body both in theory and by means of a specific case drawn from contemporary discussion of black female embodiment. Taking the centrality of race and gender in an account of embodiment seriously, I trace the recurrence of nature/culture and somatophobic/biophilic dichotomies in debates about black female hair practices that pit "natural" approaches against those that have been colonized by white norms, unless sublated by liberal language of choice and bodily autonomy. Within this debate, central questions are raised about the relationship between the natural and the emancipatory. Echoing long traditions in mainstream and feminist theory, this opposition fails to grasp how even the most "natural" perceptions of the body are produced by discipline. The final section examines recent feminist accounts of raced-gendered embodiment attuned to the complex ways that culture coerces women to engage in time-consuming normative bodily practices that produce their sense of a natural femininity.

Ancient Somatophobes and Magnificent Manly Modern Monsters

From its ancient roots and transformation in Christian thought through the modern period, the Western philosophical tradition has been somatophobic, not only asserting a separation and hierarchy between soul and body but, as feminist theorists have argued, using masculine-feminine difference to produce that distinction and mark its relation of power (Spelman 1982). Although not all thinkers in every age saw the body as the same inescapable prison, each age did "construct the body as something apart from the true self (which is conceived as soul, mind, spirit, will, creativity, freedom) . . . and as undermining the best efforts of the self" (Bordo 1993, 5). Even modern views of the body, which were less phobic, marked by Enlightenment notions that held the body to be simply one object among others to be studied, grasped by reason, and controlled, retained the soul/body separation and hierarchy. Hobbes presents an often-noted mechanistic account of the body, in which the body consists of matter in motion that responds to various internal and external stimuli. Yet Hobbes retained the Platonic notion that the soul must rule the body, drawing an analogy between sovereignty and rule over the body politic. Indeed, the state is but an artificial body for Hobbes; sovereignty, its vaunted soul.

Feminist theorists have noted the long-standing connection between the denigration of the body and the denigration of women. Plato, for example, understood "woman" as she who was "quintessentially body-directed" and held that to live a life overly concerned with the vile body was to act like a woman.[1] Significantly, in a world where the mind and rationality are highly valued, "ideal rationality is articulated in direct opposition to qualities typical of the feminine" (Gatens 1996, 50). Classical thinkers associated the mind and the soul, that is, the essence of the self with characteristics ascribed only to men. By contrast, the body, the irrational, and all deemed inessential matter were associated with femininity. This is certainly true of Aristotle. In his infamous account of human reproduction, for example, man provides the (active) soul that bestows life, and woman supplies only the (passive) matter.[2]

It is little surprise that philosophical systems that made sharp value-laden distinctions between mind and the body and characterized woman as inescapably bound to the body, existing to tend to its needs, fostered and upheld the oppression of women (Spelman 1982, 125). As Bordo (1993, 5) states, "[I]f, whatever the specific historical context of the (mind/body) duality, *the body* is the negative term and if woman is *the body*, then women *are* that negativity," however defined in specific context, whether as "distraction from knowledge, seduction away from God, capitulation to sexual desire, violence or aggression, failure of will, even death." Women are what must be suppressed. The figure of woman as body allowed actual women to be problematically and often dangerously mischaracterized, but it also allowed for a mischaracterization of man's relationship to the male body. Male thinkers, from Aristotle to the existentialists, make an all-important—some have even said magical—move with regard to their understanding of the relationship between the male subject and his body. Whereas "the female sex becomes restricted to its body," the "male body, fully disavowed, becomes, paradoxically, the incorporeal instrument of an ostensibly radical freedom" (Butler 1999, 16).

Male embodiment figures prominently in the works of some Western theorists. Hobbes, for example, was markedly concerned about the dangers posed by and the safety of the male body in a world of rough equality, which contributed to life that was nasty brutish and short. Yet acknowledging the threats posed by embodied male desires did little to guarantee equitable treatment of women. As Moira Gatens (1996) notes, Hobbes privileged the concerns of the male body over those of the female body and sought to create a powerful state solely to protect and enhance the power and safety of men. Hobbes ([1651] 1996, 7) states as much when he proclaims, "For by art is created that great LEVIATHAN . . . which is but an artificial man, though of greater stature and strength than the natural for whose protection and defense it was intended and in which the sovereignty is an artificial soul, giving life and motion to the whole body." He conceives the modern body politic, then, as the product of fear, designed to minister to, manage, and govern the needs and desires that arise out of the bodies of male subjects. Those needs and desires are understood to be products of nature that must be governed by the products of human culture. Gatens points out that Hobbes's idea of the body politic as of a work of "creative artifice," analogous to the creation of man by God, explicitly uses the male body image. In constructing the mechanical operations of the body politic, from ratiocination through voluntary action, the sovereign modeled male appetites and aversions in all its machinations.

Feminist scholars have argued that the modern body politic is not only symbolically male but also literally so: by using male bodies as the models for the lives its legal and political arrangements are designed to enhance and protect, political systems marginalize the concerns of women. Gatens argues, for example, that modern states accord little attention to issues such as abortion, rape, and maternal allowances. Female embodiment continues to present an obstacle to political participation when the model citizen is understood to be a male unburdened by reproduction and child care. According to Gatens, such gendered obstacles to participation would disappear if the state were constructed on a different model of human embodiment.

Feminist Somatophobia and Biophilia in the Twentieth Century

Some twentieth-century feminist theorists have been as somatophobic as ancient thinkers, although they tended to share the modern faith that the body could be overcome. They characterized the female body as deficient, and they, too, saw women as more bound to and bound by their bodies than men, although unlike their male predecessors they genuinely lamented this fact. They saw the female body as a significant factor in women's oppression. For Simone de Beauvoir, women's liberation depended on their release from the more mundane aspects of life—from the concerns of the body—so that they might take part in body-transcendent acts of freedom. She awaited the day when women's bodies would cease to be the obstacles that they had been owing to a combination of the situation in which men placed them and women's own efforts to fashion their bodies as objects of the male gaze. Far more somatophobic than Beauvoir, Shulamith Firestone envisioned women's capacity to bear children as an impediment and placed faith in technology to help overcome the natural deficiencies of the female body. Construing the female body as deficient by nature, Firestone insisted that transcending that nature was a prerequisite for women's liberation.

Despite their shared use of the term *transcendence*, Beauvoir offered a far more nuanced account of women's embodiment than Firestone. With her famous statement that "one is not born, but rather becomes, a woman," Beauvoir ([1949] 1989, 267) drew attention to the complex forces that produced women as immanent. Insisting that "nothing about the body is given a priori" (9), Beauvoir demonstrated how science colludes in the naturalization of social roles. By denying contingency and ignoring specificity (xxiv), women's subordination is constructed as a "natural condition that seems beyond the possibility of change." But "in truth, however, the nature of things is no more immutably given than is historical reality" (xxv). Beauvoir was ruthless in her criticism of scientists who suggested that ovaries, the uterus, hormones, chromosomes, menstruation, or pregnancy dictate women's destiny. She was equally scathing about philosophical musings that defined femininity as a "Platonic essence," debunking these products of the philosophical imagination as "male fantasies" (xix) that contributed to culture-specific efforts to make women conform to those male dictates. "Man defines woman in relation to himself, she is not regarded as an autonomous being; she is what he decrees, 'the sex'. She appears to man as an essentially *sexual* being because he has produced her as such" (xxii). Beauvoir examined science, religion, law, philosophy, psychology, literature, culture, and education in order to trace complex modes of gender power used by men to produce women as Other. Deploying differential treatment—or "sex discrimination"—as she candidly called it, men "produce in women moral and intellectual effects so profound that they appear to spring from [women's] nature" (xxxii). Comparing the active processes that produce passivity, docility, and subordination in women with the mechanisms that produce the oppression of blacks and Jews, Beauvoir drew parallels between racialization and feminization. And she noted that the accomplishment of these ends was the work of whole civilizations: "Civilization as a whole produces this creature, intermediate between male and eunuch, which is described as feminine" (267).

Keenly attuned to the pervasive effects of visual economies, intellectual systems, and material culture, Beauvoir provided a phenomenology of the intricate processes that "divide humanity into two classes of individuals whose clothes, faces, bodies, smiles, gaits, interests and occupations are manifestly different" (xx). Pointing out that these differences are always structured by power, Beauvoir cautioned against romanticizing sexual difference. Claiming freedom for themselves, men have used sexual difference to condemn women to "immanence (*en soi*): a brutish life of subjection to given conditions" (xxxv). Beauvoir demanded that this form of oppression be recognized as the injustice it is and warned women not to be confused by the double-speak of a democratic age in which men proclaim women equal while also acting to ensure that women can never be equal" (xxxii). She warned women against the equivocations of equal rights discourses grounded in abstract notions of equality that posed intractable dilemmas: women either had no grounds for complaint because they are already equal (regardless of their material circumstances) or were told that demanding greater equality was futile because their social condition simply reflected the "inherent limits set by nature" (xxxii).

In contrast to such "equality in difference" accorded women by men, Beauvoir encouraged women to claim freedom, to struggle against the negative conditions of existence, to grapple with contingency, ambiguity, and potentiality and make an intentional commitment to live. Taking freedom as her project, Beauvoir envisioned "a situation of equal possibilities" (5), and encouraged individuals to transcend fixed status restrictions imposed on bodies and to make of themselves what they will. The resulting "differences should not be taken as essential oppositions or ossified identities, but reflected the way particularity develops in and through mediation of each subject's finite context and relations" (39). By enacting freedom, she suggested that women and men might institute new modes of reality, reorganize ways of seeing, transform oppressive aspects of past practices, or indeed, come together to constitute political collectivities in the service of freedom.

Beauvoir argued that throughout history men had monopolized transcendence and forced women into immanence and passivity, yet achieving that result required a rigorous regime of body fashioning. In her portrayal of the female adolescent in Western patriarchal culture, Beauvoir noted that "the lie to which the adolescent girl is condemned is that she must pretend to be an object, and a fascinating one" (357). The transformation of feminine flesh in adolescence is deadening: "nothing is more astonishing than to discover suddenly a young girl's physiognomy . . . when it assumes its feminine function; its transcendence is laid aside, and imitates immanence; the eyes no longer penetrate, they reflect; the body is no longer alive, it waits; every gesture and smile becomes an appeal" (357–358). In her dawning awareness that her body is an object for others, the adolescent girl begins the process of making her body into an object, rather than use her body as a tool for discovering and apprehending the world. She begins to become an object by wearing makeup, doing her hair, and making her body passive, restricting its free movement.

Beauvoir's analysis of the complex social forces involved in becoming a woman suggested that both sex and gender were socially produced, an insight later developed by feminist thinkers, including Iris Marion Young and Judith Butler. Although Beauvoir insisted that it was civilization and not "biological, psychological or economic fate" that produced the feminine, in *The Second Sex* the female body itself—its burdensome biological functions and processes, such as urination and menstruation, the frustrating complexity of its mysterious vagina as well as female desire—seemed to work in tandem with civilization's considerable efforts to create the feminine. Following Freud, Beauvoir seemed to suggest that for boys, the penis is a plaything, and urination is "like a free game" (273). For girls, the vagina is taboo and urination a messy bother. For Beauvoir, feminine urination is a minor inconvenience that girls soon overcome as they use their bodies as tools for apprehending the world, much as little boys do. By contrast, the body of the adolescent girl seems to turn completely against her, doing all it can to lead her away from the path of freedom. She begins to experience her body as a burden, as sick. "The body of a woman–particularly that of a young girl—is a "hysterical" body . . . Because her body seems to suspect her, and because she views it with alarm, it seems to her to be sick: it is sick" (332). The adolescent girl "feels that her body is getting away from her, it is no longer the straightforward expression of her individuality; it becomes foreign to her; and at the same time she becomes for others a thing" (308). As Iris Young (1990, 29) commented on Beauvoir's account, menstruation and other phenomena "weigh down the woman's existence by tying her to nature, immanence and the requirements of the species at the expense of her own individuality." As a theorist of freedom, then, Beauvoir eagerly anticipated a day when women would use their bodies as instruments to transcend immanence and achieve freedom.

By contrast, Firestone (1997, 23) believed that men and women "were *created* different, and not equally privileged." She saw humanity as inherently unequal: "half the human race must bear and rear the children of them all" (23). For Firestone, women were "at the continual mercy of their biology"—from menarche to menopause, for example, they were plagued by menstruation and all manner of "female ills" (23). The only cessation of such female ills occurred when women experienced the barbarism of childbirth and the drudgery of wet nursing and child care. Furthermore, according to Firestone, women's bodies—specifically their reproductive functions—forced them to be dependent on men. Accepting at face value the female inferiority constructed by science, Firestone painted a grim picture of women's prospects.

Yet Firestone suggested that scientific innovation could redress natural inequality. "To grant that the sexual imbalance of power is biologically based is not to lose our case . . . we are no longer just animals . . . Humanity has begun to transcend Nature; we can no longer justify the maintenance of a discriminatory sex class on grounds of its origin in Nature" (24). Humanity possesses the tools to surmount the natural inequality of the sexes. Indeed, in-vitro reproduction could free women from the onerous burden of pregnancy and birthing children. Whereas Beauvoir called for a reorientation in women's use of their bodies, Firestone envisioned the use of technology to transcend the body outright. She understood that technology had the potential to be used against women, but this did not shake her faith in the progressive possibilities of technological developments, such as artificial reproduction and menstrual suppression, to free women from their bodily imprisonment.

"Biophilic" feminists such as Adrienne Rich (1976) and Luce Irigaray (1985) rejected the notion that the female body is naturally deficient. They presented the distinctiveness of women's bodies as something to celebrate and as the potential foundation for women's liberation. "I have come to believe," said Rich, ". . . that female biology—the diffuse, intense sensuality radiating out from clitoris, breasts, uterus, vagina; the lunar cycles of menstruation; the gestation and fruition of life which can take place in the female body–has far more radical implications than we have yet come to appreciate" (39–40). She encouraged women to connect with "our great mental capacities, hardly used," but also "our highly developed tactile sense; our genius for close observation; our complicated, pain-enduring, multi-pleasured physicality" (174). Rich encouraged women to think through "the miracle and the paradox of the female body," including its capacity to bear the pain of childbirth. She challenged Firestone's characterization of women's reproductive capacities as the root of their oppression, suggesting that Firestone saw childbirth only as it had been constrained by patriarchy (72). Distinguishing between motherhood under patriarchy as an oppressive institution and women's capacity to create life, Rich argued that women should refuse patriarchal oppression and embrace the capacity to give birth as a source of power. Contrasting the power of the womb to create life with male understanding of power as "power over," Rich suggested that women had resources that men lacked. Men would never possess the power to bear and nourish life.

Whereas Rich sought to revalue the female body, Irigaray analyzed the symbolic construction of the feminine in language as the root of women's oppression. According to Irigaray, misogynous metaphors had misled Beauvoir to diagnose women as men's inessential Other. Instead, "phallogocentric language" constructed women according to the logic of the same. As a consequence, the feminine was radically absent from a discourse structured in accordance with *l'homme(o)sexualité*. Within a discourse that privileges male genitalia—that which is external and visible—female genitalia exist as "nothing to be seen." She is relegated to the status of "lack," "atrophy," and attributed "penis envy," since the penis is the only recognized sex organ of any worth (Irigaray 1985, 323). Liberated from that system, the female body could engender a new way of thinking about being in the world, an unprecedented female-defined account of feminine subjectivity. Irigaray suggests that feminine morphology could undergird an entirely new "imaginary and symbolic system, morphologically suited to feminine corporeal reality" (Braidotti 2011, 94, 108). Far from finding the female body lacking with regard to sex and sexuality, Irigaray (1985, 326) theorizes its multiplicities: "*woman has sex organs just about everywhere.*" A new ontology built on "the sex which is not one" could introduce a radical economy of sexual pleasure. "Caressing the breasts, touching the vulva, opening the lips, gently stroking the posterior wall of the vagina, lightly massaging the cervix, etc., evoke a few of the most specifically female pleasures" (326). Envisioning social relations that prize plurality, difference, and multiplicities could offer new resources for politics and social justice.

Whether somatophobes or biophiles, these feminist thinkers came under criticism for overemphasizing the biological as a determinant of women's "nature." By replicating the nature/culture split, both groups offered a problematic ground on which to stake the project of women's liberation. Moreover, neither group attended to racialization in the production of differentiated modes of embodiment.

Racialized Embodiment, Somatophobia, and Black Liberation

As a tradition born in the West, Afro-Modern thought has had to contend with hatred of the black body in particular, with how both the literal enslavement of the black body and its symbolic construction functioned to nullify the black soul for much of colonial history. In contrast to traditional philosophy and white feminist theory, Afro-Modern thought and black feminist theory trace the intricate effects of racialization on embodiment, both in relation to immanence and the possibilities of transcendence.

Angela Davis (1983) has provided a searing account of how racial hierarchy complicates women's relationship to her body and its capacities, as well as her status as object—in particular her status as passive object—within white supremacist patriarchal culture. Davis traces one of the distinct characteristics of black female embodiment to black women's experiences within the slave system. Because women and men performed similar productive labor within the slave system, they developed equal consciousness of both their productive capacities—the power of their bodies—and their oppression. The exploitation of their labor power compelled them to exercise their bodies' power. It produced an "I can" in relation to their bodies' task orientation in the world. Because women performed the same productive labor as men, they had no reason to view themselves as the weaker sex. Davis regards this lack of a gendered division of labor in slavery as the deciding factor in women's participation in broader slave resistance. They did not simply summon their powers for their captors; they exercised it in service of resistance as well. Davis suggests that the persistent exploitation of black women's labor links enslaved women to black women today: "The enormous space that productive labor occupies in black women's lives today follows a pattern established during the very earliest days of slavery" (5).

In addition to the violent expropriation of their labor power, Davis argues that mass sexual violence in slavery constituted a gender-specific terrorist assault designed to thwart black women's awareness of their unique powers. Sexual assault by white masters and overseers reduced the potentially transcendent black female being to mere biological existence. "Aspiring with his sexual assault to establish her as an *animal*, he would be striving to destroy her proclivity towards resistance" (Davis 1995, 212). Systemic sexual assault is an extraordinarily brutal method of forcing women into immanence, and as such unlikely to produce the same relationship to immanence that Beauvoir chronicled based on the experiences of bourgeois French women in the twentieth century. Moreover, the terroristic sexual assault arose within a social context in which enslaved women were alienated from other aspects of femininity as depicted by Beauvoir. "The slave woman was first a fulltime worker for her owner, and only incidentally a wife, mother and homemaker" (Davis 1983, 5). Thus rape, coerced reproduction, and enforced child neglect as well as the labor exploitation in slavery produce a distinctive experience of immanence for black women. Different situations produce different embodied effects with profound consequences for subjectivity. Like Beauvoir, however, Davis suggests that enslaved women were not perpetually condemned to immanence. They came to subjectivity ("retrieved their humanity," as she puts it) in physical acts of resistance. Indeed, Davis insists that enslaved women found the will to resist in their discovery of their physical powers; the cultivation of their strength was linked to their profound suffering and capacity for endurance.

bell hooks has also devoted considerable attention to racialized embodiment, arguing that the black female sexual body, like the black female laboring body, is always thought to be active, never at rest as a passive object. Following Sander Gilman, hooks (1997) emphasizes that the black presence in North America allowed whites to desexualize the white body, while still sexualizing their world by displacing sexuality onto black bodies. By the eighteenth century, black sexuality came to denote deviant sexuality, and the black female body stood as the icon of black sexuality as a whole. From Sarah Bartman to Josephine Baker to Beyoncé today, the fascination with black female buttocks as a sign of deviant sexuality continues. This symbol of black deviance has been embraced and resignified by blacks themselves, who have launched an effective counterdiscourse against the normative (white) culture and the (cult) of thinness, which are construed as pathological. Although black popular culture has intervened to challenge the status of black buttocks as ugly, it has not succeeded in challenging the status of the black female buttocks as sexualized sign.[3] hooks suggests that the US racist/sexist cultural landscape professes black female sexuality to be "more liberated," while also insinuating that it is simply incapable of restraint.

According to hooks (1997), black women's bodies are not simply accessible but also aggressive active objects. Black women have never been encouraged to strive for passivity as a mode of black femininity. Fashion magazines do not depict black female bodies as images of beauty, but as oddly contorted, monstrous, and grotesque. Black female sexuality thus flips the dynamic of male conquest Beauvoir discussed. The man is actively conquered by this black feminine monster, complete with her grotesque sexual parts; he is not ensnared by feminine passivity. The black female body cannot fashion itself as a passive object and be seen; it can only appear as a sexual object in this active, aggressive way. Yet despite her activity, hooks claims, this activity does not bring about transcendent subjectivity. Although many black female entertainers assert that their presentation of aggressive sexuality constitutes sexual liberation, hooks challenges that view. Ironically, the black female being must adopt a persona of active, aggressive, grasping sexual empowerment despite the particulars of their situation. Tina Turner, for example, adopted such a stage persona for commercial success, at the same time that she experienced abuse and humiliation at the hands of her partner (hooks 1997, 119). Constructed as licentious, aggressive, and free, black female bodies are afforded few protections in racist patriarchal culture.

Given the pervasive impact of racialization on black women's experience of immanence and its constriction of their possibilities of transcendence, it is perhaps ironic that the same ambivalence toward the body that characterizes Western feminism also surfaces in some of the contemporary debates in black feminism. Somatophobia countered by biophilia surfaces in ongoing discussions about hair styles in relation to projects to reclaim, revalue, and indeed, liberate the black body.

Kinky hair stands as a major marker of blackness. Given the strong association between long, straight hair and normative white femininity, black women have perhaps suffered the most with regard to how this aspect of the black body deviates from the normative white one. A perennial debate among black women in popular discourse replays the opposition in twentieth-century Western feminist thought between those who reproduce somatophobia by turning to technology to liberate women from their bodies and those who, by contrast, embrace and glorify a "natural" female body. Those who support the use of culture and technology to modify black hair in some ways endorse a form of black-body transcendence (Banks 2000; Byrd and Tharps 2001; Craig 2002). When supplemented by the requisite adoption of a repertoire of normative gestures and forms of body comportment, hair modification enables transcendence of the marginalized black body and entry into interracial public space (Alcoff 2006; Ford 2013). Proponents of hair straightening would rarely identify themselves as somatophobic regarding the black body. Their critics, however, have no problem identifying them as such. According to these critics, true love of the black self or the black soul is incompatible with interventions to change the "natural" black body. Indeed, according to critics of hair modification, celebrating all distinctive aspects of black embodiment is a necessary step, even foundational, to black emancipation.

Just as Susan Bordo notes that the political terrain of body politics can shift dramatically in feminist discourses, dominant discourses about black hair have undergone important shifts from an understanding developed in the 1960s and 1970s of the black female body as a terrain colonized by white power to an understanding of black female hair practices as simply reflecting individual choices and preferences in a "postracial" era. In this depoliticized environment, those who would never chemically straighten their hair nonetheless see the decision to straighten as a choice and not as an act of resistance against white norms. This liberal individualist discourse precludes conceiving the black female body as a product of disciplinary power. Thus it forecloses important understandings of the politics of the body. To understand how profoundly constricting this liberal individualist discourse is, I turn to recent feminist accounts of embodiment that illuminate disciplinary practices, and to the complex relationship between "body work" and emancipation.

FROM THE BODY POLITIC TO THE POLITICS OF THE BODY: DISCIPLINARY POWER AND THE QUEST FOR PROPERLY EMBODIED FEMININITY

Feminist thinking about women and embodiment has been influenced by (without being wholly indebted to) discussions about the nature, techniques, and proper objects of power associated with Michel Foucault. Although Foucault is often credited with developing a political account of the body, North American feminist activists and theorists preceded him in that conceptualization. Susan Bordo (1993) points out that early twentieth-century activists organized for the "right" to ignore fashion, and activists in the late 1960s protested against the Miss America Pageant and the sexual objectification of women. Both these efforts to politicize dress, adornment, and the sexualization of women's bodies followed Mary Wollstonecraft (1792) in recognizing the social construction of femininity. Whether produced as delicate and domestic or as hypersexualized, feminist thinkers called attention to processes that produce "a socially-trained docile body." Feminists were innovators in developing a political understanding of the coercion operating in feminine body practices, whether involving grooming, comportment, physical movement, or occupation of space relative to the male. Bordo credits feminists with transforming the metaphor of the body politic into a pronounced politics of the body. And she notes that feminists need an effective analysis of the politics of the body to avoid anodyne liberal discourses about individual choice, preferences, and autonomy. She turns to Foucault's analysis of discipline to shore up an understanding of the female body as a colonized space, a view that feminist theorists advanced in the sixties and seventies.

For Foucault, in contrast to Hobbes, power as sovereignty was too limited a conception to encompass the processes involved in producing "docile subjects." The order established by the liberal social contract masked the disciplines and micropowers that operate on the body to produce a self-regulating subject. "The man described for us, whom we are invited to free, is already in himself the effect of a subjection more profound than himself" (Foucault 1977, 30). An adequate account of power, according to Foucault, must include the microphysics of power and the political anatomy of the body, as well as the resistances they produced.

Feminist scholars have argued that Foucault tended to speak of an ungendered (and unraced) body, paying little attention to biopower's disparate effects on men and women. Although differing in their emphasis, several feminist scholars have drawn insights from Foucault to analyze gendered and sexed bodies and desires. Judith Butler pays particular attention to the effects of discourse on the materialization of gendered and sexed bodies; Sandra Bartky and Susan Bordo emphasize the disciplining effects of both routine and extreme feminine bodily practices. Categorizing interiority and the body itself as effects of power's operation, Butler theorizes gender as performative and citational, the result of repetition of stylized acts prescribed by cultural norms over time. Bartky and Bordo analyze a host of cultural practices that produce docile, properly sculpted, feminine bodies and women's desire to attain and preserve feminine ideals.

Making a radical break from feminist demarcations of naturally sexed bodies from socially constructed genders, Butler ([1990] 1997) argues that the ideology of gender produces dichotomously sexed bodies that masquerade as natural. Taking seriously Foucault's caution that sex cannot provide the secret of being, Butler (1997, 415) insists that there is no true sex identity to be found within the subject and that it is a mistake to conceive gender as "passively scripted on the body." For Butler, gender is "an identity tenuously constituted in exterior space through a stylized repetition of acts" (402). These acts are corporeal; they involve gestures that "style flesh." Thus gender produces "the stylization of the body," which comes to be understood as natural sex. For Butler, then, "one is not simply a body, but in some very key sense one does one's body, and indeed, one does one's body differently from one's embodied predecessors and successors as well" (404). Binary sex difference is a "performative accomplishment which the mundane social audience, including the actors themselves, come to believe and to perform in the mode of a belief" (402).

Butler holds that gender is citational practice that refers to long-established norms. Those who refuse those norms, improvise too freely, or attempt subversion face harsh punishments. Regulative discourses determine socially acceptable behavior for two binary genders, structuring the repertoire for gender performance, and coercing compliance. Sufficient repetition of stylized gender acts generates the illusion that a sexed body is natural and provides the ground on which gender builds culturally specific modes of difference. Compulsory heterosexuality is at stake in the performance of gender. Indeed, Butler suggests that the prohibition of homosexuality underlies culture's insistence on the illusion of two discrete genders.

For Butler as for Foucault, where there is power there is resistance. The potential for agency, resistance, and subversion lies in the very practices that constitute us as gendered subjects. Thus Butler brings Foucault into feminist theory by conceptualizing gender as at once a disciplinary power and a micropolitics of the body. Her critics have argued that she shares with Foucault a tendency to overemphasize resistance without giving enough attention either to the disparity between normative performances and acts of resistance, or to the potential co-optation of resistant practices.

Other feminist scholars influenced by Foucault focus more on the power of feminine body practices, not only in in shaping the female body, but also in crafting feminine desires and aspirations. Sandra Bartky, for example, emphasizes that women's lives have changed with the modernization of patriarchal power. Women have more freedom of movement than ever before, more access to paid work, and even more sexual liberty. Yet many women continue to yearn for particular modes of femininity that are painful (e.g., spike heels) and subordinating, (e.g., according men first priority in the home and in the workplace). Bartky seeks to explain how deinstitutionalized and dispersed disciplinary power continues to produce not only conformity to a normative feminine body, but a desire to conform as well. Modern patriarchal domination produces a "machinery of power that explores [the female body], breaks it down and rearranges it" (Bartky 1990, 63). More than ever before, power produces properly embodied femininity, "a practiced and subjected" feminine body, that is a feminine body of a certain size and configuration, trained in a repertoire of gestures both in movement and at rest and trained to display the surface of the body as primarily ornamental (75).

Bartky appropriates Foucault's account of power in the context of self-surveillance to explain how and why women take up tiresome, time-consuming, and expensive feminine bodily practices in an era when official institutions no longer issue explicit directives or employ physical coercion to discipline the female body. Because there are no authoritative institutions in Western nations with the power to impose femininity on female bodies, it appears that femininity is either entirely voluntary or natural. Foucault's account of the panopticon as a means to transform surveillance technology into behavioral conformity offers an alternative account of women's relation to femininity. Bartky suggests that women take up feminine bodily practices because "a panoptical male connoisseur resides within the consciousness of most women . . . Woman lives her body as seen by another, by an anonymous patriarchal other" (72). Although Foucault provides an analysis of power as it operates in particular institutions vested with disciplinary authority—prisons, hospitals, barracks, schools—Bartky argues that women are disciplined by a panoptical gaze that is completely deinstitutionalized. For Bartky, a woman who wears makeup and watches what she eats has much in common with the inmate of the panopticon: she is a self-policing subject. Her self-surveillance is a form of patriarchal discipline.

Susan Bordo also draws upon Foucault's insights to analyze the politics of appearance, uncovering the power at play in bodily practices, including dieting, exercising, and eating disorders. Normative feminine bodily practices in Western culture train the female body in docility and obedience to specific gender ideals. Following Foucault in arguing that the body is a surface on which the commitments of culture are inscribed, Bordo (1993, 174) suggests that various feminine disorders—hysteria, agoraphobia, and anorexia—involve "conventional constructions of femininity . . . in extreme hyperliteral form." Those who suffer these disorders are deeply inscribed with an ideological construction of the ruling feminine mystique in hyperbolic, caricatured terms (168). For Bordo, then, routine feminine bodily practices, designed to produce the docile feminine body, and feminine disorders exist along a continuum.

By keeping both this continuum and the culture in which it is situated in view, the defects of the medical model of anorexia become apparent. The medical model diagnoses anorexics as suffering from a problem of perception. The model holds that women who think they must lose weight because their bodies are too big fail to perceive their bodies accurately. The medical approach, however, fails to acknowledge that women live in a culture that equates feminine slenderness with competence and self-control, and feminine curvaceousness with vapidity. The anorexic does not misperceive her body; on the contrary, she perceives all too well the dominant model of what a woman's body should be. For Bordo, anorexia is an effort to make the body speak; it is a profoundly embodied understanding of what the culture demands of women. In addition, Bordo argues that in the obsessive pursuit of slenderness, women evince the traditional feminine concern for the body, including denying their own appetites in order to satisfy the needs of others, while also manifesting the self-control required to gain entry to the masculine public space. By exercising such extreme bodily discipline, anorexic women exhibit the traditionally masculine virtues of control and mastery considered requirements for membership in the public sphere. Thus, anorexia turns the ideal of male self-control inward to regulate the traditionally feminine terrain of care for and about the body. Anorexia speaks a language that embraces masculine and feminine regulatory regimes. For this reason, anorexic women may take pleasure in what they are able to make their bodies say. But Bordo cautions that they are not in charge of the language, syntax, and vocabulary in which their bodies speak. These are given by a sexist and misogynous culture, and this severely limits the potential of this particular act of resistance.

Feminist scholars such as Judith Butler, Sandra Bartky, and Susan Bordo, like many of their predecessors in the feminist tradition, link their analyses of gender oppression with discussions of the potential for resistance or even emancipation. In much of the Western feminist tradition, bodily self-realization is associated with liberation. Anthropologist Saba Mahmood (2001) has called this association into question, challenging the idea that all subjects have a universal desire to resist prevailing norms, and criticizing the feminist presumption that women's agency should be conflated with resistance. Mahmood (2001, 206) calls attention to biases within the humanist tradition, which posit a universal desire for autonomy that is always latent, just under the surface, "[T]he slumbering ember that can spark to flame in the form of an act of resistance when conditions permit." Although she applauds poststructuralist critiques for their considerable effort to decenter the autonomous sovereign subject, Mahmood suggests that poststructuralism still falls squarely within the humanist tradition: it still centers an emancipatory subject. Uncoupling self-realization from the idea of an autonomous will and from emancipation, Mahmood insists that agency is not simply a synonym for resistance to domination, but an embodied capacity for action that relations of subordination may enable and create.

Investigating disciplinary practices within the women's mosque movement in Cairo, Egypt, Mahmood suggests that devout Muslim women actively seek to embody virtues associated with feminine passivity and submissiveness. Aspiring to cultivate such virtues as shyness and modesty, they employ their bodies in service to this goal. Indeed, they explicitly undertake bodily practices in an effort to shape their souls. Adopting language that has a marked similarity to Butler's, Mahmood emphasizes that Muslim women in the mosque movement adopt distinctive disciplinary techniques to embody shyness. In keeping with a theory of performativity, engaging in certain forms of conduct produces an inner sense of virtue.

> To begin with, what is striking here is that instead of innate human desires eliciting outward forms of conduct, it is the sequence of practices and actions one is engaged in that determines one's desires and emotions. In other words, action does not issue forth from natural feelings but *creates* them. Furthermore, in this conception it is through repeated *bodily acts* that one trains one's memory, desire and intellect to behave according to established standards of conduct . . . Taking the absence of shyness as a marker of an incomplete learning process, Amal further develops this quality by synchronizing both outward behavior and inward motives until the discrepancy between the two is dissolved.
>
> (Mahmood 2001, 213–214)

Rather than cast these gendered performances as oppressive, Mahmood suggests that they are a source of satisfaction. Piety practices involve bodily acts as a form of soul craft, which enable practitioners to achieve the inner character to which they aspire.

Recent accounts of embodiment that draw on Foucault's notions of discipline and normalization concur that women's understandings of their bodies, desires, and aspirations are produced in particular situations permeated by social norms that continue to advantage some and disadvantage others (Ahmed 2004). They agree that there is no natural body to be apprehended outside culture. The performance of certain acts from a very early age produces a sense of self. Those acts are grounded in racialized and gendered norms that reflect structures of power. Both bodies and subjectivities are socially mediated, structured in accordance with a politics of the body that is both racist and sexist. These scholars also agree that racializing and gendering processes produce women (and men) who take pleasure in raced-gendered performances. They disagree, however, about whether such pleasure taking is problematic.

Certain strands of postcolonial scholarship add an additional dimension to discussions about the pleasures disciplined bodies may take in raced-gendered performances and the subjectivities that flow from them. Philosopher Achille Mbembe (2003, 39-40) has coined the term *necropower* to capture the effects of racialized regimes on bodies of color, because both disciplinary power and the concept of biopower are "insufficient to account for contemporary forms of subjugation of life to the power of death." Mbembe notes that states have deployed weapons against the colonized "in the interest of maximum destruction of persons . . . creating *death-worlds*, new and unique forms of social existence in which vast populations are subjected to conditions of life conferring upon them the status of the living dead" (40). He argues that late modern colonial occupation combined disciplinary, biopolitical, and necropolitical power with the consequence that today, in many artificially resource-deprived postcolonial African states, the only thing available for distribution is death. Bodies devalued precisely because of their subordination are subjected to forms of precarious existence that culminate in disproportionate violence and premature death. Conduct inscribed by racist, sexist norms produces hierarchies of bodies that distinguish those who kill from those who are targeted for death, just as they produce subjectivities of some who believe they are entitled to kill with impunity and some who believe their lot is to suffer.

Drawing insights from Mbembe, Melissa Wright (2011) has suggested that contemporary *femicide*—the murder of women because they are women—must be understood in terms of necropolitics. Focusing on the murder of women in Cuidad Juarez, Mexico, Wright demonstrates how young women working in the maquiladoras were not only murdered with impunity, but blamed by local and national officials for their own deaths. Trading on misogynist notions that "good women" did not work outside the home, elected officials suggested that the women, who were murdered while returning home from factory jobs that required them to work late shifts, deserved the fate that befell them because they were "public women," a euphemism for sex workers. Rather than acting to secure the safety of working women or finding and prosecuting particularly brutal murderers, government officials circulated a discourse that justified femicide for women who had the temerity to brave the public streets in order to make a living. In this perverse necropolitics, government officials characterized working women's deaths as a kind of cleansing that restored the health of the body politic from its contamination by public women.

African American activists have long called attention to the brutal necropower sanctioned by white supremacy. From the pioneering anti-lynching campaigns of Ida B Wells to the recent mobilizations against the murders of unarmed black youths Trayvon Martin, Mike Brown, and Freddie Gray activists have denounced racist conduct on the part of civilians and police that enable them to murder with impunity. Antiracist feminist activists have raised outcries about not only the forms of disinvestment and neglect that occasioned the murders of Sakia Gunn and Renisha McBride, but also the racialized pattern of providing disproportionate state support for the sexual practices, sexual and reproductive health, reproductive relations, and caregiving and caretaking that are necessary to sustain life for some bodies over those of others. The state's support for the development and nurture of some bodies rather than others includes shielding some bodies from violence, while utterly failing to protect others. Myriad inequities, noxious practices, and racist institutions sustain conduct that enables white citizens to engage in necropower to the permanent detriment of people of color. Living in the shadow of violence enacted with impunity affects black citizens' ability to do and to become all that they could be and to convert their resources into political, economic, and social wellbeing (Threadcraft 2014). Poverty, inadequate security, and a disproportionately violent and punitive social climate affect both African American women and men. Yet, as Angela Davis and bell hooks note, black women have also been subjected to unique sexual and reproductive subordination. Constrained by economic forces and violence, they provide uncompensated or abysmally low-wage caring labor for white children. Subject simultaneously to economic and caretaking exploitation, and denied reproductive freedom through coerced reproduction in slavery, sterilization abuse, and the targeted provision of long-acting, debilitating, birth-control measures, such as Norplant and Depo Provera in the contemporary era, black women's subjectivity has been shaped by a host of practices that have more in common with Mbembe's necropolitics than Foucault's normalization.

Both Mbembe and Wright examine the role of the state in the production of properly embodied death. But they pay insufficient attention to the state's role in producing properly embodied forms of something less than death and something greater than what is necessary to produce death, *overkill*. Work at the intersection of trans studies and the analysis of the criminal justice system illuminates how centralized and diffuse power sanctions and sustains this overkill against colored bodies and against the bodies of those who transgress sanctioned gender performance. *Captive Genders: Trans Embodiment and the Prison Industrial Complex* explicitly counters the dominant LGBT progress narrative that begins with the Stonewall uprising and culminates in marriage equality; challenges the presumption of mainstream of prison studies that the body of the prisoner is male; and, critiques the discipline of trans studies for failing to attend to the role of the prison-industrial complex in producing and enforcing heterosexuality and normative gender presentation. In his introductory chapter "Fugitive Flesh: Gender Self-Determination, Queer Abolition, and Trans Resistance," Eric A. Stanley argues that prison abolition must be at the center of struggles for gender self-determination. He defines gender self-determination as the right to express the gender one feels at present through a set of body and embodied practices. He emphasizes that meaningful gender self-determination requires a social context in which changing one's gender presentation does nothing to negate past and future presentations. Falling far short of that ideal, "gender trespassing" in the current context makes one disproportionately vulnerable to state violence, surveillance, policing, and imprisonment, much as colored embodiment does. Indeed, Stanley suggests that one of the most volatile points of contact between the state and the body occurs in the domain of gender enforcement--in the state's efforts to ensure that there is no gender trespassing. Gender-nonconforming youth are subject to scrutiny, punishment, and isolation from parents, teachers, and peers. They are disproportionately thrown out of their families and foster-care services. Possessing limited opportunities for formal employment, gender non-conforming youth often take refuge in a parallel economy, where they experience recurrent poverty and state supervision. In the context of such extreme vulnerability, gender non-conforming youth, particularly those of color, confront forms of interpersonal violence best characterized as "overkill." As Lori Saffin has noted:

> Most victims of gender-based violence suffered multiple bullet wounds, or a combination of strangling, stabbing and beating. In a number of cases victims appeared to have been shot, stabbed or bludgeoned, even after death. The extreme violence used by assailants suggests that the attacks were motivated by intense rage and that the purpose of these attacks was not simply to terminate life, but to punish and torture for gender-non-conformity.
>
> (Saffin 2011, 145)

These murders often go unsolved, unpunished, and unrecognized by the mainstream press and the communities in which they take place. Occurring below the threshold of visibility, the phenomenon of overkill demonstrates that sovereign necropower must be understood to operate not only through hyper-surveillance but also through

Conclusion

Feminist theorists have illuminated profound racial and gender bias in traditional philosophical accounts of embodiment. They have traced the androcentrism in views that privilege mind, soul, spirit, or reason over matter and emotion. And they have demonstrated connections between misogyny and somatophobia. Although they have offered insightful accounts of women's embodiment as a product of patriarchal control and sexist disciplinary practices, I have argued that white feminist theorists have not succeeded in fully escaping somatophobia, celebrations of cultural mastery over "nature," or the presumption that bodies can be explained without attending to processes of racialization. By considering black feminist theorists' analyses of the critical role played by racialization and gendering in the production of raced-gendered bodies and performances, I have shown why notions of unmarked bodies are thoroughly inadequate. I have also suggested that optimistic notions of transcendence, autonomy, individual choice, and personal fulfillment fail to give full weight to the negative effects of discipline enacted through racist and sexist conduct. Turning to Mbembe's conception of necropower, I have argued that the politics of the body are inseparable from social practices that shore up racist, sexist regimes. Discussions of embodiment must move beyond concerns with individual freedom and voluntary choice to engage seriously systemic questions of justice.

Notes

1. In fact, so thoroughly entwined were Plato's hatred of the body and his misogyny that he was often able to make remarkably nonsexist remarks regarding women and their potential contributions to society when he was not thinking about the body. Conversely, however, when he did think of the body, his thoughts returned almost immediately to women and those same thoughts immediately veered towards the misogynistic. See Spelman (1982, 119).
2. Correspondingly, in his account of social life, women care for the needs of the body and men participate in the all important realm of freedom—that is, the life of the polis. For a full account, see Susan Moller Okin, *Women in Western Political Thought* (Princeton, NJ: Princeton University Press, 1979), 82.
3. It should be noted that with Bartman this fascination extended to her genitals and that this also arguably continues. See Judy Chicago's curious presentation of the inherent difference in the black female vagina in "The Dinner Party," where the vagina is not Beauvoir's bleeding wound, or even Chicago's own intricate flower, but a collection of African masks. See also Kara Walker's counterclaim that though the black vagina looms larger than life, it is perfectly ordinary and nothing to fear in her work *A Subtlety*.

References

Ahmed, Sara. 2004. *The Cultural Politics of Emotion*. New York: Routledge.
Alcoff, Linda. 2006. *Visible Identities: Race, Gender, and the Self*. New York: Oxford University Press.
Banks, Ingrid. 2000. *Hair Matters: Beauty, Power, and Black Women's Consciousness*. New York: New York University Press.
Bartky, Sandra Lee. 1990. *Femininity and Domination: Studies in the Phenomenology of Oppression*. New York: Routledge.
Beauvoir, Simone de. 1989. *The Second Sex*. New York: Vintage.
Bordo, Susan. 1993. *Unbearable Weight: Feminism, Western Culture and the Body*. Berkeley: University of California Press.
Braidotti, Rosi. 2011. *Nomadic Subjects Embodiment and Sexual Difference in Contemporary Feminist Theory*. New York: Columbia University Press.
Butler, Judith. [1990] 1997. "Performative Acts and Gender Constitution: An Essay in Phenomenology and Feminist Theory." In *Writing on the Body: Female Embodiment and Feminist Theory*, edited by Katie Conboy, Nadia Medina, and Sarah Stanbury, 401–418. New York: Columbia University Press.
Butler, Judith. 1999. *Gender Trouble: Feminism and the Subversion of Identity*. New York: Routledge.
Byrd, Ayana D., and Lori L. Tharps. 2001. *Hair Story: Untangling the Roots of Black Hair in America*. New York: St. Martin's Griffin.
Craig, Maxine Leeds. 2002. *Ain't I A Beauty Queen? Black Women, Beauty, and the Politics of Race*. New York: Oxford University Press.
Davis, Angela Y. 1983. *Women, Race and Class*. New York: Vintage.
Davis, Angela Y. 1995. "Reflections on the Black Women's Role in the Community of Slaves." In *Words of Fire: An Anthology of African-American Feminist Thought*, edited by Beverly Guy-Sheftall, 199–218. New York: New Press.
Firestone, Shulamith. 1997. *The Second Wave: A Reader in Feminist Theory*. Edited by Linda Nicholson. New York: Routledge.
Foucault, Michel. 1977. *Discipline and Punish: The Birth of the Prison*. Translated by Alan Sheridan, London: Penguin.
Ford, Tanisha C. 2013. "SNCC Women, Denim and the Politics of Dress." *Journal of Southern History* 79 (3): 625–658.
Gatens, Moira. 1996. *Imaginary Bodies: Ethics, Power and Corporeality*. London: Routledge.
Hobbes, Thomas. (1651) 1996. *Leviathan*. New York: Oxford University Press.
hooks, bell. 1997. "Selling Hot Pussy: Representations of Black Female Sexuality in the Cultural Marketplace." In *Writing on the Body: Female Embodiment and Feminist Theory*, edited by Katie Conboy, Nadia Medina, and Sarah Stanbury, 113–128. New York: Columbia University Press.
Irigaray, Luce. 1985. *The Sex Which Is Not One*. Ithaca, NY: Cornell University Press.
Mahmood, Saba. 2001. "Feminist Theory, Embodiment, and the Docile Agent: Some Reflections on the Egyptian Islamic Revival," *Cultural Anthropology* 16 (2): 202–236.
Mbembe, Achille. 2003. "Necropolitics." *Public Culture* 15 (1): 11–40.
Okin, Susan Moller. 1979. *Women in Western Political Thought*. Princeton, NJ: Princeton University Press.
Rich, Adrienne. 1976. *Of Woman Born: Motherhood as Experience and Institution*. New York: Norton.

Saffin, Lori A. 2011."Identities under Siege: Violence against Transpersons of Color." In *Captive Genders: Trans Embodiment and the Prison Industrial Complex*, edited by Eric A. Stanley and Nat Smith, 141–164. Baltimore, MD: AK Press.

Spelman, Elizabeth V. 1982. "Woman as Body: Ancient and Contemporary Views." *Feminist Studies* 8 (1): 109–131.

Stanley, Eric A. 2011 "Introduction: Fugitive Flesh: Gender Self-Determination, Queer Abolition, and TransResistance." In *Captive Genders: Trans Embodiment and the Prison Industrial Complex*, edited by Eric A. Stanley and Nat Smith, 1–14. Baltimore, MD: AK Press.

Threadcraft, Shatema. 2014. "Intimate Injustice, Political Obligation, and the Dark Ghetto." *Signs: Journal of Women in Culture and Society* 39 (3): 735–760.

Wollstonecraft, Mary. 1792. *A Vindication of the Rights of Woman: with Strictures on Political and Moral Subjects*. London: J. Johnson.

Wright, Melissa W. 2011. "Necropolitics, Narcopolitics, and Femicide: Gendered Violence on the Mexico-U.S. Border." *Signs* 36 (3): 707–731.

Young, Iris Marion. 1990. *Throwing like a Girl and Other Essays in Feminist Philosophy and Social Theory*. Bloomington: Indiana University Press.

CHAPTER 11

EXPERIENCE

JUDITH GRANT

EXPERIENCE AND EPISTEMOLOGY IN FEMINIST THEORY

THE concept of "experience" became important in Anglo-American feminist theory during the second half of the twentieth century. Anglo-American feminist theorists used the idea of experience, and in particular, "woman's experience," as a foundational epistemology that complemented various political analyses of patriarchy and personal politics. In contrast to nineteenth-century Anglo-American feminisms that were directed toward the creation of compensatory correctives to the exclusion of women from political, philosophical, social theories, rights claims and practices, "second wave" feminist theorists built new theories from the ground up. Second-wave Anglo-American feminist theorists began with critiques of existing theories and worked from the point of view that the grounding for new feminist theories ought to begin from female experience, which would be the basis for feminist theoretical knowledge claims. This would separate feminist theory from patriarchal theory developed exclusively from the male point of view. Subsequently, the central role given to experience by Anglo-American feminists became a key bone of contention in several important debates in twentieth-century feminist theory. These debates took place among Anglo-American feminisms and between Anglo-American feminism and so-called French feminist theory. One might argue that they also played a role in the split between queer theory and feminist theory.[1]

Although the reliance on experience is often pointed to as one of the major differences between Anglo-American and French feminisms, it is not precisely correct to say that the idea of experience is wholly absent from French feminism. Rather, the influence of existential, psychoanalytic, and structuralist theories meant that "experience" was not used in the same way in French theory. Rather, it was understood to be mediated by interpretation; whether one's own interpretation, as in the case of memory and other distortions of the psyche, or because the subject itself existed in a power structure that made any idea of raw experience problematic. While Anglo-American feminisms began with women's experience as a way to identify and combat patriarchy, feminists working with French theories began with the patriarchal power structure itself and then used it to problematize the reliability of female experience as a corrective to gendered power imbalances.

For example, Simone de Beauvoir's extraordinarily important book *The Second Sex* advances a concept of experience that does not locate it as an epistemological foundation in her feminist theory. Indeed, the French title of volume 2 of this work is best translated as "lived experience" (*L'experience vecue*). In the book as a whole, Beauvoir argues that the social construction of the meaning of woman and femininity create a situation in which Woman occupies the subject position of the "Other," as against Man who is defined as the true human subject. Thus positioned as object, women lack the sovereignty that Sartre and other existentialists assumed to be part and parcel of the human experience. This means, she argued, that freedom and authenticity are impossible for women, and in fact indicates that their status as human subjects is also called into question. Beauvoir writes about experience not as an epistemology, but as a phenomenology intended to chronicle life as an Other. The problem of experience informs her work in that she suggests that the female experience of subjection alters her ability to act on, or even to recognize, the choices and freedoms that are the very hallmarks of the existentialist vision of what it means to be a human being.

For Beauvoir, experiences drawn from women's situation as Other are suspect as knowledge claims insofar as they remain untouched by critical reflection. "Woman can be defined by her consciousness of her own femininity no more satisfactorily than by saying that she is female, for she acquires this consciousness under circumstances dependent upon the society of which she is a member" (Beauvoir 1989, 49). Turning her attention to the development of the structure of patriarchy itself, Beauvoir illuminates the manifold ways that patriarchy reproduces the macrolevel, mythic existences of women's lives at the level of the quotidian and of the construction of subjectivity itself. Thus, the subject position of femininity into which the narrative of patriarchy places women, potentially distorts the self-understandings that women have about their own lives. Beauvoir's work illustrates the ways in which French feminist theory moved away from epistemology because of a loss of faith in an authentic subject. As a result, the use of women's life experience was significant as evidence of patriarchy, but not useful as the basis for an epistemological foundation for feminist theory.

Origins and Development

The origin of the feminist theoretical use of experience in the Anglo-American case is quite different. The origin and development of the term is evident in the books, pamphlets and manifestos written by the members of various grassroots groups who founded 1970s radical feminism (e.g., Firestone 2003; Koedt 1973, *Notes from the Second Year* 1970).

Both "experience" and the category "woman" were related to early feminist theorizing about patriarchy as a political system of male domination. Likewise, experience figures importantly in the second-wave notion that the "personal is political." Indeed, *experience, woman, patriarchy*, and *personal politics* are interrelated terms occurring in the initial moments of Anglo-American feminist theory, and thus understanding experience demands some investigation of the other terms.

Patriarchy was conceptualized as an invisible but all pervasive, political and socially constructed system of male and masculinist domination. Because the power of patriarchy was everywhere, it was not located in the kinds of tangible political institutions that had formed the basis for political action in the first half of the twentieth century. No socialist movements or rights claims could thwart patriarchy because it was reproduced on the level of the mind and ideology, as well as in the everyday actions and rituals of men and women. For radical feminists, patriarchy was a way to name the dualistic hierarchy of gender as a system of power rather than a biological, natural phenomenon. Patriarchy was the name for the political system that structurally reproduced the domination of all women across time, space, beliefs, culture and class, (Lerner 1987). The resulting "sex-class" was, as Shulamith Firestone wrote, "so deep as to be invisible" (Firestone 2003, 63). In defining patriarchy and the resultant "sexual politics," Kate Millett wrote that sex itself was, "something of a status category" that was governed by the political system, patriarchy. Because patriarchy as male domination manifested on all levels of existence, it followed that the politics of patriarchy had to include a politics of everyday life. Feminists called this "personal politics," because patriarchy's power, or at least the reproduction of that power, was most deeply effective in the areas of sexuality and the domestic sphere.

The gendered nature of everyday life became central in second-wave feminism, and was theorized as a principal site of women's oppression. Indeed, personal politics became one of the major hallmarks of all versions of second-wave feminism, both Continental and Anglo-American. Kate Millett (2000, 24) wrote, "[I]t may be imperative that we give some attention to defining a theory of politics which treats of power relationships on grounds less conventional than those to which we are accustomed." Patriarchy, Millett continued, demanded that one expand the idea of politics to include personal life, understanding daily practices as, "a set of stratagems designed to maintain a system" (23–59). This understanding of patriarchy as a political system operated in a host of early radical feminist writings about the politicization of sexuality, romance and the domestic sphere. Anne Koedt's (1973) early essay, "The Myth of the Vaginal Orgasm," for example, was a political analysis of what had up until then been a solely psychological discourse about the female sexual response. Similarly, Ti-Grace Atkinson (1974, 19–20) wrote that sexual intercourse was a political institution whose function was to support and reproduce patriarchy. Finally, a large literature coming from socialist and Marxist feminists about housework can be attributed to the new attention to the patriarchal political system and subsequent attention to the quotidian, the experience of everyday life (Dalla Costa 1974; Delphy 1984; Weeks 2011, 96–98, 236–251).

Since patriarchy was held up as the power structure that yielded the ruling ethos governing all known societies, it followed that patriarchal domination applied to all women regardless of class. Notions of patriarchy became considerably more nuanced as feminist theory developed. Socialist feminists, for example, questioned the transhistoricity of the term (Rowbotham 1973; Hartmann 1979; Eisenstein 1978). But at the outset, this simple version of patriarchy created the possibility of this trans-class claim, a claim that was extraordinary coming from a group of women with roots in the Marxist left. One pamphlet reads, "One tends to forget that they are *women* that they belong to their husbands or fathers (owners) and that they are used by their owners in the same or equally degrading ways as other women" (quoted in Grant 1993, 29).

All of this points to the ways that feminist theory was developing on its own terms, and how it was foregrounding the importance of its own categories of analysis, including that of experience. For if patriarchy was everywhere, then there was no bias-free method of analysis that could be relied upon. Even the class analysis of Marxism was suspect. All theory, all science, all religion was constructed under patriarchy, and functioned in service to its ideological and material reproduction. Apropos of this point, woman-of-color feminist Audre Lorde (2007) would later write that "the master's tools cannot dismantle the master's house." Thus, second-wave feminists concluded that women's own experiences were the most reliable point of view from which to theorize. In a succinct and often-quoted statement of this conclusion, the manifesto of the radical feminist group Redstockings proclaimed, "We regard our personal experiences and our feelings about that experience as the basis for an analysis of our common situation. We cannot rely on existing ideologies as they are all products of male supremacist culture. We question every generalization and accept none that are not confirmed by our experience" (Crow 2000, 224); Similarly, the 1977 "Combahee River Collective: A Black Feminist Statement," the manifesto of a black feminist socialist group declares, "We have spent a great deal of energy delving into the cultural and experiential nature of our oppression" since racial politics itself does not allow "most black women to look more deeply into our own experiences" (Eisenstein 1978, 362). The use of female experience as the basis for feminist theory had become so hegemonic in feminist theory by 1974, that Julie Mitchell (2000, xvi) wrote in the introduction to the 2000 edition of *Psychoanalysis and Feminism* that she had explicitly retreated from the use of structuralist analysis in the final version of her original book because she had felt compelled to use the reigning feminist category of personal experience as a grounding rather than root her claims in male theorists' notions of structure. Mitchell's solidarity with Anglo-American feminism's developing affinity to the notion of women's experiences as a foundation to theory building is telling and illustrative of the use of the term *experience* both in theory and as evidence of one's feminist political commitments.

The idea of patriarchy posits a subconscious acquiescence and ritualized reproduction of the primacy of all things male and masculinist taking place both at the level of structure and of daily life. Feminist activists understood that it was not just the experience of living as a subject under patriarchy that was important; it was the crucial addition of self-conscious reflection about that experience that enabled female experience to be transformed into feminism. It was from the point of view of female experience coupled with consciousness-raising about patriarchal power that feminist theory began to emerge. Consciousness-raising groups were important as political and theoretical tools. In these groups, women spoke to each other about their unique personal experiences. The goal was to weave those personal narratives into common stories of women's gendered lives to demonstrate that the problems women experienced were not wholly personal, and that the solutions were not psychological but would come from politics (Crow 2000, 113–116). In an important two-part essay published in 1982, Catharine MacKinnon argued that the old radical-feminist tool consciousness-raising was, in fact, a feminist methodology and integral not just to feminist activism, but to feminist theory itself. MacKinnon argued that the mind and the body are both enmeshed in female oppression, and that feminism must address these simultaneously at the level of practice. For MacKinnon (1982, 1991), sexuality in particular was the link between the operation of patriarchy on the body and consciousness. In order to see the world as free subjects, women needed to unite and create themselves as feminist subjects through discussion and analysis of their situations from a point of view that was critical of patriarchy. Consciousness-raising, MacKinnon (1991, 101) argued, creates a shared reality by transforming the experience of the individual woman into a social experience of being female.

The desire to conceptually identify a feminist universal rooted in women's experiences explains the turn to "feminist standpoint theory." Feminist standpoint theory represents a move to a more sophisticated understanding of the female experience. While feminist standpoint is still an epistemologically based theory, standpoint theorists set to work on a more nuanced idea of the difference between female and feminist points of view, and also began to tackle the theoretical implications of the differences among women. Nancy Hartsock is one of the major founders of standpoint theory, and her work is in many ways paradigmatic of the genre. Hartsock interpreted a selection of texts on democracy to make a case that notions of power/empower operated along male/female lines displaying a gendered standpoint, in order to pose the question as to whether there was a "feminine or female" way of exercising power (1984, 2). She began with a critique of exchange models that, she argued, falsely understood the world as made up of "free and equal individuals interacting on the basis of self-interest" (50). These ways of looking at the world mask structures of domination and falsely pose power and exchange as fixed moments in time rather than as process. Further, this way of looking at the world falsely inflates the role of economic production as against those activities that reproduce economic structures, such as those that take place in the sphere of reproduction. The effect is that behaviors and activities taking place in the market sphere are incorrectly conceptualized as definitive of human identity. To the extent that theories of power, such as those articulated by Harold Lasswell, Robert Dahl, Nelson Polsby, and Talcott Parsons, have been embedded in what Hartsock argued were basically market-based ideas of human nature, they completely ignored other systems of domination, such as capitalism and patriarchy. The idea of the rational individual voluntary actor is thus exposed as an ideological myth.

Because market based theories of power understand humans as discreet actors in continual struggle with one another, they find it difficult to account for community and cooperation, and therefore collective action becomes a theoretical problem for them. Hartsock concludes that collective action and community are seen as problems because of the epistemological premises that undergird market-based thinking—namely, the assumption of rational man as an individualist, appetitive, voluntarist actor. This thinking is, she argues, a replication and universalization of the capitalist's point of view (96). To counter this, Hartsock suggests an appropriation of Marxist theorist Georg Lukacs's idea of "standpoint." Noting a similar problem having to do with epistemology in its connection to revolutionary action, Lukacs had argued that revolutionary praxis needed to be grounded in a proletarian perspective. This idea was hugely problematic in Marxism, as the proletariat was not yet constituted as a self-conscious class, and Lukacs admitted that therefore class consciousness would have to be imputed to it (Lukacs 1972). Lukacs's standpoint theory does not, therefore, emanate from worker's experience, but from the Communist Party's imputation of the alleged interests of the proletariat. Despite this, Hartsock deployed Lukacs in arguing for a feminist standpoint.

Looking to a series of women who wrote about power (Hannah Arendt, Dorothy Emmet, Hanna Pitkin, and Bernice Carroll), Hartsock argued that they were linked in that they "argue against the understanding of power as dominance or domination; to attempt to point to other meanings of the term more associated with ability, capacity, competence." She concluded that it is significant that "a large proportion of the theorists who make these moves and express these concerns are women" (224–225). This is suggestive, she contended, of the idea that theories of power are gendered, because gender is a "world-view-structuring experience" (231). Hartsock's major example of a system of domination that mitigates against wholly individual action (in addition to class oppression), is the patriarchal system of sexual and erotic domination described by feminism. Women's position with regard to the reproduction of labor, sexual victimization, childbearing, and childrearing have, she argued, resulted in a fundamentally different standpoint with regard to power. Hartsock was careful to call this a "feminist" rather than a "female" standpoint on the grounds that the female experience contains regressive elements, and she wished to highlight the liberatory potential of the alternate (female) theories of power she had identified (232).

As Hartsock's work illustrates, standpoint theory sought to theorize experience in concrete and historicized ways, while still retaining the idea of a female point of view. That is, even though alternative theories of power are disproportionately written by women, they are not exclusively gendered in this manner. And even among those written by women, theories of power vary considerably. Importantly, standpoint theory recognized and sought to understand female differences as they existed inside a female universal, the latter being crucial. As Sandra Harding asked, if standpoint theory does not assume some feminine universality, "then just what is feminist about standpoint theories?" (1991, 175). The difficulty lay in conceptualizing the multiplicity of the female experience while still maintaining a notion of Woman that did not dissolve into the kind of individualism eschewed by Hartsock. Standpoint theorist Patricia Hill Collins wrote from the position of woman-of-color feminism, acknowledging difference within race (itself a difference), saying that she was developing a black *women's* not a black *woman's* standpoint. Collins sketched the contours of an "Afrocentric feminist epistemology," which, she argued, would reflect a "Black women's standpoint rooted in the everyday experiences of African American women." Black women, Collins argued, while not providing a superior or truer version of reality, did provide an authentic partial perspective of a subjugated knowledge. She wrote, "Each group speaks from its own standpoint and shares its own partial, situated knowledge" (Hill Collins 2008, 236). Similarly, Bettina Aptheker (1989, 12) wrote, "I began then, with this idea: women have a consciousness of social reality that is distinct from that put forth by men. That is, women have a distinct way of seeing and interpreting the world . . . a way of seeing, which is common to themselves as women in that it is distinct from the way the men of their culture or group see things. All women share this *process* of distinction."

As Hartsock and other standpoint thinkers acknowledged, two major categories of practice systematically gendered the world. One was that women as subjects are socialized to be mothers and caregivers. This socialization as caregiving could somehow reflect a female and then a feminist point of view. One idea of revaluing feminine virtues linked women to peace and care. Carol Gilligan's *In A Different Voice* was in the forefront of such thinking, making the argument that women's connection to mothering leads them to think of claims about social justice from the point of view of caring about particular individuals as opposed to abstract rationalist principles found in theories about the rule of law and justice. Importantly, Gilligan reinterpreted theories on human moral development initially developed by Lawrence Kohlberg from a particular feminist point of view. Kohlberg's had argued that boys outpaced girls in moral development as they more quickly came to grasp principles of universal justice. His conclusions were based on data gathered from questions relating to a hypothetical moral dilemma in which children were asked to pit individual human need against rules. Kohlberg measured moral development according to how children solved hypothetical moral dilemmas, arguing that boys systematically favored resolutions in favor of rules about justice. Gilligan did not criticize the data, but rather the experiment itself. Why was the assumption that abstract rules should score higher than concerns about caring for individuals? If a gender difference existed, it was, she argued, the result of the gendered experience of socialization. Little girls, socialized to be mothers and caregivers, had a "different" moral voice, which Gilligan labeled an "ethics of care" (Gilligan 1982). Other theorists, such as Adrienne Rich and Sara Ruddick, also pointed to male/female difference as it pertained to the experience of motherhood (Donovan 2007; Rich 1995; Ruddick 1995), suggesting that these different ways of knowing and being were undervalued from the patriarchal standpoint, and sometimes suggesting that the feminine principles were superior. It can be argued that this "difference feminism" itself harkens back to early radical formulations of the connection between women and nature (Griffin 2000; Ortner 1974), although certainly the theorists of motherhood were far more inclined toward social constructivism, eschewing the spiritualist leanings of the earlier feminine difference ideas. This care/justice debate has continued to be important in such areas as democratic theory, animal rights, and disability studies (Tronto 1993; Donovan 2012; Garland 1997).

A second set of practices that was used to talk about women's universal experience was the idea that female sexual objectification contributed to the destruction of female agency. Indeed, the idea of female sexuality took center stage in the eighties and led to the unfolding of three major issues that are connected to the feminist use of experience: (1) the feminist sexuality debates, (2) the ongoing debate between modernist epistemologists and poststructuralists, and (3) the rise of queer theory.

Sexuality Debates as Turning Point

"Sexuality debates" is the shorthand name given to a series of issues that began in feminism but expanded into a far-reaching international conversation about sexual desire and victimization. Indeed, an idea that sexuality included elements of danger for women was present in second-wave feminism from the beginning. Radical feminists had linked lust, rape, violence against women, and sexual objectification to women's subordinate position in society generally. Radical feminists, such as Susan Brownmiller, began more detailed explorations of the link between sexuality and violence and between sexuality and power. Brownmiller's groundbreaking 1975 book, *Against Our Will: Men, Women and Rape*, was a history and theory of rape that reconceptualized it as a crime of power and violence as opposed to a sex crime. Rape, Brownmiller argued, was not an act of the uncontrolled sexual desire by a man whose passions had been stoked by an alluring woman, it was an act of power and aggression that was most often sexually enacted by men, most often upon women. Rape was always about domination, and even male-on-male rape reinforced the patriarchal link between male violence and gendered hierarchy insofar as it was a crime in which one man treated another man as though he were a sexually subservient woman. Rape, Brownmiller argued, was best understood as an institutionalized, widely used, and accepted tool of patriarchal oppression, not as an individual sex crime. In a sweeping analysis, Brownmiller analyzed rape as a tool of wars, pogroms, racism, and prison life, all the while driving home the point that rape was one of the institutionalized pillars of patriarchy.

But Brownmiller's book contained a second, equally important argument that bore on the question of female experience. She argued that an important part of feminine socialization was not only learning how to survive as prey, but also learning how to eroticize and aestheticize the experience of one's own victimization. Brownmiller (1975, 343) wrote that "women are trained to be rape victims." Brownmiller's view is an example of feminist renarrativizing that begins from a feminist interpretation of female experience, and at the same time problematizes the trustworthiness of that experience as truth. Thus, if women enjoyed rape fantasies or participating in pornographic representations of themselves, it was because of patriarchal socialization. It was a kind of truth, but it was truth from an unadulterated patriarchal point of view, and thus not an expression of authentic female agency. This was the masochistic subject position of women, and it was evidence of the reproduction of patriarchy in every day life on the very level of everyday experience. Brownmiller's extraordinary analysis illustrates the way that feminist interpretations of female experience were used to provide evidence of patriarchy, and at the same time were used to question the truth status of some female experiences. By the time of the 1980s sexuality debates, the powerful analysis of the link between normative desire and violent sexuality had become the basis for the idea of "rape culture," and figured importantly in a wide variety of feminist political activities ranging from critiques of advertising to the battered women's movement to the rise of rape crisis centers, and ultimately, to the feminist movement against pornography. But the slide between feminist truth and women's truth, and the status of the idea of experience became increasingly problematic.

Feminist writers Andrea Dworkin and Catharine MacKinnon are arguably the main theorists of the antipornography movement within feminism. Accepting the radical feminist ideas that normative sexuality and sexual violence were on a continuum, and that female socialization formed female desire as masochistic, they turned their attention to the ways in which personal experience was linked to state institutions, regulations, and cultural representation. In *Intercourse*, Dworkin (1987) wrote about the political nature of sexual intercourse that "[a]ny act so controlled by the state cannot be private in the ordinary sense . . . In that sense, intercourse has never occurred in private." Rather, she wrote, social institutions, including religion and the police, "have had too much to do with establishing the terms of the act itself: not just what people do and do not do; but also what people know, how consciousness and self-consciousness are formed" (148). In this work, Dworkin sees state and social regulations of sexuality as epistemologically implicated in the construction of gender. "In each act of intercourse, a society is formed . . . Gender is what the state seeks to control: who is the man here? Which is the woman? How to keep the man on top, how to keep the man the man; how to render the woman inferior in fucking so that she cannot recover herself from the carnal experience of her own subjugation" (1987, 148–149). Thus, experience of sexual intercourse was, for Dworkin, highly regulated and the central mechanism for the reproduction of gender as a hierarchy. It was also a principal means of gendered subject formation.

Along with sexual intercourse itself, pornography came under scrutiny as major conduit for the reproduction of male domination. Dworkin and MacKinnon advanced a definition of pornography, not as obscene material, but as material that systematically degrades women by making violence sexy and sex violent. Moreover, pornography was not simply a representation of the coupling of violence and sex, it was in and of itself an act of sexual violence. At the height of the antipornography movement, Dworkin and MacKinnon famously worked on several local civil ordinances that reframed pornography as a type of discrimination against women. These ordinances ultimately failed to pass constitutional muster, but are significant in the history of feminism, as they represented an attempt to transform an entire body of law according a feminist critique (MacKinnon and Dworkin 1997). MacKinnon (1993, 16–17) conceptualized pornography, not as speech, but as an action that was harmful to women. "With pornography, men masturbate to women being exposed, humiliated, violated, degraded mutilated, dismembered, bound, gagged, tortured. In the visual materials, they experience this *being done* by watching it *being done*. What is real here is not that the materials are pictures, but that they are part of a sex act. The women are in two dimensions, but the men have sex with them in their own three-dimensional bodies." That is, "[t]o express eroticism is to engage in eroticism . . . To say it is to do it, and to do it is to say it" (MacKinnon, 33). Pornography, MacKinnon contended, was not "only words," but was in and of itself an action that was harmful to women.

While the work of Dworkin and MacKinnon presents many rich avenues for further discussion such as this very provocative idea that pornography is not representation but is in and of itself a sex act, the point for our purposes here is to focus on how this analysis used the idea of experience. That the analysis relied on an interpretation of women's sexuality that, in turn, relied upon women's experience and was in fact at odds with the experiences of many women was the point of contention. Women who purported to enjoy pornography, who participated in the adult industry, even when they did so willingly or as business owners; women who claimed to find prostitution empowering, or who advanced any of a number of other so-called "pro–sex" arguments, were conceptualized as insufficiently feminist. Their experiences counted as evidence of oppression, but not as truth.

It was at this moment in the history of feminism that the contradictory claims about experience came to a head, resulting in profound divisions inside feminism and ultimately contributing to the creation of the offshoot, queer theory. The work of Gayle Rubin is of key importance here. Rubin identified herself as a lesbian feminist and a practitioner of sadomasochism (SM). While Dworkin and MacKinnon were advancing their theories about how female sexuality was akin to masochism, and how this female masochism was a lynchpin of patriarchal domination, Rubin and like-minded feminists were advancing the incompatible view that patriarchy could be combated by freely acting on one's sexual desires, that wide-ranging sexual pluralism ought to be encouraged, and that sadomasochism and the eroticization of power relations were a way to be freed from patriarchy. In objecting to the use of SM as a metaphor that implicitly damned it as a sexual practice, Rubin ultimately abandoned feminist theory as a tool for understanding sexuality.

Significantly, Rubin's arguments against Dworkin, MacKinnon and other antipornography feminists did not employ an idea of women's experiences, and indeed, did not begin from the point of view of the female subject position at all. Rather, Rubin turned her attention to the practice of sexuality itself. For Rubin, Dworkin, and MacKinnon arguments rooted in experience and identity were proof that feminist theory was not equipped to deal with questions of desire, and that the quagmire of experience as truth had to be rejected. Rubin argued that sexuality had its own history, its own hierarchies and normativities. Gender, she wrote, is an outcome of sexuality, a point that Judith Butler (2006) would reiterate and expand on a few years later in *Gender Trouble*. Further, while feminism is a good theory to understand marriage, kinship, heterosexual relations, and so on, Rubin held that it is not especially good at understanding sexual practices that take place outside heterosexuality. Rubin thus became interested in how heterosexuality became the privileged sexuality. Queer theory's break with feminism occurs precisely at this moment when feminist arguments about the link between male sexual violence and pornography directly attack certain experiences of female pleasure.

Rubin makes her famous argument in, "Thinking Sex: Notes for a Radical Theory of the Politics of Sexuality," a paper first presented in 1982 at Barnard College, and subsequently published in 1984 in Carole Vance's edited collection, *Pleasure and Danger: Exploring Female Sexuality* (1984). In it, Rubin turns to Michel Foucault's claim that desire is not connected to preexisting biological entities but is socially produced in historically specific practices. Foucault's work, Rubin argues, "points to a major discontinuity between kinship-based systems of sexuality and more modern forms" ([1982] 2011, 146). Nonreproductive sexualities may have emerged from kinship structures, but have ultimately acquired their own autonomy as systems (178). Rubin constructs a narrative that posits hierarchies of kinds of sexualities, noting that "reproductive heterosexuals are alone at the top of the erotic pyramid" (149). In the essay, Rubin directly attacks feminist antipornography analysis, saying it errs in implying that "sadomasochism is the underlying essential 'truth' toward which all pornography tends" (169). This mistake is in part due to feminism's tendency to reduce all problems to problems of gender, Rubin contends, and she counters by challenging "the assumption that feminism is or should be the privileged site of a theory of sexuality. Feminism is the theory of gender oppression, but not necessarily of sexual oppression. To automatically assume that it is the theory of sexual oppression is to fail to distinguish between gender, on the one hand, and erotic desire on the other" (177–178). Antipornography feminism participates in the demonization of marginal sexual practices and the reproduction of hierarchies of sexuality that center reproductive sex. Here Rubin specifically takes Catharine MacKinnon to task for subsuming sexuality under feminism (179). "To the extent that these overlap with erotic stratifications, feminist theory has some explanatory power. But as issues become less those of gender and more those of sexuality, feminist analysis becomes misleading, and often irrelevant . . . In the long run, feminism's critique of gender hierarchy must be incorporated into a radical theory of sex" (180).

Feminism and Critical Theory

The intellectual journey of feminist theory over the several decades of the second wave leading up to the beginning of queer theory is one way to understand the narrative power and problems with the idea of "experience." The question of whether experience can be trusted as a truth claim are evident in other twentieth-century discussions of the status of experience in a wide range of theories and disciplines predating feminism. These include positivism, historicism, and anthropology (Comte 1988; Thompson 1966; Levi-Strauss 1971). The question is also of profound significance in debates about the status and truth of personal experience in psychoanalysis, insofar as the practice of psychoanalysis is largely concerned with renarrativizing memory and personal experience. Likewise, the existentialist concept of "authenticity" relies at least in part on being able to make a distinction between a truthful and a false sense of self that in turn is based on judgments and actions related to one's own experiences. Another example is provided by ethnography, a methodology that raises questions about experiential reportage (Smith 1989), as does the practice of oral history (Echols 1989). Similar questions about the status of experience are raised in anthropology, a discipline committed to the proposition that knowledge and experience are not monolithic, but rather are reliant on the cultural perspectives of both the observer and the population being studied. Looked at in this fashion, one can see that the question of the truth of experience has been debated and conceptualized at great length over the course of intellectual history.

However the most helpful way to contextualize feminist theory inside the sweep of these discussions is to understand it as a kind of critical theory. For the fraught relationship with experience evidenced in feminist theory parallels a similar phenomenon in critical theory overall. Like that twentieth-century European tradition, feminist theory shares an attention to the connection between knowledge and power, the importance of daily life experiences, and an explicit link between theory and social justice. Critical theory emerged in the twentieth century as the Left turned its collective attention to ideology and consciousness as central problems of power. The failure of the working class to achieve revolutionary class-consciousness (Lenin 1987), and the remarkable ability of totalitarian regimes to attain popular support in the cases of fascism and national socialism (Horkheimer and Adorno 2007) had much to do with the global Left's new interest in the power of ideology, subject formation, and consciousness. As against "traditional theory," which pretended to be a neutral tool of knowledge, German philosopher Max Horkheimer defined critical theory, first, as having social justice as its goal, and, second, as being self-conscious about its own place in the stream of history, theory, and power. Whereas traditional theory supports the world as it is, while claiming neutrality, critical theory's categories of analysis emerge as "critical of the present" (Horkheimer 1972, 218). Yet from the perspective of traditional theory, critical theory appears "to be subjective and speculative, one-sided and useless. Since it runs counter to prevailing habits of thought, which contribute to the persistence of the past and carry on the business of an outdated order of things. it appears to be biased and unjust" (218).

Horkheimer began a tradition in critical theory that was certainly pertinent to both Continental and Anglo-American feminists in the attention to daily life, consciousness formation, questions of identity and authenticity, knowledge in its relationship to power, and the idea of experience. At this founding moment of critical theory in the work of Horkheimer, experience is acknowledged, though rejected, as an important potential site of critical knowledge claims. Against the idea of subjugated knowledge as foundational in building a worker-centered theory, Horkheimer writes that "the situation of the proletariat is, in this society, no guarantee of correct knowledge. The proletarian may indeed have experience of meaninglessness in the form of continuing and increasing wretchedness and injustice of his own life," but "even to the proletariat the world superficially seems quite different than it really is" (213–214). Pushing the point further, he continues, "If critical theory consisted essentially in formulations of the feelings and ideas of one class at any given moment, it would not be structurally different from the special branches of science. It would be engaged in describing the psychological contents typical of certain social groups; it would be social psychology" (214). Similarly, a critique of experience figures heavily in Antonio Gramsci's (1971) notion that dominant ideologies are experienced as "common sense," and in the later structuralist ideas of Althusser (2001) to the effect that ideology is a lived practice wherein our minds become colonized through the practices of everyday life.

Although Anglo-American feminist theory diverges from most critical theory in its embrace of the experiential, many of its ideas echo the notion that power and domination are reproduced under the surface in practices, and thus parallels the analysis in critical theory as a whole. There is a shared understanding that power is reproduced according to a script that is rewritten daily in the performance of activities involving even the most intimate, mundane, and seemingly benign details of human life. Personal life practices, along with speech itself, reproduced ideologies of power and constructed consciousness and experience. Feminist and other critical theorists understood everyday life to be the principal conduit for the reproduction of that power, whether gendered or not. The philosophical question faced by feminism lay in whether female experience really could be the basis for meaningful critique and theory building. Indeed, this was a question faced by all critical theorists in one form or another, and the rejection of experientialism and the turn to structure that is evident in feminism parallels the same schism in the rest of critical theory.

European feminists had the advantage of deep familiarity with decades of writing by nonfeminist critical theorists who had worked precisely on this issue of the reproduction of power on the levels of everyday life, the mind, language, and mythic ritual, all of whom had rejected the idea of the foundational role of experience. Certainly, this was largely the point of the structuralist and poststructuralist works of Althusser, Foucault, Lacan, Derrida, Levi-Strauss, and many others who had already become famous critical theorists in Europe, but who had yet to be widely translated or accepted into the English-speaking world during the early stages in the development of second-wave Anglo-American feminist theory. Likewise, German critical theory of the interwar and postwar periods had paid a great deal of attention to the problem of the reproduction of the sustaining ideologies that undergirded more overt systems of power, such as capitalism, the liberal state, and, of course, fascism and national socialism (e.g., Horkheimer and Adorno 2007; Benjamin 1996, 1999, 2002). Seen in this light, the Anglo-American idea of patriarchy developed in the 1970s anticipates the North American embrace of many European ideas having to do with the importance of the personal and the ubiquitous invisibility of power. These ideas would become virtually hegemonic in academic critical theory circles throughout the 1980s.

In practice, revolutionary socialism and fascism were largely European questions, though the events of May 1968, decolonization, race-based civil rights movements, and protests against the Vietnam War all highlighted the issues of ideology and personal politics. Thus, despite not being intellectually located in European structuralism, Anglo-American feminist theory's ideas of patriarchy and personal politics aligned with European critical theory in positioning personal life and ideology as essential to political theory. Anglo-American feminism did not let go of epistemology in the second-wave moment, as much European critical and feminist theory had already done. This, along with its very different understanding of the role of experience, is the crux of the historic division between Anglo-American and Continental feminisms. Anglo-American feminism also retained key elements of humanism. Certainly, to the extent that a goal of human equality was embedded in feminism, there was a latent humanism, but the real link was the retention of the humanist epistemological, subject-centered analysis. Indeed, the foremost problem in Anglo-American feminism, that of essentialism, was the same problem that had plagued humanism, and the same one that had been pointed out by early structuralists. In short, it is as difficult to talk about a universal category Woman as it had been to talk about a universal Man or Human. And just as Reason had been pointed to as culpable in humanist epistemologies, experience, which occupied the same role in Anglo-American feminisms, was linked to the problem of essentialism.

Still, Anglo-American feminists were politically committed to inclusion, and very well aware that feminist theory had to include concrete, flesh and blood women on whose very bodies, and in whose minds, patriarchy was being enacted. Feminism was not, after all, only a set of theories, but was also a politics with clear revolutionary goals. Feminists acknowledged varied perspectives among individual women as well differences stemming from race, class, historical position, and so on. Differences among women challenged the universality of the category Woman, and problematized woman's identity as the basis for feminist analysis and activism. Therefore one might say that while, on the one hand, it fell within humanist traditions, on the other, it was also embedded in the ongoing critique of humanism that had been occurring throughout the early twentieth century in Europe. Just as universalist humanist theories confronted the problem that concrete individual humans differed from any abstraction "human," so, too, individual women had divergent, even contradictory, experiences from those attributed to Women. The very experience that was called upon to prove the oppression of women and the basis of feminism, gave rise to a problem of authenticity, familiar in the humanist tradition as a crisis of the subject. In short (as Beauvoir had written in the 1940s), it is difficult to tell the difference between true, pristine women's experience as against an ideologically colonized experience that is merely a reproduction of the patriarchal. And, as later poststructural theorists observed, there was something about the very notion of a subject that was suspect, as the very category seemed to rest on a static understanding of identity that ignored the excess that was not captured by a unified subject. Anglo-American feminist theory mirrored Western philosophy to the extent that both used experience as an epistemological foundation. But it also shared problems with humanism in attempting to shape a coherent, universal category from among particulars. In humanism, the problem became how to resolve the infinite particularity of individuals into a universal notion of the Human. The same issue recurred in feminism in the issue of resolving multiple female experiences into a social category of Woman.

French Feminism, by contrast, appears closer to critical theory on the question of experience by virtue of its relationship to existentialism and structuralism. Of course, existentialism does not typically fall under the umbrella of critical theory, but there are significant affinities, particularly in the work of Sartre, that proved to be a kind of bridge between the Marxist critical theories of the mid-twentieth century and both postmodernism and feminism in its final third. Like Adorno and Horkheimer, Sartre understands that questions of social morality are connected to the social and to power. But he retains a stubborn faith in the possibilities of individual will, choice, and authenticity. Sartre holds that individuals can correctly perceive their situations, their subjective positions in power structures, and can then make choices to act on those in a free and authentic way. Sonia Kruks has argued that existentialism anticipated philosophical arguments usually attributed to poststructuralists. Kruks (2001, 9) writes, "Sartre arguably anticipates Derrida in insisting that the subject's 'presence to self' is never possible. It is, rather, he says, 'a way of not coinciding with oneself, of escaping identity.'" Beauvoir is important, Kruks notes, because with her idea that woman is not only "other" but also a subordinate, she is able to subvert the Sartrian idea that individual freedoms are not only autonomous but equal (37–39).

Joan W. Scott's (1991) canonical essay "The Evidence of Experience" is of paramount importance to this discussion. In the essay, Scott locates the feminist use of experience within a wider context of intellectual history and theory. In an incisive analysis of several major historians, including R. G. Collingwood, John Toews, and E. P. Thompson, Scott argues that historians have problematically used "experience" to establish the authoritative nature of their histories in a variety of ways (783–786). E. P. Thompson's *The Making of the English Working Class*, for example, used experience as a "unifying phenomenon" to bind the category "class" (Scott 1991, 784–786). Second, Thompson erred in conceptualizing experience as something internal; as a feeling. In "The Poverty of Theory and Other Essays," Thompson wrote that "people do not only experience their own experience as ideas, within thought and its procedures . . . they also experience their own experience as *feeling*" (quoted in Scott 1991, 786). Scott argues that the first mistake Thompson makes is to tautologically employ experience as foundational to an ontological category, and that "the problem Thompson sought to address isn't really solved. Working class 'experience' is now the ontological foundation of working class identity, politics, history" (786). Second, his understanding of experience as an internal expression of consciousness, rather than as the material on which consciousness acts, wrongly shifts theorists away from asking the key materialist question of how experiences are produced (778–782). Scott makes plain that her objections to the foundational status of experience in E. P. Thompson are the same as her objections to the use of experience in feminist theory and other social movements based on "identity." When used as a foundational source of evidence, experiences are treated as permanent and transcendent rather than historical, contingent, and contested. Scott writes in the mode of poststructuralism that "[i]t is not individuals who have experience, but subjects who are constituted through experience. Experience in this definition then becomes not the origin of our explanation, not the authoritative (because seen or felt) evidence that grounds what is known, but rather that which we seek to explain, that about which knowledge is produced" (780). In this, she argues, feminist uses of the concept are identical to that of some historians. "They take as self-evident the identities of those whose experience is being documented and thus naturalize their difference. They locate resistance outside its discursive construction and reify agency as an inherent attribute of individuals, thus decontextualizing it. When experience is taken as the origin of knowledge, the vision of the individual subject (the person who had the experience or the historian who recounts it) becomes the bedrock of evidence on which explanation is built" (777). Rather, Scott argues, we should not look to discover truth in experience, but look to it as a place to find the material that must then be interpreted in light of imbrication of the social and the personal, all the while recognizing that there is no one single narrative of any one experience (794–795). In fact, experience is always already an interpretation, and what counts as experience is neither self-evident nor straightforward but is always contested, and thus is always a political act (797).

Conclusion

This concept of experience has been in important in a wide variety of theories and methodologies. Defenses and critiques of it have been especially fraught in modernity because of the centrality of the roles of the individual and reason. These have linked and foregrounded agency and problems of knowledge. While these issues are evident in numerous examples and multiple disciplines, as this chapter shows, they are perhaps especially pronounced in philosophical systems that understand themselves to be linked to social justice goals. In these, the problems of agency, subject formation, and teleology are, perhaps, justifiable responses to the longing for certainty; for the ability to ground movement political actions and goals in some authoritative location, where oppression can be undeniably located, and the solution to it can be certain and clear. So, too, the problems of silencing oppressed groups and manipulating their desires and goals have contributed to the ubiquity of the idea of experience as a way to counter systems of power that seem to so overwhelm the self. Feminist theory plays a rich role in the history of the concept of experience, demonstrating as it does the important reasons for the ubiquity of experience in social theory, and the problems inherent in its use. One important observation is that feminist theory's important role in the discourse of experience has consistently been virtually ignored in many histories and analyses of experience by nonfeminist thinkers (e.g., Jay 2006). Perhaps this does indeed point to the reality of a male point of view, even if the recourse to female experience as a rejoinder is not always the ideal solution.

Note

1. "French feminism" is a contentious term. As it is used in the United States and Britain, the appellation refers to the theoretical stance of a body of theorists rather than to a national

affiliation (Delphy 1995). Indeed, Sylvie A. Gambaudo (2007, 96–97) suggests that "Alice Jardine (1982) and Toril Moi (2002) are largely responsible for the use of the term 'French feminism', the one for the coining of the term and the other for further limiting its use to a few selected authors. Jardine detected the emergence of French feminist thought out of the intellectual scene of the 1980s France ... the publication of Toril Moi's *Sexual/Textual Politics* in 1985 made official division between Anglo-American feminists and French feminists. Anglo-American feminists ... would be invested in seeking woman-centered perspective and in defining woman's identity they believe women have been denied. French feminists ... on the other hand, would be indebted to Simone de Beauvoir and would believe that woman does not have an identity as such but that the feminine can be identified where difference and otherness are found." As Gambaudo notes, French feminism is not a term that is indigenous to France, and diverse sectors of activism and theory have been collected into this monolithic understanding. The important point for the current discussion is that the theoretical tendency that has unfortunately come to be known as "French feminism" does represent a rejection of the idea of experience as foundational.

References

Adorno, Theodor. 1981. *Negative Dialectics*. 2nd ed. New York: Bloomsbury.
Agamben, Giorgio. 1998. *Home Sacer: Sovereign Power and Bare Life*. Redwood City, CA: Stanford University Press.
Althusser, Louis. 2001. "Ideology and the Ideological State Apparatus." In *Lenin and Philosophy*. New York: Monthly Review Press.
Aptheker, Bettina. 1989. *Tapestries of Life: Women's Work, Women's Consciousness and the Meaning of Daily Experience*. Amherst: University of Massachusetts Press.
Atkinson, Ti-Grace. 1974. *Amazon Odyssey*. New York: Putnam.
Barrett, Michelle. 2014. *Women's Oppression Today*. Brooklyn, NY: Verso Reprint.
Beauvoir, Simone de. 1989. *The Second Sex*. New York: Vintage.
Benjamin, Walter. 1996. *Selected Writings, Volume 1, 1913–1926*: The Belnap Press of Harvard University Press.
Benjamin, Walter. 1999. *Selected Writings, Volume 2, 1927–30*: The Belnap Press of Harvard University Press.
Benjamin, Walter. *Selected Writings, Volume 2, part 2, 1931-1934*, 1999: The Belnap Press of Harvard University Press.
Benjamin, Walter. 2002. *Selected Writings, Volume 3, 1935–1938*. The Belnap Press of Harvard University Press.
Brownmiller, Susan. 1975. *Against Our Will: Men, Women and Rape*. New York: Ballantine.
Butler, Judith. 2006. *Gender Trouble*. New York: Routledge.
Cixous, Helene. 1976. "Laugh of the Medusa." *Signs* 1 (4): 875–893.
Comte, Auguste. 1988. Introduction to *Positivist Philosophy*. Edited by Frederick Ferre. Wall Township, NJ: Hackett.
Crenshaw, Kimberlé. 1991. "Mapping the Margins: Intersectionality, Identity Politics and Violence against Women of Color." *Stanford Law Review* 43 (6): 1241–1299.
Crow, Barbara. 2000. *Radical Feminism: A Documentary Reader*. New York: New York University Press.

Dalla Costa, Maria. 1974. *The Power of Women and the Subversion of the Community*. Bristol, England: Falling Wall Press.

Davies, Tony. 2008. *Humanism: The New Critical Idiom*. London: Routledge.

De Certeau, Michel. 2011. *The Practice of Everyday Life*. Berkeley: University of California Press.

Delphy, Christine. 1984. *Close to Home: A Materialist Analysis of Women's Oppression*. Amherst: University of Massachusetts Press.

Delphy, Christine. 1995. "The Invention of French Feminism: An Essential Move." *Yale French Studies* 87: 190–221

Donovan, Josephine. 2007. *The Feminist Care Tradition in Animal Ethics*. New York: Columbia University Press.

Donovan, Josephine. 2012. *Feminist Theory: The Intellectual Traditions*. New York: Continuum.

Dworkin, Andrea. 1987. *Intercourse*. New York: MacMillan.

Echols, Alice. 1989. *Daring to Be Bad: Radical Feminism in America (1967–1975)*. Minneapolis: University of Minnesota Press.

Eisenstein, Zillah. 1978. *Capitalism Patriarchy and the Case for Socialist Feminism*. Cambridge, MA: Monthly Review Press.

Evans, Sara. 1980. *The Roots of Women's Liberation in the Civil Rights Movement and the New Left*. New York: Vintage.

Firestone, Shulamith. 2003. *The Dialectic of Sex: The Case for Feminist Revolution*. New York: Farrar, Straus, and Giroux.

Foucault, Michel. 1995. *Discipline and Punish: The Birth of the Prison*. 2nd ed. New York: Vintage.

Friedan, Betty. 2013. *The Feminine Mystique*. 50th anniversary ed. New York: W. W. Norton.

Gambaudo, Sylvie. 2007. "French Femnism versus Anglo-American Feminism: A Reconstruction." *European Journal of Women's Studies* 14 (2): 93–108.

Garland-Thomson, Rosemary. 1997. *Extraordinary Bodies: Figuring Physical Disability*. New York: Columbia University Press.

Gilligan, Carol. 1982. *In a Different Voice: Psychological Theory and Women's Development*. Cambridge, MA: Harvard University Press.

Goldman, Loren. 2015. "Pragmatism." In *The Encyclopedia of Political Thought*, edited by Michael T. Gibbons. Hoboken, NJ: Wiley.

Grant, Judith. 1993. *Fundamental Feminism: Contesting the Core Concepts of Feminist Theory*. New York and London: Routledge.

Gramsci, Antonio. 1971. *Selections from the Prison Notebooks*. New York: International Publishers Company.

Griffin, Susan. 2000. *Women and Nature: The Roaring Inside Her*. Berkeley, CA: Counterpoint Press.

Halberstam, Judith. 1998. *Female Masculinity*. Durham, NC: Duke University Press.

Harding, Sandra. 1991. *Who's Science? Whose Knowledge? Thinking from Women's Lives*. Ithaca, NY: Cornell University Press.

Harding, Sandra, and Merle Hintikka, eds. 2003. *Discovering Reality: Feminist Perspectives in Epistemology, Metaphysics and the Philosophy of Science*. 2nd ed. Springer Publishing.

Hartmann, Heidi. 1979. "The Unhappy Marriage of Marxism and Feminism: Towards a More Progressive Union." *Capital and Class* 3 (2): 1–33.

Hartsock, Nancy. 1984. *Money, Sex and Power: Toward a Feminist Historical Materialism*. Boston: Northeastern University Press.

Hartsock, Nancy. 1999. *The Feminist Standpoint Revisited, and Other Essays*. New York: Basic Books.

Hawkesworth, Mary. 1989. "Knowers, Knowing, Known: Feminist Theory and Claims of Truth." *Signs* 14 (3): 533–557.
Heberle, Renee. 2006. *Feminist Interpretations of Theodor Adorno*. State College: Penn State University Press.
Hegel, G. W. F. 1976. *The Phenomenology of Spirit*. Oxford: Oxford University Press.
Hill Collins, Patricia. 2008. *Black Feminist Thought: Knowledge Consciousness and the Politics of Empowerment*. New York: Routledge.
Hochschild, Arlie. 1989. *The Second Shift: Working Parents and the Revolution at Home*, New York: Penguin.
Horkheimer, Max. 1972. *Critical Theory*. New York: Herder and Herder.
Horkheimer, Max, and Theodor Adorno. 2007. *Dialectic of Enlightenment*. Redwood City, CA: Stanford University Press.
Jameson, Frederic. 1990. *Postmodernism or the Cultural Logic of Late Capitalism*. Durham, NC: Duke University Press.
Jardine, Alice. 1982. *Gynesis: Configurations of Woman and Modernity*. Ithaca, NY: Cornell University Press.
Jay, Martin. 2006. *Songs of Experience. Modern American and European Variations on a Universal Theme*. Berkeley. University of California Press.
Johnson, Pauline. 1994. *Feminism as Radical Humanism*. Boulder, CO: Westview Press.
Kafka, Franz. 2012. *The Complete Stories*. New York: Schocken.
Koedt, Anne. 1973. "Myth of the Vaginal Orgasm." In *Radical Feminism*, edited by Anne Koedt. New York:, Times Books.
Kruks, Sonia. 2001. *Retrieving Experience: Subjectivity and Recognition in Feminist Politics*. Ithaca, NY: Cornell University Press.
Lenin, V. I. 1987. *Essential Works of Lenin*. Mineola, NY: Dover.
Lerner, Gerda. 1987. *The Creation of Patriarchy*. Oxford: Oxford University Press.
Levi-Strauss, Claude. 1971. *The Elementary Structures of Kinship*. Boston: Beacon Press.
Locke, John. 1996. *An Essay Concerning Human Understanding*. Indianapolis, IN: Hackett.
Lorde, Audre. 2007. "The Master's Tools Will Never Dismantle the Masters House." In *Sister Outsider: Essays and Speeches*. Berkeley: Crossings Press, 110–114.
Lukacs, Georg. 1972. *History and Class Consciousness*. Cambridge, MA: MIT Press.
MacKinnon, Catharine. 1982. "Feminism, Marxism, Method and the State: An Agenda for Theory." *Signs* 7 (3): 515–544.
MacKinnon, Catharine. 1991. *Toward a Feminist Theory of the State*. Cambridge, MA: Harvard University Press.
MacKinnon, Catharine. 1993. *Only Words*. Cambridge, MA: Harvard University Press.
MacKinnon, Catharine, and Andrea Dworkin. 1997. *In Harm's Way: The Pornography Civil Rights Hearings*. Cambridge, MA: Harvard University Press.
Millett, Kate. 2000. *Sexual Politics*. Champaign: University of Illinois Press.
Mitchell, Juliet. 2000. *Psychoanalysis and Feminism: A Radical Reassessment of Freudian Psychoanalysis*. Rev. ed. New York: Basic Books.
Moi, Toril. 2002. *Sexual/Textual: Feminist Literary Theory*. New York and London: Routledge.
Notes from the Second Year. 1970. Radical Feminism, http://library.duke.edu/digitalcollections/wlmpc_wlmms01039/.
Ortner, Sherry. 1974. "Is Female to Male as Nature Is to Culture?" In *Women, Culture and Society*, edited by M. Z. Rosaldo and L. Lamphere, 68–87. Redwood City, CA: Stanford University Press.

Rich, Adrienne. 1995. *Of Woman Born: Motherhood as Experience and Institution*. New York: Norton.
Rowbotham, Sheila. 1972. *Women, Resistance and Revolution: A History of Women and Revolution in the Modern World*. New York: Vintage.
Rowbotham, Sheila. 1973. *Woman's Consciousness, Man's World*. New York: Penguin.
Rubin, Gayle. (1982) 2011. "Thinking Sex: Notes for a Radical Theory of the Politics of Sexuality." In *Deviations: A Gayle Rubin Reader*, 137–181. Durham, NC: Duke University Press. Originally presented as a paper at Barnard College, New York.
Rubin, Gayle. 2011. *Deviations: A Gayle Rubin Reader*. Durham, NC: Duke University Press.
Ruddick, Sara. 1995. *Maternal Thinking: Towards a Politics of Peace*. Boston: Beacon Press.
Sartre, Jean-Paul. 2007. *Existentialism Is a Humanism*. New Haven, CT: Yale University Press.
Scott, Joan. 1991. "The Evidence of Experience." *Critical Inquiry* 17 (4): 773–797.
Smith, Dorothy. 1989. *The Everyday World as Problematic*. 2nd ed. Boston, MA: Northeastern University Press.
Spivak, Gayatri. 1988. "Can the Subaltern Speak?" In *Marxism and the Interpretation of Culture*, edited by Cary Nelson and Lawrence Grossberg. London: MacMillan.
Thompson, E. P. 1966. *The Making of the English Working Class*. New York: Vintage.
Tronto, Joan C. 1993. *Moral Boundaries: A Political Argument for an Ethic of Care*. New York and London: Routledge.
Carol S. Vance. 1984. *Pleasure and Danger: Exploring Female Sexuality*. Boston: Routledge and Kegan Paul.
Weeks, Kathi. 2011. *The Problem with Work: Feminism, Marxism, Antiwork Politics and Postwar Imaginaries*. Durham, NC: Duke University Press.

CHAPTER 12

FEMINIST JURISPRUDENCE

JULIET A. WILLIAMS

Introduction

LEGAL scholar Wendy W. Williams opens her canonical law review article "The Equality Crisis: Some Reflections on Culture, Courts, and Feminism" with this rueful observation: "To say that courts are not and never have been the source of radical social change is an understatement" (Williams [1982] 1991, 15). What does Williams's assessment imply about the radical potential of feminist jurisprudence? Today, it appears that even many feminists dismiss the possibility of a truly transformative feminist jurisprudence. As legal scholar Martha Chamallas observes, feminists appear to "distrust legal reforms because of the tendency of such reforms to tame radical impulses, and they charge that the reforms produce doctrines that reproduce prevailing conservative or neoliberal ideologies, rather than challenge them" (Chamallas 2013, 409). The assumption that the imagination of legal scholars is of necessity constrained by conventional legal reasoning, coupled with the related impression of legal scholarship as being more concerned with practical strategy than theoretical imagination, might explain the notable marginalization of feminist jurisprudence in general surveys of feminist theory (Nicholson 1997; Kemp and Squires 1997; Zerilli 2006; McCann and Kim 2013). To others, the very possibility of a feminist jurisprudence may seem downright oxymoronic, given the highly suspicious regard for state power characteristic of feminist theorists. As political theorist Wendy Brown (1995, 169) pithily remarks, "Whether one is dealing with the state, the Mafia, parents, pimps, police, or husbands, the heavy price of institutionalized protection is always a measure of dependence and agreement to abide by the protector's rules." In policy arenas ranging from welfare reform to sexual violence, feminist thinkers have disclosed the many ways that protectionist state interventions can mask and enable the retrenchment of masculine power and male dominance (Ferguson 1984; Brown 1995; Smith 2007; Bumiller 2008). Feminist theorists have been particularly critical of the individualism that structures Anglo-American legal systems, and the attendant limitations of rights-based discourse as a liberatory paradigm (Brown 1995).

The already uneasy relationship between feminist jurisprudence and feminist theory no doubt has been further strained by the fact that prominent feminist legal scholars have emerged as some of feminism's most progressive—and most searing—critics. Janet Halley's provocatively subtitled 2006 book, *Split Decisions: How and Why to Take a Break from Feminism*, warns that feminism has been lured into complacency by prioritizing the quest to obtain power over the task of critiquing it. Against the rise of "governance feminism," Halley encourages critical thinkers not just to turn away from the legal regime as a primary addressee, but to reject as well the unduly cabined vision of social justice produced by what Halley sees as feminism's defining investment in the idea that the "sexual subordination of women by men" is the primary social injustice (Halley 2006, 125). Legal scholar Martha Fineman also voices skepticism about the current state of feminism, calling for a closer examination of "the ways that a focus on identities can narrow or constrict the critical imagination" (Fineman 2013, 108). To be sure, Fineman offers a very different kind of analysis than the sort proffered by conservative commentators who condemn identity politics as dressed-up navel-gazing. In contrast, Fineman suggests that identity-driven analyses, including feminist approaches, become problematic when they fail to push critique of the status quo far enough, settling for a focus on identity, which leads, Fineman contends, to partial and dangerously distorted understandings of the scope and effects of injustice. Reflecting on the direction of recent academic feminism, Fineman (2013, 108) wonders, "Why isn't the fact that we routinely incarcerate children, regardless of their gender, the issue, and not the fact that incarcerated boys and girls are differently disadvantaged in a system that treats everyone inhumanly?".

As these debates indicate, feminist jurisprudence is not only a field marked by diversity and internal contestation; it is a location from which scholars have sought to push the boundaries of feminist theory. To be sure, much feminist jurisprudential thought has been and continues to be centrally concerned with addressing specific instances of gender inequality in employment, education, and the social organization of the family, but in so doing, feminist jurisprudence is a place where the very the meanings not just of "equality" and "justice," but of "gender" itself, are vigorously contested. Rather than a watered-down or inherently compromised domain of feminist thought, feminist jurisprudence deserves recognition as a vital site for original and generative feminist theorizing.

To make this case, the chapter offers an overview of the development of feminist jurisprudential thought in the United States. Feminist jurisprudence often is traced to the 1970s, the period when the Supreme Court first declared the Constitution to provide substantial protection against discrimination on the basis of sex. In a series of watershed cases, a feminist jurisprudence centered on equality claims gained official recognition and led to truly historic changes in the law and public policy. On the heels of these momentous changes, the field of feminist legal theory was roiled by the so-called difference debates, as legal scholars reckoned with the limits of asserting "sameness" as the basis for challenging sex-based inequalities. By the end of the 1980s, these debates had reached a stalemate. At first glance, it may seem that the heyday of feminist jurisprudence was over, to be followed by a period of fragmentation, if not outright dissolution. However, I argue that we have witnessed since the 1990s the emergence of a number of significant critical debates that have propelled feminist jurisprudence beyond its focus on the sameness/difference paradigm, while at the same time influencing the course of feminist theorizing outside the legal academy.

From Women's Rights to Feminist Jurisprudence

For much of US history, law has played a principal role in maintaining relations of gender *in*equality. Guided by the English common law tradition, the founding legal regime established women's subordination to men. As political scientist Judith Baer (2009) notes, the women's rights activists who signed the Declaration of Sentiments and Resolutions at the historic 1848 conference in Seneca Falls, New York, "identified law as an instrument of male supremacy." The Declaration of Sentiments pointed to numerous instances of "legal sexism," such as restricting voting rights to (some) men, and denying married women the right to make contracts, keep earned wages, and own property by pronouncing wives "civilly dead" (Baer 2009). Denied standing in court, wives were denied legal recourse should they suffer a violation. In the latter part of the nineteenth century, married women finally began to gain legal personhood, though even in granting limited access to citizenship rights, the courts affirmed their enduring belief in women's natural subordination to men. The dominant ideology of "separate spheres" established a firm limit on egalitarian thinking. In 1873, the Supreme Court endorsed the constitutionality of a state law barring married women from entering the legal profession on the grounds that the "paramount destiny and mission of women are to fulfill the noble and benign offices of wife and mother" (*Bradwell v. Illinois*, 141).

It would take nearly a century after the *Bradwell* decision for the Court to begin to seriously rethink its approach to Constitutional sex-discrimination cases. In its landmark 1971 decision in *Reed v. Reed*, the Court established that laws treating one sex differently from the other would be subject to a higher than usual standard of review; no longer would mere convenience be considered a sufficient rationale for treating otherwise similarly situated men and women differently. The outcome of the *Reed* case attested not simply to shifting judicial attitudes about the nature of gender differences, but more specifically to the transformative impact of demanding that the courts extend the prevailing logic of race discrimination law into the realm of sex equality jurisprudence. As legal historian Serena Mayeri (2011, 10) explains, "reasoning from race became a centerpiece of feminist legal advocacy." Although it was not as rigorous as the "strict scrutiny" brought to consideration of race-based classifications, by 1976 the Court had made explicit a new standard requiring that any sex-based classification bear a "substantial" relationship to an "important" governmental purpose. Moving forward, equal treatment was to be regarded as the default position, absent a convincing reason for proceeding otherwise.

As courts brought an increasingly critical eye to sex-based classifications, numerous policies and practices that long had enjoyed the legitimating imprimatur of constitutionality were stricken. As Wendy Williams recounts, throughout the 1970s,

> the Supreme Court insisted that women wage earners receive the same benefits for their families under military, social security, welfare, and workers compensation programs as did male wage earners; that men receive the same child care allowance when their spouses died as women did; that the female children of divorce be entitled to support for the same length of time as male children, so that they too could get the education necessary for life in the public world; that the duty of support through alimony not be visited exclusively on husbands; that wives as well as husbands participate in the management of community property; and that wives as well as husbands be eligible to administer their deceased relatives estates.
>
> (W. Williams [1982] 1991, 17)

In the wake of this seismic shift, feminist legal theorists entered a period of intense reflection about the meaning—and limits—of equality as a feminist ideal.

During the 1980s, the so-called sameness-difference debates dominated discussion in the field. Some feminist legal scholars sought to press forward by continuing to demand that women and men be treated as equal in the eyes of the law—a strategy that had proven remarkably successful in the preceding decade. Others, however, were critical of the underlying premise that women must prove they are "just like men" in order to have their rights recognized (Finley 1986; Littleton 1987). The intensity of debates over sameness and difference in this period speaks to the challenge posed by what Martha Minow (1990) aptly calls the "difference dilemma": how to acknowledge differences between men and women without falling back on an endorsement of stereotypical accounts of gender difference. One possible path around this dilemma was charted by thinkers who shifted feminist inquiry in this period from a focus on how to achieve equality within the current social order to consideration of the relations of power that produce gender as inequality in the first place (MacKinnon 1987). As a result, while feminist jurisprudence may have had its origins in "an essentially liberal attack on the absence of women in the public world," the field soon became a ground on which feminist legal scholars would propound "a radical vision of the transformation of the world" (Scales 1986, 44–45).

This period of extraordinary feminist intellectual foment in the legal academy is most often remembered as a time of intense debate between two opposing camps: those advocating "equal treatment" and those demanding greater attention to the differently "gendered realities" of men and women (Baer 2009). But this familiar narrative has done a disservice in obscuring the complexity—and radical possibilities—of feminist jurisprudence (Colker 1987; Franklin 2010). At the height of these debates, historian Joan Scott (1988, 48) implored commentators to "stop writing the history of feminisms as a sort of oscillation between demands for equality and affirmations of difference," for, as she warned, "[t]his approach inadvertently strengthens the hold of the binary construction, establishing it as inevitable by giving it a long history." As I demonstrate in the remainder of this chapter, in the decades since the 1980s, feminist legal scholars have taken up Scott's charge, challenging feminist theory to move beyond its familiar boundaries. In the remainder of this chapter, I focus on three arenas of feminist legal discourse that have been proven particularly generative in this regard: intersectionality, gender and sexuality, and masculinities.

Intersectionality

Sociologist Leslie McCall (2005, 1771) remarks that "feminists are perhaps alone in the academy in the extent to which they have embraced intersectionality." The term *intersectionality* is used broadly today to describe approaches to social analysis that in some way address "the relationships among multiple dimensions and modalities of social relations and subject formation" (McCall 2005, 1771). But if intersectionality has emerged as a dominant feminist research paradigm, the term also has come to stand for a powerful critique of much of what has counted as feminist theory in the past, particularly during the period associated with the second wave.[1] Intersectionality demands a feminism theorized from a recognition of differences *among* women, rather than an insistence on a shared, essential womanhood—a premise that too often underwrites a false universalism that positions white middle- and upper-class heterosexual women as the exemplary feminist subject.

Intersectionality theory is deeply indebted to the writings of woman of color feminists and critical race theorists (Davis 1983; Moraga 1983; Smith 1983; Spelman 1988; Harris 1990; Collins 1990). Legal scholar Kimberlé Crenshaw commonly is credited with coining the term *intersectionality*. Crenshaw's two canonical law review articles, "Demarginalizing the Intersection of Sex and Race" (1989) and "Mapping the Margins" (1991), have stimulated scholarly inquiry into the politics of complex identity. In "Demarginalizing," Crenshaw (1989, 140) sets forth a trenchant critique of the underlying logic of US antidiscrimination law, charging that a legal framework that defines race discrimination and sex discrimination as separate categories "erases Black women in the conceptualization, identification and remediation of race and sex discrimination." In "Mapping the Margins," Crenshaw extends her use of intersectional analysis beyond the realm of antidiscrimination law to address the silencing, erasure, and marginalization of "multiply-burdened" subjects in social, cultural, and activist contexts. Reflecting on these articles more recently, Crenshaw explains that her early writings sought to

> uncover the paradoxical dimension of the sameness/difference rationales that undergirded antidiscrimination law more broadly. By these logics, Black females are both too similar to Black men and white women to represent themselves and too different to represent either Blacks or women as a whole. Although Black male and white female narratives of discrimination were understood to be fully inclusive and

universal, Black female narratives were rendered partial, unrecognizable, something apart from standard claims of race discrimination.

(Cho, Crenshaw, and McCall 2013, 790–791)

Although Crenshaw's articulation of intersectionality arose in the context of a critique of antidiscrimination law, she emphasizes that she never intended intersectional analysis to be "limited to securing legal reforms that would grant greater inclusion to differently defined subjects" (Cho, Crenshaw, and McCall 2013, 791). Nonetheless, some recent commentators suggest that the origins of Crenshaw's formulations in the context of contestation of antidiscrimination doctrine, particularly as it affects black women, may impose certain limits on the concept's serviceability as a central feminist analytic (Nash 2008; Puar 2011; Wiegman 2012, 247–250). American Studies scholar Jennifer Nash warns that intersectionality scholarship "must begin to broaden its reach to theorize an array of subject experience(s)" if it wishes to transcend parochialism and provide a more "nuanced" "conceptualization of identity that captures the ways in which race, gender, sexuality, and class, among other categories, are produced through each other, securing both privilege and oppression simultaneously" (Nash 2008, 10). However, the richness of the research literature inspired by Crenshaw's discussion can leave little doubt of intersectionality's capacity to continue to propel feminist theory in new and important directions, for example, by draqwing attention to the implication of masculinity, whiteness, and sexual orientation in the production of "racialized modes of gender normativity" in the law (Carbado 2013, 8).

Gender and Sexuality

Since the 1980s, feminist legal scholarship has explored the complex and intertwined relationship between gender and sexuality. Since the 1970s, the scope of sex discrimination law has broadened significantly, now reaching such previously unregulated offenses as sexual harassment (Mackinnon 1979; Schultz 1998). Nonetheless, courts have insistently distinguished sex discrimination from sexual orientation discrimination—a distinction that has left many victims of sexualized harassment without remedy. In asserting a categorical distinction between sexual harassment and sexual-orientation harassment, courts have been compelled to delicately parse treatment that arises from an individual's perceived gender nonconformity and treatment that emanates from perceived sexual nonconformity. In cases presented by effeminate men identified as gay, this type of analysis has appeared particularly strained.

In emphasizing the interrelationship between gender and sexuality, feminist legal theorists pose a challenge not just to a particular approach to sex discrimination adjudication, but also to a broader habit, now widely institutionalized in the US academy, of demarcating a boundary between the field of gender and the field of sexuality. This boundary authorizes the institutional separation of programs dedicated to women's, gender, or feminist studies, on the one hand, and those committed to the study of sexuality, LGBT studies, and queer studies, on the other. (Even the increasingly common use of the "gender and sexuality" rubric reinforces the irreducible exclusivity of these two domains by acknowledging intellectual proximity while simultaneously refusing the possibility of transcendence). The widely accepted imperative to mark the distinction between gender and sexuality studies was perhaps most famously articulated by anthropologist Gayle Rubin in her canonical 1984 article, "Thinking Sex: Notes for a Radical Theory of the Politics of Sexuality." In "Thinking Sex," Rubin charges feminists with failing to reckon with sexuality in the campaign to address sexism and gender inequality. Citing legal scholar Catharine Mackinnon's characteristically uncompromising proclamation that "sexuality is the linchpin of gender inequality," Rubin offers a compelling counterpoint, contending that "[t]he cultural fusion of gender with sexuality has given rise to the idea that a theory of sexuality may be derived directly out of a theory of gender" (MacKinnon 1982, 533; Rubin 1984, 169). In Rubin's view, too many feminists have been conscripted into policing sexuality to protect women from the threat of sexual subordination, effectively displacing sexual liberation as a fundamental feminist goal. Rubin (1984, 170) proclaims it nothing less than "essential to separate gender and sexuality analytically to reflect more accurately their separate social existence" and issues an urgent call for "an autonomous theory and politics specific to sexuality."

To be sure, Rubin rightly identifies not just the analytic conflation produced when sexuality is regarded as merely derivative of gender, but also the problematic political effects of this subordinating assumption. But what about the potential harms produced by an equally categorical insistence on the analytic separation of gender and sexuality? Twenty-five years after Rubin's provocative call to liberate sexuality studies from the tyranny of feminist judgment, sociologists Kristin Schilt and Laurel Westbrook (2009, 441) observe that "the relationship between heterosexuality and gender oppression remains undertheorized in social science research.". This critical neglect suggests that the salutary effort to "think sex" apart from gender can all too easily ossify into a counterproductive imperative if it discourages efforts to interrogate the mutually constitutive operation of gender and sexuality in social life.

These costs have been forcefully addressed by feminist legal theorists, who have made a compelling case for the theoretical and practical value of thinking gender and sexuality dialogically (Hunter 1991; Case 1995; Valdes 1995; Franke 1997; Koppelman 2001; Abrams 2010). Pushing back against judicial decisions that treat gender discrimination and sexuality discrimination as autonomous phenomena, legal scholar Mary Ann Case highlights the hidden gender stereotyping that operates under cover of actions seemingly directed at matters of sexuality. For example, she describes a case in which an "effeminate" man who was perceived to be gay was fired from his job as pre-school teacher for wearing an earring. The plaintiff's claim of sex discrimination was denied in court on the grounds that he was fired because of his sexuality, not his gender. Case demonstrates how, in this instance, the courts' conflation of gender and sexual orientation led to the denial of relief. Thus, Case argues for "disaggregating" sex, gender, and sexuality as analytic categories, not by way of asserting an inherent distinction among these identity markers, but, rather, to draw attention to the overlaps that are masked when analysis of gender or sexuality is undertaken in isolation.[2] In this context, to insist on the analytic distinction between gender and sexuality serves not to reinforce their independence, but rather to disclose their simultaneity. Taking this logic one step further, legal scholar Katherine Franke suggests that the wrong of sexual harassment resides not merely in the fact that a behavior is sexual but that it is also sexist. From Franke's perspective, "sexual harassment is a technology of sexism. It is a disciplinary practice that inscribes, enforces, and polices the identities of both harasser and victim according to a system of gender norms that envisions women as feminine, (hetero)sexual objects, and men as masculine, (hetero)sexual subjects" (1997, 693). Using the term "hetero-patriarchy" to characterize the cooperation of heteronormativity and male privilege, Franke emphasizes the mutually reinforcing nature of homophobia and gender norms (Franke 1997, 739).[3]

In the wake of sustained feminist critique, sexual-orientation discrimination increasingly is being understood by courts to involve gender stereotyping, and hence to constitute a prohibited form of sex discrimination in violation of Title VII (Chamallas 2013, 246). Feminist legal theorists' insistence on acknowledging the interconnection between gender and sexuality has been extended to analysis of other issues as well, such as same-sex marriage. Case (2010, 1233), for example, suggests that opposition to marriage equality emanates not just from homophobia but also from a desire to preserve and protect traditional gender roles: "The fact that recognition of same-sex marriage and elimination of enforced sex roles are as inextricably intertwined as the duck is with the rabbit has long been clear to opponents of both, from David Blankenhorn to the pope." More generally, legal scholar Kathryn Abrams (2010, 1135) contends that, in the present moment, "analysis of and organizing around gender and sexuality may be suffering not from too much convergence but from too little"—a point Abrams makes in response to Halley's suggestion, discussed earlier, that we take a break from feminism to make room in which the interests of others, including queer-identified people, can be heard and addressed. Abrams offers several examples of missed opportunities for coalition among feminist, gay and lesbian, and queer activists who presumably share an interest in "resisting state-supported efforts at gender normalization" (Abrams 2010, 1137). On the one hand, Abrams notes the failure to engage feminist critiques of marriage in the debate spurred by the passage in California of Proposition 8 banning same-sex unions. At the same time, she considers how the campaign to "clean up" Times Square in New York mobilized the image of "vulnerable women in need of protection" as a strategy to shut down the "queer sexual cultures" occupying prime urban real estate, a strategy that failed to elicit significant opposition from women's advocates. These examples suggest a need to move beyond a reactive defense of the autonomy of gender and sexuality, and to appreciate the critical possibilities afforded not only by thinking gender and sexuality apart, but also together.

Masculinities

In recent decades, masculinities studies has risen in prominence within the academy (Carrigan et. al. 1985; Connell 1995; Kimmel 1996; Messner 2002; Gardiner 2002;

Wiegman 2002a; Wiegman 2002b; Pascoe 2007). This development has evoked apprehension in some quarters. Some have warned that the rise of masculinities studies threatens to displace women as the central subjects of feminist analysis while reinforcing the authority of men in the field of gender scholarship (Modleski 1991). Others, including some feminist legal scholars, are especially wary of giving men prominence in the campaign for gender equality, pointing, as a cautionary tale, to former civil rights lawyer Ruth Bader Ginsburg's strategy of pursuing claims on behalf of male plaintiffs to challenge the constitutionality of sex-based classifications in the law, an approach some believe enabled the Court to adopt an unduly narrow, formalistic vision of equality.[4]

These warnings, occasioned by the formalization of masculinities studies as an academic field, obscure the fact that there is nothing particularly new about addressing men and masculinity in feminist studies; indeed, explorations of male dominance lies at the very heart of feminism (Levit 1996, 1038). More to the point, as sociologist Michael Kimmel rightly observes, feminists' resistance to engaging men's lives and experiences ultimately may do more to sustain than to subvert masculinized power. Reflecting on a historical tendency to marginalize men in feminist studies, Kimmel concludes, "The failure to include men-as-gendered in our work meant that men remained the unexamined center, the invisible pole around which gender dynamics revolved. Not 'naming' men and masculinity reinscribed their dominance" (2010, xiv). As Kimmel's work powerfully demonstrates, masculinities studies scholarship can make a valuable contribution to feminist research in illuminating the complex and ambivalent ways men get conscripted into the project of patriarchy. It is important to note as well, however, that an account of contemporary masculinities must include, but certainly cannot be limited to consideration of male bodies (Halberstam 1998).

In recent years, a growing number of feminist legal scholars have turned their attention to masculinities (Levit 1998; Dowd 2010; Cooper and McGinley 2012; Fineman and Thomson 2013). Moving beyond the sameness/difference debates, these scholars have shifted attention from "the notion of women being measured by male standards (and thus put in the strange position of having to assert that they were just as good at masculinity as men were), to decentering masculinity as the norm against which all behaviors were to be measured, and thus to deconstructing masculinities" (Kimmel 2010, xv). Imploring feminists "to ask the man question," legal scholar Nancy Dowd riffs on Simone de Beauvoir's famous formulation with a call to rethink the very practice of feminist jurisprudence (2010). In her well-known 1990 treatise on feminist legal methods, legal scholar Kathleen Bartlett explains:

> In law, asking the woman question means examining how the law fails to take into account the experiences and values that seem more typical of women than of men, for whatever reason, or how existing legal standards and concepts might disadvantage women. The question assumes that some features of the law may be nonneutral in a general sense, but also "male" in a specific sense. The purpose of the woman

question is to expose those features and how they operate, and to suggest how they might be corrected."

(Bartlett 1990, 837)

Importantly, Dowd's investment in asking the man question arises not from an interest in parity for its own sake, rather from a commitment to unpacking the workings of male privilege. Dowd's useful "distillation" of the primary theoretical insights of masculinities scholarship underlines several significant points of overlap with leading feminist approaches to gender. Perhaps most importantly, Dowd emphasizes that masculinities scholars regard masculinity "as a social construction, not a biological given," echoing the strong anti-essentialist tendency in feminist theory. At the same time, however, Dowd calls on feminist scholars to move beyond reductive and essentializing conceptions of male privilege. As an alternative, she demonstrates the critical purchase of a "multiple masculinities" perspective that recognizes the significant differences among men (2010, 57–58, 60). As Dowd explains, it is possible to at once acknowledge that all men enjoy a "patriarchal dividend" emanating from "the dominance of men in the overall gender order," while also accounting for the high price men play for this privilege in areas ranging from mental and physical well-being to vulnerability to extreme forms of violence. Indeed, this recognition is critical both to understand the resilience of male privilege, and to encourage challenges to it.

Legal scholar Nancy Levit similarly gestures at the productive possibilities of greater interchange between feminist legal theorists and masculinities scholars. Diagnosing feminism as having "stalled" at the point of serious critical engagement with men and masculinities, Levit (1996, 1040) demands greater attention to the operation of male privilege in the present. She explains, "The focus of feminist scholarship has been almost exclusively on the ways in which men subjugate women, rather than on exploring the complex system of structures and beliefs that impel the perpetual dominance of men. To the extent that men unthinkingly accept the dominant ideology, transformation is only possible through an understanding of the methods of cultural transmission and replication" (1085). To this end, Levit proposes that we take a closer look at the ways in which law constructs masculinity. In so doing, she aims "to make visible how the treatment of men by various legal doctrines reinforces stereotypic notions of maleness" (1054). Levit provides numerous vivid examples, including rape law's normalization of male sexual aggression by treating the absence of strenuous physical resistance as a sign of consent, and the way the courts' refusal to recognize sexual-orientation discrimination as a form of sex discrimination renders invisible the harms men suffer as victims of male-on-male sexual harassment (1056, 1072). In these ways, Levit contends, the legal regime "reinforces social stereotypes of men as tough, sexually aggressive, and impervious to pain," while helping to maintain "a cultural climate in which men cannot express their humiliation, their sense of invasion, or their emotional suffering" (1072).

The preceding suggests that the turn to "deconstructing masculinities" can be undertaken not by way of superseding feminist analysis but, rather, to address some of feminism's unfinished business. The same surely can be said of the other strands of feminist legal analysis considered here as well. In each of these areas, it should be clear that feminist jurisprudence is neither intellectually derivative nor limited to the realm of applied thinking; rather, it is an engine of original thought and a source of the continued vitality of feminist theory more broadly.

Notes

1. For an important challenge to common narratives of the second wave, see Thompson (2002).
2. Confusingly, in an article published in the same year, Katherine Franke declares "the disaggregation of sex from gender" to be "the central mistake of sex discrimination law." Here, Franke is referring to the tendency of sex discrimination law to regard "sex as a product of nature, while gender is understood as a function of culture" (2). This distinction problematically reifies the truth of sexual difference by naturalizing gender, "[S]ex equality jurisprudence has uncritically accepted the validity of biological sexual differences. By accepting these biological differences, equality jurisprudence reifies as foundational *fact* that which is really an *effect* of normative gender ideology" (2). Franke's ultimate point is that sex discrimination protection is unduly cabined by assumptions about "real" sex differences; in other words, the supposed fact of a real sex difference becomes a justification for differential treatment (12). Franke calls this view "sexual realism." In this case, the "disaggregation" Franke refers to is not the positing of a conceptual distinction between sex and gender, which Franke herself relies on (in the same way Case does)—but rather, the way the distinction is drawn, i.e. positing sex as natural and gender as socially constructed, thereby denying the ways in which the sexed body, too, is a social construction.
3. Franke attributes the term "hetero-patriarchy" to Francisco Valdes (1995).
4. But see Franklin (2010), who makes the compelling case that litigator Ginsburg's "decision to press the claims of male plaintiffs was grounded not in a commitment to eradicating sex classifications from the law, but in a far richer theory of equal protection involving constitutional limitations on the state's power to enforce sex-role stereotypes" (216).

References

Abrams, Kathryn. 2010. "Elusive Coalitions: Reconsidering the Politics of Gender and Sexuality." *UCLA Law Review* 57: 1135–1147.
Baer, Judith A. 2009. "Feminist Theory and the Law." *The Oxford Handbook of Law and Politics*. Oxford Handbooks Online. URL: http://www.oxfordhandbooks.com/view/10.1093/oxfordhb/9780199208425.001.0001/oxfordhb-9780199208425-e-25.
Bartlett, Katherine T. 1990. "Feminist Legal Methods." *Harvard Law Review* 103: 829–88.
Bradwell v. Illinois, 83 U.S. 130 (1873).
Brown, Wendy. 1995. *States of Injury: Power and Freedom in Late Modernity*. Princeton, NJ: Princeton University Press.
Bumiller, Kristin. 2008. *In an Abusive State: How Neoliberalism Appropriated the Feminist Movement Against Sexual Violence*. Durham, NC: Duke University Press.
Carbado, Devon. 2013. "Colorblind Intersectionality." *Signs* 38 (4): 811–845.

Carrigan, Tim, Bob Connell, and John Lee. 1985. "Toward a New Sociology of Masculinity." *Theory and Society* 14 (5): 551–604.

Case, Mary Ann. 1995. "Disaggregating Gender From Sex and Sexual Orientation: The Effeminate Man in the Law and Feminist Jurisprudence." *Yale Law Journal* 105: 1–107.

Case, Mary Ann. 2010. "What Feminists Have to Lose in Same-Sex Marriage Litigation." *UCLA Law Review* 57: 1199–1233.

Chamallas, Martha. 2013. *Introduction to Feminist Legal Theory*. 3rd ed. New York: Wolter Kluwer Law and Business.

Cho, Sumi, Kimberlé Williams Crenshaw, and Leslie McCall. 2013. "Toward a Field of Intersectionality Studies: Theory, Applications, and Praxis." *Signs* 38 (4): 785–810.

Colker, Ruth. 1987. "The Anti-Subordination Principle: Applications." *Wisconsin Law Journal* 3: 59–80.

Collins, Patricia Hill. 1990. *Black Feminist Thought: Knowledge, Consciousness, and the Politics of Empowerment*. New York: Routledge and Chapman and Hall.

Cooper, Frank Rudy, and Ann C. McGinley, eds. 2012. *Masculinities and the Law: A Multidimensional Approach*. New York: New York University Press.

Connell, R. W. 1995. *Masculinities*. Berkeley: University of California Press.

Crenshaw, Kimberlé. 1989. "Demarginalizing the Intersection of Race and Sex: A Black Feminist Critique of Antidiscrimination Doctrine, Feminist Theory, and Antiracist Politics." *University of Chicago Legal Forum* 140: 139–167.

Crenshaw, Kimberlé. 1991. "Mapping the Margins: Intersectionality, Identity Politics, and Violence Against Women of Color." *Stanford Law Review* 43: 1241–1299.

Davis, Angela Y. 1983. *Women, Race, and Class*. New York: Vintage.

Dowd, Nancy E. 2010. *The Man Question: Male Subordination and Privilege*. New York: New York University Press.

Ferguson, Kathy. 1984. *The Feminist Case Against Bureaucracy*. Philadelphia, PA: Temple University Press.

Fineman, Martha Albertson. 2013. "Feminism, Masculinities, and Multiple Identities." *Nevada Law Journal* 13: 619–639.

Fineman, Martha Albertson, and Michael Thomson, eds. 2013. *Exploring Masculinities: Feminist Legal Theory Reflections*. Surrey, England: Ashgate Publishing.

Finley, Lucinda M. 1986. "Transcending Equality Theory: A Way Out of the Maternity and the Workplace Debate." *Columbia Law Review* 86: 1118–1182.

Franke, Katherine M. 1997. "What's Wrong with Sexual Harassment?" *Stanford Law Review* 49: 691–772.

Franklin, Cary. 2010. "The Anti-Stereotyping Principle in Constitutional Sex Discrimination Law." *New York University Law Review* 85: 83–172.

Gardiner, Judith Kegan. 2002. *Masculinity Studies and Feminist Theory*. New York: Columbia University Press.

Halberstam, Judith. 1998. *Female Masculinity*. Durham, NC: Duke University Press.

Halley, Janet. 2006. *Split Decisions: How and Why to Take a Break from Feminism*. Cambridge, MA: Harvard University Press.

Harris, Angela. 1990. "Race and Essentialism in Feminist Legal Theory." *Stanford Law Review* 42: 581–616.

Hunter, Nan. 1991. "Marriage, Law, and Gender: A Feminist Inquiry." *Law & Sexuality* 1: 9–30.

Kemp, Sandra, and Judith Squires. 1997. *Feminisms*. New York: Oxford University Press.

Kimmel, Michael. 1996. *Manhood in America: A Cultural History*. New York: Free Press.

Kimmel, Michael. 2010. Foreword to *Masculinities and the Law: A Multidimensional Approach*, edited by Frank Rudy Cooper and Ann C. McGinley, xiii-xvii. New York: New York University Press.

Koppelman, Andrew. 2001. "Defending the Sex Discrimination Argument for Lesbian and Gay Rights: A Reply to Edward Stein." *UCLA Law Review* 49: 519–537.

Levit, Nancy. 1996. "Legal Ideology and the Social Construction of Maleness." *UCLA Law Review* 43: 1038–1116.

Levit, Nancy. 1998. *The Gender Line: Men, Women, and the Law*. New York: New York University Press.

Littleton, Christine A. 1987. "Reconstructing Sexual Equality." *California Law Review* 75 (4): 1279–1337.

Mackinnon, Catharine. 1979. *Sexual Harassment of Working Women*. New Haven, CT: Yale University Press.

Mackinnon, Catharine. 1982. "Feminism, Marxism, Method and the State: An Agenda for Theory." *Signs: Journal of Women in Culture and Society* 7: 515–544.

Mackinnon, Catharine. 1987. *Feminism Unmodified*. Cambridge, MA: Harvard University Press.

Mayeri, Serena. 2011. *Reasoning from Race*. Cambridge: Harvard University Press.

McCall, Leslie. 2005. "The Complexity of Intersectionality." *Signs: Journal of Women in Culture and Society* 30 (3): 1771–1800.

McCann, Carole R., and Seung-kyung Kim. 2013. *Feminist Theory Reader: Local and Global Perspectives*. 3rd ed. New York: Routledge.

Messner, Michael. 2002. *Taking the Field: Women, Men and Sports*. Minneapolis: University of Minnesota Press.

Minow, Martha. 1990. *Making All the Difference: Inclusion, Exclusion and American Law*. New York: Cornell University Press.

Modleski, Tania. 1991. *Feminism without Women: Culture and Criticism in a "Postfeminist" Age*. New York: Routledge.

Moraga, Cherie, and Gloria Anzaldúa. 1983. *This Bridge Called My Back: Writings by Radical Women of Color*. New York: Kitchen Table/Women of Color Press.

Nash, Jennifer C. 2008. "Re-Thinking Intersectionality." *Feminist Review* 89: 1–15.

Nicholson, Linda, ed. 1997. *The Second Wave: A Reader in Feminist Theory*. New York: Routledge.

Pascoe, C. J. 2007. *Dude You're a Fag: Masculinity and Sexuality in High School*. Berkeley: University of California Press.

Puar, Jasbir. 2011. "'I Would Rather Be a Cyborg Than a Goddess': Intersectionality, Assemblage, and Affective Politics." *Transversal*. August. http://eipcp.nt/transversal/0811/puar/en.

Reed v. Reed, 404 U.S. 71.

Rubin, Gayle. 1984. "Thinking Sex: Notes for a Radical Theory of the Politics of Sexuality." In Carole Vance, ed. *Pleasure and Danger*. New York: Routledge.

Scales, Ann. 1986. "The Emergence of Feminist Jurisprudence: An Essay." *Yale Law Journal* 95: 1373–1403.

Schilt, Kristen, and Laurel Westbrook. 2009. "Doing Gender, Doing Heteronormativity: 'Gender Normals,' Transgender People, and the Social Maintenance of Heterosexuality." *Gender & Society* 23: 440–464.

Schultz, Vicki. 1998. "Reconceptualizing Sexual Harassment." *Yale Law Journal* 107: 1683–1805.

Scott, Joan A. 1988. "Deconstructing Equality-versus-Difference; or, the Uses of Poststructuralist Theory for Feminism," *Feminist Studies* 14 (1): 33–50.

Smith, Anna Marie. 2007. *Welfare Reform and Sexual Regulation*. New York: Cambridge University Press.

Smith, Barbara, ed. 1983. *Homegirls: A Black Feminist Anthology*. New York: Kitchen Table/Women of Color Press.

Spelman, Elizabeth. 1988. *Inessential Woman: Problems of Exclusion in Feminist Thought*. Boston: Beacon Press, 1988.

Strailey v. Happy Times Nursery School, Inc., 608 F.2d 327 (9th Cir. 1979).

Thompson, Becky. 2002. "Multiracial Feminism: Recasting the Chronology of Second Wave Feminism." *Feminist Studies* 28: 337–360.

Valdes, Francisco. 1995. "Queers, Sissies, Dykes, and Tomboys: Deconstructing the Conflation of 'Sex,' 'Gender,' and 'Sexual Orientation' in Euro-American Law and Society." *California Law Review* 83 (1): 56–71.

Wiegman, Robyn. 2002a. "Unmaking: Men and Masculinity in Feminist Theory." In *Masculinity Studies and Feminist Theory*, edited by Judith Kegan Gardiner, 31–59. New York: Columbia University Press.

Wiegman, Robyn. 2002b. "The Progress of Gender: Whither 'Women'?" In *Women's Studies on Its Own*, edited by Robyn Wiegman, 106–140. Durham, NC: Duke University Press.

Wiegman, Robyn. 2012. *Object Lessons*. Durham, NC: Duke University Press.

Williams, Wendy W. 1991. "The Equality Crisis: Some Reflections on Culture, Courts, and Feminism." Reprinted in *Feminist Legal Theory: Readings in Law and Gender*, edited by Katharine T. Bartlett and Rosanne Kennedy, 15–34. San Francisco: Westview Press.

Zerilli, Linda. 2006. "Feminist Theory and the Canon of Political Thought." In *The Oxford Handbook of Political Theory*, edited by John S. Dryzek, Bonnie Honig, and Anne Phillips, 106–124. NY: Oxford University Press.

CHAPTER 13

FEMINIST STANDPOINT

KRISTEN INTEMANN

Introduction

SANDRA Harding originally distinguished "standpoint feminism" from "feminist empiricism," describing the latter as the view that instances of male bias are merely cases of "bad science" that could be eliminated if scientists more rigorously adhered to empiricist methods and norms for scientific research (Harding 1986; 1991, 111–120). In contrast, standpoint theory maintained that such biases could occur even in cases where traditional scientific methodologies were followed. As a result, correcting for bias required a new conception of objectivity, as well as mechanisms for recognizing the ways in which power structures can shape and limit what we know. Since then, both feminist empiricism and standpoint theory have become increasingly more nuanced as philosophies of science, and it now appears that the two views have more similarities than differences (Intemann 2010b). This article will elucidate and defend a version of standpoint theory referred to as *feminist standpoint empiricism* (Intemann 2010b). While largely compatible with feminist empiricism, feminist standpoint empiricism offers additional important resources for producing science that is not only epistemically adequate but also more socially responsive.

The Historical Development of Standpoint Theory

Standpoint feminism originated in the 1970s among Marxist feminists, who were interested in understanding how hierarchical structures, such as capitalism and patriarchy, shape and limit our knowledge practices (Smith 1974; Hartsock 1983; Rose 1983; Harding 1986; Hill Collins 1991; Harding 1993). As an epistemological view, it was motivated by the increasing numbers of women entering the sciences, who were able to identify sexist and androcentric biases in science that had largely gone unnoticed (e.g., Hrdy 1986; Harding 1986; Gero and Conkey 1991). Feminists began looking at the hierarchical power structures that shaped the production of scientific knowledge and sought to explain why, for example, the underrepresentation of women in science was not only a political injustice but might also hinder, distort, or limit the production of scientific knowledge.

Early standpoint theorists argued that there was something distinctive about the experiences of women in virtue of their socially constructed roles within a capitalistic patriarchal society (Smith 1974; Hartsock 1983; Rose 1983; Harding 1986). Gender socialization, including the gendered division of labor, tended to give rise to experiences that provided resources for identifying problematic assumptions in the theories and frameworks widely held by those in power, who were likely to benefit from justifying existing social inequalities (Rosaldo 1980). They argued that the experiences of women could play a crucial role in challenging dominant assumptions and helping to generate knowledge "for women," including knowledge that could be used for liberatory purposes (Hartsock 1983; Harding 1986). The central claim of the early standpoint theorists, then, was that knowledge was generated from a particular standpoint, and that a feminist standpoint, informed by the experiences of women, was epistemically advantaged.

Early formulations of this view were taken to be implausible not only by nonfeminists but also by other feminist theorists. Standpoint theory has been interpreted as the claim that women have a distinct way of knowing that is different from that of men. As a result, standpoint feminists have been charged with reinforcing gender stereotypes and falsely assuming that all women have some sorts of universal shared experiences or interests in virtue of being oppressed (Bar On 1993; Hekman 1997; Haack 1998). This sort of essentialism seems particularly problematic because of the ways in which sexism also intersects with other forms of oppression, such as racism, classism, and heterosexism. As a result, some standpoint theorists have stressed that the notion of a feminist "standpoint" must be understood in a way that captures the differences among women and the ways in which sexism intersects with other systems of oppression. For example, some argued that experiences produced by the intersections of sexism with racism, ethnocentrism, and nationalism could also produce distinctive and important epistemological resources (Garcia 1989; Narayan 1989; Hill Collins 1991).

Standpoint theorists have also been interpreted as claiming that women always have an automatic epistemic privilege in virtue of being oppressed (Hekman 1997; Haack 1998; Pinnick et al. 2003). That is, they have been understood as claiming that membership in an oppressed group is sufficient to give women a less distorted view of the world and that this epistemic advantage would be present in any epistemological context. This is dubious because there are cases of members of oppressed groups having a *less* accurate view of the world, because they have either internalized their oppression or lack the educational resources useful for achieving certain kinds of knowledge. Moreover, it is difficult to see how oppressed groups would have an epistemic advantage in every epistemological context. In some areas of knowledge (e.g., theoretical physics), the experiences one has in virtue of one's social position appear to be irrelevant to the content of the theories or the evidence at stake. This concern has led some standpoint theorists to emphasize that the main aim of standpoint theory is not to give an epistemological account of knowers or of what it is to know something; rather, standpoint theory is a methodological resource for understanding power structures and producing knowledge that is more likely to benefit marginalized groups (Smith 1997; Rolin 2009; Kourany 2012). Understood in this way, it is a methodological approach that may be beneficial in some contexts more than others.

Finally, there are concerns that the view is necessarily committed to some form of epistemological or moral relativism (Code 1991; Harding 1991; Longino 1993; Clough 2003; Pinnick et al. 2003). Standpoint theory has been interpreted as claiming that knowledge can only be generated from a particular "perspective" and that which theories or claims are true or justified depends on whether one happens to adopt a "feminist perspective." This would be troubling, not only to those who find such relativism implausible, but particularly to standpoint feminists, who clearly wanted to argue that some claims and value judgments—in particular, feminist value judgments (e.g., that sexist oppression is bad)—are better or more justified than others (Clough 2003). Thus, some have also argued that standpoint theory is inherently inconsistent in arguing that all knowledge is generated from a particular standpoint while simultaneously claiming that knowledge produced from a feminist standpoint is *better* in some sense (Antony 1993; Longino 1993). This tension is not thought to rise for feminist empiricist views, because feminist empiricism takes empirical adequacy to be a criterion for choosing between competing knowledge claims in a way that better grounds the objectivity of knowledge.

Thus, contemporary standpoint theorists have acknowledged that for the view to be successful, the theory must better articulate the notion of a "standpoint" in a way that (1) does not essentialize women or oppressed groups, (2) clarifies the potential epistemic benefits while recognizing that such benefits are not automatic, (3) avoids a pernicious form of epistemological or moral relativism, and (4) resolves the tension between the claim that knowledge is somehow relative to a standpoint and the claim that some standpoints are better than others (Wylie 2003; Crasnow 2006; Rolin 2006; Harding 2008; Rolin 2009; Intemann 2010b). At the same time, insofar as standpoint theorists have clarified their claims in ways that address these concerns, it has become increasingly difficult to see how standpoint feminism offers distinct epistemological resources as a philosophy of science, particularly as it appears to have much in common with feminist empiricist views (Campbell 1998; Intemann 2010a, 2010b). Indeed, many contemporary standpoint theorists have endorsed the importance of empirical adequacy as a standard for evaluating theories, claims, and models (Wylie 2003; Intemann 2010b). Thus, the central challenge is whether feminist standpoint theory can be understood so as to address the objections it has historically faced while demonstrating that it offers unique resources that warrant its adoption over other, arguably less controversial, feminists epistemologies. In the next section, I offer an interpretation of the central tenets of standpoint theory that attempts to address this challenge.

Feminist Standpoint Empiricism: An Interpretation and Defense

Several interrelated theses have been advanced by standpoint theorists. These will be articulated slightly differently here than they have been elsewhere (Wylie 2003; Harding 1993; Harding 2004; Crasnow 2006; Rolin 2006; Intemann 2010b; Crasnow 2014 Intemann and de Melo-Martín 2014a) but will help to unpack the notion of a standpoint in ways that can address the objections the view has historically faced, while highlighting the unique resources the view has to offer. The central tenets to be discussed are

1) *the situated-knowledge thesis,* which holds that social location systematically influences our experiences, shaping and limiting what we know, such that knowledge is contextually generated from a standpoint or an epistemic community that achieves a critical group consciousness through a process of transformative criticism governed by shared standards of evaluation;
2) *the empirical adequacy thesis,* which holds that the achievement of a standpoint requires that participants share a commitment to empirical adequacy but that how this is understood is contextually determined by the other cognitive aims that constitute a context of inquiry (including political aims);
3) *the normative commitment thesis,* the view that the achievement of a feminist standpoint requires a commitment to challenge, rather than reinforce, systems of oppression in order to arrive at a group consciousness of how power structures and influences the world (including epistemic practices);
4) *the methodological thesis,* which holds that scientific research ought to proceed by studying from the margins out, so as to understand how existing power structures shape and limit knowledge production, as well as phenomena under investigation;
5) *the epistemic advantage thesis,* the view that inquiry that achieves a feminist standpoint is epistemically advantaged (at least in some contexts).

This article explores and defends each of these five main tenets.

The Situated-Knowledge Thesis

The situated-knowledge thesis asserts that social position shapes and limits what we can know because it influences the kind of experiences we have. Historically, systems of oppression (such as racism, sexism, heterosexism, classism, and colonization) have influenced the material circumstances of individuals (such as their living conditions, their opportunities, and their treatment in a variety of social situations). As a result, individuals who occupy different social locations have, to some extent, different experiences. In this way, standpoint theorists take knowledge to be embodied rather than acquired through a universal, disembodied, rational mind. Different bodies are subjected to different material conditions and forces that can give rise to different experiences and thus to different evidence and beliefs.

Which social categories shape experience are not homogeneous within a particular social group. Women, for example, will have different experiences in virtue of their positioning by race, class, geographical location, and so on. Nonetheless, membership in certain groups is relevant to the kinds of experiences one has in virtue of the fact that certain social categories shape social, economic, political, and other material circumstances. Of course, which social categories shape experience is a contingent matter. If, for example, racism ceased to exist, then race would no longer shape our experiences in the same ways. Thus, the particular social categories that have epistemic significance can change over time.

Because experiences are socially situated, knowledge is achieved from a particular standpoint. What exactly is a standpoint? A standpoint is not merely one's perspective in virtue of the sorts of experiences one has from a particular social location. Standpoint theorists endorse the claim, widely held by many feminist epistemologists, that the locus of knowledge is at the level of communities, rather than individuals (Harding 1986; Longino 1990; Nelson 1990; Code 1991). Thus, a standpoint is something achieved by a group. Individuals may contribute to the achievement of a standpoint, but this is something that individuals cannot accomplish on their own.

A standpoint is a group consciousness that occurs through a process of transformative criticism, by reflecting on and evaluating the experiences and beliefs of the individuals that constitute an epistemic community (Wylie 2003; Rolin 2006; Intemann 2010b). The consciousness-raising groups of the 1970s provide an example of how groups of women were able to reflect on their individual experiences and collectively identify patterns they were not able to recognize on their own (Smith 1997). Individual women had experiences, such as being groped by a male coworker, which they had previously interpreted as accidental, imagined, or deserved. But, when multiple women in the group reported similar experiences, their individual interpretations became inconsistent with the pattern of collective experiences. As a group, women were able to see patterns in their experiences, identify relationships between those patterns and oppressive arrangements, and achieve an understanding of how systems of oppression limit and shape their knowledge. But, equally important to generating this knowledge were the differences in their experiences. For example, the ways in which some African American women experience sexual harassment may be different from white women in virtue of different stereotypes about African American women's sexuality. Similarly, sexism that emerged in an office setting may be fundamentally different than at a construction site. This is because gendered norms and expectations are different in relation to race and class. Thus, understanding such phenomena as sexual harassment or sexism in the workplace required a critical analysis from a diverse group of women and men to help understand these intersecting dimensions. For this reason, standpoint theorists maintain that epistemic communities are more objective, or more epistemically robust, when they include participants from diverse social categories.

For this sort of transformative criticism to occur there must be some shared values or standards about what constitute good reasons for accepting a claim, hypothesis, or explanation (Longino 1990, 2002; Rolin 2006; Borgerson 2011). Feminist empiricists take empirical adequacy to be a necessary standard for all epistemic communities (Longino 1990, 2002; Solomon 2001; Clough 2004; Borgerson, 2011). While standpoint feminists can agree that empirical adequacy is an important theoretical virtue (Campbell 1998; Wylie 2003; Intemann 2010b), they have a potentially different understanding of empirical adequacy that may distinguish them from some feminist empiricists.

The Empirical Adequacy Thesis

Like feminist empiricists, feminist standpoint theorists maintain that a central aim of inquiry is to provide empirically adequate theories, models, and explanations. At the same time, standpoint feminists insist that empirical adequacy is not a neutral criterion for theory choice that is independent of other values held (Intemann and de Melo Martín 2014a, 2014b). That is, judgments about whether a claim is empirically adequate depend on additional assumptions and standards about what data needs to be accounted for in a particular case, how we should understand an empirical success, and when it is reasonable to revise background assumptions or make ad hoc adjustments to claims in order to account for countervailing data.

Consider, for example, the integrated assessment models that are used to measure and predict climate-change impacts. Whether a model of climate impacts can be said to be empirically adequate depends on judgments about what data we believe a model needs to explain and predict. A model may be consistent with data about, for example, the observed global average temperature record. It may also be able to make successful novel predictions (such as about sea-level rise, an increase in extreme weather events, glacial retreat, or the number of acres of farmland that will no longer be farmable because of increased salinity in the soil). The model may not, however, be able to explain or predict changes in indigenous hunting practices or the loss of linguistic traditions. This is because such models often do not recognize cultural practices as phenomena that need to be explained or predicted (Schnieder et al. 2000; Agarwal 2002). Thus, whether a model is empirically successful depends on additional value judgments about what we take to be an impact that an empirically successful model must account for.

Similar disagreements arise in research on the safety of genetically modified organisms ([GMOs]; de Melo-Martín and Meghani 2008; DeFrancesco 2013). For standpoint theorists, whether the hypothesis that GMOs are safe is empirically adequate depends on additional assumptions about what constitutes a risk to human health or the environment, what sorts of risks are acceptable, whether the potential risks and benefits are justly distributed (e.g., whether they will disproportionately impact marginalized groups negatively), and how much empirical evidence is needed to accept that GMOs are safe. Those who have different conceptions about what constitutes a risk, or how much empirical data is needed will disagree about whether there is adequate empirical evidence for GMO safety.

Thus, judgments about empirical adequacy depend on additional shared standards and assumptions about the cognitive aims of inquiry. Some of these aims and standards will be social, ethical, and political value judgments about what features of the world we take to be salient or important to project. These assumptions will be relevant to determining whether a model or theory accounts for the *relevant* data or is able to make empirical predictions of *the right kind*.

It is not clear whether all feminist empiricists would agree. Some feminist empiricists seem to take empirical adequacy as a politically value-neutral criterion that trumps other considerations (e.g., Solomon 2001; Borgerson 2011). Longino, however, seems to recognize that different values and interests may produce different understandings of empirical adequacy (Longino 2002, 155). And, feminist empiricists also acknowledge that social and political values may help constitute the aims of inquiry (Longino 1990, 86–87). Thus, some feminist empiricists might agree that the social and political aims of research might constitute further shared standards that help participants understand and apply the virtue of empirical adequacy.

But, for some feminist empiricists, this may lead to tension. Longino has argued that the kind of diversity needed for objectivity is a diversity of values and interests among participants. Inquirers with diverse values and interests provide a system of checks and balances to ensure that the idiosyncratic values or interests of scientists do not inappropriately influence scientific reasoning. But if ideal epistemic communities comprise members with diverse values and interests, there is a sense in which they may not share a standard of empirical adequacy (Intemann and de Melo-Martín, 2014b). Those with different interests and values may all claim to value empirical adequacy, but they may have different ideas about what that means. For example, creationists and evolutionary theorists both claim to value empirically adequate theories, but the other values that they take to be constitutive of inquiry lead to different assumptions about the data an empirically adequate theory must account for (Intemann and de Melo-Martín, 2014b). Hence, it appears that members of an epistemic community must share more standards than just empirical adequacy to be able to make judgments about what constitutes empirical success and which theories are empirically adequate. Of course, if participants share ethical and political commitments, this would decrease the sort of diversity that Longino considers necessary for objectivity.

This tension does not arise for standpoint feminist empiricists for two reasons. First, standpoint feminist empiricists claim that it is diversity of social positions, rather than diversity of values that is necessary for achieving objectivity. This is partly because standpoint feminists take experiences to be embodied and because social categories track power relations in ways that are epistemically significant. Given historical systems of oppression, individuals from diverse social positions and backgrounds are likely to have had different experiences, and these experiences can provide access to evidence that has implications for the plausibility of background assumptions, models, and methods. Second, feminist standpoint theorists claim that achieving a standpoint involves sharing a certain sort of political commitment. It requires a commitment to producing knowledge that benefits marginalized groups and challenges systems of oppression. Thus, feminist standpoint empiricism can be seen as a branch of feminist empiricism that takes social diversity rather than diversity of values and interests to be epistemically beneficial for promoting objectivity and involves a particular political commitment. I now examine this political commitment in greater detail.

The Normative Commitment Thesis

Achieving a *feminist* standpoint requires a commitment to particular social and political aims of inquiry—namely, a commitment to understand and challenge systems of oppression (Wylie 2003; Harding 2004; Intemann 2010b; Crasnow 2014 Intemann and de Melo Martín 2014a). According to Harding (2004, 31), a feminist standpoint "intends to map the practices of power, the ways the dominant institutions and their conceptual frameworks create and maintain oppressive social relations." Adopting a feminist standpoint involves revealing the ways in which gender, race, class, sexuality, ability, and colonization have shaped and influenced objects of investigation, including scientific practices themselves. This includes understanding how hierarchical power structures (e.g., patriarchy or racism) shape or limit research questions, conceptual frameworks, methodological decisions, models, background assumptions, or interpretations of data.

A feminist standpoint, then, takes one of the aims of inquiry to be producing knowledge that is *knowledge for* marginalized groups in order to counteract, remove, or minimize the ways in which oppressive systems limit the health, well-being, or life prospects of the members of these groups (including their ability to participate in the production of knowledge). Thus, some have argued that standpoints require a kind of activism (Hundleby 1997; Intemann 2010b; Crasnow 2014). They require understanding and revising our epistemic practices so as to identify, understand, and ultimately abolish the ways in which systems of oppression limit knowledge production. It is this normative commitment that also grounds the methodological thesis (see the next section).

What justifies the adoption of this political commitment for feminist standpoint empiricists? It is justified insofar as there are good reasons to support more general ethical claims made by feminists. Feminists maintain that oppression is bad and ought to be abolished. Moreover, scientific knowledge is a resource for understanding and addressing social problems, generating interventions, and developing public policies and has great potential to address injustices caused by oppression (Kourany 2003; Kourany, 2010). As such a resource, scientific knowledge is a public good that ought to be equitably distributed, in particular, to benefit those who are least well off (Pogge 2009 Daniels 2007; Kourany 2010; Kitcher 2011). Marginalized groups have priority because they are disproportionately affected by social problems. Marginalized groups in resource-poor countries in the global South are disproportionately affected by health and environmental problems (such as climate change and pollution) in virtue of their material circumstances, the nature of their economies, their lack of resources with which to mitigate these problems, and existing inequalities. Moreover, it is often the case (as with climate change) that marginalized groups bear less responsibility for the existence of these problems. Thus, there are compelling ethical reasons to adopt the political commitment that is necessary for achieving a feminist standpoint.

At the same time, it should be noted that the normative commitment involved in feminist standpoint empiricism should be understood broadly to allow for multiple conceptions of what counts as challenging systems of oppression or producing knowledge that benefits marginalized groups. There may be different ways to understand who is marginalized (Intemann and de Melo-Martín, 2014a). For example, one might be marginalized in virtue of belonging to a group that historically has been underrepresented in science, is the least well off in terms of resources or opportunities, or is the most seriously affected by a particular problem. Moreover, the values and interests of members of marginalized groups can conflict, so that there may be disagreement about how to prioritize or weigh competing interests. Thus, political commitment to challenging systems of oppression must be broadly understood to incorporate a plurality of ways to understand these values and interests, as well as how they might best be promoted in science. Critical discussion of these differences and disagreements is a necessary and important part of the process of achieving a feminist standpoint. At the same time, some values and interests will simply be incompatible with the general political commitment that standpoint feminism requires. Thus, it is not the case that an epistemic community would be necessarily more objective or more likely to achieve a feminist standpoint with the inclusion of those who do not value the needs and interests of marginalized groups or who do not share an interest in challenging systems of oppression.

The Methodological Thesis

The political commitment required to achieve a feminist standpoint also gives rise to a methodological commitment when carrying out empirical investigations. The methodological thesis of standpoint feminism asserts that research ought to proceed by "studying-up," or studying from the margins out, so as to understand how existing power structures shape and limit knowledge production, as well as the scientific phenomena under investigation (Crasnow 2006; Harding 2008; Intemann 2010b; Intemann and de Melo-Martín, 2011). Studying from the margins out requires researchers to work with members of marginalized groups to identify and frame scientific problems, identify the full range of stakeholders affected by a problem, consider the ways in which the traditional conceptual frameworks may fail to serve the interests of different groups, investigate the ways the problem may manifest differently for different social groups, and examine how systems of oppression may play a role in or contribute to the problem.

When researchers fail to study from the margins out, they may produce knowledge, interventions, technologies or policies that neglect the needs and circumstances of marginalized groups. For example, researchers who were aiming to reduce cervical cancer morbidity and mortality focused their research and clinical trials on women in North America and Western Europe (Intemann and de Melo-Martín 2010). The resulting human papilloma virus (HPV) vaccines that were targeted to high-risk HPV-types that are less common in the areas where the incidence of cervical cancer morbidity and mortality is the highest: Sub-Saharan African, Southeast Asia, and Latin America. Moreover, the economic and cultural conditions in those areas make it very difficult for the resulting vaccines to be used effectively (Intemann and de Melo-Martín 2010; de Melo-Martín and Intemann, 2011). This is because the vaccines are quite expensive and require refrigeration, and these populations also need access to healthcare professionals to administer the vaccine in three doses over several months. Thus, the vaccines are less likely to benefit those who are at greatest risk of developing and dying from cervical cancer.

Similarly, climate change researchers have often (unintentionally) neglected the interests of marginalized groups. General circulation models have been highly successful in predicting average global climate changes, but their ability to predict the specific changes that are likely to occur in particular geographic regions, information that is crucial for developing local adaptation strategies (Oreskes and Smith 2010). As mentioned, models that measure the impact of climate change often neglect to measure those things that are valued by members of marginalized groups (e.g., cultural practices, or dependence on the global North; Agarwal, 2002). In addition, many climate impact models are aggregate cost-benefit models that neglect to measure the distribution of impacts over graphical areas or social groups. Thus, while a model may show that world food supply will not be decreased overall by climate change, it may obscure the fact that agricultural opportunities in certain regions in the global South will decrease while food production in the north will increase. As a result, research may fail to produce important information that is crucial to the development of just adaptation and mitigation policies (Agarwal 2002; Intemann 2011).

Practically speaking, what, specifically, does the methodological thesis require? First, studying from the margins out requires identifying and working with marginalized groups to set research agendas and define research problems. University researchers may wish to study a behavior intervention to address dental problems in Native American communities. But a Native community may see food scarcity as its most pressing issue. Thus, investigations related to food scarcity may be more important and ultimately more important than addressing dental problems. Indeed, successful prevention of dental problems may necessitate addressing larger food-scarcity issues as lack of access to affordable nutrious food may also contribute to dental decay.

Second, studying from the margins out involves using axes of oppression as categories of analysis in scientific investigations. It requires researchers to identify stakeholders affected by a particular scientific problem and examine the ways the problem may manifest differently for different social categories. For example, biomedical researchers ought to consider such questions as: What health problems are most significant to members of marginalized groups? Does a particular disease or health problem manifest or operate differently for those of different sexes, ethnicities, classes, or geographical locations? Are there social, political, economic, or biological differences among these groups that might be relevant to understanding the epidemiology of a disease? Do differences among these groups affect the effectiveness of possible solutions to this particular health problem? What differences in social conditions exist that present challenges or require trade-offs in addressing the disease burden? Using these sorts of categories of analysis ensures that the framing of research problems, choice of methodologies, selection of data, and interventions developed are more likely to be responsive to and effective for the needs of marginalized groups.

Third, studying from the margins out requires researchers to reflect critically about their choice of a conceptual framework and methodologies in relation to both the social and epistemic aims of research. Anderson (2004), for example, has discussed the work of sociologists who reconceptualized what should constitute a harm experienced by children of divorce. Using a feminist lens, such research employed a broader conception of potential harms that included harms that might come from women staying in inegalitarian households, which had previously been ignored. Crasnow (2014) has highlighted the work of criminologist Elizabeth Stanko (1997) who investigated the various strategies women employ to avoid assault. Rather than employing a traditional framework for behaviors that count as "defensive strategies," Stanko began by asking her subjects to give an account of "things that we do to keep safe." As a result, she elicited a broader range of descriptions of what constitutes self-defense, such as choosing a place to live, deciding when and where to walk, choosing a time to do errands, deciding what to wear and so on. Studying from the margins out requires that researchers critically reflect on the social and political aims of their research and consider which methodologies or conceptual frameworks are most likely to further those goals.

Fourth, studying from the margins out requires a critical evaluation of evidentiary standards, including what kinds of data should be collected, what constitutes good evidence, and how much evidence is needed to accept a hypothesis, explanation, or model. Kristin Shrader-Frechette (1997), for example, has argued that hydrogeological models that predict the dispersion of radioactive nuclear waste material may not be "good enough" to accept the predictions they yield, given the risks posed to those potentially exposed to contaminated ground water. In biomedical research, the evidence of the efficaciousness of a drug in a highly controlled, randomized, clinical trial may not be sufficient to know whether a drug will be effective in practice, particularly for marginalized groups who commonly have conditions that are treated as exclusionary criteria in drug testing (Intemann and de Melo-Martín 2010). Insofar as there are empirical studies on race and sex differences that produce data that may conform to implicit biases, it may be that a higher bar of evidence is needed before results are made public so as to avoid falsely perpetuating negative stereotypes (Kitcher 1993). In each of these cases, the needs and interests of marginalized groups should help inform what standards of evidence are adopted, since these groups are likely to be effected by such decisions.

The approaches that are required by the methodological thesis aim to ensure that research will proceed in a way that is responsive to the needs of marginalized groups, but also to confront the sorts of biases and limitations that might make such research challenging. The experiences of members of marginalized groups are often precisely those that are likely to be neglected in virtue of the resources that are required to engage in scientific practices. Thus, overcoming biases will require mechanisms for securing those neglected experiences and interests.

The Epistemic Advantage Thesis

The epistemic advantage thesis holds that epistemic communities that achieve a feminist standpoint have epistemic advantages. This can now be understood as the claim that epistemic communities that (1) comprise those from diverse social positions, (2) share a broad political commitment to producing knowledge that challenges systems of oppression, (3) critically reflect on and expose the ways in which power structures limit and shape knowledge, (4) begin research from the experiences, interests, and values of members of marginalized groups, and (5) engage in a process of transformative criticism governed by a set of shared standards (including empirical adequacy) will have epistemic benefits. These benefits will now be identified.

First, it is important to note that for feminist standpoint empiricists, what constitutes an "epistemic benefit," is deeply connected to the social and political benefits that research done from a feminist standpoint will produce. As noted earlier, feminist standpoint theorists take the political and social aims of inquiry to be partly *constitutive of* (as opposed to distinct from) the cognitive or epistemic aims of inquiry. The aim of inquiry is not merely to produce true or empirically adequate beliefs about the world, but to do so in ways that challenge oppression, promote social justice, and produce the sorts of knowledge, interventions, policies, and technologies that are needed to address social needs. Insofar as feminist standpoint research advances this aim, or produces knowledge that is more responsive to the needs and interests of marginalized groups, this is understood as an epistemic advantage. Moreover, as mentioned, the political aims of inquiry guide how the virtue of empirical adequacy is understood and applied in particular research contexts. The extent to which research produces social benefits is the extent to which it advances its epistemic or cognitive aims, and vice versa. Feminist standpoint empiricism therefore rejects the view that the epistemic aims of research are wholly distinct from the social or political aims of research. For this reason, it may be best to understand the epistemic advantage thesis as the claim that communities of inquirers that achieve a feminist standpoint will yield several benefits with both epistemic and social dimensions.

Identification and Challenging of Power Structures That Limit Participation

First, communities that achieve a feminist standpoint are more likely to be able to identify the ways in which systems of oppression limit the participation of members of marginalized groups and to pursue inquiry in ways that remove or challenge these barriers. It exposes and challenges the ways in which social injustice can also contribute to epistemic injustice (Fricker 2007). Because a feminist standpoint employs a critical stance, the epistemic communities that adopt it are more likely to secure the participation of those who have historically been excluded from scientific inquiry.

It is not just that feminist standpoint communities seek greater diversity, but that they do so in ways that simultaneously challenge the ways in which certain interests dominate scientific inquiry. This is particularly important in the current context, as commercial interests increasingly shape research agendas, control the publication of results, and influence the selection of methodologies (Reiss 2010; Intemann and de Melo-Martín 2014a). Communities that achieve a feminist standpoint will be able to counter these influences.

Correction and Minimization of Bias

A second benefit that feminist standpoints yield is that they are more likely to counteract the problematic biases that arise in particular research contexts. Feminist standpoint theorists reject the view that bias occurs when values or interests influence scientific reasoning or practices. It is not the presence of values per se that is a problem; rather, some values are privileged because they serve the interests of those in power, and not because they are supported by good reasons that are widely accepted by the stakeholders affected by the research. Bias occurs when such values influence scientific reasoning or practices in ways that serve the interests of those in power rather than the community-endorsed epistemic and social aims of research. Thus, a feminist standpoint is "strongly objective" in Harding's terms because the diversity of inquirers and the political consciousness that is achieved reduce or minimize these negative influences.

Standpoint feminists' commitment to the participation of marginalized groups and to challenging systems of oppression make it more likely that such biases will be identified and counteracted. Communities of standpoint inquirers are likely to involve more rigorous critical reflection because their experiences are often precisely those that are most needed in identifying problematic background assumptions and revealing the limitations of research questions, models, or methodologies. Epistemic communities that do not involve the participation of marginalized groups may be unknowingly insulated from criticism that might arise from individuals with different relevant experiences and evidence.

Enhancement of Creativity and Epistemic Pluralism

Third, by securing the participation of marginalized groups, diverse epestimic communities are more likely to discover new ways of framing research questions, develop novel conceptual frameworks, and employ alternative methodologies. It is not merely that the inclusion of marginalized groups will add new knowledge to what is already known. Standpoint theorists have argued that members of oppressed groups sometimes have special experiences that result from their location as "insider-outsiders" (Hill Collins, 1991). Members of oppressed groups must understand the assumptions that constitute the worldviews of dominant groups in order to successfully navigate the world. At the same time, they often have experiences that conflict with dominant views and generate alternative views about how the world works (Wylie 2003, 34–35). This insider-outsider perspective can introduce new conceptual schemes, advance alternative methodologies, and reframe research questions in ways that offer resources for reinterpreting what is known as well as generating knew knowledge.

Consider, for example, a female biomedical researcher who grew up in Sub-Saharan Africa and is now working in the United States on a new HIV vaccine. To be successful as a biomedical researcher, she must learn and conform to what is taken to be authoritative knowledge in her field; that is, she must know the relevant biological theories related to the causal mechanisms of HIV transmission, understand how various interventions might affect or control those mechanisms, and master the accepted methodological practices for drug testing in clinical trials. Yet to the extent that her experiences as a Sub-Saharan African woman conflict with the assumptions widely endorsed by US biomedical researchers, she will recognize that those assumptions may problematic or partial (Hill Collins 1991, 49–51). For example, in virtue of her experiences living in Sub-Saharan Africa, she may be aware that a vaccine under development will likely not work for the populations with the highest incidence of HIV. She may know that the vaccine technology favored by molecular biologists in the United States requires refrigerating the vaccine, which will be expensive and difficult to do in many contexts in rural Africa. She may realize that an HIV vaccine will be particularly ineffective for women because of the cultural, social, and economic barriers for women that do not exist for men. She may also be aware that clinical-trial evidence that a vaccine is efficacious is not evidence that the drug will be effective among the general population because she understands the different conditions that exist in Sub-Saharan Africa and in highly controlled clinical trials conducted in the United States. She may also be able to see that the way a research problem is being framed actually hinders the aims of the research. For example, she may recognize that Western researchers are framing the problem as a only question of whether a particular vaccine will trigger an immune response that will block HIV infection, when it might be alternatively framed as a question of how to block HIV infection in those populations who are most at risk. In other words, her unique position as an insider-outsider provides her with both the expertise and experience to recognize the limitations of current assumptions, methodologies, and models and to identify alternative approaches that may better serve the aims of the research. Because she is an insider she has the relevant expertise to be able to understand and identify the assumptions that are being made in her field. Yet as an outsider, or member of a group that has been historically excluded from such research, she has had experiences that allow her to identify the limitations and problems with some of those assumptions. In this way, scientific communities that include members of oppressed groups whose experiences are relevant to the research are more likely to generate new explanations, models, theories, and approaches.

Science That Is More Socially Responsive

The standpoint commitment to challenge rather than reinforce systems of oppression and to study from the margins out are more likely to produce the kind of knowledge that will be responsive to the needs and interests of marginalized groups. As has been seen in the HPV case, there are multiple ways of addressing scientific problems but not all of them are equally effective in improving the lives and conditions of marginalized groups. Because feminist standpoint empiricism makes certain political and social aims of inquiry explicit and requires researchers to be attentive to those aims throughout the research process, it is more likely to produce socially responsive knowledge.

OBJECTIONS AND RESPONSES

It is now possible to see how this interpretation of feminist standpoint theory, as a branch of feminist empiricism, has the resources to respond to several objections standpoint theory has historically faced.

Is The Notion of a Standpoint Essentialist?

On the interpretation I have defended, a standpoint is not something that automatically results from being a member of a particular social group. It is a political consciousness that is achieved, in degrees, by an appropriately diverse group that employs a particular critical stance. Moreover, the inclusion of inquirers from marginalized groups is not itself sufficient to achieve a standpoint or to give rise to the epistemic benefits just described. The mere presence of a member of an oppressed group is not sufficient to achieve the sort of conscious, critical reflection that is required to achieve a standpoint. For diversity to yield epistemic advantages, the community must engage in critical reflection and the criticisms of insider-outsiders must be taken seriously. In other words, there must be some sort of equality of intellectual authority and uptake of criticism.

In addition, this interpretation does not assume that members of marginalized groups all have a set of uniform or monolithic experiences, values, or interests. Indeed, it is the differences among participants that give rise to a more rigorous process of transformative criticism. While the notion of a standpoint does assume that there is something particularly beneficial about the inclusion of experiences and interests that have been historically excluded, it does not suppose that those experiences will be similar to each other.

Is the Claim That *All* Research Should Aim to Achieve a Feminist Standpoint?

Feminist standpoint empiricism is not committed to the claim that *all* scientific research should aim to challenge systems of oppression or benefit marginalized groups (although some may argue that this kind of research ought to be prioritized). The claim, rather, is that when the problems under investigation are ones that affect disadvantaged groups or that may involve hierarchical power structures, achieving a feminist standpoint can yield a variety of epistemic and political benefits.

Whether a feminist standpoint is always useful or likely to yield epistemic advantages is itself an empirical question. There may be research contexts in which the object of inquiry is far removed from anything impacted by systems of oppression and therefore not likely to affect marginalized groups any differently; in these cases it is less clear that attempts to achieve a feminist standpoint would yield the same benefits that it might in other research contexts. The inclusion of insider-outsiders only yields epistemic benefits when their experiences are relevant to the research context. The experience of living in Sub-Saharan Africa may be relevant to HIV or climate-change research but less relevant to evaluating background assumptions in organic chemistry.

At the same time, it should be noted that relevance is often difficult to know a priori, in advance. As the history of science has shown, even areas of research that do not appear to relate to marginalized groups may suffer from distorting biases that could be addressed by achieving a feminist standpoint. This is particularly the case when models or analogies are employed that, for instance, rely on gender stereotypes or represent ungendered phenomena. For example, the use of the "lock and key" metaphor to understand human biological reproductive processes reinforced gender stereotypes of the female as passive and noncontributing to causal process, which was both politically problematic and ultimately empirically inadequate (Martín 1991). Thus, using the sort of critical lens that feminist standpoint empiricism advocates may be beneficial in a wide variety of research contexts, including those that may first appear to be politically neutral.

Moreover, even in cases in which the content of science may not be related to addressing social problems or developing technologies, interventions, and policies, the practice of science may itself be influenced by systems of oppression in ways that decrease the social diversity of the inquirers. There are studies showing that demographic diversity among researchers may produce greater creativity and result in research with higher impacts within the scientific community (McLeod and Lobel 1992; Freeman and Huang 2014). Thus, even in cases in which the methodological thesis, for example, is less applicable, adopting the other tenets of feminist standpoint empiricism may yield benefits.

Can This View Avoid Pernicious Relativism?

Perhaps the most worrisome concern is that feminist standpoint empiricism might be committed to some form of epistemological or moral relativism. While this is a concern that many have had with standpoint theory (Haack 1998; Clough 2003; Pinnick 2003), it is also likely to be a concern for nonstandpoint feminist empiricists, because of way empirical adequacy has been articulated here. Traditionally, empirical adequacy or empirical success has been understood to be an independent check on scientific reasoning, helping to ensure that our theories and models track "the way the world really is." The concern is that if feminist values and political commitments are allowed to help determine what the evidence is, then we will simply end up with theories and models that reflect the way we *wish* the world would be (given our politics) rather that the way the world *actually is*. Oftentimes, the example of "Lysenko science" is used to demonstrate how disastrous it can be when politics are allowed to influence judgments of evidence (Haack 1998; Douglas 2009). Indeed, creationists often dismiss the empirical data pointed to by evolutionary theorists because it is not consistent with their other values, such as a worldview that is consistent with a literal interpretation of the Bible. Thus, there is concern that feminist standpoint empiricism is committed to the view that whether one believes a theory is justified or not is solely dependent on the political values that one holds.

It is true that feminist standpoint empiricism is committed to the claim that political values can legitimately operate as background assumptions in determining what features of the world an empirically adequate theory must account for, and how much evidence is needed to constitute an empirically successful theory. But this does not entail that feminist values, by themselves, determine what the data are. Feminist political values may give us reasons to think that climate change models ought to account for specific impacts (such as to cultural traditions) or for the distribution of impacts among resource-poor and resource-wealthy countries. However, feminist values do not determine what the outcomes of such investigations will be. Feminist values may also give us reasons to think that HIV-positive individuals should not be excluded from clinical trials for an HPV vaccine (even though HIV infection is a complicating health factor), since those who are at high risk for cervical cancer are also more likely to be HIV positive—and we want to make sure that a drug is efficacious for those most at risk. Nonetheless, this does not determine whether a vaccine will be efficacious for a particular group that is tested.

Moreover, even insofar as our understanding of empirical adequacy is dependent upon certain other aims of inquiry, including social and political aims, this is only a problem if those social and political aims cannot themselves be justified with good reasons. Yet no feminist theorists would argue that such value judgments are unjustified as they presumably take their own political and value commitments to be supported by good reasons. Although it is beyond the scope of this chapter to provide a full account of how ethical and political values are justified, I hope to have provided some justification for the political commitment advocated here. For these reasons, feminist standpoint empiricism need not be committed to epistemological or moral relativism.

Is Feminist Standpoint Empiricism Logically Inconsistent?

A final objection to feminist standpoint theory is that it is logically inconsistent (Antony 1993; Longino 1993). On the one hand, the situated knowledge thesis claims that all knowledge is socially situated and produced from a particular standpoint. On the other hand, standpoint theorists claim that some standpoints are epistemically better than others. If all knowledge is situated to a particular standpoint, then what standards can a standpoint theorist use to claim that a feminist standpoint is epistemically superior?

To claim that knowledge is produced from a particular standpoint does not entail that that there are no shared values or standards of evaluation among different standpoints. Nonfeminist empiricists, feminist empiricists, and standpoint theorists might all share certain broad cognitive aims, such as furthering understanding of the world, correcting for distorting biases, maintaining logical consistency, promoting creativity and theoretical pluralism, and perhaps even producing scientific knowledge that helps address pressing social needs. Standpoint theorists attempt to defend the thesis of epistemic advantage on grounds that nonstandpoint theorists would accept; that is, they aim to point to consequences of their approach that would be seen as beneficial even by those who do not share all their cognitive aims and values. They can appeal to other shared cognitive or ethical values to defend their approach.

Conclusion

I have attempted to elucidate and defend a version of standpoint theory, feminist standpoint empiricism, understood as a branch of feminist empiricism. Like other feminist empiricist views, it takes epistemic communities to be the locus of knowledge and objectivity. Knowledge is produced through a group process of transformative criticism that is governed by a set of shared standards. Among these shared standards is a commitment to empirical adequacy. However, feminist standpoint empiricists do not maintain that empirical adequacy is independent of other social and cognitive aims of inquiry. These other aims are important in identifying the features that empirically adequate theories must account for, how much evidence is needed to establish empirical success, and when it is reasonable to revise other background assumptions in light of potentially countervailing evidence. Achieving a feminist standpoint further requires the adoption of a broad political aim of inquiry: to challenge systems of oppression and improve the conditions and life prospects of marginalized groups. While some pluralism with respect to how this political commitment is understood is reasonable, members must share this broad political aim and utilize methodologies that enable them to further it. Particularly important to maximizing objectivity in this process are mechanisms for ensuring that participants in an epistemic community are from diverse social positions with diverse experiences. I have not defended the claim that *all* epistemic communities ought to aim to achieve a feminist standpoint. There may be areas of research in which the phenomenon under investigation has little relation to human beings or their interests. But, insofar as marginalized people are affected by research, I have argued that epistemic communities that achieve a feminist standpoint are likely to yield several epistemological and political benefits.

References

Anderson, E. 2004. "Uses of Value Judgments in Science: A General Argument; with Lessons from a Case Study of Feminist Research on Divorce." *Hypatia* 19 (1): 1–24.

Antony, Louise. 1993. "Quine as Feminist: The Radical Import of Naturalized Epistemology." In *A Mind of One's Own: Feminist Essays on Reason and Objectivity*, edited by Louise Antony and Charlotte Witt, 185–226. Boulder: Westview Press.

Agarwal, A. 2002. "A Southern Perspective on Curbing Global Climate Change." In *Climate Change Policy: A Survey*, edited by S. H. Schneider, A. Rosencrantz, and J. O. Niles, 375–391. Washington DC: Island Press.

Bar On, B. 1993. "Marginality and Epistemic Privilege." In *Feminist Epistemologies*, edited by L. Alcoff and E. Potter, 83–100. New York: Routledge.

Borgerson, K. 2011. "Amending and Defending Critical Contextual Empiricism." *European Journal for Philosophy of Science* 1 (3):435–449.

Campbell, R. 1998. *Illusions of Paradox: A Feminist Epistemology Naturalized*. Lanham, MD: Rowman and Littlefield.

Clough, S. 2003. *Beyond Epistemology: A Pragmatist Approach to Feminist Science Studies*. Landham, MD: Rowman and Littlefield.

Clough, S. 2004. "Having It All: Naturalized Normativity in Feminist Science Studies." *Hypatia* 19 (1): 102–118.

Code, L. 1991. *What Can She Know? Feminist Theory and the Construction of Knowledge*. Ithaca, NY: Cornell University Press.

Crasnow, S. 2006. "Feminist Anthropology and Sociology: Issues for Social Science." In *Handbook of the Philosophy of Science. Vol. 15, Philosophy of Anthropology and Sociology*, edited by S. Turner and M. Risjord, 827–860. Amsterdam: Elsevier.

Crasnow, S. 2014. "Feminist Perspectives." In *Philosophy of Social Science*, edited by N. Cartwright and E. Montuschi. New York: Oxford University Press.

Daniels, N. 2007. *Just Health: Meeting Health Needs Fairly*. Cambridge, UK: Cambridge University Press.

de Melo-Martín, I., and K. Intemann, 2011. "Feminist Resources for Biomedical Research: Lessons from the HPV Vaccines." *Hypatia: A Journal of Feminist Philosophy* 26 (1): 79–101.

de Melo-Martín, I., and Meghani, Z. 2008. "Beyond Risk: A More Realistic Risk-Benefit Analysis of Agricultural Biotechnologies." *EMBO Reports* 9 (4): 302–306.

DeFrancesco, L. 2013. "How Safe Does Transgenic Food Need to Be?" *Nature Biotechnology* 31: 794–802.

Douglas, H. 2009. *Science, Policy, and the Value-Free Ideal*. Pittsburgh, PA: University of Pittsburgh Press.

Freeman, R. B., and W. Huang, 2014. "Collaborating with People like Me: Ethnic Co-Authorship in the U.S." *National Bureau of Economic Research Working Paper*, No. 19905. http://www.nber.org/papers/w19905 (accessed April 6, 2014).

Fricker, M. 2007. *Epistemic Injustice: Power and the Ethics of Knowing*. New York: Oxford University Press.

Garcia, A. M. 1989. "The Development of Chicana Feminist Discourse, 1970-1980." *Gender and Society* 3 (2): 217–238.

Gero, J. M., and M. W Conkey. 1991. *Gendering Archaeology: Women and Prehistory*. Malden, MA: Blackwell-Wiley.

Haack, S. 1998. *Manifesto of a Passionate Moderate*. Chicago: University of Chicago Press.

Harding, S. 1986. *The Science Question in Feminism*. Ithaca, NY: Cornell University Press.

Harding, S. 1991. *Whose Science? Whose Knowledge?* Ithaca, NY: Cornell University Press.

Harding, S. 1993. "Rethinking Standpoint Epistemology: What Is Strong Objectivity?" In *Feminist Epistemologies*, edited by L. Alcoff and E. Potter, 49–82. New York: Routledge.

Harding, S. 2004. "A Socially Relevant Philosophy of Science? Resources from Standpoint Theory's Controversiality." *Hypatia* 19 (1): 25–47.

Harding, S. 2008. *Sciences from Below: Feminisms, Postcolonialities, and Modernities*. Raleigh, NC: Duke University Press.

Hartsock, N. 1983. "The Feminist Standpoint: Developing the Ground for a Specifically Feminist Historical Materialism." In *Discovering Reality*, edited by M. B. Hintikka and S. Harding, 283–310. Dordrecht, The Netherlands: Kluwer Academic Publishing.

Hekman, S. 1997. "Truth and Method: Feminist Standpoint Theory Revisited." *Signs* 22 (2): 341–365.

Hill Collins, P. 1991. "Learning from the Outsider Within." In *Beyond Methodology: Feminist Scholarship as Lived Research*, edited by M. M. Fonow and J. A. Cook, 35–59. Bloomington: Indiana University Press.

Hrdy, S. B. 1986. "Empathy, Polyandry, and the Myth of the Coy Female." In *Feminist Approaches to Science*, edited by R. Bleier, 119–146. New York: Pergamon Press.

Hundleby, C. 1997. "Where Standpoint Stands Now." *Women & Politics* 18 (3): 25–43.

Intemann, K. 2010a. "Standpoint Empiricism: Rethinking the Terrain in Feminist Philosophy of Science." In *New Waves in Philosophy of Science*, edited by P. D. Magnus and J. Busch, 198–225. Houndmills, UK: Palgrave MacMillan.

Intemann, K. 2010b. "25 Years of Feminist Empiricism and Standpoint Theory: Where Are We Now?" *Hypatia* 25 (4): 778–796.

Intemann, K. 2011. "Putting Feminist Research Principles into Practice: Objectivity and Social Justice in Climate Change Studies." In *The Handbook of Feminist Research: Theory and Praxis*, 2nd ed., edited by Sharlene Hesse-Biber, 495–510. Thousand Oaks, CA: Sage Publishing.

Intemann, K., and I. de Melo-Martín. 2010. "Social Values and Evidentiary Standards: The Case of the HPV Vaccine." *Biology and Philosophy* 25 (2): 203–213.

Intemann, K., and I. de Melo-Martín. (2014a). "Commercialized Science: Can Feminist Conceptions of Objectivity Help?" *European Journal of Philosophy of Science* 4 (2):135–151

Intemann, K., and I. de Melo-Martín. 2014b. "Are There Limits to the Obligations Scientists Have to Dissenters?" *Synthese* 191 (12): 2751–2765.

Kitcher, P. 2011. *Science in a Democratic Society*. (Amherst, NY: Prometheus Books.

Kitcher, P. 1993. *The Advancement of Science*. Oxford: Oxford University Press.

Kourany, J. 2003. "A Philosophy of Science for the Twenty-First Century." *Philosophy of Science* 70 (1): 1–14.

Kourany, J. 2010. *Philosophy of Science after Feminism*. New York: Oxford University Press.

Kourany, J. 2012. "The Place of Standpoint Theory in Feminist Science Studies." *Hypatia* 24: 209–218.

Longino, H. 1990. *Science as Social Knowledge* (Princeton, NJ: Princeton University Press.

Longino, H. 1993. "Subjects, Power, and Knowledge: Description and Prescription in Feminist Philosophies of Science." In *Feminist Epistemologies*, edited by L. Alcoff and E. Potter, 101–120. New York: Routledge.

Longino, H. 2002. *The Fate of Knowledge*. Princeton, NJ: Princeton University Press.

Martin, E. 1991. "The Egg and Sperm: How Science Has Constructed a Romance Based on Stereotypical Male-Female Roles." *Signs* 16 (3): 485–501

McLeod, P. L., and S. A. Lobel 1992. "The Effects of Ethnic Diversity on Idea Generation in Small Groups." *Academy of Management Proceedings* August 1 (1): 227–231.

Narayan, U. 1989. "The Project of Feminist Epistemology." In *Gender/Body/Knowledge: Feminist Reconstructions of Being and Knowing*, edited by S. Bordo and A. Jaggar, 256–272. Rutgers, NJ: Rutgers University Press.

Nelson, L. H. 1990. *Who Knows? From Quine to a Feminist Empiricism*. Philadelphia, PA: Temple University Press.

Oreskes, Naomi, David Stainforth, and Leonard A. Smith. 2010. "Adaptation to Global Warming: Do Climate Models Tell Us What We Need to Know?" *Philosophy of Science* 77: 1012–1028.

Pinnick, C., N. Koertge, and R. F. Almeder, eds. 2003. *Scrutinizing Feminist Epistemology*. New Brunswick, NJ: Rutgers University Press.

Pogge, T. 2009. "The Health Impact Fund and Its Justification by Appeal to Human Rights." *Journal of Social Philosophy* 40 (4): 542–569.

Reiss, J. 2010. "In Favour of a Millian Proposal to Reform Biomedical Research." *Synthese* 177 (3): 427–447.

Rolin, K. 2006. "The Bias Paradox in Feminist Standpoint Epistemology." *Episteme* 1 (2): 125–136.

Rolin, K. 2009. "Standpoint Theory as a Methodology for the Study of Power Relations." *Hypatia* 24 (4): 218–226.

Rosaldo, M. Z. 1980. *Knowledge and Passion: Ilongot Notions of Self and Social Life*. Cambridge, UK: Cambridge University Press.

Rose, H. 1983. "Hand, Brain, and Heart: A Feminist Epistemology for The Natural Sciences. *Signs*, 73–90.

Schnieder, S. H., K. Kunz-Duriseti, and C. Azar. 2000. "Costing Non-Linearities, Surprises, and Irreversible Events." *Pacific and Asian Journal of Energy* 10 (1): 81–106.

Shrader-Frechette, K. 1997. "Hydrogeology and Framing as Having Policy Consequences." *Philosophy of Science* 64: S149–S160.

Smith, D. 1974. "Women's Perspective as a Radical Critique of Sociology." *Sociological Inquiry* 44 (1): 7–13.

Smith, D. 1997. "Comments on Hekman's 'Truth and Method: Feminist Standpoint Theory Revisited.'" *Signs* 22 (2): 392–398.

Solomon, M. 2001. *Social Empiricism*. Cambridge, MA: MIT Press.

Stanko, Elizabeth A. 1997. "Conceptualizing Women's Risk Assessment as a 'Technology of the Soul.'" *Theoretical Criminology* 1 (4): 479–499.

Wylie, A. 2003. "Why Standpoint Matters." In *Science and Other Cultures: Issues in Philosophies of Science and Technology*, edited by R. Figueroa and S. Harding, 26–48. New York: Routledge.

CHAPTER 14

GENDERED DIVISIONS OF LABOR

MARY BETH MILLS

IT is hard to overestimate the significance of divisions of labor for the formulation and development of feminist theory. The artificial separation of key life activities into gendered spheres—production versus reproduction, paid versus unpaid work, public versus private domains—and the oppressive effects of these divisions have motivated and informed a wide range of feminist research, activism, and philosophy. The daily lived experiences of gendered inequalities—particularly of women's unequal access to public life and their legal, economic, and social dependence within the patriarchal household—inspired some of the earliest advocates for women's rights, including Mary Wollstonecraft, Susan B. Anthony, Charlotte Perkins Gilman, and Emma Goldman. Second-wave feminism identified the patriarchal division of labor by sex as a crucial impediment to women's psycho-social liberation. Similarly, long-term engagements with critical Marxist studies have been important for feminist interrogations of the ways patriarchy and capitalism converge to harness women's domestic reproductive labor for the support and maintenance of a productive labor force (Folbre 1994; Gibson-Graham 1996; Hartmann 1979; Hartsock 1983).

Studies of gender and of divisions of labor remain a critical focus of analysis in contemporary feminist theorizing, even as the terrain of these inquiries has shifted significantly in recent decades. In particular, scholars have sought to move beyond the Eurocentric and universalizing assumptions that characterized much earlier feminist thinking. These changes are most clearly represented in an important shift in vocabulary—from long-standing interest in "the sexual division of labor" to an increasing focus on the many and diverse "gendered divisions of labor." In the rest of this chapter, I examine how this recognition of diversity and complexity informs feminist analyses of gendered labor on a global scale. In particular, this scholarship attends not only to the variety of lived experiences to which gendered hierarchies of labor and value give rise, but also to the ways in which gender intersects with other forms of inequality (class, race/ethnicity, nationality, and sexuality, among others) in complex and often contradictory ways.

More than a change in terminology, then, the phrase *gendered divisions of labor* articulates the commitment of contemporary feminist theorizing and research to globally engaged, comparative, and interdisciplinary scholarship. In turn, the incorporation of transnational, postcolonial, and intersectional perspectives has enabled powerful new directions of feminist research, the results of which have both complicated and enlivened the debates about the limits to and opportunities for gender equality in a globally connected world.

I begin by discussing briefly some of the ways in which the concept of gendered divisions of labor engages with wider themes of contemporary feminist theorization. I then review how scholars have sought to examine the empirical workings of gendered divisions of labor in their diverse local and global manifestations. Here I pay particular attention to three interrelated phenomena: the recruitment of a feminized wage labor force in the service of contemporary global industry; the commodification of reproductive labor, particularly in relation to transnational mobility; and the gendered effects of economic restructuring and related forms of neoliberalization. Throughout the chapter, I seek to show how research into gendered divisions of labor and their global entanglements offers critical insights for feminist analysis. In varied ways, the investigation of gendered divisions of labor allows for a fuller understanding, not only of the gendered inequalities that shape contemporary lives and livelihoods, but also of the barriers these pose to the pursuit of a more liberatory future. Ultimately, the study of gendered divisions of labor reveals their artificiality and human constructedness. As such, they can be unmade and reimagined. How best to do so and what the results might look like are among some of the more exciting questions that continue to animate feminist theory and practice around the world.

Theorizing Gendered Divisions of Labor

The concept of gendered divisions of labor builds upon several key developments in recent feminist scholarship, three of which I focus on here. First, the concept incorporates new theorizations of gender and gender hierarchies as the dynamic products of cross-culturally varied and historically contingent processes. It also reflects the critical contributions of intersectional and postcolonial analyses. And, lastly, it draws on Marxist-feminist analyses, particularly studies of social reproduction, and the questions these raise about the easy conflation of capitalism(s) and patriarchy(ies) as well as the artificial gendering of different spheres of human activity. The significance of these diverse directions of feminist insight emerges from a closer analysis of each component of the term *gendered divisions of labor*.

The idea of *gendered* divisions of labor relies on the understanding that gender is not a fixed or essential feature of the sexed body but, rather, comprises complex systems of meanings, practices, and identities. Although gender is linked to sex and sexuality, these are not isomorphic categories. Moreover, they encode norms and identities that are highly diverse as well as historically and culturally contingent. Consequently, in any given context, feminist scholars must ask what it means to identify or to be identified as a man or a woman (or as some other potentially available—or transgressive—category of person). The content of such identities and the relative value associated with them cannot be assumed but must instead be understood in relation to complex processes of social and cultural construction (Ortner and Whitehead 1981; Ross and Rapp 1981; Scott 1986). Gender systems are, in effect, discursive formations that shape and are shaped by matrices of power; as such they are also continually articulated and negotiated through intersubjective performances, which, in turn, produce, reproduce, and at times contest these same patterns of domination (Butler 1990).

Like the culturally and historically constructed systems of gender with which they articulate, then, *gendered* divisions of labor can be analyzed on at least three levels: the symbolic or ideological meanings they produce and reproduce; the normative (or transgressive) social roles and relationships they rely on or make possible; and the diverse lived experiences of individual self-identity and motivation that they mobilize. While all these dimensions can contribute to patterns of gender hierarchy, they may not do so in parallel or consistent ways. This leaves room for ambiguity and for potential conflict to arise between, for example, idealized meanings of masculinity and femininity and the kinds of employment available to actual men and women in a particular economic setting. Similarly, as new kinds of work are made possible or old jobs transformed (as with the advent of new technologies), these changes may prompt employers to recruit men and women for different, often segregated, tasks, a process that frequently serves to reinforce hierarchical gender meanings and roles but can also open up challenges to them. Meanwhile, men's and women's actual experiences of employment may not conform easily or meaningfully to the gendered norms and identities that shape their lives in non-work settings, prompting some individuals to think about themselves, as well as about the significance of gendered differences, in new ways. Such slippages and contradictions between different dimensions of gender are part of what makes *gendered* divisions of labor highly variable processes, rather than fixed or uniform structures.

Not only do the meanings and social value associated with gender difference vary tremendously, so do the ways in which men and women understand what they do as work and how they expect (or are expected) to contribute to their societies and households.[1] Hence, it is crucial to conceptualize gendered *divisions* of labor in the plural. Moreover, just as gender inequalities take varied forms, they also interact with other meaningful dimensions of social and cultural identity to generate complex and contested hierarchies of value. Here, the concerns of postcolonial and intersectional scholarship have played a critical role in moving studies of gender and labor toward a recognition that the organization of tasks by gender is but one among many potentially relevant dimensions of difference and inequality (Lowe and Lloyd 1997; Stoler 2002). A fully realized concept of gendered *divisions* of labor requires the analysis of how different hierarchies of value converge and diverge with gendered processes of inequality. It also allows for research into the way these dynamics may vary within and across different societies. In other words, gendered divisions of labor are always shaped by social systems of power and hierarchy, systems that increasingly stretch across globally dispersed sites of production and reproduction. Consequently, understanding gendered *divisions* of labor in any given context necessarily requires the examination of how gender difference interacts with other hierarchies of value, including those rooted in diverse hierarchies of class, race, age, or nationality. While these intersecting forms of power shape gendered *divisions* of labor in varied ways, the result is a widespread association of the most marginalized populations with the most devalued and feminized forms of labor (regardless of whether the work is performed by men or by women).

Not surprisingly, then, studying gendered divisions of *labor* necessarily involves the actual empirical investigation of how, specifically, people produce and consume value in their daily activities of life and livelihood. In other words, research into gendered divisions of *labor* makes visible patterns of production and consumption that connect the lives of men and women as they are recruited and disciplined into transnationally linked but often highly segmented labor forces. The resulting inequalities cannot be viewed as the isolated effects of specific cultural communities or national societies; rather, they reveal the extent to which, in today's world, everyday lives are shaped by regimes of capitalist accumulation that mobilize diverse forms of gendered labor across globally differentiated scales of value. Of particular interest to feminist scholarship has been the ways in which these gendered divisions of labor mark the global proliferation of value hierarchies between productive and reproductive activities. Associations with masculine breadwinning and individual self-reliance privilege public "productive" labor as the engine of formal economic wealth and well-being (Folbre 1994); in contrast, even when reproductive labor is performed by hired service workers, it retains its feminized status, thereby justifying, if not naturalizing, the low wages and insecure conditions that dominate in such occupations. Furthermore, in recent decades these ideological distinctions and the gendered assumptions that underlie them have found renewed justification in neoliberal principles and practices that privilege the responsible "productive" citizen. By contrast, feminist analyses of gendered divisions of *labor* reveal the shifting and unstable dimensions of such distinctions, blurring the lines between productive and reproductive labor, paid and unpaid work, public and private sectors, and formal and informal economies (Bakker and Silvey 2008). These insights build on and contribute to Marxist-feminist theorizing about the complex and contested ties between capitalist labor relations and patriarchal household divisions of labor (Gibson-Graham 1996; Hartmann 1979). A focus on gendered divisions of *labor* enables close attention to the slippages between productive and reproductive value and the significance of both for flexible accumulation in the global economy (Mills 2003). In a variety of ways, then, gendered divisions of *labor* expose the links and interdependencies between capitalist production and social reproduction, highlighting the artificial distinctions of gendered spheres alongside the oppressive hierarchies of labor value that they support.

Transnational Industry and the Feminization of Labor

Bearing in mind the complex meanings of the concept and its diverse theoretical underpinnings, I turn now to the rich body of empirical research that traces gendered divisions of labor around the globe. Among the most prominent and productive veins of inquiry in this literature are feminist analyses of global industrialization, in particular, the massive recruitment of cheap, flexible, and largely female labor forces. This process of labor "feminization" has been most closely associated with export-oriented industries, such as textiles, electronics, food processing, and other low-wage commodity manufacturing. Touted as important avenues for economic development, these industries have grown into a dense global network of "gendered commodity chains" (Dunaway 2014), linking widely dispersed production sites with distant consumers.

For the past several decades, it has been clear to feminist scholars that this "new international division of labor," as it was initially called (Nash and Fernandez-Kelly 1983), deployed gender hierarchies alongside a range of other inequalities (such as those tied to race/ethnicity, nationality, rural-urban divisions, age, and even marital status) to position members of some populations as cheap and cheaper labor for global capital. Over the past several decades, these processes of transnational capital accumulation have expanded into a vast "global assembly line" in which factories, located primarily in the global South, employ marginalized and feminized workers to produce inexpensive commodities for consumers, primarily in the global North.[2] Once associated largely with the production of cheap commodity goods—food, clothing, appliances—these globally dispersed production processes increasingly extend to "pink collar" labor, such as data entry and clerical services (Freeman 2000), and to the outsourcing of customer service through offshore call centers (Patel 2010). Across the board, however, the close relationship between global industry and gender inequality has remained a constant theme. Whether located in the textile and electronics factories of free-trade zones, small urban sweatshops, or hi-tech call centers, global capital relies on a gendered division of labor in which women dominate in jobs with the lowest levels of pay and authority, while men occupy most of the positions at the supervisory and managerial ranks.

In country after country, these arrangements draw on patriarchal assumptions to define women as the preferred labor force. Women are desired not only for their "nimble" dexterity—the seemingly "natural" byproduct of doing household tasks such as sewing, cleaning, and cooking—but also, and primarily, for their deferential femininity. These patriarchal assumptions commonly include the expectation that women are in the workforce only until marriage, or if they are already married, only to supplement household income, thereby justifying the low wages, limited job security, and minimal benefits that characterize working conditions all along the global assembly line. For example, in a comparative analysis of Chinese and Mexican export factories, Melissa Wright (2006) argues that day-to-day managerial authority and labor discipline relies on discursive practices that she calls the "myth of the disposable third world woman." While it may be expressed slightly differently in relation to local gender idioms, this myth undergirds capital's reliance on patriarchal models of household labor to define women's work as not only "cheap" but also as lacking the capacity to produce social and economic value. Therefore, anything women do (whether for a wage or not) is "worthless" (at least in terms of market value) and so, literally, is worth less. Such beliefs serve to naturalize patterns of inequitable pay and other forms of women's subordination in the work force as a whole; importantly, they also support daily performances of masculine authority and control that actively secure the logics of gender hierarchy both on and off the shop floor (Wright 2006).

Around the world, then, hierarchical gender ideologies work in complex but persistent ways to cheapen the direct costs of labor to capital by defining certain segments of the population (notably women and children) as workers of lesser value (Elias 2004; Enloe 1989; Marchand and Runyon 2000; Wright 2006). In tracking these pervasive and persistent themes of patriarchal domination, feminist scholars have also been careful to note how such patterns are themselves products of distinctly gendered histories of capitalist and state development. For example, the weaving, spinning, and other textile industries that drove the industrial revolution in eighteenth- and nineteenth-century Europe and North America all gained momentum by employing women (particularly young unmarried women) to create a highly flexible, inexpensive, and easily disciplined labor force (Dublin 1979; Rose 1991; Tilly and Scott 1978). At the same time, metropolitan patriarchy joined forces with the racialized hierarchies of empire to mobilize the labor of colonized subjects for imperial profit, both in the colonies and as enslaved or bonded laborers transported elsewhere (Stoler 1985, 2002). Contemporary patterns of feminized labor are rooted in and continue to reflect many of the same ethnically segmented and gendered divisions of labor that were central to early capitalist and colonial extraction.

Despite striking similarities, both past and present, the specific, local entanglements between gender hierarchies and global industry are complex and multisided. The lived experiences of ethnicized, racialized, and gendered subjects within transnational circuits of labor recruitment and capital accumulation are never as uniform as common patterns of ideological devaluation might suggest. Wide-ranging scholarship documents the diversity of local arrangements and forms of labor value operating within contemporary gendered divisions of industrial labor. The variability and flexibility of gender meanings themselves aid in their discursive manipulation for labor recruitment and workplace discipline. For example, in some cases, women's status as unmarried and subordinate "daughters" is what identifies them to employers as an attractively cheap and flexible pool of labor (Drori 2000; Pun 2005; Wolf 1992). In other contexts, women's roles as wives and mothers are used to justify their lower wages and limited job security (Kondo 1990; Lamphere 1987; C. K. Lee 1998). Monolithic images of an ideal (i.e., docile) feminized labor force for transnational industry find expression in a range of disciplinary arrangements. Salzinger (2003) notes how shop-floor regimes on the United States–Mexico border vary between those that hypersexualize women workers into objects of masculine consumption and paternalistic control and those that minimize gendered identities to focus on workers' carefully monitored compliance with piece-rate production quotas. Numerous fine-grained studies of specific factories, free-trade zones, and their feminized work forces have enabled feminist researchers, not only to show the pervasive role that gendered hierarchies play in global patterns of labor recruitment and discipline, but also to explore how actual conditions shaping gendered divisions of labor intersect with dominant discourses, local histories, and production processes in sometimes surprising and unpredictable ways.

One result has been growing interest not just in how gender hierarchies serve the interests of global capital but also in how local communities, women and men, receive and negotiate their insertion within feminized (and racialized) labor relations. While acknowledging the coercive and disciplinary power of capitalist employers and state authorities, researchers have also explored why it is that women and men can willingly enter into exploitative labor relations and stay on the job despite harsh and inequitable conditions (Enloe 1989; Tsing 2009). They often do so, as studies from around the world have shown, to achieve other goals—goals related to kinship and family obligations as well as to personal desires, such as those driven by new consumption practices, or for greater control over courtship and sexuality (Lynch 2007; Mills 1999; Wallis 2013). Independent wage incomes are frequently a source of increased household bargaining power, enabling women to negotiate for greater control over such matters as the use of their wages by parents or other household members, the timing of courtship and marriage decisions, as well as the division of childrearing and other domestic responsibilities (Hewamanne 2008; A. Lee 2004; Ong 1987). Consequently, although women's entry into global industrial wage work subjects them to exploitative and devalued forms of labor, it also often sets the stage for a (sometimes) dramatic reworking of household divisions of labor and the distribution of authority along age and gender lines.

Not surprisingly, then, as women and their kin come to rely on new sources of wage income, their own actions and desires may sustain their recruitment into a feminized labor force. Nevertheless, women's new experiences of autonomy as independent earners can also enable transformations of identity and desire. In other words, the processes of labor feminization do not serve only the interests of capital accumulation. They can enable the articulation of new needs and aspirations on the part of workers and their communities. Particularly dramatic examples of this include women's participation in labor rights organizing, despite the often severe obstacles these efforts face. In free-trade zones and other sites of global production, women workers are frequently on the front lines, challenging harsh working conditions or unpaid wages and other abuses (Collins 2003; Hensman 2011; Kim 1997; Mills 2005; Mosoetsa and Williams 2012). In other contexts, women's experiences of wage employment can prompt the pursuit of newly imaginable opportunities and identities on an individual basis. Here, feminist scholarship documents the creativity and experimentation that women's globalized labor can encourage. For example, pink-collar workers in the Caribbean parlay their savings earned in low-wage data-entry jobs into more lucrative "suitcase" trading ventures, traveling to the United States to bring back goods for resale, often to fellow employees

(Freeman 2000). In Thailand, the autonomy and independence that young wage workers experience living on their own or in dormitories allows some women the freedom to explore same-sex erotic desire or even to build new identities for themselves as transgender "toms," masculine-identified females, or "dees," the toms' feminine partners (Sinnott 2004).[3] All along the global assembly line, women have used their experiences to negotiate greater control over their lives in different ways: from the timing of marriage and choice of partner to engagement with exciting cultures of commodity consumption and modernity, to opportunities for social mobility, either for themselves or for their children and other family members. While this kind of creative agency may not always directly challenge the constraints faced by feminized labor within a global labor force, it does destabilize any comfortable assumptions about the naturalness of such gendered divisions of labor. In addition, it highlights how the lived experience of gendered inequalities can produce complex local arenas of contestation, even as they are subject to the forces of a globally interconnected political economy (Tsing 2009).

Global Care Chains and the Commodification of Reproductive Labor

Around the world, hierarchies of gender, race, and nationality intersect to secure the cheap and flexible labor necessary to sustain global commodity chains. The transnational mobility of goods made possible by these low-cost production regimes is accompanied by a parallel mobility of people whose labor is increasingly necessary to processes of social reproduction, particularly in the global North. In the world's wealthiest societies as well as in many of those identified as "middle" or "emerging" economies, migrant workers from distant parts of the world constitute a pool of vulnerable, feminized labor concentrated in the lowest-wage sectors (Gottfried 2013; Hochschild 2003a; Kwong 1997). As sweatshop garment sewers, restaurant workers, domestic servants, or insecure construction and manual laborers, immigrants (with or without legal documentation) supply many of the essential support services needed to sustain global hierarchies of power and privilege. In so doing, their transnational migration extends the processes of labor feminization and marginalization beyond the production of global commodities into global chains of commodified reproduction.

The gendered divisions of labor entailed in and supported by these transnational labor flows are especially well documented in studies of what are now widely called *global care chains* (Hochshild 2003a; Yeates 2012). Transnational migration generates a steady stream of women and men, often from disadvantaged regions of the world, who can provide the low-cost reproductive services (cleaning, cooking, caring for children and elders) necessary to household maintenance in the global North. Immigrant women in particular provide a feminized and racialized support structure for privileged households in many parts of the world—whether they are Sri Lankan or Indonesian maids in Saudi Arabia (Gamburd 2000; Silvey 2006); Filipina domestic workers in Hong Kong, Taiwan, or Italy (Constable 2006; Lan 2006; Parreñas 2001); or Mexican and Latina housecleaners in the United States (Hondagneu-Sotelo 2001; Romero, 1992). The concept of *global care chains* exposes how complex inequalities—themselves rooted in global hierarchies of gender, class, race, and nationality—structure the highly individualized and intimate conditions of employment within private households. Around the world, employers of domestic labor are often professional women actively pursuing careers that may in fact challenge gender barriers in their own societies; yet by paying other women to perform their own domestic chores, they reinforce existing gender hierarchies that tie femininity to reproduction. In such arrangements, productive labor remains clearly divided from reproductive labor, and the value of the latter may be even further diminished by its displacement onto the bodies of ethnically and legally marginalized women (Hochschild 2003a; Parreñas 2008). Mirroring the gendered and racialized hierarchies of the global assembly line, global care chains reproduce patriarchal household divisions of labor while shifting at least some of the costs of social reproduction from households and economies in the global North to those in the global South.

Nevertheless, many of the women (and men) who provide transnational service labor are themselves motivated by globally inflected desires for social mobility. Shrinking job opportunities, declining middle-class incomes, and other uncertainties, driven perhaps by economic or political crises, can push even skilled workers in the global South—including nurses, technicians, and teachers—to seek work abroad, where they can earn much more as nannies, gardeners, and cooks (Constable 2006; Kilkey et al. 2013). While these migrants can experience downward class mobility working as low-wage labor in the world's high-cost societies, such moves can enable significant improvements in quality of life (well beyond basic reproduction costs) for the families left behind. Overseas wages can boost the status and well-being of households left behind through better housing and other material purchases as well as better and more years of schooling for children (sometimes including university education). In some cases, migrant-sending households may hire their own local domestic servants, particularly to help with the responsibilities of the absent mothers. In such cases, global care chains extend their hierarchies of value to incorporate the cheaper labor of even less mobile women and children, often from marginalized minority groups. In a variety of ways, then, gendered and ethnic hierarchies proliferate along the global care chain—reflecting and reinforcing both local and global relations of inequality.

Similar hierarchies of value expand out beyond global care chains and into other arenas of the postindustrial service economies of the global North. For example, in the world's wealthier nations forms of labor that Linda McDowell (2013) calls "interactive service employment" can quite literally embody global hierarchies of gender, race, class, and nationality. In these service-driven economies, many tasks that were formerly accomplished through private, domestic interactions are now commodified services, available for purchase. The visibility and desirability of commodified personal services have expanded dramatically, from various kinds of food provision (restaurants, fast food, and catering services) to beauty services, fitness training, clothing and cosmetic retail, body grooming, child care, pet care, and even more intimate services, such as sex work (Hochschild 2012). Not surprisingly, many forms of service employment remain relatively low-wage and insecure, devalued by their association with private, reproductive tasks. However, as McDowell (2013) shows, these inequalities go beyond hierarchies of reproductive versus productive labor; rather, the relative value of interactive service labor is linked to the kind of body that provides it. Bodily markers such as height, weight, skin tone, hair, and dress—as well as attitudinal performances and other forms of "emotional labor" (see also Hochschild 1983)—all become part of the exchange. As a result, what one looks like, one's bodily and emotional comportment, all become measures of labor value in a service economy, "part of why some workers get hired and others do not for particular sorts of interactive work" (McDowell 2013, 9). As interactive service exchanges come to dominate much of everyday life in northern societies, the standards of attractiveness and bodily value they encode overlap with and reinforce many of the same divisions at work in other arenas of the global economy (see also Otis 2012). Gendered, classed, and racialized inequalities define some bodies as more or less employable, as more or less valuable, and relegate others to even less desirable, marginalized positions.

Neoliberal Gendered Divisions of Labor

One of the intriguing features of feminized/racialized care chains and service work is their ability to enable exceptional autonomy for some women and men, even as many others remain bound by their subordinate and marginal positions. A number of scholars note how these experiences of autonomy and constraint parallel the processes and principles of contemporary neoliberalism. The latter privileges "productive" citizens who are self-reliant and independent over less successful citizens whose "irresponsible" lack of productivity is considered less deserving of social value (Weeks 2011). Neoliberal hierarchies of valued versus devalued citizenship map readily onto the gendered/racialized hierarchies of productive (paid, masculine, white) and reproductive (unpaid, feminine, minority) labor that characterize much of today's globally interconnected political economy (Tsing 2009). Viewed from this angle, gendered divisions of labor offer intriguing insights into the global reach of neoliberal biopolitics (Ong 2006).

Studies of the gendered effects of structural adjustment and other neoliberal development policies offer some particularly revealing examples of these processes, particularly in the global South (Benería 2003). For the past several decades, institutions such as the International Monetary Fund (IMF) and the World Bank have required governments seeking development loans to dramatically reduce or eliminate supports for health, education, and related public services. These conditions, often referred to as "structural adjustment" policies, seek to promote growth through privatization and market exchange. In reality, they have had devastating and often sharply gendered effects on target communities, effects that follow from neoliberalism's deeply patriarchal assumptions about gendered divisions of labor. When publically funded social supports disappear, restructuring policies must rely for their success on private households' ability to absorb these costs of social reproduction. Ultimately, such approaches presume the availability of unpaid domestic labor (i.e., women) to make do with less (Benería and Feldman 1992; Gill 2000; Susser 1997; Thomas-Emeagwali 1995). At the same time, neoliberal structural adjustment policies tend to diminish the security of formal wage employment, pushing many households into the informal economy and into livelihoods that are predominantly feminized: vending and hawking (Clark 1994; Seligmann 2001), subcontracting and industrial homework (Benería and Roldan 1987; Staples 2006; Zhang 2001), artisanal craft production (Grimes and Milgram 2000; Tice 1995), domestic service (Adams and Dickey 2000; Gill 1994; Goldstein 2013), and sex work (Cabezas 2009; Kelly 2008).

The advent of microfinance development programs offers a further neoliberal twist to this picture. Quite literally banking on women's marginalized labor, microfinance programs fund informal economic ventures that are almost always touted as platforms for women's "empowerment." In line with this goal, microcredit loans typically require recipients to cultivate values and attitudes closely resembling neoliberal principles of self-reliance, responsibility, discipline, and productivity. The rapid spread of microfinance reflects the enormous appeal these programs hold among both development policymakers and antipoverty activists and NGOs. Yet, in addition to the ethical questions some raise about the appropriateness of extracting profits from the world's poor (even if some of these profits are rolled back into more loans), empirical studies of microfinance programs have also questioned their effectiveness in challenging gender hierarchies. Among some of the concerns raised are circumstances in which microcredit programs cannot ensure that women retain control of their loans, allowing, instead, male family members to take charge of the money. Similarly, attendance at mandatory loan meetings can conflict with women's domestic responsibilities, leading at times to increased rates of domestic violence and other marital tensions. It is also not uncommon for microfinance to reinforce power divisions within receiving communities, as women from more powerful families may be able to influence the distribution of loans in ways that benefit their own interests and that allow them to cultivate other women as loyal clients. A growing literature now addresses the successes and failures of the microcredit phenomenon as well as its unstable and, at times, deeply conventional gendered effects (Bateman, 2011; Elyachar 2005; Karim 2011; Rahman 1999).

Many of the same gendered hierarchies that accompany and support structural adjustment and related aspects of neoliberalization in the global South are also evident in other analyses. For example, feminist scholars have done much to unpack the patriarchal assumptions embedded in neoliberal modes of governance and the making of the "responsible" citizen-subject (Bernal and Grewal 2014; Fraser 2013; Weeks 2011). These principles of neoliberalism are deeply embedded in the gendered logics of postindustrial service societies that continue to value and reward productive (read, masculine) arenas of economic activity over those linked to social and domestic (read, feminine) reproduction.

The resulting gender hierarchies follow two distinct patterns. First, with respect to interactive service labor,

> the associations between femininity, caring emotions, waste, smells, desire and fleshy embodiment act in concert to code these forms of work as 'naturally' women's work, reinforcing low rates of pay, flexible forms of provision, low levels of organization and precarious attachments to the labour market.
>
> (McDowell 2013, 215)

For men and women positioned within the lower levels of the economy, then, these patterns of feminization converge with neoliberal norms of productivity to generate an increasing divide between those citizens deemed most employable and those left largely out of the work force. In both the United Kingdom and the United States, for example, decades of neoliberal economic restructuring, along with the shift of most manufacturing to offshore production, has displaced the blue-collar and unionized jobs that once supported a viable working-class model of manly breadwinning. The result is a growing underclass of alienated and unemployable working-class men, including many from racialized minorities, whose tough and assertive styles of masculinity are incompatible with the "feminized" skills of empathy and care required for the only kinds of jobs they are likely to find: low-wage service work (McDowell 2003; Bourgois 1995). Meanwhile, poor women may have the feminine attributes to qualify for service positions, but such jobs are rarely sufficient to ensure a secure livelihood, especially if a woman is trying to provide for children as a single parent (a not uncommon byproduct of the unstable and insecure incomes of male partners). In the United States, neoliberal welfare "reform" has further stigmatized reliance upon public support as a mark of irresponsible citizenship. This sharpens the social and economic obstacles for poor women who face impossible demands both to work "productively" for wages (in low-wage and inflexible jobs) and to uphold their reproductive duties as responsible mothers (Collins and Mayer 2010).

The gendered assumptions of neoliberalism take on a second, slightly different, dynamic as they play out in the upper echelons of contemporary societies. For many middle-class and elite women and men, entry into managerial and professional occupations confirms their class and educational privilege as responsible, productive citizens. At the same time, professional positions, whether held by men or women, retain their ties to historically masculine qualities of intellectual ability and value production, thereby securing the status of their occupants as deserving agents of neoliberal productivity (McDowell 1997). At root, however, the wealth and social recognition that accrue to professional occupations rest on the reproductive and service labor of more marginalized women and men. Moreover, neoliberal values of self-reliance and individualism serve to justify and explain the persistence of gender, race, and class inequalities as matters of personal responsibility, leaving unquestioned the ideological and structural conditions that produce and reproduce these hierarchies across time and place. In a variety of ways, then, the divisions of labor in postindustrial service economies work to sustain ideological and gendered hierarchies between productive and reproductive labor, even as some individuals are freed to move beyond these distinctions in their own lives.

New Directions, Envisioning Alternatives

Gendered divisions of labor—their dynamism, multiplicity, and complex, global intersectionality—offer rich terrain for feminist analysis. The scholarship discussed earlier makes visible the oppressive effects of specific gendered inequalities. It also illuminates how the latter intersect with other hierarchies of value—along lines of ethnicity, race, class, nationality, sexual preference, and more—to structure the lives and livelihoods of women and men in different and unequal ways around the world. Thinking in terms of many gendered divisions of labor (rather than a singular sexual division of labor) enables feminist research to address these interconnections on local and global scales and to explore their links to diverse processes of domination and emancipation. The variety of lived experiences to which gendered hierarchies of labor give rise also complicate any easy division between public and private, production and reproduction, or paid labor and unpaid labor. In so doing, gendered divisions of labor and the scholarship that examines them shed new light on the assumptions supporting neoliberal models of power and governance, problematizing social policies and economic practices that continue to rely on such flawed ideological distinctions.

Much remains to be done to explore the full complexity and diversity of gendered divisions of labor and their global entanglements. In addition to the research discussed here, new directions of inquiry demonstrate the ongoing energy of this field of analysis, generating new and critical insights for debates about gender, labor, and inequality. For example, emerging research on the trafficking of global labor incorporates the experiences of both women and men, including but not limited to the trafficking of sexual labor. This research tracks the complex intersections of coercion and agency as well as the complicated roles that state and NGO actors often play in reinforcing inequalities that perpetuate trafficking rather than counter it (Agustin 2007; Cheng 2010; Kempadoo 2005; Kwong 1997; Mahdavi 2011; Moland 2012). Other work explores the limits to and opportunities for challenging gender hierarchies in those few employment contexts—such as modeling (Mears 2011) or fertility clinics (Almeling 2011)—where women's compensation is generally higher than men's. Despite higher pay rates, in both of these cases gender norms are reproduced as much as they are challenged. A number of intriguing studies have also documented the power of gender hierarchies to reproduce themselves in complex but not always uncontested ways when women enter into nontraditional occupations such as mining, computer programming, banking, or law (Fisher 2012; Fitzsimons 2002; Fletcher 1999; Leiper 2006; Rolston 2014; Wormald 2000). Far less work documents the gendered dynamics of men's entry into feminine jobs—nursing, preschool, and other "caring" professions (but see Cameron and Owen 1999; Williams 1993). Similarly, researchers have only begun to explore how the advent of legal marriage equality and the growing visibility of alternative family forms may (or may not) influence the gendering of domestic divisions of labor (Bernstein and Reimann 2001; Heaphy et al. 2013; Hicks 2011; Moore 2011). More focused attention to these and related areas of research can enhance understanding of how gendered hierarchies persist in divisions of labor and of the openings for contestation that can and do arise.

Additional promising research tackles the problematic staying power of gender hierarchies in the workplace, despite the efforts of several decades of equality legislation and educational achievement. For example, wage differentials continue to disadvantage women in most national workforces, including those of the global North. Although some wage gaps are shrinking, nowhere have these inequalities disappeared. The power of cultural expectations about women's primary domestic obligations continue to translate into diminished economic opportunities, even as women move into the labor force in ever larger numbers in most countries.. Moreover the persistence of conventionally gendered household divisions of labor is well documented by the "double" and even "triple" shifts that await many women at the end of their workday (Hochschild 1997, 2003b).[4] These concerns have contributed to a range of policy debates and in some cases—most notably, in parts of North America and Western Europe—generated new social initiatives regarding flexible time, family-friendly labor laws, and similar state-based interventions. Best known here are the efforts in several European states to promote shared family leave, which requires both parents to take time out of the paid work force (Lundqvist 2011; Sümer 2009). Although many such programs are still in the early stages of implementation, observers note some difficulty in enlisting the full participation of eligible fathers due to continuing perceptions that men who prioritize family over work will diminish their longer-term career prospects (Haas and Hwang 2008).

These social and policy experiments offer intriguing directions for additional research and for exploring the possible transformation of both actual practices and the gendered meanings of household labor divisions, at least in some of the world's wealthier societies. To the extent that these experiments are limited to specific national and relatively wealthy social contexts, they bely the extent to which the everyday reproduction of such privileged households is already reliant upon the raced, classed, and gendered inequalities of other more globally dispersed divisions of labor—that is, on the feminized labor of global commodity chains and global care chains. Nevertheless, these and other feminist engagements with gendered divisions of labor will continue to offer important insights into the problems and challenges of gender inequalities. Indeed, research into the gendered divisions of labor in global care chains reveal that the pursuit of greater gender equity for some (i.e., women in the global North) may come at the cost of heightened inequalities for others (often, in the global South). At the same time, feminist investigations into the global scope of gendered labor relations may open up new ways of understanding not only these complex sources of gender inequality but also the dynamic ways in which women's and men's lived experiences can produce unlooked for and unpredictable avenues for change and challenge. Research into gendered divisions of labor offers productive avenues for connecting these geographically dispersed patterns of subordination and conflict. As such, gendered divisions of labor will remain a crucial focus of analysis, not least for anyone interested in the possibilities of transnational organizing and of a more truly "global feminism" (Ferree and Tripp 2006; Moghadam 2005). Such projects of solidarity have the potential to bring together and support diverse populations in their struggles to overcome forms of inequality and experiences of marginalization, even if these inequalities may not be fully shared or similarly comprehended.

Critical engagements with gendered divisions of labor enable scholars and activists to interrogate the divisive and exploitative structures that proliferate within and across contemporary societies. Indeed, feminist thinking about gender and labor has long driven theoretical insights into and political challenges to oppressive social norms and practices. Given our present interconnected, yet highly segmented, world, understanding gendered divisions of labor in all their global diversity has never been more critical to feminism's emancipatory vision. For many, this includes striving for societies, households, and workplaces in which gender does not determine or shape access to resources or frame expectations about appropriate roles and behaviors (e.g., Folbre 2001; Gornick and Meyers 2008). Such a liberatory future would not privilege breadwinning over care-giving; rather, all people would engage in (and be supported by state institutions to undertake) both productive and reproductive tasks as equally valued and value-producing activities, a model of social engagement that philosopher Nancy Fraser calls the "universal caregiver" (Fraser 2013, 135). However, achieving such ungendered and holistic (non)divisions of labor will require not only addressing the material and structural barriers posed by global relations of inequality but also transforming ideological discourses about gender and value on a similarly global scale. Clearly, these are daunting challenges. But feminist explorations of gender and labor can and will continue to offer critical insights on which to build. In this vein, the investigation of gendered divisions of labor will remain central to the feminist imagination and to its pursuit of more fully human lives and livelihoods.

Notes

1. Cross-cultural research offers ample evidence against claims for a universal, homogeneous human sexual division of labor. See, among others, Du (2002); Friedl (1978); Lepowsky (1993); MacCormack and Strathern (1980); Rosaldo and Lamphere (1974.
2. While the categories of "global North" and "global South" are themselves problematic, I use these phrases to avoid the moralizing judgments and politicized histories encoded in other widely used terms such as: "First" and "Third Worlds" or "developed" and "under-" or "lesser-developed" nations.

3. Similar patterns of sexual experimentation may be much more common features of the global assembly line than the existing literature would suggest and warrant more focused research. Transgressive performances of gender and sexuality are frequently stigmatized or go unrecognized within the normatively gendered regimes of labor discipline in global factories.
4. Time-use studies offer continuing evidence that women's reproductive labor exceeds that of men in many household divisions of labor. See recent work by Birch et al. (2009); Cooke (2009); and Treas and Drobnič (2010).

References

Adams K. M., and S. Dickey, eds. 2000. *Home and Hegemony: Domestic Service and Identity Politics in South and Southeast Asia*. Ann Arbor: University of Michigan Press.

Agustin, L. M. 2007. *Sex at the Margins: Migration, Labour Markets and the Rescue Industry*. London and New York: Zed Books.

Almeling, R. 2011. *Sex Cells: The Medical Market for Eggs and Sperm*. Berkeley: University of California Press.

Bakker, I., and R. Silvey. 2008. *Beyond States and Markets: The Challenges of Social Reproduction*. Abingdon and New York: Routledge.

Bateman, M., ed. 2011. *Confronting Microfinance: Undermining Sustainable Development*. Sterling, VA: Kumarian Press.

Benería, L. 2003. *Gender, Development, and Globalization: Economics as if All People Mattered*. New York: Routledge.

Benería L., and S. Feldman, eds. 1992. *Unequal Burden: Economic Crises, Persistent Poverty and Women's Work*. Boulder, CO: Westview Press.

Benería L., and M. Roldán. 1987. *The Crossroads of Class and Gender: Industrial Homework, Subcontracting, and Household Dynamics in Mexico City*. Chicago: University of Chicago Press.

Bernal, V., and I. Grewal, eds. 2014. *Theorizing NGOs: States, Feminisms, and Neoliberalism*. Durham, NC: Duke University Press.

Bernstein, M. and Reimann, R., eds. 2001. *Queer Families, Queer Politics: Challenging Culture and the State*. New York: Columbia University Press.

Birch, R. E., A. T. Le, and P. W. Miller. 2009. *Household Divisions of Labour: Teamwork, Gender and Time*. Basingstoke and New York: Palgrave Macmillan.

Bourgois, P. 1995. *In Search of Respect: Selling Crack in El Barrio*. New York: Cambridge University Press.

Butler, J. 1990. *Gender Trouble: Feminism and the Subversion of Identity*. New York: Routledge.

Cabezas, A. L. 2009. *Economies of Desire: Sex and Tourism in Cuba and the Dominican Republic*. Philadelphia, PA: Temple University Press.

Cameron, C., P. Moss, and C. Owen. 1999. *Men in the Nursery: Gender and Caring Work*. London and Thousand Oaks, CA: Paul Chapman.

Cheng, S. 2010. *On the Move for Love: Migrant Entertainers and the U.S. Military in South Korea*. Philadelphia: University of Pennsylvania Press.

Clark, G. 1994. *Onions Are My Husband: Survival and Accumulation by West African Market Women*. Chicago: University of Chicago Press.

Collins, J. L., and V. Mayer, 2010. *Both Hands Tied: Welfare Reform and the Race to the Bottom in the Low-Wage Labor Market*. Chicago: University of Chicago Press.

Collins, J. L. 2003. *Threads: Gender, Labor, and Power in the Global Apparel Industry*. Chicago: University of Chicago Press.

Constable, N. 2006. *Maid to Order in Hong Kong: An Ethnography of Filipina Workers*. Ithaca, NY: Cornell University Press.

Cooke, L. P. 2009. *Gender-Class Equality in Political Economies*. New York: Routledge.

Drori, I. 2000. *The Seam Line: Arab Workers and Jewish Managers in the Israeli Textile Industry*. Stanford, CA: Stanford University Press.

Du, S. 2002. *"Chopsticks Only Work in Pairs": Gender Unity and Gender Equality among the Lahu of Southwest China*. New York: Columbia University Press.

Dublin, T. 1979. *Women at Work: The Transformation of Work and Community in Lowell, Massachusetts, 1826–1860*. New York: Columbia University Press.

Dunaway, W. A., ed. 2014. *Gendered Commodity Chains: Seeing Women's Work and Households in Global Production*. Stanford, CA: Stanford University Press.

Elias, J. 2004. *Fashioning Inequality: The Multinational Company and Gendered Employment in a Globalizing World*. Aldershot, UK, and Burlington, VT: Ashgate.

Elyachar, J. 2005. *Markets of Dispossession: NGOs, Economic Development, and the State in Cairo*. Durham, NC: Duke University Press.

Enloe, C. 1989. *Bananas, Beaches and Bases: Making Feminist Sense of International Politics*. Berkeley: University of California Press.

Ferree, M. M., and A. M. Tripp, eds. 2006. *Global Feminism: Transnational Women's Activism, Organizing, and Human Rights*. New York: New York University Press.

Fisher, M. S. 2012. *Wall Street Women*. Durham, NC: Duke University Press.

Fitzsimons, A. 2002. *Gender as a Verb: Gender Segregation at Work*. Aldershot, UK, and Burlington, VT: Ashgate.

Fletcher, J. K. 1999. *Disappearing Acts: Gender, Power and Relational Practice at Work*. Cambridge, MA: MIT Press.

Folbre, N. 1994. *Who Pays for the Kids? Gender and the Structures of Constraint*. London and New York: Routledge.

Folbre, N. 2001. *The Invisible Heart: Economics and Family Values*. New York: New Press.

Fraser, N. 2013. *Fortunes of Feminism: From State-Managed Capitalism to Neoliberal Crisis*. London and New York: Verso.

Freeman, C. 2000. *High Tech and High Heels in the Global Economy: Women, Work and Pink-Collar Identities in the Caribbean*. Durham, NC: Duke University Press.

Friedl, E. 1978. "Society and Sex Roles." *Human Nature* 1: 8–75.

Gamburd, M. R. 2000. *The Kitchen Spoon's Handle: Transnationalism and Sri Lanka's Migrant Housemaids*. Ithaca, NY: Cornell University Press.

Gibson-Graham, J. K. 1996. *The End of Capitalism (as We Knew It): A Feminist Critique of Political Economy*. Oxford: Blackwell.

Gill, L. 1994. *Precarious Dependencies: Gender, Class and Domestic Service in Bolivia*. New York: Columbia University Press.

Gill, L. 2000. *Teetering on the Rim: Global Restructuring, Daily Life and the Armed Retreat of the Bolivian State*. New York: Columbia University Press.

Goldstein, D. M. 2013. *Laughter out of Place: Race, Class, Violence, and Sexuality in a Rio Shantytown*. Berkeley: University of California Press.

Gornick, J. C., and M. K. Meyers. 2008. "Creating Gender-Egalitarian Societies: An Agenda for Reform." *Politics & Society* 36 (3): 313–349.

Gottfried, H. 2013. *Gender, Work, and Economy: Unpacking the Global Economy*. Cambridge and Malden, MA: Polity Press.

Grimes, K. M., and B. L. Milgram, eds. 2000. *Artisans and Cooperatives: Developing Alternative Trade for the Global Economy*. Tucson: University of Arizona Press.

Haas, L., and C. P. Hwang. 2008. "The Impact of Taking Parental Leave on Fathers' Participation in Childcare and Relationships with Children: Lessons from Sweden." *Community, Work & Family* 11 (1): 85–104.

Hartmann, H. 1979. "The Unhappy Marriage of Marxism and Feminism: Towards a More Progressive Union." *Capital & Class* 3: 1–33.

Hartsock, N. 1983. *Money, Sex, and Power: Toward a Feminist Historical Materialism*. New York: Longman.

Heaphy, B., C. Smart, and A. Einarsdottir. 2013. *Same Sex Marriages: New Generations, New Relationships*. Basingstoke, UK: Palgrave Macmillan.

Hensman, R. 2011. *Workers, Unions, and Global Capitalism: Lessons from India*. New York: Columbia University Press.

Hewamanne, S. 2008. *Stitching Identities in a Free Trade Zone: Gender and Politics in Sri Lanka*. Philadelphia: University of Pennsylvania Press.

Hicks, S. 2011. *Lesbian, Gay, and Queer Parenting: Families, Intimacies, Genealogies*. New York: Palgrave Macmillan.

Hochschild, A. R. 1983. *The Managed Heart: Commercialization of Human Feeling*. Berkeley: University of California Press.

Hochschild, A. R. 1997. *The Time Bind: When Work Becomes Home and Home Becomes Work*. New York: Metropolitan Books.

Hochschild, A. R. 2003a. *Global Woman: Nannies, Maids, and Sex Workers in the New Economy*. New York: Metropolitan Books.

Hochschild, A. R. 2003b. *The Second Shift*. New York: Penguin.

Hochschild, A. R. 2012. *The Outsourced Self: Intimate Life in Market Times*. New York: Metropolitan Books.

Hondagneu-Sotelo, P. 2001. *Domestica: Immigrant Workers Cleaning and Caring in the Shadows of Affluence*. Berkeley: University of California Press.

Karim, L. 2011. *Microfinance and Its Discontents: Women in Debt in Bangladesh*. Minneapolis: University of Minnesota Press.

Kelly, P. 2008. *Lydia's Open Door: Inside Mexico's Most Modern Brothel*. Berkeley: University of California Press.

Kempadoo, K. ed. 2005. *Trafficking and Prostitution Reconsidered: New Perspectives on Migration, Sex Work, and Human Rights*. Boulder, CO, and London: Paradigm Publishers.

Kilkey, M., D. Perrons, and A. Plomien with P. Hondagneu-Sotelo and H. Ramirez. 2013. *Gender, Migration and Domestic Work: Masculinities, Male Labour and Fathering in the UK and USA*. Basingstoke, UK, and New York: Palgrave Macmillan.

Kim, S-K. 1997. *Class Struggle or Family Struggle? The Lives of Women Factory Workers in South Korea*. Cambridge: Cambridge University Press.

Kondo, D. 1990. *Crafting Selves: Power, Gender, and Discourses of Identity in a Japanese Workplace*. Chicago: University of Chicago Press.

Kwong, P. 1997. *Forbidden Workers: Illegal Chinese Immigrants and American Labor*. New York: New Press.

Lamphere, L. 1987. *From Working Daughters to Working Mothers: Immigrant Women in a New England Industrial Community*. Ithaca, NY: Cornell University Press.

Lan, Pei-Chia. 2006. *Global Cinderellas: Migrant Domestics and Newly Rich Employers in Taiwan*. Durham, NC: Duke University Press.

Lee, A. 2004. *In the Name of Harmony and Prosperity: Labor and Gender Politics in Taiwan's Economic Restructuring*. Albany: State University of New York Press.

Lee, C. K. 1998. *Gender and the South China Miracle: Two Worlds of Factory Women*. Berkeley: University of California Press.

Leiper, J. M. 2006. *Bar Codes: Women in the Legal Profession*. Vancouver: University of British Columbia Press.

Lepowsky, M. 1993. *Fruit of the Motherland: Gender in an Egalitarian Society*. New York: Columbia University Press.

Lowe, L., and D. Lloyd, eds. 1997. *The Politics of Culture in the Shadow of Capital*. Durham, NC: Duke University Press.

Lynch, C. 2007. *Juki Girls, Good Girls: Gender and Cultural Politics in Sri Lanka's Global Garment Industry*. Ithaca, NY: ILR Press / Cornell University Press.

Lundqvist, Å. 2011. *Family Policy Paradoxes: Gender Equality and Labour Market Regulation in Sweden 1930–2010*. Bristol: Policy Press.

MacCormack, C., and M. Strathern, eds. 1980. *Nature, Culture and Gender*. Cambridge: Cambridge University Press.

Mahdavi, P. 2011. *Gridlock: Labor, Migration, and Human Trafficking in Dubai*. Stanford, CA: Stanford University Press.

Marchand M. H., and A. S. Runyan, eds. 2000. *Gender and Global Restructuring: Sighting, Sites and Resistances*. London and New York: Routledge.

McDowell, L. 1997. *Capital Culture: Gender at Work in the City*. Oxford and Malden, MA: Blackwell.

McDowell, L. 2003. *Redundant Masculinities?: Employment Change and White Working Class Youth*. Malden, MA: Blackwell.

McDowell, L. 2013. *Working Lives: Gender, Migration and Employment in Britain, 1945-2007*. Oxford: Wiley-Blackwell.

Mears, Ashley. 2011. *Pricing Beauty: The Making of a Fashion Model*. Berkeley: University of California Press.

Mills, M. B. 1999. *Thai Women in the Global Labor Force: Consuming Desires, Contested Selves*. New Brunswick, NJ: Rutgers University Press.

Mills, M. B. 2003. "Gender and Inequality in the Global Labor Force." *Annual Review of Anthropology* 32: 41–62.

Mills, M. B. 2005. "From Nimble Fingers to Raised Fists: Women and Labor Activism in Globalizing Thailand." *Signs: Journal of Women in Culture and Society* 31 (1): 117–144.

Moghadam, V. M. 2005. *Globalizing Women: Transnational Feminist Networks*. Baltimore, MD: Johns Hopkins University Press.

Moland, S. 2012. *The Perfect Business? Anti-Trafficking and the Sex Trade along the Mekong*. Honolulu: University of Hawai'i Press.

Moore, M. 2011. *Invisible Families: Gay Identities, Relationships, and Motherhood among Black Women*. Berkeley: University of California Press.

Mosoetsa, S., and M. Williams, eds. 2012. *Labour in the Global South: Challenges and Alternatives for Workers*. Geneva: International Labour Office.

Nash, J. C., and M. P. Fernández-Kelly, eds. 1983. *Women, Men, and the International Division of Labor*. Albany, NY: State University of New York Press.

Ong, A. 1987. *Spirits of Resistance and Capitalist Discipline: Factory Women in Malaysia.* Albany, NY: State University of New York Press.

Ong, A. 2006. *Neoliberalism as Exception: Mutations in Citizenship and Sovereignty.* Durham, NC: Duke University Press.

Ortner, S., and H. Whitehead, 1981. *Sexual Meanings: The Cultural Construction of Gender and Sexuality.* Cambridge and New York: Cambridge University Press.

Otis, E. M. 2012. *Markets and Bodies: Women, Service Work, and the Making of Inequality in China.* Stanford, CA: Stanford University Press.

Parreñas, R. S. 2001. *Servants of Globalization: Women, Migration and Domestic Work.* Stanford, CA: Stanford University Press.

Parreñas, R. S. 2008. *The Force of Domesticity: Filipina Migrants and Globalization.* New York: New York University Press.

Patel, R. 2010. *Working the Night Shift: Women in India's Call Center Industry.* Stanford, CA: Stanford University Press.

Pun, N. 2005. *Made in China: Women Factory Workers in a Global Workplace.* Durham, NC, and Hong Kong: Duke University Press/Hong Kong University Press.

Rahman, A. 1999. *Women and Microcredit in Rural Bangladesh: An Anthropological Study of the Rhetoric and Realities of the Grameen Bank Lending.* Boulder, CO: Westview Press.

Rolston, J. S. 2014. *Mining Coal and Undermining Gender: Rhythms of Work and Family in the American West.* New Brunswick, NJ: Rutgers University Press.

Romero M. 1992. *Maid in the U.S.A.* London and New York: Routledge.

Rosaldo, M. Z., and L. Lamphere, eds. 1974. *Woman, Culture, and Society.* Stanford, CA: Stanford University Press.

Rose, S. O. 1991. *Limited Livelihoods: Gender and Class in Nineteenth-Century England.* Berkeley: University of California Press

Ross, E., and R. Rapp. 1981. "Sex and Society: A Research Note from Social History and Anthropology." *Comparative Studies in Society and History* 23 (1): 51–72.

Salzinger, L. 2003. *Genders in Production: Making Workers in Mexico's Global Factories.* Berkeley: University of California Press.

Scott, J. W. 1986. "Gender: A Useful Category of Historical Analysis." *American Historical Review* 91 (5): 1053–1075.

Seligmann, L. J., ed. 2001. *Women Traders in Cross-Cultural Perspective: Mediating Identities, Marketing Wares.* Stanford, CA: Stanford University Press.

Silvey, R. 2006. "Consuming the Transnational Family: Indonesian Migrant Domestic Workers to Saudi Arabia." *Global Networks* 6 (1): 23–40.

Sinnott, M. 2004. *Toms and Dees: Transgender Identity and Female Same-Sex Relationships in Thailand.* Honolulu: University of Hawai'i Press.

Staples, D. E. 2006. *No Place Like Home: Organizing Home-Based Labor in the Era of Structural Adjustment.* New York and London: Routledge.

Stoler, A. L. 1985. *Capitalism and Confrontation in Sumatra's Plantation Belt, 1870–1979.* New Haven, CT: Yale University Press.

Stoler, A. L. 2002. *Carnal Knowledge and Imperial Power: Race and the Intimate in Colonial Rule.* Berkeley: University of California Press.

Sümer, S. 2009. *European Gender Regimes and Policies: Comparative Perspectives.* Farnham, UK and Burlington, VT: Ashgate.

Susser I. 1997. "The Flexible Woman: Regendering Labor in the Informational Society." *Critical Anthropology* 17: 389–402.

Thomas-Emeagwali, G., ed. 1995. *Women Pay the Price: Structural Adjustment in Africa and the Caribbean*. Trenton, NJ: Africa World Press.

Tice, K. E. 1995. *Kuna Crafts, Gender, and the Global Economy*. Austin: University of Texas Press.

Tilly, L. A., and J. W. Scott. 1978. *Women, Work, and Family*. New York: Holt, Rhinehart and Winston.

Treas, J., and S. Drobnič, eds. 2010. *Dividing the Domestic: Men, Women, and Household Work in Cross-National Perspective*. Stanford, CA: Stanford University Press.

Tsing, A. 2009. "Supply Chains and the Human Condition." *Rethinking Marxism: A Journal of Economics, Culture, and Society* 21 (2): 148–176.

Wallis, C. 2013. *Technomobility in China: Young Migrant Women and Mobile Phones*. New York: New York University Press.

Weeks, K. 2011. *The Problem with Work: Feminism, Marxism, Antiwork Politics, and Postwork Imaginaries*. Durham, NC: Duke University Press.

Williams, C. L., ed. 1993. *Doing "Women's Work": Men in Nontraditional Occupations*. Newbury Park, CA: Sage Publications.

Wolf, D. L. 1992. *Factory Daughters: Gender, Household Dynamics, and Rural Industrialization in Java*. Berkeley: University of California Press.

Wormald, J. 2000. *Gender and Policing: Comparative Perspectives*. Basingstoke, UK and New York: St. Martin's Press.

Wright, M. 2006. *Disposable Women and Other Myths of Global Capitalism*. New York: Routledge.

Yeates, N. 2012. "Global Care Chains: A State-of-the-Art Review and Future Directions in Care Transnationalization Research." *Global Networks* 12 (2): 135–154.

Zhang, L. 2001. *Strangers in the City: Reconfigurations of Space, Power, and Social Networks within China's Floating Population*. Stanford, CA: Stanford University Press.

CHAPTER 15

GOVERNANCE

KI-YOUNG SHIN

INTRODUCTION

THE concept of *governance* entered the political vernacular when Plato appropriated the Greek verb κυβερνάω (*kubernáo*)—"to steer"—as a metaphor for the central task of a political leader (*Republic* 8.551c). As the *Oxford English Dictionary* notes, the term has long been used to characterize "the action or manner of governing," "the state of being governed," or indeed, "good order." Whereas *government* is a descriptive term that refers to the official institutions of a state, the term *governance* has had a normative cast since its inception, signifying forms of rule that produce desired ends. If Plato aligned governance with the task of producing justice, construed as harmonious order within the souls of citizens and across the segments of society, the ascendance of neoliberalism in the final quarter of the twentieth century aligned the goals of the state with distinctly economic ends—efficiency, profit maximization, privatization, and deregulation. In response to neoliberal imperatives, discourses on governance have changed dramatically over the past four decades. This chapter provides a sketch of three recent approaches to governance: the Foucauldian conception of governmentality; discourses devised by public administration specialists and international institutions, such as the United Nations, the World Bank, and the International Monetary Fund to promote "good governance"; and feminist critiques of governmentality and governance, including feminist efforts to adopt the language of good governance for social justice ends.

GOVERNMENTALITY

In developing his analytics of modern power, the French poststructuralist theorist Michel Foucault differentiated between, on the one hand, discipline as a strategy of power concerned with individuals and, on the other hand, governmentality as a strategy of power concerned with populations. Emerging in about 1800, with such practices as census taking and the regulation of economic markets, governmentality involves "an explosion of numerous and diverse techniques for achieving the subjugation of bodies and the control of populations" (Foucault 1978, 140; see also Miller chapter 4 in this volume). Emphasizing the "protection of life" rather than the threat of death, governmentality obliterates the classical boundaries between public (*polis*) and private (*oikos/* household), as the state undertakes the regulation of health, sexuality, bodies, dispositions, and desires as part of its legitimate terrain. Moreover, the political technologies associated with the "conduct of conduct" produce individual identities—resisting identities according to Foucault, but identities also invested in particular orders of desire (Foucault 1994, 237).

According to Foucault, governmentality has been evolving as a modern technology of power since the long eighteenth century. Governmentality, rather than concentrating power in the official institutions of state, is diffused through manifold "capillaries"— power-knowledge constellations that permeate professions (law, medicine, education, psychology, social work), institutions (courts, families, hospitals, prisons, schools, the market, the military), and processes (discipline, normalization, socialization) (Foucault 1977). In the neoliberal era, states diffuse power by devolution, allocating responsibilities to supranational, regional, and subnational organizations; by "contracting out" responsibilities to private firms and corporations; and by fostering the exercise of autonomy as a duty to manage oneself according to neoliberal principles, such as rational and responsible "choice" (Novas and Rose 2000; Rose 2001). Foucauldian discourses call attention to the central contradictions of neoliberal governmentality: power proliferates under the guise of privatization; heightened surveillance accompanies self-regulation; the responsible management of risk confronts individuals with impossible choices; and the manifold technologies of governance foster profit-generating consumption far more than meaningful freedom.

Governance as Praxis

In contrast to Foucault's critical account of governmentality, a descriptive discourse on governance has surfaced since the 1970s to characterize the changing role of government in an era of neoliberal globalization. Within the arenas of public administration and political science, governance refers to a shift from a government-centered, top-down administration to dispersed power through public-private partnerships that involve civil society, the market, and a host of private voluntary actors in governing activities. Studies of governance emphasize the decentering of the state's role in decision-making and administration. In contrast to traditional state theories that accord the official institutions of the state a monopoly on power over the people within its territorial boundaries, governance studies recognize that governmental institutions share power with other organizations, such as corporations, commissions, civil-society groups, and nongovernmental organizations (NGOs). Rather than being the exclusive preserve of government, governance suggests a broader concept that refers to different types of coordinated activities among multiple "stakeholders" toward the achievement of common goals. Indeed, governance refers to "all processes of governing, whether undertaken by a government, market, or network, whether over a family, tribe, formal or informal organization, or territory, and whether through laws, norms, power, or language" (Bevir 2012, 1).

Several works have been published in recent years that trace the emergence and expansion of governance (e.g., Bervir 2011; Levi-Faur 2012; Kjær 2004; Bevir 2012). Anne Mette Kjær (2004), for example, provides an overview of governance discourses in public administration and public policy, international relations, the European Union (EU), and comparative politics, as well as the criteria for "good governance" proposed by the World Bank. Mark Bevir (2011) surveys changing practices and policy innovations associated with governance, including the changing role of the state, transnational and global governance initiatives, and the reliance on markets and networks, as well as public management, budgeting, and finance. He also explores the dilemmas of "managing" governance and the challenges governance poses to democracy and citizenship, particularly in relation to capacity building, regulation, and sustainable development. Providing a chronology of governance discourse, Rod Rhodes (2012) compares network governance ("a modernist and empiricist approach") with metagovernance (an effort to bring the state back into governance debates), and interpretive governance (an examination of the beliefs and practices of the actors who design and implement new governing rules). Although there is some variation in approaches to governance, analysts and proponents tend to highlight several defining characteristics: the role of multiple actors, nonhierarchical processes, and proliferating levels of governance.

Multiple Actors

In the public policy and public administration literature, the ascendency of governance is attributed to public-sector reforms that have taken place in Western democracies since the 1980s. Describing a shift from hierarchy to market and network, analysts hail the positive roles taken by multiple market and civil-society actors in governing activities. Public administration scholars, in particular, describe partnerships between the government and nonstate actors as a positive step, as governments contract out management responsibility and service delivery to private- and voluntary-sector actors in policy areas as diverse as health, education, combat support, and prisons (Pierre and Peters 2000). Instead of dictating policy and regulating the actions of governmental agents, the hybrid, coordinated practices of governance facilitate collaboration among public, voluntary, and private actors working together in networks and partnerships. As the state negotiates with other actors, using metagovernance strategies to steer them, the state is rendered a less important actor, constrained by its dependence on others (Bevir 2012). Indeed, arguing that government's top-down authority is harmful and inefficient, proponents of the "new public management" advocate for a bigger role in governing networks for market actors and civil organizations.

Discussions of governance also reflect efforts to rethink the nation-state as the fundamental unit of international politics, as the emergence of supranational institutions challenge the Westphalian model that has been sacrosanct since the seventeenth century. Comparative politics and international relations scholars link the emergence of governance discourses to supranational organizations, whether this be the creation of the bureaucracies of the EU or the growing role of the United Nations. In the twenty-first century, international nongovernmental organizations (INGOs), multinational corporations, and nonstate EU organizations, as well as subnational governments, are all crucial players in shaping and implementing EU policies. Similarly, the United Nations has assumed important supranational responsibilities with respect to various global policy issues, such as climate change, democratization, development, humanitarian relief, human rights, nuclear proliferation, peacemaking, refugees, poverty alleviation, and women's rights. Under UN auspices, many transnational actors work in partnerships and networks without particular reliance on national governments—and in spaces of organized conflict, where no government has sovereign control over contested territory.

In contrast to older accounts of government that envision sovereignty as monolithic and operating exclusively through the rule of law predicated on a monopoly of coercive forces, governance draws attention to different mechanisms of decision-making, involving distinctive cohorts of actors who intercede with relative autonomy, operating as committed volunteers and partners whose relationships are based on mutual trust. While some social scientists suggest that public-sector reforms have created a differentiated polity characterized by a hollowed-out state that fumbles to control the massive proliferation of networks (Bevir 2012), others argue that the central state still dominates policymaking and implementation, though it does so through new policy instruments (Jessop 2004). The debates on the role of the state reflect the changing relationship of state and society in various nations, in particular, in geographical regions where political actors are increasingly constrained by mobilized and organized elements in society, including private firms, NGOs, and nonprofit service providers. Thus, governance discourses bring renewed attention to governing technologies and mechanisms as well as to the role of multiple actors with different interests and resources who participate in changing governing practices.

Governing Mechanisms

Political scientists have long debated the comparative merits of various models that attempt to explain how governments actually operate, contrasting the *rational actor model*, which posits the state as a unified actor that adopts policies to maximize hierarchically ordered values, with an *organizational process model*, which emphasizes that multiple fractious agencies within the state compete for scarce resources in their desire to pursue agendas distinctive to their missions, and a *bureaucratic politics model*, which adds the specific political interests of particular leaders to complicate the competition among governmental agencies (Allison 1971). In governance studies, discussions of governing mechanisms draw metaphors from economics and cybernetics, in contrast to models that focus on the institutions of state. Fixed institutional settings (government agencies) are displaced by self-regulating processes (drawn from claims about markets) and fluid nodes within networks (the structure of information technology). In his discussion in *Governance without Government*, for example, James Rosenau (1992, 5) uses "the setting of prices in a market place" as an example of "a self-regulating aggregation that facilitates order: sellers are concerned with receiving the highest amount for their goods and buyers seek to pay the lowest possible amount, but the result of their individual bargains is normally an orderly and stable system-wide market for the commodity." Rosenau (2002, 72) suggests that, similar to the operations of the market, governance involves "steering mechanisms ... [that] enable systems to preserve their coherence and move toward desired goals." In contrast to the steering mechanisms of governments, which rely on sovereignty, constitutional and statutory law, and hierarchical institutions to exact compliance, governance relies on traditional norms, informal agreements, shared premises, and other informal processes that provide horizontal modes of steering (72). Rod Rhodes (1996, 660), the founder of the Anglo-governance school, turns to cybernetic models rather than markets to conceptualize the "self-organizing, interorganizational networks" that characterize governance, emphasizing interdependence among organizations; shifting and opaque boundaries between the public, private, and voluntary sectors; continuing interactions driven by shared purposes, rooted in trust and regulated by rules negotiated and agreed by network participants who have significant autonomy and little accountability to the state. In situating governance in formal and informal networks that operate outside the state, both Rosenau and Rhodes call for empirical studies that "explore how the informal authority of networks supplements and supplants the formal authority of government" in order to understand the limits to the state and "develop a more diverse view of state authority and its exercise" (Rhodes 2012, 33). Focusing on informal coordination within shifting governing networks, scholars suggest that the process of governing need not be consciously undertaken by a hierarchically organized set of actors, much less involve a coherent set of public values. Markets and networks of actors pursuing individual and corporate interests can govern, produce coordination, and make decisions through fluid and changing processes of rule that structure virtually all social organizations and spheres.

Governing Levels

With the shift from fixed institutions to fluid processes, governance scholars focus on multilevel, hybrid, and multijurisdictional governing arrangements. As Rosenau (1992, 2–3) notes, "[A]uthority is undergoing continuous relocation—both outward toward supranational entities and inward toward subnational groups; [thus] it becomes increasingly imperative to probe how governance can occur in the absence of government."

Although multiple levels of governance and overlapping jurisdiction have been a staple in studies of federal political systems since the eighteenth century, attention to multilevel governance has gained new traction as political rhetoric in the EU explicitly refuses the language of federalism.

GOOD GOVERNANCE AS A PROBLEM FOR DEMOCRACY

As the shift away from the state and the reliance on market mechanisms suggest, contemporary governance discourses are a product of neoliberal restructuring, which triggered public-sector reform, either through voluntary policies introduced by president Ronald Reagan in the United States, prime minister Margaret Thatcher in the United Kingdom, and the new austerity regime of the EU since 2008 or involuntarily through structural adjustment programs imposed by the International Monetary Fund (IMF) and the World Bank as a condition for loans. Despite evidence that structural adjustment and austerity measures result in the economic dislocation and impoverishment of growing numbers of people, governance discourses routinely endorse cutting back the state, privatization, and deregulation as the most effective means to manage public resources and foster "development." Indeed, *good governance* has become a catchphrase in the international development literature, urging neoliberal agendas to guide nations in the global South toward viable economies and effective political systems. In the words of the International Monetary Fund (1997, v), "promoting good governance in all its aspects, including by ensuring the rule of law, improving the efficiency and accountability of the public sector, and tackling corruption, are essential elements of a framework within which economies can prosper."

Critics of global restructuring have pointed out that the rhetoric of good governance can mask neo-imperialist policies and practices. When efficiency becomes the fundamental priority, governance can impair participation, democratic inclusion, and social well-being (Kjær 2004, 15). In marked contrast to the language of fluid, self-organizing and self-regulating networks, governance can subject states to the coercive hierarchy of international financial institutions that are politically unaccountable. As Mark Bevir has noted,

> [G]overnance agendas have generally privileged markets and networks over hierarchies. These actors have tended to undermine the values associated with representative and responsible government, since decisions are regularly made not by elected representatives but by unelected officials and non-governmental actors.
>
> (Bevir 2012, 108, 116)

Traditionally, administrative accountability has depended on clear lines of authority; while representative entities rely on electoral mechanisms of accountability. But networks are devoid of either of these mechanisms. Premised on the collaboration of members of self-governing and self-regulating organizations, networks lack an overt center that provides coordination and control, making it difficult to specify who is responsible to whom for what (Kjaer 2004; Pierre and Peters 2000).

Some proponents of governance attempt to include participatory mechanisms within "collaborative governance" as a means to supplement the electoral accountability of public officials (Bevir 2012). In these models, citizens play a more active role in policy-making or service delivery during all stages of the policy process. From initial discussions over the agenda to project completion, relevant stakeholders come together for face-to-face discussions as policies are developed. However, these models still suffer a democratic deficit as decisions about who counts as a stakeholder, and who represents various stakeholders in the process, are never open to democratic contestation. Even in participatory governance networks, some participants are more equal than others.

As a consequence of the neoliberal roots of governance, approaches to it are notoriously insensitive to and uninterested in structural inequalities within and across nations. Although governance emphasizes coordinated management directed toward particular policy outcomes, it pays little attention to the structural characteristics of the system to be governed. Self-organizing among fluid networks to enable the pursuit of diverse interests appears to be a remarkably disembodied process. The purportedly equal nodes in the governance network seem impervious to hierarchies of power grounded in class, race, ethnicity, and gender. Feminist analysis of the new discourses on governance draws attention to these lacunae and offers alternative mechanisms to appropriate the rhetoric of good governance for feminist ends.

Feminist Engagement with Governance

Some feminist scholars have bemoaned the co-optation of feminist projects by neoliberal governance (Fraser 2009; Eisenstein 2010), and others have condemned "governance feminism" tout court (Halley 2006; Bernstein 2010). Some feminist political scientists, however, engage governance directly, investigating its operations and effects (e.g., Meyer and Prügl 1999; Banaszak, Beckwith, and Rutch 2003; Rai 2003; Rai and Waylen 2008; Waylen 2008a; Bedford 2013; Gülay, Prügl and Zwingel 2013). Offering critiques of the gendered and raced nature of various modes of governance, feminist scholars have documented the complex effects of governmentality and neoliberal governance on women's lives and livelihoods and on gender power dynamics in the contemporary world.

Gendered Effects of Governmentality

Although Foucault identified sexuality, health, and welfare as crucial sites of governmentality, both in relation to interventions "to make live or let die" and as modes of subjectification, he was markedly unconcerned with sexed embodiment and gender power. When sex, gender, and sexuality are deployed as analytical categories, however, the coercive dimensions of neoliberal governmentality become clear. In the United States, for example, Anna Marie Smith (2002, 2007) has documented how one public-sector reform—welfare "reform"—subjected poor women to mandatory workfare; mandatory paternity identification; mandatory DNA testing; mandatory drug testing; mandatory adoption counseling; and punitive "family caps," which lowered benefit levels for families into which a new child is born while they are receiving Temporary Assistance to Needy Families. Under the guise of cutting back the state, neoliberal governmentality infringed the privacy and reproductive rights of poor women, exposed them to increased threats of domestic violence, impaired their ability to care for their dependent children, and forced them into low-waged work that generated income well below the poverty level (see also Soss, Fording, Schram 2011).

Neoliberal commitments to privatization coexist with a menacing regulation of intimate life; governmentality links sexuality, reproduction, and citizenship through new pronatalist and anti-abortion initiatives, constructing the womb not only as a setting for political debate, but also as a site for political intervention (Miller 2007). In contrast to liberal claims that the private sphere lies beyond the reach of the state, women's reproductive organs are "publicized," claimed as legitimate targets of public regulation and concern. Abstinence-only sex education programs in schools condemn sexual activity outside wedlock, while also denying teens access to information about birth control and abortion. While the freedom of the economic sector is proclaimed, the state and its capillary circuits encroach on the most intimate decisions, sentencing some young women of color to mandatory birth control as a condition of probation, while committing other young pregnant women to incarceration for practices the state deems "abusive" to an unborn child. Within these naturalized circuits, women citizens enter the public sphere on markedly different terms than their male counterparts. They are public, in the sense that they are subjects of collective concern and interest, subject to regulation in the collective interest, but sorely lacking in the beneficial aspects of privacy associated with negative liberty.

Feminist Critiques of Governance Praxis

Feminist theorists have demonstrated that modern states have actively shaped gender relations through governing institutions and rules as well as discourses (Landes 1988; Pateman 1988; Hawkesworth 2012; see also Rupp and Thomsen chapter 44 in this volume.). More recently, feminist scholars have also analyzed the gendered dimensions of processes and relations within systems of governance (Chappell 2013). As states have changed under the regime of neoliberal globalization, some feminist scholars have shifted their analytic lens from the state-centric approach to more complex governing networks. Operating in a web of relationships that span local and global markets and other nonstate institutions, the state remains a crucial actor, but not necessarily the dominant actor, and it is no longer (if it ever was) autonomous from other social forces (Chappell 2013).

In taking note of some contributions of the governance turn, feminists have preserved a critical distance: none have become strong proponents of neoliberal governance. Noting that governance studies fail to grasp the continuing reality of gender inequality and women's marginalization in political life, in public-private partnerships, in markets, and in self-organizing networks, feminist scholars have emphasized that governance scholarship seems impervious to unequal social relations and forces. Far from being seduced by the focus in governance studies on the state's relationship to social actors, such as the market and civil society—a longtime concern of feminist inquiry—feminists insist that the governance paradigm must be augmented in order to explain power differentials, exclusion, and misrepresentation of social groups that are defined in terms of gender, race, and class in new governance regimes (Sauer 2011; Waylen 2008a, 2008b).

In *Women's Movements Facing the Reconfigured State*, Banaszak, Beckwith, and Rucht (2003) employed a gender perspective to analyze changes in governance practices in the EU and the United States as power has been delegated to supranational institutions, transnational organizations, subnational governments, independent agencies, and the private sector. Through a series of case studies, they examine how women's movements have contributed and responded to changes in state powers and policy responsibility in North America and Western Europe. Focusing on changes in Western welfare states that figure prominently in governance scholars' analyses of public-sector reform, they conceptualize the state's "reconfiguration" as an amalgam of four specific transformations. Three of these processes occur within the state, involving horizontal and vertical shifts of power and policy responsibility—namely, *uploading*, *downloading*, and *lateral loading*:

> Structural changes imply a relocation of formal state authority and/or a transfer of state policy responsibilities from one governmental level or branch to another. This relocation can first occur in a vertical direction by shifting power, which was mainly concentrated at the level of the nation-state, upward or downward. Much state authority has been *uploaded* to supranational organizations such as the European Union ... Vertical reconfiguration of formal state decision-making powers is also evidenced by *downloading*, that is, by the relocation of national state authority or responsibilities for specific tasks to substate, provincial, or regional governments.
>
> (Banaszak, Beckwith, and Rucht 2003, 4)

Another aspect of state reconfiguration alters relations between the state and society as states *offload* certain responsibilities by withdrawing from particular functions or by delegating tasks to actors in civil society (Banaszak, Beckwith, and Rucht 2003, 7).

State reconfiguration also involves shifts of power across the traditional representative spheres of the state, particularly the legislative and executive arenas. Banaszak, Beckwith, and Rucht point to a weakening of the power of elected state spheres, and a growing reliance on other nonelected state bodies to make policy (lateral loading).

"The national state maintains its decision-making powers, yet policy decisions increasingly occur in the courts, quasi-nongovernmental organizations (quangos), and executive agencies of government" (5). The consequence of lateral loading for feminist activists is palpable: "[e]lectoral politics allow activists greater influence over the framing of issues. When issues move from the Parliament to the administration, they tend to become more invisible and depoliticized" (5). In comparison with uploading and downloading, Banaszak, Beckwith, and Rucht suggest, lateral loading and offloading eventually reduces social movement influence (6).

Offloading also has negative consequences for proponents of women's rights. As welfare states offload traditional responsibilities for social provision onto nonstate venues, such as the community, family, market, or intermediary organizations, women increasingly bear the burdens of caring for the aged and disabled(Bashevkin 1998). Thus, feminist analysis demonstrates that purportedly "gender-blind" state reconfiguration has significant consequences for gendered divisions of labor and the attendant power relations. Specifically, offloading resurrects women's role as naturalized care providers in communities and families.

In "From State Feminism to Market Feminism," Johanna Kantola and Judith Squires (2012) also investigate the gendered effects of new governance regimes. Over the course of the twentieth century, women's rights activists lobbied their governments to create various forms of national machinery to address women's concerns, including ministries of women's affairs, women's bureaus within various government agencies, and women's units within multiple departments, especially those dealing with health, education, employment, and welfare. Amy Mazur and Dorothy McBride (1995) used the term "state feminism" to characterize the government agencies that were created in response to demands from the women's movement and staffed by feminist policymakers. Kantola and Squires suggest that the concept of state feminism no longer adequately captures the complexity of emerging feminist engagements with new forms of governance. As "governments have opted for differing degrees of neoliberal market reform with different consequences for women's policy agencies," a new terminology is needed to draw attention to the changing contours of equality policymaking and implementation (383).

They coin the term "market feminism" to analyze "the ways in which feminist engagements with public policy agendas are increasingly mediated via private sector organizations according to the logic of the market" (383). According to Kantola and Squires, the move from state feminism to market feminism impacts both the political *practices* and policy *priorities* of women's policy agencies. Whereas state feminism turned on a modernist bureaucratic state and a cohesive national women's movement to fuel the dynamic pursuit of gender equality, market feminism must operate "in the context of governing styles in which boundaries between and within public and private sectors have become blurred, entailing contracting, franchising and new forms of regulation, including new public management" (386). For this reason, "market feminism seeks to promote gender equality by turning to the channels and mechanisms offered by the market," which include increasing engagement with nongovernmental organizations that have stepped into the gap created by offloaded policies. Women's movement activists must deal with changing priorities, as well as the rise of the rhetoric of economic efficiency, as they pursue gender equality (390). In the field of domestic violence, for example, feminist activists have shifted their arguments from the rhetoric of rights to physical safety to an economic calculus of the cost of domestic violence in terms of days lost at work and declining productivity. Although Kantola and Squires are critical of these developments, they note that new governance provides different opportunities for women's groups. Rather than cling to state feminist strategies, they urge feminists to attend to market operations and to think creatively about new approaches to gender-equality policy and implementation.

Working at the intersection of feminist international relations and international political economy, Shirin Rai and Georgina Waylen (2008) offer a far more critical appraisal of the effects of global governance on gender equality. They note that the political shift from government to governance is directly tied to the deregulation of a gendered, global, capitalist economy, altering gendered social relations that structure modes of production, exchange, and consumption, as well as ideas and ideologies. The essays in their collection demonstrate the systemic effects of neoliberal globalization on domains as diverse as agriculture, employment, intimacy, macroeconomics, trade, international law, security policy, and violence against women. Within these diverse policy arenas, the shift to governance can have unintended and contradictory effects. For example, marketization and trade policies over the past four decades have "pushed" men to migrate to cities for industrial employment in nations as diverse as China and Mexico, leaving women in rural areas increasingly responsible for agricultural production. To fulfill these demands, women often rely on their daughters for assistance in the fields and in the home, something that contributes to growing levels of female illiteracy despite official government commitment to the education of girls. In addition to illuminating these gendered effects, the essays offer concrete suggestions for remedying these growing inequities—solutions that foreground interventions by national and international institutions, as well as democratic mobilization (see also Marchand and Osorno Velázquez chapter 22 in this volume).

Engaging Governance: From Civil Society to NGOization

As new governance regimes have emerged over the past four decades, feminist activists have been positioning themselves to take advantage of the shifting relations among the state, market, and civil society within nations and through transnational activism. As noted, the advent of governance transforms civil society from actor in the realm of nonstate action, voluntary association, and individual pursuit of private interests (as it is positioned within liberal political theory) to partner in the putatively horizontal relations of power that characterize the new global order (Alvarez 1999). As a form of voluntary organization closely tied to marketization and to neoliberal agendas for "democratization," "global civil society" emerged in the wake of a bipolar global world order after the demise of the Soviet system, marking a resurgence of capital flows to an emerging nonstate, "voluntary" sector (Anheier, Glasius and Kaldor 2001). The donors helping to fund civil society organizations include huge foundations, such as the Soros Open Society Institute and the Ford Foundation, and the governments of Western nations.

Feminist analyses emphasize that civil society—like governance mechanisms and markets—is a thoroughly gendered and raced space (Fraser 1992; Dawson 1994). As Barbara Einhorn and Charlotte Sever (2003, 167) have pointed out, whether construed as "informal political activity," as a "space between state and household," as a "defining characteristic of liberal democracies," as a "third point in society's triangle of state, market, and voluntary, non-profit sector," as "the mobilization of citizens outside governmental arenas," as a "space for political resistance," or as an "idealized space for dissident groups," civil society is "structured by gendered relations of unequal power, and its institutions—trade unions, religious organizations, dissident political movements—are male dominated. "Feminist civil society," then, specifically refers to those voluntary associational activities aimed at undermining male domination and promoting the empowerment or status of women (Beckwith 2000). As a strategy for social change in the era of neoliberal globalization, feminist civil society involves women's self-organization to undermine social practices and norms that devalue women and keep them subordinate (Weldon 2004, 5). Addressing a wide array of social, political, and economic issues, including many that are not easily resolved via legislation (e.g., the gendered division of labor in the family or women's triple shift), feminist civil society enables discussion and critique of dominant views and generates ideas and strategies that can lead to social change.

"Feminist civil society" is neither fully outside nor fully inside national and international political arenas. In the newly independent states created from the former Soviet bloc, 63 percent of the women's organizations received all of their funding from Western foundations (Hrycak 2002, 71–77). In the late 1990s, as Aili Tripp (2003) pointed out, 40 percent of USAID (United States Agency for International Development) funds in Africa were going to civil society organizations. Funders of civil society organizations are explicit about their motivations. They seek to promote organizations that can serve as a counterweight to the state, monitoring and challenging state practices, generating proposals for reform, and pressuring for democratization.

The NGO forums, organized in conjunction with the four UN-sponsored World Conferences on Women, are perhaps the best examples of feminist civil society as a "counter-public of women." Running parallel to the official intergovernmental conferences and consisting of those feminist activists who choose (and who can afford) to participate, NGO forums are an "inchoate form of a more democratic and participatory global governance," which gesture toward alternatives to existing hierarchical structures dominated by nation-states and international organizations. While NGO forums are exhilarating sites of debate, performance, mobilization, information sharing, petition gathering, brainstorming, and, sometimes, solidarity building, they remain at some remove from democratic practice and consensual decision-making. As Rosalind Petchesky has pointed out, NGO forums are neither representative nor accountable assemblies. "There is no reliable mechanism for representing the voices of the oppressed; those who claim to speak for them are not "representative" in any systemic sense. An infinitesimal fragment of the world's women are represented at, much less participate in UN Conferences, and those who do participate are divided by region, class, race/ethnicity, culture, positioning within global capitalism, and access to power and resources (Petchesky 2003, 25).

In contrast to these global gatherings of women, a second construction of transnational feminist civil society focuses on a much narrower framework, NGOs. The term *nongovernmental organization* is itself the progeny of the United Nations, adopted by the UN when it agreed to provide a mechanism for citizen-based organizations to participate in the Economic and Social Council. As defined by the UN, "NGO" applies only to private, nonprofit groups (Tinker 1999, 89). Created to make claims on behalf of those who are excluded from official institutions of national and transnational governance, however, "NGOs are a special set of organizations that are private in form, but public in purpose" (Weiss and Gordenker 1996). Moreover, NGOs include an enormous array of organizational types and sizes, ranging from grassroots or community-based organizations to service or advocacy organizations that are largely dependent on private donors to giant nonprofit organizations that are funded mainly through public resources—some having budgets larger than those of some poor countries (e.g., International Red Cross, CARE International; Petchesky 2003, 28).

By 1945, the international women's movement had created twenty-five INGOs that were involved in efforts to shape UN practices and agendas. By 1975, that number had grown to fifty (Stephenson 1995, 135). Despite the claims found in the literature on globalization from below concerning the "populist" character of NGOs, "most NGOs in membership or headquarters reflect rather than counteract prevailing hegemonic structures of the world system" (Stephenson 1995, 138). Feminist NGOs also fall under that indictment. Most come from or are funded by rich Western nations. Carolyn Stephenson has traced the changing character of women's international NGOs over the course of the twentieth century. Prior to 1915, most women's NGOs were religious in origin and orientation. From 1916 to 1970, the character of women's NGOs shifted as women's professional organizations came to dominate the field. Prior to 1977, less than 10 percent of women's NGOs were headquartered outside the United States or Europe. Of the thirty new women's NGOs launched in the 1980s, however, more than half were headquartered in the global South (Stephenson 1995, 138).

Feminist INGOs have played a number of significant roles in the development of a women's rights agenda at the UN. They have organized, educated, and lobbied to ensure that women are included in UN offices and decision-making circles. They also played a central role in the creation of International Women's Year, the Decade for Women, and the UN World Conferences on Women; this, in turn, contributed to a new spate of transnational feminist organizing. In a sense, then, feminist INGOs were not only constitutive of but also gave birth to an increasingly vibrant transnational feminist civil society. INGOs have also played key lobbying and monitoring roles, pressuring for UN Conferences, then pressing intergovernmental conference participants to produce concrete Platforms for Action, and then using them to leverage nations to change their laws and structures to conform to the UN platform (Stephenson 1995, 150).

In addition to feminist INGO activism at the United Nations, the UN system (the UN Development Programme [UNDP], UN Development Fund for Women [UNIFEM], and the World Bank) has stimulated the emergence of a new development agenda that requires a "gender perspective." International agencies "exert pressure and provide incentives in favor of gender policies," significantly increasing the demand for "gender experts" (Rios Tobar 2003). To meet this demand, the growth of women's NGOs over the past twenty-five years has been exponential. In China, for example, 5,800 new women's NGOs were created in the two years immediately preceding the 1995 Beijing World Conference on Women (Howell 2003). Women's organizations now constitute the largest organized sector in many African nations—indeed, the largest proportion of human rights organizations in Africa are women's rights organizations (Tripp 2003). A study conducted by the Chilean Centro de Estudios de la Mujer (Center for the Study of Women) found that 38.4 percent of the feminist activists surveyed were employed in NGOs (Rios Tobar 2003).

The proliferation of feminist NGOs in all regions of the world is both a bid for feminist participation in governance and also, more importantly, a reaction to severe cutbacks in state provision. In Eastern and Central Europe, for example, "grassroots groups have stepped in to fill the gap left when welfare and social services previously provided by the state were privatized or ruthlessly culled" by incoming regimes (Einhorn and Sever 2003). Provision of healthcare services, poverty relief, domestic violence shelters, and HIV/AIDS hotlines are desperate efforts to take up the slack left by the retreat of the state from welfare and social provision (Einhorn and Sever 2003). NGOs pick up problems that states in fiscal crisis or under the mandate of structural-adjustment policies disdain. Working on soft money and without job security, NGO staff offer cheaper means to alleviate poverty or provide healthcare than do state employees (Lang 1997). Funded by Western foundations, governments, and INGOS, "NGOization" gives rise to "contractual bureaucracies responding to policy directives remote from the people they serve" (Rowbotham and Linkogle 2001, 6).

Even as they provide a counterforce to the resurgence of capitalism and the ascendancy of the neoliberal agenda, NGOs prove emblematic of the shift from government to governance. Small, professionalized organizations that are not subject to democratic control, NGOs are accountable to their funders as much if not more than to the constituencies they serve. Their funding is short term and subject to movement offshore with little advance warning. Indeed, Marcela Rios Tobar (2003) has noted that as Chile moved forward with the project of democratization, the withdrawal of funds from Chilean feminist NGOs by Oxfam (the United Kingdom and Canada) as well as Dutch, German, and French funders created a crisis of funding, contributing to the unemployment of feminist policy experts and the demobilization of feminism as a force in some policy debates.

NGOization, however, need not imply a weakening of state power. In some nations of the world, states regulate and monitor NGOs, requiring registration or licensing that can be revoked if the government disapproves certain forms of NGO activity. In China, for example, feminist civil society emerged in the context of marketization, with the assistance of major international donors, such as the Ford Foundation; yet the existence of NGOs is carefully monitored by the state (Howell 2003). All NGOs must register with the government and be "sponsored" by state apparatus.[1] Negotiating these intricate boundaries of the permissible, the "new women's organizations" in China have nonetheless created a "new public sphere of critical reflection and dialogue about gender issues," and they are addressing an array of previously neglected issues, including exploitive working conditions; the plight of women workers laid off from collective and state-owned enterprises, who face sex discrimination in labor market; growing sex discrimination in employment; sexual harassment; the expansion of the sex industry; violence against women; trafficking in women; lesbian and gay existence; and women's studies (Howell 2003).[2]

With the bulk of NGO funding coming from Western sources, the advocacy strategies, mobilizing tactics, policy models, and substantive agenda of feminist civil society has had a decidedly Western cast. Indeed, women's rights advocates in socialist and former socialist states have complained that Western biases may distort understanding of the scope of feminist activism and of the strategies conducive to success in these contexts (Einhorn and Sever 2003; Hrycak 2002; Hsiung and Wong 1999). East/West partnerships created to train feminist activists in the Commonwealth of Newly Independent States, for example, assume the validity of a Western model of feminist activism and promote a "Western agenda," providing funding for rape crisis centers, business incubators, microenterprise and microfinance, gender studies centers, and women's leadership training.[3] Established women's councils are largely bypassed in these new partnerships, and a "maternalist orientation," deployed by many of the women's rights activists negotiating nationalist agendas, is actively repudiated (Hrycak 2002, 71–77). Under such conditions, feminist civil society may seem less open, participatory, and democratic and more imperialist. Indeed, claiming concern over undue Western influence, Vladimir Putin passed a law to increase monitoring of NGOs by Russia's Justice Ministry in 2006, and issued a presidential decree eliminating tax-exempt status from 90 percent of the NGOs operating in Russia with the support of funds from foreign donors in 2008. In so doing, Putin not only made it much more difficult for NGOs to operate; he also heightened the restrictions on the only political sphere that women dominate in contemporary Russia (Johnson and Saarinen 2013). For feminist activists, then, "partnership" in the putatively horizontal relations of power that characterize the new global order may be short term, easily revocable, and far from idealized notions of mutual trust and shared purposes.

Gendered Governance Networks

References to self-organizing systems and self-regulating networks in governance suggest a world in which race, ethnicity, and gender play no role. Yet, feminist scholars have demonstrated that informal networks are every bit as gendered and raced as are government institutions and markets (Hawkesworth 2003). Indeed, the very creation of feminist civil society was necessary because women and women's issues have been and continue to be sorely neglected by governments and governance. In addition to using their positional power inside political institutions, the power of seniority, and the power that accrues from holding the majority of seats in government to thwart the incursion of women in governance and the advancement of women in society, some men have actively organized forces of reaction against feminism, committing themselves to the restoration of "traditional" gender relations. Despite the doctrinal differences that distinguish them, Christian fundamentalists in the United States; Jewish fundamentalists in Israel; and Islamic fundamentalists in some countries in Africa, the Middle East, and South Asia share the belief that traditional relations between men and women are divinely ordained and must be preserved. Appealing to various scriptures (the Bible, the Quran) for justification, they advocate the equal dignity of men and women in the context of gender-differentiated roles that accord greater power to men both in the public sphere and within the home. Characterizing their stance as "pro-family," these conservative forces have mobilized in particular nation-states and in international forums to promote heterosexual marriage and the role of women as mothers and dependents in a hierarchical family structure. Taking aim at women's movement activists and their policy agenda, they have not only attacked gender equality as "anti-family and unnatural" but also attempted to undermine or reverse recent policy gains (Chappell 2006, 514).

Tracing the emergence of a "loosely structured transnational conservative patriarchal network" within United Nations circuits, Louise Chappell (2006, 493) notes that "these international conservative actors rely explicitly or implicitly on a patriarchal concept of power to shape their understanding of the relationship between men and women," insisting that men and women have different roles and different functions. In addition to the Vatican and Christian Right NGOs, the network includes a number of governments, such as Iran, Egypt, Libya, Saudi Arabia, and the United States during George W. Bush administration. Organized to counter women's movement gains, this conservative coalition became visible in 1993 at the Vienna Conference on Human Rights. It was better organized and even more visible at the Cairo Conference on Population and Development in 1994, raising a host of objections to proposed language concerning women's reproductive autonomy. In 1995, the network succeeded in preventing sexuality rights from being included in the Beijing Platform for Action. In addition to using delaying tactics to block change, the coalition has persuaded governments to register reservations concerning pro-women provisions, thwarted the emergence of international protocols concerning sexual rights, and blocked any reference to abortion as a family planning device. During debates about the nature of crimes against humanity and the jurisdiction of the International Criminal Court at the Statute of Rome Conference, the conservative network succeeded in adding "a rider to the definition of forced pregnancy to ensure that it could not be interpreted as diluting anti-abortion laws at the national level" (Chappell 2006, 493). At the Beijing Plus 10 meetings at the United Nations in 2005, the Bush administration played the leading role in efforts to thwart the extension of women's rights, "attempting to reopen and amend the Platform for Action to emphasize that it confers no international legal rights and imposes no legally binding obligations on states under international law" (Chappell 503). The unique combination of the Christian Right NGOs and the Vatican acting in consort with the governments of Islamic states, such as Saudi Arabia and Iran; Arab states, such as Egypt and Libya; and the world's one remaining superpower, the United States, has heightened the influence of this network in international conferences. NGOs are restricted to lobbying governments for changes to texts before each conference, but the active support of government delegations for the network's conservative agenda affords opportunities to influence deliberations within the international meetings themselves.

The coalescence of these powerful forces in opposition to women's equality raises important issues about the likelihood of progress toward equitable politics in this era of neoliberal governance. At a minimum, these fundamentalist forces have kept women's rights activists on the defensive for nearly two decades, precluding development of a more expansive agenda internationally. As Louise Chappell (2006, 518) notes, "[T]he women's movement was locked into defending what had already been achieved within the confines of formal equality, rather than pursuing more expansive goals, including those to address differences among women."

Informal mechanisms can also sustain invisible but entrenched power relations that advantage men and exclude women from core power groups in various networks (Franceschet 2011; Mackay 2011; Bjarnegård 2013; Waylen 2014). Conceptualizing governance networks as a form of clientelist politics, Elin Bjarnegård (2013, 29) has suggested that maleness constitutes a precondition for male bonding within clientelist homosocial networks,

> "For men, it is almost always considered advantageous to build networks with other men. Men are still more often found in important societal and political positions that are vital in gaining access to resources and information exchange. In addition, men often perceive other men to be more competent and reliable and more like themselves—and therefore more comfortable to cooperate with. Male networking is seen as maximizing network predictability. For women, homosocial capital is simply not a valid currency with which to attain political power."

Building on Eve Sedgwick's (1985) conception of homosociality as a preference for members of one's own sex and theories of social capital, Bjarnegård considers homosociality to be an invaluable political asset for male politicians and activists, a form of political capital that helps men secure their positions of power. "There is thus, in a sense, a political capital that can be used to gain and maintain power but that is only, or predominantly, reserved for men and to which only certain men have access" (3). As evidenced by "old boys' networks," homosocial capital enables social bonding and fosters trust within the group. "The clientelist context specifically carries with it incentives for individuals to accumulate homosocial capital. Clientelism per se can be understood as a form of uncertainty reduction in an otherwise unpredictable political environment, and homosocial capital is the currency needed to buy clientelist predictability" (11). Emphasizing that homosocial capital is a prerequisite for inclusion, Bjarnegård suggests that governance networks operate in accordance with informal practices and resources that, although they may not have been designed with this explicit aim, prove to systematically exclude women and other social groups (21). Bjarnegård's analysis of exclusive and gendered homosocial capital moves beyond de jure segregation to show how informal mechanisms can be gendered in favor of (hegemonic) men even in cases where the formal rules exist to promote gender equality.

Conclusion

The concept of governance offers new perspectives on the state and the operation of power in an era of neoliberal globalization. New actors in governance networks, new governing mechanisms grounded in informal rules and self-organized coordination, multilevel and multisphere governance regimes—all pose new challenges for gender-inclusive politics. Yet, governance theories are relatively underdeveloped in taking into account structural inequality of participants, accountability mechanisms, and the reconciliation of efficiency and democracy. Feminist analyses draw attention to these deficits, while illuminating subtle, informal gendering processes in governance that are seldom considered in mainstream approaches.

In principle, new forms of governance offer women multiple channels for accessing policymaking and implementation. However, more access is not readily transformed into more power and a greater voice. Although transnational feminist activism has spurred the UN and its affiliated agencies to play a catalytic role in advancing a women's rights agenda, women are not yet equal participants in most governance regimes.[4] Over the past four decades, feminists have developed their own strategies to degender the nation-state (state feminism, quotas, gender mainstreaming, formal equality institutions, etc.), but these efforts presuppose that the state—as the de facto dominant actor in policymaking and implementation—is willing and able to promote gender justice. With the neoliberal reconfiguration of the state and the devolution of many responsibilities to the market and civil society, feminists face new challenges in dealing with far-reaching changes in governmentality and governance.

Notes

1. The All China Women's Federation (ACWF), the state apparatus developed by the Chinese Communist Party, to mobilize women to meet the needs of the revolution, not only sponsors fifty thousand women's organizations across China; since the UN World Conference on Women in Beijing, it has also taken to calling itself, and sometimes acting like, an NGO. For differing accounts of the ACWF as an NGO, see Howell 2003; Hsiung and Wong 1999.
2. Feminist civil society is vulnerable to changing state priorities, however. On March 6, 2015, the Chinese government arrested ten feminist activists who were planning demonstrations

against sexual harassment and domestic violence to coincide with the March 8 celebration of International Women's Day. Although five activists were released within forty-eight hours, Li Tingting, Wei Tingting, Zheng Churan, Wu Rongrong, and Wang Man were imprisoned until April 13. Their arrests and detention caused many Chinese feminist activists to go into hiding.

3. To counter Western influence, Vladimir Putin passed a law in 2006 to increase monitoring of NGOs by the Russian Justice Ministry, and in 2008, he issued a presidential decree eliminating tax-exempt status from 90 percent of the NGOs operating in Russia with the support of funds from foreign donors. In so doing, Putin not only made it much more difficult for NGOs to operate; he also heightened the restrictions on the only political sphere that women dominate in contemporary Russia (Guenther 2011).

4. The notable exceptions would be the Nordic States, where women have approximated parity in elective offices for two decades; women hold more than 50 percent of the seats in the Rwandan parliament.

References

Allison, Graham. 1971. *Essence of Decision*. Boston: Little Brown.
Alvarez, Sonia. 1999. "Advocating Feminism: The Latin American Feminist NGO 'Boom.'" *International Feminist Journal of Politics* 1 (2): 181–209.
Anheier, Helmut, Malies Glasius, and Mary Kaldor. 2001. *Global Civil Society*. Oxford: Oxford University Press.
Banaszak, Lee Ann, Karen Beckwith, and Dieter Rucht. 2003. "When Power Relocates: Interactive Changes in Women's Movements and States." In *Women's Movements Facing the Reconfigured State*, edited by Lee Ann Banaszak, Karen Beckwith, and Dieter Rucht, 1–29. New York: Cambridge University Press.
Bashevkin, Sylvia. 1998. *Women on the Defensive: Living through Conservative Times*. Chicago: Chicago University Press.
Beckwith, Karen. 2000. "Beyond Compare? Women's Movements in Comparative Perspective." *European Journal of Political Research* 37: 431–468.
Bedford, Kate. 2013. "Gender, Institutions, and Multilevel Governance." In *The Oxford Handbook of Gender and Politics*, edited by Georgina Waylen, Karen Celis, Johanna Kantola, and Laurel S. Weldon, 627–653. Oxford: Oxford University Press.
Bernstein, Elizabeth. 2010. "Militarized Humanitarianism Meets Carceral Feminism: The Politics of Sex, Rights, and Freedom in Contemporary Antitrafficking Campaigns." *Signs: Journal of Women in Culture and Society* 36 (1): 45–72.
Bevir, Mark. 2011. *The Sage Handbook of Governance*. Los Angeles, CA: Sage.
Bevir, Mark. 2012. *Governance: A Very Short Introduction*. Oxford: Oxford University Press.
Bjarnegård, Elin. 2013. *Gender and Politics: Explaining Male Dominance in Parliamentary Representation*. Gender and Politics Series. Basingstoke, UK: Palgrave Macmillan.
Caglar, Gülay, Elisabeth Prügl, and Susanne Zwingel. 2013. "Introducing Feminist Strategies in International Governance." In *Feminist Strategies in International Governance*, edited by Gülay Caglar, Elisabeth Prügl, and Susanne Zwingel, 1–18. London and New York: Routledge.
Chappell, Louise. 2006. "Contesting Women's Rights: Charting the Emergence of a Transnational Conservative Counter-Network." *Global Society* 20 (4): 491–520.

Chappell, Louise. 2013. "The State and Governance." In *The Oxford Handbook of Gender and Politics*, edited by Georgina Waylen, Karen Celis, Johanna Kantola, and Laurel S. Weldon, 603–626. Oxford: Oxford University Press.

Dawson, Michael. 1994. "A Black Counterpublic? Economic Earthquakes, Racial Agenda(s), and Black Politics." *Public Culture* 7: 195–224.

Einhorn, Barbara, and Charlotte Sever. 2003. "Gender and Civil Society in East Central Europe." *International Feminist Journal of Politics* 5 (2): 163–190.

Eisenstein, Hester. 2010. *Feminism Seduced: How Global Elites Use Women's Labor and Ideas to Exploit the World*. Denver, CO: Paradigm Publishing.

Franceschet, Susan. 2011. "Gendered Institutions and Women's Substantive Representation: Female Legislators in Argentina and Chile." In *Gender, Politics and Institutions: Towards a Feminist Institutionalism*, edited by Mona Lena Krook and Fiona Mackay, 58–78. London: Palgrave Macmillan.

Fraser, Nancy. 1992. "Rethinking the Public Sphere: A Contribution to the Critique of Actually Existing Democracy." In *Habermas and the Public Sphere*, edited by Craig Calhoun, 109–142. Cambridge, MA: MIT Press.

Fraser, Nancy. 2009. "Feminism, Capitalism and the Cunning of History." *New Left Review* 56 (March–April): 97–117.

Foucault, Michel. 1977. *Discipline and Punish: The Birth of the Prison*. Translated by Alan Sheridan. New York: Vintage Books.

Foucault, Michel. 1978. *The History of Sexuality*. Vol. 1. New York: Vintage Books.

Foucault, Michel. 1994. *Dits et écrits IV*. Paris: Gallimard.

Guenther, Katja M. 2011. "The Possibilities and Pitfalls of NGO Feminism. Insights from Post Socialist Europe." *Signs: Journal of Women in Culture and Society* 36 (4): 863–887.

Halley, Janet. 2006. *Split Decisions: How and Why to Take a Break from Feminism*. Princeton, NJ: Princeton University Press.

Hawkesworth, Mary. 2003. "Congressional Enactments of Race-Gender: Toward a Theory of Raced-Gendered Institutions." *American Political Science Review* 97: 529–550.

Hawkesworth, Mary. 2012. *Political Worlds of Women: Activism, Advocacy, and Governance in the Twenty-First Century*. Boulder, CO: Westview Press.

Howell, Jude. 2003. "Women's Organizations and Civil Society in China: Making a Difference." *International Feminist Journal of Politics* 5 (2): 191–215.

Hrycak, Alexandra. 2002. "From Mothers' Rights to Equal Rights: Post Soviet Grassroots Women's Organizations." In *Women's Activism and Globalization: Linking Local Struggles and Transnational Politics*, edited by Nancy Naples and Manisha Desai, 64–82. New York: Routledge.

Hsiung, Ping-Chun, and Yuk-Lin Renita Wong. 1999. "Jie Gui—Connecting the Tracks: Chinese Women's Activism Surrounding the 1995 World Conference on Women in Beijing." In *Feminisms and Internationalism*, edited by Mrinalini Sinha, Donna Guy, and Angela, 126–153. Woollacott. Oxford: Blackwell.

International Monetary Fund. 1997. *Good Governance: The IMF's Role*. Washington D.C: IMF.

Jessop, Bob. 2004. "Multi-Level Governance and Mulit-Level Metagovernance." In *Multi-Level Governance*, edited by Ian Bache and Matthew Flinders, 49–74. Oxford: Oxford University Press.

Johnson, Janet Elise, and Aino Saarinen. 2013. "Twenty-First Century Feminisms under Repression: Gender Regime Change and the Women's Crisis Center Movement in Russia." *Signs: Journal of Women in Culture and Society* 38 (3): 543–567.

Kantola, Johanna, and Judith Squires. 2012. "From State Feminism to Market Feminism?" *International Political Science Review* 33: 382–400.

Kjær, Anne Mette. 2004. *Governance*. Cambridge, UK: Polity Press.

Landes, Joan B. 1988. *Women and the Public Sphere in the Age of the French Revolution*. Ithaca, NY: Cornell University Press.

Lang, Sabine. 1997. "The NGOization of Feminism." In *Transitions, Environments, Translation*, edited by Joan Scott, Cora Kaplan, and D. Keates, 101–120. New York: Routledge.

Levi-Faur, David, ed. 2012. *The Oxford Handbook of Governance*. Oxford: Oxford University Press.

Mackay, Fiona. 2011. "Conclusion: Towards a Feminist Institutionalism." In *Gender, Politics and Institutions: Towards a Feminist Institutionalism*, edited by Mona Lena Krook and Fiona Mackay, 181–196. London: Palgrave Macmillan.

McBride Stetson, Dorothy, and Amy Mazur. 1995. *Comparative State Feminism*. Thousand Oaks, CA: Sage.

Meyer, Mary Keysor, and Elisabeth Prügl. 1999. *Gender Politics in Global Governance*. Lanham, MD: Rowman & Littlefield Publishers.

Miller, Ruth. 2007. "Rights, Reproduction, Sexuality and Citizenship in the Ottoman Empire and Turkey." *Signs: Journal of Women in Culture and Society* 32 (2): 347–374.

Novas, Carlos, and Nikolas Rose. 2000. "Genetic Risk and the Birth of the Somatic Individual." *Economy and Society* 29 (4): 485–513.

Pateman, Carole. 1988. *The Sexual Contract*. Redwood City, CA: Stanford University Press.

Petchesky, Rosalind. 2003. *Global Prescriptions: Gendering Health and Human Rights*. London and New York: Zed Books.

Pierre, Jon, and B. Guy Peters. 2000. *Governance, Politics, and the State*. New York: St. Martin's Press.

Rai, Shirin, ed. 2003. *Mainstreaming Gender, Democratizing the State? Institutional Mechanisms for the Advancement of Women, Perspectives on Democratization*. Manchester: Manchester University Press.

Rai, Shirin M., and Georgina Waylen, eds. 2008. *Global Governance: Feminist Perspectives*. Basingstoke, UK: Palgrave Macmillan.

Rhodes, Rod A. W. 1996. "The New Governance: Governing without Government." *Political Studies* 44: 652–667.

Rhodes, Rod A. W. 2012. "Waves of Governance." In *The Oxford Handbook of Governance*, edited by David Levi-Faur, 33–48. Oxford: Oxford University Press.

Rios Tobar, Marcela. 2003. "Paradoxes of an Unfinished Transition: Chilean Feminism in the Nineties." *International Feminist Journal of Politics* 5 (2): 256–281.

Rose, Nikolas. 2001. "The Politics of Life Itself." *Theory, Culture, and Society* 18 (6): 1–30.

Rosenau, James N. 1992. "Governance, Order, and Change in World Politics." In *Governance without Government: Order and Changes in World Politics*, edited by James N. Rosenau and Ernst-Otto Czempiel, 1–29. Cambridge: Cambridge University Press.

Rosenau, James N. 2002. "Governance in a New Global Order." In *Governing Globalization: Power, Authority and Global Governance*, edited by David Held and Anthony McGrew, 70–86. Cambridge, UK: Polity Press.

Rowbotham, Sheila, and Stephanie Linkogle. 2001. *Women Resist Globalization: Mobilizing for Livelihood and Rights*. London: Zed Press.

Sauer, Birgit. 2011. "Governance as Political Theory: Through the Lens of Gender. A Response to B. Guy Peters." *Critical Policy Studies* 5 (4): 454–457.

Sedgwick, Eve Kosofsky. 1985. *Between Men. English Literature and Male Homosocial Desire*. New York: Columbia University Press.

Smith, Anna Marie. 2002. "The Sexual Regulation Dimension of Contemporary Welfare Law." *Michigan Journal of Gender and Law* 8 (2): 121–218.

Smith, Anna Marie. 2007. *Welfare Reform and Sexual Regulation*. Cambridge: Cambridge University Press.

Soss, Joe, Richard C. Fording, and Sanford F. Schram. 2011. *Disciplining the Poor: Neoliberal Paternalism and the Persistent Power of Race*. Chicago: University of Chicago Press.

Stephenson, Carolyn. 1995. "Women's International Non-Governmental Organizations at the United Nations." In *Women Politics and the United Nations*, edited by Ann Winslow, 135–154. Westport, CT: Greenwood Press.

Tinker, Irene. 1999. "Non-governmental Organizations: An Alternative Power Base for Women?" In *Gender Politics in Global Governance*, edited by Elisabeth Prugl and Mary K. Meyer, 88–104. Lanham, MD: Rowman and Littlefield.

Tripp, Aili Mari. 2003. "Women in Movement: Transformations in African Political Landscapes." *International Feminist Journal of Politics* 5 (2): 233–255.

Waylen, Georgina. 2008a. "Gendering Governance." In *Politics, Gender, and Concepts: Theory and Methodology*, edited by Gary Goertz and Amy Mazur, 114–135. Cambridge: Cambridge University Press.

Waylen, Georgina. 2008b. "Transforming Global Governance: Challenges and Opportunities." In *Global Governance: Feminist Perspectives*, edited by Shirin M. Rai and Georgina Waylen, 254–275. Basingstoke, UK: Palgrave Macmillan.

Waylen, Georgina. 2014. "Informal Institutions, Institutional Change and Gender Equality." *Political Research Quarterly* 67 (1): 212–223.

Weiss, Thomas, and Leon Gordenker. 1996. *NGOs, the UN, and Global Governance*. Boulder, CO: Lynner Rienner.

Weldon, S. Laurel. 2004. "Democratic Policymaking on Violence against Women in the Fifty US States." *International Feminist Journal of Politics* 6 (1): 1–28.

CHAPTER 16

HEALTH

AMANDA J. GRIGG AND ANNA KIRKLAND

INTRODUCTION

FEMINIST theorizing about health is both everywhere and curiously absent at the same time. Health has long been a prominent focus for feminist activists, but the subject remains comparatively neglected in the canon of feminist theory. Health has not been a popular topic in Anglo-American political theory more broadly, except in a line of liberal political theory that considers whether a right to healthcare exists. There is, in addition, a lot of attention to health by scholars of social movements and of the history of medicine and disease, but much of this work is not written from a feminist perspective. Much of French theorist Michel Foucault's work is certainly about health, including its sites (such as the clinic) and practices (such as surveillance and discipline), as well as health as a concern of the state in its governance of the whole population (his concept of *biopolitics*), and his work has been influential for feminist scholars. Foucault did not take gendered features of health as a particular focus, however.

Not only is the topic of health covered unevenly in theoretical academic disciplines, but it is also the subject of a vast professional field with distinct research traditions that are often difficult to mesh with theoretical perspectives. The medical and public health professions, particularly in the contemporary United States, attract women in large numbers as practitioners and promote research on women with attention to race and gender as variables of interest. Researchers doing quantitative work on such issues as gender disparities across medical outcomes, for example, have a difficult time designing empirical research studies that deconstruct gender categories rather than employ them as variables or markers (Kuhlmann and Babitsch 2002). Women and gender are all over health, in other words, but what exactly this abundance means is far from clear.

Feminist theory has been most explicit in considering health in bioethics and in disability studies frameworks, but these are small subfields that are sometimes estranged from each other. Feminist bioethics, nearly all of which is written by feminist philosophers, has taken up moral problems in healthcare, most commonly associated with the beginning and ending of life. Feminist bioethics has not had the interdisciplinary reach that would enable it to serve as the foundation for a unified feminist theory about health, perhaps because much of it is conducted within the fairly narrow range of the analytic philosophical method or because it tends to be institutionally housed in hospital ethics centers or in bioethics programs, rather than taught widely in undergraduate curricula. Feminist disability theorists have written extensively and in great detail about the hegemony of the normal and the healthy, offering a powerful corrective to feminist framings that pay too much homage to avoiding disease and advancing women up the hierarchy of the healthy, instead of questioning health itself. There is some overlap between feminist bioethics and feminist disability studies, to be sure (Asch and Geller 1996), but the two subfields often diverge based on their closeness to mainstream medicine and hospital ethics work (bioethics) or their challenge to medical judgments (disability theory).

Overall, it is clear that feminist theory and what is called "women's health" are not well integrated, and that disability theory perspectives are distant from both. So, while our chapter began by noting the curious combination of attention and inattention to health in feminist theory, we argue that there has been much critical theorizing about health in works that would probably not appear on most undergraduate reading lists for a course titled Feminist Theory. Before moving to a discussion of the feminist theory of *Our Bodies, Our Selves*, we pinpoint a few exemplary (but by no means exhaustive) works of feminist theory that have served as important way points to thinking about health, albeit for disconnected audiences. We spend the rest of our chapter pulling theorizing out of popular and academic sources and evaluating its somewhat less conventional trajectories, and we close with an assessment of what has been gained from feminist engagement with health and also what ground has been lost.

Divergent Disciplinary Roots for Feminist Thought about Health

Feminist Bioethics

One of the greatest debates in the field of bioethics has been over the existence of a right to health and, later, a right to healthcare (Buchanan 1984; Daniels 1984; Fried 1976; Jones 1983). Proponents of healthcare as a right often argued from the perspective of distributive justice, suggesting that equal access to healthcare is a requirement of a just society. Critics of extending rights to health or to healthcare responded that inequalities in health are not unjust unless they result from intentional violations of an individual's rights and, later, that the policies required to insure equal healthcare would constitute unacceptable violations of individual liberty (Daniels 1985; Menzel 2003). Once the scholarly consensus that there should indeed be a right to healthcare had formed, debate began over how to specify the scope of services to be included in a decent minimum of care (Hadorn 1992; Engelhardt Jr. and Rie 1986). More recent efforts have viewed healthcare as a limited good and sought better means of distributing it (Russell et al. 1996). Still others have addressed the philosophical challenges confronted in attempts to fulfill the right to healthcare (Menzel 2003).

While these debates over health as a right are valuable, scholars in this debate—nearly all of them white, male philosophers—tend to assume that health is a preexisting good, a fixed, transferable entity with inherent value. This assumption obscures how health produces the social order, as feminist and critical social scientists of medicine and health have pointed out (Metzl and Kirkland 2010). To invoke health is to invoke authority—the power to regulate and to define normal and abnormal, good and bad. Further, experiences of health and within the healthcare system vary dramatically depending on one's identity and position in society. Viewing health purely as a good obscures the less desirable of these experiences, reducing the story of what is wrong to the lack of health or healthcare rather than examining the sources of hierarchy or suffering.

Where mainstream bioethicists have largely framed health as a good to be distributed, feminist bioethicists have illuminated the ways in which health can produce and reinforce harms, particularly to marginalized groups. Dorothy Roberts argues that one of feminism's main contributions to medical ethics has been in adding a political dimension to the analysis of moral issues. Feminist ethics, she argues, "refuses to overlook the role of social problems in ethical deliberations; rather, it identifies and criticizes the ways in which the practice of medicine contributes to oppression based on gender" (Roberts 1996, 116). The groundbreaking works of feminist bioethics including Susan Wolf's edited volume *Feminist Bioethics: Beyond Reproduction* and Susan Sherwin's *No Longer Patient* (the first book-length work of feminist bioethics) have done exactly that. As Sherwin points out, medical ethics tends to presuppose the existing authority and institutional structures of medicine, narrowly focusing on particular challenges of private encounters between doctors and patients, including consent and confidentiality. A feminist approach, however, attends to "the politics of the relationship between the practice of medicine and the social order" (Roberts 1996, 121).

Feminist bioethics now boasts its own governing body (founded in 1992) and an international peer-reviewed journal (first published in 2008; Scully et al. 2010). The relative insularity of the field seems to have become an impediment to the robust extension of the topics of feminist bioethics, however. The 2010 collection *Feminist Bioethics: At the Center, on the Margins* illuminates the somewhat precarious current state of feminist bioethics. The editors suggest that feminist bioethics is at a "defining point in its 20-year history" caught between incorporation into mainstream bioethics and solidification as marginal/outsider (Scully et al. 2010, 3). The collection highlights the impact feminist bioethics has had on mainstream bioethics, including pushing bioethics beyond concerns about the doctor-patient relationship and challenging several dominant methodologies. It also acknowledges the challenges facing the field. In an early chapter of the book, Richard Twine (2010) argues that feminist bioethics ignores the majority of feminisms, focusing on feminism based in care ethics, and thus takes itself out of the conversations taking place in feminist theories such as postmodernism. Feminist bioethics has also had relatively little to say about how racialization and gendering work together in bioethics and healthcare. Scholars such as Dorothy Roberts (2011), whose work targets these intersections, have reached wider audiences and thus show a way forward for feminist bioethics. Greater theoretical range, broader methodologies, increased sophistication about the intersections with race, ethnicity, and transnationalism, and a wider conception of the bioethical will help make feminist bioethics more useful for theorizing about health.

Feminist Disability Theory

Disabled women had been making the case for integrating feminism and disability studies well before these arguments appeared in the flagship feminist journals (Finger 1983; Fine and Asch 1988). Susan Wendell's foundational call for an integration of feminist theory and disability theory, "Toward a Feminist Theory of Disability," appeared in the feminist philosophy journal *Hypatia* in 1989 and was reiterated in her 1996 book, *The Rejected Body: Feminist Philosophical Reflections on Disability*. More recently, writing in *Signs*, Rosemarie Garland-Thomson (2005) has renewed the argument that we ought to pay more attention to theoretical intersections with disability studies. These arguments go well beyond the end-of-life or beginning-of-life debates within bioethics and theorize health as social and political, not merely as a good to be properly distributed.

Wendell's 1989 arguments about why feminists should theorize about and through disability were remarkably prescient in terms of today's problems: the burdensome demands of around-the-clock work schedules, electronic devices that pressure us to be and stay on task, and the harmful effects of health moralism and of blaming the individual for illness and disability. Wendell begins by describing two of her own experiences: first, becoming chronically ill in 1985 and, second, searching the philosophical literature on disability and finding that almost all of it focused on the questions of when it was permissible to let a disabled person die and of how disabled a fetus or infant needs to be before it is permissible to let it die or prevent its being born (1989, 104). If these were the questions that bioethics had about disabled people, they are certainly not the questions of feminist disability theory. Wendell's argument for feminist disability theory is rooted in the similar theoretical problems that feminist thought and disability studies share. Do we want sameness or difference? Which is better, promoting independence or raising up dependency? Is integration or separation more empowering?

A feminist disability perspective emphasizes that, just as much of the world has been constructed by men, with men's needs and habits as the unquestioned norm, it has also been built for able bodies. "In the split between the public and the private worlds," Wendell observes, "women (and children) have been relegated to the private, and so have the disabled, the sick and the old (and mostly women take care of them)." She continues, "The public world is the world of strength, the positive (valued) body, performance and production, the able-bodied and youth. Weakness, illness, rest and recovery, pain, death and the negative (de-valued) body are private, generally hidden, and often neglected" (Wendell 1989, 111). Feminist theorists, such as Simone de Beauvoir and Dorothy Dinnerstein, have explored the patriarchal culture's urge to control the body; Wendell draws on this heritage, arguing that fear rooted in lack of control is also central to the devaluing of disabled bodies, and women's disabled bodies in particular.

It is particularly important to resurrect Wendell's article as we think about health in feminist theory because she puts chronic illness at the center of her proposed feminist disability studies perspective. A woman who is disabled because of an exhausting chronic illness is a very different spokesperson from the more visible disabled man, perhaps disabled as the result of an accident, who uses a wheel chair but does not identify as unhealthy. Wendell's focus on chronic illness, fatigue, and what she calls "the pace of life" as themselves disabling is similar to critiques of health as a moralizing discourse that valorizes youthful energy and blames people for their health failures (Metzl and Kirkland 2010).

Feminist theorizing about health would do very well to recover Wendell's critique of how the language of fighting, strength, vigor, positivity, and energy—even when mustered in woman-focused or feminist causes, such as breast-cancer or anti-rape activism—re-inscribes the deserving woman as the one who is able to keep up with and juggle it all, happily. Unfortunately, because chronic illness has never been a primary focus in disability studies, and because feminist theory has yet to engage with disability studies to the degree Wendell and Garland-Thomson have suggested, the research syntheses suggested here have not happened in feminist theory. Moreover, perhaps because the medical world and the disability studies world remain antagonistic, the more medically and quantitatively focused study of women's health continues to regard disability as a regrettable medical problem to avoid rather than as a socially created, gendered problem.

Feminist Social Science Approaches to Health

A great deal of research on health topics by feminist social scientists—more than we can do justice to in this chapter—has been conducted by anthropologists and sociologists, much of it focused on transnational connections or on sites beyond the industrialized West. These scholarly conversations are quite separate from feminist bioethics or feminist disability studies, but they take up many of the same questions from a different methodological and disciplinary perspective. Feminist health anthropologist Marcia Inhorn (2006) has surveyed this vast literature and argues that women all over the world share similar concerns about their health. For example, Inhorn finds that women frequently express concern that it is predominantly male medical professionals and government agencies that hold power over their health, defining what their problems are and what interventions are needed to address them. Other shared concerns and insights include the overemphasis on women's reproductive capacity and their status as mothers, the increasing medicalization of women's lives, and the socially constructed and culturally dependent nature of ideas of health and sickness.

Inhorn cites several large international programs aimed at promoting children's health in poor countries through training their mothers about conditions like diarrhea or how to prevent the transmission of HIV/AIDS during breastfeeding that work *on* or *through* women as mothers. And yet, as she points out, what women identify as their "most serious and troublesome reproductive health conditions, such as cervical cancer, pelvic inflammatory disease and accompanying infertility, miscarriage and stillbirth, fistulas, uterine prolapses, and pain during sexual intercourse, continue to be relatively ignored in these initiatives" (Inhorn 2006, 351). Inhorn also notes that there are similar examples from women right here in the United States. For instance, while the Centers for Disease Control and Prevention (CDC) honed in on bacterial vaginosis (BV) as their main concern in preventing prematurity and low birth weight in pregnant African American residents of Harlem, the women themselves described entirely different sources of stress in their pregnancies: "among other things, inadequate housing, community violence, exhausting, low-wage labor, disrespectful interactions in public health care settings, lack of social support from partners, lack of access to healthy foods, and toxic waste dumping in the community" (Inhorn 2006, 350).

Famous US-focused books, such as Emily Martin's *The Woman in the Body* and Rayna Rapp's *Testing the Woman, Testing the Fetus*, have explored the meanings of many of the major topics considered central to women's health, such as menstruation, childbearing, amniocentesis, and menopause, using techniques like interviewing and participant observation. One criticism has been that this focus on reproduction further reproduces an ideology of womanhood as essentially rooted in body parts, such as the uterus and breasts, and their biological goings-on. As medical sociologist Hannah Bradby puts it, "The reluctance of feminist theory to grapple with embodied aspects of sex difference in relation to gendered ideas, together with medical sociologists' fascination with obstetrics, gynecology and midwifery, has perhaps left undisturbed a Victorian core of thinking that gendered illness patterns are a matter of reproductive physiology" (2012, 73). Bradby points out, for example, that feminist work on gender and health could do much more to destabilize "the fixity of a biologically-determined sex difference," such as drawing upon "models associated with post-structural thought, such as networks and cyborgs, [which] have yet to make their mark in our discipline's record of published research" (2012, 73).

Perhaps because feminists in fields such as anthropology are commonly focused on questions of global power and colonialism, these aspects of feminist theory have not been neglected as they have been within feminist bioethics, for example. Feminist social scientists, such as Miriam Ticktin (2008), have taken a political and transnational approach to gender and health, focusing on the connections between colonialism, antipathy toward Muslims in France, and the invocation of women and girls' human rights. Ticktin's book, *Casualties of Care: Immigration and the Politics of Humanitarianism in France*, draws on postcolonial feminist theory to interrogate why Western humanitarian impulses favor the "recognizably gendered, racialized, and sexualized bodies of women and girls from the global South" (2011, 18). Ticktin's work reminds us that tales of women's and girls' bodily suffering can certainly get a lot of attention, but the terms of that attention may not be empowering and must be considered within a broad theoretical and critical framework.

Feminist Health Activism in the United States: 1969 to the Present

Within the feminist movement of the last fifty years in the United States, health issues—particularly reproductive rights and, more recently, disease-specific issues, such as breast cancer—have been among the most prominent galvanizing issues for activists. We argue that feminist theories about health emerged in perhaps the most centrally feminist way possible: from richly descriptive and highly politicized accounts by women articulating what it is like to experience one's body as the site of power struggle. In this section, we identify three prominent themes in feminist theorizing about health as they have emerged from different phases of activist engagement (or disengagement, as we note). We argue that while feminist contributions to understanding health have been uniquely powerful, several significant weaknesses and omissions leave feminist theories of health somewhat diminished. And although our focus is on the United States, Inhorn's global ethnographies of women's health show that the themes we identify are important to women around the world.

First, feminists managed to *politicize the body and the idea of health* during what is termed the *second wave of feminism*, roughly from the late 1960s to about 1980. To politicize the body is to show how it is created, understood, and experienced in everyday life through power relations, and is not simply a biological substrate or an instrument for the mind. On this view, health is not just an obviously good scientific thing to get more of or to redistribute more fairly. Health is part of these power relations, and a great deal of feminist energy has gone toward dismantling sexist views of the female body as a damaged or inferior version of the male body, of women as uniquely susceptible to physical harm or mental disturbance, and to redirecting respect and curiosity toward women's body differences on their own terms and not as departures from the male standard.

Second, feminist thought about health has consistently *given priority to structures as determinative of health, rather than individual psychological or biological processes*. Feminist thinkers have maintained the distinction between individual biomedicalization—that is, locating health in the physical processes of the body and the psycho-physical process of the mind and thus looking to fix the individual to promote health—and larger social structures, particularly those that perpetuate racial, gender, and economic inequality and that counterpose the enlightened West to supposedly irrational, exotic, disease-ridden foreign places. Third, we note a *loss or failure to maintain these critiques in the face of the growing power of health as virtuous self-regulation and achievement*. In fact, the new embrace of health promotion is in many ways an elevation of the feminine over the masculine, but in a disempowered form in which self-monitoring, anxiety, obedience, and moralism predominate. Women as a group are considered model health citizens for adopting these practices as compared to men, who are more likely to resist, ignore, and push past health admonitions.

Resistance, Inclusion, Achievement: Shifting Conceptions of Health

Much of our discussion in this half of the essay is rooted in a historicized understanding of women's health politics in the United States since the late 1960s. The fuller history includes such important moments as the consolidation of the male-dominated medical profession and the displacement of laywomen as care providers or J. Marion Sims's development of gynecological surgery through experimentation on slave women. We do not attempt a full discussion of everything that has contributed to feminist theorizing about health, however; instead, we target the most important ideas from the last half-century and discuss how they have changed and what they offer or fail to notice. Sheryl Burt Ruzek's *History of the Women's Health Movement* and Sandra Morgen's *Into Our Own Hands* do an excellent job telling the longer story of the rise and fall of feminist radicalism in health. Michelle Murphy's *Seizing the Means of Reproduction: Entanglements of Feminism, Health, and Technoscience* is unique in its biopolitical examination of the radical women's health movement of the 1970s, tracing contradictory entanglements with transnational histories of the Cold War and American imperialism as feminist health techniques moved about the globe.

There are very clear eras in feminist activism about health that are marked by dramatic shifts in the organization of women's health work and in national politics. **The era of resistance** is associated with the feminist movement of the 1960s and 1970s, and is generally characterized as focusing on reproductive rights (a necessary precursor to the broader goals of gender equality) and critiquing and even rejecting the medical institution. This era is also criticized for failing to include the voices of marginalized women. The 1980s and 1990s saw an expansion beyond reproduction issues, to include such issues as AIDS, domestic violence, and breast cancer, as well as a detachment from the broader feminist movement as groups formed issue-specific organizations. We term this period **the era of inclusion**. By the late 1980s the women's health movement was working closely with institutions that previous activists had rejected, as evidenced by the movement to include women in federally funded medical trials, for example, and to promote women's inclusion in the medical profession and in positions of public health administration (Epstein 2007). Although it has not been marked by as dramatic a shift as between the eras of resistance and inclusion, we argue that we've now entered an **era of achievement**, in which women and gender are clearly at the center of health discourses, and women are even held up as the highest achievers of wellness and self-care and tasked with doing more to achieve high health status for themselves and their families.

Though it is impossible to pinpoint the exact beginning of the women's health movement, we begin our history in 1969, a year that saw the first meetings of what would become the Boston Women's Health Collective, as well as the publication of Barbara Seaman's landmark book *The Doctor's Case against the Pill*. In the years that followed, the movement quickly gained momentum. By 1970, Congress was holding hearings on the safety of the pill. In 1971, self-help gynecology, perhaps the most revolutionary invention of the movement, was born, and 800 women assembled for the nation's first Women's Health Conference (Ruzek, 1978). The central argument of the women's health movement's founders was that medical institutions were patriarchal and operated as tools of social control over women's bodies. Activists drew attention to the ways that medicine shaped ideas about the female body. They argued that medical ideas about women's bodies were often the result of sexist, racist elite culture, and were thus far from scientifically objective. The male-dominated medical profession did not deserve the deference and obedience it got, in other words. The exposure of mainstream medicine's gendered power structure inspired women to engage in self-help healthcare and to establish independent, women-run, feminist health services. Carol Downer led sessions across the country in which she taught women to use a speculum to see their own cervix, and to diagnose yeast infections and treat them with yogurt. Together these efforts helped women take control of their own health.

These more radical and independent sites for feminist health activism ran into trouble, however. Were they inclusive and democratic enough, and could they operate without adopting a standard business model with managers and employees? Should they organize themselves to be suitable recipients of grant funding, with the strings and requirements that come with that? Over time, the institutions that feminist health activists had created became more mainstream, more businesslike, more appealing to funding agencies and private benefactors, and more oriented toward getting their organizations and leaders represented in the government settings where critical decisions about healthcare are made. Arguments against capitalism and against participation in the mainstream medical community receded, and a women's health movement emerged that was well adapted to the much more conservative political climate as President Ronald Reagan took office.

By the 1980s and 1990s, activists had achieved significant success in this type of mainstream leverage and representation at the federal level, including the creation of the National Institutes of Health Office of Research in Women's Health and significant increases in federal funding for breast cancer research (Baird et al. 2009). Women's health activists formed successful nonprofits, worked in federal agencies, and formed lobbying organizations. The success, professionalization, and mainstreaming of the breast cancer movement over the last twenty years is one of the best examples of a new form of single-issue success. Including women as subjects in medical studies and funding breast cancer research were not divisive partisan issues, and they did not invoke the battle lines that the more contentious issues like contraception and abortion did. During this period, the most radical arm of the movement, feminist health clinics, were on the decline, and more traditional political organizations were on the rise. The more radical feminist health critics, however, had won some important victories, and explicit sexism and racism, and the exclusion of women and minorities from medical research were widely considered improper. Treatments that activists had critiqued, including routine radical mastectomies and unnecessary episiotomies, had become far less common. As Baird, Davis, and Christensen emphasize in their history of the women's health movement, "One does not need to be a feminist in order to support women's health, and given the antifeminist temperament in the United States in the 1990s, this severance contributed to the success of the women's health movement" (Baird et al. 2009, 14).

Each era's politics assumed a theoretical account of health that shifted over time. Resistance to the patriarchal medical models meant that feminist activists had to redefine health, and their rejection of mainstream models gave them the freedom to define it more broadly, with a better chance to include the perspectives from radical women of color, who wanted health to include economic redistributions, or radical separatists, who wanted to train women to provide abortions without dependence on professionals. Health meant systemic empowerment for lower-status groups. The more mainstream politics of inclusion would get more women and women's issues represented in powerful places, but it required trying to change the definitions of health from within, by shifting resources and emphasis, not by radically changing how the federal health bureaucracies and professions conceptualized health (as freedom from disease and the dysfunction of body parts and systems). The contemporary period is much more about achieving health than being included in or resisting it. The definition of health has been broadened but, paradoxically, in a narrow way: it now includes both avoiding disease and reaching full flourishing across the entire life span, but only within the individual's body and mind.

Politicizing the body and the idea of health

The feminist urtext of health activism is undoubtedly the Boston Women's Health Collective's *Our Bodies, Our Selves*. Work on the book began in 1969 at a socialist feminist conference in Boston. Over the course of their discussion, participants in one workshop discovered that they each had a "doctor story," a story about a physician who had been sexist, paternalistic, or had treated their information seeking with contempt (Norsigian et al. 1999, 35). They decided to continue meeting to try to develop a list of recommended doctors. When they found that every doctor's name suggested was met with a complaint, they decided to do their own research on women's health and to share it with one another at weekly meetings. The group became the Boston Women's Health Book Collective, and their research became *Our Bodies, Ourselves*. The initial editions of the book covered issues of interest to the young, white, middle-class founders, predominantly reproductive issues, but quickly expanded to include chapters on menopause, nutrition, poverty, and occupational safety. The tone of *Our Bodies, Ourselves* was radical, criticizing "[t]he prohibitive cost of medical care, the racist and inferior treatment of poor people and black people, the profit and prestige-making institutions of the 'health industry' (hospitals, medical schools, drug companies, etc.), the total neglect of the public or preventative protection [and] the fee-for-service, pay-as-you-die economic base upon which most medical practice is based" (Boston Women's Health Book Collective 1971, 137).

It is difficult to overstate the influence of *Our Bodies, Ourselves*, sometimes lovingly referred to as the bible of women's health (Scott 1999). Within its first year of publication, *Our Bodies, Ourselves* was adopted as a text by colleges and medical schools (Morgen 2002). A revised version, published in 1976, quickly became a national bestseller. Today, the book has been donated to thousands of women's health clinics and as of 2006 had been translated into twenty languages and had sold over four million copies (Davis 2002, 223-224). The group's success was not without problems. As the group grew, tensions emerged among staff members. Conflicts arose over the unequal influence of certain members and the sustainability of a nonhierarchical structure. Notably, though the creators intended to include the voices of all women, they have acknowledged that early editions presumed that middle class white-women could represent all women, and that during later efforts to make the book more inclusive differences in race, class, and sexual preference led to conflict within the collective (Boston Women's Health Book Collective 1998, 22).

Our Bodies, Ourselves is a classic example of feminist theorizing through embodied experiences, wrestled with and shared collectively (and not always without conflict, especially over the presentation of lesbian and transgender issues and the representation of women of color, among the authors and in the text). *Our Bodies, Ourselves* clearly argues that control over what is termed *health* and women's healthcare is critical for women's freedom from gender oppression (see e.g., Boston Women's Health Collective 1970, 6-8). It does this through a focus on the embodied experiences that set women apart from men and that have been under considerable paternalistic medical control: menstruation, sex, conception and preventing conception, abortion, childbirth, and menopause, as well as certain diseases that are closely connected to sexual activity or to women's reproductive organs. Davis (2002) notes that the first few editions were very much a product of the sixties and of the young, white, college-educated, new mothers who wrote them. The early editions emphasized sexuality and reproduction, and topics included anatomy, childbirth, birth control, the postpartum period, abortion, and sexually transmitted diseases. In the late 1970s menopause was included, and in 1984 occupational health was added (Bonilla 2005).

From the beginning, the Boston Women's Health Collective combined medical information about women's health with political arguments for greater bodily autonomy. For the collective and many other activists, control of one's lives required control of one's own body. This was particularly so for women since so much of a woman's life (from first menstruation to menopause) was under the scope of predominantly male medical authority. The first edition of *Our Bodies, Ourselves* began by arguing that having "basic information about how our bodies work" would ensure that women were no longer "at the total mercy of men who are telling us what to feel when we don't or what we don't feel when we do." Such information was characterized as "a weapon without which we cannot begin the collective struggle for control over our own bodies and lives" (Boston Women's Health Collective 1970, 10). The Collective spoke of "reclaiming" sex as "familiar and ours" (16) and claimed the right not to be "intimidated and frightened into doing things we're not sure of" to prevent pregnancy (71). Critiquing contemporary childbirth practices, the authors mourn the shift from midwifery to hospital delivery, where women are "seen as 'sick'" and thus lose control over their birthing experience (128). They encourage women, in addition to educating themselves about pregnancy and childbirth, to demand "the right to shape our experiences whether in the hospital or at home" (128). As evidenced by its early work, the Collective was well aware of the links between women's experiences of health and broader social and political institutions.

Prioritizing structures over individual psychological or biological processes

The second critical feminist insight we highlight is related to the politicization of the body, but it represents the turning outward of that insight. Although health can be influenced by individual biology, exercise, or a genetic predisposition to a disease, social, political and economic institutions also fundamentally shape it. Health is situated within institutions—professions; credentialing processes; economic and business structures, such as insurance companies; and the like—and these institutions themselves are gendered, hierarchical, and unequal in ways that can be oppressive. Health is a feature of communities and can be imperiled by violence, discrimination, pollution, inferior housing, and lack of employment and livable wages. Understanding health through this lens draws attention to potential solutions to health problems that go beyond treating individuals with medicine to call for broader social and political change. The early feminist health activists making these structural arguments were often women of color, whose activism extended beyond health into welfare rights, criminal justice issues, or housing, for example (Nelson 2003).

There has long been awareness that sexism and racism can have real effects on health. In a 1991 report, the American Medical Association's Council on Ethical and Judicial Affairs called on physicians to consider whether their personal biases were affecting the medical care they provided (1991). The council has documented significant gender disparity in the access to kidney transplants, diagnosis and treatment of cardiac disease, and diagnosis of lung cancer. Medical researchers regularly investigate how doctors treat individual patients and the role of race and gender in those interactions. Studies suggest that race plays a role in physician decisions to prescribe pain medication, for example, leaving nonwhite patients less likely than white patients to have their pain adequately treated (Burgess et al. 2008). Former National Insttitues of Health director Bernadine Healy argued that women's historic exclusion from the research on cardiac issues created a problematic male standard in medical scholarship and practice. As a result, women's heart disease has historically been recognized and treated aggressively only when it resembles that of men (Healy 1991). The critical question has been whether this sexism and racism in health will be understood as the individualized faulty reasoning of a few errant providers, or whether the problem will be defined more broadly.

Feminists, particularly among women of color, have argued for decades in favor of the broader structural view. Helen Rodriguez-Trias, a doctor, feminist health activist, and founding member of the Committee to End Sterilization Abuse, framed health as structural in this way: "I try not to just talk in terms of narrow health issues or, just about healre and lack of access to health care. I try to emphasize the need to improve health conditions: where we work, where we live, what our environment is like, what are the chances of you or someone in your family being victimized by violence, traumatized by violence? What are your chances of tranquility unless your kids are safe in school and at home? All of these elements in life are determinants and definers of our health" (quoted in Ketenjian 2012a, 91). Byllye Avery, the founder of the National Black Women's Health Project, recalls the role of antiviolence in her organization's definition of health (quoted in Ketenjian 2012b, 98). In early meetings of the National Black Women's Health Project, the women often discussed psychological well-being, including experiences of domestic violence, rape, and incest. Avery explains, "These things kind of gnaw, they really rob us of our power and keep us from being all of who we are. So back in the early 1980s when women really started coming together, we declared that violence was the number one health issue for black women, just before the CDC (Centers for Disease Control and Prevention) and all the rest of them determined that violence was a health issue" (98).

The efforts of women of color in the reproductive rights movement to supplement the struggle for abortion access with strategies to protect the freedom to *have* children provide one well-known example of the structural turn in feminist health (Roberts 1997). This meant demanding an end to forced sterilization and calling for access to childcare, healthcare, and a living wage (Nelson 2003). Prominent women of color criticized the mainstream, white-dominated women's health movement for failing to take up the reproductive justice issues most important to their communities, and that tension has never really dissipated. Angela Davis, writing in 1981, noted that "over the last decade the struggle against sterilization abuse has been waged primarily by Puerto Rican, black, Chicana, and Native American women. Their cause has not yet been embraced by the women's movement as a whole" (141). Writing more recently, Andrea Smith argues that the pro-choice versus pro-life framework of reproductive rights marginalizes women of color, poor women, and women with disabilities. Specifically, she argues that neither frame questions the systems in which reproductive decisions are made and that both ignore the "economic, political, and social conditions that put women in this position [seeking to end a pregnancy] in the first place" (Smith 2005, 134).

In the decades since, women of color activists have continued to lead the charge linking reproductive rights to environmental justice, welfare reform, and economic injustice, among other social-justice issues (Price 2010). One ongoing feminist effort is to move from the language of "choice," which centers the autonomous, private, empowered self, to the language of "reproductive justice," which signals a more comprehensive and political account of individuals and communities struggling for power over reproductive issues that extend beyond the right to choose an abortion. For example, one activist group, Asian Communities for Reproductive Justice (ACRJ), defines reproductive justice as "the complete physical, mental, spiritual, political, economic, and social well-being of women and girls [that] will be achieved when women and girls have the economic, social and political power and resources to make healthy decisions about our bodies, sexuality and reproduction for ourselves, our families and our communities in all areas of our lives" (ACRJ 2005, 1). Scholars documenting these more structural accounts of what health requires have also noted that reproductive freedom for African American women includes the concern about maternal death during pregnancy, childbirth, and the period right after childbirth and the high infant-mortality rate for African American babies, as well as the sterilization concern (Barbee and Little 1993, 191–192).

They also point out the vulnerability of poor women to invasion of their privacy when they apply for welfare benefits or are waiting in the emergency room (Barbee and Little 1993, 186). Social service agencies often enter women's lives at the point that they seek healthcare for themselves or their children, and as they receive scrutiny for domestic violence, substance abuse, or child abuse and neglect (Roberts 2001). While these interventions may be necessary and helpful, they can also be stigmatizing, criminalizing, and disruptive in ways that the women find disempowering. Within this structural frame, health is part of a system of social control and domination; it is structurally enabled and unevenly distributed; and health seeking often brings poor women and their families under state power in ways that would not happen for women with good private insurance.

Despite feminist efforts to make these arguments over many years, this more structurally embedded conception of health has not taken hold. In fact, health has become ever more individualized, and race and gender are commonly treated as individual variables that can contribute to health disparities. Once health disparities are identified, the next step is often to try to educate or target disadvantaged individuals to get them to do things to become healthier. Thus inclusion of gendered and raced individuals in medical studies coincides with medicalization and treatment of individual patients. Documenting disparities among raced and gendered individuals falls far short of a structural account, however, which locates the source of the problem in widespread social conditions of inequality and links individual remedies to the eradication of social injustices.

Neoliberalism's emphasis on personal responsibility in combination with the scientific discourse on genetic determinism have strengthened the trend toward individualized medicine. Proponents of new genetic technologies suggest that risk factors for disease are not just linked to a person but can be traced to her very DNA. Warning of the neo-eugenic implications of these approaches, Dorothy Roberts (2009, 2011) calls attention to the manifold structural issues occluded by efforts to provide genetic explanations for diseases that are more deadly or prevalent in racial minorities, such as childhood asthma (2011). Studies have repeatedly linked the higher rates of asthma in children of racial minorities to environmental factors. Notably, these environmental factors include exposure to insect particles in poorly maintained public housing units and exposure to outdoor pollution in poor neighborhoods near highways (Krieger et al. 2000). Feminist scholars point out that these environmental risk factors are the result of social and political systems that systematically disadvantage particular groups. Despite the compelling evidence of environmental determinants of illness, the University of California, San Francisco has dedicated an entire lab to exploring the genetic links between race and childhood asthma (Roberts 2011).

Postfeminism and the growing power of health as virtuous self-regulation and achievement

The structures and institutions of feminist organizing have changed at the same time that the idea of health has changed. Feminist critique was sharpest when it pointed out how sexist, racist, and heteronormative conceptions of health were used to subordinate women, objectify and harm their bodies, disregard their experience, and deny their expertise. By drawing attention to rampant abuses and offering alternatives, feminist theorists and activists significantly altered the understandings of women's bodies and women's health, as well as of the paternalist relationship between doctors and patients.

The past few decades have also brought significant changes that are at a great remove from feminist objectives for women's health. What women in affluent nations are supposed to be doing to care for themselves and others these days is telling: making their own organic baby food, for instance; exercising regularly; getting routine mammograms and other wellness screenings; and monitoring their weight and cholesterol levels. Women are awash in exhortations about health, and many of them come from women, focus on women, and address women as mothers and responsible caretakers.

Women heed these messages well. In the United States, women go to the doctor more often than men, use more supplements and alternative remedies than men, and avoid risky behaviors more than men (Beal 1998; Courtenay 2000, 2003; Kronenberg et al. 1997; Starfield et al. 2005). Research suggests that the duty to monitor one's health has itself become feminized, and that perception, combined with the medicalization of almost universal female life events (menstruation to menopause) has resulted in women making up the majority of healthcare consumers (Owens 2008). In the United States, for example, women are 25 percent more likely than men to have seen a physician in the past year. Men are 40 percent more likely than women to have skipped recommended cholesterol screenings (Murray-Law 2011). When men have wives, they are healthier, an effect associated with a wife's reminders to take medicine, get that bump checked out, and so on (Atzema et al. 2011; Parker-Pope 2011). One recent study found that found that men with strong beliefs in stereotypical or hegemonic masculinity (associated with power, confidence, self-reliance, and invulnerability) are half as likely as men with more moderate ideas of masculinity to receive preventative care, suggesting that the feminization of health-seeking may make it seem unmanly (Springer and Mouzon 2011).

Sarah Moore (2010) argues convincingly that feminists still mistakenly hold the view that sexism in health means that women are presented as sick. According to Moore, in the current context sexism persists but no longer renders women sickly. Instead women are understood to be exemplars of health maintenance. As she puts it, "Once associated with masculine attributes, the 'healthy body' is now more likely to be described in conventionally feminine terms: as the result of constant bodily awareness, openness about symptoms, risk-reduction, and readiness to seek and attend to medical advice" (Moore 2010, 96). Moore emphasizes that "the new paradigm of health is potentially just as damaging as the old model of health that feminists fought against," for both men and women (Moore 2010, 97). Paula Gardner (2007) shows how the newest promotions for antidepressants such as Zoloft borrow the language of feminist activism, but in the interest of consumerism. "Candyce," a case presented on the American Psychiatric Association website, "considers herself a survivor" of rape and sexual assault and credits Zoloft, therapy, and a "strong support system" for her recovery (Gardner 2007, 544). Tasha Dubriwny's book length treatment of "the vulnerable empowered woman" offers a sustained critique of the media framing and public rhetoric that creates a neoliberal, postfeminist woman who monitors her own risks and buys the right products to care for herself (2013).

The feminist ideal of women as self-empowered caretakers of their own health and as experts in knowing and defining health has given way to a form of *women-centered healthism* that shares some features with feminism, but lacks its structural critique and politicized edge. *Healthism* is the critical term for health as an ideology of private self-betterment, often pursued through holistic and alternative approaches to traditional medicine but nonetheless individualized and commercialized (Crawford 1980). There is much *about* women in the new healthism, and many women are involved with it. Nonfeminist political and social theorists are also devoting attention to the contemporary pressures to care for and produce ourselves as responsible, healthy citizens (Rose 1999). These new operations of power in health are gendered and racialized and work through the repetition of gendered practices and habits—as such, they stand in need of sustained feminist investigation.

Conclusion

Feminist theorizing and activism about health have produced some of the most popular and searing accounts of the politicized body. As the influence of health in contemporary life grows, the accounts and critiques of health presented by feminist scholars and activists become increasingly valuable. Unfortunately, although some academic disciplines have been influenced by these feminist insights, they have not been broadly adopted in all fields and certainly do not figure prominently in health education. Although "women's health" is a highly visible political tagline, contemporary debates rarely question definitions of health, the power (and potential negative effects) of health discourses, or the role structural inequalities play in shaping health outcomes and experiences in health systems. In addition, although feminist activists produced some of the most discerning analyses of women's health decades ago, much of the contemporary women's health activism is no longer linked to the feminist movement, and may even explicitly disavow it. Feminist theoretical and activist interventions in relation to health are being eroded and undermined.

An exception to this trend seems to be feminist disability theory, which has enjoyed recent vitality in the spaces where feminist bioethics seems to have receded. Yet, mainstream women's health curricula tend not to focus on disability. Greater attention to feminist disability theory could help integrate some of the greatest insights of feminist activists and scholars into the mainstream discussion of women's health. These insights include politicizing the body, questioning notions of health, and drawing attention to the structural factors shaping health outcomes. Some of the most promising work on the politics of health is coming from the intersections of disciplines, including Miriam Ticktin's study of health and gendered humanitarianism under conditions of colonialism and race discrimination, Dorothy Roberts's work in bioethics and critical race theory, and Tasha Dubriwny's work in feminist thought and rhetorical studies of contemporary discourses of health. Thus, it seems that feminist theories of health would do well to lean on what has consistently been the foundation of feminist theory more generally: interdisciplinary encounters with sites of power and gendered, raced, classed bodies, where feminism does not mean simply amplifying whatever women want in health, but rather interrogating the social production of medicalized health desires and needs.

Suggestions for Further Reading

Dubriwny, Tasha N. *The Vulnerable Empowered Woman: Feminism, Postfeminism, and Women's Health*. New Brunswick, NJ: Rutgers University Press, 2013.
Inhorn, Marcia C. "Defining Women's Health: A Dozen Messages from More Than 150 Ethnographies." *Medical Anthropology Quarterly* 20, no. 3 (2006): 345–378.
Moore, Sarah E. H. "Is the Healthy Body Gendered? Toward a Feminist Critique of the New Paradigm of Health." *Body & Society* 16, no. 2 (2010): 95–118.
Morgen, Sandra. *Into Our Own Hands: The Women's Health Movement in the United States, 1969–1990*. New Brunswick, NJ: Rutgers University Press, 2002.
Nelson, Jennifer. *Women of Color and the Reproductive Rights Movement*. New York: New York University Press, 2003.
Roberts, Dorothy. *Fatal Invention: How Science, Politics, and Big Business Re-create Race in the Twenty-First Century*. New York: New Press, 2011.
Scully, Jackie Leach, Laurel E. Baldwin-Ragaven, and Petya Fitzpatrick, eds. *Feminist Bioethics: At the Center, on the Margins*. Baltimore, MD: Johns Hopkins University Press, 2010.
Seaman, Barbara, and Laura Eldridge, eds. *Voices of the Women's Health Movement*. 2 vols. New York: Seven Stories Press, 2012.
Ticktin, Miriam. *Casualties of Care: Immigration and the Politics of Humanitarianism in France*. Berkeley: University of California Press, 2011.
Wendell, Susan. *The Rejected Body: Feminist Philosophical Reflections on Disability*. New York: Routledge, 2013.

References

Asch, Adrienne, and Gail Geller. 1996. "Feminism, Bioethics and Genetics." In *Feminism and Bioethics: Beyond Reproduction*, edited by Susan M. Wolf, 318–350. New York: Oxford Univeristy Press.

Asian Communities for Reproductive Justice. "A New Vision for Advancing Our Movement for Reproductive Health, Reproductive Rights and Reproductive Justice." 2005. Accessible at http://strongfamiliesmovement.org/assets/docs/ACRJ-A-New-Vision.pdf.

Atzema, Clare L., Peter C. Austin, Thao Huynh, Ansar Hassan, Maria Chiu, Julie T. Wang, and Jack V. Tu. 2011. "Effect of Marriage on Duration of Chest Pain Associated with Acute Myocardial Infarction before Seeking Care." *Canadian Medical Association Journal* 183 (6): 663–669.

Baird, Karen L., Dana-Ain Davis, and Kimberly Christensen. 2009. *Beyond Reproduction: Women's Health Activism, and Public Policy*. Madison, NJ: Fairleigh Dickinson University Press.

Barbee, Evelyn L., and Marilyn Little. 1993. "Health, Social Class and African-American Women." In *Theorizing Black Feminisms: The Visionary Pragmatism of Black Women*, edited by Stanlie M. James and Abena P.A. Busia. Hoboken, NJ: Taylor & Francis.

Beal, Margaret W. 1998. "Women's Use of Complementary and Alternative Therapies in Reproductive Health Care." *Journal of Nurse-Midwifery* 43 (4): 224–234.

Bonilla, Zobeida E. 2005. "Including Every Woman: The All-Embracing 'We' of *Our Bodies, Ourselves*." *National Women's Studies Association Journal* 17 (1): 175–183.

Boston Women's Health Book Collective. 1970. "Women and Their Bodies: A Course." Boston, MA: Boston Women's Health Book Collective. http://www.ourbodiesourselves.org/uploads/pdf/OBOS1970.pdf.

Boston Women's Health Book Collective. 1971. *Our Bodies, Ourselves: A Book by and for Women*. New York: Simon and Schuster.

Boston Women's Health Book Collective. 1998. *Our Bodies, Ourselves for the New Century*. New York: Touchstone.

Bradby, Hannah. 2012. *Medicine, Health and Society*. London: Sage Publications.

Buchanan, Allen E. 1984. "The Right to a Decent Minimum of Health Care." *Philosophy and Public Affairs* 13 (1): 55–78.

Burgess, Diana Jill, Megan Crowley-Matoka, Sean Phelan, John F. Dovidio, Robert Kerns, Craig Roth, Saha Somnath, and Michelle van Ryn. 2008. "Patient Race and Physicians' Decisions to Prescribe Opoids for Chronic Low Back Pain." *Social Science and Medicine* 67 (11): 1852–1860.

Council on Ethical and Judicial Affairs, American Medical Association. 1991. "Gender Disparities in Clinical Decision Making." *Journal of the American Medical Association* 266 (4): 559–562.

Courtenay, Will H. 2000. "Constructions of Masculinity and Their Influence On Men's Well-Being: A Theory of Gender and Health." *Social Science and Medicine* 50: 1385–1401.

Courtenay, Will H. 2003. "Key Determinants of the Health and Well-Being of Men and Boys." *International Journal of Men's Health* 2 (1): 1–30.

Crawford, Robert. 1980. "Healthism and the Medicalization of Everyday Life." *International Journal of Health Services* 10 (3): 365–388.

Daniels, Norman. 1984. "The Right to a Decent Minimum of Health Care." *Philosophy and Public Affairs* 13 (1): 55–78.

Daniels, Norman. 1985. *Just Health Care*. New York: Cambridge University Press.

Davis, Kathy. 2002. "Translating *Our Bodies, Ourselves*." *European Journal of Women's Studies* 9 (3): 223–247.

Dubriwny, Tasha N. 2013. *The Vulnerable Empowered Woman: Feminism, Postfeminism, and Women's Health*. New Brunswick, NJ: Rutgers University Press.

Engelhardt, Tristram H., Jr., and Michael A. Rie. 1986. "Intensive Care Units, Scarce Resources, and Conflicting Principles of Justice." *Journal of the American Medical Association* 255 (9): 1159–1164.

Epstein, Steven. 2007. *Inclusion: The Politics of Difference in Medical Research*. Chicago: University of Chicago Press.

Fine, Michelle, and Adrienne Asch. 1988. *Women with Disabilities: Essays in Psychology, Culture, and Politics*. Philadelphia, PA: Temple University Press.

Finger, Anne. 1983. "Disability and Reproductive Rights." *Off Our Backs* 13 (9): 18–19.

Fried, Charles. 1976. "Equality and Rights in Medical Care." *Hasting Center Report* 6 (1): 29–34.

Gardner, Paula. 2007. "Re-gendering Depression: Risk, Web Health Campaigns, and the Feminized Pharmaco-Subject." *Canadian Journal of Communication* 32 (3): 537–555.

Garland-Thomson, Rosemarie. 2005. "Feminist Disability Studies." *Signs* 30 (2): 1557–1587.

Hadorn, David C. 1992. "The Problem of Discrimination in Health Care Priority Setting." *Journal of the American Medical Association* 268 (11): 1454–1459.

Healy, Bernadine. 1991. "The Yentl Syndrome." *New England Journal of Medicine* 325 (4): 274–276.

Inhorn, Marcia C. 2006. "Defining Women's Health: A Dozen Messages from More Than 150 Ethnographies." *Medical Anthropology Quarterly* 20 (3): 345–378.

Jones, Gary E. 1983. "The Right to Health Care and the State." *Philosophical Quarterly* 33 (132): 279–287.

Ketenjian, Tania. 2012a. "Helen Rodriguez-Trias." In *Voices of the Women's Health Movement*, edited by Barbara Seaman and Laura Eldridge, 90–96. New York: Seven Stories Press.

Ketenjian, Tania. 2012b. "Taking Our Bodies Back." In *Voices of the Women's Health Movement*, edited by Barbara Seaman and Laura Eldridge. New York: Seven Stories Press.

Krieger, James W., Lin Song, Timothy K. Takaro, and James Stout. 2000. "Asthma and the Home Environment of Low-Income Urban Children: Preliminary Findings from the Seattle–King County Healthy Homes Project." *Journal of Urban Health* 77 (1): 50–67.

Kronenberg, F., J. O. Leary Cobb, D. McMahon, S. Workman, L. Cushman, C. Wade, and P. Factor. 1997. "Women and Alternative Medicine: Patterns of Use Nationally and by African-American, Hispanic and Caucasian Women." *Menopause* 4 (4): 239.

Kuhlmann, Ellen, and Birgit Babitsch. 2002. "Bodies, Health, Gender: Bridging Feminist Theories and Women's Health." *Women's Studies International Forum* 25: 433–442.

Menzel, Paul T. 2003. "How Compatible Are Liberty and Equality in Structuring a Health Care System?" *Journal of Medicine and Philosophy* 28 (3): 281–306.

Metzl, Jonathan M., and Anna Kirkland. 2010. *Against Health: How Health Became the New Morality*. New York: New York University Press.

Moore, Sarah E. H. 2010. "Is the Healthy Body Gendered? Toward a Feminist Critique of the New Paradigm of Health." *Body & Society* 16 (2): 95–118.

Morgen, Sandra. 2002. *Into Our Own Hands: The Women's Health Movement in the United States, 1969–1990*. New Brunswick, NJ: Rutgers University Press.

Murphy, Michelle. *Seizing the Means of Reproduction: Entanglements of Feminism, Health, and Technoscience*. Duke University Press, 2012.

Murray-Law, Bridget. 2011. "Why Do Men Die Earlier?" *Monitor on Psychology* 42 (6): 58–63.

Nelson, Jennifer. 2003. *Women of Color and the Reproductive Rights Movement*. New York: New York University Press.

Norsigian, J., Diskin, V., Doress-Worters, P., Pincus, J., Sanford, W., & Swenson, N. 1999. The Boston women's health book collective and our bodies, ourselves: A brief history and reflection. *Journal of the American Medical Womens' Association*, 54, 35–39.

Owens, Gary M. 2008. "Gender differences in health care expenditures, resource utilization, and quality of care" *Journal of Managed Care Pharmacy* 14.3: S2.

Parker-Pope, Tara. 2011. "The Nagging Effect: Better Health for Married Men." In *Well: The New York Times*.

Price, Kimala. 2010. "What Is Reproductive Justice? How Women of Color Activists Are Redefining the Pro-Choice Paradigm." *Meridians* 10 (2): 42–65.

Roberts, Dorothy E. 1996. "Reconstructing the Patient: Starting with Women of Color." In *Feminism in Bioethics*, edited by Susan M. Wolf, 116–143. New York: Oxford University Press.

Roberts, Dorothy. 1997. *Killing the Black Body: Race, Reproduction, and the Meaning of Liberty*. New York: Pantheon.

Roberts, Dorothy. 2001. *Shattered Bonds: The Color of Child Welfare*. New York: Basic Books/Civitas.

Roberts, Dorothy. 2009. "Race, Gender, and Genetic Technologies: A New Reproductive Dystopia?" *Signs: Journal of Women in Culture and Society* 34 (4): 783–804.

Roberts, Dorothy. 2011. *Fatal Invention: How Science, Politics, and Big Business Re-create Race in the Twenty-First Century*. New York: New Press.

Rose, Nikolas. 1999. *Powers of Freedom: Reframing Political Thought*. New York: Cambridge University Press.

Russell, Louise B., Marthe R. Gold, Joanna E. Siegel, Norman Daniels, and Milton C. Weinstein. 1996. "The Role of Cost-Effectiveness Analysis in Health and Medicine." *Journal of the American Medical Association* 276 (14): 1172–1177.

Ruzek, Sheryl Burt. *The women's health movement: Feminist alternatives to medical control*. New York: Praeger, 1978.

Scott, Rebecca Lovell. 1999. "Review Essay: Women's Health." *National Women's Studies Association Journal* 11 (1): 185–192.

Scully, Jackie Leach, Laurel E. Baldwin-Ragaven, and Petya Fitzpatrick. 2010. *Feminist Bioethics: At the Center, on the Margins*. Baltimore, MD: Johns Hopkins University Press.

Sherwin, Susan. 1996. "Feminism and Bioethics." In *Feminism and Bioethics: Beyond Reproducion*, edited by Susan M. Wolf, 47–66. New York: Oxford University Press.

Smith, Andrea. 2005. "Beyond Pro-Choice versus Pro-Life: Women of Color and Reproductive Justice." *National Women's Studies Association Journal* 17 (1): 119–140.

Springer, Kristen W., and Dawne M. Mouzon. 2011. "'Macho Men' and Preventative Health Care: Implications for Older Men in Different Social Classes." *American Sociological Association* 52 (2): 212–227.

Starfield, Barbara, Leiyu Shi, and James Macinko. 2005. "Contribution of Primary Care to Health Systems and Health." *Milbank Quarterly* 83 (3): 457–502.

Ticktin, Miriam. 2008. "Sexual Violence as the Langauge of Border Control: Where French Feminist and Anti-Immigrant Rhetoric Meet." *Signs* 33 (4): 863–889.

Twine, Richard. 2010. "Broadening the Feminism in Feminist Bioethics." In *Feminist Bioethics: At the Center, on the Margins*, edited by Jackie Leach Scully, Laurel E. Baldwin-Ragaven, and Petya Fitzpatrick, 45–59. Baltimore, MD: Johns Hopkins University Press.

Wendell, Susan. 1989. "Toward a Feminist Theory of Disability." *Hypatia* 4 (2): 102–124.

CHAPTER 17

IDENTITIES

NADINE EHLERS

My recommendation is not to solve this crisis of identity, but to proliferate and intensify the crisis.
   —Judith Butler, "The Force of Fantasy: Feminism, Mapplethorpe, and Discursive Excess"

Feminism is not self-identical, which means that her temporal order is not teleological; her subjectivity is irreducible to the political emplottment of either mine or yours.
   —Robyn Wiegman, "Feminism's Apocalyptic Futures"

THE question and problematic of identity have been integral to feminist inquiry, theorizations, and activism. Yet, in the new millennium, feminist theory might be said to have traveled toward post-identitarian models of inquiry—where the focus is explicitly *not* on identity and the politics in which identity is bound up but, rather, on thinking about somatic life, affect, time, space, and materiality as organizing principles or concepts. For example, the field of feminist new materialism turns matter/the material into a theoretical object. Feminist theorists, such as Elizabeth Grosz (2004), Karen Barad (2007), Rosi Braidotti (2002, 2007), and Vicky Kirby (1997, 2008), among others, have, in what has been named the material turn, called for a more positive feminist engagement with biology and materiality. In doing this, they consider how matter, rather than simply being *formed through* the workings of language, culture, power, and discourse, has agency and is *formative*. According to Samantha Frost, new materialism as a theoretical paradigm asks feminist thinkers to include in their analyses an acknowledgement of the "forces, processes, capacities, and resiliencies with which bodies, organisms, and material objects act both independently of and in response to discursive provocations and constraints" (2011, 70). In thinking through such ideas, feminist new materialists question the distinction between nature and culture, explore the intra-actions between the body, the self, and the world, and ask how matter contributes to the workings of power. For Grosz, discussions such as these are imperative, precisely because "all theorists interested in the relations between subjectivity, politics, and culture, need to have a more nuanced, intricate account of the body's immersion and participation in the world if they are to develop political strategies to transform the existing regulation of bodies" (Grosz 2004, 2). In short, the concerns of materialist inquiry are at odds with the previous focus of feminist inquiry on the cultural realm and categories of identification.

Postmillennial feminist theories, as might be imagined, raise an interesting set of provocations and complications, particularly as they pertain to the question of identity in feminism. Given that feminist theory and activism has been centrally concerned with the politics of identity, we might ask where feminist discussions of identity would go from here—in the wake of postmillennial modes of inquiry—when identity seems to have all but disappeared as an area of concern. To begin asking such questions, however, it is necessary to first trace how identity has been conceptualized and theorized in various forms of feminist thought—to appreciate the complex ways identity has been framed, understood, and contested in the feminist past and present. Although there is infinite complexity and heterogeneity in the feminist work on identity, in what follows I mark out several strands of thought. My tracing is broadly a historiography—a particular writing of feminist histories of thinking about identity. However, the ways feminism has thought about identity—particularly, the identity of women—do not fit into a neat linear narrative. As Judith Butler notes in the quote with which I open above, there is a crisis of identity, and this is never more clear than when we recognize the competing theories of identity within feminist work. Despite this, stories generally have to follow some form of logic, and while I offer an incomplete map of some of the theories of identity within feminism, I am at the same time conscious of Robyn Wiegman's warning that feminisms' "temporal order is not teleological" and that any emplottment is problematic (2000, 809). Clare Hemmings (2005, 118) goes further, to argue that any attempt to "get the story straight" would be—using the words of Gayatri Spivak—an act of "epistemic violence." Thus, in my telling of how feminism has thought about identity, it is important to note that there is no clear trajectory; there are competing theories within—and links across—each of the broad time periods and rubrics of thought I trace out, and that all feminist theories of identity are themselves marked by contradictory possibilities and imaginings for/of the self.

With such caveats in mind, the term *identity* is usually used within feminism to refer to a woman's conscious sense of herself—a sense of who she is (Weedon 2003, 112). In a broader social understanding, the term refers to the "fact" of being who or what a person is. As Susan Hekman (1999, 5) notes, "To declare that something or someone has a particular identity is to claim, simultaneously, that it is identical to other entities that possess that identity and that, as a particular thing, it possesses unique qualities, that is, an identity." It is precisely this idea—that those who are claimed by and who claim the identity woman are identical to other women and that women possess some unique qualities that identify them *as* women and separate them from men—that has been the focal point of feminist inquiry and a subject of fierce debate.

During eighteenth- and nineteenth-century first-wave feminism, the central question was whether or not women's identity was the same as or different from men's.

Many early liberal feminists argued that women were, indeed, essentially the same as men, that men and women shared a common human identity, and that this, in turn, required that women be granted the same social rights as men. They relied on the Western humanist supposition that the body and mind are distinct and that the body is a superficial rather than constitutive element of the self: bodily features are contingent characteristics of the self, they argued, whereas the mind merits more attention and is superior to the body. If, as many early feminists insisted, consciousness and the capacity for reason were located in the mind, and following François Poulain de la Barre's famous 1670 declaration that "the mind has no sex," then women's bodies—their sexual difference—should not be used as justification for denying their full participation in the social sphere and access to equal rights. For example, Mary Astell's *A Serious Proposal to the Ladies* (1694), Mary Wollstonecraft's *A Vindication of the Rights of Woman* (1792), and Harriet Taylor Mill's "The Enfranchisement of Women" (1851) sought to break any supposed deterministic link between corporeal characteristics, mental capacities, and social role: any particularity of women's gender identity should not eclipse their human identity, which was seen as commensurable with men's owing to the shared possession of reason. However, at the same time that many women were fighting to have their identities seen as equal to men's and inconsequential to social life, other women, particularly in the United States, fought to highlight the contradictions and assumptions (political, economic, cultural) inherent in the use and meaning of the term *woman*. This questioning is perhaps most clearly evidenced through Sojourner Truth's (1797–1883) challenging lament that noted certain women's relegation outside dominant understandings of female identity and presaged what would come to be the fundamental question of Western feminism: what, exactly, is a woman?: "I have ploughed, and planted and gathered into barns, and no man could head me!" And ain't I a woman?" Women abolitionists highlighted the interrelatedness of gendered and racial oppression and exclusion based on supposed corporeal truth: for instance, Elizabeth Cady Stanton argued that "the prejudice against color, of which we hear so much, is no stronger than that against sex. It is produced by the same cause, and manifested very much in the same way. The negro's skin and the woman's sex are both *prima facie* evidence that they were intended to be in subjection to the white Saxon man" (Stanton [1860] 1881, 681). Regardless of differences between forms of feminist thinking during this time, first-wave feminism largely argued that women and men are in essence identical and rallied against the subordination of women's identity to men's.

The theorization of women's subordination to men was perhaps most clearly articulated in Simone de Beauvoir's *The Second Sex*, which explored the notion of women's radical otherness. For Beauvoir, "She is defined and differentiated with reference to man and not he with reference to her; she is incidental, the inessential as opposed to the essential. He is the Subject, he is the Absolute—she is the Other" (1972, 16). Gender and female identity were not, however, to be seen as the expression of biological sex according to Beauvoir, but, rather, as constructed within a particular cultural framework. Famously, she insisted:

> One is not born, but rather becomes a woman. No biological, psychological or economic fate determines the figure that the human female presents in society; it is civilization as a whole that produces this creation, intermediate between male and eunuch who is described as feminine.
>
> (1972, 295)

In making such an argument, Beauvoir posited an early social constructionist view of gendered identity and, critically, uncoupled biological sex from the creation of gendered identity: identities that we define as feminine are seen purely as the product of history and culture rather than an essence or natural propensity.[1] The ultimate aim of *The Second Sex* was to show the artificiality of female identity in order that it might be rejected. In doing so, this work foreshadowed debates regarding female identity that persisted through the twentieth century and provided a vocabulary for analyzing the social constructions of femininity and a structure for critiquing those very constructions.

While feminist activism and scholarship during the eighteenth century and into the mid-nineteenth century emphasized the ultimate similarity and equality of men and women, in the late 1960s, feminists began pushing beyond the early quest for political rights and took on the issue of women's identity as a self-conscious feminist concern. Discussions within feminist work from the late 1960s to the late 1980s—in what has become known as second-wave feminism—generally revolved around two central questions: is identity (femaleness and femininity) an essential, fixed characteristic of women, located in the body, experience, or the psyche?; or is it historically and culturally specific and socially formed?

Liberal feminists during this time largely followed earlier feminist views, downplaying issues of identity to instead focus on achieving formal equality between men and women. They renewed the struggle for equal rights and the removal of barriers to recognition in the workforce, the family, and before the law. Like their liberal feminist predecessors, they were guided by the claim that all individuals are rational and governed by free will, and that reason, because it is universal, transcends gender. Women had been confined, however, to the identity of mother and housewife (a view that would be subsequently contested by feminists of color), behind what Betty Friedan in *The Feminine Mystique* called "the doors of all those pretty suburban houses" ([1963] 1983, 200). Only women's full participation in the public arena, politics, and the economy would enable their social status to become equal to men's, and the only way to achieve this would be to refuse to identify with the disempowering roles of wife and mother that they were socialized to assume. Ultimately, then, as Hekman has argued, liberal feminists limited their attention to women's political identity and attempted "to fit women into the universal category of 'citizen'" (Hekman 2000, 290). As a consequence, many critics have charged liberal feminism with maintaining a normative (and humanist) mind/body dualism—in which the mind is privileged over and to the exclusion of the body—and shown, as Alison Jaggar does in *Feminist Politics and Human Nature* (1983), that "the rational, free, and autonomous self that liberals favor is not neutral between the sexes. On the contrary, it is a 'male' self" (Tong 2008, 37). Moreover, in focusing on white, middle-class, heterosexual women, liberal feminism largely universalized women's identity, advancing the idea that there is such an entity as the homogenous woman, who shares the same concerns and experiences as all other women. It was on the basis these criticisms, then, that alternative theories of identity were formulated in other second-wave approaches.

For socialist feminists, class was the defining feature of patriarchal oppression. In the early second wave, many socialist feminists continued to be influenced by the work of Marx and saw women as a "class" that was subjugated by and to capitalist patriarchy.[2] Identity was not their main focus, except insofar as they saw women's identity as being marked by *false consciousness*—a term Friedrich Engels used to characterize the way the working class is compelled, through ideology, to formulate mental representations of the social relations around them in ways that systematically conceal or obscure the realities of subordination, exploitation, and domination that those relations embody. The key for feminists following this tradition of thought was to show how ideological assumptions about women's role in society (often marked by unpaid and unacknowledged domestic labor) were reproduced through written and visual media, to attack subordination as a product of inequalities caused by capitalism, and revolutionize women's consciousness. By the 1970s, however, socialist feminists had turned to other theorists to understand the status and identity of women. The work of Louis Althusser was particularly appealing, specifically his 'On Ideology and Ideological State Apparatuses: Notes Towards and Investigation' (1971), which argued that sets of institutions—religion, the family, culture, the media—produce and reproduce social states of knowledge and, indeed, social subjects. For Althusser, ideological state apparatuses function through ideology, which *interpellates* (or calls into being) and *produces* individuals who understand themselves as possessing a particular identity. Socialist feminists added the dimension of gender to that of class to critically consider how all social texts, practices, and institutions played a role in calling women into being, in ways that make them useful to the capitalist mode of production. Feminist critics, however, charged theory rooted in the Marxist tradition with phallocentrism, because it posits a universal representation of humanity that is actually masculine. For Mia Campioni and Elizabeth Grosz (1991, 367), "This phallocentrism is not eradicated or removed simply by admitting to charges of 'sex-blindness,' by adding women's oppression to a whole set of other oppressions.... Rather... it entails 'seeing women first.'"

Radical feminism more squarely addressed "women first" and, thus, provided alternative theorizations of gendered identity. What set this form of feminism apart from liberal and socialist/Marxist feminisms was the conviction that (a) women's oppression was seen as the most primary and fundamental form of oppression, (b) this oppression marked out shared global determinants of women's lives, and (c) women should not be seen as the same as men. Instead, their identities should be understood as fundamentally different, and the political goal should be liberation (that is, radical social change) from patriarchal control. The shared determining factors of women's lives created what radical feminists saw as a common sisterhood bound by a common female identity: women were united by their commonalities, which primarily stemmed from the appropriation of women's bodies within patriarchy (whether for labor, reproduction or other uses, or in terms of sexuality). As such, the body was seen as integral to both women's oppression and their shared identity. For Shulamith Firestone, for instance, this was both because of the patriarchal appropriation of female bodies and because women were inescapably tied to biology, particularly prior to the advent of birth control: "menstruation, menopause, 'female ills,' constant painful childbirth, wetnursing and care of infants all of which made them dependent on men for survival" ([1970] 1981, 8). Rather than aiming to become like men, the end goal of radical feminism, according to Firestone, should be the elimination of sex distinction (and the gendered identities built on sexual difference) and the pursuit of androgynous identities.

The tendency within much radical feminist work toward essentializing a female nature and identity was consolidated by an influential strand of thought, subsequently designated by scholars as "cultural feminism" (Alcoff 2006, 137). For Mary Daly, a key cultural feminist, essential femaleness was located in women's capacity for motherhood, in their sexuality, and in their daily experience of victimization through patriarchal power (Weedon 2003, 116). For Adrienne Rich, another proponent of cultural feminism, the essential identity of women was to be found in the "female consciousness" (1979, 18) that, she argued, is largely located in the female body. However, while the female body has been used to constrain and delimit women's identity, Rich claimed it could be reappropriated by feminists—revalidated and used as the vehicle to liberate women. According to Rich, despite the fact that "patriarchal thought has limited female biology to its own narrow specifications," feminists "will come to view our physicality as a resource rather than a destiny. We must touch the unity and resonance of our physicality, our bond with the natural order, the corporeal ground of our intelligence" (1977, 121). In "Compulsory Heterosexuality and Lesbian Existence" (1984), Rich argued that a key way to reclaim women's identities was through embracing a lesbian orientation. Rather than confine lesbianism to sexual practice, Rich argued that women—if freed from patriarchal control—were naturally "woman-identified," existing on what she called a "lesbian continuum." In her understanding, lesbianism had been limited within patriarchal knowledge systems to a clinical definition and should instead include female friendship—a recognition that would initiate the possibility of what she called "a female erotic." Importantly, however, theory and poetry written by feminists of color problematized and ultimately rejected the universalizing tendencies found in cultural feminism. These feminists insisted that focusing on a binary opposition between men and women was too simplistic and that the category and identity of "woman" was internally divided: differences among women based on race needed to be specifically addressed—differences that would, in turn, lead to alternative understandings of identity (a point that I return to later).

Another key development in feminist theorizing of identity during the 1970s and 1980s was the turn to psychoanalysis. Feminists were attracted to psychoanalysis because, as a theoretical paradigm, it rejected biological determinism. Freud, for instance, argues that gender is a result of psycho-sexual development rather than being innate, and is precarious because it is based on repression. Freud's theory was clearly patriarchal, as he took the male body as the norm and saw the female body and feminine identity and sexuality as governed by lack and penis envy (based on this lack). Feminists, however, attempted to reread Freud through re-interpreting the meaning and centrality of the penis. For example, Juliet Mitchell's *Psychoanalysis and Feminism* (1975) repositioned the penis as a *symbol* of masculine power within patriarchal systems.

An influential branch of feminist psychoanalysis was Anglo-American feminist object relations theory, represented by the work of Nancy Chodorow (1978), Jane Flax (1980), Dorothy Dinnerstein (1976), and Jessica Benjamin (1988), among others. This area of scholarship sought to explain how gendered identity was inscribed in the psyche as a consequence of the emotional relationship between parents and children. Chodorow (1978), in her classic *The Reproduction of Mothering: Psychoanalysis and the Sociology of Gender*, draws on the earlier work of Melanie Klein and neo-Freudian theorists, such as D. W. Winnicot, to argue that women's primary role as the caretaker of infants and young children is key to the development of gendered identity. She assumes the identification of girls with the mother, which enables her to argue that girl children develop a stronger bond with the mother, the result of which is that they become less individuated and have more flexible ego boundaries. This, in turn, creates the psychical preconditions that enable girls and women to become subordinate to men. Boys, on the other hand, are socialized by the mother to differentiate, and to develop a masculine identity based on the father, according to Chodorow. But, because of the father's absence (based on his conventional role as breadwinner) and boys' separation from the mother, boys develop an identity that is independent and autonomous, one that represses feminine dimensions of identity, so that boy children learn to devalue women and femininity. Chodorow posited, however, that because this process was social, altered conditions—such as greater involvement from the father—could transform gender norms, the sexual division of labor, and, theoretically, the contours of gendered identity. For Benjamin, masculine identity is also formed through a disavowal of femininity, but she focused on the relationship of domination and subordination that leads to a "breakdown of the necessary tension between self-assertion and mutual recognition that allows self and other to meet as sovereign equals" (1988, 12). Relations of domination and subordination are prevalent, she argues, because of heterosexual gender complementarity (which is based on notions of gendered identity difference), and subjects become bound by love to oppressive social relations. These relations will not be transformed through changing caretaking roles, however, according to Benjamin. Instead, it requires attention to social roles and "cultural representations" (Benjamin 1988, 217), since "the core feature of the gender system—promoting masculinity as separation from and femininity as continuity with the primary bond—is maintained even when mother and father participate equally in that bond" (Benjamin 1988, 217).[3]

Despite the fact that liberal, socialist, radical, and psychoanalytic feminisms were marked by tensions over the category and identity woman, for women of color each of these versions of feminism shared a common failure to adequately account for *difference*. The seminal collection of US black feminist thought compiled by Gloria T. Hull,

Patricia Bell Scott, and Barbara Smith (1982) highlighted in its very title—*All the Women Are White, All the Blacks Are Men, But Some of Us Are Brave*—that mainstream feminism had persistently focused on one oppressed identity (woman) as a means for unification, obfuscating other forms of oppression. For black feminists in the United States, the supposed shared common identity woman was inherently problematic precisely because it obscured the internal subdivisions within that very category and, as bell hooks argues, "ignored the complexity of women's experience" (1981, 190).

Two clear arguments pertaining to identity emerge through the work of black feminism. First, black feminists have insisted that identity is *multifaceted*. By this I mean that they showed that one is never simply a woman but, rather, that one's sense of self—and the experience of everyday life—is always marked and conditioned by other categories of identity, such as race, class, and sexuality. Black feminists labored specifically, however, to foreground how race and institutionalized racism leads to particularities in black women's experience, and they demanded that these particularities be recognized as structuring features of identity for black women: as Pearl Cleage (quoted in Collins 1990, 22) has stated, black women "are a unique group, set undeniably apart because of race and sex with a unique set of challenges."[4] Second, black feminists argued that identity is *intersectional*, a term critical race legal theorist Kimberlé Crenshaw used to describe "the various ways in which race and gender interact to shape the multiple dimensions of Black women's experiences" (1991, 1244). Identity and oppression are not simply multifaceted in such an understanding. Instead, mutually reinforcing axes of race, gender, class, and sexuality form identity simultaneously (and in inextricable ways), and oppression also works in an intersectional sense to constitute what Patricia Hill Collins (1990) refers to as a "matrix of domination." For the authors of the Combahee River Collective's "A Black Feminist Statement" ([1977] 1995), such an understanding has historically been integral to black feminist thought, for, as they insist, "There have always been black women activists—some known, like Sojourner Truth, Harriet Tubman, Frances E.W. Harper, Ida B. Wells-Barnett, and Mary Church Terrell, and thousands upon thousands unknown—who had a shared awareness of how their sexual identity combined with their racial identity to make their whole life situation and the focus of their political struggles unique" (Combahee River Collective 1995, 233).

Chicana and Latina feminists in the United States—such as Gloria Anzaldúa (1987), Ana Castillo (1994), Norma Alarcón (1995), and Cherríe Moraga (1995), among others—lent further complexity to feminist theories of multifaceted and intersectional identities by foregrounding the dilemmas of mestiza and borderland subjects. In *Borderlands/La Frontera: The New Mestiza* (1987), Anzaldúa introduced the term *mestizaje* to refer to the state of existing in an identity beyond the binary (of either-or)—where one straddles multiple cultures, forms of oppressions, and understandings of self: the mestiza, Anzaldúa argues, experiences "mental and emotional states of perplexity . . . [and] undergoes a struggle of the flesh, a struggle of borders, an inner war" (1987, 77–78). She called for a "new mestiza," which she described as an individual who is aware of their conflicting—yet meshing—identities, who embraces this conflict, and who uses the "new angles of vision" that come with this awareness to challenge binary thinking in Western knowledge systems.[5]

Across the Atlantic, black British feminists problematized the very category "black" by highlighting the complexities of black female disaporic identities in a context where black—as a descriptor—is used as an identity category to refer to individuals from diverse ethnic and racial groups. For black feminists in Britain, a key focus in the theorizing of identity has been to map out the ways that nationalism and national identity in Britain has consistently been associated with whiteness / white identity, to the exclusion of black subjects, and many black British feminists explore how a self-conscious black identity evolves among women who come from very different historical, economic, and geographical backgrounds. As Heidi Safia Mirza has noted, "Life histories as diverse as African-Caribbean, Iraqi-Kurd, black South African and African-Indian Kenyan reveal the organic, complex interweaving of past-present experience in the recovery of diasporic subjectivity" (1997, 16). In Australia, black feminists, such as Aileen Morton-Robinson, Roberta Sykes, Jackie Huggins, and Melissa Lucashenko, have analyzed the construction of black women's identities in the context of settler society. For Lucashenko, "What you call patriarchy, I call one aspect of colonisation: for all their commonalities, for all your hoping and wishing it, our oppressors are not interchangeable" (1994, 22). Additionally, Australian black feminists have shown that, while the Western way of conceiving identity insists that gender should be a primary defining feature, Indigenous women have often privileged nongendered markers of self-identification, such as cousin, keeper of secrets, or elder.

Together, then, women of color feminisms have challenged the essentialism, ethnocentrism, and ahistoricism found within segments of feminist theory and shown, as hooks notes, that "race and class identity create differences in quality of life, social status and lifestyle that take precedence over the common experience women share—differences that are rarely transcended" (1984, 4). Indeed, women of color have highlighted the inadequacy of the identity category woman and worked toward "changing the calculus of who was and who was not included" (Wiegman 2012, 63).

Many of the concerns pertaining to identity that have been raised by women of color in the United States, the United Kingdom, and Australia have been reiterated by "Third World" and postcolonial feminists. Third World feminism, for instance, asserts the *difference* of the identities of Third World women from dominant Western feminist viewpoints of these women—which have increasingly controlled how Third World women are represented.[6] Theorists such as Chandra Talpade Mohanty (1991b), Uma Narayan (1997), and Minoo Moallem (2006) have charged Western feminists with both feminist imperialism and discursive colonization, claiming that they have constructed a singular composite identity for Third World women and defined them as passive victims of an ahistorical and monolithic patriarchy. This discursive colonization, Third World feminists argue, homogenizes the identities of Third World women, measures them against Western norms, values, and customs, and strips them of any agency. For Mohanty, however, "The crucial point that is forgotten is that women are produced through these very relations [their complex lived situations] as well as being implicated in forming these relations" (1991, 59). Gayatri Spivak, perhaps one of the most prominent postcolonial feminist theorists, takes a deconstructive approach to the question of postcolonial identity.[7] For Spivak, postcolonial subjects have historically had their identities marked by what she calls "radical alterity," in that they have been defined as Other and relegated to the margins of Western society and knowledge systems. She argues that it is imperative to deconstruct the imperial logic and essentializing operations that regulate the lives of postcolonial subjects but that, in a double-bind situation, it may simultaneously be necessary for postcolonial subjects to adopt what she calls "strategic essentialism." Spivak uses this term to describe the ways marginalized groups may need to use essentialism—that is, the flattening of differences in identification—as a short-term tactic to forge a sense of collective political identity in order to secure certain political ends. She cautions, however, that such strategic essentialism should work against fixing (or stabilizing this identity) and always critique the essentialism at play (by both dominant culture and resistance operations). As she states, "Since one cannot not be an essentialist, why not look at the ways in which one is an essentialist, carve out a representative essentialist position, and then do politics, according to the old rules, whilst remembering the dangers in this?" (1990, 45)[8]

Spivak is part of a broader poststructuralist feminist position that has waged a forceful critique of identity and attempted to go beyond both the goal of extending rights to women and that of recognizing the differences among women. Influenced most prominently by the work of Michel Foucault, Jacques Derrida, and Jacques Lacan, poststructuralist feminist approaches have critiqued identity at the epistemological level and introduced conceptual struggles over the very notion of identity. At the root of poststructuralist feminist thought was the claim that, despite wide differences in other forms of feminist approaches to the question of identity, *all* relied on the humanist subject—that has some kind of fixed characteristics—to engender solidarity. For instance, feminists who focused on equality for women assumed there was a group of individuals who could be named as belonging to a homogenous group who had been oppressed within patriarchal culture. Even when other feminists called into question the universalist and essentialist category woman—by showing differences based on race, class, sexuality, and ethnicity—their own group concepts (such as woman of color or lesbian) homogenized differences that were internal to those groups. Such forms of feminist politics and thought have subsequently been referred to as "identity politics," and they have been widely critiqued in other arenas of feminist scholarship.[9] For instance, according to Susan Hekman,

> Identity politics ... made embracing a specific fixed identity a precondition for political action.... Women claiming a political identity as African-American women, Asian women, Chicanas, and so on do not enter the political arena asserting those identities as provisional and constructed, but, rather, as fixed and true. Identity politics is not about identities as fictions, but identities as truths.
>
> (1999, 4)

As such, the claim from many feminist critics is that feminism itself has tended to carry the legacy of Enlightenment humanist thought, precisely because it has maintained that there is such an identity—a self—that can be recognized as belonging to the (albeit internally subdivided) identity category "women." For some, poststructuralist thought offered an opportunity to "move beyond the dilemmas" created by a politics focused on claiming an identity (Hekman 1999, 4), while for others it "reinforced critiques that had already been directed at the 'essentialism,' ethnocentrism and 'ahistoricism' of branches of feminist theory" (Brooks 1997, 16).

While poststructuralist thinking comprises disparate theories, these share an insistence on (a) showing that all identity categories silence or exclude certain differences, (b) denaturalizing and deconstructing identity, and (c) highlighting that any idea of the "authentic" subject is the product/construct of humanist discourse itself. In deconstructing identity, poststructuralist feminists, such as Teresa de Lauretis, Eve Sedgwick, Luce Irigaray, and Judith Butler, among others, emphasize there is no "true" identity woman: rather than reflect a preexisting "truth"—to be found in biology or essence of self—any reference to the identity "woman" is always already bound up in certain relations of power and forms of knowledge that have produced the very identity we call woman. Rather than reflect any kind of truth, they argue that the identity woman is a construct of language, discourse, and cultural practices. As such, for Ladelle McWhorter, instead of expressing any kind of internality, identities are,

> reified personality types, coagulations of comportments and communicative styles, social positions carrying certain penalties and privileges, ways of distinguishing oneself from others, ways of orienting oneself in the world, ways of designating the practices and relationships that have the most significance in one's daily life.
>
> (1999, 85)

What does it mean, though, to argue that identities—and in this case gendered identities—are the products of language, discourse, and cultural practices? For Foucault, there is no pre-social essential self who is then acted upon by power and denied by social, economic, or political structures. Instead, individuals are the embodied effect of relations of power because power "produces reality: it produces domains of objects and relations of truth" (1991, 194). Taken in terms of gender, poststructuralists have argued that no-one is born gendered. Rather, the gender categories and identities *male* and *female* pre-exist the individuals' entrance to the world. These identities are associated with certain traits, dispositions, and normative modes of behavior, and these, in turn, are repeatedly articulated in dominant knowledge systems and the practices of daily life. When individuals are born into the world, where ideas about gendered identities already exist, they are reared in relation to these ideas and must come to understand themselves as gendered—according to these ideas. Gender, as de Lauretis has argued, quoting Foucault, is then "the set of effects produced in bodies, behaviours, and social relations" (1987, 3) and individuals are *engendered*. The identity woman, in this understanding, is not a unique feature of individuals but a subject position that must be *assumed*. It is for this reason that poststructuralist theorists use the term *subjectivity* (denoting the ways individuals are subjected to and participate in forming themselves in relation to dominant cultural knowledges, discourses, and practices) rather than the term "identity" (which suggests there is a self that exists apart from culture and that is then oppressed within the cultural realm).

For French feminists working in the psychoanalytic tradition, it became imperative to analyze the role of language in the formation of gendered subjectivity. Despite wide-ranging differences in their theories, a common strand of thought in their work is the notion that language privileges masculinity while denigrating all traits associated with femininity—which has consequences for how masculine subjectivity and feminine subjectivity are understood and lived. Hélène Cixous, for instance, highlighted that femininity is always associated with powerlessness in the binary oppositions that structure patriarchal discourse and language:

> Activity/Passivity
> Sun/Moon
> Culture/Nature
> Day/Night
> Father/Mother
> Head/Emotions
> Intelligible/Sensitive
> Logos/Pathos.
> (Cixous and Clément 1987, 63)

Importantly, however, masculinity and femininity only have meaning in relation to one another so that, as Judith Squires has argued, "the question of gender then becomes primarily linguistic or discursive rather than material or social" because "its meaning is generated within linguistic structures" (1999, 60).[10] Julia Kristeva (1986) proposes a theory of the "subject-in-process": rather than seeing identity as a fixed essence and subjectivity as a "truth," for Kristeva the self is constituted in language and subject to both the laws of the Symbolic Order (the realm of shared cultural meaning) and the unconscious. According to Kristeva, however, language becomes a site of potential radical change precisely because it is social. For Luce Irigaray (1985), who also argues that Western thought is founded on the exclusion of the feminine, change is to be found in the development of a "female imaginary" which, she argues, would enable women to assume a subjectivity in their own right and to express a feminine identity on their own terms. This possibility emerges because the Symbolic Order is itself open to change.[11]

For other poststructuralist feminist thinkers, the work of these French feminists did not go far enough to problematize the concept of woman, and it failed to account for the intersectionality of identity and the multiple relations of power (race, class, ethnicity, etc.) that condition the formation and regulation of identity. For Judith Butler, this French feminist theory, despite its complications of "woman," still problematically maintains the sex/gender distinction—which assumes that gendered identities will inevitably be built on sexed bodies that are supposedly natural and ontologically different.[12]

Critiquing this idea is central to Judith Butler's approach in both *Gender Trouble: Feminism and the Subversion of Identity* ([1990] 1999) and *Bodies That Matter: On the Discursive Limits of "Sex"* (1993). She begins by arguing that, rather than being stable and signifying an interior depth (and "truth"), gendered identity is wholly a social production that is performatively constituted. As she defines it, this means that, "what we take to be an internal essence of gender is manufactured through a sustained set of acts, posited through the gendered stylization of the body" (1999, xv). Rather than being an expression of what one *is*, gender is something that one *does*. This is because the production of a gendered identity relies on the repetition—through time—of acts, norms, bodily comportments, and stylizations that are seen to represent gendered identity. And this doing of gender—the repetition of gendered acts over time—has the effect of *producing* (rather than representing) a gendered identity: only enactments of gendered identity "constitute the illusion of an abiding gendered self" (Butler 1999, 179). To be socially understood as a feminine subject, then, an individual must reproduce the norms associated with femininity, and it is this activity that *makes* her gendered a woman: "there is no gender identity behind the expressions of gender . . . identity is performatively constituted by the very 'expressions' that are said to be its results" (Butler 1999, 33). Perhaps most importantly, Butler dissolves the sex/gender distinction. She shows that gendered identities are arbitrarily related to sexed bodies (so, for instance, there is no necessary relationship between feminine gender and the female body) but, more that this, she argues that rather than being natural, the body/sex is also an effect of power and discourse and the *product* of the gendered system. It is the discourse of heterosexuality, she argues, that requires the gender binary (division into masculine and feminine subjects), and this, in turn, regulates how the body/sex can be understood and how it is materialized: rather than being "natural" (and distinct from culture), the body/sex is always already gender from the start. By this she means that the body can only be understood through discourse and, because the discourse of heterosexuality requires binary gender, the body/sex can only also be interpreted and lived as a binary—as only existing (in any socially viable sense) as two distinct kinds. Bodies, for Butler, are constituted as sexed based on gendered performativity.[13] Resistance to gendered normalization, according to Butler, is to be found within the very discursive field that produces subjectivity: through working the weaknesses in the norms that form us as subjects.

Given that gender is performative, the appropriate response to feminist identity politics for Butler involves two things. First, feminists should understand *woman* as open-ended and "a term in process, a becoming, a constructing that cannot rightfully be said to originate or end . . . it is open to intervention and resignification" (Butler 1999, 43). That is, feminists should not try to define *woman* at all. Second, the category of woman "ought not to be the foundation of feminist politics" (Butler 1999, 9). Rather, feminists should focus on providing an account of how power functions and shapes our understandings of womanhood not only in society at large but also within the feminist movement. Such suggestions, needless to say, caused considerable objections among many feminist writers and activists: "How, it was asked, could women organize together and develop new positive identities if there were no essence of womanhood on the basis of which women could come together in the spirit of sisterhood?" (Weedon 1997, 170). To say that feminism should not use the category "woman" as the foundation for feminist politics, however, is not same thing as saying that gender does not exist and does not remain a political concern. As Butler herself has been at pains to note,

> It is no longer clear that feminist theory ought to settle the questions of *primary* identity in order to get on with the task of politics. Instead, we ought to ask, what political possibilities are the *consequence* of a radical critique of the categories of identity. What new shape of politics emerges when identity as a common ground no longer constrains the discourse of feminist politics. And to what extent does the effort to locate a common identity as the foundation for a feminist politics preclude a radical inquiry into the political construction and regulation of identity itself?
>
> (1999, xxix; my italics)

Butler and other poststructuralist feminist theorists refute the objections to this kind of a revised politics on several fronts. First, it must be clear that "to deconstruct is not to negate or dismiss, but to call into question and, perhaps, most importantly, to open up a term, like the subject, to reusage or redeployment that previously has not been authorized" (Butler 1992, 15). This means that to question the identity "woman" *occasions the possibility* of reimagining what gender might *mean* and how it might be *lived*. Second, it is both possible to recognize the contingency of gender while at the same time struggling against the terms that regulate and constrain gendered life. And third, poststructuralist theorists seek to imagine other forms of solidarity that might be cultivated, such that, rather than rallying around a supposed common identity individuals might instead rally around common goals (that are not linked necessarily to identity—such as childcare needs, the mitigation of violence, etc.).

In making these various claims, poststructuralist feminist theory clearly changed the terrain of feminist thought and, indeed, called for a revision of feminism itself. It continued, however, with concerns that have marked much of feminist thought from its earliest days: that is, to critique gendered identity and the politics it is bound up in. Across the various approaches I have traced out here, we see that identity has been indispensible to feminist political discourse. At the same time, however, the concept of identity has troubling implications for models of selfhood, political inclusiveness, and possibilities for politics itself and pathways of resistance. What becomes clear despite these wide-ranging differences in approach, though, is the imperative to understand how identity is formed through and subject to (1) power relations, (2) systems of knowledge and regimes of representation, (3) interpersonal relations, and (4) geopolitical particularities and histories.

Yet, as I mark in the opening of this piece, much feminist theorizing in the new millennium has taken a decided step away from the question of identity and the concerns I list here. In taking this step, these feminist scholars have rejected what they see as the poststructuralist focus on epistemology and moved instead toward a focus on ontology—a move from the critique of how things are *known* (through language, discourse, knowledge systems) to the study of what *is* (of that which exists outside of language, discourse, and knowledge systems). For some, this has meant a need to focus on "the reality of matter, space, and time" (Grosz 2004, 3), while for others it has meant directing sustained attention to the realm of affect.[14] According to feminist new materialists specifically, poststructuralism has put too much focus on language to the detriment of matter. Note Barad, who states that "language has been granted too much power. The linguistic turn, the semiotic turn, the interpretative turn, the cultural turn: it seems that at every turn lately every 'thing'—even materiality—is turned into a matter of language or some other form of cultural representation" (2003, 801).[15] In response, one strand of feminist new materialism has taken the materiality of the human body as the object of renewed interest and, thereby, extended late twentieth-century feminist interest in the corporeal (see, for example, Diprose 1994; Grosz 1994). These accounts do not deny that earlier feminists have addressed issues of biology, but, as Elizabeth Wilson has noted,

> Despite the intensive scrutiny of the body in feminist theory . . . certain fundamental aspects of the body, biology, and materiality have been foreclosed. After all, how many feminist accounts of the anorexic body pay serious attention to the biological functions of the stomach, the mouth or the digestive system? . . . How many feminist discussions of the sexual body have been articulated through biochemistry?
>
> (2004, 8)

Her argument, then, is that discussions of the biological have been *sealed off from* or *constituted against* the cultural in much feminist scholarship, and it is this that feminist new materialism seeks to rectify.[16] Thus, the focus has shifted from identity to the biological functioning of the body because, for new materialists, "no adequate political theory can ignore the importance of bodies in situating empirical actors" (Coole and Frost 2010, 19).[17] Likewise, feminist affect theory has witnessed a shift in focus: from *being* (which is predicated on a sense of identity) to *belonging* (which presumes not a shared identity but a common sense of identification with others). For instance, Clare Hemmings has explored how "rage, frustration, and desire for connection" (2012, 148) along with affective dissonance—between one's sense of self and the social possibilities afforded to oneself—can become the basis of connection with others.[18]

These are bold, exciting new directions that have rejuvenated feminist scholarship. At the same time, however, we still live in a world that is less than ideal and occupy a social arena in which masculinist norms and humanist assumptions continue to hold sway. We live in bodies that are identified by knowledges about those very bodies and, as individuals, we are compelled to identify with and understand our sense of self through these knowledges. In the context of such ongoing realities, addressing gendered power relations and the question of gendered identity still seems to be important. Such a need is at the forefront of, for example, feminist disability scholarship (which explores how gendered norms intersect with biomedical and broader social understandings of disability to condition the lives of people marked as disabled; see Hall 2011) and feminist science and technology scholarship (which examines how new technologies are simultaneously reproducing gendered forms of labor [see, for instance, Cooper and Waldby 2014] and altering our concepts of and possibilities for identity and identification: that is, changing our understandings of who we "are"). For all the obvious need to expand attention beyond the narrow rubric of identity, feminists also cannot afford to ignore enduring inequalities that are based on the social construction, acceptance, and reproduction of the notion of identity, the fact that identities continue to be formed in relation to some supposed biological truth (whether that be based on sex, sexuality, or race), and the reality that individuals continue to be constrained based on those identities. Whatever limits, contestations, and problematizations might exist in relation to the concept, it appears unlikely, then, that feminist concerns around identity will—or can—be abandoned.

Notes

1. Beauvoir thus introduces what has come to be called the sex-gender distinction.
2. This is not to say that socialist/Marxist feminism does not have a much longer history. In the first instance, it emerged as a parallel to early liberal feminism, and was initiated by, among others, Rosa Luxemburg (1870–1919) and Carla Zetkin (1857–1933) in Germany, Alexandra Kollontai (1873–1952) in Russia, Emily Pankhurst (1858–1928) in Britain, and Emma Goldman (1869–1940) in the United States. For a detailed analysis, see Rosemarie Tong (2008); Valerie Bryson (2003).
3. Note that I discuss what is known as French feminism, or French psychoanalytic theory, in reference to poststructuralist thought below.
4. Patricia Hill Collins focuses on how shared experiences among black women lead to a distinct standpoint. This, then, might be seen as a *mitigated* account of essential black female identity. Hazel Carby opposes such a view. Rather than see racism and sexism as in any way fixed or transhistorical, she insists that we examine how they are historical practices that are enmeshed with changing social, political, and economic practices. It is these always altering practices, she argues, that function to maintain power in a given context and society (1989, 18).
5. "Living on borders and in margins, keeping intact one's shifting and multiple identity and integrity, is like trying to swim in a new element, an 'alien' element. . . . The 'alien element' has become familiar—never comfortable, but home" (Anzaldúa 1987, iii).
6. The use of the term *Third World women* by Western feminists has been widely critiqued. Mohanty uses the term interchangeably with "women of color." She argues that "what seems to constitute 'women of color' or 'third world women' as a viable oppositional alliance is a common context of struggle rather than color or racial identifications. Similarly, it is third world women's oppositional political relation to sexist, racist, and imperialistic

7. I address this position in more detail later in relation to poststructuralist feminist thought. To explain this position, Spivak states, "Deconstruction does not say there is no subject, there is no truth, there is no history. It simply questions the privileging of identity so that someone is believed to have the truth. It is not the exposure of error. It is constantly and persistently looking into how truths are produced" (1996, 28). It should also be noted that Spivak rejects the term *Third World feminist*. In a 1989 interview titled "Naming Gayatri Spivak," she addresses the issue directly when she says, "My work would not be an undermining of names but an acknowledgement of the vulnerability that there is nothing but naming . . . I think the historicizing of the inevitable production of names is a much more productive enterprise than a counter-name calling" (1989, 85–86).

Note: item 6 continues at top: structures that constitutes our political commonality" (1991a, 7). Many feminists prefer to characterize this perspective as transnational feminism. See Aihwa Ong (1999).

8. Spivak does not specifically address what she means by "one cannot not be an essentialist"; however, one reading might be that in the very act of writing or naming oneself, identity has to be essentialized.
9. For Sonia Kruks (2000, 85), "What makes identity politics a significant departure from earlier, pre-identitarian forms of the politics of recognition is its demand for recognition on the bases of the very grounds on which recognition has been denied: it is *qua* women, *qua* blacks, *qua* lesbians that groups demand recognition." For a further critique of identity politics, also see Wendy Brown, who argues that all appeals to political justice on the basis of identity have to struggle with the paradox of acting from a subject position—an identity—that it also opposes. This, she calls, a "wounded attachment" (1995). The primary critique of identity politics is that, while these forms of feminism deconstructed a collective female identity, they reasserted another form of collective identity, where, despite the recognition of difference, women were called on to privilege one aspect of their identity as the site for political struggle. For a counter view, see Linda Alcoff (2006).
10. The broader implications of such thinking are that (a) the relationship between gendered identity and biological sex is arbitrary and, therefore that (b) it becomes possible to imagine in terms other than only two genders. These points are not taken up in French feminism, but are the focus of Judith Butler's work, which I discuss later.
11. These feminists are known for their project of *l'écriture féminine*, which is the attempt to write from or to discursively embody the position of woman in order to challenge women's positioning in phallogocentric culture. It is the expression of the female body and sexuality in writing, an expression that cannot be coded or theorized.
12. As Butler claims, "Central to each of these views . . . is the notion that sex appears within hegemonic language as a *substance*, as, metaphysically speaking, a self-identical being. This . . . conceals the fact that 'being' a sex or a gender is fundamentally impossible" (1999, 25).
13. While I am unable to address this here, an essential part of Butler's project is to show that sexed (and gendered) identities are constructed through the violent rejection of identities that are deemed to *not* matter; that is, those identities that do not count or are not intelligible within the heterosexual matrix.
14. While I am unable to go into particularities here, for Sara Ahmed (2008, 38, n5), affect theory and new materialism share a reliance on distinguishing between nature and culture (which are imagined as distinct). She sees affect theory, for instance, as describing emotion as cultural and affect as biological, and she sees new materialism as insisting that there is a reality to matter that is unfixed from the cultural domain. According to Stacy

Alaimo and Susan Hekman, on the other hand, feminist new materialism "accomplishes what the postmoderns failed to do: a deconstruction of the material/discursive dichotomy that retains both elements without privileging either" (2008, 6).

15. This charge has been the focus of must feminist debate and counter-debate. See, for instance, Ahmed (2008).
16. Again, many feminists have refuted this argument (see, for instance, Ahmed [2008]).
17. The idea that we can describe or "know" the ontological *tout court* has been seen as problematic in many criticisms of feminist new materialism. See, for instance, Nikki Sullivan (2012).
18. Many of these new viewpoints echo the sentiment offered by Lawrence Grossberg, who has claimed: "I want to recognize that people live identity but ask whether you need to live belonging as always bound up necessarily with difference and negativity.... [T]here's always the potential for the actualization of other imaginations, of other ways of belonging, of identification, of community" (2010, pp. 324–325).

REFERENCES

Ahmed, Sara. 2008. "Open Forum Imaginary Prohibitions: Some Preliminary Remarks on the Founding Gestures of the 'New Materialism.'" *European Journal of Women's Studies* 15 (1): 23–39.

Anzaldúa, Gloria. 1987. *Borderlands/La Frontera: The New Mestiza*. San Francisco: Aunt Lute Books.

Alarcón, Norma. 1995. "The Theoretical Subject(s) of This Bridge Called My Back and Anglo-American Feminism." In *Making Face, Making Soul/Haciendo Caras: Creative and Critical Perspectives by Feminists of Color*, edited by Gloria Anzaldúa. San Francisco: Aunt Lute Books.

Alcoff, Linda. 2006. *Visible Identities: Race, Gender, and the Self*. Oxford and New York: Oxford University Press.

Althusser, Louis. 1971. "On Ideology and Ideological State Apparatuses: Notes Towards An Investigation." In *Lenin and Philosophy and Other Essays*. Translated by Ben Brewster. New York: Monthly Review Press.

Astell, Mary. (1694) 2002. *A Serious Proposal to the Ladies*. Parts I and II. Edited by P. Springborg. Ontario: Broadview Literary Texts.

Barad, Karen. 2003. "Posthumanist Performativity: Toward an Understanding of How Matter Comes to Matter." *Signs* 28 (3): 801–831.

Barad, Karen. 2007. *Meeting the Universe Halfway: Quantum Physics and the Entanglement of Matter and Meaning*. Durham, NC: Duke University Press.

Beauvoir, Simone de. 1972. *The Second Sex*. Harmondsworth: Penguin.

Benjamin, Jessica. 1988. *The Bonds of Love*. New York: Pantheon.

Braidotti, Rosi. 2002. *Metamorphoses: Towards a Materialist Theory of Becoming*. Cambridge: Polity.

Braidotti, Rosi. 2007. "Feminist Epistemology after Postmodernism: Critiquing Science, Technology, and Globalization." *Interdisciplinary Science Reviews* 32 (1): 65–74.

Brooks, Ann. 1997. *Postfeminisms: Feminism, Cultural Theory and Cultural Forms*. London and New York: Routledge.

Brown, Wendy. 1995. *States of Injury: Power and Freedom in Late Modernity*. Princeton, NJ: Princeton University Press.

Bryson, Valerie. 2003. *Feminist Political Theory: An Introduction*. Basingstoke and New York: Palgrave Macmillan.

Butler, Judith. 1990. "The Force of Fantasy: Feminism, Mapplethorpe, and Discursive Excess." *differences* 2 (2): 105–125.

Butler, Judith. 1992. "Contingent Foundations: Feminism and the Question of Postmodernism." In *Feminists Theorize the Political*, edited by Judith Butler and Ann W. Scott, 3–21. New York: Routledge.

Butler, Judith. 1993. *Bodies That Matter: On the Discursive Limits of "Sex."* London: Routledge.

Butler, Judith. (1990) 1999. *Gender Trouble: Feminism and the Subversion of Identity*. 2nd ed. London: Routledge.

Campioni, Mia, and Elizabeth Grosz. 1991. "Love's Labour Lost: Marxism and Feminism." In *A Reader in Feminist Knowledge*, edited by Sneja Gunew, 366–397. London and New York: Routledge.

Carby, Hazel. 1989. *Reconstructing Womanhood: The Emergence of the Afro-American Woman Novelist*. New York: Oxford University Press.

Castillo, Ana. 1994. *Massacre of the Dreamers: Essays on Xicanisma*. Albuquerque: University of New Mexico Press.

Chodorow, Nancy. 1978. *The Reproduction of Mothering: Psychoanalysis and the Sociology of Gender*. Berkeley: University of California Press.

Cixous, Helene, and Catherine Clément. 1987. *The Newly Born Woman*. Translated by Betsy Wing. Minneapolis: University of Minnesota Press.

Combahee River Collective. 1995. "A Black Feminist Statement." In *Words of Fire: An Anthology of African-American Feminist Thought*, edited by Beverly Guy-Sheftal, 232–240. New York: New Press.

Collins, Patricia Hill. 1990. *Black Feminist Thought: Knowledge, Consciousness, and the Politics of Empowerment*. New York: Routledge and Chapman and Hall.

Coole, Diana and Samantha Frost. 2010. "Introducing the New Materialisms." In *New Materialisms: Ontology, Agency, and Politics*, edited by Diana Coole and Samantha Frost. Durham, NC: Duke University Press.

Cooper, Melinda, and Catherine Waldby. 2014. *Clinical Labor: Tissue Donors and Research Subjects in the Global Bioeconomy*. Durham, NC: Duke University Press.

Crenshaw, Kimberlé. 1991. "Mapping the Margins: Intersectionality, Identity Politics, and Violence against Women of Color." *Stanford Law Review* 43 (6): 1241–1299.

Dinnerstein, Dorothy. 1976. *The Mermaid and the Minotaur: Sexual Arrangements and Human Malaise*. New York: Harper & Row.

Diprose, Rosalyn. 1994. *The Bodies of Women*. London and New York: Routledge.

Firestone, Shulamith. (1970) 1979. *The Dialectic of Sex: The Case for Feminist Revolution*. New York: Bantam.

Flax, Jane. 1980. "Mother-Daughter Relationships: Psychodynamics, Politics, and Philosophy." In *The Future of Difference*, edited by H. Eisenstein and Alice Jardine, 20–40. New Brunswick, NJ: Rutgers University Press.

Foucault, Michel. 1991. *Discipline and Punish: The Birth of the Prison*. Translated by Alan Sheridan. London: Penguin.

Friedan, Betty. (1963) 1983. *The Feminine Mystique*. New York: Laurel.

Frost, Samantha. 2011. "The Implications of the New Materialism for Feminist Epistemology." In *Feminist Epistemology and Philosophy of Science: Power in Knowledge*, edited by H. E. Grasswick. London and New York: Springer.

Grossberg, Lawrence. 2010. "Affect's Future: Rediscovering the Virtual in the Actual." In *The Affect Theory Reader*, edited by Melissa Gregg and Gregory J. Seigworth, 309–338. Durham, NC: Duke University Press.

Grosz, Elizabeth. 1994. *Volatile Bodies: Toward a Corporeal Feminism*. Bloomington: Indiana University Press.

Grosz, Elizabeth. 2004. *The Nick of Time: Politics, Evolution, and the Untimely*. Durham, NC: Duke University Press.

Hall, Kim, Q., ed. 2011. *Feminist Disability Studies*. Bloomington: Indiana University Press.

Hekman, Susan. 1999. "Identity Crises: Identity, Identity Politics, and Beyond." *Critical Review of International Social and Political Philosophy* 2 (1): 3–26.

Hekman, Susan. 2000. "Beyond Identity: Feminism, Identity, and Identity Politics." *Feminist Theory* 1 (3): 289–308.

Hemmings, Clare. 2005. "Telling Feminist Stories." *Feminist Theory* 6 (2): 115–139.

Hemmings, Clare. 2012. "Affective Solidarity: Feminist Reflexivity and Political Transformation." *Feminist Theory* 13 (2): 147–161.

hooks, bell. 1981. *Ain't I a Woman: Black Women and Feminism*. Boston: South End Press.

hooks, bell. 1984. *Feminist Theory: From Margin to Center*. Boston: South End Press.

Hull, Gloria. T., Patricia Bell Scott,. and Barbara Smith,. 1982. *All the Women Are White, All the Blacks Are Men, But Some of Us Are Brave*. Old Westbury, NY: Feminist Press.

Irigaray, Luce. 1985. *This Sex Which Is Not One*. Translated by C. Potter and C. Burke. Ithaca, NY: Cornell University Press.

Jagger, Alison. 1983. *Feminist Politics and Human Nature*. N.J.: Rowman & Allanheld.

Kirby, Vicky. 1997. *Telling Flesh: The Substance of the Corporeal*. London and New York: Routledge.

Kirby, Vicky. 2008. "Natural Convers(at)ions: Or, What if Culture Was Really Nature All Along?" In *Material Feminisms*, edited by Stacy Alaimo and Susan Hekman, 214–236. Bloomington: Indiana University Press.

Kristeva, Julia. 1986. *The Kristeva Reader*. Edited by Toril Moi. Oxford: Blackwell.

Kruks, Sonia. 2000. *Retrieving Experience: Subjectivity and Recognition in Feminist Politics*. Ithaca, NY: Cornell University Press.

Lauretis, Theresa de. 1987. *Technologies of Gender: Essays on Theory, Film, and Fiction*. London: Macmillan.

Luchashenko, Melissa. 1994. "No Other Truth?: Aboriginal Women and Australian Feminism." *Social Alternatives* 12 (4): 21–25.

McWhorter, Ladelle. 1995. *Bodies and Pleasures: Foucault and the Politics of Sexual Normalization*. Bloomington: Indiana University Press.

Mill, H. T., 1998. *The Complete Works of Harriet Taylor Mill* Edited by Jo Ellen Jacobs. Bloomington: Indiana University Press.

Mirza, Heidi Safia. 1997. Introduction to *Black British Feminism: A Reader*, edited by Heidi Safia Mirza. New York and London: Routledge.

Mitchell, Juliet. 1975. *Psychoanalysis and Feminism*. Harmondsworth: Penguin.

Moallem, Minoo. 2006. "Feminist Scholarship and the Internationalization of Women's Studies." *Feminist Studies* 32 (2): 332–351.

Mohanty, Chandra Talpade. 1991a. "Introduction: Cartographies of Struggle: Third World Feminism and the Politics of Feminism." In *Third World Women and the Politics of Feminism*, edited by C. Mohanty, A. Russo, and L. Torres, 1–50. Bloomington: Indiana University Press.

Mohanty, Chandra Talpade. 1991b. "Under Western Eyes: Feminist Scholarship and Colonial Discourses." *Third World Women and the Politics of Feminism*, edited by C. Mohanty, A. Russo, and L. Torres, 51–80. Bloomington: Indiana University Press.

Moraga, Cherrie. 1995. "From a Long Line of Vendidas: Chicanas and Feminism." In *Making Face, Making Soul/Haciendo Caras: Creative and Critical Perspectives by Feminists of Color*, edited by Gloria Anzaldúa. San Francisco: Aunt Lute Books.

Narayan, Uma. 1997. "Contesting Cultures: 'Westernization,' Respect for Cultures and Third-World Feminists." In *The Second Wave: A Reader in Feminist Theory*, edited by Linda Nicholson, 396–423. London and New York: Routledge.

Ong, Aihwa. (1999) 2006. *Flexible Citizenship: The Cultural Logics of Transnationality*. Durham, NC: Duke University Press.

Rich, Adrienne. 1977. *Of Woman Born*. New York: Bantam.

Rich, Adrienne. 1979. *On Secrets, Lies, and Silence: Selected Prose 1966–1979*. New York: W. W. Norton.

Rich, Adrienne. 1984. "Compulsory Heterosexuality and Lesbian Existence." In *Desire: The Politics of Sexuality*, edited by A. Snitow, C. Stansell, and S. Thompson, 212–241. London: Virago.

Spivak, Gayatri Chakravorty. 1989. "Naming Gayatri Spivak." Interview. *Stanford Humanities Review* I (i): 84–97.

Spivak, Gayatri Chakravorty, and Sarah Harasym. 1990. *The Post-Colonial Critic: Interviews, Strategies, Dialogues*. New York: Routledge.

Spivak, Gayatri Chakravorty. 1996. "Bonding in Difference, Interview with Alfred Arteaga (1993–94)." In *The Spivak Reader*, edited by Donna Landry and Gerald MacLean, 15–28. New York and London: Routledge.

Squires, Judith. 1999. *Gender in Political Theory*. Cambridge: Polity Press.

Stanton, Elizabeth Cady. (1860) 1881. "Mrs. Stanton's Address to Legislature in 1860." In *History of Woman*, vol. 1, edited by E. C., Stanton, Susan Anthony, and M. J. Gage, 679–685. New York: Fowler and Wells, Publishers.

Sullivan, Nikki. 2012. "The Somatechnics of Perception and the Matter of the Non/Human: A Critical Response to New Materialism." *European Journal of Women's Studies* 19 (3): 299–313.

Tong, Rosemarie. 2008. *Feminist Thought: A More Comprehensive Introduction*. Boulder, CO: Westview Press.

Weedon, Chris. 1997. *Feminist Practice and Poststructuralist Theory*. Cambridge, MA: Blackwell.

Weedon, Chris. 2003. "Subjects." In *A Concise Companion to Feminist Theory*, edited by Mary Eagleton, 111–132. Malden, MA: Blackwell.

Wiegman. Robyn. 2000. "Feminism's Apocalyptic Futures." *New Literary History* 31: 805–825.

Wiegman, Robyn. 2012. *Object Lessons*. Durham, NC: Duke University Press.

Wilson, Elizabeth. 2004. *Psychosomatic: Feminism and the Neurobiological Body*. Durham, NC: Duke University Press.

Wollstonecraft, Mary. (1792) 1998. *A Vindication of the Rights of Woman*. New York: Norton.

CHAPTER 18

INSTITUTIONS

CELESTE MONTOYA

INSTITUTIONS are a central component of feminist analysis, although they are not always discussed as such. In common vernacular, the term *institutions* has a relatively narrow focus and is often used to discuss formal organizations, such as government institutions, institutions of higher learning, medical institutions, and legal institutions. Within this narrow conceptualization, institutions might serve as the focus or target of feminist analysis and critique, as these formal structures are the site of gender inequality and injustices. And, indeed, there is much important work to this end. Some scholars, however, have pushed for a broader conceptualization of institutions, instead defining them as the rules (both formal and informal) that structure behavior. As such, institutions are not merely one target for analysis, but really are at the very heart of feminist analysis. The centrality of institutions became particularly pronounced as feminist scholars began to shift away from analysis of women and sex roles towards a broader conceptualization of gender as "the pervasive ordering of human activities, practices, and social structures" and as "part of the processes that also constitute class and race, as well as other lines of demarcation and domination" (Acker 1992, 567). In recent years, application of the term *institution* to a variety of phenomena has become so widespread that it is difficult to establish what exactly an institution is.

How feminist scholars have used "institutions" in their research, is in no small part determined by their varied understandings of gender. For example, early liberal feminists frequently focused on sex as a biological category and gender as a product of socialization. Liberal feminist scholars have investigated gender differences within institutions, but have treated institutions themselves as gender neutral. Conceiving institutions in the context of patriarchy, the overarching system of power that organizes society to advantage men, radical feminists have challenged claims of gender neutrality, suggesting instead that institutions entrench male power and are important sites for contestation. Socialist feminists situate institutions within larger structures of constraint such as race, class, gender, and nationality that limit individual choice and action in systemic ways. Emphasizing discursive and performative aspects of institutions, postmodern and poststructural feminist scholars probe fundamental categories of identity as cultural and social productions. Intersectional feminist scholars build on some of these schools of thought, while emphasizing the simultaneity of multiple oppressions. Taking a constructivist approach to gender, intersectional feminists suggest that gender is constituted in and through race, class, sexuality, and other social vectors of power. An intersectional approach to institutions investigates not only how institutions are gendered, but also how they are also raced, classed, and enmeshed in complex geopolitical formations. Emphasizing the importance of intersectional institutional analysis, Patricia Hill Collins (1993, 30) has noted that "removing any one piece from our analysis diminishes our understanding of the true nature of relations of domination and subordination."

Theorizing gender as an analytical category, Joan Scott (1986, 1067) has conceptualized gender as "a constitutive element of social relationships based on perceived differences between the sexes, and. a primary way of signifying relationships of power." Using gender as an analytical category, in this essay, I compare four leading feminist approaches: "gender within institutions," "gendered institutions," "gender as an institution," and "institutions as producers of gender." I focus on scholarship in the fields of law, sociology, political science, communication, and history that has explicitly used the language of institutions. I also explore the contributions and benefits that feminist theorizing has had on the study of institutions and the role that institutional analysis might have in feminist scholarship. By discussing historical trends as well as recent innovations, I hope to illuminate how feminist approaches to institutions create possibilities to enhance understanding and to challenge systems of inequality. I draw attention to current limitations in the field, particularly the shallow explorations of intersectionality, and argue for the benefits of an intersectional approach to institutional analysis while also suggesting the benefits of institutional analysis to the intersectional study of gender.

STRUCTURE, INSTITUTIONS, AND ORGANIZATIONS

As mechanisms of social order that regulate human behavior within particular communities, structures, institutions, and organizations are often conflated. Yet there are subtle distinctions among these concepts, and the explanatory force attributed to each varies across disciplinary fields and ideological formations.

Working within a Marxian framework, Iris Marion Young and R.W. Connell analyze gender and institutions as a part of structure. According to Young (2002, 20), structure "denotes the confluence of institutional rules and interactive routines, mobilization of resources, and physical structure, which constitute the historical givens in relation to which individuals act." Indeed, structures "connote the wider social outcomes that result from the confluence of many individual actions within given institutional relations." Conceptualizing structures as practices that have been institutionalized over time, which create patterns of constraint on individual choice, R. W. Connell (1987, 93) notes that structure may not be immediately visible in social life but these foundational relations underlie the surface complexity of interactions and institutions. Structural analysis is a mode of inquiry that investigates these constraining practices and probes their complex dynamics. As conventions created by humans, structures are amenable to change; but, once entrenched, they gain a potent hold over the popular imagination. And, once "naturalized," structures gain impressive stability that makes them enormously difficult to transform.

For structural analysts, institutions are embedded in structures, which shape larger, broader, and deeper patterns of social interaction. Yet, there are also suggestions of a two-way or cyclical relationship between structures and institutions: structures underlie and inform the creation and possibilities of institutions; but as products of human action, structures also result from and are the consequence of institutions. Within the context of structural analysis, institutions are never "neutral"; they reflect and reproduce structural inequalities.

Barbara Risman (2004) explicitly differentiates between structures and institutions, noting that institutions usually refer to particular aspects of society, ranging from social institutions like the family to organizations such as corporations or government agencies. Suggesting that the concept of structure is trivialized if it is located, Risman argues that structure, and more specifically gender as structure, is more deeply embedded within social relations, operating as a basis for stratification "not just in our personalities, our cultural rules, or institutions but in all these, and in complicated ways" (Risman 2004, 12). Noting that agency has a role in relation to institutions and structures, Risman points out that gendered institutions depend on individuals' willingness to "do gender." When individuals refuse to perform in accordance with gender conventions, they can change institutions. Structure is not so easily changed without more dramatic and widespread societal shifts.

This comparative difficulty in changing structure versus institutions has been discussed in relation to stability or "stickiness." Created to serve particular purposes, institutions and the behaviors and relations they regulate can change as the intentions and purposes of those who created them change. Indeed, institutions can be targeted for transformation by those who are dissatisfied with their objectives or operations. Because structures operate independently of individual intention, evolving through customary practices over long expanses of time, their points of origin and their purposes are often far murkier. Whether operating through systemic divisions of labor, ability, responsibility and power or articulated in absolute prohibitions, taboos, legislation, hiring decisions of private corporations, or informal mechanisms of social control, structures such as race, class, and gender are often called "natural" or "given." Once naturalized, structures become very difficult to change. They must be denaturalized and politicized before change is possible. Thus it is sometimes said that institutions can be reformed, but transforming structure requires something much bigger, such as a revolution.

Where structural analysis emerged in the context of socialist theory, and institutional analysis is a hallmark of empirical inquiry that often characterizes itself as "value free," organizational analysis grew out of Max Weber's conception of the progressive disenchantment of the world, which gave rise to bureaucracy as a mode of rational, law-guided, and impersonal governance. Although in popular usage "institutions" are often conflated with "organizations," "foundations," and "associations," organizational studies, particularly in the fields of sociology, economics, political science, and public administration distinguish between institutions and organizations. Douglass North (1990) advanced one of the most useful and compelling distinctions between these concepts, suggesting that institutions establish the rules of the game, while organizations are best understood as the players that operate in accordance with and implement those rules.

Within social science research, differences between structures, institutions, and organizations can also be understood in relation to different levels of analysis. Structural analysis involves macro-level investigation; institutional and organizational studies entail meso-level research. Within feminist scholarship, researchers have examined how organizational processes structure inequality with profound effects on the experiences, behavior and treatment of people within and beyond those organizations. To understand these differential outcomes, some scholars investigate the institutions, both formal and informal, that shape and regulate behavior. Other scholars seek to illuminate how institutional rules and organizational processes are embedded in the larger and historically relevant structures such as gender, race, and class. To clarify these varying levels of analysis, consider various possibilities for investigating inequality in education. One method for examining inequality in education might involve an organizational study of a school or multiple schools, focusing on demographics, behavior, treatment, performance, and experiences of administrators, faculty, staff, and students. An institutional study might examine the rules (formal and informal) that shape the demographics, behavior, treatment, performance and experiences of the various actors. A structural analysis might investigate how educational institutions and organizations reflect and reinforce the power hierarchies that exist within the larger society.

Gender and Institutions

Feminist scholars have theorized gender as both structure, conceiving it as a fundamental ordering of society, and as an institution, a reiterative and performative process. Gender as an "institutionalized" social process connotes a more dynamic, less "sticky," though still constrained, understanding than does gender as structure. In the words of Sally Kenney (2012, 16), "Gender is not a thing sitting passively ... but an institutionalized process of meaning creation that is contested in different ways.... [Although it] is a tenacious social category, it is continually reinscribed and its content changed."

The evolution of feminist understandings of gender coincided with the development of "new institutionalism" in the social sciences. Joan Acker's (1992, 567) conceptualization of gender as the pervasive ordering of human practices bears stark resemblance to Douglass North's (1990, 3) description of institutions as the rules that structure human interaction, whether political, social, or economic. The powerful symmetry in these definitions, along with the growth of feminist research in the social sciences help explain the emergence of scholarly inquiry that posits gender as an institution, as well as the analysis of gendered institutions.

In contrast to structural accounts that foreground the stability of gender, institutional analyses conceive gender as a dynamic process that is produced and reproduced within particular contexts. In the 1970s, liberal feminist empiricists initiated studies of "gender in institutions" and "sex in institutions," which treated institutions as neutral entities and examined how women and men fared within them. By the late 1990s, much of the feminist institutions literature focused on "gendered institutions," a more radical conceptualization that sees institutions themselves as constituted in and through gender. Overlapping with the study of gendered institutions are discussions of "gendering institutions," which emphasize that institutions play a crucial role in producing and reproducing gender.

In the following sections, I focus on these different ways of using institutions in feminist analysis. Although there are substantial areas of overlap in these approaches, it is useful to isolate discrete trajectories and emphases for analytical purposes. It is important to note that there have been temporal evolutions in the study of institutions, of gender, and of gender and institutions, yet not all differentiations in approaches are temporal in nature. Ideology also plays an important role. Liberal feminist empiricist and socialist feminist standpoint approaches coexist in feminist scholarship, fueling ongoing debates within the study of social, economic, and political institutions. Contention and disagreement have been and remain a vital part of academic and social movement work.

Gender (Sex) in Institutions

An early focus of feminist institutional studies, particularly those conducted by liberal feminist empiricist scholars, was not as much about gender as it was about biological sex. In particular, this type of work notes the participation or, more frequently, the lack of participation of women in certain institutions or organizations, particularly social, economic, political, religious, financial, and academic institutions. Ester Boserup's (1970) groundbreaking study of the many ways that women were left out of development, development organizations, as well as development as a process, provides one powerful example of an early study that adopted a gender (sex) "in" institutions approach. Her work inspired a wave of activism within development organizations to ensure that women were brought into all aspects of development. Documenting the presence and absence of women across an array of institutions, these studies rely on quantitative indicators to measure women's participation or underrepresentation.

Beyond measuring women's presence and absence, some liberal feminist scholars have investigated gender socialization and "appropriate" gender roles within various institutional sites (e.g., legislatures, judiciaries, the military, education, workplace, family, religious organizations). Using qualitative and ethnographic methods, these studies document women's stories and analyze inequalities and hidden injuries that women experience within and across these sites. Whether quantitative or qualitative, studies of sex or gender "in" institutions, clearly distinguish between attributes of individuals and aspects of institutions. Actors within institutions have genders and may have gendered expectations, but institutions do not. Treating institutions as neutral sites in which inequalities play out, liberal feminist scholars link inequities to external biases that infiltrate institutions. When institutions are viewed as neutral, the solution to inequality appears simple: increase the number of women within the institution and create mechanisms to ensure that women are treated the same as their male counterparts. Equality does not require radical transformation of institutions; equal opportunity and equal treatment are sufficient to create gender equity. Within this liberal, individualist frame, institutions are not the problem. On the contrary, institutions that mandate laws and regulations guaranteeing equal opportunity and equal treatment are the prescribed solution.

Liberal feminist strategies for addressing gender (sex) inequality in institutions typically emphasize anti-discrimination policies or (narrowly defined) positive action policies aimed at integrating women into previously male-dominated institutions. Such strategies have included and continue to include campaigns for equal suffrage; equal pay; nondiscrimination in hiring, promotion, and educational opportunities; and gender quotas and gender mainstreaming that focus on incorporating women into institutions and institutional decision-making bodies without seeking to change the institutions themselves.

There have been many critiques of the "add women and stir" approach, as liberal feminist strategies are often referred to by detractors. First and foremost, critics point out the limitations of treating institutions as entirely exogenous to societal structures and immune to power hierarchies. By masking institutional gender power, the women-in-institutions approach fails to analyze women's treatment within institutions, women's effectiveness, their attrition, or the institutional dynamics that contribute to persistent inequities.

Another important limitation of the women-in-institutions approach is the failure to undertake intersectional analysis. When "women" within institutions are viewed exclusively in opposition to men, there is little room to explore the differences among women (or among men for that matter) grounded in race, class, sexuality, or citizenship. When sex/gender is deemed the only relevant dimension of institutional analysis, critical issues are left unexamined. When women enter male-dominated institutions, which women are allowed in? Which women succeed? What happens to women and men who refuse to conform to hegemonic conceptions of gender? Pay inequity provides one example of how much information is lost when gender is considered the only important vector of analysis. In the United States, much attention has been given to the fact that "women" earn approximately 77 cents for every dollar earned by a "man." Feminist organizations have launched recurrent pay equity campaigns, lobbying governments to pass legislation to redress gendered pay inequity. But discussions of average women's pay mask more inequities than they reveal. When pay data are disaggregated by race (a fairly simplistic, positivist approach to intersectionality that is compatible with the "gender/sex in institutions" approach), a far more complex account of inequality comes into view. When average white male earnings are held as the baseline, for every dollar earned by a white man, white women earn 78 cents; black men earn 73 cents; black women earn 64 cents; Latinos earn 61 cents and Latinas earn 54 cents (Current Population Survey, 2013 Annual Social and Economic Supplement). Although official data on LGBTQ earnings are sparse, scholars and advocates emphasize that employment discrimination creates a pay gap for LGBTQ individuals that exacerbates inequities grounded in gender, race, and ethnicity (Arabsheibani et al., 2007).

Another limitation of the liberal feminist approach is the emphasis (or perhaps overemphasis) on women's "choices" regarding participation within certain institutions. As manifested in current popular US discourses about women "opting out" or "leaning in," and in the US women and politics literature about women's electoral success "when they run," these claims situate the problem of women's absence in relation to the choices of individual women. Emphasizing that women candidates are just as likely as men to win elections, Richard Fox and Jennifer Lawless (2004), draw attention to an "ambition gap," which deflects attention away from sexist practices within political parties that prevent women from securing nominations. Similarly, Cheryl Sandburg's best-seller *Lean In* attributes the dearth of women in corporate board rooms to women's self-defeating behavior rather than to sex discrimination by corporations. Her voluntarist solution, then, is that women simply need to "lean in" more at work. Although these explanations raise important questions about internalized oppression—that is, how the acceptance of misogynous claims about women's lesser abilities might curb women's career ambitions and performance at work—they mask all the ways that institutions (political, economic, and social) actively discriminate against women and create inhospitable environments based on hegemonic (frequently white, heterosexual, cisgendered, able-bodied) masculine norms.

Because of these important limitations, much of the work on gender and organizations has evolved beyond the "women/gender in" approach. Although it has not been entirely abandoned and, indeed, seems to be the most palatable approach within conservative paradigms, much of the work has evolved to more complex understandings. While there is much to be found in looking at women/gender in institutions, it is best used as a starting point, as one layer of a multilayered and nuanced assessment.

Gendered Institutions

The study of gender *in* institutions, suggests that gender is distinct from institutions. This treatment of institutions as exogenous to societal structures is fairly common in neo-institutional studies. Many feminist scholars (along with other scholars engaged in critical studies), however, have argued that institutions are not neutral stand-alone entities and that they are very much embedded in societal hierarchies. "To say that an institution is gendered, then is to recognize that construction of masculinity and femininity are intertwined in the daily culture of the institution rather than existing out in society or fixed within individuals which they then bring whole to the institution" (Kenney 1996, 456). Within the study of "gendered institutions," gender is not an individual variable, but an organizing principle of institutions (Acker 1992; Lorber 1995). "Seeing social institutions as gendered provides a critical perspective, in which the relevant question becomes not why are women excluded but to what extent have the overall institutional structure, and the character of particular institutional areas been formed through gender (Acker 1992, 568).

Although the analysis of "gendered institutions" is markedly distinct from the study of "sex/gender in institutions," feminist scholars have advanced multiple accounts of the nature of "gendered institutions" and prospects for degendering them. Reflecting different feminist ideological and epistemological traditions, the contemporary literature on gendered institutions offers a range of insights into feminist institutionalisms.

Power and Patriarchy

One of the key contributions of radical, socialist, and postmodern feminist theory is the emphasis on power. While institutional studies do not always discuss power, feminist studies of institutions bring power to the center of institutional analysis (Kenny and Mackay 2009). Most feminist institutionalists argue that institutions reflect and contribute to power dynamics that reinforce and magnify the position of their creators. Institutional rules and norms privilege certain forms of behavior and certain actors over others (Thelen 2003; Chappell 2010). Feminist scholars bring to the study of institutions a critical lens that seeks to make visible gendered power relations and the processes that support and undermine them (Lovenduski, 2011).

Although feminists foreground power in their analysis of institutions, they differ in their conceptualizations of power. For radical feminists, gender is a system of male domination, a fundamental organizing principle of patriarchal society, at the root of all other systems of oppression. Focused on patriarchal power, radical feminists reject liberal feminist prescriptions for increasing the presence of women in institutions as inadequate. According to radical feminists, it is not enough to increase the numbers of women in male-dominated institutions because those institutions were created by and for men, and serve as a means of maintaining males' power advantage. Within a radical feminist framework, emphasis is placed on the masculine character of various institutions. Spurred by this insight, feminist political scientists have explored how masculinity structures the presidency, the military, the law, Congress, global finance, and international institutions. Even "feminine" institutions have been deemed patriarchal when they reinforce rigorous and oppressive gender roles. Feminist sociologists have emphasized that social institutions such as the family, the church, and the transnational care economy, which involve the energy of millions of women, are nonetheless patriarchal, privileging male interests while placing women in subordinate roles.

Working with a more dynamic and intersectional conceptualization of gender, as a process constructed and reproduced through the intersection of sex, race, sexuality, ideology, and experiences of oppression under patriarchal capitalism (Calas and Smircich 2006, 302), socialist feminists conceive gender itself as an institution as well as a key component of other institutions (social and political). Socialist feminists conceptualize power as less fixed and static than radical feminist accounts of patriarchy suggest. As Louise Chappell (2010) notes, "The notion of gender as a process is particularly useful as it draws attention to the constantly shifting nature of gender power relations within institutions." By shifting the focus beyond an analysis of patriarchy, socialist feminists avoid the problematic notion that male power underpins all modes of oppression. Although the socialist feminist intersectional understanding of power has only intermittently been translated into the empirical institutional analyses, socialist feminist presuppositions have been very influential in feminist sociological and political studies.

Challenging totalizing explanations, postmodern and poststructuralist feminist scholars have theorized institutions in relation to the production, normalization, and performance of identities within particular power/knowledge systems. Understanding gender as an institution and gendered institutions as products of discourse and performative practices, Judith Butler (1993, 2) has noted that "performativity must be understood not as a singular or deliberate 'act,' but, rather, as the reiterative and citational practice by which discourse produces the effect that it names."

Influenced by Michel Foucault's conceptions of *governmentality* and *biopower*, feminist poststructuralist scholars have investigated the means by which institutions, particularly medico-juridical institutions, produce raced, gendered, and sexualized subjects who experience individual identity in particular ways. Tracing the intended and unintended consequences of state efforts not only to regulate the conduct of individuals but also to manage whole populations, poststructuralist feminists map the means by which disciplinary mechanisms specific to particular institutions produce self-regulating subjects—subjects whose desires and interests have themselves been shaped by practices of individualization and normalization. Operating through schools, hospitals, mental health clinics, therapeutic practices, court proceedings, military training, public-health measures, prisons, and everyday surveillance, biopower involves "an explosion of numerous and diverse techniques for achieving the subjugations of bodies and the control of populations" (Foucault 1977, 140). Emphasizing the "protection of life" rather than the threat of death, biopower obliterates classical boundaries between public and private, as state institutions undertake the regulation of health, welfare, sexuality, bodies, dispositions, and desires as part of their legitimate terrain. While legitimating a vast expansion of the reach of the state, biopower masks this extension of power by using the mechanism of rights to produce disciplined subjects who believe themselves to be self-regulating and therefore "free." According to poststructuralist feminists, the regulation of sexuality and reproduction plays a central role in normalizing and naturalizing the identities of political subjects (Miller 2007; Smith 2002, 2007).

Institutional Dynamism

Just as conceptions of power vary with differing feminist ideological and epistemological approaches, so too do assumptions about the degree to which gendered institutions are changeable. While some feminist scholars emphasize the intransigency of stable patriarchal institutions, others see gendered institutions as more open to change, either because institutions are seen as neutral or because they are seen as malleable. Yet other scholars address both institutional constraints and changeability within a dialectical context. R. W. Connell (1987), for example, notes that particular institutions establish gender regimes that are dynamic, complex, constantly negotiated, and powerfully constrained.

One of the continuing debates within feminist movements is about whether or how much to engage the state. Some radical feminists insist that the state is deeply embedded in unyielding structures of oppression, promulgating rules and distributing resources to entrench male power and privilege. Thus, they advocate autonomous feminist organizing to avoid cooptation by patriarchal institutions. A precursor to the conceptualization of gendered institutions, Catharine MacKinnon (1982, 1989) was one of the first to characterize the state and its most powerful product, the law, as inherently male. In MacKinnon's analysis, the state "coercively and authoritatively constitutes the social order in the interests of men through legitimating norms, forms, relation to society, and substantive policies" (1989, 162). According to MacKinnon, as a site that institutionalizes male norms, perceptions, and desires as the "natural" order of things, the state has not been, and never will be, a site for liberation. This sentiment is echoed in the works of many feminist activists who caution against engagement with the state or articulate a high degree of skepticism about the prospects for progressive state-led change. The skepticism of radical feminists, and particularly radical feminists of color, helps to illuminate entrenched racial and gender power within institutions, the role of institutions in perpetuating privilege and disadvantage, and the enormity of the challenges facing those who seek to eradicate systemic inequalities.

In contrast to radical feminist suspicion of power-laden state institutions as a source of liberation, the liberal feminist assessment of state institutions as gender-neutral suggests the possibility of progressive change once feminists infiltrate the state. Feminist scholars who understand the state as a series of dynamic organizations in which both internal and external players can act to challenge oppressive rules also advocate engagement with the state as a strategy to foster societal change that might eventually affect unequal structures.

To be fair, very few feminist scholars fit easily at either extreme end of this rather simplified and one-dimensional continuum. Even MacKinnon (1979), who developed such a powerful critique of the intransigent character of the male state, does not wholly reject the law, as her work to conceptualize sexual harassment as a form of sex discrimination makes clear. And although some feminist scholars continue to emphasize women's participation within institutions somewhat uncritically, many recognize gendered impediments that women face in these institutions. Criticizing simplistic dismissals of institutions and institutionalists, Sally Kenney (2012) has argued persuasively that "liberal feminists" have been unfairly denigrated. To demonstrate the importance of a nuanced "gendered institutional" approach, Kenney has developed a sophisticated comparative study of the judiciary that emphasizes the difference women make when they serve as judges and justices in national and international courts.

Many feminist institutionalists acknowledge that shifting power dynamics within institutions is not only extremely difficult, but also somewhat rare. Their increasing attention to informal institutions reflects growing understanding of the stickiness of institutional power dynamics. Awareness of competing agendas within institutions has also helped explain how hard-won mandates for progressive change in institutions can be undermined by street-level bureaucrats who find ingenious mechanisms to comply with the letter of the law while perpetuating informal practices that sustain inequality. Nonetheless, there is some optimism within the new institutionalism literature, particularly in the feminist new institutionalism literature, about "institutional dynamism." Although new institutionalist scholars readily acknowledge that institutions are created through and reinforce power relations that privilege some at the expense of others, they have demonstrated that institutions can provide opportunities—intended or unintended—for marginalized groups to enact change (Thelen 2003; Chappell 2006). Some scholars argue that the mere act of uncovering this dynamism opens up the possibility of alternatives (Driscoll and Krook 2009). Other scholars focus on policy entrepreneurs and activists who work to "regender" institutions as crucial sources of change (Beckwith 2005; Chappell 2006). Yet others identify exogenous shocks as a potent mechanism for altering gendered institutions. Such shocks may be rare and may operate independently of individual agency, but they can initiate irreversible change.

A good deal of feminist literature probes the complex relation between structure and agency in relation to institutional change. Meryl Kenny (2007, 94), for example, argues that "while institutions constrain practice, defining possibilities for actions, institutions are themselves constituted from moment to moment by these practices." By contextualizing and historicizing the study of institutions, it is possible to discern patterns of stability and instability. Where structures afford unquestioned stability in "settled times," instabilities associated with war, natural disasters, and economic crisis can create new possibilities for social change agents to foster institutional change (Kenny 2007, 92). Lee Ann Banaszak and Laurel Weldon (2011) suggest that conflicts between formal and informal institutions may also contribute to possibilities for institutional change.

Formal versus Informal Institutions

Within political science, the focus on informal institutions is comparatively new. Traditionally focused on formal institutions, political scientists have been slow to appreciate the importance of informal institutions. Feminist political scientists have played an important role in pressing the discipline to recognize that informal mechanisms can play a key role in maintaining and reproducing power even in the midst of institutional reform (Mackay et al. 2010; Hellsten et al. 2006). Where formal institutions are consciously designed and operate according to codified, clearly specified rules (Chappell and Waylen 2013), informal institutions are "socially shared rules, usually unwritten, that are created, communicated, and enforced outside of officially sanctioned channels" (Helmke and Levitskey 2004, 727). Although they are sometimes referred to as "social institutions" or "culture," Banaszak and Weldon (2011, 268) suggest that "informal institutions are communicated, enforced, and sanctioned through nonofficial channels."

Informal gendered institutions help explain gaps between the goals of new laws and policies designed to promote equality and their implementation within existing institutions. While formal and informal rules can operate in tandem, supporting and reinforcing each other, they can also conflict. Formal rules designed to establish gender equality can be sabotaged or undermined by informal institutions committed to traditional gender hierarchies. Echoing radical feminist cautions about the persistence of patriarchy, multiple feminist institutional analyses have demonstrated that changing formal rules may be insufficient to produce meaningful equality because powerful informal institutions mediate their effects (Banaszak and Weldon 2011). In countries where equal employment laws have been adopted, for example, women have formal protections against workplace discrimination; yet, economic parity is far from a reality. Understanding the multiple informal practices within the workplace that undermine women's full participation is pivotal if equal outcomes are to be realized. Similarly, huge gaps exist between legislation designed to eliminate violence against women and the persistence of the everyday practices that subject women to physical, psychological, and sexual violence (Montoya 2013). The global movement to eliminate violence has helped to achieve the passage of numerous antiviolence laws; yet persistent norms concerning "acceptable" violence and the characteristics of a "sympathetic" victim combine to ensure that successful prosecution of sexual assault and intimate partner violence is rare. To realize the objectives of equality and antiviolence policies, then, informal institutions must also be transformed. Thus, nuanced institutional analyses are important not only to feminist scholarship, but also for feminist social justice mobilizations to produce systemic change.

Institutions as Producers of Gender

In addition to discussions of gender as an institution, gender *in* institutions, and gendered institutions, some feminist scholars have characterized institutions as integrally involved in the production of gender. Far from being neutral entities, institutions create and maintain gender privilege and disadvantage, not only through law, but also through institutional processes and practices that create separate spheres for men and women of various races and ethnicities and distribute political opportunities on the basis of race and gender.

Many institutional scholars have pointed out that institutions influence gender roles. Iris Marion Young (2002), for example, has discussed the role that legal rules and cultural norms play in constraining gender performance and in punishing nonconformity, asserting that "feminist and queer theories need conceptual tools to describe the rules and practices of institutions that pressure differing roles for men and women" (21). Mike Savage and Anne Witz (1993) made a stronger claim, suggesting that all institutions are implicated in the shaping gender relations, not only in the private sphere where well-defined gender roles have been a hallmark of family life, but also in public workplaces and governing institutions, where job segregation by sex has been the norm.

Some scholars have gone still further. Joan Scott (1988) noted that the attributes associated with men and women and deemed as masculine and feminine vary across time, culture, race, *and* institutions. Other scholars have demonstrated that institutions, whether public and private, social and political, or formal and informal, play critical roles in the construction of gender (Connell 1987; Savage and Witz 1993; Kenney 1996). Carole Pateman (1998, 248), for example, has traced the means by which nascent welfare states constructed (white) "male independence" as the criterion for public citizenship, while simultaneously making it impossible for women to meet that criterion. States created "three elements of 'independence' . . . related to the masculine capacity for self-protection: the capacity to bear arms, the capacity to own property and the capacity for self-government." States used mandatory male military service, conscription, and militia duty as means to construct men as "bearers of arms." Women, on the other hand, were "unilaterally disarmed," barred from military service and from combat duty, as men were assigned responsibility for the "protection of women and children." Through laws governing freedom of contract, states created the most fundamental property owned by "free men," the property in their own person and in their labor power. By constructing women as the property of their fathers or husbands, states denied women the right to freely contract their labor. By structuring marriage laws to guarantee men perpetual sexual access to their wives, states denied married women autonomous ownership of their bodies. Moreover, by creating the category "head-of-household" and restricting it to men, states created men's capacity for governance, not only of themselves but of their "dependents." The state created and reinforced women's identity as "dependent" directly and indirectly, even as it used dependency to legitimate women's exclusion from political life. Defined by the state as dependent, regardless of their actual earnings or wealth, women were declared "trespassers into the public edifice of civil society and the state (248).

Beyond laws that produced women as "apolitical" by barring them from political engagement and "dependent" by rendering their arduous contributions to subsistence invisible, political and economic institutions have fostered employment rules and norms that shore up gendered divisions of labor that construct women as primary caregivers and men as primary bread winners, whether or not they actually contribute to household income. More recent policies, such as those pertaining to maternity leave, reinforce these gendered relations. Institutions, however, also have the capacity to reshape and transform gender relations in more progressive and liberating fashions. For example, by creating incentives that require men to take parental leave in order to maximize the benefit allowed for heterosexual families, Sweden has attempted to change gendered responsibilities for child care. And in so doing, Swedish political institutions have intervened profoundly into defining characteristics of gender in the contemporary era.

By demonstrating key roles played by institutions in producing gender, feminist scholars have sought to "denaturalize" gender. By showing in concrete cases how institutions create divisions of labor, power, and desire, feminist analyses illuminate prospects for gender transformation.

INTERSECTIONAL INSTITUTIONAL ANALYSIS

Intersectional analyses emphasize the mutual constitution of gender, race, class, sexuality, and other categories of oppression within institutions. Although socialist and postmodern feminists have noted the importance of investigating multiple vectors of power, most studies of gendered institutions have focused on institutional practices that disadvantage women without fully engaging the implications of the insight that gender is inseparable from race, class, ethnicity, sexual orientation, and other socially constructed hierarchies of difference (Hawkesworth 2003). Even when multiple dimensions of difference are acknowledged, they are seldom incorporated into a systematic intersectional institutional analysis.

Although discussion of the simultaneity of oppressions has a long history in black feminism, the term *intersectionality* was introduced in the 1980s as a heuristic term "to focus attention on the vexed dynamics of difference and the solidarities of sameness in the context of antidiscrimination and social movement politics" (Cho, Crenshaw, and McCall 2013, 787). Kimberlé Crenshaw (1989, 1991) conceptualized intersectionality in order to demonstrate how "single-axis thinking," that is, exclusive focus on race or class or gender, undermines legal thinking, disciplinary knowledge production, and struggles for social justice. In her studies of the failure of the US courts to address discrimination experienced by black women, Crenshaw demonstrated both how to conduct more sophisticated analyses of inequality and oppression and identified the intellectual and social justice benefits that would accrue from intersectional analysis. From the outset, the theorizations of intersectionality and intersectional studies focused on the critical role of institutions in creating and preserving inequalities. In the words of Patricia Hill Collins (1993, 29–30), "racism, sexism, and elitism all have concrete institutional locations."

Intersectional analysis is important not only to "understand" the operations of power within institutions, but also to assess strategies appropriate to change them. Just as feminist investigations of gendered institutions illuminate the impact that institutions have on lived experiences of men and women, intersectional analyses reveal that gendering processes are also raced, classed, and enmeshed in other salient categories of oppression. Far from sustaining a false sense of institutional neutrality, intersectional analysis identifies the many groups of people rendered invisible or substantively harmed by institutional practices that claim to be colorblind, gender-blind, and indifferent to sexual orientation and disability. As Crenshaw noted, intersectional analysis can demonstrate that institutions deemed "women-friendly" may in fact be harmful to some women, as well as to some men and to those who reject gender binaries altogether.

Institutions that seek to combat violence against women provide a pivotal example of the need for more inclusive and intersectional institutional analysis. In "Mapping the Margins: Intersectionality, Identity Politics, and Violence against Women of Color," Crenshaw (1991) pointed out that while many women face similar obstacles in leaving violent relationships, women of color may face unique hurtles because of the multiple dimensions of oppression that circumscribe their lives. Institutionalized racism may exclude women of color from effectively utilizing the state services or protections. Xenophobia institutionalized in policies that bar immigrant women from welfare provisions may make it impossible for immigrant women to seek an escape from a violent household. Heternormative understandings of violence (whether formalized in law or upheld informally by legal, medical, or shelter personnel) may prevent those identifying or perceived as queer or transgender from accessing help. Furthermore, laws designed to help victims of violence might actually hurt certain groups of vulnerable populations. Mandatory arrest policies, for example, are oblivious to long histories of racism within the criminal justice system, which results in the arrest of battered women along with their assailants and leaving women of color at risk of losing their children if they seek police assistance. Mandatory arrest policies may also subject some women to ostracism within communities of color, severing their access to resources vital to their survival. Indeed, mandatory arrest may also culminate in deportation of women with tenuous immigration status.

Policies designed to address the oppression of marginalized groups may worsen the situation of the worst off, when intersectional complexities are not explicitly considered. For example, in recent years European antiviolence policies have increasingly highlighted gender-based violence within migrant and ethnic/racial minority communities. As policy discourse "culturalizes" violence, "dowry deaths," "honor killings," and "female genital mutilation" become the focus of public attention as domestic violence in majority communities becomes invisible. While intended to help marginalized groups, framings that suggest that violence is "imported" from elsewhere reinforce and exacerbate racist and xenophobic tendencies within European Union member nations, while they fail to provide any tangible measures, such as better immigration policies or culturally sensitive public services that actually help migrant women and racial/ethnic minority women (Montoya 2013; Montoya and Agustin 2013). Constructing violence as a problem of the foreign "other," from whom "brown women" must be saved (Spivak 1988), discourses that culturalize violence damage not only "brown men" who are targeted for police intervention, but also "brown women" whose agency is eradicated by unrelenting rhetoric of victimization. As state institutions position themselves to save brown women from "death by culture" (Narayan 1997), the racism and xenophobia that constitute so much of the violent oppression experienced by immigrant women are rendered invisible.

Dean Spade (2013, 1031) has pointed out that resistance conceived through single-axis frameworks can never transform legal institutions, which have been complicit in the foundational violence of slavery, genocide, and heteropatriarchy. This insight has lessons for scholars as well as activists. Intersectional institutional analysis is necessary to generate scholarship that illuminates the complexity of power dynamics within and beyond institutions, just as it is necessary to envision and enact systemic institutional transformation. Feminist studies of institutions have charted important directions for future research, but much more scholarly attention is needed to theorize intersectional institutional analysis, develop methodologies capable of grappling with the messiness of complexity, and investigate the intersecting power dynamics of the manifold institutions that circumscribe contemporary life.

References

Acker, Joan. 1992. "From Sex Roles to Gendered Institutions." *Contemporary Sociology* 21 (5): 565–569.

Arabsheibani, G. Reza, Alan Marin, and Jonathan Wadsworth. 2007. "Variations in Gay Pay in the USA and in the UK." In *Sexual Orientation Discrimination: An International Perspective*, edited by M.V. Lee Badgett and Jefferson Frank, 44–61. New York: Routledge.

Banaszak, Lee Ann, and Laurel Weldon. 2011. "Informal Institutions, Protest, and Change in Gendered Federal Systems." *Politics & Gender* 7 (2): 262–273.

Beckwith, Karen. 2005. "A Common Language of Gender." *Politics & Gender* 1 (1): 128–137.

Boserup, Ester. 1970. *Women's Role in Economic Development*. London: Earthscan.

Butler, Judith. 1993. *Bodies That Matter*. New York and London: Routledge.

Calas, Marta B., and Linda Smircich. 2006. "From the 'Woman's Point of View' Ten Years Later: Towards a Feminist Organization Studies." In *The SAGE Handbook of Organization Studies*, edited by Stewart R. Clegg, Cynthia Hardy, Thomas B. Lawrence, and Walter R. Nord, 284–346. London: Sage Publications.

Chappell, Louise. 2006. "Moving to a Comparative Politics of Gender." *Politics & Gender* 2 (2): 221–263.

Chappell, Louise. 2010. "Comparative Gender and Institutions: Directions for Research." *Perspectives on Politics* 8 (1): 183–189.

Chappell, Louise and Georgina Waylen. 2013. "Gender and the Hidden Life of Institutions." *Public Administration* 91 (3): 599–617.

Cho, Sumi, Kimberlé Williams Crenshaw, and Leslie McCall. 2013. "Toward a Field of Intersectionality Studies: Theory, Applications, and Praxis." *Signs* 38 (4): 785–810.

Collins, Patricia Hill. 1993. "Toward a New Vision: Race, Class, and Gender as Categories of Analysis and Connection." *Race, Sex & Class* 1 (1): 25–45.

Connell, R. W. 1987. *Gender and Power: Society, the Person, and Sexual Politics*. Redwood City, CA: Stanford University Press.

Crenshaw, Kimberlé Williams. 1989. "Demarginalizing the Intersection of Race and Sex: A Black Feminist Critique of Antidiscrimination Doctrine, Feminist Theory and Antiracist Politics." *University of Chicago Legal Forum*, 140: 139–167.

Crenshaw, Kimberlé Williams. 1991. "Mapping the Margins: Intersectionality, Identity Politics, and Violence against Women of Color. *Stanford Law Review* 43 (6): 1241–1299.

Driscoll, Amanda, and Mona Lena Krook. 2009. "Can There Be a Feminist Rational Choice Institutionalism?" *Politics & Gender* 5 (2): 238–245.

Foucault, Michel. 1977. *"Discipline and Punish: The Birth of the Prison.* Translated by Alan Sheridan. New York: Vintage Books.

Fox, Richard L., and Jennifer L. Lawless. 2004. "Entering the Arena? Gender and the Decision to Run for Office." *American Journal of Political Science* 48 (2): 264–280.

Hawkesworth, Mary. 2003. "Congressional Enactments of Race-Gender: Toward a Theory of Race-Gendered Institutions." *American Political Science Review* 97 (4): 529–550.

Hellsten, Sirkku, Anne Maria Holli, and Krassimira Daskalova. 2006. *Women's Citizenship and Political Rights.* Basingstoke: Palgrave Macmillan.

Helmke, Gretchen, and Steven Levitsky. 2004. "Informal Institutions and Comparative Politics: A Research Agenda." *Perspectives on Politics* 2 (4): 725–740.

Kenny, Meryl, and Fiona Mackay. 2009. "Skeptical Notes on Feminism and Institutionalism." *Politics & Gender* 5 (2): 271–280.

Kenny, Meryl. 2007. "Gender, Institutions, and Power: A Critical Review." *Politics* 27 (2): 91–100.

Kenney, Sally J. 1996. "New Research on Gendered Political Institutions." *Political Research Quarterly* 49 (2): 445–466.

Kenney, Sally J. 2012. *Gender and Justice.* New York and London: Routledge.

Lorber, Judith. 1995. *Paradoxes of Gender.* New Haven, CT: Yale University Press.

Lovenduski, Joni. 2011. Foreword to *Gender, Politics, and Institutions: Towards a Feminist Institutionalism*, edited by Mona Lena Krook and Fiona Mackay, vii–xi. Basingstoke: Palgrave Macmillan.

Mackay, Fiona, Meryl Kenny, and Louise Chappell. 2010. "New Institutionalism through a Gender Lens: Towards a Feminist Institutionalism?" *International Political Science Review* 21 (5): 573–588.

MacKinnon, Catherine A. 1979. *Sexual Harassment of Working Women: A Case of Sex Discrimination.* New Haven: Yale University Press.

MacKinnon, Catharine A. 1982. "Feminism, Marxism, Method, and the State: An Agenda for Theory." *Signs: Journal of Women in Culture and Society* 7 (3): 515–544.

MacKinnon, Catharine A. 1989. *Toward a Feminist Theory of the State.* Cambridge, MA: Harvard University Press.

Miller, Ruth. 2007. "Rights, Reproduction, Sexuality and Citizenship in the Ottoman Empire and Turkey." *Signs: Journal of Women in Culture and Society* 32 (2): 347–374.

Montoya, Celeste. 2013. *From Global to Grassroots: The European Union, Transnational Advocacy, and Combating Violence against Women.* New York: Oxford University Press.

Montoya, Celeste, and Lise Agustin Rolandsen. 2013. "The Othering of Domestic Violence: The EU and Cultural Framings of Violence against Women." *Social Politics* 20 (4): 534–557.

Narayan, Uma. 1997. "Cross-Cultural Connections, Border Crossings, and 'Death by Culture': Thinking about Dowry-Murders in India and Domestic Violence-Murders in the United States." In *Dislocating Cultures: Identities, Traditions, and Third World Feminism.* New York: Routledge.

North, Douglass. 1990. *Institutions, Institutional Change and Economic Performance.* Cambridge: Cambridge University Press.
Pateman, Carole. 1998. "The Patriarchal Welfare State." In *Feminism, the Public and the Private*, edited by Joan Landes, 241–274. New York: Oxford University Press.
Risman, Barbara J. 2004. "Gender as Social Structure." *Gender & Society* 18 (4): 429–450.
Savage, Mike, and Anne Witz. 1993. *Gender and Bureaucracy.* Oxford: Blackwell.
Scott, Joan Wallach. 1986. "Gender." *American Historical Review* 91 (5): 1053–1075.
Scott, Joan Wallach. 1988. *Gender: A Useful Category of Historical Analysis.* New York: Columbia University Press.
Smith, Anna Marie. 2002. "The Sexual Regulation Dimension of Contemporary Welfare Law: A Fifty State Overview." *Michigan Journal of Gender and Law* 8 (2): 121–218.
Smith, Anna Marie. 2007. *Welfare Reform and Sexual Regulation.* Cambridge: Cambridge University Press.
Spade, Dean. 2013. "Intersectional Resistance and Law Reform." *Signs* 38 (4): 1031–1055.
Spivak, Gayatri Chakfravorty. 1988. "Can the Subaltern Speak?" In *Marxism and the Interpretation of Culture*, edited by Cary Nelson and Lawrence Grossbert, 271–313. London: Macmillan.
Thelen, Kathleen. 2003. "How Institutions Evolve: Insights from Comparative Historical Analysis." In *Comparative Historical Analysis in the Social Science*, edited by James Mahoney and Dietrich Rueschemeyer, 208–240. Cambridge: Cambridge University Press.
Young, Iris Marion. 2002. *Inclusion and Democracy.* New York: Oxford University Press.

CHAPTER 19

INTERSECTIONALITY

BRITTNEY COOPER

In the nearly three decades since black feminist legal scholar and critical race theorist Kimberlé Crenshaw coined the term *intersectionality*, a host of debates within feminist theory have ensued about what the term means, the breadth of its intellectual history and genealogies, and the scope of its political possibility. Though intersectionality has taken on a kind of "citational ubiquity" (Wiegman 2012) in academic circles, giving the sense that "everyone" does intersectional work, there seems to be less agreement about what exactly intersectionality is and a growing sense that despite its expansive academic reach, the framework does not sufficiently attend to a range of critical questions. In this chapter, I provide both an overview of Crenshaw's articulation of intersectionality and a sense of the broader genealogies of black feminist thought from which it emerges. I map the most significant recent arguments against intersectionality in the work of three feminist theorists: Jennifer Nash, Robyn Wiegman and Jasbir Puar. I then attend to the work of theorists who take up intersectionality as a kind of feminist methodology and consider whether this approach solves the problems attributed to intersectional approaches.

Intersectionality emerged in the late 1980s as an analytic frame capable of attending to the particular positionality of black women and other women of color both in civil rights law and within civil rights movements. It is the most visible and enduring contribution that feminism, and in particular black feminism, has made to critical social theory in the last quarter century. Coined and elaborated by Crenshaw in a pair of essays published in 1989 and 1991, the term *intersectionality* asserted an analytic frame that disrupted the tendency in social-justice movements and critical social theorizing "to treat race and gender as mutually exclusive categories of experience and analysis (Crenshaw 1989)." In "Demarginalizing the Intersection of Race and Sex: A Black Feminist Critique of Antidiscrimination Doctrine, Feminist Theory and Antiracist Politics," Crenshaw exposed the problems of this "single-axis" analysis when set against the backdrop of "the multidimensionality of Black women's experiences." "This single-axis framework," she argued, "erases Black women in the conceptualization, identification and remediation of race and sex discrimination by limiting inquiry to the experiences of otherwise-privileged members of the group" (1989, 140). Calling attention to the manner in which the single-axis framework erased the experiences of black women also exposed the larger challenge that "these problems of exclusion cannot be solved simply by including Black women within an already established analytical structure" (140). The "intersectional experience," Crenshaw averred, "is greater than the sum of racism and sexism," meaning that "any analysis that does not take intersectionality into account cannot sufficiently address the particular manner in which Black women are subordinated" (140). These observations demanded a total "recasting and rethinking" of existing policy frameworks (140).

In her 1991 article, "Mapping the Margins: Intersectionality, Identity Politics and Violence against Women of Color," Crenshaw revisited intersectionality with respect to its relationship to social constructionist ideas about identity and cultural battles over identity politics. She made clear that intersectionality should not be taken as "some new, totalizing theory of identity" (1991, 1244). Rather intersectionality demonstrated "the need to account for multiple grounds of identity when considering how the social world is constructed" (1245). Explicitly expanding her framework to include both black and Latina women, Crenshaw talked about the relationship between "structural intersectionality" and "political intersectionality." Structural intersectionality referred to a convergence of "race, gender, and class domination" wherein social interventions designed to ameliorate the results of only racism, or sexism, or poverty would be insufficient to address the needs of a woman of color marginalized by the interaction of all three systems of power. For instance, in addressing domestic violence, "intervention strategies based solely on the experiences of women who do not share the same class or race backgrounds will be of limited help to women who face different obstacles because of race and class" (1246). Political intersectionality, on the other hand, looked outward to "highlight that women of color are situated within at least two subordinated groups that frequently pursue conflicting political agendas" (1252).

Taken together, Crenshaw's essays catalyzed a tectonic shift in the nature of feminist theorizing by suggesting that black women's experiences demanded new paradigms in feminist theorizing, creating an analytic framework that exposed through use of a powerful metaphor exactly what it meant for systems of power to be interactive, and explicitly tying the political aims of an inclusive democracy to a theory and account of power. As an account of power, intersectionality attended to the particular forms of subjugation and subordination that characterized black women's intersecting and multiplicative (King 1986) experiences of racism and sexism within the law.

After more than a quarter century of traversing feminist academic terrain, there is an increasing concern that intersectionality has outlived its analytic usefulness. Some argue, implicitly rather than explicitly, that its overarching investment in speaking about the social conditions of US black women's lives militates against its ability to offer a broadly applicable set of theoretical propositions. Others are disillusioned with intersectionality's inability to fully account for all the exigencies of identity in the face of multiple and proliferating categories of social identity, such as sexuality, nation, religion, age, and ability, in contemporary intersectional discourses. Yet, the political import of paradigms that make the interactive process of social marginalization visible cannot be denied. The institutional transformation of the status of women of color feminisms within the academy is a direct result of the political work that intersectional frames do. Thus, there is a tension about what it might mean to jettison or move *beyond* intersectionality's theoretical concerns without jettisoning a commitment to its social-justice aims.

Sirma Bilge (2013) notes that "like other 'traveling theories' that move across disciplines and geographies, intersectionality falls prey to widespread misrepresentation, tokenization, displacement, and disarticulation. Because the concept of intersectionality emerged as a tool to counter multiple oppressions, there are multiple narratives about its orgins, as well as tensions over the legibility of its stakes" (410). Thus, I want to begin with an intellectual genealogy of works by black women thinkers that laid the intellectual groundwork from which Crenshaw launched intersectionality.

Genealogies

The idea that patriarchy interacts with other systems of power—namely, racism—to uniquely disadvantage some groups of women more than others has a long history within black feminism's intellectual and political traditions. As early as 1892, Anna Julia Cooper wrote, "[T]he colored woman of to-day occupies, one may say, a unique position in this country.... She is confronted by both a woman question and a race problem, and is as yet an unknown or an unacknowledged factor in both" (134). The "woman question" was nineteenth-century shorthand for talking about the full inclusion of women as legally recognized human beings entitled to property rights and all other rights attaining to citizens. The "race problem" was nineteenth-century shorthand for discussing the cementing of Jim Crow segregation in the post-Reconstruction era. Black women endured the ignobility of both systems, often while confronting crushing poverty too. Even after significant milestones had been reached in the broader women's movement, black women often found themselves excluded from employment opportunities reserved for white women.

In 1940, Cooper's colleague and contemporary Mary Church Terrell penned a self-published autobiography with the title *A Colored Woman in a White World*, with the opening lines, "This is the story of a colored woman living in a white world. It cannot possibly be like a story written by a white woman. A white woman has only one handicap to overcome—that of sex. I have two—both sex and race. I belong to the only group in this country, which has two such huge obstacles to surmount. Colored men have only one—that of race" (Terrell [1940] 2005, 29) Terrell argued that these "two such huge obstacles" constituted the "double-handicap" of race and sex (29). She positioned herself in relationship to white women, whose struggles for equal rights had fomented an epic battle in the latter half of the nineteenth century and the first two decades of the twentieth century, and also to black men, whose failure on the basis of racism to attain what Ida B. Wells frequently called "manhood rights" has formed the basis of the long black freedom struggle. The idea that racism and sexism and patriarchy acted in tandem to duly disadvantage black women in the body politic became a mainstay of early feminist theorizing among black women. Over and over again, black women formulated new ways to think and talk about how racism and sexism dovetailed to wall them out of the benefits of citizenship.

In the early 1940s, while she was a student at Howard University Law School, the only woman in her class, famed civil rights activist Pauli Murray coined the term "Jane Crow." Murray (1987, 183) characterized the male-centered legal culture she encountered in the law school as a culture of "discriminatory sex bias," a system of "Jane Crow," which she understood to be "a twin evil" of Jim Crow. In the 1970s, Murray had come to think more specifically about how Jane Crow or sexual bias against black women showed up within the confines of the law. In a groundbreaking essay, "Constitutional Law and Black Women" (Murray, n.d.) she drew a range of parallels between the treatment of blacks and the treatment of women in the law. She concluded that "Black women have an important stake in the present movement to make the guarantee of equal rights without regard to sex the fundamental law of the land" (45). The use of the race-sex analogy became one of Murray's signal contributions to legal thought and civil rights activism (Mayeri 2011).

Because Murray felt that sexism functioned analogously to racism, she believed that cases brought under the Equal Protection Amendment (the 14th) could alleviate sex discrimination against all women. Though she did not fully factor in that the law was incapable of accounting for black women's unique position vis-à-vis Jane Crow, she laid the groundwork for legal interventions that emerged two decades later in Crenshaw's work and the work of other critical race theorists.

In 1970, echoing Terrell's concept of the "double-handicap" of race and sex, Frances Beale argued that black women were caught in a kind of "double jeopardy" of being both black and female. She described "the black woman in America . . . as a 'slave of a slave,'" placed in that position because black women often became the "scapegoat for the evils that this horrendous system has perpetrated on black men (Beale [1970] 1995, 148)." By the mid-1970s the Combahee River Collective was arguing that "the major systems of oppression are interlocking." Most importantly they argued, "the synthesis of these oppressions creates the conditions of our lives" (1995, 232).

By the late 1980s, Deborah King revisited Beale's concept of double jeopardy and Beverly Lindsay's concept of triple jeopardy, which attempted more explicitly to account for class and to include the experiences of Native American, Chicana, and Asian American women. King (1988, 47) argued that these frameworks fell into the trap of taking an "additive approach" that "ignor[ed] the fact that racism, sexism, and classism constitute three, interdependent control systems," something that could be better captured in a term like *multiple jeopardy*. "Multiple," she argued referred "not only to several, simultaneous oppressions but to the multiplicative relationships among them as well" (47).

Taken together, this body of proto-intersectionality theorizing advanced the idea that systems of oppression—namely, racism, classism, sexism, and heterosexism—worked together to create a set of social conditions under which black women and other women of color lived and labored, always in a kind of invisible but ever-present social jeopardy. Crenshaw built on and brought together this body of black feminist theorizing, when she encountered the legal conundrum of black women who were discriminated against as black women, not only as women and not only as blacks. What she named "intersectionality," encapsulated and expanded a body of work about a set of social problems that black women thinkers had been grappling with and attempting in various shapes and forms to name for nearly a century. In this regard, Crenshaw's bringing together of critical race theory with the work of such black feminist theorists as Anna Julia Cooper, Gloria Hull, Barbara Smith, and the women of Kitchen Table Press, as well as the work of Paula Giddings, represented the very kind of interdisciplinarity that has become a hallmark of black feminist theorizing. In the twenty-five years since the publication of these two germinal essays, Crenshaw has continued over the course of several articles to sharpen her intersectional analysis. For instance, she argued in "From Private Violence to Mass Incarceration: Thinking Intersectionally about Women, Race, and Social Control" (2012), that with regard to the growing problem of black and Latina women and mass incarceration, "not only is there no one way that racially marginalized women are subject to overlapping patterns of power, but also women of color are certainly not intersectionality's only subjects when it comes to social punishment" (1425). Thus, she argues, "intersectional dynamics are not static, but neither are they untethered from history, context, or social identity" (1426). But the core of her work remains about mapping the manner in which power dynamics interact to make black women marginalized by social systems like mass incarceration invisible.

Intersectional Feminisms

Crenshaw used a discrete set of problems that black women encountered when bringing antidiscrimination lawsuits against their employers to point to the broader challenge of the law's insufficiency to remedy harm done to people placed along multiple axes of marginalized identities. Although she did not intend it to, her framework, which is at base an account of structural power relationships, offered a way to begin talking about the interaction of these systems of power in the formation of identity. To return to Combahee, black women noted that interactive systems of power "formed the conditions" of their lives. And insofar as material conditions bear some relationship to how one identifies in the world and moves through the world, intersectionality's implications for reconceptualizing identity have had far-reaching consequences, in particular for the development of feminist studies in the academy.

However, the disjuncture between theories of identity and the intellectual project of intersectionality led to a range of unfortunate consequences as the theoretical framework traveled to other disciplines. The most egregious of these consequences is the tendency to treat intersectionality as a feminist account of identity, despite Crenshaw's (1991, 1244) very clear assertion that the framework did not constitute some "new, totalizing theory of identity." So while Crenshaw used intersectionality to demonstrate certain fissures in identity politics and the ways that these kinds of group politics were frequently unable to meet the needs of certain putative members of the group, the theory has been accused of fomenting unhelpful and essentialist kinds of identifications.

In the original formulation of intersectionality, Crenshaw demonstrated that black women's experiences, while intersectional, were not reducible to intersectional treatments of race and sex, or to any other category, for that matter. Intersectionality was a first, formative step that allowed for recognition of the black female subject within juridical structures of power, where she had heretofore remained invisible and illegible, and thus unable to obtain any kind of justice. Crenshaw's argument was that *failure* to begin with an intersectional frame would always result in insufficient attention to black women's experiences of subordination. She did not argue for the converse, namely, that intersectionality would fully and wholly account for the range or depth of black female experiences. Intersectionality constituted a specific paradigm or framework for understanding black women's subordinated social position and the situated effects of mutually constructing systems of power and oppressions within black women's lives. Never did her work indicate that intersectionality was an effective tool of accounting for identities at any level beyond the structural. More recently, she has argued that "at the same time that intersectionality transcends an exclusive focus on identity or mere categorization, the lived experiences of racially marginalized women and girls are shaped by a range of social and institutional practices that produce and sustain social categories and infuse them with social meanings" (2012, 1426).

The implicit distinction being made here between personal kinds of identity and structural identities is an important one. The law conceptualizes people through the structural identities of gender, race, sexual orientation, or national origin. These kinds of identities are different from personal identities of the sort that refer to personal taste, personality traits, gender performativity, or intimate and filial relationships. If Crenshaw's account of intersectionality is implicated in the project of identity politics at all, it is implicated at the structural level rather than the personal level. However, as an analytic tool it has been erroneously taken up in some feminist academic circles as a totalizing account of identity, and it has proved insufficient for such projects. That in no way implicates the merits of intersectional paradigms, but rather calls into question the epistemic routes through which it has traveled to other places and whether these routes make sense.

In one of the earliest major critiques of intersectionality, legal scholar Peter Kwan argued:

> Intersectionality does not pack much of an epistemological punch. In other words, although intersectionality illuminates the ways in which victims of multiple forms of oppression must be recognized as such on their own terms, in and of itself intersectionality tells us little about the fiscal, emotional, psychological, and other conditions nor the subjectivity of those caught in the trajectories of intersecting categories. Intersectionality tells us, for example, that the condition and subjectivity of and

hence the legal treatment of Black women is not simply the sum of Blackness and femaleness, but it does not shed much light on what it is nevertheless. Narratives are often used to fill this gap. But narratives provide only empirical data on which the theoretical work remains to be done.

(Kwan 2000, 687)

Kwan is right on one level: knowing about the various intersections that constitute a person's structural position does not mean in fact *knowing* that person as an individual. But Kwan's real critique of intersectionality seems to be not of Crenshaw's articulation, but rather of black feminist standpoint theory, which is invested in an affirmative articulation of a black women's epistemological point of view. Intersectionality is not beholden to a particular epistemological viewpoint. While it brings into focus marginalized people practicing what Nancy Hartsock might call "subjugated knowledges," and while the relations of power intersectionality exposes might be most articulable through the framework of subjugated knowledges, intersectionality does not tether black women to a certain epistemological standpoint. By the time Kwan penned his essay at the end of the 1990s there had already been more than a decade of scholarly dissent among black feminists about the role of standpoint theory in circumscribing and ghettoizing black women's experiences and black feminist knowledge production (Carby 1987; Smith 1998). Still, intersectionality is dogged by critiques of its alleged epistemological and identitarian investments.

Take for instance, the work of black feminist theorist Jennifer Nash. In an essay called "Rethinking Intersectionality," Nash (2008, 4) outlines four central problems or "unresolved questions" with intersectionality: "[T]he lack of a clearly defined intersectional methodology, the use of black women as prototypical intersectional subjects, the ambiguity inherent to the definition of intersectionality, and the coherence between intersectionality and lived experiences of multiple identities." In raising these questions, Nash's "hope is not to dismantle intersectionality" but rather to expose intersectionality's underlying assumptions in order to help scholars "dismantle essentialism," "craft nuanced theories of identity and oppression," and "grapple with the messiness of subjectivity" (4). Current articulations of intersectionality are situated in Nash's work in opposition to the aforementioned goals.

Nash defines intersectionality as "the notion that subjectivity is constituted by mutually reinforcing vectors of race, gender, class, and sexuality" (2). She further argues that one of the theoretical and political purposes that intersectionality serves for feminist and antiracist scholarship is "to subvert race/gender binaries in service of theorizing identity in a more complex fashion" (2). This definition of intersectionality and articulation of its goals reveals two significant misreadings of intersectionality. The first is that the framework never claimed to be an affirmative assertion about how subjectivity is constituted, but was rather a claim about how certain aspects of one's identity could make them invisible as subjects within the law. The second problem, which is not unique to Nash's work but is, rather, indicative of how intersectionality is now discussed in some feminist circles, is that "vectors of race, gender, class, and sexuality," are conflated with a discussion of remedying "racism, sexism, and classism." One set of phrases points to identity categories; the other points to systems of power. Intersectionality is thus assessed as failing to account fully for identity issues from the view that its goal is to "subvert race/gender binaries *in service of theorizing identity in a more complex fashion*" (emphasis added) (2). Undoubtedly, this is how the project of intersectionality has been taken up in feminist studies, and undoubtedly, intersectionality would be found wanting as an epistemological system since it was meant to be a provisional solution to a more specific problem. Nowhere in the genealogies of thought that came to constitute intersectionality do black women ever put forth the interlocking nature of racism and sexism as the basis for understanding their identity wholly. In fact, they assert just the opposite—namely, that the operations of racism, sexism, and sometimes classism make them civically and juridically *unknowable*. In this case, the solution to the problem of unknowability is not being *known* but being *knowable*. Therefore, we should not conclude that frameworks that attempt to solve the problem of "unknowability," or what we might call *juridical illegibility* (Carbado 2013, 815), are attempting to help us know anyone. These frameworks attempt to make some aspect of people's identity *legible*. They attend to the problem of recognition rather than a problem of subjectivity.

Existing structures recognize and provide property rights and protections for a standard white, male, property-owning, heterosexual, able-bodied subject. But bringing into view lives that have been occluded by obtrusive structures, such as racism and sexism, does not then mean that the people living them are now known. It means that the structures making them invisible are now clear and that the negative impact of those structures must be addressed. Feminist theorists must reject any misrepresentations of intersectionality that suggest that the search for a theoretical frame that fully encompasses the bounds of articulable identities takes priority over a framework that sustains critiques of the institutional power arrangements that make those identities invisible and illegible. Intersectionality's most powerful argument is not that the articulation of new identities in and of itself disrupts power arrangements. Rather, the argument is that institutional power arrangements, rooted as they are in relations of domination and subordination, confound and constrict the life possibilities of those who already live at the intersection of certain identity categories, even as they elevate the possibilities of those living at more legible (and privileged) points of intersection. Thus, while intersectionality should be credited with "lifting the veil," to invoke Du Bois's metaphor of the racial "color line," we should remain clear that the goal of intersectionality is not to provide an epistemological mechanism to bring communities from behind the veil into full legibility. It is rather to rend the veil and make sure that no arguments are articulated to support its reconstruction. Thus political commitments which grow out of intersectionality are rooted in a critical demeanor of vigilance, my riff on Koritha Mitchell's notion of a "critical demeanor of shamelessness," (2014) with regard to challenging the ever-shifting machinations of systems that seek to reinstantiate and reinscribe dominance.

Barbara Tomlinson (2013, 1000) takes issue with critics, such as Nash, whose work suggests that "intersectionality's critique of structural power interferes with its more important use for developing general theories of identity." Tomlinson writes,

"Diminishing the role of power in identity formation, such critics demonstrate a desire for individual self-invention, as if history and power no longer have claims on us, as if the significance of identities lies in expressions of subjectivity" (1000). This set of concerns is markedly different "for scholars concerned with antisubordination," for whom "the experience and subjectivity of specific identities is not really the focus of the argument but rather a proxy or tool to examine and counter structural justice and subordination" (1000). Tomlinson issues a scathing indictment in the form of a warning: "which meaning of identity we are interested in depends on the work we want our work to do" (1000).

The stated desire among intersectionality's most pointed critics to "not dismantle it" has everything to do with their recognizing that intersectionality is institutionally important for providing the language and justification for a diverse academy. Robyn Wiegman (2012), for example, makes clear that she agrees with the central thrust of Jennifer Nash's argument and that she has many reservations about intersectionality herself. Nonetheless, we are told that to take her concerns as "an indictment of intersectional analysis is to hear a judgment I do not intend" (250). Rather, Wiegman is concerned not "with measuring the value of the promise that intersectionality makes but with the lessons at stake in fully inhabiting them" (250). Moreover, she argues that Nash's work "brings to the foreground the significance of the institutional setting in which intersectionality has garnered its critical authority, such that a theory of marginalization can become dominant even when the majority of those represented by its object of study have no access to the ameliorative justice its critical hegemony represents" (299). This assessment of intersectionality's broad critical reach seems very much to indict it for an inability to achieve "ameliorative justice" on behalf of black women (and perhaps other marginalized groups of color) that it claims to represent. To suggest that intersectionality possesses "critical hegemony" in a world where hegemony always signals a problematic relationship of dominance that needs to be dismantled runs counter to Wiegman's (and Nash's) assertions that they are not interested in "judging" or "dismantling" the project of intersectionality. But the fear, it seems, is that to fully "inhabit" the lessons of intersectionality is to prevent ourselves from attending to groups whose experience of marginalization is not akin to black women's or to suggest erroneously that black women are always, in every case, marginalized. This kind of intersectional conundrum as articulated by Nash and echoed by Wiegman is a skepticism about "whether all identities are intersectional or whether only multiply marginalized subjects have an intersectional identity" (Nash 2008; Wiegman 2012). Carbado (2013) responds to this particular quibble about which identities are intersectional essentially by noting that *all* identities are intersectional. The theory applies in cases where we are talking about multiply jeopardized or marginalized subjects, but "the theory [also] applies where there is no jeopardy at all. Thus it is a mistake to conceptualize intersectionality as a 'race to the bottom'" (814). The theory seeks to map the top of social hierarchies as well. By suggesting that intersectionality has a range of problems to which it cannot attend, some critics artificially circumscribe the limits of what the theory can perform. This need to displace intersectionality while claiming a desire to keep it intact in some greatly altered form is absolutely a function of market-driven, neoliberal forms of academic knowledge production and the sense that academics must always say something new. It is therefore bizarre when critics suggest that it is intersectionality itself, and not the impulses seeking to displace intersectional frames, that acts as a tool of neoliberal collusion, despite a continuing need for its political project within institutions.

The argument that the way intersectionality accounts for identity and its indebtedness to stable intact categories reproduce juridical structures that collude with neoliberal and imperialist projects emerges in the work of Jasbir Puar. In her groundbreaking *Terrorist Assemblages: Homonationalism in Queer Times*, Puar (2007, 212) argues for new formulations of identity that don't begin and end with intersectionality: "As opposed to an intersectional model of identity, which presumes that components—race, class, gender, sexuality, nation, age, religion—are separable analytics and can thus be disassembled, an assemblage is more attuned to interwoven forces that merge and dissipate, time, space, and body against linearity, coherency, and permanency." Puar deploys Gilles Deleuze and Felix Guattari's (2001, 6) conception of assemblage, which they define as a "multiplicity" that has "neither subject nor object, only determinations, magnitudes, and dimensions." They go on to say that "there are no points or positions . . . such as those found in a structure, tree, or root. There are only lines." In other words, assemblage is a way of describing relationships between constitutive entities that does not assume either an overarching system or structure, or a shared set of roots or genealogies. Puar suggests that this conception is more favorable than intersectionality, which

> demands the knowing, naming, and thus stabilizing of identity across space and time, relying on the logic of equivalence and analogy between various axes of identity and generating narratives of progress that deny the fictive and performative aspects of identification: you become an identity, yes, but also timelessness works to consolidate the fiction of a seamless stable identity in every space.
>
> (Puar 2007, 212)

One immediate problem with this account is that the black body has never been conceived as being capable of linearity and coherency, and certainly not of permanency, particularly when it comes to institutionalized and official knowledges. Moreover, since the earliest days of intersectional theorizing, Patricia Hill Collins (1998) has stridently rejected the logic of equivalence that inheres in some work on intersectionality, writing that "continuing to leave intersectionality as an undertheorized construct contributes to old hierarchies (and some new ones) being reformed under . . . a new myth of equivalent oppressions" (211). She says, "[I]f all oppressions mutually construct one another, then we're all oppressed in some way by something—oppression talk obscures unjust power relations" (211). Moreover, Rebecca Clark-Mane (2012, 92) argues that this logic of equivalence, this "flattening and proliferation of difference," is part of syntax of whiteness that inheres in third-wave or contemporary feminist theorizing. So a "stabilizing" of black identity across time and space might be politically attractive in the US context insofar as it creates the conditions for the protection of one's rights as a citizen. But this would require leaving an analysis not only of race as identity but also of racism as a system of power at the forefront of analyses of intersectionality, a point I will return to shortly.

Puar (2007, 215) continues her indictment of intersectionality by arguing that "intersectionality privileges naming, visuality, epistemology, representation, and meaning, while assemblage underscores feeling, tactility, ontology, affect, and information." Because assemblages attempt to "comprehend power beyond disciplinary regulatory models," in Puar's estimation they are more adept at "work[ing] against narratives of U.S. exceptionalism that secure empire, [by] challenging the fixity of racial and sexual taxonomies that inform practices of state surveillance and control" (215). Although Puar contends (like Nash and Wiegman) that she does not want to do away with intersectionality but only to supplement and complicate it through the introduction of the assemblage, the claims that intersectionality is complicit with US imperialism, that it is overly beholden to what Wiegman terms the "juridical imaginary," and that it replicates taxonomies of violence are nothing short of devastating. Moreover, to recast the desire of marginalized US subjects for state-based recognition as a collusion with empire suggests a troubling misunderstanding of the differing material realities of those who benefit from empire and those whose lives and labor and marginalization buttress the foundation of violence upon which the empire is built.

Yet, Puar writes, "as a tool of diversity management and a mantra of liberal multiculturalism, intersectionality colludes with the disciplinary apparatus of the state—census, demography, racial profiling, surveillance—in that 'difference' is encased within a structural container that simply wishes the messiness of identity into a formulaic grid" (212). In Puar's formulation, state recognition is an inherently limiting thing to want, because the desire for recognition vis-à-vis official channels reinscribes the authority of the state. But if, in the case of racialized others in the United States. for instance, the state is already interpellating identities in violent ways, then asking for recognition on different terms constitutes not collusion but dissent from various forms of state-based violence, both physical and discursive. Crenshaw (2012, 1452) argues in the case of mass incarceration that "some of the discursive spaces most vulnerable to neoliberal occupation have been those where feminist and antiracist commitments have been weakened by their failure to address the intersectional dimensions of violence and social control." In other words, to lose sight of structural systems of power and their varied interactions is to enable "neoliberal occupation" of putative social justice discourses. To suggest, for instance, that the desire for intersectional recognition in the law means that working-class communities of color are acquiescing to the overpolicing and surveillance of their bodies and communities assumes that lack of recognition and the invisibility that comes with it somehow constitutes a form of "protection" for black and brown people. That kind of analysis also suggests that intersectionality is implicated in obscuring rather than exposing the massive kinds of state surveillance that characterizes life in communities of color. This is simply not the case. Where protection of one's body is tied to being a recognizable category, the idea that people of color should not want categorizations and the protections they afford is short-sighted. And because intersectionality can consider a range of different ways in which modes of power intersect in these instances, it offers tools for dismantling these systems not reifying them.

Because US-based intersectionality does seek to understand circulations of juridical power, it would be problematic to impose dominant US identity categories in other national or transnational contexts. But if it is true that intersectionality's primary concern is to expose the way circulations of power enable or disable articulations of identity, rather than to offer better language through which to express and make subjectivity legible, then the suggestion that intersectionality colludes with rather than exposes power seems to be misplaced. Puar (2012) returns to this critique of intersectionality as a tool of US imperialism in another essay, called "I'd Rather Be a Cyborg Than a Goddess: Becoming Intersectional in Assemblage Theory." Here, she argues that intersectionality falls victim to certain "geopolitical problems":

> [T]ransnational and postcolonial scholars continue to point out that the categories privileged by intersectional analysis do not necessarily traverse national and regional boundaries nor genealogical exigencies, presuming and producing static epistemological renderings of categories themselves across historical and geopolitical locations. Indeed many of the cherished categories of the intersectional mantra, originally starting with race, class, gender, now including sexuality, nation, religion, age, and disability, are the product of modernist colonial agendas and regimes of epistemic violence, operative through a western/euro-american epistemological formation through which the whole notion of discrete identity has emerged.
>
> (Puar 2012, 54)

In other words, intersectionality relies on the production and reproduction of fixed identity categories that are tethered to the apparatuses of the nation-state, which is itself a problematic category and social formation, in order to make any interventions. Essentially, the argument here is that in seeking to remedy one kind of epistemic violence—namely, that against black women—intersectionality proliferates a variety of other kinds of violence against other women of color subjects.

Puar (2012) offers her own intervention to remedy the limitations of intersectionality through recourse again to the Deleuzean notion of assemblage. Intersectional identities, she tells us, "are the byproducts of attempts to still and quell the perpetual motion of assemblages, to capture and reduce them, to harness their threatening mobility" (50). I want to register two concerns about this move. First, I concur with Devon Carbado (2013) that formulations such as Kwan's cosynthesis and Puar's assemblages are "no more dynamic than intersectionality" because they all grow out of a common problem: "[T]here are discursive limitations to our ability to capture the complex and reiterative processes of social categorization. The very articulation of the idea that race and gender are co-constitutive, for example discursively fragments those categories—into race and gender—to make that point. The strictures of language require us to invoke race, gender, sexual orientation, and other categories one discursive moment at a time" (816). To then suggest that this amounts to a reproduction of the fixity of these categories is false.

Second, Puar argues that intersectional identities "attempt to quell" the "mobility" of assemblages. To acknowledge that fixity is an essentializing fiction does not deny either the very real realities of fixed or declining social positions or the ways that the matrix of domination (Collins [1990] 2000), acts very much like a spider's web that captures and immobilizes its prey. The concept of mobility should itself be problematized as being the property of certain embodied subjects. Intersectionality makes the disciplinary apparatus of the state visible and theorizes the way legal constructions continually produce categories of bodies existing outside the limits of legal protection. In other words, the ways in which juridical structures affix narratives of criminality to black male bodies (or brown bodies), for instance, Trayvon Martin and Jordan Davis, on the basis of a very particular race-gender schema, works to limit the mobility of these kinds of bodies in public and private space. In the end, even Puar concedes these realities and opts for some unarticulated possibility of bridging the two frameworks:

> [To] dismiss assemblage in favor of retaining intersectional identitarian frameworks is to miss the ways in which societies of control apprehend and produce bodies as information, ... to render intersectionality as an archaic relic of identity politics then partakes in the fantasy of never-ending inclusion of capacity-endowed bodies, bypassing entirely the possibility that for some bodies—we can call them statistical outliers, or those consigned to premature death, or those once formerly considered useless bodies or bodies of excess—discipline and punish may well still be the primary mode of power apparatus.
>
> (Puar 2012, 63)

THE PARADIGMATIC BLACK FEMALE SUBJECT

This tension about the way intersectionality purportedly limits the ability of scholars to develop frameworks that more fully account for subjectivity leads to a central question: What is the status of the black female subject in a world where the theoretical paradigm that has made her the most visible is indicted for making the identities of other marginalized groups invisible? Because Crenshaw constructed the intersectional proposition on the ground of black women's erasure in civil rights law, intersectionality has come to stand in as a kind academic and/or theoretical pronoun, whose antecedent is, or has at different turns been, black women, the black woman, and the black female experience. It is has also become central to the intellectual scope of black feminism as an institutional project. Literary scholar Valerie Smith (1998, xxiii) has argued that "there is no black feminism without intersectionality."

There is therefore no denying that institutional endorsement of intersectional frameworks has made unprecedented space for the intellectual production of academic works by and about black women. However, unsubstantiated claims that intersectionality must always be about black women presume, as Devon Carbado (2013, 813) notes, that black women cannot "function as the backdrop for the genesis and articulation of a generalizable framework about power and marginalization." As Carbado goes on to explain, "many of the articles on intersectionality focus squarely on black women or on race and gender. Surely, however, that is not, in itself, a problem. It is becoming increasing[ly] unspeakable (dubbed theoretically backward, monopolistic, identitarian, categorically hegemonic, etc.) to frame theoretical and political interventions around black women. . . . It is part of a larger ideological scene in which blackness is permitted to play no racial role in anchoring claims for social justice" (814). Indeed, there is disagreement among feminist scholars about whether this is in fact the case. Nikol Alexander-Floyd (2012, 19) argues that "intersectionality research must be properly understood as the purview of scholars investigating women of color." She rejects the view that this is an endorsement of essentialism because intersectionality allows women of color to "contest and refashion" embattled identity categories. To the extent that intersectionality makes systems of power that disadvantage other groups visible, the idea that its theoretical and analytic scope should be limited to women of color seems parochial. But we should caution against any moves to evacuate or relegate to the margins women of color from the intellectual trajectories of their own knowledge production. And we should recognize that part of what it means to have women of color doing knowledge production is that their particular positionality enables a different view of the way that many other groups move through power structures and not just themselves.

Still for feminist scholars such as Wiegman, black women anchor intersectionality to a kind of particularity that seems difficult to overcome. As intersectionality circulates in the academy, Wiegman argues that

> the particularity of black women's identity position functions as the formative ground for a critical practice aimed at infinite inclusion. The leaps engaged here are most arresting if set in slower motion. On what terms, for instance can the commitment to particularity take paradigmatic shape without sacrificing its force as a counter to universalizing tendencies? Or more to the point, how can particularity retain the specificity it evokes when the destination it inscribes is to render practice not simply coherent but comprehensive in its analytic capacity and scope? Both of these questions point to the tension between intersectionality as a commitment to the particularity of black women's minoritization and its redeployment as the means to claim paradigmatic mastery over both the experiences of women of color and identity's historical, social, political, and psychic complexity as a whole.
>
> (Wiegman 2012, 242)

It seems that what Wiegman points to is a problem of what she terms the "redeployment" of intersectionality rather than a problem of the framework itself. Moreover, it is intersectionality that exposed the limitations of single-axis frameworks that presumed a kind of paradigmatic mastery over experience. Still, she and Puar are correct that it is unfair to saddle intersectionality with the challenge of accounting for the experience of all groups. The problem is that critiques of the epistemological limitations of intersectionality frequently cast intersectionality as something either that has been achieved or something that is wholly unachievable. This discourse in which intersectionality "is 'hailed' and 'failed' simultaneously" is part of a neoliberal push in which "some elements of intersectionality are taken into account, but only to be declared lapsed or obsolete, to be set aside for something better" (Bilge 2013, 407). In either case, the search is for some new paradigm that can do what intersectionality cannot do. But we should remain skeptical of newer approaches to identity that take as their centerpiece a fundamental belief that the particularity of black women's experiences exempt black women from being the foundation on which broadly applicable theoretical frames can be built. This desire to move on from intersectionality bears the spectre of a troubling desire to *move on* from discussions of black women. That kind of move matters not simply theoretically but also institutionally, since it would have the effect of using a theory rooted in the experiences of black women as the sine qua non of feminism's achievement of institutional diversity while potentially marginalizing black women in the academy who have made space for themselves largely based on the intellectual cachet afforded to intersectionality.

According to Wiegman, it is intersectionality's relationship to a paradigmatic black female subject that creates the need for a new analytic frame. Intersectionality is mired in an analytic impasse whereby "its figural resolution as a comprehensive, inclusive, and multidimensional approach to the intersections of race and gender not only renders 'Black women's experience' paradigmatic, but stakes intersectional reason on the force of the protocols of paradigmatic reading it hones" (248). It seems here that this is really an argument against the use of experience as the basis for theorizing, because no experience can be taken as paradigmatic without apparently doing violence to the experiences of people who are differently placed. But intersectionality does not argue that black women's experiences are wholly paradigmatic for all experiences of social marginalization. Rather, it captures the parts of black women's common experiences and suggests that these experiences illumine the experiences of others marginalized vis-à-vis intersecting categories. Moreover, black feminist engagements with and critiques of standpoint theory and its attendant epistemologies are as old as intersectionality itself (Carby 1987; Collins 1998; Smith 1997). Yet Wiegman (2012, 250) concludes that "in exacting its obligation to the figure that compels its analysis [the black woman], intersectionality becomes enthralled to an object of study that must conform to the shape of its critical desires, which is to say to the shape of the authority it draws from her perspective and social position in order to confer on her the very epistemological priority and legal autonomy it promises to her." In other words, intersectionality prescribes what it claims to only name or describe. But Carbado (2013) warns that those who falsely impose these kinds of limits on intersectionality are the ones who are prescribing what they claim only to describe. Moreover, all of these critics accede to the politics of diversity and inclusion that buttress calls for intersectionality—hence their reluctance to move on from it. In response to such reluctance, Tomlinson (2013, 996) warns that "critics assume that their task is to critique intersectionality, not to foster intersectionality's ability to critique subordination." At the risk of being too prescriptive of the task of the feminist critic, I would add the caveat that those feminist theorists who claim an investment in challenging structures of power that lock marginalized subjects out should rethink the role of their criticism regarding intersectionality.

Because intersectionality's biggest success within feminist studies is largely estimated to be its exposure of the nonessentialist nature of gender identity, its role in helping us to understand racial formation remains nebulous. The fact that intersectionality has seemingly successfully named and exposed the problem of racism and white privilege in feminism has emboldened a new generation of scholars to become postintersectional. Like post-feminist discourses that positively invoke feminism and cite the prevalence of feminist discourses to prove that there is no longer a need for feminism, post-racial discourses use the neoliberal language of diversity to prove that we are either beyond racism or that racism happens in individualist and isolated incidences. Broad systemic racism is no longer a problem, and one of the ways that we continue to promote racism is to remain invested in the fictive category of race and racialized discourses. The desire to become *post*intersectional is bound up with these post-racial and post-feminist moves. Postintersectional discourses and analyses take the pervasiveness (or citational ubiquity) of intersectionality in the academy (and now also in feminist social media) to be evidence that it has achieved its goals, become outdated, and beckons for something new. Further, they insist that a continued focus on the outmoded categories that inhere in intersectional analysis elides other peoples and problems and prohibits progress. The turn to intersectionality as methodology is one concrete way that intersectionality has attempted to get beyond its implicit connections to a black female embodied subject.

INTERSECTIONALITY AS METHODOLOGY

One way in which scholars have attempted to demonstrate the broader usefulness of intersectionality beyond its import for black women is by employing it as a research paradigm. In her book *Not Just Race, Not Just Gender: Black Feminist Readings,* literary scholar Valerie Smith (1998, xv) rejects black feminism as a "biologically grounded positionality," arguing instead that black feminism vis-à-vis intersectionality "provide[s] strategies of reading simultaneity." She proposes that the critic can "read intersectionally in the service of an antiracist and feminist politics that holds that the power relations that dominate others are complicit in the subordination of black and other women of color as well" (xvi). This kind of intellectual maneuver is meant to remove black feminism from all attempts by earlier black feminist critics to situate black feminism on the ground or *standpoint* of black women's experience. In making it, Smith echoes the work of black feminists such as Ann duCille and Hazel Carby (1987, 10), who argued that "black feminist criticism cannot afford to be essentialist and ahistorical, reducing the experience of all black women to a common denominator and limiting black feminist critics to an exposition of an equivalent black 'female imagination.'" In response to critics who questioned whether or not this approach to intersectionality disappears black women from view, Smith attempts to hold in tension a desire "to avoid notions of identity that are timeless, transparent, or unproblematic in favor of those that are, in Stuart Hall's words, 'never complete, always in process, and always constituted within, not outside representation', alongside a need to "acknowledge the strategic need to claim racial, gendered, sexual and class identities as meaningful in specific ways in the name of struggle and resistance to institutional violence and exploitation" (1998, xvii). In this regard her critique anticipates Puar (2007, 216) who argues that "intersectionality and its underpinnings—an unrelenting epistemological will to truth—presupposes identity and thus disavows futurity, or, perhaps more accurately, prematurely anticipates and thus fixes a permanence to forever [whereas] assemblage, in its debt to ontology and its espousal of what cannot be known, seen, or heard, or has yet to be known, seen or heard, allows for becoming beyond or without being."

Smith runs squarely into the challenge that many of her successors have noted as well—there is a fundamental tension between intersectionality's theoretical and intellectual possibilities and its use as a tool of institutional transformation. But unlike her successors, Smith's adoption of intersectionality as a reading strategy is a useful corrective to approaches which attempt to circumscribe the usefulness of intersectionality on the grounds that it cannot epistemologically account for the intersectional identities that it has made visible. Smith (1998, xxiii) reminds us that the primary usefulness of intersectionality, whether as a tool of achieving institutional diversity or as a kind of black feminist reading strategy, is that "by addressing the multifarious ways in which ideologies of race, gender, class, and sexuality reinforce one another, reading intersectionally can illuminate the diverse ways in which relations of domination and subordination are produced."

Smith's ability to wrest intersectionality from the clutches of essentialist ghettoization suggest that battles over the potential essentialism of black feminist perspectives have shaped intersectionality's traversal through the academy. These debates about the ways that black feminist criticism had the potential to render black female identities static have existed within black feminist criticism at least since 1987, when Hazel Carby suggested that, at best, black feminism should be understood as a "locus of contradictions." But what Smith reminds us of again is that intersectionality is most useful not as an account of all the intricacies of the subjectivity of any intersectional group, but rather it is useful for exposing the operations of power dynamics in places where a single axis approach might render those operations invisible.

In the fields of sociology and political science, Leslie McCall (2005) and Ange-Marie Hancock (2007), respectively, have also argued for intersectionality as a rubric that can shape social science research protocols. Attempting to remedy the failure of intersectionality researchers to clarify a methodology for intersectionality, McCall argues that in sociology, intersectional research paradigms are indicative of what she terms the *intracategorical* approach. Researchers using this approach "tend to focus on particular social groups at neglected points of intersection . . . in order to reveal the complexity of lived experience within such groups." McCall (2005, 1786) advocates for a move toward an intersectional approach that facilitates "intercategorical complexity," which "focuses on the complexity of relationships among multiple social groups within and across analytical categories and not on complexities within single social groups, single categories, or both."

In a follow-up essay about intersectionality as methodology, McCall and Averil Clarke clarify what intersectional methodologies make possible in the field of social science research. In social science, intersectionality facilitates what the authors call "different interpretations of the same facts," by both incorporating and specifying "the overlap of multiple social dynamics" (Clarke and McCall 2013, 351). "These different interpretations and their normative implications," they argue, "are the logical outcomes of intesectionality's beginnings in women of color's critique of the dominant descriptions of gender and racial inequality, and in their production of new knowledge at the intersection of multiple vectors of scholarship, identity, structure, and social activism" (351). For instance, Clarke (2013, 353) has used the intercategorical approach to challenge traditional sociological understandings of fertility as being tied to class, using the experiences of educated black women to demonstrate that "when it comes to the achievement of low fertility, a race-based deprivation in romance differentiates the experiences of black women with college degrees from similarly educated White and Hispanic women. The advantages of class in desired family formation practices are thus distinctly racialized." Moreover, "this conclusion, buttressed by detailed analysis of group differences, augments and modifies the conclusions of studies that elevate the role of class-based explanations" (Clarke and McCall, 353).

Hancock (2007) argues that within political science, intersectionality can be useful not solely as a "content specialization" but as a research paradigm. Mapping a similar set of concerns in political science as those outlined by McCall (2005) in sociology, Hancock (2007) notes a shift in political science from single or unitary categorical approaches, to explorations of multiple approaches (i.e., examinations of race and gender) to finally intersectional approaches or the interaction of categories such as race and gender. Within political science, intersectionality as a research paradigm makes at least two important methodological interventions. It "changes the relationship between the categories of investigation from one that is determined a priori to one of empirical investigation," which could make a difference for instance in "large-n quantitative studies," which might "assume that race operates identically across entire cities, states, and nations when placed in interaction with gender or class" (2007, 67). Additionally, "intersectionality posits an interactive, mutually constituted relationship among these categories and the way in which race (or ethnicity) and gender (or other relevant categories) play a role in the shaping of political institutions, political actors, the relationships between institutions and actors and the relevant categories themselves" (67).

These paradigmatic approaches open up useful new avenues for thinking about how various social identity categories co-constitute and are constituted by other categories and for asking new kinds of questions in empirical and social-science-based approaches to research. But they also raise concerns about the status of the black female subject relative to these research paradigms. For instance, there is a way in which despite the many adaptations of Western political thought, white men are never disappeared from

Western intellectual traditions. Within the history of Western feminism, white women are in no danger of being disappeared as architects of feminist theory. Yet, the move toward postintersectional frames shows a resurgence of hesitancy to deal with racism. Nikol Alexander-Floyd (2012, 2) situates her skepticism toward these instrumentalist approaches to intersectionality within "two competing currents [that] shape the contemporary moment: a postmodern avoidance of identity and a postfeminist deployment of feminism focused on incorporation and formal equality." She argues that postmodern approaches to identity, in their insistence that we all "have ruptured identities and fragmented bodies," "delegitimize the study of racism, sexism, and the structural bases of inequality" (2). Moreover, the convergence of post-feminist and post-racial discourses has created a kind of "post-Black feminist" sensibility that "emphasizes gender and racial representation while short-circuiting more far-reaching social and political change" (2). In this regard, I think that the calls to become postintersectional and to move beyond intersectionality are akin to and give false intellectual heft to broader political suggestions that the election of Barack Obama has thrust us into a post-racial era. These institutional and political moves index an increasing discomfort with talking about racism. Race, removed from an overarching framework of talking about racism, is fine as such conversations merely signal diversity and mark a sense that we are progressing to a time when such categories will become devoid of meaning.

Alexander-Floyd takes both McCall and Hancock to task for using rhetorical strategies that reframe intersectionality in ways that disappear black women from a body of scholarship that emerges from the intellectual production and political activism that they created. According to Alexander-Floyd (2012, 13), McCall's focus on complexity "advances a post-black feminist politics that disappears black women." For Alexander-Floyd, the "issue is one of subjugation, not complexity," but McCall's categorical approach, "unmoors intersectionality from women of color's lives and their multifaceted marginalization as its focus" (11). Moreover, Alexander-Floyd demonstrates that McCall, in her rejection of the centrality of narratives to the "intracategorical approach" that defines black feminism, reinstantiates positivist research frames despite "explicit epistemological challenges that black women, along with feminists in general, have made to the positivist approach" (13). Alexander-Floyd's critiques sound a note of concern similar to Smith's, but she concludes that black women should remain at the center of intersectional paradigms.

In tandem with what she terms McCall's "bait-and-switch" approach to the knowledge production of black women, Alexander-Floyd indicts Hancock for the "universalizing tendency" of her work. Citing Hancock's argument for intersectionality as a general research paradigm, Alexander-Floyd (2012, 15) notes that "the re-visioning of intersectionality that Hancock presents, however, is designed to give it greater appeal in the discipline in ways that undermine black women and other women of color and intersectionality's potentially transformative power." She argues that the universalizing tendency in Hancock's work constitutes a post–black feminist reading of intersectionality that disappears black women. For instance, one of the key ways that Hancock's work represents a universalizing tendency is "through its privileging of dominant modes of knowledge production in the discipline. The relegation of intersectionality to a content specialization, as opposed to a research paradigm, voids its standing as a vibrant, complex body of knowledge, implicitly suggesting that its knowledge is naïve or nonempirical" (17). Sirma Bilge (2013, 413) has noted that there is now a troubling move to diminish the import of the racial foundations of intersectionality by coopting its genealogy and declaring the concept to be the "brainchild of feminism" rather than the "brainchild of *black* feminism." "Such reframing makes intersectionality a property specifically of feminism and women's/gender studies," and erases the intellectual labor of its black women creators. Wiegman does not erase this history. Instead, she suggests that the depth of intersectionality's connections to black feminism saddles it with a kind of baggage—racial baggage—that makes its movement to other spaces problematic. Alexander-Floyd's point about the ways in which a desire to "universalize" intersectionality disappears black women as a material matter while also curtailing and taming its potential to disrupt problematic relations of power is a powerful one. Thus, she rejects all pretense of universal inclusion and stakes her territory on the ground of black female particularity.

The broader challenges raised by Alexander-Floyd's critique of intersectionality's traversal through the social sciences reflect issues about the way in which intersectionality works not just as theory but as praxis. And certainly, we must recognize the manner in which postintersectional moves are deeply tethered to investments in a faulty post-racial idea. The status of racial others within academic spaces remains fragile, especially in the era of the neoliberal university, with its increasing commitments to diversity at the rhetorical level but decreasing commitments at the level of funding for faculty in departments and programs in women's and gender studies and ethnic studies. To suggest as Puar does that intersectionality is a tool of a neoliberal agenda rather than a tool that works against it is a line of thinking that should be vigilantly guarded against. Still, questions remain: Does intersectionality need to have a more universal utility in order retain relevance in the academy? Do we really want to argue that theories about black women should only travel in limited amounts? Is this not an essentializing fiction that limits black women as much as it limits the import of our knowledge production? And if it achieves citational ubiquity but is found not to be broadly applicable, is not intersectionality guilty of the charge of doing violence to other marginalized peoples? These remain challenging questions, but what we must hold front and center is that in its relationship to dominant institutions (be they juridical, academic, or social), intersectionality has a teleological aim to expose and dismantle dominant systems of power, to promote the inclusion of black women and other women of color and to transform the epistemological grounds upon which these institutions conceive of and understand themselves. If it can be found to be doing this work, whether politically, analytically or methodologically, then it should be understood not only as a continued boon to feminist theorizing but also to feminist movement-building. At the same time, intersectionality does not deserve our religious devotion. It has particular goals. To the extent that intersectional frames have made clear a need for new paradigms that more fully explicate the lived realities of women of color, across a range of identity positions, the framework does not preclude the development of new ways of thinking about identity. But as a conceptual and analytic tool for thinking about operations of power, intersectionality remains one of the most useful and expansive paradigms we have.

References

Alexander-Floyd, Nikol. 2012. "Disappearing Acts: Reclaiming Intersectionality in the Social Sciences in a Post-Black Feminist Era." *Feminist Formations* 24 (1): 1–25.

Beale, Frances. (1970) 1995. "Double Jeopardy: To Be Black and Female." In *Words of Fire: An Anthology of African American Feminist Thought*, edited by Beverly Guy-Sheftall, 146–155. New York: New Press.

Bilge, Sirma. 2013. "Intersectionality Undone: Saving Intersectionality from Feminist Intersectionality Studies." *Du Bois Review* 10 (2): 405–424.

Carbado, Devon. 2013. "Colorblind Intersectionality." *Signs: Journal of Women in Culture and Society* 38 (4): 811–845.

Carby, Hazel. 1987. *Reconstructing Womanhood: The Emergence of the Afro-American Woman Novelist*. New Haven, CT: Yale University Press.

Clarke, A.Y., and L. McCall. 2013. "Intersectionality and Social Explanation in Social Science Research." *Du Bois Review* 10 (2): 349–363.

Collins, Patricia Hill. (1990) 2000. *Black Feminist Thought: Knowledge, Consciousness and the Politics of Empowerment*, 2nd ed. New York: Routledge.

Collins, Patricia Hill. 1998. *Fighting Words: Black Women and the Search for Justice*. Minneapolis: University of Minnesota.

Cooper, Anna Julia. 1988. *A Voice from the South by a Black Woman of the South*. New York: Oxford University Press.

Crenshaw, Kimberlé Williams. 1989. "Demarginalizing the Intersection of Race and Sex: A Black Feminist Critique of Antidiscrimination Doctrine, Feminist Theory, and Antiracist Politics." *University of Chicago Legal Forum* 1989: 139–167.

Crenshaw, Kimberlé Williams. 1991. "Mapping the Margins: Intersectionality, Identity Politics, and Violence against Women of Color." *Stanford Law Review* 43 (6): 1241–1299.

Crenshaw, Kimberlé Williams. 2012. "From Private Violence to Mass Incarceration: Thinking Intersectionally about Women, Race, and Social Control." *UCLA Law Review* 59: 1419–1472.

Deleuze, Gilles and Felix Guattari. 2001. *A Thousand Plateaus: Capitalism and Schizophrenia*. London: Athlone Press.

Hancock, Ange-Marie. 2007. "When Multiplication Doesn't Equal Quick Addition: Examining Intersectionality as a Research Paradigm." *Perspectives on Politics* 5 (1): 63–79.

Kwan, Peter. 2000. "Complicity and Complexity: Cosynthesis and Praxis." *DePaul Law Review* 49: 687.

King, Deborah. 1986. "Multiple Jeopardy, Multiple Consciousness: The Context of Black Feminist Ideology." *Signs: Journal of Women in Culture and Society* 14: 42–72.

Mayeri, Serena. 2011. *Reasoning from Race: Feminism, Law and the Civil Rights Revolution*. Cambridge, MA: Harvard University Press.

McCall, Leslie. 2005. "The Complexity of Intersectionality." *Signs: Journal of Women in Culture and Society* 30 (3): 1771–1800.

Mitchell, Koritha. 2014. "No More Shame! Defeating the New Jim Crow with Antilynching Activism's Best Tools." *American Quarterly* 66 (1): 143–152.

Murray, Pauli. 1987. *Song in a Weary Throat*. New York: Harper & Row.

Murray, Pauli. n.d. "Constitutional Law and Black Women," in American Law and the Black Community: Viewed By Black Women Lawyers. Boston University Afro-American Studies Program, Occasional Paper No. 1.

Nash, Jennifer. 2008. "Re-Thinking Intersectionality." *Feminist Review* 89: 1–15.

Puar, Jasbir. 2007. *Terrorist Assemblages: Homonationalism in Queer Times*. Durham and London: Duke University Press.

Puar, Jasbir. 2012. "I'd Rather Be A Cyborg Than a Goddess: Becoming Intersectional in Assemblage Theory." *Philosophia* 2 (1): 49-66.

Smith, Valerie. 1998. *Not Just Race, Not Just Gender: Black Feminist Readings*. New York: Routledge.

Terrell, Mary Church. (1940) 2005. *A Colored Woman in a White World*. Amherst, MA: Prometheus Books.

Tomlinson, Barbara. 2013. "To Tell the Truth and Not Get Trapped: Desire, Distance, and Intersectionality at the Scene of Argument." *Signs: Journal of Women in Culture and Society* 38 (4): 993–1017.

Wiegman, Robyn. 2012. *Object Lessons*. Durham and London: Duke University Press.

CHAPTER 20

INTERSEXUALITY, TRANSGENDER, AND TRANSSEXUALITY

TALIA MAE BETTCHER

INTRODUCTION

FEMINISM recognizes multiple forms of oppression beyond sexism and illuminates how these different oppressions can be deeply intermeshed; yet specific issues arise when trans and intersex experience are theorized because they foreground different forms of sex/gender-based oppression. Trans and intersex are, far from mere feminist topics, "political locations" that reveal discrete forms of oppression and resistance, which demonstrate that sex/gender-based oppression is not reducible to sexist oppression. Placing trans and intersex experience at the center of analysis raises important concerns about how the intersecting oppressions of women, intersex people, and transsexual/transgender people are to be understood.

In this chapter, I engage in a historical retrieval, examining the early roots of intersex and trans politics and theory, arguing that a particular explanatory account, the "beyond-the-binary model," which came to dominate transgender politics in particular, sidesteps rather than adequately addresses an important radical feminist argument about the connection between resistant identities and oppression. As a consequence, the beyond-the-binary model has foreclosed a genuinely intersectional trans feminism and intersex feminism, leaving the former mired in a politically impoverished individualism. From the outset, the beyond-the-binary model was, in part, a reaction to specific vices in Janice Raymond's radical feminism. By returning to and resisting multiple troubling aspects of Raymond's work, I offer a more sophisticated account of transphobia in the radical feminist argument, which illuminates unique dimensions of trans and intersex oppression, and lays the groundwork for genuinely intersectional trans and intersex feminisms.

Preliminaries

Since at least the 1990s, *transgender* has been used as an umbrella term to group together a number of "gender variant people" such as transsexuals, cross-dressers, and drag queens (Bettcher 2014b). It also refers more narrowly to people who live permanently in a gender "opposite" to birth-assigned sex. *Transsexual* was originally used in a medical context to refer to individuals with gender identities incongruent with the sex assigned at birth who sought medical technologies to alter their bodies. The term has recently been used to flag opposition to the politics of transgender. The term *trans** has recently been deployed because of worries that *transgender* has failed to be sufficiently broad. I will use the expression *trans* as a means to preserve neutrality on the politics surrounding certain transsexual/transgender debates.

The expressions *hermaphrodite* and *intersex* have a long history, and both have been used in medical and activist ways (Chase 1998b). The more recent, controversial expression "individuals with disorders of sex development," while it is apparently pathologizing, notably avoids any commitment to the view that such people are in-between male and female (for discussion of the controversy, see Dreger and Herndon 2009; Karkazis 2008; Reis 2009; Holmes 2009). I use the expression *people with intersex conditions*, or *intersex people* for short, to avoid attributing an identity category, and I follow Dreger and Herndon (2009, 200) in defining "intersex" context specifically as "variations in congenital sex anatomy that are considered atypical for females or males." In all cases I recognize that both the meaning and the range of application of these expressions are subject to contestation. Finally, I take intersex and transsexualism/transgender to be distinct phenomena. Some transsexual individuals have claimed transsexuality as a kind of intersex condition. As far we as we know, such claims have not been substantiated.

Both transgender and intersex politics/theory emerged in the United States during the heady 1990s. Transgender politics/theory was articulated by theorists such as Sandy Stone (1991), Kate Bornstein (1994), and Leslie Feinberg (1992), while the latter was driven largely through the work of Cheryl Chase and the Intersex Society of North American (formed in 1993).[1] Both transgender and intersex politics arose in reaction to the problematic medicalization of, respectively, transsexual and intersex people.

Under the influence of John Money, a model for the treatment of intersex individuals emerged in the mid-1950s, and moved quickly into dominance (Karkazis 2008). This model held that rather than gonads or chromosomes, gender of rearing was the most reliable factor in determining the gender identity of an intersex individual, as long as the gender was properly assigned before the ages of eighteen to twenty-four months (Dreger and Herndon 2009, 202; Reis 2009, 135). This required parental consistency in the gender of rearing and a lack of confusion in the child created by knowledge of their intersex past. In practice, this led to clinicians deceiving patients about their intersex conditions (Dreger and Herndon, 2009, 202; Reis 2009, 145–148). Central to this model was the view that medical interventions on the body were necessary to facilitate the appropriate identity development and overall happiness of the patient (Karkazis 2008). Crudely put, this involved the view that "congruent" genitals were necessary to successful gender-identity development (Dreger and Herndon 2009, 202). This intervention involved genital surgery (to approximate the genitalia of the assigned gender), gonadal removal (if the gonads disagreed with the assigned gender), and subsequent hormone therapy when the patient reached the age of puberty (202). The gender of rearing was largely determined by the likelihood of surgical success, and, as a consequence, most intersex infants were socially and surgically assigned female (202).

In 1966, the same year Harry Benjamin published the landmark *The Transsexual Phenomenon*, the Johns Hopkins Hospital of Johns Hopkins University became the first to offer a program for sex-reassignment surgery (with Money as the lead), ushering in an era of large-university gender-identity clinics that would last to the end of the seventies (Meyerowitz 2002, 218). Specific treatment criteria for genital reconstruction surgery began to be formulated to guard against the specter of "surgery on demand," including psychological evaluations to determine long-standing "cross-gender" identification, living full-time as the "opposite" gender for a period of time, and taking hormones for a period of time prior to surgery (Meyerowitz 2002, 224). Patients were selected partly based on their ability to pass (as nontranssexual), willingness to fade into the background of everyday life, and compliance with a heteronormative lifestyle (Meyerowitz 2002, 225). Criteria were further refined and standardized in 1979 in the Harry Benjamin Standards of Care, and in 1980, "transsexualism" was added to the DSM-III as a mental disorder. The core idea, championed by Harry Benjamin, was that while the gender identity of transsexuals was pathological, it was impervious to alteration. If the mind cannot be changed, according to this logic, the body must be changed to alleviate the suffering of the patient (Benjamin 1966, 91).

In opposing this medical model, transgender politics attempted to subsume transsexuality under an umbrella of "gender variance." The effect was to yield depathologized conceptions of transsexuality that replaced the "trapped in the wrong body" metaphor with "trapped in the wrong culture." Recently, there have been some modest gains on this front. The Harry Benjamin International Gender Dysphoria Association (HBIGDA) became the World Professional Association of Transgender Health in 2006, and in 2013, the newer DSM-V replaced the diagnostic category *gender identity disorder* with *gender dysphoria*.

Intersex activism has also had some success, though it has diverged significantly from its earlier ties with transgender activism. In opposing the Money protocols, intersex politics aimed to end the era of secrecy and shame and, most of all, to end these nonconsensual surgeries. In 2005, the Lawson Wilkins Pediatric Endocrine Society and the European Society for Pediatric Endocrinology held a consensus-building meeting that, according to Dreger and Herndon, "resulted in a hopeful degree of movement toward providing more psychosocial care, peer support, truth telling, informed consent, and outcomes data," while the Consortium on the Management of Disorders of Sex Development developed clinical guidelines for a patient-centered model of care (Dreger and Herndon 2009, 205). Although the deployment of "disorders of sex development" remains controversial, there is clearly a new willingness among clinicians to move away from the Money protocols (207). In 2008, the Intersex Society of North America (ISNA) closed its doors, transferring assets to the newly formed nonprofit organization Accord Alliance (219).

Radical Feminism Unanswered

In a decade dominated by the enormously influential work of Judith Butler (1990), early transgender and intersex theory/politics were inevitably facilitated by the queer theory and politics of the day. Yet the genealogy is also longer and more complex. From the beginning, there were some trans thinkers who worried that trans theory and politics were too closely wedded to queer theory and politics (Namaste 2000; Prosser 1998; Rubin 1998). Consequently, the relation between trans theory/politics and queer theory/politics developed in a way that was both symbiotic and tense. Intersex theory/politics, while queer-inflected, arose in very close relation to the newly emerging *trans* theory/politics. Cheryl Chase (1998a, 196–197) speaks of a political/theoretical context inhabited by organizations, such as Transgender Nation, and of individuals, such as Kate Bornstein, Leslie Feinberg, Sandy Stone, and Susan Stryker, who, Chase says, played a significant role in shaping her politics after she moved to San Francisco in 1992.

Moreover, while both intersex theory and transgender theory almost invariably cite queer-theoretical work (principally Butler's), it's important to note that they derive from other feminist sources. Stone's (1991) founding "Posttranssexual Manifesto" is largely informed by the works of Donna Haraway (1991) and Gloria Anzaldúa (1987). Bornstein's (1994) *Gender Outlaw* is clearly indebted to Stone's work. Bornstein also draws significantly on the groundbreaking feminist ethnomethodological work of Suzanne Kessler and Wendy McKenna (1978, 7), who had undermined the sex-gender distinction long before Butler arrived on the scene. Similarly, Chase (1998a, 201) cites the importance of feminist thinkers, such as Anne Fausto-Sterling, Suzanne Kessler, and Alice Dreger.

While aided by feminist theory, however, transgender studies/politics developed as a very strong *reaction* against a version of feminism, primarily lesbian separatism, which viewed trans women in hostile ways. That hostility had a long history. In 1973, there was heated controversy over Beth Elliott's participation in the West Coast Lesbian Conference at the University of California, Los Angeles (UCLA) not long after she had been expelled from the Daughters of Bilitis in San Francisco (Stryker 2008). At UCLA, Robin Morgan (1973, 32) publicly denounced Elliott "as an opportunist, an infiltrator, and a destroyer with the mentality of a rapist." Then, in 1977 controversy raged over Sandy Stone's participation in Olivia, an all-woman's music collective (Stryker 2008, 105). Stone was subsequently singled out in Janice Raymond's influential *Transsexual Empire* (1979, 101–103). And in 1991, the same year Stone published her manifesto, Nancy Jean Burkholder was denied entrance to the Land at Michigan Womyn's Music

Festival, leading to trans protests the following year and the formation of Camp Trans in 1994 (Koyama 2006, 699).

Underlying this hostility is the premise that trans women are actually men. Two, possibly inconsistent, claims, often blurred together, motivate that position. The first is the essentialist view that chromosomes determine sex (Raymond 1979, 114). This obviously undercuts the feminist view that "one is not born a woman." It does, however, reflect the traditional ("everyday") sense in which "woman" is understood as referring to "adult, female human being," where "female" denotes a biological characteristic. The second, more sophisticated view reflects a decidedly political sense of "woman," insisting that one's history with respect to sex role privilege and oppression determines sex (Raymond 1979, 116). The latter view appears more important in Raymond's work, as she acknowledges that a person born with an intersex condition who did not have XX chromosomes but did have a history of oppression as a woman would be "practically, a woman" (115). And the latter view is crucial to lesbian feminism and the woman-identified woman as a political project of self-definition (Radicalesbians 1988). In this view, women have long had their self-identities colonized by men. The solution is to become woman-identified, to begin to see oneself through the loving eyes of another woman. Crucially, this involves a political *redefinition* of one's self-identity. Indeed, categories such as "woman/women" can be shed in favor of "womon/womyn." Little wonder, then, that Raymond was intent upon criticizing Money's view that gender identity is fixed by the age of two, a view that would make the development of liberatory identities impossible (Bettcher 2014b).

Given that Raymond allows for the possibility of self-definition, the question arises of why it is not possible for trans women to self-define as women. Drawing analogies with race, Raymond argues that one's history of oppression/privilege places ethical constraints on the possibilities of self-definition. Just as it would be questionable for a white person to claim to be black as a way of resisting racism, so it is questionable for a man to define himself as a woman to adopt a pro-feminist stance (Raymond 1979, 116). Since a person who has been assigned male at birth and who has had the history of a male in society has not been subject to a lifetime of sexist oppression, the possibilities of self-definition that accrue to the category "woman" aren't available to him. An appeal to woman-identification *could not possibly* have the same meaning of resistance for a man because he has not experienced sexist oppression in the first place—the oppression from which the necessity for meaningful resistance arises. To the extent that "woman" is used politically to name a horizon of possibilities for self-redefinition that arise out of and are constrained by a history of sexist oppression, "woman" is not an available category for individuals who have not had that history. Indeed, for a man to claim a resistant category of womonhood or feminist lesbianism seems altogether beyond the pale. I will call this the *radical feminist argument*.

Unfortunately the argument, already buried in an ocean of hostile representations of trans women, was subsequently de-emphasized in what appears to have been a deeper plunge into essentialism. In her introduction to the 1994 edition of *The Transsexual Empire*, Raymond pointed to the importance of history—but this time to the history of bodily events (as determined by XX chromosomes)—menstruation, childbirth, and certain bodily cycles and life changes came to the fore (Raymond 1994, xx). While Raymond denied any essentialism, one wonders what she would say about individuals who did not experience such a history but were nonetheless raised as girls and subjected to sexist oppression. Germaine Greer adopted similar logic in her critique of male-to-female transsexuals in *The Whole Woman* (1999). There she argued that intersex individuals with complete androgen insensitivity syndrome (CAIS) are male despite the fact that most individuals with the CAIS condition are raised as female and self-identify as females (Greer 1999, 74–79). According to Greer, that they don't experience the type of bodily events listed by Raymond makes them ineligible for womanhood (and for femaleness), despite the fact that such individuals experience sexism from a very young age. This dismissive attitude evoked responses by many in the CAIS community as well as by sexologist Milton Diamond, which were subsequently mocked by Greer in the book's second edition (Dreger and Herndon 2008, 215).

Although some individuals with intersex conditions had to contend with such identity-invalidating attitudes from feminists, this confrontation played a much more formative role in trans theory/politics. The feminists who critiqued the medical protocols for the treatment of people with intersex conditions, *allied* themselves with intersex activism and contributed to the theoretical context of its development. Chase reached out to Kessler in 1993, leading to a correspondence between the two. Around the same time, Anne Fausto-Sterling's "The Five Sexes" was published, and Chase wrote a letter to the editor, praising the article and announcing the formation of the group that would soon become ISNA. Chase also found a devoted ally in Alice Dreger a few years later (Karkazis 2008).[2] There was, however, no such ally to be found in the person of Janice Raymond. To be sure, there is a perverse sense in which the emerging transgender politics of the nineties endorsed many of the points that Raymond herself had made. There was agreement that the medical model of transsexuality serves to perpetuate sexist norms (Raymond 1979, 92; Stone 1991, 290), and that transsexuality is not a pathological condition but arises, rather, as a consequence of an oppressive gender system (Raymond 1979, 115; Bornstein 1994, 118). There was even agreement that bodily dysphoria, which motivates surgical intervention, would disappear in a culture that had no gender oppression (Raymond 1979, 119; Bornstein 1994, 70). But Raymond represented the hostile face of feminism *in opposition to which* trans studies and politics arose. Her transphobia had to be named and analyzed. This process generated efforts to articulate a notion of trans oppression and resistance that did not reduce to sexist oppression. In carving out a space for (post)transsexual resistance, Stone confronted both the medical model *and* Raymond's feminist starting point.

Raymond's transphobia was named a crime of "totalization," and fear of "borderdwellers," which in combination transform insistence on a sharp gender binary into a source of oppression (Stone 1991, 208; Bornstein 1994, 74). When Raymond (1979, 155) represents postoperative trans people as synthetically hermaphroditic, she construes trans women as hybrids who take up feminine stereotypes while retaining aspects of masculine sex role and privilege (165). She contrasts such integration (the putting together of parts) with integrity, represented as the transcendence of sex roles altogether

(163–164). Trans studies/politics responded to Raymond's claims concerning the replication and perpetuation of harmful sex roles. Drawing on Haraway and Anzaldúa, Stone *celebrated* the mixture of incongruent parts. In contrast to Raymond's representation of "post-operative" trans women as "synthetic hermaphrodites," who were inescapably male, Stone challenged the gender binary:

> But the transsexual currently occupies a position which is nowhere, which is outside the binary oppositions of gendered discourse. For a transsexual, as a transsexual, to generate a true, effective and representational counter-discourse is to speak from outside the boundaries of gender, beyond the constructed oppositional nodes which have been predefined as the only positions from which discourse is possible.
>
> (Stone 1991, 230)

For Stone, this means that transsexuals ought not construct plausible histories of their past. Instead, they ought to own their transsexual pasts and integrate that into their current self-identities. In the case of male-to-female transsexuals, such an embrace involves accepting one's male past, and by implication, accepting both one's history as oppressor and as oppressed, in much the way that Anzaldúa's (1987) mestiza is a mixture. In opposing Raymond's adherence to strict binarism, Stone also managed to sidestep the radical feminist argument by moving beyond the binary, a move exemplified in Bornstein's politics:

> Years earlier, when I went through my gender change from male to female, I glided through life under the commonly accepted assumption: I was finally a real woman! That worked for me until I ran into a group of politically smart lesbians who told me that I wasn't allowed to co-opt the word "woman." Woman was not a family word that included me. My answer to this exclusion was to call myself a gender outlaw: I wasn't a man, I wasn't a woman.
>
> (Bornstein 2010)[3]

Although there are different variants of the beyond-the-binary model, a common denominator is a characterization of sharp splits between two oppositional gender extremes as the source of oppression. As articulated by intersex theorist/activist Chase,

> The insistence on two clearly distinguished sexes has calamitous personal consequences for the many individuals who arrive in the world with sexual anatomy that fails to be easily distinguished into male or female. Though the male/female binary is constructed as natural and presumed to be immutable, the phenomenon of intersexuality offers clear evidence to the contrary and furnishes an opportunity to deploy "nature" strategically to disrupt heteronormative systems of sex, gender, and sexuality.
>
> (Chase 1998a, 189)

This model has left many unhappy as it invalidates trans people who identify within the binary. As Namaste (2005, 7) notes, "Most transsexuals I know, and most I have interviewed, describe themselves as men or women. And there is a sense in which this position cannot be understood in relation to the question posed, 'What is the significance of the challenge to the two-gendered dichotomous system that transsexual and transgendered people raise?' Because transsexuals seek to have a different embodied position within that system." It likewise invalidates the many intersex people who identify within the binary. In Herndon's (2006) words, "At ISNA, we've learned that many intersex people are perfectly comfortable adopting either a male or female gender identity and are not seeking a genderless society or to label themselves as a member of a third gender class . . . Intersex people don't tell us that the very concept of gender is oppressive to them. Instead, it's the childhood surgeries performed on them and the accompanying lies and shame that are problematic." Moreover, it appears to represent such people as being in some ways political retrograde. Henry Rubin (1998, 276) remarks, "Queer appropriations and the new movement among some transgenders to resignify themselves in a queer register carry an implicit critique of transsexuals who choose not to queer their identities. These more traditional transsexuals . . . choose to 'play it straight'—to pass, to assimilate. They refuse the confessional strategy of coming out." In a similar vein, Morgan Holmes critiques the feminist work of Sharon Preves by saying that Preves's position "lacks compassion for those who do not maintain a critical relationship to the operation of gender norms or of heteronormativity. For this reader, it *feels* as though having been identified as a statistical outlier, I and others like me, it seems to say, cannot be permitted to want simply to be like all the other girls and boys" (Holmes 2008, 15). To characterize "their position as a normative capitulation misses the point: they are seeking a place where they will no longer be called upon to support other people's ideals" (16).

Underlying trans reactions to Raymond's hostility is the belief that the *only* mode of resistance is one that celebrates identities beyond the binary. To formulate an alternative that avoids the marginalizing effects of the beyond-the-binary model, I would suggest a return to Raymond's view to examine transphobic aspects that are not adequately captured by the arguments advanced by the pioneers of the beyond-the-binary model. Consider the following well-known passage from Raymond:

> All transsexuals rape women's bodies by reducing the real female form to an artifact, appropriating this body for themselves. However, the transsexually constructed lesbian-feminist violates women's sexuality and spirit, as well. Rape, although it is usually done by force, can also be accomplished by deception. It is significant that in the case of the transsexually constructed lesbian-feminist, often he is able to gain entrance and a dominant position in women's spaces because the women involved do not know he is a transsexual and he just does not happen to mention it.
>
> (Raymond 1979, 104)

Raymond suggests that the sheer act of surgically altering one's body to a female form constitutes an act of rape (cf. 108, 118). This is clearly an extreme transphobic claim, but one that requires additional theorization. The claim that postoperative male-to-female transsexuals are, from their *sheer* existence, inherently rapists was not fully addressed in the beyond the binary model. The frequently deployed representation of trans women as *deceptive* has also escaped scrutiny (102, 104, 116, 119). Raymond's conflation of deceptiveness with sexual violence (104, 112) articulates a particular kind of transphobic invalidation that confronts trans people on a daily basis. By understanding the nature of this transphobia, and how trans people contest it, it is possible to answer the radical feminist argument.

INTERSECTIONALITY FORECLOSED

Although Kimberlé Crenshaw (1989) coined the term *intersectionality*, the concept was inherent in early writings of women of color who critiqued feminism as racially biased (e.g., Combahee River Collective 1981). Emphasizing the mutual constitution of racial and sexist oppression and the importance of investigating systems of advantage and disadvantage, the concept of intersectionality seems to provide an attractive basis for trans feminism. Certainly, intersectionality is key to Emi Koyama's coalitional trans feminism. In her manifesto, Koyama (2003, 244) defines trans feminism as "primarily a movement by and for trans women who view their liberation to be intrinsically linked to the liberation of all women and beyond." She later recognized the importance of trans feminism for trans men (who have lived part of their lives as woman). Not only does her trans feminism concern both trans-specific oppression and sexist oppression and the ways in which these oppressions can be integrally linked, Koyama (2006) also argued that any form of trans feminism which fails to centralize other forms of oppression (such as racism and classism) through an intersectional lens does so at its own peril. Julia Serano (2007) also defended a form of trans/feminism that foregrounds the intersection of trans oppression ("oppositional sexism") and the oppression of women ("traditional sexism").

But how is the intersection between sexist and trans oppression to be understood? The beyond-the-binary model cannot sustain such an intersection. The central formulation of the model claims that trans (and intersex) people are positioned problematically with respect to the binary categories man/woman and male/female. A specific version notes that there are intersex and transgender people who do not fit neatly into the binary categories, therefore the insistence that every person be categorized as either a male/man or female/woman is a source of oppression. A general version suggests that the very categories male/man and female/woman are inherently oppressive and ought to be rejected. But in developing a politics based on rejecting gendered binaries, this model precludes the possibility of an intersectional trans or intersex feminism.

A broad rejection of identity-based politics makes it difficult to launch a trans feminist politics in the absence of the categories "trans" and "woman." And trans women who have been fighting to hang on to their self-identity in a hostile culture have been dismayed by discourses that evaporate their identity. It is possible to advance a critique similar to that raised by Paula Moya (1997), by suggesting that there is a distinction between oppressive identity categories grounded in essentialist views of gender and race and resistant ones, which are open-ended political projects, grounded in real social locations. Indeed, the presumption that an anti-identity stance is a good political strategy runs afoul of intersectional concerns. As Cathy Cohen notes,

> Class or material privilege is a cornerstone of much of queer politics and theory as they exist today. Queer theorizing that calls for the elimination of fixed categories of sexual identity seems to ignore the ways in which some traditional social identities and communal ties can, in fact, be important to one's survival.
>
> (Cohen 2005, 34)

Cohen endorses a politics "built not exclusively on identities but rather on identities as they are invested with varying degrees of normative power" (37). This idea seems likewise applicable to trans theory and politics. Within that frame, a trans feminist politics must provide for the possibility of "trans woman" as a resistant identity.

Trans as resistant identity raises interesting conundrums, however. Consider, for example, when trans and intersex women are recognized as hybrid or "in-between" categories, they are subjected to a particular form of discrimination. For example, the categorical liminality of a trans woman might be recognized by referring to her as "it." This denial of personhood is oppressive. But in this instance, she is not oppressed as a woman, because she is not even recognized as one. Alternately, a trans woman may be recognized as a woman, which also constitutes a form of trans oppression insofar as her liminal status has been erased precisely by thrusting her into one of two hegemonic categories. In this case, she is oppressed first through the erasure of her liminal status, and second through standard forms of sexism once she is regarded as woman. In neither instance can *trans woman* (or *intersex woman*) be properly understood as a resistant category on par with, say, *woman of color*, however. For to place oneself in the category woman, and hence in the binary, is *precisely to be complicit in trans or intersex oppression*. What she ought to claim, by way of resistance, is a categorically liminal status (not the category "woman"). In this respect, there is a fundamental disanalogy between trans or intersex feminism and say, black feminism (in which "black woman" can serve as a resistant identity). Something more than analogy is needed as a basis for trans and intersex feminism.

This theoretical inadequacy haunts Gayle Salamon's (2010) recent discussion of trans feminism and women's studies. According to Salamon, "If it is to reemerge as a vital discipline, women's studies must become more responsive to emerging genders. Genders beyond the binary of male and female are neither fictive nor futural but are embodied and lived. Women's studies has not yet taken account of this and is thus unable to assess the present state of gender as it is lived" (95). In her view, it's not merely an empirical matter that trans identities have not yet been incorporated into women's studies—in that long line of adjective-identities finally recognized within the category of women (e.g., lesbian, black, disabled, and so forth). Rather, the nonbinary nature of many trans identities threatens the stability of "woman" as a coherent category. Thus, rather than reckoning with lived subjectivities beyond the binary, women's studies harnesses transgender phenomena as "the constitutive outside of binary gender" to preserve the coherence and persistence of the category "woman" (98).

Intersex activists and theorists have raised related concerns about feminist theorizing and teaching on intersex issues (see Rosario 2006).[4] Koyama and Weasel (2002, 176) write, "Too often, exploration of the political and practical issues relating to intersex lives have been marginalized in feminist scholars' use of intersex existence in support of their theoretical and pedagogical deconstructions." They point specifically to Fausto-Sterling's famous "The Five Sexes," noting that the article continues to be used frequently in classrooms as a way to "deconstruct" the gender binary, despite Fausto-Sterling's subsequent departure from it, while the voices of intersex people are seldom presented (171).

Similar complaints have made in trans studies. Both Jay Prosser (1998, 47–55) and Viviane Namaste (2000, 13–14) raised serious concerns about Butler's use of transsexuality as nothing more than a theoretical tool or rhetorical device to make her points. Butler's (1993) discussion of Venus Xtravaganza's death in the film *Paris Is Burning* came under particular fire for allegorizing her death while obscuring the basis for the violence—violence against a transsexual sex worker. Namaste has continued to press her concerns against Butler's (2004) recent claims about "undoing gender," as well as "Anglo American Feminism" more generally. According to Namaste (2009), "Anglo American Feminism" has for the past twenty years asked "The Transgender Question"—that is, it has asked questions about trans people's lives in order to answer its own epistemological questions, rather than investigate questions posed in collaboration with actual trans people to produce knowledge that improves the life of trans people. Namaste's view sheds light on Salamon's complaint that trans people have be used as the constitutive outside binary gender to bolster women's studies own agenda.

In may be, however, that trans and intersex identities (e.g., trans women and some women with intersex conditions) have not been added to the category woman, in part, because the beyond-the-binary model *has foreclosed that possibility*. Once such a model is endorsed, we have seen, it isn't possible to *add* trans people to the category, never mind explore any of the intersectional possibilities that might arise were they to be "added."

It is worth noting that that there has *not* been a parade of adjectives acknowledged under the category woman. Rather than merely adding "lesbian" to "woman, " a lesbian feminist paradigm was created that saw lesbianism (women loving woman) as the literal answer to sexism. Rather than merely adding "woman of color" to "woman," the entire framework of intersectionality came to overhaul women's studies. Rather than add queer sexuality, Butler's queer theory opened possibilities for a radically free-floating feminism. In aiming for a genuinely intersectional trans feminism, then, perhaps a transformative model might be preferable. By theorizing trans in ways that *do not* rely on the beyond-the-binary model, it is possible to move beyond nonbinary subjectivities as flattened theories and tired tropes to see real flesh and blood people who live outside the binary.

Trans Feminism Unmoored

To provide a basis for trans feminism, the first order of business is to answer the radical feminist argument. Such a response would begin by noting that many trans women do experience sexist oppression after transitioning, and many trans women transition quite early. As a consequence, it seems possible for trans women to become "women" (in the radical feminist sense) after a time. The problem, however, is that that a trans woman still couldn't *begin* her transition by self-defining as woman. And she certainly couldn't so self-define well *before* her transition. And that raises a problem in thinking through the idea that trans women are oppressed as trans most of their lives.

One possibility is to turn to the "wrong body" account to validate trans identities. The wrong-body model is premised on the assumption that gender identity is not only inalterable but also innate (Bettcher 2014a). There are two possible variations. The first stipulates that innate gender identity determines one's sex/gender even prior to genital reconstruction surgery. One is always a woman: "gender confirmation" surgery simply changes the wrong body into the right body. A weaker view is that one begins as a transsexual (as a kind of quasi-intersex condition) and then, through "sex-change" surgery, becomes a woman. It is not clear that either variant of the wrong-body model can sustain the claim that one is a woman, however, particularly if it is assumed that sex/gender is determined by chromosomes. Even if a more sophisticated conception of sex/gender is adopted, it is difficult to see how a postoperative transsexual woman is going to be perceived as more than a mix of sex features. More importantly, once "woman" is understood in a feminist sense as naming a social category, the appeal to an innate gender identity violates basic feminist principles by presupposing that the category woman is *not* a social one.

What is needed is an underlying account of trans oppression out of which woman can emerge as a resistant category from the very beginning. Koyama (2003, 250) explicitly grounds the validity of any self-identity in a prior political vision: "Trans liberation is about taking back the right to define ourselves from medical, religious, and political authorities. Transfeminism views any method of assigned sex as socially and politically constructed, and advocates a social arrangement in which one is free to assign her or his own sex (or non-sex, for that matter)." Thus, Koyama contrasts nonconsensual sex assignment with a liberated view according to which sex is voluntarily chosen. Koyama is quite right to condemn the nonconsensual surgical alteration of intersex infants and sex reassignment in medical contexts. But there are problems with the alternative construction of sex as freely chosen, a form of voluntarism that is incompatible with understandings of the power of regulative gender and sexual norms and which is incapable of providing an adequate conception of gender oppression.

To see this, consider a variant of the beyond-the-binary model that we have not yet discussed. According to "the expressive variant," various forms of gender expression are restricted in a system that expects all males to be highly masculine and all females to be highly feminine. Liberation, in this view, requires that all forms of gender expression be recognized as acceptable. The problem, particularly when it's framed generally, is that the sheer existence of gender norms that regulate certain forms of expression are insufficient to yield an account of gender oppression. Marilyn Frye (1983) shows why norms forbidding men from being emotionally vulnerable do not by themselves constitute the *oppression of men*. Such norms need to be examined within the larger social context to determine who is advantaged and who is disadvantaged by them.

To provide a compelling account of trans and intersex oppression, it is not enough to claim there are people who are unhappy with their sex assignment at birth. Even men may have some grounds for complaint with the way sex is socially constituted. This does not, by itself, yield a theory of oppression, since when considered within a larger context, it's clear that men are ultimately advantaged by this system. By contrast, the ways in which intersex people are indeed oppressed are evident. The problem is that her account doesn't provide any specificity with regard to *trans oppression*. Both non-trans women and intersexuals may be likewise viewed as oppressed as a consequence of the nonconsensual nature of sex-assignment. They, too, may wish to change this. While it is useful to find common cause, there is also a danger in collapsing different types of oppression and representing certain people as oppressed when they are not.

And there are deeper worries. The view that it's acceptable to express whatever gender one wants because it "feels right" simply cannot be sustained in any serious form of feminism. Cressida Heyes (2003, 1111–1114) raises legitimate worries about a transgender politics, which proclaims all individual gender expression good. She rightly observes that gender is not merely an aesthetic style or the expression of an isolated self. It is relational and embedded in systems of oppression. For example, forms of masculinity involve interacting with women in particular ways. Certain forms of masculinity involve misogyny. Such gender behavior *is* morally problematic. And what is missing from accounts that merely tout gender freedom of expression, Heyes argues, is a rich "ethics of transformation," which distinguishes progressive transformations from those that are oppressive, marginalizing, or hegemonic (1111–1113).

Just as there are concerns about the relational nature of gender expression, so there are concerns about the relational nature of gender identity. Is *any* gender identity valid? Koyama (2003, 245) writes, "It is our belief that each individual has the right to define her or his own identity and to expect society to respect it." But certainly Koyama would not countenance gender identities that were built on sexist views of the world. And once we grant these ethical constraints, the radical feminist argument that self-definition is subject to constraints arising out of one's history of oppression gains a clear foothold. Simply *saying* that one has the right to define oneself as a woman simply doesn't address political concern about the resistant force (or lack thereof) of one's self-definition. What we need is an account of trans oppression out of which the category woman can arise as a resistant option. To accomplish that, we now return to the transphobic representations of trans women as deceivers that we earlier found in Raymond's work.

Reality Contested

What is needed, I believe, is a deeper account of the sort of resistance at work in trans identities. I want to show that trans uses of "woman" can be seen as resistant uses that emerge out of and respond to a form of oppression that is, in some sense, prior to the resistant identities. In doing so, I will also show that this form of oppression opens up clear possibilities for understanding the intersections of trans, intersex, and sexist oppressions.

Issues around "identity-invalidation" are often inherent in the actual lives of trans people. Transsexuality is about having one's sex doubted, challenged, or impugned in manifold daily transactions. It's about going out on a date and worrying about when to tell one's date that one is trans. It is about harassment by the police who treat trans prostitutes as "really men." It is about the risks of "being exposed as a man" in a commercial sexual encounter. It is about how pervasive identity-invalidation contributes to HIV-prevalence among trans women (cf. Bettcher 2014a).

Identity-invalidation is not the *only* social obstacle that trans people face, but it is an *extremely* expansive and important one (Bettcher 2014a). Rather than focusing on broad notions of identity-specific oppressions (oppression of trans people, oppression of women), therefore, I prefer to start "one level down" in the order of abstraction by examining significant organized practices of violence and domination that inhere in various different social practices and institutional settings, selecting people according to the mechanics of the practices. By abandoning any monolithic account of trans oppression, it is possible to focus on the cross-institutional phenomenon of identity invalidation.

Reality enforcement is one treacherous form of identity invalidation; it turns "appearance/reality" incongruence into a perceived misalignment between the public gender presentation and the private sexed body (Bettcher 2014a). It is not *merely* that a trans woman is called a man. It is that she is called "*really* a man who *appears* to be a woman," where *sartorial practices provide social content to such locutions*. This appearance-reality contrast is manifested in two ways, both to the detriment of trans identity. When a trans person passes as non-trans, the possibility of exposure as "really" a different gender is established; and if such an exposure occurs, the trans person is viewed as a deceiver. By contrast, when it's known that the trans person is trans, the trans person is often viewed as merely playing make-believe, a practice that again is said to involve deception or self-delusion.

Exposure of trans people as deceivers is the point of "reality" enforcement, which is often accompanied by graphic genital verification: somebody physically exposes a trans person's genitals. Such practices are clearly abusive. But even in the absence of physical abuse, certain *discursive* practices deploy euphemism to invalidate trans identity. For example, a trans woman might be asked whether she has had "the surgery" or not. That question clearly concerns whether the trans woman has a penis. Such privacy invading questions are never asked of cisgendered people, and questions about genitalia are not normally demanded in polite conversation, the euphemistic quality of the query does not mitigate the sexually invasive character of the question.

But if trans people are deceivers in "misaligning" public gender presentation with private genital status, it follows that cis people are truth-tellers in correctly aligning public gender presentation with private genitalia, and that therefore public gender presentation systematically communicates private genital status in a euphemistic way (Bettcher 2014a). Yet, we've already seen that demands for information about genitalia are abusive. Therefore *the entire system* of communicating genital status through public gender presentation must be viewed as inherently abusive. Thus, even cis people are subject to this abuse in their daily disclosures of genital status through gender presentation. What makes it particularly abusive is that it is a form of *mandatory boundary violation*. Trans people oppose this systematically abusive system by refusing the mandate to disclose their genital status. Such opposition comes into immediate conflict with violent forces that aim to secure public disclosure of genital status, of course, often through violent means of reality enforcement. In this way the mandatory quality of the system becomes visible. What makes trans identities *resistant*, in my view, is not only a stand against reality enforcement but transformative practice in many trans subcultures where public gender presentation is re-signified. In such contexts, gender presentation simply provides no information at all about genital status. It no longer *means* genital status.

In their everyday sense, *man* and *woman*, and the entire binary gender system are sustained by the practice of communicating private genital status through public presentation (Bettcher 2009). Euphemistic references to trans women as "really a man, disguised as a woman" depend upon and shore up links between gender performance and genitalia. When trans subcultures deploy "woman" with new meaning, they engage in transformative practices that resist trans and intersex oppression. By disrupting hegemonic gender signification, various features (such as possessing a penis) thought to count against a trans woman being a woman no longer do. Within trans subcultures, being a trans woman is a sufficient condition for being a woman. Within such resignifications, trans identities are *resistant* not merely in their opposition to dominant concepts, but by disabling the capacity of gender euphemisms to communicate genital status. Once gender presentation no longer communicates genital status, it is not clear just what one is doing when one performs gender or why gender performance is undertaken, much less mandated (Bettcher 2009). In such transformative contexts, terms such as *woman* and *man* can function to illuminate the significance of the presentation, particularly when underwritten by narratives that elucidate what *woman* means to the person who uses it. When viewed in this way, resistant meanings are afforded to "women" and "men" that flow from *prior* trans resistance to the structure of reality enforcement (the enforcement of a sexually abusive system). Any identity category predicated upon a gender presentation that does not communicate genital status is resistant in this way.

It is worth noting that the beyond-the-binary model capitulates to this abusive representational system. As part of its commitment to the politics of visibility, it endorses the view that passing (as non-trans) is ultimately deceptive. As Stone (1991, 298) has noted,

"Transsexuals who pass seem able to ignore the fact that by creating totalized, monistic identities, forgoing physical and subjective intertextuality, they have foreclosed the possibility of authentic relationships. Under the principle of passing, denying the destabilizing power of being 'read,' relationships begin as lies." Similarly, Bornstein (1994, 76) has suggested that "Raymond and her supporters bring up the subject of deception. Personally, I agree that hiding, and not proclaiming one's transsexual status is an unworthy stance." Within the frame of resistant identities, by contrast, trans people who come out merely fall prey to the other side of the bind, obeying the mandate to "disclose the truth" about genitals.

The traditional "trapped in the wrong body" discourse can be viewed as resistant insofar as it inverts the appearance/reality contrast. Rather than suggesting a man disguised as a woman, it posits a woman trapped in a body that appears to be a man's (Bettcher 2014a). To be sure, the account is limited in that it does not attend to the intersection of multiple oppressions. But *both* the beyond-the-binary account's partial complicity in trans oppression *and* the resistant character of the long-standing "wrong body" discourse flip a script that sees the former as resistant and the latter as reactionary. The identity-invalidation dimension of oppression illuminates complementary aspects of oppression and resistance in the beyond-the-binary model.

When situated in relation to Kessler and McKenna's (1978) ethnomethodological approach to gender, this theoretical perspective offers new insights into the intersections among trans, intersex, and sexist oppression. Kessler and McKenna build upon Harold Garfinkel's insight that "biological sex" is often treated as a moral notion. In cases of genital amputation, Garfinkel (1967, 127) noted, we speak of penises and vaginas *to which we are entitled* or *were meant to have*. I will call this *moral genitalia*. Kessler's and McKenna's (1978) conceptualization of "cultural genitalia" supplements moral genitalia (the genitalia to which one is entitled) with an analysis of the genitalia one is presumed to have on the basis of gender performance in public (154). In everyday life, gender attribution turns on how one is dressed, the make-up one wears, the accessories one sports, how one moves in public space, that is, on the basis of cultural genitalia. What enables them to wed moral and presumed genitalia together is their view that once a genital/gender attribution is made, it becomes very difficult to overturn that initial attribution (17).

The frequency and severity of "reality enforcement," however, demonstrates that Kessler's and McKenna's convictions about the stability of cultural genitalia fail to withstand scrutiny (Bettcher 2014a). For trans people, the cultural genitalia imputed from gender performance can come apart from disclosed moral genitalia. That is why even transsexuals who have had genital reconstruction surgery are viewed as deceptive. As their surgically constructed genitalia are dismissed as fraudulent, they are charged with deception about their *moral* genitalia. Oppressive reality enforcement makes clear that public gender presentation communicates moral genitalia (2014a). When radical feminists of Raymond's ilk lapse into essentialist appeals to chromosomes as the invariant determinants of sex, they do so as a way to challenge postoperative trans women's *moral genitalia*.

In the case of intersex theory, Suzanne Kessler again figures prominently. She has argued that "the belief that gender consists of two exclusive types is maintained and perpetuated by the medical community in the face of incontrovertible physical evidence that this is not mandated by biology" (1990, 25). Responding to Fausto-Sterling's "modest proposal" for the existence of five sexes, Kessler argued (and Fausto-Sterling [2000, 134] came to agree) that rather than multiplying categories beyond the binary, it is important to "expand" the existing categories so as to defeat the equation of gender with genitals (Kessler 1998, 90). Drawing on her notion of cultural genitalia, Kessler insists: "There is no sex, only gender, and what has primacy in everyday life is the gender that is performed, regardless of the flesh's configuration under the clothes" (1998, 90). Arguing against the early intersex activist desire to promote a pan-intersex identity (Chase 1998a), Kessler suggests that a better strategy is to adapt the two binary categories, expanding them in ways that make genitals irrelevant. Kessler's strategy is congruent with the desire among some individuals with intersex conditions to refuse "intersex" as an identity category. And it parallels practices in trans subcultures that resignify the meaning of "man" and "woman."

What is odd in Kessler's strategy, however, is that the *actual* genitalia of intersex people (or of anybody for that matter) do not count as "cultural genitalia." Physical embodiment is dismissed because it purportedly does not figure prominently in gender attribution in "everyday life." But as reality enforcement and intimacy demonstrate, exposed bodies do play a very important part in *our intimate* lives. Although intimacy is often relegated to the private sphere, our private lives are very much a part of the everyday. Kessler's mistake is to conflate the everyday with the public.

Nakedness itself can be viewed as a social construct, where the intimate presentation of a person is structured in accordance with moral boundaries related to certain body parts (breasts, buttocks, genitals)—boundaries that determine what count as violations of privacy and decency (Bettcher 2012). Clearly, there are at least two different kinds of socially constituted nakedness, male and female, associated with distinct moral boundaries. For "women," nakedness is more highly regulated in many cultures (e.g., toplessness is prohibited). And moral boundaries pertaining to privacy are thoroughly gendered. For example, a male voyeur who secretly observes a naked female will be guilty of violating her privacy; a female who is exposed involuntarily to a naked male will have her decency boundaries violated. Norms in Anglo-American cultures often construct moral boundaries that position men as violators and women as violated (Bettcher 2012).

Indeed, such intimate modes of self-presentation are central to the notion of moral genitalia. That is, moral genitalia are integrally related to sex-differentiated bodily privacy/decency boundaries (Bettcher 2012). It is within this context that Raymond constructs trans women as inherently rapists. Viewing them as morally male, she situates them within a male boundary-structure of nakedness, which overrides surgically constructed female embodiment. Invalidating their gender identities by insisting that trans women inescapably fall within male boundaries of nakedness, Raymond construes trans women as the personification of rape.

Attending to gender presentation in intimate contexts also reframes the nonconsensual surgeries performed on intersex infants, which provide a person with a socially-constituted mode of intimate self-presentation. Given the non-consensual nature of surgery on intersex infants, these operations could be construed not only as a violation of physical integrity, but also as a kind of *sexual* violation. Such a reframing illuminates claims made by some intersex people. For example, Preves (2003, 73) cites one woman who said, "I was forced to be surgically mutilated and medically raped at the age of fourteen." Intersex children often find themselves subjected to *abusive* genital scrutiny (Preves 2003, 66–73). As Chase (2003, 240) noted, "This misplaced focus on gender distorts the perspective of clinicians in many ways that are harmful to patients. Intersex patients have frequently been subjected to repeated genital examinations, which creates a feeling of freakishness and unacceptableness." When issues of intimacy and privacy are taken into account, John Money's protocols constitute a system of violence analogous to "reality enforcement." They conveniently secure the alignment of public gender presentation with private self-presentation, thereby ensuring that genitals are ever communicated through public gender presentation. In so doing, the Money protocols perpetuate the abusive system of genital representation that oppresses trans and intersex people whose identities do not require any "genital congruence."

The oppressive dynamics of identity invalidation and reality enforcement provide one basis for coalition among intersex and trans activists and suggest possibilities for understanding the intersections of intersex, trans, and sexist oppressions. The differential structuring of female and male forms of nakedness constitute women—particularly white, privileged women—as "the violated" (Bettcher 2012). The public communication of private genital status is central to the manipulative character of compulsory heterosexual sexuality, which accredits certain nonverbal gestures and behaviors such as attire, accepting drinks, dinner or a movie as communicating consent to sexual encounters (Bettcher 2007). Hegemonic assumptions about such tacit communication link sexual violence to this system of genital representation, illuminating connections between violence against trans and intersex people and violence against women. And these connections provide a ground for coalition among intersex, trans women and non-intersex, non-trans women—a coalition grounded in resistance against multiple modalities of sexual violence. Perhaps transformative conceptions of womanhood generated within trans politics can contribute to gendered identities that are not only resistant, but genuinely coalitional. As Stone (1991, 299) has suggested, "Perhaps it's time to begin laying the groundwork for the next transformation." But perhaps *this time* the next transformation will give rise to a new kind of feminism.

Notes

1. For far more detailed accounts of the development of intersex politics, see Chase (1998a); Karkazis (2008).
2. Oddly, however, Karkazis omits any reference to the transgender politics in San Francisco that Chase cites as so important to her development.

3. I don't know what argument convinced Bornstein that she wasn't a woman, but I suspect it was at least a *good* one—probably something like the radical feminist argument discussed earlier.
4. For a full discussion, see Rubin (2010).

References

Anzaldúa, Gloria. 1987. *Borderlands/la Frontera: The New Mestiza*. San Francisco: Spinsters Aunt Lute.

Benjamin, Harry. 1966. *The Transsexual Phenomenon*. New York: Julian Press.

Bettcher, Talia Mae. 2007. "Evil Deceivers and Make-Believers: Transphobic Violence and the Politics of Illusion." *Hypatia* 22 (3): 43–65.

Bettcher, Talia Mae. 2009. "Trans Identities and First-Person Authority." In *You've Changed: Sex Reassignment and Personal Identity*, edited by Laurie Shrage, 98–120. Oxford: Oxford University Press.

Bettcher, Talia Mae. 2012. "Full-Frontal Morality: The Naked Truth about Gender." *Hypatia* 27 (2): 319–337.

Bettcher, Talia Mae. 2014a. "Trapped in the Wrong Theory: Rethinking Trans Oppression and Resistance." *Signs* 39 (2): 43–65.

Bettcher, Talia Mae. 2014b. "Feminist Perspectives on Trans Issues." *The Stanford Encyclopedia of Philosophy*. Spring 2014. Edward N. Zalta, ed. http://plato.stanford.edu/archives/spr2014/entries/feminism-trans/

Bornstein, Kate. 1994. *Gender Outlaw: On Men, Women, and the Rest of Us*. New York: Routledge.

Bornstein, Kate. 2010. "The Trouble with Tranny" *Out* online. November 14, 2010. http://www.out.com/entertainment/2010/11/14/trouble-tranny-0

Butler, Judith. 1990. *Gender Trouble: Feminism and the Subversion of Identity*. New York: Routledge.

Butler, Judith. 1993. *Bodies That Matter: On the Discursive Limits of Sex*. New York: Routledge.

Butler, Judith. 2004. *Undoing Gender*. New York: Routledge.

Chase, Cheryl. 1998a. "Hermaphrodites with Attitude: Mapping the Emergence of Intersex Political Activism." *GLQ* 4 (2): 189–211.

Chase, Cheryl. 1998b. "Affronting Reason." In *Looking Queer: Body Image and Identity in Lesbian, Bisexual, Gay, and Transgender Communities*, edited by Dawn Atkins.

Chase, Cheryl. 2003. "What Is the Agenda of the Intersex Patient Advocacy Movement?" *Endocrinologist* 13 (3): 240–242.

Cohen, Cathy J. 2005. "Punks, Bulldaggers, and Welfare Queens: The Radical Potential of Queer Politics?" In *Black Queer Studies: A Critical Anthology*, edited by Patrick Johnson and Mae G. Henderson, 21–51. Durham, NC: Duke University Press.

Combahee River Collective. 1981. "A Black Feminist Statement." In *This Bridge Called My Back: Writing by Radical Women of Color*, edited by Cherríe Moraga and Gloria Anzaldúa, 210–218. New York: Kitchen Table.

Crenshaw, Kimberlé. 1989. "Demarginalizing the Intersection of Race and Sex: A Black Feminist Critique of Anti-Discrimination Doctrine, Feminist Theory, and Antiracist Politics." *University of Chicago Legal Forum* 140: 139–167.

Dreger, Alice D., and April M. Herndon. 2009. "Progress and Politics in the Intersex Rights Movement: Feminist Theory in Action." *GLQ* 15 (2): 199–224.

Fausto-Sterling, Anne. 1993. "The Five Sexes: Why Male and Female Are Not Enough." *Sciences* (March/April): 20–24.

Fausto-Sterling, Anne. 2000. *Sexing the Body: Gender Politics and the Construction of Sexuality.* New York: Basic.

Feinberg, Leslie. 1992. *Transgender Liberation: A Movement Whose Time Has Come.* New York: World View Forum.

Frye, Marilyn. 1983. *The Politics of Reality: Essays in Feminist Theory.* Berkeley, CA: Crossing Press.

Garfinkel, Harold. 1967. *Studies in Ethnomethodology.* Oxford: Polity Press.

Greer, Germaine. 1999. *The Whole Woman.* New York: Anchor Books.

Haraway, Donna. J. 1991. *Simians, Cyborgs, and Women: The Reinvention of Nature.* New York: Routledge, 149–182.

Herndon, April. 2006. "Why Doesn't ISNA Want to Eradicate Gender?" ISNA online. http://www.isna.org/faq/not_eradicating_gender

Heyes, Cressida. 2003. "Feminist Solidarity after Queer Theory: The Case of Transgender." *Signs* 28 (4): 1093–1120.

Holmes, Morgan. 2008. *Intersex: A Perilous Difference.* Selinsgrove, PA: Susquehanna University Press.

Holmes, Morgan. 2009. "Introduction: Straddling Past and Future." In *Critical Intersex,* edited by Morgan Holmes, 1–12. Burlington, VT: Ashgate.

Karkazis, Katrina. 2008. *Fixing Sex: Intersex, Medical Authority, and Lived Experience.* Durham, NC: Duke University Press.

Kessler, Suzanne J. 1990. "The Medical Construction of Gender: Case Management of Intersexed Infants." *Signs* 16 (1): 3–26.

Kessler, Suzanne J. 1998. *Lessons from the Intersexed.* New Brunswick, NJ: Rutgers University Press.

Kessler, Suzanne, and W. McKenna. 1978. *Gender: An Ethnomethodological Approach.* New York: John Wiley.

Koyama, Emi. 2003. "The Transfeminist Manifesto." In *Catching a Wave: Reclaiming Feminism for the 21st Century,* edited by Rory Dicker and Alison Piepmeier, 244–259. Boston: Northeastern University Press.

Koyama, Emi. 2006. "Whose Feminism Is It Anyway? The Unspoken Racism of the Trans Inclusion Debate." In *The Transgender Studies Reader,* edited by Susan Stryker and Stephen Whittle, 698–705. New York: Routledge.

Koyama, Emi, and Lisa Weasel. 2002. "From Social Construction to Social Justice: Transforming How We Teach about Intersexuality." *Women's Studies Quarterly* 30 (3/4): 169–178.

Meyerowitz, Joanne. 2002. *How Sex Changed: A History of Transsexuality in the United States.* Cambridge, MA: Harvard University Press.

Morgan, Robin. 1973. "Lesbianism and Feminism: Synonyms or Contradictions?" *The Lesbian Tide* (May–June).

Moya, Paula M. L. 1997. "Postmodernism, 'Realism,' and the Politics of Identity." In *Feminist Genealogies, Colonial Legacies, Democratic Futures,* edited by M. Jacqui Alexander and Chandra Talpade Mohante, 125–150. New York: Routledge.

Namaste, Viviane, K. 2000. "'Tragic Misreadings': Queer Theory's Erasure of Transgender Subjectivity." In *Invisible Lives: The Erasure of Transsexual and Transgendered People.* Chicago: University of Chicago Press.

Namaste, Viviane, K. 2005. *Sex Change, Social Change: Reflections on Identity, Institutions, and Imperialism.* Toronto: Women's Press.

Namaste, Viviane, K. 2009. "Undoing Theory: The 'Transgender Question' and the Epistemic Violence of Anglo-American Feminist Theory." *Hypatia* 24 (3): 11–32.

Preves, Sharon E. 2003. *Intersex and Identity: The Contested Self.* New Brunswick, NJ: Rutgers University Press.

Prosser, Jay. 1998. *Second Skins: The Body Narratives of Transsexuality.* New York: Columbia University Press.

Radicalesbians. 1988. "The Woman Identified Woman." In *For Lesbians Only: A Separatist Anthology*, edited by Sarah Hoagland and Julia Penelope, 17–21. London: Onlywomen.

Raymond, Janice. 1979. *The Transsexual Empire: The Making of the She-Male.* Boston: Beacon Press.

Raymond, Janice. 1994. *The Transsexual Empire: The Making of the She-Male.* With a new introduction on transgender. New York: Teachers College Press.

Reis, Elizabeth. 2009. *Bodies in Doubt: An American History of Intersex.* Balimore, MD: Johns Hopkins University Press.

Salamon, Gayle. 2010. *Assuming a Body: Transgender and Rhetorics of Materiality.* New York: Columbia University Press.

Rosario, Vernon A. 2006. "An Interview with Cheryl Chase." *Journal of Gay & Lesbian Psychotherapy* 10 (2): 93–104.

Rubin, David. 2010. *Intersex before and after Gender.* dissertation. Emory University.

Rubin, Henry. 1998. "Phenomenology as Method in Trans Studies." *GLQ* 4 (2): 145–158.

Serano, Julia. 2007. *Whipping Girl: A Transsexual Woman on Sexism and the Scapegoating of Femininity.* Emeryville, CA: Seal Press.

Stone, Sandy. 1991. "The *Empire* Strikes Back: A Posttranssexual Manifesto." In *Body Guards: The Cultural Politics of Gender Ambiguity*, edited by Julia Epstein and Kristina Straub, 280–304. New York: Routledge.

Stryker, Susan 2008. *Transgender History.* Berkeley, CA: Seal Press.

CHAPTER 21

MARKETS/MARKETIZATION

MARIANNE H. MARCHAND AND ROCÍO DEL CARMEN OSORNO VELÁZQUEZ

Introduction

THE market is a central element in our vocabulary.[1] We refer to it on a daily basis, when we mention that we have to go to the (super)market to get groceries or to its virtual counterpart online, the Internet, which specializes in selling discounted products.[2] Given its ubiquity, it is difficult to think of our lives without the presence of the market. Markets have been around for centuries, since before the Christian era. In medieval Europe, feudal lords would grant towns the right to hold a market in exchange for payment of a fee or tax. Hence, the emergence of "market towns" that became bustling economic hubs in their regions. But markets are not just a European phenomenon; they have existed on different continents, predating their appearance in medieval Europe. In pre-industrial times, markets fulfilled important roles in terms of exchange and storage, as was the case in Babylonia (Garraty and Stark 2010; van der Spek, van Leeuwen, and van Zanden 2015). Markets are therefore not exclusively a capitalist phenomenon, although with the emergence of capitalist economies the market has become the central concept of economic thought, policy, and activity. As Michael Parkin (2014, 44) comments, "In ordinary speech, the word *market* means a place where people buy and sell goods such as fish, meat, fruits, and vegetables . . . In economics, a **market** is any arrangement that enables buyers and sellers to get information and to do business with each other."

Markets are both a physical and spatial arrangement, where people meet face to face, and a central concept in economic theory for analyzing the workings of economies. Both articulations have contributed to the centrality of the market in our way of doing and thinking. With the emergence of post-Keynesian, neoliberal (or neoclassical) economics as well as neoliberal globalization, the market has become a dominant force in virtually all spheres of life. The encroachment of the capitalist market upon noneconomic spheres is known as "marketization." As Bob Jessop has noted:

> Any discussion of economization or marketization presupposes a field of social relations that is not yet (or is no longer) oriented to economic activities and/or organized along market principles of one kind or another. This could be because the (market) economy is not yet disembedded from the wider ensemble of social relations and/or because sets of social relations that are not currently organized in terms of market principles are subordinated to, penetrated by, or colonized by, such principles.
>
> (Jessop 2012, 5)

This chapter examines how markets are gendered, as spatial and conceptual constructions, and how feminists have theorized markets and market behavior. It also demonstrates how marketization or the encroachment of market principles upon noneconomic spheres of human activity is itself a gendering practice that transforms relations between women and men of particular races, ethnicities, classes, and geopolitical locations.

Feminists Theorize Markets

Neoclassical economic theory suggests that the purpose of the market is to benefit individual consumers by rewarding producers who maximize efficient utilization of the earth's scarce resources. Economists propose that precisely because the market is a self-regulating system, guided by an "invisible hand" that operates through free competition, it should be the principal means of determining the allocation of productive resources (Gilpin 2001, 23–24). Within this intellectual tradition, theorists suggest not only that the market is not gender biased but also that it is gender neutral. Indeed, neoclassical economic theorists insist that gender inequity is incompatible with basic market principles: gender inequity is inefficient; it fails to maximize productivity capacity (Braunstein 2007, 5). According to these theorists, the existence of gender inequality reflects differences in the choices men and women make about investment in human capital, occupational selection, and labor-force participation (Bridges and Nelson 1989, 617). Any resulting inefficiency in the labor market is a function of institutions being "'sticky' in the sense of failing to change in response to changing economic incentives, or because of market failures" (Braunstein 2007, 6; Folbre 1994).

Feminist scholars have pointed out that neoclassical economic theory is tied to a particular form of market relations, associated with capitalism as it emerged in Europe from the fifteenth to eighteenth centuries. Like other aspects of Western modernity, the theoretical framework of neoclassical economics contains marked androcentric biases. It "presumes that humans are autonomous, impervious to social influences, and lack sufficient emotional connection" (England 1993, 37). In addition, neoclassical theory accentuates the separation of public and private, an artifact of modernity that is implicated in the construction and perpetuation of raced and gendered divisions of labor, which are profoundly inequitable. Focusing exclusively on the formal (structured and regulated) sector of the economy, neoclassical economics reflect "unexamined assumptions about gender roles [that] lead to a sharp disjuncture of views about the household and the market, and these assumptions result in an inability to see how conventional arrangements perpetuate women's systematic subordination to men" (England 1993, 49).

To challenge mainstream economic accounts of markets, feminist scholars have theorized markets and marketization from a range of multidisciplinary and transdisciplinary perspectives. Feminist anthropologists have analyzed the gendered nature of physical markets, their relation to the subsistence and informal (unstructured and unregulated) sectors of the economy, and the diverse roles of market women (and men). In *Gossip, Markets, and Gender,* for example, feminist anthropologist Tuulikki Pietilä demonstrates that markets in Tanzania are gendered spaces, but that, in contrast to the male-dominant markets of Western capitalism, women are the main producers, traders, and consumers:

> Indeed Kilimanjaro is one of the few places in Tanzania and greater East Africa with a long history of regularly held markets, where women have traditionally gathered to exchange and market produce. The old system in which neighboring marketplaces form a rotating market ring continues today.
>
> (Pietilä 2007, 16)

In many parts of the world, women have performed central roles in the functioning of local markets and continue to do so. As a site of social as well as economic interaction, these markets are multifunctional spaces, where people engage in much more than selling and buying: "the women of a family usually go to the nearest market on the day it is held in order to acquire foodstuffs and to do other errands such as taking maize to be milled. Others are attracted to the market in order to meet people or perhaps send a message through a market woman to someone living farther away" (Pietilä 2007, 21). Despite their prevalence across the global South, market women exist below the threshold of intelligibility for mainstream economic theory.

In addition to analyzing the gendered biases underpinning the conceptualization of markets in economic theory, some feminist economists have called attention to the inadequacy of formal market models to capture the complexity of economic behavior.[3] Feminist economists and feminist political scientists, specializing in international political economy have investigated markets' embeddedness in social relations and relations to other nonmarket sectors. Indeed, in their groundbreaking work *Beyond Economic Man: Feminist Theory and Economics*, Marianne Ferber and Julie A. Nelson suggest that male dominance in the academic profession of economics has had important consequences for the content and the methodology of the field:

> The most obvious point to be made about gender and the social construction of economics is that historically, and continuing to the present day, men have dominated the community of scholars who have created the discipline. Equally important, gender also affects the construction of the discipline in terms of the standpoint from

which the world is perceived, and the way the importance and relevance of questions are evaluated.

(Ferber and Nelson 1993, 2)[4]

Although market women have been the norm in many societies, Western economists have privileged a conception of *homo economicus*, man as the rational economic maximizer, who acts intentionally to improve his condition. Economists' conviction that men are workers and women are not, has contributed to their neglect of the informal sector that secures the livelihoods of the majority of the world's population. It has also rendered invisible the role of the liberal democratic state in producing *homo economicus* by restricting or reclassifying women's labor. Recent scholarship by feminist historians has demonstrated that the capitalist market is far less "autonomous" than the neoclassical model suggests. Rather than operating independently from the state, certain gendered market dynamics have been engineered by state action.

In Europe, over the course of the nineteenth century, the industrial revolution introduced new modes of production that separated workplaces from homes. Although factories employed men and women, and factory housing was often adjacent to worksites, bourgeois theory envisioned a spatial separation between two distinct social spheres, the productive or public and the reproductive or private. Women, in particular middle-class women, were increasingly barred from the public sphere, not only as workers but also as participants in politics and the professions. In France, for instance, women were excluded by law and emerging practice from political clubs and associations, and legislative assemblies, as well as from coffee houses, educational institutions, the professions, the practice of science, and the worlds of art and cultural production (Davidoff 1998). By 1850, in Anglo-American nations, women were excluded from the leadership of unions. Although poor women always worked outside the home, repeated efforts were launched in the nineteenth century to bar women from factories, mines, and other skilled crafts. As feminist labor historians have demonstrated, the invention of the "male breadwinner" and the quest for a "family wage" were well-orchestrated attempts to mask the pronounced presence of women in the industrial labor force and to remove women from desperately needed waged labor (Anderson 2000; Landes 1988). Defining women by their familial relationships, placing women under the legal guardianship of men, and denying them the right to enter into contracts, effectively precluded women from selling their labor freely in the marketplace. In this way, bourgeois law produced *homo economicus* as an exclusively male identity.

Political theorist Carole Pateman (1998) has traced the means by which nascent welfare states constructed the myth of the male "breadwinner." Through laws governing freedom of contract, states created the most fundamental property owned by "free men," the property in their own person and in their labor power. By constructing women as the property of their fathers or husbands, states denied women the right to freely contract their labor. By structuring marriage laws to guarantee men perpetual sexual access to their wives, states denied married women autonomous ownership of their bodies.

Moreover, by creating the category "head-of-household" and restricting it to men, states created men's capacity for governance, not only of themselves but of their "dependents." Pateman points out that census classifications in Britain and Australia officially recognized the male worker as "breadwinner" and his wife as his "dependent," regardless of her contributions to household subsistence and income. In the second half of the nineteenth century, in Britain and Australia, women's domestic labor was reclassified from a form of productive activity to a mode of dependency. This reclassification was coupled with efforts to remove married women from the paid labor market on the belief that women workers depressed men's wages. The campaign for a "family wage" paid to the male "breadwinner"—actively promoted by the trade union movement—enshrined the principle of unequal pay for women in law, as it simultaneously masked women's presence in the industrial and agricultural labor force and rendered their role as family providers invisible. In 1912, 45 percent of the male workers in Australia were single, yet they were paid the family wage; while women workers, one-third of whom were supporting dependents, were paid 46 percent to 50 percent less than the male wages based on the legal fiction that they were not breadwinners. Thus the state created and reinforced women's identity as "dependent" directly and indirectly, even as it used dependency to legitimate women's exclusion from political life. Defined by the state as dependent, regardless of their actual earnings or wealth, women were declared "trespassers into the public edifice of civil society and the state" (Pateman 1998, 248).

In challenging the androcentric focus of the discipline of economics, feminist economists have suggested that neoclassical economics has constructed an unrealistic dualistic model of the market vis-à-vis the family or household (Ferber and Nelson 1993, 1; see also Suzanne Bergeron's chapter in this volume). As Paula England has noted, economists' dichotomous treatment of markets and households contributes to errors in interpreting both markets and home life:

> In the family, individuals (particularly men) are presumed to be altruistic. Thus, empathic emotional connections between individuals are emphasized in the family whereas they are denied in analyzing markets. I will argue that these assumptions exaggerate both the atomistic, separative nature of behavior in markets and the connective empathy and altruism within families.
>
> (England 1993, 37)

In contrast to neoclassical economists, feminist economists have emphasized that the productive sector and the market are embedded in geographically- and historically-specific social relations. As Drucilla Barker and Susan Feiner (2004, 20) have noted, Western capitalism is the suppressed premise in the neoclassical model, "The economy of the market is the familiar public economy of supply and demand, production for exchange, profit, and class conflict. The economy of the household constitutes the "other" economy of domestic relationships in which people are reproduced through expenditures of time, affection, and money."

To expand the framework to encompass economic dimensions of households and the reproductive sphere, feminist economists have explored new questions concerning markets: How do masculinist presuppositions structure research findings about the market? In particular, how does the centrality of notions about the rational actor making decisions on utilitarian principles entrench binary constructions of a "masculine" market and a "feminine" household that obscure critical dimensions of and relations between these spheres? How is unpaid care work sustaining the market economy?

Such questions have also driven the field of market sociology, which examines networks among market actors, how markets have become institutionalized, and the performance of market actors in relation to specific technologies and artifacts. Social relations among market actors involve "trust, friendship, power and dependence," which are central to the functioning of markets (Fligstein and Dauter 2007, 6.9). Yet these relationships are often occluded by economists' preoccupation with self-interest and preference maximization. Feminist scholars suggest that culture plays a critical role in market behavior and exchanges, not only in relation to particular modes of production and consumption, but also in assigning meaning and worth, and producing signifiers for products and exchange (Fligstein and Dauter 2007).

Rather than positing universal market relations and behavior, feminist scholars have called attention to cultural and historical variation in markets as well as to change over time and place. Feminist political economists, for example, have addressed the gendered nature and implications of globalization and the shift toward neoliberal economic policies over the past four decades. To illuminate the dynamics of gendered globalization, V. Spike Peterson has suggested that market behavior spans the reproductive, productive, and virtual sectors of the global political economy:

> In essence, the RPV [reproductive, productive, and virtual sectors] framing brings the conceptual and material dimensions of "social reproduction," non-wage labor, and informalization *into relation with* the familiar but increasingly global, flexibilized, information-based and service-oriented "productive economy," as well as with the less familiar but increasingly consequential "virtual economy" of financial markets, commodified knowledge, and the exchange less of goods than of signs.
>
> (Peterson 2003, 38)

According to feminist scholars, analyzing economic phenomena such as markets and processes of marketization requires an approach grounded in relational thinking that emphasizes the embeddedness, connectedness, and mutually constructive character of these three economic spheres. Moreover, relational thinking extends to gender analysis itself, combining a focus on ideological dimensions, such as gendered representations and valorizations with social (gender) relations and the mechanisms through which gender is inscribed on bodies of men and women (Marchand and Runyan 2011, 11). Marchand and Runyan adopt the terminology of "gendered global restructuring(s)" instead of globalization to capture the multidimensional processes of transformation, which can lead to crises in social reproduction and human securities, as well as a "hyper-commodification of care, labor, migration, development, and even food" (Marchand and Runyan 2011, 13).

Globalization, Neoliberal Policies, and Markets

Since the 1980s, markets have undergone important transformations due to the introduction of neoliberal economic policies as part of overall processes of (global) restructuring. Although "Reagonomics" and "Thatcherism" refer to voluntary adoption of policies that deregulate the private sector, privatize national industries and utilities, and cut back the state and state provision in advanced economies, in the global South neoliberal (global) restructuring was introduced through structural adjustment programs, or SAPs, imposed by international financial institutions as a condition for loans to assist with debt management. Structural adjustment programs have had multiple gendered effects, as cuts in state provision, privatization, export production, and migration have affected men and women differently. As subsidies for food and transportation have been reduced or eliminated, families and households, especially those living under or near the poverty line, had to adjust their consumption patterns and daily life in general. Many households resorted to coping and survival strategies, ranging from more women and children entering the labor market to men taking on extra work or a second job (Benería and Feldman 1992; Moser 1993). As women have assumed additional responsibilities to make up for cuts in state provision, such as to healthcare, their "triple burden" of reproductive labor, including subsistence activities, waged employment and community management has grown increasingly onerous (Moser 1993). These transformations continued steadily on a global scale during the 1990s and the early twenty-first century.

With the liberalization and deregulation of domestic markets, states and international organizations such as the World Bank, the International Monetary Fund, and the World Trade Organization prioritized production for the market, particularly the international market. Together with transformations in processes of production, including outsourcing and offshoring, these policies led to the creation of global value chains, also referred to as global commodity or production chains. In the realm of food production, the emergence of such global value chains had a major impact on rural areas in the global South, but also affected the agricultural sector in the global North. Agricultural industrialization—that is, bringing industrial production processes to agriculture, which entails major restructuring of the countryside in the global South and North—has been central to these global value chains. As agribusiness displaces family farms, women's and men's involvement in food production has changed. Where women had long been involved in subsistence production, caring for the livestock and raising vegetables for home consumption, restructuring food production has increasingly led to their employment in agribusinesses, working for the export sector, a process which is part of the "feminization of agriculture" (Ramamurthy 2010). As Stephanie Barrientos's research on women's seasonal labor in the Chilean fruit sector demonstrates, the insertion of women into global agricultural value chains may have contradictory effects:

> At one level they are a marginalised and "invisible" group, yet they play a key role at the forefront of one of Chile's key export sectors. At another level they are the most heterogeneous, flexible and insecure workers in the sector, yet at the height of the season they are able to earn higher wages than most men. These two levels are, I believe, interconnected in that their "invisibility" is partially facilitated by the heterogeneity and flexibility of their employment; and the fact that they can earn higher wages is facilitated by the degree of export specialisation in the central regions.
>
> (Barrientos 1997, 78)

Increased focus on nontraditional agricultural exports has also affected the position of male farmers and farm workers. In her study of the production of hybrid cotton in South Asia, for example, Priti Ramamurthy found complex transformations in patterns of production and reproduction. As prices for hybrid cotton have increased, male small landholders have shifted from laboring as farm workers to become self-employed farmers who take on the cross-pollination of cotton shrubs. In the hopes of earning higher income and assuring upward mobility for their families, these men are taking on work previously done by women and children. The contracting-out system of farm production thus contributes to the feminization of male farmers, even as they justify this shift with claims that they do this work more efficiently (Ramamurthy 2010). Many of these farmers have traded the farmhand's dependence on an employer for the farmer's dependence on large transnational companies, which provide the needed seeds and credit while also imposing strict quality requirements to conform to export standards set by the World Trade Organization—requirements that tend to privilege northern agribusiness (Ramamurthy 2010).

The increasingly complex realities for women and men in agriculture have been called "new rurality" by Latin American specialists, who suggest that decades of neoliberal policies have had a significant impact on the countryside, forcing households dependent on smallholdings to look for multiple coping and survival strategies, ranging from working for agribusinesses; performing jobs in nonagricultural sectors, such as commerce, industry, and the informal sector, to increasing reliance on additional household income, especially in the form of remittances from migrant family members (Burkham 2012). Such multiple coping strategies by smallholders or family farms are not just a phenomenon in the global South. Increasingly, European family farms have resorted to seeking alternative sources of income, through rural tourism projects, by transforming farmlands into environmental preservation and management areas, and by using farms as daycare centers or for other social activities.

As Marchand and Runyan (2011) argue, global restructuring is multidimensional and touches on all aspects of everyday life. Transformations have occurred not only in the countryside of the global South but also in industrial production and the service sectors. Moreover, the privatization of care work, in particular in the global North, has engendered the emergence of a global care chain (Ehrenreich and Hochschild 2002). The creation of feminized jobs in the global North in the service sector and through the global care chain is intricately connected to the feminization of migration, whereby more women are migrating, and for reasons other than family reunification.

Marketization and the Re-Gendering of Labor Markets

In her plenary address to the 1995 United Nations World Conference on Women in Beijing, Noeleen Heyzer (1995), then director of UNIFEM, the United Nations Development Fund for Women, noted, "Women work two-thirds of the world's working hours, but earn only one-tenth of the world's income and own less than one-tenth of the world's property." The striking disparity between hours worked and remuneration received reflects various factors. Two-thirds of the work women do is unwaged (compared to one-quarter of men's work). Occupational segregation by sex concentrates women in the lowest-waged and least secure positions. Slightly more than 20 percent of all economically active women are employed in the industrial sector, while 75 percent are employed in the far less well-paid service sector.[5] Women are overrepresented in the subsistence and informal (unstructured and unregulated) sectors of the economy and underrepresented in the formal sector, where pay levels are higher, and fringe benefits may be provided. Women also constitute three-quarters of the part-time labor force, working for very low pay without any job security and little hope of upward mobility. Women continue to suffer systemic pay discrimination. Even in nations with equal pay legislation on the books, women earn less than men. Women also make up the majority of those enmeshed in coerced labor. Of the twelve million people worldwide involved in forced labor—from sweatshop workers to sex slaves—women and girls constitute 98 percent of those in forced sexual exploitation and 56 percent of those in forced industrial labor (Seager 2009, 56, 63–66).

Feminist economists, political economists and labor specialists have sought to make visible women's complex and changing relations to both formal and informal labor markets. And they have sought to assess the effects of marketization on diverse markets. As the discussion of global restructuring indicates, women's participation in formal labor markets has been increasing in many parts of the world even as the informal sector has experienced growth in relation to the formal economy (Kabbeer, Milward, and Sadarshan 2013, 14). To examine diverse markets and the effects of marketization, it is useful to analyze specific economic sectors individually.

Agricultural Production

Across much of the global South, women are responsible for subsistence, producing the food that sustains the household. Because this form of subsistence production is often subsumed under the rubric of housework, it tends to be omitted from official counts of farm labor, raising questions about the reliability of statistics about gendered divisions of labor in agriculture. In official statistics, women comprise 40 percent of the agricultural labor force worldwide, rising to 67 percent in developing countries and 80 percent in Sub-Saharan Africa (Seager 2009, 68).

In the twenty-first century, the agricultural labor force continues to shrink, following a trend of the past several centuries, and the nature of farm labor is changing with the consolidation of a corporate-led global agrosystem. Changes in agricultural production introduced by international trade agreements and loan repayment policies have affected women in agriculture in multiple ways (Sachs and Alston 2010). As many countries in the global South shift from subsistence crops to the production and processing of nontraditional export crops in order to generate the revenue to repay international debt, new gendered divisions of labor emerge. Mechanization deployed to produce cash crops tends to reduce men's farm labor, but not women's. Mechanization may create new economic opportunities for men, while also shifting the site of male labor further from home. "At the same time, women's farm work increases because of the loss of men's help in subsistence production and the loss of control over crops that may have started to be profitable. Commercialization of agriculture often reduces the land available for subsistence crop production, and leaves women to cultivate ever-more marginal lands" (Sachs and Alston 2010, 278).

In some regions,

> "corporate employers prefer women laborers for the production of new export crops, such as flowers in Colombia, grapes in Chile, and green beans in Kenya. Because employers can pay women less and hire them in less stable forms of employment, women's employment conditions can be kept largely invisible, and women workers are easily replaceable by the many other women seeking supplementary income"
>
> (Sachs and Alston 2010, 278).

When governments cut subsidies and supports for traditional agricultural crops and commodities, many family farms or subsistence farmers can no longer maintain their livelihoods through farming. Unable to subsist on the land, many men migrate to urban areas or across international borders in search of work, contributing to "the feminization of agriculture, a development compounded by the increasing use of women's labor in migrant worker arrangements and by the increasing corporatization of agriculture, which has resulted in the further co-option of women's (often invisible) labor" (Sachs and Alston 2010, 279). The feminization of agriculture is also reflected in the increasing numbers of women migrating to work as temporary laborers in the horticultural sector, for instance, through the Mexican-Canadian Seasonal Agricultural Workers' Program (Becerril 2004, 2011; Preibisch and Grez 2010).

Industrial Production

Agriculture is not the only economic sector undergoing feminization. Over the past three decades, more and more women have been recruited to the formal and informal labor force, supplementing the work they do in the home and in the production of subsistence. In export processing zones across the global South, for example, women constitute 70 percent to 90 percent of factory workers, producing textiles, leather goods, toys, electronic goods, and pharmaceuticals (Wichterich 2000). Export processing zones approximate a new form of extraterritoriality, existing within the borders of particular states, but exempt from taxes, tariffs, national labor laws, and environmental regulations. With official and unofficial bans on labor unions, working hours are long, and working conditions are often hazardous. As transnational corporations have increasingly moved to outsourcing labor, 200 million women are employed by subcontractors. Working in textile and pharmaceutical production, small numbers of women employees work in their employers' homes, garages, or workshops for very low wages. To meet production deadlines, mandatory overtime without compensation is often required. The tolls such working conditions take are manifold. Long hours at work impose strains on family life, as women workers have little time to perform the domestic chores expected of them. Some families find it difficult to withstand the strains. In Salvador, for example, 80 percent of the married women in the garment industry are living without their husbands (Brooks 2007). Thus, global restructuring is changing family formations: 52 percent of poor households are now headed by women, compared to 20 percent in the 1990s, and 10 percent in the 1970s (Poster and Salime 2002). The health effects of work in the export processing zones are also palpable. Women working in export processing zones have twice the normal rate of miscarriages and deliver twice as many underweight babies. Poor lighting, eye strain, and repetitive stress syndrome combine to impair the performance of women factory workers after comparatively short periods. The average work life for women factory workers in Thailand, for example, is five years. Job-induced problems with eye-hand coordination provide managers with a reason to fire workers. Nor is Thailand atypical. In Central America, a woman factory worker is let go after an average of seven years (Wichterich 2000).

The feminization of labor markets involves more than a shift to a majority female labor force in certain sectors of the global economy. It also encompasses the informal and flexible conditions of employment that have long been associated with women workers, including part-time and temporary jobs, low wages, and no benefits. In 1975, 80 percent of economically active workers were eligible for unemployment compensation; in 1995, only 25 percent of economically active workers qualified for that benefit (Wichterich 2000). Both men and women workers have been subjected to "informalization" and "flexibilization" as the conditions of labor are feminized, although women remain the vast majority (more than 75 percent) of part-time workers.

Saskia Sassen (2002) has pointed out that one manifestation of informalization is home-based work, which reintroduces the household as important economic space not only for outsourced workers in subcontracting facilities in export-processing zones, but also for telecommuting professional workers, and for growing numbers of domestic workers and self-employed. Similar to the effects of deregulation, home-based work increases flexibility while reducing costs of labor, as infrastructure expenses (physical space, utilities, equipment) are passed on to the workers themselves.

The Service Sector

The feminization of the labor force and of the conditions of labor is also related to the kinds of work characteristic of the twenty-first-century global economy, in particular, the shift to a service economy. Although male-dominated services in finance and information technology can be highly remunerated, women-dominated services, such as child care, paraprofessional healthcare, retail sales, or cleaning services, tend to be paid very poorly. The vast majority of women service workers earn subsistence-level wages or less, which contributes to the feminization of poverty (Wichterich 2000). More than 70 percent of the poor globally are women.

The economic restructuring involved in the transition to a market-based service economy has been particularly tough on women workers. In 1990, prior to the collapse of state socialism in Russia, women held 60 percent of the highly skilled positions in fields such as medicine and chemistry. In the transition to a market economy, 80 percent of women workers lost their jobs. After a decade of severe economic dislocation, the job opportunities available to many women were far less attractive than the positions they had lost. Taking positions as hairdressers, cosmeticians, secretaries, and sex workers, many Russian women experienced a significant decline in wages. Before 1990, Russian women earned 70 percent of the average male wage; in 2000, they earned 40 percent of the average male wage (Wichterich 2000). The intensification of sex segregation in the labor force in recent decades has contributed to a growing wage gap between male and female workers. In Western nations, women earn 10 percent to 25 percent less than average male earnings; in the global South, as in Russia and the former Soviet states, women earn 30 percent to 60 percent to less than the average male wage.

Migration

High levels of unemployment in their home nations and the demand for workers in affluent nations have made the feminization of migration another feature of contemporary marketization. More than 100 million women, drawn predominantly from poor nations, constitute a mobile labor force crossing the globe in search of livelihoods (International Labour Organization 2010). Certain migratory circuits have been well mapped: from South Asia to the Middle East, former Soviet states to Western Europe, Mexico and Central America to Canada and the United States, and Africa to Europe (Ehrenreich and Hochschild 2002). Women now comprise 48 percent to of the international migrant flows worldwide, although the proportion of women migrants varies across regions. In the global North, women constituted 52 percent to of all migrants in 2013, compared to 43 percent to in the global South (Department of Economic and Social Affairs 2013).

Migrating women are not a new phenomenon. African women experienced forced migration through the slave trade from the sixteenth to the nineteenth centuries, and many European women migrated in search of better economic opportunities from the eighteenth to the twentieth centuries. In the current era, the sheer number of women migrants, the very long distances they travel, and their migration without family members are distinctive, however. Women migrant workers in Middle East, for example, increased from 8,000 in 1979 to 100,000 in 1999 (Moghadam 2005, 71). Some 3.8 million Filipinas are currently working overseas as maids, nannies, nurses, and entertainers, composing more than 70 percent of the migrant labor force from their country. They are working in 180 nations, spanning Asia (especially Hong Kong and Singapore), the Middle East, North America, and Europe (Briones 2009; Parreñas 2001a, 2001b). The remittances they send home are a mainstay of the Philippine economic system, providing the government with its largest source of foreign currency, totaling more than US$12 billion a year in 2006 (Barber 2011). Among other things, these remittances are used by the Philippine government to cover "the $1.8 billion in annual interest on loans accumulated with lenders, including the International Monetary Fund and the World Bank" (Rosca 1995, 524). In addition to generating foreign currency, the migration of Filipinas helps solve the problem of unemployment in the Philippines. Absent this migrant labor, unemployment in the Philippines would increase by 40 percent (Castles, de Haas, and Miller 2012).

The increase in female migration from the global South to the global North over the last five decades has been integrally related to the erosion of gendered divisions in both public and private life that located feminized work (unpaid, unskilled, reproductive, and naturalized activities, such as child care) in families and households (Peterson 2003). The feminization of migration is characterized not only by an increase in female migrants, but also by changing reasons for women's migration (Castles, de Haas, and Miller 2012, 16). Although a good deal of female migration was initially associated with family reunification, more recent migration involves their insertion in transnational labor markets. As married men have migrated for work, women have taken on waged labor and increased their involvement in community activities, contributing to Moser's "triple burden." Women's waged employment has also spurred economic strategies that transcend national labor markets, as social reproduction is not only "contracted out" but "offshored" (Hondagneu-Sotelo and Avila 1997; Pessar 2003, 26). Transnational migrant women increasingly provide paid domestic services, such as nannies, home-care helpers, and domestic workers, as well as professional care services, such as nursing. Transnational migration has become a private solution to a public problem for both women from poor countries and their (female) employers in rich countries (Ramírez, García, and Míguez 2005, 8). As a result, the proportion of dual-wage-earning transnational migrant households has increased. Escalating rates of male unemployment in sending countries has also underscored the centrality of women's contributions to households budgets (Pessar 2003, 32). In many cases, migrant women have become primary income providers for their households. In the twenty-first century, more and more women are migrating not to accompany or join family members, but to earn money to send back to their families (Paiewonsky 2007; Morrison et al. 2008; Kunz 2011, 135). Indeed, whether considered in terms of Maghrebian women working in the European Union (Sorensen 2004; Musette et al. 2006; de Haas 2008) or Philippine, Indonesian, and Sri Lankan women, who comprise 60 percent to 80 percent of the total flow of labor migration from their countries (Omelaniuk 2005), domestic workers have become emblems of contemporary global migration.

With the feminization of migration household arrangements have changed dramatically: in the global South, fewer families now reflect a traditional nuclear family model, if they ever did, as aunts or grandmothers take care of children whose mothers have migrated abroad (Bergeron 2011, 76). Migrant women who have left their children back home are experiencing a reconfiguration of maternity—transnational motherhood. As transnational providers, migrant women face spatial separation from their children over long periods of time. To cope with this situation, they try to sustain family connections by cultivating emotional ties through letters, phone calls, remittances, and gifts (Hondagneu-Sotelo and Avila 1997; Zinn, Hondagneu-Sotelo, and Messner 2005, 317).

As 55 percent of the global labor force, women are heavily concentrated in the more "invisible" activities, such as domestic work and in lower-paying jobs (Morton, Klugman, Hanmer, and Singer 2014). Migrant women are often inserted in labor-intensive jobs such as entertainment and hospitality (clubs, restaurants, hotels), trading and entrepreneurship (small business, self-employment), or sex work (including trafficked women; UNFPA 2006; Kunz 2011, 136).

Migration plays a major role in restructuring labor markets (Castles 2011, 314), contributing to "flexibilization" (Peterson 2003; Bergeron 2011). A product of neoliberal globalization, flexibilization condemns migrant women to extensive working hours, low wages, and jobs that are devalued as "low skilled." Marketization associated with neoliberalism is thoroughly gendered, privileging certain kinds of skills and economically resourceful migrants, even as it deskills and devalues others, typically to the detriment of women from the global South (Barber 2011, 144).

The Global Care Economy

Given the vital economic importance of the remittances provided by migrant workers, the governments of sending states have been actively promoting the marketization of care work, taking the lead in negotiating labor contracts with the governments of receiving states in Asia, the Americas, Europe, and the Middle East. Among the provisions of these labor contracts are a number of significant violations of women's rights, including extensive curtailment of reproductive freedom, the freedom to marry and engage in sexual relationships of one's own choosing, freedom of movement, and freedom of domicile. The contracts also violate a number of fair-labor practices. Feminist scholars have pointed out that the terms of these overseas domestic employment contracts bear startling resemblance to the conditions of indentured servitude. Under the terms of these contracts, domestic workers become dependents of their employers. The Singapore contract, for example, requires domestic workers to live in the household of their employers. They are not allowed to bring family members to their host nation. They are allowed one day off a month—after they have completed a three-month probationary period. They may not leave the country during the period of the contract (typically two years) without the written permission of their employers. They are forbidden to marry any citizen or permanent resident of Singapore. They must submit to pregnancy tests every six months. Moreover, the contract stipulates that they will be fired and deported should they become pregnant (Bakan and Stasiulis 1997; Chang and Ling 2011; Constable 1997; Daenzer 1997; Parreñas 2001b).

In stark contrast to celebrations of individual freedom and mobility, a peculiarly gendered form of indenture is emerging at the heart of productive relations in the global service economy. Moreover, this prescribed mode of gender subordination is negotiated and enforced through the cooperative action of sending and receiving states. In contrast to capitalist notions of individual freedom to contract their labor power, governments structure the foreign domestication of transnational women workers, who leave their own children to care for the children of foreigners and who leave their own homes to assume domestic responsibilities in the households of foreign men and women. Government-negotiated contracts transform overseas domestic workers from autonomous adults and citizens in the sending nation into dependents excluded from all rights of citizenship in the receiving nation, as they are denied control over the conditions of their lives and work, over decisions concerning love, marriage, reproduction, and physical mobility, and excluded from rights of political participation in both nations during the terms set by their contracts.

Millions of women throughout Africa, Asia, Central America, and Latin America are migrating to meet the need for reproductive labor in more affluent nations. "Pulled by the 'care deficit' in wealthier nations and pushed by poverty in their home states," women migrants involved in the global care economy contribute to a "global transfer of emotional resources" (Ehrenreich and Hochschild 2002, 8). The transnational commodification of care thus appears to be a distinctive aspect of the contemporary era. In the words of Barbara Ehrenreich and Arlie Hochschild (2002, 4),

> "In an earlier phase of imperialism, northern countries extracted natural resources and agricultural products—rubber, metals, and sugar, for example—from lands they conquered and colonized. Today, while still relying on third world countries for agricultural and industrial labor, the wealthy countries also seek to extract something harder to measure and quantify, something that can look very much like love."

It would be a mistake, however, to romanticize the commodification of care. Overseas domestic workers often face abusive and exploitive working conditions. Indeed, a British study of 755 overseas domestic workers revealed that 88 percent had experienced psychological abuse by their employers; 38 percent had suffered physical abuse; 11 percent had been subjected to sexual assault; and most were underfed and overworked, required to work seventeen hours per day (Chang 2000, 138).

The Commodification of Sex

Sex work and sexual trafficking also help illuminate the gulf between the simulacrum of love and the real thing. High rates of poverty and unemployment have long served as triggers for increasing numbers involved in sex work. The exponential growth in transnational sexual work in the last three decades of the twentieth century has more proximate causes, however. The Vietnam War generated a vibrant sex industry in Thailand and Japan, where American, Australian, and Korean soldiers were sent for rest and relaxation. When the supply of soldiers dwindled after the war, sex tourism in Thailand was launched as a global business venture. The Thai government developed marketing schemes to make Thailand the preferred destination of sex tourists. Burgeoning tourism attracted two million tourists in 1981, four million in 1988, seven million in 1996—two-thirds of whom were unaccompanied men. In the early twenty-first century, some five million men visit Thailand annually generating 656 billion baht (in US dollars, $26.2 billion) in revenue. Sustaining this booming economy are young Thai women who service ten to eighteen clients a day to repay the cost of their "purchase" from their parents, plus the expense of their room and board (Bales 2002, 219–220).

The Thai model of sex tourism has been replicated by governments in the global South whose immiserated economies encourage them to promote the commodification of women as sex workers as a strategy for survival (Sassen 2002, 273). This appears to be an unintended side-effect of World Bank and International Monetary Fund's recommendations to promote tourism as an economic solution to the troubles of poor countries. Catering to the market demands of affluent tourists, sex tourism has been adopted as a development strategy by nations experiencing widespread poverty and unemployment (Sassen 2002, 269). It is certainly a lucrative strategy, generating remittances of $70 billion in 1998.

Sex tourism involves complicated public-private partnerships, however, because sex work remains illegal in most nations. Although government officials may be eager for the revenue generated by this illegal enterprise, their support for such ventures often takes the form of non-enforcement of existing criminal laws. The global traffic in women, then, turns on a suspect partnership involving government corruption and transnational criminal networks. Consider, for example, the significant increase in sexual trafficking of women from Armenia, Russia, Bulgaria, Croatia, and Ukraine to Europe during the last decade of the twentieth century. With women's unemployment in these states running 70 percent to 80 percent during the economic restructuring in the 1990s and without any safety net to rely on during the "shock transition," pressing financial need motivated some women to enter prostitution. Promising transportation, visas, local accommodations, and the cell phones essential for meeting clients and providing inaccurate information concerning the legality of sex work in most European nations, criminal networks secure the attention of prospective sex workers. The UN estimates that the four million people trafficked in 1998 generated $7 billion for criminal networks. Traffickers in Ukrainian and Russian women, for example, earned $700 to $1000 for every woman delivered to a European destination. Expected to service fifteen clients a day on average, sex workers in Europe generate $215,000 a month for the gangs that control trafficked women (Sassen 2002, 268). Once sex workers are in the hands of criminal traffickers, their "freedom" to contract is severely compromised. Working illegally in their host nations and having their passports confiscated by sex traffickers, transnational sex workers become a transnational underclass, cut off from civil protections and political life in both the sending and receiving states. Although the terms of their employment are onerous, they have lost the putative freedom of every worker—to quit.

Affective Labor

As the marketization of everyday life has expanded with neoliberal, global restructuring, emotions, too, have been commodified, constructed as interchangeable and measurable things that can be exchanged in the market and sold as skills (Arruzza 2014). Arlie Hochschild first drew attention to emotional labor in *The Managed Heart* (1980) through her examination of the work of flight attendants, who are required to perform warmth, empathy, and solicitude as part of their daily work regimen. Building on Hochschild's insights, Michael Hardt and Antonio Negri (2004, 96) conceptualize affective labor as a subcategory of "immaterial labor," which entails human contact and interaction that produce and manipulate affects: "a feeling of ease, well-being, satisfaction, excitement or passion." As the global care economy makes clear, growing numbers of people purchase affective services that were once provided by families, friends, and communities. Affective labor blurs the boundaries between productive and reproductive labor, as the private realm and the production of life itself are marketized. Johanna Oksala (forthcoming) adds,

> "Affective labor not only identifies qualitative changes in today's waged work, but it also, inadvertently, eradicates the differences between such varied laborers as child bearers, child rearers, hospitality industry workers, wedding planners, and Walmart greeters. Affective labor includes at least four different kinds of labor that traditional Marxist analyses have sharply distinguished with the help of the distinctions between productive and unproductive labor and production and reproduction."

Commercial surrogacy is emblematic of the blurred boundaries endemic to marketization of affective labor. Commercial surrogacy is a means of producing a child by contract between a gestational mother (a woman in whose womb a fertilized egg is implanted) and an adoptive family (the family that contracts to raise the child as its own). Whether or not the gestational mother is also the biological mother who provides the egg for artificial insemination and implantation, by signing the surrogacy contract a woman agrees to carry a child to term for a couple who will then adopt the child. The government in India is one of many states that have chosen not to pass any regulations pertaining to surrogacy, thereby allowing the practice to flourish. In India, as in several US states such as California, surrogacy remains a "private" matter, negotiated by contracting parties through an intermediary—a fertility clinic or a law firm—that screens egg and sperm donors, arranges a "match" with an adoptive couple and regulates agreements according to their own criteria, "without state interference," even though adoption is, by definition, a state-regulated means of family formation.

In "Commercial Surrogacy in India: Manufacturing a Perfect Mother-Worker," Amrita Pande (2010) explores norms and practices operating in surrogacy hostels that produce not only healthy babies for adoption but profound subordination in the form of "selfless mothers," whose rights are suspended for the duration of pregnancy and who do not negotiate the payment received. Pande notes that commercial surrogacy has become a temporary occupation for some poor rural women, who agree to bear a child as a survival strategy. The fiction of selfless and devoted mother, then, coexists precariously with economic motives that fuel the transaction. Unlike most economic-livelihood strategies, however, commercial surrogacy is highly stigmatized in India: "The parallels between commercial surrogacy and sex work in the Indian public imagination make surrogacy a highly stigmatized labor option ... As a consequence, almost all the surrogates in this study decided to keep their surrogacy a secret from their community and very often from their parents" (Pande 2010, 975). Dire economic circumstances combined with severe social stigma are far from ideal conditions under which to negotiate a labor contract. Further heightening the power imbalance in surrogacy negotiations, "the surrogacy contract, which lays out the rights of the surrogates, is in English, a language almost none of the surrogates can read."

Neoclassical economics envisions the contract as an emblem of freedom, the mechanism by which equal self-determining actors form agreements of mutual advantage. It is difficult to extend that image of voluntary self-determination among free agents to women driven by economic exigencies to sign a contract written in a language they do not speak. The terms of the contract accord the power to the surrogacy hostel and the adoptive parents. The hostel dictates how the surrogates will live during their pregnancy, what they will eat, what exercise they will take, the number of hours of bed rest daily, the schedule of medical procedures, and the moment at which they will deliver the baby into the hands of the adopting couple. The contract also specifies that neither the hostel nor the adoptive family can be held responsible if any harm comes to the surrogate over the course of her pregnancy. Her rights as a claims-making citizen, entitled to seek redress of grievances, are terminated by contract. As Pande (2010, 976) points out, the contract establishes the "transient role and disposability of the women, not just as workers but also as mothers." It affirms the essence of a master-servant relationship, specifying the terms according to which the surrogate satisfies the needs of the adoptive parents, rendering her needs, interests, and putative equality thoroughly irrelevant. The stigma surrounding commercial surrogacy helps to ensure that the inequities encoded in the contract remain a well-kept secret. Insulated from public scrutiny, commercial surrogacy contracts reduce women citizens of a democratic nation to a means for generating life. Whether the metaphors for this mode of reproduction are drawn from nature or from technology—the soil that nourishes the seed, the fetal environment, the incubator—women are conceptualized as inert beings that require monitoring and control.

As a mechanism of commercial exchange, the surrogacy contract produces servility. The selfless mother signs away her rights of personhood in order to serve the needs of the child-seeking couple, and in so doing generates considerable profit for those who construct and enforce the terms of the contract. To insulate certain social relationships from marketization, some states have banned commercial surrogacy; others prohibit any payment for egg donation, sperm donation, or gestational services.

Financialization and Gendering Global Finance

In many parts of the global South and the global North, finance has traditionally been seen as a masculine domain—despite women's presence in the field. In Mongolia, for example, women have traditionally dominated banking and finance; yet they are perceived as anomalies by senior IMF officials who work with the Mongolian banking sector.[6] Being reduced to an anomaly, however, is far more benign than some characterizations of women in finance. In her study of financial crises, Marieke de Goede (2000, 59) notes that women were discursively "locate[d] . . . in the realm of madness" in economics analyses "based on gendered dichotomies which defy the often assumed neutral or scientific nature of financial discourse." Indeed, "Lady Credit" has been said to lure men away from their banking and financial dealings. Gendered discourses also circulated widely during the financial crisis of 2008, where heightened levels of testosterone or cortisol were blamed for the crisis, prompting calls to "de-masculinize" or feminize the financial sector to reduce risk-taking behavior (Coates and Herbert 2008; Kristof 2009). Thus, finance and banking remain highly masculinized realms, where women are made invisible, denied pay equity, confronted with glass ceilings, and sometimes forced to deal with sexual harassment.[7]

An additional dimension of gendered finance pertains to women's inequitable access to banking and financial instruments. As a consequence of legal changes in the nineteenth century that defined women as legal dependents, it was difficult or impossible for women to hold property, open bank accounts or get credit. In advanced economies, it was not until the twentieth century, and in some cases the 1960s, that states redressed this inequity under pressure from the feminist movement. In the global South, women's access to credit varies by nation and region. In many Latin American countries, women are not legally obstructed from having property or opening bank accounts. In various Sub-Saharan countries, however, inheritance laws prevent women from access to property, most notably land, which, in turn, impairs their capacity to provide collateral for loans.

Access to credit, property, banking, inheritance, and other legal rights for women were placed on the international development agenda during the UN decade for women (1975–1985). Grassroots organizations, such as the Self-Employed Women's Association, or SEWA, in India and the Bangladesh Rural Development Committee, or BRAC, both founded in the 1970s, provided early models of microfinancing institutions that targeted women, advancing an integrated approach that provided financial services and built human and social capital (Lairap 2004, 98). As Josephine Lairap has noted, these "empowerment" models lost ground in the 1980s and 1990s, as many organizations adopted a minimalist approach, focusing primarily on providing of financial services, such as credit, savings facilities, and insurance within a profit-making framework (Lairap 2004). With the dwindling of donor funds and government subsidies earmarked for women's empowerment, the Grameen Bank established a model for a minimalist approach. This change ensured the financial sustainability of microfinancing institutions, but negatively affected the empowerment of women, who had benefited from training sessions to build self-esteem, human capital, and social capital, while also providing information on health issues, nutrition, and gender violence (Lairap 2004). As the international community shifted to microfinance as an important development tool in the global South, this profit-generating tool became increasingly integrated into the global financial system.

With the integration of microfinance into the global financial system, poor women in the global South were "financialized," targeted as a source of profit from the interest they paid on commercial loans. Women were celebrated as good financial risks, because of their high payment compliance. Indeed, under the Grameen Bank model, loans were awarded to small groups of women, creating a system of social pressure to ensure that members of the group would repay their loans. Within these credit collectives, poor women assume responsibility for improving their own welfare. "One big achievement of microfinance is that it makes the poor assume the responsibility for reducing their poverty and inequalities they face. This has led to the poor internalising the norm and becoming self-disciplined.... They are conforming to the requirement of financial and market discipline in order to continue to get access to credit" (Lairap 2004, 268).

Within the domain of microfinance, neoliberal economic policies have served as a vehicle for a market-oriented biopolitics. Marketization and financialization—the expansion of finance and financial logic to nonfinancial spheres—have transformed everyday life, as well as individuals' subjectivities and practices. Even the poorest of the poor have been disciplined and normalized as rational economic maximizers, who pursue individual self-interest according to the rules of the market and financial sector. As feminist social scientists have demonstrated, however, transforming impoverished women into *homo economicus* falls far short of improving their lives or mitigating their poverty.

Conclusion

Feminist scholarship reveals that markets are gendered, both as social spaces and as theoretical constructs. Women are important market actors, as producers, traders, and consumers. Yet, economic theory has made gender invisible in its conceptualization of markets even as it perpetuates neoclassical notions that markets are the (masculine) realm of rational behavior, altogether distinct from the (feminized) private sphere of affect and intimacy. In their analyses of neoliberal economic policies and global restructuring, feminist scholars have traced the gendered dimensions of the flexibilization of labor markets and the marketization of previously noneconomic spheres. Although men and women experience these dynamic processes differently, neoliberal policies heighten inequalities, while miring the majority of workers in jobs that are low paid and not very secure or stable. Although some men and women have benefited exponentially from processes of marketization and financialization, the mutually constitutive socioeconomic and political transformations of global restructuring have reinforced and exacerbated existing inequalities and engendered new inequalities related to gender, race, ethnicity, age, sexuality, class, national origin, and geopolitical location.

Notes

1. We wish to greatly thank Mary Hawkesworth for her wonderful support and feedback on this chapter.
2. In Spanish, the equivalent of eBay is called mercadolibre.com, and in Dutch, it is marktplaats.nl (*mercado* or *marktplaats* meaning "market").
3. As the *Elgar Compendium to Feminist Economics* (Peterson and Lewis 1999) shows, markets have not been the focus of many feminist economists' analyses. The *Compendium* does not even include an entry for the term *market*. Many feminist economists accept the neoclassical definition of the market, but challenge its central position in economic thought.
4. The number of women in the field of economics has trailed behind the social sciences and the natural sciences. Although women have gained ground recently, they remain markedly underrepresented in the economics profession. According to the National Science Foundation Survey of Earned Doctorates, women earned 34 percent of economics PhDs in 2011, compared to 46 percent of all doctorate degrees, the lowest percentage of the social sciences. In 2012, in colleges and universities in the United States, women were 28 percent of assistant professors of economics, 22 percent of associate professors with tenure, but less than 12 percent of full professors (Romero 2013).
5. Employment in the manufacturing sector has been declining, and employment in the service sector has been growing in all regions of the world since 1990. According to the International Labor Organization, the percentage of workers employed in services increased from 33.6 percent in 1991 to 43.8 percent in 2008, as the percentage employed in manufacturing fell to less than 30 percent. There are higher proportions of men than women in the better paid manufacturing sector in all but four economies for which data are available—Honduras, Macau, China, and Morocco (van der Hoeven 2009).

6. Personal communication, June 3, 2001.
7. For a collection of news stories on these issues, see "Bankers Behaving Badly: Sex, Harassment, Racism, Embarrassing E-Mails, & Outrageous Extravagance," http://projects.exeter.ac.uk/RDavies/arian/scandals/behaviour.html.

References

Anderson, B. 2000. *Joyous Greetings: The First International Women's Movement, 1830-1860.* New York: Oxford University Press.

Arruzza, C. 2014. "The Capitalism of Affects." *Public Seminar 1* (2). http://www.publicseminar.org/2014/08/the-capitalism-of-affects.

Bakan, A., and S. Stasiulis, eds. 1997. *Not One of the Family: Foreign Domestic Workers in Canada.* Toronto: University of Toronto Press.

Bales, K. 2002. "Because She Looks Like a Child." In *Global Woman: Nannies, Maids, and Sex Workers in the New Economy*, edited by B. Ehrenreich and A. Hochschild, 207–229. New York: Henry Holt and Company.

Barber, P. 2011. "Women's Work Unbound: Philippine Development and Global Restructuring." In *Gender and Global Restructuring*, 2nd ed., edited by M. Marchand and A. S. Runyan, 143–162. New York and London: Routledge.

Barker, D., and S. Feiner. 2004. *Liberating Economics: Feminist Perspectives on Families, Work, and Globalization.* Ann Arbor: University of Michigan Press.

Barrientos, S. 1997. "The Hidden Ingredient: Female Labour in Chilean Fruit Exports." *Bulletin of Latin American Research* 16 (1): 71–81.

Becerril, O. 2004. "Políticas laborales de género, trabajo transnacional y experiencias vívidas: trabajadores y trabajadoras agrícolas migrantes en Canadá." *Antropología. Boletín Oficial del Instituto Nacional de Antropología e Historia* 74 (1). https://revistas.inah.gob.mx/index.php/antropologia/article/view/2994/2895.

Becerril, O. 2011. "A New Era of Seasonal Mexican Migration to Canada." *Focal Point: Dialogue, Research and Solution* website. http://www.focal.ca/publications/focalpoint/467-june-2011-ofelia-becerril-quintana-en.

Benería, L., and S. Feldman, eds. 1992. *Unequal Burden: Economic Crises, Persistent Poverty and Women's Work.* Boulder, CO: Westview Press.

Bergeron, S. 2011. "Governing Gender in Neoliberal Restructuring: Economics, Performativity, and Social Reproduction." In *Gender and Global Restructuring*, 2nd ed., edited by M. H. Marchand and A. Sisson Runyan, 66–77. New York and London: Routledge.

Braunstein, E. 2007. "The Efficiency of Gender Equity in Economic Growth: Neoclassical and Feminist Approaches." The International Working Group on Gender, Macroeconomics and International Economics. Working paper 07. http://www.mtnforum.org/sites/default/files/publication/files/1556.pdf. Accessed February 6, 2015.

Bridges, W., and R. Nelson. 1989. "Markets in Hierarchies: Organizational and Markets Influence on Gender Inequality in a State Pay System." *American Journal of Sociology* 95 (3): 616–658.

Briones, Leah. 2009. *Empowering Migrant Women: Why Agency and Rights Are Not Enough.* Farnham, Surrey, England: Ashgate.

Brooks, E. 2007. *Unraveling the Garment Industry: Transnational Organizing and Women's Work.* Minneapolis: University of Minnesota Press.

Burkham, J. M. 2012. "The City Will Come to Us: Development Discourse and the New Rurality in Atotonilco El Bajo, Mexico." *Journal of Latin American Geography* 11 (1): 25–43.

Castles, S. 2011. "Migration, Crisis, and the Global Labour Market." *Globalizations* 8 (3): 311–324. doi:10.1080/14747731.2011.576847.

Castles, S., H. de Haas, and M. Miller. 2012. *The Age of Migration*, 5th ed. New York and London: Guilford.

Chang, G. 2000. *Disposable Domestics*. Boston: South End Press.

Chang, K., and L. H. Ling. 2011. "Globalization and Its Intimate Other: Filipina Domestic Workers in Hong Kong." In *Gender and Global Restructuring*, edited by M. Marchand and A. S. Runyan, 30–47. London and New York: Routledge.

Coates, J. M., and J. Herbert. 2008. "Endogenous Steroids and Financial Risk Taking on a London Trading Floor." *Proceedings of the National Academy of Science* 105 (16): 6167–6172. http://www.pnas.org/content/105/16/6167.full.pdf+html.

Constable, N. 1997. *Maid to Order in Hong Kong*. Ithaca, NY: Cornell University Press.

Daenzer, P. 1997. "An Affair between Nations: International Relations and the Movement of Household Service Workers." In *Not One of the Family*, edited by A. Bakan and D. Stasiulis, 81–118. Toronto: University of Toronto Press.

Davidoff, L. 1998. "Regarding Some 'Old Husbands' Tales': Public and Private in Feminist History." In *Feminism, the Public and the Private*, edited by J. Landes, 164–194. New York: Oxford University Press.

de Haas, H. 2008. *Irregular Migration from West Africa to the Maghreb and the European Union: An Overview of Recent Trends*. Geneva, International Organization of Migration. http://www.heindehaas.com/Publications/de%20Haas%202008%20MRS-32_EN.pdf.

De Goede, M. 2000. "Mastering 'Lady Credit': Discourses of Financial Crisis in Historical Perspective." *International Feminist Journal of Politics* 2 (1): 58–81. doi: 10.1080/146167400407019.

Department of Economic and Social Affairs. 2013. "The Number of International Migrants Worldwide Reaches 232 Million." *Population Facts* 2: 2–5. United Nations / Department of Economic and Social Affairs. http://esa.un.org/unmigration/documents/The_number_of_international_migrants.pdf.

Ehrenreich, B., and A. R. Hochschild, eds. 2002. *Global Woman: Nannies, Maids, and Sex Workers in the New Economy*. New York: Henry Holt and Company.

England, P. 1993. "The Separate Self: Androcentric Bias in Neoclassical Assumptions." In *Beyond Economic Man: Feminist Theory and Economics*, edited by M. A. Ferber and J. A. Nelson, Chicago, IL: University of Chicago Press.

Ferber, M. A., and J. A. Nelson, eds. 1993. *Beyond Economic Man: Feminist Theory and Economics*. Chicago, IL: University of Chicago Press.

Fligstein, N., and L. Dauter. 2007. "The Sociology of Markets." *Annual Review of Sociology* 33: 6.1–6.24. http://sociology.berkeley.edu/sites/default/files/faculty/fligstein/ANRV316.pdf. Accessed March 14, 2015.

Folbre, N. 1994. *Who Pays for the Kids? Gender and the Structures of Constraint*. London and New York: Routledge.

Garraty, C. P., and B. L. Stark, eds. 2010. *Archaeological Approaches to Market Exchange in Ancient Societies*. Boulder: University of Colorado Press.

Gilpin, R. 2001. *Global Political Economy: Understanding the International Order*. Princeton, NJ: Princeton University Press.

Hardt, M., and A. Negri. 2004. *Multitude: War and Democracy in the Age of Empire*. London: Penguin Press.

Heyzer, N. 1995. Plenary address. United Nations World Conference on Women in Beijing. *Women's International Network News* 21 (4): 27–37.

Hondagneu-Sotelo, P., and E. Avila. 1997. "'I'm Here but I'm There': The Meanings of Latina Transnational Motherhood." *Gender and Society* 11 (5): 548–571.

Hochschild, A. 1983. *The Managed Heart: Commercialization of Human Feeling*. Berkeley and Los Angeles, CA: University of California Press.

Hondagneu-Sotelo, P. ed. 2003. *Gender and U.S. Immigration: Contemporary Trends*. Berkeley: University of California Press.

International Labour Organization. 2010. *International Labor Migration: A Rights-Based Approach*. Geneva: International Labour Organization. http://www.ilo.org/wcmsp5/groups/public/—-ed_protect/—-protrav/—-migrant/documents/publication/wcms_208594.pdf.

Jessop, B. 2012. "Understanding the "Economization" of Social Formations." In *The Marketization of Society: Economizing the Non-Economic* by Uwe Schimank and Ute Volkmann Welfare Societies Conference Paper, p. 5. Research Network Welfare Societies. Bremen: University of Bremen. http://welfare-societies.com/uploads/file/WelfareSocietiesConferencePaper-No1_Schimank_Volkmann.pdf. Accessed February 12, 2015.

Kabeer, N., R. Sudarshan, and K. Milward, eds. 2013. *Organizing Women Workers in the Informal Economy: Beyond the Weapons of the Weak*. London: Zed Books.

Kristof, N. D. 2009. "Mistresses of the Universe." *New York Times*, February 7. http://www.nytimes.com/2009/02/08/opinion/08kristof.html?_r=0.

Kunz, R. 2011. "The 'Making Women Productive' Strategy: Uncovering Gender Sightings, Sites and Resistances to Global Restructuring in rural Mexico." In *Gender and Global Restructuring*, 2nd ed., edited by M. Marchand and A. S. Runyan, 163–182. New York and London: Routledge.

Lairap, J. 2004. "The Disciplinary Power of Microcredit: Some Preliminary Evidence from Cameroon." PhD thesis. University of Amsterdam.

Landes, J. 1988. *Women and the Public Sphere in the Age of the French Revolution*. Ithaca, NY: Cornell University Press.

Landes, J., ed. 1998. *Feminism, the Public and the Private*. New York: Oxford University Press.

Marchand, M. H., and A. Sisson Runyan, eds. 2011. *Gender and Global Restructuring: Sightings, Sites and Resistances*. 2nd ed. New York and London: Routledge.

Moghadam, V. 2005. *Globalizing Women: Transnational Feminist Networks*. Baltimore, MD: Johns Hopkins University Press.

Morrison, A., M. Schiff, and M. Sjöblom. 2008. *The International Migration of Women*. Washington, DC, and New York: The World Bank and Palgrave Macmillan. http://www-wds.worldbank.org/external/default/WDSContentServer/WDSP/IB/2007/12/10/000020953_20071210115624/Rendered/PDF/417880PAPER0Mi101OFFICIAL0USE0ONLY1.pdf.

Morton, M., J. Klugman, L. Hanmer, and D. Singer. 2014. *Gender at Work: a companion to the world development report on jobs*. Washington, DC: World Bank Group. http://documents.worldbank.org/curated/en/2014/02/19790446/gender-work-companion-world-development-report-jobs

Moser, C. 1993. *Gender Planning and Development: Theory, Practice and Training*. London: Routledge.

Musette, M. S., Y. Alouane, M. Khachani, and H. Labdelaoui. 2006. *Summary Report on Migration and Development in Central Maghreb*. Geneva: International Labour Office. http://www.ilo.org/wcmsp5/groups/public/—-ed_protect/—-protrav/—-migrant/documents/publication/wcms_201461.pdf.

Oksala, Johanna. Forthcoming. "Affective Labor and Feminist Politics." *Signs: Journal of Women in Culture and Society* 41 (3).

Omelaniuk, I. 2005. "Gender, Poverty Reduction and Migration." Washington, DC: The World Bank Group. http://siteresources.worldbank.org/EXTABOUTUS/Resources/Gender.pdf

Paiewonsky, D. 2007. "The Feminization of Migration." Working Paper. The United Nations International Research and Training Institute for the Advancement of Women/INSTRAW. Santo Domingo, Dominican Republic. http://www.wunrn.com/news/2009/05_09/05_18_09/051809_feminization_files/Feminization%20of%20Migration-INSTRAW.pdf.

Pande, A. 2010. "Commercial Surrogacy in India: Manufacturing a Perfect Mother-Worker." *Signs: Journal of Women in Culture and Society* 35 (4): 969–992.

Parreñas, R. 2001a. *Servants of Globalization: Women Migration and Domestic Work*. Redwood City, CA: Stanford University Press.

Parreñas, R. 2001b. "Transgressing the Nation-State: The Partial Citizenship and 'Imagined Community' of Migrant Filipina Domestic Workers." *Signs: Journal of Women in Culture and Society* 26 (4): 1129–1154.

Parkin, M. 2014. "The Economic Problem." In *Economics*. 11th ed., 31–46. New York, NY: Pearson Education.

Pateman, C. 1998. "The Patriarchal Welfare State." In *Feminism, the Public and the Private*, edited by J. Landes, 241–274. New York: Oxford University Press.

Pessar, P. 2003. "Engendering Migration Studies: The Case of New Immigrants in the United States." In *Gender and U.S. Immigration: Contemporary Trends*, edited by P. Hondagneu-Sotelo, 20–42. Berkeley: University of California Press.

Peterson, J., and M. Lewis. 1999. *Elgar Compendium to Feminist Economics*. Cheltenham, UK, and Northampton, MA: Edward Elgar. http://www.elgaronline.com/view/9781858984537.xml.

Peterson, V. S. 2003. *A Critical Rewriting of Global Political Economy: Integrating Productive, Reproductive and Virtual Economies*. London: Routledge.

Pietilä, T. 2007. *Gossip, Markets, and Gender: How Dialogue Constructs Moral Value in Post-Socialist Kilimanjaro*. Madison: University of Wisconsin Press.

Poster, W., and Z. Salime. 2002. "The Limits of Micro-Credit: Transnational Feminism and USAID Activities in the United States and Morocco." In *Women's Activism and Globalization: Linking Local Struggles to Transnational Politics*, edited by N. Naples and M. Desai, 189–219. New York and London: Routledge.

Preibisch, K., and E. Encalada Grez. 2010. "The Other Side of 'El Otro Lado': Mexican Migrant Women and Labor Flexibility in Canadian Agriculture." Special Issue. *Women in Agriculture*. *Signs: Journal of Women in Culture and Society* 35 (2): 289–316.

Ramamurthy, P. 2010. "Why Are Men Doing Floral Sex Work? Gender, Cultural Reproduction and the Feminization of Agriculture." *Signs: Journal of Women in Culture and Society* 35 (2): 397–424.

Ramírez, C., M. García, and J. Míguez. 2005. *Remittances, Gender and Development*. UN International Research and Training Institute for the Advancement of Women (UN-INSTRAW). Working paper. http://reliefweb.int/report/world/crossing-borders-remittances-gender-and-development.

Romero, J. 2013. "Where Are the Women?." *Econ Focus*, 2nd quarter, p. 12. https://www.richmondfed.org/publications/research/econ_focus/2013/q2/pdf/profession.pdf.

Rosca, N. 1995. "The Philippines Shameful Export." *The Nation*, April 17: 522–527.

Sachs, C., and M. Alston. 2010. "Global Shifts, Sedimentations, and Imaginaries: An Introduction to the Special Issue on Women and Agriculture." *Signs: Journal of Women in Culture and Society* 35 (2): 277–288.

Sassen, S. 2002. "Global Cities and Survival Circuits." In *Global Woman: Nannies, Maids, and Sex Workers in the New Economy,* edited by B. Ehrenreich and A. R. Hochschild, 254–274. New York: Henry Holt and Company.

Seager, J. 2009. *The Atlas of Women in the World.* 4th ed. Brighton, Vt.: Earthscan.

Sorensen, N. 2004. "Migrant Remittances as a Development Tool: The Case of Morocco." Working paper 2. Migration Policy Research. Geneva: International Organization of Migration.

United Nations Population Fund State of World Population. 2006. *State of World Population 2006: A Passage to Hope: Women and International Migration.* New York: United Nations Population Fund (UNFPA). http://www.unfpa.org/sites/default/files/pub-pdf/sowp06-en.pdf.

van der Hoeven, R. 2009. "Labor Market Trends, Financial Globalization and the Current Crises in Developing Countries." United Nations / Department of Social and Economic Affairs. Working paper 99 / ILO Trends: Econometric Models. http://www.un.prg/development/desa/papers/2010.

van der Spek, R. J., B. van Leeuwen, and J. L. van Zanden, eds. 2015. *Markets from Ancient Babylonia to the Modern World.* London: Routledge.

Wichterich, C. 2000. *The Globalized Woman: Reports from a Future of Inequality.* London: Zed Books.

Zinn, M. B., P. Hondagneu-Sotelo, and M. A. Messner, eds. 2005. *Gender through the Prism of Difference.* 3rd ed. New York and Oxford: Oxford University Press.

CHAPTER 22

MATERIALISMS

ELIZABETH WINGROVE

Introduction

In a 1994 interview with Judith Butler, Gayle Rubin questioned the "explanatory potency" of psychoanalytic paradigms for understanding sexual deviance by elaborating what such approaches ignore: "I do not see how one can talk about fetishism, or sadomasochism, without thinking about the production of rubber, the techniques and gear used for controlling and riding horses, the high polished gleam of military footwear, the history of silk stockings, the cold authoritative qualities of medical equipment, or the allure of motorcycles and the elusive liberties of leaving the city for the open road" (Butler and Rubin 1994, 78–79). For Rubin, contemplating the "rich complexity of erotic meaning and conduct" opens up a world of dense materiality, where resource extraction, industrial manufacture, interspecies intimacies, international trade and war, scientific technologies, and movement within and across built environments are all implicated in the forms that desire takes. And it is an aesthetically rich materiality: highly polished, coldly authoritative, alluring. While her particular concern remains the limitations of psychoanalytic theory, Rubin's expressive appeal to the historical specificities of social, economic, and topographical context captures a broader predicament animating contemporary feminist theory: In what ways does an attention to materiality inform and (re)direct feminist analysis? Does such attention require particular analytic approaches and not others? And just how capacious can the category of "the material" be?

Given what Sonia Kruks (2010, 258) characterizes as the "essentially contested" status of materialism in contemporary feminist theory, these questions would seem to be unresolved, and unresolvable. I don't intend to try to remedy that state of affairs. I mean instead to consider some of the ways in which feminists have used materialism to frame questions, articulate demands, and undermine certainties. What, in short, are they talking about when they're talking about materiality? As I will address shortly, the "matter" referred to varies, depending on who is doing the talking. But there is a consistency across approaches, inasmuch as the call for a material analysis is regularly presented or heard as an appeal to what is actual, or "real": a sensuous or affective dimension, rooted in time and space, standing, if not fast, then relatively firm as a site for or agent of continuity and change. Alternatively viewed as counterpoise to, base for, or endlessly entangled with the constitutive force of representational (ideological, linguistic, literary, cognitive) processes and practices, materialism in feminist theory stakes a claim for the level(s) of analysis on which sex/gender—as a system, a phenomenological event, a subjective state, a regulatory fantasy—is best approached. Setting to the side the vexed issue of whether this appropriation of the "real" is warranted or the charge justified, my interest is to consider the interpretive claims it makes possible. What are the properties of materialism's "real," and how do they set the terms for understanding difference, agency, domination, freedom, and other enduring feminist concerns?

My point of entry is two established and distinct fields of feminist materialist inquiry, each of which emphasizes the need to ground analysis in material "realities." The first, historical materialist feminisms (hereafter HMF) can be traced to feminism's early engagement with Marx and Marxism. Deeply influenced by Marx's insistence on the historical primacy of the production and reproduction of physical life yet deeply unsatisfied with how sex/gender was addressed in that account, feminists in the 1960s and 1970s began to pursue a wide-ranging inquiry into the limits and possibilities of understanding sexual inequality, oppression, and difference through the categories of labor, class, and capitalism. Since that time the scope and contours of HMF have changed, largely in response to its reception by women of color and others who have urged attention to multiple axes of oppression, the changing conditions of global and postmodern capitalism, and the provocations associated with the "linguistic turn." A recurrent subject of debate on this last score has been whether or how HMF's long-standing attentions to ideology—systems of ideas and beliefs embedded within and critical to sustaining productive and reproductive relations—adopt or adapt poststructuralist approaches.

The second field I will consider is feminist new materialisms (hereafter FNM). Drawing variously from the insights and provocations of science and technology studies, Deleuzian philosophies of immanence, feminist technoscience, object-oriented ontology, and systems theory (among other new and old intellectual projects), FNM's common core is a commitment to rethinking matter: the stuff of which humans, nonhumans, and nature are comprised should be understood not as given or passive but instead as dynamic and agentic, contributing both content and form to processes of world formation. From this perspective, feminist theory's sturdy suspicion of essentialism has obstructed inquiry into vital realms: investigations into bodily and natural matter are necessary, FNM insists, not to find originating causes but to explore the biological and ecological sites where relations of power take shape and agency is forged. Such exploration suggests in turn a suspicion of the power accorded to discourse, even as FNM scholars remain deeply engaged with poststructuralist theory.

In both cases, a materialist orientation provides a conceptual framework that specifies not only the phenomena to be interrogated—for example, the sexual division of labor, the breaching of boundaries between the biological and the technological—but also an interpretive grammar. For HMF, to speak of materiality is to speak of structural logics and constitutive contradictions, systematic relationality, and social totalities. For FNM, by contrast, to speak of materiality is to speak of contingencies, web-like meshes and multidirectional flows that suggest fluctuating connections and a rich "messiness" whose complexity and indeterminacy preclude the notion of a totality. These distinct, even oppositional framings of how materiality sets the terms for feminist analysis will be my touchstone in what follows.

Historical Materialist Feminisms (HMF)

At a most basic level, materiality in the Marxian framework adapted by HMF refers to the subsistence needs of the human body and the "sensuous activities" undertaken to meet those needs (Marx 1998). These activities are insistently relational: responding to the imperatives of physical survival gives rise to social relations, relations to the natural world, and likewise a relationship to self, which is to say, consciousness. Social structures—the repetition, aggregation, and enforcement of these activities as they assume patterned, durable forms—thus reflect a systematic relationality whose historically unequal and unfree character is the centerpiece of Marxian critique. Applying these concepts to the analysis of capitalism, Marx argued that the systematic relationality of productive relations instantiates exploitation (through the extraction of surplus value in the form of wage labor), domination (through the practices of workplace and state-sponsored discipline and violence), and alienation (through producers' lack of control over the processes and products of their labor). Otherwise put, under conditions of capitalism, the "sensuous activities" through which consciousness, community, and world are generated sustain oppression, and likewise, a transformation in these same activities is necessary if we are to live otherwise.

The notion of a materiality that is at once bodily, systematically relational, historically contingent, and riven with power has been compelling to many feminist theorists, despite the shortcomings of the Marxist framework. Its most obvious failure is to subject the "sensuous activities" performed by women—in particular, the labor of reproduction (giving birth, caring for children, maintaining a home, etc.)—to historical materialist critique. Addressing this failure has taken HMF in diverse directions. Some have retained a primary focus on the inseparability of contemporary capitalist and patriarchal relations, arguing that women's unpaid and underpaid labor is critical to processes of capital accumulation, which are in turn critical to sustaining men's dominance over women (e.g., Vogel 1983; Gimenez 1978). Others have pursued alternative accounts of exploitation, domination, and alienation, approaches that take their bearings directly from the sex/gender relations that organize women's reproductive labor.

The approach taken by Christine Delphy, for example, begins from the materiality of women's labor as it takes place in the "family mode" (Delphy 1984, 69). Unlike the "industrial mode" analyzed by Marx, the goods produced and services performed in the "family mode" are unremunerated. Additionally, domestic labor isn't "fixed," either in terms of its hours or its scope; it takes place within an intimate space marked by relations of love and loyalty, as well as force; and it remains almost exclusively the labor of women, whether or not they are also engaged in waged work outside the home. However functional for capitalism domestic labor might be, Delphy insists, its particularities cannot be explained through a Marxian analysis. Labor that is free, unfixed, personal, and feminized can only be understood as a function of the social relations between men and women, that is to say, as a function of patriarchy. The ubiquity of these relations motivates Delphy's (in)famous conclusion that women "constitute a class," as well as her less quoted claim that "as a category of human beings who are destined by birth to become members of this class, [women] constitute a caste" (71).

While Delphy's account has been criticized on various fronts, her understanding of the explanatory potency of materialism highlights several interpretive commitments central to HMF. First, its *de*naturalizing of women's "sensuous activities" makes those practices legible as labor. Neither a manifestation of an essential or eternal feminine nature nor an inevitable result of biological function, "women's work" as performed in both the household and workplace must instead be understood in terms of the historically articulated relations of power and expropriation it both sustains and reflects. This understanding was central to the Wages for Housework Campaign, started in Italy in 1972, which Silvia Federici underscores must be grasped as a "political perspective" rather than a "thing": "[W]hen we struggle for wages *we struggle unambiguously and directly against our social role*" (1975, 5; emphasis in original). That such work is often "caring" work, embedded in affective ties and occasioned by the realities of human (inter)dependence and vulnerability, does not make it any less laborious or ill-suited to the category of labor. On the contrary, these aspects of "women's work"—once disentangled from the ideological stranglehold of naturalized femininity—point directly to the distortions of labor (technically, labor power) as a commodity and thus to the need for a more collective organization of both reproductive and productive relations. Precisely the apparent impossibility of meeting the demand underscores its radical potential: the fight for wages for housework means "revolutionizing—in the process of struggling for it—all our family and social relations" (1–2).

A similar commitment animates Federici's (2012) more recent consideration of the politics of "the commons"—collectively held or accessed environmental (e.g., oceans, forests) and sociocultural (e.g., the Internet, cities) goods—which she insists must be conceptualized from the perspective of feminist analyses of reproductive relations and labor: any struggle for a "right to the commons" can only be coincident with a struggle to transform the relations through which life is sustained. From a related, autonomous Marxist perspective, Kathi Weeks (2011) moves from denaturalizing women's work to denaturalizing work altogether, taking the domestic labor disputes of the 1970s as a critical point of departure for questioning the experience, organization, and meaning of work in a postindustrial, post-Fordist era. In this context, Weeks argues, where (social) reproduction makes up an increasingly large percentage of waged work, the struggle to transform the relations and practices of reproductive labor becomes a struggle against work itself, together with the twinned fantasies of overcoming alienation through "better" work and achieving freedom and equitability through hyperproduction (13).

Denaturalizing feminized labor has long been central to HMF analyses of women's waged work. Interrogating the relationship between a sexual division of labor in the household and women's position in market-oriented production processes, feminist scholars have shown how the presumption of women's primary duties as homemakers and caretakers sustains the fiction that their labor is for subsistence (i.e., that it does not produce exchange-values), regardless of the capital it in fact generates (Mies 1982). In addition the naturalization of "women's work" has rationalized their lower wages as a "supplement" to men's primary, family-sustained wages (Fernández-Kelly 1983) their status as temporary, part-time, and "unskilled" workers (Mohanty 2003), and their positioning in the global economy, both as participants in new (and old) "industrial modes" of production and as "new agents of development" (Rankin 2001; Keating, Rasmussen, and Rishi 2010). In short, an HMF approach highlights how the "sensuous activities" performed by women in the agricultural sector, on the shop floor, and as entrepreneurs are subject to the patriarchal imperatives long operative in domestic labor relations.

A second aspect of the explanatory potency of an HMF approach is its insistence on oppression as the starting point of analysis. As Delphy puts it: "[M]aterialism is not one possible tool, among others, for oppressed groups; it is *the* tool, precisely in so far as it is the only theory of history for which oppression is the fundamental reality, the point of departure" (1984, 87; emphasis in original). In making this statement, Delphy both distances a feminist materialist approach from Marxism, which has "reduced materialism to an analysis of the capital mode of production alone," and identifies oppression as the linchpin of a sex/gender system. Less its cause than the hook that holds it together *as* a system, the oppressive relations that organize sexual divisions of labor, within and outside the household, remain the bedrock of HMF, even when it proceeds on what would seem to be an *im*material level of analysis.

Consider, for example, the pivotal role materialism has played in the development of standpoint theory. As articulated by Nancy Hartsock, women's "experiences" of productive and reproductive labor make possible an epistemic perspective from which the constitutive perversions and contradictions of contemporary social relations become legible (Hartsock 1997). Paralleling Marx's analysis of the proletariat's position in capitalist relations of exchange, it is women's oppression—the devaluation, misrecognition, and expropriation of their labor—that grounds the claims of feminist standpoint to provide a superior account of social relations: superior because it recognizes the power and hierarchy that sustain those relations, and because, in so doing, it recognizes the distortions that have kept the "sensuous activities" of women inaccessible to analysis. In developing this latter dimension, Hartsock makes an "excursion" into the "materialist psychology" of object relations theory that shifts the focus of her analysis to the psychic world of personality, where the self-relations (i.e., consciousness) shaped by the sexual division of labor and attendant "frameworks of thought" (e.g., "abstract masculinity") take center stage (471–472). But the "fundamental reality" of oppression remains key in her account, providing as it does the material context that secures the distinction between a diverse multiplicity of perspectives corresponding to a diversity of social locations and *a* feminist standpoint corresponding to a position in the sexual division of labor.

The apparent singularity of feminist standpoint brings me to a third aspect of HMF's analytic approach, which concerns its approach to difference. The dichotomous rendering of oppressor/oppressed suggested by that singularity (and conjured by Delphy in her rhetorical choice to name patriarchy "the main enemy") appears to many to be overly simplifying if not ham-fisted, flattening interclass differences between women and ignoring or minimizing the "interlocking systems" of power that make race, ethnicity, sexuality, and nation critical to any account of oppression. On the one hand, Delphy's dichotomous framing is to some extent a political choice, motivated by her insistence on identifying men as the systematic beneficiaries of the exploitation of women's labor, as well as identifying a pervasive desire to "exempt" them from responsibility for women's oppression (1984, 154). A similarly political insistence on identifying the systematic beneficiaries of racism, heterosexism, nationalism, and so on is evident in the work of feminists of color and others who emphasize multiple axes of oppression. Indeed, these scholars and activists have been vital to the development of standpoint theory, leveraging and complicating a materialist approach in which oppression remains the "fundamental reality" to be confronted (Collins 1990, 2003; Narayan 2004; Sandoval 2004). Here, naming the benefits attached to whiteness, heterosexuality, "first world" citizenship, and the like unavoidably raises the specter of the zero-sum relationship of oppressor and oppressed (e.g., Joseph 1981); it also fends off the flattening singularity of that dichotomy, both by characterizing these benefits as "privilege" (evoking granted or unearned advantage rather than the direct exercise of power) and by underscoring the multiplicity of oppressive systems in play.

On the other hand, recognition of that multiplicity forces a reconsideration of the distinction I highlighted earlier, between a diversity of perspectives and *a* standpoint. I would underscore that at issue is precisely the materialist commitments that animate HMF analysis. The difference between diverse perspectives corresponding to a range of social locations and *a* standpoint corresponding to a particular social location hinges on the analytic priority accorded to structurally secured relations, rooted in "sensuous activities," through which consciousness, community, and world are reproduced. Absent that account of oppression's systematic and naturalized character, the critical claims of standpoint are difficult to distinguish from demands to recognize and accept difference. When, by contrast, a materialist framework guides the analysis, "difference" becomes a social relational production that requires explanation. From this perspective, the capacity of HMF to attend to multiple axes of oppression hinges on whether and how racism, heterosexism, nationalism, and so on, can be conceptualized as systemic wholes, sustained—in all their historical and geographic variation—by the productive and reproductive relations that make up social structures.

The properties of HMF's material "real" thus include the capacity to generate differences. The resonance between this aspect of feminist materialism and feminist poststructuralist approaches has been addressed by Lisa Disch (2015), who retraces the emergence of what she calls "constructivist materialism" in Delphy's evolving critique of the sex/gender couplet. While Disch highlights how Delphy's theoretical re-articulations steadily whittle away the material "substrate" of anatomical sexual difference in favor of a wholly constructivist account, I want to underscore how another material "substrate"—the imperatives of bodily survival—stands fast in HMF's approach to difference. From this perspective, the systemic relationality of productive and reproductive practices remains the cornerstone of constructivist claims. Indeed, such constructivism emerges as the necessary corollary to the axiomatic claims that "sensuous activities" must be denaturalized and that oppression is the "fundamental reality" of the social relations those activities generate. Inasmuch as domination produces differences ("that matter"), they are a material reality.

But to underscore the material "real" of difference in an HMF framework risks conjuring up the much-debated (in)compatibility between materialist and discursive approaches to sex/gender's constructed realities. Alternatively celebrated, assailed, and diagnosed as feminist theory's deceptive "common sense," the notion that a materialist approach remains in opposition to those focused on representation has had an extraordinary staying power (Hemmings 2011; see also Wingrove 1999). While, as I indicated earlier, this claim has been mobilized both to assert and to contest HMF's appeal to a sensuous, worldly "real," it is likewise true that an attention to "words" as well as "things," as Michelle Barrett (1992) staked out the options some time ago, has always punctuated HMF theory. Initial challenges to the presumed-but-undertheorized role of ideas, beliefs, symbols (in short, representational forms) in materialist approaches came from feminists influenced by Louis Althusser's foregrounding of ideology's generative (rather than "merely" distorting) effects; they also came from feminists of color who disputed the universalizing components of a sex/gender ideology rooted in the experiences of white Western women, for example, "dependency" and "domesticity" (Carby 1982). Subsequent challenges have incorporated these early insights even as their interventions are differently framed, as attempts to, in Rosemary Hennessy's formulation, "make use of postmodern notions of the subject" (1992, 3) or, in Kathleen Canning's, to "rewrit[e] key concepts of political and historical vocabulary" in the wake of the "encounter between feminism and poststructuralism" (1994, 373).

Put otherwise: both before and after the linguistic turn, what HMF scholars are talking about when they're talking about materiality includes the power of representational processes, practices, and forms. This does not, of course, settle the issue of the relative autonomy (so to say) of linguistic and symbolic structures and systems vis-à-vis the "sensuous activities" that are central to HMF's material "real," even as those activities remain the site of and occasion for signifying practices. But it does suggest that the discussion might be more productively focused on those aspects of HMF's explanatory potency I have highlighted here, namely, on the imperatives to denaturalize sex/gender systems such that they become legible as historical and political productions, to center oppression as that which demands explanation and action, and to parse difference as the outcome of, rather than the occasion for, relations of domination, exploitation, and alienation. The question then becomes: how does the analysis of signifying practices enable, confirm, impede, or challenge these interpretive imperatives?

Feminist New Materialisms (FNM)

While I have suggested that, for HMF, the material phenomenology of signification has been a subject of recurrent interest and debate, scholars associated with FNM are committed to challenging the very distinction between materiality and representation. The challenge has been framed in various ways: as a response to the unintended consequences of feminist theory's insistence that women be "transport[ed] from the category of nature to the realm of culture" (Alaimo 2008, 239), as a corrective to the excesses of poststructuralist and other discursive approaches, through which "language has been granted too much power" (Barad 2003, 801) and as a call to attend to the hybrid organism/machine, human/animal, and physical/virtual couplings presented as both metaphor and historical articulation (of Cold War-era science, politics, and technology) in the "political myth" of the cyborg (Haraway 1991). Each framing reflects a suspicion of theoretically impoverishing binaries that oppose sociocultural forces to materiality, which in this scheme remains legible only "as a given or a mere effect of human agency" (Barad 2003, 847). The challenge is to develop feminist analyses attentive to dynamic, multidirectional processes that are, to borrow from Anne Fausto-Sterling, "100 percent nature and 100 percent nurture," a monistic proportionality that underscores the singular rather than dualistic character of the world (Fausto-Sterling 2005, 1510).

The divergent figures of breached borders and always already entangled agencies suggest some of the variation in FNM's points of entrée. More generally, there is a notable heterogeneity of approaches and intellectual resources mobilized within and across the field. But there is also a great deal of overlap and convergence among them. In particular, FNM scholars share an interpretive commitment to disrupt the humanistic orientation that informs much feminist theory, an orientation presented as inseparable from investments in a knowing and doing agent who is sovereign, self-constituting, and unitary. While feminist theorists have long interrogated the masculinist assumptions that sustain this fantasy of an autonomous subject, FNM pushes beyond critiques of its gendered particularity to argue for a posthumanist alternative, which is to say, an account that refuses the dualisms of mind/body, nature/culture, and subject/object on which the Western account of human "exceptionalism" (in its feminine or masculine guises) relies, even as it often retains a rhetorical investment in figures of agency, doers, and deeds. Such an alternative orientation enables feminist theorists to develop both a better account of women's lives and futures (because more attentive to the "reality" of our embodied, embedded, and integrated condition) and a better politics (because more attuned to the ruinous, worldly consequences of ignoring those realities).

Central to FNM's posthumanist orientation is an understanding of matter as a co-constituting force, an "actant" that participates in processes of world formation. Here co-constitution does not mean the additive outcome of two (or more) entities' discrete contributions, such that one might, for example, determine which aspects of sexual difference are owing to the physiological body and which aspects are owing to cultural, social, or political forces and actions. On the contrary, a conceptualization of nature and culture as wholly entwined makes such an approach incoherent. What is needed is a different way of thinking and representing materiality (and culture) such that the dynamic, interactive, and historically contingent processes of their mutual constitution or becoming can be grasped. Among early and influential formulations of this agency-that-is-not-one is Haraway's "material-semiotic actor," which she introduces to portray "the object of knowledge as an active part of the apparatus of bodily production" (1991, 208). More recently Karen Barad's neologistic "intra-action"—which displaces the notion of "individual agencies that precede their interaction" with an understanding of "the mutual constitution of entangled agencies"—has been adopted by a wide range of FNM scholars (2007, 33).

The imperative to deconstruct dualisms that mystify the world points to the need for what might be called a metaphysical intervention. While the materialism of HMF aims to denaturalize essential, transcendental, or otherwise immovable truths by subjecting them to the material "real" of historical social relationality, the materialism of FNM aims to ontologize the contingency and provisionality of the distinction (matter/ideas) in play. From this perspective, demystifying naturalist ideologies entails a more subtle, critical, and complex understanding of being. Culture and politics are not inscriptions on the surfaces of bodies but rather dynamic presences in their deep layers. More than a site for such inscriptions, the corporeal body becomes an historically textured force that both initiates and responds in unruly ways. Perhaps most insistently, the relationality through which the world is transformed extends beyond the human to encompass organic and inorganic matter, a networked agency—regularly portrayed as an "assemblage" (borrowing from Gilles Deleuze) or "mangle" (introduced by Andrew Pickering)—that makes (human and worldly) being always and forever a collective and highly contingent affair.

Such an ontology does not, in and of itself, dictate a feminist politics; its explanatory potency for FNM scholars lies rather in how it changes the coordinates for any such politics. Perhaps most forcefully, it demands a different orientation toward physical embodiment and worldly embeddedness, an orientation that upends any reliance on "a fixed, essential, material basis for human nature, a basis which renders biological determinism meaningful" (Tuana 1997, 57) and that likewise underscores the need for feminist engagements with science and technology. The material "real" of FNM also provides potent confirmation that a "coherent inner self, achieved (cultural) or innate (biological) is a regulatory fiction that is unnecessary—indeed, inhibitory—for feminist projects of producing and affirming complex agency and responsibility" (Haraway 1991, 135).

While reframing dilemmas of sexual difference, gender identity, relations of hierarchy, and social transformation as immanent within the very processes through which existence comes into being—which is to say, ontologizing feminist dilemmas—is sometimes represented as a radical break from feminism's historical "flight from nature" (Alaimo 2008), others emphasize continuity with earlier feminist projects. Elizabeth Wilson, for example, has suggested that "there has [n]ever been a fully human feminism, a feminism that only now comes into contact with the inorganic, the animalistic, or the artificial" (Kirby and Wilson 2011, 228). In a related vein, Peta Hinton and Iris van der Tuin find in FNM inquiry "not a defensive break with a feminist past [b]ut instead an indeterminacy that animates and denaturalizes the familiar coordinates of second-wave feminist political work, and renders its texts and practices wholly relevant to a feminist present and future" (2014, 3).

At the same time, networked agency—a crucial property of FNM's material "real"—pushes the analysis beyond the familiar coordinates of much feminist theory. In her exploration of Hurricane Katrina's devastation of New Orleans in 2005, for example, Nancy Tuana posits an "interactionist ontology" in pursuing how the economic, political, technological, biological, and racial forces that collectively constituted a "natural disaster" exemplify the "viscous porosity" between humans and their environment (Tuana 2008). "Seeing through the eye of Katrina," Tuana writes, "transformed an essay that was focused on women's embodiment to the embodiment of levees, hurricanes, and swamps as well as the embodiment of women and men." The "core" of her essay, she continues, is "the centrality of an interactionist ontology as the lens through which we must be feminists and do our feminism" (190). Through this lens, gender no longer proves useful as an analytic category, even as it might remain useful or even indispensible as a descriptive term, to designate the persons called women or men (see Scott 1986). The conclusion follows not only from the wide array of organic and inorganic materialities whose interactions (or intra-actions) exceed gender's analytic reach and yet are central to how feminism must be done; more fundamentally, it follows from gender's enmeshment in false binaries (biology/culture, essential/constructed) that will inevitably "mischaracterize" the "material-semiotic matrix" (Tuana 1997, 57).

Avoiding such mischaracterizations is an interpretive imperative for FNM: it is also an ethical imperative, inasmuch as a failure or refusal to confront both the scope and the limits of networked agency is also a failure or refusal to address critical relations of power and responsibility. The power relations in question concern knowledge production practices and the postures of mastery and control that follow from them. On the first score, FNM argues that the distinctions between subject and object or human and nonhuman are produced through our very practices of investigation. What Barad refers to as "agential cuts," or the specific intra-actions that make distinctions between what is ontologically inseparable and in so doing, materialize bodies marked by the differentiating cuts, are acts of world-making or materialization for which we must be accountable (Barad 2003, 815). This is not to say we do so as willful "choosers:" on the contrary, our always entangled agency makes the notion of "choosing" where to cut deeply suspect. Shorn of the usual causal account that would tie intended (or unintended) human actions to discrete external effects, taking responsibility for our intra-actions entails a re-orientation toward the world as dynamic, unruly, and always differential becoming, and to ourselves as an agential part of that "material becoming." The ethical demand is thus to recognize "responsibility to intervene in the world's becoming, to contest and rework what matters and what is excluded from mattering" (827).

This account of responsibility in no way denies oppressive relations as a worldly fact; neither does it operate within those familiar coordinates of feminist theory. Indeed, on this score FNM's explanatory potency is its interrogation of the terms in which oppression and resistance to it are conceived. For many FNM scholars, at issue is an unwarranted confidence in human agency that misleads both those who analyze power and those who wield or would wield it. Here an understanding of how, in the terms used above to discuss HMF, the "sensuous activities" through which consciousness, community, and world are generated must refuse the "regulatory fiction" of a unified, autonomous agent. At issue is not only the false assumption of the self's internal coherence but, more pressingly for politics, a failure to see how that assumption is sustained through relations with a sovereign power whose illusory unity remains an effect of collective, contingent, and deeply affective intra-actions. Effacing their own (and others') generative role in producing that unity, individuals' who would resist it reproduce the fantasy of autonomous agency, an imagined property of the ruler that they now claim for themselves (Frost 2010). In addition to reproducing and "inflating" a deeply destructive if ultimately chimerical sovereign power, the paradoxical result of efforts to claim such an agency is that individuals remain, in Samantha Frost's formulation, "alienated from the ways in which they are in fact effective, that is, from the complex interdependencies through which all actions take place" (2010, 173).

Critical to this account is recognizing the "the role played by the body as a visceral protagonist within political encounters" (Coole and Frost 2010, 19). Here the challenge to the political actor's aspirations to autonomous agency resonates with FNM critiques of the "material autonomy" of living organisms (Hird 2004a, 87): the "reality" of political agency as a contingent and heterogeneous assembly parallels the "reality" of material organisms as contingently bounded. Scholars differ in their accounts of the (dis)continuity between feminist theory's historical engagement with a corporeal politics and a more recent alignment between critiques of a mind/body dualism and inner/outer (or organism/environment) distinctions (Grosz 2004; Ahmed 2008; Coole and Frost 2010). But what seems clear is that FNM's metaphysical intervention orients feminist analysis to corporeality as a site not only of political and cultural imposition or transformation, but also of political possibility tied to the agential capacity of bodily matter.

Consider, for example, Elisabeth Grosz's account of Darwin's model of evolution as a "striking response to various theories of oppression" (2008, 40). His model reveals that environmental input is always "the force or impetus that propels the individual to processes, not of remediation (remediation literally involves undoing what cannot be undone), but of self-transformation" (Grosz 2008, 40). While the general notion that past experiences of injustice spur future actions to overcome it would seem a commonplace, Grosz's resituating of this dynamic within the context of living systems and the adaptions on which their survival depends shifts the terms of analysis: overcoming injustice is first and foremost a process of self-overcoming, as organisms pursue strategies of survival "whose success can only be measured by the degree to which they induce transformation in the criteria by which natural selection functions" (41). The priority relationship has changed, from an analysis of oppression as the central "fact" to be explained to an analysis of how evolution and growth are generated by that "fact" and remain central to its becoming otherwise. To be clear, Grosz is not lauding the felicitous generativity of oppression: she is rather suggesting that we understand responses to it in terms of evolutionary rather than revolutionary processes, a difference in temporal framing that marks the distance between purposive, collective action and the unpredictable eruptions that emerge through individual transformations and in turn affect the life of the species. Politics must attempt to "mobilize" the self-overcoming of individuals and groups that is "incessantly if slowly at work in the life of all species." From this perspective, "social forces borrow the energy and temporality of natural systems for political modes of resistance and overcoming" (41).

If in HMF analyses politics often appears either as confrontation or conformity, in FNM it seems more akin to metamorphosis, a vision of fluid if angular transformations whose unity borrows from a monistic ontology of matter, form, and meaning. While politics as collaborative "action in concert" becomes difficult to see in a world of mangles and assemblages, that world also promises an agential vitality, borne of the recognition that human sovereignty is a destructive fantasy and expanded by an attunement to affinities that cross-cut the ecological and technological terrain. While the ethical orientation countenanced by much FNM writing is one of humility, responsibility, and witness, its political sensibility is decidedly more exuberant and expectant.

A final dimension of FNM's approach I want to highlight is its approach to difference. Like HMF, the properties of FNM's material "real" include its capacity to generate differences. Unlike HMF, which situates difference at the level of social relational activities and structures, FNM understands the proliferation of difference to be intrinsic to the intra-active processes of "naturecultures," and the denial or containment of this multiplicity to be the result of social relational activities and structures. On the one hand, this conclusion emerges from FNM scholars' engagement with the natural sciences, a productive entanglement in which long-standing feminist attentions to the cultural forces at play in scientific research converge with an approach to biological organisms and matter more generally as complex, open systems. Of particular interest has been the variability and abundance of behaviors and processes in the natural world through which reproduction takes place; the relevance (or irrelevance) of sex and sexuality to those processes; and the contortions undertaken by researchers to impose a stable form—most centrally, sexual dimorphism—on what remains unpredictable, mutable, and always "emergent" (Hird 2004b). Attending in non-pathologizing ways to what Joan Fujimura refers to as the "awkward surplus"—data obtained in research projects that fail to conform to researchers' initial assumptions—reveals fluidity rather than binaries (Fujimura 2006). In short, natural scientific inquiry performed or analyzed from a critical feminist perspective confirms that "we may no longer be certain that it is nature that remains static and culture that evinces limitless malleability" (Hird 2004a, 88).

On the other hand, the conclusion that the generation of difference is immanent within materiality has also emerged from FNM's philosophical investigations of embodiment and being, which, while regularly inspiring, complementing, and complicating feminist science studies, unfold on a different level of analysis. Rosi Braidotti, for example, identifies "neo-materialism" as a "method, a conceptual frame, and a political stand that refuses the linguistic paradigm" (Dolphijn and van de Tuin 2012, 21). Here difference is conceptualized not as a social relational production to be transformed but rather as a "fact and a factor of our situated, corporeal existence." Toward this end, sexual difference must be rethought outside the "binary machine" on which gender systems depend in order to make legible the productive diversity that distinguishes sexed bodies and is generated by them (Braidotti 2013, 99). From this perspective, confirming the reality of sexual difference is paradoxically crucial in displacing the oppositional binary of sameness/otherness that disciplines and devalues all differences: to allow sexual difference "actually to *differ*," as Dolphijn and Van der Tuin write, is to pursue a "practical philosophy in which difference *in itself* comes to being" (2012, 141). No longer different from, difference "*in itself*" points to an abundance of ways and forms of being that challenges global capitalism's celebratory, homogenizing embrace of diversity, and remains true to the material "real" of FNM.

Situating race and racism within this practical philosophy—probing how race might be conceptualized as difference "*in itself*"—remains an uncommon practice. While FNM scholars regularly reference race as a category of interest and relevance, it does not typically emerge as a matter of central analytic concern. An exception is Arun Saldanha's account of "phenotypic assemblage," which draws on FNM (most specifically, on Grosz's notion of "corporeal feminism") to pursue racial being or becoming as spatialized phenomena located in "*movements between* human bodies, things, and their changing environment" (Saldanha 2006, 19; emphasis in original). The biological aspect of agency revealed in this approach—how phenotype might "resist its 'performance,' " as Saldanha puts it—seems to reside in the necessary and perpetual remaking of biological matter, a contingent but not arbitrary process that casts racialization as creative, dynamic, and emergent (12). A related claim is made by Richard Hames-García, whose exploration of race as "intra-active phenomena" encompassing phenotypic particularities concludes with a call for the "creative elaboration of racial standpoints" (Hames-García, 2008, 327–328).

From this perspective, the usefulness and even intelligibility of the familiar coordinates of feminist theory become, again, suspect. Intersectionality, for example, appears too "gridlike" to accommodate either the multidirectional enmeshments that characterize an assemblage or the imperative to "star[t] from the presumption of mutual constitution" (Hames-Garcia 2011, 11; Grosz 1994, 19–20). More generally, the shift in levels of analysis—from the institutional and discursive durabilities of racialization processes to "chain[s] of contingency, in which the connections between [race's] constituent components are not given but made viscous through local attractions"—introduces challenges to the analysis of racism (Saldanha 2006, 18). In the absence of the "regulatory fiction" of autonomous and unified agents, investigating the laws, policies, and practices undertaken by white men (and white women) is no longer a self-evident route to take. Likewise, the imperative to pursue "what race *can be*" when it is "no longer stifled by racism"—a vision of proliferating racial phenomena—decenters oppression as a critical optic (Saldanha 2006, 21; emphasis in original). This is of course not to say that FNM-inspired inquiry into the materiality of race denies the persistence of racism; it is rather to suggest that, in directing analysis away from overly static structures, the "real" of race testifies to contingent materialities that fit poorly with the totalizing figure of oppression. Taking its bearings from molecular as well as evolutionary rhythms, an anti-racist politics must take shape by "building upon a gradual, fragmented, and shifting sense of corporeal difference" (21).

A commitment to exploring "difference *in itself*" does not characterize the work of all FNM scholars. Indeed, as I've intimated, there is a noteworthy distance between inquiry into how biological materiality persistently confounds scientific attempts to typologize, dimorphize, and otherwise stabilize it, and inquiry into how a philosophical framework of "neomateriality" enables alternative valuations of difference. That distance underscores, again, the wide range of analytic approaches that inform FNM scholarship, which are sometimes mutually informing and sometimes occasion debate or silence among those who share FNM's common commitment to rethinking matter. Perhaps it should be acknowledged that "feminist new materialisms" (along with "historical materialist feminisms") is not only a capacious field of inquiry; it's also a somewhat flabby signifier. Complicating the matter further is Sara Irni's suggestion that a "politics of materiality" threads through transdisciplinary feminist debate, a politics that reflects both power relations between disciplines and the affective states they occasion (Irni 2013). Irni's account offers one way to parse some of the contrapuntal dimensions of FNM. But such a melodic discordance is also in keeping with a core insight of FNM, that knowledge production practices will perforce reflect and enact the fundamental indeterminacy that animates natureculture.

Conclusion

It is possible to trace an inaugural moment of FNM to a critique that speaks directly to HMF. In her "Cyborg Manifesto" (1985) and "Gender for a Marxist Dictionary" (1987), Haraway identifies the insufficiency of Marx's materiality to address the "breached boundaries" between the biological and the technological and the human and the animal as an incitement to pursue a new materialist imaginary. Haraway signals shared analytic preoccupations when she writes that the material conditions of postmodern times require a remapping of "the territories of production, reproduction, and imagination." In appealing to the sites and forms of HMF's material "real," Haraway raises the possibility that precisely those aspects of HMF analyses I highlighted above—its commitments to denaturalize, to center oppression, and to approach difference in those terms—must be rethought in light of a changed materiality.

But those aspects of FNM that I have highlighted here—its commitments to see nature anew, to center agency, and to approach difference in those terms—are not best characterized as continuations or elaborations of that earlier hail to HMF. While several FNM scholars have addressed Marx's work and the ontology said to sustain his account of exploitation and alienation (Colebrook 2008; Edwards 2010; see also Bennett 2001; Cheah 2010) there has been very little direct engagement with HMF analyses. Likewise, the reception of FNM among feminists committed to ongoing adaptations of historical materialist methods has been, on the whole, less than enthusiastic. While FNM's insistence on overcoming a "nature-phobic" strand in feminist theory has been celebrated, the accompanying tendency toward what Lena Gunnarsson describes as the "political glorification of indeterminate dynamism" has been questioned on epistemological and political, as well as rhetorical, grounds (Gunnarsson 2013, 9; see also Washick and Wingrove 2015).

The difference between an analytic focus on the systemic dimensions of oppression and the "sensuous activities" through which they are reproduced, and an analytic focus on the untapped potential for living otherwise in a universe sustained and transformed by "intra-action" is at once a matter of interpretive disposition and aesthetic sensibility. It is also, as Jane Bennett has recently suggested, a matter of political judgment: "[I]s it better," she asks, "in this place at this time, to focus on the trappings of the system or to emphasize the possibility of 'laying down a path by walking' out from it?" (2015, 21). At the same time, as Kathy Ferguson has recently suggested, forging an encounter between different feminist approaches to materiality need not be an occasion to choose between them, but rather to "provoke the advocates of both materialisms to consider potential political weaknesses in their projects, weaknesses that could be supplemented by other kinds of material engagements." (2015, 18) And on this score, Ferguson continues, the "conversation" will be "more fruitful when located within specific material circumstances rather an abstract world of argument" (18). In other words, staying close to our material, instead of our materialism, might provide the opportunity (if not the imperative) to make legible simultaneously constitutive contradictions and local contingencies, systemic relationality and assembled agency, and the durability of structures and the "messiness" of the world.

References

Ahmed, Sara. 2008. "Open Forum Imaginary Prohibitions: Some Preliminary Remarks on the Founding Gestures of the 'New Materialism.'" *European Journal of Women's Studies* 15 (1): 23–39. doi:10.1177/1350506807084854.
Alaimo, Stacy. 2008. "Trans-corporeal Feminisms and the Ethical Space of Nature." In Alaimo and Hekman, *Material Feminisms*, 237–264.
Alaimo, Stacy, and Susan Hekman, eds. 2008. *Material Feminisms*. Bloomington: Indiana University Press.
Barad, Karen. 2003. "Posthumanist Performativity: Toward an Understanding of How Matter Comes to Matter." *Signs* 28(3): 801–831. doi:10.1086/signs.2003.28.issue-3.
Barad, Karen. 2007. *Meeting the Universe Halfway: Quantum Physics and the Entanglement of Matter and Meaning*. Durham, NC: Duke University Press.

Barrett, Michèle. 1992. "Words and Things: Materialism and Method in Contemporary Feminist Analysis." In *Destabilizing Theory: Contemporary Feminist Debates*, edited by Anne Phillips and Michèle Barrett, 201–220. Redwood City, CA: Stanford University Press.

Bennett, Jane. 2001. "Commodity Fetishism and Commodity Enchantment." *Theory & Event* 5 (1). doi:10.1353/tae.2001.0006.

Bennett, Jane. 2015. "Ontology, Sensibility, and Action." Critical Exchange. *Contemporary Political Theory* 14 (February): 20–27. doi:10.1057/cpt.2014.19.

Braidotti, Rosi. 2013. *The Posthuman*. Cambridge and Malden, MA: Polity.

Butler, Judith, and Gayle Rubin. 1994. "Sexual Traffic." *Differences: A Journal of Feminist Cultural Studies* 6 (2–3): 62–99.

Canning, Kathleen. 1994. "Feminist History after the Linguistic Turn: Historicizing Discourse and Experience." *Signs* 19 (2): 368–404.

Carby, Hazel V. 1982. "White Woman Listen! Black Feminism and the Boundaries of Sisterhood." In *The Empire Strikes Back: Race and Racism in 70's Britain*, edited by Center for Contemporary Cultural Studies, 212–235. London: Routledge.

Cheah, Pheng. 2010. "Non-Dialectical Materialism." In Coole and Frost, *New Materialisms Ontology*, 70–91.

Colebrook, Claire. 2008. "On Not Becoming Man: The Materialist Politics of Unactualized Potential." In Alaimo and Hekman, *Material Feminisms*, 52–84.

Collins, Patricia Hill. 1990. *Black Feminist Thought: Knowledge, Consciousness, and the Politics of Empowerment*. Vol. 2, *Perspectives on Gender*. Boston: Unwin Hyman.

Collins, Patricia Hill. 2004. "Learning from the Outsider Within: The Sociological Significance of Black Feminist Thought." In Harding, *Feminist Standpoint Theory Reader*, 103–126.

Coole, Diana, and Samantha Frost. 2010. *New Materialisms: Ontology, Agency, and Politics*. Durham NC: Duke University Press.

Delphy, Christine. 1984. "The Main Enemy" and "A Materialist Feminism is Possible." In *Close to Home: A Materialist Analysis of Women's Oppression*, edited by Diana Leonard, 57–77. Amherst: University of Massachusetts Press.

Disch, Lisa. 2015. "Christine Delphy's Constructivist Materialism: An Overlooked 'French Feminism,'" *South Atlantic Quarterly* 114:4 (forthcoming).

Dolphijn, Rick, and Iris van der Tuin. 2012. *New Materialism: Interviews and Cartographies*. Ann Arbor, MI: Open Humanities Press.

Edwards, Jason. 2010. "The Materialism of Historical Materialism." In Coole and Frost, *New Materialisms*, 281–298.

Fausto-Sterling, Anne. 2005. "The Bare Bones of Sex: Part 1—Sex and Gender." *Signs* 30 (2): 1491–1527. doi:10.1086/signs.2005.30.issue-2.

Federici, Silvia. 1975. *Wages against Housework*. Bristol, UK: The Power of Women Collective and Falling Wall Press.

Federici, Silvia. 2012. *Revolution at Point Zero: Housework, Reproduction, and Feminist Struggle*. Oakland, CA: PM Press.

Ferguson, Kathy E. 2015. "Engaging New and Old Materialisms." Critical Exchange. *Contemporary Political Theory*. 14 (February): 17–20. doi:10.1057/cpt.2014.19.

Fernández-Kelly, María Patricia. 1983. *For We Are Sold, I and My People: Women and Industry in Mexico's Frontier*. SUNY Series in the Anthropology of Work. Albany: State University of New York Press.

Frost, Samantha. 2010. "Fear and the Illusion of Autonomy." In Coole and Frost, *New Materialisms*, 158–177.

Fujimura, Joan H. 2006. "Sex Genes: A Critical Sociomaterial Approach to the Politics and Molecular Genetics of Sex Determination." *Signs* 32 (1): 49–82. doi:10.1086/signs.2006.32.issue-1.

Gimenez, Martha. 1978. "Structural Marxism on 'The Woman Question.'" *Science and Society* 42 (3): 301–323

Grosz, Elizabeth. 1994. *Volatile Bodies: Toward a Corporeal Feminism*. Bloomington: Indiana University Press.

Grosz, Elizabeth. 2004. *The Nick of Time: Politics, Evolution, and the Untimely*. Durham, NC: Duke University Press.

Grosz, Elizabeth. 2008. "Darwin and Feminism: Preliminary Investigations for a Possible Alliance." In Alaimo and Hekman, *Material Feminisms*, 23–51.

Gunnarsson, Lena. 2013. "The Naturalistic Turn in Feminist Theory: A Marxist-Realist\ Contribution." *Feminist Theory* 14 (1): 3–19. doi:10.1177/1464700112468567.

Hames-García, Michael. 2008. "How real is race?" In Alaimo and Hekman, *Material Feminisms*, 308-349.

Hames-García, Michael. 2011. *Identity Complex: Making the Case for Multiplicity*. Minneapolis: University of Minnesota Press.

Haraway, Donna Jeanne. 1991. *Simians, Cyborgs, and Women: The Re-Invention of Nature*. London: Free Association.

Harding, Sandra, ed. 2004. *The Feminist Standpoint Theory Reader: Intellectual and Political Controversies*. New York: Routledge.

Hartsock, Nancy C. M. 1997. "The Feminist Standpoint: Developing the Ground for a Specifically Feminist Historical Materialism." In *Feminist Social Thought: A Reader*, edited by Diana Tietjens Meyers, 461–484. New York: Routledge.

Hemmings, Clare. 2011. *Why Stories Matter: The Political Grammar of Feminist Theory*. Durham: Duke University Press.

Hennessy, Rosemary. 1992. *Materialist Feminism and the Politics of Discourse*. New York: Routledge.

Hinton, Peta, and Iris van der Tuin. 2014. Preface to *Women: A Cultural Review* 25 (1): 1–8. doi: 10.1080/09574042.2014.903781.

Hird, Myra J. 2004a. "Naturally Queer." *Feminist Theory* 5 (1): 85–89. doi:10.1177/1464700104040817.

Hird, Myra J. 2004b. "Feminist Matters: New Materialist Considerations of Sexual Difference." *Feminist Theory* 5(2): 223–232. doi:10.1177/1464700104045411.

Irni, Sari. 2013. "The Politics of Materiality: Affective Encounters in a Transdisciplinary Debate." *European Journal of Women's Studies* 20 (4): 347–360. doi:10.1177/1350506812472669.

Joseph, Gloria. 1981. "The Incompatible Menage à Trois: Marxism, Feminism, and Racism." In *Women and Revolution: A Discussion of the Unhappy Marriage of Marxism and Feminism*, edited by Lydia Sargent. Boston, 91-107. MA: South End Press.

Keating, Christine, Claire Rasmussen, and Pooja Rishi. 2010. "The Rationality of Empowerment: Microcredit, Accumulation by Dispossession, and the Gendered Economy." *Signs: Journal of Women in Culture and Society* 36 (1): 153–176. doi:10.1086/652911.

Kirby, Vicki, and Elizabeth A. Wilson. 2011. "Feminist Conversations with Vicki Kirby and Elizabeth A. Wilson." *Feminist Theory* 12 (2): 227–234. doi:10.1177/1464700111404289.

Kruks, Sonia. 2010. "Simone de Beauvoir: Engaging Discrepant Materialisms." In Coole and Frost, *New Materialisms*, 258–281.

Marx, Karl. 1998. "Theses on Feuerbach." In *The German Ideology, Including Theses on Feuerbach*, by Karl Marx and Friedrich Engels, 569–574. Amherst, NY: Prometheus Books.

Mies, Maria. 1982. *The Lace Makers of Narsapur: Indian Housewives Produce for the World Market*. London and Westport, CT: Zed Press. http://hdl.handle.net/2027/[u]:uc1.b4558467.

Mohanty, Chandra Talpade. 2003. *Feminism without Borders: Decolonizing Theory, Practicing Solidarity*. Durham, NC: Duke University Press.

Narayan, Uma. 2004. "The Project of Feminist Epistemology: Perspectives from a Nonwestern Feminist." In Harding, *Feminist Standpoint Theory Reader*, 213–224.

Rankin, Katharine N. 2001. "Governing Development: Neoliberalism, Microcredit, and Rational Economic Woman." *Economy and Society* 30 (1): 18–37. doi:10.1080/03085140020019070.

Saldanha, Arun. 2006. "Reontologising Race: The Machinic Geography of Phenotype." *Environment and Planning D: Society and Space* 24 (1): 9–24. doi:10.1068/d61j.

Sandoval, Chela. 2004. "U.S. Third World Feminism: The Theory and Method of Differential Oppositional Consciousness." In Harding, *Feminist Standpoint Theory Reader*, 195–210.

Scott, Joan W. 1986. "Gender: A Useful Category of Historical Analysis." *The American Historical Review* 91 (5): 1053. doi:10.2307/1864376.

Tuana, Nancy. 1997. "Fleshing Gender, Sexing the Body: Refiguring the Sex/Gender Distinction." *Southern Journal of Philosophy* 35 (S1): 53–71.

Tuana, Nancy. 2008. "Viscous Porosity: Witnessing Katrina." In Alaimo and Hekman, *Material Feminisms*. 188–213. doi:10.1111/j.2041-6962.1997.tb02207.x.

Vogel, Lise. 1983. *Marxism and the Oppression of Women: Toward a Unitary Theory*. New Brunswick, NJ: Rutgers University Press.

Washick, Bonnie, and Elizabeth Wingrove.2015. "Politics That Matter: Thinking about Power and Justice with the New Materialists." Critical Exchange. *Contemporary Political Theory* 14 (February): 1–17. doi:10.1057/cpt.2014.19.

Weeks, Kathi. 2011. *The Problem with Work: Feminism, Marxism, Antiwork Politics, and Postwork Imaginaries*. Durham, NC: Duke University Press.

Wingrove, Elizabeth. 1999. "Interpellating Sex." *Signs* 24 (4): 869–893.

CHAPTER 23

MICROPHYSICS OF POWER

JOHANNA OKSALA

Introduction

POWER is a pivotal concept for feminist theory. While feminists strongly disagree on a host of issues, most of them take it for granted that feminism is at least somehow concerned with power relations between men and women. As a political project, feminism aims to alter or eradicate these power relations; as a theoretical project, it aims to expose and understand them.

For the early feminist writers, such as Mary Astell and Mary Wollstonecraft, slavery provided a model for theorizing power. Astell (1996, 18), a contemporary of John Locke, asked sarcastically, 'If all Men are born Free, how is it that all Women are born Slaves?" Wollstonecraft's major polemic *A Vindication of the Rights of Woman* adapts the terms of contemporary political debate on slavery.[1] Throughout the eighteenth century, feminist writers criticized marriage as a form of slavery. The power relations between men and women were viewed as relations of domination and coercion similar to the relations between slave owners and slaves. Until late into the nineteenth century the legal and civil position of a wife in most Western nations resembled that of a slave. Like a slave, she was her husband's possession in the sense that she had no legal existence apart from him, and he was also entitled to punish her physically.

By the time the second-wave feminist movement emerged in the 1960s and 1970s, the legal and civil position of women in most nations had dramatically improved, yet the power imbalances between men and women seemed to persist. Feminists began to extend the concept of equality beyond the earlier movement's emphasis on formal equality in the civil and political sphere. The models for theorizing power that many of the pioneering feminist theorists of this era turned to were derived from either liberalism or Marxism. Within a liberal feminist frame, power relations were viewed as relationships between individuals who were formally recognized as equals, and yet their relationships involved, to a greater or lesser extent, forms of coercion, discrimination and/or ideological manipulation. Socialist feminists, on the other hand, analyzed power in relation to gendered divisions of labor, men's appropriation of women's unwaged domestic and sexual labor, and the complex intersections of capitalism and patriarchy.

Liberal feminists tended to view power as a resource or a capacity that was unequally distributed among men and women. Their aim was to create equal opportunities for women to acquire political and economic power. Betty Friedan (1968, 454), the author of the feminist classic *The Feminine Mystique* (1963), for example, argued that women "need political power" meaning equal access to political institutions (on liberal approaches, see also, e.g., Okin 1989). Feminists also appropriated Marxist analyses of capitalism for their critique of patriarchy: the domination of the working class by the bourgeoisie provided a model for the analysis of the domination of women by men. In the 1970s, feminist theory in Western Europe to a large extent became dominated by Marxism and the parallel questions of class and gender oppression (on feminist appropriations of Marx, see, e.g., Mitchell 1971; Vogel 1983; MacKinnon 1983).

The problems of both of liberal and Marxist models of theorizing power soon came to fore, however. Liberal feminists' understanding of power as a resource or a capacity seemed to downplay domination and did not recognize sufficiently the relational character of power. Women's lack of power could not be understood in isolation and independently of their relationships to men. The Marxist-feminist attempts to model gender oppression on the model of class oppression proved problematic too. Women did not form a unified class with similar interests and needs; instead, the intersections of class, gender, and racial oppression seemed to call for more specific and historically varied analyses than what was allowed by the framework of class antagonism between capital and the proletariat.

At this theoretical and political crossroads Michel Foucault's conception of power opened up completely new avenues for feminist theory. Foucault introduced his conception of power in *The History of Sexuality*, volume 1, in the form of short propositions over merely three pages (Foucault 1978, 94–96). However, he elucidated and developed his account in a number of essays, lectures, and interviews throughout the rest of his life (see, e.g., Foucault 1982, 2000, 2003). Although his understanding of power is often presented as a unified theory and labeled "productive power" or "a microphysics of power," it is in fact a multifaceted analysis of the historically shifting rationalities and technologies of power that have appeared and disappeared in Western societies. Foucault introduced and distinguished several different modalities of power, such as disciplinary power, biopower, pastoral power, juridical power, and governmentality in order to show how the exercise of power has taken historically varied forms, and how the technologies and practices of power have been rationalized or organized in different ways in different societies and at different points in time.

In this chapter, my aim is to explicate the key features of Foucault's conception of productive power—disciplinary power, biopower, governmentality, and resistance—and to examine the ways they have been taken up and disputed by feminist scholars. Although Foucault had little interest in the feminist politics of his time, his theorization of the various rationalities and technologies of power both opened up new resources for feminist critique, and has been controversial among feminists. His account has deepened our theoretical understanding of the constitution of gendered subjectivity and provided stimulus for political critiques of gender normalization, biopolitics, and neoliberalism. It has also challenged some of the most basic assumptions of feminist theory, however, such as the idea of woman as an emancipatory political identity, and the belief that women would have privileged critical insight into patriarchal societies.

Productive Power

Foucault's rethinking of power was initially targeted against liberal and Marxist conceptions of power, the two dominant conceptual models in the 1970s that were central also in feminist theory. For Foucault, the problem was the "economism" in these theories: both traditions viewed power through economic models (see, e.g., Foucault 2003, 88). Power was conceived in the liberal model as a possession or a resource; it was regarded as something that could be possessed, lost, and traded in the way that one trades merchandise. Against this view, Foucault argued that power exists only when it is exercised. It is not like a thing that one owns but is always relational. It is an action in a relationship. He also criticized the excessive focus in the liberal tradition on contracts, rights, the law, and legitimatization. It was not possible to account for the subtle operations and mechanisms of modern power within this conceptual framework. There were forms of power, such as disciplinary power, that do not function according to the dichotomous distinction between legal and illegal but use much more subtle distinctions, by operating on the sliding scale of healthy/sick and normal/abnormal, for example.[2]

The Marxist model reduced power relations to economic relations too, albeit in a different way: power relations were antagonistic relationships between two preexisting classes defined in terms of their relation to the means of production. Foucault argued instead that power relations form a dense network that traverses the whole of society rather than a dual structure of rulers and the ruled or employers and the employed. A generalized formula that pitted the bourgeoisie and its interests against the proletariat, for example, reduced the multiplicity and variety of power relations to a simplistic opposition between two classes. Foucault insisted that one should not start by looking for the center of power, or, for the individuals, institutions, or classes that rule, but should rather construct a "microphysics of power" that focuses on the extremities: families, workplaces, everyday practices, and marginal institutions.[3] One has to analyze power relations from the bottom up, not from the top down, and to study the myriad ways in which the power relations operate in different but intersecting capillary networks.

The idea of a microphysics of power resonated strongly with the feminist credo that the personal was political. The second-wave feminists saw it as vitally important to expose power relations in what was considered the private sphere, not only in what was considered the public and properly political sphere. Feminist concerns had to be extended to areas of female experience formerly viewed as private, natural, and apolitical, such as sexuality, child care, control over one's own reproductive life, and the gendered division of labor in housework. The feminist establishment of sexual politics as a central area of struggle required a conception of power that was able to account for its capillary forms in everyday practices and habits, in other words, for its microphysics.

Apart from the idea that power is relational, capillary, and diffuse, Foucault's conception of power also provided another major insight for feminism: power relations are productive of the subjects embedded in them. His perhaps most important theoretical contribution for feminist theory has been his idea of *productive power*, the idea that power does not operate primarily through repression, prohibition, and censorship, but is essentially productive. Being a subject, a socially recognized individual with intelligible intentions, desires, and actions, is only possible within the power/knowledge networks of a society. In other words, the subjects over whom the power network is defined cannot be thought to exist apart from it. Individuals do not enter the public, political arena as fully formed subjects who then demand rights and represent interests. The supposedly personal or private aspects of their being are already traversed by power relations, which not only restrain them but also produce them as certain kinds of subjects.

The consequences of the idea of productive power for feminist theory were momentous: it formed the starting point of what has undoubtedly been the most influential appropriation of Foucault's thought for gender theory—namely, Judith Butler's *Gender Trouble* (1990). The book opens with troubling questions. If we accept Foucault's argument about productive power and acknowledge that subjects are produced by power relations, does this not imply that the subject of feminism, "women," is produced by the very same oppressive power relations that it aims to theorize and eradicate? Would "women" even exist if society was not structured by sexist power relations? Who are the subjects that feminism aims to liberate?

> Foucault points out that juridical systems of power *produce* the subjects they subsequently come to represent . . . If this analysis is right, then the juridical formation of language and politics that represents women as "the subject" of feminism is itself a discursive formation and effect of a given version of representational politics. And the feminist subject turns out to be discursively constituted by the very political system that is supposed to facilitate its emancipation.
>
> (Butler 1990, 2)

Butler thus takes on Foucault's idea of productive power and asks what the consequences of it are for feminist politics. She insists that it implies that it is not enough to try to include more women in politics or to seek to represent their interests more effectively. We have to ask more fundamentally who these women are: how the very identity and the category of women are constituted through practices of power. This implies reconsidering the viability of feminist identity politics. The problem is not merely that the category of women denies the differences among women and thereby inadvertently privileges one group of women. More fundamentally, we have to pose critical questions about the desirability of embracing an oppressive identity that excluded women from politics in the first place.

Butler's critique had also devastating consequences for those feminist epistemologies that had invested in the idea that women's experiences could provide a critical standpoint on patriarchal society.[4] Instead of having a special vantage point on power due to their marginalization, women and their experiences had to be understood as effects of power. Joan Scott's important essay "The Evidence of Experience" (1991) developed this idea further and has arguably been one of the most influential contributions to the dismissal of first-person accounts of experience in feminist theory in recent decades. Scott's key claim is that women's experience cannot function either as evidence or as a starting point for feminist analysis because of its derivative and ideological status. She denies the usefulness of documenting women's subjective experiences as evidence for feminist theoretical or political claims and urges us to turn instead to the history of concepts (on feminist critiques of Scott's argument, see, e.g., Alcoff 2000; Kruks 2001; Oksala 2014).

It is no exaggeration to say that *Gender Trouble* caused a paradigm shift in the way that the intertwinement of power, feminist emancipation, and the female subject was theorized. It was subjected to extensive feminist commentary, and Butler responded to the criticism in the books that followed *Gender Trouble* (Butler 1993, 1997, 2004). The book was formative for the key ideas behind queer politics: the identities of gay and lesbian—as well as of heterosexual—are not essential or authentic identities, but are culturally constructed through normative discourses and power relations regulating the "healthy" and "normal" expressions of sexuality. This does not mean that homosexuality does not "really" exist. Just because something is constructed through practices of power does not mean that it is not real. People are defined by and must think and live according to such constructions. The aim of sexual politics, however, cannot be simply to find one's true identity through a scientific study of the various aspects of the sexual body, for example. Sexual bodies as well as the sexual identities they are supposed to cause and found are constructed through the oppressive power relations that our politics must attempt to challenge and to resist. The goal of queer feminist politics therefore has to be more complicated than simple liberation from power and the affirmation of one's homosexuality and gender identity: practicing freedom entails questioning and even denying the identities that are imposed on us as natural and essential by making visible their cultural construction and dependence on the power relations that are operative in society (on projects delineating "queer feminism" with the help of Foucault's work, see, e.g., Winnubst 2006; Huffer 2010; Sawicki 2013).

Disciplining the Female Body

Feminist theorists have also developed important appropriations of disciplinary power to study the different ways that women shape their bodies—from cosmetic surgery to dieting and eating disorders—and analyzed these everyday practices as disciplinary technologies in the service of patriarchal, normalizing power. These normative feminine practices train the female body in docility and obedience to cultural demands, while at the same time they are paradoxically experienced in terms of "power" and "control" by the women themselves.

Sandra Bartky's seminal and much anthologized 1988 article, "Foucault, Femininity and the Modernization of Patriarchal Power," was one of the first appropriations of Foucault's idea of disciplinary power to explicitly feminist issues (for other influential feminist appropriations of Foucault's idea of disciplinary power, see, e.g., Bordo 1989, 1993). It gives a compelling account of the way in which a docile feminine subject is constructed through the internalization of disciplinary habits. The key claim that Bartky adopts from Foucault is that an adequate understanding of women's oppression requires an appreciation of the extent to which not only women's lives, but their very subjectivities are constructed through an ensemble of disciplinary habits.

In *Discipline and Punish* Foucault argues that discipline was a historically specific technology of power that emerged in the eighteenth century and operated through the body. In disciplinary practices, habits and patterns of behavior are broken down and constructed in new ways that are more productive for the aims of modern industrial societies. Discipline consists of various techniques, which aim at making the body both docile and useful. In the eighteenth century, claims Foucault, bodies of prisoners, soldiers, workers, and school children were subjected to a new kind of discipline to make them more useful for mass production and, at the same time, easier to control. The functions, movements, and capabilities of their bodies were broken down into narrow segments, analyzed in detail, and recomposed in a maximally effective way. Disciplinary power does not mutilate or coerce its target, but through detailed training reconstructs the body to produce new kinds of gestures, habits, and skills. Individuals literally incorporate the objectives of power, which become part of their own being. The human body becomes a machine, the functioning of which can be optimized, calculated, and improved through the internalization of specific patterns of behavior.[5]

Bartky (1988, 64) acknowledges the strengths of Foucault's analysis but contends that he is blind to those disciplines that produce a modality of subjection that is particularly feminine. She analyzes habits, such as dieting and fitness regimes, as disciplinary practices aimed at producing an ideal feminine body that are imposed on women. These disciplinary practices of femininity aim at an exhaustive and perpetual regulation of the body's size and contours, its appetite, posture, gestures, and comportment, as well as the appearance of each of its visible parts. Expert discourses on how to walk, talk, style one's hair, care for one's skin, and wear makeup create habits conducive to the requirements of submissive femininity: feminine movement, as well as feminine faces, is trained to the expression of deference. The rationality of these disciplinary practices can thus only be understood in the light of patriarchal domination. They subjugate women by normalization, by constructing them as particular kinds of subjects, not simply by taking power away from them. Feminist analysis must recognize these individual practices of feminine beauty as aspects of a large and systematic disciplinary regime—an oppressive and inequitable system of sexual subordination. The rationality of this disciplinary apparatus is clear: it aims at turning women into "the docile and compliant companions of men just as surely as the army aims to turn its raw recruits into soldiers" (Bartky 1988, 75).

The question of why women agree to partake in these practices and actively acquire such oppressive and painful habits clearly troubles Bartky. She acknowledges that "no one is marched off for electrolysis at gunpoint, nor can we fail to appreciate the initiative and ingenuity displayed by countless women in an attempt to master the rituals of beauty" (1988, 75). She explains the compelling character of these practices by emphasizing how they are tied to powerful sanctions and rewards. Refusal to take part in these practices in a world dominated by men means that women face a very severe sanction: the refusal of male patronage. This can mean the loss of badly needed intimacy or even of decent livelihood (76). The disciplinary technologies of femininity are also taken up and practiced by women against the background of a pervasive sense of bodily deficiency: a sense of shame is a central component of normative feminine experience and a measure of the extent to which all women have internalized patriarchal standards of bodily acceptability (71). A generalized male gaze structures woman's consciousness of herself as a bodily being, and women become self-policing subjects committed to a relentless self-surveillance. The rewards importantly include sexual attractiveness: to possess a feminine body is usually essential to a woman's sense of herself as a sexually desiring and desirable subject (78). Pain, constriction, tedium, semistarvation, and constant self-surveillance are preferable to desexualization and the loss of a socially recognized identity.[6]

Instead of being explicitly coerced into adopting disciplinary practices or freely choosing them as the preferred means of self-expression, women thus internalize them as normative habits that become an integral part of their gender identity. The explanatory power of habit as the mundane basis of gender oppression lies exactly in the way it forms a conceptual bridge between coercion and free volition, the two untenable extremes in the debates on the nature of gender. Feminist accounts of gender have attempted to challenge forms of essentialism, but they have equally rejected gender voluntarism: one is not born a woman, one becomes one, but not through a deliberate choice. Disciplinary practices form the normative mechanism that produces a stable and enduring pattern of being and creates an illusion of a permanent gender core or essence. It is like a second nature, which unlike the first nature, allows for historical and cultural variation and change while also incorporating the permanence and stability that characterize our experience of gendered identity.

Biopower and Governmentality

While Foucault's conception of power has influenced feminist theory significantly, it has also been subjected to strong criticism. One of the key issues that his feminist critics have raised concerns the restrictive scope of his microphysics of power. The charge is that the attention to a microphysics of power—the specific everyday practices and techniques of power—fails to address the more general, structural issues of power and therefore to provide a macro-level analysis of domination. Amy Allen (1996), for example, has argued that an adequate feminist theory of power should include both micro-level and macro-level analyses. The micro-level analysis would examine a specific power relation between two individuals or groups of individuals. The macro-level analysis, on the other hand, should focus on the background to such particular power relations. It must examine the cultural meanings, practices, and larger structures of domination that make up the context within which a particular power relation is able to emerge (Allen 1996, 267). A feminist analysis of power relations that remained solely on the micro level would be seriously inadequate because power relations studied in isolation from their cultural and institutional context can be easily perceived as anomalies, and not as part of a larger system of domination such as sexism (268). She argues that while Foucault's analysis of power makes a considerable contribution for feminist theory on the micro level, it falls short on the macro level: it does not "give us any assistance in examining deep structures of domination" (280).

Foucault's conception of biopower and his lectures on governmentality can be read as providing resources to respond to such concerns. While the analyses of disciplinary power were restricted to specific institutional contexts, the ideas of biopower and power as governmentality widened the scope of his rethinking of power to the domain of the state and the broader rationalities underlying practices of governing.

Foucault introduced the influential concept of biopower at the end of *The History of Sexuality*, volume 1. He argues that this power over life evolved in two basic forms: one was the disciplinary power that centered on the body as a machine, and the other was the *biopolitics of the population*, which focused on the species body (Foucault 1978, 139). *Biopolitics* is concerned with the regulatory control of propagation, birth, and mortality as well as the level of health and life expectancy, for example. The era of biopolitics is marked by the explosion of numerous and diverse techniques for achieving the control of populations: techniques that coordinate medical care, normalize behavior, rationalize mechanisms of insurance, and rethink urban planning, for example. The aim is the effective administration of bodies and the calculated management of life through means that are scientific and continuous.

Biopower further illustrates the idea of productive rather than repressive power. Biopower is not repressive or destructive but appears as essentially protective of life. While being explicitly concerned with health and well-being, biopower is an extremely effective form of social control that takes over the management of the life of individuals from the time before their birth until they die. Foucault's key claim is that the West has undergone a very profound transformation of the mechanisms of power since the seventeenth century. Violent sovereign power operating as a power to seize and destroy has been gradually complemented and partly replaced by biopower, a form of power that exerts a positive influence on life, "that endeavors to administer, optimize, and multiply it, subjecting it to precise controls and comprehensive regulations" (Foucault 1978, 137). Physical violence and appropriation are no longer the predominant forms of power, but are merely some elements among others, working toward a new objective under a new rationality. Biopower is bent on generating and ordering forces: the aim is to increase them rather than to impede or destroy them. In short, its logic or rationality is not violent appropriation of life and possessions, but positive production.

In his last lecture in the series "Society Must Be Defended" (1975–1976), Foucault discusses the phenomenon of state racism in Nazi Germany as an example of paradoxes in the exercise of modern biopower. He notes that Nazi Germany could in many ways be seen as the extreme development of biopower: there was no other state in which "the biological was so tightly, so insistently, regulated" (Foucault 2003, 259). However, he poses the question of how a political system so completely centered upon biopower and the optimization of life could unleash such murderous power and in fact utilize the old sovereign right to kill (254). His answer was biological racism, which provided a way of separating the different groups that exist within a population and then establishing a biological relationship among them. This was not an adversarial relationship between enemies—the inferior group was not the enemy threatening the nation's existence. It was rather a biological relationship of abnormality: the inferior group had to be eliminated as a biological threat to the population and its improvement. The death of inferior races would make life in general healthier. The objective to improve life for its own sake could thus legitimize killing within the rationality of biopower. The logic of biological racism was the condition that makes killing acceptable in biopolitical societies.

Biopolitics has been an extremely fertile idea for feminist theory: the power over reproduction and within the institution of the family have traditionally been central feminist concerns. A prime example of biopower would not be a repressive institution such as a prison or a labor camp, but a caring facility such as a psychiatric hospital or a maternity clinic. While the overt aim of maternity clinics is the well-being of mothers and babies, they also have aims and effects that are more problematic: the medicalization of pregnancy and the intensification of the social control of family life, for example. Foucault's analysis of biopower as a particularly modern form of power has supported feminist criticism of medicalization and of the bioscientific control of reproduction (on feminist engagements with Foucault, familial power, and biopolitics, see, e.g., Feder 2007; Deutscher 2010; Taylor 2012; see also chapter 4 on Biopolitics in this volume).

Ladelle McWhorter (2009) appropriates Foucault's idea of biopolitics and racism in her provocative book *Racism and Sexual Oppression in Anglo-America*. Her key argument is that we can only understand the emergence of the modern nuclear family in the United States within the biopolitical context of the eugenics movement. She shows how the eugenic concern with the purity and health of the population transmuted after WWII into a concern to protect the traditional family. She contends that "in the postwar years, *family* would become the semantic substitute for *race*" (2009, 250). "The family" of the family values movement fulfilled the same objectives as the pure and healthy race of eugenics movement had done some decades earlier: it provided a normalizing model for what kinds of people should reproduce, how many children they should have, and under what kinds of conditions normal children should be raised, for example. For McWhorter, biopower would be impossible without the organizing forces of race and sexuality, and vice versa, race and sexuality require biopower (181).

Commentators sometimes read Foucault's lectures on the history of governmentality "Security, Territory and Population" (1977–1978) and "The Birth of Biopolitics" (1978–1979) as a major turning point in his thought. After his study of disciplinary power in the context of the prison, and productive power in connection with the emergence of modern sexuality, these lectures effect a shift to more traditional political theory in their concern with the development of the modern administrative state. In these lectures *government* becomes Foucault's preferred term for power, while *governmentality* functions as his main theoretical tool for analyzing the rationality, techniques, and procedures of power in modernity.[7] He wanted to articulate and to reveal, through historical analysis, the development of a specific type of political rationality and a power technology that were fundamental to the exercise of modern state power. He identified the historical conditions—such as Christian pastoral power and the birth of political economy—that have produced the modern administrative state: a historically specific form of power with a distinct rationality.

Foucault's genealogy of the modern state culminates in an analysis of neoliberal governmentality in the lecture series "The Birth of Biopolitics."[8] In these lectures neoliberalism is crucially treated as a form of governmentality, a rationality of governance that produces new kinds of political subjects and a new organization of the social realm. It is not reducible to a set of economic policies, such as limiting the regulation of capital, maximizing corporate profits, and dismantling the welfare state. As a form of governmentality neoliberalism extends beyond economic policy, or even the economic domain as traditionally conceived. A fundamental feature of neoliberal governmentality is not just the eradication of market regulation, for example, but the eradication of the border between the social and the economic: market rationality—cost-benefit calculation—must be extended and disseminated to all institutions and social practices.

Contemporary feminist political scholarship is strongly focused on critiques of neoliberalism, compellingly demonstrating how neoliberalism hinders feminist political goals and initiatives (see, e.g., Eisenstein 2009; Griffin 2009; Walby 2011). Foucault's analysis of neoliberalism as a form of governmentality and his understanding of the fundamental link between power and the subject have offered new perspectives for this critique. Many of the most recent feminist appropriations of Foucault's work have focused on his lectures on neoliberal governmentality.[9]

Johanna Oksala (2013) argues that Foucault's thought provides a more nuanced diagnostic approach to neoliberalism than does traditional socialist welfare feminism because it enables us to account for neoliberalism's constitutive effects. These effects include both new forms of the subject and new limitations on what are understood as viable and rational political options in today's society. A Foucauldian approach shows that the impact of neoliberalism is not limited to the dismantling of the welfare state: as a form of governmentality, neoliberalism is not only constitutive of our conceptions of politics and political action, but also of ourselves as political subjects. This implies that the feminist subject, too, as well as our understanding of feminist politics are shaped and constituted by our current neoliberal governmentality. In other words, "women," "feminism," and "feminist politics" are not natural, apolitical entities that are simply affected by certain empirical changes in society. They are fundamentally shaped and constituted by these changes and by our conceptions and background beliefs about the social world. Assessing the impact of neoliberal governmentality therefore requires rethinking how our conceptions of female subjectivity, citizenship, political action, and feminist liberation, for example, have themselves changed due to the impact of neoliberal hegemony (Oksala 2013, 39).

Resistance

Another central point of contention in feminist discussions of Foucault's conception of power has been his understanding of resistance. Many of his feminist critics have argued that his account of power does not allow for resistance, either because of its lack of an explicit normative framework and/or because of its lack of a robust theory of the subject. Nancy Fraser, for example, has pointed to the debilitating lack of normative grounding in his analyses. Since all social relations appear to be power relations, there seems to be no possibility of progress in the sense that social relations would become less oppressive. "Because Foucault has no basis for distinguishing, for example, forms of power that involve domination from those that do not, he appears to endorse a one-sided, wholesale rejection of modernity as such" (Fraser 1989, 32–33). Moreover, if we accept the claim that power is constitutive of the subject, we seem to be unable to account for agency—the subject's ability to resist forms of power and to make autonomous choices, rather than simply capitulate to normalization. Lois McNay (1992, 12), for example, notes that Foucault's account of power leads to "an oversimplified notion of gender as an imposed effect" and permits "no explanation of how individuals may act in an autonomous and creative fashion despite overarching constraints." (For other influential feminist critiques of Foucault from the late 1980s and early 1990s that engage with these issues, see, e.g., Diamond and Quinby 1988; Sawicki 1991; Ramazanoglu 1993.)

For Foucault, power does not form a deterministic system of overbearing constraints, however. Because it is understood as an unstable network of practices, where there is power, there is always resistance. When Foucault introduces his influential conception of power in the form of short propositions in *The History of Sexuality*, volume 1, he explicitly states the inseparability of resistance and power. The fifth proposition contends: "Where there is power, there is resistance" (Foucault 1978, 95). What makes his position contested—and original—is the way he understands the relationship between power and resistance. Immediately after stating their interdependence, he adds, "yet or rather consequently, this resistance is never in a position of exteriority to power" (95). He forbids us to think that resistance is outside power and also denies that we could ever locate it in a single point: "There is no single locus of great Refusal, no soul of revolt, source of all rebellions, or pure law of the revolutionary" (95). To view the relationship between power and resistance as external would mean misunderstanding the relational character of power. Because power is not something that an individual acquires, holds, or gives away, its existence depends on resistance: since power exists only in a relation, resistance must be located in these very same power relations.

This understanding of resistance as an effect of power, or as its self-subversion, has led feminist theorists sympathetic to Foucault's account of power to insist that the technologies of power that constitute forms of the gendered subject are never completely successful. Judith Butler (1997, 93), for example, argues that for Foucault resistance inevitably appears in the course of subjectivation that exceeds the normalizing aims by which it is mobilized or through convergence with other discursive regimes. This inadvertently produced discursive complexity undermines the teleological aims of normalization. Insofar as power always accidentally produces resistance, even the most disciplined subject can be engaged in it.

What still appears as a problem in Foucault's account is how the subject is able to deliberately instigate resistance. For his critics, the main problem would not be admitting that some strategies of power are too complex to always succeed, and, inevitably, there will be failures. They would insist that these failures do not yet constitute resistance, however. Our idea of resistance implies an intentional strategy, a deliberate attempt to subvert power. On the basis of Foucault's understanding of both power and the subject, it is not evident how the normalized subject, constituted by power, is capable of engaging in resistance and, furthermore, on what grounds such an attempt could be advocated or justified.

Foucault's late texts on power, the Enlightenment, and the practices of the self are important in this context and provide his fullest account of resistance, but the project was cut short by his untimely death. In an interview given in 1984 shortly before his death Foucault admits that when he first became interested in the problem of power, some of the concepts and ideas linked with it were ill defined and unclear. It was only later that he developed a clearer sense of the problem. He goes on to distinguish between power and domination: whereas power relations are always fluid and can be reversed, states of domination are static power relations that have been ossified through institutions. While we can never eradicate all power relations, we can, and we should, eradicate domination (Foucault 1997, 299). His late essays on the contemporary legacy of the Enlightenment further problematize the idea that his thought was a one-sided, wholesale rejection of modernity devoid of any normative grounding. Foucault (1997, 312) rejects what he calls "the blackmail of the Enlightenment," the idea that one has to be either for or against the Enlightenment. He suggests that the Enlightenment should, rather, be understood and appropriated as a philosophical *ethos* that translates into concrete practices of freedom, as well as a permanent critique of our own era.

From a feminist perspective perhaps the most interesting attempts to rethink resistance are the two last volumes of *The History of Sexuality*, which study ancient ethical practices and technologies of the self. In his late interviews and lectures Foucault also significantly discusses their relevance for the contemporary art of living. A key theme is the deliberate work that the subjects perform on themselves: the forms of understanding subjects create about themselves and the ways they form themselves as subjects through historically changing technologies of the self. While Foucault's earlier genealogical studies investigated the ways the power/knowledge apparatus constitutes the subject, in his late work the emphasis is on the subject's own role in implementing or refusing forms of subjectivity.

His late work thus brings into focus a new component of the constitution of the subject—modes of relation to oneself—and thus presents a more elaborated understanding of the subject than is found in his earlier writings.[10] Foucault advocates "a politics of ourselves" that does not attempt to find an authentic or true self but aims at a creative transformation of ourselves. The practices of the self are importantly practices of freedom because they are attempts to resist normalization by approaching our lives as material for ethical and political transformation. In his rare but important comments in interviews with the gay press, Foucault (1997, 163) argued, for example, that the gay movement did not need scientific knowledge about sexuality but an art of life: "We don't have to discover that we are homosexuals . . . we have to create a gay life. To *become*."

While the initial feminist reaction to Foucault's late work was largely negative, criticizing it for being individualistic, masculinist, and even narcissistic (e.g., Soper 1993, 35–36; also McNay 1992), more recently it has been appropriated for imaginative attempts to sketch a feminist art of life and to develop concrete ways to resist patriarchal power and gender normalization (see, e.g., McWhorter 1999; Taylor and Vintges 2004). Feminist theorists have argued that consciousness raising, for example, can be viewed from a Foucauldian perspective as practice of freedom. Margaret McLaren (2004, 230) points out how feminist consciousness raising exemplifies the type of self-transformation Foucault refers to in his discussion of practices of the self because it draws on the rules, methods, and customs of one's culture, but with the explicit aim of transforming cultural conventions about gender. Mariana Valverde (2004, 82) also contends that a Foucauldian perspective on these practices is particularly illuminating because it refuses to view them as forms of confession (see also Taylor 2009, 229–230). Viewed as technologies of the self, the aim of the feminist practices of consciousness raising is not the exposure of deep inner self or an original and authentic womanhood, but rather the problematization of the normalized self (see also Sawicki 1991, 44). In other words, consciousness-raising practices can be understood as practices of freedom in the sense that their goal is not a naturalization of identity, but its critical deconstruction.

In *Self-Transformations: Foucault, Ethics, and Normalized Bodies*, Cressida Heyes (2007) acknowledges that there is a particular difficulty in such feminist projects of self-fashioning. It is problematic to assess the co-optation of feminist practices of the self by the very disciplinary technologies that structure gender normalization. She argues that Foucault's late thought can nonetheless provide important tools for rethinking our relationship to ourselves as normalized individuals and suggests that we have to rejects all teleological accounts of self-development and instead adopt "new practices that remain open to forms of becoming not yet imagined" (11). Despite the pervasiveness of the techniques of gender normalization, it is thus possible to engage in creative and critical feminist practices of the self that refuse the habituated trajectories. Heyes describes feminist practices of self-transformation as being "a kind of therapy." These practices are both ethical and spiritual and they require techniques that are "somatic, meditative, artistic as well as communal" (108). The ethical challenge that Heyes poses to feminists is no less than to develop "a new art of embodied living" (11).

Amy Allen (2008) also takes up the idea of the feminist politics of ourselves in *The Politics of Ourselves*. She begins by noting that the idea of a politics of ourselves seems to entail two distinct claims. First, it suggests that the self is not a natural entity but a political one, always constituted by power relations. Second, implicit in Foucault's idea of practices or technologies of the self is an appeal to a notion of autonomy, understood as the capacities for critical reflection and self-transformation. She notes that these two sides of the politics of our selves are often thought to be incompatible with each other: "It has been assumed that thinking of the self as political in the first sense, as constituted by power, makes politics of the self in the second sense impossible, because it reveals agency, autonomy, and critique to be nothing more than illusions, power's clever ruses" (2). Allen argues that Foucault's thought is helpful in showing how subjection and autonomy are always deeply intertwined and how both aspects of the politics of ourselves are therefore essential.

As Allen argues, an adequate understanding of gendered forms of subjectivity is crucial for any feminist theorizing of gender subordination as well as the attempts to transform it. We have to recognize that even our innermost selves are always constituted in social and political practices incorporating gendered power relations. Without an adequate acknowledgement of how widespread and systematic power relations are and how profoundly they constitute the subjects' interests, desires and capacities for critical reflection we will not be able to understand the extent and the recalcitrance of gender oppression. Foucault's account of productive power has contributed significantly to this task: his microphysics of power has deepened our theoretical understanding of the constitution of gendered subjectivity through disciplinary practices of power, and his lectures and essays have provided stimulus for contemporary feminist critiques of gender normalization, biopolitics, and neoliberalism.

However, we also have to maintain an adequate understanding of agency and feminist resistance. Conceptions of subjectivity that fail to account for the possibility of some measure of reflection and autonomy will make it impossible to theorize feminist transformations—transformations of the self as well as political transformations. Our theoretical understanding of resistance, moreover, has to translate into concrete practices of resistance. Sandra Bartky (2002, 14) has voiced the concern that an insurmountable gap lies between feminist theory and practice: we have produced sophisticated theories without any corresponding political practice. Feminist theory should not become a mere intellectual game with no connection to real lives or experiences.

I have attempted to show that Foucault's understanding of power provides some limited resources for the feminist theorization of resistance and, moreover, suggests models for corresponding political practices. If we accept the theoretical implications of Foucault's idea of productive power for gendered forms of the subject, then we have to also recognize the need to engage in transformative practices of the self that target the constitutive effects of power. While Foucauldian practices of the self do not, by themselves, necessarily imply any radical political movements, the reverse is nevertheless true: radical political movements such as feminism necessarily imply practices of the self. Feminism as a political project must aim at profound social transformation, not merely at some quantitative gain such as increase in women's power, political rights, or social benefits, for example. It has to aim to change who we are—both as men and as women. Such transformation requires politics that is able to question and transform the political institutions, cultural representations, and values that shape and structure our subjectivities, but it also requires self-transformation—political practices that aim to change our singular experiences.

Notes

1. Moira Ferguson (1996, 125) shows how *A Vindication of the Rights of Woman* contains more than eighty references to slavery and that the constituency Wollstonecraft champions—white, middle-class women—is constantly characterized as slaves.
2. In *Discipline and Punish* Foucault famously showed how the supposedly free political subject of liberalism was in fact materially constructed through concrete and detailed disciplinary techniques. He argued that the establishment of an explicit, coded and formally egalitarian juridical framework, made possible by the organization of a parliamentary, representative regime in the 18th century, was accompanied by the development and generalization of disciplinary mechanisms. They constituted "the other, dark side of these processes" of democratic progress (Foucault 1991, 222).
3. Foucault (1991, 26) introduces the term "microphysics of power" in *Discipline and Punish*.
4. Many of the seminal articles on feminist standpoint theories, such as the papers by Dorothy Smith, Nancy Hartsock, Hilary Rose, and Patricia Hill Collins are collected in Harding's *The Feminist Standpoint Theory Reader* (2004).
5. Foucault (1991, 135) argues that in the seventeenth century a soldier, for example, for the most part still learned his profession in actual fighting in which he proved his natural strength and inherent courage. But by the eighteenth century, a soldier had become a fighting machine, something that could be constructed through correct training.
6. In her 2002 article "Suffering to Be Beautiful," Bartky acknowledges that two themes were underdeveloped in the earlier paper. First, she wants to respond to the criticism that she had undertheorized the pleasure women take in turning themselves into properly feminine subjects, by spelling out in more detail the nature of these pleasures. The second theme she neglected was the psychic ambivalence connected to these disciplinary practices (Bartky 2002, 4). For a discussion on how the disciplinary technologies of gender discussed by Bartky have changed due to neoliberalism, see Oksala (2011).
7. Foucault's notion of *governmentality* emerged in the fourth lecture of the series "Security, Territory, Population" in the year 1978. The word *governmentality* is not only ugly—as Foucault himself (2007, 115) noted—it is also ambiguous. As Michel Senellart (2007, 387–388) explains, its meaning progressively shifts from a precise, historically determinate sense connected to the governance of the modern state, to a more general and abstract meaning. Whereas in the 1978 lectures it denotes the techniques of government that underpin the formation of the modern state, from 1979 onward it receives a more general meaning: "I have proposed to call governmentality . . . the way in which one conducts

the conduct of men, ... a proposed analytical grid for ... relations of power" (Foucault 2008, 186).
8. The lectures provide an explicit analysis of the neoliberal program in its two forms. The initial German form was represented by the proponents of the Freiburg School of economists, such as Walter Eucken and Wilhelm Röpke, also called *Ordoliberals* after the journal *Ordo*. It was strongly linked to the critique of Nazism and, after the War, to postwar reconstruction. The other, American form was the neoliberalism of the Chicago School, which was derived from the former but was in some respects more radical.
9. In her recent introduction to *Foucault Studies* Special Issue: *Foucault and Feminism*, Cressida Heyes (2013, 10) writes that if there are any trends in the last decade of the scholarship on Foucault and feminist theory, "they crystallize around three themes: Foucault's account of subjectivity and of desubjectivation as it relates to his methods of genealogy and critique, and especially to his last (and less well explored) work on ethics; reevalutions of his work on sexuality and the attempt to delineate a 'queer feminism'; and the growing conversation around Foucault's lectures on neoliberalism and their relations to biopolitics." Three of the five essays in the special issue engage directly with Foucault on neoliberalism. See McWhorter (2013); Oksala (2013); Sawicki (2013).
10. As Gilles Deleuze (1988, 101) argued, Foucault's fundamental idea was that of a dimension of subjectivity derived from power/knowledge apparatus without being dependent on it. The constituted subject is capable of turning back upon itself: of critically studying the processes of its own constitution, but also of deliberately subverting them and effecting changes in them.

References

Alcoff, L. 2000. "Phenomenology, Post-Structuralism, and Feminist Theory on the Concept of Experience." In *Feminist Phenomenology*, edited by Linda Fisher and Lester Embree, 39–56. Dordrecht: Kluwer Academic Publishers.

Allen, A. 1996. "Foucault on Power: A Theory for Feminists. " In *Feminist Interpretations of Michel Foucault*, edited by Susan J. Hekman, 265–282. University Park: Pennsylvania State University Press.

Allen, A. 2008. *The Politics of Our Selves. Power, Autonomy and Gender in Contemporary Critical Theory*. New York: Columbia University Press.

Astell, M. 1996. *Political Writings*. Edited by Patricia Springborg. Cambridge: Cambridge University Press.

Bartky, S. 1988. "Foucault, Feminity and the Modernization of Patriarchal Power." In *Feminism and Foucault: Paths of Resistance*, edited by Irene Diamond and Lee Quinby, 61–85. Boston: Northeastern University Press.

Bartky, S. 2002. *"Sympathy and Solidarity" and Other Essays*. Lanham, MD: Rowman & Littlefield.

Bordo, S. 1989. "The Body and the Reproduction of Femininity: A Feminist Appropriation of Foucault." In *Gender/Body/Knowledge*, edited by Allison Jaggar and Susan Bordo, 13–33. New Brunswick, NJ: Rutgers University Press.

Bordo, S. 1993. "Feminism, Foucault and the Politics of the Body." In *Up against Foucault*, edited by Caroline Ramazanoglu, 179–203. London: Routledge.

Butler, J. 1990. *Gender Trouble*. London and New York: Routledge.

Butler, J. 1993. *Bodies That Matter: On the Discursive Limits of Sex*. London and New York: Routledge.

Butler, J. 1997. *The Psychic Life of Power: Theories in Subjection*. Redwood City, CA: Stanford University Press.

Butler, J. 2004. *Undoing Gender:* London and New York: Routledge.

Deleuze, G. 1988. *Foucault*. London: Athlone Press.

Deutscher, P. 2010. "Reproductive Politics, Biopolitics, and Auto-Immunity: From Foucault to Esposito." *Journal of Bioethical Inquiry* 7 (2): 217–226.

Diamond, I., and L. Quinby, eds. 1988. *Feminism and Foucault: Reflections on Resistance*. Evanston. IL: Northwestern University Press.

Eisenstein, H. 2009. *Feminism Seduced: How Global Elites Use Women's Labor and Ideas to Exploit the World*. Boulder, CO: Paradigm Publishers.

Feder, E. K. 2007. *Family Bonds: Genealogies of Race and Gender*. Oxford: Oxford University Press.

Ferguson, M. 1996. "Mary Wollstonecraft and the Problematic of Slavery." In *Feminist Interpretations of Mary Wollstonecraft*, edited by Maria J. Falco, 125–149. University Park: Pennsylvania State University Press.

Foucault, M. 1978. *The History of Sexuality, Vol. 1, An Introduction*. Translated by Robert Hurley. London: Penguin.

Foucault, M. 1982. "The Subject and Power." *Michel Foucault: Beyond Structuralism and Hermeneutics*. Edited by Hubert Dreyfus and Paul Rabinow, 208–226. Hemel Hempstead: Harvester.

Foucault, M. 1991. *Discipline and Punish: The Birth of the Prison*. Translated by Alan Sheridan. London: Penguin.

Foucault, M. 1997. *Ethics, Subjectivity and Truth: Essential Works of Foucault 1954–1984*. Vol. 1. Edited by Paul Rabino. Translated by Robert Hurley and others. New York: New Press.

Foucault, M. 2003. *Society Must Be Defended: Lectures at the Collège de France 1975–1976*. Edited by Mauro Bertani and Alessandro Fontana. Translated by David Macey. London: Penguin.

Foucault, M. 2007. *Security, Territory, Population: Lectures at the Collège de France 1977–78*. Edited by Michel Senellart. Translated by Graham Burchell. Basingstoke: Palgrave Macmillan.

Foucault, M. 2008. *The Birth of Biopolitics: Lectures at the Collège de France 1978-79*. Edited by Michel Senellart. Translated by Graham Burchell (Basingstoke: Palgrave MacMillan.

Fraser, N. 1989. *Unruly Practices: Power, Discourse and Gender in Contemporary Social Theory*. Cambridge: Polity Press.

Friedan, B. 1963. *The Feminine Mystique*. Harmondsworth, UK: Penguin.

Friedan, B. 1968. 'Our Revolution Is Unique." In *American Political Thought*, 5th ed., edited by Kenneth M. Dolbeare and Micheal S. Cummings, 450–455. Washington, DC: CQ Press.

Griffin, P. 2009. *Gendering the World Bank: Neoliberalism and the Gendered Foundations of Global Governance*. Basingstoke: Palgrave Macmillan.

Harding, S. ed. 2004. *The Feminist Standpoint Theory Reader*. New York and London: Routledge.

Heyes, C. 2007. *Self-Transformations: Foucault, Ethics and Normalized Bodies*. Oxford: Oxford University Press.

Heyes, C. 2013. Introduction to *Foucault Studies*. Special Issue: *Foucault and Feminism* 16: 3–14.

Huffer, L. 2010. *Mad for Foucault: Rethinking the Foundations of Queer Theory*. New York: Columbia University Press.

Kruks, S. 2001. *Retrieving Experience: Subjectivity and Recognition in Feminist Politics*. Ithaca, NY: Cornell University Press.
MacKinnon, C. 1983. "Feminism, Marxism, Method, and the State." *Signs* 8(4): 635–658.
McLaren, M. 2004. "Foucault and Feminism: Power, Resistance, Freedom." In *Feminism and the Final Foucault*, edited by Dianna Taylor and Karen Vintges, 214–234. Urbana and Chicago: University of Illinois Press.
McNay, L. 1992. *Foucault and Feminism*. Cambridge: Polity Press.
McWhorter, L. 1999. *Bodies and Pleasures: Foucault and the Politics of Sexual Normalization*. Bloomington: Indiana University Press.
McWhorter, L. 2009. *Racism and Sexual Oppression in Anglo-America: A Genealogy*. Bloomington: Indiana University Press.
McWhorter, L. 2013. "Post-Liberation Feminism and Practices of Freedom." *Foucault Studies*. Special Issue. *Foucault and Feminism* 16: 54–73.
Mitchell, J. 1971. *Women's Estate*. Harmondsworth: Penguin.
Okin, S. 1989. *Justice, Gender and the Family*. New York: Basic Books.
Oksala, J. 2011. "The Neoliberal Subject of Feminism." *Journal of the British Society for Phenomenology* 42 (1): 104–120.
Oksala, J. 2013. "Feminism and Neoliberal Governmentality." *Foucault Studies*. Special Issue. *Foucault and Feminism* 16: 32–53.
Oksala, J. 2014. "In Defense of Experience." *Hypatia* 29 (2): 388–403.
Ramazanoglu, C. 1993. *Up against Foucault: Explorations of Some Tensions between Foucault and Feminism*. London and New York: Routledge.
Sawicki, J. 1991. *Disciplining Foucault: Feminism, Power, and the Body*. London and New York: Routledge.
Sawicki, J. 2013. "Queer Feminism: Cultivating Ethical Practices of Freedom." *Foucault Studies*. Special Issue: *Foucault and Feminism* 16: 74–87.
Scott, J. 1991. "The Evidence of Experience." *Critical Inquiry* 17: 773–797.
Senellart, M. 2007. "Course Context." In *Michel Foucault: Security, Territory, Population: Lectures at the College de France 1977-78*, edited by Michel Senellart, translated by Graham Burchell, 370–401. Basingstoke: Palgrave Macmillan.
Soper, K. 1993. "Productive Contradictions." In *Up against Foucault*, edited by Caroline Ramazanoglu, 29–50. London and New York: Routledge.
Taylor, C. 2009. *The Culture of Confession from Augustine to Foucault: A Genealogy of the "Confessing Animal."* New York and London: Routledge.
Taylor, C. 2012. "Foucault and Familial Power." *Hypatia* 27 (1): 201–218.
Taylor, D., and K. Vintges, eds. 2004. *Feminism and the Final Foucault*. Urbana: University of Illinois Press.
Valverde, M. 2004. "Experience and Truth Telling in a Post-Humanist World: A Foucauldian Contribution to Feminist Ethical reflections." In *Feminism and the Final Foucault*, edited by Dianna Taylor and Karen Vintges, 67–90. Urbana and Chicago: University of Illinois Press.
Vogel, L. 1983. *Marxism and the Oppression of Women: Toward a Unitary Theory*. New Brunswick, NJ: Rutgers University Press.
Walby, S. 2011. *The Future of Feminism*. Cambridge: Polity Press.
Winnubst, S. 2006. *Queering Freedom*. Bloomington: Indiana University Press.
Wollstonecraft, M. 2001. *A Vindication of the Rights of Woman*. New York: Random House.

CHAPTER 24

MIGRATION

RHACEL SALAZAR PARREÑAS AND CAROLYN CHOI

More than thirty years ago, Maria Mies insightfully observed the links between the expansion of capitalism and the ideology of the housewife in her detailed study of lace makers in Narsapur, India (Mies 1982). Their productive labor as home-based workers upheld the notion that women belong in the home. According to Chandra Mohanty (1988, 73), this ideological construction provided "the necessary subjective and socio-cultural element for the creation and maintenance of a production system that contributes to the increasing pauperization of women, and keeps them totally atomized and disorganized as workers." We begin with the classic study of Mies to make a similar argument about the discussion of contemporary women's migration. In this chapter, we argue that the contradictory location inhabited by homeworkers thirty years ago is not a thing of the past. As we will show, an ideology of female domesticity continues to stall the gender advancements that migration grants women.

It is easy to assume that the independent migration of women challenges the "gendered configurations of space and motion" (Freeman 2001, 1018). After all, women are no longer just following their husbands when they migrate, as they did in the early 1980s and 1990s (Hondagneu-Sotelo 1994). Instead, they migrate independently of them, sometimes ahead of them (George 2005), and sometimes to a different destination altogether (Parreñas 2001). For instance, a migrant husband can be based in Saudi Arabia while his wife relocates to the United Arab Emirates. More significantly, migration signals that women are not only working outside but far away from their homes, suggesting the breakdown of the "ideology of the housewife" (Parreñas 2001). According to various scholars, migration liberates women. They argue that women, for instance from Mexico, Sri Lanka, and the Dominican Republic, achieve a certain amount of gender autonomy in migration (Hondagneu-Sotelo 1994; Gamburd 2000; Grasmuck and Pessar 1991). More specifically, it is argued that migrant women's greater participation in the public sphere as household mediators and wage earners allows them to increase their power in the household.

However, a closer look at the position of migrant women shows a limit to the reconstitution of gender in their experiences. Taking, for instance, their labor market participation, one would easily see that migrant women's labor usually retains the ideology of women's domesticity—as nimble-fingered electronics production workers, domestic workers, or nurses or some other form of care worker. Such jobs retain the assumption of women's natural aptitude for caring and nurturing. In fact, most independent women migrants are domestic workers. This is true in Sri Lanka, the Philippines, and Indonesia, the three largest source countries of domestic workers (Parreñas 2008). In the case of the Philippines, more than half of the 2.8 million women migrant contract workers who work outside the country are employed as domestic workers (Parreñas, forthcoming).

To move away from a colonialist view of gender, that is, the view that women in more developed countries have greater autonomy and freedom, we wish to complicate our feminist analysis of migration and trouble the assumption that the movement of women to more developed countries signals their liberation. Instead, we propose that the migration of women be viewed as a movement from one patriarchal system to another. We build from a previous argument made by Rhacel Parreñas (2001) in her study on migrant Filipina domestic workers in Rome and Los Angeles, which found that migrant Filipina domestic workers flee from the patriarchal system of the Philippines only to enter the patriarchal system of various receiving countries. Upon migration, they escape the double day, the daily pressures and cultural monitoring of their actions as "dutiful daughters," the threat of domestic violence, or the impoverishment of single motherhood. Yet, they enter a country with a patriarchal system that usually designates housework to women; hence the demand for their labor as domestic workers. This framework, however, does not advance the argument that migrant women face a static set of gender inequalities in home and host societies. Instead, it acknowledges that while migration may allow women to negotiate the gender constraints they face in the home society, this comes at the cost of them having to confront a different set of gender constraints in the host society.

In this chapter, we argue that women's migration results in the simultaneous retention and rejection of the ideology of female domesticity. This contradictory construction of gender emerges in the experiences of three groups of migrant women: migrant domestic workers, transnational mothers, and, lastly, marriage migrants. Our chapter is not exhaustive but representative of the largest groups of migrant women. It is also inclusive of different groups of migrant women including women who migrate for work, those who migrate for love and romance, and those who migrate for adventure. These groups are not mutually exclusive; for instance, a domestic worker can migrate for work but also adventure and a marriage migrant can relocate for both money and romance. Lastly, we look at the constitution of gender solely by examining the experiences of women, as opposed to comparing the experiences of men and women.

We are aware that our approach might be dismissed as theoretically incomplete, as it has long been argued in the literature on gender and migration that focusing exclusively on women could easily fall trap to the long-dismissed sex role theory, which establishes that women and men learn and play out different sex roles (Hondagneu-Sotelo 1999). As Pierrette Hondagneu-Sotelo contends, a sole focus on women ultimately marginalizes immigrant women because it retards "our understanding of how gender as a social system contextualizes migration processes for all immigrants" and, at the same time, stifles our ability to theorize "about the ways in which constructions of masculinities and femininities organize migration and migration outcomes" (Hondagneu-Sotelo 1999, 566).

In contrast to such views, we insist that gender's constitution can be examined with a sole focus on women. In taking a women-centric approach, we argue that migrant women are troubled by gender constraints throughout the process of migration. In documenting gender constraints and how women negotiate these constraints, our discussion does not require an analysis of men's experiences. Finally, an intersectional analysis that documents the mutual constitution of race, class, and gender in the experiences of migrant women, which we will also examine in this chapter, can be achieved without comparing the experiences of men and women.

Migrant Domestic Work

Of the estimated 86 million migrant workers worldwide, most are unskilled laborers (International Labor Organization 2005). Women make up 49 percent of the international migrant labor force, and the majority (83 percent) of "unskilled" female migrants are employed as domestic workers (International Labor Organization 2013).[1] The disproportionate representation of migrant women in domestic work signals that the "ideology of the housewife" indeed haunts their productive labor activities. The category of migrant domestic worker broadly refers to noncitizens employed as paid workers in private households. According to sociologist Cameron McDonald (2011), this categorization includes a wide range of workers including nannies, au pairs, elder caregivers, and housecleaners. Considering the majority of independent female migrants end up doing domestic work, the labor migration of women is arguably a movement from one household to another, illustrating the limits to the gender advancements that women achieve in migration. This suggests that women do not escape the ideology of female domesticity but only maintain it upon migration with their continuous performance of housework.

Notably, many states recognize the dependence of families on the labor of migrant domestic workers and accordingly allocate visas to domestic workers. This is the case across Asia, where domestic workers qualify for two-year legal residency in various states, including Hong Kong, Singapore, and Malaysia, as well as in Gulf Cooperative Council countries, where states also grant domestic workers legal residency for two years (Asia Pacific Forum on Women and Development 2010; Human Rights Watch 2010). Likewise, various Western countries, including Canada and Italy, grant working visas to domestic workers. In contrast to destinations in Asia and the Middle East, Canada and Italy grants migrant domestic workers the opportunity to transition to permanent residency. Under Canada's Live-In Caregivers Programme two years of continuous employment with a sponsoring family qualifies the migrant domestic worker to apply for "landed status." In Italy, migrant domestic workers can transition from holding a *permesso di soggiorno* (permit to stay) to a *carta di soggiorno* (residence card) after their continuous contribution to social security and payment of taxes for five years. The latter is equivalent to attaining permanent residency.

The migration of domestic workers represents a global movement of women that occurs in various spheres: global (South to North) or regional (East to West or South to South). The frequent *routes* of migration for domestic workers include their movement from Mexico and Central America into the households of working families in the United States (Hondagneu-Sotelo 2001), Sri Lankan women to Greece and West Asia (Gamburd 2000), Indonesians to East and West Asia (Silvey 2004; Lan 2006; Constable 2007), Ethiopian women to West Asia (Mahdavi 2011), Polish women to Germany and Italy (Lutz 2011), Caribbean women to Canada and the United States (Bakas and Stasiulis 1997), and Filipino care workers to more than 165 destinations across the globe (Parreñas 2001; Pratt 2012).

The retention of the ideology of female domesticity in migrant domestic work is also reflected in the legal incorporation of migrant domestic workers as family dependents and not independent workers. In many countries, the incorporation of migrant domestic workers places them in the liminal category of being "one of the family." For example, this is legally the case with au pairs, who by law are not considered workers but family helpers who receive an allowance instead of a wage (Anderson 2009). Yet, even if not legally inscribed, familial assumptions underlie the status of other types of domestic worker—nannies, elderly caregivers, and housecleaners. For instance, visa requirements for domestic workers in Asia and the Gulf states not only tie them to a citizen sponsor but also require them to reside in the home of their citizen sponsor (Asia Pacific Forum on Women and Development 2010; Human Rights Watch 2010; Parreñas 2001). In other words, the working visa of domestic workers does not render them an independent worker but rather a family dependent who is tied to a citizen-sponsor. To give a few examples, migrant domestic workers in Canada must work continuously for one sponsoring family for two years in order to qualify for landed status whereas a domestic worker in Taiwan is given a nonrenewable six-year contract that ties them to an employer-sponsor (Goldring and Landolt 2013; Valiani 2013). In the Gulf Cooperative Council nations, a domestic worker is bound to a *khafeel* and required to work as a condition of their legal residency (Goldring and Landolt 2013; Valiani 2013).

While other migrant contract workers share with domestic workers an employer sponsored legal status, domestic workers experience an aggravated relation of unequal dependency with their sponsor due to the live-in residency requirement. These two conditions combined reinforce the idea that domestic workers are family members and not workers. Feminist labor scholars have long argued that the construction of domestic workers as "one of the family" results in the nonrecognition of domestic work as labor and consequently leads to the justification of lower wages and the solicitation of unpaid labor by employers (Romero 2002; Rollins 1985).

The culture of maternalism, or the notion that women are natural caregivers, leads to unequal gender divisions of labor in the family. In a 2002 United Nations report, sociologist Ann Orloff lamented, "Across the developed countries, there is surely variation in the quality of the work itself, as well as in the exact mix of paid and unpaid work but the basic pattern is the same: men specialize in paid work while doing little unpaid, mainly caregiving, labour, and women do the bulk of unpaid work, increasingly in combination with paid work" (2002, 4). To get around this burden, some wealthier women have turned to low wage labor to relieve themselves of the second shift. States assist families in accessing low wage labor with the institution of *au pair* and other migrant care work programs. While the culture of maternalism creates a demand for low wage labor via foreign employment, it also shapes the incorporation of migrant workers by imposing terms and conditions that do not contradict this culture. State incorporation of migrant domestic workers as sponsored migrants not independent workers therefore gives them the status of quasi-family member.

As "one of the family," migrant domestic workers are legally incorporated as "shadow mothers," or what Cameron McDonald (2011) describes as a "puppet" of the working mother. Their presence is considered none other than an extension of the woman. As such, they are there to maintain the traditional gender order in the family and ease the impacts of women's labor market participation to this order. The constitution of domestic workers as "shadow mothers," one that is solidified in their conditional residency as family members upon migration, confirms that a culture of maternalism haunts migrant domestic workers by creating demand for labor but simultaneously relegating their legal status to a quasi-family member. The idea that women should take care of their own children and their own parents and do their own cooking and cleaning, regardless of their income contributions to the family, is a manifestation of the nonrecognition of domestic work as genuine labor by employers and the state. This affects not only the women of the household but also the women they hire to perform domestic work. Consequently, society struggles to recognize the labor performed by paid domestic workers, resulting in limited labor rights and a murky legal status for the migrants who do this work.

The continued ideological stranglehold of maternalism results in a paradoxical situation for migrant domestic workers: states recognize the need for their labor, but refuse to grant them independent legal status, transforming them into quasi family members. This paradox facilitates the simultaneous marketization and familialization of domestic work, which emerges from Arlie Hochschild's notion of a "stalled gender revolution," a stall that insists care work remains women's unpaid labor despite the increase in their paid labor activities (Hochschild and Machung 1989; Parreñas 2001; McDonald 2011). This tells us that states' immigration governance of migrant domestic workers as "one of the family" retains not just the familialization of care but also the designation of this labor as unpaid work to women.

Transnational Mothering

The gender stall in women's migration also manifests in their family life as visible in the gender tensions that constitute the experiences of transnational mothers. Pierrette Hondagneu-Sotelo and Ernestive Avila (1997) define "transnational mothering" as the reconstitution of the organizational arrangement of motherhood to accommodate the temporal and spatial separations forced by migration. Transnational mothering is not an exception but is instead a normative feature of the experiences of migrant women, including among others, Ukranian migrant mothers employed as domestic workers in Italy (Solari 2006), Polish migrants in Germany (Lutz 2011), migrant women in the United States from Mexico (Dreby 2010), El Salvador (Abrego 2009), and Honduras (Schmalzbauer 2005), and migrant women in the Philippine diaspora (Parreñas 2005). In the Philippines, nongovernmental organizations in the early 2000s estimated that more than 9 million children, a figure representing approximately 27 percent of the overall youth population, are growing up in the Philippines with at least one parent working outside the territorial boundaries of the nation (Parreñas 2005). Since then, that estimate has been increased to 10 million children (Madianou and Miller 2012). Considering the disproportionate number of women leaving the Philippines every year, we can assume that a sizeable number of them are children of migrant mothers. Numerous factors facilitate the formation of transnational families among migrant women. Structural factors that promote its formation include the conditions of employment in domestic work, migration laws that disqualify temporary migrant workers from family reunification, and the low wages of migrant women workers; cultural factors include the extended kinship base that provides child-care support for prospective migrant women and the extended history of women's employment in various sending countries of migration (Parreñas 2001).

Transnational mothering is either a short-term or a long-term arrangement. In Austria, transnational mothers from Romania and Slovakia are separated from their children for a short duration as they circulate between home and host country. Slovakians interchangeably spend two weeks in the home and in the host country, while Romanians spend one month in each site (Bauer 2013). In contrast, migrant Filipinas spend a longer period being away from their children. A study on transnational families that Rhacel Parreñas conducted in the Philippines in 2000 and 2001 shows that in ten years, migrant mothers spent on average less than six months with their now young adult children (Parreñas 2005). Geraldine Pratt (2012) likewise found that participants in Canada's Live-in Caregivers Programme are separated from their children for five to six years before their children have the opportunity to reunite with them in Canada. In their study of Filipino transnational families in the United Kingdom and Philippines, Madianou and Miller (2012) likewise found an extended duration of separation beyond a decade in some families.

Imposing geographical distance on mothers and children, the practice of transnational mothering ruptures the ideological foundation of a traditional family, as it questions not only the idea that biological mothers should raise their children exclusively but also that mothers and children should reside together. This arrangement radically reshapes common ideas of appropriate mothering. First, it expands "definitions of motherhood to encompass breadwinning that may require long-term physical separations" (Hondagneu-Sotelo and Avila 1997, 562). Second, it involves mothering from a distance, which some would interpret as abandonment of one's conventional mothering duties, though others would insist not. Relying on advancements in telecommunication, women compress time and space and use the Internet, telephone, and postal mail to nurture their children from afar and not up close. Regular communication—whether through telephone calls, remittances, letters, voice recordings, emails, SMS messages, or photographs—allows mothers simultaneously to be "here and there," a process described by Madianou and Miller (2012) as a mediation of relationships.

Transnational mothering seems to suggest a disruption of the traditional gender division of labor in the household. This disruption, according to Mirca Madianou (2012), results in ambivalent sentiments among migrant mothers, who feel liberated from the traditional duties of nurturing their children up close but personally fulfilled by their fulfillment of such duties unconventionally from afar. Regardless of the personal sentiments of women, a key to understanding transnational mothering is that it does not redefine mothering but instead reconstitutes its performance from occurring up close to taking place from a distance. Although it is understood that there are different personal meanings to the experience of mothering, transnational mothers have not completely shaken off their continued responsibility to care for children. As Parreñas (2005) has argued, it is the advancements in communication technology that facilitate the retention of traditional gender norms because they enable women to continuously perform their nurturing duties in the family. Joanna Dreby (2006, 2010) likewise noticed the greater emotional involvement expected of mothers than fathers in Mexican transnational families. As she states, "mothers' relationships with their children in Mexico are highly dependent on demonstrating emotional intimacy from a distance, whereas fathers' relationships lie in their economic success as migrant workers" (Dreby 2006, 34). Leisy Abrego (2009) similarly observed that Salvadoran transnational mothers firmly maintained their caregiving responsibilities from a far via their selfless commitment to their children's well being. Men, she noted, did not.

Although transnational mothers might redefine mothering as breadwinning for themselves, we should recognize that children and the society back home might not necessarily accept such efforts. Indeed, they may reject such a redefinition. The backlash confronting migrant mothers in various home societies indicates this to be the case. In the Philippines, the public sees children of transnational mothers as victims who have been abandoned by their mothers. The public dismisses women's migration, seeing it as not just bad for the welfare of children but dangerous to the sanctity of the family. Interestingly, the public does not disdain migrant fathers as they do migrant mothers. In the Philippines, the prevailing view is that if a parent must migrate, it is better for the father to do so than the mother. The negative view associated with women's migration seems to haunt migrant mothers not only in the Philippines but also in many other sending countries of domestic workers, including Poland and Romania.[2] In Poland, for instance, public discourse labels the children of migrant women as "Euro-orphans," meaning children who have been orphaned by the outflow of migrant mothers to Western Europe (Urbanksa 2009). Newspaper reports in Poland and Romania likewise depict transnational mothering, negatively. A newsprint article on Euro-orphans, for instance, quotes the Minister of Education in Poland as blaming failing test scores and growing truancy on parental migration. As she notes, "Kids get into trouble with the law, have social problems, behavior and attitude problems in school, and absences" (*Chicago Tribune*, 2008). Likewise, an article in the *New York Times* describes the outmigration of women as a "national tragedy" that has triggered social upheaval in Romania. The article blames not only the collapse of the Romanian family but also the abandonment and delinquency of children on the migration of women (Bifelski 2009). In this article, the migration of mothers is said to result in severe psychological difficulties among children and even suicide for a number of them. Notably, increasing evidence suggests that media reports about the delinquency and difficulties of the children of migrant mothers are not based on concrete studies (Slany et al. 2010; Urbanska 2009). In fact, studies do not support the negative assertions frequently associated with women's migration. Instead, studies show that the maintenance of transnational families results neither in children's poorer performance in school nor in their increased criminal activities (Parreñas 2005; Urbanska 2009).

How do we explain the vilification of migrant mothers in countries such as the Philippines and Poland? Why is there a moralistic compulsion to equate their migration with the abandonment of children? We could speculate that national identity is frequently tied to the idea of women as the reproducers of the nation. Hence, we see the tendency to naturalize mothering as a reaction against the social transformations encouraged by women's labor and migration in countries as diverse as the Philippines, Poland, and Romania. We could also assume that the family in its traditional sense remains a central institution that defines the cultural identity of a nation. The backlash against migrant mothers in countries as disparate as the Philippines and Poland attests to the limits in the gender advancements achieved by transnational mothers. Breadwinning has not eased their nurturing responsibilities in the family. Their efforts to become breadwinners have even resulted in their vilification as "bad mothers," suggesting a stall in the reconstitution of gender facilitated by women's migration in the contemporary global economy.

Marriage Migration

The reconstitution of gender norms is further complicated when women migrate independently for marriage. Like women's labor migration, marriage migration to developed countries may signal women's liberation through escaping cultural monitoring, parental surveillance, filial obligations, and economic restraints. Recent works on contemporary marriage migration highlight migrants' enhanced sense of agency in their decision to choose romantic partners and spouses and by gaining an upper hand in marriage negotiations and family life (Constable 2003; Faier 2009). Although women may flee their domestic obligations at home, upon migration they become subordinate to the expectations of their husband's home as a wife and mother. This suggests that marriage migration does not lead to the breakdown of the "ideology of the housewife" but, rather, to its continuation through the movement from one patriarchal home to yet another.

Contemporary marriage migration reflects a female-dominated migration flow where women enter through family reunification and formation (Belanger and Linh 2011). The earliest accounts of marriage migration to the United States were in the form of "picture brides" where foreign women were sent to marry unwedded Japanese and Korean migrant workers in the western frontier (Glenn 1988; Jameson 1976; Sinke 1999; Enns 2005). Later in the twentieth century, the advent of international marriage agencies facilitated the rise of the "mail-order bride" phenomenon, where women seeking marriage abroad would be displayed in catalogs for the selection of men in other countries. In recent years, the development of Internet-based international marriage agencies through technological advancement has greatly broadened the scope of marriage migration with women from Southeast Asia, East Asia, Central Asia, and Latin America matched with men from mostly developed countries[3].

Since gaining visibility in the past few decades, feminists, popular media, and policymakers have critiqued the phenomenon of mail-order brides as women marrying out of economic desperation and selling themselves into servitude. These views are lodged in Western feminist paradigms of gender inequality that ignore cultural specificities of gender and view Third World women as subordinate to men. These feminist assumptions underlie contemporary anti-trafficking discourses on mail-order brides as examples of "trafficking in women" and victims of sexual and economic slavery. Anti-trafficking organizations often include mail-order brides in their classifications and conflate them with prostitutes. Such views on mail-order brides have informed national and global policies on marriage migration that have further hindered the movement of women for marriage. For example, in a United States Senate (2004) hearing on "bride trafficking," foreign brides were described as coming from "countries where women are oppressed ... where domestic violence against women is condoned, if not encouraged" (7). Such reports are not based on any hard empirical data but rather individual cases of abuse and violence that are made representative of all marriage migrants. The accounts of trafficked brides furthermore affirms the essentalizing, universalizing, and orientalist tendencies of feminist and anti-trafficking discourses that view women from the Third World as "condensed symbols of oppression, subordination and victimhood" (Mohanty 2003).

At its core, the retention of ideology of female domesticity in marriage migration is rooted in the preservation of gendered roles in traditional institutions of marriage. Many men from developed countries participating in romance "introduction" agencies openly seek out family-minded women with traditional feminine values who are willing to assume the traditional gendered division of labor and carry out reproductive work in the home. Nicole Constable (2003) observed that Western men with a history of failed relationships with Western women desire "good old-fashioned" relationships where roles are "separate but equal." Felicity Schaeffer's (2013) male romance-tour participants additionally voiced their preferences for Latinas over Western women, saying that Latinas have "better genes" as lovers and mothers and are more "authentic" in their regard for feminine values than Western women. These men seek an alternative to feminist-minded Western women, who are viewed as career hungry and not family oriented. However, sometimes men's desires for "traditional women" are ideologically opposed to the desires of migrant women who aspire for cosmopolitan modernity. As Schaeffer (2013) found in her study, Mexican professional women often view transnational marriages as opportunities to work, occupy consumer spaces, and experience heightened mobility and "equitable love." This was also true for mainland Chinese women married to infirm Taiwanese war veterans who migrate for marriage but also for better work opportunities in Taiwan. These women therefore must negotiate their modern cosmopolitan desires with men desiring more traditional wives in transnational arrangements of love and marriage (Lu 2012).

In countries like South Korea and Taiwan, the "ideology of the housewife" and other traditional gender norms are maintained through state-mandated biopolitical projects for population control. In East Asia, low birth rates and sharp population ageing have led to rapid demographic changes and a restructuring of the family order. The increasing rates of educated and working single women refusing traditional roles (Belanger 2010) and moving into urban centers have created "bride shortages" in rural areas. As a response, governments have turned to marriage migration as a solution to the female deficit with migrant women replacing Korean women in rural households. By replacing local women with foreign women, the state facilitates the retention of the ideology of women as the biological reproducers of the nation. From the state's perspective, migrant brides allow nations to continue and maintain patriarchal family structures in spite of national women's increasing urbanization, social mobility, and migration. In the past few decades, marriage migration has become a visible presence in ethnically homogenous countries, comprising 15 percent of the population in Taiwan and 8 percent in South Korea in 2009 (Belanger 2010).

In the ethnically homogenous nations of East Asia, government-sponsored assimilation projects serve to ethnicize migrant mothers and their children into Korean subjects and erase the mother's cultural identity. Minjeong Kim (2013) describes the process of ethnicizing migrant mothers for "ethnicized maternal citizenship," in which migrant wives must express mother-citizen practices according to the husband's ethnic and cultural identity (6). The projects are often couched in the rhetoric of "multiculturalism" that celebrates cultural difference by assimilating the wife into the husband's dominant cultural identity. In Korea, Japan, and Hong Kong, deepening concerns about the incompetent childrearing of migrant mothers have led state governments to create "multicultural" centers for women geared toward "cultural" and language education.

Some centers sponsor mothering workshops aimed at educating migrant women in the proper way of being an ethnic housewife and raising their children as ethnic citizens (Faier 2009; Newendorp 2008; Kim, 2013). In one Korean mothering class, women are given "cultural lessons" entrenched in gendered and ethnocentric rhetoric; they are guided through demonstrations of tea ceremony and cloth dyeing and taught the basics of feminine topics and expressions on shopping as well as dealing with in-laws. These examples attest to the notion that marriage migration not only reinstates gender but also racial and ethnic constraints on migrant women. These ethnic assimilationist projects serve to integrate migrant women into the nation as docile reproducers of national citizens.

For older marriage migrants, gender norms are maintained in their social reproductive labor of domestic and care work. In Taiwan, marriages between divorced mainland Chinese women and elderly Taiwanese veterans are common—as a mutually beneficial strategy that supports women's desires for business or their children's education and men's desires to invest in old-age security (Lu 2012). Melanie Lu (2012) demonstrates the mutual and equalizing features of these marriages through her notion of the couples' "reciprocity of care"—reversal of roles that show veterans doing domestic and care work for their wives while the wives are working to supplement their husbands' pensions. While reciprocal care relations transgress gender roles through enabling women's labor participation, these arrangements do not ultimately nullify other gender constraints faced in women's migration. Mainland Chinese migrant wives still undergo gendered constraints in their daily family lives, enduring cultural monitoring, caretaking responsibilities, downgraded labor options, lack of kin, and vulnerabilities related to their precarious legal status. For example, although men tend to assume domestic and care work, family and community members still place cultural and social expectations on migrant wives to perform domestic duties in the home. Furthermore, women working outside the home experience structural constraints in the labor market. Migrant women with work experience and education may only find low-wage jobs that fill labor shortages, further retaining the operation of traditional gender norms. Ironically, many mainland Chinese wives become paid care workers in the commercial care market in Taiwan and provide docile and subservient labor to others (Lu 2012, 248). Finally, migrant women are further constrained by their murky legal status. In Taiwan, marital law renders foreign women legally dependent on their husbands, which can rescind the financial independence accorded them by their labor market participation. In Taiwan, Chinese migrant women married to Taiwanese veterans are only entitled to a three-year temporary visa, with significant periods of delay for naturalization. In addition, while the husband may entitle his wife to his inheritance and pension, many veterans die before their mainland wives obtain citizenship leaving them to face deportation.

Traditional gender ideologies are further maintained in the legal incorporation of marriage migrants in the host country. Immigration laws in many receiving states simultaneously work toward upholding traditional family order while excluding "undesirable" groups. Schaeffer (2013) points out that the institution of marriage is based on the system of coverture whereby women's rights are dependent on their husbands (36–37).

In the United States, South Korea, Taiwan, and other destination countries contemporary immigration policies on international marriages increasingly reflect the terms of coverture; migrant women under a conditional status must rely on their citizen spouses for financial and legal support for at least the first two years until the husbands petitions for her naturalization (Schaeffer 2013; Kim 2013; Belanger 2010). A woman's status is further jeopardized at the local level when the husband's families monitor and confiscate her passports and IDs (Choo 2013). Consequently, these policies serve to exacerbate women's dependency on their husbands and leave women vulnerable to abuse. In Taiwan, an immigrant spouse married for less than two years can only get a divorce without facing deportation if she gives birth to a Taiwanese child (Friedman 2012).

Marriage migrants from the educated and upwardly mobile classes in developing countries are often viewed as exercising more autonomy and entering into more equitable marriage relations. These educated and professional middle-class women are viewed as exceptions to the "typical 'mail-order brides' popularly thought to marry men ... out of poverty and desperation" (Schaeffer 2013: 54). As "modern" women living in a developing country, they turn to foreign men and lifestyles as an escape from the patriarchal structures and traditional systems of family (Schaeffer 2013; Kelsky 2001; Kim 2013). Middle-class women from developing countries, therefore, will sometimes see themselves as "marrying down" to a man in the developed world if he is not from the "executive" class. The higher status of these women is viewed as giving them the power to negotiate equitable relations in marriage and also the luxury to "fall in love." This assumption overlooks the fact that "average" men of the developed world still possess more economic and legal power than the middle-class woman, which can lead to very unequal relations. Furthermore, middle class migrant women still maintain the ideologies of the housewife upon migration as Western men specifically look to Mexican women being better wives and mothers (Schaeffer 2013). While social standing can negotiate individualized relationships, it can also facilitate the retention of traditional gender roles and norms.

Conclusion

This chapter examined the reconstitution of gender in contemporary women's migration through an empirical analysis of migrant domestic work, transnational mothering, and women's marriage migration. More specifically, it complicated contemporary feminist arguments about the gender configurations in women's migration as a disruption to the old gender order as well as the association of women's migration with upward mobility and the eventual rejection of female domesticity. A number of contemporary feminist scholars argue that women's independent migration leads to their greater autonomy and ultimately to a breakdown of the "ideology of the housewife." Upon migration women supposedly escape patriarchal pressures and responsibilities, threats of domestic violence, and female impoverishment. In addition, women supposedly redefine motherhood with their newfound role as wage earners and household mediators. For example, the sending of remittances has shown to impact women's power and public participation in home countries. As observed by Belanger and Linh (2011), sending communities of female marriage migrants in rural Vietnam began to prefer female births over male births due to women's increased power via remittances.

Whereas the dominant paradigm in the study of women's migration asserts that migrant women's labor participation and practice of choice in marriage markets has led to significant advancements in gender, our review of the literature also finds that women's positions as agents and pioneers of globalization do not translate to their equal standing vis-à-vis men. We still find that women's migration is a movement from one system of gender inequality to another. A deeper understanding of women's migration shows us that migrant women face limits to the reconstitution of gender in their everyday experiences of migration. One of the major pull factors for women's migration has been to meet the need for domestic labor produced by the gender advancement among professional women in the First World. In turn, migrant women enter a country with a patriarchal system that designates housework to women corresponding to the high demand for domestic work worldwide. Such pathways insist on women's natural inclination for care and affirm their primary place in the home. Additionally, women's movement away from their families does not necessarily relieve them of their traditional duties of mothering. Instead, women are expected to negotiate gender constraints in their home society from afar as they confront gender constraints in the host society. For example, in the large sending country of the Philippines, the public remains suspicious of migrant women and their "neglected" households despite women surpassing men in the number of overseas labor migrants (Parreñas 2005). The retention of traditional gender norms is further corroborated in studies that include transnational fathers. On separate occasions, Dreby's (2006, 2010) and Abrego's (2009) observations on Latin American transnational families showed migrant fathers to have less involvement in their children's lives due to their own gendered expectations of economic success. In the Philippines and Eastern Europe, public furor over the "abandonment" of children conflated with fears of increasing juvenile delinquency has condemned women's migration and reaffirmed the preference for the father's movement (Parreñas 2005; Bifelski 2009). The migrant or domestic father's retention of traditional gender norms in contemporary migration suggests that women's movement only serves to recuperate existing gender norms for the continued performance of mothering from afar.

The reconstitution of gender norms becomes aggravated when women migrate for marriage. From its inception, cross-cultural marriage migration has faced harrowing criticism as the sale and commodification of Third World brides. Western antitrafficking discourses conflate marriage migrants with trafficked persons. In response to narrow definitions, contemporary feminist writings have worked to confront sensationalized and case-based representations of violence and abuse in marriages through an understanding of the gendered heterogeneity of cross-cultural marriages. These works highlight women's agency in their selection of spouses as well as their upper-handedness in their relationships with men from developed countries. Yet, marriage migration remains a slippery slope for women from developing countries. Although some studies highlight women's choice in marital selection and their upward mobility via marriage, women's marriage migration serves to stall the gender advancements migration affords women. While women are indeed not naïve in their decisions to marry, ideological gaps exist between migrant women's desires for modernity and developed world men's desires for women of yesteryear and tradition. In fact, many husbands (as well as state governments) seek out "traditional" and family-minded women who will carry out reproductive labor at home.

In conclusion, we argue that women's migration results in the simultaneous retention and rejection of the ideology of female domesticity. We built on contemporary feminist works that focus on the agency, upward mobility, and movement of migrant women to show how gender constraints exist in the form of legal and social controls both in the sending and receiving countries. We also drew from an intersectional perspective to see how race, class, and gender are constituted in women's experiences of migration. It becomes evident in their experiences that beyond personal rewards and moments of socioeconomic uplift, migrant women are still being subject to the processes of racialization, feminization/domestication, and criminalization in host and home societies. These hurdles constrain the advancements enabled by the independent migration of women and thereby stall the gender revolution instigated by women's migration.

Notes

1. Domestic workers migrate to carry out cleaning and caring labor (Anderson 2000) in countries with official labor recruitment programs for domestic workers, including Canada (Bakan and Stasiulis 1997; Pratt 2004); Denmark (Stenum 2008); Italy (Parreñas 2001); Spain (Escriva and Skinner 2008); Taiwan (Lan 2006), Singapore (Yeoh and Huang 1998; Yeoh and Huang 1999); the Middle East (Gamburd 2000), including Saudi Arabia (Silvey 2004, 2009), the United Arab Emirates (Mahdavi 2011) and Israel (Shamir 2010); and to those without such programs, including Germany (Lutz 2011; Slaney, Kontos, and Liapi 2010) and the United States (Hondagneu-Sotelo 2001; Cohen 1995), Germany and Italy (Slaney et al. 2010). Filipino women migrate to work in more than 160 countries (Parreñas 2001).
2. In Poland, the children of domestic workers are commonly referred to as *Euro Orphans*, a term suggesting the "abandonment" of children for the care of families in Western Europe.
3. These flows include: Filipina and Vietnamese to Asian men (Wang 2007; Choo 2013; Faier 2009; Belanger 2010; Kim, 2013; Suzuki 2003), divorced Chinese women to rural Taiwan men (Lu 2012; Friedman 2012), Pakistani brides to co-ethnic British born (Charsley, Benson, and Van Hear 2012), Eastern European women to Western European men (Charlsey and Liversage 2013), Asian urbanites to white men (Thai 2008; Kelsky 2001; Constable 2003), and professional Latinas to US men (Schaffer 2013).

References

Abrego, L. 2009. "Economic Well-Being in Salvadoran Transnational Families: How Gender Affects Remittance Practices." *Journal of Marriage and Family* 71: 1070–1085.

Anderson, B. 2000. *Doing the Dirty Work? The Global Politics of Domestic Labor* London: Zed Books.

Anderson, B. 2009. "What's in a Name? Immigration Controls and Subjectivities: The Case of Au Pairs and Domestic Worker Visa Holders in the UK." *Subjectivity* 29: 407–424.

Asia Pacific Forum. 2010. *The Right to Unite: A Handbook on Domestic Worker Rights across Asia*. Chiangmai, Thailand: Asia Pacific Forum on Women, Law and Development.

Bakan, A., and D. Stasiulis, eds. 1997. *Not One of the Family: Foreign Domestic Workers in Canada*. Toronto: University of Toronto Press.

Bauer, G. 2013. "Migrant Care Workers in Austria: Balancing Formal and Informal Care Across Borders," Presented at *Family Life in the Age of Migration and Mobility: Theory, Policy and Practice*, Norrkoping, Sweden. September 2013: 16–20.

Belanger, D. 2010. "Marriage with Foreign Women in East Asia: Bride Trafficking or Voluntary Migration?" *Population and Societies* 469: 1–4.

Belanger, D., and T. G. Linh. 2011. "The Impact of Transnational Migration on Gender and Marriage in Sending Communities of Vietnam." *Current Sociology* 59 (1): 59–77.

Bifelski, D. 2009. "In Romania, Children Left behind Suffer the Strains of Migration." *New York Times*. February 14, 2009. See http://www.nytimes.com/2009/02/15/world/europe/15romania.html. Accessed June 8, 2009.

Charsley, K., B. Storer-Church, M. Benson, and N. Van Hear. 2012. "Marriage-Related Migration to the UK." *International Migration Review* 46 (4): 861–890.

Charsley, K., and A. Liversage, 2013. "Transforming Polygamy: Migration, Transnationalism and Multiple Marriages among Muslim Minorities." *Global Networks* 13 (1): 60–78.

Chicago Tribune. 2008. "Poland Sees Host of Problems among 'Euro-Orphans.'" September 21.

Choo, H. Y. 2013. "Migrant Women, Feminist Advocacy, and Gendered Morality in South Korea." *Gender & Society* 27 (4): 445–468.

Constable, N. 2007. *Maid to Order in Hong Kong: Stories of Migrant Workers*. 2nd. ed. Ithaca, NY: Cornell University Press.

Constable, N. 2003. *Romance on a Global Stage: Pen Pals, Virtual Ethnography, and "Mail Order" Marriages*. Berkeley and Los Angeles, CA: University of California Press.

Dreby, J. 2006. "Honor and Virtue: Mexican Parenting in the Transnational Context." *Gender & Society* 20: 32–60.

Dreby, J. 2010. *Divided by Borders: Mexican Migrants and Their Children*. Berkeley and Los Angeles: University of California Press.

Enns, C. 2005. *Hearts West: The True Stories of Mail-Order Brides on the Frontier*. Guilford, CT: Globe Pequot Press.

Escriva, A., and E. Skinner. 2008. "Domestic Work and Transnational Care Chains in Spain." In *Migration and Domestic Work: A European Perspective on a Global Theme*, edited by Lutz, Helma, 113–126. Aldershot, UK: Ashgate.

Faier, L. 2009. *Intimate Encounters. Filipina Women and the Remaking of Rural Japan*. Berkeley and Los Angeles: University of California Press.

Freeman, C. 2001. "Is Local: Global as Feminine: Masculine? Rethinking the Gender of Globalization." *Signs* 26 (4): 1007–1037.

Friedman, S. 2012. "Adjudicating the Intersection of Marital Immigration, Domestic Violence, and Spousal Murder: China-Taiwan Marriages and Competing Legal Domains." *Indiana Journal of Global Legal Studies* 19 (1): 221–255.

Gamburd, M. 2000. *The Kitchen Spoon's Handle*. Ithaca, NY: Cornell University Press.

George, S. 2005. *When Women Come First: Gender and Class in Transnational Migration*. Berkeley and Los Angeles: University of California Press.

Glenn, E. N. 1988. *Issei, Nisei, Warbride: Three Generations of Japanese American Women in Domestic Service*. Philadelphia, PA: Temple Unviersity Press.

Goldring, L., and P. Landolt, eds. 2013. *Producing and Negotiating Non-Citizenship: Precarious Legal Status in Canada*. Toronto, Ontario: University of Toronto Press.

Grasmuck, S., and P. Pessar. 1991. *Between Two Islands: Dominican International Migration*. Berkeley and Los Angeles: University of California Press.

Hochschild, A., and A. Machung. 1989. *The Second Shift*. New York: Viking Penguin.

Hondagneu-Sotelo, P. 1994. *Gendered Transitions*. Berkeley and Los Angeles: University of California Press.

Hondagneu-Sotelo, P. 1999. "Introduction: Gender and Contemporary U.S. Immigration." *American Behavioral Scientist* 42 (4): 565–576.

Hondagneu-Sotelo, P. 2001. *Domestica*. Berkeley and Los Angeles: University of California Press.

Hondagneu Sotelo, P., and E. Avila. "'I'm Here but I'm There': The Meanings of Latina Transnational Motherhood." *Gender & Society* 11 (1997): 548–571, 331.

Human Rights Watch. 2010. *Slow Reform: Protection of Migrant Domestic Workers in Asia and the Middle East*. New York: Human Rights Watch.

International Labor Organization. 2005. "Facts on Labor Migration." Geneva, Switzerland: International Labor Organization.

International Labor Organization. 2013. *Domestic Workers across the World: Global and Regional Statistics and the Extent of Legal Protection*. Geneva, Switzerland: International Labor Organization.

Jameson, E. 1976. "Imperfect Unions Class and Gender in Cripple Creek." *Frontiers: A Journal of Women's Studies* 1 (2): 89–117.

Kelsky, K. 2001. *Women on the Verge*. Durham, NC: Duke University Press.

Kim, M. 2013. "Citizenship Projects for Marriage Migrants in South Korea Intersecting Motherhood with Ethnicity and Class." *Social Politics* 20(4): 455–481.

Lan, P. 2006. *Global Cinderellas*. Durham, NC: Duke University Press.

Lu, M. C. 2012. "Transnational Marriages as a Strategy of Care Exchange: Veteran Soldiers and Their Mainland Chinese Spouses in Taiwan." *Global Networks* 12 (2): 233–251.

Lutz, H. 2011. *The New Maids: Transnational Women and the Care Economy*. London: Zed Books.

Madianou, M. 2012. "Migration and the Accentuated Ambivalence of Motherhood: The Role of ICTs in Filipino Transnational Families." *Global Networks* 12 (3): 277–295.

Madianou, M., and D. Miller. 2012. *Migration and New Media: Transnational Families and Polymedia*. London and New York: Routledge.

Mahdavi, P. 2011. *Gridlock: Labor, Migration and Human Trafficking in Dubai*. Redwood City, CA: Stanford University Press.

McDonald, C. 2011. *Shadow Mothering*. Berkeley and Los Angeles: University of California Press.

Mies, M, 1982. *Lace Makers of Narsapur: Indian Housewives Produce for the World Market*. London: Zed Books.

Mohanty, C. 1988. "Under Western Eyes: Feminist Scholarship and Colonial Discourses." *Feminist Review* 30: 61–88.

Mohanty, C. 2003. *Feminism without Borders*. Durham, NC: Duke University Press.

Newendorp, N. D. 2008. *Uneasy Reunions: Immigration, Citizenship, and Family Life in Post-1997 Hong Kong*. Redwood City, CA: Stanford University Press.

Orloff, A. 2002. "Women's Employment and Welfare Regimes Globalization, Export Orientation and Social Policy in Europe and North America." Social Policy and Development Programme Paper No. 12, 1–39. Geneva: United Nations Research Institute for Social Development.

Parreñas, R. 2001. *Servants of Globalization: Women, Migration and Domestic Work*. Redwood City, CA: Stanford University Press.

Parreñas, R. 2005. *Children of Global Migration: Transnational Families and Gendered Woes*. Redwood City, CA: Stanford University Press.

Parreñas, R. 2008. *The Force of Domesticity: Filipina Migrants and Globalization*. New York: New York University Press.

Parreñas, R. Forthcoming. *Servants of Globalization: Women, Migration and Domestic Work*. 2nd. ed. Redwood City, CA: Stanford University Press.

Pratt, G. 2004. *Working Feminism* Philadelphia, PA: Temple University Press.

Pratt, G. 2012. *Families Apart: Migrant Mothers and the Conflicts of Labor and Love*. Minneapolis: University of Minnesota Press.

Romero, M. 2002. *Maid in the USA*. New York: Routledge.

Rollins, J. 1985. *Between Women*. Philadelphia, PA: Temple University Press.

Schaeffer, F. A. 2013. *Love and Empire: Cybermarriage and Citizenship across the Americas*. New York: New York University Press.

Schmalzbauer, L. 2005. "Searching for Wages and Mothering from Afar: The Case of Honduran Transnational Families." *Journal of Marriage and Family* 66: 1217–1231.

Shamir, H. 2010. "The State of Care: Rethinking the Distributive Effects of Familial Care Policies in Liberal Welfare States." *American Journal of Comparative Law* 58 (4): 953–986.

Silvey, R. 2004. "Transnational Migration and the Gender Politics of Scale: Indonesian Domestic Workers in Saudi Arabia, 1997-2000." *Singapore Journal of Tropical Geography* 25 (2): 141–155.

Silvey, R. 2009. "Transnational Rights and Wrongs: Moral Geographies of Gender and Migration." *Philosophical Topics* 37(1): 75–91.

Sinke, S. 1999. "Migration for Labor, Migration for Love: Marriage and Family Formation Across Borders." *OAH Magazine of History* 14 (1): 17–21.

Slaney, K., M. Kontos, and M. Liapi, eds. 2010. *Women in New Migrations: Current Debates in European Societies*. Krakow, Poland: Jagiellonian University Press.

Solari, C. 2006. "Professionals and Saints: How Immigrant Careworkers Negotiate Gendered Identities at Work." *Gender & Society* 20: 301–331.

Stenum, H. 2008. "Au Pair in Denmark: Cheap Labour or Cultural Exchange." Copenhagen: FOA Trade and Labour.

Suzuki, N. 2003. "Transgressing 'Victims': Reading Narratives of 'Filipina Brides.'" *Critical Asian Studies* 35 (3): 399–420.

Thai, H. C. 2008. *For Better or for Worse: Vietnamese International Marriages in the New Global. Economy* Rutgers, NJ: Rutgers University Press.

Urbanksa, S. 2009. "Mothers of the Nation as a Target of Public Therapy: Transnational Parenting and Moral Panic in Poland." Paper presented in Mosaics of Transnational Spaces Workshop. Krakow, Poland. May 9.

United States Senate. 2004. "Human Trafficking: Mail-Order Bride Abuses." *Human Trafficking Data and Documents* Paper 49. Committee on Foreign Relations. July 13.

Valiani, S. 2013. "The Shifting Landscape of Contemporary Canadian Immigration Policy: The Rise of Temporary Migration and Employer-Driven Immigration." In *Producing and Negotiating Non-Citizenship: Precarious Legal Status in Canada*, edited by L. Goldring and P. Landolt, 55–70. Toronto. Ontario: University of Toronto Press.

Wang, H. 2007. "Hidden Spaces of Resistance of the Subordinated: Case Studies from Vietnamese Female Migrant Partners in Taiwan." *International Migration Review* 41 (3): 706–727.

Yeoh, B., and S. Huang. 1998. "Negotiating Public Space: Strategies and Styles of Migrant Female Domestic Workers in Singapore." *Urban Studies* 35 (3): 583–602.

Yeoh, B., and S. Huang. 1999. "Spaces at the Margin: Migrant Domestic Workers and the Development of Civil Society in Singapore." *Environment and Planning A* 31 (7): 1149–1167.

CHAPTER 25

MILITARIZATION AND WAR

KATHY E. FERGUSON AND SHARAIN SASHEIR NAYLOR

INTRODUCTION

WHEN the Women's Studies Department at the University of Hawai'i first submitted a request to offer the class Women, War and the Military in 1986, there were problems. First, while the university committee had immediately liked the proposal for a class called Women and Madness, they stumbled over one named Women, War and the Military, unable to see the relevance of the latter. Second, there were almost no resources other than Cynthia Enloe's *Does Khaki Become You?* (1983), Mady Segal's early sociological analysis of women in the military (1982), Judith Stiehm's collection about women's roles and responsibilities in war (1983), and some critical readings of the relation between masculinity and war by Marc Fasteau (1974).

Things have changed. The 1980s saw the emergence of an extensive and growing feminist literature on militarization and war. It was preceded by considerable attention to the subject during the first wave of the women's movement: organizations such as the Women's Peace Party; the Women's International League for Peace and Freedom; the No-Conscription League; and numerous anarchist, socialist, syndicalist, and progressive groups, including such well-known individuals as Emma Goldman, Rosa Luxemburg, Helen Keller, and Jane Addams, wrote, spoke, and organized to oppose war and militarization. However, the return to engagement with war and militarism in feminism's second wave was not, for the most part, building on the earlier feminist work but, more commonly, on the intellectual tools and political resources available in the late twentieth century.

Enloe's cleverly titled book *Does Khaki Become You?* launched her groundbreaking investigations into the global patterns of women's military participation along with states' mobilization and naturalization of patriarchal gender practices. In 1987, Carol Cohn's pathbreaking *Signs* article, "Sex and Death in the Rational World of Defense

Intellectuals," offered a discursive analysis of the sexualized and gendered means of enunciation in the world of war planners. Also in 1987, Jean Bethke Elshtain's *Women and War* challenged the "congealed typifications" of peaceful women and violent men, asking how those images became dominant, and at what price (xiv). Sara Ruddick's *Maternal Thinking: Toward a Politics of Peace* (1989), in contrast, sought to build a feminist peace politics on the standpoint made available by the labor of mothering, while avoiding the essentialism that Elshtain rightly rendered problematic. They and subsequent scholars have invited us to see that militaries, wars, and war systems depend on women's labor and on patriarchal gendering and sexualizing practices to function and even to exist at all.

Today, there is a plenitude of rich interdisciplinary, transnational scholarship expanding and transforming the questions we can ask, the frames of analysis we can employ, and the practical connections we can make with global feminist activism. Feminist work in this broad arena has been stimulated by many factors, including at least these elements: the expanding energies and engagements of feminist theories; the growth in interdisciplinarity and global scope of feminist scholarship; and the devastating impact of armed conflict, along with the mixed opportunities available to women in military institutions. Much of this scholarship has inherited as well as expanded the initial questions raised by Enloe, Cohn, Elshtain, and Ruddick thirty years ago. Where are the women? How are wars and militarizing practices gendered? What is the relation of gender and sexuality to the making of war and peace?

Two Central Dilemmas

Two dilemmas (at least) dwell within this scholarship, two related intellectual and political tensions that need to be mediated and mined rather than resolved or ignored in feminist research and activism. The first has to do with the questions we ask, the second with the goals that we seek. We think of the first dilemma as the *women and* approach versus the *gendering of* frame. Early women's studies classes tended to employ the *women and* approach, bringing women into areas of study where they were previously neglected: women and politics, women and crime, women and art, and so forth. Sometimes mocked as an "add women and stir" approach, *women and* gradually gave way to *gendering of* questions, wherein gender as a material and semiotic practice provides a lens of analysis. We think of the second dilemma as the *let us in* agenda versus the *set us free* demand. This tension is primarily political: do feminists want women to be included within the existing structures of power and opportunity, or do we want to subvert and transform those institutions in a more radical way? The two dilemmas are connected: asking how women can be incorporated more fairly and equally into existing institutions tends to support demands to reform those institutions, while asking how those institutions create and reflect gendering and sexualizing practices tends to give rise to more radical efforts to transform those practices. The two projects also stand in tension, since advocates of transforming militaries and societies often view efforts at reform as dangerous capitulations to war and militarization, while the reformers tend to view the radicals as impractical and counterproductive. Recognizing that we must both live in the world at hand, and struggle toward the world that could be, we argue for cultivating these tensions as productive and enduring: we should retain both frames of analysis and pursue both political agendas, looking for bridges as well as recognizing incompatibilities. Both frames of inquiry can create important new knowledge, and can learn productively from each other; similarly, both political goals can sometimes benefit from each other's engagements, even though their goals are contradictory.

"Bringing Women In" versus "Gendering Our Thinking"

Asking Enloe's question—where are the women?—at first seems deceptively straightforward, a simple recovery operation wherein women's voices are brought forward and missing data are filled in to make a more complete picture. While some feminists may mock this as the "add women and stir" approach to scholarship, such scorn is misplaced. These studies are often based on interviews and ethnographies, providing data that can be useful to a variety of analyses. Women soldiers typically find themselves in a contradiction: since soldiering is so fully associated with masculinity, female soldiers are at best anomalies, neither properly female nor credibly soldierly. Exploring these contradictions, including listening to the women and men who inhabit them, can lead to an analysis that goes beyond simply adding women to the existing military institutions or war practices, to provoke a more radical rethinking of those institutions and practices.

Some of the best work on women in the military is created by journalists, filmmakers, or other nonacademic writers, and thus might not come to the attention of university-based researchers. For example, journalist Helen Benedict's fine book *The Lonely Soldier: The Private War of Women Serving in Iraq* (2010) interviews US women who fought in the war in Iraq. Playwright and film director Zsa Zsa Gershik, in *Secret Service: Untold Stories of Lesbians in the Military* (2005), interviews lesbian soldiers in the US military prior to and during the restrictions imposed by the federal Don't Ask, Don't Tell policy. The 2008 documentary film *Lioness*, produced and directed by Meg McLagan and Daria Sommers, interviews US women combat veterans about their military duty in Iraq. The 2012 documentary film *The Invisible War*, written by Kirby Dick and produced by Amy Ziering and Tanner King Barklow, interviews women veterans about rape and sexual assault in the US military (Dick 2012). These books and films lack a strong theoretical frame but give their interviewees plenty of room to speak and reflect. The soldiers' own insights into their troubled military service suggest badly needed reforms in military training and sexual assault prevention, and at the same time reveal the deep patriarchy that such reforms must confront.

Other studies that focus on women in militaries but lack the liveliness provided by interview data are still informative, but offer less intellectual and political engagement for feminist theory. In *Gender and the Military: Women in the Armed Forces of Western*

Democracies, Helen Carreiras (2006) investigates the factors that affect women's participation in the militaries of NATO countries. Darlene Iskra, Stephen Trainor, Marcia Leithauser, and Mady Wechsler Segal, in "Women's Participation in Armed Forces Cross-Nationally: Expanding Segal's Model," (Iskra et al. 2002), go beyond NATO countries to look at women in militaries in the global South. While informative, these studies tend to employ a conventional positivist epistemology and to focus more on policy than on the frameworks that generate and legitimize policies, so their reach is limited. Without the chorus of voices gained from interviews, studies of women in armed forces lack thick descriptions of wars and militaries, and thus offer little insight into the daily imbrication of these soldiers into the military itself or the larger militarized society. Further, studies relying on substantial interview data invite an intersectional dimension to inquiry, since the women who speak in these films and interviews are never generic women, but are always already located within racial, economic, sexual, national, religious, and geographic stratifications. Without grounding in the multidimensional particulars of women's lives and labors, intersectionality tends to slip away and women from the dominant groups tend to slide into place as the unnamed representatives of all women.

Alongside work that looks at women's role in militaries is the literature on women's roles and circumstances in societies at war. The famous 1980 documentary film *The Life and Times of Rosie the Riveter* by Connie Field (Field et al. 1980) and the edited text of interviews in Sherna B. Gluck's *Rosie the Riveter Revisited: Women, the War, and Social Change* (1987) bring women's voices to bear on the sudden opening and abrupt closing of economic opportunities for women in the United States during the 1940s. Maureen Honey expands this inquiry to include more African American women's voices from publications in the World War II–era black press in *Bitter Fruit: African-American Women in World War II* (1999). While the women who speak and write in Gluck's and Honey's work look to the military and the war-time economy for opportunity, their understanding of patriarchy, capitalism, and systemic racism in the military and the larger society complicates their relation to those opportunities. They both look to be included within the dominant institutions on better terms, and challenge the makeup of those institutions. Another crucial angle on women's relation to war looks at the gendering of policy choices surrounding "guns versus butter," as women are disproportionately harmed when budgets for health, education, housing, food, and transportation programs shrink so that war budgets can grow (Benería and Blank 1989).

A host of studies start with a recovery or integration project but go beyond the limits of those approaches. Enloe is rightly famous for combining a close empirical and historical study of women's roles in military and other institutions with a critical assessment of the patriarchal, racist, capitalist, and colonial context within which militaries operate. Enloe's book *Maneuvers* (2000), for example, has chapters on military wives, nurses, prostitutes, and other laborers, an approach that starts with "where are the women?" and ends up with "how is this gendered?" Judith Steihm's book *Arms and the Enlisted Woman* (1989) also bridges the inclusion of women with reframing questions around gender. Based on extensive interviews, Steihm looks at the hardships military women face while also questioning the sex/gender system and the military as an institution. Studies examining women's lives in societies where armed conflict takes place on their own lands, not on distant shores, readily segue from "women in" to the "gendering of" the wars and war systems. Using data from 2009–2010, Wenona Giles (2013, 80) follows the consequences of war on the gendering of relocation: women and children are 80 percent of 27.5 million displaced persons, and women are half of refugees. Dyan Mazurana discusses the economic consequences of men's displacement from the work force of a war-ravaged land, as in Somalia, where the UN High Commissioner for Refugees estimates that by the end of the 1990s, 90 percent of the work force was made up of women (2013, 164). Ruth Jacobson (2013, 234) follows the consequences of women's loss of land rights in postconflict situations such as Mozambique as well as their ability to set up income-generating projects across warring groups in Kosovo (239).

The bridge between the two frames emerges when, as Enloe (2007, 1) insists, we cultivate thorough-going "feminist curiosity" to properly inquire into those spaces and practices in which women are both captive and absent:[1] captive in the sense that they are present in circumscribed, subordinate roles; absent in that they are underrepresented in prevailing accounts and struggle to find a voice. Spurred by feminist curiosity, the question, "where are the women?" readily becomes "how are the women?"—that is, how does it come to be that bodies and voices of women are knitted into/excluded from militarized arrangements? "Where are the women?" segues into the larger and more complex question, "how are war and militarization gendered?" Cohn's and Elshtain's examples have led feminist scholarship to look past the presence or absence of women to unravel the gendering and sexualizing of narrative practices, material bodies, local/regional/global institutions, state formations, and language codes. Thus, the seemingly innocuous question, "where are the women?" provokes other questions, including, "where and how are the men in wars and militarized societies?" Once women's presence or absence becomes a question rather than a fact, then inevitably men's presence or absence, as well as the inadequacy of the gender binary to contain such questions, also becomes problematic. We are further provoked to think about how those arrangements came to be as well as how they might be changed.

"Let Us In" versus "Set Us Free"

A second tension within feminist analyses of war and militarization is overtly political.[2] Do we aim to reform militaries and militarized social orders so that women are treated fairly and equally within them, or do we aim to transform militaries and societies so that violence is minimized while justice and equality are fostered? Lynne Segal (2008, 21) notes, "more women than ever are serving in many of today's armies, with feminists rather uncertain on how to relate to this phenomenon." Segal lays out the dilemma: do we battle "to improve the conditions for the women inside [today's armies]" or "confront the practices of warfare itself" (23)? The distinction between "let us in" and "set us free" is endemic to most struggles for social change, but is particularly thorny in the context of war and militarization. Women who enter militaries as soldiers or align with militaries as wives, mothers, or workers are subject to the same (or worse) patriarchal arrangements as other women, including pervasive sexual violence and labor exploitation; how can feminists not care about that? Yet these women soldiers, wives, mothers, and workers are also contributing to the militarization of their societies, by their presence implicitly supporting the war-making apparatus and making wars easier to fight. Reforms that would treat them more fairly and equitably or even protect them from assault by their fellow soldiers may undermine the more radical transformative goals by making militaries work more smoothly and rendering war-making easier to accept.

A strong example of the "let us in" approach is found in Sarah Ziegler and Gregory Gunderson's (2005) *Moving Beyond G.I. Jane: Women and the US Military*. They suggest reforming the military by experimenting with all-female units, creating gender-neutral standards for calibrating the requirements of physical training, and other alterations that likely appear minor to critics but would be world-shaking to military leaders. They aim to make "a compelling argument for the full inclusion of women in all aspects of military life" (17). In contrast, efforts to transform, rather than reform, militarized arrangements often focus on changing the economic, political, and social assemblages that produce militarization. Some of the strongest examples of fundamental opposition to militarization come from formerly colonized peoples. As Shigamatsu and Camacho (2010, xv) argue in *Militarized Currents*, "Colonial histories constitute the conditions of possibility for ongoing forms of militarization." Their objective is not to make militarization more palatable but to "advance the current value of indigenous, people of color, and feminist-oriented demilitarizing coalitions as critiques of and alternatives to militarized worlds of the twenty-first century" (xvii). Gwen Kirk's (2008, 294) analysis of the relation of environmental protection to US military presence in the Philippines, South Korea, and Okinawa concludes, "there is a fundamental contradiction between environmental security and military security." Struggles for sovereignty in neocolonial places generally call for ending militarized occupations, as the "No Bases" movement indicates (Lutz 2006).

Yet another aspect of this question emerges when we ask *which* militaries matter: the militaries of established states are often tools to establish and protect colonial investments and empires, while armed insurgencies are likely to contest those colonial arrangements. Girls and women typically join armed resistance movements in much greater numbers than they join state armies: many women want to fight for their communities' revolutions; others arm themselves for protection or revenge; still others are forcibly recruited or turn to rebel factions to escape domestic or state violence (Holzner 2011, 46; Mazurana 2013). The informal hierarchies of insurgencies, compared to the stricter administrative hierarchies of state militaries, are more likely to allow or compel women and girls to join. Between 10 percent and 30 percent of all fighters in the war in Sierra Leone in the last decade of the twentieth century, for example, were girls and women, most of whom had been abducted and brutalized prior to becoming combatants and, often, "bush wives" (Coulter 2008, 55–58), As Coulter (2008) argues with regard to the female fighters in Sierra Leone, and Utas (2005) argues with regard to Liberia, these women "maneuvered in the field of local social relations" as well as the postconflict context of humanitarian aid organizations in ways that "defy the neat dichotomy of victim/perpetrator" (Coulter 2008, 67).

Yet guerrilla organizations often draw on patriarchal understandings of women as "mothers of the nation" or as sexual resources for male fighters. Women who join resistance groups, like women in state militaries, often find themselves in a war on two fronts, battling the alleged enemies of their community or nation while struggling against male dominance within their own forces. Further, when guerrilla forces win, they often become the official militaries of new governments, pushing the women back out to "normalize" the society by returning them to subordinate domestic roles. Rebel women in postconflict situations may be feared as hyperviolent or scorned as damaged goods in some civilian contexts, as Coulter documents in Sierra Leone. In contrast, as in Nicaragua after the Sandinista victory or Vietnam after the defeat of the United States, they may be honored as veterans of the revolution and at least some of them recruited into positions of leadership in the postconflict society (Enloe 1983, 170–172; Randall 1995, 793–805). Studying both women in war and gendering of militarization brings up latent questions of feminisms' relation to violence: many of us support, albeit with reservations, anticolonial armed struggles, while others reject armed resistance in all contexts. Revolutionary feminists may ally themselves with armed rebellions, while feminists who are pacifists likely reject both sites of organized violence.

Conceptual Resources

Feminist theory offers many conceptual resources for addressing these dilemmas. Here we sketch needed understandings of gender and intersectionality, which are crucial to most feminist thinking, then explore three concepts that are central to the topic at hand: war, militarization, and securitization. We also gesture toward other important concepts that are related to our central inquiry, including peace and antiwar movements, neoliberalism, war economies, and revolution, but fall outside our main trajectory of analysis.

Gender

We use the concept of *gender* to name a complex set of practices that are emergent, variable, and often contradictory. These practices appear in identities, institutions, and discursive systems, which of course also interact in vast assemblages. Restraining our focus to contemporary patriarchal societies, we view gender as "*a social system which structures hierarchical power relations*" (Cohn 2013, 5). The word "system" here does not mean a stable structure but a network of interconnected, dispersed nodes and relations, some deeply entrenched, others more fleeting, all interacting in various ways.

This approach to gender includes many levels of analysis. One level focuses on identities, that is, practices by which people create gendered self-understandings, constitute themselves as male or female, or perhaps contest that binary division altogether. It's important to see gender identities as performative, not given, as fluid and mutually constitutive with other vectors of self-understanding. Our understandings of identity need to stretch past "what's in our heads" and bring the materiality of bodies into our thinking so that we can contest the persistent residue of mind/body dualisms and instead understand identities as always embodied. For some time, feminists tended to avoid talking about bodies out of understandable anxiety over re-energizing the patriarchal dismissals of women's bodies as weak and inferior. More recent work in feminist theorizing of war insists on a different approach: engaging body-brain-culture relations[3] rather than sidestepping them. Christine Sylvester, for example, calls for feminist analysis of war to incorporate new materialist analyses of bodies into our understandings of war:

> Writing instead of the reciprocities of body and mind, relays, and comminglings—giving the body some credit as the unit that senses and feels and thinks about its surroundings—is more sensible than saying that the body is out of the picture, to all intents and purposes, when it comes to emotional activities of all kinds, including war activities.
>
> (Sylvester 2013, 6)

Much contemporary feminist work on war and militarization follows Sylvester's lead, locating identities as themselves assemblages of body-mind-society relations and thus expanding and complicating the dynamic energies and feedback loops that knit gendered and sexualized identity practices into war systems.

A second level of theorizing gender focuses on institutions, that is, structured relationships that create social order by organizing activities around gender (and other) lines. For example, "women's work" in many societies situates them differently in relation to war than do typical labors assigned to/expected of men. In many societies, it is women's job to collect water and firewood, which, in a war zone such as Darfur, means leaving camps or villages to walk, often miles, through insecure territory, subject to assault, kidnapping, and rape (DeLargy 2013, 70). Domestic economic structures in many war-making societies famously pull women into paid labor and soldiering as, in Marx's term, a "reserve army" that is available but dispensable at the same time. Societies that view women as men's property, and allocate control over women's sexuality to fathers, brothers, and husbands, set up women to be "high value targets" in attacking the enemies' honor and the coherence of their communities. The infamous rape camps where Serbian soldiers systematically raped Bosnian women until they were pregnant and then forced them to bear the children regarded as "mixed blood," and the thousands of Tutsi women raped during the Rwandan genocide, are among the most infamous examples. Focusing on gender and sexuality as they work within militarized institutional contexts allows feminist researchers to analyze divisions of labor and power that both create and disguise gendered patterns.

A third level of theorizing about gender attends to codes, that is, to discursive arrangements that make it possible for meanings to emerge and to be comprehensible. Gendered and sexual symbolizations insinuate themselves into all sorts of codes, calling on both familiar and disruptive metaphors to make and circulate meaning. Certainly, the familiar association of masculinity with activity and war, while femininity is linked with passivity and peace, is a codification feminist thinkers have problematized in order to cultivate our curiosities about militarization and war. For instance, discursive practices that code women in terms of their sexual availability to men commonly reduce women soldiers to "dykes, bitches or whores" (Gershick 2005; Ness 2008). The fraught symbolic association of women/mothers with the essence of nations or communities does a great deal of work in militarized imaginaries. In her study of war and rape in Bangladesh, Mookherjee (2008, 37) points out the versatility of cultural codes intertwining mothers and nations: "The ideology of woman as mother is a dominant symbolic imagery through which the position of the woman becomes visible in national projects. It becomes crucial for national mobilization processes." These symbolic associations can work in multiple ways. Commonly, when women are encoded as the "collective 'womb'" of the society, as Angela Raven-Roberts (2013, 50) writes about Sudan, women are both attacked by enemy soldiers and, subsequently, shamed and blamed for acting in complicity with the enemy. In a different twist on the encoding of actual women as expressions of a spiritualized national mother, Mookherjee explores efforts by the government of Bangladesh to create "a very public discourse of rehabilitation of raped women;" while the state's goal was to show itself as progressive and modern toward the women who represent the nation, these women often faced rejection and hardship within their communities (2008, 49). Feminist successes in establishing rape as a war crime, rather than a timeless expression of fixed male sexuality, require disrupting the naturalization of heteronormativity and rape as well as the codification of women-as-nation in order to politicize sexual assault within militarized contexts.

Intersectionality

The concept of intersectionality is widely recognized as one of the key contributions of feminist theory to critical thinking. It is a productively open-ended idea calling for us to analyze different dimensions of phenomena in terms of their mutually constitutive relations with one another, looking at networks of interactive processes rather than hierarchies of discrete factors. Many early intersectional analyses focused on identity, while others have brought intersectionality to bear on institutions and social structures (Davis 2008, 68). Viewed expansively, intersectionality expresses both the determination of feminists of color that race, class, sexuality, and other vectors of power be theorized simultaneously with gender and the sensibility in postmodern feminism that power is best thought of as assemblages of connections rather than hierarchies of cause and effect (Davis 2008, 71).

Explorations of intersectionality as identity and as structure are both productive for feminist analyses of war and militarization. In her analysis of war-produced refugees, Giles (2013, 100) finds that for humanitarian interventions to have a chance at success, the specific contours of identities within each crisis situation demand attention: "We need to understand the intersectionality of the multiplicity of identities and differences that comprise the population in a humanitarian disaster, including race, class, gender, cast, ethnicity, age, religion." Cohn and Jacobson (2013, 115) point to the implicit racializing of the war on terror and argue that within the US government's war on terror, feminists find a discursive strategy that "has erased women's diverse political histories in favor of a racialized narrative of Islamic oppression and of 'rescue' by the forces of modernity." In this case, an intersectional analysis is required to interrogate calls to "protect women" in order to see exactly which women are alleged to need protecting from which men, and for what purposes.

In a different use of intersectionality, V. Spike Peterson (2008) applies the concept toward institutions rather than identities, looking at the intertwining of reproductive, productive and virtual economies to understand how they co-constitute one another in financing wars. Pamela DeLargy also cultivates an intersectional approach to the effects of war on medical institutions and on women's health. Her approach pushes past the obvious deaths and mutilations that are direct consequences of armed conflict to look at the various intersections of war with medical services, to understand the different ways that people in war zones lose their access to healthcare. In Rwanda, East Timor, and the rebel-held areas of Syria, healthcare facilities were destroyed; in El Salvador, healthcare workers were specifically targeted; in Liberia, healthcare workers fled the country during the war (DeLargy 2013, 75). The consequences of these attacks on the medical system are generational: immunizations are unavailable; contagious diseases become epidemics; chronic illnesses cannot be treated. Contraception and abortion are unavailable and/or unsafe. Women and infants are endangered: "the risk of maternal death in countries with ongoing or recent armed conflicts is almost twice as high as the risks in peaceful countries" (75). By pushing intersectionality to look at the assemblages of relations among structures and organizations as well as identities, the concept has become more productive for analyses of war and militarization.

War

Feminist explorations of war have rethought it on many levels. V. Spike Peterson (2008, 8) asks, "But what exactly *is* war?" This quest for a definition is much more than that: it marks a terrain that has become unsettled, so that there is no clear object or neat demarcations to confine war to its place. Joshua Goldstein (2001, 3) defines war as "*lethal intergroup conflict*" and usefully extends his definition to "the *war system* as the interrelated ways that societies organize themselves to participate in potential and actual wars" (italics in original). By connecting war to systems of war, Goldstein helps to bridge war to broader processes of militarization.

James Der Derian (2001) importantly calls our attention to the "interwar," indicating both the collapsed times between wars that become part of the wars, and the collapsed distance between war and representations of war, so that the ways that militaries fight and the ways that fighting is represented look the same. Cohn (2013, 21) agrees, emphasizing that women's experiences in pre and postconflict situations make it impossible to think of war "as a discrete event with a clear location and a distinct beginning and end." Laura Sjoberg (2013, 24) points out the common obstacles to feminist scholarship and to policymaking when the gendering of war and conflict is sidelined: "Epistemological, ontological, and methodological barriers have often prevented this [feminist] work from attracting a 'mainstream' audience in the discipline or the attention of the policy world." The inability to pin war down leads feminists and other critical theorists to focus on process and context, to ask not just "what is a war?" but "how is a war?" Feminist researchers have called attention to militaries' organization of women's sexuality as a key component in producing soldiers and organizing war, rather than an alleged natural by-product of male sexuality. US military officials have collaborated with local authorities, for example, to administer the systems of prostitution around US bases in Korea, the Philippines, and Okinawa (Moon 1997; Sturdevant and Stultzfus 1992). The Indian military literally recruited and imported prostitutes to Kashmir to service Indian soldiers, combining sexual labor with military labor, even to the point of giving the women "basic military training" and counting them as "members of the military" (Raven-Roberts 2013, 47). Fighters from various factions in wars in Sierra Leone force girls and women into domestic and sexual service, combining "war time rape with essentially indentured servitude" (Raven-Roberts 2013, 47). These relationships generate long-term, often diasporic consequences for their participants, especially the mixed-race offspring who represent the violation of borders that the war was intended to defend, and the women whose bodies are interdigitated with national bodies. As Grace Cho (2008, 22) remarks, "The Yankee whore who was the body of a fractured nation is entombed in the body of the GI bride." The organization of sexuality, as a resource and a weapon, thus becomes a part of our understanding of war, not an unfortunate externality to the main event.

While there is much debate over whether we are now seeing "new wars" or continuations of old wars, there are characteristic adjustments in thinking that late twentieth-century and twenty-first-century wars require of feminist researchers (Chan 2011; Kaldor 1999; Peterson 2008). War systems are made even more complex by the workings of neoliberal globalization, which has "profoundly altered the ability of states to regulate economic and political activities more generally, and the conduct of war more specifically" (Peterson 2008, 8). First, wars have become privatized: as corporate and nonstate interactional actors multiply and grow in power, governments do not fully control the conduct or the funding of war. Peterson (2008, 8) accordingly urges feminists to investigate the gendering of "transnational financing of new wars." Second, wars have become virtual: the sanitized representations of digitalized battlefields, drone strikes, and force multipliers make netcentric war appear less bloody, even though, as Sylvester (2013, 66) remarks, "War is [still] about injuring bodies." "New wars" may reduce the numbers of imperial troops needed for high-tech combat operations, but they still rely on aerial bombardment and tank assaults as well as widespread surveillance and "targeted" assassinations that wipe out communities. Further, the digitalization of war blurs distinctions between war and domestic policing, between terrorism and migration, between data mining and private communications. As Jairus Grove (2014, 34) remarks regarding new wars, "War as we know it may be coming to an end but a permeating militarization is just getting started." The privatization and digitalization of war raises enormous questions about brave new genderings that feminist theorists have just begun to ask.

Militarization and Securitization

When Goldstein slides from war to the war system, he is creating a bridge between wars and militarization and securitization. Enloe has defined militarization as "a step by step process by which a person or thing gradually comes to be controlled by the military or comes to depend for its well-being on militaristic ideas" (Enloe 2000, 3). Michael Sherry's (1995, ix) definition adds a bit to Enloe's: "The process by which war and national security became consuming anxieties and provided the memories, models, and metaphors that shaped broad areas of national life." Building on these understandings, feminist analyses link militarization to related global trajectories, including colonization and securitization. Feminists in the global South weave colonization into militarization, framed through a gendered analysis, in order to critique and challenge the ongoing imposition of militarized order by US and European militaries, plantation economies, missionary zeal, patriarchal family arrangements, colonial education, and global tourism (Ferguson and Turnbull 1999; Lutz 2001). Feminists also put pressure on practices of making people and nations "secure" to include such matters as having enough to eat, clean water to drink, safe households to live in, safe schools to attend and roads to travel—the practices of daily living that are differentially gendered. Feminists examine how things are securitized, under what conditions, for whom: some populations and interests are destabilized and rendered vulnerable, while others are implicitly authorized and protected from challenge. While both colonization and securitization are contested concepts, they feed back into global militarization in complex and intimate ways.

Taking militarization as a process of producing a kind of order opens up the analysis to "memories, models and metaphors" that produce hegemonic frames of understanding while implicitly disqualifying others. Judith Butler (2004, 5), for example, pushes US readers to examine *"what we can hear"* (italics in original) when we situate ourselves critically within a post-9/11 world. By insisting on the question, *"What makes for a grievable life?"* (italics in original) Butler (2004, 20) makes the militarization of affect detectable in the work that must go on so that some deaths are marked with names and stories, while others, such as hundreds of thousands of war dead in Iraq, Afghanistan, and Palestine, are thrown outside the dominant zone of grievability in the US political imaginary. Similarly, in Lina Hoshino's powerful film *Living Along the Fenceline* (co-produced and co-directed with Gwyn Kirk and Deborah Lee) women from Texas, Puerto Rico, Hawai'i, Guam, the Philippines, Korea, and Okinawa reveal the militarization of communities that, while not officially considered war zones, are securitized and colonized in the name of security and protection (Hoshino et al. 2011). These women offer alternative ideas of peace and security, reflecting grassroots practices of local and indigenous communities, to challenge prevailing militarized assumptions and practices ("Living Along the Fenceline—the film," 2011).

Feminist interventions into traditional security studies intend a self-reflexive, critical feminist scholarship that places gender as the focal category of analysis while resisting normativizing practices and agendas within the discipline. "Securitization," Joanna Nyman (2012, 53) states, "was developed as a theory for identifying security issues once they are moved out of the traditional military sector" into other arenas. A feminist analysis of security studies, in addition to using gender as a category of analysis, transverses the ontological, epistemological, and methodological boundaries of traditional (classical and realist/neorealist based) theorizations to call attention to the day-to-day experience of (in)security while critiquing the nation-state and abstract concepts of strategic discourse. This work reframes the application of securitization theory in areas of study to include migration (Giles 2013; Doty 1996, cited in Nyman 2012, 52), food (Jenkins 2011), the environment (Mackenzie 2009, cited in Nyman 2012, 52), energy (Nyman 2014, 2012), gendered technologies (Wilcox 2009), HIV/AIDS (Elbe 2006, 2005, cited in Nyman 2012, 52), trafficking (Lobasz 2009), sex workers (Moon 1997), land reform (Jacobson 2013, 232–236), tourism (Ferguson and Turnbull 1999; Gonzalez 2013), and political economy (Raven-Roberts 2013; True 2010, 2012), among other issues. Broadly speaking, Laura Shephard (2013, 3) explains, critical security studies researchers challenge conventional security studies methodologies and "endeavour to challenge and unsettle anything that is taken for granted in the research process, including their own assumptions and politics." All these incursions into traditional security studies carry feminist curiosities into militarization/securitization to interrogate what counts as security and insecurity (Hansen 2000; Parashar 2013).

Feminist security studies (FSS) is a newly emerging subfield within international studies that attempts to radicalize critical security studies in response to the more familiar classical, realist/neorealist, neoliberal conceptions of security. Since the earliest feminist interventions in security studies, four major moves mark the development of feminist security studies. Initially, feminists questioned the irrelevance and nonexistence of women in international security studies. Second, feminists questioned whether or not the state truly protects women in times of war and peace as it claims to do. Third, feminist security theory challenged the unreflective link between women and peace. More recently, new theorizations of masculinity and security are developing in order to challenge assumptions that centering gender only addresses women (Blanchard 2003, 1290). Soumita Basu (2013, 456) concludes, "much of what we now describe as FSS has come to focus on armed conflicts, and matters of international peace and security (generally understood), but feminist scholarship offers radical imaginings of security through the employment of gender." Recently, feminist research on security themes "has focused mostly on empirical analysis of women and/in wars, UN resolution 1325 and peacekeeping, human security, and postconflict reintegration and development" (Parashar 2013, 441).

As with most sites of inquiry, FSS is also a site of struggle over the practices and goals of research projects. To achieve publications, get jobs and develop careers, as well as to have an impact on the larger field of security studies, some feminists focus on getting their work accepted in their disciplines. Others object to this disciplining; as Carol Cohn (2011, 583) comments, "My motivation centers on problems in the world I want to change—not on a field of academia I want to change." Some FFS scholars call for a more ethnographic, participatory research agenda that allows insecure populations of study to participate in the framing of their experiences through their narratives (Wibben 2011). In solidarity with this call, Laura McLeod (2013, 462) urges researchers to "reconsider, develop, and refine our conceptualization of (feminist) security issues" using our "emotions experienced during ethnographic explorations to provide powerful and productive insights about what constitutes a feminist security concern, and how they are represented." Critics of efforts to "let us in" to existing academic fields charge that such efforts interfere with transnational and transdisciplinary work. Claire Wilkinson (2007) finds securitization theory by FSS scholars remains too Western-centric and problematic when used to study non-Western states. Parashar laments the appearance of disciplinary camps:

> Feminists are increasingly comfortable only in scholarly spaces inhabited by the familiar and the like-minded. While too invested in trying to make ourselves relevant to [the] mainstream, we are losing sight of the relevance we could have to understanding one another, to acknowledging and bridging differences, and to broader commitments of feminist politics. We are operating in fenced terrains of (in)securities where we actively construct camps (to find a sense of belonging and acceptance) and choose to ignore the existence of those different and beyond.
>
> (Parashar 2013, 442)

Noting the continued marginalization of the Pacific in FSS, Teresia Teaiwa asks, "How can feminists still be reproducing such hierarchies of knowledge and authority in the twenty-first century?" (Teaiwa and Slatter 2013, 442). These debates indicate that tensions between "let us in" and "set us free" are often reproduced within the very structures and debates intended to address them.

LOCATIONS OF RESEARCH/ACTIVISM

A further question for feminist teachers and researchers requires the examination of the production and circulation of the research itself. Where does it originate? How does it circulate? What are the goals? Who is the intended audience? Activist groups, often in partnership with academics, often push past "let us in" questions and tackle more challenging "set us free" agendas. At the same time, activists often recognize and sympathize with the pull of military recruitment on members of working class, rural, and Third World communities (Teaiwa 2008).

Researchers inside and outside of universities share their labor through a small and changing number of organizations and networks, including the following:

- The Consortium on Gender, Security and Human Rights at the University of Massachusetts, Boston, directed by Carol Cohn
- The Resistance Studies Network at the University of Gothenburg, Sweden;
- ISIS International in Manila, the Philippines
- International Women's Network against Militarism (IWNAM) and their US-based arm, Women for Genuine Security
- The Women in Conflict Zones Research Network at York University, Canada
- New Profile: A Movement to Demilitarize Israeli Society
- The Feminist Security Studies subfield within The International Studies Association

While not comprehensive, this list shows the global reach of feminist scholarship and activism and may encourage further global cross-fertilization of antimilitarist struggles.

Future Directions

It is arguable that feminist scholarly and activist engagements with war and militarization are the most urgent of our many demanding issues, in that so many other pressing concerns stem from and loop back into the complex devastation that war and militarization bring. Poverty, neoliberal economic change, environmental destruction, family and community violence, racial and class injustice, educational erosion, contortions of our political and scholarly imaginations—all these and other critical beacons for feminist curiosities are wired into global assemblages of war and militarization. Our recommendations for future directions for feminist work reflect our conviction that war and militarization are critical spindles for a wide array of feminist projects.

First, we argue for retaining and interrogating (rather than ignoring or resolving) the tensions between "women and war"/"gendering of war" as well as "let us in"/"set us free." In our class Women, War and the Military, we've held on to the *women and* part of our curriculum, rather than switch entirely to the *gendering of* focus, for both pedagogical and analytic reasons. Many of our students are soldiers, partners of soldiers, or children of soldiers; investigations of women within military institutions often speak directly to our students and encourage them to ask further and bigger questions. At the same time, some students are anti-militarization activists from indigenous and local communities who struggle with the tension between understanding the military as an economic opportunity among their people while articulating a radical challenge to militarization.

We encourage teaching and research that build bridges between the more reformist and the more radical approaches, exploring the connections and the incompatibilities.

Examples of the both/and approach exist in both activist and academic arenas. For example, Cohn has consistently brought together the perspectives of women and men within military institutions and radical critiques of those institutions. She talks about how the "deep cultural divide between military and civilian" worlds affects her research (2006, 100) and notes that her academic colleagues are as surprised to learn of "intelligent, thoughtful military officers" as military personnel are to hear of fair-minded academics (99). Annica Kronsell (2006, 119) similarly argues in her work on women and men in the Swedish military that "women in minority positions within institutions of hegemonic masculinity should not be brushed off as irrelevant for feminist knowledge production." These women make hegemonic masculinity visible and thus are "an extremely important source of knowledge" (118). Respect for and engagement with those inside as well as outside the war system acknowledges the leaky boundaries such divisions inevitably entail while enhancing the insights and surprises available to feminist researchers.

Yet another example of both/and approaches is reflected in the work of New Profile, a feminist organization whose goal is "to 'civil-ize' Israeli society" (Segal 2008, 24). This radicalized demilitarizing process, as Lynne Segal explains, requires a transformative agenda that takes them into multiple related issues and communities:

> They research and write about the costs of the militarized nature of Israeli society, exposing the links between militarism and violence against women, monitoring the military mythology that enters the media and educational curriculum, organizing youth groups and summer camps, creating traveling exhibitions and, aligned with the Israeli Coalition of Women for Peace and the wider women's peace movement internationally, speak out on any platforms they can use in the service of peace.
>
> (Segal 2008, 26)

At the same time, New Profile has launched the movement called Gun-Free Kitchen Tables, a political initiative that has a seemingly narrow and "inside-the-system" focus: to persuade police and legal authorities to enforce the law, already on the books, prohibiting security personnel from taking their guns home from work. This deceptively reformist campaign has had significant successes in publicizing violence against women in their homes while simultaneously challenging the proliferation of small arms in Israeli society ("Gun Free Kitchen Tables Activity Report" 2011). This dynamic interaction of reformist and transformational activisms offers a powerful model of both/and thinking to guide feminist antimilitarist thinking/practice.

Second, we urge feminist scholar/activists to (continue to) ground our work in specific places and times, to cultivate specificity and attend to past (and often forgotten) struggles. The eclectic first wave of the feminist movement hosted a remarkable range of antiwar and antimilitarist ideas and actions, including the Women's International League for Peace and Freedom, the anarchist No-Conscription League, and many more. Connecting contemporary work more broadly to feminist histories can tap neglected resources for analysis and struggle. Being historically and geographically specific can encourage us "to envisage emancipatory possibilities that are context-specific, realizable, and flexible, and yet cognizant of the need to transform oppressive matrices of structural power" (Basu 2013, 456).

Third, we enthusiastically endorse intersectional framing of questions, taking intersectionality to include not just identities but ways of theorizing power and resistance, discourses and materialities. A capacious intersectionality incorporates masculinity studies and queer theory, bringing in varieties of masculinity and sexuality. Attention to men and masculinity is crucial for several reasons, not least of which is that men are victimized and bribed by militarization, too. Lynne Segal (2008, 21) insists, "The gendered nature of warfare must also encompass the costs of war to men, whose fundamental vulnerability to psychological abuse and physical injury is often downplayed, whether in mainstream accounts of warfare or in more specific gender analysis." Further, hegemonic masculinities usually make use of class/race/gender/sexual intersections to articulate and reflect national interests, requiring fluid analysis of intersecting threads of power (Mookherjee 2008, 37). Danny Kaplan, for example, draws on feminist and queer theory to analyze the sexual dynamics of the Israeli army, as does Aaron Belkin for the US military. Both analyze complex relations of power and eros that complicate straightforward identifications of soldiering with aggressive masculinity and the rejection of all things coded feminine (Belkin 2012; Kaplan 2003).

Fourth, we want to continue and expand feminism's transnational reach and its capability for fostering global antimilitarist alliances. A transnational reach, broadly conceived, can take feminist researchers into sites of inquiry that go far beyond disciplines and subdisciplines to embrace a necessarily eclectic set of venues. Butler (2004, 47) suggests, "A feminist opposition to militarism emerges from many sources, many cultural venues, in any number of idioms; it does not have to—and finally, cannot—speak in a single political idiom, and no grand settling of epistemological accounts has to be required." With Butler, we call for "an international coalition of feminist activists and thinkers" (48) that works from our common vulnerability and shared capacity to reinvent ourselves-in-relation. "We do not need to ground ourselves in a single model of communications, a single model of reason, a single notion of the subject before we are able to act" (48). As Teiawa suggests, perhaps we can no longer afford "taking a combative approach" to disagreements with those whom "we might otherwise consider friends and allies" (Teaiwa and Slatter 2013, 449). It is more important, in a world saturated with war and militarization, to use the resources of feminist theory and activism to work together for a less violent world.

Notes

1. This felicitous wording comes from Teresa de Lauretis, *Alice Doesn't: Feminism, Semiotics, Cinema* (Bloomington: Indiana University Press, 1984), 14.

2. "Let us in" versus "set us free" was a common idiom in second-wave feminism. The earliest documented use we find comes from Barbara Deckard, *The Women's Movement* (New York: Harper and Row, 1975), 336. While the metaphor of waves is a contested one, it is useful for indicating basic periodization of women's movements.
3. We owe this productive concept of "body-brain-culture" relations to William Connolly, *Neuropolitics: Thinking, Culture, Speed* (Minneapolis: University of Minnesota Press, 2002).

References

Basu, S. 2013. "Emancipatory Potential in Feminist Security Studies." *International Studies Perspectives* 14: 455–458.

Belkin, A. 2012. *Bring Me Men: Military Masculinity and the Benign Facade of American Empire, 1898–2001*. New York: Columbia University Press.

Benedict, H. 2010. *The Lonely Soldier: The Private War of Women Serving in Iraq*. Boston: Beacon Press.

Benería, L., and R. Blank. 1989. "Women and the Economics of Military Spending." In *Rocking the Ship of State: Toward a Feminist Peace Politics*, edited by A. Harris and Y. King, 191–203. Boulder, CO: Westview Press.

Blanchard, E. M. 2003. "Gender, International Relations, and the Development of Feminist Security Theory." *Signs* 28: 1289–1312.

Butler, J. 2004. *Precarious Life: The Powers of Mourning and Violence*. London: Verso.

Carreiras, H. 2006. *Gender and the Military: Women in the Armed Forces of Western Democracies*. London: Taylor & Francis.

Chan, S. 2011. "On the Uselessness of New Wars Theory: Lessons from African Conflicts." In *Experiencing War*, edited by C. Sylvester, 94–102. New York: Routledge.

Cho, G. M. 2008. *Haunting the Korean Diaspora: Shame, Secrecy, and the Forgotten War*. Minneapolis: University of Minnesota Press.

Cohn, C. 1987. "Sex and Death in the Rational World of Defense Intellectuals." *Signs* 12: 687–718.

Cohn, C. 2006. "Motives and Methods: Using Multi-sited Ethnography to Study US National Security Discourses." In *Feminist Methodologies for International Relations*, edited by Brooke A, Ackerly, Maria Stern, and Jacqui True, 91–107. Cambridge: Cambridge University Press.

Cohn, C. 2011. "Feminist Security Studies": Toward a Reflexive Practice." *Politics and Gender*. 7: 581–586.

Cohn, C. 2013. "Women and Wars: Toward a Conceptual Framework." In *Women and Wars*, edited by C. Cohn, 1–35. Cambridge: Polity Press.

Cohn, C., and R. Jacobson. 2013. "Women and Political Activism in the Face of War and Militarization." In *Women and Wars*, edited by C. Cohn, 102–123. Cambridge: Polity Press.

Coulter, C. 2008. "Female Fighters in the Sierra Leone War: Challenging the Assumptions?" *Feminist Review* 88: 54–73.

Davis, K. 2008. "Intersectionality as Buzzword: A Sociology of Science Perspective on What Makes a Feminist Theory Successful." *Feminist Theory* 9: 67–85.

DeLargy, P. 2013 "Sexual Violence and Women's Health in War." In *Women and Wars*, edited by C. Cohn, 54–79. Cambridge: Polity Press.

Der Derian, J. 2001. *Virtuous War: Mapping the Military-Industrial-Media-Entertainment Network*. Boulder, CO: Westview Press.

Dick, K. 2012. Director. *The Invisible War*. Sausalito, CA: Roco Films.
Doty, R. L. 1996. *Imperial Encounters: The Politics of Representation in North-South Relations*. Minneapolis: University of Minnesota Press.
Elbe, S. 2005. "AIDS, Security, Biopolitics." *International Relations* 19: 403–419.
Elbe, S. 2006. "Should HIV/AIDS Be Securitized? The Ethical Dilemmas of Linking HIV/AIDS and Security." *International Studies Quarterly* 50.
Elshtain, J. B. 1987. *Women and War*. New York: Basic Books.
Enloe, C. 1983. *Does Khaki Become You? Militarisation in Women's Lives*. Boston: South End Press.
Enloe, C. 2000. *Maneuvers: The International Politics of Militarizing Women's Lives*. Berkeley: University of California Press.
Enloe, C. 2007. *Globalization and Militarism: Feminists Make the Link*. Lanham, MD: Rowman & Littlefield.
Enloe, C. 2000. *Bananas, Beaches and Bases: Making Feminist Sense of International Politics*. Updated ed. Berkeley: University of California Press.
Fasteau, M. 1974. *The Male Machine*. New York: McGraw-Hill.
Ferguson, K. E., and P. Turnbull. 1999. *Oh, Say, Can You See? The Semiotics of the Military in Hawai'i*. Minneapolis: University of Minnesota Press.
Field, C., M. Ziebarth, and M. Frank. 1980. *The Life and Times of Rosie the Riveter*. Berkeley, CA: Clarity Films.
Gershick, Z. Z. 2005. *Secret Service: Untold Stories of Lesbians in the Military*. Los Angeles: Alyson Books.
Giles, W. 2013. "Women Forced to Flee: Refugees and Internally Displaced Persons." In *Women and Wars*, edited by C. Cohn, 80–101. Cambridge: Polity Press.
Gluck, S. B. 1987. *Rosie the Riveter Revisited: Women, the War, and Social Change*. Boston: Twayne Publishers.
Goldstein, J. S. 2001. *War and Gender: How Gender Shapes the War System and Vice Versa*. Cambridge: Cambridge University Press.
Gonzalez, V. V. 2013. *Securing Paradise: Tourism and Militarism in Hawai'i and the Philippines*. Durham, NC: Duke University Press.
Grove, J. 2014. "Dangerous Algorithms: The Globalization of Drones, Bots, and Informatics." Presented at the International Studies Association. Toronto, Canada.
"Gun Free Kitchen Tables Activity Report." 2011. January-December. Haifa, Israel: Isha L'Isha Feminist Center.
Hansen, L. 2000. "The Little Mermaid's Silent Security Dilemma and the Absence of Gender in the Copenhagen School." *Millennium: Journal of International Studies* 29: 285–306.
Holzner, B. M. 2011. "Wars, Bodies, and Development." In *Experiencing War*, edited by C. Sylvester, 42–63. New York: Routledge.
Honey, M. 1999. *Bitter Fruit: African American Women in World War II*. Columbia: University of Missouri Press.
Hoshino, L., G. Kirk, and D. Lee. 2011. *Living Along the Fenceline*. Petaluma, CA: Many Threads. http://www.alongthefenceline.com/filmmakers.html. Accessed April 6, 2014.
Iskra, D., S. Trainor, M. Leithauser, and M. W. Segal. 2002. "Women's Participation in Armed Forces Cross-Nationally: Expanding Segal's Model." *Current Sociology* 50: 771–797.
Jacobson, R. 2013. "Women 'After' Wars." In *Women and Wars*, edited by C. Cohn, 215–241. Cambridge: Polity Press.

Jenkins, R. 2011. "Women, Food Security and Peacebuilding: From Gender Essentialism to Market Fundamentalism." open Democracy online. http://www.opendemocracy.net/5050/rob-jenkins/women-food-security-and-peacebuilding-from-gender-essentialism-to-market-fundamenta. Accessed April 12, 2014.

Kaldor, M. 1999. *New and Old Wars: Organized Violence in a Global Era*. 3rd ed. Redwood City, CA: Stanford University Press.

Kaplan, D. 2003. *Brothers and Others in Arms: The Making of Love and War in Israeli Combat Units*. New York: Harrington Park Press.

Kirk, G. 2008. "Environmental Effects of U.S. Military Security: Gendered Experiences from the Philippines, South Korea, and Japan." In *Gender and Globalization in Asia and the Pacific: Method, Practice, Theory*, edited by K. E. Ferguson and M. Mironesco, 294–317. Honolulu: University of Hawaii Press.

Kronsell, A. 2006. "Methods for Studying Silences: Gender Analysis in Institutions of Hegemonic Masculinity." In *Feminist Methodologies for International Relations*, edited by B. A Ackerly, M. Stern, and J. True, 108–128. Cambridge: Cambridge University Press.

Lobasz, J. K. 2009. "Beyond Border Security: Feminist Approaches to Human Trafficking." *Security Studies* 18: 319–344.

Lutz, C. 2001. *Homefront: A Military City and the American Twentieth Century*. Boston: Beacon Press.

Lutz, C. 2006. "Empire Is in the Details." *American Ethnologist* 33: 593–611.

Mackenzie, M. 2009. "Securitization and Desecuritization: Female Soldiers and the Reconstruction of Women in Post-Conflict Sierra Leone." *Security Studies* 18: 241–261.

Mazurana, D. 2013. "Women, Girls, and Non-State Armed Opposition Groups." In *Women and Wars*, edited by C. Cohn, 146–168. Cambridge: Polity Press.

Mcleod, L. 2013. "Ethnographic Explorations and Fragmented Senses of Feminist Insecurity." *International Studies Perspectives* 14: 459–462.

Mookherjee, N. 2008. "Gendered Embodiments: Mapping the Body-politic of the Raped Woman and the Nation in Bangladesh." *Feminist Review* 88: 36–53.

Moon, K. H. S. 1997. *Sex among Allies: Military Prostitution in U.S.-Korea Relations*. New York: Columbia University Press.

Ness, N. V. 2008. "Perceived as 'Dykes, Whores, Bitches': 1 in 3 Military Women Experience Sexual Abuse." *The Women's International Perspectives*. http://thewip.net/2008/05/07/perceived-as-dykes-whores-bitches-1-in-3-military-women-experience-sexual-abuse/. Accessed January 9, 2015.

Nyman, J. 2012. "Securitization Theory." In *Critical Approaches to Security: An Introduction to Theories and Methods*, edited by L. Shepherd, 51–62. New York: Routledge.

Nyman, J. 2014. "Red Storm Ahead: Securitisation of Energy in US-China Relations." *Millennium: Journal of International Studies* 43(1): 43–65.

Parashar, S. 2013. "Feminist (In)securities and Camp Politics." *International Studies Perspectives* 14: 440–443.

Peterson, V. S. 2008. "'New Wars' and Gendered Economies." *Feminist Review* 88: 7–20.

Randall, M., ed. 1995. *Sandino's Daughters: Testimonies of Nicaraguan Women in Struggle*. New Brunswick, NJ: Rutgers University Press.

Raven-Roberts, A. 2013. "Women and the Political Economy of War." In *Women and Wars*, edited by C. Cohn, 36–53. Cambridge: Polity Press.

Ruddick, S. 1989. *Maternal Thinking: Toward a Politics of Peace*. Boston: Beacon Press.

Segal, L. 2008. "Gender, War and Militarism: Making and Questioning the Links," *Feminist Review* 88: 21–35.

Segal, M. W. 1982. "The Argument for Female Combatants." In *Female Soldiers—Combatants or Noncombatants? Historical and Contemporary Perspectives*, edited by N. L. Goldman, 267–290. Westport, CT: Greenwood Press.

Shepherd, L. J., ed. 2013. "Introduction: Critical Approaches to Security in Contemporary Global Politics." In *Critical Approaches to Security: An Introduction to Theories and Methods*, 1–8. London: Routledge.

Sherry, M. S. 1995. *In the Shadow of War: The United States Since the 1930s*. New Haven, CT: Yale University Press.

Shigematsu, S., and K. L. Camacho, eds. 2010. "Introduction: Militarized Currents, Decolonizing Futures." In *Militarized Currents: Toward a Decolonized Future in Asia and the Pacific*, xv–xlviii. Minneapolis: University of Minnesota Press.

Sjoberg, L. 2013. *Gendering Global Conflict: Toward a Feminist Theory of War*. New York: Columbia University Press.

Stiehm, J. 1983. *Women and Men's Wars*. Oxford: Pergamon Press.

Stiehm, J. 1989. *Arms and the Enlisted Woman*. Philadelphia, PA: Temple University Press.

Sturdevant, S. P., and B. Stultzfus. 1992. *Let the Good Times Roll: Prostitution and the U.S. Military in Asia*. New York: New Press.

Sylvester, C., ed. 2013. *War as Experience: Contributions from International Relations and Feminist Analysis*. New York: Routledge.

Teiwai, T. 2008. "Globalizing and Gendered Forces: The Contemporary Militarization of Pacific/Oceania." In *Gender and Globalization in Asia and the Pacific: Method, Practice, Theory*, edited by K. E. Ferguson and M. Mironesco, 318–332. Honolulu: University of Hawaii Press.

Teaiwa, T., and C. Slatter. 2013. "Samting Nating: Pacific Waves at the Margins of Feminist Security Studies." *International Studies Perspectives* 14: 447–450.

True, J. 2010. "The Political Economy of Violence Against Women: A Feminist International Relations Perspective." *Australian Feminist Law Journal* 23: 39–59.

Utas, M. 2005. "West-African Warscapes: Victimcy, Girlfriending, Soldiering: Tactic Agency in a Young Woman's Social Navigation of the Liberian War Zone." *Anthropological Quarterly* 78: 403–430.

Wibben, A. T. R. 2011. *Feminist Security Studies: A Narrative Approach*. New York: Routledge.

Wilcox, L. 2009. "Gendering the Cult of the Offensive." *Security Studies* 18: 214–240.

Wilkinson, C. 2007. "The Copenhagen School on Tour in Kyrgyzstan: Is Securitization Theory Useable Outside Europe?" *Security Dialogue* 38: 5–25.

Zeigler, S. L., and G. G. Gunderson. 2005. *Moving Beyond G.I. Jane: Women and the U.S. Military*. Lanham, MD: University Press of America.

Further Reading

Abu-Lughod, L. 2013. *Do Muslim Women Need Saving?* Boston: Harvard University Press.

Balzacq, T., ed. 2010. *Securitization Theory: How Security Problems Emerge and Dissolve*, New York: Routledge.

Hudson, V. M., and A. M. den Boer. 2005. *Bare Branches: The Security Implications of Asia's Surplus Male Population*. Cambridge, MA: MIT Press.

Lorentzen, L. A., and J. Turpin, eds. 1998. *The Women and War Reader*. New York: New York University Press.

True, J. 2012. *The Political Economy of Violence Against Women*. New York: Oxford University Press.

Waller, M. R., and J. Rycenga, eds. *Frontline Feminisms: Women, War and Resistance*. New York: Routledge, 2001.

Weber, C. "Why Is There No Queer International Theory?" *European Journal of International Relations*. 1354066114524236. April 3, 2014.

CHAPTER 26

NATURE

STACY ALAIMO

INTRODUCTION

DESPITE the word's many positive associations with bucolic pastoral traditions, sublime wilderness areas, harmonious ecologies, and healthy lifestyles, *nature* has been and continues to be a thorny term for feminist theory. This is because *nature*, in at least two broad senses, has been enlisted by Western philosophical and cultural traditions to define and denigrate the female half of the human species. First, the idea that there is such a thing as the "nature" of something is a type of *essentialism*, a philosophical or commonsensical belief in some sort of essence, core identity, or characteristic that defines an individual or group as such. An essentialist notion of say, *woman's nature*, would assert a quintessence of *woman*, that could, presumably be delineated. Both sexism and racism have been fueled by essentialist beliefs that women, as well as other groups, such as people of African descent or indigenous peoples, are inferior due to their unchanging, core "natures," which exist in a realm apart from histories of colonialism, economic systems, ideologies, or other social and discursive formations. This is a convenient idea: it segregates the social and economic forces in such a way as to preclude the question of whether the supposed "nature" of particular social groups has been fashioned precisely in order to justify or fortify the oppression of those groups. When females are deemed inferior by their very nature, for example, that corseted construction leaves little breathing space, and even less room for argument. And while such views may seem outlandishly outdated in the twenty-first century, a quick trip to a local park or playground may exhibit how widespread gender essentialism still is; contemporary feminist movements seem to have had little impact on everyday discussions of children's behavior. Girls do such and such because they are girls; boys act as they do because they are boys. Such tired and circular pronouncements assume that we already know what it means, in terms of attitudes, predilections, talents, energies, or behaviors, to be a boy or a girl. And sadly, we often do, to the extent that gender is tenacious, pervasive, and self-replicating.

Second, the concept of "nature," in the sense of the vast biophysical world that is not human and not cultural, is a foundational term for a set of dualisms that are fundamental to how Westerners make sense of things. These persistent dualisms, which still shape commonsensical arguments, attitudes, and beliefs are hardly complimentary toward women. Instead, they place both women and nature on the wrong side of the tracks of these and other oppositions: subject/object, knower/known, active/passive, reason/emotion, mind/body, civilized/primitive, culture/nature, man/woman. These dualisms not only tag male and female with positive and negative valences, however; they also, in an intersectional grid, extend to racialized others, indigenous peoples, non-Western peoples, the colonized, and the lower classes, marking them with all that the white, Euro-American subject repudiates in himself. Indeed, movements such as Social Darwinism, which drew on the evolutionary idea of the survival of the fittest, naturalized political oppression and even the attempted genocide of particular groups by way of arguing that some peoples inhabit a "primitive" nature and others a lofty, civilized culture. The photographer Edward S. Curtis, for example, who took hundreds of photographs of American Indians at the start of the twentieth century, believed they were a race that was doomed to vanish, not because of genocidal campaigns but due to their inherent inferiority.

But to complicate matters, consider that the term *nature* has been used, paradoxically, both to disparage people, including American Indians and women, who are supposedly "closer" to it, and to promote what is alleged to be "natural." The history of feminism reveals many instances in which women's freedoms have been curtailed by the condemnation of such things as higher education for women or birth control as unnatural. Perhaps there is some sort of twisted logic here in that such "unnatural" activities could elevate women from their "naturally" inferior state as more bodily, less rational. Within this cultural matrix, where both *nature* and the *unnatural* have been wielded against women, gay people, people of color, and non-Western people, what is a feminist to do? Feminist theorists, activists, writers, and artists have forged divergent paths through this overdetermined territory—distancing themselves from the conceptual ground of nature, allying with nature, subverting the nature/culture dualism, and undertaking profound redefinitions of nature, materiality, environment, and the human. The fact that the overstuffed concept of nature has posed so many challenges has placed feminist thought and practice at the forefront of innovative theories that trace the entanglements and interconnections between the human and the more-than-human world. Feminist theorists have reconceptualized nature in robust and profound ways, most recently in science studies, material feminisms, and feminist posthumanisms.

Social Construction and the Feminist Flight from Nature

The postmodern feminist artist Barbara Kruger, known for her boldly captioned photographs that critique misogyny and consumerism while mimicking the style of advertisements, offers one work in particular that epitomizes what I have called the "feminist flight from nature" (Alaimo 2000). Kruger depicts an upside down woman's face, lying on the ground, with leaves covering her eyes. The photo suggests that being associated with the earth has meant that women are linked to something mute, passive, lowly, even vulnerable—as the woman's head looks like it is at risk of being stepped on. Significantly, the woman is displayed for the viewer, but she cannot, herself, see. The feminist caption, however, "We Won't Play Nature to your Culture," spoken by a politicized group, the "we," refuses to assume the position of the object-like head. Refusing to "play nature," has meant both the critique of gender essentialism and the critique of how *woman* has been aligned with nature, rather than culture.

Against the essentialist philosophy that such a thing as "woman's nature" exists, feminist theory has argued that the concept of "woman" is not natural but cultural, not timeless, but historical, not predetermined but the result of socialization. As Simone de Beauvoir famously noted in her feminist classic *The Second Sex*, "one is not born, one becomes a woman," meaning that social forces profoundly shape what humans born as females will become (Beauvoir 1952, 301). Indeed, the concept of *gender*, which, arguably, is the most significant concept to arise from feminist theory, contrasts gender, that is, the cultural ideals, norms, and roles defined as masculine and feminine, with biological sex, which is (usually) "male" or "female." In "The Traffic in Women," Gayle Rubin draws upon, extends, and critiques Marxist theory when she proposes that gender is a production of culture: "Sex as we know it—gender identity, sexual desire and fantasy, concepts of childhood—is itself a social product. We need to understand the relations of its production and forget, for awhile, about food, clothing, automobiles, and transistor radios" (Rubin 1990, 80). While here "sex" is known through its already gendered forms, Rubin's theory is notable for emphasizing the production of gender from sex. Rubin argues that every society has what she terms a "sex/gender" system, "a set of arrangements by which the biological raw material of human sex and procreation is shaped by human social intervention and satisfied in a conventional manner" (Rubin 1990, 80). Rubin's model of the sex/gender system suggests an underlying opposition between nature and culture as she distinguishes biological substance as distinct from what culture fabricates from that substance. This makes sense, of course, as a system parallel to Marxist models of production, which usually conceive of nature as a resource.

In its broadest sense, the concept of social construction, which argues that categories of gender and race are culturally fabricated, historical, and contingent, has been utterly invaluable for arguments against misogyny and racism. And yet, it is important to note how the domain of "nature," as a repository of essentialisms, remains intact within many of these models. Monique Wittig, in an essay whose title, "One Is Not Born a Woman," echoes Simone de Beauvoir, does distinguish nature as reality from nature as concept when she argues, "We have been compelled in our bodies and in our minds to correspond, feature by feature, with the *idea* of nature that has been established for us" (Wittig 1992, 9; italics in original). Nonetheless, she still holds the concept of nature responsible for oppressive alterations, "distorted to such an extent that our deformed body is what they call 'natural,' what is supposed to exist as such before oppression. Distorted to such an extent that in the end oppression seems to be a consequence of this 'nature' within ourselves (a nature which is only an *idea*)" (ibid.). Wittig concludes this essay by arguing, famously, that lesbians are not women, "either economically or politically or ideologically," since "what makes a woman is a specific social relationship to a man" (Wittig 1992, 20). Insofar as the concept of nature has been used to warp bodies and control social and sexual relations, dispensing with the very idea of nature, then, is key for feminist and lesbian freedom.

In *Undomesticated Ground: Recasting Nature as Feminist Space*, I trace such "feminist flights from nature," arguing that this is a predominant trajectory in feminist theory, from Mary Wollstonecraft, Simone de Beauvoir, and Juliet Mitchell to Monique Wittig and poststructuralist feminisms (Alaimo 2000). Juliet Mitchell, in "Women: The Longest Revolution," for example, suggests that the further we move away from nature, in a teleology of progress, the freer we will be, "The liberation of women under socialism will not be 'rational' but a human achievement, in the long passage from Nature to Culture that is the definition of history and society" (Mitchell 1990, 70). The feminist flight from nature is, as I see it, problematic in at least three ways. First, it leaves the nature/culture dualism intact, along with the entire constellation of dualisms that have associated women with emotion, corporeality, and animality. The concept of *nature*, insofar as it has been ideologically saturated, requires more thorough deconstruction; otherwise, it retains its bite. Moving "woman" to the more privileged side of the binary does nothing to subvert the structure that upholds misogyny, racism, and colonialism. Moreover, we may do well to wonder who is left behind in the bad conceptual neighborhood of nature once particular groups of females are relocated. Second, feminists who are also environmentalists or "animal people" (as Joy Williams puts it) may reject well-worn, transcendent paths to liberation that depend on the domination of nonhuman life. Shifting from "nature" to "culture" is not exactly a desirable conceptual endpoint for environmentalists, who critique the master narratives that underwrite the exploitation of the natural world. Third, as the final section of this essay will discuss, the very notion of nature as something distinct from culture and human activity has become unthinkable in the twenty-first century, as climate change, mass extinction, genetic engineering, and pollution can no longer be ignored. While there are plenty of lively creatures, beings, and interactions, there is no such thing as a separate domain of nature in the anthropocene.

Social constructionist, poststructuralist, and postmodernist feminist theories have, for the most part, promoted "gender minimizing" rather than "gender maximizing" feminisms, to use Ann Snitow's terms (Snitow 1990). That is, they argue against gender essentialisms in order to minimize the impact of the very notion that some characteristics, abilities, activities, roles, or values are more feminine and others are more masculine. Interestingly, while many of these arguments explicitly or implicitly undertake a flight from nature, there is another tradition of gender-minimizing feminisms, from the late nineteenth through the twentieth centuries that imagines "nature" as an undomesticated ground for feminism (Alaimo 2000). Antoinette Brown Blackwell and Elizabeth Burt Gamble drew from Charles Darwin's *Descent of Man*, asserting that evolution entails radical and ceaseless change—in the vast chronological landscape of evolution, ideas about what is "male" and what is "female" are mere trifles, subject to transformation. Marxist-feminist theorists of the 1930s in the United States suggested their own model of social construction. In a strange twist on the history of feminist claims that women are created by culture, not nature, writers such as Mary Inman and Rebecca Pitts turn toward nature to condemn the social "manufacturing" of females, arguing that it is oppressive because it is "unnatural." In such formulations, it is culture that enforces rigid notions of gender, while nature is imagined as a space utterly free from such confining concepts, values, and roles. (Alaimo 2000, 16). Mary Austin's turn-of-the-century story "The Walking Woman" takes the masculinist mythology of the American West and recasts it, reveling in the southwestern desert as an untamed space, where the law and the landmarks fail, where Euro-American women can disidentify from sedimented gender categories. Thus feminists have sought to free themselves from confining notions of womanhood by distancing themselves from the category of nature but also by imaginatively reinhabiting nature as undomesticated, liberatory space.

Environmental Feminisms

Both the feminist flight from nature and the feminist excursion to nature as an undomesticated ground seek to release women from gendered scripts, roles, and values. These modes of feminism, especially those that seek to distance women from the cultural idea of nature and the natural, do not, for the most part, forward environmentalist objectives. Indeed, many feminists would identify neither as environmentalists nor as advocates for nonhuman animals. Feminism, as a social movement and as a body of academic theory has, for the most part, remained within the domain of the human, the cultural, the social, and the political. But for feminists who are also environmentalists and "animal people," the overcoded, overwrought term *nature* poses additional challenges. Some feminists have chosen to embrace the cultural associations between "woman" and "nature" in order to forge explicitly environmentalist positions. Activists, writers, artists, and theorists have argued on behalf of animals and the environment from a feminist stance. Rather than distance themselves from nature or animals, ecofeminists tend to ally themselves with the creatures that have been oppressed by the same, or parallel, forces. In solidarity, ecofeminist discourse sometimes echoes the popular gendering of the earth as female, as in the prevalent trope of "Mother Earth" or "Mother Nature." Lorraine Anderson's collection of women's prose and poetry about nature is entitled *Sisters of the Earth* and includes such sections as "Our Kinship with Her," "Her Pleasures," "Her Wildness" and "Her Rape" (Anderson 1991). Susan Griffin's *Woman and Nature: The Roaring inside Her,* unites woman and nature into one being, the eponymous "her" (Griffin 1978). Such figurations raise concerns about whether positive assertions that link woman to nature end up reiterating the ideological linkages that are detrimental to members of both groups. Does the idea that the earth is a "mother" encourage humans to expect to be coddled and loved unconditionally by the planet? Does personification consolidate complicated ecological systems, plants, animals, and other living creatures to one godlike being? Such figures may be comforting, but aside from the absurdity of imagining the planet as female, the personified image of the planet domesticates the profound scientific and epistemological challenges of contending with a multitude of geological, biological, chemical, ecological, and other emergent—and messy—processes. Feminists may also question whether the loaded discourse of nature and the natural can be productively reinhabited. What does it mean to feel like a "natural woman"? Would one be hiking, gathering, skinny dipping, barefoot and pregnant, without reason, language, or culture? Moreover, it is difficult to imagine that the trope of Mother Nature does not naturalize heterosexism and the definition of women as primarily reproductive creatures. Catriona Sandilands critiques the "neoconservative aroma" of the discourse of "motherhood environmentalism": "a return to patriarchal and heterosexual 'family values' will restore not only a healthy (natural) family but a healthy (natural) planet" (Sandilands 1999, xiii). It is possible, of course, to cast "mother nature" as queer, as a bitch, or as a butch in a playful and subversive mode of cultural politics, but then it is hard to imagine how such figurations would serve environmental ends. Broadly, the affirmative mode of ecofeminism shares the dilemmas of other gender-maximizing feminisms. For example, although extending a feminist ethics of care to animals and the environment may be effective ethically and politically, it does risk reinforcing gendered divisions of labor that make women responsible for virtuous but unpaid work. Furthermore, in terms of intersectionality, it is not only lesbian, gay, bisexual, intersex, transgender, and queer peoples who are positioned in especially awkward ways with regard to the figuration of a heteronormative, gendered nature, but also people of color who live within ideological landscapes in which "nature" has been loaded with racism. For example, African Americans in the United States must confront a horribly virulent history of racist associations with animality and a degraded nature. This history makes identification with *nature* a hazardous prospect, indeed.

Finally, when ecofeminists unite women and nature, there is the danger, as Val Plumwood has warned, that they pose as "angels in the ecosystem" (1993, 9). Women living in industrialized countries contribute to environmental devastation and cruelty toward animals every time we turn on a light, drive a car, buy clothes, or order a hamburger. The idea that values and virtues that have been seen as feminine could help make the environment healthier and the world less cruel to living creatures does not, in the least, absolve actual women of the effects of their everyday actions. Whether and in what circumstances it is beneficial to ally "woman" and "nature," and to align environmentalism with feminism, is I believe, a perpetually open question that must contend, within each particular historical moment and specific cultural context, with a string of potentially volatile associations, discourses, and histories.

Notwithstanding the many perils of affirming connections between woman and nature, ecofeminist theory has contributed invaluable analyses and critiques of the parallel and interconnected epistemologies, ideologies, discourses, and other cultural productions that have denigrated, oppressed, and exploited females and the environment. Key texts here include Carolyn Merchant, *The Death of Nature: Women, Ecology, and the Scientific Revolution* (1980); Annette Kolodny, *The Lay of the Land* (1984); Susan Griffin, *Woman and Nature: The Roaring Inside Her* (1989); Carol J. Adams, *A Sexual Politics of Meat: A Feminist Vegetarian Critical Theory* (1990); and Greta Gaard, *Ecofeminism: Women, Animals, Nature* (1993). Ecofeminists critique how capitalism and patriarchy, or even a fear or hatred of the body, have harmed women, animals, and the earth. Val Plumwood, in *Feminism and the Mastery of Nature*, critiques instrumental reason, denial of difference, dualism as a logic of colonization, and the masculinist position of mastery. She warns that after "much destruction, mastery will fail, because the master denies dependency on the sustaining other; he misunderstands the conditions of his own existence" (Plumwood 1994, 195). Plumwood encourages us to "remake reason" as something other than mastery, which implies "creating a democratic culture beyond dualism, ending colonizing relationships and finding a mutual, ethical basis for enriching coexistence with earth others," as well as creating "social formations built on radical democracy, co-operation and mutuality" (Plumwood 1994, 196).

Catriona Sandilands in *The Good-Natured Feminist: Ecofeminism and the Quest for Democracy* also positions ecofeminism as a vital democratic project. *The Good-Natured Feminist* shows "the specific trajectory of ecofeminism as a politics toward a radical democratic vision and the more general movement of radical democracy toward a horizon informed by the specific struggles of ecofeminism" (1999, xxi). She concludes by noting, drawing on Noel Sturgeon's *Ecofeminist Natures*, that "ecofeminism marks a political intervention that is radically deconstructive and viscerally constructive, for all its contradictions and vicissitudes" (Sandilands 1999, 210). One of the valuable contributions Sandilands makes in the book is her concept of the "ethics of the Real," which "involves the production of a relation between human and nonhuman nature in which a democratic conversation is simultaneously valorized and recognized as always already incomplete" (Sandilands 1999, 181). She explains that the ethics of the Real involves a double movement: "in the search for new metaphoric relations in which nature can appear differently, there also needs to be a point in an ethical relationship at which the ill fit is explicitly recognized, preventing metaphoric closure and opening the need for ongoing conversation" (Sandilands 1999, 181). One of the ethical and political problems then, of portraying nature as female—as mother or sister—is that nature's otherness and unknowability are obscured or tamed. Sandilands notes wryly, "For nature to appear in feminist politics it must, in a sense, become a feminist itself, and thereby be known not just as an ally but as a female person whose interests are in fact met completely by feminist politics" (Sandilands 199, 197). Clearly "nature," in all its impossibly diverse, heterogenous, and emergent manifestations would gain little from this sort of alliance with feminism.

The concept of nature within postcolonial feminisms and indigenous feminisms requires its own discussion, one that would carefully attend to specific, non-Western cultural traditions, since the very term *nature*, with all its cultural baggage, may not even have a corresponding term within other cultures. Such an account would be beyond the scope of this chapter. Nonetheless, it is important to consider that the way the West has divided up the world conceptually is only one way that it could be understood.

Moreover, although traditional ecological knowledges. or TEK, are a vital part of indigenous cultures, those cultures may or may not gender those knowledge practices. Elvira Serrano, Sebastian Boillat, and Stephan Rist, in "Incorporating Gender in Research on Indigenous Environmental Knowledge in the Tunari National Park in the Bolivian Andes," map out the complicated system in which mountains, elevation, temperature, humidity, and stars are seen as gendered beings, each with male and female expressions (low mountains are female and high ones are male, for example). They explain that the

> underlying rationale seems to be related to the idea that the differences expressed as 'gendered qualities of all 'being-things' that compose the world have come together in order to produce and reproduce life in all its aspects. As long as the differences give place to a dynamic interplay, the polarity (including gender differences) rather than being a problem, is seen as a primordial condition of maintaining life and livelihoods based on complementarity, which is made possible only through the existence of differences.
>
> (Serrano, Boillat, and Rist 2006, 321)

Whether or not indigenous or non-Western cultures imbue something akin to nature with gender, the forces of colonization, capitalism, and globalization have harmed many non-Western peoples and their environments. In some cases, when women are involved in subsistence practices, for example, they may be at the forefront of perceiving and contesting environmental degradation, such as the Chipko movement in northern India, which began in 1973, where women literally hugged trees to prevent loggers from destroying them. Vandana Shiva has written extensively about indigenous knowledges, globalization, biopiracy, water, food, oil, biopolitics, biodiversity, and biotechnology and has forged feminist, postcolonialist environmental positions in such books as *Staying Alive: Women, Ecology, and Development* (Shiva 2010). While Shiva, who is both a scientist and a popular writer, is notable for her environmental activism and for her many influential books, many other feminist scholars have also critiqued globalization and "development" from environmental perspectives. By 1994, for example, the range of feminist work in this area compelled one group of scholars—Rosi Braidotti, Ewa Charkiewicz, Sabine Häsler, and Saskia Wieringa—to construct a synthesis of these positions in *Women, the Environment, and Sustainable Development: Towards a Theoretical Synthesis* (Braidotti et. al, 1994).

Donna Haraway and Feminist Science Studies

One particularly rich field of feminist inquiry in terms of investigating how the concept of nature has been gendered is feminist science studies. Because it crosses the chasm between the humanities and the sciences, science studies must attend to nature as both a cultural conception and as a material entity. Thus science studies scholarship has been crucial for the models of new materialism and material feminisms that are discussed here. Before discussing material feminisms, however, it is important to distinguish Donna Haraway's work, which has persistently reconfigured the concept of nature as a mode of feminist theorizing. (Indeed, the subtitle of one of her collections is "the reinvention of nature" [1991b].) Moreover, in terms of the organization of this chapter, the preceding sections coalesce around whether feminists have distanced themselves from the concept of nature, recast nature as an undomesticated ground for gender-minimizing feminisms, or allied themselves with nature and nonhuman animals. Much of Haraway's work, however, inhabits the border zones where the distinctions between nature and culture are rendered absurd. Haraway's explicit political commitments to feminism, antiracism, queer politics, environmentalism, and nonhuman creaturely lives are promoted through her inventive figurations that deconstruct the dualisms set out in the beginning of this chapter.

In "A Manifesto for Cyborgs," first published in the *Socialist Review* in 1985, Haraway asserts that the figure of the cyborg can "suggest a way out of the maze of dualisms in which we have explained our bodies and our tools to ourselves" (Haraway 1991b, 39). Although much of the scholarship that took up the cyborg subsequent to Haraway's manifesto emphasized technology, Haraway does not privilege the technological over the biological, but instead insists that the cyborg merges the human with both machine and animal. In "The Promise of Monsters," "nature" does not exist as some essential, eternal, or exploitable material or form but instead is "artifactual," something made, but "not entirely by humans; it is a co-construction among humans and nonhumans" (Haraway 1991a, 297). Haraway populates her work with "material-semiotic" actors, human and nonhuman alike. She depicts "naturecultures" where materiality and meaning are co-extensive. One of her figurations, the "oncomouse," for example, a creature genetically engineered to be prone to human cancers, bred for use in cancer research, cannot be considered exclusively natural nor exclusively cultural.

Her masterpiece of intersectional modes of analysis, science studies, cultural studies, and animal studies, *Primate Visions: Gender: Race, and Nature in the World of Modern Science* (Haraway 1989), analyzes nonhuman primates as border creatures. Haraway begins the book by asking, "What may count as nature for late industrial people?" She then explains that apes and monkeys "have a privileged relation to nature and culture for western people: simians occupy the border zones between those potent mythic poles" (Haraway 1989, 1). While *Primate Visions* engages in extensive research, rigorous modes of analysis, and often devastating critiques, it also aims to open up less harmful modes of thinking: "I want readers to find an 'elsewhere' from which to envision a different and less hostile order of relationships among people, animals, technologies, and land. Like the actors in the stories that follow, I also want to set new terms for the traffic between what we have come to know historically as nature and culture" (Haraway 1989, 15). Haraway's work suggests a paradoxical ontology, as the "elsewhere" is, in a sense, the world we already inhabit. Her figurations—the cyborg, the oncomouse, the primate, and the companion species (to be discussed later)—are discovered, already existing in the world, but are also rewritten in poetic and inventive ways so as to catalyze new modes of knowing, acting, and being. Her work inhabits what *is* in such a way as to orient particular naturecultures toward what could be.

Queer Natures

Haraway tells a story about going to the lake with a friend and her husband who, upon seeing four ducks, assumed they were two "reproductive, heterosexual pairs:" "It quickly sounded like they had a modest mortgage on the wetlands around that section of the lake and were about to send their ducklings to a good school to consolidate their reproductive investment" (Haraway 2003b, 129). Wryly, Haraway notes that she, on the other hand, "held that the ducks were into queer communities" (129). Haraway then critiques both positions, declaring that "the ducks deserved our recognition of their *nonhuman* cultures, subjectivities, histories, and material lives" (129). Although Haraway warns against applying human categories such as "queer" to nonhuman creatures, the fact that the concept of nature has long been imbued with heteronormativity has meant that both ordinary people and the scientists who study animal behavior have expected or assumed that nonhuman animals are "heterosexual," despite much evidence to the contrary. Thus, documenting, defining, and performing "queer natures," remains a significant feminist project, as the rest of this section will explore. It is important to point out, however, that even as several feminist scholars have undertaken the project of "queering" nature, in part by emphasizing how both human and nonhuman creatures do not fit within binary categories of sex and gender, one eminent feminist theorist, Elizabeth Grosz, develops a Darwinian feminism that insists upon an ontological sexual difference between male and female. Reading Luce Irigaray through Charles Darwin, for example, Grosz argues that "sexual difference is ineliminable, the force that proliferates all social and natural relations" (Grosz 2011, 168). Grosz argues for the primacy of sexual difference: "sexual difference is not just one social difference among many but that form of difference that makes all other lived differences possible, the engine of all lived differences" (168). Myra J. Hird, critiquing Grosz, points out that "most organisms are not differentiated by sexual difference," and that "most organisms do not reproduce through sexual reproduction" (Hird 2012, 224).

Bruce Bagemihl's massive book *Biological Exuberance: Animal Homosexuality and Natural Diversity* includes a "wondrous bestiary" which documents same sex behaviors, including "courtship, affectionate, sexual, pair-bonding, and parenting" in countless different species of mammals and birds, often accompanied by rather adorable illustrations of same-sex animal sex (Bagemihl 1999). Joan Roughgarden's *Evolution's Rainbow: Diversity, Gender, and Sexuality in Nature and People,* discusses same-sex sex, gender diversity, transgender, and categories of sexual difference beyond male and female. White throated sparrows, for example, have four "genders," two male and two female. Species of fish are especially complicated, with their "sequential, simultaneous, and criss-crossing hermaphroditism" (Roughgarden 2004, 89, 35). Myra J. Hird also contends that the nonhuman world is queer indeed. See, for example, her chapter, "Sex Diversity in Nonhuman Animals," in *Sex, Gender, and Science* (Hird 2004b); the coedited collection with Noreen Giffney, *Queering the Nonhuman* (Hird and Giffney 2008); and her lively essay, "Naturally Queer," which includes the astonishing fact that *Schizophyllum*, a genus of fungi, includes "28,000 sexes" (Hird, 2004a). In "Eluding Capture: The Science, Culture, and Pleasure of 'Queer' Animals," I note the sense of wonder often provoked by the remarkable variance of gender, sex, reproduction, and childrearing arrangements among animals. By eluding human conceptual categories or modes of capture, "queer" animals dramatize emergent worlds of desire, action, agency, and activity, in which "nature" is always already populated by diverse animal cultures. (Alaimo 2010b, 67). In fact, the very cultural achievements that humans have used to distinguish themselves from nonhuman animals—language and tools—are, it turns out, not only accomplishments of which other primates can boast, but skills that they have used to enhance their sexual pleasure (Bagemihl 1999, 66–71; Alaimo 2010b, 60–63). For bonobos and many other species, sex is not merely some sort of natural instinct for heterosexual reproduction but a pleasurable, sociable, cultural, even creative practice. Queer, but not, perhaps, "natural."

In their introduction to the collection *Queer Ecologies: Sex, Nature, Politics, Desire*, Catriona Mortimer-Sandilands and Bruce Erickson present an important genealogy of queer ecologies, ranging from Darwin, Kraft-Ebbing, and Olmsted to Kinsey, Foucault, and the scholarship on cultural geography, ecofeminism, and environmental justice. They trace these genealogies not only through theory but through literature, film, environmental movements, and queer politics. They assert that "the task of a queer ecology is to probe the intersections of sex and nature with an eye to developing a sexual politics that more clearly includes considerations of the natural world and its biosocial constitution, and an environmental politics that demonstrates an understanding of the ways in which sexual relations organize and influence both the material world of nature and our perceptions, experiences, and constitutions of that world" (Mortimer-Sandilands and Erickson 2010, 5). This is an ambitious project, especially given that queer politics rarely considers environmentalism and that most environmentalisms would see GLBTIQ issues as irrelevant at best. Irrelevance would be preferable, perhaps to the sense that queer people are adversaries. Ladelle McWhorter entitles her essay in this collection, "The Enemy of the Species." She explains that queer, dark-skinned, and disabled people "were held to be, literally, biological enemies of the human species, pollutants and pathogens whose very presence posed a physical and possibly mortal threat not only to individuals but to the species as a whole" (McWhorter 2010, 76). Giovanna Di Chiro, examining actual pollutants, takes on a similar dynamic, in which queer and environmental orientations are at odds in her essay, "Polluted Politics? Confronting Toxic Discourse, Sex Panic and Eco-Normativity" (Di Chiro 2010). Di Chiro critiques mainstream environmentalist rhetoric about how "toxic chemical pollution is responsible for the undermining or perversion of the 'natural,'" and especially the flood of estrogenic chemicals that put "at risk the future existence of *natural* masculinity" (Di Chiro 2010, 201). The rhetoric surrounding hormone disruptors reveals a particularly vexing fault line for queer ecologies, in which gender normativity serves as the baseline for assessing environmental harm. Determining queer, green ways of intervening in these rhetorics is crucial at this particular cultural moment, given that hormone disruptors, like many manufactured substances, are becoming more prevalent in the biophysical world, that many species these substances could affect are already endangered, and that the movements for the recognition of transgender, intersex, and agendered peoples are only now beginning to gain momentum. The fundamental conflict, however, may be deeper than rhetoric, in that the conservation of species that currently exist entails a reproductive trajectory, and such trajectories are bound up with the very sort of heteronormative reprosexuality that has harmed humans.

Dianne Chisholm's essay, "Biophilia, Creative Involution and the Ecological Future of Queer Desire, concludes *Queer Ecologies* on an affirmative note, with an analysis of the nature writing of Ellen Meloy. Chisholm presents Meloy as counterpoint to Lee Edelman's *No Future*, in which "'life' is the ideological enemy that queer desire ought to, critically and clinically, annihilate" (Chisholm, 2010, 377). Chisholm argues that Meloy's "biophilic compositions demonstrate the ecological future of queer desire." Chisholm presents Meloy as writing a "nature" that is not heteronormative but instead, "a paradigm of queer—nonreproductive, nonfiliative, anti-sexist, thoroughly perverse, and wildly anarchic—desire" (2010, 377). Chisholm's analysis of Meloy's work may also suggest the wild desire performed by Beth Stephens and Annie Sprinkle in their recent performance pieces as self-proclaimed "ecosexuals." Stephens and Sprinkle offer "SexEcological walking tours," for example, that teach "25 ways to make love to the earth." They have also created collaborative performance art ecosex weddings around the world, in which they have married the Applachian mountains, the dirt, the sky and the sea. (Stephens and Sprinkle 2014, n.p.) Their playful, sexy performances make environmentalism a bit less dour, offering abundant pleasure rather than what we expect from environmentalism—virtuous self-deprivation shadowed by a horizon of impending doom. But Stephens and Sprinkle also counter the tendency within queer theory to oppose naturalized reprosexuality of heteronormativity by grimly embracing the negation of futurity. For environmentalists, concerned about such things as climate change and the massive extinction of nonhuman creatures, the invocation of the future remains invaluable; environmental ethics and politics must orient themselves toward the future, since the survival of so many other creatures is at stake. Well aware of the grief and pain wrought by environmental devastation, such as the mountaintop removal Stephens documents in her film *Goodbye Gauley Mountain: An Ecosexual Love Story* (2013), Stephens and Sprinkle nonetheless creatively stage (I must draw upon Chisholm again) "a paradigm of queer—nonreproductive, nonfiliative, anti-sexist, thoroughly perverse, and wildly anarchic—desire" (2010, 377). And they invite everyone to join the festivities.

Material Feminisms, Feminist Posthumanism and the Anthropocene

In this final section, the key term, *nature*, with its long and vexing history within feminism, feminist theory, and queer theory, morphs into other terms or becomes dispersed, distributed, or otherwise transformed. Several overlapping forces have decomposed the concept of nature, including the extraordinary, anthropogenic physical, chemical, biological, and climatic alterations of the planet. Even the most casual glance at "nature" in the twenty-first century would reveal that the idea it is something unchanging, something external to and untouched by human culture, is an absurd relic. Indeed, scholars in environmental studies have long argued that both the concept of "wilderness" and wilderness spaces themselves are, to some degree constructed by humans. Bruno Latour, in *We Have Never Been Modern* (1993), demonstrates that the division between "nature" and "society" is untenable, as we live among a proliferation of hybrids, such as the hole in the ozone layer. Hybrids require more integrated academic modes of inquiry: "the ozone hole is too social and too narrated to be truly natural; the strategy of industrial firms and heads of state is too full of chemical reactions to be reduced to power and interest; the discourse of the ecosphere is too real and too social to boil down to meaning effects. Is it our fault if the networks are *simultaneously real, like nature, narrated like discourse, and collective like society*?" (Latour 1993, 6, italics in original). Donna Haraway, as discussed earlier, has been indefatigable in her project to refigure the concept of nature. Haraway's boundary creatures, like Latour's hybrids, have been especially good to think with in this regard. Haraway, however, also undertakes a profoundly intersectional mode of analysis as she considers how gender, race, and sexuality are part of the "traffic" in nature. Moreover, even when social constructionist models of feminist theory held sway, Haraway insisted that nature had its own agency and that nonhuman creatures should be allowed to participate, somehow, in the stories told about them. Somewhere around the turn into the twenty-first century, a chorus of theorists began to voice their frustration that models of social construction enabled discursive analysis and critique but discouraged engagement with lived, biological bodies and the actions and significations of the nonhuman world. The prevailing feminist critiques of essentialism were themselves critiqued for being disciplining, constraining scholarly injunctions. Feminist theorists debated, for example, whether or not bodies really did matter in Judith Butler's *Bodies That Matter: On the Discursive Limits of Sex* (1993). Whether, how, and to what extent Butler accounted for materiality will not be resolved here. The crucial thing for this discussion is that in the wake of the linguistic turn, scholars in feminist theory sought alternative methods that could engage with material as well as cultural and discursive domains.

Nature as a concept, then, gives way to the broader designation of materiality, which encompasses human bodies, nonhuman bodies, and the wide biophysical world. As feminist science studies scholar Cecilia Äsberg, puts it, "materialities beckon us . . . from inside the humanities and the natural sciences in an age when transgenic biotechnology and patented genes, wildlife conservation and anthropocene rhetorics, in-vitro meat and in-vivo foetal imaging, embryo selection and consumer custom-made pharmacology are the *post-natural* orders of the day" (Äsberg, 2013, 5). Shifting to materiality from nature, within a postnatural multiverse may allow feminist theory to leave some cultural baggage behind, and it may foster new lines of inquiry, assemblages, and alliances that were previously volatile, awkward, or retrogressive. Even without the term *nature*, however, essentialisms may still operate through other means, such as through the genetic reductionism that is so prevalent in popular culture. Nonetheless, shifting from nature to materiality may perform cultural work, especially in so far as the materiality is understood as something agential.

The terms, territories, groupings, overlaps, and fault lines between the theoretical positions in what could be called the "material turn" (as opposed to the linguistic turn) are still being worked out, but the list of theories that one could consider is long indeed: actor-network theory, new empiricism, thing theory, object-oriented ontology, affect theory, new vitalism, somatechnics, new materialism, material feminism, posthumanism. While all of these theories may be relevant for feminism—moreover, while feminist theory may be invaluable for them all—this chapter focuses on material feminism and feminist posthumanism, since those two fields are particularly important for tracing what used to be known as "nature." Material feminisms and other new materialisms emerge from poststructuralist, postmodern, and social constructionist theories in that they value modes of discursive critique and the attention to how economics, ideologies, and other social and cultural forces shape knowledge practices. But they insist that there must be ways to make sense of how material and nonhuman entities act, signify, and affect social, cultural, and economic processes. Some science studies scholars have been explicit about the need for methods that can reveal how economics, discourses, ideologies, and other cultural systems affect what we know about the world and, at the same time, that can allow aspects of material reality to register. (See Andrew Pickering's 1995 *The Mangle of Practice* for one robust model.) Feminists need to know both about how, for example, the idea that women tend to be malingerers or hypochondriacs affects research and treatment protocols for autoimmune diseases, which are often difficult to diagnose, as well as how estrogen may cause or exacerbate particular autoimmune diseases. More to the point, it would be useful to know both how estrogen operates within bodies and how gendered conceptions have shaped what sorts of information about estrogen is and isn't available. Considering the interactions *between* cultural conceptions, medical research, and the biochemistry of lived bodies complicates matters further since it is impossible to know what estrogen is apart from how it is known within particular scientific captures that are already structured by economic and ideological forces. The nature/culture divide cannot be reinstalled here or elsewhere. *Estrogen* is *simultaneously* a group of compounds that does things in bodies, a cultural term saturated with gendered and often heterosexist meanings, something that enables big Pharma to profit from the lives of nonhuman animals, and something that science, in Susan J. Hekman's terms, has "disclosed" (Hekman 2010).

Whereas various forms of feminism analyzed how social and political forces, structures, inequities, and ideologies have material effects on bodies, material feminisms theorize how the social and the material interact and how bodies (and substances and environments) have their own forces. For feminists, LGBTIQ people, persons with disabilities, and others, grappling with how corporeal processes, desires, orientations, abilities, and harms accord with or diverge from social categories, norms, and discourses is a necessary epistemological-political undertaking. For some people, it is a matter of survival. Even though many of the theories described in the collection *Material Feminism* (Alaimo and Hekman 2008) hardly seem distinctly feminist in that they often do not speak directly to the questions of sex or gender, they still have their roots in feminism as a social movement via their insistence that the human body is a site that is simultaneously political, ontological, and epistemological. As Hekman puts it, "women have never been allowed to jettison the body and the biological; they have not been allowed to become the disembodied knowers of the Cartesian tradition" (2010, 25).

The introduction to the collection *Material Feminisms* states, "The theorists assembled here have been working to revise the paradigms of poststructuralism, postmodernism, and cultural studies in ways that can productively account for the agency, semiotic force, and dynamics of bodies and natures. The most daunting aspect of such a project is to radically rethink materiality, the very 'stuff' of bodies and natures" (Alaimo and Hekman 2008, 6). Material feminisms rethink nature, corporeality, and materiality in ways that make it ludicrous to imagine the substance of the world as a repository, a static vault for retrograde cultural formulations, or as a passive, plastic resource for the exploits of culture. Material feminisms, precisely because they recast nature and the environment in ways that stress them as agential, emergent, and intertwined with whatever it is we have been demarcating as exceptionally human or cultural make it possible for feminists to engage with all that has been imagined as distinct from culture without reinstalling gender, race, or other essentialisms. Donna Haraway, Karen Barad, and other feminist and environmental theorists develop models of material agency that do not depend on a (human) subject. Whereas a commonsensical notion of agency could be that of someone acting on something else in a unidirectional fashion, conceptions of material agency often involve "interaction" or "intra-action." In her essay on the environmental, chemical, ethical, and political dimensions of Hurricane Katrina and its aftermath, Nancy Tuana advocates "interactionism": "The point is that material agency in its heterogenous forms, including irreducibly diverse forms of distinctively human agency, interact in complex ways. Agency in all these instances emerges out of such interaction; it is not antecedent to them" (2008, 196). Similarly, Karen Barad explains agency as "*'doing' or 'being' in its intra-activity*" (Barad 2007, 178; italics in original). *Intra-activity* is a key term for Barad, in that, drawing on Neils Bohr, she insists that "relata" "do not precede their relations; rather relata—within—phenomena emerge through specific intra-actions" (Barad 2007, 140). Barads's "agential realism," rejects representationalism in favor of a notion of performativity in which discourse and materiality are not external to each other but are, instead, "mutually implicated in the dynamics of intra-activity" (Barad 2007, 146).

In *Bodily Natures: Science, Environment, and the Material Self* (Alaimo 2010a), I analyze the environmental health and environmental justice movements, including the citizen scientists who must discern, track, and negotiate the unruly substances that move across bodies and places. Nature is neither external nor eternal, but instead, the immediately present, ever-changing, materiality of the world and ourselves. Thinking materiality as agential, thinking bodies as continually transforming, and thinking across the bodies and places in ways that highlight their interactions, culminates in what I call *trans-corporeality*. Trans-corporeality entails a radical rethinking of the physical environment and human bodily existence by attending to the transfers across those categories. Trans-corporeality begins with the subject in place, where the materiality of xenobiotic substances, consumer products, invisible flows and networks cut through the ostensible outline of the self, transforming the human subject into a posthuman subject who is always already the very stuff of the world. As a type of material feminism, trans-corporeality is indebted to Judith Butler's conception of the subject as immersed within a matrix of discursive systems, but it transforms that model, insisting that the subject cannot be separated from networks of intra-active material agencies (drawing on Karen Barad) and thus cannot ignore the disturbing epistemological quandaries of risk society (drawing on Ulrich Beck). Thinking the subject as a material being, not as a transcendent, utterly rational subject but as a being subject to the agencies of the compromised, entangled world, enacts an environmental posthumanism, insisting that what we are as bodies and minds, is inextricably interlinked with the circulating substances, materialities, and forces of the wider world.

While some scholarship that is part of the material turn, including some feminist theories, continues to be concerned solely with the human animal, I would contend that once the human is conceptualized as a material creature that has happened to appear as a being in the same way that other beings have happened and who continues to exist as the very stuff of intra-acting agencies—not a creature made exceptional by his reason, independence, and transcendence—then the grounds for ignoring or dismissing the lives, the suffering, and the concerns of other creatures make little sense. For me, then, material feminisms and other theories of the material turn would or should be critical posthumanist theories as well, in that they inhabit a zone inimical to human exceptionalism. Haraway's figuration of the companion species, for example, radically redefines the human as such, arguing that the human coevolved with dogs and other species (Haraway 2003a). Similar to Barad's concept of intra-action, Haraway stresses that *human* cannot be understood as prior to or separate from dogs: "Dogs are about the inescapable, contradictory story of relationships—co-constitutive relationships in which none of the partners pre-exist the relating, and the relating is never done once and for all. Historical specificity and contingent mutability rule all the way down, into nature and culture, into naturecultures" (Haraway 2003a, 12). Rosi Braidotti's voluminous works also stress a posthumanist sense of materiality and relationality as an ethical practice. She argues in *The Posthuman* that "the ethical imagination is alive and well in posthuman subjects, in the form of ontological relationality. A Sustainable ethics for non-unitary subjects rests on an enlarged sense of inter-connection between self and others, including the nonhuman or 'earth' others" (Braidotti 2013, 190). Feminist theory, long a site for innovative interdisciplinary work, long critical of the concept of Man, may well be a generative field for the transformation of the humanities into the posthumanities. Conversely, posthumanism may transfigure feminist scholarship. Cecilia Äsberg, Redi Koobak, and Ericka Johnson advocate posthumanist feminist practices that would "*re-tool* the humanities so as to meet up with the on-going transformations of our worlds." They argue that forging posthumanist theories and methodologies is crucial for feminist research: "it may help us inhabit, in simultaneously critical, creative, and reciprocal manners, the meaningful materialities of emerging naturecultures . . ., the new, unsettled Self-Other relations pertaining to gendered and sexualized, aged and racialized, human and nonhuman ideals of embodiment—and the inclusions and exclusions they engender" (Äsberg, Koobak, and Johnson 2011, 228). One of the boldest performances of an "an enlarged sense of inter-connection between self and others" as Braidotti puts it, may well be Eva Hayward's essay, "More Lessons from a Starfish: Prefixial Flesh and Transpeciated Selves." Hayward writes of transsexuality as a "mutuality," a "shared ontology," with the starfish, as both regenerate "as an act of healing": "Trans-morphic as zoomorphic—if we can understand the cut as an act of love, then can we not imagine that "like a starfish" it is an enactment of trans-speciating? We, transsexuals and starfish, are animate bodies; our bodies are experienced and come to be known through encounters with other animate bodies" (Hayward 2008, 81). This is a palpable, dazzling, posthumanist figuration, as the shared ontology with the starfish, culminates in a "transspeciated self," a self who is, who knows, through an encounter with another species. Hayward's work demonstrates how the history of feminist and queer modes of writing at the chasm of the subject/object divide, as an animated material being, may flourish as a newly transfigured posthumanism.

It is fitting to conclude with a meditation on the anthropocene. The *Anthropocene* is a recently coined term that describes the current geological epoch, in which human activities have altered the planet to such an extent that these changes register on a vast geological time scale. The anthopocene began around 1800, when the steam engine was adopted and fossil fuels began to be used extensively. Since this chapter focuses on nature, the crucial, and rather obvious point to be made here is that with the human alteration of the planet's biology, chemistry, climate, landscapes, and ecological systems, there can be said to be no more "nature" in existence. As Claire Colebrook puts it, "The literal truth of the Anthropocene era is that man is not a being within the world, nor a fragment of life, but has existed as a geological force that has irrevocably altered a world that is no longer an earth, but is now an imbricated man-world complex" (Colebrook 2012, 198). Colebrook uses the term *man* deliberately, with a feminist edge, recalling a long history of man's naming of himself as such. I would note that the predominant, not feminist, discourse about the anthropocene sometimes sports a triumphant tone, as Man remarks on his spectacular achievement by viewing it from a safe position, above and beyond the marked earth. Scholarship in feminist epistemology and feminist science studies, for example, Haraway's critique of the "conquering gaze from nowhere," the "view of infinite vision," and the "god trick" of an unmarked, disembodied perspective," are potent resources for examining the implications of particular accounts of the anthropocene, especially those that shore up a delusional notion of an intact Man, who observes the ruins from a cold distance (Haraway 1991b, 188, 189). The posthuman, trans-corporeal subject, one who is utterly in and of the very stuff of the world, who does not transcend but engages in knowledge practices as a situated, political, and material being, is the subject adequate for the ethical predicaments of the anthropocene, which involve nothing short of everyday incalculable considerations of how even the most minute actions have effects on the future of life itself. For the trans-corporeal subject of the anthropocene there can be no refuge from alarming reckonings with the perplexing accountabilities that occupy multiple scales.

One of the paradoxes of the concept of the anthropocene for material feminisms and for feminist posthumanisms is that at the same moment new materialisms stress the interactive agencies of the material world and posthumanism erodes models of human exceptionalism, the "anthropocene" elevates humans to an unrivaled status as the species that has made the most lasting mark on the world. Simultaneously imagining a feminist posthumanism and a feminist account of the anthropocene is rather bewildering. The University of Milwaukee's C21: Center for 21st Century Studies, in their call for papers for a conference on "anthropocene feminism" put forth the following questions:

> First, how has feminism anticipated the concept of the Anthropocene, and what might it yet have to offer: how can feminism help us to historicize, challenge, or refine the concept of the Anthropocene? . . . Second, and equally important, is there (or should there be) an Anthropocene feminism? How should feminism in an Anthropogenic age take up an altered relation to—an increased attention to or concern for—the nonhuman world? (C21 2014, n.p.).

These are vital questions, which have yet to be answered, but there is certainly the potential for the anthropocene to alter feminism's engagement with "nature," and for feminism to recast the concept of the anthropocene.

Claire Colebrook has written several stunning essays about the anthropocene, including "Not Symbiosis, Not Now: Why Anthropogenic Climate Change Is Not Really Human," in which she contends, "The figural and critical truth of the Anthropocene is that just as there is no pure earth that might be reclaimed, so there is no thought that is not already contaminated and made possible by the very logic of man that ecology might seek to overcome" (Colebrook 2012 198–199). Specifically, Colebrook points to the recent theoretical turns that coincide with material feminisms and feminist posthumanisms: "these turns 'back' to bodies, matters, historicity, ecology and the lived," calling them "reaction formations or last gasps." (Colebrook 2012, 193). She asks, "What if all the current counter-Cartesian, post-Cartesian or anti-Cartesian figures of living systems (along with a living order that is one interconnected and complex mesh) were a way of avoiding the extent to which man is a theoretical animal, a myopically and malevolently self-enclosed machine whose world he will always view as present for his own edification? (193). Surely, the history of the concept of *nature* exemplifies the way in which "man" as a "malevolently self-enclosed machine" has viewed the world as "present for his own edification," as he casts the other as a passive, silent object or resource. But when Colebrook warns that recent theories intended to remedy this wretched state of affairs are part of the same system, she leaves us in a terribly bleak place. And though we could conclude with a question meant to provoke anthropocene feminist theories—what knowledge practices, what modes of life, what forms of ethics or politics are possible and desirable within an anthropocene epoch?—it is also fitting to remain, at least for a moment, squarely within the bleak landscape of the anthropocene that Colebrook paints. Because, if a chapter that begins with nature and concludes with the anthropocene does not make its readers quake, well, then, it is just another product of the "self-enclosed machine."

References

Adams, Carol. 1990. *A Sexual Politics of Meat. A Feminist-Vegetarian Critical Theory*. New York: Continuum.
Alaimo, Stacy. 2000. *Undomesticated Ground: Recasting Nature as Feminist Space*. Ithaca, NY: Cornell University Press.
Alaimo, Stacy. 2010a. *Bodily Natures: Science, Environment, and the Material Self*. Bloomington: Indiana University Press.
Alaimo, Stacy. 2010b. "Eluding Capture: The Science, Culture, and Pleasure of 'Queer' Animals." In *Queer Ecologies: Sex, Nature, Politics, Desire*, edited by Bruce Erickson and Catriona Mortimer-Sandilands. Bloomington: Indiana University Press, 51–72.
Alaimo, Stacy, and Susan J. Hekman. 2008. "Introduction: Emerging Models of Materiality in Feminist Theory." In *Material Feminisms*, edited by Alaimo and Hekman. Bloomington: Indiana University Press, 1–22.
Anderson, Lorraine. 2003. *Sisters of the Earth: Women's Prose and Poetry About Nature*. Vintage.
Åsberg, Cecilia. 2013. "The Timely Ethics of Posthumanist Gender Studies." *Feministische Studien* 1: 7–12.
Åsberg, Cecilia, Redi Koobak, and Ericka Johnson. 2011. "Beyond the Humanist Imagination." *NORA: Nordic Journal of Feminist and Gender Research* 19 (4): 218–230.
Bagemihl, Bruce. 1999. *Biological Exuberance: Animal Homosexuality and Natural Diversity*. New York: St. Martin's Press.
Barad, K. 2007. *Meeting the Universe Halfway: Quantum Physics and the Entanglement of Matter and Meaning*. Durham, NC: Duke University Press.
Butler, Judith. 1993. *Bodies That Matter: On the Discursive Limits of Sex*. New York: Routledge.
Braidotti, Rosi. 2013. *The Posthuman*. Cambridge: Polity Press.
Braidotti, Rosi, Ewa Charkiewicz, Sabine Häusler, and Saskia Wieringa. 1994. *Women, the Environment and Sustainable Development: Towards a Theoretical Synthesis*. London: Zed Books.
C21: Center for 21st Century Studies. 2104. Call for papers. Anthropocene Feminism Conference. http://c21uwm.com/anthropocene/
Chisholm, Dianne. 2010. "Biophilia, Creative Involution, and the Ecological Future of Queer Desire." In *Queer Ecologies: Sex, Nature, Politics, Desire*, edited by Bruce Erickson and Catriona Mortimer-Sandilands. Bloomington: Indiana University Press, 359–383.

Colebrook, Claire. 2012. "Not Symbiosis, Not Now: Why Anthropogenic Climate Change Is Not Really Human." *Oxford Literary Review* 34 (2): 185–209.

de Beauvoir, Simone. 1952. *The Second Sex*. Translated and edited by H. M. Parshley. New York: Random House.

Di Chiro, Giovanna. 2010. "Polluted Politics? Confronting Toxic Discourse, Sex Panic, and Eco-Normativity." In *Queer Ecologies: Sex, Nature, Politics, Desire*, edited by Bruce Erickson and Catriona Mortimer-Sandilands. Bloomington: Indiana University Press, 199–230.

Grosz, Elizabeth. 2011. *Becoming Undone: Darwinian Reflections on Life, Politics, and Art*. Durham, NC: Duke University Press.

Haraway, Donna. 1989. *Primate Visions: Gender, Race, and Nature in the World of Modern Science*. New York: Routledge.

Haraway, Donna. 1991a. "The Promise of Monsters: A Regenerated Politics for Inappropriate/d Others." In *Cultural Studies*, edited by Lawrence Grossberg, Cary Nelson, and Paula Treichler. New York: Routledge.

Haraway, Donna. 1991b. "Situated Knowledges: The Science Question in Feminism and the Privilege of Partial Perspective." In *Simians, Cyborgs, and Women: The Reinvention of Nature*. New York: Routledge.

Haraway, Donna. 2003a, *The Companion Species Manifesto: Dogs, People, and Significant Otherness*. Chicago: Prickly Paradigm Press.

Haraway, Donna, 2003b. The *Haraway Reader*. New York, Routledge.

Hird, Myra J. 2004a. "Naturally Queer." *Feminist Theory* 5 (1): 85–89.

Hird, Myra J. 2004b. *Sex, Gender, and Science*. New York: Palgrave MacMillan.

Hird, Myra J. 2012. "Digesting Difference: Metabolism and the Question of Sexual Difference." *Configurations* 20 (3): 213–237.

Hird, Myra Noreen Giffney, ed. 2008. *Queering the Nonhuman*. Farnham: Ashgate.

Hayward, Eva. 2008. "More Lessons from a Starfish: Prefixial Flesh and Trans-speciated Selves." *WSQ: Women's Studies Quarterly* 36 (3–4): 64–85.

Hekman, Susan. 2010. *The Material of Knowledge: Feminist Disclosures*. Bloomington: Indiana University Press.

Latour, Bruno. 1993. *We Have Never Been Modern*. Cambridge, MA: Harvard University Press.

McWhorter, Ladelle. 2010. "Enemy of the Species." In *Queer Ecologies: Sex, Nature, Politics, Desire*, edited by Bruce Erickson and Catriona Mortimer-Sandilands. Bloomington: Indiana University Press.

Mitchell, Juliet. 1989. "Women: The Longest Revolution" Karen V. Hansen and Irene J. Philipson, *Women, Class, and the Feminist Imagination*. Philadelphia: Temple University Press.

Pickering, Andrew. 1995. *The Mangle of Practice: Time, Agency, and Science*. Chicago: University of Chicago Press.

Plumwood, Val. 1994. *Feminism and the Mastery of Nature*. New York: Routledge.

Roughgarden, Joan. 2004. *Evolution's Rainbow: Diversity, Gender, and Sexuality in Nature and People*. Berkeley: University of California Press.

Rubin, Gayle. 1990. "The Traffic in Women: Notes on the 'Political Economy' of Sex." Reprinted in *Reader*, edited by Karen V. Hansen and Ilene J. Philipson, *Women, Class, and the Feminist Imagination, a Socialist-Feminist*. Philadelphia: Temple University Press.

Sandilands, Catriona. 1999. *The Good Natured Feminist: Ecofeminism and the Quest for Democracy*. Minneapolis: University of Minnesota Press.

Sandilands, Catriona Mortimer, and Bruce Erickson. 2010. "Introduction: A Geneaology of Queer Ecologies." In *Queer Ecologies*, edited by Mortimer-Sandilands and Erickson. Bloomington: Indiana University Press, 1–50.

Serrano, E., S. Boillat, S. Rist. 2006. "Incorporating Gender in Research on Indigenous Environmental Knowledge in the Tunari National Park in the Bolivian Andes." In *Gender and Sustainable Development: Case Studies from the National Centre of Competence in Research (NCCR) North-South*, edited by Premchander and Müller. Bern: Geographica Bernensia/University of Bern, 329–351.

Shiva, Vandana. 2010. *Staying Alive: Women, Ecology, and Development*. Cambridge, MA: South End Press.

Snitow, Ann. 1990. "A Gender Diary." In *Conflicts in Feminism*, edited by Marianne Hirsch and Evelyn Fox Keller. New York: Routledge, 9–43.

Stephens, Elizabeth, and Annie Sprinkle. 2014. SexEcology. http://sexecology.org.

Stephens, Elizabeth. 2013. *Goodbye Gauley Mountain: An Ecosexual Love Story*. DVD. Fecund Arts.

Tuana, Nancy. 2008. "Viscous Porosity: Witnessing Katrina." In *Material Feminisms*, edited by Alaimo and Hekman. Bloomington: Indiana University Press, 188–213.

Wittig, Monique. 1992. *The Straight Mind and Other Essays*. Boston: Beacon Press.

CHAPTER 27

NORMS AND NORMALIZATION

DEAN SPADE AND CRAIG WILLSE

The concepts of the "norm," and processes of "normalization" are significant for feminist theory and activism. Feminist theories and activisms seek to dismantle conditions of heteropatriarchy, and to do so they provide an analysis of those conditions and the logics that sustain them. Feminisms approach cultural "common sense" about gender and sexuality critically, exposing how the putative facts about gender, bodies, family structures, and work roles are historically contingent and culturally constructed, as well as both harmful and open to transformation. Much of what feminists challenge are arrangements that have been deemed "natural," such as gender role assignments supposedly rooted in immutable bodily difference. Feminist methodologies and interventions vary with regard to which norms they interrogate. For example, liberal feminisms have taken aim at workplace inequality, examining normalized practices of labor division within families and wage labor systems to propose methods of increasing women's access to participation in wage labor systems. Meanwhile, anticapitalist feminists have argued that such interventions are not enough, and feminists must interrogate and dismantle patriarchal norms that structure the entire framework of racialized-gendered wage labor system rather than just seeking participation in them. Regardless of these differences among feminist interventions, the concept of the norm is crucial to a broad range of feminist inquiries and challenges, including inclusion and equality-seeking models and radical transformative approaches.

Where heteropatriarchal conditions (such as women doing the bulk of unpaid domestic labor) are cast as "natural" preferences or capacities, feminists argue that coercive racialized gender norms about motherhood, rather than anyone's fundamental nature, disproportionately force women into that work. Where rigid standards of body and appearance endanger health, feminists identify "beauty norms" as a serious concern, shifting attention to studying the enforcement of such norms and dismantling them rather than trying to get women to meet them or blaming women for being concerned with them. Understanding the ways that ideas and rules about gender structure the world as norms allows feminists to study how these norms are invented, enforced, and lived; how processes of normalization work. It facilitates inquiries into how norms are internalized, so that we enforce them on ourselves and each other, despite the fact that such enforcement limits our realm of possibility or causes us suffering. Gender, itself, comes to be understood as a set of norms, rather than as a natural division among people.

Simone de Beauvoir's foundational interventions in *The Second Sex* expose how a range of myths about women's biology and psychology, along with mythological female-ideal roles, such as the virgin and the mother, establish and maintain the norm of maleness and consign women to the role of "other." Beauvoir (2011, 283) famously claims, "One is not born, but rather becomes, a woman." This statement opposes the idea of an essential womanhood or femininity, arguing that gender is constructed and enforced by social indoctrination. Judith Butler (1990, 33) describes gender as "the repeated stylization of the body, a set of repeated acts within a highly rigid regulatory frame that congeal over time to produce the appearance of substance, of a natural sort of being." Butler argues that "the body is not a mute facticity" (129). For Butler, gender is not itself a truth, but is instead a matrix of norms and repeated practices: "If the inner truth of gender is a fabrication and if a true gender is a fantasy instituted and inscribed on the surface of bodies, then it seems that genders can be neither true nor false, but are only produced as the truth effects of a discourse of primary and stable identity" (136). "Femininity is thus not the product of a choice, but the forcible citation of a norm, one whose complex historicity is indissociable from relations of discipline, regulation, punishment" (Butler 1993, 232). Butler shows that gender is a set of congealed, repeated practices that produce a field of regulation in which all people are compelled to perform in order to survive (Butler 1997, 20). She describes the task of feminist theory as such: "A political genealogy of gender ontologies, if it is successful, will deconstruct the substantive appearance of gender into its constitutive acts and locate and account for those acts within the compulsory frames set by the various forces that police the social appearance of gender" (Butler 1990).

The chapter that follows makes three related moves. First, we review Michel Foucault's conception of disciplinary norms and the normalization of populations to illuminate the centrality of interrogating norms and normalization to feminist inquiry and activism. We then demonstrate this feminist critique through the example of feminist criticism of same-sex marriage advocacy. Finally, we look at how concern with norms and normalization guides feminist criticism and self-reflection within social movement spaces and organizations to produce transformative understandings of collectivity.

Disciplinary Power and the Norm

The work of Michel Foucault is particularly useful for tracing how the concepts of "norm," "normativity," and "normalization" relate to feminist theories and activisms.

Foucault's work intervenes in accepted accounts of how power works. Foucault argued that we often think of power as repressive, as a top-down dynamic in which those who hold power tell the powerless what they are forbidden from doing. However, this view of power hides how power actually operates. Feminist theorists and activists have extensively used Foucault's alternative account to understand both how systems of gender and sexuality operate and what resistance struggles might look like.

Foucault argued that modern power is productive rather than repressive. The regulation of sexuality offered a key example. Foucault observed that people often think that the Victorian period was a time when repression of sexuality increased, what Foucault termed the "repressive hypothesis" (1990). This "common sense" story tells us that during this period new rules and regulations were created to control, for example, women's sexuality and masturbation in children, asserting a new code of silence and secrecy around sexuality. If one accepts the repressive hypothesis, the liberatory response is to "free" sexuality and ourselves by speaking openly about sexuality, including and especially our practices and desires that are considered deviant. Foucault argued that this story misses the real operation of power in the context of the new forms of regulation of sexuality that emerged during the Victorian period. Foucault described how the period that is often associated with increased sexual repression actually witnessed an explosion of discourse about sexuality. Rather than information about sexuality being silenced, such information proliferated as new scientific practices that named, described, and classified sexual acts as well as personas or identities associated with them. He famously described the invention of the homosexual, arguing that sodomy, which had been a criminalized practice among many others, was newly understood to signify a type of person who had a certain type of childhood and bore specific physical and mental characteristics (Foucault 1990). New treatments and practices were invented to manage and prevent sexually deviant behaviors and change, control and intervene on the newly invented deviant types. Sexuality became central to how identity was understood, and enormous amounts of writing and talking about sexuality were required in order to make this happen. Rather than sex being silenced by a repressive kind of power that forbids, Foucault (1990) showed that sexuality was newly regulated through an incitement to speak about sex and sexual deviation; to know oneself and others as defined by sexuality; and to be hypervigilant about sex, sexuality, and the characteristics newly associated with deviant sexuality. Through this example, Foucault demonstrated this kind of productive power, arguing that power operates by generating knowledges about the world that shape the world. Foucault's description of power as productive rather than repressive draws our attention to the mechanisms that produce and enforce norms. Bodies, subjectivities, and their relations in space come to be in relation to norms of embodiment, behavior, and thought. Norms generate a magnetic pull in the productions of biopower.

Gender and sexuality theorists have extensively used these insights to analyze disciplinary power, power that establishes norms of good behavior and ideas about proper and improper categories of subjects. Disciplinary practices congeal in certain institutional locations such as the school, the factory and the clinic, where proper behavior is codified at the level of detail, and subjects are formed to police ourselves and each other according to these norms (Foucault 1990). Feminist activists and scholars have accounted for the development of this kind of normalizing power, and how this power works both through institutions (including families, schools, and hospitals) and through the internalization of these norms within the subjects of those institutions. The invention of various categories of proper and improper subjects, such as categories of sexual deviants, is a key feature of disciplinary power. Creating these types or categories of people requires establishing and maintaining guidelines and norms that guide the process of diagnosing or labeling.

Feminists have examined invented types like "the hysterical woman," "the welfare queen," "the good mother," "the slut," "the bitch," and many other normalizing figures. The existence of these categories relies on the constant reproduction and enforcement of racialized gender norms that govern sexual behavior, speaking styles, diet, emotional range, punctuality, manners, dress, and much more. Discourses in the social and medical sciences, popular media, criminal and immigration systems, education, and social services industries produce and uphold these norms and the stories that elicit belief in these types of people. The norms produced in these discourses are enforced through institutions that diagnose, evaluate, take formal or informal disciplinary action, or require trainings, as well as through social or internal approval or shaming. Through these processes, we learn to be appropriately afraid of being labeled in particular ways, and we learn what ideals to strive to become. We learn the norms that govern being a proper man or woman, girl or boy, soldier, worker, parent, student, member of our racial group, consumer, patriot, or member of our racial, ethnic, religious, and/or subcultural group. These norms and codes of behavior reach into the minute details of our bodies, thoughts, and behaviors. Feminists have, for example, extensively critiqued how the beauty industry produces voluminous products and media to promote those products to alter every minute aspect of women's bodies, from cuticles to labia shape to body hair and odors. These industries thrive when women internalize these norms, learn to be hypervigilant about their conformity, and relentlessly chase beauty ideals that are for the most part unacheivable. Disciplinary norms keep us in our places by helping us know how to be ourselves properly and establishing internal and external monitoring systems.

Foucault's examination of disciplinary power can be read to suggest that as disciplinary norms become internalized, more directly coercive or violent means of social control are replaced by self-regulation, so that "soft" control replaces direct violence. Anticolonial feminist theorists, including Ann Laura Stoler, Rey Chow, and Gayatri Chakravorty Spivak, have critiqued this historicization, arguing that direct violence and threats of violence accompany disciplinary norms (Stoler 1995, 2002; Chow 2002; Spivak 1988). Violent enforcement of these norms operates alongside internalization of them. One example is the enforcement of racialized and class-specific gender norms in women's prisons in the United States. US prisons have long forced women to participate in "rehabilitation" programs that aim to train them as domestic workers or to do the type of unpaid domestic labor that is typically considered "women's work." Inside carceral systems women's rehabilitation and readiness to leave prison has often been judged based on performance of gendered norms such as appearing passive, humble, meek, vulnerable, and prepared for roles as house cleaner and child-care provider. Women who are perceived to be aggressive or unfeminine, especially black women, who are consistently cast as outside standards of femininity that center whiteness, receive increased punishment and increased likelihood of having their parental rights terminated in the related child welfare system (Roberts 2002, vi). The racialized gender norms enforced by the criminal punishment and child-welfare systems overlap with those in the outside world, and are internalized by women in these systems to varying degrees just as by those outside. But these standards are also enforced in an exceptionally violent context using means of coercion that are very direct, such as keeping people in cages in isolation from their homes and communities; denying healthcare and adequate nutrition; subjecting people to conditions that amount to torture, such as solitary confinement and sexual violence; and terminating parental rights (Arkles 2009; Idaho Department of Corrections 2009; Special Rapporteur of the Human Rights Council 2011, 19, sect. J; Mogul, Ritchie, and Whitlock 2011, ch. 5; Bureau of Justice Statistics 2012, 18–19, 30–31).

Scholars and activists have also documented the ways that systems and institutions that create norms of mental health and categorizations of deviance use both "soft" and "hard" control to enforce racialized gender norms (Scholinsky 1998; Jackson 2002; Bird n.d.; Metzl 2009; Kanani 2011; Haritaworn 2013; LeFrancois, Reaume, and Menzies 2013). Violating gender norms makes people vulnerable to being labeled mentally ill and potentially being imprisoned, experiencing forced medication, or other loss of bodily autonomy and subjection to violence (Metzl 2009). Similarly, rehabilitation is often assessed according to a person's compliance with gender norms. Feminist theorists in trans studies have particularly examined this with regard to mental health diagnoses that are about failing to meet gender norms, such as gender identity disorder and gender dysphoria (Wilson, Griffin and Wren 2002; Spade 2003; Wilchins 1997). These diagnoses produce categories of "healthy" and "unhealthy" ways of being gendered, pathologize people whose gender identities or expressions deviate from the rigid norms of the binary gender system, and create systems of vigilance where people, especially children, must be subject to surveillance for signs of variance and "treated" to correct as needed. The creation, maintenance, and enforcement of these norms is wrapped up in systems of scientific expertise and authorizes particular professionals as gatekeepers, and can include forced or denied medication and other healthcare treatments, including "reparative therapies" and involuntary psychiatric imprisonment. Gender norms, then, operate both through constant internal enforcement in each of us as we daily prepare our appearances, modulate our voices and gaits, and feel shame about our bodies as we move through all the institutions of social control and deviance management that are authorized to intervene directly on the bodies of those categorized as violating these norms.

Much feminist theorizing and activism can be understood to be resistance to disciplinary power and the enforcement of racialized gender norms. Feminist resistance to this kind of control often focuses on opposing norms that center maleness; gender binarism; whiteness; heterosexuality; Christianity; and standards of beauty, health, intelligence, and reason that produce violent hierarchies of value. One key intervention of these strategies is to expose norms as norms, denaturalizing them. When feminists show that women are not naturally sexually passive and vulnerable, but, rather, are perceived as such and coerced to be so in a culture dominated by severe sexual violence, the romance myth, and the privileging of male sexuality, they are exposing gender norms and challenging them, arguing that things could be another way. When activists form consciousness-raising groups that encourage people to question standards about how they perceive their own bodies and identities and replace those norms with other ideas that they consider better, they are engaging with disciplinary power. White feminist activists and intellectuals in the 1970s are a commonly cited example of this type of work, but it was taken up broadly at that time by Puerto Rican, Black Power, lesbian and gay, and women of color groups, among others. Such groups examined white beauty standards, heterosexism, monogamy, hierarchical governance styles, and other norms and proposed alternatives ranging from natural hairstyles to polyamory to vegetarianism to collective governance structures. In all these movements, discussion of gender roles, beauty myths, and sexual violence played an important part.

Critique of media representations of women is another example of feminist resistance to disciplinary norms. The famous Bechdel test, proposed by artist Alison Bechdel, is a well-known example of this kind of critique. The test asks whether a work of fiction features at least two women who talk to each other about something other than a man (Associated Press 2013). The test is a commentary on the fact that in most representations of women in fiction, women's relationships with men are prioritized over all other relationships. Women are consistently depicted as solely interested in heterosexual love and romance, and their lives are only important with regard to how they relate to men. The Bechdel test is a popular critical tool and commentary on how media representations enforce harmful gender norms.

Feminist media critique can also be seen in feminist scholarship and activism about welfare policy. Black feminists, in particular, have extensively analyzed how deviant mythological types of black women invented and circulated by white scientists, scholars, media producers, and politicians are mobilized in debates about welfare policy (Neubeck and Cazenave 2001; Mink 1990; Sparks 2003). Patricia Hill Collins has named these "controlling images." The figure of the "welfare queen" was famously invoked by Ronald Reagan in a 1976 speech but was based in long-standing discourses dating back to the chattel slavery system in the United States about black women as sexually immoral, overly reproductive, irresponsible, greedy, and unfeminine. This image has consistently been portrayed in welfare debates. Black feminist scholars and activists have attacked this portrayal, exposing how it is invented by various institutions of expert knowledge, how its circulation demonizes and harms black women and black populations more broadly, and how it becomes enforced by individual caseworkers in welfare offices on a daily level to deny black families government services (Ernst, Nguyen, and Taylor 2013). Feminists have observed how racialized gender norms circulate in the welfare debate and in the broader context of debates about women's roles in the workforce and in domestic labor. While the myth of the "welfare queen" and the policies it is used to promote portray black mothers as lazy and undeserving if they do not work outside the home for a wage or in "workfare" while raising small children, white women are often encouraged to give up wage labor and be stay-at-home moms. Gender norms about labor roles portray an ideal of white motherhood that drastically contrasts with the way black motherhood in interpreted, and different forms of coercion apply to enforce these norms. Examination of these roles, the norms that govern them, and the institutions and arrangements that enforce them is a central task for feminism.

Foucault's description of disciplinary power as productive rather than repressive can help develop feminist perspectives on how resistance can be mounted against heteropatriarchy. When we imagine power as primarily repressive, we often imagine that to make change the main thing is to go to those who "have power" and are at the top of the hierarchy, and take over their roles and/or convince them to pass new rules and laws forbidding the prior behavior. So, for example, we might prioritize passing laws to make sex discrimination, rape, domestic violence, sexual orientation discrimination, and gender identity discrimination illegal. These actions, according to a view of power as repressive, should work to make the operations of heteropatriarchy stop. Interestingly, many of these things have happened in the United States. Yet sexual violence and intimate-partner violence remain endemic; the wage gap has not been eliminated; people still work in highly gendered labor roles (such as 90 percent of secretaries are women) that correlate to pay inequity; parenting roles remain highly gendered and parenting labor remains inequitably divided; and, in general, rigid gender norms remain vibrantly alive and violently enforced. Some would even argue that the passage of such laws exacerbates heteropatriarchal conditions because it serves as a mask for these conditions, creating an illusion of equality and of the government as the protector and guarantor of equality, meanwhile apparatuses of racialized-gendered violence, such as the child-welfare, criminal punishment, and immigration enforcement systems, expand. By reconceptualizing how power works and attending to different forms of power, we can account for the seeming contradictions of systems where control occurs in multiple intersecting ways, including through processes of norm creation and enforcement that help us all see, experience and reproduce ourselves and the world according to racialized gender hierarchies.

BIOPOLITICS AND THE NORM

Discipline was not the only model of power that Foucault described. Foucault also analyzes what he calls "biopolitics," and an understanding of biopolitics and its relationships to discipline is important for understanding the significance of the concepts of norms and normalization to feminist theories and activisms. While Foucault's model of disciplinary power helps elucidate the ways that norms and processes of normalization in terms of gender, sexuality, and race operate in systems of heteropatriarchy, Foucault also offers a statistical sense of norm that operates at the level of population. Foucault uses the term "biopolitics" to describe normalization at the level of populations. Whereas the objective of disciplinary power is to invest in and shape individuals' subjectivities, bodies, behaviors, and interactions, biopolitical power shapes at the general level of population composition. Foucault points to the emergence of state-based statistical gathering practices and the emergence of demographic sciences as evidence of the emergence of biopolitics.

Foucault also points to the ways that processes of normalization are central to biopolitical projects. For Foucault, the consolidation of a population also involves identifying and eliminating the "weak" elements in that population. Weak here designates anything that seems to interfere with or threaten the growth of the population, especially figured in terms of a national population and its relationship to the economy of the state (Clough and Willse 2011). Foucault uses the term "state racism" to describe the process of identifying and cutting out weak elements. This "cutting out" occurs both indirectly through social abandonment, and more directly through mass killing. While Foucault emphasizes that the racism he uses implies the "human race" and he is not thinking only of racialized categories of life, analysis of the racial state and racial capitalism, following David Theo Goldberg (2001) and Cedric Robinson (2000), among others, reminds us that racial subordination is central to the project of nation-state making, and hence to a biopolitics of the population as well.

Biopolitics as a racial project of homogenization that requires killing off weak elements means that eugenic projects, far from an aberration of modern society, are central to any modern state. To understand this claim, we can look to how Foucault writes that the norm travels between the realms of disciplinary and biopolitical power:

> In more general terms, we can say that there is one element that will circulate between the disciplinary and the regulatory, which will also be applied to the body and population alike, which will make it possible to control both the disciplinary order of the body and the aleatory events that occur in the biopolitical multiplicity. The element that circulates between the two is the norm. The norm is something that can be applied both to a body one wishes to discipline and a population one wishes to regularize.
>
> (Foucault 2003, 253)

Foucault also argues that sexuality serves as a kind of hinge between individuals and the population, suggesting that this may explain why sexuality achieves such a important and contested status in modern societies. Rey Chow has amended Foucault's history of sexuality, arguing that it might be better framed as a description of the "ascendancy of whiteness." In so doing, Chow draws out the centrality of processes racialization submerged in Foucault's account and highlighted by critical feminist interventions. With this in mind, we can understand the emergence of the women's birth control movement in the United States in the early twentieth century in relation to race population control strategies. Following both emancipation and new waves of immigration, fears of a "race suicide" circulated among white elites in the United States (Haraway 1984/85, 57). Margaret Sanger's campaign to provide women with information and means for birth control was not simply a feminist project. Rather, it was meant to provide tools for poor white women and women of color to curb what was seen as their hyperreproductivity, a reproductivity that threatened to outnumber the children borne of the proper elements of US society, middle-class and wealthy white women. Here, then, we see the collusion of norms of behavior, including new norms of "empowerment," to use a modern phrase, in women taking control of their bodies by using birth control with statistical norms of the racial and class composition of the US society. These are exactly the subtle forms of state racism Foucault argues characterize the modern state, a kind of positive eugenics of growing the right kind of population by cutting out in advance the wrong kinds. Here we see processes of norming at the level of individual discipline and the normalization of population forms and patterns. Feminists have used terms like "population control" and "ethnic cleansing" to talk about this kind of normalization of the population, where the growth of certain elements is encouraged while attempts are made to reduce the prevalence of subpopulations that are considered undesireable.

Less subtle versions of this have persisted as well, as evidenced in the history of forced sterilization of indigenous, black, and Puerto Rican women in US health clinics. Sterilization has been a regular practice in US prisons as well, emphasizing again feminists' insistence that directly violent forms of domination and control have accompanied the emergence of disciplinary regimes of self governance. Bringing a biopolitical analysis forward helps keep the violence of modern normalization in view.

Applying an Analysis of Norms and Normalization When Strategizing Change: Case Study on Heteropatriarchy and Same-Sex Marriage Advocacy

Foucault's emphasis on norms, categorization, and processes of normalization are vital insights for feminist resistance strategies. Foucault's work draws attention to some significant traps that people and groups resisting heteropatriarchy can fall into if we employ an oversimplified understanding of power. When power is conceived of as repressive, the imagined solution is often to redeem what is repressed and have that despised identity or category become accepted, tolerated, or even supported. To follow Foucault's famous example of homosexual identity, from the perspective of the repressive model of power, it would make sense to attempt to move homosexuality out of being labeled criminal and deviant and toward being understood as a normal and acceptable variation with sexual practice and identity. Indeed, this has been one strategy of gay rights reformers in the United States—to get sodomy decriminalized, to remove the bar to military service for gays and lesbians, and to advocate for sexual orientation non-discrimination laws and for same-sex relationships to be recognized as the same as heterosexual relationships by allowing same-sex couples to marry. These reforms seek to change laws understood to repress homosexuality, and to instead establish in law that gay and lesbian people and their relationships must be treated the same as heterosexual people and relationships. Such reforms purport to achieve equality by having the authority of law (where power is understood to reside) come down on the side of "gays are the same" rather than "gays are different and bad." This model seeks to punish discriminators and eliminate legal distinctions.

When processes of normalization are considered, change seekers can assess whether a particular approach will have the transformative impact they hope. Gayle Rubin's famous 1984 essay "Thinking Sex" helps illustrate how the project of becoming accepted, or being declared the same as heterosexuals, is at odds with feminist approaches to dismantling sexual hierarchies created by heteropatriarchal regimes of normalization. Rubin describes how systems that hierarchically rank sexual practices change as part of maintaining their operations of control. Sexuality is divided into those practices that are considered normal and natural—what she calls the "charmed circle"—and those that are considered bad and abnormal—the "outer limits." Practices sometimes cross from the outer limits to the charmed circle. Unmarried couples living together, or, perhaps, homosexuality when it is monogamous and married, have moved in mainstream US culture from being highly stigmatized to being considered acceptable (see Figure 27.1).

These shifts, however, do not eliminate the ranking of sexual behaviors. In other words, the shifts do not challenge the existence of a charmed circle and outer limits—they do not disrupt a system in which people are coerced and shamed into engaging in certain practices and not others. Freedom and equality are not achieved when a practice crosses over to being acceptable. Instead, such shifts strengthen the line between what is considered good, healthy, and normal and what remains bad, unhealthy, stigmatized, and criminalized. The line moves to accommodate a few more people, of whom society suddenly comes to approve, adjusting the system and keeping it in place. The legal marriage system—along with its corollary criminal punishment system, with its laws against lewd behavior, solicitation, indecency, and the like—enforces the line between which sexual practices and behaviors are acceptable and rewarded, and which are contemptible and even punishable (Extein 2013; Pittman 2013; Center for HIV Law and Policy 2013).

The trouble with the strategy to "get the law to say gay is the same" is that it promotes equality within the oppressive frame of heteropatriarchy. Rather than questioning the terms and categories through which sex, love, and romance are disciplined and controlled, this approach embraces such terms and categories and reproduces them. Critique of romance and marriage as cultural institutions central to the subjection of women, the creation of harmful gender roles, and cultivation of sexual violence is part of the bedrock of feminist thought. As feminists have attacked the institution of marriage, they have both attacked the romantic myths that accompany it and hold it up, and drawn attention to the structural violence in the way that marriage as a legal institution is used to distribute such basic needs as healthcare and immigration status.

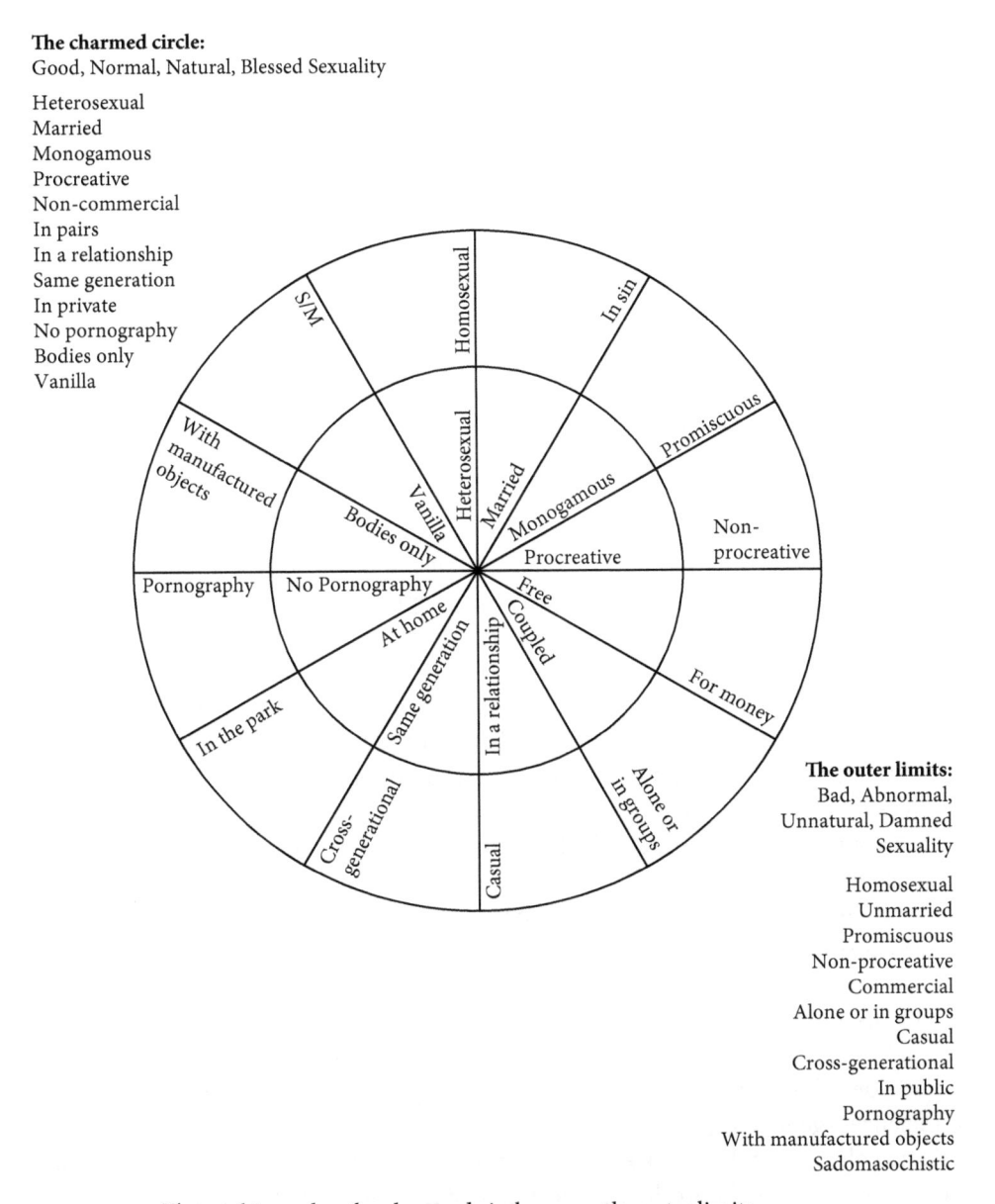

The charmed circle:
Good, Normal, Natural, Blessed Sexuality

Heterosexual
Married
Monogamous
Procreative
Non-commercial
In pairs
In a relationship
Same generation
In private
No pornography
Bodies only
Vanilla

The outer limits:
Bad, Abnormal,
Unnatural, Damned
Sexuality

Homosexual
Unmarried
Promiscuous
Non-procreative
Commercial
Alone or in groups
Casual
Cross-generational
In public
Pornography
With manufactured objects
Sadomasochistic

FIGURE 27.1 The sex hierarchy: the charmed circle versus the outer limits.

Source: Rubin (1984).

As part of seeking entrance into marriage, gay rights advocates have taken up messaging that is deeply invested in these same myths and reproduces them. Same-sex marriage advocacy has included talking points about how children benefit from having married parents, about how expressing love through marriage is important to human dignity, about how married love is the most important relationship people can have, about how the marital family is the proper place for care to happen. Feminists have fought to remove stigma from unmarried childbirth, to expose marriage as a form of social control rather than a voluntary bond based in love, to expose marriage as a key site of sexual and gender violence and labor exploitation, to break stereotypes that declare women "selfish" if they are not willing or able to endlessly provide care labor in the marital family, and to expose how marriage is a site where women are forced into unpaid care labor while governments and employers reap the benefits of the workforce being reproduced by this uncompensated work. Roles and categories that feminists have critiqued and worked to denaturalize, such as "good wife," "romantic couple," and "legitimate family," have been embraced by same-sex marriage advocacy. Rather than being concerned with the harmful norm enforcement entailed in the maintenance of these categories, these advocacy efforts have sought to prove that gay and lesbian people can also occupy these roles and carefully follow the norms they require.

Feminist scholars and activists have imagined a break from the norms of romance and the marital family, but same-sex marriage advocacy has introduced a new celebration of the traditional trappings of the institution of marriage, complete with blood diamonds, white gowns and destination weddings in colonized locales. Feminists have dared to imagine a world in which sexuality and reproduction was not tied to the couple form or the marital family, in which the moral enforcement of sexuality through the figures of "slut," "mistress," "adulterer," and "faithful spouse" might fall away, in which people would not spend their lives believing that being unmarried is a personal failure, or remain in harmful marriages because of emotional and economic coercion. Further, they have dared to imagine a world in which immigration status, healthcare, and other life necessities are not conditioned on entering into the state-approved family form. Such imaginings and proposals challenge the disciplinary norms of marriage and the romance myth, and are deeply at odds with a project that identifies liberation not by questioning norms and exposing their operations to dismantle them, but by being considered normal.

In addition to analyzing the limits of same-sex marriage advocacy from the perspective of disciplinary norms, feminist scholars and activists have also articulated how such advocacy abandons feminist analysis of the ways that marriage is used to manage populations. Specifically, feminist analysis has exposed how marriage is an apparatus of racialized-gendered population control—a key tool of anti-black racism, xenophobia, and colonialism that ensure that black people, native people, immigrants, and other racialized people are controlled, subjected to significant state violence, displaced, and disposed of.

Since the founding of the United States, regulating family formation has been key to anti-black racism and violence (Spillers 1987; Hartman 1997; Willse and Spade 2013). Slaves were not allowed to marry. Denying the family ties of slaves was essential to slavery—ensuring that children would be born enslaved and maintaining black people as property rather than persons. Sexual violence against black women was central to the system of racial chattel slavery. After emancipation, the US government scrambled to control black people, coercing marriage among newly freed black people and criminalizing them for adultery as one pathway of recapturing them into the convict lease system. After *Brown v. Board of Education*, which challenged formal, legal segregation, illegitimacy laws became a favored way to exclude black children from programs and services (Mayeri 2011).

The idea that married families and their children are superior was and remains a key tool of anti-black racism. Black families have consistently been portrayed as pathological and criminal in academic research and social policy based on marriage rates, most famously in the Moynihan Report (US Department of Labor: Office of Policy Planning and Research 1965). Anti-poor and anti-black discourse and policymaking frame poverty as a result of the lack of marriage in black populations. President Bill Clinton's 1996 dismantling of welfare programs, which disproportionately harmed black families, was justified by an explicit discourse that said that poverty results from unmarried parenthood (Personal Responsibility and Work Opportunity Reconciliation Act 1996). Under both President George W. Bush and President Barack Obama, "healthy marriage promotion" initiatives have been used to encourage low-income women to marry, including at times offering cash incentives (Silag 2003; Olson 2005). Demonizing, managing, and controlling black people by applying racist and sexist marital family norms to justify both brutal interventions and "benign neglect" has a long history in the United States, and remains standard fare.

Enforcement of gender and family formation norms has also been central to the processes of colonization of North America by European settlers. Colonizers often portray invasion as rescuing colonized populations from their backward gender and family systems. Forcing indigenous people to comply with European norms of gender, sexuality and family structure and punishing them for not doing so has been a key tool of US settler colonialism in North America. Marriage has been an important tool of land theft and ethnic cleansing aimed at disappearing indigenous people in many ways. The US encouraged westward settlement by promising male settlers 160 acres to move west, plus an extra 160 if they married and brought a wife (Matthew n.d.). At the same time, the United States criminalized traditional indigenous communal living styles, burning longhouses where indigenous people lived communally, eliminating communal landholding methods, and enforcing male individual ownership. Management of gender and family systems was and is essential to displacement and settlement processes. Enforcing gender norms in boarding schools as part of a "civilizing mission," and removing children from native communities through a variety of programs that persist today are key tools of ethnic cleansing and settlement in the United States (Morgensen 2010; Smith 2005; Rifkin 2011).

The racialized-gendered ethnic cleansing that produced and produces the United States, of course, requires not only the displacement and erasure of indigenous people but also racialized-gendered population control at the borders. Since its origins, US immigration law has put in place mechanisms for regulating those migrants it does allow in, always under threat of deportation, and labeling other migrants "undesirable" to make them both more exploitable and easier to purge. Keeping out poor people, people with stigmatized health issues, and people of color has been urgent an national priority. Marriage has been one of the key valves of that control. The Page Act of 1875, the first restrictive federal immigration law in the United States, sought to keep out Asian women, hoping to prevent Asian laborers in the United States from reproducing, but allowed the immigration of Asian merchants' wives (Abrams 2005). Marriage continues to be a deeply unjust tool of immigration control in the United States, with marital family ties being one of the few pathways to immigration. One impact of this system is that it keeps people trapped in violent and harmful sexual and family relationships because their immigration status depends on it (Dutton, Orloff, and Haas 2000).

Given these analyses of marriage as a key tool of normalization at the population level, feminists have questioned the wisdom of same-sex marriage advocacy which, rather than challenging the ways that marriage regulates access to property, healthcare, and immigration status to maintain white supremacist and colonial arrangements, embraces marriage and an institution and seeks to slightly reform it so that those who may benefit from it within gay and lesbian populations can get their piece of the action. Marriage operates as a tool of population regulation, cultivating the life of the desired population, and producing conditions of vulnerability, ranging from lack of access to healthcare to imprisonment and deportation, for those marked as disposable or threatening.

NORMS AND NORMALIZATION IN FEMINIST RESISTANCE FORMATIONS

Analysis of norms and normalization processes allow feminists opportunities to evaluate the impact of heteropatriarchy across several scales—our individual psyches, our immediate interactions with other individuals, our experiences of coercive institutions, and the broad management of populations by multiple, overlapping structures and methods of governance. In addition to helping feminists assess these conditions and evaluate various resistance strategies to see how they might participate in or dismantle various norms, an analysis of norms and normalization also draws our attention to our own methods of organizing ourselves. Biopolitics and state racism, and the processes of normalization they require, are not limited to governments. Any group that imagines a good way of life and the kinds of people who would live that life and be the ideal subjects of that life is creating and enforcing norms. Various social movements, including the nationalist anticolonial and antiracist movements of the 1960s and 1970s in the United States, often imagined a revolutionary subject that was, by default, male, and often reproduced heteropatriarchal gender and family formation norms in discourses about restoring power and ownership to those subjects (Combahee River Collective 1980; Yuval-Davis 1997; Kaplan et al. 1999; Anzaldua 1987; Grewal and Kaplan 1994; Moraga 1983; Mohanty 1988). In the mid-sixties, women in the civil rights and student movements made key interventions when they spoke out against being relegated to "second sex" status by men in the movement (Evans 1979). Black feminists and other feminists of color have analyzed how white feminism and white women's movements have imagined white women as the subjects of feminism, have centered their needs and struggles as the issues feminism is concerned with, falsely universalizing white women's experience as "women's experience" in ways that collaborate with and reproduce white supremacy (Moraga and Anzuldua 1981; Sandoval 2000). These analyses of the production and enforcement of racialized gender norms within resistance movements draw attention to both disciplinary and biopolitical processes of normalization as well as to their intersections.

At the disciplinary level, these analyses ask activists to consider the ways that we create social movement culture. What are our meetings and social spaces like? Who speaks and whose perspectives are privileged? What behaviors move people into leadership roles or get people kicked out? What norms about valued bodies, gender expressions, ways of having sex or forming families are enforced in the movement culture and how are they enforced? In contemporary movement spaces, we can see the impacts of these feminist inquiries. Contemporary social movement organizations frequently utilize "anti-oppression" curricula with members to address harmful dynamics within groups. Increasingly, feminist and queer organizing meetings begin with individuals identifying what pronouns they prefer to be referred by and what accessibility needs they have for the meeting. These innovations are the results of trans people and people with disabilities advocating for analyses of how these spaces reproduce ableist and transphobic norms and what might be done in the immediate context of a meeting to begin to shift these dynamics.

At the level of population, feminist activists have asked and continue to ask difficult questions about how to build processes into our work that address the tendency of groups to create internal enemies, people who can be expelled, denied, or forgotten in the name of the health or well-being of the life being cultivated. The systems of distribution that we seek to replace, whose exclusions and expulsions feminist scholars and activisms have documented carefully, must not be replaced with systems that, though using perhaps altered norms, still sort the population into those who will live and those who must die. Tools developed particularly in women of color feminist scholarship and organizing contexts that address this are critiques of institutionalization, critiques of hierarchy and a value for horizontal structures, consensus decisionmaking, and ongoing processes of self-reflection (see Nepon, Redfield, and Spade 2013; INCITE! 2007). These tools aim to disrupt forms of governance that establish norms and ignore or exclude those for whom the norms produce harm. These tools operate on an assumption that even the most well-intentioned individuals and groups will enforce harmful norms that make some people vulnerable, and that the processes of coming to understand, denaturalize and "unlearn" such norms is an ongoing one that requires ongoing vigilance and adaptation, facilitated by consistently working to critically reflect on processes of normalization. These tools represent lessons learned from the pitfalls of often rigid, norm-enforcing ideologies enforced within social movements.

Feminist prison-abolition work represents a vibrant location where feminist scholars and activists are deeply engaging an analysis of state racism and developing innovative social movement infrastructure. Scholars and activists have traced how the rise of the antiviolence movement in the US corresponded with a historical prison boom (INCITE! 2006; Ritchie 2012; Munshi 2010). White feminist antiviolence activists, in particular, embraced approaches to domestic and sexual violence that centered criminalization (Bumiller 2008). Women of color, immigrant, and indigenous feminists critiqued this turn, arguing that increased policing further endangered their communities and failed to get to the root causes of sexual and gender violence, and that feminist analysis of gender violence was being coopted to justify devastating racially targeted prison expansion (Crenshaw 1991; Smith 2005). Meanwhile, the prison-abolition movement in the United States has been growing, asserting a deeply transformative claim that prisons do not resolve violence, but *are* violence, and that imprisonment cannot be reformed to become just, safe or fair but instead must be abolished (Stanley et. al. 2012; Davis 1998). This claim significantly challenges the criminalization-centered approach to gender and sexual violence, which purports to resolve such violence by using the state's most coercive powers to neutralize harmdoers and convince potential harmdoers not to engage in violence. Feminist prison abolitionists argue that the institutional logics of state violence, in particular carceral control, were adopted by antiviolence movement organizations when they began to collaborate with state strategies of increased prosecution and enhanced criminal penalties, at least in part because the federal government made funding available to domestic violence agencies willing to focus on prosecution strategies. Feminist abolitionists assert an opposing view about resolving violence, one centered in prevention, healing, resolution, and root causes (Creative Interventions 2012; Generation Five 2007; INCITE! and Critical Resistance 2001).

Particularly importantly, they contend that violence should be resolved without processes centered in shaming, labeling and exiling people. These processes are analyzed by such scholars and activists using wisdom from the disability justice movement, prisoners' rights movement and antiracist movements, among others, about how such processes relentlessly enforce racialized gender norms and disproportionately target vulnerable populations with state violence. They refute that such processes produce safety, and instead presume the existence of large apparatuses of caging and punishment to be inherently racist in Foucault's sense—designed to produce, label and bring on the death of those cast by harmful systems of meaning and control as "threats." These feminist abolitionists look for the root causes of gender and sexual violence not in bad individuals who need to be exiled but in the larger processes of normalization that produce uneven distributions of life chances, including the punishment system itself. Further, they imagine that people doing harm are not dangerous outsiders to be contained or extinguished (as imagined by the criminal punishment system) but are the people we already know, often intimately. They argue that we need not throw anyone away. Instead, feminist antiviolence work can be focused on preventing harm by addressing the root causes of violence and the reasons someone has engaged in violence if it has already happened, figuring out what s/he needs to never do it again, and addressing the reasons a survivor of violence was vulnerable and what s/he needs to be safe from experiencing this harm again.

This reimagining of the core work of the antiviolence movement is significant for feminist engagement with norms and normalization in several ways. First, it engages a critique of the feminist processes that produce internal enemies and justify exiling them for the safety of the population. Second, it imagines and experiments with alternative approaches while centering an awareness of the tendency to produce killable populations and a detailed analysis of the institutional modes and normalization processes that sort the population into those whose lives will be cultivated and those who are disposable. Third, while it asserts a bold vision of an alternative society that does not exile "dangerous others," it takes seriously the reality that norms and normalization are functions of human socialization and interdependency, and seeks to engage ongoing reflection and processes of democratization to address the harms produced by that tendency rather than imagining that it can be ultimately resolved. Feminist prison abolition work, for that reason, represents a site of engaged feminist critique of processes of norms and normalization that is deploying lessons learned in prior feminist experiments.

References

Abrams, K. 2005. "Polygamy, Prostitution, and the Federalization of Immigration Law." *Columbia Law Review* 105 (3): 641–716.

Anzaldua, G. 1987. *Borderlands/La Frontera: The New Mestiza*. San Francisco: Aunt Lute Books.

Arkles, G. 2009. "Safety and Solidarity across Gender Lines: Rethinking Segregation of Transgender People in Detention." *Temple Political and Civil Rights Journal* 18 (2): 515–560.

Associated Press. 2013. "Swedish Cinemas Take Aim at Gender Bias with Bechdel Test Rating." *The Guardian*. November 6. Accessed May 3, 2014. http://www.theguardian.com/world/2013/nov/06/swedish-cinemas-bechdel-test-films-gender-bias.

Beauvoir, Simone de. 2011. *The Second Sex*. New York, NY: Vintage Books.

Bird, P. Y. n.d. "Wild Indians: Native Perspectives on Hiawatha Ayslum for Insane Indians." Accessed May 3, 2014. http://www.power2u.org/downloads/NativePerspectivesPeminaYellowBird.pdf.

Bumiller, K. 2008. *In an Abusive State: How Neoliberalism Appropriated the Feminist Movement against Sexual Violence*. Durham, NC: Duke University Press.

Bureau of Justice Statistics. 2012. "Sexual Victimization in Prisons and Jails Reported by Inmates, 2011–12." Accessed May 3, 2014. http://www.bjs.gov/content/pub/pdf/svpjri1112.pdf.

Butler, J. 1990. *Gender Trouble: Feminism and the Subversion of Identity* New York: Routledge and Chapman & Hall.

Butler, J. 1993. *Bodies That Matter: On the Discursive Limits of "Sex."* New York: Routledge.

Butler, J. 1997. *The Psychic Life of Power: Theories in Subjection*. Redwood City, CA: Stanford University Press.

Center for HIV Law and Policy. 2013. "State HIV Laws." The Center for HIV Law and Policy website. Accessed May 4, 2014. http://www.hivlawandpolicy.org/state-hiv-laws.

Chow, R. 2002. *The Protestant Ethnic and the Spirit of Capitalism*. New York: Columbia University Press.

Clough, P. T., and C. Willse. 2011. *Beyond Biopolitics: Essays on the Governance of Life and Death*. Durham, NC: Duke University Press.

Combahee River Collective. 1980. "Combahee River Collective Statement." In *Home Girls: A Black Feminist Anthology*, edited by B. Smith, 264–274. New Brunswick, NJ: Rutgers University Press.

Creative Interventions. 2012. "Creative Interventions Toolkit." Accessed May 6, 2014. http://www.creative-interventions.org/tools/toolkit/.

Crenshaw, K. W. 1991. "Mapping the Margins: Intersectionality, Identity Politics, and Violence against Women of Color." *Stanford Law Review* 43 (6): 1241–1299.

Davis, A. 1998. "Racialized Punishment and Prison Abolition." In *The Angela Y. Davis Reader*, edited by J. James, 264–274. Oxford: Blackwell Publishers.

Dutton, M., L. Orloff, and G. A. Haas. 2000. "Characteristics of Help-Seeking Behaviors, Resources, and Services Needs of Battered Immigrant Latinas: Legal and Policy Implications." *Georgetown Journal on Poverty Law and Policy* 7 (2) (Summer): 245–305.

Ernst, Rose, Linda Nguyen, and Kamilah C. Taylor. 2013. "Citizen Control: Race at the Welfare Office." *Social Science Quarterly* 94 (5): 1283–1307.

Evans, S. 1979. *Personal Politics: The Roots of Women's Liberation*. New York: Random House.

Extein, A. 2013. "Why Queers Should Care about Sex Offenders." *Huffington Post*. June 8. Accessed May 4, 2014. http://www.huffingtonpost.com/andrew-extein-msw/why-queers-should-care-about-sex-offenders_b_3386970.html.

Foucault, M. 1990. *The History of Sexuality*. Vol. 1, *An Introduction*. Translated by R. Hurley. New York: Random House.

Foucault, M. 2003. *Society Must Be Defended: Lectures at the College de France, 1975-1976*. Translated by D. Macey. New York: Picador.

Generation Five. 2007. *Toward Transformative Justice: A Liberatory Approach to Child Sexual Abuse and other forms of Intimate and Community Violence*. Generation Five online. Accessed May 6, 2014. http://www.generationfive.org/wp-content/uploads/2013/07/G5_Toward_Transformative_Justice-Document.pdf.

Goldberg, D. T. 2001. *The Racial State*. Malden, MA: Blackwell Publishers.

Grewal, I., and C. Kaplan, eds. 1994. *Scattered Hegemonies: Postmodernity and Transnational Feminist Practices*. Minneapolis: University of Minnesota Press.

Haraway, D. 1984/85. "Teddy Bear Patriarchy: Taxidermy in the Garden of Eden, New York City, 1908-1936." *Social Text* 11 (Winter): 20–64. doi:10.2307/466593.

Haritaworn, J. 2013. "Beyond 'Hate': Queer Metonymies of Crime, Pathology and Anti/Violence." *Jindal Global Law Review* 4 (2): 44–78.

Hartman, S. V. 1997. *Scenes of Subjection: Terror, Slavery, and Self-Making in Nineteenth-Century America*. New York: Oxford University Press.

Idaho Department of Corrections. 2009. "Procedure Control No. 325.02.01.001: Prison Rape Elimination." Accessed May 3, 2014. http://www.wcl.american.edu/endsilence/documents/prea_doc_idaho.pdf.

INCITE! Women of Color Against Violence, ed. 2006. *Color of Violence: The INCITE! Anthology*. Cambridge, MA: South End Press.

INCITE! Women of Color Against Violence, ed. 2007. *The Revolution Will Not Be Funded: Beyond the Non-Profit Industrial Complex*. Cambridge, MA: South End Press.

INCITE! Women of Color Against Violence and Critical Resistance. 2001. Statement on Gender Violence and the Prison Industrial Complex. incite-national.org. and criticalresistance.org. Accessed May 6, 2014. http://www.incite-national.org/sites/default/files/incite_files/resource_docs/5848_incite-cr-statement.pdf.

Jackson, V. 2002. "In Our Own Voice: African-American Stories of Oppression, Survival and Recovery in Mental Health Systems." *International Journal of Narrative Therapy & Community Work* 2. Accessed May 3, 2014. http://www.power2u.org/downloads/InOurOwnVoiceVanessaJackson.pdf.

Kanani, N. 2011. "Race and Madness: Locating the Experiences of Racialized People with Psychiatric Histories in Canada and the United States." *Critical Disability Discourse 3*. Accessed May 3, 2014. http://pi.library.yorku.ca/ojs/index.php/cdd/article/viewFile/31564/31232.

Kaplan, C., N. Alcaron, and M. Moallem, eds. 1999. *Between Woman and Nation: Nationalisms, Transnational Feminisms, and the State*. Durham, NC: Duke University Press.

LeFrancois, B. A., G. Reaume, and R. J. Menzies. 2013. *Mad Matters: A Critical Reader in Canadian Mad Studies*. Toronto: Canadian Scholars Press.

Matthew, S. n.d. "Northwest Homesteader: A Curriculum Project for Washington Schools." Center for the Study of the Pacific Northwest. University of Washington. Accessed March 25, 2014. Available at http://content.lib.washington.edu/curriculumpackets/Northwest_Homesteader.pdf.

Mayeri, S. 2011. "What's Wrong with Illegitimacy? A Brief History." Address at American University Washington College of Law: The New Illegitimacy Conference. March 15. Transcript on file with author.

Metzl, J. M. 2009. *Protest Psychosis: How Schizophrenia Became a Black Disease*. Boston: Beacon Press.

Mink, G. 1990. "The Lady and the Tramp: Gender, Race, and the Origins of the American Welfare State." In *Women, the State, and Welfare*, edited by L. Gordon, 92–122. Madison: University of Wisconsin Press.

Mogul, J. L., A. J. Ritchie, and K. Whitlock. 2011. *Queer (In)Justice: The Criminalization of LGBT People in the United States*. Boston: Beacon Press.

Mohanty, C. T. 1988. "Under Western Eyes: Feminist Scholarship and Colonial Discourse." *Feminist Review* 30: 61–88. doi:10.1057/fr.1988.42.

Moraga, C. 1983. *Loving in the War Years: Lo Que Nunca Paso por Sus Labios*. Boston: South End Press.

Moraga, C., and G. Anzuldua, eds. 1981. *This Bridge Called My Back: Writings by Radical Women of Color*. New York: Kitchen Table/Women of Color Press.

Morgensen, S. L. 2010. "Settler Homonationalism: Theorizing Settler Colonialism within Queer Modernities." *GLQ: A Journal of Lesbian and Gay Studies* 16 (1–2): 105–131. doi:10.1215/10642684-2009-015.

Munshi, S. 2010. "Negotiations of Safety within Logics of Security: Section 287(g) and Domestic Violence against Immigrant Women." Paper presented at the Association of Asian American Studies Annual Conference. April 7–11.

Nepon, E., E. Redfield, and D. Spade. 2013. "From the Bottom Up: Strategies and Practices for Membership Based Organizations." Sylvia Rivera Law Project. Accessed May 6, 2014. http://srlp.org/from-the-bottom-up-strategies-and-practices-for-membership-based-organizations/.

Neubeck, K. J., and N. A. Cazenave. 2001. *Welfare Racism: Playing the Race Card against America's Poor*. New York: Routledge.

Olson, S. 2005. "Marriage Promotion, Reproductive Injustice, and the War against Poor Women of Color." *Dollars & Sense* 257. Accessed May 4, 2014. http://www.dollarsandsense.org/archives/2005/0105olson.html.

Personal Responsibility and Work Opportunity Reconciliation Act 1996. http://www.gpo.gov/fdsys/pkg/BILLS-104hr3734enr/pdf/BILLS-104hr3734enr.pdf.

Pittman, N. 2013. "Raised on the Registry: The Irreparable Harm of Placing Children on Sex Offender Registries in the US." *Human Rights Watch*. Accessed May 4. 2014. http://www.hrw.org/reports/2013/05/01/raised-registry.

Rifkin, M. 2011. *When Did Indians Become Straight: Kinship, the History of Sexuality and Native Sovereignty*. New York: Oxford University Press.

Ritchie, B. E. 2012. *Arrested Justice: Black Women, Violence, and America's Prison Nation*. New York: New York University Press.

Roberts, D. 2002. *Shattered Bonds: The Color of Child Welfare*. New York: Civitas Books.

Robinson, C. 2000. *Black Marxism: The Making of the Black Radical Tradition*. Chapel Hill: University of North Carolina Press.

Rubin, G. 1984. "Thinking Sex: Notes for a Radical Theory of the Politics of Sexuality." In *Pleasure and Danger: Exploring Female Sexuality*, edited by C. S. Vance. Boston: Routledge and Kegan Paul.

Sandoval, C. 2000. *Methodology of the Oppressed*. Minneapolis: University of Minnesota Press.

Scholinsky, D. 1998. *Last Time I Wore a Dress*. New York: Riverhead.

Silag, G. 2003. "To Have, to Hold, to Receive Public Assistance: TANF and Marriage Promotion Policies." *Journal for Gender, Race and Justice* 7 (2): 413–438.

Smith, A. 2005. *Conquest: Sexual Violence and American Indian Genocide*. Cambridge, MA: South End Press.

Spade, D. 2003. "Resisting Medicine/Remodeling Gender." *Berkeley Women's Law Journal* 18 (1): 15–37.

Spade, D. and Willse, C. "Marriage Will Never Set Us Free." http://www.organizingupgrade.com/index.php/modules-menu/beyond-capitalism/item/1002-marriage-will-never-set-us-free. Portions of pages 562–564 of this chapter are taken from this previously published article.

Sparks, H. 2003. "Queens Teens and Model Mothers: Race, Gender and the Discourse of Welfare Reform." In *Race and the Politics of Welfare Reform*, edited by S. F. Schram, J. Soss, and R. Fording, 188–189. Ann Arbor: University of Michigan.

Special Rapporteur of the Human Rights Council. 2011. "Interim Report of the Special Rapporteur of the Human Rights Council on Torture and Other Cruel, Inhuman or Degrading Treatment or Punishment." United Nations General Assembly. Accessed May 3, 2014. http://solitaryconfinement.org/uploads/SpecRapTortureAug2011.pdf.

Spillers, H. 1987. "Mama's Baby, Papa's Maybe: An American Grammar Book." *Diacritics* 17 (2): 64–81.

Spivak, G. S. 1988. "Can the Subaltern Speak?" In *Marxism and the Interpretation of Culture*, edited by C. Nelson and L. Grossberg. Chicago: University of Illinois Press.

Stanley, E. A., D. Spade, A. J. Ritchie, J. L. Mogul, and K. Whitlock. 2012. "Queering Prison Abolition, Now?" *American Quarterly* 64 (1): 115–127. doi:10.1353/aq.2012.0003.

Stoler, A. L. 1995. *Race and the Education of Desire: Foucault's History of Sexuality and the Colonial Order of Things*. Durham, NC: Duke University Press.

Stoler, A. L. 2002. *Carnal Knowledge and Imperial Power: Race and the Intimate in Colonial Rule*. Berkeley: University of California Press.

US Department of Labor. Office of Policy Planning and Research. 1965. *The Negro Family: The Case for National Action*. Accessed May 4, 2014. http://www.dol.gov/dol/aboutdol/history/webid-meynihan.htm.

Wilchins, R. A. 1997. *Read My Lips: Sexual Subversion and the End of Gender.* Riverdale, NY: Magnus Books.

Willse, C., and D. Spade. 2013. "Marriage Will Never Set Us Free." Organizing Upgrade online. Accessed March 25, 2014. http://www.organizingupgrade.com/index.php/modules-menu/beyond-capitalism/item/1002-marriage-will-never-set-us-free.

Wilson, I., C. Griffin, and B. Wren. 2002. "The Validity of the Diagnosis of Gender Identity Disorder Child and Adolescent Criteria." *Clinical Child Psychology and Psychiatry* 7 (3): 335–351. doi:10.1177/1359104502007003003.

Yuval-Davis, N. 1997. *Gender and Nation.* Thousand Oaks, CA: SAGE Publications, Inc.

CHAPTER 28

PERFORMATIVITY AND PERFORMANCE

MOYA LLOYD

In 1990, a book was published that changed feminist theory profoundly. The book was *Gender Trouble*, and its author was Judith Butler. The transformations it wrought on feminist understandings of the relationship between sex and gender centered on the effect of one of its central concepts. The concept in question was *performativity* or, more accurately, *gender performativity*, for performativity has a history that predates and exceeds the work of Butler. It originates initially in speech act theory, specifically, in the work of English philosopher J. L. Austin (1962), where it is used to denote a specific kind of linguistic utterance: words that "do" things. It is this notion that words could do things—that communication is a type of action—that was to prove hugely influential both within and outside feminism, giving rise to one of the main fault lines dividing current theories of performativity—namely, that between those who treat performativity as a formal quality of language and those who construe it as a social, cultural, or corporeal practice.[1] In what follows, we will see examples of both strands of thinking at work in feminist theory.

Performativity is not the only analytical frame relevant to this chapter. The metaphor of performance has also been used widely to understand gender. There are at least two main, sometimes interrelated, traditions of performance theory that are relevant to feminist thinking. The first derives from performance studies broadly conceived and understands "acts" in dramatic or theatrical terms. The other found in (feminist) sociology, conceives of gender ethnomethodologically as a "performance or accomplishment achieved in everyday life" (Brickell 2003, 159). While there is some overlap in vocabulary, with, for instance, performance studies using *performative* as the adjective form of *performance*, and the theory of gender performativity referencing gender "performances," conceptually, performance and performativity tend to connote different things, have distinct theoretical origins, and have diverse implications in relation to gender.

This article divides broadly into two parts. In the first, I examine how performativity and performance have been used to understand gender. In the second part, I focus on what might be termed *linguistic performativity* and how it has been taken up within feminism to understand pornography and hate speech. Since *Gender Trouble* is *the* pivotal text in feminist discussions of gender performativity, it is where I begin. Of necessity, this exploration will require us to examine some of Butler's earlier writings, in which the traces of an alternative configuration of the performativity-performance nexus may be discerned. For although Butler is best known for her philosophically grounded understanding of performativity in *Gender Trouble* and beyond, her first forays into the field drew from feminist phenomenology and performance studies.

Gender Performativity

A common characteristic of Anglo-speaking feminism throughout the 1970s and 1980s was the effort to differentiate between sex and gender. As one classic formulation contended, "'Sex' is a biological term," connoting "the differences between individuals that make them male and female," while "'gender' is a psychological and cultural one" referencing the features ascribed to men and women (Oakley [1972] 2005, 7). From this perspective, sex was regarded as the fixed biological bedrock upon which culturally variable gender, masculinity, and femininity, was constructed. Feminists drew attention to the category of gender not in order to do away with or to replace the category of sex (see Nicholson 1994); rather, they stressed the difference between sex and gender in order to challenge both biological determinism, the idea that the differences between men and women are natural and cannot be changed, and the sexism they saw following from that position. Their diverse understandings of the relation between sex and gender aside, they proposed that the constructed nature of gender renders it contestable and perhaps even ultimately eliminable. Few of these feminists challenged, in fact most of them took for granted, the naturalness of sex. Indeed, many regarded the sexed body as *the* factor that united all women.

In *Gender Trouble* Butler interrogates this relation between sex and gender, and, in particular, seeks to show that sex is just as constructed as gender. Radically and controversially, in fact, Butler rejects the assumption that sexual difference is the foundation upon which gender is erected. Building on arguments derived from, among others, Michel Foucault (1978), Adrienne Rich (1980), and Monique Wittig (1981), she conceptualizes gender as the "apparatus" that produces sexual difference (Butler 1990, 7).[2] It is in the context of her discussion of how subjects acquire gendered identities within the terms of what she calls the "heterosexual matrix" (34), or the "law of heterosexual coherence" (138), now generally described as heteronormativity, that Butler deploys the idea of performativity.

The concept of performativity, as noted, originally stems from the speech act theory of J. L. Austin. A revised and influential version was also developed by Jacques Derrida ([1972] 1988), whose idea of performativity as a quality of language emerges out of his critical reading of Austin. Although Butler will eventually draw explicitly from

Derrida as well as engage with Austin, the idea of *gender* performativity has rather different beginnings. It arises initially out of Butler's changing assessments of Simone de Beauvoir's idea that "one is not born, but rather becomes, a woman" ([1949] 1983, 295; see Butler 1986 1988, 1989; see Lloyd 2007), and so is part of Butler's exploration of what she terms, in an article prior to the publication of *Gender Trouble*, a "politics of performative gender acts" (1988, 530).

Two claims of Beauvoir's that Butler focuses on in these writings are relevant to our discussion. The first is that the body is not a "natural fact" but an "historical idea" that only gains *meaning* from being "signified within an historically specific discourse." Butler reads this as implying that gender is an idea that the body assumes "*as if* it were its natural form" (1989, 254: my emphasis). We might see in this reading of Beauvoir the first stirrings of Butler's own view that sex is gendered. The second is the claim that one becomes a woman. It is in the process of investigating what this involves that Butler's notion of gender performativity begins to take shape.

According to Butler, for Beauvoir gender is not "only a cultural construction imposed upon identity," but to "become" a woman is also "a process of constructing ourselves." Butler (1986, 36) parses this as meaning that becoming a woman entails "a purposive and appropriative set of acts" leading to the assumption of a "certain corporeal style." Or, as she puts it in a later piece, in words she will later use to describe her own theory, for Beauvoir gender is "an identity instituted through a *stylized repetition of acts*" (1988, 519; original emphasis; see also Butler 1990, 140). Additionally, although the idea of self-construction might appear to imply both that we can shape our gender in any way we like and that we can become any gender we want, actually this is not the case, since, Butler notes, Beauvoir never envisaged any genders "beside 'man' and 'woman.'" To Butler (1986, 47), this suggests that Beauvoir understands gender as limited by the binary system men/women, a system that is a historical construct, not an "ontological necessity." It is within the terms of this gender system that certain persons become women, a process that involves "interpreting a cultural reality laden with sanctions, taboos, and prescriptions" (40), a view Butler will later recast as a process of engagement with constraining gender norms, although she does not yet describe this mode of "enacting and re-enacting received gender norms" as performative (48).

The issue that concerns Butler is how Beauvoir conceives of "acts." Butler (1988, 519) takes Beauvoir to be adopting and recasting "the doctrine of constituting acts from the phenomenological tradition." The problem with this tradition, Butler alleges, is that it relies on individualist assumptions, since it focuses on the particular subject enacting—becoming—their gender. From a feminist perspective, Butler charges, this approach risks overlooking the systemic nature of women's oppression *and* neglecting the collective dimensions of gendered performances. To redress this deficiency, Butler (1988, 519) turns to an alternative tradition of acts, "acting in the theatrical sense," or performance.

Within the context of a theatrical performance, the staging of a play, for example, acts are a shared, collective experience encompassing actors and the audience; actors embody roles that are scripted and rehearsed; although scripts might be enacted in different ways by different actors, nevertheless those enactments are always constrained to some degree by the terms of the script. Butler suggests that thinking of gender as an act in this way. To consolidate her argument, she consults the work of social anthropologist Victor Turner. Butler (1988, 526) derives from Turner the idea that human life as ritual social drama depends on the repetition of social performances, a repetition that is simultaneously "a reenactment and re-experiencing of a set of meanings already socially established," but one that also secures their legitimation. Butler conjectures that the same is true of gender; it, too, is a "ritualized, *public* performance" (1988, 526n9;: my emphasis), and not, as is often assumed, an individual expression of an inner gender identity. The effect of gender is produced by the repetition of particular bodily gestures, activities and movements, and these repeated gender performances are the mechanisms whereby the dualistic, heteronormative (or presumptively heterosexual) structure of sex and gender is perpetuated and an individual gender identity created.

Butler, at this stage, tethers her account of gender performativity to performance theory rather than to the linguistic philosophy of either Austin or Derrida (see also Loxley 2007).[3] When she suggests that gender reality is *performative*, "real only to the extent that it is performed" (1988, 527), she is contending that gender is "real" only insofar as it is sustained through repeated social performances understood theatrically or dramaturgically.[4] By the time *Gender Trouble* appears, however, Butler's work has undergone a number of important modifications that bear on her discussion of gender performativity. Little remains of her initial reading of Beauvoir as some kind of performative theorist *avant la lettre*; all explicit references to a phenomenological theory of constituting acts have disappeared in this text; and the only direct reference to Turner is hidden in a footnote (Butler 1990, 169n71).[5] Instead, much of the language used in her earlier discussion and many of the key assertions are now presented as features of Butler's own account of gender performativity that, for example, gender is a form of "ritual social drama" (1990, 140; see also 1988, 526); that gender identity is an effect of the "*stylized repetition of acts*" rather than the expression of an inner core (1990, 140); that such acts are fundamentally somatic; and that it is the repetition of these acts that maintain compulsory heterosexuality. Nevertheless, there are some important changes.

The essence of Butler's (1990) account of performativity in *Gender Trouble* is her claim that "gender is always a doing, though not a doing by a subject who might be said to pre-exist the deed." Indeed, she writes a little further on, "There is no gender identity behind the expressions of gender; that identity is performatively constituted by the very 'expressions' that are said to be its result" (25). Instead of Turner or Beauvoir, Butler now iterates this notion by way of Nietzsche, specifically his claim in *On the Genealogy of Morals* that "there is no 'being' behind doing, effecting, becoming" (quoted in Butler 1990, 25). Gender is performative, for Butler, in that it *only* exists in the "doing," in the replication of the corporeal repertoire (actions, gestures, movements) that renders one masculine or feminine. This notion of gender performativity also has radical implications for how the subject is understood. Butler jettisons the conception of an autonomous agent able to implement his/her goals and projects at will; instead, it is the repeated doing of fleshly acts that constitutes the gendered subject as a gendered subject. In other words, for Butler, doing gender is not performed by an already fully fledged gendered subject who consciously directs his/her own activities. Doing gender is the means by which a gendered subject is produced.

The anti-essentialist account of subjectivity that follows from apprehending gender as performative also has implications for how agency is theorized. For Butler, it, too, inheres in the repetitions constituting the gendered subject, repetitions that generate the *illusion* of a stable gender identity. Calling on Esther Newton's (1972) anthropological study of female impersonators, *Mother Camp*, Butler proposes that gender shares the same imitative structure as drag. *All* gender performances, she suggests, masculine or feminine, gay or straight, are a form of impersonation. It is just that some *appear* to be natural—namely, those in which sex, gender, and desire converge in the way determined by compulsory heterosexuality; that is, in which masculinity follows from a male body and femininity from a female body, and both issue in sexual desire for the opposite sex and gender. They appear that way because, by repeating specific gestures, actions, and movements, they reproduce a rough approximation of what idealized heterosexual gender is supposed to look like. By somehow exposing the artificiality of gender, as the drag artist does in "his" parody of femininity, it is possible to disclose the performative or constituted nature of gender. This is why in *Gender Trouble* Butler (1990) argues that "the task is not whether to repeat" the practices constitutive of gender; it is "*how* to repeat" so that "through a radical proliferation of gender" it is possible to "*displace* the very gender norms that enable the repetition itself" (148; first emphasis mine, second in the original).

Critics came out in force in response to Butler's arguments. Some took her to be advocating a volitional politics (Rothenberg and Valente 1997), often centered on the idea drawn from her discussion of drag and parody that, as Elspeth Probyn (1995, 79) puts it, "we can have any whatever type of gender we want" and that "we wear our genders as drag." (See also Martin 1992; Hawkes 1995.) They read her, in other words, as suggesting that the individual performs gender in the same way that an actor takes on a role on the stage. Others took the opposite tack. They believed that the theory of gender performativity entailed a mode of determinism that meant subjects were inextricably caught in power relations they were unable to resist or transform (Weir 1996). These reservations about the conception of agency that gender performativity apparently entailed also led to concerns about the view of the subject it seemed to imply (Benhabib 1995; Assiter 1996).

In *Bodies That Matter*, Butler (1993) revisits the question of how political action to undermine gender norms is doable even when there is no "'doer' behind the deed" (1990, 25). She explicitly reorients her understanding of performativity by way of Derrida's discussion of Austin. In contrast to the language-based forms championed by Austin and Derrida, Butler's original innovation in relation to performativity was to see it as a form of a bodily enactment or style of the flesh—that is, as *nonverbal* (see Walker 2003). This was, as observed, an understanding of performativity partially indebted to a theatrical conception of acts. From *Bodies That Matter*, however, Butler's account of performativity shifts course. It is now increasingly presented in linguistic terms.

In "Signature Event Context" ([1972] 1988), Derrida takes issue with certain features of Austin's account. After setting out the general conditions for successful, or what Austin (1962), in *How to Do Things with Words*, calls "happy," performatives, Derrida then sketches a distinction between serious and nonserious uses of language. It is this distinction that troubles Derrida. Nonserious uses, for Austin (1962, 22), include words pronounced by an actor on a stage, for instance, or "in soliloquy." Austin describes these words as "hollow or void," as "*parasitic* upon" ordinary speech, and as "*etiolations* of language" (22, original emphases). Derrida ([1972] 1988, 18) demurs: he sees them as no different from ordinary speech. *Any* performative utterance, whether on stage or in life, succeeds, he contends, only by repeating "a 'coded' or iterable utterance." Its success depends, in other words, on its being a *citation*.

Taking her lead from Derrida, Butler proposes that both sex and gender are similarly citational. She thus writes, for example, that "the norm of sex only takes hold to the extent that it is 'cited'" (1993, 13), as when, for instance, a doctor announces a child's sex at its birth (7), and that femininity is the effect of "the forcible citation of a norm" (232); behavior is identifiable as feminine precisely because it reiterates—cites—the fleshly styles (acts, gestures, movements) that historically have come to signify femininity (wearing makeup, sitting with legs crossed, or, in a different cultural context, wearing a veil).

One particular consequence of this turn to Derrida for Butler's argument is noteworthy in the light of her earlier work. It concerns the rejection of any linguistic distinction between "real life" and "the stage," both of which for Derrida, contra Austin, rest on the same structure of citationality, a position Butler also accepts. The move to understanding "performativity as citationality," as Butler now labels her discussion of performativity, has particular implications for its theatricality. She (1993) returns to the idea of an "act" to explain. Acts, understood from the perspective of performativity are not "singular," "deliberate," or freely chosen, and as such cannot be "simply equated with performance" understood dramaturgically (13, 225, 94). The "actions" constitutive of gender are, by contrast, reiterative actions, repetitive actions, actions that "echo [...] prior actions" (227). Moreover, they are compulsory, enforced actions, involving "regularized and constrained repetition," and the "embodying" of gender norms (95, 231). She continues that it is "in relation to such a *compulsory citationality* that the theatricality of gender is also to be explained" (232; my emphasis). It is not that all gender is dramaturgical or staged; it is not a role put on and taken off by a preexisting self or actor. A citation will appear to be theatrical, she now asserts, to the degree that it "*mimes and renders hyperbolic* the discursive convention" by which it is governed (232; original emphasis), whether through a "hyperbolic 'performance'" of death in ACT UP "die-ins," or by a "hyperbolic display" of femininity at a drag ball or AIDS benefit (233).

Such hyperbolic gestures are important for Butler not only in terms of her exploration of the relation between performativity and theatricality; they are also important in respect of the possibilities for agential change. They offer an opportunity, she suggests, to work "*the weakness in the norm*" (1993, 237)—that is, to contest the terms of heteronormativity. Butler invokes a second aspect of Derrida's argument here: that no sign is ever tied indelibly to any particular context but always has the capacity to split from one situation to be reiterated in any number of others, such that its meaning shifts in the process. Gender norms, Butler proposes, may be similarly "decontextualized" and resignified or reworked. Agency, for Butler, is thus not an inborn property of the individual. It is a possibility integral to the performative practice of citation that supports and maintains the regulatory force of gender norms. The critical potential of drag, though nothing can be guaranteed, rests on its ability to challenge the taken-for-granted nature of heterosexual performativity by demonstrating that "heterosexual regimes" are unable to "contain their own ideals" (237), as when, at its most simple, a (gay or straight) male "does" femininity.

While Butler is widely credited with introducing the idea that gender is a form of "doing," and that gender might be conceptualized as a performance, in fact, she is not the first to make these claims. In the next section, I consider three thinkers whose work, although theoretically distinct from Butler's, nevertheless anticipates Butler's in a number of important ways.

Gender as Performance, Gender as "Doing"

According to Greg Smith (2011, 125), the first person to introduce the concept of social performance to sociology was Erving Goffman (1959, 1976). His ethnomethodological account was to have a significant influence in sociology in general, but also on the development of feminist sociology specifically (see West 1996; Deegan 2014). In *The Presentation of Self in Everyday Life* (1959), drawing on the metaphor of a theatrical performance ("life as theatre"), Goffman explores the ways in which social interactions are structured, concentrating on the "enacted and displayed aspects of our everyday 'performances'" (Smith 2011, 137). The gist of Goffman's argument is that the self is an effect of its "performances" to others. In social interactions, "interactants" will endeavor to manage their "impressions" so as to create the right effect on their "audience." To convey what he means by this, Goffman talks of the "scripts" the actors use, of "belief in the part one is playing" (28), of "dramatic realization"—the capacity to "express . . . what he wishes to convey" (40)—of setting, "scenery," and "stage props" (32), and so forth.

What concerns Goffman (1959, 246) is not the "aspects of theatre that creep into everyday life" but "the structure of social encounters." Although the individual is to some degree able to "manage" the impressions she/he is attempting to create by manipulating elements of the performance, by, for example, donning garb that makes the performance of a particular role more convincing, or by moving in the "right" way, she/he nevertheless does not have full freedom to act. Individuals are not able to stage performances just as they wish or to define situations in any way they please; rather, social conventions—or what he (1974) later called "frames"—exist within which those individual performances take place, including "shared vocabularies of body idiom" (Goffman 1963, 35; see also Lloyd, 1999, 119–121; Brickell 2003, 160; Smith 2011, 138-140).

Although Goffman did not address questions of gender directly in *The Presentation of Self in Everyday Life*, he did in later work, where he posits what appears to be a social constructionist—or anti-essentialist—account of sex and gender. So, he argues, for instance, that arrangements between the sexes that seem to be an effect of natural biological differences between them—he uses segregated toilet facilities as an example—are, in fact, ways of "producing" sex difference (1977, 316) and that the placement of all infants into one or other "sex class" may be characterized as a form of sociological "sorting" (302–303). Goffman (1976) characterizes gender as a "behavioral style," "stylization," "ritual-like" display and as a mode of enactment. At times, the language used, together with his repudiation of the idea that there is an "underlying reality" to gender, or anything that "lies behind or underneath" expressions of femininity or masculinity (77)—is resonant of Butler's later theory of gender performativity. At other points, however, Goffman's argument clearly moves in a different direction from Butler's, as, for example, when he talks of the "apparent optionality" (71) of gender displays or performances, a position that has the effect, according to one set of scholars, of "segregating gender display from the serious business of interaction" and of obscuring the ways that gender is an "ongoing activity embodied in everyday interaction" (West and Zimmerman 1987, 130).

It is to the account developed by Candace West and Don Zimmerman (1987), the scholars just alluded to, that I now want to turn. Dissatisfied with standard theorizations of the sex-gender relationship, in "Doing Gender" West and Zimmerman develop what they refer to as an "ethnomethodologically informed ... understanding of gender as a routine, methodical and recurring accomplishment" (126); gender as a form of interactional or social "doing."[6] Their thesis rests not on the standard dualistic sex/gender division familiar from feminism but on a tripartite classification that differentiates among "sex" (understood as "a determination made through the application of socially agreed upon biological criteria for classifying persons as females or males," for example, chromosomes or genitalia); "sex category" (which is "established and sustained by the socially required identificatory displays that proclaim one's membership in one or the other category" but which allow claiming membership in the other sex category when the "sex criteria" are lacking, say, where a male might pass as female); and "gender" ("the activity of managing situated conduct in light of normative conceptions of attitudes and activities appropriate for one's sex category" (West and Zimmerman 1987, 127).

From Goffman they draw the idea that gender is some form of "socially scripted dramatization" of idealized gender displays (West and Zimmerman 1987, 130). Concerned, however, about Goffman's tendency to separate gender from interaction proper, West and Zimmerman treat "doing gender" as a continuous and inescapable feature of daily social interaction. In an argument that seems to prefigure Butler's later discussion of drag as highlighting the constituted character of gender identity, the authors invoke Harold Garfinkel's study of Agnes, a male-to-female transsexual, in order to explore the connections among sex, sex category, and gender. For West and Zimmerman, "Agnes's case makes visible what culture has made invisible—the accomplishment of gender"—because to pass as female both before and after her surgery Agnes had through social intercourse to learn how to "do," to *perform*, femininity (1987, 131).

Gender performance has a number of characteristics for West and Zimmerman. As noted, it is interactional. Further, because society is organized around sex difference "doing gender is unavoidable" (1987, 137). There is no time, that is, when we *cannot* do gender. Following Goffman, gender performance is also considered to be dependent on the construction of a series of "institutionalized frameworks" (137) through which so-called essential sex differences are produced and enacted. Moreover, in yet another move that seems to anticipate Butler's contention that sex is an effect of gender, West and Zimmerman note that: "doing gender also renders the social arrangements based on sex category accountable as normal and natural, that is, legitimate ways of organizing social life" (146).

Finally, gender performance is "accountable." By this they mean that it can be assessed in terms of whether or not a particular performance conforms to "normative conceptions of masculinity or femininity." Every gender performance is "*at the risk of gender assessment*" by others (West and Zimmerman 1987, 136; original emphasis). When "we do gender appropriately," we "sustain, reproduce, and legitimate the institutional arrangements" based on sex category. When, however, our gender performance is "inappropriate," then, "we as individuals," rather than the institutional arrangements within which we operate, "may be called to account" (146). All in all, "a person's gender is not simply an aspect of what one is, but more fundamentally, it is something that one *does*, and does recurrently, in interaction with others" (140; original emphasis).

There is no published evidence that Butler had recourse to the work of West and Zimmerman; yet there are several parallels between their respective works: both see gender as a form of "doing"; both apparently consider gender to naturalize the idea of binary sex; and both note the connections between gender and compulsory heterosexuality, though Butler pursues this insight further. This has led one commentator to speculate that had West and Zimmerman been reading Austin "at the time, they might have called this ["Doing Gender"] an analysis of the performative character of gender" (Connell 2009, 105). But they did not. For all the similarities, however, there are important differences between them.

The theoretical frameworks from which they derive their ideas vary significantly. West and Zimmerman draw primarily from ethnomethodological sources, including, most notably, Goffman and Garfinkel but also the writings of Suzanne Kessler and Wendy McKenna (1978). By contrast, Butler works within a theoretical framework influenced by Continental philosophy, incorporating ideas from Nietzsche, Foucault, and Derrida, among others. Moreover, Butler has, more than once, differentiated her approach to gender from that of Goffman, on whose work West and Zimmerman expressly build, on the grounds that Goffman's view of the self is opposed to hers. He, Butler suggests, operates according to some sort of "behaviorist model," in which "'expressions' are said to construct or fashion a social self" (1995, 134; see also Butler 1988); whereas she is concerned with the way that the "interiority" of the subject is "a publically regulated and sanctioned form of essence fabrication" (1988, 528).

So far, we have concentrated on how the twin concepts of performativity and performance have been employed to understand gender, identifying two particularly important approaches: an account of gender performativity and an understanding of gender as a form of social performance or interactional doing. This has revealed some of the diverse ways in which performance has been understood—that is, both in theatrical and in ethnomethodological terms—and performativity theorized, both as a "gestural style" (Sedgwick 2003, 6) and, particularly in its deconstructive mode, in more strictly linguistic terms. I suggested at the outset that there are two principal ways in which *performativity*, specifically, has been relevant for feminist theory. The first, just covered, in terms of gender performativity; the second, in terms of the capacity of speech, broadly conceived, to harm, wound, degrade, or humiliate its addressees. Within feminism, discussion has centered primarily on pornography as a mode of speech that subordinates women. In the next section, I examine these feminist debates, starting with the work of Catharine MacKinnon. To set the context for the arguments that follow I return very briefly to Austin's account of performative speech acts in *How to Do Things with Words*.

Performativity and Language

The focus for Austin is the *pragmatics* of speech, that is, language as action upon the world. In defining language as performative, Austin emphasizes that certain forms of speech perform the action they describe, as when we say "I bet" or "I promise." Austin distinguishes three types of speech act, a distinction that will become particularly pertinent to feminist discussions. The three sorts of speech act are the *locutionary*, the *illocutionary*, and the *perlocutionary*. A locutionary utterance he defines as "the act *of* 'saying something'" (1962, 94; my emphasis)—that is, making a meaningful statement. An illocutionary act entails "the performance of an act *in* saying something" (94; my emphasis), a saying that is *simultaneously* a doing (as in the two examples "I bet" and "I promise" previously given). Finally, a perlocutionary speech act is an utterance that "will often, or even normally, produce certain *consequential* effects" on others (101; my emphasis), where, in other words, an ensuing effect is produced *by* saying something (see also Langton 1993; Loxley 2007). For Austin, simply put, words perform actions and, as a result, a stark differentiation between speech and conduct is untenable.

The Performativity of Pornography

In *Feminism Unmodified*, MacKinnon (1987, 130) puts forward the view that pornography is a "form of 'speech'" that is also "a kind of act." Elaborating in *Only Words*, she (1994) notes that pornography is "constructing and performative rather than merely referential or connotative" (15). Although MacKinnon (1994, 86–87) develops her account independently of Austin, she acknowledges that, like him, she is advancing an account of "doing things with words" that undermines the dichotomy between speech and conduct. It is not the content of pornography that concerns her but what pornography enacts; not what it says but what it does. Pornography equates to "subordinating women through sex" (20). It is a form of "sexual abuse *as* speech" (7) that "violates women" (1987, 192); constructs "the social reality of gender, the force behind sexism, the subordination in gender inequality" (1987, 166); and "makes women into objects" (1987, 182). In short, it "makes the world a pornographic place" (1994, 17).

Pornography, for MacKinnon, is not, as it has conventionally been understood, a matter of obscenity, free speech, or morality. Akin to hate speech, it is rather a matter of social inequality, inequality that is "substantially created and enforced—that is *done* through words and images" (1994, 9; original emphasis). Pornography is a "constitutive practice" (MacKinnon 1987, 173) that produces gender inequality by constructing the abuses suffered by women (rape, battery, sexual harassment, and prostitution) as sex. It "sexualizes" these abuses and "thereby celebrates, promotes, authorizes, and legitimizes them." In so doing, it constructs women "as what men want from sex" (171) and in the process "institutionalizes the sexuality of male supremacy."[7] As such, pornography "eroticizes hierarchy . . . [and] sexualizes inequality" (172). MacKinnon's contention, however, is that pornography does more than only subordinate women (as if that were not enough).

Drawing from the work of Andrea Dworkin, MacKinnon (1987) contends that it also silences them. As the "speech of men," pornography stops women—subordinated by its texts and images—from speaking out, rendering their speech "impossible, and where possible, worthless" (209, 181). It does so, she speculates, by creating a hostile environment in which they are reluctant to protest the violence against them by, for example, reporting rape; when women do speak, pornography produces a context in which their words are often distrusted, and it silences them by evacuating meaning from their words, as when a woman's no is taken to mean yes (see also West 2013). MacKinnon (1994) illustrates this by recounting the plight of Anita Hill. Hill alleged that then Supreme Court nominee Clarence Thomas had sexually harassed her with inappropriate talk, including about pornographic films. Hill testified to this effect during Thomas's Senate confirmation hearings, and MacKinnon reports that "much of the response was disbelief, the reaffirmation of the silence of 'nothing happened.'" "When speech is sex" (44), women's speech lacks the authority, plausibility, and influence of men's speech.

In her paper "Speech Acts and Unspeakable Acts," feminist philosopher Rae Langton (1993, 299), responding to claims that MacKinnon's argument is "philosophically incoherent," sets out to assess whether the dual claim that pornography both subordinates women and silences them is philosophically defensible. First, Langton determines whether speech can, in fact, subordinate. Her answer is that it can, provided the speech in question fulfills three criteria: that it *ranks* a particular group of people as inferior, that it *legitimates* discriminatory behavior toward them, and that it unjustly *deprives* them of important powers. Langton considers what happens when a legislator in apartheid Pretoria utters the words "Blacks are not permitted to vote" (302). The effect, she observes, is to deny the right to vote to black South Africans and, thus, to subordinate them.

To count as a subordinating illocution, pornography needs to operate in the same way. It must have what Langton, invoking Austin, calls *verdictive* and *exercitive* force. For Austin (1962, 151), verdictives (from verdict) involve giving an estimate, appraisal, or reckoning of some kind; they *rank*. Exercitives involve the "exercising of powers, rights, or influence," described by Langton as "actions of ordering, permitting, prohibiting, authorizing, [and] enacting law;" they *legitimate*. As Langton (1993) understands them, exercitives also—and this will become relevant later on—"confer powers and rights on people, or *deprive* people of powers and rights" (304; my emphasis). For Langton, both exercitives and verdictives are "authoritative"—delivered by someone with the appropriate (formal or informal) authority, such as the legislator in Pretoria in her example. In Austinian parlance, this is one of their "felicity" conditions.

Langton (1993, 307) concludes from her assessment of MacKinnon's work that pornography is verdictive insofar as it "ranks women as sex objects." Moreover, it is exercitive in that it "legitimates sexual violence" against women. In these senses, it subordinates. That is, pornography is an "*illocutionary act* of subordination" (308; original emphasis). The issue is whether it constitutes authoritative speech. Langton asks, "Do its speakers have authority?" (311). The answer depends on whether or not pornography is believed to be the utterance of a powerless minority or fringe element of society, or whether, as MacKinnon proposes, "pornography's voice is the voice of the ruling power" (311). Langton notes simply that this is a question that cannot be "settled from the philosopher's armchair" since it is "empirical" (312, 329). Nevertheless, she concludes on the basis of her evaluation that pornography may indeed subordinate, and that therefore the claim is philosophically coherent.

What, though, of the contention that pornography silences women? "If speech is action," Langton (1993) notes, "then silence is failure to act." As she, rather than MacKinnon construes it, the issue here is whether pornography impedes women from "doing things with their words" (314). What primarily interests Langton are occasions of "illocutionary disablement," when the right words are spoken, "with the appropriate intention," but the speaker fails to perform the illocutionary act intended (315), when they are somehow prevented or *disabled* from doing so. If, she surmises, the ability to perform illocutionary acts is a feature of authority or power, then the inability to do so is indicative of a lack of authority or power. Does pornography render women's speech acts "unspeakable"? MacKinnon suggests it does. For Langton, the question is, how? What happens to prevent a woman's no from "achieving its intended purpose" (323)—that is, to refuse sex?

Langton (1993, 324) interprets MacKinnon's claim that pornography silences women to mean that the "*felicity conditions for women's speech acts are set by the speech acts of pornography*" (original emphasis). The words of the pornographer, like the words of the legislator, are "words that set conditions" that determine the rules of the linguistic game and decide what kinds of speech is possible. *If* pornography works in this way, and again, Langton suggests this is only verifiable empirically, then it is authoritative in that it distributes certain linguistic rights and powers. It thus fulfills the third criterion: it is a class of illocution that *deprives* women of the ability to utter certain kinds of speech act.

By silencing women, pornography also subordinates them. For Langton, the claim that pornography silences women is thus also philosophically defensible.

I want to return briefly to MacKinnon and to the political and legal solutions she has put forward to deal with pornography. As is well known in feminist and legal circles, MacKinnon, together with Andrea Dworkin, was involved in drafting a number of local antipornography civil rights ordinances in the United States, beginning in 1983. These ordinances defined pornography as "a form of discrimination on the basis of sex" that subordinates women "through pictures/and or words," including in ways that dehumanize them or present them "as sexual objects" who "enjoy humiliation or pain" or experience "sexual pleasure in rape, incest, or other sexual assault" (MacKinnon 1987, 262n1). The purpose of the legislation was not to criminalize the production, sale, or consumption of pornography; rather it was to allow women to sue for damages from pornographers for *demonstrable harm* done to them by pornographic material and to petition for a future ban on material proven to be harmful. (For a critique of the anti-pornography legislation, see Strossen 2000.)

The fact that MacKinnon champions the legal regulation of pornography is often interpreted through the lens of the First Amendment to the US Constitution protecting free speech.[8] Some critics, most notably Ronald Dworkin (1985), railed against this, suggesting that for the ordinance to censor pornography as it was proposed doing entailed a denial of free speech. Plenty of feminist ink has already been spilt rebutting Ronald Dworkin's case (see Langton 1990, 1993; Hornsby 1993; West 2003 by way of example), and I do not want to reprise that controversy here. I want, instead, to look at an alternative critique advanced by Judith Butler in *Excitable Speech* (1997).

Hate Speech and the Politics of Performativity

One consequence of the line of reasoning presented by MacKinnon and supported by Langton (among others)—namely, that pornography silences women—is that in the current pornography-imbued climate, freedom of speech for women may be meaningless. The "purposes of the First Amendment, premised upon conditions presumed and promoted by free speech," MacKinnon ([1985], 2009, 309) writes, "do not pertain to women because they are not our condition." This is a condition, she continues, in which the "free speech of men silences the free speech of women." The standard defense of the First Amendment is that in a democratic society all viewpoints have the right to be expressed in the "free market place of *ideas*." Langton, building on MacKinnon, takes issue with this. Free speech, she (1993, 328) surmises, is not about ideas; freedom of speech is "good" when it "*enables people to act*" (original emphasis). If women are unable, as Austin put it, to "do things with words," unable to act, then for Langton "that ... is not free speech" (327).

In *Excitable Speech: A Politics of the Performative*, Butler (1997) engages the antipornography views of MacKinnon and Langton, as well as the critique of assaultive speech—or "words that wound"—proposed by a prominent group of critical race theorists.[9] She does not offer an orthodox free-speech defense of pornography, however. Instead, she draws her critique from the linguistic approaches of Austin and Derrida. There are several points of connection between Butler and her opponents—the stress on the performativity of language, its centrality to the construction of reality in inegalitarian and exclusionary ways, and the implied connections between language and subjectivity/identity—but they divide significantly over the best strategy for dealing with wounding words and subordinating speech. What is required to combat "hate speech" (broadly construed), Butler contends, is not its legal regulation but "talking back," a strategy extrapolated from the idea that, structurally, speech and conduct are always dissociable.

Butler is interested in what it means to claim that language has the capacity to harm. What concerns her is the idea that pornography and hate speech, in and of themselves, directly and immediately enact the subordination of oppressed groups or persons. She sets out to demonstrate that contra the claims of MacKinnon and Matsuda et al., subordinating speech is perlocutionary rather than illocutionary. For Austin, the two were distinguished by the fact that they operated, as Butler puts it, according to different temporal logics: illocutions require the simultaneity of word and deed and perlocutions require only that an utterance bring about certain effects. Truncating a longer argument, Butler (1997, 51) avers in Derridean fashion that for *any* performative to succeed (illocutionary or perlocutionary), it has to repeat or recite a "*prior and authoritative set of practices*" (original emphasis). Every speech act "exceeds the instance of its utterance" (3) and has a past, present, and future iterative context. Pornography and hate speech are no different. They are citational. They refer to "already existing discursive practices, to already circulating images and encoded trauma" (Passavant and Dean 2001, 377). So, although an individual illocutionary speech act might enact its effects as it is uttered, its *force* (its capacity for success) derives from its historicity, from its repetition over time.

Butler (1997, 16) is also concerned about what she terms "the sovereign conceit" that she alleges is at work in the writings of MacKinnon and the critical race theorists. As she notes of the former, when MacKinnon contends that pornography subordinates women, she "engages a figure of the performative, a figure of sovereign power that governs how a speech act is said to act—as efficacious, unilateral, transitive, generative" (74). The allegation is that hate speech and pornography *always* attain their harmful, subordinating effects in ways that are, to borrow from Lisa Schwartzman (2002, 423), "immediate and fully predictable." Again, Butler disagrees: hate speech and pornography do not "always work" (19). In fact, they can sometimes take on a meaning unlike that intended by their speaker because of the "excitability" of language. In corroboration, she presses into service Austin's differentiation between "felicitous" and "infelicitous" speech acts—that is, speech acts that succeed and those that, for various reasons, fail.

In *How to Do Things with Words*, Austin (1962), lists a number of conditions that are necessary for happy performatives, as well as the different forms of "misfires" and "abuses" to which they may be prone. Infelicities happen for Austin when certain of the conventions that govern the performative are breached; for instance, when the person conducting a marriage service (the purser in Austin's illustration) is legally ineligible to do so (16). Derrida understands this to mean that Austin construes the risk of performative failure as *extrinsic* to the utterances themselves when, as Derrida has it, it is *intrinsic* to language, "its internal and positive condition of possibility" (Derrida [1972] 1988). Failure, in other words, is not circumstantial; it is structurally inherent in language as a feature of its iterability. By implication, any term can potentially be wrested from its context and made to connote differently. Butler concurs. This insight is important politically for her because she sees the failure of hate speech and pornography as performatives as the occasion for a critical response to them (Butler 1997, 19).

To explain how Butler allies these insights borrowed from Derrida with an interpretation of Louis Althusser's idea of interpellation (when "hailing"—or calling—someone constitutes the person as a subject) to suggest that noxious speech can be resignified. (Recall that MacKinnon thought that pornography was a means by which women were subjectivated.) Instead of identifying censorship as the solution to sexually and racially assaultive speech, Butler argues that egregious words can be appropriated and recited to counter their historical associations and that interlocutors to that speech can refuse its subordinating interpellations by, for instance, taking up a pernicious designation as a self-description. In this way, the damaging potential of hate speech and pornography can be defused. Changes in meaning of the term *queer* shed light on what she intends here. Once employed as an abusive term to stigmatize and shame those to whom it was addressed, restaged as "part of an affirmative practice" (Butler in Olson and Worsham 2000, 759), it has become an expression celebrating and legitimizing homosexuality (Butler 1993).

One important consequence that follows from Butler's discussion concerns where the responsibility for hate speech and pornography lies. In rejecting a legal solution, Butler appears to reject the idea that individuals should be prosecuted for uttering wounding words on the twofold ground that to do so reduces the widespread structural and institutional dimensions of sexism and racism to individual acts of speech. And she ignores that any individual utterance is itself always already a recitation of existing racist or sexist language. Not surprisingly, some critics worry that Butler appears to be absolving those deploying hate speech and pornography of legal culpability (Mills 2003).

Conclusion

Feminist theory operates throughout a range of different subject disciplines. The same is true of the discussions of performativity and performance outlined in this chapter. Butler's theorization of gender as performative had a radical impact on feminist theory, in gender and sexuality studies and in queer theory, with its anti-essentialist characterization of the subject and its particular account of agency (indeed, in 2009 she defined performativity *as* an "account of agency" [i]). Indeed, *Gender Trouble* is routinely taken to be one of the originating texts of queer theory, and gender performativity, one of its inaugural ideas.[10] Moreover, gender performativity as a framework has been used as a lens through which to inform readings of diverse cultural texts, from the BBC television series *The Office* (Tyler and Cohen 2007) to Samuel Beckett's *Rockaby* (Jones 1998) to explorations of transgender issues (Chávez 2010) to theorizations of the performance of sexuality in geographical space (Bell et al. 1994; Valentine 1996) to studies of gender practices at work (Martin 2003) and to investigations of the relation between gender performativity and rape law (Loizidou 1999), among many other things. This is not to suggest, of course, that everyone accepted or endorsed Butler's approach. In fact, it has been and continues to be the subject of some controversy.

While its reach in terms of influence is perhaps not as great as Butler's idea of gender performativity, West and Zimmerman's proposal that gender is a form of "doing" nevertheless helped to shape the debates in feminist sociology and gender studies. Described as "groundbreaking" by Francine Deutsch (2007, 106), "Doing Gender" was, in 2009, "the most cited article ever published in *Gender & Society*" (Jurik and Siemsen 2009, 72). Echoes of West and Zimmerman's work are discernible in studies of female-to-male transsexuals and transgendered persons (Dozier 2005), explorations of the connections between "doing gender" and "doing heteronormativity," when so-called gender normals interact with transgender people (Schilt and Westbrook 2009), and investigations of the role of female surgeons (Cassell 1997). There have also been, in response to the critical charge that "doing gender" is principally an account of gender conformity, attempts to extend their framework to the notion of "undoing gender" (Deutsch 2007).

The importance of MacKinnon's critique of pornography for feminism cannot be underestimated either. While some feminists rejected the argument that pornography subordinates women in the radical sense deployed by MacKinnon (see, for instance, Cornell 2000), and others challenged MacKinnon's definition of pornography (Strossen 2000), her view nevertheless helped to shift the discussion away from the conventional view that pornography offends to the position that pornography directly (performatively) harms, silences, and oppresses women. One of the most fecund developments in relation to MacKinnon's writings was in the realm of feminist philosophy where numerous authors (Hornsby 1993; Hornsby and Langton 1998; McGowan 2003, 2005; Maitra 2009), including Langton (1990, 1993), began to explore pornography through Austin's speech act theory,[11] and some of the more recent texts are critically indebted to both MacKinnon and Langton.

It was, in part, the arguments put forth by these two authors that prompted *Excitable Speech*, which in turn sparked considerable debate in feminist and gender circles. Commentators challenged the accuracy of Butler's readings of MacKinnon, Austin, et al., (Jenkins 2001; Schwartzman 2002), and registered concern that Butler had underestimated the degree of difficulty of resignifying certain particularly entrenched forms of racial or gender slur (Lloyd 2007). Additionally, questions were posed about why MacKinnon's own discussion of pornography did not count as an example of resignification for Butler (Jenkins 2001), and about whether Butler's account either adequately addressed the "authority" of hate speech "in the empirical world" (Schwartzman 2002) or the possibility of resistance (Mills 2000).

Although much more could be said here about the significance of each individual approach, what ought to be clear is that exploration of the two concepts, performance and performativity, significantly transformed feminist theory's apprehension of gender in ways that cannot now be undone.

Notes

1. For general discussion of the concept of performativity in philosophy, social and political theory, including the work of J. L. Austin, Jacques Derrida, and Judith Butler, see Loxley (2007) and Lloyd (2011).
2. For further discussion of Butler's account of sex and gender, see Lloyd (2007).
3. In her 1988 article Butler also makes explicit reference to texts in performance studies by Bruce Wilshire, and Richard Schechner, as well as to Turner.
4. She does, however, recognize that there is a difference between theatrical performances of gender and gender performances in nontheatrical contexts, where the risks attaching to the performance may be much higher (see 1988, 527).
5. The index gives a second reference to Turner (allegedly on page 2); however, this appears to be a proofing error because there is no mention of Turner at that point in the text.
6. For West and Zimmerman, conventional understandings do not address the difficulties sometimes attendant on ascribing biological sex to a body or to the apparent fixity of gender from an early age. Additionally, they often do not recognize that the relation of biology to culture is more complex than often assumed.
7. MacKinnon's discussion also extends to children, though for the purposes of this article I have focused on how it relates to women.
8. In fact her reference point is the Fourteenth Amendment—the equal protection amendment.
9. One of Butler's targets is the volume *Words That Wound*, written by critical legal scholars Mari Matsuda, Charles R. Lawrence III, Richard Delgado, and Kimberlé Williams Crenshaw (1993).
10. The other academic routinely identified as inaugurating the field of queer studies is Eve Kosofsky Sedgwick. Sedgwick develops an idea of "queer performativity" out of the work of Austin and explores its operation in literary texts, including the work of Henry James (see, for example, Sedgwick 2003).
11. As we have seen MacKinnon understands pornography to be performative. But as noted, she does not deploy Austin's technical vocabulary, such terms as "illocutionary" or "perlocutionary," to do so; yet as Langton (1993: 307) notes, her account rests on the use, in particular, of illocutionary verbs such as "promote," "authorize," "legitimate" to expose what pornography does.

References

Assiter, Alison. 1996. *Enlightened Women: Modernist Feminisms in a Postmodern Age*. London and New York: Routledge.

Austin, J. L. 1962. *How to Do Things with Words*. 2nd ed. Oxford: Oxford University Press.

Beauvoir, Simone de. (1949) 1983. *The Second Sex*. Translated by H. M. Parshley. Harmondsworth: Penguin.

Bell, David, Jon Binnie, Julia Cream, and Gill Valentine. 1994. "All Hyped Up and No Place to Go." *Gender, Place and Culture: A Journal of Feminist Geography* 1 (1): 31–47.

Benhabib, Seyla. 1995. "Feminism and Postmodernism: An Uneasy Alliance." In *Feminist Contentions: A Philosophical Exchange*, Seyla Benhabib, Judith Butler, Drucilla Cornell, and Nancy Fraser, 17–34. London: Routledge.

Brickell, Chris. 2003. "Performativity or Performance? Clarifications in the Sociology of Gender." *New Zealand Sociology* 18 (2): 158–178.

Butler, Judith. 1986. "Sex and Gender in Simone de Beauvoir's *Second Sex*." *Yale French Studies* 72: 35–49.

Butler, Judith. 1988. "Performative Acts and Gender Constitution: An Essay in Phenomenology and Feminist Theory." *Theatre Journal* 40 (4): 519–531.

Butler, Judith. 1989. "Gendering the Body: Beauvoir's Philosophical Contribution." In *Women, Knowledge, and Reality: Explorations in Feminist Philosophy*, edited by Ann Garry and Marilyn Pearsall, 252–262. Boston: Unwin Hyman.

Butler, Judith. 1990. *Gender Trouble: Feminism and the Subversion of Identity*. London: Routledge.

Butler, Judith. 1993. *Bodies That Matter: On the Discursive Limits of "Sex."* London: Routledge.

Butler, Judith. 1995. "For a Careful Reading." In *Feminist Contentions: A Philosophical Exchange*, Seyla Benhabib, Judith Butler, Drucilla Cornell, and Nancy Fraser, 127-143. London: Routledge

Butler, Judith. 1997. *Excitable Speech: A Politics of the Performative*. London: Routledge.

Butler, Judith. 2009. "Performativity, Precarity, and Sexual Politics." *Revista de Antropología Iberoamericana* 4 (3): i–xiii.

Cassell, Joan. 1997. "Doing Gender, Doing Surgery: Women Surgeons in a Man's Profession." *Human Organization* 56 (1): 47–52.

Chávez, Karma R. 2010. "Spatializing Gender Performativity: Ecstasy and Possibilities for Livable Life in the Tragic Case of Victoria Arellano." *Women's Studies in Communication* 33 (1): 1–15.

Connell, Raewyn. 2009. "Accountable Conduct: 'Doing Gender' in Transsexual and Political Retrospect." *Gender & Society* 23 (1): 104–111.

Cornell, Drucilla, ed. 2000. *Feminism and Pornography*. Oxford: Oxford University Press.

Deegan, Mary Jo. 2014. "Goffman on Gender, Sexism, and Feminism: A Summary of Notes on a Conversation with Erving Goffman and My Reflections Then and Now." *Symbolic Interaction* 37 (1): 71–86.

Derrida, Jacques. (1972) 1988. "Signature Event Context." In *Limited Inc*. Evanston, IL: Northwestern University Press.

Deutsch, Francine M. 2007. "Undoing Gender." *Gender & Society* 21 (1): 106–127.

Dozier, Raine. 2005. "Beards, Breasts, and Bodies: Doing Sex in a Gendered World." *Gender & Society* 19 (3): 297–316.

Dworkin, Ronald. 1985. *A Matter of Principle*. Cambridge, MA: Harvard University Press.

Foucault, Michel. 1978. *The History of Sexuality. Vol. 1, An Introduction*. Translated by Robert Hurley. Harmondsworth: Penguin.

Goffman, Erving. 1959. *The Presentation of Self in Everyday Life*. Harmondsworth: Penguin.

Goffman, Erving. 1963. *Behavior in Public Places: Notes on the Social Organization of Gatherings*. New York: The Free Press.

Goffman, Erving. 1974. *Frame Analysis: An Essay on the Organization of Experience.* Cambridge, MA: Harvard University Press.

Goffman, Erving. 1976. "Gender Display." *Studies in the Anthropology of Visual Communication* 3 (2): 69–174.

Goffman, Erving. 1977. "The Arrangements between the Sexes." *Theory, Culture, & Society* 4 (3): 301–331.

Hawkes, Gail. 1995. "Dressing-Up: Cross Dressing and Sexual Dissonance." *Journal of Gender Studies* 4 (3): 261–270.

Hornsby, Jennifer. 1993. "Speech Acts and Pornography." *Women's Philosophy Review* 10: 38–45.

Hornsby, Jennifer, and Rae Langton. 1998. "Free Speech and Illocution." *Legal Theory* 4, 21–38.

Jenkins, Fiona. 2001. "The Heeding of Differences: On Foreclosure and Openness in a Politics of the Performative." *Constellations* 8 (3): 364–375.

Jones, Christine. 1998. "Bodily Functions: A Reading of Gender Performativity in Samuel Beckett's *Rockaby*." In *Samuel Beckett: A Casebook*, edited by Jennifer M. Jeffers, 179–202. London: Routledge.

Jurik, Nancy C., and Cynthia Siemsen. 2009. "'Doing Gender' as Canon or Agenda: A Symposium on West and Zimmerman. *Gender & Society* 23 (1): 72–75.

Kessler, Suzanne, and Wendy McKenna. 1978. *Gender: An Ethnomethodological Approach.* New York: Wiley.

Langton, Rae. 1990. "Whose Right? Ronald Dworkin, Women, and Pornographers." *Philosophy and Public Affairs* 19 (4): 311–359.

Langton, Rae. 1993. "Speech Acts and Unspeakable Acts." *Philosophy and Public Affairs* 22 (4): 293–330.

Lloyd, Moya. 1999. "The Body." In *Contemporary Social and Political Theory: An Introduction*, Fidelma Ashe, Alan Finlayson, Moya Lloyd, Iain MacKenzie, James Martin and Shane O'Neill., 111–130. Buckingham: Open University Press.

Lloyd, Moya. 2007. *Judith Butler: From Norms to Politics.* Cambridge: Polity.

Lloyd, Moya. 2011. "From Linguistic Performativity to Social Performance: The Development of a Concept." In *Routledge International Handbook of Contemporary Social and Political Theory*, edited by Gerard Delanty and Stephen P. Turner, 270–279. London: Routledge.

Loizidou, Elena. 1999. "The Trouble with Rape: Gender Matters and Legal Transformations," *Feminist Legal Studies* 7 (3): 275–297.

Loxley, James. 2007. *Performativity.* London: Routledge.

MacKinnon, Catharine A. 1987. *Feminism Unmodified: Discourses on Life and Law.* Cambridge, MA: Harvard University Press.

MacKinnon, Catharine A. 1994. *Only Words.* London: Harper Collins Publishers.

MacKinnon, Catharine A. (1985) 2009. "From *Pornography, Civil Rights, and Speech*." In *Doing Ethics: Moral Reasoning and Contemporary Issues*, 2nd ed., edited by Lewis Vaughn, 299–311. New York: W. W. Norton

Maitra, Ishani. 2009. "Silencing Speech." *Canadian Journal of Philosophy* 39 (2): 309–338.

Martin, Biddy. 1992. "Sexual Practice and Changing Lesbian Identities." In *Destablising Theory: Contemporary Feminist Debates*, edited by Michèle Barrett and Anne Phillips, 93–119. Cambridge: Polity.

Martin, Patricia Yancey. 2003. "'Said and Done' versus 'Saying and Doing': Gendering Practices, Practicing Gender at Work." *Gender & Society*, 17 (3): 342–366.

Matsuda, Mari J., Charles R. Lawrence III, Richard Delgado, and Kimberlé Williams Crenshaw. 1993. *Words That Wound: Critical Race Theory, Assaultive Speech, and the First Amendment*. Boulder, CO: Westview Press.

McGowan, Mary Kate. 2003. "Conversational Exercitives and the Force of Pornography." *Philosophy and Public Affairs* 31 (2): 155–189.

McGowan, Mary Kathryn. 2005. "On Pornography: MacKinnon, Speech Acts and 'False' Construction." *Hypatia* 20 (3): 23–49.

Mills, Catherine. 2000. "Efficacy and Vulnerability: Judith Butler on Reiteration and Resistance." *Australian Feminist Studies* 15 (32): 265–279.

Mills, Catherine. 2003. "Contesting the Political: Foucault and Butler on Power and Resistance." *Journal of Political Philosophy* 11 (3): 253–272.

Newton, Esther. 1972. *Mother Camp: Female Impersonators in America*. Chicago: Chicago University Press.

Nicholson, Linda. 1994. "Interpreting Gender." *Signs: Journal of Women in Culture and Society* 20 (1): 79–105.

Oakley, Ann. (1972) 2005. "The Difference between Sex and Gender." In *The Ann Oakley Reader: Gender, Women and Social Science*, 7–12. Bristol, UK: Policy Press.

Olson, Gary A., and Lynn Worsham. 2000. "Changing the Subject: Judith Butler's Politics of Radical Resignification." *JAC: A Journal of Composition Theory* 20 (4): 727–765.

Passavant, Paul, and Jodi Dean. 2001. "Laws and Societies." *Constellations* 8 (3): 376–89.

Probyn, Elspeth. 1995. "Lesbians in Space: Gender, Sex, and the Structure of Missing." *Gender, Place and Culture: A Journal of Feminist Geography* 2 (1): 77–84.

Rich, Adrienne. 1980. "Compulsory Heterosexuality and Lesbian Existence." *Signs: Journal of Women in Culture and Society* 5 (4): 531–560.

Rothenberg, Molly Anne, and Joseph Valente. 1997. "Performative Chic: The Fantasy of a Performative Politics." *College Literature* 24 (1): 295–304.

Schilt, Kristen, and Laurel Westbrook. 2009. "Doing Gender, Doing Heteronormativity: 'Gender Normals,' Transgender People, and the Social Maintenance of Heterosexuality." *Gender & Society* 23 (4): 440–464.

Schwartzman, Lisa H. 2002. "Hate Speech, Illocution, and Social Context: A Critique of Judith Butler." *Journal of Social Philosophy* 33 (3): 421–441.

Sedgwick, Eve Kosofsky. 2003. *Touching Feeling: Affect, Pedagogy, Performativity*. Durham and London: Duke University Press.

Smith, Greg. 2011. "Erving Goffman." In *The Wiley-Blackwell Companion to Major Social Theorists*, vol. 2, *Contemporary Social Theorists*, edited by George Ritzer and Jeffrey Stepnisky, 125–154. Oxford: Wiley Blackwell.

Strossen, Nadine. 2000. *Defending Pornography: Free Speech, Sex, and the Fight for Women's Rights*. New York: New York University Press.

Tyler, Melissa, and Laurie Cohen. 2007. "Management in/as Comic Relief: Queer Theory and Gender Performativity in *The Office*." *Gender, Work, and Organization* 15 (2): 113–132.

Valentine, Gill. 1996. "(Re)negotiating the 'Heterosexual Street': Lesbian Productions of Space." In *BodySpace: Destabilising Geographies of Gender and Sexuality*, edited by Nancy Duncan, 146–155. London: Routledge.

Walker, Julia A. 2003. "Why Performance? Why Now? Textuality and the Rearticulation of Human Presence." *Yale Journal of Criticism* 16 (1): 149–175.

Weir, Allison. 1996. *Sacrificial Logics: Feminist Theory and the Critique of Identity*. London: Routledge.

West, Candace. 1996. "Goffman in Feminist Perspective." *Sociological Perspectives* 39 (3): 353–369.

West, Caroline. 2003. "A Free Speech Argument against Pornography." *Canadian Journal of Philosophy* 33 (3): 391–422.

West, Caroline. 2013. "Pornography and Censorship." *The Stanford Encyclopedia of Philosophy*. Fall 2013 edition. Edward N. Zalta. ed. http://plato.stanford.edu/archives/fall2013/entries/pornography-censorship/ (accessed October 13, 2014).

West, Candace, and Don H. Zimmerman. 1987. "Doing Gender." *Gender & Society* 1 (2): 125–151.

Wittig, Monique. 1981. "One Is Not Born a Woman." *Feminist Issues* 1 (2): 47–54.

CHAPTER 29

THE PERSONAL IS POLITICAL

RENEE HEBERLE

During the Chinese revolutionary war of 1949 against the Nationalist forces of Chiang Kai-Shek, organizers of the Chinese Communist Party encouraged peasants to publically "speak bitterness" against landlords who abused them. These sessions of public witnessing sometimes ended in brutal violence against the personages of the landed class, but they also led to a revolutionary taking of the means of production, the land (Farquar and Berry 2004).

In 1962 at the Port Huron meeting of the national council of Students for a Democratic Society, Tom Hayden, primary author of the Port Huron Statement, said, "It is time for a reassertion of the personal. A new Left must give form to . . . feelings of helplessness and indifference so that people may see the political, social, and economic sources of their private troubles and organize to change society" (quoted in Echols 1984, 29). Hayden's invocation of a connection between the personal and the political was a call to move from the alienated condition of liberal individualism to an empowered and participatory mode of collective action. On the terms of the New Left, the personal and the private referred to the individual, and the political and the public to the collective. Being political referred to developing a structural analysis of what liberalism and capitalist culture attributes to individual suffering or failure.

Martin Luther King invoked the ideal of the "beloved community" in speeches and in his writings. For King, nonviolent action was simultaneously a form of witnessing and revolutionary action; the beloved community would be the result. Civil rights activists of the 1960s struggled to enact through organization and relationships of solidarity the beloved community that King imagined. This was known as a "prefigurative" politics and identified the voices of the oppressed as the authentic voices of revolutionary change.[1]

In the mid-1960s as black activists in the Student Non-Violent Coordinating Committee (SNCC) became increasingly disenchanted with the privilege of white participants, as the Black Power movement and black nationalism became more influential among activists, the phrase "look to your own oppression" became a way for white students to carry what they had experienced and learned from civil rights activism into the movement for democracy on college campuses.

In the community action projects, funded by the federal government under Lyndon B. Johnson but taken up by student activists disillusioned with activism on campuses, the phrase "let the people decide" became a mantra for community organizers. The organizer was there to identify issues and bring people together, facilitating but not leading collective action. The authenticity of the claims made was at stake. Outsiders coming in to impoverished communities brought abstract knowledge to bear. Those who lived in impoverished communities had experiential, or personal, knowledge of the history and dynamics of poverty and racism that formed those communities.

THERE are innumerable references to and discussions of the phrase *the personal is political* in theoretical, activist, and even fictional writing from the last sixty years. It is associated with second-wave feminism but no single political movement or theory can lay claim to its meaning.[2] This chapter identifies several contexts in which it appears and some of the meaning(s) it has accrued over time. Identity politics, debates about experience and authenticity, and critical reframings of the public and the private carry traces of this apparently simple catchphrase. Its influence and fluctuating meanings are inscribed in the history of new social movements and newer counterpublics.[3] Some argue it inspired a "personalized" politics in a way that breeds disunity and fractured sensibilities about the functions and effects of institutionalized and structural injustices and inequalities. A more optimistic evaluation, however, is that it authorizes a radically expanded space for politicized and politicizing reflection on the part of the subject/citizen, and more capacious interpretive frameworks for challenging illegitimate forms of power and dominance.

HISTORICAL EMERGENCE

Second-wave feminism was not the first or only twentieth-century social movement to invoke the spirit of the phrase *the personal is political*. Feminism did, however, introduce it into the popular lexicon, and it became a crucial, albeit deeply and sometimes fiercely contested, reference point for feminist politics. I therefore begin with a brief account of the experiences and thinking of women who planted the seeds of the second wave of feminist politics in the United States.

Sara Evans's history of white Southern women's experiences in the civil rights movement through the 1960s traces the journey of the phrase into second-wave feminist discourse and activism. Her work focuses particularly on women as organizers in the SNCC and then with the Southern Student's Organizing Committee (SSOC).[4] The personal is political resonated deeply with women who, through their political organizing experiences in the civil rights movement, became painfully aware of how their daily activities and personal lives were shaped by unstated assumptions about male superiority and prerogative.

Evans describes young civil rights activists as creating a way of life as much as a set of ideas. They ate together, slept together, had sex, formed intimate relationships, and worked in very close proximity with and, often under threat, in hostile neighborhoods and rural communities. The movement was their life (Evans 1979, 42). Early SNCC organizers were committed to enacting the "beloved community," invoked by Martin Luther King, of nonviolent social justice activists. The organizing environment itself was thus intensely personal and political; activists aspired to enact a model of the egalitarian and democratic world in which they wanted to live. The "beloved community" invoked ethical claims, calling on activists to create relationships of solidarity that would go beyond the abstract unity inspired by shared analysis or by leadership based on traditional rhetorical skills or the intellectual mastery of issues.

This commitment did not ultimately create expanding or long-term political unity. Rather, it became a generative space of sometimes harsh and painful conflict that would, over the long term, inform understanding of the significance of sex and sexism as it entwined with race and racism among women and men in both SNCC and SSOC. Many who were involved in the organizing of the civil rights movement would ultimately become involved in radically differentiated political movements, black nationalism, second-wave feminism, and a reinvigorated Students for a Democratic Society (SDS) among them. The differentiated social movements that emerged out of the civil rights and student movements of the 1960s would reflect variations on the theme that the personal is political.

In the environment of civil rights organizing, where the personal was inevitably politicized in an immediate sense, white women were often assigned or assumed to be responsible for traditionally female tasks such as housekeeping, filing or organizing the office, typing the press releases rather than writing them, and making the coffee. And the presence of white women in the movement was imbued with racial and sexual significance. White women could not travel to most communities with black men and sex between black men and white women in the movement was fraught, associated as it was with a challenge to white masculinity and with the standing threat from white men to torture and murder black men, especially those who appeared to associate with white women for any reason. Unlike their white male companions, white women organizers had to challenge roles forced on them by political friends and enemies alike. They contended with assumptions about female behavior, goals, and responsibilities that were not only a part of the general culture, but, as they recognized with some distress, imbued in their subjectivity. The tenacity of traditional racialized, bourgeois roles for white women kept them in the safer counties, less likely to be registering voters, and more likely to be sexualized by men in the movement. Young white women had, of necessity, to forge a new sense of self, to redefine the meaning of being a woman quite apart from the flawed, disempowering images they had inherited (Evans 1979, 57).

Black women did not experience the sexualization of relationships in the same way, nor did they experience the protective "chivalry" white women came to despise. Black women's immediate conflicts were often with the white women, not the men, in the movement. In this sense, the personal was political in that the personal relationships white women formed with black men were both personal and political to black women. Those relationships constituted a deeply felt personal affront to some black women even as they could simultaneously be interpreted in the context of resistance to miscegenation, one of the most closely held and dangerous of "racial traditions" in the United States. Whatever the "truth" of the personal relationships that developed in SNCC, black women themselves were alternatively marginalized or reified; ultimately, they were assumed to be detached from such matters. Black women made critical claims about these issues in the moment and as the feminist movement emerged with a predominantly white cast of visible figures and set of issues predominantly associated with white women's lives, articulated critiques of the race-blindness of what became mainstream feminist discourse (Joseph and Lewis 1999).

In short, the personal is political was enacted in the gendered and sexed dynamics of the civil rights movement, the Black Power movement, and the student movement. *The personal is political* was thus invoked as a challenge within and among those movements to see the limits of their own vision as to what constitutes the "political." It simultaneously signified a quest for authenticity in one's pursuit of justice. In some of its original invocations, the phrase *the personal is political* announced the imperative for reflexivity about one's own position of privilege or oppression in any given context. It called for avoiding imposing one's values on others as a means of creating a participatory democracy. And finally, it indicates that each person has at least a thread of their identity ensnared in oppressive relationships; that no one can claim to be "free" from alienation or oppression as a subject or as an objectified other. The organizing principle of new social movements, "look to one's own oppression," called for self-reflection that would lead to revelations of complicity with or victimization by oppressive relationships on the part of each individual. Ultimately *the personal is political* would inspire women to insist that what had been thought of as, alternatively, moral issues (sex) or trivial offenses (sexism) in everyday interactions were symptoms of oppressive norms and structural forces.

The Personal Is Political and the Second Wave of Feminism

In 1965, Casey Hayden and Mary King, two white women from the South who were deeply embedded in civil rights activism early on in the movement, wrote what they called a "kind of memo." Their immediate purpose was to open dialogue, particularly with the black women in SNCC, about women's place in the organization and in society at large. The language of the personal figures prominently in the memo, both as the subjective reason Hayden and King were speaking to the issue of sex caste, but also because the transformation of the personal was, for movement activists at the time, said to be a path to radical and progressive political transformation.

> Having learned from the movement to think radically about the personal worth and abilities of people whose role in society had gone unchallenged before, a lot of women in the movement have begun trying to apply those lessons to their own relations with men. Each of us probably has her own story of the various results, and of the internal struggle occasioned by trying to break out of very deeply learned fears, needs, and self-perceptions, and of what happens when we try to replace them with concepts of people and freedom learned from the movement and organizing.
>
> (Hayden and King 1965)

The memo eloquently describes the personalized struggles of women to confront the deeply subjective constraints of femininity. The reference to each woman having her own story of internal struggle as a woman in relationship to men invokes the spirit that would infuse consciousness-raising among radical feminist groups later in the decade.

Hayden and King's memo had little immediate effect. However, it circulated nationally among women in the New Left movements and continued to inspire women to organize women's workshop sessions at meetings. Finally, a hostile response to a working document produced by a women's liberation workshop by a majority of the men at a 1967 meeting of the SDS inspired women activists to begin to meet independently of the established Left organizations. A subsequent meeting of the National Conference for New Politics (NCNP) in Chicago confirmed that women would not see their demands for equality and recognition met in the male-dominated New Left movements. Women began to organize independently as women against sex oppression.[5]

Women-only meetings would eventually come to be more formally organized as consciousness-raising groups. Radical feminists, many of whom had been deeply involved in the New Left, insisted that women's oppression must be seen as independent of and even prior to racial and class oppressions.

Among radical feminists "the personal is political" became a method and a claim. This occurred in the context of consciousness-raising groups, which became the means to the end of politicizing women's understanding of what they had normally experienced and normatively identified as personal problems. Over a few years, even as consciousness-raising groups proliferated, feminists became skeptical of this method of politicizing otherwise privatized issues, as did Carol Williams Payne when she wrote about her group becoming more like a social club than a political organization; she described consciousness-raising as becoming an end in itself (Koedt 1973, 282–284). Jo Freeman famously critiqued the acclaimed "structurelessness" of consciousness-raising groups. She identified the egalitarian method of sharing personal problems to see what individuals in a group had in common as a "developmental" moment—but one to which participants became too attached. Freeman argued that attempting to sustain a structureless group will always lead to a group with informal structure in the form of elites, friendship groups, and "stars" identified not by the group but by the media or other external influences, outside the control of the group. As this occurs, participants begin to take things "personally," and the "personal is political" takes on an entirely new and negative meaning as destructive and unacknowledged power relationships develop within and around the group (Koedt 1973, 285–299). In organizational terms the personal became political as radical egalitarianism devolved into conflicts over prerogative and visibility. Nonetheless, over time consciousness-raising groups became sites of feminist reinventions of the personal and discoveries of systemic oppression related to normative masculinity and femininity. They were places where gender and sex became contested references related to social justice rather than politically neutral roles or activities that existed outside of power relationships (Snitow 1983).

In the early 1970s, radical feminists organized specifically against sexual violence in the many forms it adopts, including prostitution, pornography, violence against women, sexual assault and rape, and sexual harassment (Gavey 2009). The damage done by a patriarchal order to the possibilities of women's sexuality became a theory and a political claim that the male use and abuse of women's sexuality is the fount of women's oppression. As the movement grew beyond the early small-group models of discussion and activism, arrangements and institutions long buried in the space of the private, constructed on the terms of modern liberalism, were identified as a source of suffering for women, no matter their background.

Inspired by the necessity to expose the collective harms they discovered in consciousness-raising groups, to raise public consciousness and to provoke political responses, such as legislation and funding for organizational purposes, Radical feminists organized speak-outs. The earliest speak-outs were about abortion rights, organized to highlight the white maleness of the legislative bodies that were deciding the future of women's reproductive lives and the harm done by criminalizing abortion.[6] Speak-outs were initially understood as politicizing the personal because women came into public spaces, the streets, town halls, and capitol buildings to tell of experiences otherwise obscured by liberalism's romance with the privacy of sex, sexuality, reproduction, and familial relationships and arrangements, no matter how exclusionary, exploitative, abusive or violent. Speak-outs were organized to show that abuse and violence are not personal aberrations, but rather the norm for millions of women and children (stories of survival of child sexual abuse were also told in these forums). They were a reincarnated version of the Chinese revolutionary tradition of speaking bitterness (see chapter epigraph). They sought recognition of historical and collective failures to render a just society. This iteration of the phrase the personal is political anticipates public empathy with otherwise individualized suffering obscured by the demands of privacy. The publicizing of the harm constitutes a kind of shaming as a means to inspire fairer and more just responses to otherwise covert violence.

Speak-outs and other public actions ruptured the appearance that all was well in the home, the obstetrician's office, the workplace, or on the streets (barring the stranger or the pathological individual who threatened or "violated" women). Annual "Take Back the Night" speak-outs and marches were organized as assertions of a woman's right to appear in public, at whatever time of day or in whatever configuration of style and attitude she chose, without being targeted for rape or assaultive speech.[7] Unlike consciousness-raising groups in their ideal form, speak-outs were not about deliberating the significance and meaning of experiences in the interest of building political arguments or creating a deliberative space that could generate political action. Speak-outs publicized sexualized and gendered harms and injustice, showing that they are not about the immoral or abnormal behaviors of deviant individuals but normatively masculinist prerogatives and entitlements. The recognition that otherwise personal suffering was not an effect of personal failure or perception, but of relationships of power and dominance, inspired women to argue for reforms in rape law and marital law, and domestic violence became a statutory criminal offense. By the late 1980s it was possible for wives to claim rape by men who were their husbands (Hasday 2000) and for women to claim sexual harassment as discrimination, not merely "flirting" in the workplace (Mackinnon 1986); and the fact that "stranger rape" was the exception to the rule of sexual assault of women and girls by friends and relatives was not dismissed as propaganda against the traditional family or the romance of seduction (Estrich 1987). In this decade the personal became political in the sense that personal suffering was made public; subsequently, the personal became a space where society would begin seeing and naming criminal behavior, not just worrying about dysfunctional relationships.

As sexuality came to the forefront of second-wave feminist concerns, like earlier commitments to radical egalitarianism, it was generative of conflict. By the 1980s sexuality became one of the most contested areas among feminists, to the point where that era is identified as the era of the "sex wars" (Ferguson 1984). Feminists were torn about whether to focus only on the dangers of sex and sexuality and the material facts of male and masculinist dominance, coercion, and physical violence, or to simultaneously elaborate the pleasures of sex and sexuality as potentially liberatory, and thus political, whether enacted with men or women, monogamously or promiscuously, in private or in public (Russell 1990; Snitow, Stansell, and Thompson 1983; Vance 1984). Either way one turned to understand sexuality, the personal is political became ever more salient as the debate itself illustrated that sex and sexuality, traditionally codified in moral terms related to individual desires and behaviors and veiled by liberal commitments to "privacy," are governed by relationships of power, inequality, and interests (Rubin 1975).

As the white women Sara Evans and Alice Echols described were alienated from male dominated organizations that trivialized or dismissed their presence and participation, black women were redefining the "personal is political" in reaction to different kinds of stereotypes of "the strong (asexual) matriarchal black woman." When the National Black Feminist Organization (NBFO) issued a statement of purpose in 1973, it asserted that black women were a part of the women's liberation movement, that their seeming exclusion was only a construction of the white, male-dominated media. As noted earlier, however, black women and white women were situated quite differently historically and experientially within the organizations of the Left in the 1960s and 1970s. Ultimately, while the NBFO did identify as part of women's liberation, black women in large part organized separately from white women's groups throughout the 1970s. Some understood their fight to be more linked with anti-imperialist women's struggles than with white women in the United States. Others did not agree with the increasingly separatist strategies white women were adopting in order to organize as autonomously or "freely" from men (Allen 2000). For black women the personal is political eventually transformed into claims about identity and what came to be referred to as "identity politics." The struggle to claim a political identity in solidarity with black men as oppressed by white supremacy and as women against masculinist myths of manhood framed the political lives of black feminists (Wallace 1978; Hull, Smith and Scott 1982).

The differentiated terms on which black feminists took up *the personal is political* was elaborated in the context of confronting the family as a political institution. The radical feminist critique, which politicized the family as an institution by arguing it could and should be radically transformed or even abolished if women's liberation was to be attained, did not resonate with black feminists. Black women were less invested in this critique of the family and the terms of bourgeois masculinity that framed its legitimate presence. The legacy of slavery and Jim Crow had left many families in black communities fractured and fragile; the brutal separations of lovers, the prohibition of slave marriage, the selling away of children, and the intentional disempowerment and material impoverishment of black people since Reconstruction made the very existence of a family a radical idea and also led to the emergence of significant alternative forms of family (Collins 2000). Twentieth-century black women were not escaping the constraints of white middle-class conformity and suburbia; they criticized the state not for incentivizing and enforcing oppressive nuclear family values, but for being complicit in destroying the potential for stable relationships among African American people and thus destroying black children's futures. In this case, the "personal" space of the family was critiqued as "political" for black women and white women, but for essentially different reasons that required very different strategies on the part of activists. The report "The Negro Family: the Case for National Action," overseen by Daniel Patrick Moynihan for the US Department of Labor in 1965, identified the predominance of female headed households in black families as creating a "matriarchal" society that diminished the likelihood of black men committing to fatherhood. The report displaced white responsibility for the condition of African American communities and neighborhoods onto the "culture" of black women, families, and communities in the name of "rethinking" welfare policy. The report encouraged the proliferation of "culture of poverty" arguments that attributed the failure of black communities to thrive to pathologies in family structure. This discursive construction of "cause and effect" illustrates the double burden black women experience politicizing the terms on which family is understood in the context of social-welfare liberalism (Giddings 1984; Hull, Scott, and Smith 1993; hooks 1982).

In 1983 the Combahee River Collective (CRC), a group of black lesbian socialist women, translated *the personal is political* explicitly into a claim about the relationship between identity and experience. "Black women have always embodied, if only in their physical manifestation, an adversarial stance to white male rule and have actively resisted its inroads upon them and their communities in both dramatic and subtle ways." Further,

[t]his focusing upon our own oppression is embodied in the concept of identity politics. We believe that the most profound and potentially most radical politics come directly out of our own identity, as opposed to working to end somebody else's oppression. In the case of black women this is a particularly repugnant, dangerous, threatening, and therefore revolutionary concept because it is obvious from looking at all the political movements that have preceded us that anyone is more worthy of liberation than ourselves. We reject pedestals, queenhood, and walking ten paces behind. To be recognized as human, levelly human, is enough."

(reprinted in Hull, Smith, and Scott 1993, pp. 13-22)

This manifesto suggests that in their very existence, black women manifest resistance to white male rule. This echoes (albeit tangentially) Marx's claim that the working class, brought into existence by capitalism, will undo capitalism. As a socialist feminist organization the Combahee River Collective describes their analysis of the politics of black women's situation as a critical reformulation. It does not present feminism, as some radical and cultural feminists did, as an autonomous theoretical or practical approach that would exhaustively capture sex oppression. It thus introduced feminism to what Kimberlé Crenshaw would, in 1989, name as the approach or method of intersectional analysis. This idea is elaborated when the statement directly addresses the idea that the personal is political. It gives an account of the multiple oppressions that black women experience. "A political contribution which we feel we have already made is the expansion of the feminist principle that the personal is political. In our consciousness-raising sessions, for example, we have in many ways gone beyond white women's revelations because we are dealing with the implications of race and class as well as sex. Even our black women's style of talking/testifying in black language about what we have experienced has a resonance that is both cultural and political" (CRC, in Hull, et al. 1993) It is by embodying an oppressed race, class and gender, in the very form of their existence that black women are everything that threatens white, male, class-based rule. Here, the personal is political in a literal sense; it is in the personhood of the oppressed. It is a complex and embedded (in political history and differentiated contexts) sense of the "personal" that the manifesto describes.

In 1981 Bernice Johnson Reagon delivered what would become a widely read and anthologized speech about coalition in what had become the age of "identity politics." She understood, as did the early radical feminist groups, the personal as political as a means to an end of organizing for social change. Her metaphor for consciousness-raising groups, or what had by the early 1980s become known as, identity-based groups, was "home." But she destabilizes the idea of "home," reminding those at the Women's Music Festival, particularly white women, that if they attempted to keep their home homogenous, not only would they fail to make social change but would also become an easy target, marked for destruction. Staying at "home" (in this case as womyn-identified women) would become a practice of exclusion and mimic the politics that inspired the movement in the first place (Reagon 1981). Ultimately, Reagon's rhetoric invoked the personal as political as an inspirational source of activism rather than as a constative utterance. The personal is not the same as the political, but it never ceases to potentially become political—that is, a place of contestation over power and the terms of inclusion. Shane Phelan (1990) makes a similar argument as she critiques the tendency of feminists to aspire to authenticity in self and relations, thus losing site of the power relationships that cut across the category "woman."

Like Reagon in "Turning the Century," Audre Lorde, in an address titled "The Master's Tools Will Never Dismantle the Master's House," given in 1984, says it is through acknowledging the dangerousness of racial differences that her predominantly white audience may find their creativity. But that danger lives in the self as much as it does in social relationships.

> I agreed to take part in a New York University Institute for the Humanities conference a year ago, with the understanding that I would be commenting upon papers dealing with the role of difference within the lives of American women: difference of race, sexuality, class, and age. The absence of these considerations weakens any feminist discussion of the personal and the political.
>
> (Lorde 1984, 110)

She goes on to say:

> Racism and homophobia are real conditions of all our lives in this place and time. I urge each one of us here to reach down into that deep place of knowledge inside herself and touch that terror and loathing of any difference that lives there. See whose face it wears. Then the personal as the political can begin to illuminate all our choices.
>
> (Lorde 1984, 110)

Lorde calls for critical work on the self; she elaborates a transformative process of confrontation with biased aspects of the self too deeply rooted in and by historical circumstance and experience to be obvious. Thus the personal as identity or subjectivity is a space of politics in itself requiring attention for those who aspire to lead a just and ethical life.

Thus far we have seen that *the personal is political* is a claim about expanding the spaces that politics might be found, a proscriptive analytic, a prescriptive set of norms, a method for getting to a theory, and a means to self-transformation toward effective coalition-building and political struggle. It would become the starting point for internal critique and conflict among feminists and inspire the exploration of the self and subjectivity. Its mutability meant it would be taken up in different ways by different groups of feminists as it circulated in very different contexts and among different groups of women. The Redstockings Manifesto issues one classic interpretation:

> Because we have lived so intimately with our oppressors, in isolation from each other, we have been kept from seeing our personal suffering as a political condition. This creates the impression that a woman's relationship with her man is a matter of interplay between two unique personalities, and can be worked out individually. In

reality, every such relationship is a class relationship, and the conflict, between individual men and women are political conflicts that can only be solved collectively.

(quoted in Crow 2000, 223)

As seen in the Combahee manifesto, *the personal is political* also informed what in the 1980s came to be called "identity politics." In addition to inspiring theory and practices that challenge the private/public divide.

"Identity politics" and "identity and difference" were common references in feminist theorizing and practice by the late 1980s. In "Identity: Skin, Blood, Heart," Minnie Bruce Pratt (1984, 148-202) writes about her personal identity as a networked force field, littered with ethical and political pitfalls. She takes up Lorde's challenge in her everyday life and chronicles the experience. Her essay ultimately argues that an ethical individual will, with each encounter with "difference," acknowledge and reflect on a lesson that emerges from the personal being political; that is that our identities are like a tapestry of tightly mingled threads, each of which may be alternatively threatening or subordinated in any given context. The autobiographical accounts in *Yours in Struggle* (1984) do not seek authenticity in the self, nor do they attempt to gather up all of the particularities and differences of the personal in order to establish once and for all a unity as a necessary precondition for politics. According to Chandra Mohanty and Biddy Martin (2003), Pratt's accomplishment is in her resistance to the conflation of her personal experience, as such, with "the political" in such a way that the political significance of her identity is exhausted by unitary claims about her victimization. One could also describe Pratt's essay as elaborating a kind of life-long consciousness-raising session as she navigates through and resists a world constituted by differences, internal and external to her self, created through histories of relationships of dominance and power. Her essay reflects Reagon's wariness about the desire to recreate "home" in our political lives when "homes" are necessarily constituted through the exclusion of otherness and difference and therefore resistant to the agonistic quality of coalition building and political change.

Kimberlé Crenshaw argues that feminist research should start from the assumption that identities forged in oppressive relationships do not exist parallel to one another but as intersecting forces. Instead they "intersect" in the subjective and objective lives of women as subjects and it is this point of intersection that feminism should struggle to articulate. Her work builds on many insights feminist activists and thinkers developed in the 1980s about identity, while highlighting blind spots about the "personal" in some feminist organizing against domestic violence and anti-discrimination law. Crenshaw challenges liberalism's imperative to empty social and cultural, or "identity differences," of meaning in order to achieve a society of tolerance and, ultimately, sameness. But she goes on to say, "Yet implicit in certain strands of feminist and racial liberation movements, for example, is the view that the social power in delineating difference need not be the power of domination; it can instead be the source of social empowerment and reconstruction" (Crenshaw 1991, 242). The politics of difference here does not have to be left to the sorting powers of the dominant class. It is subject to the concrete reclamation Lorde calls for when she says political power lies in acknowledging buried fears of being different or encountering difference. Crenshaw describes the differences between women of color and white women in the context of domestic violence. As in the discussion earlier of the differences in the personal experiences of black women and white women in the family, Crenshaw identifies the ways antiviolence discourses and strategies on the part of feminist and anti-racist groups form in such a way as to render the experiences of women of color unintelligible. She uses the language of "location," "experience," and "identity" rather than "personal" to invoke the specificity of the subject of her analysis (women of color).

The examples that Crenshaw brings to bear illustrate the racist and classist distributions of state resources subsequent to the elision of women of color from predominant constructions of the problem. It is not merely a "personal" or privatized problem, though it is certainly that, but is intertwined with issues of citizenship, racist policing strategies, the sexualization of black female bodies, and criminalization of black male bodies respectively, and access to resources more generally. To construct the issue of rape and domestic violence as about rescuing women from the traditional constraints of liberal privacy in the middle-class nuclear family elides the intersecting ways citizenship status, race, religious values, and resources alter the meanings of and the reactions to the harms done to women in various sites in which they live, work, play or wander.

THE PERSONAL IS POLITICAL AND THE PRIVATE/PUBLIC DISTINCTION

The phrase *the personal is political* as an axiomatic reference has influenced feminist theorizing from standpoint theory, which asks how lived experience inflects knowledge production and perceptions of reality (Hartsock 1983), to body politics, which interrogate how embodied characteristics or behaviors are symptomatic of gendered, sexed, and racialized constructions of difference (Young 1998), to critical social psychology that assumes interpersonal relations are effects of power relationships, not a neutral process of socialization or role-development (Henley 1981). Preconceptions governing the sense of personhood, or pertaining to our self, are politicized in the sense that they are shown to be effects of, not causes of, constructions of gendered, sexed, and racial differences. Liberal constructions of what is appropriately available for political contestation have been challenged by feminisms inspired by the possibilities of contesting oppressively personalized and individuated conditions of life. Feminist critiques of the public/private divide have argued for reconfigurations of the relationship between the personal and political that do not reify either term as unchangeable and sacred. We should keep in mind that the personal as a particular space of individualized and/or familial "privacy" is unique to Western modernity. Feminist literature that built on the personal being politicized shows that there is nothing primeval, organic, or immutable about the personal. It is never and never has been immune to public/political intervention, scrutiny, judgment, sanction, or misrecognition.

Linda Nicholson (1989) identifies the phrase as a significant rebuttal of liberal and Marxist theories, both of which assume the family to be an ahistorical fact, ontologically prior to and distinct from the sphere of politics and economic relations of production. John Locke situates the equalitarian space of his polity up against the "naturally" patriarchal space of the family. Marxism projects the possibility that the personal, defined as the capacity to consciously produce the whole of nature in freedom, will ultimately be unbound from the bourgeois mythology about the home as the space of freedom and autonomy. Liberalism distinguishes the bases for relationships in the family, those being nature, honor, and duty, from those of the polity, reason, contract, and self-interest. Marx and Marxism understand that production moved, with the advent of capitalism, from the household to the factory and that, in fact, there was nothing sacred or natural about the condition of the family in capitalism. However, in the Marxist analyses of that movement the family becomes an anachronism whose justifications are historically rendered irrelevant by the imperatives of capital.

Nicholson's purpose is to argue that the "personal" as that which is private or non-political must be understood to be in a historical dynamic with what is considered political at any given time. Nicholson argues for the historicity of that which is personal or privatized, critiquing those feminist approaches that seek out causative origins of "patriarchy," or gendered and/or sexed conditions of inequality and domination. The personal as "privacy" is unique to Western modernity. As a response to patriarchal norms that reify the public/private distinction as natural and necessary to the future of a stable democratic republic, the personal is political was taken up as a critique of the public/private divide. Feminists argue that nothing considered "personal" should be immune to judgment about its collusion with oppression or harm or injustice.

Conclusion

The Vagina Monologues is one relatively recent (late 1990s) incarnation of *the personal is political*. The movement begun by Eve Ensler's play insists on talking about the vagina in public and without shame, about what happens to "it," what "it" likes and does not like, and why as a body part "it" has been subject to such bizarre claims and damaging treatment over the ages and across time. The international success of *The Vagina Monologues* may be due, in part, to the fact that it renders public that body part that has been alternatively violently objectified or mystified by patriarchy while also being a source of pleasure. The originality of the play is in putting an otherwise "hidden" or "secret" body part, rather than a marginalized identity, at the center of political attention. It acknowledges the vagina as mutable in its significance and as having political standing as a measure of the freedom (and even pleasures) that should be available in the world. Radical feminist groups reintroduced women to their vaginas. But they did not introduce the vagina with the public as an audience. Critiques of the *Vagina Monologues* (not so much the international movement that has taken it up as a rallying cry) focus our attention back onto the potential for essentialism and artificial unity in "woman" or in this case, in identifying through a body part held in common, implicit in the phrase, the personal is political. Further, Christine Cooper points out that most configurations of the monologues performed use "the raped Bosnian woman" to stand in for "traditional societies" and third- (or second-) world brutality (Cooper 2007, 745). *The Vagina Monologues* is not some kind of endgame in the history of *the personal is political*; while identifying through the vagina carries the historical baggage of the patriarchal identification of "woman" with the body and sexuality, it also acts as a rhetorical reclamation of a body part that has, in part because of the "personal" and "private" (secret and hidden) quality of its existence, been available to be vilified culturally and destroyed physically.

There are many other questions to be raised about how *the personal is political* plays in the contemporary context. It does not resonate in the same way as when it was invoked in the name of political resistance to covert dominance and oppression. Challenges to uproot, disrupt, disclaim, or disaggregate normative identity formations, assumptions, and relationships have become claims to rights for marginalized persons and groups (e.g., gay liberation now means the right to same-sex marriage). In another iteration, the original meanings of the phrase have disappeared into "choice feminism." In "choice feminism," the personal is political because an individual woman now has a choice about enacting femininity; her style and decisions are "choices" and therefore, in themselves, are empty of political content aside from the triumphalist contrast with a less enlightened past (Marso 2010).

At the most basic-level, second-wave feminism was (is?) about showing that those choices that liberalism and now neoliberalism think of as personal are actually socially constructed and often constraints on our capacities. Much of the ire it raises among public commentators about feminism (from Rush Limbaugh to those who advocate choice) is that it dares to judge what "ought to be" left to personal preferences. It judges as Linda Hirschman did in 2005 when she made an argument that women with high-powered educations should stay in the workforce and shape the world differently than it is. It judges as womyn-identified women did when they challenged self-identified feminists who were intimate with men to reflect on whether they were attuned to the dynamics of compulsive heterosexuality as an institution (Rich 1986). It judges as radical feminists did when they protested the Miss America Pageant in Atlantic City in 1968. Feminism is a political movement in that it makes judgments about a world in which staying home, sleeping with men, or competing for public recognition and resources on the basis of skin tone and shiny teeth (made so by smearing Vaseline on the teeth, which also made the smile slide more easily across the face), are not "real" choices (whatever that may mean). It demands we question whether we are making choices, falling off the log of habit or second nature, or defending ourselves from sanction and abuse. Feminism is about judging "personal behavior" in that it assesses the context in which that personal behavior is naturalized and normative. The question is not about whether feminism makes "correct" judgments. It is about feminism exposing otherwise unseen or untouchable sites for judgment. Feminism makes us pay attention to the discursive and material context of "choices" rather than assume the choice is self-evident based on individual desire or purpose (Marzo 2010).

Through the influence of new social movements and radical rethinking of the "personal," the significance of equality and justice was brought into the space of the personal. Inequality does not just have socioeconomic impacts on communities affected by discrimination, oppression, exclusion, marginalization, and violence. It renders the personal, as related to the person and personhood, necessarily political. The influence of liberal individualism has trivialized the meaning of this recognition. The accusation of "political correctness" suggests claims of harm are, instead, neurotic symptoms. There is obviously a difference between taking discrimination personally as a personal "offence" that should be compensated for and politicizing that personalized or individualized experience by showing how it is informed by normative assumptions and un-thought relationships of dominance. Politicizing acts of discrimination will highlight not the impact on the individual and demands for compensation, but the implications for the way we as a now global community have lived (survived) and will live together. As heterosexual relationships are no longer the invisible norm, but instead something that require explanation (the peculiar questions asked about homosexuality could be turned on heterosexuality to good rhetorical effect: Is there a heterosexual gene? What makes heterosexual intimacy more "real"?), the world changes and not only because individuals will live with less fear. Rather, it changes because the formation of the "personal" is never untouched by the meaning and significance of what is recognizable, legitimately present and valued, or rendered possible in the public/political spaces we inhabit together.

Notes

1. In her history of the influence of the civil rights movement on second-wave feminists, Sara Evans calls this "personal politics."
2. Linda Nicholson notes, "[M]any hippies believed 'the personal is political' ... with the emergence of the women's liberation movement ... it became a slogan" (1988, 5).
3. New Social Movements refer to the emergence of multiple organized liberation movements in the 1960s and 1970s. The appellation refers to organizations that do not take class conflict as the singular or fundamental point of departure for analysis of social and political oppressions. An emphasis on "identity" and the constitutive qualities of race, gender, sexuality, ability, and ethnicity expanded the possibilities for understanding dominance and subordination in the social order.
4. SSOC was founded when white activists were no longer welcome in SNCC.
5. It is worth noting that at the 1967 meeting of the NCNP, Todd Gitlin referred to the acceptance of the meeting of black demands for control of SNCC as the "castration" of the white male. "Castrated whites will not create a movement worthy of alliance" (Echols 1984, 313). Echols mentions this with little comment. However, the unconscious identification of the movement as essentially male and the implication that black men were castrating white men are both profoundly insulting to white and black women and to the history of torture and castration Black men experienced at the hands of white slaveholders and mobs. It is

telling that the joking comment made by Stokely Carmichael in the tense aftermath of an early presentation of women's claims at a SNCC meeting that "the position of women in SNCC is prone" has traveled so much further in historical memory. Alice Echols tells us that Carmichael was parodying his own sexism, not making a misogynist claim about women in the movement (Echols 1984, 31). The distorted meaning of Carmichael's comment travels as evidence of the sexism in the leadership of SNCC, while Todd Gitlin's very straightforwardly racist and sexist comment escapes notice.
6. The New York City-based radical feminist group, Redstockings, organized a protest and speak out during the legislative hearing about the legalization of abortion in New York State.
7. The first Take Back the Night rally was in Philadelphia in 1977. The mission of the now international event has transformed to contest the terms of violence more generally, but sustains its original focus of sexual violence and women's freedom of movement.

References

Allen, Pam. 2000. *Free Space: A Perspective on the Small Group in Women's Liberation.* New York: Times Change Press.

Collins, Patricia Hill. 2000. Black Feminist Thought: Knowledge, Power and the Politics of Empowerment. New York: Routledge.

Cooper, Christine. 2007. "Worrying about Vaginas: Feminism and Eve Ensler's *Vagina Monologues.*" Signs: A Journal of Women and Culture 32 (3): 727–758.

Crenshaw, Kimberlé. 1989. "Demarginalizing the Intersection of Race and Sex: A Black Feminist Critique of Anti-Discrimination Doctrine, Feminist Theory, and Anti-Racist Politics." *University of Chicago Legal Forum* 140: 139–167.

Crenshaw, Kimberlé. 1991. "Mapping the Margins: Intersectionality, Feminism, and Violence Against Women." *Stanford Law Review* 43 (6): 1241–1300.

Crow, Barbara A. ed., 2000. *Radical Feminism: A Documentary Reader.* New York: New York University Press.

Echols, Alice. 1984. *Daring to Be Bad: Radical Feminism in America, 1967-1975.* Minneapolis: University of Minnesota Press.

Ensler, Eve. 2000. *The Vagina Monologues.* New York: Dramatists Play Service.

Estrich, Susan. 1987. *Real Rape.* Harvard University Press.

Evans, Sara. 1979. *Personal Politics: The Roots of Women's Liberation in the Civil Rights Movement and the New Left.* New York: Knopf.

Farquar, Mary, and Chris Berry. 2004. "Speaking Bitterness: History, Media and Nation in Twentieth Century China." *Historiography East and West* 2 (1): 116–143.

Ferguson, Ann. 1984 "Sex War: The Debate Between Radical and Libertarian Feminists" in *Signs: A Journal of Women and Culture*, 106-112.

Gavey, Nicola. 2009 "Fighting Rape." In *Theorizing Sexual Violence*, edited by Renee Heberle and Victoria Grace, 96–124. New York: Routledge.

Giddings, Paula. 1984. *When and Where I Enter: The Impact of Black Women on Race and Sex in America.* New York: William Morrow.

Hartsock, Nancy. 1983. *Money, Sex and Power: Toward a Feminist Historical Materialism.* Boston: Northeastern University Press.

Hasday, Jill Elaine. 2000. "Contest and Consent: A Legal History of Marital Rape." *California Law Review* 88 (5): 1373–1506.

Henley, Nancy M., and Clara Mayo, eds. 1981. *Gender and Non-Verbal Behavior*. New York: Springer-Verlag.

Hirshman, Linda. 2005. "Homeward Bound." *American Prospect*. November 21.

hooks, bell. 1982. *Ain't I a Woman? Black Women and Feminism*. New York: Pluto Press.

Hull, Gloria, Barbara Smith, and Patricia Bell Scott, eds. 1993. *All the Men Are Black, All the Women Are White, but Some of Us Are Brave*. New York: Feminist Press at City University of New York.

Joseph, Gloria and Jill Lewis. 1999. *Common Differences: Conflicts in Black and White Feminism*. Boston: South End Press.

Koedt, Anne. 1973. *Radical Feminism*. New York: Quadrangle Press.

Lorde, Audre. 1984. "The Master's Tools Will Never Dismantle the Master's House." In *Sister Outsider: Essays and Speeches*, 110–113. Berkeley: Crossing Press.

MacKinnon, Catharine. 1986. *Sexual Harassment of Working Women: A Case of Discrimination*. New Haven, CT: Yale University Press.

Marso, Lori. 2010. "Feminism's Quest for Common Desires." *Perspectives in Politics* 8 (1): 263-269.

Mohanty, Chandra, and Biddy Martin. 2003. "What's Home Got to Do with It?" In *Feminism without Borders: Decolonizing Theory, Practicing Solidarity*, edited by Chandra Mohanty, 85-105. Durham, NC: Duke University Press.

Moynihan, Daniel Patrick. 1965. *The Negro Family: The Case for National Action*. Washington, DC: Office of Policy Planning and Research, United States Department of Labor.

Nicholson, Linda. 1989. *Gender and History: The Limits of Social Criticism in the Age of the Family*. New York: Columbia University Press.

Phelan, Shane. 1990. "The Jargon of Authenticity: Adorno and Feminist Essentialism." *Philosophy and Social Criticism* 16 (1): 39–54.

Pratt, Minnie Bruce. 1984. *Yours in Struggle*. New York: Long Haul Press.

Reagon, Bernice Johnson. 1981. "Coalition Politics: Turning the Century." In *Home Girls: A Black Feminist Anthology*, edited by Barbara Smith, 343–356. New Brunswick: Rutgers University Press.

Rich, Adrienne. 1986. "Compulsory Heterosexuality and Lesbian Existence." In *Blood, Bread and Poetry*, 23–75. New York: Norton.

Rubin, Gayle. 1975. "The Traffic in Women: Toward a Political Economy of Sex." In *Toward an Anthropology of Women*, edited by Rayna Reitner, 235–283. New York: Monthly Review Press.

Russell, Diane H. 1990. *Rape in Marriage*. Bloomington: Indiana University Press.

Snitow, Ann, Christine Stansell, and Sharon Thompson. 1983. *Powers of Desire: The Politics of Sexuality*. New York: Monthly Review Press.

Vance, Carol, ed. 1984. *Pleasure and Danger: Exploring Female Sexuality*. London: Pandora.

Wallace, Michelle. 1978. *Black Macho and the Myth of the Superwoman*. New York: Doubleday.

Young, Iris. 1998. "Polity and Group Difference: A Critique of the Ideal of Universal Citizenship." In *Feminism and Politics*, edited by Anne Phillips, 401–429.

CHAPTER 30

POLICY

EMANUELA LOMBARDO AND PETRA MEIER

When discussing policy, we automatically add the word "public" to it, focusing attention on public policy. The word "public" that is so spontaneously added to the concept of policy, however, has long been contested by feminist scholars, who have raised important questions about what is public, how the public relates to the private, and how the public/private dichotomy masks political dimensions of both spheres, questions initially encapsulated in the slogan "the personal is political." This chapter examines how feminist scholars theorize the concept and subject of policy and how they challenge the existing knowledge about it.

Feminist critiques of the division between public and private are a key challenge and contribution to theorizing policies. In contrast to traditional conceptions of policymaking as exclusively related to the public domain (Parsons 1995), feminist theorists such as Pateman (1989; 1983), Fraser (1997), Okin (1991), and Benhabib (1992) redefined the contours of the public by demonstrating the androcentric bias inherent in the dominant definition, showing how it ignored many issues of concern to women, and how it contributed to the reproduction of gender inequality and inequalities structured by other social hierarchies. Feminist theories of the public broadened the notion of public policies, the consequences they might have, and the subjects that policies and policy studies must address to include such issues as domestic violence, the reconciliation of paid labor and care work, and reproductive rights.

Over the course of the last three decades, feminist policy studies has grown as a field (Hawkesworth 1994; Lombardo, Meier, and Verloo 2013; Mazur 2002; Mazur, and Pollack 2009; Orloff and Palier 2009). While it is difficult to delineate its boundaries and the scholars belonging to it precisely, the field began when feminist activists and scholars challenged the lack of attention to sex and gender in policymaking, politicized the absence of women from policymaking, and called attention to the complex ways that gender structured the operation of multiple policy fields (Lombardo, Meier, and Verloo 2013). Advanced by scholars from a broad range of disciplines, such as anthropology, economics, geography, history, law, medicine, political science, public administration, and sociology, the field evolved, studying both the process and content of policy and policymaking, the institutions and actors involved, and the challenges at stake in order to further "gender+ equality," a concept that situates gender always in relation to other axes of inequality. Scholars have different foci, ranging from an emphasis on the concerns, needs, and positions of women to the adoption of gender as an analytical category that investigates how power permeates socially constructed relations and institutions, to discursive and intersectional approaches that go beyond gender altogether.

This chapter explores how feminist scholars theorize the concept and subject of policy. In the absence of a corpus of feminist theory on policy, it brings together some of the existing work theorizing policy and related matters, thereby contributing to a more comprehensive feminist theoretical reflection on policy. We do not pretend to review the feminist literature on policy exhaustively; rather, we rely on literature that is particularly helpful in taking a theoretical stance on the *concept* of policy. The chapter draws on work by some scholars who do not necessarily label themselves policy studies scholars. It also situates feminist policy studies in relation to policy studies that is typically labeled traditional and/or mainstream. This chapter highlights insights that feminist theorization adds to the study of public policy, the new conceptualizations and framings they generate, the research questions they raise, and how this helps to advance feminist theory on policy.

Feminist theories take a critical stance toward their object of study and the way it is approached. They also adopt a normative standpoint in that they strive for transformation, attempting to promote gender+ equality. At the heart of feminist theorizing is a concern for issues of power, its articulation in and through the object of study and the attempts to study it. Taking an intersectional approach, feminists theorize hierarchies of power and dimensions of domination grounded in different social structures and markers. The concept of gender+ encapsulates these encompassing equality commitments.

The chapter starts, in the section "The Concept of Policy," by presenting the main conceptualization of policy and of non-feminist theoretical approaches to it. The second section, "The Constructivist Turn," discusses the constructivist turn in both non-feminist and feminist theoretical approaches to policy, tracing how the latter demonstrate that policies are "gendered" and "gendering" constructions, embedded in underlying norms that tend to perpetuate unequal power hierarchies between women and men. Since the focus of most feminist theorizations of policy, implicitly or explicitly, has been on power, section 3, "Power and Transformation," addresses feminist approaches to power and their contribution to theorizing policy. Section 4. "The Quality of Policy: Feminist Criteria for Policy," shows how feminist theorizing of policy improves the quality of policies. This is relevant to feminist thinking because its main concerns are to produce policies that can promote greater equality. The conclusion summarizes the main contributions of feminist theorizing on policy and indicates future directions for work in this field.

The Concept of Policy

Public policy is defined by Dye (1972, 2) as "anything a government chooses to do or not to do," including both decisions to act or not to act, and that involves the definition and selection of goals as well as the means to achieve them (Anderson 2006). Public policy, then, is the output of processes of policymaking in which governments at different levels, ranging from regional to international, plan, formulate, adopt, implement and evaluate interventions aimed at addressing those problems that political actors have defined and selected as relevant in specific social contexts. Public policy is the output of policymaking in the sense that it is the product of governmental activity to address societal problems, through interventions delivered on a variety of issues (Hogwood and Gunn 1984). Public policies on all areas, from budget to health, are, in this respect, an output of policymaking processes.

A major contribution of feminist scholars to policy studies—and political science—is broadening the notion of what is and should be public and, therefore, what falls under the remit of public policy. Feminist scholars have contributed in different ways to expanding the notion of what is public and what, therefore, are important policy issues. The nature of the (policy) issues on which they have focused—dealing with violence, care, or the body—has allowed feminist thinking to scrutinize policies through gender and intersectional lenses that illuminates biases in existing policies and unequal relations between women and men. By challenging claims of policy neutrality and universality, feminist scholars pose fundamental challenges to the public/private dichotomy on which policies have been traditionally based (Pateman 1983; Okin 1991). By shoring up a division between the public and private spheres and allocating the public domain to men, while restricting women to the private sphere, public policies not only neglect issues considered private, but circumscribe the equal citizenship of women. In a now classic debate, feminist scholars have demonstrated that the two spheres are deeply interrelated with each supporting and maintaining the other. Thanks to feminist struggles for a broader definition of the political, new policy issues such as violence against women, reproductive rights, the sharing of care work between the sexes, as well as equal work and equal political representation for women and men have been added to the political agenda (Mazur 2002).

Public policies are developed through processes in which various policy actors *frame* specific problems and engage in political debates in efforts to set the political agenda, formulate and adopt particular policy alternatives to address a problem, implement the decisions adopted, and evaluate different aspects of policies. These processes are not sequential and some policy proposals are truncated (i.e., put on the agenda but never adopted, or adopted but not implemented or evaluated). Yet, each of these dimensions creates opportunities and challenges for specific policy problems and the actors affected (Parsons 1995). For instance, adopting a policy program against gender violence can open opportunities to protect victims and prevent violence, or may do little to solve the problem of violence because of either inadequate conceptualization or ineffective implementation of the program. Evaluation of such programs can detect what works well or what went wrong.

To study policy, scholars often distinguish three basic components: (1) general policy goals, (2) the concrete policy instruments used to implement them, and (3) the even more specific operational settings in which these instruments are used (Hall 1993). Although critics have questioned this artificial and inaccurate characterization, policy-making tends to be studied as a *cycle*, comprising a set of steps ranging from problem definition to evaluation (Parsons 1995). Public policy is also typically conceived in the literature as intentional, as "a purposive course of action followed by an actor or set of actors in dealing with a problem or matter of concern" (Anderson 2006, 6).

Policy studies scholars have employed various theoretical models to explain how public policies are made (see Enserink et al. 2013; Parsons 1995). Rational actor models assume that governments are unified actors committed to a coherent set of policy goals and use objective information to identify the best means to achieve established policy aims (Simon 1957). By contrast, incrementalist models assume that policies involve small adjustments to the status quo that emerge from the negotiations of self-interested actors seeking to maximize their advantage (Lindblom 1959). Such models emphasize bounded rationality due to decision-makers' limited information and information-processing capacity, as well as the pressure of multiple issues vying for attention at the same time. As a result, incremental decision-makers cannot "optimize," but only "satisfice" their objectives (Enserink et al. 2013). Bureaucratic politics models (sometimes called *garbage-can* models by their detractors) consider policies as the result of competing and erratic organizations, populated by partisan actors who seek to solve problems opportunistically, devising solutions as particular opportunities open without much substantive rationality involved (Cohen et al. 1972). Emphasizing the partisan political interests involved in policymaking, this model also suggests intensive bargaining among elites and/or interest groups (Lindblom 1959; Dahl 1994).

Because governments play a primary role in policymaking, mainstream policy models often focus on institutions, studying the diverging roles of legislatures, executives, bureaucracies, and courts in the policy cycle (Parsons 1995; Hogwood and Gunn 1984). More recently, neo-institutionalists have examined the importance of institutions, broadly construed as rules, routines, and cultures, as key factors in the making of policies (March and Olsen 1984, 1989). Within this framework, the policymaking process and the actors involved in it, as well as the actual output, are shaped and constrained by existing institutions, which operate according to powerful conventions in specific historical contexts, deploying long-established routines.

Feminist theorists have developed institutionalist studies that deepen the analysis of power in formal and informal policy institutions, showing an interest not merely in analyzing and describing how institutions work, but also critically evaluating their inadequacies from the standpoint of equal citizenship (Krook and Mackay 2011). Attuned to the role of institutions in cementing gendered power relations that disadvantage women, feminist institutionalism conceives of institutions as objects to study and challenge, as battlegrounds over gendered norms and power relations.

Suggesting that policy involves more than actors bargaining over their interests, constructivist (or discursive) models investigate how social meanings enable and constrain policymaking through debates in which actors and institutions structure arguments intended to persuade others in the hope of achieving a shared understanding of problems to be addressed. Within this frame, the policymaking process is also an interactive learning process (Fischer and Forrester 1993; Hall 1993; Hajer 1995). Diverging arguments are based not only on different interests but often on different belief systems (Sabatier 1987) or policy paradigms as well (Hall 1993).

The Constructivist Turn

Gendered Policies, Gendering Subjects

As social constructions that reflect particular conceptions of reality, public policies define what problems are to be put on the agenda and how they are framed. Mainstream public policy research typically construes social construction in relation to issue definition and agenda setting, investigating how a "problem" first enters a government's policy agenda through the interaction of multiple social groups concerned with the issue, each framing the problem in relation to prevailing political conditions and opportunities available at a given historical moment (Elder and Cobb 1984; Allison 1971; Etzioni 1976). Some public policy scholars also embrace constructivism as an epistemological and analytical framework. Graham Allison (1971) argued that policy problems are not objectively discovered "out there." On the contrary, certain conceptual lenses frame policy issues in different ways, subjectively constructing social reality. For this reason, policy analysts must be critically aware of the multiple policy frames that shape policymakers' and policy actors' views of the world, as well as the "biasing effects of their own assumptions or backgrounds" on the policies they study (Hogwood and Gunn 1984, 119).

Public policy studies share this elementary constructivist component with feminist theories that conceptualize gender as a social construction (see Hawkesworth 2013). Yet feminist theories differ from the constructivist public policy literature by challenging mainstream analysts' conception of policy actors as abstract, disembodied, gender-neutral individuals who target undifferentiated publics with policies proposed to meet social needs unconstrained by race, class, ethnicity, or gender. Deploying gender as an analytical tool (Scott 1986), feminist studies investigate the ways in which policies structure the organization of labor, intimacy, and citizenship within particular nations, consolidating norms and institutions that construct hierarchical gender relations that advantage some men, while disadvantaging women in accordance with critical demarcations of class, race, and sexual orientation. Far from abstract, disembodied subjects, feminist scholars insist on the mutual constitution of race, gender, and other hierarchies of power in ways that inequitably allocate benefits and burdens to supposedly equal citizens. Critical race feminists and feminist poststructuralist approaches have underlined the importance of going beyond gender, because a focus on female and male roles can constrain the analysis—and limit the capacity for more transformative approaches—that challenges binaries and other categorical frames that fix people in specific roles. Postmodern feminist theorists such as Haraway (1991) and Braidotti (2011) have challenged the unitary identity of gendered subjects, suggesting instead a subjectivity that is multiple, nomadic, partial, contradictory, situated, and continuously changing. Criticizing the binary construction of sexual difference, for example, Donna Haraway (1991, 180) noted, "One is too few, and two is only one possibility," and called for a fluid post-gender world beyond rigid categories.

Within a feminist perspective, policies that are biased along axes of gender, race, sexuality, and class contribute to the production of specific intersectional subjects. Thus, feminist analyses of gendered-raced policies have given rise to investigations of policy as racing-gendering practice. Although conceptually distinct, accounts of gendered+ and gendering+ policies can be seen as complementary or opposed depending on the epistemological perspective that scholars adopt.

Various feminist approaches have conceptualized policies as gendered, some focusing on biases against women incorporated within policies whether in terms of exclusion or disparate impact, others examine the division of power and responsibility between men and women, while others investigate more complex intersectional distributions of advantage and disadvantage. Feminist scholars have demonstrated that policies can be gendered in quite different ways: particular policies may be deemed the terrain of a particular gender (e.g., defense-, finance-, and taxation-policy agencies are predominantly staffed by men; welfare and early childhood education bureaucracies are staffed largely by women). Alternatively, policies may be based on, and reinforce, male and heterosexual power advantage (e.g., marriage policies that define men as heads of household while also shoring up heteronormativity or military policies that exclude women and GLBTQ people from service; Hawkesworth 1994, 105).

Policies have been conceptualized as gendering+, as producing gendered and raced systems of power that structure individuals' self-understanding, opportunities, legal status, and aspirations. Haney-Lopez (1996), for example, demonstrated how US laws pertaining to indigenous peoples, slavery, antimiscegenation, and immigration affected not only citizenship rights but the very composition of the United States as a "white" nation. Poststructuralist feminists examine policies as discourses that construct women and men, producing certain desires and ambitions that shape the conditions of everyday life as well as future opportunities (Bacchi 1999, 2009b, forthcoming). Employment policies in many nations, for example, construct men as breadwinners and women as caregivers, reflecting and reinforcing attributes associated with Western raced and classed conceptions of masculinity and femininity that were consolidated in the nineteenth century.

Feminist scholars point out that gendered policies reproduce male norms that masquerade as neutral, operating to systematically disadvantage women (Hawkesworth 2013; Lombardo, Meier, and Verloo 2013). Through gendered exclusions, policies may position women as inferior, abnormal, or deviant. Policies that appear inclusive may have adverse impacts or disparate effects on women. Parental-leave policies, for example, may constrain women's participation in the labor market (Blofield and Haas 2013); so, too, may insufficient, poor-quality, or absent childcare and early childhood education policies. Gendered policies also generate and sustain different models of care, a universal male breadwinner model produces women as dependents, sustaining a markedly different system of gender power than a caregiver parity model, or a universal caregiver model (Fraser 1994; Sainsbury 2013).

Feminist political theorists have illuminated the gendered dimensions of political concepts such as power, citizenship, and politics that mainstream theorists posit as gender-neutral (Jones and Jonasdottir 1988), opening new avenues of investigation and providing new analytical tools for the theorization of public policies and their complex effects. In contrast to mainstream conceptions of individuals as disembodied subjects who share an invariant rationality, for example, feminist scholars have called attention to androcentric bias in particular conceptions of reason that have profound influence, not only on the history of Western political thought, but also on national security, defense, and economic policies (Cohn 1987; Brown 1988; Hawkesworth 1994; Shanley and Pateman 1991).

Where empirical studies of gendered+ policies draw attention to disparate impact and detrimental effects, discursive policy analysis illuminates how specific policies constitute the categories *women* and *men* (Bacchi 1999; Kantola 2006). Conceiving policies as discursive gendering+ practices, Bacchi (forthcoming) emphasizes that feminist policy scholars must scrutinize the constitutive effects of policies, investigating gendering, racializing, heteronorming, classing, disabling, and third-worldizing effects. Following Butler's (1990, 1993) discussion of the performative power of discourses to delimit the meanings and practices of sex and sexuality within a given society, feminist scholars have expanded their examination of policy effects on the construction of masculine and feminine bodies to consider heteronormative policy dimensions that enable homophobia and constrain the citizenship of LGBTQ people in contemporary societies (Cooper 2004; Rubin 1993; Rich 1993; Butler 1993; Lind 2013).

Framing Policies: Norms and (Un)Intentionality

To examine gendering effects, a growing body of feminist discursive policy studies explores how policies are framed, the values and norms that inform specific frames, and their consequences for gender equality. Envisioning policy as a discursive field in which various actors deploy very different conceptions of men, women, gender, and equality in their efforts to define policy problems and solutions, discursive feminist policy analysts excavate the worlds of meaning constructed in and through policy documents (Bacchi 1999; Ferree 2012; Ferree et al. 2002; Kantola 2006; Lombardo, Meier, and Verloo 2009; Verloo 2007). Investigating how particular policy frames privilege and marginalize subjects, foregrounding some while rendering others invisible, feminist discursive policy studies seek to make public the tacit norms and unintended consequences neglected in mainstream policy analysis.

Mainstream studies of policy frames acknowledge their constitutive power, and advocate modes of analysis attuned to intensive contestations over meaning and their implications for individual subjectivity (Schön and Rein 1994; Hall 1993; Fischer and Forrester 1993; Fischer and Gottweis 2012; Hajer 1995). Yet even the most critical versions of mainstream discursive policy studies fail to include gender in their approach. To correct such persistent oversights, feminist scholars place special emphasis on how policy frames reveal discursive contestations over *norms* about the meaning of *gender* (Bacchi 1999; Ferree et al. 2002; Kantola 2006; Verloo 2007; Lombardo, Meier, and Verloo 2009; Ferree 2012). Feminist discursive studies excavate normative assumptions deeply embedded in public policy frames that legitimize particular gendered+ subjectivities and relations, endorse distinct roles and rules of conduct for particular men and women, and structure life opportunities (Ferree 2012; Bacchi 2009b).

Attention to tacit norms moves feminist discursive approaches to policy beyond mainstream methods attuned to the intentional, conscious interventions to shape policies that dominate the public policy literature (Anderson 2006; Howlett and Cashore 2014). Keenly aware that sexist, ethnocentric, racist, and heteronormative norms are often most powerful when they operate at an unconscious level, feminist scholars investigate *unintentional* and *nonexplicit* norms that frame policy problems and solutions in ways that generate unintended as well as intended consequences (Bacchi 2009b). Policy discussions that prioritize labor-market productivity, for example, may frame policies to reconcile work/family balance as means to enhance productivity, totally occluding issues of gender equality and citizenship rights. By conceptualizing policy frames as unintentional representations of reality, Bacchi (1999, 2009b), Verloo (2007), and Lombardo, Meier, and Verloo (2009) draw attention to aspects of social reality that are illuminated (or neglected) due to widely shared sociocultural biases. By making visible the routines and practices that structure people's consciousness, which are often acquired through processes of socialization in unequal societies (Giddens 1984), these feminist discursive analyses create the possibility for policy actors to formulate policies in more gender-, class- or race-conscious ways than they originally intended. By unmasking claims of neutrality, they press policymakers to explicitly address implicit biases that infiltrate their policy constructions.

These feminist theoretical interventions make clear that multiple approaches are required to grapple with gendered and gendering effects in policy. Policies can and should be studied as deliberate efforts to achieve particular aims as, for instance, when policymakers who defend a pro-life ideology intend to design and implement policies that restrict women's access to abortion rights. Yet policies should also be analyzed as interventions with unintended effects, as when policymakers seek to promote gender equality by creating programs that help to reconcile work and family responsibilities that inadvertently have the effect of reproducing traditional roles (Bacchi 2009b; Meier et al. 2007). Given that manifold forms of bias infiltrate and structure actors' assumptions and perceptions in ways they are not necessarily aware of, policy analysts must be reflexive about their own gendered and intersectional policy frames (Bacchi 2009b).

In sum, although feminist theories share with much of the public policy scholarship a focus on how policy is subjectively constructed, rather than objectively "discovered" in social realities, and therefore direct sustained attention to the study of policy frames, feminist scholars emphasize dimensions of policy that are routinely neglected in mainstream approaches. Feminist scholars emphasize that policies do not construct gender-neutral but rather gendered+ meanings and effects. Feminists also insist that policies embody norms that are not necessarily intentional, but result from processes of gendered socialization. These tacit norms can have a profound influence in structuring gender roles and relations that perpetuate systems of advantage and disadvantage. Within feminist theorizations of policy, some commonalities exist that bridge empirical studies of gendered policies and poststructuralist analyses of the gendering of subjects through policies. Despite their different emphases and methodologies, feminist policy studies concur directly or indirectly that power relations are central to processes that define and accredit particular policy problems and solutions.

Power and Transformation

Transforming Gendered Power

Feminist concerns with gender and intersectional biases, privileges, and exclusions, and with the inequalities that policies produce or counteract, place power at the core of feminist policy analysis. Yet power, like other theoretical concepts, can be conceptualized variously. Feminist scholars tend to view power somewhat differently from conceptions accredited in mainstream policy studies.

Within mainstream approaches to public policy, power is often construed in relation to the operating practices of political institutions (legislatures, executives, bureaucracies, and courts) and the rules, norms, and mechanisms that enable actors to achieve their objectives in policymaking processes. In general, state institutions tend to be the focus of analysis (March and Olsen 1984, 1989), within which actors use power to shape the political agenda and to take decisions (Cobb and Elder 1972). Pluralists expanded the frame somewhat to investigate power games that actors play in the processes of negotiation and bargaining within and beyond state institutions, especially during policy implementation (Bardach 1977). Following the three dimensions of power conceptualized by Lukes (2005), mainstream policy studies conceive power as a tool or a relation that policy actors in institutional and other processes use to make policies and to achieve specific political goals. Power may be manifested by putting an issue of concern on the agenda, "winning" a negotiation process, adopting specific policies (or preventing their adoption), or accessing policy resources. Policy actors are commonly conceived as gender-neutral subjects; gender is deemed extraneous to explanations of how power operates in agenda setting and in the negotiation, implementation, or evaluation of specific policies.

Feminists differ from mainstream policy scholars both in their demonstration of the centrality of gender+ to adequate explanations of policymaking and in their embrace of a transformative agenda. Rather than simply trying to describe and explain policymaking, feminist scholars seek to promote gender+ equality. Interest in the transformative aspects of power marks feminist policy studies as both an empirical and a normative project. Feminist policy scholars seek to scrutinize the extent to which policies, the process in which they emerge, and the institutions and actors involved constitute and reproduce gender power relations; and to consider how these institutions, processes, and policies could be changed to contribute to a more gender+ equal society.

This transformative emphasis has inspired feminist policy studies to analyze the messy complexity of subjects and structures rather than search for parsimonious explanations of policymaking. Feminists are concerned with the power of institutions, actors, and policies to shape and affect people who are differently positioned in relation to race, ethnicity, gender, and sexuality. They are also interested in demonstrating how policymaking produces or counteracts specific social hierarchies, structuring differing substantive opportunities and life chances. The subject of feminist policy studies is necessarily an embodied one, whose gender intersects with class, race and ethnicity, sexuality, and other social hierarchies and whose complexity and specificity must be taken into account to generate policy explanations attuned to unequal power relations in existing societies. In marked contrast to mainstream policy studies, feminist approaches connect power and social structures with gender+ subjects. Power, in feminist theorizing, has a structural component that is reproduced through the social practices, structures, and routines that create unequal roles between women and men in areas such as labor, intimate relations, and citizenship. Feminist policy analysis strives to unveil and transform those unequal relations.

Calls for a transformative and gender+ conscious concept of power have been a staple of feminist scholarship. Whether conceptualizing gendered power relations that routinely advantage men and disadvantage women (Hartsock 1983; MacKinnon 1987; Fraser 1989, 1993; Brown 1988, 1995; Okin 1989; Butler 1990, 1993; Young 1990; Allen 1999) or developing an account of domination that recognizes the mutual constitution of multiple modes of marginality (Young 1990) or analyzing the comparative import of cultural norms and socioeconomic structures and practices to women's subordination (Fraser 1993) or construing power as a resource that must be more equally distributed (Okin 1989), feminist theorists have unveiled power mechanisms that are both explicit and implicit in formal and informal policy practices (Rai 2010; Waylen 2010; Hawkesworth 2003). The aim of this criticism is normative: feminists criticize power inequalities in order to transform them into more equal relations between women and men.

Between Domination and Empowerment

A conceptualization of power frequently discussed in the feminist literature distinguishes between "power over," "power to," and "power-with" (Allen 1999). According to Allen, this critical approach affords "an analysis of power that will prove useful for feminist theorists who seek to comprehend, *critique*, and *contest* the subordination of women" (Allen 1999, 121; emphasis ours). Within feminist policy studies, this conception positions established policy in many nations as an instrument of domination. Policy fits well with Allen's definition of *power over* as "the ability of an actor or set of actors' to constrain people's choices in a way that works to the other's disadvantage" (Allen 1999, 123, 125). Many policy domains exemplify this dynamic. Consider, for example how employment, childcare, and other care policies are framed in ways that contribute to men's domination in the labor market and women's underrepresentation or withdrawal from the market after having children (see Blofield and Haas 2013, 705). Power over is also manifest in policies that restrict women's access to abortion (Mottier 2013), or refuse to recognize diversity in family forms (Razavi 2013). Power as the domination of men over women is also apparent in the formal and informal policy practices of the men in political parties that marginalize female party members, exclude them from decision-making, or perpetuate gendered divisions of labor in party activities that allow men to monopolize decision-making, while assigning subordinate roles and less important portfolios to women, then failing to introduce gender quota policies that could promote women's numerical representation (Verge and De la Fuente 2014). Across multiple policy terrains in many nations, policy operates as a mechanism of male domination that constrains women's autonomy, decision-making, and opportunities.

Policy can also be a site of contestation, where feminists challenge male domination, seeking to promote empowerment and the "power that women do have" at an individual level (Allen 1999, 122). Struggles over substantive representation illustrate this dynamic, where political representatives propose policies against gender violence or to liberalize abortion and improve the state provision and quality of gender-inclusive care (Celis and Childs 2008). Efforts to eliminate policies that foster or sustain male domination can also take the form of "collective power," which brings diverse individuals together to pursue feminist aims (Allen 1999, 122). When feminists, sometimes in alliance with other social movements, pursue specific equality projects (Walby 2011), collective activism has the power to "change the major frames and the content of a policy" (Sauer 2010, 215). Indeed, through collective action, feminists have added new frames to the agenda on issues such as "women's social inequality, women's political underrepresentation, women's rights, and gender hierarchies" (ibid.). Comparative research documents how alliances of feminist activists, policymakers, parliamentarians, and academics have been of crucial importance to the successful passage of gender-equality policies, generating political debates on gender issues and promoting social change (Walby 2011; McBride and Mazur 2010).

Feminist scholars have been especially interested in the "dynamic interplay between domination and empowerment, between power and counterpower" (Allen 1999, 18). In addition to investigating concrete ways that men dominate women, feminists have also examined how some women dominate others on the basis of their race, class, ethnicity, age, or sexual orientation. And they have documented strategies of empowerment at individual and collective levels, while also tracing the appropriation of discourses on empowerment by proponents of neoliberalism and oppressive development policies.

Feminist theorists have also discussed the conditions required for nonhegemonic collectives to exercise transformative power. Distinguishing social groups or "publics" in terms of their "relative power," Fraser (1997, 167; 1989) defines hegemonic groups as those who are "able to set the terms of debate for many of the rest," and "counterhegemonic publics" as those opposed to hegemonic groups, who often experience difficulties in proposing their interpretation of policy problems in the political arena. According to Fraser, the social arena, the site of intensive debates over the definition of people's needs, is characterized by unequal conditions that favor the "interests of dominant social groups and work to the disadvantage of subordinate or oppositional groups" (Fraser 1997, 164). For this reason, successful articulation of feminist definitions of needs requires the construction of more equal arenas of public deliberation in which counterhegemonic groups can voice their issues. As Fraser (1997, 135) states, "struggling for women's autonomy" requires "collective control over the means of interpretation and communication sufficient to permit us to participate on a par with men in all types of social interaction, including political deliberation and decisionmaking."

Feminist poststructuralist theories also discuss the dynamics of normalization and contestation of power. Bacchi (1999, 2009a, forthcoming) notes that policies normalize particular representations of women and men, and designate certain issues as problematic and others as "non-problems." What is represented as an important policy problem and what is silenced in policy discourses often reflect gendered power assumptions that underlie the worldview of powerful male policymakers. Similarly, Rönnblom (2009) emphasizes that power and conflict are permanent features of politics. Thus, when policy discourses construct some issues as unquestioned and some goals as universally shared, feminists should investigate how power is being used to mask dissent. When policymakers characterize economic growth as an unquestioned good, for example, they limit the sphere of contestation, removing certain radical social critiques and environmental concerns from the realm of public debate. Although hegemonic power reproduces prevailing economic, gender, heteronormative, and racial hierarchies through long-established discourses and practices, some policy actors routinely contest these practices and seek to subvert them. Butler (1990, 1993), following Foucault (1980), emphasizes the possibility of subversion, noting that power is productive; it enables and constrains, yet also produces resistance. For Butler, feminist subjects are constrained by power structures reproduced in heterosexist cultural norms, but they are also capable of resisting and subverting those norms, introducing changes in reiterative practices.

In sum, feminists theorize power in order to transform unequal power relations and create a gender+ equal society. Feminist scholars interrogate gendered policies and institutions to identify and counteract inequalities that sustain complex social hierarchies. Advancing a transformative conception of power, feminist policy scholars analyze policies that promote and sustain male domination, introduce new issues to the public agenda, foster debate over the meaning of people's needs, challenge the views of hegemonic groups, and seek to empower nonhegemonic groups to articulate their policy concerns. In so doing, feminist policy scholarship enables individual and collective challenges to established power hierarchies, the transformation of unequal social structures, the empowerment of women, and the promotion of greater equality. In advocating social transformation, empowerment, and integration of gender+ equality into policymaking, feminist policy scholars have argued that changes of this magnitude would improve the quality of public policy. In making that case, they have developed innovative criteria for assessing the quality of policies.

The Quality of Policy: Feminist Criteria for Policy

Feminists have proposed several ways to transform gendered policies, dismantle power inequalities, and empower women. In so doing, they have argued that making policies more inclusive, more gender conscious, and more attuned to intersectional norms that foster social justice would simultaneously improve the quality of public policies. Like all normative concepts, the concept of quality is open to contestation, and feminist scholars have advanced multiple interpretations of what the quality of policy means. Yet, despite their differences, feminists identify criteria for evaluating the quality of public policies that go well beyond evaluation criteria developed in mainstream policy studies. These include the integration of gender and intersectionality in assessment mechanisms in order to foster the empowerment of disadvantaged groups and social transformation to achieve a more equitable distribution of opportunities, burdens, and benefits.

A number of feminist policy studies have addressed the criteria for assessing the quality of policy from a gender+ perspective, as well as the best means to evaluate gender equality policies. Drawing on comparative research on the "quality of gender equality policies in Europe" (www.quing.eu), Krizsan and Lombardo (2013, 77) propose a two-dimensional model to conceptualize the quality of policies on gender equality: "The first dimension links quality to procedural aspects: empowerment of women's rights advocates at different stages of the policy process, and transformation with reference to prevailing contextual legacies. The second dimension is more substantive, and includes genderedness, intersectionality and the structurally transformative focus of policies." This conceptualization was inspired by Ferree and Gamson (2003), who identified empowerment as a key goal to achieve gender equality and suggested that empowerment must involve dimensions of autonomy (freedom to make life choices) and authority (participation in making decisions about the group). To operationalize autonomy, Ferree and Gamson investigate how states control the self-determination of women through the content of policies. They measure authority in terms of women's involvement in decision-making. Progressive policies promote empowerment through procedural mechanisms that increase women's participation in decision-making, and they have substantive outcomes that heighten women's autonomy. As articulated by Krizsan and Lombardo (2013), policies can be assessed procedurally in relation to the incorporation of women's rights advocates at all stages of the policy process, and they can be assessed substantively in relation to their transformation of the status quo by fostering gender and intersectional equality.

To assess the quality of policies, Armstrong, Walby, and Strid (2009) have stressed the importance of assessing policies not only individually but also holistically, examining the interconnectedness of policy areas, instruments, and levels. To analyze the quality of policies on employment and care holistically, for example, would require not only assessing employment policies from a gender perspective, but also considering minimum wage laws, which disproportionately affect women workers. Integrating a gender lens into the evaluation of all policy domains is a constitutive criterion of gender mainstreaming.

As formulated by the Council of Europe (1998), gender mainstreaming requires that all public policies be analyzed to assess their gendered impacts. Whether the focus is budget, finance, transportation or national security, policies must be evaluated and altered to eliminate gender bias and promote gender equity. Some feminist scholars have advocated gender mainstreaming as the best means to transform unequal policy structures, processes, and content (Rees 1998; Verloo 2005; Mazey 2000; Rai 2003; Walby 2005; Squires 2005). Yet gender mainstreaming has generated intense feminist theoretical debates concerning which vision of gender equality is to be mainstreamed (inclusion, difference, or transformation; Walby 2005), as well as which criteria of quality are to be used in assessing the substantive effects of gender mainstreaming (Lombardo and Meier 2006).

Adopting an explicit intersectional approach, a few studies have suggested that diversity rather than gender must be mainstreamed if all unequal relations in society are to be eliminated (Squires 2005). Tactics to facilitate diversity mainstreaming have included development of deliberative practices in citizen's forums, and opening spaces for debates about diverse women's and men's visions of equality (Squires 2005). Proposals for intersectional mainstreaming are grounded in feminist criticisms of particular governments' gender mainstreaming policies, which have reproduced heterosexual and white cultural hegemony. Explicit attention to intersectionality is designed to prevent the illusion that equality has been mainstreamed when only elite women's interests have been advanced (McRobbie 2009).

The proliferation of feminist intersectional analyses over the last two decades indicates extensive feminist theoretical interest in addressing intersecting systems of power that sustain complex inequalities (for an overview, see Collins and Chepp 2013). Within feminist policy studies, Verloo (2013) has identified multiple challenges that must be addressed to remedy intersecting inequalities: policy analysts must expose stigmatizing effects of policies on minoritized groups, identify existing policy instruments that can be deployed to address complex inequalities (e.g., integrate mechanisms embedded in immigration, gender equality, and labor legislation), develop new diversity mainstreaming mechanisms, and devise procedural means to include diverse groups in policymaking processes so that they can express specific equality concerns.

According to Bacchi (forthcoming), to operationalize intersectionality in public policies, it is imperative to focus on "how a *range of social dynamics*—gendering, racializing, heteronorming, disabling, and so on—*interact*" (Dhamoon 2011). Feminists have identified various methodologies for analyzing the interaction of such complex social dynamics designed to illuminate material and discursive constraints and opportunities within particular policy domains (Rolandsen 2013; Krizsan, Skjeie, and Squires 2012; Walby and Verloo 2012; Hankivsky et al 2011; Hawkesworth 2003; Crenshaw 1989). But they concur that attention to intersectionality or gender+ provides a key criterion for evaluating the quality of public policy. And they note that a verbal commitment to intersectional analysis is never sufficient. Powerful forces within organizations seek to resist or undermine efforts to redress gender and intersectional inequalities. Even policies that explicitly aim at more egalitarian transformation can be undermined during the implementation process by bureaucrats who believe that their professional commitment to neutrality (i.e., to treat all citizens the same) is incompatible with the goals of gender+ mainstreaming (Benschop and Verloo 2011; Lombardo and Mergaert 2013).

Beyond the problem of how best to address resistances within organizations charged with the implementation of gender+ mainstreaming, feminist policy scholars have also debated how to deploy the concept of empowerment as a constitutive criterion of policy quality. Feminist scholars have advocated the participation of women's organizations and other disadvantaged civil society groups in policymaking processes as a criterion for good quality policies for two main reasons (Fraser 1989; Ferree et al. 2002; Verloo 2005; Goetz 2009). First, participation allows women and other nonhegemonic groups to make choices about their lives, which increases their political authority and the likelihood that their interests and concerns will be given consideration in policies (Kabeer 1999; Ferree and Gamson 2003). Second, feminist studies have found that participatory policy processes lead to better quality policy outputs in general (Weldon 2002; Outshoorn and Kantola 2007; McBride and Mazur 2010). Feminist scholars have analyzed who is present in policymaking processes, who is left out, who holds key positions, and who is marginalized, and they have investigated the mechanisms of exclusion and marginalization (Kabeer 1999). They have also advocated creation of new deliberative spaces for the expression and empowerment of counterhegemonic publics (Fraser 1997). The creation of spaces for nonhegemonic voices to articulate their equality concerns, according to Verloo (2005), can promote more transformative ways of mainstreaming gender into policies. That said, neither all women nor all members of socially disadvantaged groups are committed to gender and intersectional equality. Thus there remains a gap between procedural mechanisms to foster democratic inclusion in decision-making and substantive outcomes that foster equality.

Feminist theorists conceive policies as transformative when they address the roots of inequality and generate changes in the social structures that produce or maintain inequalities (Walby 2011; Connell 1987; Verloo 2007). Structurally transformative policies address both individual discrimination and structural power hierarchies that are at the core of group inequalities (Mazur 2002; Weldon 2009; Walby 2009). Yet to produce long-lasting changes in the unequal power relations between men and women, and between hegemonic and nonhegemonic groups, proponents of social justice must be empowered. Comparative research on the quality of gender-equality policy in Europe has documented the importance of empowering advocates of gender+ transformation. To secure the substantive results associated with progressive public policy, Krizsan and Lombardo propose the empowerment of women's rights advocates committed to changing unequal social structures and achieving a more gender-equal society. Krizsan et al. (2010) emphasize empowerment of social groups as an alternative to upward mobility of individual citizens.

In contrast to mainstream policy approaches, feminist policy scholars define the quality of policy in terms of three criteria: integrating gender and intersectionality analytics into policy assessment, empowerment of disadvantaged groups, and social transformation to foster gender+ equality. These criteria reflect feminist efforts to broaden the concept of policy and the realm of concerns that public authorities should address to include matters that were formerly considered private, such as gender violence and reproductive rights. They call attention to the inaccuracy and inadequacy of imagining citizens as gender-neutral, disembodied individuals—imaginings that mask systemic disadvantages that policies impose on embodied subjects, replicating gender, race, ethnic, class, and heteronormative biases. To avoid the reproduction of privilege, they emphasize the importance of taking gender and intersectionality into account when constructing, formulating, adopting, implementing, and evaluating policies. These criteria also place a great emphasis on power, with its constraining and enabling functions, pressing policymakers to become more aware of and to challenge the mechanisms of gender+ domination and hegemonic dynamics. These criteria assess public policy in relation to feminism's overarching goal to transform unequal social relations into equal ones by addressing the structural roots of inequality. In demonstrating how mainstream policy studies fail to grapple with fundamental injustices created and sustained by inequitable public policies, feminist conceptions of the quality of policy also encourage analysts, activists, and policymakers to develop a more reflexive approach to policy that would increase their awareness of existing biases, and increase the possibility of improving the quality of policies (Bacchi 2009b).

Conclusion

Over the last several decades, feminist research has critically examined policymaking processes and public policies, pinpointing several major problems and flaws. This research demonstrates unrealistic normative or theoretical assumptions underlying policy(making), as well as gendered power inequalities within policy processes that are (re)produced through public policies. To rectify these problems, feminist scholars have developed new conceptualizations and framings that enable more sophisticated policy studies, and they have identified criteria by which to assess progressive policy change.

Grounded in both feminist theory and feminist policy studies, a feminist theory of policy has both normative and empirical dimensions. Spanning multiple methodological approaches, it reflects the rich feminist literature on policy, explores how gender+ inequalities are related to each other, and identifies strategies to transform existing power relations and promote more egalitarian political systems.

Needless to say, more work needs to be done on this topic. Future research could move beyond identification of the criteria for quality policy to deploy these criteria in assessing policies across the world. Beyond ranking states, feminist policy research could spell out further when and under what conditions policy transformation succeeds, identifying key obstacles to success, and theorizing strategies to overcome these obstacles. Empirical research of this order could deepen understanding of criteria for good quality policy, and the mechanisms required to foster it. Harnessing feminist insights into subconscious social biases, unintentional gender+ harm, and unintended consequences of policies to produce more equitable policy outcomes would generate far more sophisticated accounts of policymaking processes, the actors involved, and the broader contexts in which social transformation takes place. Future research can—and should—take a feminist theory of policy in many directions that will challenge core concepts and theories, thereby ensuring that feminist policy studies remain critical and reflexive in their approach to social transformation.

Acknowledgments

We wish to thank Lisa Disch and Mary Hawkesworth for their helpful and supportive comments, and Mary Hawkesworth also for her thorough and competent editing of a former draft of this chapter.

References

Allen, A. 1999. *The Power of Feminist Theory. Domination, Resistance and Solidarity*. Boulder, CO: Westview Press.
Allison, G. 1971. *Essence of Decision: Explaining the Cuban Missile Crisis*. Boston: Little Brown.
Anderson, J. E. 2006. *Public Policymaking*. 6th ed. Boston / New York: Houghton Mifflin Company.
Armstrong, J., S. Walby, and S. Strid 2009. "The Gendered Division of Labour: How Can We Assess the Quality of Employment and Care Policy from a Gender Equality Perspective." *Benefits: The Journal of Poverty and Social Justice* 17 (3): 263–275.
Bacchi, C. L. 1999. *Women, Policy, and Politics: the Construction of Policy Problems*. London: Sage.

Bacchi, C. L. 2009a. *Analysing Policy: What's the Problem Represented to Be?* Frenchs Forest, New South Wales: Pearson.
Bacchi, C. L. 2009b. "The Issue of Intentionality in Frame Theory: The Need for Reflexive Framing." In *The Discursive Politics of Gender Equality: Stretching, Bending and Policymaking*, edited by E. Lombardo, P. Meier, and M. Verloo, 19–35. London/New York: Routledge.
Bacchi, C. L. Forthcoming. "Policies as Gendering Practices: Re-Viewing Categorical Distinctions." *Journal of Women, Politics and Policy*.
Bardach, E. 1977. *The Implementation Game*. Cambridge, MA: MIT Press.
Benhabib, S. 1992. *Situating the Self: Gender, Community and Postmodernism in Contemporary Ethics*. Cambridge: Polity Press.
Benschop, Y., and M. Verloo. 2011. "Gender Change, Organizational Change, and Gender Equality Strategies." In *Handbook of Gender, Work, and Organization*, edited by E. Jeanes, D. Knights, and P. Yancey Martin, 277–290. Oxford: Wiley-Blackwell.
Blofield, M., and L. Haas. 2013. "Policy Outputs." In *The Oxford Handbook of Gender and Politics*, edited by G. Waylen, K. Celis, J. Kantola, and L. Weldon, 703–726. Oxford: Oxford University Press.
Braidotti, R. 2011. *Nomadic Subjects. Embodiment and Sexual Difference in Contemporary Feminist Theory*. New York: Columbia University Press.
Brown, W. 1988. *Manhood and Politics. A Feminist Reading in Political Theory*. New York: Routledge.
Brown, W. 1995. *States of Injury: Power and Freedom in Late Modernity*. Princeton, NJ: Princeton University Press.
Butler, J. 1990. *Gender Trouble. Feminism and the Subversion of Identity*. New York: Routledge.
Butler, J. 1993. *Bodies that Matter: On the Discursive Limits of "Sex."* New York: Routledge.
Celis, K., and S. Childs, eds. 2008. *Representation Journal of Representative Democracy*. Special issue on the substantive representation of women 44 (2).
Cobb, R. W., and C. D. Elder. 1972. *Participation in American Politics: The Dynamics of Agenda Building*. Boston: Allyn and Bacon.
Cohen, M., J. March, and J. Olsen. 1972. "A Garbage Can Model of Organizational Choice." *Administrative Science Quarterly* 17 (1): 1–25.
Cohn, C. 1987. "Sex and Death in the Rational World of Defense Intellectuals." *Signs: Journal of Women in Culture and Society* 12: 687–718.
Collins, P. H., and V. Chepp. 2013. "Intersectionality." In *The Oxford Handbook of Gender and Politics* edited by G. Waylen, K. Celis, J. Kantola, and L. Weldon, 57–87. Oxford: Oxford University Press.
Connell, R. 1987. *Gender and Power*. Redwood City, CA: Stanford University Press.
Cooper, D. 2004. *Challenging Diversity: Rethinking Equality and the Value of Difference*. Cambridge: Cambridge University Press.
Crenshaw, K. W. 1989. "Demarginalizing the Intersection of Race and Sex: A Black Feminist Critique of Antidiscrimination Doctrine, Feminist Theory and Antiracist Politics." *University of Chicago Legal Forum* 139–167.
Dahl, R. 1994. "A Democratic Dilemma: System e\Effectiveness versus Citizen Participation." *Political Science Quarterly* 109 (1): 23–34.
Dhamoon, R. K. 2011. "Considerations on Mainstreaming Intersectionality." *Political Research Quarterly* 64 (1): 230–243.
Dye, T. R. 1972. *Understanding Public Policy*. Englewood Cliffs, NJ: Prentice Hall.

Elder, C. D., and R. W. Cobb. 1984. "Agenda-Building and the Politics of Aging." *Policy Sciences Journal* 13 (1): 115–129.

Enserink, B., J. F. Joop, F. M. Koppenjan, and I. S. Mayer. 2013. "A Policy Sciences View on Policy Analysis." In *Public Policy Analysis*, edited by W. A. H. Thissen and W. E. Walker, 11–40. New York: Springer.

Etzioni, A. 1976. *Social Problems*. Englewood Cliffs, NJ: Prentice Hall.

Ferree, M. M. 2012. *Varieties of Feminism. German Gender Politics in Global Perspective*. Redwood City, CA: Stanford University Press.

Ferree, M. M., and W. A. Gamson. 2003. "Gendering of Governance and Governance of Gender: Abortion Politics in Germany and the USA." In *Recognition Struggles and Social Movements*, edited by B. Hobson, 35–63. Cambridge: Cambridge University Press.

Ferree, M. M., W. A. Gamson, J. Gerhards, and D. Rucht. 2002. *Shaping Abortion Discourse: Democracy and the Public Sphere in Germany and the United States*. Cambridge: Cambridge University Press.

Fischer, F., and F. Forrester. 1993. *The Argumentative Turn in Policy Analysis and Planning*. Durham, NC: Duke University Press.

Fischer, F., and H. Gottweis, eds. 2012. *The Argumentative Turn Revisited: Public Policy as Communicative Practice*. Durham, NC: Duke University Press.

Foucault, M. 1980. *Power/Knowledge: Selected Interviews and Other Writings 1972–1977*. New York: Pantheon Books.

Fraser, N. 1989. *Unruly Practices: Power, Discourse and Gender in Contemporary Social Theory*. Minneapolis: University of Minnesota Press.

Fraser, N. 1993. "Beyond the Master/Subject Model: Reflections on Carole Pateman's Sexual Contract." *Social Text* 37: 173–181.

Fraser, N. 1994. "After the Family Wage: Gender Equity and the Welfare State." *Political Theory* 22 (4): 591–618.

Fraser, N. 1997. *Justice Interruptus: Critical Reflections on the "Post-Socialist" Condition*. London: Routledge.

Giddens, A. 1984. *The Constitution of Society: Outline of the Theory of Structuration*. London: Macmillan.

Goetz, A. M., ed. 2009. *Governing Women: Women's Political Effectiveness in Contexts of Democratization and Governance Reform*. New York: Routledge.

Hajer, M. 1995. *The Politics of Environmental Discourse: Ecological Modernization and the Policy Process*. Oxford: Clarendon Press.

Hall, P. 1993. "Policy Paradigms, Social Learning, and the State: the Case of Economic Policymaking in Britain." *Comparative Politics* 25 (3): 275–296.

Haney-Lopez, I. 1996. *White by Law*. New York: New York University Press.

Hankivsky, O., S. de Leeuw, J. Lee, A. B. Vissandjée, and N. Khanlou, eds. 2011. *Health Inequities in Canada: Intersectional Frameworks and Practices*. Vancouver: University of British Columbia Press.

Haraway, D. 1991. *Simians, Cyborgs and Women: the Reinvention of Nature*. London: Free Association.

Hartsock, N. 1983. *Money, Sex, and Power: Toward a Feminist Historical Materialism*. Boston: Northeastern University Press.

Hawkesworth, M. 1994. "Policy Studies within a Feminist Frame." *Policy Sciences* 27 (2–3): 97–118.

Hawkesworth, M. 2003. "Congressional Enactments of Race-Gender: Toward a Theory of Raced-Gendered Institutions." *American Political Science Review* 97 (4): 529–550.

Hawkesworth, M. 2013. "Sex, Gender and Sexuality: From Naturalized Presumption to Analytical Categories." In *The Oxford Handbook of Gender and Politics*, edited by G. Waylen, K. Celis, J. Kantola, and L. Weldon, 31–56. Oxford: Oxford University Press.

Hogwood, B., and L. Gunn. 1984. *Policy Analysis for the Real World*. Oxford: Oxford University Press.

Howlett, M., and B. Cashore. 2014. "Conceptualizing Public Policy." In *Comparative Policy Studies. Conceptual and Methodological Challenges*, edited by I. Engeli and C. Rothmayr Allison, 17–34. Houndmills: Palgrave Macmillan.

Jones, K. B., and A. G. Jònasdòttir, eds. 1988. *The Political Interest of Gender*. London: Sage.

Kabeer, N. 1999. "Resources, Agency, Achievements: Reflections on the Measurement of Women's Empowerment." *Development and Change* 30 (3): 435–464.

Kantola, J. 2006. *Feminists Theorize the State*. Basingstoke: Palgrave Macmillan.

Krizsan, A., H. Skjeie, and J. Squires, eds. 2012. *Institutionalizing Intersectionality*. Basingstoke: Palgrave Macmillan.

Krizsan, A., T. Dombos, E. Kispéter, L. Szabó, J. Dedić, M. Jaigma, R. Kuhar, A. Frank, B. Sauer, and M. Verloo, 2010. *Framing Gender Equality in the European Union and Its Current and Future Member States. Deliverable No. 61: Final LARG Report*. Vienna: Institute for Human Sciences.

Krizsan, A., and E. Lombardo. 2013. "The Quality of Gender Equality Policies: A Discursive Approach." *European Journal of Women's Studies* 20 (1): 77–92.

Krook, M. L., and F. Mackay. eds. 2011. *Gender, Politics and Institutions. Towards a Feminist Institutionalism*. Houndmills: Palgrave Macmillan.

Lind, A. 2013. "Heteronormativity and Sexuality." In *The Oxford Handbook of Gender and Politics*, edited by G. Waylen, K. Celis, J. Kantola, and L. Weldon, 189–213. Oxford: Oxford University Press.

Lindblom, C. 1959. "The Science of Muddling Through." *Public Administration Review* 19 (1): 79–88.

Lombardo, E., and P. Meier. 2006. "Gender Mainstreaming in the EU: Incorporating a Feminist Reading?" *European Journal of Women's Studies* 13 (2): 151–166.

Lombardo, E., P. Meier, and M. Verloo, eds. 2009. *The Discursive Politics of Gender Equality. Stretching, Bending and Policymaking*. London / New York: Routledge.

Lombardo, E., P. Meier, and M. Verloo. 2013. "Policy Making." In *The Oxford Handbook of Gender and Politics*, edited by G. Waylen, K. Celis, J. Kantola, and L. Weldon, 679–702. New York: Oxford University Press.

Lombardo, E., and L. Mergaert. 2013. "Gender Mainstreaming and Resistance to Gender Training: A Framework for Studying Implementation." *NORA Nordic Journal of Feminist and Gender Research* 21 (4): 296–311.

Lukes, S. 2005. *Power: A Radical View*. 2nd updated ed. Basingstoke: Palgrave Macmillan.

MacKinnon, C. A. 1987. *Feminism Unmodified. Discourses on Life and Law*. Cambridge, MA: Harvard University Press.

March, J., and J. Olsen. 1984. "The New Institutionalism: Organizational Factors in Political Life." *American Political Science Review* 78 (September): 734–749.

March, J., and J. Olsen. 1989. *Rediscovering Institutions: The Organizational Basis of Politics*. New York: Free Press.

Mazey, S., ed. 2000. "Introduction: Integrating Gender: Intellectual and 'Real World' Mainstreaming." *Journal of European Public Policy* 7 (3): 333–345.
Mazur, A. 2002. *Theorizing Feminist Policy*. Oxford: Oxford University Press.
Mazur, A., and M. A. Pollack. 2009. "Gender and Public Policy in Europe: An Introduction." *Comparative European Politics* 7 (1): 1–11.
McBride, D., and A. Mazur, eds. 2010. *The Politics of State Feminism: Innovation in Comparative Research*. Philadelphia, PA: Temple University Press.
McRobbie, A. 2009. *The Aftermath of Feminism. Gender, Culture, and Social Change*. London: Sage.
Meier, P., E. Peterson, K. Tertinegg, and V. Zentai. 2007. "The Pregnant Worker and Caring Mother: Framing Family Policies across Europe." In *Multiple Meanings of Gender Equality: A Critical Frame Analysis of Gender Policies in Europe*, edited by M. Verloo, 109–140. Budapest: CEU Press.
Mottier, V. 2013. "Reproductive Rights." In *The Oxford Handbook of Gender and Politics*, edited by G. Waylen, K. Celis, J. Kantola, and L. Weldon, 214–235. Oxford: Oxford University Press.
Okin, S. M. 1989. *Justice, Gender and the Family*. New York: Basic Books.
Okin, S. M. 1991. "Gender, the Public and the Private." In *Political Theory Today*, edited by D. Held, 67–90. Cambridge: Polity Press.
Orloff, A., and B. Palier. 2009. "The Power of Gender Perspectives: Feminist Influence on Policy Paradigms, Social Science, and Social Politics." *Social Politics* 16 (4): 405–412.
Outshoorn, J., and J. Kantola, eds. 2007. *Changing State Feminism*. Basingstoke: Palgrave Macmillan.
Parsons, W. 1995. *Public Policy: An Introduction to the Theory and Practice of Policy Analysis*. Northampton: Edward Elgar.
Pateman, C. 1983. "Feminist Critiques of the Public/Private Dichotomy." In *Public and Private in Social Life*, edited by S. I. Benn and G. F. Gaus, 281–303. London: Croom Helm and St. Martin's Press.
Pateman, C. 1989. *The Disorder of Women*. Cambridge: Polity Press.
Rai, S., ed. 2003. *Mainstreaming Gender, Democratising the State? Institutional Mechanisms for the Advancement of Women*. Manchester: Manchester University Press.
Rai, S., ed. 2010. *Journal of Legislative Studies*. Special Issue. *Ceremony and Ritual in Parliament* 16.
Razavi, S. 2013. "Households, Families, and Social Reproduction." In *The Oxford Handbook of Gender and Politics*, edited by G. Waylen, K. Celis, J. Kantola, and L. Weldon, 289–312. Oxford: Oxford University Press.
Rees, T. 1998. *Mainstreaming Equality in the European Union: Education, Training and Labour Market Policies*. London: Routledge.
Rich, A. 1993. "Compulsory Heterosexuality and Lesbian Existence." In *The Lesbian and Gay Studies Reader*, edited by H. Abelove, M. A. Barale, and D. M. Halperin, 227–254. New York/London: Routledge.
Rolandsen, L. 2013. *Gender Equality, Intersectionality and Diversity in Europe*. Basingstoke: Palgrave Macmillan.
Rönnblom, M. 2009. "Bending towards Growth: Discursive Constructions of Gender Equality in an Era of Governance and Neoliberalism." In *The Discursive Politics of Gender Equality. Stretching, Bending and Policymaking*, edited by E. Lombardo, P. Meier, and M. Verloo, 105–120. London/New York: Routledge.

Rubin, G. 1993. "Thinking Sex: Notes for a Radical Theory of the Politics of Sexuality." In *The Lesbian and Gay Studies Reader*, edited by H. Abelove, M. A. Barale, and D. M. Halperin, 3–44. New York/London: Routledge.

Sainsbury, D. 2013. "Gender, Care, and Welfare." In *The Oxford Handbook of Gender and Politics*, edited by G. Waylen, K. Celis, J. Kantola, and L. Weldon, 313–336. Oxford: Oxford University Press.

Sabatier, P. 1987. "Knowledge, Policy-Oriented Learning, and Policy Change: An Advocacy Coalition Framework." *Science Communication* 8 (4): 649–692.

Sauer, B. 2010. "Framing and Gendering." In *The Politics of State Feminism: Innovation in Comparative Research*, edited by D. McBride and A. Mazur, 193–216. Philadelphia. PA: Temple University Press.

Schön, D., and M. Rein. 1994. *Frame Reflection: Towards the Resolution of Intractable Policy Controversies*. New York: Basic Books.

Scott, J. 1986. "Gender: A Useful Category of Historical Analysis." *American Historical Review* 91 (5): 1053–1075.

Shanley, M. L., and C. Pateman, eds. 1991. *Feminist Interpretations and Political Theory*. Cambridge: Polity Press.

Simon, H. A. 1957. *Administrative Behavior: A Study of Decision-Making Processes in Administrative Organization*. New York: Palgrave Macmillan.

Squires, J. 2005. "Is Mainstreaming Transformative? Theorizing Mainstreaming in the Context of Diversity and Deliberation." *Social Politics* 12 (3): 366–388.

Verge, T., and M. De la Fuente. 2014. "Playing with Different Cards: Party Politics, Gender Quotas and Women's Empowerment." *International Political Science Review* 35 (1): 67–79.

Verloo, M. 2013. "Intersectional and Cross-Movement Politics and Policies: Reflections on Current Practices and Debates." *Signs* 38 (4): 893–915.

Verloo, M. 2005. "Displacement and Empowerment: Reflections on the Concept and Practice of the Council of Europe Approach to Gender Mainstreaming and Gender Equality." *Social Politics* 12 (3): 344–365.

Verloo, M., ed. 2007. *Multiple Meanings of Gender Equality: A Critical Frame Analysis of Gender Policies in Europe*. Budapest: CEU Press.

Walby, S., and M. Verloo, eds. 2012. Special Issue Intersectionality and the Equality Architecture in Europe. *Social Politics* 19 (4): 433–621.

Walby, S. 2005. "Gender Mainstreaming: Productive Tensions in Theory and Practice." *Social Politics* 12 (3): 1–25.

Walby, S. 2009. *Globalization and Inequalities: Complexity and Contested Modernities*. London: Sage.

Walby, S. 2011. *The Future of Feminism*. Cambridge: Polity.

Waylen, G. 2010. "Researching Ritual and the Symbolic in Parliament." *Journal of Legislative Studies* 16 (3): 352–365.

Weldon, L. 2002. "Beyond Bodies: Institutional Sources of Representation for Women in Democratic Policymaking." *Journal of Politics* 64 (4): 1153–1174.

Weldon, L. 2009. "Intersectionality." In *Politics, Gender and Concepts*, edited by G. Goertz and A. Mazur, 194–218. Cambridge: Cambridge University Press.

Young, I. M. 1990. *Justice and the Politics of Difference*. Princeton, NJ: Princeton University Press.

CHAPTER 31

POLITICS

LINDA M. G. ZERILLI

Introduction

On the face of it, the very idea of feminist theory seems unthinkable without politics. Did not feminist theory originate in the context of the first and second waves of the feminist movement? And is not feminist theory itself "political"? Does it not eschew any aspiration to neutrality and make partisan claims about explicitly political things such as power, justice, and rights?

To treat feminist theory as always already political risks occluding the different ways in which feminists think about politics. It also risks falsely unifying plural conceptions of what theory is and how it relates to political practice. Far from providing a single definition on which all feminists can agree, what counts as political is itself a matter of feminist contestation and debate. However they may coalesce on the need to redefine politics to make visible that which has remained largely hidden in traditional (masculinist) conceptions of politics, feminists diverge in their understanding of what a feminist theory of politics would include. Not unlike the traditional and mostly male thinkers they criticize, feminists, too, bring their own diverse and at times unacknowledged assumptions about politics to bear on theoretical refigurations of inherited concepts.[1]

"The Personal Is Political"

The temptation to see unity in diversity when it comes to feminist theories of politics is perhaps nowhere more apparent than in accounts of the well-known slogan of second-wave feminism, "the personal is political." Typically taken to capture a feminist consensus about what politics is, this famous rally cry seems to state that what has been heretofore considered a private issue is by definition a public matter. Thus housework, sexuality, reproduction, child care, and so on, are all to be redefined as intrinsically political activities deserving of our collective concern. When stated in such a broad way, this understanding of the slogan as the core claim of feminists of all stripes can seem unobjectionable. In reality, it harbors a number of problems that go to the heart of the issue at hand, namely, whether feminists do in fact share an understanding of what counts as politics.

Although it would come to define at least two generations of Western (especially American) feminism, the phrase "the personal is political" originated in a specific response to the ridicule that second-wave feminists encountered in the context of their early attempt at organizing around gender discrimination. Attributed to New York radical feminist Carole Hanisch in an essay of the same title,[2] the claim to the personal being political was initially an attempt to refute the idea that the 1960s early feminist practice of consciousness raising was just "therapy" or little more than yet another expression of the proverbial "female complaint."[3] Rejecting such psychologizing explanations, especially as they called into question the need for autonomous feminist groups in the context of the New Left, Hanisch defended consciousness raising as an attempt to move away from subjectivizing accounts of oppression and toward a political critique of male power. Accordingly, it was not simply an anonymous capitalist "system" but also individual men who benefited from the gendered division of labor and the ideological privatization of women's misery.

In important ways, then, feminists call into question the naturalized distinction between public and private realms that has been foundational to the contractual basis of liberalism and the "sexual contract" (i.e., men's property in women) that underwrites it (Pateman 1988). Far from gender neutral, this distinction presupposes structural forms of injustice that render oppression invisible by concealing it in highly individualized conceptions of gender roles (Okin 1979; Elshtain 1981). The respective mapping of masculine and feminine roles onto public and private spheres hides the coercive manner in which gender-based segregation is created and enforced (Brown 1998; Zerilli 1994; Di Stefano 1991). Consciousness raising was a tool for illuminating the public character of private desires and private identities, revealing them to be expressions of a pervasive structure of gender power.

As it was taken up in second-wave practices of speaking and acting, "the personal is political" was not a description of how things already were (i.e., already *political*) but a transformative claim about how they ought to be seen. It was, in other words, by means of publically declaring a private practice such as housework to be political that it actually came to be political and to be seen as such. Even Christine Delphy, who understood housework to be inherently exploitative by virtue of men's expropriation of women (and others') unwaged labor in the home, would argue that it had to be politicized to be seen as such. By understanding "the personal is political" to be a mere description of what already is the case, we would miss the very predicative moment of second-wave feminist politics, the moment, that is, when a relation of power became political in being taken up as a matter of common concern. Nothing is political in itself: it is the very act of making public claims that has the power to transform an issue from something personal into something political.

Another way of thinking about early second-wave attempts to remap the terrain of politics is to consider Kate Millet's famous argument in *Sexual Politics*. Like Hanisch,

Millet calls our attention to the "frequently neglected political aspect" of something that has been heretofore considered "personal" (Millet 1969, xiii), in this case the sexual relations between men and women. It might seem, therefore, that Millet is simply making visible a political relation that existed all along. In certain respects, of course, one might say that (hetero)sexuality was always already political, awaiting its discovery by an insightful feminist theorist. And, further, that Millet's rhetorical brilliance is to open our eyes to what has been there all along. But this would be to miss the radically transformative work of feminist theory when it becomes part of collective practice.

When it is taken up in the speech and action of readers, for whom the text is no mere set of abstract arguments but an occasion to exchange opinions and engage in collective action on a matter of common concern, a work of theory can become a presentation of "new forms/figures of the thinkable," to borrow Cornelius Castoriadis phrase (1997, 271). When US second-wave feminists introduced such formulations as the "personal is political" or the "sex/gender distinction" (whose mutability and instability became the focus of considerable empirical feminist scholarship), "the personal is political," and similar formulations associated with the Second Wave, can be seen as creative theoretical efforts to refigure experience in terms that made it newly thinkable, that is, mutable and amenable to change. Millet's book was at the center of a firestorm on the state of gender relations and was read and debated by thousands of women seeking to make sense of their own experience and develop new ways of being in the world. The same was true for Simone de Beauvoir's *The Second Sex*, which, too, became a lightening rod for critical discussions of femininity. The point is not simply that *Sexual Politics* or *The Second Sex* and their authors became famous, but that the texts served as a common object for feminist public-opinion formation about the social, economic, and political conditions of women's lives. Strictly speaking, one might say that as works of feminist theory, both texts are not intrinsically political books; they *became* political once they were taken up in the speech and action of (emerging) feminists.

Politics as Power

If the restriction of the term "political" to collective speech and action seems strange, that is because we have come to think of politics not only as something that is a property of an object (or a practice) but also as synonymous with power: where there is power, there is politics. This definition or rather equation of politics with power is compelling insofar as it facilitates our ability to recognize in the most ordinary conditions of daily life relations that are not naturally given but historically constituted and subject to change. But such an equation is also misleading: as we well know, the mere fact of power relations does not automatically issue in political consciousness and change. Furthermore, the identification of politics with power—be it the tradition's idea that to wield power from above is to act politically or more modern conceptions, such as that of Michel Foucault, where power is not exercised simply in a top-down manner but is more or less everywhere—leads to impasses for feminist theory. One of these impasses is the difficulty such a definition presents for conceptualizing politics as a practice of resisting unjust power. What enables one to see relations of power, in which one group subordinates another, as unjust and open to change?

In their groundbreaking work on new social movements and the future of the New Left, *Hegemony and Socialist Strategy*, Chantal Mouffe and Ernesto Laclau bring out the difference between relations of "oppression," on the one side, and relations of "subordination" on the other. An anthropological view of human nature and a unified subject, they argue, leads us to think that where there is subordination there is oppression: "[I]f we can determine *a priori* the essence of the subject, every relation of subordination when it denies it [e.g., its natural freedom] becomes a relation of oppression" (Laclau and Mouffe [1985] 2001, 153). But if we reject this "essentialist perspective," we need to explain how relations of unequal power come to be seen by subordinated subjects to *be* oppressive. That some individuals and groups are "subjected to the decisions of another—an employee with respect to an employer, for example, or in certain forms of family organization the woman with respect to the man"—constitutes a relation of power over another, subordination (153). For this relation of power to be seen as a relation of oppression—as unjust and potentially open to change, rather than as natural and timeless—is a political matter. Just as the personal *becomes* political, a relation of subordination becomes one of oppression when it is transformed into "the site of an antagonism" (153).

Laclau and Mouffe's arguments are specific to the era of democratic politics that emerged with the eighteenth-century revolutions. They argue that the transformation of women's subordination into oppression, into a site of antagonism, was inextricably connected with the emergence of a "different discursive formation"—namely, the democratic discourse, with its idea of "the rights that are inherent to every human being" (Laclau and Mouffe [1985] 2001, 154). Mary Wollstonecraft's *Vindication of the Rights of Woman*, for example, "determined the birth of feminism through the use made in it of the democratic discourse, which was thus displaced from the field of political equality between citizens to the field of equality between the sexes" (Laclau and Mouffe [1985] 2001, 154). Whether Wollstonecraft merely applied the logic of democratic rights discourse to women as disenfranchised subjects or actually transformed its meaning is a matter of some debate (Maione 2012). What is clear, however, is that Wollstonecraft's ability to bring into view the centuries-long subordination of women as something that was oppressive, hence unjust, involved a radical transformation of a so-called natural relation between man and woman into a social and political antagonism. That not only the *Rights of Woman* but also its author herself became the subject of countless public debates, however, is what made Wollstonecraft's brilliant insights into the private reality of gender power truly political. In other words, her texts were taken up by acting subjects in the public space. And in taking up her texts, women became speaking subjects in a public space that had for the most part excluded them, thereby transforming the character of public space and of what counts as a public matter by virtue of their action and speech.

Crossing Borders

We can better appreciate the ways in which what comes to count as political involves a deeply interactive and intertextual practice of putting feminist theory texts to work in diverse practical contexts by turning briefly to the US second-wave classic on women's health *Our Bodies, Ourselves* (*OBOS*). Originally written as a set of discussion papers and published under the name of the Boston Women's Health Book Collective in 1973, *OBOS* went on in seven editions to sell four million copies. Kathy Davis explains:

> *OBOS* was a lively and accessible manual on women's bodies and health. It was full of personal experience and contained useful information on issues ranging from masturbation (how to do it) to birth control (which methods were available and how to use them) to vaginal infections, pregnancy, and nursing. It combined a scathing critique of patriarchal medicine and the medicalization of women's bodies with an analysis of the political economies of the health and pharmaceutical industries. But above all, *OBOS* validated women's embodied experiences as a resource for challenging medical dogmas about women's bodies and, consequently, as a strategy for personal and collective empowerment.
>
> (Davis 2007, 1–2)

What makes *OBOS* of interest to our discussion here is not only how the text was originally written (as discussion papers for meetings, public protests, or collective local action) but also how it has been taken up by feminists across the world as a political rallying point for articulating differences and commonalities. Translated into multiple languages (including French, German, Italian, Spanish, Hebrew, Arabic, Russian, Telugu, Polish, Korean, Serbian, Bulgarian, Armenian, among others) the book's most remarkable feature, writes Davis, is "its ability to speak to a wide variety of women at different times and in disparate circumstances and social, cultural, and political contexts" (2007, 6). More precisely, this ability to speak across contexts has itself been an interactive global process of interpretation through which *OBOS* has been understood and deployed to articulate at once shared and divergent conceptions of feminist politics.

Tracking multiple receptions of the book across time and space, Davis explores what Adrienne Rich (1986) coined "the politics of location," the idea that the specificity of one's location constitutes the ground from which feminists form political identities and make political claims. As it is also expressed in various ideas of "locational feminism" (Friedman 2001), "feminist conjuncturalism" (Frankenberg and Mani 1993), "postmodern geographies" (Kaplan 1996), "diasporic space" (Brah 1996), and "theory from the borderlands" (Anzaldúa 1987), the politics of location builds on the basic claim of feminist standpoint theory—namely, that political activism has an epistemological basis and that critical epistemology has a basis in political activism. As Nancy Hartsock famously put it, "[W]omen's lives make available a particular and privileged vantage point on male supremacy, a vantage point that can ground a powerful critique of the phallocratic institutions and ideology that constitute the capitalist form of patriarchy" (1983, 231). Although Hartsock was careful to use the term "feminist" rather than "women's standpoint," emphasizing the "achieved character and liberatory potential" (232) of standpoint as a political concept, she tended to theorize it as singular and unitary. Critics have held that feminist standpoint theory takes white middle-class Western women as the default subject of political struggle and change (Collins 1999).

Whatever the shortcomings of early standpoint theory, it opened up a new way of thinking about politics by insisting on location, rather than an interiorized conception of identity, as crucial to understanding power. Whereas the early second-wave feminism of Millet and Beauvoir relied on a "temporal rhetoric of awakening, revelation, and rebirth," as these were captured in the idea of consciousness raising, argues Susan Sanford Friedman, third-wave feminism is organized around a "spatial rhetoric of location, multipositionality, and migration" (2001, 5). As we shall see, this spatialized conception of politics envisions "*feminist political alliances* across lines of difference rather than through a shared identity as women" (Davis 2007, 9; italics in original). More precisely, identity is now understood as constituted along multiple axes or lines of difference (race, ethnicity, class, religion, and sexuality, etc.) that undercut the "individualist telos of developmental models" (Friedman 2001, 8), according to which consciousness is raised and subjection is seen as oppression. In this "new geographics of identity," argues Friedman, identity is "a crossroad of multiple situated knowledges" (2001, 8).

Friedman's conception of "locational feminism" may well overstate the difference between a temporal and a spatial rhetoric for articulating feminist politics, and is arguably overly generalizing when it comes to interpreting the dominant idiom of the Second Wave (which surely was not One) as temporal rather than spatial. Nevertheless, her account helps us to see how difficult it has been for feminism to deal with differences without folding them into a single concept of women's identity or feminist political consciousness that follows more or less one path of liberation. The question would be how plural identities could be brought into a spatialized political rhetoric that recognizes the need to "articulate" differences into what Laclau and Mouffe call the "chains of equivalence" that make possible collective action in the absence of shared identity (1985, 127–129). The idea, in other words, is not what women share qua women but rather how common projects emerge through specific practices of struggle located in time and space without losing track of the basis of feminist politics—namely, plurality.

Although the differences among women have always formed the irreducible basis of feminist politics, concerns about the practical consequences thought to flow from acknowledging plurality have haunted feminism throughout its history. As we shall see when we turn to the US debates over "identity politics," feminists have struggled to square their commitment to recognizing diversity with the worry that differences will tear feminism apart. This worry expresses the view that if feminism is a political movement that speaks in the name of women, then women must represent a specific sociological group with shared interests based on a shared identity. Absent such prepolitical commonality, feminism would have no collective subject in whose name it could speak.

Thinking about "the subject of feminism" as identical with the sociological group called "women" places tremendous pressure on feminists to seek commonality or sameness as the condition of feminist politics, both within and across national boundaries. It is a problem for recognizing differences that, far from unique to feminism, reflects feminism's entanglement in an inherited model for thinking about politics along the lines of kinship or the family. The traditional modeling of political communities as families is exemplified in the notion of a people bound by blood and gathered within the territorial confines of a nation-state. Within feminism, the kinship claim has taken the form of a "sisterhood," a kind of communal belonging based in something essentially given and shared. Although the idea of feminism as a sisterhood in the strict sense of a biologically based political affinity of women across time and space has been more the exaggerated creation of its eager critics than actual political actors, the temptation to think about feminist political communities as having to be grounded in something unifying and given, like kinship, has been difficult to shake.

The kinship metaphor that structures feminist critiques of women's shared oppression underwrites certain iterations of global feminism. The latter term, as Friedman explains, "arose in relation to the common Second Wave feminist assumption of a universal patriarchy and the promotion of a global sisterhood united in its resistance to world-wide male dominance. Global feminism, often represented by Robin Morgan's anthology *Sisterhood Is Global*, usefully insisted that feminists in the West look beyond their particular national and western conditions to the status of women in the so-called second and third worlds." Notwithstanding this salutary call to move beyond the parameters of the US nation-state for theorizing oppression and political strategizing, the idea of a global feminism based on a global sisterhood "became subject to critique, especially by women in non-western settings, for isolating gender from the context of other concerns such as colonialism (and its aftereffects), national identity, race, and class, and for assuming a homogeneous sisterhood of women united together against men" (Friedman 2001, 13).

Although characterizations of the Second Wave as wholly captive to totalizing notions of gender power and oppression should be questioned, it seems right to say that feminists today are more likely to reject "notions of monolithic patriarchy and sisterhood in favor of locational heterogeneity and idiomatic particularity in transnational context" (Friedman 2001, 25). Feminism takes root in local contexts but also in relation to global ideas and practices that travel and, in traveling, are reinterpreted and rearticulated in relation to local conditions—just as *Our Bodies, Ourselves* was. To get a better understanding of how identity has figured in feminist politics, we turn now to what has been the most criticized, if also often misunderstood, way of thinking about feminism along lines of commonality—namely, "identity politics."

Identity Politics

Reading the vast literature on identity politics, both within and outside feminism, one is struck not only by the elasticity of definition—identity politics means everything from the canon wars that wracked American universities in the 1990s, to French language rights in Canada, to the parochialism of white middle-class American feminism, to the celebration of Martin Luther King Jr. day—but also by the remarkable collusion of liberal, conservative, and leftist critics, for whom identity politics (a.k.a. multiculturalism) represents all that went wrong with progressive politics in the second half of the twentieth century. Indeed, "the phrase 'identity politics,'" as Cressida Heyes (2002) observes, is a 'punching bag for a variety of critics', a kind of 'blanket description that invokes a range of political failings', but most commonly a failure to move outside the narrow circle of a particular oppressed group and join with diverse others in the struggle for justice based on universal political ideals.

According to Todd Gitlin, for example, identity politics has destroyed the "historic ideals of the Left: a belief in progress through the unfolding of a humanity present—at least potentially—in every human being" (1996, 85). "The cant of identity underlies identity politics," continues Gitlin (1996, 126), "which proposes to deduce a position, a tradition, a deep truth, or a way of life from a fact of birth, physiognomy, national origin, sex, or physical disability." In Gitlin's account, the identity politics of the 1970s and 1980s, as it was extended into the multiculturalism of the 1990s, represents the turn away from the universalism (i.e., class basis) of radical politics. Gitlin claims that by 1969 no one wanted anything to do with the democratic politics of the traditional Left because "identity groups was where the action was ... [T]he American Indian Movement seized the former prison island of Alcatraz in San Francisco Bay on Thanksgiving Day in 1969. In Northern cities, Puerto Rican groups organized. In the West and Southwest, Chicanos were doing the same—Cesar Chavez's farm workers in California, ... antiwar Chicano Moratorium in Los Angeles, ... In California, young Chinese Americans insisted on their distinct needs as an interest group" (Gitlin 1996, 134–135).[4]

Why don't the forms of organizing that Gitlin describes as instances of identity politics count as forms of democratic practice? Don't they share the defining feature of democratic movements: action in concert? We should resist the tendency to ascribe the practice of identity politics to minority racial, sexual, and ethnic groups and to women. At a minimum we should ask how one would characterize the political practice of rich white people, especially men, in the United States, if not as a form of identity politics. As C. Wright Mills showed long ago in *The Power Elite*, the rich practice a form of politics that is constructed around their cultural identities. To say, for example, that when CEOs of the Fortune 500 companies lobby Congress on an economic matter, they practice interest politics not identity politics is to beg the question. Why is that any different from African Americans demanding a Martin Luther King national holiday or a family wage? Why is it different from women demanding maternity leave and equal pay? Why is it different from Cesar Chavez organizing for the rights of farm workers?

Critics of identity politics are blind to these similarities because they think of identity not as something formed in the crucible of history but instead, to cite Gitlin again, as the voluntary celebration of "a fact of birth, physiognomy, national origin, sex, or physical disability." They also think of these facts as something that their idealized liberal or Left subject does not share. Black people have race, whites don't. Women have gender, men don't. And so on.

What this definition of identity politics leaves out is the politically constituted character of identity. Although not every aspect of identity is political, identity politics is a response to those aspects of being born into group membership that have been made political. Understanding this distinction, the German Jewish émigré political theorist Hannah Arendt sees that the danger to democracy lies in the temptation not only to treat identity as a deep transhistorical truth about oneself and one's group but also to deny one's membership in a group that has been singled out for discrimination. As Arendt writes of her stance toward being a Jew in Hitler Germany, "I considered the only adequate reply to the question, Who are you? to be: A Jew. That answer alone took in the reality of persecution" (1968, 17). For Arendt, "counter[ing] the command: 'Step closer, Jew'" with "the statement: I am a man" is "nothing but a grotesque and dangerous evasion of reality." "Unfortunately," says Arendt, "the basically simple principle in question here is particularly hard to understand in times of defamation and persecution: the principle that one can resist only in terms of the identity that is under attack. Those who reject such identifications on the part of a hostile world may feel wonderfully superior to the world, but their superiority is then truly no longer of this world" (Arendt 1968, 18).[5]

Likewise, Beauvoir, speaking in *The Second Sex* of a similar temptation in relation to patriarchy, argues that the woman who would deny her existence as a woman will not, despite her protestations, be taken for a human being. "To decline to accept such notions of the eternal feminine . . . does not represent a liberation for those concerned, but rather a flight from reality" (1989, xvii). Unlike a man who "never begins by presenting himself as an individual of a certain sex; it goes without saying that he is a man," the woman who would speak at all must not only "admit, provisionally, that women do exist," she must say: "I am a woman; on this truth must be based all further discussion" (xvii).

Beauvoir and Arendt teach that there are times in history when identity is political and must be articulated politically. Thus the question is not, is taking political account of identity antithetical to democratic or feminist values?, but rather, when does an ascribed cultural identity become political? For Arendt and Beauvoir respectively, the answer "I am a Jew" or "I am a woman" can be either a political act that takes up the identity that is under attack to contest oppression or a pose that serves to reinscribe it. What matters is the context, the political conditions in which such an answer is given. Examining the historical contexts in which a particular identity becomes political, we can see how the denial of one's identity in contexts in which it is under attack can be a profoundly apolitical act and a dangerous evasion of reality. Reading Gitlin's happy humanist account one is tempted to conclude that the only answer it would have allowed to the question, "who are you?" is, "why I'm a human being. I don't know why you continue to mistake me for a woman or a Jew."

Although it has come to stand for everything that went wrong with second-wave feminism and like-minded political movements of the time (e.g., Black Power, gay and lesbian liberation, Native American liberation), identity politics, then, was initially a mode of organizing around and revaluing oppressed and stigmatized identities (Young 1990). The aim was not to celebrate "difference" as such but to transform the conditions of its production and continued marginalization. In this sense, identity politics was connected with the consciousness raising discussed earlier; it was a means for seeing in long-standing practices of subordination unjust oppression and cause for political organizing. For example, as told in the Combahee River Collective's classic statement, in 1977, of black feminist identity politics, being continually reprimanded for talking too much or too loud was a mechanism of patriarchal and racist social control, a means for making African-American girl-children both "'ladylike' and . . . less objectionable in the eyes of white people . . . In the process of consciousness-raising, actually life-sharing, we began to recognize the commonality of our experiences and, from the sharing and growing consciousness, to build a politics that will change our lives and inevitably end our oppression" (Combahee River Collective 1982, 15). Feminist critics such as Wendy Brown, Judith Butler, and Marion Tapper argue that identity politics creates a defended self that is invested in its own injury, seething with *resentment*, and ultimately hostile to differences. (Tapper 1993; Brown 1995; Butler 1990). As part of the larger "regulatory practice of identity" (Butler 1990, 32), identity politics becomes complicit as well in the disciplinary apparatus of the state, which serves as the sole addressee of political identity qua injury claims. Furthermore, as Susan Bickford summarizes—without endorsing—these feminist critiques, "[T]he assumption of morally pure and powerless victims eliminates the possibilities for democratic disagreement. Rather than articulating political claims in contestable ways, victims wield 'moral reproach' against power" (Bickford 1997, 115).

Although identity politics may "run the risk of further entrenching normalizing conceptions of identity and the power of regulatory apparatuses to enforce and police them," counters Bickford (1997, 118), we would be mistaken to assume that this must be the case in any identity-based claim (Young 1990). Even more suspect is the idea that any political use of identity necessarily expresses the self-defeatist logic of rancor. Instead, reclaiming stigmatized identities as political identities can involve what bell Hooks calls a "legacy of defiance, of will, of courage" (1989, 9). And there is a difference between feelings of anger at injustice that lead to political action and simmering resentment at suffering that can lead to a self-destructive retreat from the world (Lorde [1980] 1984; Bickford 1997, 125). Finally, modeling feminist politics on kinship, which many critics impute to every iteration of identity politics, is precisely what the most prominent voices of identity politics *themselves* characterize as a problematic way of thinking about political alliances (Reagon [1983] 2011; Combahee River Collective 1982; Bickford 1997, 23). Sisterhood is a limiting concept for feminist politics, for it conceals divisions and struggles even within identity groups seen as homogenous from those "outside" them (Anzaldúa 1987; Moraga 1983). As Audre Lorde succinctly put it, "By and large within the women's movement today, white women focus upon their oppression as women and ignore differences of race, sexual preference, class, and age. There is a pretense to a homogeneity of experience covered by the word *sisterhood* that does not in fact exist" ([1980] 1984, 122).

Just as it is important to recognize that the political claim to identity arose in the wake of the failure of liberal democracy and various progressive movements to include the people each claimed to represent, so, too, is it crucial to see that the emergence of politicized identities did not begin as a narrow claim to identity, as if identity were somehow an unproblematic category in need only of social recognition. It began as a claim to participate equally in politics, to be seen and heard in the space of appearances that was the grassroots struggle (Young 1999). Rather than think of identity as that which identity politics takes for granted as already shared, the common basis on which politics proceeds, we might think of it as that which can be created in the practice of politics as a *public* persona: "who" rather than "what" someone is, to borrow Arendt's useful distinction (1989, 184). Though rooted in the "what" of the identity that one shares with others by membership in a particular group marked by race, gender, class, ethnicity, or sexuality, the "who" is something that comes into being only in and through politics and in the public space that Arendt calls the common world.[6] "It is the space between them that unites them, rather than some quality in each of them," as Margaret Canovan (1985, 634) puts the Arendtian difference between a politics built around "what" someone is (i.e., on identity) and one based on "who" someone is (i.e., on world building). Identities come to be politicized identities not only insofar as they are marginalized or disenfranchised but also insofar as the "what" is transformed into the "who" in the in-between space of the common world.

In recent years, several feminist critics have turned to Arendt to articulate a conception of politics attuned to the historical contexts in which politicized identity involves a creative if precarious form of world-building (Benhabib 2000; Bickford 1995; Dietz 1995; Disch 1994; Honig, 1995; Orlie 1995; Zerilli 2005). For them, the space of the "who" is not the safe "home" of a sisterhood but the always uncertain and risk-ridden space of feminism as a motley of alliances and coalitions. Shared identities do not guarantee shared politics but only an occasion to engage in practices of world building, which are always fraught with uncertainty. When you seek out coalitions with others, as Bernice Johnson Reagon argued long ago, you engage in a precarious practice of politics whose outcome cannot be known in advance of relinquishing the safe, home-like space of a fantasized "sisterhood" and putting oneself on the line with others who are very different from you, could work together with you, but could also "kill you" (Reagon [1983] 2011; Bickford 1997, 123).

To think of identity politics in the explicitly political terms of the "who" is to challenge the critiques lodged, respectively, by leftist critics such as Gitlin, for whom the obsession with difference has led to a loss of interest in the commonalities that undergird the "we" of a collective political movement (Gitlin 1996, 177), and feminist critics such as Brown, for whom this obsession undermines the otherwise legitimate grievances and collective world building of politicized identities. The question left unanswered by these and other critics of identity politics, writes Bickford, "is more like: in a context of inequality and oppression, *how* are multiple 'we's' to be democratically part of the same public thing? What can make possible democratic communication with differently placed others?" (1997, 117). Keeping our eye on the demand to be a participator in government broadly construed, we can better appreciate the real challenge that identity politics and more broadly feminism poses to conventional conceptions of politics: the idea that participation is secondary to representation for politics is little more than a means to an end.

POLITICS AS A MEANS TO AN END

The fear that differences will tear feminism apart expresses the tenacious sense that feminism must be grounded in a unified subject whose interests it represents (Butler 1990) and, further, that this subject is identical with the sociological group called women (Zerilli 2005). When we think about politics in accordance with this representational model, it is easy to find in the differences among women both the challenge of political organizing and an uneasy sense of impending crisis. If women are not a homogenous group with similar interests, then there is no unified subject in whose name feminism speaks; it becomes hard to imagine the need or possibility of feminism as a political movement at all. Might not other political movements that represent other interests just as well represent those of women as they are divided along lines of race, ethnicity, and class, to name but three categories of difference?

The idea that the point of politics is to represent the interests of a particular group (e.g., women, blacks, gays and lesbians, small business owners, the middle class, etc.) presupposes that those interests can be known in advance of the practice of politics qua representation itself. It also assumes that politics has a purpose, which is to say, a goal of some sort—in short, politics is a (mere) means to an end. The powerful hold of this instrumentalist conception of politics on the thinking of many feminists is not unique to feminism but expresses the dominant modern view of democratic politics as primarily a means to pursue individual and group interests. On this view, political speech and action are directed at attaining a good of some sort and are valuable only to the extent that they achieve their goal-oriented end. Feminist struggles for reproductive rights, for example, are valuable insofar as they result in changes in law and legislation that provides better access to contraception, family planning, abortion, and the like. As Mary Hawkesworth's work on transnational coalitions for reproductive justice has shown, however, such struggles create networks of relations among political actors that exceed the success or failure of any particular stated goal (Hawkesworth 2012). Keeping our eye on the emergence of these networks, we can better appreciate feminist politics as a practice of world building and freedom.

So commonplace is this instrumentalist view of politics that it seems almost impossible to question it without falling into a kind of circular logic by which politics is the justification of its own activity. But what activity is that, we might ask? And why would we so much as engage in politics if it were not a means to an end of some sort, something tangible like legislation securing wage parity between men and women, affordable child care, and so on? Although such concrete objectives surely are an important part of feminist politics, and their attainment forms the basis of why particular individuals might engage in politics in the first place, we would miss the world-building aspects of speech and action if we reduced politics to the realization of stated goals. The activities of Boston Women's Collective mentioned earlier, for example, were organized around the achievement of certain goals having broadly to do with women's health and well being. Their critique of the medicalization of women's bodies—that is, the social construction of the female body as an unruly object to be brought under the control of (male) experts—gave rise to a network of relations among women (both local and global) that far exceeded any particular policy objective that was the intended aim of their political organizing. Even failed attempts to change policy or to secure reproductive rights for all women contributed to this world-building practice, the creation of a worldly in-between in which women developed the ability to form, share, and debate opinions with others. This is how political actors can at once constitute and transcend the success or failure of the particular political movements in which they are engaged, how they learn to engage in political activities in the broadest sense, discover what their shared interests are, and make common cause with others.

Put somewhat differently, it is the activity of politics itself that brings into being the shared interests thought to unite a sociological group and to be the prior basis of politics. The "subject of feminism," then, is not "women" as a sociological group, but "women" in whose name feminist political actors speak. Keeping this distinction in mind we can better understand why the acknowledgment of differences among women need not lead to a crisis of feminism. Feminists can speak in the name of women without assuming a shared identity (and interests) of women as a social group. This speaking can include biological males, self-identified men, and non-gender-normative identities such as transgender and LGBTQ individuals. One does not have to "be" a woman to call oneself a feminist or fight in the name of feminism and, further, identities themselves are refigured in the very practice of politics itself. Identities, though they surely play a role in why someone initially gets involved in politics, are activated in the practice of politics as politically significant in the form of the public persona, the "who" mentioned above.

Finally, to think about feminist politics outside a means-ends instrumental idiom is not to relinquish the idea that political activity can strive for and achieve certain goals. As noted earlier, it is to question the view, first, that the attainment of the goals exhausts the meaning of feminist politics and, second, that to act politically we must be able to control the outcome of our actions, foretell in advance what their consequences will be. This view of politics as excluding unpredictability forgets that whenever we act, we do so into a context of other human wills and intentions that we can never fully know in advance. We can never know with certainty how other political actors will take up our actions; political action always exceeds political actors' predictions and control (Arendt 1989, 289; Zerilli 2005, 18).

Politics as a Practice of Freedom

Rather than think of politics as a mean to an end, many grassroots feminist organizations, such as the Boston Women's Collective, have conceptualized politics as a practice of freedom understood as "action in concert" and the freedom to begin anew, to create new forms of being in common. The interdependence of politics and freedom departs radically from the negative idea of freedom as that which politics is supposed to guarantee or secure, a realm independent from politics. On this view, which has historically been associated with liberalism, freedom begins where politics ends, where we are free from politics (in the private realm, for example). Such a view is premised on the idea of freedom as freedom of the will, which is to say on the idea of sovereignty. As the political realm is characterized by plurality, not sovereignty, freedom is seen as existing outside politics and as that which it is the business of a liberal politics to protect and defend.

Although feminists have been critical of the ideal of sovereignty, seeing in it androcentric relations of gender power, many remain entangled in the inherited negative or will-based conception of freedom that underwrites it. To depart from this conception of freedom as based in the will is to take leave of sovereignty as the measure of freedom, where I am most free when I am most independent of others, whose own wills stand as obstacles to my freedom. A nonsovereign conception of freedom entails moving from the I-will to the I-can, and this I-can is only possible with the help of others. The long-standing problem of freedom in feminism, then, cannot be addressed at the level of the autonomy of the individual subject but must involve the creation of the worldly conditions that allow individuals to do what they may will. Women's freedom involves transforming the conditions of the common world; it is fundamentally a problem of political action.

In "The Meaning of Freedom," for example, Angela Y. Davis strongly contests the liberal conception for its highly individualist understanding of freedom and argues for a practice of freedom as an engaged collective form of political participation that belongs to a genuine democracy in which women and practically disenfranchised populations engage in common projects aimed at the transformation of real social conditions (Davis 2012). For Davis, freedom is not granted or secured by the state, housed in constitutionally guaranteed rights, or experienced as something that begins where politics ends. It is an ongoing active practice of claiming one's rights in concert with others and, in the process, transforming the lived conditions of oppressed identities.

The creative or inaugural aspect of feminist politics understood as a practice of freedom has been crucial to the formation of feminism's ability to put forward alternative ways of engaging with others in public fora and to refiguring the boundaries of the public and the private realms. When understood as action in concert, politics qua freedom is a practice that can emerge in spaces or in relation to activities that have been heretofore considered nonpolitical, just as the second-wave account of consciousness raising held. Such a conception of politics is implicit in the grassroots character of feminist efforts to defamiliarize what counts as a matter of common concern and the spaces in which politics can take place. As already indicated, feminist politics has involved a challenge to the traditional institutional conceptions and spaces of politics, according to which politics is what happens in, say, the Houses of Congress or in protests that take place in officially sanctioned public spaces such as the National Mall in Washington DC.

Conclusion

Like the worries associated with democratic politics in multicultural societies, the debates over the category of women and the fear that differences will tear feminism apart can be interpreted in terms of the distinction between an understanding of politics as life with and among one's kin versus an understanding of politics as life with and among strangers. "There is nowhere you can go and only be with people who are like you. It's over. Give it up," advises Bernice Johnson Reagon ([1983] 2011, 344). Precisely because feminist—like democratic—politics consists in an ongoing attempt to live with and among strangers, that is, in the context of plurality, it cannot be based on pre-given notions of what we share by virtue of being born into a particular group or into a particular nation and culture. The temptation to make shared experience the definitive criterion both for membership in a group and for pursuing a politics based on an ascribed identity is caught in a disturbing feature of liberal humanism, namely, the idea that political affiliation can only be based on the logic of sameness: I recognize you as a member of my feminist community to the extent that I find myself in you. The question, then, would be how to articulate political relations of commonality that do not reproduce these relations of dominance, that enable different groups to work together politically, and that respect the plurality of individual differences between members of the same social group.

Although identity has been argued here to be something other than what critics of identity politics claim, we have seen that the difference between the "what" and the "who" of identity actually relies on a radical refiguration of politics from an identity- or subject-based relation to a spatial relation centered on world building. Feminist politics is based not on something inside acting subjects but on the creation of a common space in-between them that unites them. To think of politics in terms of space rather than identity is to take leave of the Western tradition of political thought that sees politics as a substance that inheres in certain activities or even in human beings themselves—that is, the idea of "man" as a political being (*zoon politikon*), with "political" understood as something that belongs to man's essence. Political, we have seen, is no more the essence of what it is to be human than it is a substance or property that inheres in any particular activity or thing. Politics is the activity of relating to others in a space characterized by plurality and by distance and proximity, the space of the common world that is created through action and speech.

Thinking about politics in terms of the spaces and practices of freedom allows us to account for the unexpected emergence of politics in registers and idioms of life heretofore seen as nonpolitical or private. This inaugural character of feminist politics is easy to overlook when we think about politics in the instrumental terms described above. Looking for the traditional objects of political activity, we risk blinding ourselves to political activity itself, namely, the speech and action that is not necessarily materialized into a stable object such as law, policy, or any material good. And though feminist politics conceptualized as a practice of freedom surely aims at the transformation of the conditions of women's lives (and thus at these objects), it also creates relations among speaking and acting subjects that exceed the success or failure of any particular material transformation and provide the intangible but crucial basis, the worldly in-between of human relationships, for advancing new struggles.

Notes

1. As other chapters in this volume address feminist views of the state, socialist feminist work on redistributive politics, transnational and critical race feminist approaches to reproductive politics, and feminist postcolonial views of politics, in this chapter I focus only on what it means to call something political, not on the myriad ways in which politics can be manifested. My approach, then, is by no means intended to be exhaustive of what politics has meant in feminist practice and theory but is instead aimed at clarifying how we might think about the kind of activity that politics is.
2. Strictly speaking, the term itself, writes Hanish, was not her own: "I'd like to clarify for the record that I did not give the paper its title, 'The Personal Is Political.' As far as I know, that was done by *Notes from the Second Year* editors Shulie Firestone and Anne Koedt after Kathie Sarachild brought it to their attention as a possible paper to be printed in that early collection. Also, 'political' was used here in the b[r]oard sense of the word as having to do with power relationships, not the narrow sense of electoral [*sic*] politics" ([1969] 2006, 1).
3. As Hanish would later explain, "[T]hey [members of the Southern Conference Educational Fund] belittled us to no end for trying to bring our so-called 'personal problems' into the political arena. According to Hanisch, "The paper actually began as a memo that I wrote in February of 1969 while in Gainesville, Florida. It was sent to the women's caucus of the Southern Conference Educational Fund (SCEF) a group for whom I was a subsistence-paid organizer doing exploratory work for establishing a women's liberation project in the South. The memo was originally titled, 'Some Thoughts in Response to Dottie's Thoughts on a Women's Liberation Movement', and was written in reply to a memo by another staff member, Dottie Zellner, who contended that consciousness-raising was just therapy and questioned whether the new independent WLM was really 'political'.... This was not an unusual reaction to radical feminist ideas in early 1969."
4. A similar attack on identity politics and multiculturalism can be found in the pragmatist antiphilosopher Richard Rorty's latest work, *Achieving Our Country: Leftist Thought in Twentieth Century America*. Although Rorty does not accept Gitlin's metaphysics of humanity approach to building a Left for the new millennium, he shares Gitlin's frustration with the emergence of a Left that is narcissistically obsessed with identity and that pursues cultural—in contrast to real—politics. Although Rorty claims to attend to issues of difference, his prescriptions for political action are dismissive of race, sexuality, ethnicity (indeed, of everything that is not reducible to the economic). Like Gitlin, Rorty contrasts his ideal of the pre-sixties reformist Left, which "proclaimed that all of us—black, white, and brown—are Americans, and that we should respect each other as such," against the contemporary "cultural Left" which "urges that America should not be a melting-pot, because we need to respect each other in our differences" (Rorty 1998, 100). Like Gitlin, Rorty holds to an image of the pre-sixties Left that is at odds with the historical record. There is not a word about

New Dealers who were segregationists. Not a word about labor unions that excluded racial minorities and discriminated against women. Rorty's Left liberalism has no place for these accounts because they point to the particularities that cannot be incorporated in his communal subject, the "We" that is to achieve "our country."

5. Arendt sees that a focus on identity can lead to a loss of worldly reality. The sense of belonging to an oppressed group, based on expulsion from the world or the denial of one's rightful place in it, can generate in the oppressed a sense of being a pariah people and thus worldless. What becomes all-important is not care for the world but the survival of the group. "In such a state of worldlessness," writes Arendt, "it is easy to conclude that the element common to all men is not the world but 'human nature' of such and such a type" (Arendt 1968, 16). Thus forms of identity politics that model group relations on kinship, brother and sisters who share a social, cultural, and political genealogy, tend to reduce relations with others to the sentimental terms of compassion and pity, shared suffering.

6. To have a "common world" is not to share a worldview, and this common world exists only where there is a plurality of worldviews. Arendt writes:

> [T]he reality of the public realm relies on the simultaneous presence of innumerable perspectives and aspects in which the common world presents itself and for which no common measurement or denominator can ever be devised. For though the common world is the common meeting ground of all, those who are present have different locations in it . . . Being seen and heard by others derive their significance from the fact that everybody sees and hears from a different position. This is the meaning of public life . . . . Only where things can be seen by many in a variety of aspects without changing their identity, so that those who have gathered around them know they see sameness in utter diversity, can worldly reality truly and reliably appear.
>
> (Arendt, 1989, 57)

Our sense of what is common can appear only when it is seen from different perspectives. Consequently, the loss of competing perspectives results not in a world that is more shared but in a loss of what we have common.

References

Anzaldúa, Gloria. 1987. *Borderlands/La frontera*. San Francisco, CA: Spinsters/Aunt Lute Foundation.
Arendt, Hannah. 1968. "On Humanity in Dark Times: Thoughts about Lessing." In *Men in Dark Times*. New York: Harcourt, Brace & Co., 3–32.
Arendt, Hannah. 1989. *The Human Condition*. Chicago: University of Chicago Press.
Beauvoir, Simone de. (1949) 1989. *The Second Sex*. Edited by H. M. Parshley. New York: Vintage.
Benhabib, Seyla. 2000. *The Reluctant Modernism of Hannah Arendt*. Lanham, MD: Rowman and Littlefield.
Bickford, Susan. 1995. "In the Presence of Others: Arendt and Anzaldúa on the Paradox of Public Appearance." In *Feminist Interpretations of Hannah Arendt*, edited by Bonnie Honig, 313–336. University Park, PA: Pennsylvania State University Press.

Bickford, Susan. 1997. "Anti-Anti-Identity Politics: Feminism, Democracy, and the Complexities of Citizenship." *Hypatia* 12 (Autumn): 111–131.
Brah, Avtar. 1996. *Cartographies of Diaspora: Contesting Identities*. New York: Routledge.

Brown, Wendy. 1995. *States of Injury: Power and Freedom in Late Modernity*. Princeton, NJ: Princeton University Press.

Brown, Wendy. 1998. *Manhood and Politics*. Totowa, NJ: Rowman and Littlefield.
Butler, Judith. 1990. *Gender Trouble*. New York: Routledge.
Canovan, Margaret. 1985. "Politics as Culture: Hannah Arendt and the Public Realm." *History of Political Thought* 6 (3): 617–642.
Castoriadis, Cornelius. 1997. "Logic, Imagination, Reflection." In *World in Fragments: Writings on Politics, Society, Psychoanalysis, and Imagination*, edited by David Ames Curtis, 246–272. Redwood City, CA: Stanford University Press.
Collins, Patricia Hill. 1999. *Black Feminist Thought: Knowledge, Consciousness, and the Politics of Empowerment*. New York: Routledge.
Combahee River Collective. 1982. "A Black Feminist Statement." In *But Some of Us Are Brave*, edited by Gloria T. Hull, Patricia Bell Scott, and Barbara Smith, 13–22. New York: The Feminist Press at CUNY.
Davis, Angela Y. 2012. "The Meaning of Freedom." In Angela Y. Davis, *The Meaning of Freedom: And Other Difficult Dialogues*. San Francisco, CA: City Lights, 135–152.
Davis, Kathy. 2007. *The Making of Our Bodies, Ourselves*. Durham. NC: Duke University Press.
Dietz, Mary G. 1995. "Feminist Receptions of Hannah Arendt." In *Feminist Interpretations of Hannah Arendt*, edited by Bonnie Honig, 17–50. University Park, PA: Pennsylvania State University Press.
Disch, Lisa Jane. 1994. *Hannah Arendt and the Limits of Philosophy*. Ithaca, NY: Cornell University Press.
Di Stefano, Christine. 1991. *Configurations of Masculinity: A Feminist Perspective on Modern Political Theory*. Ithaca, NY: Cornell University Press.
Elshtain, Jean Bethke. 1981. *Public Man, Private Woman: Women in Social and Political Thought*. Princeton, NJ: Princeton University Press.
Frankenberg, Ruth and Lata Mani. 1993. "Crosscurrents, Crosstalk: Race, 'Postcoloniality' and the Politics of Location." *Cultural Studies* 7 (2): 292–310.
Friedman, Susan Sanford. 2001. "Locational Feminism: Gender, Cultural Geographies, and Geopolitical Literacy." In *Feminist Locations: Global/Local/Theory/Practice in the 21st Century*, edited by Marianne DeKoven, 13–36. New Brunswick, NJ: Rutgers University Press.
Gitlin, Todd. [1969] 2006. *The Twilight of Common Dreams: Why America Is Wracked by Culture Wars*. New York: Metropolitan.
Hanish, Carole. "The Personal Is Political: The Women's Liberation Classic with a New Explanatory Introduction." http://www.carolhanisch.org/CHwritings/PIP.html.
Hartsock, Nancy. 1983. *Money, Sex, and Power: Toward a Feminist Historical Materialism*. New York: Longman.
Hawkesworth, Mary. 2012. *Political Worlds of Women: Activism, Advocacy, and Governance in the Twenty-First Century*. Boulder, CO: Westview.
Heyes, Cressida. 2002. "Identity Politics," *Stanford Encyclopedia of Philosophy*. http://plato.stanford.edu/entries/identity-politics/

Honig, Bonnie. 1995. "Toward an Agonistic Feminism: Hannah Arendt and the Politics of Identity." In *Feminist Interpretations of Hannah Arendt*, edited by Bonnie Honig, 135–166. University Park, PA: Pennsylvania State University Press

Hooks, Bell. 1989. *Talking Back: Thinking Feminist, Thinking Black*. Boston: South End Press.

Kaplan, Caren. 1996. Questions of Travel: Postmodern Discourses of Displacement. Durham: Duke University Press.

Laclau, Ernesto, and Chantal Mouffe. (1985) 2001. *Hegemony and Socialist Strategy*. London: Verso.

Lorde, Audre. (1980) 1984. "Age, Race, Class, and Sex: Women Redefining Difference." In *Sister Outsider: Essays and Speeches*, 114–231. Trumansburg, NY: Crossing Press.

Maione, Angela. 2012. *Revolutionary Rhetoric: The Political Thought of Mary Wollstonecraft*. Diss., Northwestern University.

Millet, Kate. 1969. *Sexual Politics*. New York: Equinox Books.

Moraga, Cherríe. 1983. Preface to *This Bridge Called My Back: Writings by Radical Women of Color*, edited by Cherríe Moraga and Gloria Anzaldúa. New York: Kitchen Table: Women of Color Press.

Morgan, Robin, ed. 1970. *Sisterhood Is Powerful*. New York: Vintage.

Okin, Susan Moller. 1979. *Women in Western Political Thought*. Princeton, NJ: Princeton University Press.

Orlie, Melissa. 1995. "Forgiving Trespasses, Promising Futures." In *Feminist Interpretations of Hannah Arendt*, edited by Bonnie Honig, 337–356. University Park, PA: Pennsylvania State University Press.

Pateman, Carole. 1988. *The Sexual Contract*. Redwood City, CA: Stanford University Press.

Reagon, Bernice Johnson. (1983) 2011. "Coalition Politics: Turning the Century." In *Home Girls: A Black Feminist Anthology*, edited by Barbara Smith, 343–356. New York: Kitchen Table Press.

Rich, Adrienne.1986. "Notes toward a Politics of Location." In *Blood, Bread, and Poetry*, 210–232. New York: W. W. Norton.

Rorty, Richard. 1998. *Achieving Our Country: Leftist Thought in Twentieth Century America*. Cambridge, MA: Harvard University Press.

Tapper, Marion. 1993. "Resentment and Power." In *Nietzsche, Feminism, and Political Theory*, edited by Paul Patton, 130–143. New York: Routledge.

Young, Iris Marion. 1990. *Justice and the Politics of Difference*. Princeton, NJ: Princeton University Press.

Zerilli, Linda M. G. 1994. *Signifying Woman: Culture and Chaos in Rousseau, Burke, and Mill*. Ithaca, NY: Cornell University Press.

Zerilli, Linda M. G. 2005. *Feminism and the Abyss of Freedom*. Chicago: University of Chicago Press.

CHAPTER 32

POP CULTURE/VISUAL CULTURE

REBECCA WANZO

In the 1960s and 1970s, student movements, the Civil Rights Movement, women's liberation, gay liberation, and decolonization movements raised fundamental challenges to Western academic institutions. Social justice activists posed new questions for scholarly investigation and demanded the creation of academic programs to address areas of inquiry omitted from traditional disciplines. African studies and African American studies, ethnic studies, LGBTQ studies, and women's studies were born of these political mobilizations. As these new intellectual projects developed over the ensuing decades both within established disciplines and in new interdisciplinary sites, they challenged myths about the neutrality and disinterestedness of academic inquiry. Some of the most radical challenges to disciplines came from feminist scholars working in the fields of popular culture, visual culture, and cultural studies. Rejecting "the canon" as an objective archive of the world's greatest art, for example, some scholars began investigating canonicity as a mechanism of exclusion. Others raised fundamental questions about what counts as "art" and whose views matter in establishing aesthetic criteria.

By probing questions of inclusion and exclusion, feminist scholars suggested that much could be learned about the politics of knowledge production, the criteria determining aesthetic value, and the complex interaction between art and society, popular works and cultural reception, "ways of seeing," and "ways of knowing." Feminist scholars were particularly interested in examining practices of representation, how canonical art, literature, and film explored issues of gender and sexuality. When feminist scholars of color intervened in these fields, feminist scholarship also began addressing how race and imperialism affected cultural productions. Feminists now routinely address how cultural productions (visual arts, performing arts, literature, advertising, fashion, technology) influence social relations, gendered and raced interactions, individual identities and desires. While carefully avoiding simplistic claims about cultural productions "causing" social problems, feminist scholars sought to illuminate how hegemonic ideologies operate through cultural production and how individuals and groups are affected by, resist, and, at times, transform cultural productions.

This chapter provides an introduction to key themes and approaches in feminist studies of popular and visual culture. Popular culture and visual culture are not identical, of course. Everything that is popular is not visual, and many objects of visual culture research fall well beyond the category of the popular. Nonetheless, examining feminist studies of visual and popular culture in tandem is useful in raising fundamental questions about the nature and functions of representation, the ideological content of cultural production, and how power circulates in images and texts.

Concepts and Analytic Strategies

Feminist scholars working in multiple disciplines have made significant contributions to visual and popular culture studies, most notably art history, communications, film studies, history, literature, media studies, musicology, performance studies, philosophy, and sociology. Although an exhaustive overview of these contributions is impossible in one chapter, it is possible to identify certain shared assumptions and analytical frames.

By analyzing "representations," feminist scholars seek to make naturalizing assumptions visible and subject them to criticism. Whether the assumptions pertain to race, gender, sexuality, or the nature of existence itself, feminists seek to identify whose perspectives are incorporated into the normative view and whose are omitted. Following a long line of critical theorists, feminist scholars explore how cultural representations create and fix meaning, how they structure desires and fears, and draw boundaries between self and other.

To analyze visual and textual representations, feminist scholars have borrowed and adapted concepts from continental philosophy. G. W. F. Hegel's ([1807] 1967) account of identity formation as "pure self-recognition in absolute otherness," which suggests that we come to know ourselves not only by comparing ourselves with others but by engaging in intensive struggle against others whom we imagine to be a threat, has played a critical role in shaping discussions of the operation of power in representational practices. Karl Marx's (Marx and Engels [1846] 1970) insight that what is taken as common sense often reflects the interests of the dominant class and requires "ideology critique" to unmask vested interests has also been formative. Structural linguist, Ferdinand de Saussure (1966) challenged notions that there is an essential relation between words and things, "signifiers" and "signified," arguing that meaning is established by relationships of difference and distinction within a linguistic system, which is itself a system of opposites and contrasts. Rejecting referential theories of language that suggest that words are labels for independently existing things, Saussure suggested that language is constitutive: signifying processes create meaning through the interplay of relationships of selection and combination, through the juxtaposition of similarities and differences within a grammatical structure without necessarily referring to anything outside the language.

For Saussure, the task of structural analysis was to reveal the rules and conventions that structure meaning within particular linguistic systems.

Jacques Derrida's theory of deconstruction moves the site of fluidity in meaning to the ambiguity of language itself. He revised Saussure, arguing that the arbitrariness is not only between signifier and signified but that the signifier always leads to another signified. Derrida proposed the concept of *"différance"* to suggest that meaning is elusive, always deferred, never fully present but, rather, simultaneously absent and present. In contrast to the structuralist focus on the relation between the signifier and the signified, Derrida's (1976, 25) poststructuralism suggests that the continual deferment of meaning establishes relations only among signifiers: "the indefinite referral of signifier and signifier . . . gives the signified meaning no respite . . . so that it always signifies again." Neither context nor connotation can fully control the meaning of signifiers, which carry with them traces of meanings from other contexts. Within this deconstructive framework, evidence itself is linguistic, unstable, and unfixed, but attention to contradictions, lacunae, false totalities, and homogenizations within particular relations of signification can provide an opening for efforts to trace multiplicities of meaning, deconstruct binary oppositions, and overthrow the hierarchies and privilege they attempt to establish.

In addition to tools designed to analyze perception, representation, and the construction of meaning through images and texts, "cultural studies" has been influenced by the critical theory tradition that developed from the works of Frankfurt School thinkers (Adorno, Horkheimer, Marcuse, and Benjamin) and was transformed by scholars in the Centre for Contemporary Cultural Studies in Birmingham, England, notably, Raymond Williams and Stuart Hall. Whereas the Frankfurt School examined the power of mass media to seduce the public to compliance with authoritarian rulers or to be distracted by consumption, the Birmingham School emphasized a dialectical relationship between power and resistance, conceptualizing popular culture as a site where power is both established and destabilized. Leni Riefenstahl's *Triumph of the Will*, a propaganda film depicting the 1934 Congress at Nuremberg, helps illuminate the stakes of popular culture for Frankfurt School theorists. For these thinkers, Riefenstahl's grand orchestral score; groundbreaking aerial photography; montages of images depicting the German nation rising again, the presence of cherub-cheeked blonde children; and representations of a seemingly humble Adolph Hitler being greeted by an adoring, hopeful crowd manifest the power of cinematic techniques to produce generic pleasures that romanticize and naturalize fascist domination. Frankfurt School theorists warned that new technologies were tools of distraction for the masses. In "The Culture Industry: Enlightenment as Mass Deception," Theodor Adorno and Max Horkheimer ([1944] 2002, 94) argued that mass media infects "everything with sameness." The culture industry encourages people to think they have individual choice when their pleasures are channeled into predictable, mind-numbing pleasures. Consumers are also transformed by the market, imitating what they consume, becoming something "they recognize as false" (Adorno 2002, 136).

In his important essay "The Work of Art in the Age of Mechanical Reproduction," Walter Benjamin (1968) suggested that technological innovation such as photography and film was changing the relation of audience to art. Although mass media—particularly film—can circulate fascist aesthetics by their power to mesmerize viewers, they also offer the possibility for the masses to participate in the production of revolutionary art. Following Benjamin, scholars in the Birmingham School insisted on the complexity of cultural production, rejecting the top-down model of ideological production and consumption proposed by Adorno and Horkheimer. While they continued to focus on the ways in which ideology circulates, they also illuminated practices of resistance and explored how consumers actively produced meaning as well.

Continental philosophy and critical theory traditions often ignored race, gender, and sexuality, and feminist scholars appropriated analytical strategies to examine how representations naturalized the meaning of "woman" and "other." They sought to discover whether women writers and artists produced alternative representations, whether there was a distinctive "*écriture feminine*" (women's writing; Cixous 1976) or a "feminist aesthetics," and if so, how it related to the complex material realities of diverse women's experiences, desires, and resistances across time and space.

"Women's Texts": Pleasure, Danger, and Reclamation

Many feminist scholars interested in representation have worked to reclaim the works of women writers and artists, pressing for their inclusion in the respective canons of their fields and interrogating the structures and forces that have kept women from being included in canons or valued in other contexts. In her influential essay "Why Have There Been No Great Women Artists?" Linda Nochlin ([1971]1988) argued that the infrastructure of art production produced a dearth of great women artists. Within the art world, men established the criteria for great art and positioned themselves as the judges of great works, consigning women artists to invisibility. Nochlin eschewed the idea that there is something that links women artists as women, and cautioned feminists not to make "excuses" or puff "mediocrity" in an effort to claim the value of women's works. Nochlin was particularly interested in preserving a conception of the aesthetically "good," which she tied to the use of innovative and accomplished techniques—techniques that required access to education and apprenticeships routinely denied to women. Drawing contrasts between women artists and women writers, Nochlin claimed that women were able to produce great literature because women writers were not inhibited by the same problems of infrastructure.

Feminist literary theorists were less sanguine about the treatment of women writers by the literary establishment. In their efforts to reclaim the works of women writers, some feminist literary critics turned to the popular "women's texts" that Nochlin cautioned against. Jane Tompkins, for example, championed the sentimental authors of the nineteenth century, who were excluded from the literary canon for many decades. Tompkins sought to "demonstrate the power and ambition of novels written by women," and to contest the erasures perpetuated when "popular" is deployed as a derogatory term. Tompkins noted that "the popularity of novels by women has been held against them almost as much as their preoccupation with 'trivial' feminine concerns":

> Because I think it is morally and politically objectionable, and intellectually obtuse, to have contempt for literary works that appeal to millions of people simply *because* they are popular, I chose to discuss three works of popular fiction in order to demonstrate the value of these texts: to explore the way that literature has power in the world, to see how it connects with the beliefs and attitudes of large masses of readers so as to impress or move them deeply.
>
> (Tompkins 1986, xiv)

Although feminist theorists have not been the only ones to claim the popular as a site of research, feminist scholars emphasize that the popular has been a place where women have had (slightly) more access as cultural producers, particularly in ghettoized areas of production. Although some feminist literary critics have investigated the aesthetics of women's popular works, others have analyzed what popular fiction reveals about identity, pleasure, and power. Some have investigated why women's writing seems to cause cultural anxiety.

Anxieties about women's consumption of "women's texts" are quite old. In the nineteenth century many preachers and writers railed against women reading novels, fearing that it eroded sound moral judgment. Defenders of public morals were concerned about men too, but they suggested that women were more vulnerable, particularly to representations of romance and sexuality. Critics wishing to uphold the patriarchal social order were particularly worried that "women's texts" encouraged women to break free of normative models prescribing appropriate work, social relations, and subordination for women. Feminist critics, on the other hand, have worried that women's texts reinforced these models. Many popular texts for women, from sentimental fiction and romance novels to soap operas, "woman's films," and "chick flicks" both challenge and reinscribe dominant norms.

When feminist studies of popular culture came of age in the 1980s, scholars approached women's consumption practices with sophistication, understanding them both as sites of indoctrination and as sites of resistance. In 1980, Ann Barr Snitow called romance novels "porn for women," utilizing nineteenth-century debates that never truly went away about the dangers of women's consumption of pulp fiction. In contrast, texts such as Ien Ang's *Watching Dallas* (1985) and Tania Modleski's *Loving with a Vengeance* (1984) took the political possibilities of consuming "women's texts" seriously. Janice Radway's *Reading the Romance* (1984) was perhaps the most groundbreaking of these works. In the 1970s, Harlequin Romances began producing a large number of paperback romances that were wildly successful. In 1972, Avon Books published Kathleen Woodiwiss's historical romance, *The Flame and the Flower*, giving birth to the "bodice-ripper"—historical fiction featuring women with heaving bosoms, and alpha men with chiseled chests who had a habit of raping the heroines before settling down for happily ever after. In *Reading the Romance*, Radway combined a history of the genre, an exploration of the conditions of production and circulation, ethnography with a community of fans, and a psychoanalytic interpretation of the ways that pleasure worked for readers. She argued that reading romance novels afforded women a way of negotiating patriarchy, creating space for their interpretations of the violent and abusive treatment the "heroes" bestowed on the heroines, and allowing women to carve out time for themselves in the midst of heavy demands on their time and attention. Radway's attentiveness to the conditions of production, consumption, and examination of texts in relation to their content and their reception provided a powerful model for other scholars, launching important methodological work on fan culture.

Much of the scholarship on fan culture explores the gendered nature of fandom, while some demonstrate the instability of heteronormative performance and desire. In her analysis of *Star Trek* fans and fan fiction, *NASA/Trek* (1997), for example, Constance Penley discovered that many heterosexual women were writing slash fiction (fan fiction depicting same sex romantic and sexual relationships), inventing romantic and sexual relationships between the leading male characters, Captains Kirk and Spock. Rather than reading these narratives as queer, however, Penley argued that these texts were heteronormative, suggesting that fan fiction afforded women an opportunity to recast these male characters in relationships governed by heterosexual dynamics. In *Textual Poachers* (2003), Henry Jenkins (1992) drew upon Michel de Certeau's *The Practice of Everyday Life* ([1980] 1984) to analyze fan fiction, suggesting that readers could best be understood as "travelers," who bring their own histories to every text they consume. Both Penley and Jenkins treated readers as theorists in their own right, who fashioned their interpretation of texts in relation to their own self-definition. For women in particular, reading practices created possibilities for creative resistance of hegemonic norms, culminating in their adoption of the role of artist/author, crafting fan fiction for consumption by other fans.

People have expressed concerns about the effects of popular culture in every medium. Every form of mass media has been regulated with an eye to content that could be bad for consumers. Concerns were especially pronounced with respect to matters of gender and sexuality. The Hays Code, adopted by the motion picture industry in 1930, provides an excellent example of cultural anxieties about representations of sexuality. Through the Hays Code, the motion picture industry policed itself, attempting to ban "licentious or suggestive nudity" or "sex perversion," among other things, for decades. The publication of Frederic Wertham's *Seduction of the Innocent* (1954) spurred the creation of the Comics Code. Although Wertham was primarily concerned with the violence in crime and horror comics, which he believed contributed to juvenile delinquency in young males, he was also troubled about sexual representation in comics. Indeed, he argued that Batman and Robin modeled a sexual relationship and that lesbian content and sexual bondage were the subtext in *Wonder Woman*. (Wertham was right about *Wonder Woman* in terms of subtext, if not about the danger: *Wonder Woman*'s creator publicly supported bondage and was in a polyamorous relationship with two women who contributed to the comic; Lepore 2014). Wertham's concerns about effects on masculinity would be echoed in later regulations over music, television, and video games. Anxieties over what happens when people consume texts and images would continue to be endlessly debated by scholars. Scholars of gender and race would particularly explore how identity can structure audience perception.

(Feminist) Ways of Seeing

Power relations govern interpretation, consumption, inclusion, and erasure; hence the issue of power has been at the center of studies of visual culture. John Berger's (1972) influential television series and subsequent book *Ways of Seeing* explained that the allegedly objective practice of seeing is shaped by our belief systems. Of particular use to feminist theorists was his argument that the "high art" tradition so prized by art historians as a manifestation of the progress of Western civilization structured perception in ways that objectified and sexually commodified women. Drawing comparisons between "the female nude" and pornographic images, Berger argued that consumption of "great" art trained viewers to adopt the "male gaze." Marita Sturken and Lisa Cartwright (2001) elaborated on Berger's account in their discussion of "practices of looking":

> Through looking we negotiate social relationships and meanings. Looking is a practice much like speaking, writing, or signing. Looking involves learning to interpret and, like other practices, looking involves relationships of power. To willfully look or not is to exercise choice and influence. To be made to look, to try to get someone else to look at you or at something you want to be noticed, or to engage in an exchange of looks, entails a play of power.
>
> (Sturken and Cartright 2001, 10)

Debates concerning the "gaze" or the "look" have been among the most influential and controversial in the study of representation.

In 1975, Laura Mulvey published "Visual Pleasure and Narrative Cinema," the most cited and reprinted essay in feminist film theory and one of the most cited essays in all of film studies, which also explored the idea of the male gaze explicated in Berger. Through psychoanalytic readings of the woman's presence in Hollywood film—using Hitchcock's *Vertigo* as a prime example—Mulvey argued that "in a world ordered by sexual imbalance, pleasure in looking has been split between active/male and passive/female. The determining male gaze projects its fantasy on to the female figure which is styled accordingly." For Mulvey, male pleasures are embedded in the camera work in classical Hollywood cinema. The camera structures how audiences perceive and identify. According to Mulvey, the "bearer of the look" is always male, and the film is structured so that viewers identify with the male gaze, as women are reduced to "spectacle." Hollywood films might feature handsome men, but in Mulvey's account they do not function as erotic objects. Like a number of other feminist theorists of representation who emerged in the 1970s, Mulvey was influenced by the psychoanalytic theories of Jacques Lacan, who brought structural linguistics and anthropology to Freudian psychoanalysis, and his discussion of a "mirror stage" in identification shaped her argument that viewers identify with these male protagonists as "the more perfect, more complete, more powerful ideal ego conceived in the original moment of recognition in front of the mirror" (1975, 11–12). Mulvey suggests that the camera positions women characters as sites of anxiety that must be controlled in the narrative space. Within Hollywood cinema, the narrative trajectory affords women only three options: to be demystified, to be punished or saved, or to function as reassuring fetish objects.

"Visual Pleasure and Narrative Cinema" generated intense debate, opening new vistas for the interpretation of representation and identification in film studies. Many scholars contested Mulvey's framework, arguing that identification is more complicated than Mulvey suggests. While Mulvey later revised her theory and argued that women might also take pleasure as masochists, many critics pointed out that Mulvey missed the possibility that filmgoers could develop identificatory attachments to characters other than the protagonist and to characters who differ significantly from them. Indeed, some scholars suggested that women, people of color, queer subjects, non-westerners (and those at the intersections of these groups) might have radically different practices of identification than the elite, white male whose perspective provided the ground for psychoanalytic theory. Moreover, the complexities of film structure—including the generic coherence of classic Hollywood cinema—allow for more varied practices of spectatorship than Mulvey suggested in her original groundbreaking essay.

Although many scholars have addressed specific deficiencies of Mulvey's account of spectatorship over the past four decades, her theorization of the gendered, structuring possibilities of the camera has remained influential, generating manifold examinations of practices of looking and modes of visual objectification. The concept of the "male gaze" continues to inform studies of visual culture that explore the ways in which normative male subject positions function as the ideal viewer.

Many ongoing conversations about the gaze challenge the subject/object split in identification, and related assumptions about stable identity categories and desires. Contesting Mulvey's claims about "scopophilia," which tie the gaze to notions of male pleasure rooted in the objectification of women, Gaylyn Studlar (1988) suggested an alternate interpretation of classic Hollywood films. Arguing that objectification is not always what produces pleasure in male subjects, Studlar traced masochism as an operative principle in Hollywood films, which feature men submitting to powerful women who possess what men lack. According to Studlar male viewers can experience great pleasure from these films. Mary Ann Doane (1982) also made major interventions in feminist film studies by focusing on female spectators, particularly in the context of the woman's film. Describing women's spectatorship as a "masquerade," Doane argues that women possess an ability to pretend they are the "Other," temporarily identifying with those who differ radically from themselves. Suggesting that men also have this flexibility in identification, Carol Clover (1992) investigated identification in slasher films. She argued that the structure of horror narratives encourages men to identify with the "final girl," the heroine who survives at the end to stalk the monster. Indeed, Clover demonstrated that the slasher film—often understood as one of the most misogynist genres with its predilection for the stalking and murder of scantily clad young women—has an investment in gender bending, and can thus interpellate audiences in a variety of ways.

One of the contentious questions surrounding issues of identification is what triggers it. Is identification evoked by sameness, difference, an ideal, or a fantasy? Does identification require, as Anne Friedberg (1990) argued, "recognition," and if so, must recognition involve "an implicit confirmation of the ideology of the status quo?" Jackie Stacey (1987) addressed the question of whether viewers find pleasure in sameness or difference in her discussion of a lesbian spectator. In her analysis of a number of films, Stacey sought to disrupt the association of gender identification with heterosexuality, arguing that these film narratives "tempt the woman spectator with the fictional fulfillment of becoming an ideal feminine other, while denying complete transformation by insisting upon differences between women" (1987, 61). Stacey's analysis asks whether a lesbian subject must identify consistently with some variation of a "woman" or "man" or whether she could engage in shifting practices of identification.

Taking issue with approaches that presuppose a white viewer, black feminist scholars bell hooks (1992) and Jacqueline Bobo (1995) have suggested that black female film spectators can derive pleasure from representations not made for them. They claimed that African American women viewers use their own cultural frameworks to interpret negative representations, developing oppositional viewing practices. The conceptualization of oppositional viewing practices has been particularly generative for more recent work in queer, feminist, and postcolonial film studies.

These oppositional interpretive practices are rooted in a long history of black spectators' understanding of how their own status as "objects of the gaze" affects the roles they inhabit socially and politically. As W. E. B. Du Bois noted in *The Souls of Black Folk*, "this sense of always looking at one's self through the eyes of others" ([1903] 1994, 2) was not merely an individualized psychological burden; this otherness conferred by the gaze affected the status of African Americans as citizens. Within colonial contexts and drawing from psychoanalysis and existentialism, Frantz Fanon (1967) explored how colonized people were objects negotiating their relationship to other objects, constantly struggling with being dehumanized and fetishized under the colonial gaze.

But not only racialized others are victimized by the western gaze. Michel Foucault (2010) has argued that prevailing knowledge-power constellations entrench "regimes of truth," which affirm representations that perpetually reinscribe identity categories defined by these power relations. For example, mainstream discourses that imbue white, straight, middle-class men with authority construct women, people of color, the disabled, and the queer as inferior or deviant, and sometimes as threats to the prevailing order. Scholars from Du Bois to Foucault have shown that the hegemonic gaze is not only produced and circulated through mass media; wherever texts exist, from medical records to public policy, damaging objectification can occur.

Feminist scholars have also explored how stereotypes about gender and sexuality circulate in law, policy, and popular culture with devastating effects. In fact, public-policy discourse and popular representations can be mutually constitutive. For example, public-policy documents like the Moynihan Report (1965) perpetuated a narrative of an emasculating "black matriarch," and attributed black poverty to the pathology of the black family, as opposed to structural inequality. This representation had a relationship to the stereotypes of the loud and emasculating Sapphire in US popular culture. In 1976, Ronald Reagan evoked an omnipresent "welfare queen" who abused public assistance, and this fictive bogeywoman informed what Ange Marie-Hancock (2004) has termed the "politics of disgust" and the punitive welfare reform legislation in 1996 that abolished entitlements to social benefits regardless of need. Drawing upon the work of postcolonial scholar Edward Said, Lila Abu-Lughod has demonstrated how "Orientalist" discourses shape and sustain homogenizing representations of Middle Eastern women as uneducated and oppressed by the burqa. These distorted and distorting representations were used as pro-war propaganda to legitimate the US invasion of Afghanistan and the "war on terror" (Abu-Lughod 2002; Cloud 2004). Long-standing representations of gender prescribe sex-appropriate dress for children, naturalizing a prohibition against boys wearing dresses that did not always exist and that imposes unique harms on transgender children (Paoletti 2012). In the case of a disabled body, Rosemarie Garland-Thompson has noted that the objectifying look that makes women a spectacle transforms into a "stare . . . framing her body as an icon of deviance" (1997, 26).

Theorizing representation in popular and visual culture is thus not only about media such as film and television—although they are essential to circulating meanings. Because visuality permeates contemporary life and textual representation is ubiquitous, representational analysis affords tools that foster critical resistance. Although the concept of "the male gaze" is problematic, and feminist scholars have cautioned against making generalizations about the identity and desires of the one who looks, attention to and analysis of the circulation of the gaze is warranted. In hierarchical social systems, the "look" has power and subordinated people experience the historical and cultural weight of looks. For this reason, feminist scholars continue to examine the mechanisms through which looking and being looked at occur. Theorists who are concerned with the power of media in contemporary life investigate the complex means by which hegemonic ideology is reproduced and the spaces in which consumers of culture resist its force and envision alternative possibilities.

REPRESENTATION AND INJURY: THE CASE OF PORNOGRAPHY

Few genres have solidified the idea of a male gaze more than pornography, a contentious topic in the history of feminist theory. The "porn wars" of the late 1970s and the 1980s are closely associated with the work of Andrea Dworkin (1989) and feminist legal scholar Catharine MacKinnon, who argued that pornography harmed women. In *Only*

Words, MacKinnon (1996) focused on the material conditions of pornography production, suggesting that impoverished women were often coerced into sex work by economic exigencies, and that low-income women were forced into sex work by abusive male partners. Beyond multiple forms of physical coercion in the production of porn, MacKinnon argued that textual and visual pornographic representations are performative. Pornography not only capitalizes on women's abjection, it produces it. According to MacKinnon, "social inequality is substantially created and enforced—that is, done—through words and images. Social hierarchy cannot and does not exist without being embodied in meanings and expressed in communications" (MacKinnon 1996, 13). Drawing parallels with "Whites Only" signs under Jim Crow laws, MacKinnon argued that pornography is not only an idea or representation, it causes behavior:

> With pornography, men masturbate to women being exposed, humiliated, violated, degraded, mutilated dismembered, bound, gagged, tortured, and killed. In the visual materials, they experience this *being done* by watching it *being done*. What is real here is not that the materials are pictures, but that they are part of a sex act.
> (MacKinnon 1996, 17)

Although she acknowledges that pornography does not cause all violence against women, MacKinnon sees it as a pivotal act in a system of domination.

MacKinnon's argument raises an important question about causality. Her claim that "sooner or later" pornography consumers will attempt to dominate women (1996, 19) will strike many readers as demonstrably false. She connects pornography to a wide-ranging set of examples of gender and sexual domination: teachers may treat women students unequally, male doctors may molest anesthetized women or enjoy watching and inflicting pain on women in childbirth, and men may write nasty things about women on bathroom walls. But many men and women consume pornography without causing harm to others, which provides empirical grounds to challenge MacKinnon's generalization.

In contrast to anti-porn feminists, who frame pornography as injurious to women, pro-porn or "pro-sex" feminists argue that pornography can provide an outlet for producing varied, complex, resistant narratives about sexuality. As the editors of *The Big Feminist Porn Book* suggest,

> "[F]eminist" porn uses sexually explicit imagery to contest and complicate dominant representations of gender, sexuality, race, ethnicity, class, ability, age, body type, and other identity markers. It explores concepts of desire, agency, power, beauty, and pleasure at their most confounding and difficult, including pleasure with and across inequality, in the face of injustice, and against the limits of gender hierarchy and both heteronormativity and homonormativity. It seeks to unsettle conventional definitions of sex, and expand the language of sex as an erotic activity, an expression of identity, a power exchange, a cultural commodity, and even a new politics.
> (Taorimo et al. 2013, 9–10)

For these theorists, pornography can "do" things too: it can be a progressive political force—when it is properly "feminist." Other theorists of sexuality have pressed the argument further to claim that representations of sex can be pleasurable even when they do not have "good" politics. A woman may have sexual fantasies of being dominated, or a man may have fantasies of dominating women, without those fantasies bleeding over into their interpersonal or professional relationships.

Yet this research assumes that men are the exclusive audience for porn. Gay porn, lesbian porn, sado-masochistic porn, and the general fetishistic taxonomy of pornography attract varieties of spectators, demonstrating the genre's potential to push back against normative models of sexuality. As Linda Williams has suggested, there is a reason that lesbians initially spearheaded the feminist fight against MacKinnon: a genre in which "women's bodies are the object of knowledge" manifests complex and conflicted negotiations with knowledge/pleasure (1999, ix).

At the same time, pornography, like other forms of popular culture, is a powerful tool for circulating idealized representations of the body, representations that women (and perhaps to some extent, gay men) feel pressure to replicate in their lives (Duggan and McCreary 2004). Pubic hair waxing, procedures such as labioplasty, and products for women of color to bleach their vaginas in the early twenty-first century have largely been attributed to an increased circulation of pornographic images, which construct new models of what an ideal vagina should look like. Advertising has also perpetuated narrow ideals of beauty and Hollywood has circulated a wide variety of stereotypes about women. In short, pornography does not escape the work of ideology.

Representation, Reality, and Agency

The relation between representation and reality is another contentious question that surfaces in the porn debates and in many other contexts in feminist studies of visual and popular culture. Although some analysts claim that textual and visual representations "reflect" reality, capture the "truth" about social relations, or achieve verisimilitude, others suggest that this is far too simple a view. On the one hand, cultural productions are a product of the moment in which they are produced, and it is important to situate a representation historically, culturally, and geopolitically. On the other hand, the content of a representation may be far removed from what people experience as "reality;" representations can also be a site of fantasy. Stuart Hall may have described the relation of representation to fantasy best in his discussion of the popular:

> [P]opular culture, commodified and stereotyped as it often is, is not at all, as we sometimes think of it, the arena where we find who we really are, the truth of our experience. It is an arena that is profoundly mythic. It is a theater of popular desires, a theater of popular fantasies. It is where we discover and play with the identifications

of ourselves, where we are imagined, where we are represented, not only to the audiences out there who do not get the message, but to ourselves for the first time.

(Hall 1993, 113)

Although some cultural producers attempt to capture something they describe as "real"—consider *cinema verité* as an example—representations can exceed the intentions of their creators, serving as sites of anxieties, hopes, and profound disconnection from people's everyday experiences. Theorists of race and imperialism have often argued, for example, that the many representations that circulate about whiteness, blackness, the "third world," or the "Oriental," are projections and fantasies about identity. At the same time, audiences may become attached to a representation—no matter how stereotypical—because the performer's talent speaks to them in some way. Recognition, like identification, is complicated.

Most theorists of representation describe cultural productions as historically situated, and they seek to explicate what the text "does"—what narrative it tells—in cultural context. Recent scholarship explores how textual and visual representations speak to varied experiences even when they do not transparently *reflect* experience. Representations can be sites of aspiration, but the models they present may not suggest progressive or emancipatory political possibilities. Quite often, representations present ideals or fantasies that are impossible or cruel stereotypes; and consumers can have various responses to these images. For this reason, it is difficult, if not impossible, to prove a precise relation between representation and reality. When a teenage girl watches films depicting glamorous, underweight women and develops an eating disorder, or when a young, suburban white male's only knowledge of black people comes from pernicious media stereotypes and he discriminates against African Americans, it is not possible to declare the representations the cause of their perceptions. Many people consume these same depictions, but do not develop eating disorders or discriminatory behavior. Representations matter, but their effects are varied and diffuse.

It is not only difficult to ascertain the agency and resistance practiced by consumers of texts, it is also often challenging to discern the agency of cultural producers. Following theorists such as Roland Barthes (1977) and Michel Foucault (1984) who problematized the idea of "intent" and the "author function" in interpretation, scholars recognize that searching for a secret, singular meaning ignores the ways in which cultural productions are the products of discourse. In addition, all cultural producers are constrained by conditions of production. In mass media, editors, directors, performers, producers, and other specialists shape the final product. In research concerned with addressing the politics of a performer, feminist scholars often struggle to discern how much of a voice the performer had in the final product. These performances are also constrained by market considerations.

Some performances often aim at representing something that speaks to the lived experiences of some audience members, but that very quest for authenticity may produce a "stock character," or worse, the production team may invoke a "generic formula" designed to manipulate the audience, commodify an identity, or control aspects of resistance. Public performances are strategic, and market considerations often are central to those strategies. It is not a simple matter to sort out what an actor seeks to achieve in a performance, how that relates to the author or the director's intent, much less, how the performance will be received by the public. The existing archive of interviews, and when available, private correspondence can provide clues to the intentions underlying a performance, but these clues cannot resolve a host of questions about the relation between representation and reality.

Nonetheless, artists, critics, and consumers often gesture to the "authentic" and the "real" in assessing a performance and in judging its effects on audiences. The gesture toward the real can be recognizable to audiences, who typically contrast a realistic representation with more idealized, fantastic, and stereotypical representations. But, as Stuart Hall has noted, the "real" may be a fantasy that expresses desire. Audiences may "see" something "real" and recognizable even as they know the performance has been produced under a number of constraints. The history of African American performance provides a powerful example. In *Love and Theft*, Eric Lott (1993) demonstrates how minstrel culture in the nineteenth century United States came to be perceived as an "authentic" representation of black masculinity. As a consequence, black performers would have to perform these caricatures to be hired. Despite the racism embedded in these characterizations, some African American audiences might come to see hints of "racial sincerity" in these performances, to borrow a phrase from anthropologist John Jackson (2005). From the legendary African American stage performer Bert Williams, to Blaxploitation films in the 1970s, to representations of the "gangsta" and "strong black women" in late twentieth-century US culture, a number of scholars who study black performance have described a consistent use of stereotypes and complex identity politics in the entertainment marketplace. Even as these representations may reinforce pathological, heteronormative, and reductive narratives of black men and women, scholars have also argued that many of these performers have addressed African American experiences, fantasies, and wounds, despite constraints placed by market demands.

The constraints of industry and audience expectations are particularly acute where actresses and music performers are concerned. Although writers must contend with genre expectations and publishing infrastructure, these pale in comparison to the constraints associated with the Hollywood "starlet" and the pop music star performer who must grapple with demands for youth, beauty, sexuality, and spectacle. Quite apart from individual talent, performers must craft a public persona shaped by the marketplace they enter. What the audience sees is the product of collective enterprise. For example, in *Gender Politics and MTV: Voicing the Difference*, communications scholar Lisa A. Lewis examined how popular women performers in the 1980s negotiated the constraints on women's musicianship. Although the performers demonstrated "increasing sophistication about issues of representation and self-presentation" over time, their efforts to craft public personae as artists and authors were powerfully shaped by both industry and audience expectations (1990, 78). These pop music stars are illustrative of a major bone of contention in feminist studies of representation, namely the question of whether or not we can discern progressive political possibilities in sexual representations in popular culture.

Feminist and Post-Feminist Approaches: Challenging Hegemonic Norms

Few topics encapsulate the interpretive challenges of representation more than depictions of sexuality. Both within and beyond feminist studies the meanings of sexual representation are diffuse and contradictory. Many third wave feminists, for example, have circulated a common narrative that depicts second wave feminists as "anti-sex." Representing themselves as a new generation that came of age in the 1990s, third wave feminists suggest that only they have succeeded in representing women's sexuality as self-affirming and free from the taint of the male gaze. This narrative ignores straight and lesbian women's work in the 1970s that explicitly explored sexuality, as well as popular cultural productions like the feminist comics *It Ain't Me Babe* and *Women's Comix*, which represented women enjoying sex, challenging conventional notions of women's sexuality. Although third-wave feminist theorists often describe themselves as rescuing feminism from prudish second wavers, their caricature of second-wave feminists' representations of women's sexuality is not supported by the historical record.

That said, there has been an increased emphasis on the study of media representation of women since the 1990s and a concomitant concern about the power of women to represent themselves as sexual subjects. Within this literature, feminist and queer theorists have focused on sexual performance as a means to challenge hegemonic norms and to manifest feminist agency.

The sexual performances of pop stars and film actresses have provided an important site for the analysis of representations of women's sexuality that challenge gender stereotypes. In her treatise on the "feminist pin-up" throughout US history, Mary Ann Buszek (2006) has shown that even nineteenth-century female performers produced carefully constructed nude pictures of themselves to challenge narratives about women in the public sphere. Contesting interpretations of Asian American women as demeaned sexualized objects in popular culture, Celine Parrenas Shimizu (2007) has advanced an alternative account of "productive perversity" in their performances. Investigating representations of black women in pornography, Mireille Miller-Young (2014) has argued that black women can be "self-fashioning" sexual subjects in the porn industry, and she has suggested that it is time to move beyond the politics of respectability that position representations of black women's sexuality as inescapably injurious. Examining how girls and women play with gender and sexuality in cyberspace, new media scholars have remained attentive to negative representations, but have also advanced analyses that explore the progressive possibilities of gender bending and self expression online. Many third- and fourth-wave feminist scholars of representation focus on the potential of "sex positive" representations to challenge hegemony.

Some feminist scholars take a less sanguine view. Susan J. Douglas, for example, has characterized much of the popular performance of sexuality in the 1990s and early twenty-first century as "enlightened sexism"—a kind of "post"-feminist representation of women that covers its sexism with "fantasies of power":

> Enlightened sexism is feminist in its outward appearance (of course you can be or do anything you want) but sexist in its intent . . . [It] takes the gains of the women's movement as a given, and then uses them as permission to resurrect retrograde images of girls and women as sex objects, bimbos, and hootchie mamas still defined by their appearance and their biological destiny.
>
> (Douglas 2010, 10)

For Douglas, pop stars who are scantily clad and singing about girl power demonstrate little real attentiveness to political issues. Sexual exhibition is the beginning and end of their activism. In television shows and films that feature powerful women who can dominate men physically and mentally, sexy attire and delicate white female performativity combined with power may provide pleasure for all kinds of gazes, but it also depicts their attractiveness as being part of that power. The stars of such shows are certainly not 200-pound women body builders wearing comfortable shoes.

The question of whether or not a particular text is "feminist" raises complex issues, but Douglas's critique provides an important framework for thinking about the criteria used in making such judgments. There are many different feminisms, which makes a litmus test impossible. Any single criterion will fail to recognize the variety of feminist viewpoints. In the era often described as "post-feminist," struggles for legal, social, economic, and political equality are sometimes displaced by a celebration of individual choice. As Angela McRobbie has noted, in the allegedly "post-feminist" era, people draw "on a vocabulary that includes words like 'empowerment' and 'choice,'" and "these elements are then converted into a much more individualistic discourse" than previous discourses of feminist activism (2008, 1). Within a "choice" frame, feminism is compatible with any desires and endeavors freely chosen by a woman. If a woman chooses to dress in a man's suit and tie, it can be considered feminist because this attire queers gender performance and resists cultural mandates about femininity. Plastic surgery to sculpt a body to look more like Barbie can be feminist, if it satisfies a woman's desire to realize her ideal form of embodiment. Submissiveness can be a feminist stance as an articulation of free will and self-discipline. Destabilizing gender norms, body modification as performance art, submission as a means to explore sexual pleasure, and consensual BDSM (bondage/domination/sadism/masochism) as a manifestation of trust within sexual play have all been proclaimed feminist acts in the context of popular culture. On the other hand, donning a suit and tie to make fun of trans men, refashioning one's body to conform to a Barbie aesthetic on the grounds that women should look like that, and performing submissiveness as a way to model appropriate womanly behavior would be decidedly non-feminist acts.

The distinction between feminist and nonfeminist acts in these instances seems to turn on individual intention. Yet, intent alone cannot determine the meaning of an act. As poststructuralist theorists have emphasized, the creator of a text cannot entirely control its meaning. Once in circulation, texts "do" things and have meanings well beyond the conscious intentions of their authors. Individuals routinely say that they do not intend a representation to be racist, sexist, or homophobic, but their intentions are not dispositive. Others may experience the representation as racist, sexist, or homophobic because it circulates in a culturally freighted realm of representation whose oppressive legacies cannot be expunged by an author's or artist's intention. Within a particular sociocultural milieu that bears the traces of centuries of racial and sexual practices, a text will have meaning and will circulate those meanings quite independent of the creator's wishes.

Douglas's critique of enlightened sexism raises another difficult issue. Under what conditions can sexualized representation move into the terrain of emancipatory politics? When paired with claims to "girl power" or feminism can sexualized images escape regulatory sexual discourses that have operated to control women's appearance and behavior? With a hint of feminist politics—the mere reference to equality—can sexual representation achieve a revolutionary stance? When some proclaim a work to be feminist and others dispute that claim, are they "policing" the borders of feminism? Or is there room to debate the substance of claims concerning the advancement of women's equality and the cultivation of women's agency in relation to specific "feminist" projects? Scholars in the field of feminist visual and popular culture have struggled with these questions, albeit not always explicitly. The question is not whether a particular cultural production is political—no cultural production exists outside of politics. The question concerns the criteria for revolutionary or progressive representation—an enormously difficult topic for feminist theorists, as for other critical theorists. Desire to transcend the confines of hegemonic ideology may be pronounced, but accomplishing that objective often remains elusive. Cultural studies theorists suggest that popular texts constantly negotiate the push-pull between reinforcing ideology and manifesting resistance.

Angela McRobbie, the most influential feminist theorist of the Birmingham School, has illuminated the dialectic between ideology and resistance in popular culture over the course of her career. In her pioneering essay, "Rock and Sexuality," coauthored with Simon Frith, McRobbie acknowledges the possibility of rock as a liberatory site for sexual expression, but also argues that sexism in rock music is so systemic that there is little freedom for women in the structure of the industry or in practices of consumption (1978). Exploring the possibilities for agency for girls and women in popular culture, McRobbie called attention to youth subcultures, addressing the invisibility of girls in studies of youth subculture, highlighting the misogyny in boys' cultures of "resistance," and demonstrating that girls negotiated their spaces within youth cultures differently than boys. Developing an analytical framework that focused on class and capitalism, while also attending to the intersections of gender, class, and racism, McRobbie investigated the production and consumption of teen magazines. Noting the important role these texts played in the lives of consumers, McRobbie traced the emotional pull of "romantic individualism," an ideology that both affirmed girls' individuality and encouraged girls to relinquish that individuality when "in love." Manifesting a staunch commitment to heteronormativity, teen magazines like *Jackie* privileged the heterosexual couple and rejected female community as an empowering site for girls. Despite these reinscriptions of hegemonic culture, McRobbie cautioned against the view that girls would "swallow its axioms without question" (2000, 114). In recognizing the power of ideology but acknowledging spaces for negotiation and thoughtful consumption practices, McRobbie advanced a cultural studies model that sought to trace both the circulation of ideology and the mobilization of resistance.

Representation in New Media

No medium has offered the utopian possibilities of resistance as much as new media. The Internet has enabled an exponential increase in the production and circulation of visual and textual representation. Although the "digital divide" of class and geopolitical region affects who has access to producing and consuming content, the Internet has been a powerful place for contention production untethered to corporations and building global communities. The concept of "new media" has been loosely defined as a blending of computer and media technologies. In combining media with the new possibilities of interaction, storage, access, and production, media becomes "new" (Manovich 2001).

For feminists, cyberspace offered new possibilities for theorizing the body and for proliferating the ways women could represent themselves in a public sphere. The possibilities of gender play and a disembodied self seemed to offer utopian possibilities for cyber-representation. Hailed as a realm of "disembodied pleasure" (Plant 1998), cyberspace offered opportunities to escape from gender and racial hierarchies and heteronormativity. But new technologies have also enabled the proliferation of traditional gender representation in Internet pornography, video games, and social media. Thus cyberspace is also a space of contradiction, offering means to transcend embodiment, while also heightening mechanisms of surveillance and shoring up normative and pathologizing representations of women. The "new" information and communication technologies did not change the conditions under which meanings of gender and race are produced. Nevertheless, social media does provide new opportunities for female authorship in blogging, life journals, social networking, YouTube, and other outlets, which allow audiences access to subjectivities that address experiences and desires in new ways. The fourth wave of feminists in the twenty-first century see themselves as mobilizing politics through new media, embracing "hashtag" activism on twitter, and other forms of commentary and protest that give a broad range of people access to production, consumption, and connections with others.

The Internet also offers the opportunity for people to circumvent corporations or persuade corporations to come to them. For example, the most famous fan fiction in history is an online serial novel called *Master of the Universe* by E. L. James. Inspired by the best-selling teen-vampire romance series *Twilight* (Meyer 2005), James resituated the main characters, placing them in a BDSM relationship. She later changed the characters' names and published the series as the *Fifty Shades* trilogy, which sold millions of copies worldwide, and was quickly optioned by Hollywood for a series of movies (2012). Despite this impressive popular success, there has been widespread criticism of the writing quality in these texts, which suggests that the *Fifty Shades* series would not have been published by a traditional publisher if James had not gained a following online.

Fifty Shades provides one of the most prominent examples of new media's transformative effects on the conditions of production, opening new spaces for women and empowering them to control production and circulate atypical representations in the marketplace. Yet this series idealizes abusive "heroes" and submissive women just as some of the earlier romance novels did, suggesting that a woman controlling content does not necessarily lead to emancipatory or revolutionary representations. Although one of the primary concerns of feminist theorists of visual and popular culture has been to expose and analyze power and resources necessary to produce and circulate representations, they have consistently acknowledged that a female producer will not necessarily produce a feminist text. And yet more opportunities for women to engage in cultural production do increase the odds that more varied representations of women will emerge.

The complex interdisciplinary field of media, visual, and popular culture is compelling for feminist scholars because it addresses the interplay of ideology, desire, inequality, and pleasure—long omitted from serious consideration in traditional disciplines. Some critics have charged that feminist interpretations of visual and textual representation fall into two traps: "over-reading" and overstating the revolutionary possibilities of feminist texts. The "over-reading" accusation suggests that some texts are "just" popular or easily interpreted, or that feminist analyses read "too much" into texts. However, every cultural production can and should be situated in the time and context in which it is produced, and neither high culture nor popular culture is empty of signification or untouched by discourse. Feminist analyses of visual and textual representations—including those that are popular—often capture important dimensions of people's everyday experiences in complex social worlds.

Despite claims that the study of representation holds little importance given what happens in the "real" world, the terrain of representation is very much about real things—what we see and long for, what we give into and resist. Much of the early history of gender and representation examined dichotomous constructions of women (e.g., virgin/whore) and normative models of masculinity and femininity. A good deal of recent cultural production by and for women has sought to redress that misogynous history, providing alternatives to the representations of women in classic and contemporary works. The desires expressed within women's cultural production are often not "feminist" and fall far short of revolutionary art, but this realm of representation often illustrates complex battles over agency and power that are at the heart of feminist struggles to redress inequality.

REFERENCES

Abu-Lughod, Lila. 2002. "Do Muslim Women Really Need Saving? Anthropological Reflections on Cultural Relativism and Its Others." *American Anthropologist* 104 (3): 783–790.
Ang, Ien. 1985. *Watching Dallas: Soap Opera and the Melodramatic Imagination*. London; New York: Methuen.
Barthes, Roland. 1977. *Image, Music, Text*. Translated by Stephen Heath. New York: Hill and Wang.
Benjamin, Walter. 1968. *Illuminations*. Translated by Harry Zohn. New York: Harcourt Brace, and World.
Berger, John. 1972. *Ways of Seeing*. New York: Penguin.
Bobo, Jacqueline. 1995. *Black Women as Cultural Readers*. New York: Columbia University Press.
Buszek, Maria Elena. 2006. *Pin-up Grrrls: Feminism, Sexuality, Popular culture*. Durham NC: Duke University Press.
Certeau, Michel de. (1980) 1984. *The Practice of Everyday Life*. Berkeley: University of California Press.
Cixous, Helene. 1976. "The Laugh of the Medusa." Translated by Keith Cohen and Paula Cohen. *Signs* 1 (4): 875–893.
Cloud, Dana. 2004. "'To Veil the Threat of Terror': Afghan Women and the 'Clash of Civilizations' in the Imagery of the U.S. War on Terrorism." *Quarterly Journal of Speech* 90 (3): 285–306.
Clover, Carol. 1992. *Men, Women, and Chainsaws: Gender in the Modern Horror Film*. Princeton, NJ: Princeton University Press.
Derrida, Jacques. 1976. *Of Grammatology*. Translated by Gayatri Chakravorty Spivak. Baltimore, MD: Johns Hopkins University Press.
Doane, Mary Ann. 1982. "Film and the Masquerade: Theorising the Female Spectator." *Screen* 23 (3–4): 74–88.
Douglas, Susan J. 2010. *Enlightened Sexism: The Seductive Message That Feminism's Work Is Done*. New York: Times Books.
Du Bois, W. E. B. (1903) 1994. *The Souls of Black Folk*. New York: Dover.
Duggan, Scott J., and Donald R. McCreary. 2004. "Body Image, Eating Disorders, and the Drive for Muscularity in Gay and Heterosexual Men: The Influence of Media Images." *Journal of Homosexuality* 47 (3–4): 45–58.
Dworkin, Andrea. (1981) 1989. *Pornography: Men Possessing Women*. New York: Dutton.
Fanon, Frantz. 1967. *Black Skin, White Masks*. New York: Grove Press.
Foucault, Michel. (1969) 2010. *The Archaeology of Knowledge and the Discourse on Language*. Translated by R. Swyer. New York: Vintage Books.
Foucault. Michel. 1984. The Foucault Reader. Edited by Paul Rabinow. New York: Pantheon.
Friedberg, Anne. 1990. "A Denial of Difference: Theories of Cinematic Identification." In *Psychoanalysis and Cinema*, edited by E. Ann Kaplan. New York: Routledge.
Frith, Simon, and McRobbie, Angela. 1978. "Rock and Sexuality." *Screen Education* 29 (3–19).

Garland Thompson, Rosemarie. 1997. *Extraordinary Bodies: Figuring Physical Disability in American Culture and Literature*. New York: Columbia University Press.

Hall, Stuart. 1993. "What Is This 'Black' in Black Popular Culture?" *Social Justice* 20 (1–2): 104–114.

Hancock, Ange-Marie. 2004. *The Politics of Disgust: The Public Identity of the Welfare Queen*. New York: New York University Press.

Hegel, G.W.F. 1807/1967. *The Phenomenology of Mind*. Trans. J.B. Baillie. New York: Harper Colophon Books.

hooks, bell. 1992. *Black Looks: Race and Representation*. Boston, MA: South End Press.

Horkheimer, Max, and Theodor W. Adorno. (1944) 2002. *Dialectic of Enlightenment: Philosophical Fragments*. Translated by Edmund Jephcott. Redwood City, CA: Stanford University Press.

Jackson, John. 2005. *Real Black: Adventures in Racial Sincerity*. Chicago: University of Chicago Press.

James, Erika Leonard. 2012. *Fifty Shades of Grey*. New York: Random House.

Jenkins, Henry. 1992. *Textual Poachers: Television Fans and Participatory Culture*. New York: Routledge.

Lepore, Jill. 2014. *The Secret History of Wonder Woman*. New York: Alfred A. Knopf.

Lewis, Lisa A. 1990. *Gender Politics and MTV: Voicing the Difference*. Philadelphia, PA: Temple University Press.

Lott, Eric. 1993. *Love and Theft: Blackface Minstrelsy and the American Working Class*. New York: Oxford University Press.

MacKinnon, Catharine A. 1996. *Only Words*. Cambridge, MA: Harvard University Press.

Manovich, Lev. 2001. *The Language of New Media*. Cambridge, MA: MIT Press.

Marx, Karl, and Friedrich Engels. (1846) 1970. *The German Ideology*. New York: International Publishers.

McRobbie, Angela. 2000. *Feminism and Youth Culture: From Jackie to Just Seventeen*. New York: Routledge.

McRobbie, Angela. 2008. *The Aftermath of Feminism: Gender, Culture, and Social Change*. London: Sage Publications.

Meyer, Stephenie. 2005. *Twilight*. New York: Little, Brown and Company.

Miller-Young, Mireille. 2014. *A Taste for Brown Sugar: Black Women in Pornography*. Durham: Duke University Press.

Modleski, Tania. 1984) *Loving with a Vengeance*. New York: Methuen.

Mulvey, Laura. 1975. "Visual Pleasure ad Narrative Cinema." *Screen* 16 (3): 6–18.

Nochlin, Linda. (1971) 1988. *Women, Art, and Power: and Other Essays*. New York: Harper and Row.

Paoletti, Jo B. 2012. *Pink and Blue: Telling the Boys from the Girls in America*. Bloomington: Indiana University Press.

Penley, Constance. 1997. *NASA/Trek: Popular Science and Sex in America*. London and New York: Verso.

Plant, Sadie. 1998. "Coming across the Future." In *Virtual Futures: Cyberotics, Technology, and Posthuman Pragmatism*, edited by Joan Dixon Broadhurst and Eric J. Cassidy, 30–36. London: Routledge.

Radway, Janice. 1984. *Reading the Romance*. Chapel Hill: University of North Carolina Press.

Saussure, Ferdinand de. 1966. *Course in General Linguistics*. Translated by W. Baskin. New York: McGraw-Hill.

Shimizu, Celine Parreñas. 2007. *The Hypersexuality of Race: Performing Asian/American Women on Screen and Scene*. Durham, NC: Duke University Press.

Snitow, Ann. (1980) "Soft-Porn Culture: Punishing the Liberated Woman." *New Republic* 183 (9): 25–29.

Stacey, Jackie. 1987. "Desperately Seeking Difference." *Screen* 28 (1): 48–61.

Studlar, Gaylyn. 1988. *In the Realm of Pleasure: Von Sternberg, Dietrich, and the Masochistic Aesthetic*. Urbana: University of Illinois Press.

Sturken, Marita, and Lisa Cartwright. 2001. *Practices of Looking: An Introduction to Visual Culture*. New York; Oxford: Oxford University Press.

Taorimo, Tristan, Celine Parrena Shimzu, Constance Penley, and Mireille Miller-Young. 2013. *The Big Feminist Porn Book: The Politics of Producing Pleasure*. New York: Feminist Press.

Tompkins, Jane. 1986. *Sensational Designs: The Cultural Work of American Fiction, 1790–1860*. New York: Oxford University Press.

Wertham, Fredric. 1954. *Seduction of the Innocent*. New York: Rinehart and Co.

Williams, Linda. 1999. *Hard Core: Power, Pleasure, and the "Frenzy of the Visible."* Berkeley: University of California Press.

Woodiwiss, Kathleen E. 1972. *The Flame and the Flower*. New York: Avon Books.

CHAPTER 33

POSTHUMAN FEMINIST THEORY

ROSI BRAIDOTTI

Introduction

It is commonly accepted that European feminism, in its liberal as well as socialist variations, is connected to humanist values and ideals. Since the Enlightenment, the activist energy and egalitarian aspirations of women's movements have shaped multiple reforms in society, which also affected law, morals, academic knowledge, and scientific production in order to reflect more adequately the experience and concerns of women. The political passions and innovative epistemologies of feminist movements, however, were never indexed solely on the interests of women, but rather contained explicit blueprints for the improvement of the human condition as a whole. In so doing, women's movements renewed the shared understanding of the basic unit of reference for our common humanity. This made them humanist at an almost visceral level, positing women's liberation as human liberation.

That intrinsic connection to humanism, however, was never without critical distance (Soper 1986). Especially since the second feminist wave of the 1970s, feminist interdisciplinary knowledge production took to task the universalism, the binary structure of thought, and the teleological vision of progress that are built into the humanist project of human emancipation. Over the last thirty years in particular, under the influence of poststructuralism and deconstruction, an anti-humanist wave has redefined the relationship between feminism and humanism.

The argument I want to defend here is that both the humanist legacy and the anti-humanist reaction are very important genealogical sources for posthuman feminism, but by no means the only ones. The posthuman turn is triggered by the convergence of feminist anti-humanism, on the one hand, and anti-anthropocentrism, on the other. Both these strands enjoy strong support in feminism, but they refer to different genealogies and traditions. Anti-humanism focuses on the critique of the humanist ideal of

"Man" as the universal representative of the human, while anti-anthropocentrism criticizes species hierarchy and advances ecological justice. The term *posthuman feminist theory* marks the emergence of a new type of discourse that is not merely a culmination of these two strands of thought, but is also a qualitative leap in a new and more complex direction. This shift of perspective also moves feminist debates away from the explicit anti-humanism supported by poststructuralist theories since the 1980s and inaugurates an array of different posthumanist perspectives circulating in the current era. In other words, the genealogical timelines of the posthuman are neither linear nor sequential.

In this chapter, I will first illustrate feminist attempts to emancipate feminism from classical humanism; then I will explore the multiple roots of posthuman feminism, and in conclusion, I will outline the key features of posthuman feminist theory today.

Feminism Is Not (Only) a Humanism

Even before the emergence of the posthuman, the second feminist wave entered a series of radical negotiations with the legacy of humanism, which had provided its historical grounding. This means that the contemporary outburst of scholarship on the posthuman is by no means the first or the most original critique of humanism available in critical theory. This movement rather needs to acknowledge the pioneering efforts accomplished by feminist theory and to give it credit for developing concepts and methods that have encouraged critical distance from humanism.

For instance, in her watershed 1983 text, Alison Jaggar produced one of the very first taxonomies of feminist philosophy: *Feminist Politics and Human Nature*. She introduced a classification of the main schools of feminist thought: socialist, Marxist, liberal, and radical and explored their respective redefinitions of what and who counts as human. Although the actual term *humanism* does not occur very often in that canonical work, the idea of overcoming received notions of the human is built into Jaggar's political and theoretical program.

The monumental work of Simone de Beauvoir (1973), which was first published in English in 1953, had already positioned feminist humanism as a secular tool of critical analysis, the source of moral responsibility and the motor of political freedom. Influenced by, but moving beyond a Marxist philosophy of history and liberation, Beauvoir remained a rationalist at heart. She never questioned the validity of universal reason but rather upheld humanistic universalism—in a socialist frame—and used its conceptual tools to critique the treatment of the depreciated "others," starting from the second sex but ultimately addressing humanity as a whole. This generous humanistic universalism, combined with Beauvoir's finer phenomenological analyses of women's lived experience, based on social constructivist premises, laid the grounds for feminist political ontology in the twentieth century. The key ideas are the feminist humanist principle that "woman is the measure of all things" and the notion that to account for herself, the feminist philosopher needs to take into account the situation of *all* women.

A female humanity thus emerges, endowed with universal valence. This produces theoretically a nondialectical vision of self-other relations and politically a bond of solidarity among women, which the second feminist wave in the 1960s turned into the principle of political sisterhood.

Allegiance to socialist humanism was also a feature of anticolonial thinkers, postcolonial theory, and race theory in the first half of the twentieth century. It played a significant role in national liberation movements throughout the world, notably in Africa and Asia, as testified by Andre Malraux's (1934) seminal text *Man's Fate (La Condition Humaine)* and, more recently, by Nelson Mandela's (1994) life and work. A fairly consistent non-European school of liberatory humanism emerges from Toussaint Louverture (2011, first published in 1794–1798), Franz Fanon (1967), Aimé Césaire (1955) in the previous century, and in the work of Edward Said (2004), Paul Gilroy (2000), Vandana Shiva (1988), and others today. I shall return to them later.

In my critical assessment, the achievement of humanist feminism was twofold: it invented a new genre of both academic and public writing, and it introduced fundamental new concepts. Crucial among the latter is a new brand of materialism, of the embodied and embedded kind (Braidotti 1991, 2013). Focus on embodied female subjects establishes the premises for new and more accurate analyses of power. Being-women-in-the-world is the starting point for all critical reflection on the status of humanity and for a jointly articulated political praxis (Harding 1986; Haraway 1988). These are based on the radical critique of masculinist universalism and are dependent on an activist and equality-minded brand of feminist Humanism.

As for the new genre, the motif that women's liberation is also human liberation produces a mixture of critique and creativity, negative criticism and utopian imagination. Joan Kelly (1979) labeled it "the double-edged vision of feminist theory," which infuses oppositional consciousness with empowering creativity, combining reason with the imagination. This highly imaginative tradition of thinking also fueled the production of a new literary genre: feminist science-fiction, which, as I will argue later on, set a different genealogical line for posthuman feminism.

The immediate result of this new alliance between critical reason and the creative imagination was a change of paradigm, which resulted in a proliferation of new feminist scholarship. By the end of the 1980s, the epistemologist Sandra Harding (1991) and the philosophers Genevieve Lloyd (1984) and Jean Grimshaw (1986) were in a position to adopt more specific and original categories of thought to do justice to the theoretical creativity of the new feminist movement (Eisenstein 1983). References to human nature and the human were replaced with original feminist concepts that reflected the multifaceted specificities of the female condition in all its diversity but kept a firm focus on women's lived experience. The clearest expression of this focus is "standpoint feminist theory" (Harding 1986), which stresses women's embodiment, experience, and the collective nature of feminist knowledge production. Standpoint theory not only covers a broader range of feminist positions on difference by privileging the diversity of lived experiences by marginal subjects, but also intersects productively with postcolonial and anti-racist thought (Harding 1993; Collins 1991; Alcoff and Porter 1993).

By 1998, Alison Jaggar and Iris Young had so much original feminist material at hand that they could edit a full-fledged companion to feminist philosophy, covering every major school and tradition of philosophical thought, all monotheistic and a few other religions, and the different theoretical constituencies within feminism itself. This shift and expansion of theoretical and methodological perspective took barely a decade, and it left a great deal of humanist aspirations behind, prioritizing instead the concept of radical difference and the diversity of women's experience.

But this narrative cannot be linear, as I noted at the outset. In the midst of these developments, singular dissonant texts stand out on their own, disrupting new master narratives and sowing the seeds of unprogrammed futures. One of these is without doubt Shulamith Firestone's 1970s masterpiece *The Dialectic of Sex*, the first feminist techno-utopia of the twentieth century.[1] Like all thinkers of her generation, including Beauvoir herself (to whom, incidentally, Firestone's book is dedicated), Firestone rests on a Marxist view of revolution built on a Hegelian philosophy of history. Contrary to the humanist feminists, however, she consistently pushes the program for women's liberation to its logical Marxist conclusion—namely, the making of a new humanity that will be technologically enhanced and freed from natural needs. First and foremost among the natural chains that need to be broken is the duty to procreate biblically and women's sole social responsibility for the rearing of children. Firestone actively calls for reproductive technologies to intervene as the factor that could break up the nuclear bourgeois family and liberate women and men for better and more productive aims—namely, the building of a socialist system and a new shared sense of what it means to be humans in a classless, sex-egalitarian, and anti-racist society. Covering the issue of racism as well as sexism, Firestone also engages with ecology and environmentalism, arguing for the need of a radically different approach to our natural and built habitat. In this regard Firestone combines the two defining features of posthuman thought that I indicated at the start of the chapter: the feminist critique of humanism, on the one hand, and a postanthropocentric approach to ecology and animal rights, on the other.

The stunning originality of this almost prophetic vision is, moreover, expressed in a style that combines incisive analytical insights with soaring flights of the imagination, establishing the feminist genre I mentioned earlier. Shulamith Firestone stands alone, in some ways contextually bound, and in others, way ahead of her time, in foreseeing what technology was about to become in our world. It would take almost thirty years for this posthumanist, pro-technology but also radical ecological message to be heard. In this respect Firestone counts single-handedly as one of the initiators of posthuman feminist thought.

Feminist Anti-Humanism

Anti-humanism is linked to humanism by rejection. As a movement of thought, it developed throughout the 1980s thanks to the new social movements and the youth cultures of the day: feminism, decolonization and anti-racism, antinuclear and environmental movements. In the context of the Cold War, they challenged both the unfulfilled promises of Western democracies, notably, their claim to respect universal human rights, and the utopias of the Marxist tradition. Edward Said pointed out (2004) that in the United States anti-humanism grew out of revulsion for and resistance to the Vietnam War.

Anti-humanism constitutes the core of the feminist critiques of "Man" as the alleged "measure of all things," for being androcentric, exclusionary, hierarchical, and Eurocentric. Feminists differed, however, on what strategies to adopt in order to deal with the checkered legacy of European humanism. The radical wing resolutely rejected humanism, while other critical feminists (Benhabib and Cornell 1987) charged that the West did not live up to this ideal and produced a highly selective and exclusionary version of humanism, which needed to and could be corrected.

Two notions have driven anti-humanism forward since the 1980s: the rejection of universalism and the critique of hierarchical binary thinking. Faith in the unique, self-regulating, and intrinsically moral powers of human reason is the core of the humanistic creed, which asserts European superiority as a standard for both individuals and their cultures, while upholding the exceptionalism of the human species. Anti-humanists maintain that, its pretense to universality notwithstanding, humanism historically developed into a hegemonic civilizational model, which shaped the idea of Europe as coinciding with the universalizing powers of self-reflexive reason. In addition, they argue that the alleged universalism of the Eurocentric paradigm of "Man" rests on entrenched dualisms. It implies the dialectics of self and other, and a binary logic of identity and otherness that distributes differences along a scale of asymmetrical power relations. This reduces the notion of "difference" to pejoration: it spells inferiority and social and symbolic disqualification for those who get branded as "others." They are the human and nonhuman referents of negative difference: the sexualized, racialized, and naturalized others, which is to say women and LGBT; blacks, postcolonial and non-Europeans; but also animals, plants, and earth others—who are reduced, both socially and symbolically—to the less than human status of disposable bodies.

The dominant norm of the subject—the former "Man" of classical Humanism—was positioned at the pinnacle of a hierarchical scale that rewarded the ideal of zero-degree of difference.[2] This norm is used to justify the deployment of rational epistemic and social violence that marks "others," whose social and symbolic existence is unprotected. This makes Eurocentrism into more than just a contingent matter of attitude: it is a structural element of our cultural practice, which is also embedded in both theory and institutional and pedagogical practices (Braidotti 2013).

The lessons of race and postcolonial theories (Brah 1996; Hall 1996; Harding 1993; hooks 1990; Ware 1992; Crenshaw 1995; Spivak 1999; and Young 2004) are of the greatest importance to add political inflection as well as higher degrees of complexity to this philosophical understanding of difference. Because the history of these "others" in Europe and elsewhere has been one of lethal exclusions and fatal disqualifications, these "others" raise crucial issues of power, domination, and exclusion.

On this point the intersections between feminism and race or postcolonial theory are intense and mutually enriching, though not without tensions. Crucial to both political movements is the recognition of the historical limitations of the emancipatory programs that were postulated on the humanist principle of human progress through the deployment of universal and social and scientific practices. We shall see later, however, how race and postcolonial theorists hold onto some aspects of humanism as an unfulfilled project relocate it outside the Western tradition, and develop its subversive and anti-racist potential. This neo-humanist tradition is in dialogue but also in disagreement with the posthuman turn.

Poststructuralist Feminism

The "death of Man," announced by Foucault (1970) formalized an epistemological and moral crisis that went beyond binary oppositions, cutting across different poles of the political spectrum. Poststructuralist theorists called for insubordination from received humanist ideals. They targeted the humanistic arrogance of continuing to place Man at the center of world history and, more specifically, the implicit assumption that what is "human" about humanity is connected to a sovereign ideal of "reason" as Enlightenment-based rationality and science-driven progress. Even Marxism, under the cover of a master theory of historical materialism, continued to define the subject of European thought as unitary and hegemonic and to assign him (the gender is no coincidence) a royal place as the motor of human history.

Poststructuralist feminism is a precursor of posthuman theory in that it proposes a radical form of anti-humanist thought. Feminists such as Luce Irigaray (1985a, 1985b) pointed out that the allegedly abstract ideal of Man as a symbol of classical Humanity is very much a male of the species: it is a he. Moreover, he is white, European, handsome, and able-bodied. Feminist critiques of patriarchal posturing through abstract masculinity (Hartsock 1987) and triumphant whiteness (hooks 1981; Ware 1992) argued that this Humanist universalism is objectionable not only on epistemological but also on ethical and political grounds (Lloyd 1984, 1996). Feminist phenomenologists reject universalism (Young 2004; Sobchack 2004) by emphasizing the carnal nature of thought and hence its embedded and embodied structure (Braidotti 2011a, 2011b).

Anticolonial thinkers adopted a similar but distinct critical stance by questioning the primacy of whiteness in the humanist ideal as the moral, intellectual, and aesthetic canon of perfection. Regrounding such lofty claims in the history of colonialism, anti-racist and postcolonial thinkers explicitly questioned the relevance of the Humanistic ideal in view of the obvious contradictions imposed by its Eurocentric assumptions, but at the same time, they did not entirely cast it aside. In an immanent critique of humanism, they held Europeans accountable for the uses and abuses of this ideal by looking at colonial history and the violent domination of other cultures, but still upheld its basic premises. Frantz Fanon, for instance, wanted to rescue humanism from its European perpetuators, arguing that we have betrayed and misused the humanist ideal. As Sartre astutely put it in his preface to Fanon's *Wretched of the Earth* (1963), the future of humanism lies outside the

Western world, bypassing the limitations of Eurocentrism. The "bellicose dismissiveness" of other cultures and civilizations is exposed, following Edward Said, as "self-puffery, not humanism and certainly not enlightened criticism" (2004, 27). As Paul Gilroy (2000) noted, the reduction to subhuman status of nonWestern others was a constitutive source of ignorance, falsity and bad faith for the dominant subject who is responsible for the epistemic as well as social dehumanization of the "others" they produced. By extension, the claim to universality by scientific rationality was challenged on both epistemological and political grounds (Spivak 1999), all knowledge claims were recognized as expressions of Western culture and of its drive to mastery. This position results in a critical form of neo-humanism that refers to non-Western sources and tends to strike a skeptical note in relation to posthuman theory, though it often intersects with it.

Feminist philosophies of sexual difference (Irigaray [1984] 1993; Cixous 1997) embraced the concept of difference with the explicit aim of making it function differently.[3] Reading through the spectrum of the critique of dominant masculinity, they also stressed the ethnocentric nature of European claims to universalism. They advocated the need to open up to the "others within" (Kristeva 1991) in such a way as to relocate diversity and multiple belongings to a central position as a structural component of European subjectivity (Braidotti 1991). They recast political subjectivity along a more complex line of interrogation that includes class, race, sexual orientation, and age, targeting the main tenets of equality-minded feminism. Irigaray's provocative question, "equal to whom?" (1994), could be taken as the war cry for the following generation that refused to take equality as homologation or reduction to a masculine standard of Sameness.

As a consequence, poststructuralist feminist philosophers were anti-humanist in that they critiqued from within all the unitary identities predicated upon phallologocentric, Eurocentric, white supremacist and standardized views of what constitutes the humanist ideal of "Man." They also argued, however, that it is impossible to speak in one unified voice about women, indigenous peoples, and other marginal subjects (Johnson 1998). The emphasis falls instead on issues of diversity and differences among them and on the internal fractures of each category.

This militant anti-humanism intersects productively with postcolonial and critical race perspectives, which hold humanism accountable for its racist connotations and racialized bias. They reject the universalist pretense of white supremacy (hooks 1990), and propose instead non-Western forms of radical neohumanism (Shiva 1997; Collins 1991; Narayan 1989) that allow us to look at the "human" from a more inclusive and diverse angle: new recompositions of humanity after humanism. This does not however necessarily make them posthuman in the postanthropocentric sense of the term.

Planet Haraway

But again, this narrative cannot be linear. Disruptive voices challenged and complicated emerging paradigms. The most prominent in the 1980s was Donna Haraway's *Primate*

Visions (1990), followed by her path-breaking "Manifesto for Cyborgs," (1985) the first feminist postanthropocentric social theory text of the twentieth century. Haraway is a non-nostalgic posthuman thinker: her conceptual universe is the high-technology world of informatics and telecommunications and a postanthropocentric universe of companion species (2003). First and foremost among 's insights is that contemporary technologies (1997) are enacting a qualitative shift in our understanding of how the human is constituted in its interaction with nonhuman others, which opens up postanthropocentric premises in feminist theory.

Haraway (2006) moves beyond the legacy of both humanism and feminist antihumanism and sets a new agenda. She builds on the poststructuralist critique of binary oppositions and challenges specifically the long-standing association of female with nature (Ortner 1974), introducing instead a nature-culture continuum. Although she does not rely on a linguistic frame of reference and thus does not engage in deconstructive methods, she makes the unique move of initiating a crossover dialogue between science and technology studies, socialist feminist politics, and feminist neomaterialism through the figure of the cyborg. A hybrid, or body-machine, the cyborg is a connection-making entity, a figure of interrelationality, receptivity, and global communication that deliberately blurs categorical distinctions (human/machine, nature/culture, male/female, Oedipal/non-Oedipal). The cyborg exemplifies how Haraway combines competence in contemporary biosciences and information technologies with a firm program of social justice and critique of capitalist abuses.

As Haraway's representation of a generic feminist humanity, the cyborg answers the question of how feminists reconcile the radical historical specificity of their embodied experience with the insistence on constructing new values that can benefit humanity as a whole. The cyborg is both a postanthropocentric and postmetaphysical construct that offers a new political ontology, taking into account technological mediation while staying focused on the project of constructing an ecologically accountable, feminist, classless, sex-egalitarian, and anti-racist society. The stunning originality of Haraway's vision, combining analytical insights with striking images and formulations, added a glorious new page to the feminist techno-utopia genre. As such, Haraway too counts as one of the singular initiators of posthuman feminist thought.

The Postanthropocentric Turn

By the late 1990s, it begins to be possible to speak of the posthuman turn in feminist theory as a strand of work that pays increasing attention to postanthropocentric perspectives. A feminist consensus is reached about the seemingly simple notion that there is no "originary humanicity" (Kirby 2011, 233). This turn occurred in response to political developments, including growing public awareness of the climate-change issue; the accompanying notion that we have entered a new geologic era (the Anthropocene), where human activities are having world-changing effects on the earth's ecosystem; and the limitations of economic globalization (Grewal and Kaplan 1994). The postanthropocentric is situated at the intersection of different and at times disconnected strands of feminist thought.

The main strand involved the theoretical fallout from the poststructuralist antihumanist generation. The key notion of embodiment gets reworked on the basis of neomaterialist understandings of the body, drawn from the neo-Spinozist philosophy of Gilles Deleuze and Félix Guattari. Embracing their version of vital bodily materialism, while rejecting the dialectical idea of negative difference, this theoretical approach changes the frame of reference. It differs from the more linguistically oriented branch of poststructuralism that relies on semiotics, psychoanalysis, and deconstruction to undo gender (Butler 2004). A more complex vision of the subject is introduced in a materialist process ontology that foregrounds an open, relational self-other entity framed by embodiment, sexuality, affectivity, empathy, and desire as core qualities. Social constructivist binary oppositions were replaced by a nature-culture continuum that, following but also moving beyond Foucault (1977), envisaged power as both a restrictive (*potestas*) and productive (*potentia*) force.

The shift to a monistic ontology resulted in overcoming the classical opposition "materialism/idealism" and moving toward a dynamic brand of materialist vitalism and "vibrant matter" (Bennett 2010). Deleuzian feminists built on monistic philosophy to spell out a "vital politics," premised on the idea that matter, including the specific slice of matter that is human embodiment, is intelligent and self-organizing and not dialectically opposed to culture, nor to technological mediation, but rather continuous with them (Braidotti 1994; Grosz 1994; Colebrook 2000, 2004; MacCormack 2008). They explored the potential of contemporary vital thought, arguing for feminist reappraisals of contemporary technoscientific culture in a nonreductive frame. The switch to vital material definitions of "matter" as a self-organizing force stresses processes, vital politics, and nondeterministic evolutionary theories (Grosz 2011).

This approach helps us update the feminist politics of location in terms of radical immanence, with special emphasis on the embedded and embodied, affective and relational structure of subjectivity (Braidotti 2006, 2013). By extension, it helps redefine old binary oppositions, such as nature/culture and human/nonhuman, paving the way for a nonhierarchical and hence more egalitarian relationship to the species. The emphasis on rational and transcendental consciousness—one of the pillars of humanism and the key to its implicit anthropocentrism—is replaced by process ontology. This shift also supports a collaborative vision of the evolution of species that rests on the displacement of anthropocentrism.

A younger generation of scholars generated a wave of materialist scholarship on the body as a dynamic process of embodied interactions that emphasize the relational nature of the subject. Their explorations of embodied materialism led to a serious reconsideration of what counts as "matter" for materialist feminist thought, which produced many interrelated strands of posthuman feminist theory. "Matter-realist" feminists (Fraser, Kember, and Lury 2006) developed alongside neomaterialist feminism (Braidotti 1991; Dolphijn and Tuin 2012; Alaimo and Hekman 2008; Coole and Frost 2010; Kirby 2011).

This neomaterialist line of thought also developed transversal nomadic subjectivity (Braidotti 1991, 1994) as well explicit discourses about the nonhuman in terms of the animal and the earth (Grosz 2004) but also technological others (Haraway 1985), and thus furthered the nonanthropocentric strand of feminist thought. Thus, feminist philosophy in this period opens up a number of perspectives, which I consider to be the stepping stones to feminist posthumanism.

A second genealogical strand emerges from the convergence of feminist science studies with cultural studies and media theory. Feminist epistemology and science studies had always been strong (Haraway 1990; Stengers 1997) and by the turn of the millennium, joined forces with cultural studies (McNeil 2007) to assess the impact of new technologies on social relations of power (Terranova 2004), focusing specifically on the effects of the fast-growing field of reproductive technologies on women (Braidotti 1994; Rapp 2000). These sociocultural analyses of science and technology gathered momentum as priority research areas, producing a discursive boom in feminist theory of political subjectivity (Bryld and Lykke 1999; Smelik and Lykke 2008; Parisi 2004; Colebrook 2014a, 2014b; Alaimo 2010; Hird and Roberts 2011). At the same time, comparative literature ceased to be the main forum for these debates, as Spivak (2003) lucidly noted.

New media and global cultural studies, under the impact of the ethical turn (Zylinska 2009; MacCormack 2012), provided related genealogical sources. As the Birmingham school of cultural studies mutated into a new generation of British scholars, Marxist humanism was slowly replaced by more complex materialist approaches that registered the transformations induced by contemporary science and technology. The understanding of "Life" as a symbiotic system of codependence and coproduction (Margulis and Sagan 1995) also alters the terms of human interaction with what used to be called "matter," which now needs to be approached as a self-organizing vital system. Insofar as advanced capitalism has grasped this logic of exploitation of living matter (Rose 2007), as well as the high degrees of mediation humans are caught in today, it has become capable of unprecedented forms of the manipulation of life. This has important implications for feminist science studies, which converge with media and cultural studies to produce sharper analyses of the political economy of globalized capital. For instance, Franklin, Lury and Stacey (2000) and Smelik and Lykke (2008), in response to these fast-changing circumstances, map out the new convergence between science and media, producing a wave of scholarship that contributes to a de facto displacement of the centrality of the human, through studies of molecular biology (Fox-Keller 2002; Franklin 2007) and computational systems (Lury, Parisi, and Terranova 2012). These studies are marked by a new methodology that replaces the critiques of representation, which were canonical in feminist cultural studies throughout the 1990s, with a more materialist orientation, approaching technology as a social and scientific practice as well as a cultural phenomenon (McNeil 2007; Stacey 2010; Ferrando 2013).

Ecofeminists (Plumwood 1993, 2003) had already pioneered geo-centered perspectives (Mies and Shiva 1993), and now this perspective takes off across a broader interdisciplinary field. Animal studies begins from the mid-1990s to be a serious topic, questioning the metaphorical use and abuse of animals in literature and culture, as well as their ruthless economic and physical exploitation (Midgley 1996). Ecofeminists also draw a structural analogy between the exploitation of human females and that of other species, calling for a transspecies process of liberation from capitalist male aggression. Vegetarian and animal rights activists (Adams 1990; Donovan and Adams 1996, 2007) evolve into radical vegan activism (MacCormack 2014), while a more liberal feminist line develops in support for the human rights of animals and other living species (Nussbaum 2006).

Parallel to these developments, feminist scholars' interest in Darwin, which had been scarce (Beer 1983), starts to grow proportionally by the end of the millennium (Rose and Rose 2000; Carroll 2004; Grosz 2011). Again, multiple strands of research develop like variations on a posthuman theme. For instance, new studies of primatology (de Waal 1996, 2009) stressed the gendered nature of social virtues, such as solidarity and empathy, emphasizing the positive role of females in evolutionary history.

Explicit references to the posthuman condition begin to circulate in feminist texts from the 1990s on (Braidotti 1994; Balsamo 1996; Hayles 1999; Halberstam and Livingston 1995). The advantages of this change of perspective for a theory of feminist subjectivity become evident with the advent of what has become known as the "ontological" or "onto-epistemological" turn, which allows the inclusion of nonhuman agents in the constitution of subjects of knowledge and politics. Exemplary of this development is the work of Barad (2003, 2007), who coins the term "agential realism" to signify this enlarged and, in my terms, postanthropocentric vision of subjectivity.

The "affective turn" emerges in a series of feminist critical variations, firstly in conjunction with Derridian deconstruction (Wolfe 2003, 2010; Kirby 2011) and then within phenomenology (Ahmed 2006) and psychoanalysis (Clough 2007), but also with neo-Spinozist and Deleuzian monism (Lloyd 1994; Gatens and Lloyd 1999; Braidotti 2002; Massumi 2002; Protevi 2009; Grosz 2011). These perspectives converge on the notion that it is now both possible and desirable to expand the relational capacity of humans to all other species, in a planetary embrace that allows feminists theorists to address global issues like climate change, while pursuing the struggle for equality and social justice. The politics of the affective turn is debated as a crucial issue and special emphasis is placed on the specific materiality of race and ethnicity within feminist neomaterialism (Ahmed 2004; Hemmings 2011). The next and somehow obvious step in this discursive expansion is "Anthropocene feminism" (Grusin forthcoming) that becomes more prominent as posthumanism comes into its own.

What these new developments make possible is sustained reflection on the human-nonhuman continuum not only at the theoretical and methodological levels, but also institutionally. Coinciding with the reorganization of universities along neoliberal economic lines (Braidotti 2013), the question of what vision of the human is implicit in the academic practice of the humanities results in the formation of new transdisciplinary alliances between, for instance, ecofeminism and social history. These perspectives displace the traditional institutional location of gender and women's studies in the humanities and social science faculties, reopening the issue of the relationship between the "two cultures" within feminism itself. The immediate consequence of the formulation of these new posthumanistic and postanthropocentric perspectives is a renewal of meta-methodological studies on inter- and transdisciplinarity itself as the preferred hybrid feminist approach (Buikema, Lykke, and Griffin 2011; King 2011, 2012; Birke, Bryld, and Lykke 2004; Asberg and Lykke 2010).

Postanthropocentric feminist theory is on firm ground in contesting the arrogance of anthropocentrism and the "exceptionalism" of the Human as a transcendental category, but it also has to confront some crucial issues, notably human agency in ethical and political terms and the specificity of human language. This shift of perspective involves in fact both methodological and political consequences. Methodologically, posthuman feminist theory abandons the social constructivist approach and the deconstructive political strategies of poststructuralism and embraces monism and vitalist ontologies (Ansell Pearson 1999). Postmodernist theory, while still relying to a certain extent on a social constructivist method, did acknowledge the importance of nonhuman or inhuman factors (Lyotard 1989) in the constitution of subjectivity, as evidenced by psychoanalytic accounts of the unconscious. It seldom questioned, however, the centrality of anthropomorphic subjects in processes of subjectivation that involve negotiations with social and symbolic systems.

Politically, postanthropocentrism produces a different scheme of militant engagement and a nondialectical politics of human liberation. It assumes that political agency need not be critical in the negative sense of oppositional and that, in the pursuit of countersubjectivities, it may rely on process ontologies. The emphasis on the politics of autopoiesis, the coproduction of self-organizing systems and collective self-styling, involves complex and continuous negotiations with dominant norms and values and, hence, also multiple forms of accountability (Braidotti 2006). I have argued for an activist embrace of *zoe*: nonhuman life as a way forward. Becoming-earth (geocentered) or becoming-imperceptible (*zoe*-centered) approaches are more radical breaks with established patterns of thought resting on the pejorative naturalization of differences. They introduce a radically imminent planetary dimension that defines difference positively as a virtual and vital resource (Bonta and Protevi 2004; Grosz 2011).

Disloyalty to our species, moreover, is no easy matter. The real difficulty in releasing our bond to Anthropos and developing critical postanthropocentric forms of identification is affective. How one reacts to taking distance from our species depends to a large extent on the terms of one's engagement with it, as well as one's assessment of and relationship to contemporary technological developments. In my work I have always stressed the technophilic dimension (Braidotti 2002) and the liberating and even transgressive potential of these technologies, in contrast to those who attempt to index them to either a predictable conservative profile, or to a profit-oriented system that fosters and inflates hyperconsumeristic possessive individualism (Macpherson 1962). But loyalty to one's species has some deeper and more complex affective roots, which cannot be shaken off at will. It involves an anthropological exodus that is especially difficult emotionally, and it can entail a sense of loss and pain. This effort however cannot be dissociated from an ethics and politics of inquiry that demands respect for the complexities of the real-life world we are living in.

The Posthuman Condition
and Feminist Politics

These theoretical shifts do not occur in a vacuum, but rather resonate with fast-changing conditions in advanced capitalism. Foremost among them are the high degrees of technological mediation that shake up established mental habits, as Donna Haraway put it, the machines are so alive, whereas the humans are so inert! (Haraway 1985).

The displacement of the centrality of human agency through massive interventions of network systems and increasingly intrusive technologies is one of the factors that make capitalism into a postanthropocentric force. It also accounts for its inhumane aspects (Agamben 1998) and structural injustices, including increasing indebtedness (Deleuze and Guattari 1977). The "global obscenities" (Eisenstein 1998) of an economic system that relies on "bio-piracy" (Shiva 1997) also engenders a "necro-political" governmentality (Mbembe 2003) through technologically mediated wars and counterterrorism.

As I have argued elsewhere (Braidotti 2002, 2006), advanced capitalism is a spinning machine that actively produces differences for the sake of commodification and consumption. It is a multiplier of deterritorialized differences and a producer of quantitative options. Global consumption knows no borders and a highly controlled flow of consumer goods, information bytes, data, and capital constitutes the core of the perverse mobility of this system (Braidotti 2002, 2006). Capitalism poses as a nomadic force, while it controls the space-time of mobility in highly selective ways.

The contemporary global economy has a technoscientific structure, built on the convergence between previously differentiated branches of technology, notably, nanotechnology, biotechnology, information technology, and cognitive science. This aspect involves research and intervention upon animals, seeds, cells, and plants, as well as humans. In substance, advanced capitalism both invests and profits from the scientific and economic control and the commodification of all that lives. This context produces a paradoxical and rather opportunistic form of postanthropocentrism on the part of market forces, which happily trade on Life itself. Life, as it happens, is not the exclusive prerogative of humans.

The opportunistic political economy of biogenetic capitalism induces, if not the actual erasure, at least the blurring of the distinction between the human and other species, when it comes to profiting from them. Seeds, plants, animals, and bacteria fit into this logic of insatiable consumption alongside various specimens of humanity. The uniqueness of Anthropos is intrinsically and explicitly displaced by this equation.

But the complexity is even greater, as I argued before. What constitutes capital value today is the informational power of living matter itself, transposed into data banks of biogenetic, neural, and mediatic information about individuals, as the success of Facebook demonstrates at a more banal level. These practices reduce bodies to their informational substrate in terms of energy resources, or vital capacities, and thereby levels out other categorical differences. The focus is on the accumulation of information itself, its immanent vital qualities and self-organizing capacity. "Data mining" includes profiling practices that identify different types or characteristics and highlights them as specific strategic targets for capital investments, or as risk categories. The capitalization of living matter produces a new political economy, which Melinda Cooper (2008) calls, "Life as surplus." It introduces discursive and material political techniques of population control of a very different order from the administration of demographics, which preoccupied Foucault's work on biopolitical governmentality (1997). Today, we are undertaking "risk analyses" not only of entire social and national systems but also of whole sections of the population in the world risk society (Beck 1999). Informational data is the true capital today, supplementing but not eliminating classical power relations (Livingston and Puar 2011).

The theoretical insight is clear: living "matter" is a process ontology that interacts in complex ways with social, psychic and natural environments, producing multiple ecologies of belonging (Guattari 2000). A change of paradigm about the human is needed to come to terms with these new insights. Human subjectivity in this complex field of forces has to be redefined as an expanded relational self, engendered by the cumulative effect of all these factors (Braidotti 1991, 2011a). The relational capacity of the post-anthropocentric subject is not confined within our species, but it includes all nonanthropomorphic elements: the nonhuman, vital force of Life, which is what I have coded as *zoe*.[4] It is the transversal force that cuts across and reconnects previously segregated species, categories and domains. *Zoe*-centered egalitarianism is, for me, the core of the postanthropocentric feminist turn: it is a materialist, secular, grounded, and unsentimental response to the opportunistic transspecies commodification of Life that is the logic of advanced capitalism, which Haraway (2014) recently labeled: "capitalocene."

Queer science studies, in response to these contemporary challenges, propose a radical transversal alliance between humans and other species. This is the case for instance of Alaimo (2010), who theorizes transcorporeal porous boundaries between human and nonhuman bodies, while Hayward calls for "humanimal relations" (Hayward 2011), that is to say, transcorporal connections between humans and nonhumans, and for "transspeciated selves" (Hayward 2008). This approach makes the most of monistic ontology and argues for absolute species equality, in a very radical form of postanthropocentric thought that gives renewed energy and relevance to the ecofeminist agenda.

In the midst of such conceptual and methodological fervor, the specific genre pioneered by feminist theory—the mixture of theoretical sophistication with literary imagination—not only persisted but actually gained strength. A significant alliance between queer theorists and the science-fiction horror genre constitutes a fast-growing posthuman feminist strand. Since the 1970s, feminist writers and literary theorists of science fiction (Kristeva 1980; Barr 1987, 1993; Haraway 1992; Creed 1993) had supported the alliance between women, as the others of Man, and such other "others" as non-whites (postcolonial, black, Jewish, indigenous, and hybrid subjects) and nonhumans (animals, insects, plants, tress, viruses, and bacteria). This "Gothic" tradition of feminist theory, which generated some staggeringly original work, has a distinct posthumanist but also postanthropocentric slant, as evidenced by the ease with which it proposes relational bonds between different species and across classes of living entities. It also expresses passionate resistance to Oedipal power relations, celebrating what I have labeled "the society of undutiful daughters" (Braidotti 2012), who betray the patriarchal social contract and prefer to run with wolves (Pinkola Estès 1992).

Queer theorists, ever alert to the opportunity of exiting the Oedipalized sexual binary system, have equated the posthuman with post-gender and proposed an explicit alliance between extraterrestrial monsters and freaks, social aliens, and queer political subjects (Halberstam 1995, 2012). Queering the nonhuman is now in full swing, in a series of variations that include rethinking sexual diversity based on animal and other organic systems (Giffney and Hird 2008). An array of alternative sexualities and multiple gender systems have been proposed, but also degrees of sexual indeterminacy or indifferentiation, often modeled on the morphology and sexual systems of nonhuman species, including insects (Grosz 1995; Braidotti 1994, 2002). Post-gender sexualities have also been postulated in a radical form of postanthropocentric reflection on the extinction of the current form of human embodiment (Colebrook 2014b).

Ever mindful of the fact that the "human" is not a neutral term but rather one that indexes access to privileges and entitlements, postcolonial feminist theorists have made a strong intervention in this debate. They warn that feminists cannot mindlessly embrace the equation between the "posthuman" and post-gender without taking into account serious power differentials (Livingston and Puar 2010). New assemblages or transversal alliances need to be negotiated carefully and not taken for granted. Another significant development in this area is the recasting of disability studies in the affirmative mode of proposing "otherwise enabled" bodies that defy the expected standards of normality not merely in terms of gender normativity (Braidotti and Roets 2012).

The emphasis on living matter—including embodied human flesh—as intelligent and self-organizing offers another level of transversal theoretical alliances. By foregrounding the radical immanence of embodiment and embeddedness, posthuman feminism is in a position to strike an alliance also with extended mind theories (Clarke 1997, 2008), with distributed cognition models inspired by Spinoza via Deleuze (Deleuze and Guattari 1987; Damasio 2003) and with special emphasis on distributed affectivity (Wilson 2011). It can also strike productive dialogues with qualitative neuro-philosophies of perception and cognition (Stafford 2007; Churchland 2011), redefining sexual difference in relation to the plasticity of the brain (Malabou 2011).

The crucial question however remains: What can be the feminist political stand in relation to the productive paradoxes engendered by the posthuman condition? To what extent does the convergence of the posthumanistic and postanthropocentric perspectives complicate the issues of human agency and feminist political subjectivity? My argument is that it actually enhances it by offering an expanded relational vision of the self, and it recasts a posthuman theory of the subject as an empirical project that aims at experimenting with what contemporary, biotechnologically mediated bodies are capable of doing. Mindful of the structural injustices and massive power differentials at work in the globalized world, I rely on the feminist method of the politics of locations as the preferred form of radical immanence to produce more accurate accounts of the multiple political economies of subject-formation at work in our world. These cartographies enable nonprofit accounts of contemporary subjectivity and actualize the virtual possibilities of an expanded, relational self that functions in a nature-culture continuum, which is technologically mediated and opposed to the spirit of contemporary capitalism. They refuse to turn Life/*zoe*—that is to say, human and nonhuman intelligent matter—into a commodity for trade and profit.

Sexuality beyond Gender

The neomaterialist branch of poststructuralist feminist philosophy had emphasized the crucial notion that sexuality is an integral part of the embodied structure of the subject: one is always already sexed. Deleuzian feminists had argued against the sex-gender distinction (Gatens 1991), suggesting that sexuality is conceptualized as a general life force, which cannot be adequately contained within the dichotomous view of gender defined as the social construction of differences between the sexes. Social constructivism is also called to task by the ontological shift to a monistic view of sexuality as part of a vital materialist autopoietic system. Whereas high poststructuralist feminist theory was solidly ensconced in social constructivist methods and political strategies, thinkers of the next generation affirm and explore the ontological aspects of sexuality and sexual difference, and not only its constructed elements.

Returning sexuality to its polymorphous perversity (here in the sense of playful and nonreproductive) as an ontological force, in opposition to a gender system that privileges binary opposition and heterosexual reproductive sex, raises further questions. What happens to gender identities if sexuality is not based on oppositional terms? What happens when there is sexuality without the possibility of either heterosexual or homosexual union?

When sexuality is not theorized as caught in the sex-gender binary, it enjoys more transversal, structural, and vital connotations. Sexuality as life force provides a nonessentialist ontological structure for the organization of human affectivity and desire. This notion clearly opposes the position of the linguistic mediation school (Butler 1991), which argues that the discursive structure of gender functions as a coercive grid that constructs social relations and identities. Sexuality does get caught in gender's captive mechanisms, but it remains a constitutive force that is always already present and hence prior to gender, though it intersects with it in constructing functional subjects in the social regime of biopolitical governmentality.

Postanthropocentric feminists advocate a vision of the body as a sexually preconstituted, dynamic bundle of relations and explore the transformative potential of a different concept of the political. They (Braidotti 1994; Grosz 1994; Gatens 1996; Olkowski 1999) stress that the political advantage of this monistic and vital approach is that it provides a more adequate understanding of the fluid and complex workings of power in advanced capitalism and hence can devise more suitable forms of resistance.

In other words, sexuality as human and nonhuman precedes and exceeds the normative social apparatus of gender, which is a form of governance that can be disrupted through processes of becoming-minoritarian/becoming-woman/becoming-animal (Braidotti 2002, 2006). This implies that sexuality is a force, or constitutive element, that is capable of deterritorializing gender identity and institutions (Braidotti 1994, 2011a, 2011b). Combined with the idea of the body as an incorporeal complex assemblage of virtualities, this approach posits the ontological priority of difference and its self-transforming force, bypassing social constructivist approaches. They are the transformative counteractualizations of the multiple, always-already sexed bodies we may sustain and what they may be capable of doing.

This is what I have called the feminist becoming-woman (Braidotti 1991, 1994), then the "virtual feminine" (Braidotti 2002, 2006). On this point all vital materialist feminists concur: Grosz refers to it as "a thousand tiny sexes" (2004); Colebrook labels it "queer passive vitalism" (2014a, 2014b); Patricia MacCormack (2008, 2012) similarly draws attention to the need to return to sexuality as a polymorphous and complex visceral force, and to disengage it from both identity issues and all dualistic oppositions. Luciana Parisi's innovative adaptation of Guattari's schizo-analysis and Lynn Margulis's concept of "endosymbiosis" (Margulis and Sagan 1995) produces a schizo-genesis of sexual difference as an organic variable of autopoesis (Parisi 2004). Posthuman feminists look for subversion, not in counteridentity formations, but rather in pure dislocations of identities via the disruption of standardized patterns of sexualized, racialized, and naturalized interaction. Feminist posthuman politics is an experiment with intensities beyond binaries, that functions by "and, and," not by "either-or."

In other words, we need to experiment with intensity in order to find out what posthuman bodies can do. Because the gender system captures the complexity of human sexuality in a binary machine that privileges heterosexual family formations and literally steals all other possible bodies from us, we no longer know what our sexed bodies can do. We therefore need to rediscover the notion of the sexual complexity that marks sexuality in its human and posthuman forms. A postanthropocentric feminist approach makes it clear that bodily matter in the human as in other species is always already sexed and hence sexually differentiated along the axes of multiplicity and heterogeneity.

These experiments with what sexed bodies can do, however, do not amount to saying that in the social sphere pejorative differences no longer matter or that the traditional power relations have been resolved. On the contrary, on a world scale, extreme forms of polarized sexual difference are stronger than ever. They get projected onto geopolitical relations between the West and the rest, creating belligerent gendered visions of a "clash of civilizations" that is allegedly predicated in terms of women's and LGBT people's rights. We need to adopt a multilayered feminist politics: contain and resist the negative aspects while continuing to experiment with intensities. Posthuman feminists pursue sexuality beyond gender as the epistemological but also political side of contemporary vitalist materialism after anthropocentrism.

Conclusion: For Critical Posthuman Feminism

The strength of posthuman feminist thought is in developing affirmative ethical and political perspectives. In my work, I have proposed cross-species alliances with the productive and immanent force of *zoe*, or life in its nonhuman aspects (Braidotti 2002, 2006). This relational ontology is *zoe*-centered and hence nonanthropocentric, but it does not deny the anthropologically bound structure of the human. This shift of perspective towards a *zoe* or geocentered approach requires a mutation of our shared understanding of what it means to be human, which however needs to be qualified by grounded analyses of power relations and structural inequalities in the past and present.

Starting from philosophies of radical immanence, vital materialism, and the feminist politics of locations, I have also argued against taking a flight into an abstract idea of a "new" pan-humanity, bonded in shared vulnerability or in species supremacy. What we need instead is embedded and embodied, relational and affective cartographies of the new power relations that are emerging from the current geopolitical and post-anthropocentric order. Class, race, gender, and sexual orientations, age and able-bodiedness are more than ever significant markers of human "normality." They are key factors in framing the notion of and policing access to something we may call "humanity." Yet, considering the global reach of the problems we are facing today, in the era of that "Anthropocene," it is nonetheless the case that "we" are in *this* together. Such awareness must not however obscure or flatten out the power differentials that sustain the collective subject ("we") and its endeavor (*this*). There may well be multiple and potentially contradictory projects at stake in the recomposition of "humanity" right now. Posthuman feminist and other critical theorists need to resist hasty and reactive recompositions of cosmopolitan bonds, especially those made of fear. It may be more useful to work toward multiple actualizations of new transversal alliances, communities and planes of composition of the human: many ways of becoming-world together.

I have argued forcefully that the posthuman is not postpolitical. The posthuman condition does not mark the end of political agency, but a recasting of it in the direction of relational ontology. This is all the more important as the political economy of biogenetic capitalism is postanthropocentric in its very structures, but not necessarily or automatically more humane, or more prone to justice.

Last but not least, posthuman feminists advocate a vision of the body as a dynamic and sexed bundle of relations and rest on it to explore the transformative potential of a different concept of the political. They state the primacy of sexuality as ontological force, in opposition to a majoritarian or dominant line of territorialization—the gender system—that privileges heterosexual, familial, reproductive sex. Sexuality beyond gender is the epistemological but also political side of contemporary vitalist neomaterialism. It consolidates a feminist genealogy that includes creative deterritorializations, intensive and hybrid cross-fertilizations and generative encounters with multiple human and nonhuman others. The counteractualization of the virtual sexualities—of bodies without organs that we have not been able to sustain as yet—is a posthuman feminist political praxis.

Notes

1. *Sketch of The Analytical Engine Invented by Charles Babbage* by Ada Lovelace (1842) has to be quoted here as an equally anomalous and untimely text from the nineteenth century.
2. Deleuze calls it "the Majority subject" or the Molar center of being (Deleuze and Guattari 1987). Irigaray calls it "the Same," or the hyperinflated, falsely universal "He" (Irigaray 1985b, 1993); whereas Patricia Hill Collins calls to account the white and Eurocentric bias of this particular subject of humanistic knowledge (Collins 1991).
3. The most significant works in this tradition are the Milan's Women Bookshop elaboration of *Sexual Difference: A Theory of Socio-Symbolic Practice*. This was developed into an original critique of the history of philosophy by Adriana Cavarero in *In Spite of Plato*. In German, the significant contribution are Herta Nagl-Docekal and Herlinde Pauer-Studer, ed., *Denken der Geschlechterdifferenz: neuen fragenund perspektiven des feministische philosophie*; and Andrea Maihofer, *Geschlecht als Existenzweise. Macht, Moral, Recht und Geschlechterdifferenz*. In Spanish, the pioneering work is done by Celia Amorós in *Hacia una crítica de la razón patriarchal* and by Maria Santa Cruz, Marie-Luisa Femenias, and Anna-Maria Bach on *Mujeres y filosofía* in Latin America.
4. This is radically different from the negative definition of *zoe* proposed by Giorgio Agamben (1998), who has been taken to task by feminist scholars (Cooper 2009; Colebrook 2009; Braidotti 2013) for his erasure of feminist perspectives on the politics of natality and mortality and for his indictment of the project of modernity as a whole.

References

Adams, Carol. 1990. *The Sexual Politics of Meat: A Feminist-Vegetarian Critical Theory*. New York: Continuum.
Agamben, Giorgio. 1998. *Homo Sacer. Sovereign Power and Bare Life*. Redwood City, CA: Stanford University Press.
Ahmed, Sarah. 2004. *The Cultural Politics of Emotion*. Edinburgh: Edinburgh University Press.
Ahmed, Sarah. 2006. *Queer Phenomenology*. Durham, NC: Duke University Press.
Alaimo, Stacey. 2010. *Bodily Natures: Science, Environment and the Material Self*. Bloomington: Indiana University Press.
Alaimo, Stacey, and Susan Hekman, eds. 2008. *Material Feminisms*. Bloomington: Indiana University Press.
Alcoff, Linda, and Elizabeth Porter, eds. 1993. *Feminist Epistemologies*. London and New York: Routledge.
Ansell Pearson, Keith. 1999. *Germinal Life. The Difference and Repetition of Deleuze*. London and New York: Routledge.
Asberg, Cecilia, and Lykke, Nina. 2010. "Feminist Technoscience Studies." *European Journal of Women's Studies* 17 (4): 299–305.

Balsamo, Anne. 1996. *Technologies of the Gendered Body: Reading Cyborg Women*. Durham, NC: Duke University Press.
Barad, Karen. 2003. "Posthumanist Performativity. Toward an Understanding of How Matter Comes to Matter." *Signs* 28 (3): 801–831.
Barad, Karen. 2007. *Meeting the Universe Halfway*. Durham, NC: Duke University Press.
Barr, Marleen. 1987. *Alien to Femininity: Speculative Fiction and Feminist Theory*. New York: Greenwood.
Barr, Marleen. 1993. *Lost in Space. Probing Feminist Science Fiction and Beyond*. Chapel Hill, NC: University of North Carolina Press.
Beauvoir, Simone de. 1973. *The Second Sex*. New York: Bantam Books.
Beck, Ulrich.1999. *World Risk Society*. Oxford: Blackwell.
Beer, Gillian. 1983. *Darwin's Plots: Evolutionary Narrative in Darwin, George Eliot and Nineteenth-Century Fiction*. London: Routledge and Kegan Paul.
Benhabib, Seyla, and Drucilla Cornell, ed. 1987. *Feminism as Critique: On the Politics of Gender*. Minneapolis: University of Minnesota Press.
Bennett, Jane. 2010. *Vibrant Matter: A Political Ecology of Things*. Durham, NC: Duke University Press.
Birke, Lynda, Mette Bryld, and Nina Lykke. 2004. "Animal Performances: An Exploration of Intersections between Feminist Science Studies and Studies of Human/Animal Relationships." *Feminist Theory* 2 (5): 167–183.
Bonta, Mark, and John Protevi. 2004. *Deleuze and Geophilosophy: A Guide and Glossary*. Edinburgh: Edinburgh University Press.
Brah, Avtar. 1996. *Cartographies of Diaspora-Contesting Identities*. New York and London: Routledge.
Braidotti, Rosi. 1991. *Patterns of Dissonance: An Essay on Women in Contemporary French Philosophy*. Cambridge: Polity Press.
Braidotti, Rosi. 1994 *Nomadic Subject: Embodiment and Sexual Difference in Contemporary Feminist Theory*. New York: Columbia University Press.
Braidotti, Rosi. 2002. *Metamorphoses. Towards a Materialist Theory of Becoming*. Cambridge: Polity Press.
Braidotti, Rosi. 2006. *Transpositions: On Nomadic Ethics*. Cambridge: Polity Press.
Braidotti, Rosi. 2011a. *Nomadic Subject: Embodiment and Sexual Difference in Contemporary Feminist Theory*. Rev. 2nd ed. New York: Columbia University Press.
Braidotti, Rosi. 2011b. *Nomadic Theory*. New York: Columbia University Press.
Braidotti, Rosi. 2012. "Preface: The Society of Undutiful Daughters." In *Undutiful Daughters: New Directions in Feminist Thought and Practice*, edited by Henriette Gunkel, Chrysanthi Nigianni and Fanny Söderbäck, ix–xix. New York: Palgrave MacMillan.
Braidotti, Rosi. 2013. *The Posthuman*. Cambridge: Polity Press.
Braidotti, Rosi, and Griet Roets. 2012. "Nomadology and Subjectivity: Deleuze, Guattari and Critical Disability Studies." In *Disability and Social Theory: New Developments and Directions*, edited by Dan Goodley, Bill Hughes, and Lennard Davis, 161–178. New York: Palgrave Macmillan.
Bryld, Mette, and Nina Lykke. 1999. *Cosmodolphins. Feminist Cultural Studies of Technologies: Animals and the Sacred*. London: Zed Books.
Buikema, Rosemarie, Nina Lykke, and Gabriele Griffin, eds. 2011. *Theories and Methodologies in Postgraduate Feminist Research: Researching Differently*. London: Routledge
Butler, Judith. 1991. *Gender Trouble*. London and New York: Routledge.

Butler, Judith. 2004. *Undoing Gender*. London and New York: Routledge.
Carroll, Joseph. 2004. *Literary Darwinism. Evolution: Human Nature and Literature*. London and New York: Routledge.
Césaire, Aimé. 1955. *Discours sur le colonialisme*. Paris: Présence Africaine.
Churchland, Patricia. 2011. *Braintrust: What Neuroscience Tells Us about Morality*. Princeton, NJ: Princeton University Press.
Cixous, Hélène. 1997. "Mon Algeriance." *Les Inrockuptibles*, August 20, magazine archive nr. 115.
Clarke, Andy. 1997. *Being There. Putting Brain, Body and World Together Again*. Cambridge, MA: MIT Press.
Clarke, Andy. 2008. *Supersizing the Mind: Embodiment: Action and Cognitive Extension*. Oxford: Oxford University Press.
Clough, Patricia Ticineto, with Jean Halley. 2007. *The Affective Turn: Theorizing the Social*. Durham, NC: Duke University Press.
Colebrook, Claire. 2000. "Is Sexual Difference a Problem?" In *Deleuze and Feminist Theory*, edited by Ian Buchanan and Claire Colebrook, 110–127. Edinburgh: Edinburgh University Press.
Colebrook, Claire. 2004. "Postmodernism Is a Humanism: Deleuze and Equivocity." *Women: A Cultural Review* 15 (3): 283–307.
Colebrook, Claire. 2009. "Agamben: Aesthetics, Potentilality, Life." *South Atlantic Quarterly* 107 (1): 107–120
Colebrook, Claire. 2014a. *Death of the Posthuman*. Open Humanities Press/University of Michigan Press.
Colebrook, Claire. 2014b. *Sex after Life*. Open Humanities Press/University of Michigan Press.
Collins, Patricia Hill. 1991. *Black Feminist Thought: Knowledge, Consciousness, and the Politics of Empowerment*. London and New York: Routledge.
Coole, Diana, and Samantha Frost. 2010. *New Materialisms: Ontology, Agency, and Politics*. Durham, NC: Duke University Press.
Cooper, Melinda. 2008. *Life as Surplus: Biotechnology and Capitalism in the Neoliberal Era*. Seattle: University of Washington Press.
Cooper, Melinda. 2009. "The Silent Scream: Agamben, Deleuze and the Politics of the Unborn." In *Deleuze and Law: Forensic Futures*, edited by Rosi Braidotti, Claire Colebrook, Patrick Hanafin, 1–142. Basingstoke, UK: Palgrave Macmillan.
Creed, Barbara. 1993. *The Monstrous-Feminine: Film, Feminism, Psychoanalysis*. New York and London: Routledge.
Crenshaw, Kimberlé. 1995. "Intersectionality and Identity Politics:. Learning from Violence against Women of Color." In *Critical Race Theory*, edited by Kimberlé Crenshaw, Neil Gotanda, Gary Peller, and Kendall Thomas, 279–309. New York: The New Press.
Damasio, Antonio. 2003. *Looking for Spinoza*. Orlando, FL: Harcourt.
Deleuze, Gilles, and Félix Guattari. 1977. *Anti-Oedipus: Capitalism and Schizophrenia I*. New York: Viking Press.
Deleuze, Gilles, and Félix Guattari. 1987. *A Thousand Plateaus: Capitalism and Schizophrenia*. Minneapolis: University of Minnesota Press.
de Waal, Frans. 1996. *Good Natured*. Cambridge, MA: Harvard University Press.
de Waal, Frans. 2009. *The Age of Empathy*. New York: Three Rivers Press.
Dolphijn, Rick, and Iris van der Tuin. 2012. *New Materialism: Interviews and Cartographies*. Ann Arbor, MI: Open Humanities Press.

Donovan, Josephine, and Carol J. Adams, eds. 1996. *Beyond Animal Rights: A Feminist Caring Ethic for the Treatment of Animals.* New York: Continuum.
Donovan, Josephine, and Carol J. Adams, eds. 2007. *The Feminist Care Tradition in Animal Ethics.* New York: Columbia University Press.
Eisenstein, Hester. 1983. *Contemporary Feminist Thought.* Boston: G. K. Hall.
Eisenstein, Zillah. 1998. *Global Obscenities. Patriarchy, Capitalism and the Lure of Cyberfantasy.* New York: New York University Press.
Fanon, Frantz. 1967. *Black Skin, White Masks.* New York: Grove Press.
Ferrando, Francesca. 2013. "Posthumanism, Transhumanism, Antihumanism, Metahumanism and New Materialism: Differences and Relations." *Existenz: An International Journal in Philosophy, Religion, Politics and the Arts* 8 (2): 26–32.
Firestone, Shulamith. 1970. *The Dialectic of Sex.* New York: Bantam Books.
Foucault, Michel. 1970. *The Order of Things: An Archaeology of Human Sciences.* New York: Pantheon Books.
Foucault, Michel. 1977. *Discipline and Punish.* New York: Pantheon Books.
Foucault, Michel. 1997. *Society Must Be Defended: Lectures at the Collège de France, 1975-1976.* New York: St. Martin's Press.
Fox Keller, Evelyn. 2002. *Making Sense of Life.* Cambridge, MA: Harvard University Press.
Franklin, Sarah. 2007. *Dolly Mixtures.* Durham, NC: Duke University Press.
Franklin, Sarah, Celia Lury, and Jackie Stacey. 2000. *Global Nature, Global Culture.* London: Sage.
Fraser, Mariam, Saraha Kember, and Celia Lury, eds. 2006. *Inventive Life. Approaches to the New Vitalism.* London: Sage.
Gatens, Moira. 1991. "A Critique of the Sex/Gender Distinction." In *A Reader in Feminist Knowledge,* edited by Sneja Gunew, 139-157. London and New York: Routledge.
Gatens, Moira. 1996. *Imaginary Bodies.* New York: Routledge.
Gatens, Moira, and Genevieve Lloyd. 1999. *Collective Imaginings: Spinoza, Past and Present.* London and New York: Routledge.
Grewal, Inderpal, and Caren Kaplan, eds. 1994. *Scattered Hegemonies: Postmodernity and Transnational Feminist Practices.* Minneapolis: University of Minnesota Press.
Giffney, Noreen, and Myra J. Hird. 2008. *Queering the Non/Human.* Surrey, UK: Ashgate.
Gilroy, Paul. 2000. *Against Race: Imaging Political Culture beyond the Color Line.* Cambridge, MA: Harvard University Press.
Grimshaw, Jean. 1986. *Philosophy and Feminist Thinking.* Minneapolis: University of Minnesota Press.
Grosz, Elizabeth.1994. *Volatile Bodies: Toward a Corporeal Feminism.* Bloomington: Indiana University Press
Grosz, Elisabeth. 1995. *Sexy Bodies: The Strange Carnalities of Feminism.* London and New York: Routledge.
Grosz, Elizabeth. 2004. *The Nick of Time.* Durham, NC: Duke University Press.
Grosz, Elizabeth. 2011. *Becoming Undone.* Durham, NC: Duke University Press.
Grusin, Richard. Forthcoming. *Anthropocene Feminism.* Minneapolis: University of Minnesota Press.
Guattari, Félix. 2000. *The Three Ecologies.* London: The Athlone Press.
Halberstam, Judith, and Ira Livingston, eds. 1995. *Posthuman Bodies.* Bloomington: Indiana University Press.

Halberstam, Judith. 2012. *Gaga Femisism: Sex, Gender and the End of Normal*. Boston: Beacon Press.
Hall, Stuart. 1996. "What Is Black in Black Popular Culture?" In *Stuart Hall: Critical Dialogues in Cultural Studies*, edited by David Morley and Kuan-Hsing Chen, 468-478. London and New York: Routledge.
Haraway, Donna. 1985. "A Manifesto for Cyborgs: Science, Technology, and Socialist Feminism in the 1980s." *Socialist Review* 15 (2): 65–107.
Haraway, Donna. 1988. "Situated Knowledges. The Science Question in Feminism as a Site of Discourse on the Privilege of Partial Perspective." *Feminist Studies* 14 (3): 575–599.
Haraway, Donna. 1990. *Simians, Cyborgs and Women*. London: Free Association Press.
Haraway, Donna. 1992. "The Promises of Monsters: A Regenerative Politics for Inappropriate/d Others." In *Cultural Studies*, edited by Lawrence Grossberg, Cary Nelson, and Paula Treichler, 295–337. London and New York: Routledge.
Haraway, Donna. 1997. *Modest_Witness@Second_Millennium. FemaleMan©_Meets_ Oncomouse*. London and New York: Routledge.
Haraway, Donna. 2003. *The Companion Species Manifesto: Dogs, People and Significant Otherness*. Chicago: Prickly Paradigm Press.
Haraway, Donna. 2006. "When We Have Never Been Human, What Is to Be Done?" *Theory, Culture & Society* 23 (7–8): 135–158.
Haraway, Donna. 2014. "Anthropocene, Capitalocene, Cthulhucene". On-line talk 27 September 2014. Consulted May 4, 2015.
Harding, Sandra. 1986. *The Science Question in Feminism*. Ithaca, NY: Cornell University Press.
Harding, Sandra. 1991. *Whose Science? Whose Knowledge?* Ithaca, NY: Cornell University Press.
Harding, Sandra. 1993. *The "Racial" Economy of Science*. Bloomington: Indiana University Press.
Hartsock, Nancy. 1987. "The Feminist Standpoint: Developing the Ground for a Specifically Feminist Historical Materialism." In *Feminism and Methodology*, edited by Sandra Harding, 157-180. London: Open University Press.
Hayles, Katherine. 1999. *How We Became Posthuman. Virtual Bodies in Cybernetics, Literature and Informatics*. Chicago: University of Chicago Press.
Hayward, Eva. 2008. "More Lessons from a Starfish: Prefixial Flesh and Transspeciated Selves." *Women's Studies Quarterly* 36 (3–4): 64–85.
Hayward, Eva. 2011. "Sensational Jellyfish: Aquarium Affects and the Matter of Immersion." *Differences* 25 (5): 161-196.
Hemmings, Clare. 2011. *Why Stories Matter: The Political Grammar of Feminist Theory*. Durham, NC: Duke University Press.
Hird, Myra, and Celia Roberts, eds. 2011. "Feminism Theorises the Nonhuman." *Feminist Theory* 12 (2).
hooks, bell. 1981. *Ain't I a Woman*. Boston, MA: South End Press.
hooks, bell. 1990. "Postmodern Blackness." In *Yearning: Race, Gender and Cultural Politics*, 23-32. Toronto: Between the Lines.
Irigaray, Luce. 1985a. *Speculum of the Other Woman*. Ithaca, NY: Cornell University Press.
Irigaray, Luce. 1985b. *This Sex Which Is Not One*. Ithaca, NY: Cornell University Press.
Irigaray, Luce. (1984) 1993. *An Ethics of Sexual Difference*. Ithaca, NY: Cornell University Press.
Irigaray, Luce. 1994. "Equal to Whom?" In *The Essential Difference*, edited by Naomi Schor and Elizabeth Weed and translated by Robert L. Mazzola, 80. Bloomington: Indiana University Press.

Jaggar, Alison. 1983. *Feminist Politics and Human Nature.* Lanham, MD: Rowman and Littlefield.

Jaggar, Alison, and Iris M. Young, ed. 1998. *The Blackwell Companion to Feminist Philosophy.* Oxford and Malden: Blackwell Publishers.

Johnson, Barbara. 1998. *The Feminist Difference: Literature, Psychoanalysis, Race and Gender.* Cambridge, MA: Harvard University Press.

Kelly, Joan. 1979. "The Double-Edged Vision of Feminist Theory." *Feminist Studies* 5 (1): 216–227.

King, Katie. 2011. *Networked Reenactments: Stories Transdisciplinary Knowledges Tell.* Durham, NC: Duke University Press.

King, Katie. 2012. "A Naturalcultural Collection of Affections: Transdiciplinary Stories of Transmedia Ecologies Learning." *The Scholar and the Feminist Online*: Special issue on Feminist Media Theory: Iterations of Social Difference 10/3. Available at: http://sfonline.barnard.edu/feminist-media-theory/a-naturalcultural-collection-of-affections-transdisciplinary-stories-of-transmedia-ecologies-learning/

Kirby, Vicki. 2011. *Quantum Anthropologies: Life at Large.* Durham, NC: Duke University Press.

Kristeva, Julia. 1980. *Pouvoirs de l'horreur.* Paris: Editions du Seuil.

Kristeva, Julia. 1991. *Strangers to Ourselves.* New York: Colombia University Press.

Livingston, Julie, and Jasbir K. Puar. 2011. "Interspecies." *Social Text* 29 (1): 3–13.

Lloyd, Genevieve. 1984. *The Man of Reason: Male and Female in Western Philosophy.* London: Methuen.

Lloyd, Genevieve. 1994. *Part of Nature: Self-Knowledge in Spinoza's Ethic.* Ithaca, NY: Cornell University Press.

Lloyd, Genevieve. 1996. *Spinoza and the Ethics.* London and New York: Routledge.

Louverture, Toussaint. 2011. *Lettres à la France. Idées pour la Libération du people noir d'Haiti.* Bruyères-le-Chatel: Nouvelle Cité.

Lyotard, Jean Francois. 1989. *The Inhuman: Reflections on Time.* Oxford: Blackwell.

Lury, Celia, Luciana Parisi, and Tiziana Terranova, eds. 2012. "Topologies of Culture." *Theory, Culture & Society* 29 (4–5): 3-35

MacCormack, Patricia. 2008. *Cinesexualities.* London: Ashgate.

MacCormack, Patricia. 2012. *Posthuman Ethics.* London: Ashgate.

MacCormack, Patricia. 2014. *The Animal Catalyst.* London: Bloomsbury.

Macpherson, Crawford B. 1962. *The Theory of Possessive Individualism.* Oxford: Oxford University Press.

Malabou, Catherine. 2011. *Changing Difference.* Cambridge: Polity Press.

Malraux, André. 1934. *La Condition Humaine.* Paris: Librairie Gallimard.

Mandela, Nelson. 1994. *A Long Walk to Freedom.* Randburg, South Africa: Macdonald Purnell.

Margulis, Lynn, and Dorion Sagan. 1995. *What Is Life?* Berkeley: University of California Press.

Massumi, Brian. 2002. *Parables for the Virtual: Movement, Affect, Sensation.* Durham, NC: Duke University Press.

Mbembe, Achille. 2003. "Necropolitics." *Public Culture* 15 (1): 11–40.

McNeil, Maureen. 2007. *Feminist Cultural Studies of Science and Technology.* London: Routledge.

Midgley, Mary. 1996. *Utopias, Dolphins and Computers: Problems of Philosophical Plumbing.* London and New York: Routledge.

Mies, Maria, and Vandana Shiva. 1993. *Ecofeminism*. London: Zed Books.

Narayan, Uma. 1989. "Project of Feminist Epistemology: Perspectives from a Nonwestern Feminist." In *Gender/Body/Knowledge: Feminist Reconstructions of Being and Knowing*, edited by Alison M. Jaggar and Susan Bordo, 256-269. New Brunswick, NJ: Rutgers University Press.

Nussbaum, Marta. 2006. *Frontiers of Justice: Disability, Nationality, Species Membership*. Cambridge, MA: Harvard University Press.

Olkowski, Dorothea. 1999. *Gilles Deleuze and the Ruin of Representation*. Berkeley: University of California Press.

Ortner, Sherry B. 1974. "Is Female to Male as Nature is to Culture?" In *Woman, Culture, and Society*, edited by M. Z. Rosaldo and L. Lamphere, 68–87. Redwood City, CA: Stanford University Press.

Parisi, Luciana. 2004. *Abstract Sex: Philosophy, Bio-Technology, and the Mutation of Desire*. London: Continuum Press.

Pinkola Estés, Clarissa. 1992. *Women Who Run with the Wolves: Myths and Stories of the Wild Woman Archetype*. New York: Ballantine.

Plumwood, Val. 1993. *Feminism and the Mastery of Nature*. London and New York: Routledge.

Plumwood, Val. 2003. *Environmental Culture*. London: Routledge.

Protevi, John. 2009. *Political Affect*. Minneapolis: University of Minnesota Press.

Rapp, Rayna. 2000. *Testing Women, Testing the Foetus*. New York: Routledge.

Rose, Hilary, and Steven Rose. 2000. *Alas, Poor Darwin: Arguments against Evolutionary Psychology*. New York: Harmony.

Rose, Nicholas. 2007. *The Politics of Life Itself: Biomedicine, Power and Subjectivity in the Twentieth-First Century*. Princeton, NJ: Princeton University Press.

Said, Edward. 2004. *Humanism and Democratic Criticism*. New York: Columbia University Press.

Sartre, Jean-Paul. 1963. Introduction to *The Wretched of the Earth* by Frantz Fanon. London: Penguin Books.

Shiva, Vandana. 1988. *Staying Alive*. New Delhi: Kali for Women.

Shiva, Vandana. 1997. *Biopiracy. The Plunder of Nature and Knowledge*. Boston: South End Press.

Smelik, Anneke, and Nina Lykke, eds. 2008. *Bits of Life: Feminism at the Intersections of Media, Bioscience and Technology*. Seattle: University of Washington Press.

Sobchack, Vivian. 2004. *Carnal Thoughts*. Berkeley: University of California Press.

Soper, Kate. 1986. *Humanism and Anti-Humanism*. LaSalle, IL: Open Court Press.

Spivak, Gayatri Chakravorty. 1999. *A Critique of Postcolonial Reason: Toward a History of the Vanishing Present*. Cambridge, MA: Harvard University Press.

Spivak, Gayatri C. 2003. *Death of a Discipline*. New York: Columbia University Press.

Stacey, Jackie. 2010. *The Cinematic Life of the Gene*. Durham, NC: Duke University Press.

Stafford, Barbara. 2007. *Echo Objects: The Cognitive Work of Images*. Chicago: University of Chicago Press.

Stengers, Isabelle. 1997. *Power and Invention: Situating Science*. Minneapolis: University of Minnesota Press.

Terranova, Tiziana. 2004. *Network Culture*. London: Pluto Press.

Ware, Vron. 1992. *Beyond the Pale: White Women, Racism and History*. London: Verso.

Wilson, Elizabeth. 2011. "Another Neurological Scene." *History of the Present* 1 (2): 149–169.

Wolfe, Cary, ed. 2003. *Zoontologies: The Question of the Animal.* Minneapolis: University of Minnesota Press.

Wolfe, Cary. 2010. *What Is Posthumanism?* Minneapolis: University of Minnesota Press.

Young, Robert. 2004. *White Mythologies: Writing History and the West.* Florence, KY: Psychology Press.

Zylinska, Joanna. 2009. *Bioethics in the Age of New Media.* Boston: MIT Press.

CHAPTER 34

PREGNANCY, PERSONHOOD, AND THE MAKING OF THE FETUS

SILJA SAMERSKI

Introduction

Cultural images of pregnancy and birth mirror a society's conceptions of gender and human nature. Who counts as a member of the social community, on what grounds, and how does it come into being? As feminist research has shown, these questions are negotiated in an anthropologically and historically unique way in Western societies. Practices and notions of childbearing and personhood center around a newfangled subject: the fetus, an individual hosted in a pregnant woman's womb. Here, human beings do not come into this world by being born but by being objectified and managed as fetal individuals.

It is the achievement of feminist scholarship to have analyzed the construction of the fetal individual as a recent and culturally bounded phenomenon and to have cautioned about its impingement on women. Thereby, feminists have not only successfully foiled the public and scientific hailing of the fetus as a biological fact but also undermined predominant concepts of nature, knowledge, individuality, and human life. Thus, feminist theory has pioneered a critical understanding of sanctified "facts of life" and the respective transformation of self-perception and subjectification. The fetus, as feminist research has revealed, is not a natural given discovered by scientific progress, but rather a managed object generated by new social practices and governance techniques. As such, the fetus mirrors contemporary power relations and corresponding notions of personhood and practices of subjectification.

Fetal Politics

Since the 1980s, sociologists, anthropologists, political scientists, and philosophers have portrayed and examined contemporary fetal politics from a feminist standpoint (e.g., Duden 1993; Petchesky 1984; Rothman 1986). They have made clear that the more the fetus is hypostatized and catches public imagination, the more the pregnant woman is treated as its mere container and, eventually, as its potential adversary and threat. As soon as a woman is diagnosed as pregnant, she is woven into the filaments of professional and legal control. If she does not want to have a baby, she is treated as the site of a conflict between her and her interior—that is, the technically verified "life" inside her. If she lives in a country with permissive abortion regulations, such as Germany or the United States, she can undergo an abortion on the condition that she has submitted to educational measures that aim to change her sense of self. In Germany, professional counseling tries to ensure that women do not simply follow their wits and guts but make so called informed and responsible decisions. In the United States, several states have passed bills requiring a mandatory ultrasound prior to an abortion, to show women what they "really" are: containers and potential adversaries of a human life.

When a woman hopes to give birth, she is caught in a tight web of medicalized and professionalized prenatal care whose goal is to optimize fetal development. Sonographic scanning and laboratory tests monitor fetal growth and search for risk factors and potential abnormalities (Rapp 1999; Samerski 2009). Fetal surgery is a growing field of medical intervention, subjecting a woman to an operation for the potential benefit of her fruit (Caspar 1998). Yet, in most cases of a prenatally diagnosed abnormality, the new patient cannot be healed but only aborted. If an abnormality or a developmental risk is diagnosed, professional and legal protection of the unborn quickly turns into the opposite: so-called therapeutic abortions are routine, recommended by professionals and sometimes performed until shortly before birth.

If the fetal profile meets contemporary health standards but the pregnant woman does not comply with professionally prescribed behavior, professionals and experts might act as fetal advocates. If she does not abstain from drugs or alcohol or consent to a medical intervention, such as a cesarean section, medical professionals and jurisdiction might rob the woman of her civil rights and liberties. In the United States, a growing number of women are prosecuted because, by the standards of biomedicine, they are accused of harming or abusing their fetus. The Unborn Victims of Violence Act of. 2004 was a big step towards turning unborns into full-fledged legal persons and extending state encroachments into the female interior. In 2004, a judge in the United States stopped the deportation of a Mexican woman on the grounds that she carried an American citizen inside her (Casper and Morgan 2004). Other countries also follow this line. In 2013, the New Zealand Ministry of Health pondered assigning national health index numbers to fetuses.

Feminist Analysis and Critique of Fetal Politics

Growing uneasy over the scientific hypostatization of the fetus, its public appropriation, and the professional and legal encroachments on women, feminist scholars began to study the historical, epistemological, philosophical, and political scaffolding of modern fetal politics. Many had been active in abortion politics and the reproductive rights movement, and thus were sensitized to the disastrous effect the invention of a prenatal subject with needs and rights would have on women's autonomy. Shifting their activism "from the streets to academia" (Casper 1999, 101), they started to question the common credos about pregnancy, fetuses, biological development, and personhood. In the 1980s, feminist scholars published numerous historical, sociological, anthropological, and philosophical treatises on the power of fetal images (e.g., Petchesky 1987), on the "Captured Womb" (Oakley 1984), on the transformation of pregnancy and motherhood (e.g., Rothman 1986), on "Disembodying Women" (Duden 1993), and on the modern making of personhood and subjectivity (e.g., Franklin 1991; Morgan 2009; Morgan and Kaufman 2005; Strathern 1992) that, by now, have become classics. Their work widely influenced scholarship and political activism well beyond the topic of pregnancy and women's rights, shaking the certitudes of contemporary society. Their main topics and insights can be grouped along the following three research directions: First, observing the medicalization of pregnancy and birth and the transformation of mothers-to-be into managers of fetuses, many feminists challenged the premise that reproductive technologies empower women. They critically inquired into the growing power of science and technology to shape and interpret reality and questioned new forms of governance that do not repress women but create new subjectivities, such as the responsible pregnant woman managing fetal risks. Secondly, feminists searched for the social and cultural conditions that facilitate the construction of the fetal subject and its contemporary proof. For a rich contrast with the present, historians and anthropologists unearthed women from pre-20th century periods of history and other non-Western cultures, giving voice to their experience of pregnancy and childbearing. What struck scholars, who as enlightened feminists were accustomed to perceiving themselves in biological terms (Duden 1998) and thus expected the fetus to be an a-historical, natural fact, was this: nothing comparable to a fetal subject existed in former times or other cultures. This insight reverberates with contemporary certainties about gender and human nature and has encouraged a rethinking of the peculiarity of today's "fetal obsession." And thirdly, philosophers struggled to establish a feminist view on pregnancy and the fetus, jettisoning the Western emphasis on autonomy and individuality for the sake of concepts hinging on relationality, contextuality and everyday experience.

Fetal Politics and Pregnancy

The emergence of the fetal subject goes hand in hand with the politicization and medicalization of human reproduction. What Lisa Featherstone asserts about Australia holds true for other countries as well: in the beginning of the twentieth century, "the new medical concern for the foetus was embedded in social, political and economic discourses stressing the need for population growth" (Featherstone 2008, 454). In early prenatal care, "medical interest in the foetus resided in its potential for a new life for the white nation" (Featherstone 2008, 459). Meanwhile, the optimization and control of human reproduction is at the center of today's politics aiming at the management of "human life." Because of the advance of reproductive technologies and demography, pregnancy and childbearing have become highly politicized and hotly debated topics. In practice, medicine has almost completely captured the female womb. Pregnancy is diagnosed, managed, ceased, and partly even generated by medical experts. The main client, however, is not the woman; medical prenatal care is fixated on the fetus and supervises its development.

Some feminists, such as Laura Purdy (1996), embrace new reproductive technologies and prenatal testing as liberating women from their biological destiny, increasing their options and thus expanding female autonomy. Most feminists, however, critically examine the impact of scientific expertise and technology on pregnant women and on the cultural meaning of pregnancy and motherhood. The "making of the unborn patient" (Casper 1998), as they point out, subjects pregnant women to professional and public control. An intimate female experience—namely, the coming of a child—is turned into a matter of medical and public administration. "For making her interior a public space has also made it a space to be kept under surveillance and, ultimately, controlled" (McCulloch 2012, 17). But women are not only subordinated, but are asked to adapt their self-perception and experience to the "public fetus" ascribed to them. Fetal images, risk curves, statistical charts, and genetic test results seduce women to take a biological phantom for concrete reality, thus experiencing themselves as uterine environments.

Fetal Practices and Technologies

Feminist epistemology challenging aperspectival, universalistic truths has enabled scholars to unearth the technological, practical, and discursive construction of the fetus. In guidebooks or at the doctor's office, technological and scientific constructs mutate into quasi-natural facts or even tangible realities, and thus reify the child-to-be as an objective fetus that can be measured and diagnosed. Routinely performed in prenatal care, ultrasound testing promises a "window to the womb" and, although it aims at prenatal selection, mothers-to-be enjoy seeing their baby and come to cherish the procedure. Barbara Duden (1993) and Sarah Franklin (1991) argue, however, that ultrasound does not enable women to see their child-to-be but only to perceive the technological visualization of measuring data. It does not reveal a hidden truth, but constructs an artificial reality. Hence, drawing on Donna Haraway's theory of postmodern existence as chimera between machine and organism, anthropologists Lisa Mitchell and Eugenia Georges (1997) call the fetus women experience via coupling with the machine a "cyborg fetus." Furthermore, it is especially the medical ascription of risk that promises knowledge about the coming child and turns mothers-to-be into managers of fetal risk profiles. By calculating and attributing risks, experts attempt to anticipate and gain control of the future. For physicians and geneticists, the simple fact that a woman is pregnant carries the so-called base risk that the child might have some congenital disorder. Furthermore, the age of the mother-to-be is fed into a statistical calculation to determine her risk of carrying a child with Down syndrome. A welter of other risks can follow (Rapp 1999; Samerski 2009). Whenever risk emigrates from statistics to the doctor's office or to the sick bed, however, it undergoes a radical transformation: Physicians (and patients) interpret risk factors as "objective clinical signs of disease" (Gifford 1986, 222). Such "clinical risks" are not, strictly speaking, real risks, as Lorna Weir points out, because the future of a specific patient cannot be calculated; instead, "clinical risk comprises an unstable amalgam of incompatible forms of reasoning" (Weir 2006, 19). Unaware of this epistemological confusion, pregnant women do not realize that the health professional has merely ascribed to her the probabilistic traits of a fictive cohort of patients (Rapp 1999; Samerski 2009, 2015). Even feminist sociologists and anthropologists tend to interpret the epistemological gulf between tangible reality and statistics as a mere language problem or, at best, a discrepancy between the abstract and the concrete (Schwennesen, Koch, and Svendsen 2009; Rapp 1999). Thus, they oftentimes overlook the fictitious nature of diagnosed risks and the transforming power of their imputation. These "clinical risks" transmogrify the child-to-be into a faceless risk profile and turn the mother-to-be into its manager (Samerski 2009).

Disembodiment and Dependency on Experts

When pregnancy no longer refers to the expectation of a child but rather to a reproductive process that can be technically defined and optimized, a woman can no longer trust her senses. As Barbara Duden (1993) and Barbara Katz Rothman (1986), among others, have argued, the technological reconstruction of reality demands that she doubt her own corporeality. The rituals of prenatal care teach a woman to ascribe to herself developmental stages, risk figures, and hormone levels—technological abstractions that she is supposed to consider more real than what she feels and can see with her own eyes. Counseling and professional instructions encourage her to believe not only that the shape on the computer screen shows what is going on with her today but also that genetic models and probability calculations can predict what might happen tomorrow. Risk curves, electrophoretic gels, and chromosome charts claim to provide evidence, not only about the veiled fruit of her womb, but also about its veiled future.

Historically, quickening was a decisive moment for a pregnant woman, telling her that she was expecting a child. Today, quickening has been substituted with technological bonding (Duden 1993; Mitchell 2001; Taylor 2000). It is the ultrasound screen, a sonographic representation that forms the relation of the women to her fruit—that is the reason it has been legally installed in the United States as a compulsory educational measure for women who are willing to interrupt pregnancy. Constructing the unborn as an individual entity, the ultrasound image facilitates the bonding of a fetal manager to her managed subject. Or, as Janelle Taylor puts it, a women becomes the consumer of a fetal commodity: "Obstetrical ultrasound plays a part in constructing the fetus more and more as a commodity at the same time and through the same means that it is also constructed more and more as a person" (Taylor 2000, 415). Prenatal genetic tests ask women to ignore their senses for other reasons as well. The prenatal quality check demands a decision on the child-to-be on the basis of test results and imposes on women a new kind of pregnancy—namely, a "tentative pregnancy" (Rothman 1986). Waiting for experts to give the green light for accepting their pregnancies, women do not to turn toward the coming "thou," but push aside their bodily signs and perceptions. The effects of amniocentesis, as sociologist Barbara Katz Rothman found out in her interviews with women, "were an awesome silence from a belly growing larger—a belly to be hidden in big sweaters, not flaunted in maternity clothes. The fear of having to become the executioner of one's hopes meant that any early movement of the fetus that was felt became denied, acknowledgment of the sensation of movement was delayed, the quickening slowed, awaiting a phone call" (Rothman 1986, 261).

New Forms of Government

The professional encroachment on pregnant women and their increasing dependency on experts and technology has prompted various feminist theories to examine new forms of governance that do not exercise power through repression, but by forming new technologies of the self. The objective fetus together with its main manager, the pregnant woman, can be understood as new forms of subjectification. Neither in the case of abortion nor of medicalized prenatal care are women dictatorially treated as passive objects. On the contrary, various counseling events offer them options, require them to weigh risks, and to make responsible decisions. Pregnant women are not simply to comply with prescribed modes of behavior but to adapt their sense of self and responsibility to a biomedical redefinition of reality. Construed as an "informed and active rights bearing individual," Maria Fannin argues, the pregnant woman is addressed as "a responsible and reflective subject to use her body reasonably" (Fannin 2013, 273– 274)—where "reasonableness" is determined by biomedical definitions and professional standards. Thus, *responsibility* and *reasonableness* or *rationality* have become loaded catchwords, pressuring women to turn themselves into managers of fetal development. "Responsibility is equated with the capacity to behave rationally, the term presupposes a calculation of expected benefits and risks, and a decision to follow the path with the greatest possibility of benefit with the least risk" (Ruhl 1999, 96). Women are not coerced into conformance but are motivated to conform by making a choice, a choice defined by the instruction they receive on the risks and potential consequences of their menu of options: "with the principle of informed choice, and the ideal of the pregnant woman as an autonomous individual, the woman and her partner are constituted as responsible for the choice they are making and thereby also for the future which is created through their decision making" (Schwennesen, Koch, and Svendsen 2009, 202). Thus, a woman is burdened with a new kind of responsibility: the responsibility for the outcome of her pregnancy. If she bears a disabled child, it was her choice; after all, she decided in favor of giving birth to this risk profile. Thus, fetal politics fundamentally changes what it means to become a mother. Pregnant women are transmogrified into administrators of a prenatally generated managerial object. They are, as Anne Balsamo concludes, "both disempowered and held responsible at the same time" (Balsamo 1996, 110).

By studying the social and cultural consequences of medicalized prenatal care, feminist studies on fetal politics have substantially contributed to the theoretical analysis of new power technologies. Inspired by governmentality studies based on Michel Foucault's work that analyze the call for autonomy and self-responsibility as a new technology of governance, Barbara Duden, Sarah Franklin, Lorna Weir, and other scholars dismantle the powerful premise that scientific information, technological options, and professional care empower women. In contrast, they show how women are led into the disembodied sphere of risks, genes, and fetuses, where they are made responsible for the management of scientific and technological artifacts. Thus, as these scholars show, the other side of the new fetal subject is the new maternal subject: the pregnant woman as a responsible self-manager.

The Fetus as a Modern Construct

Most feminist scholars analyzing contemporary fetal politics and corresponding power relations do not fundamentally question the fetus as a natural entity and pregnancy as an objective fact. Hence, their accounts do not overcome the basic assumptions that have facilitated the emergence of the fetal subject in the first place. It is the excursion into either history or non-Western cultures that has enabled scholars to not only criticize the hailing of the fetus and the governmental, professional, and technical encroachment on women's bodies but also question the corresponding cultural certainties, which, unavoidably are also their own. Anthropologists and historians who delved into different realities, whether the world of the Hagen in Melanesia (Strathern 1992) or a physician's office in a eighteenth century (Duden 1993), happened to experience their own certainties as strange. Searching for anything comparable to the modern notion of the fetus, they were struck by an astonishing insight: For women in the eighteenth century or today in the Ecuadorian Andes there is no such thing as prenatal individual human life. So as not to misinterpret this observation as behind the times or unenlightened, the researcher must have the willingness for a kind of askesis (Duden 1991): to avoid the fallacy of imposing her own cultural assumptions on others, she has to jettison the certainties she has lived with so far. Hence, a researcher examining childbearing has to leave behind the natural facts about fetuses, pregnancy, and female bodies that seem evident and unquestionable in Western culture.

History: Pregnancy as a Somatic Stance and the Unborn as a Coming Child

Some of the most intriguing challenges to the quasi-natural notion of pregnancy as a symbiosis of mother and fetus were formulated by the historian Barbara Duden. Her study of women's bodies and somatic experiences in the eighteenth century, *The Woman Beneath the Skin* (1991) fundamentally questioned the existence and plausibility of the fetus as an organic fact. As Duden shows, until the eighteenth century, and for most people, well into the twentieth, there was no such thing as an individual being hosted in a pregnant woman's womb. Historically, the unborn was a liminal being whose hidden existence was only revealed at birth. Based on various historical sources, such as a physician's diary and medical textbooks, Duden argues that historically, there was no determinable, objective pregnancy. Instead, there were only women who felt pregnant. "Pregnant" was the expression for the particular mindset of the woman toward her coming child, her somatic *hexis*, or physical disposition (Duden 2000).

Barbara Duden distinguishes two different ways of knowing—namely, women's somatic knowledge *of* pregnancy and men's scholarly knowledge *about* pregnancy. Until the late nineteenth century, they coexisted. On the one hand, male theologians, physicians, philosophers, and natural historians discussed the fate of unchristened deceased newborns and studied the *signa impraegnationis* and *graviditatis* as well as the anatomy of the female womb. On the other hand, women knew of being pregnant. Citing the diary of a physician in the eighteenth century, Duden reports on the manifold stories that women tell about themselves and their bodily state. These stories were personal, subjective and diverse. For scholars, it was not possible to infer from them an objectivity of pregnancy. The stories were told by women who sensed the coming of a child, by women who were, as an old German expression captures beautifully, in "good hope." Since there was no possibility that outsiders could prove or refute a woman's narrative, her condition remained uncertain. Only birth could reveal its truth. Generally, the quickening of the child was the significant moment that brought certainty for women themselves. Then, she was truly pregnant. Women experienced their pregnancy haptically—not visually, on a screen. This haptic experience was exclusively female and had no correspondence in the male domain. Thus, it was the woman's attestation, her report of her "good hope" and of the quickening that turned her pregnancy into a social fact.

The Historical Fetus as the Emblem for the Child-to-Be

Since the eighteenth century, Duden reports, women's somatic perceptions were gradually delegitimized through the construction of scientific facts. Only then was pregnancy transformed from a female *hexis* to an entitative pregnancy with a fetus. Until then, the unborn was not seen an objective fact, but as a liminal being that was only represented symbolically. It was a traditional truth, going back to Greek antiquity, that human becoming was veiled and enclosed. Thus, in the Middle Ages, the unborn was depicted as a child coated in the female womb. This truth of the concealed and covered inwardness guided the gaze of the first dissectors: When Leonardo da Vinci or Vesalius drew the fetus, they portrayed a crouched little human in the twilight realm of becoming. Duden comments that da Vinci "depicts a fully grown little boy sitting in the center of the spheres of the matrix, a symbol for the human in the center of the universe"(Duden 1999, 20). Thus, the unborn was not the representation of a subject or object, but the allegory of the child-to-be. "The figure that in the anatomic atlases of the 16th century is called 'embryo', 'fetus' or 'child' is an ambiguous ideogram. What the early anatomical depictions showed was particularly the symbolically meaningful sphere of the becoming and being of the microcosm and the motive of the enclosed and the sheltered" (Duden 1991, 21). Despite the anatomical drawings of the womb and its skins and veins becoming ever more "realistic" in the seventeenth and early eighteenth centuries, the unborn remained an allegory. Its graphic representation symbolized the atopic, the non-dum, and the latent at its essence. It was not fully of and in this world, it was prospective, a child-to-be, and it was nascent.

In 1799, Samuel Thomas Soemmering, a German anatomist and researcher, wondered why no one yet had represented a human embryo and its development—a gap he wanted to fill. Through a new drawing technique called aperspectival mapping, he managed to construct the precursor of today's prenatal individual: an objective and motherless fetus as well as the stages of fetal development. As with sonographic depictions today, the construction of this fetus stipulated a nonhuman, a-relational, artificial perspective. Soemmering did not represent what he saw, but what he measured. He wanted "a *simulacrum of the object* and not *a facsimile of inspection as the object was seen*. He does not want 'realistic' representation, but a blueprint, a construct. The fetuses are thus projected on the 'farther shore,'" in a virtual nowhere and as no man's naked eye could ever perceive them. The simulacrum posits a new kind of objectivity: a forcefully distanced sight of the object" (Duden 1999, 13, 23). This birth of the a-relational fetus is a dramatic imposition in the history of pregnancy. Today, this fetus from the "farther shore" has become the emblem of pregnancy. Thus, what modern women are asked to ascribe to themselves, to cherish, and to experience is a technological artifact constructed through an a-human, a-relational view from nowhere.

Birth as Revelation and Beginning

Since pregnancy was ambivalent, uncertain, and hidden, birth was the significant moment of revelation. A true pregnancy could only be assured postpartum. The female womb was seen as capable of bearing various fruits, not only children: As physicians knew, "not everything that comes from the birth parts of a women is a human being" (Gottfried 1788, quoted in Duden 1999, 13). Sometimes they would breed nonhuman beings, such as mooncalves, moles, and false fruit. Referring back to Aristotle, moles were seen as concepts of the womb not having reached human form. What today would be diagnosed as an early fetus was seen as a fruit without human shape. Given the multiform fertility of the female womb, birth finally revealed the truth of the latent being (Duden 1998).

Before the medicalization of birth starting in the eighteenth century and finally taking hold in practice in the twentieth century, human beings were born into a female sphere. The parturient and a female aide, generally a midwife, made the child's passing the threshold between beyond and here. Birth, as Barbara Duden puts it, historically meant the coming of a child in the co-action of women. It was the "source of the epiphany of an expected child within a socio-somatic... activity, that started with labor, culminated in cutting the cord and was finished by afterbirth and—sometimes—with swaddling. It happened between women. Birth was a beginning" (Duden 1998, 155; my translation).

Traditionally, newborns attained social status in a rite of passage, for example, the Muslim *aquiqa*, (slaughter of a sacrificial animal at birth) Christian baptism, or Jewish bris. (male circumcision ceremony). Nevertheless, they came to the world by being born. Birth has been the unique event with which each *bios* began. Faced with the abortion debate and the extension of rights to unborns, feminist philosophers, such as Susan Sherwin (1992), Mary Anne Warren (1989), and Martha Nussbaum (2000), make strong arguments for retaining birth as the moment of human individuation and "moral significance." With birth, they argue, the infant "does become a biologically separate human being" (Warren 1989, 62). Yet Morgan refutes this argumentation, blaming it for romanticism and, more important, biological reductionism since it uses "physical autonomy... as the most important qualification for personhood" (Morgan 1996, 59). Rebecca Wilkin, along similar lines, charges that it cements male-dominated notions of autonomy and corporeal individualism. Pregnant women and breast-feeding mothers together with their infants, she objects, do to not meet this condition of physical independence. "... adherence to birth as a dividing line crystallizes individuation as the primary condition of personhood" (Wilkin 2008, 99).

This feminist debate about the justification for a dividing line testifies to the dramatic loss of the traditional meaning of birth. Historically, birth was not essentially meaningful because it would generate an independent individual, but because it was revelation and beginning. Birth marked the threshold between two heterogeneous spheres: inside and outside, invisible and visible, and beyond and here and now. Every newborn is a newcomer, an unforeseeable surprise, as philosopher Hannah Arendt wrote in 1958.

Yet decades later, Arendt's thinking on birth is about to lose cultural resonance. Within thirty years, birth has largely been reduced to the simple transition of a human life from an intrauterine to an extrauterine state—and thus to an arbitrary but negotiable dividing line. Since the advance of technological prenatal care, practices around pregnancy and birth treat the invisible as visible and the child-to-come as the child already there. As Barbara Katz Rothman reports, when prenatal examinations give the desired green light and determine the sex of the child-to-be, parents-to-be treat it as a member of the family. Pregnant women name their unborn and cherish ultrasound scans in the same way they hitherto cherished photos of the newborn. They plan the nursery, the clothes, the place at the kindergarten, and sometimes even a cesarian for a predictable delivery day. Parents-to-be do not want any surprises. Birth is not a beginning anymore, but "a critical moment in the career of a prenatally generated managerial object" (Duden 2002, 155).

The Absence of the Fetus in Non-Western Cultures

Barbara Duden's thrilling insights into the radically different meaning of pregnancy, birth, and the child-to-be that prevailed until two or three generations ago is echoed in feminist ethnographic research on pregnancy in other cultures. The absence of a fetal subject is not restricted to Western history. For women who still rely on a phenomenologically grounded reality, the unborn is not an autonomous individual; instead, it is a liminal being beyond this space and time (Gammeltoft 2007; Morgan 1997; Strathern 1992). As anthropologist Lynn Morgan shows, people consider abortion a sin in Catholic Ecuador, but for completely different reasons than in advanced technological societies. Ecuadorians are not concerned that abortion kills a human being, but rather that it mutilates a woman's body and interferes with the will of God. To the rural women Morgan interviewed, the unborn is far from being a person or otherwise comparable to the Western notion of a fetus. They call it *criatura* (creature) or *venidero* (the one to come) and imagine it as a "liminal, unripe, and unfinished creature. Nascent persons are brought into being slowly, through processes rife with uncertainty and moral ambiguity" (Morgan 1997, 324, 329). Ecuadorians see no need to technically and objectively define the beginning of life and personhood. "There was no such thing as 'the status of the fetus,'" Morgan comments, "because fetuses were not singular entities" (Morgan 2009, xiii). Women are convinced that some time during pregnancy the fruit reaches its childish form, boys earlier than girls. But even then, the *venidura* stays in the twilight of becoming and is rather a subject of assumptions and personal narratives than of bodily fact. Pregnancy belongs to the female realm, and women "use overlapping and sometimes competing discourses to make sense of their own circumstances and the will of God" (Morgan 1997, 324).

Through the increasing use of techniques like ultrasound and amniocentesis, however, the Western technologically mediated understanding of pregnancy is spreading around the globe. When women seek professionalized medical care, they are confronted with scientific objects, such as the fetus and risks, as well as with Western conceptions of health and responsibility. As feminist studies have shown, these ideas clash with local notions of what it means to be pregnant and to give birth (e.g., Kaufert and O'Neil 1993). For women not used to the Western hegemony of an instrumented reality, such as the Vietnamese women interviewed by Tine Gammeltoft, the ultrasound picture does not diminish their culturally rooted sense of uncertainty. "Women in Hanoi seem to see sonogram images as more contingent: as fleeting and transitory pictures of human beings in the process of becoming, rather than as fixed representations of a stable and firmly existing 'baby'" (Gammeltoft 2007, 145). For the recent immigrants in Canada studied by Lisa Mitchell (2001), a sonogram provides neither the pleasure of seeing the baby nor the comfort of being reassured—as it does for European and North American women.

Sources of Truth: The Epistemology of the Fetus

In the face of the historical and anthropological absence of the fetus, feminists started to question the historical, cultural, and epistemological conditions that make the fetus an unquestionable fact of our time. What made it possible for the fetus to see the light of the day? How did it become a spectral citizen and the emblem of human life? In a nutshell, the apparent obviousness and plausibility of individual "human life" in women's bellies rests mainly on two pillars: First, on the persuasive power of fetal images in a visual culture, and second, on the belief in scientific inquiry as a source of truth. Images of the fetus as well as "objective" biological facts about its development make it a certainty. The visual artifice and culturally bound credulity in these facts as well as the a-human perspective they stipulate—namely, the "god-trick of seeing everything from nowhere" (Haraway 1991, 189)—are simply ignored.

Fetal Emblems in a Visual Culture

One target of the feminist challenge is the image of the fetus that, especially in the United States, has become an omnipresent public emblem. Fetal figures appear in movies, magazines, and advertisements; clinics use the fetal form as an eye-catcher; parents-to-be bond with their unborn "baby" on the ultrasound screen; and ultrasound scans of the unborn decorate desks, refrigerators, and websites. In the United States, pro-life activists played a significant role in promoting the fetal figure in public: in their crusade against abortion, they promoted their mission with movies and fetal pictures as emblems of vulnerable human life in need of protection. After losing political and legal struggle against abortion with the US Supreme Court ruling in *Roe v. Wade* in 1973, they renewed their "commitment to a more long-term ideological struggle over the symbolic meaning of fetuses, dead or alive" (Petchesky 1987, 263).

Rosalind Petchesky (1987, 264) denounced this a strategy of antiabortionists "to make fetal personhood a self-fulfilling prophecy by making the fetus a public presence." Thus, feminists called attention to the artificiality of these images and decoded their hidden messages. Karen Newman wrote a history of fetal representations, beginning in the sixteenth century, when drawings of dissected female bodies and pregnant uteri first appeared. Focusing on the obliteration of women, Newman places these drawings in a line with modern scientific representation. This supposition of similarity and comparability, however, is problematic. Barbara Duden convincingly refutes this interpretation by arguing that before the eigthteenth century, depicted fetuses were not representations but symbols. Lynn Morgan's (2009, 188) cultural history *Icons of Life* retraces the making of fetal representations by showing how embryology and the scientific collection of fetuses "materialized the embryonic body" and the idea of biological development. In the first half of the twentieth century, however, the fetal form was not yet politicized; only later did it begin to "speak—loudly—on a range of contentious topics including gender, abortion, and reproductive technologies" (187). Nevertheless, embryologists "helped to construe the human embryo as an autonomous actor, detachable from women's bodies and motivated solely by biological forces" (188). Intermeshed with societal and political concerns about gender, race, and religion, this autonomous actor turned into a kind of projection screen, reflecting "individual and collective beliefs about individuality, motherhood, and American society" (Dubow 2011, 9).

In the 1960s, the pioneering fetal photographs of Lennart Nilsson caught broad public attention. His pictures of unborns were celebrated as an expedition into the previously hidden mysteries of the "beginning of human life." Nilsson produced a series of pictures that were supposed to show the development of a living fetus in utero. His photographs in effect "skinned" pregnant women and imparted objectivity as well as miraculousness to fetal development. Like Soemmering's first fetal representations, Nilsson's pictures promised objectivity and revelation, although they were the products of technological construction. Nilsson used dead fetuses from abortions, dressed them up, and experimented with new photo-optical techniques. He carefully arranged these objects to achieve the intended photographical effects, resulting in the famous pictures of free-floating fetuses. Karen Newman calls them an "aesthetic artifice" of the simulation of "life" (Newman 1996, 15). Like Soemmering's depictions, these fetuses were a-relational. The mother was absent, "replaced by empty space" (Franklin 1991, 195–196). "These round fetal orbs resemble nothing more than a sort of organic spacecraft floating in a void" (Franklin 1991, 196). Meanwhile, ultrasound scans tempt women to consume and incorporate these technical constructs. As Barbara Duden and others argue, women do not see their baby on the ultrasound screen, but only the visualization of measuring data. They are asked to ascribe to themselves the "disembodied realization of an optical imputation" (1999, 24).

By questioning the objectivity of fetal images and analyzing their symbolism, feminists weakened their symbolic power, deconstructing the apparent realism and objectivity of visualizations. In doing so, they not only unmasked the fetal image as an ideologeme, but also exposed the very foundation of a society increasingly sucked up by virtual reality. The habit of staring at the screen and consuming dressed-up pictures tempts a woman to equate existence with visualization. "She lives with most of her world behind glass," Barbara Duden (1993, 92) comments about the pregnant women who are so fond of the ultrasound picture "and takes for granted, for real what is shown on the screen."

Biological Facts

There is a second powerful source for the construction of prenatal human life, which is "served by its handmaiden visualization technologies" (Michaels and Morgan 1999, 4) and which feminists successfully challenged: the equation of the "beginning of human life" with biological organizational stages. Whether they are conservatives, liberals, or even feminists, they refer to biological findings to make their argument for or against fetal personhood. For decades, genetic, embryological, and neurological research has claimed to have settled the question of the beginning of human life and the moral status of the embryo and fetus—through definite scientific facts. From the distanced view of the anthropologist, Marilyn Strathern describes the attribution of personhood to cells in development as follows:

> The point at which a "human being" could be said to have emerged was presented as the point at which the individuality of the physical matter that will make up the future body and mind of a single entity could be discerned. With the establishment of the individual, in this view, comes a necessary condition for the establishment of the person, that is, an entity with potential moral claims on others. Yet, those claims seem a consequence of, rather than a cause of, its personhood. . . . No relationship with other persons, not even its parents, affects the way the issue of personhood is generally discussed."
>
> (Strathern 1992, 21)

This individual fetus hinges upon biological notions of body, organizational stages, nerve cells facilitating sensations, and genetic singularity. Thus, the plausibility of fetal individuality presupposes the common belief in the science of biology to discover objective fetal truth(s). "Biology thus not only obscures social categories, but it becomes the basis for their cultural production" (Franklin 1991, 200).

Drawing on the insights of social and feminist science studies on the social and cultural construction of scientific facts, feminist theory puts biological facts back into their place—namely, into their social and historical context. "Feminist theorizing about fetuses rests on an assumption that there is no 'natural' meaning of the fetus outside of social and cultural claims" (Casper 1999, 105). Seen in this light, the contemporary equation of unborns with persons raises a worrisome issue: fetal individuality is postulated on the basis of scientific hypotheses. The contemporary attempt to install personhood to the unborn is not based on "its alleged possession of a soul, but rather its possession of a human body and genotype" (Petchesky 1984, 334). In political debates, ethical treatises and juridical verdicts, scientific constructs, such as fertilized eggs, genes, and blastulas, are linked to socially meaningful and powerful notions, such as motherhood, children, and, above all, "human life." Outside their context of origin, technical terms such as DNA, gene, and genetic information become imbued with social and cultural meaning. "The 'biological facts' of conception, pregnancy and fetal life are not only powerful as authoritative forms of *knowledge*, they are also powerful *symbolically*, as key cultural resources in the construction of personhood" (Franklin 1991, 192). From the moment of the biological nidation of a fertilized egg—something that can only be technologically asserted—women are addressed as "mothers." As the German High Court puts it, drawing on findings of embryological research, the fusion of the genomes of two gametes produces a fixed "genetic identity" that develops not into but *as* a human being. This scientifically constructed individuality is projected into women's bellies. Pregnancy is redefined as a symbiosis between a woman and this newfangled fetal subject beyond human perception.

This production of social categories on the basis of biology, to use Franklin's terms, has momentous social consequences: First, the projection of a scientific construct into the interior female womb incapacitates women. Now a hormone test or ultrasound scan declares a woman pregnant and thereby a mother of a fetus, rendering her somatic condition and interpretation meaningless. And secondly, judges and legislators define human life and the criteria of membership on the basis of scientific facts from the laboratory. The law and rules protecting the fetus equate zygotes and biological organizational stages with concrete human beings and demand rights and human dignity for a being whose existence can only scientifically and technologically be verified. Not a vis-à-vis whom I can face and grasp but a biologically defined human life is the object of legal protection. "The obvious question, however, is whether we really mean to reduce identity—'personhood' or 'the self'—to genetic patterns or strands of a few basic chemicals?" (Hartouni 1997, 301). How, Barbara Duden asks, does this biologically substantiated approval of equality between an individual and a being without hands and feet, without head and tail impinge upon the understanding of personhood? It gets people used to the idea that judges and lawmakers decide on a biomedical basis if the dementia patient, the body ready for organ harvesting, or the dead pregnant women belong to the category of human life which is protected by law. "With this 'life,'" Duden warns, "our technological society extinguishes individual humans and creates an object, a resource which it can access managerially" (1996, 99; my translation).

FEMINIST PERSPECTIVES ON PREGNANCY AND THE UNBORN

The fetus as an individual agent residing in a female body stipulates, as Sarah Franklin puts it, an "extensive reliance on high technology." She points out that separation, not connectedness, is the basis of this "ontological construction": it involves the separation "of the fetus from the mother, and of the social from the biological.... it is a definition of personhood constructed entirely out of 'natural facts,' although they are themselves, of course, socially constructed" (Franklin 1991, 196). Some feminist theorists, such as the political scientist Eileen McDonagh, have developed strong arguments for the right to abortion on the basis of this separation. Starting with the modern notion of the fetus as an individual, they conceptualize the child-to-be as an intruder, depriving the pregnant woman of her bodily resources. Thus, when women do not consent to this intrusion, on the basis of liberal human rights, such as the laws of self-defense, the maintenance of this kidnapper cannot be morally or legally imposed on them (McDonagh 1996; see also Thompson 1971). Nevertheless, most feminists do not see the fetal agent as a source for recuperating a feminist view on pregnancy and personhood. "The entire basis of this dominant patriarchal construction prohibits the possibility of a woman-centered perspective on pregnancy, in which the term 'individual' has no meaning" (Franklin 1991, 203). Thus, feminist scholars strive to establish a view of the unborn that counters the fetus as an individual. They develop theoretical foundations for an understanding of childbearing and personhood that transcends modern Western conceptions of isolated objective identities. Mostly, they stress "relationality" as a key concept for being a person, understanding it as an antidote to the prevailing individualism (e.g., Petchesky 1984; Sherwin 1992; Whitbeck 1984). As empirical studies show, remnants of the relational notion of childbearing still exist among women—even when they routinely and delightedly submit to ultrasound scans that transmit the image of a fetal individual. As the Greek women interviewed by Georges account for, "fetal persons, like persons generally, are constituted processionally, across time, and relationally, through their connections with others, most importantly with family members, and not as autonomous and separate units." Taking up the experience of connectedness and relationality, Sherwin (2009, 146) proposes "a shift in ... [the] understanding of the nature of personhood, moving from a traditional abstract conception to one that explicitly embraces the embodied, relational reality of persons." As she strives to leave behind the assumption that persons are entities that can be defined biologically or psychologically, Sherwin calls for a "theory of personhood that acknowledges that the embodied nature of a human being is always situated in a specific social, historical context; persons are embedded within the social environments that constitute and sustain them" (49). Persons, she states, are not simply a given, but are created through social interaction: through nurturing, education, and socialization. Like Caroline Whitbeck (1984), she argues that persons are kindred beings, fellows. Finally, fully developed persons become moral agents participating in a moral community. Yet, the only relation the fetus has is the very intimate one with the pregnant woman. It resides within her body and is fully dependent on her nurturing. Apart from this existential relation, the fetus cannot have any other direct ones. But this intimate connection with the pregnant women, Sherwin argues, is not a social one. She compares fetuses with patients in persistent vegetative state and concludes: "These are not social relationships, since the limited neocortical function of the beings in question prevents any degree of reciprocal interaction" (2009, 153). Thus, to make the argument short, the fetus cannot be conceived of as a full person and a "moral agent." In the case of the woman desiring abortion, reciprocity is missing and thus "the women can determine what relational status she assigns to the human who is dependent on her for its ongoing needs" (Sherwin 2009, 160).

Despite a vast feminist literature discussing relationality, personhood, and ethics well beyond the question of pregnancy and individuation, relational theories have not succeeded in establishing a radically new vision of pregnancy, the fetus, and personhood. As in the case of Sherwin's arguments, they even cement the epistemologies and power relations they intend to counter. Thus, while respecting their feminist effort, Lynn Morgan fundamentally criticizes Sherwin's and Whitebeck's relational theory of (fetal) personhood. Their theory, Morgan argues, rests on seemingly universally valid biological explanations whose cultural and historical context is not reflected. Sherwin's argument of the inability of the fetus to have relations to others is based on biological explanations, such as the fetus's dependency on the motherly body and of its "limited neocortical function." Similarly, her concept of relationality presupposes an individual body that is understood in biological terms. Deeply embedded in Western notions of individualism, it repeats the split between natural and social, body and mind. "A wholly realized relationality hinges, in the views of Sherwin and Whitbeck, on the notion of corporeal autonomy" (Morgan 1996, 55). Thus, Morgan counters, the feminist theory of relational personhood simply repeats the kind of Western individualism that she seeks to leave behind. Arguing against the seeming naturalness of this concept, Morgan refers to non-Western views in which the body is not seen as a natural, material substance for the social making of persons, but literally as an embodiment of social relations. Marilyn Strathern's anthropological work in Melanesia demonstrates this relational existence beautifully. Persons, Strathern writes, "are not conceptualized. . . as free-standing" (1992, 125). Rather, "relations are integral to persons." Thus, she calls the Melanesians "fractal persons": "the fractal person is an entity with relationship integrally implied. Any scale of social activity mobilises the same dimensionality of person/relation" (1992, 125). Here, the natural and the social coincide. "The body and the person are thus coterminous, and the body/person is valued socially precisely *because* it is the product of specific social interaction" (Morgan 1996, 56).

Universalistic Theories, Fuzzy Realities and the Hope for New Beginnings

Has the feminist endeavor to develop a feminist theory of pregnancy, the fetus, and personhood failed? Most philosophical treatises trying to develop a consistent and universalistic new theory of pregnancy and personhood do not reflect the multifaceted experiences and perceptions of women. Instead, they tend to echo the biological and individualistic premises that downgrade women's knowledge *of* pregnancy and exalt objective, distanced knowledge *about* pregnancy—exactly the kind of epistemology—namely, the "god-trick of seeing everything from nowhere" (Haraway 1991, 189)—that has facilitated the construction of the fetal subject. Hence, based on her insights into the cultural variability of perceiving individuals and relations, Morgan proposes a rather praxeological understanding of personhood and a "pragmatic situational ethics of fetal relationality" (1996, 63). In accordance with other feminists, she considers the question of whether the fetus is a person "inherently irresolvable" (Casper and Morgan 2004, 17). Instead of developing universalistic concepts, norms, and theories, she pleads for the examination of the fuzzy and sometimes paradoxical social realities in specific political and historical contexts. Along the lines of Valerie Hartouni (1997), she argues that personhood should be seen as a negotiated, dynamic concept whose practical implications for women have to be assessed. "Personhood must be understood as an outcome of power relations, as an unstable project subject to constant negotiation and debate" (Morgan 1996, 63).

Thus, for good reasons, and in the tradition of a feminist epistemology, Morgan and Michaels propose abandoning universalistic theories in favor of a critical analysis of the present. Instead of exploring abstract questions, such as "when does personhood begin?" and "what constitutes it," they want to inquire about the condition of possibility to ask and answer them: "rather than engage these questions on their own terms, we hope to shed light on why these questions get asked, and how they get answered, by attending both to the cultural contexts out of which they arise, and to those in which they do not" (Michaels and Morgan 1999, 5).

In fact, feminist studies have been remarkably fruitful in inquiring into the political dimension as well as the cultural and epistemological foundation that have produced the specter of the fetal person. By linking theory with empiricism, that is theoretical reflections on pregnancy and personhood with historical and anthropological analysis, they not only expose the objective fetus as a modern ideologeme, but also shed a new light on the basic assumptions that structure Western societies. By putting such seemingly self-evident facts as "fetal images," "biological development," and "genetic identity" back into their cultural context, they unmask science-based dogmas as a belief system that presumes a technologically distanced view from nowhere and systematically excludes personal experience, sensory perception and relatedness. Thus, in a nutshell, feminist scholarship has shown that the conception of prenatal "human life" mirrors the techno-scientific redefinition of persons in times of managerial governance. As an object that is scientifically defined, technologically measured, and professionally administered, the fetus is a child of our time.

Despite their fundamental criticism of fetal obsession and the notion of fetal individuality, feminists, surprisingly, did not take up Hannah Arendt's thinking on the meaning of birth and natality for the human condition. Human mortality has excited philosophical thinking from its inception, but not so the fact that human beings are born—except for Hannah Arendt. She made birth the starting point for her deliberations on human action. Inherent in every birth, Arendt says, is a beginning, and this beginning is the emblem and foundation of the human ability to act. "Because they are initium, newcomers and beginners by virtue of birth, men take initiative, are prompted into action" (Arendt 1958, 177). The fact that everybody is born, Arendt says, facilitates the human capacity to act freely. By acting, individuals can create beginnings, which initiate unpredictable stories and leave tracks in the social web and in history. These stories based on free human action are unique and surprising in the same way that every newborn is an unforseeable surprise. Humans again and again marvel at the newborn, the completely new and singular: "The new always happens against the overwhelming odds of statistical laws and their probability, which for all practical, everyday purposes amounts to certainty; the new therefore always appears in the guise of a miracle." (Arendt 1958, 178).

Seen in the light of Hannah Arendt's thinking, the transformation of birth into a technical event transferring a human life from an intrauterine to an extrauterine state gains a worrisome new dimension. The loss of birth not only jeopardises women's freedom and capacities, but also disquietingly impinges upon the cultural conceptions of humankind. Following Hannah Arendt, the eradication of birth as a meaningful moment of beginning threatens the human capacity to act freely and thus dims the possibility of hope. For Arendt, birth as beginning is the origin of confidence and hope:

> The miracle that saves the world, the realm of human affairs, from its normal, "natural" ruin is ultimately the fact of natality, in which the faculty of action is ontologically rooted. It is, in other words, the birth of new men and the new beginning, the action they are capable of by virtue of being born. Only the full experience of this capacity can bestow upon human affairs faith and hope ... which Greek antiquity ignored altogether ... It is this faith in and hope for the world that found perhaps its most glorious and most succinct expression in the few words with which the Gospels announced their "glad tidings": "A child has been born unto us." (1958, 247).

Feminist analysis and theory on pregnancy succeeded in making the familiar strange. They enable readers to take a viewpoint from which the fetal individual dissolves into a phantom and thus open new possibilities to perceive, think and experience. Following Hannah Arendt, there is hope as long as human beings are born. Thus, feminist scholarship, by questioning the managerial and objective scaffolding of our time, has disseminated the possibility for hope and new beginnings.

References

Arendt, Hannah. 1958. *The Human Condition*. Chicago: University of Chicago Press.
Balsamo, Anne. 1996. *Technologies of the Gendered Body: Reading Cyborg Women*. Durham, NC: Duke University Press.
Casper, Monica. 1998. *The Making of the Unborn Patient. A Social Anatonmy of Fetal Surgery*. New Brunswick, NJ: Rutgers University Press.
Casper, Monica. 1999. "Operation to the Rescue. Feminist Encounters with Fetal Surgery." In *Fetal Subjects, Feminist Positions*, edited by Lynn M. Morgan and Meredit W. Michaels, 101–112. Philadelphia: University of Pennsylvania Press.

Casper, Monica and Lynn M. Morgan. 2004. "Constructing Fetal Citizens." *Anthropology News*, December 17–18.

Dubow, Sara. 2011. *Ourselves Unborn: A History of the Fetus in Modern America*. Oxford: Oxford University Press.

Duden, Barbara. 1991. *The Woman beneath the Skin: A Doctor's Patients in Eighteenth-Century Germany*. Cambridge, MA: Harvard University Press.

Duden, Barbara. 1993. *Disembodying Women: Perspectives on Pregnancy and the Unborn*. Cambridge, MA: Harvard University Press.

Duden, Barbara. 1999. "The Fetus on the 'Farther Shore': Toward a History of the Unborn." In *Fetal Subjects, Feminist Positions*, edited by Lynn M. Morgan and Meredit W. Michaels, 13–25. Philadelphia: University of Pennsylvania Press.

Duden, Barbara. 1996. "Das Leben als Entkörperung." In *Frauen gegen Bevölkerungspolitik: LebensBilder-LebensLügen. Leben und Sterben im Zeitalter der Biomedizin*. 89–100. Hamburg: Verlag Libertäre Assoziation.

Duden, Barbara. 2002. "Zwischen 'wahrem Wissen' und Prophetie: Konzeptionen des Ungeborenen." In *Geschichte des Ungeborenen. Zur Erfahrungs—und Wissenschaftsgeschichte der Schwangerschaft, 17.-20. Jahrhundert*, edited by Barbara Duden, Jürgen Schlumbohm, and Patrice Veit, 11–48. Göttingen: Vandenhoeck and Ruprecht.

Fannin, Maria. 2013. "The Burden of Choosing Wisely. Biopolitics at the Beginning of Life." *Gender, Place and Culture* 20 (3): 273–289.

Featherstone, Lisa. 2008. "Becoming a Baby? The Foetus in Late Nineteenth-century Australia." *Australian Feminist Studies* 23 (58): 451–465

Franklin, Sarah. 1991. "Fetal Fascinations. New Dimensions to the Medical Scientific Construction of Fetal Personhood." In *Off-Centre: Feminism and Cultural Studies*, edited by Sarah Franklin, Celia Lury, and Jackey Stacey, 109–125. London, Harper Collins.

Gammeltoft, Tine. 2007. "Sonography and Sociality: Obstetrical Ultrasound Imaging in Urban Vietnam." *Medical Anthropology Quarterly* 21 (2): 133–153.

Gifford, Sandra 1986. The Meaning of Lumps: A Case Study of the Ambiguities of Risk. In *Anthropology and Epidemiology: Interdisciplinary Approaches to the Study of health and Disease*, edited by C.R. Janes, R. Stall and Samdra M. Gifford 213–246. Dodrecht, Reidel.

Haraway, Donna. 1991. *Simians, Cyborgs and Women. The Reinvention of Nature*. New York: Routledge.

Hartouni, Valerie. 1997. *Cultural Conceptions: On Reproductive Technologies and the Remaking of Life*. Minneapolis: University of Minnesota Press.

Kaufert, Patricia, and John O'Neil. 1993. "Analysis of a Dialogue on Risks in Childbirth. Clinicians, Epidemiologists, and Inuit Women." In *Knowledge, Power and Practice: the Anthropology of Medicine and Everyday Life*, edited by M. Lock and S. Lindenbaum, 32–54. Berkeley: University of California Press.

McCulloch, Alison. 2012. "The Rise of the Fetal Citizen." *Women's Studies Journal* 26 (2), 17–25.

McDonagh, Eileen. 1996. *Breaking the Abortion Deadlock. From Choice to Consent*. New York: Oxford University Press.

Michaels, Meredith W. and Lynn M. Morgan. 1999. "Introduction: the Fetal Imperative." In *Fetal Subjects, Feminist Positions*, edited by Morgan and Michaels, 1–9. Philadelphia: University of Pennsylvania Press.

Mitchell, Lisa. 2001. *Baby's First Picture: Ultrasound and the Politics of Fetal Subjects*. Toronto: University of Toronto Press.

Morgan, Lynn M. 1997 "Imagining the Unborn in the Ecuadoran Andes". *Feminist Studies* 23, 322–350.
Morgan, Lynn M. 1996 "Fetal Relationality in Feminist Philosophy: An Anthropoligical Critique". In *Hypatia* 11, 47–70.
Morgan, Lynn M. 2009. *Icons of Life: A Cultural History of Human Embryos*. Berkeley: University of California Press.
Morgan, Lynn M., and Sharon R. Kaufman. 2005. "The Anthropology of the Beginnings and Ends of Life." *Annual Review of Anthropology* 34: 317–341.
Newman, Karen. 1996. *Fetal Positions: Individualism, Science, Visuality*. Palo Alto, CA: Stanford University Press.
Oakley, Ann. 1984. *The Captured Womb: A History of the Medical Care of Pregnant Women*. Oxford: Basil Blackwell.
Petchesky, Rosalind Pollack. 1984. *Abortion and Woman's Choice. The State, Sexuality, and Reproductive Freedom*. New York: Longman.
Petchesky, Rosalind Pollack. 1987. "Fetal Images: the Power of Visual Culture in the Politics of Reproduction." *Feminist Studies* 13 (2), 263–292.
Purdy, Laura M. 1996. *Reproducing Persons. Issues in Feminist Bioethics*. Ithaca, NY: Cornell University Press.
Rapp, Rayna. 1999. *Testing Women, Testing the Fetus. The Social Impact of Amniocentesis in America*. New York: Routledge.
Rothman, Barbara K. 1986. *The Tentative Pregnancy. Prenatal Diagnosis and the Future of Motherhood*. New York: Penguin.
Ruhl, Lealle. 1999. "Liberal Governance and Prenatal Care: Risk and Regulation in Pregnancy." *Economy and Society* 28 (1): 95–117.
Samerski, Silja. 2015. *The decision trap. Genetic education and its social consequences*. Exeter: Imprint Academic (in press).
Samerski, Silja. 2009. "Genetic Counseling and the Fiction of Choice: Taught Self-Determination as a New Technique of Social Engineering." *Signs: Journal of Women in Culture and Society* 34: 735–761.
Schwennesen, Nete, Lene Koch, and Mette N. Svendsen. 2009. "Practising Informed Choice: Decision-Making and Prenatal Risk Assessment; the Danish Experience." In *Disclosure Dilemmas. Ethics of Genetic Prognosis After the "Right to Know/Not to Know" Debate*, edited by Christoph Rehmann-Sutter and Hansjakob Müller, 191–204. Farnham, Burlington: Ashgate.
Sherwin, Susan. 1992. *No Longer Patient: Feminist Ethics and Health Care*. Philadephia: Temple University Press.
Sherwin, Susan. 2009. "Relational Existence and Termination of Lives: When Embodiment Precludes Agency". In *Embodiment and Agency*, edited by Sue Campbell, Letitia Meynell and Susan Sherwin, The Pennsylvania State University Press.
Strathern, Marilyn. 1992. *Reproducing the Future: Essays on Anthropology, Kinship and the New Reproductive Technologies*. New York: Routledge.
Taylor, Janelle. 2000. "Of Sonograms and Baby Prams: Prenatal Diagnosis, Pregnancy, and Consumption." *Feminist Studies* 26: 391–418.
Thompson, Judith Jarvis. 1971. "A Defense of Abortion." *Philosophy and Public Affairs* 1 (1): 47–66.

Warren, Mary Anne. 1989. "The Moral Significance of Birth." *Hypatia* 4 (3): 46–65.

Weir, Lorna. 2006. *Pregnancy, Risk, and Biopolitics: On the Threshold of the Living Subject.* New York: Routledge.

Whitbeck, Caroline. 1984. "A different reality: Feminist Ontology". In: Carol C. Gould. ed. *Beyond Domination: New Perspectives on Women and Philosophy.* Totowa, NJ: Rowman and Allanheld: 64–68.

Wilkin, Rebecca. 2008. "Descartes, Individualism, and the Fetal Subject." *Differences: A Journal of Feminist Cultural Studies* 19 (1): 96–126.

CHAPTER 35

PRISON

SARAH X PEMBERTON

Introduction

PRISONS are inherently coercive institutions. By design, prison deprives inmates of freedom through what Weber defined as the state's monopoly on "the legitimate use of physical force" (Weber 2009, 83). While modern states prohibit some forms of violence, such as attacks on police, they exercise and legitimate other forms of violence, such as physical force by prison guards. Through the criminal justice system, the state legitimates violence by police and prison guards who are empowered to contain nonlegitimated violence. The bars of a prison cell therefore separate the "good guys" of law enforcement from the "bad guys" who commit crimes, and it is significant that both are predominantly masculine. The vast majority of prisoners and prison guards worldwide are men (Walmsley 2012; Bureau of Justice Statistics 2008, 20), and violence has long been associated with traditional conceptions of masculinity. This relationship between law enforcement, violence, and masculinity makes prisons highly problematic for feminists.

The criminal justice system purports to fulfill a protective function, so some women's advocates have appealed to the state to intervene in sexual and domestic violence. Feminist activism around rape and battered women in the 1970s led to changes in public attitudes about gender violence and to the provision of women's shelters and rape crisis centers, but some feminists also contributed to a carceral logic by calling for more policing and harsher punishments (Gottschalk 2006, 115). For example, Susan Brownmiller's influential analysis of rape as a form of masculine domination of women concludes by recommending long prison terms for rapists (Brownmiller 1977, 379). The dominance of punitive law and order approaches in the United States since the 1970s and provision of funding to some women's groups through victims advocacy programs in the Department of Justice led to many women's advocates cooperating with, and sometimes being co-opted by, a justice system that promotes carceral expansion instead of deeper social change to end gendered violence (Gottschalk 2006, 138). However, these appeals to the criminal justice system for protection from masculine violence overlook "the man in the state" (Brown 1992). Even as some (often more privileged) women have benefited from the criminalization and imprisonment of some men who assault women, the inherent masculinism of the criminal justice and prison systems means that these institutions tend to reinforce male dominance and women's subordination. Feminist theories of the prison have therefore sought to understand how the penal system contributes to forms of gendered identity and gender inequality.

Understanding power relations in criminal punishment requires unpacking the meaning of crime. Crime is not a neutral, objective, or preexisting category but is instead socially constructed. Activities are defined as crimes through criminal law and the justice system, and penalties are imposed on people who are convicted of committing crimes. The meaning of crime is shaped by social values and power relations, so the activities that are criminalized change over time and vary among jurisdictions. Some activities that were previously crimes in the United States have been decriminalized, including sodomy and abortion (although the practice of the latter is increasingly restricted, and its status precarious in many states). Other activities vary in legal status in different jurisdictions, as is the case with prostitution, which is lawful in several counties in Nevada but criminalized elsewhere in the United States. As the changing laws about sodomy, abortion, and prostitution show, ideas about gender and sexuality partly determine the activities that are labeled as crimes. Crime is usually defined in a way that reflects the views and interests of dominant groups, so criminal law and enforcement tends to disadvantage less powerful groups such as women, people of color, and the poor, including by criminalizing behavior associated with these groups, subjecting them to more restrictions and surveillance, and by protecting wealth that was historically acquired through their exploitation, dispossession, or enslavement.

The enforcement of criminal law is also shaped by racialized and gendered power relations, which intersect to make some groups targets of police surveillance, criminalization, and imprisonment. In the United States, nearly one in fourteen black men aged 30 and 34 was in prison during 2012, compared to less than one in six hundred white women of the same age (Bureau of Justice Statistics 2013, 25). These stark disparities in incarceration rates mean that imprisonment provides a powerful lens for understanding systems of privilege, and "in most countries one can discover which are the marginalized groups in society by analysing the prison population" (Coyle 2005, 60). The complex intersections of race, gender, class, and sexuality mean that it is overly simplistic to regard any single group as the most marginalized, or any single institution as exemplifying oppression, but imprisonment is both a major indicator of and contributor to socioeconomic disadvantage (Western 2006). Practices such as racial profiling, sex segregation of prisoners, and gendered disciplinary regimes in penal institutions also mean that the prison system contributes to the construction of gendered and racialized identities (Bosworth 1999; Hill Collins 2004; Lamble 2011; Spade 2011). Prisons therefore contribute to constructing gender and racial identities, reinforce forms of socioeconomic inequality that are tied to those identities, and are a site of struggle between state violence and forms of resistance.

Prisons, Class, and Identity

Many theories of the prison focus on how imprisonment contributes to the maintenance of social order and inequality, a line of argument that originates from the work of the Frankfurt School theorist Georg Rusche. Writing in the 1930s, Rusche draws on Marxist theory to present a critical theory and economic history of punishment in Europe and North America. Rusche argues that criminal punishment upholds capitalism by protecting the property of the wealthy, deterring the poor from stealing, and enabling the exploitation of workers' labor (Rusche and Dinwiddie 1978). Historically, the development of industrial capitalism led to the use of imprisonment as a criminal penalty, and Rusche argues that prison regimes are largely determined by the labor market. When there was a shortage of labor Rusche states that prisons sought to generate a profit from convict labor, as occurred in the Auburn prison system of silent congregate work used in the nineteenth century United States (Rusche and Kirchheimer 1939, 130). By contrast, the ample supply of labor in nineteenth century Europe made convict labor unprofitable, so European prison regimes focused on deterring crime through harsh conditions and solitary confinement (Rusche and Kirchheimer 1939, 137). This theory argues that penal philosophy, prison architecture, and even details such as the quality of prison food were shaped by the capitalist economy and labor market.

Rusche's major theoretical contribution is identifying the connection between punishment and the living conditions of the poor. The penal system attempts to deter the poor from committing property crimes, but Rusche argues that this relies on the principle of "less eligibility," whereby prison conditions must be worse than the living conditions of the poorest law-abiding citizens. If prisoners have better living standards than the poor, for example, good food and pleasant living quarters, then the needy may be encouraged to commit crimes. The poorest people in capitalist societies often have low living standards, so, in practice, less eligibility requires highly unpleasant prison conditions because "unemployed masses, who tend to commit crimes of desperation because of hunger and deprivation, will only be stopped from doing so through cruel penalties" (Rusche and Dinwiddie 1978, 4). Two important implications follow from this insight about less eligibility. Firstly, imprisonment will only be an effective deterrent for property crime when the living conditions of the poor are above a bare subsistence level. If the poor are barely surviving then deterrence would require below-subsistence prison conditions, which would kill inmates. Secondly, less eligibility means that prison conditions cannot improve without first increasing living standards for the poor, thereby limiting efforts to make prisons more humane or rehabilitative. Rusche concludes that better prison conditions require the introduction of progressive policies that ensure good living standards for all (Rusche and Kirchheimer 1939, 207). Penal reform therefore becomes inseparable from broader socioeconomic justice.

Although Rusche's account of the relationship between criminal punishment and capitalism was originally published in the 1930s, these ideas did not receive widespread attention until the re-publication of his book *Punishment and Social Structure* in 1968. The rediscovery of Rusche's work spurred a surge in critical theories and histories of the prison,[1] but his economic explanation of criminal punishment was challenged by theories of the prison that focus on political institutions and ideas.[2] The most prominent of these alternative accounts is provided by Michel Foucault, who traces the rise of imprisonment to changes in political power and forms of knowledge during the late eighteenth century. Foucault rejects Rusche's argument that the central function of the prison is to uphold capitalism and enable labor exploitation, arguing instead that prisons aim to produce a modern political subject that is individualized, orderly, and self-disciplined.

In *Discipline and Punish*, Foucault rejects Rusche's focus on class while crediting him with the important insight that prisons exercise a form of power that is not repressive but productive and "linked to a whole series of positive and useful effects which it is their task to support" (Foucault 1995, 24). To explain this, Foucault presents a poststructuralist genealogy that juxtaposes two systems of political power and punishment: sovereignty and disciplinary power. Sovereign power stems from the king and punishes offenders through the public infliction of physical pain on the body, including torture and death. By contrast, disciplinary power is decentralized and uses the subtler techniques of "hierarchical observation and normalizing judgement" (Foucault 1995, 192) to induce subjects to follow a detailed set of behavioral norms. Under disciplinary power, lawbreakers are imprisoned in the attempt to make them conform to these norms. Foucault therefore links the historical transition from corporal punishment to imprisonment with late eighteenth-century political changes such as the American and French revolutions. By replacing monarchy with liberal democracy, Foucault argues that Western societies led to the introduction of disciplinary power and imprisonment: "The real, corporal disciplines constituted the foundation of the formal, juridical liberties" (Foucault 1995, 222).

Whereas Rusche maintains that prisons are unpleasant in the attempt to deter crime among the poor, Foucault argues that prisons use disciplinary power in the attempt to transform and rehabilitate offenders. Discipline works by producing "docile bodies" (Foucault 1995 135) through precise norms about spatial organization, the timetable, and activity, combined with processes of surveillance and assessment that record and rank each person. As an example of disciplinary power, Foucault refers to Jeremy Bentham's radial design for the panopticon: a prison where each prisoner occupies a solitary cell that is constantly visible to a guard in the central tower, who may or may not be watching—the prisoners cannot tell. The constant threat of surveillance makes prisoners aware that they are being assessed, leading them to internalize and self-impose the norms of conduct (Foucault 1995, 201). The logic of the panopticon is that the combination of behavioral norms and observation will transform occupants, turning a disorderly group into individualized and normalized subjects. Although Foucault acknowledges that prison regimes vary and that many are unlike the panopticon, he argues that imprisonment always involves both "the deprivation of liberty and the technical transformation of individuals" (Foucault 1995, 233).

While Foucault agrees with Rusche that the prison fails to prevent crime, he maintains that this cannot be resolved by economic redistribution. Instead, Foucault suggests that the failure of the prison is inevitable and irresolvable because, whereas prisons aim to normalize prisoners, they actually serve to label prisoners as different and stigmatize them. This tension between the goals and effects of imprisonment means that rather than normalize inmates, prisons produce a category of delinquents: "for the observation that prison fails to eliminate crime, one should perhaps substitute the hypothesis that prison has succeeded extremely well in producing delinquency . . . in producing the delinquent as a pathologized subject" (Foucault 1995, 277). The existence of delinquents then provides a justification for the intensification and extension of disciplinary power throughout society, which leads to ever more surveillance and normalization. According to Foucault, the prison's failure at its purported goals itself achieves different political ends.

Foucault's account connects prison regimes to identity because the disciplinary norms imposed by prison authorities seek to produce a particular kind of subject. Since prisons use the timetable and control of activity in the effort to instill normative identities among inmates, it becomes possible to identify this normative ideal through close examination of prison regimes. While the actual effect of imprisonment may be very different from the goal, as Foucault argues, his work opens up a rich field of analysis concerning the relationship between prison regimes and forms of identity. In addition, Foucault shows how disciplinary power produces corresponding forms of knowledge, including detailed records about each prisoner and behavioral sciences based on these observations. Fields such as criminology and psychology are revealed to be part of the exercise of disciplinary power in which prisoners are objects of study and experts outline the norms against which their behavior is assessed and modified. Foucault's work therefore suggests that it is important to challenge official and scientific knowledge about the prison by drawing on other sources of information, such as the experiences of prisoners. While Foucault was writing *Discipline and Punish,* he was also involved in circulating a counterknowledge of imprisonment through the Group d'Information sur les Prisons, which collected and disseminated French prisoner narratives.

The neoliberal direction of US penal policy since the 1980s has led scholars to question whether Foucault's account of disciplinary power and the prison remains relevant (Alford 2000; Fraser 2003), but other theories of punishment have continued his focus on the way imprisonment shapes identity and knowledge. Critical race theory identifies race as a social construct shaped by government policies and laws (Omi and Winant 1994), and the sociologist Loïc Wacquant draws on this to argue that the US prison system is a race-making institution (Wacquant 2001, 116). Wacquant explains that such practices as racial profiling and the disproportionate imprisonment of black Americans have shaped the meaning of race through "official solidification of the centuries-old association of blackness with criminality" (Wacquant 2001, 117). Moreover, racially disproportionate imprisonment has contributed to constructing racialized identities as "black" and "white," and reinforced inequality between these racialized groups. Overall, Wacquant suggests that the US prison system has succeeded slavery and Jim Crow as a new "peculiar institution" (Wacquant 2001, 98) that makes both racialized identities and racial hierarchy. Although not all scholars share this focus on the social construction of race, the view that the US prison system contributes to racialized inequality has become widespread among sociologists and legal theorists (James 1996; Mauer 2006; Western 2006; Alexander 2010).

Feminist Theories and Histories of Punishment

Although Rusche and Foucault disagree about the significance of economics, they both assume that prisoners are male and that the power dynamics in punishment are not shaped by gender. Rusche argues that prisons sought to ensure the exploitation of labor in industrial capitalism, but he does not recognize that forms of labor and pay were shaped by ideas about gender. During the nineteenth century, industrial wage labor became associated with the ideal of a male breadwinner, and women were expected to provide unpaid domestic labor within the household instead of, or in addition to, paid work for lower wages. Similarly, Foucault traces the origin of the disciplinary prison to the military ideal of discipline without recognizing that this was a masculine ideal designed for the public sphere. Foucault's claim that the rise of imprisonment in the nineteenth century accompanied the extension of political liberties overlooks the lack of political and economic rights for women and the implications for how women were normalized or punished. Because Foucault does not recognize the public sphere and prison as masculine, he overlooks the way prisons and other disciplinary institutions impose gendered norms of conduct that are designed to construct normatively gendered subjects.

Feminist scholars have provided histories of punishment that show how both definitions of crime and criminal penalties were shaped by gender and race. These feminist histories show that men and women were subjected to different forms of discipline in specific eras. For much of the nineteenth century, middle-class norms of domestic femininity relegated affluent white women to a private sphere in which discipline was provided by the family, Church, and medical profession (Freedman 1981, 10). Whereas Foucault argues that disciplinary prison regimes accompanied new political rights, women and people of color in the nineteenth century lacked the status of "individuals possessing rights and liberties" and were largely excluded from the prisons he describes (Davis 1998, 97). Gender also played an important role in defining crime, as women were criminalized and punished for sexual conduct, including the premarital or extramarital sex that was permissible for men. Women in nineteenth- century England were judged according to an exacting middle-class ideal of the domestic wife and mother, against which they were categorized either as moral and chaste or as a "moral menace" beyond redemption (Zedner 1991, 30). Similarly, in the United States, white women were evaluated against a white, middle-class ideal of moral and domestic conduct, which criminalized "fallen women" (Freedman 1981, 20). Under these race and gender-specific standards, women were frequently incarcerated for moral offenses, such as drunkenness or prostitution, whereas men were imprisoned for violent or property crimes.

These feminist prison histories show that the nineteenth-century prisons discussed by Rusche and Foucault sought to instill normative forms of gender identity. In both England and the United States, prisons used policies of sex segregation that placed men and women in different penal institutions, which enabled the use of gender-specific penal philosophies and disciplinary regimes (Rafter 1990, 10; Zedner 1991, 119). Regimes in women's prisons were strongly influenced by conceptions of middle-class femininity and centered on "restoring white women to their place as wives and mothers" (Davis 1998, 97). In England, women's prisons attempted to instill domestic femininity and moral conduct through religious education and the beneficial influence of personal relationships between offenders and female guards (Zedner 1991, 120). Women's prison reformers in the United States also sought to encourage middle-class norms of femininity by, for example, developing women's prisons that were modeled on a domestic environment and used communal "cottages" instead of individual cells (Freedman 1981, 76). These restrictive gender norms led to the punishment of women who did not conform to white, middle-class forms of femininity, including women of color and poor women who engaged in paid labor (Rafter 1990, xxxii). Not only did men and women experience different forms of penal discipline, but the very restrictive standards applied to women meant that they were often more severely regulated and punished than men (Rafter 1990, 36; Zedner 1991, 183).

Feminist histories of punishment also explore the intersection of gender and race by identifying three distinct penal institutions for women in the United States during the nineteenth century. The first set of penal institutions, often termed *reformatories*, focused on rehabilitating women who were regarded as capable of reform. Reformatories were usually found in northern states and were largely reserved for white women (Rafter 1990, 37). Secondly, there were *custodial institutions* for female prisoners viewed as less capable of reform, and black offenders in northern states were usually sent to these nonrehabilitative prisons. The third system of punishment existed in the South, where criminal law was explicitly racialized. The prison activist and scholar Angela Davis points out that here chattel slavery was replaced by penal slavery, because forced labor for convicted criminals remained legal under the Thirteenth Amendment. To continue exploiting black labor, Southern states passed discriminatory black codes that re-criminalized former slaves so that they could be re-enslaved (Davis 1998, 100). Whereas many white women who committed crimes were sent to rehabilitative institutions, black women were criminalized through racist laws and then forced to work in very severe conditions. These different forms of punishment reflected racialized conceptions of femininity, under which black women were seen as "lacking the soul that might be shaped and transformed by punishment" (Davis 1998, 99).

These feminist histories challenge the accounts of penality provided by Foucault and Rusche in several ways. Firstly, crime was defined in specifically gendered and racialized ways, because women were criminalized for activities that were legal for men (such as extra-marital sex), and black people were criminalized for activities that were legal for whites. Secondly, this literature shows the variety of penal institutions during the nineteenth century and the racialized and gendered power dynamics involved in these institutions. The criminalization of black Americans in order to re-enslave them is broadly consistent with Rusche's argument that punishment served the purposes of class control and labor exploitation, but Rusche overlooks how race framed particular people as slaveable. By contrast, white convicts were more likely to be sent to rehabilitative prisons designed to instill particular forms of identity and conduct, as Foucault argues. However, these rehabilitative institutions used highly gendered disciplinary regimes that were designed to develop normative forms of masculinity or femininity. Whereas men's US prison regimes involved industrial work, women's reformatories sought to instill feminine ideals of sexual morality and unpaid domestic labor. Only by paying attention to race and gender is it possible to understand how these forms of punishment reflect and reinforce political power and social inequality.

Like Rusche and Foucault, feminist prison histories provide insights about the ongoing power dynamics in prisons, which continue to be highly gendered. Sex-segregation policies place men and women in separate penal facilities, and prisons have gender-specific rules about personal appearance, dress, and activity (Rafter 1990, 196; Bosworth 1999). Research by the criminologist Mary Bosworth suggests that the traditional conception of white, middle-class domestic femininity is reflected in women's prison regimes through work and education programs that teach such skills as beauty, cooking, and cleaning. However, Bosworth identifies two contradictory views of the subject within contemporary women's prisons: the traditional ideal of femininity, and a universalistic conception of an autonomous and rights-bearing subject. Women's prisons therefore reflect broader tensions within modern norms of femininity, variously construed as "responsible and autonomous or passive and dependent" (Bosworth 1999, 58). Indeed, Bosworth argues that inmates exercise resistance against the prison regime through strategic appeals to either of these ideals (Bosworth 1999, 143). Not only do prisons still enforce normative gender roles, but Bosworth's research suggests that gendered prison regimes provide broader insights about gendered power relations and the constitution of the self.

Research also suggests that female prisoners continue to receive more severe punishment. Sex segregation and the relatively small number of women's prisons mean that female prisoners are usually held further from their families than male prisoners, and are often placed in higher-security institutions than necessary (Coyle 2005, 68). Since women are a minority of prisoners, they often receive less attention, leading to fewer resources and programs in women's prisons (Rafter 1990, 196; Ross 1998, 138). Female prisoners are prescribed psychiatric drugs at high rates (Ross 1998, 120), which is linked to historical stereotypes whereby "deviant men have been constructed as criminal, while deviant women have been constructed as insane" (Davis 2003, 66). Moreover, security procedures in women's prisons involve strip searches and internal cavity searches that many prisoners experience as a form of state-legitimated sexual assault (Davis 2003, 63).

This routinized and state-sanctioned sexual coercion of female prisoners is a form of "sexualized, patriarchal power" (Miller 2001, 882) that highlights the violent and masculinist nature of imprisonment.

The economic exploitation of prisoners that Rusche identified in the nineteenth century also continues to occur through prison privatization and what Davis terms the "prison industrial complex" (Davis 2003). Davis argues that the exploitation of both male and female prisoners for profit is racialized and tied to the history of chattel and penal slavery in the United States. In the present day, the economic beneficiaries of imprisonment include private prison companies, such as Corrections Corporation of America; prison employees; companies that use prisoner labor; suppliers of goods and services to prisons; investors in any of these companies and politicians who receive campaign donations from these groups (Davis 2003, 100). Given this exploitation, racism, and sexism in the prison system, Davis argues that prisons should be abolished and that disadvantaged groups should be provided with welfare, education, and healthcare instead of being criminalized (Davis 2003, 108). Although Davis's call for prison abolition has not been widely adopted, her account of the economic incentives involved in carceral expansion has been influential and led other scholars to condemn the political and economic interests around prison privatization and expansion (Hallet 2006). The attention to multiple systems of power and identity that is a consistent theme of Davis's work has also been widely adopted in recent years and become known as *intersectionality*.

Intersectional Theories of the Prison

In common with most feminist and antiracist scholarship before the 1990s, much of the feminist scholarship about prisons is largely inattentive to the experiences of women of color and the relationships among gender, race, and class. Although the feminist histories and theories of imprisonment discussed earlier show that prisons contribute to the construction of normative gender identities, most of this literature focuses on white women. Critical race analysis of the prison argues that imprisonment constructs racialized identities and inequality, but this work has concentrated on black men. Over the past two decades this lacuna has been addressed by the development of intersectionality as a conceptual framework, and the turn by leading scholars of intersectionality to a discussion of criminal justice. This intersectional scholarship is attentive to the intersections of race, gender, and class for both victims of crime and criminalized people. Much of the intersectional literature also draws on the ideas of women of color who are engaged in antiviolence or prison activism, such as the INCITE network of women of color antiviolence organizations, Critical Resistance, and Mothers Reclaiming Our Children (Mothers ROC) in California.

The centrality of gender to racialized state violence is captured in Spivak's much-cited description of British imperialism as "white men saving brown women from brown men" (Spivak 1988, 297). This phrase draws attention to how the state constructs women as vulnerable subjects in order to exercise racial violence in the name of protection. By framing men of color as posing a threat to women and simultaneously portraying white men as the protectors of women, the state appeals to gender as a way to legitimate the exercise of violence by white men against men of color. However, Spivak emphasizes that the logic of white men "saving" women of color does not make women of color safer or more politically empowered; instead, the competing ideas of womanhood provided by white men and men of color make it more difficult for the voices of women of color to be heard. Spivak shows that the state's claim to protect women of color actually serves as a pretext for coercive acts that uphold both male dominance and racial hierarchy. Intersections between gender, race, and class are context specific, so Spivak's formulation may not apply in other places and times, but her words provide an important reminder to critically assess claims that state violence protects women of color.

Since the early 1990s, there has been a growing body of intersectional feminist scholarship about imprisonment that makes three important contributions to theories of the prison. First, intersectionality scholars have analyzed how the US criminal justice system responds to violence against different groups of women in order to understand who is being protected by the penal system, against whom, and at whose expense. The most influential account of how race and gender overlap in relation to sexual violence is provided by Kimberlé Crenshaw, who coined the term *intersectionality*. In the United States, Crenshaw identifies a "dominant conceptualization of rape as quintessentially Black offender/white victim" (Crenshaw 1991, 1266) that disadvantages both black men and black women. The racist stereotype of black men as highly sexualized and potential rapists meant they were targeted for state violence, through policing and imprisonment, and for extralegal violence, such as lynchings. However, the conceptualization of rape victims as white led to a lack of attention and support for women of color, whose reports of sexual assault were seen as less credible and less important (Crenshaw 1991, 1271). Crenshaw argues that sexual violence against black women has been de-prioritized, so sexual assaults on black women receive lower priority from police and less severe sentencing for assailants (Crenshaw 1991, 1277). This shows that racism in the penal system has specifically gendered impacts, because black men are subjected to more intensive surveillance and punishment than white men, while black women receive less protection from sexual violence than white women. In Spivak's phrasing, Crenshaw's work suggests that the US penal system uses a logic of white men saving white women from black men.

The intersectional framework for analyzing violence has been extended by Patricia Hill Collins, who echoes Crenshaw's call for more attention to violence against women of color, but argues that this requires challenging the very definition of violence. Hill Collins argues that conventional definitions of violence obscure the way violence upholds gender and racial hierarchies: "Elite groups define violence in ways that legitimate their own power, use those definitions of violence to enforce hierarchical power relations, and then point to ensuing social inequality as proof of the veracity of the definitions of violence themselves" (Hill Collins 1998, 920). Against conventional definitions of violence that focus on individuals and unusual events, Hill Collins calls for a recognition of how violence affects racialized and gendered groups and of how everyday acts can be violent, as with domestic violence. In particular, Hill Collins distinguishes between violence legitimated by the state and nonlegitimated violence, arguing that physical harm is rarely labeled violence when it is perpetuated by the state. The failure to recognize state-legitimated violence means that police killings of people of color are neither widely recognized as violent nor punished; whereas the black journalist Mumia Abu-Jamal was sentenced to death for the killing of a white policeman (Hill Collins 1998, 922). Hill Collins demonstrates that the US penal system exercises racialized and gendered violence, conceals it in a self-serving definition of violence, and justifies the continuation of state violence by pointing to acts of nonlegitimated violence by marginalized groups.

Indigenous scholar Andrea Smith shares this concern with state violence, arguing that the US state both contributes to violence against Native American women and fails to protect them. Smith emphasizes that sexual victimization in Native American communities is tied to the history of colonization and the imposition of European ideas of gender such as binary sexes, heterosexuality, and European family structure (Smith 2006, 72). Colonization produced sexual violence, as indigenous people were constructed as dirty, "sexually violable and 'rapeable'" (Smith 1999, 35). The colonial state also directly contributed to sexual violence toward indigenous women as is seen in the exceptionally high rates of sexual abuse in government boarding schools for Native Americans (Smith 2005, 126). Because the US state coerces indigenous peoples and bears responsibility for causing sexual violence, Smith argues, the US justice system will not protect indigenous women: "There is a contradiction . . . in relying upon the state to solve the problems it is responsible for creating" (Smith 1999, 44).

These intersectional accounts identify the relationship between violence towards individuals and broader systems of sexual, racial, and colonial domination that intersect to make women of color at high risk of violence both from the community and from the state. The US criminal justice system is grounded in and reproduces dominant forms of power and inequality, making less effort to protect women of color from sexual violence than white women, and justifying state violence against men of color by stressing the vulnerability of white women. Moreover, Hill Collins provides a powerful challenge to dominant definitions of violence and the double-standard whereby state-legitimated violence is not recognized as violent. By arguing that the US state not only fails to protect women of color but causes racialized and gendered violence, this work calls into question the protective function of the US penal system.

Second, intersectional scholarship illuminates how the intersections of race and gender disadvantage women of color in the penal system. This work shows that in the United States women of color are incarcerated at far higher rates than white women, and often face more severe prison conditions. In 2012, black women were imprisoned at more than twice the rate of white women (Bureau of Justice Statistics 2013, 25), and black women such as Assata Shakur have been held in more severe prison conditions than other female prisoners (Davis 2003, 64). The incarceration rate of Native

Americans is not listed in official prison statistics, but indigenous scholars calculate that Native Americans are imprisoned at twice the rate of whites (Ross 1998, 89). Native American scholars, such as Luana Ross and Stormy Ogden, emphasize that the imprisonment of Native American women stems from a colonial system of law that is biased against indigenous peoples (Ross 1998 p.16; Ogden 2005, 62). Jurisdictional issues over aboriginal territory lead to more severe punishment for Native American women than for white women, because crimes committed on Indian land fall under federal criminal laws that are usually more severe than state laws (Ross 1998, 19; Ogden 2005, 62). In prisons, Native American women receive less support for their cultural and religious practices (Ross 1998, 138), are overrepresented in maximum security facilities with severe regimes (Ross 1998, 142), and experience frequent sexual assault (Ross 1998, 168).

The third major contribution of intersectional prison scholarship lies in identifying the relationships between masculinist law enforcement institutions and race and class. This literature shows that the penal system causes violence in two ways: first, law enforcement and prisons involve racialized and sexualized violence toward criminalized men and women, who are disproportionately from communities of color; second, the penal system contributes to violent domination of women and of LGBT people in the broader society because the culture of policing and prisons legitimates and spreads forms of racialized masculinity that are aggressive, sexist, and racist. This work suggests that prisons strengthen the systems of domination that disempower and victimize women.

Legal scholar Angela Harris has done important work on the relationship between masculinity and law enforcement, especially policing. Harris argues that overwhelmingly male law enforcement officials, such as police and prison guards, performatively enact a form of hypermasculinity, exercising authority by being "tough and violent" (Harris 2000, 793). The culture of hypermasculinity in law enforcement culminates in police violence. Harris emphasizes that this violence is racialized, gendered, and sexualized and includes the sexual assault of inmates by arresting officers and prison officials. Harris characterizes acts of violence toward black communities by law enforcement as "ways of doing race as well as gender" by seeking to assert "the superiority of white masculinity" (Harris 2000, 798–799). The violent hypermasculinity prevalent in law enforcement then spreads, because the aggressive, heteropatriarchal forms of masculinity used by police become associated with manliness and authority and encourage other men to be violent in order to prove their manhood (Harris 2000, 802). In short, the criminal justice system both exercises racialized and gender violence and spreads forms of masculinity that involve such violence. To change this, Harris calls for a new theory and practice of law enforcement that is less aggressive and masculinist.

Sociological research by Hill Collins also suggests that the US justice system contributes to violent and racialized forms of masculinity. Whereas white men hold "legitimate authority over mechanisms of violence" (Hill Collins 2004, 189), including the military, police, and prisons, black men tend to occupy more marginal social locations. As a result, white men often express masculine authority and violence through state-legitimated structures; whereas many black men express their masculinity by challenging the "legitimated White state violence" (165) of the justice system. Through the mass criminalization and imprisonment of young black men since the 1980s as part of the "war on drugs," prisons have played a particular role in shaping black masculinity. Hill Collins (2004, 211) argues that the imprisonment of so many young black men has reinforced gang structures in black communities, and contributed to a "thug life" image of black youth culture that is commercialized through hip-hop. Moreover, Hill Collins is concerned that because prison authorities tolerate and perpetuate violence, sexism, and homophobia, this has lead to the spread of violent, hierarchical masculinity among US prisoners and their communities. The dominant form of masculinity in many US prisons involves proving one's manhood by committing violence, including sexual assault, and by avoiding victimization, so prisoners may adopt violent masculinity in the attempt to protect themselves (Hill Collins 204, 237). Hill Collins argues that this culture in men's prisons creates a strong incentive for young black men to adopt tough, sexist, and homophobic behavior, since this is associated with higher status and less risk of being attacked. The criminal justice and prison system therefore both directly exercises racialized violence over black communities, and contributes to forms of black masculinity that involve physical and sexual violence, and domination of women.

Trans Prison Scholarship

Although earlier feminist theories of the prison have shown how the penal system shapes forms of masculinity and femininity and contributed to forms of gender inequality, this literature has not challenged binary constructions of sex and gender. Recently, these categories have come into question by queer and trans scholars, who argue that the prison system plays a significant role in enforcing ideas of binary, biological sex and normative cisgender (i.e., nontransgender) identity, thereby disadvantaging lesbian, gay, bisexual, transgender, and queer (LGBTQ) people. For much of the twentieth century LGBTQ people in the United States were criminalized through sodomy laws that regulated sex and sumptuary laws that required people to wear at least three articles of clothing associated with the gender they were assigned at birth (Mogul, Ritchie, and Whitlock 2011, 64). Although these laws no longer exist, the US criminal justice system continues to discriminate against people whose gender or sexuality is considered deviant (Mogul, Ritchie, and Whitlock 2011), and particularly harms transgender and gender-nonconforming people. Critical trans analysis by scholars such as Dean Spade and Sarah Lamble shows how this discrimination against transgender people stems from the way the US criminal justice system upholds norms of binary sex, normative cisgender identities, and heterosexuality. Moreover, this work builds on intersectional scholarship by examining how gender and sexuality intersect with class and race to especially disadvantage groups such as low-income transgender people of color.

Studies of imprisonment from queer and trans perspectives argue that the US penal system harms LGBTQ people by de-prioritizing them as victims of crime and by discriminating against them in law enforcement and imprisonment. Because official statistics about the US penal system usually do not include categories for queer and transgender people, information has been gathered by advocacy organizations such as the National Coalition of Anti-Violence Programs (NCAVP), and the National Center for Transgender Equality. This research shows that there were over two thousand bias-motivated attacks on LGBTQ people in 2013, including eighteen murders (NCAVP 2014, 8). Less than half these attacks were reported to police because many LGBTQ fear police prejudice or revictimization through unjust arrests and verbal, physical, or sexual abuse (NCAVP 2014, 47). Transgender people face particular hostility and are assaulted by police at seven times the rate of nontransgender people (NCAVP 2014, 59). A national survey of transgender people in the United States found that over 20 percent of those who interacted with police were harassed, 6 percent were physically abused, and 2 percent were sexually abused (National Center for Transgender Equality 2011, 159). This widespread abuse leads some trans scholars to conclude that "the criminal punishment system is the most significant perpetrator of violence against trans people" (Spade 2011, 90).

Transgender people are also subject to police profiling, and trans women are often arrested on suspicion of being sex workers. This police bias has led to transgender women who are not sex workers being arrested and charged for prostitution, as happened to the transgender activist and Arizona State University student Monica Jones.[3] This pattern of discrimination and violence against transgender people by police has been described as "*walking while trans*, derivative of the more commonly used term *driving while black*" (Mogul, Ritchie, and Whitlock 2011, 61). While this term captures the aspect of police discrimination based on gender identity, it obscures crucial intersections between gender, race, and class. Intersectional analysis shows that trans people are more likely to be targeted by police if they are poor and/or people of color, and black trans people are arrested and imprisoned at more than four times the rate of whites (National Center for Transgender Equality 2011, 163). Trans analysis of the US penal system therefore needs to account for the intersections between multiple systems of power.

Trans analysis of the US penal system by Dean Spade provides an intersectional account that incorporates themes from both Rusche and Foucault, emphasizing that imprisonment reinforces socioeconomic inequality and participates in the constitution of particular forms of identity. Spade argues that trans and gender-nonconforming people are criminalized and imprisoned as a result of being poor, which is frequently due to cumulative discrimination in housing, employment, and healthcare (Spade 2011, 11). Transgender people are arrested for poverty-related offenses, such as homelessness, or for engaging in survival strategies that involve illicit economies, such as sex work. Moreover, poor trans people of color are most likely to be criminalized and imprisoned (Spade 2011, 11). Institutions within the penal system are segregated based on binary sex or gender categories, so trans people are often placed in facilities that conflict with their self-identification, where they are the targets of physical and sexual violence (Spade 2011, 147). Spade argues that the underlying cause of these problems is the use of gender as a category for labeling people, determining what spaces they should use (ranging from prisons to bathrooms), and regulating their lives (Spade 2011, 123). Spade draws on Foucault's analysis of disciplinary norms (Foucault 1995) and his account of how populations are governed through categories of sex and sexuality (Foucault 1990) to explain how gender is constructed and enforced. To reduce criminalization and violence toward trans people, Spade argues that it is necessary to challenge the use of gender as an administrative category, gendered forms of disciplinary power, and other forms of domination including socioeconomic inequality, racism, and xenophobia. Perhaps most radically, Spade argues that the penal system manifests existing forms of power including sexism and racism, thus reducing violence against trans people requires working to both abolish prisons and reduce policing (Spade 2011, 90).

A similar argument for prison abolition from a critical trans perspective is developed by Sarah Lamble, who draws on research about US, English, and Canadian prisons. Lamble argues that prisons are inherently harmful to trans people because they are violent institutions that impose oppressive gender and sexual norms, through sex segregation, gender discipline, and sexual violence (Lamble 2011, 242). In addition, prisons contribute to "racism, classism, ableism, and colonial oppression" (Lamble 2011, 246) while taking resources away from services that benefit disadvantaged groups, such as education and healthcare. While some LGBTQ activists call for protection of trans rights by police, including by enforcing hate crimes laws, Lamble emphasizes that these strategies overlook the deep-rooted biases in the penal system and contribute to further criminalization and carceral expansion (Lamble 2013, 240). Instead of protecting disadvantaged communities from harm, Lamble argues, prisons only reinforce domination and inequality, including by exercising necropower: a form of slow death and living death (Lamble 2013, 244).

Trans analysis suggests that the penal system is more deeply gendered than has been previously recognized by feminist scholars. The use of sex segregation in prisons naturalizes binary sex categories, eliding the existence of intersex and trans people, as well as enabling the imposition of gender-specific discipline. The use of sex and gender as administrative categories extends to criminal justice statistics, which do not record transgender or intersex people, thus impeding efforts to demonstrate their overrepresentation among those who are arrested and imprisoned. Although many social and governmental institutions use administrative categories of gender, these categories are particularly rigorously enforced in institutions that deal with poor people, such as homeless shelters and prisons (Spade 2011, 142). Prison is one of the institutions in which gender categories and rules are most rigorously and coercively enforced, and thus where trans and queer people are most disadvantaged and vulnerable. By drawing on an intersectional feminist methodology, Spade and Lamble also show how multiple systems of power intersect to make it particularly likely that low-income trans people of color will be marginalized, victimized, and imprisoned. Both Lamble and Spade argue that prisons are inherently violent institutions that uphold racial, gender, class, and sexual hierarchies and coercively enforce normative gender identities. Moreover, this intersectional trans analysis suggests that this violence and hierarchy cannot be removed from the penal system.

Directions in Feminist Prison Scholarship

Like critical theories of the prison from Marxist, poststructuralist, and critical race perspectives, feminist theories of the prison show how imprisonment upholds systems of power and thereby contributes to forms of inequality. Whereas Rusche focuses on economic power and class inequality, and critical race theorists, such as Wacquant, focus on racialized identity and white supremacy, feminist analysis has drawn attention to the gendered aspects of punishment. Feminist histories and sociological studies of the prison show that prison regimes seek to instill normative forms of masculinity and femininity. Trans analysis of the prison extends these insights by showing how segregation based on binary sex and gender categories in criminal punishment serves to naturalize the idea of binary, biological sexes and cisgender identity, while harming trans and gender-nonconforming people. By enforcing the binary categories of man and woman and then norms of masculinity and femininity, prisons therefore contribute to constructing gender categories and identities. This research suggests that prisons play an important role in constituting the identities that sexism works upon and through. Further, the analysis of Harris and Hill Collins suggests that the enactment of violent, sexist, and homophobic forms of masculinity by law enforcement personnel encourages those who are criminalized and imprisoned to adopt similarly violent and regressive forms of masculinity. If prisons not only enforce gender categories and norms but also perpetuate aggressive forms of masculinity that involve male domination, then the prison system may do more to contribute to gendered violence than to protect women.

Many feminist insights about imprisonment stem from intersectional analyses that show how prison systems reflect and reinforce multiple interlocking systems of power and domination. This work shows that racism is gendered and that gender is racialized, so that the US penal system harms men and women of color in different ways. Whereas men of color are criminalized and imprisoned at exceptionally high rates, women of color are vulnerable to gendered and sexual violence from both the community and the state. Crenshaw's work suggests that the US criminal justice system uses a logic of white men saving white women from men of color to justify the exercise of state-legitimated violence, and both Hill Collins and Harris argue that this leads to the spread of particularly violent and sexist forms of masculinity. Perhaps unsurprisingly, intersectional and black feminist prison scholars are often particularly doubtful about the potential for reforming the penal system so that it no longer sustains gendered violence and inequality. Since the 1970s, feminist appeals to the state for protection have often added support for tough-on-crime policies that have increased the scope and punitiveness of the US justice system[4], causing soaring incarceration rates in communities of color (Gottschalk 2006, 125). The recognition that feminists have sometimes contributed—deliberately or not—to penal expansion helps to explain why the authors of several leading intersectional theories of the prison call for the abolition of prisons based on the belief that the violence, inequality, and sexism in the prison system is ineradicable (James 1996; Smith 1999; Davis 2003; Lamble 2011; Spade 2011).

Although feminist scholarship about prisons often involves the empirical analysis of the US penal system, the theoretical insights generated by this work apply far more widely because it calls into question the ideal that prisons fulfill a protective role toward women. One of the central ways that male domination operates through the modern state is by framing women as "requiring protection from the world of male violence while the superior status of men is secured by their supposed ability to offer such protection" (Brown 1992, 25). In most states the criminal justice and prison systems are the paradigmatic examples of this masculinist protection and show that the supposed protection of women relies on the exercise of state-legitimated masculine violence. Intersectional and trans scholarship identifies a clear racialized, gendered, and class hierarchy in this protection, so that those who are marginalized by multiple systems of power receive less state protection from violence and are often directly subject to violence from the state. The prison system therefore reinforces and exacerbates systems of privilege that empower affluent white men while disempowering and victimizing other groups, especially those that are multiply marginalized by gender, race, class, and sexuality. As long as the penal system continues to operate through state-legitimated violence, and as long as this violence continues to be associated with masculinity, the penal system is likely to remain masculinist and to reinforce gender inequality. Developing a feminist approach to punishment, let alone a nonracist or social justice approach, therefore requires a critical engagement with how male domination is perpetuated through law, definitions of crime, and the penal system and, perhaps, a fundamental reconceptualization of the coercive powers of the state.

Notes

1. For histories of punishment that draw on economic explanations of penality, see Michael Ignatieff (1978) *A Just Measure of Pain: The Penitentiary in the Industrial Revolution, 1750–1850*. London: Pantheon Books; Dario Melossi and Massimo Pavarini (1981) *The Prison and the Factory: Origins of the Penitentiary System*. London: Macmillan; and Adam Hirsch (1992). *The Rise of the Penitentiary: Prisons and Punishment in Early America*. New Haven, CT: Yale University Press.
2. Alternative explanations of punishment in the United States that focus on changing social and political ideas include David J. Rothman (1971) *The Discovery of the Asylum: Social Order and Disorder in the New Republic*. Boston: Little, Brown; David Rothman (1980) *Conscience and Convenience: the Asylum and Its Alternatives in Progressive America*. Boston: Little, Brown; Michael Meranze (1996). *Laboratories of Virtue: Punishment, Revolution and authority in Philadelphia 1760–1835*. Chapel Hill, NC: University of North Carolina Press; and Thomas Dumm (1987) *Democracy and Punishment: Disciplinary Origins of the United States*. Madison: University of Wisconsin Press.
3. For accounts of the arrest of Monica Jones and her conviction for "manifesting" prostitution see the ACLU interview "Arrested for Walking While Trans: An Interview with

Monica Jonesm," https://www.aclu.org/blog/lgbt-rights-criminal-law-reform-hiv-aids-reproductive-freedom-womens-rights/arrested-walking; and media reports, including the *Arizona Republic*, April 11, 2014, "Transgender Woman is Convicted of Prostitution-Related Charge," http://www.azcentral.com/story/news/local/phoenix/2014/04/12/transgender-woman-convicted-prostitution-related-charge/7633091/ andAdvocate.com, and *Advocate*, April 15, 2014, "Arizona Activist Found Guilty of 'Walking While Trans'" http://www.advocate.com/politics/transgender/2014/04/15/arizona-activist-found-guilty-walking-while-trans.

4. For example, many women's advocates supported the 1994 Violent Crime Control and Law Enforcement Act because Title IV (known as the Violence against Women Act of 1994) increased penalties for both domestic and sexual violence, and provided funding for services to support victims. However, the Act also extended the application of the death penalty (Title VI), introduced federal three strikes penalties (Title VII), provided funding to hire more police (Title I), and funding to build new prisons (Title II). Feminist support for some provisions of the bill therefore contributed to the bipartisan appeal and broader public support of a law that expanded policing and imprisonment (Gottschalk 2006, 151). Intersectional scholarship has also shown how the support provided to victims of violence through these programs is less adequate for the needs of women of color (Crenshaw 1991).

References

Alexander, Michelle. 2010. *The New Jim Crow: Mass Incarceration in the Age of Colorblindness*. New York and London: New Press.

Alford, Fred. 2000. "What Would It Matter if Everything Foucault Said about Prison Were Wrong? "Discipline and Punish" after Twenty Years." *Theory and Society* 29 (1): 125–146.

Bosworth, Mary. 1999. *Engendering Resistance: Agency and Power in Women's Prisons*. Aldershot, UK. and Brookfield, USA: Dartmouth Publishing Co./Ashgate Publishing Co.

Brown, Wendy. 1992. "Finding the Man in the State." *Feminist Studies* 18 (1): 7–34.

Bureau of Justice Statistics. 2008. *Census of State and Federal Correctional Facilities, 2005*. US Department of Justice, Washington, DC. http://www.bjs.gov/content/pub/pdf/csfcf05.pdf

Bureau of Justice Statistics. 2013. *Prisoners in 2012*. Bulletin, US Department of Justice, Washington, DC. http://www.bjs.gov/index.cfm?ty=pbdetail&iid=4842.

Brownmiller, Susan. 1977. *Against Our Will: Men, Women and Rape*. Harmondsworth, UK: Penguin Books.

Coyle, Andrew. 2005. *Understanding Prisons: Key Issues in Policy and Practice*. Maidenhead, UK, and New York: Open University Press.

Crenshaw, Kimberlé. 1991. "Mapping the Margins: Intersectionality, Identity Politics, and Violence against Women of Color." *Stanford Law Review* 43 (6): 1241–1299.

Davis, Angela. 1998. "Racialized Punishment and Prison Abolition." In *The Angela Y. Davis Reader*, edited by Joy James, 98–107. Malden, MA: Blackwell.

Davis, Angela. 2003. *Are Prisons Obsolete?* New York: Seven Stories Press.

Foucault, Michel. 1995. *Discipline and Punish: the Birth of the Prison*. New York: Vintage Books.

Foucault, Michel. 1990. *The History of Sexuality, Volume One: An Introduction* (New York: Vintage Books.

Fraser, Nancy. 2003. "From Discipline to Flexibilization? Rereading Foucault in the Shadow of Globalisation." *Constellations* 10 (2): 160–171.

Freedman, Estelle B. 1981. *Their Sisters' Keepers: Women's Prison Reform in America, 1830–1930.* Ann Arbor: University of Michigan Press.
Gottschalk, Marie. 2006. *The Prison and the Gallows: The Politics of Mass Incarceration in America.* New York: Cambridge University Press.
Hallett, Michael A. 2006. *Private Prisons in America: A Critical Race Perspective.* Urbana: University of Illinois Press.
Harris, Angela P. 2000. "Gender, Violence, Race, and Criminal Justice." *Stanford Law Review* 52 (4): 777–807.
Hill Collins, Patricia. 1998. "The Tie That Binds: Race, Gender, and US Violence." *Ethnic and Racial Studies* 41 (5): 919–938.
Hill Collins, Patricia. 2004. *Black Sexual Politics: African Americans, Gender and the New Racism.* New York and London: Routledge.
James, Joy. 1996. *Resisting State Violence: Radicalism, Gender, and Race in US Culture.* Minneapolis: University of Minnesota Press.
Lamble, S. 2011. "Transforming Carceral Logics: 10 Reasons to Dismantle the Prison Industrial Complex Using a Queer/Trans Analysis." In *Captive Genders: Trans Embodiment and the Prison Industrial Complex*, edited by Eric Stanley and Nat Smith. Edinburgh, Oakland, and Baltimore: AK Press.
Lamble, Sarah. 2013. "Queer Necropolitics and the Expanding Carceral state: Interrogating Sexual Investments in Punishment." *Law Critique* 24: 229–253.
Mauer, Marc. 2006. *Race to Incarcerate.* Rev. ed. New York: New Press.
Miller, Teresa. 2001. "Keeping the Government's Hands off Our Bodies: Mapping a Feminist Legal Theory Approach to Privacy in Cross-Gender Searches." *Buffalo Criminal Law Review* 4 (2): 861–889.
Mogul, Joey, Andrea Ritchie, and Kay Whitlock. 2011. *Queer (In)Justice: The Criminalization of LGBT People in the United States.* Boston: Beacon Press.
National Center for Transgender Equality. 2011. *Injustice at Every Turn: A Report of the National Transgender Discrimination Survey.* http://www.thetaskforce.org/downloads/reports/reports/ntds_full.pdf (accessed November 24, 2011).
National Coalition of Anti-Violence Programs. 2014. *Hate Violence against Lesbian, Gay, Bisexual, Transgender, Queer, and HIV-Affected Communities in the United States in 2013.* http://www.avp.org/storage/documents/2013_ncavp_hvreport_final.pdf (accessed June 3, 2014).
Ogden, Stormy. 2005. "The Prison-Industrial Complex in Indigenous California." In *Global Lockdown: Race, Gender and the Prison-Industrial Complex*, edited by Julia Sudbury, 57–66. New York and London: Routledge.
Omi, Michael, and Winant, Howard. 1994. *Racial Formation in the United States: From the 1960s to the 1990s.* New York: Routledge.
Rafter, Nicole. 1990. *Partial justice: Women, Prisons and Social Control.* New Brunswick, NJ: Transaction Publishers.
Ross, Luana. 1998. *Inventing the Savage: The Social Construction of Native American Criminality.* Austin: University of Texas Press.
Rusche, Georg, and Dinwiddie, Gerda. 1978. "Labor Market and Penal Sanction: Thoughts on the Sociology of Criminal Justice." *Crime and Social Justice* 10: 2–8.
Rusche, Georg, and Kirchheimer, Otto. 1939. *Punishment and Social Structure.* New York: Columbia University Press.
Smith, Andrea. 1999. "Sexual Violence and American Indian Genocide." *Journal of Religion & Abuse* 1 (2): 31–52.

Smith, Andrea. 2005. "Native American Feminism, Sovereignty, and Social Change." *Feminist Studies* 31 (1): 116–132.

Smith, Andrea. 2006. "Heteropatriarchy and the Three Pillars of White Supremacy: Rethinking Women of Color Organising." In *The Color of Violence: The INCITE Anthology*, edited by Andrea Smith, Beth Richie, and Julia Sudbury, 66–73. Cambridge, MA: South End Press.

Spade, Dean. 2011. *Normal Life: Administrative Violence, Critical Trans Politics, and the Limits of Law.* Brooklyn, NY: South End Press.

Spivak, Gayatri C. 1988. "Can the Subaltern Speak?" In *Marxism and the Interpretation of Culture*, edited by Cary Nelson and Lawrence Grossberg, 271–313. Urbana: University of Illinois Press.

Wacquant, Loïc. 2001. "Deadly Symbiosis: When Ghetto and Prison Meet and Mesh." *Punishment & Society* 3 (1): 95–133.

Walmsley, Roy. 2012. *World Female Imprisonment List (second edition).* http://www.prisonstudies.org/sites/prisonstudies.org/files/resources/downloads/wfil_2nd_edition.pdf (accessed June 19 2014).

Weber, Max. 2009. "Politics as a Vocation." In *From Max Weber: Essays in Sociology*. Oxford and New York: Routledge, 77–127.

Western, Bruce. 2006. *Punishment and inequality in America.* New York: Russell Sage Foundation.

Zedner, Lucia. 1991. *Women, Crime and Custody in Victorian England.* Oxford: Clarendon Press.

CHAPTER 36

RACE AND RACIALIZATION

ZENZELE ISOKE

Introduction

RACIALIZATION refers to an ongoing process of marking, categorizing, and reproducing human difference through the uneven distribution of life chances within specified geographic space-time continuums.[1] Within European societies and geographies that have withstood generations of colonial invasion, enslavement, and diverse modes of racial apartheid, the reproduction of difference is realized through the maintenance of fairly rigid social, economic, and political hierarchies based on skin color, phenotype, culture, and the invention and enforcement of legal fictions that reify human difference. Race as a putative biological category is one such fiction. As Toni Morrison (1997, xvi) noted in the preface to *Paradise,* race "is designed to construct artificial boundaries and maintain them against all reason and evidence to the contrary." These fictions are deadly. They determine who is eligible for personhood and who is rendered subhuman and thereby excluded from civil and political rights, including the right to freely live and to belong within sovereign political territories. Lisa Cacho (2012, 7) explains, "Racism is a killing abstraction. It creates spaces of living death and populations "dead to others." In the United States' public imaginary, the living dead include prisoners, criminals, terrorists, looters, addicts, prostitutes, and other subjects who may fall into these politically construed categories of the socially abject.

Race is produced by the application of violence. And it is evidenced by state-sanctioned or extralegal production and exploitation of group-differentiated vulnerabilities to premature death, and what some scholars have theorized as "bare life"—or human flesh that can be murdered, or rendered socially dead (Agamben 1998). Consequently, the most important and influential scholarly treatments of race and contemporary and historic processes of racialization have explored the role of violence—epistemic, physical, and structural—in the un/gendering of subjects within and across diverse spatial and temporal domains—material, symbolic, embodied, legal, and psychic. These studies document how racialization contributes to the impossibility and impairment of life, to (social) death, and to the negation of freedom and humanness.

This chapter provides an overview of conceptualizations of race and racialization that have shaped feminist writings in the past thirty years. It analyzes key categories of difference, including gender, sexuality, class, ability, and nation that have clarified the project of race-making in late modernity. It examines new genealogies of race that theorize processes of heterosexualization, neoliberalization, nationalization, and the un/making of gendered bodies and subjectivities in the field of feminist studies. Drawing on works in critical race theory, postcolonial theory, feminist post-slave studies, and feminist theory that have ignited the most generative conversations about race, the chapter is an exercise in feminist, anticolonial, and anti-racist knowledge production and political struggle.

RACIAL FORMATION THEORY AND INTERSECTIONAL APPROACHES

Sociologists Michael Omi and Howard Winant (1986) coined the term "racial formation" to describe the process by which social, economic, and political forces determine the context and importance of racial categories, which are reified through the attachment and proliferation of racial meanings. In this formative study, Omi and Winant argued that racial formations were produced through state and civic discourses that delineated certain groups as worthy of inclusion and the political rights of citizenship, in contrast to other groups, who were designated inferior and subject to limited inclusion or total exclusion. *Racialization*—the political and social practice of making race real—determines the distribution of property, the denial or enjoyment of political rights, whether or not one is or one's ancestors have been subject to coercive labor, social and political containment, forced migration, or outright extermination. Racial thinking, as well as the invention and reproduction of racial categories (white, Negro, mulatto, savage) determined which social groups could have their lives and properties protected by the law and reinforced by court decisions, and demarcate *others* whose lives were unprotected, whose lands and properties were confiscated, and whose capacities were circumscribed by indentured servitude, enslavement, incarceration, and the ongoing misery of poverty (Omi and Winant 1986, 68).

Racial formations have varied histories, shaped by specific relations of power within a given territory. In the southern United States, for example, the emergence of race was attached to juridical-political mechanisms informed by scientific racism such as the theory of hypodescent, otherwise known as the "one drop rule." The theory of hypodescent reserved the legal standing of a human being as a citizen, with rights of legal protection, ownership, and inclusion in civil society, to whites while relegating indigenous people and people of color to the status of noncitizen, and in the case of African-descendant people in the colonies, to that of chattel. For Omi and Winant, the making of racial formations can be traced to specific juridical-political devices and mechanisms that marked and valuated difference within a specific geopolitical order. Drawing attention to the role of the state, typically at the scale of the nation or "national body," Omi and Winant (2014) emphasize that dominant classes produce supposedly superior and inferior social groups. In the US context prior to the twentieth century, the "inferior" groups included "blacks," "Indians," "Mexicans," "Asians," and "women."

Omi and Winant's comprehensive theory of racial formation has been critiqued, extended, and reformulated to account for the workings of gender and class in both domestic and international contexts (Rothenberg 1992; Caldwell 2007). Writing within a critical race legal framework, Kimberlé Crenshaw developed perhaps the most profound critique of earlier articulations of racial formation, arguing that single-axis treatments of race marginalize those who are multiply burdened by sex and gender discrimination. Theorizing "intersectionality," Crenshaw emphasized how intersecting forces of racial and gender subordination work simultaneously to frame a unique set of difficulties for women of color. Thus Crenshaw challenged not only unidimensional conceptualizations of racial formation, but also the validity of hegemonic feminism whose ideological and descriptive definitions of patriarchy rendered black women's experiences invisible or unintelligible. Theorizing "matrices of domination" that included race, gender, and class oppression—later extended to include nation, ethnicity, sexuality, and age—Patricia Hill Collins (1991, 2004, 2007) also emphasized an intersectional approach. Collins argued that "controlling images" of black femininity (and, later, black masculinity) provide the ideological justification for intersecting modes of group-based subordination. Furthermore, controlling images create the paradox of new racial formation: "the new racism—the simultaneous invisibility and hyper-visibility of those racialized as black in the United States" (Collins 2004, 7). In her view, the "new racism" produces historic rates of hypersegregation in American communities, the racial containment of poor blacks and Latinos, and the growth of mass incarceration—all while the US "nation" indulges in myths of color blindness.

In later years, feminist theorist and literary critic Sally Kitch (2009) revised the original thesis advanced by Omi and Winant, arguing that gender works as a foundational organizing principle that fuels processes of racialization. Indeed, she suggested that gender binaries define modern ways of making sense of sexed bodies and gendered relationships under patriarchy. Kitch conceptualizes gender as a "force that reduces a spectrum of sexual identities and proclivities into dichotomies of sexuality and sexual difference." And she conceives "race" as "the persistent tendency toward racial dichotomization reflected in the black-white racial paradigm that normalizes the concept of racial opposites" (10). Kitch describes the making of race and gender as more or less identical processes that operate in tandem over the course of Western sociopolitical history, informing social theories that legitimate and perpetuate European patriarchy. This work, while relatively influential, did not clarify how race itself is has morphed with the recent shifts in the arrangement and distribution of capital. Gender remains tethered to biology (male-female) and therefore bound to the limits of the archive. Scholarly thinking of this kind produces a distorted view of both race and gender because it treats them as relatively stable categories of identity that are temporally isolated from social factors, including urbanization, neoliberalization, and migration—factors that determine how racialized gender hierarchies are reproduced by such practices as containment, disappearing, public killing, or the wholesale extermination of gendered bodies deemed inferior, illegal, monstrous, or terrorist.

Jasbir Puar (2007, 212), inspired by Giles Deleuze and Felix Guattari (1987) and Brian Massumi (2002), issued a resounding critique of theories of intersectionality that are overly attached to stable notions of identity, arguing that "[i]ntersectionality colludes with the disciplinary apparatus of the state—census, demography, racial profiling surveillance—in that 'difference' is encased within a structural container that simply wishes the messiness of identity into a formulaic grid." Dismissing intersectionality as a "hermeneutic of positionality" that accounts for locality, specificity, placement, and junction, Puar offers the concept of "assemblage" as an alternative. Following Deleuze and Guattari, she defines assemblage as a "series of dispersed but mutually implicated networks," which are conceptually treated as collections of dynamic multiplicities based upon complex, perpetually shifting, and spatially and temporally constituted modes of power—often enunciated as race, gender, sexuality, nationality, ability, or debility. According to Puar (2007, 215), "[I]ntersectionality privileges naming, visuality, epistemology, representation and meaning, while assemblage underscores feeling, tactility, ontology, affect and information." Moving past Puar's critique of intersectionality, and drawing from careful reading of Hortense Spillers and Sylvia Winters, Alexander Weheliye (2014, 49) writes that racializing assemblages materialize as "sets of complex relations of geographic and discursive territorialization and deterritorializations that are structured in political, economic, social, racial and heteropatriarchal dominance." He goes further, arguing that racializing assemblages "represent among other things, the visual modalities in which dehumanization is practiced and lived." Within this paradigm, race itself disciplines humanity into full humans, not-quite humans, and nonhumans. Consequently, race-gender, rather than operate as a categorization or intersection of identity and difference, actually figures into how and which kinds of human experiences can be clearly articulated within the Western notions of racialized gender—revealing the very notion of binary gender to be limited to those who are always already fully recognized and racialized as human.

Of course, intersectionality, as a structure of identity making and an affective and resistant mode of identification (including knowledge making), is not so neatly distinguishable from assemblage. Both are effects of and responses to complex modes of gendered racialization that make political movements and deeply situated writing and analysis of sub/alterity possible (see, e.g., Berger and Guidroz 2009; Isoke 2013). While "intersectionality" is considered by many to be a "dated" concept, it is the preeminent way in which complex relationships among gender, race, class, nation, sexuality, and ability and debility are both conceived and taught to undergraduate students in both feminist studies classrooms and the social sciences. Indeed, the intersectional mode of theorizing race has gained strength in contemporary feminist studies, particularly women's and gender studies departments that are heavily influenced by the social sciences, including sociology, feminist philosophy, political science, and feminist history proper (excluding strictly Foucauldian approaches). The "mutually constitutive" nature of race, gender, and sexuality is often theorized under the umbrella phrase "intersectionality," especially in the social sciences.

In tandem with assemblage theories of race and racialization, affect theory has also prodded race/gender scholars beyond the boundaries of strict social constructionism. Affect theory has sought to explain how race operates viscerally—driving human bodies toward certain modes of relationship, which reproduce the everyday intimacies that are foundational to race's realness. Sharon Patricia Holland (2012), for example, thinks through the concept of the erotic in order to understand not only race but also the psychic life of racism. Building jointly on theories of the erotic featured in the writing of Audre Lorde and Simone de Beauvoir, Holland invokes the erotic to recall how race both structures and ruptures the possibility of connection and reciprocity between human subjects:

> While race creates the possibility for blood strangers, it also employs its primary ally and enforcer, "racism," to produce the imaginary boundary between blood (us) and strangers (them). Racism transforms an already porous periphery into an absolute, thereby making it necessary to deny all kinds of crossings. Moreover, even when those crossings appear together in a quotidian scene of racist violence, for example—racism succeeds in breaking the tacit connection between them. In other words, racism irrevocably changes gendered relationship. Racism can also be described as the emotional lifeblood of race; it is the 'feeling' that articulates and keeps the flawed logic of race in its place."
>
> (Holland 2012, 6)

Affect theory has stimulated new ways of thinking with, and writing through the peculiarities of race, often requiring scholars to engage more deeply with the histories of coerced intimacies that are framed by shifting racial hierarchies within and across diverse, multiple, and convergent spatial and temporal configurations. This kind of work has required sustained practices of interdisciplinarity that privilege engagements with film, music and sound studies, literature, and the archive, as well as more conventional "scientific" sources of evidence of race, racism, and racialization.

ENTANGLEMENTS OF RACE-GENDER IN FEMINIST POSTSLAVE STUDIES AND POSTCOLONIAL THEORY

As an alternative to the notion of the mutual constitution of race, gender, and sexuality, such scholars as literary critic Hortense Spillers (1987), feminist historian Anne Stoler (1995), and critical indigenous studies legal scholar Andrea Smith (2005, 2006) locate the making and unmaking of gender in the entanglements of enslavement and colonialism. From postcolonial and anticolonial vantage points, they have theorized how the (coerced) intimacies of rape, concubinage, and sexual violence constitute simultaneously raced and rapeable bodies, lands, and cultures. These approaches emphasize that violence, intimacy, and the policing of sex helped to organize, justify, and maintain racial boundaries throughout the New World. Their painstaking reexaminations of the past illuminate how grammars and discourses of race, gender, and desire attached themselves to certain bodies—or, in the case of enslaved Africans, made bodies into flesh—across time and continents, creating hierarchies of in/humanness that are continually reenacted today (Hartman 1997).

In 1987, Hortense Spillers wrote about the New World, "That order, with its human sequence written in blood, represents for its African and indigenous peoples a sense of actual mutilation, dismemberment and exile. Under these conditions we lose at least *gender* difference *in the outcome*, and the female body and the male body become a territory of cultural and political maneuver, not at all gender-related, gender-specific" (Spillers 1987, 67). For Spillers, the making of race occurred *before* the invention of juridical-political devices to justify the political exclusion of the other, and it occurred as an effect of the un/gendering process of making slaves. For enslaved Africans, the "(un)gendering" of subjects happened on the slave ships of the Middle Passage. Embedded in both the actual experiences (unsayable) and remembrances of slavery, relationships between African male and female subjects were produced in the context of captivity, displacement, and transportation. The "making of slaves" itself required the obliteration of any conceivable gendered relationships that may have existed prior to enslavement.

It was exclusively for the sake of profit that American slavers subjected males and females to nearly identical social realities—backbreaking labor, brutality, and torture as well as distinct modes of sexual degradation that transformed captive bodies into flesh. Spillers writes, "This materialized scene of unprotected female flesh—of female flesh "ungendered"—offers a praxis and a theory, a text of living and for dying, and a method for reaching both through their diverse mediations" (62). Thus Spillers notes that notions of gender difference are often superfluous in relation to racialized subjects. She identifies the past as a fertile site through which to examine how black fe/male subjectivities are misrecognized in the present (e.g., the notorious Moynihan report). And she challenges us to imagine new insurgent grounds in which we might "radically re-write notions of female empowerment." Spillers's notion of empowerment rests in tracing how power itself creates a structure of value that produces black women as nonhuman in relation to the production of the very categories of race/gender that operate as "real" in the US political and social imaginary. Spillers argues that the "empowered" liberal female subject (read white woman) comes into being only in comparison to the enslaved women's non-being in relation to the category of the so-called raced and gendered human. This rewriting would come through locating the "interstices" of discourse and myth which have placed and continue to place black women within the realm of the "monstrous."

From a political vantage point, this perspective urges scholars to trace the multiple discourses of the "human" from which blackened subjects have been categorically excluded by virtue of their physical, material, and psychic subjugations and erasures. Blackness here is not about skin color but about social, political, and economic processes that construe certain human bodies as inherently violable. As Katherine McKittrick (2014) poetically reflects, "[B]lack is naturally malignant and therefore worthy of violation; where black is violated because black is inherently violent; where black is naturally unbelievable and is therefore naturally empty and violated; where black is naturally less-than-human and starving to death and violated; where black is naturally dysselected, unsurviving, swallowed up; where black is same and always dead and dying; where black is complex and difficult to bear and violated (17)." Within this paradigm, is not enough to simply name and describe the political violence that manufactures racial subjugation or blackness per se; rather, scholars should begin to identify simultaneous philosophical and geographic processes that scaffold racial hierarchies of humanness. The most obvious historical examples of this are captivity, enslavement, lynching, rape, and forced breeding; more contemporary examples might include national and foreign policies that foster permissible genocide, mass incarceration, biometric surveillance at the border, geographic containment, state-endorsed extrajudicial killings, and even slow death or debility (through impoverishment; poor health; malnourishment; cross-generational debt; lack of economic opportunity; or physical, mental, or emotional disablement; McKittrick 2013; Spade 2011; Puar 2011).

Ann Stoler (1995) links the making of race—specifically whiteness—with efforts to construct a respectable bourgeois European self that could be easily distinguished from colonial subjects and legitimized as fit to rule the empire. According to Stoler, "What sustained racial membership was a middle-class morality, national sentiments, bourgeois sensibilities, normalized sexuality, and carefully circumscribed 'milieu' in school and home" (105). "Europeanness," later coded "whiteness," functioned as a discourse mobilized by colonizers (in both the metropole and the colony) to distinguish themselves from the rapidly increasing population of ethnically ambiguous and "racially" hybrid subjects in the colonized territories. "Whiteness" itself was deeply contingent upon social disposition, class background, and close adherence to codes of sexual morality, accomplished through the micromanagement of European women's domestic lives. By tethering white women's supposed chastity to their class status and social standing, colonizers were able to control who was white and whose children could become citizens by virtue of their "Europeanness," distinguishing them from the Natives who would become subjects. Stoler (1995, 115) emphasized that "Europeanness was not just class specific but gender encoded. A European man could live with or marry an Asian woman without necessarily losing rank, but this was never true for a European woman who might make a similar choice to live [with] or marry a European." Stoler locates racialization not only in the subjugation, regulation, and management of the colonized, but also in the compulsion for European women to fashion a bourgeois, middle-class self. Through "good" parenting, convincing performances of bourgeois respectability, and the fulfillment of their sexual and conjugal contracts with European men, white women both secured and reproduced the colonial nation and its racial underpinnings.

Andrea Smith identifies sexual violence as a tool of both colonialism and racism. For Smith, the exercise of power and domination through racial/colonial ideologies is consolidated through the European construction of Native bodies as inherently violable through the practices of genocide and rape. Smith juxtaposes sexual violence against Native women with practices of land theft, attempts to eradicate indigenous cultures through the forced removal of Indian children from their homelands to boarding schools, and efforts to erode Native sovereignty through broken treaties. In so doing, she challenges nationalist discourses that deploy rape as a metaphor for colonial violence against indigenous peoples, arguing instead that sexual violence against Native women must be examined in its full brutality. It provides a unique demonstration of state-sanctioned violence, while also illuminating structural connections among environmental racism, population control, and the widespread appropriation of Native cultural practices by whites and other nonnatives.

Cedric Robinson and other scholars have argued that in addition to demonstrating the intricate ties between racialization and colonization, the dissemination of racial ideology—a system of meaning that is consolidated through the institutions of science, politics, and religion—coincided with the ascendancy of global capitalism. The genocide of indigenous people and the enslavement of Africans enabled the development of capitalism through accumulation by dispossession. The first slaves of the New World were the Native peoples of the Americas and the Caribbean. The decimation of the Native population through disease and overwork, however, created a sharp demand for enslaved Africans to work the land and build colonial infrastructures that would secure and maintain whiteness.

Racialization versus Biological Notions of Race

Scholars of racialization emphasize that state policies and practices subordinate, marginalize, and exclude particular groups while affirming, privileging, and securing the dominance of other groups. In marked contrast to notions of "biological" race—the discredited belief that there are naturally occurring hierarchies of humans determined by brain size, genes, morphology, phenotype, or pigmentation—racialization traces how states produce particular raced-gendered-sexualized national identities through processes that simultaneously create the dominant and the subordinate. Far from being givens in nature, races are produced through political mechanisms that create forms of inequality written on the body. Manifold social, economic, and political forces contribute to the hierarchical organization of social groups with profound implications for self-understandings, interpersonal relations, possibilities of belonging, and life prospects. But contrary to liberal notions about negative liberty (a sphere free from state intervention) and legal neutrality (the idea that the law applies equally to all), racialization calls attention to the role of the state in creating dominant and subordinate groups by means of laws, policies, norms, and practices that categorize, classify, separate, and segregate in ways that create and sustain a social order and seep into individual consciousness.

Although certain processes define racialization (the production of hierarchies of difference and their justification through appeals to notions of superiority and inferiority), racial categories themselves are not static but vary in accordance with the cultural and political imperatives of specific locales. Thus, systems of racial classification in the United States differ substantially from those in Brazil, the United Kingdom, the Middle East, South Asia, or East Asia. Racial classifications also shift over time in conjunction with processes of migration, state management of difference, litigation, and popular tolerance for "assimilation." Where some groups are allowed to "become white" (e.g., Irish, Italians, and Jews in the US context), others are rendered "unassimilable" (e.g., blacks, Asians, and Native Americans; Haney-Lopez 1996; Jacobson 1998; Ngai 2004).

State practices of racialization produce observable and widespread inequities in wealth, income, political representation in government, life expectancy, and other markers of human well-being. Yet these palpable differences are naturalized through racist ideologies that attribute unequal outcomes to physical attributes or individual effort. Racist discourses transform stratified distributions of goods, resources, honors, respect, opportunities, liberties, and life prospects into mystified notions of "just desserts." Precisely because racism naturalizes racial hierarchy, it is useful to specify state practices that create and maintain racial difference.

In *White by Law*, Ian Haney Lopez (1996, 19) points out that through the direct control of human behavior and by shaping public understanding, "law translates ideas about race [gender and sexuality] into material and societal conditions that entrench those ideas." Laws pertaining to citizenship are one of the most fundamental ways that race and gender structure national belonging. Laws define the minimal conditions that must be met to be eligible for citizenship—conditions that often turn on race, class, and gender. And changes in law over time provide clear indications of shifting processes of racialization that undergird citizenship in particular countries.

In the United States, for example, state and federal governments, from colonial times to the present, have crafted citizenship laws that envision a white "race-nation" of European ancestry and have used the law to produce a population that conforms to that vision, simultaneously creating hierarchies of citizens based on race, gender, ethnicity, and sexuality (Stevens 1999). From the earliest days of settlement in North America, British colonists used the law to draw lines of inclusion and exclusion based on a racial conception of membership. In 1662, ten years before the British government awarded the Royal Africa Company the sole privilege of supplying African labor to the colonies, Virginia passed legislation to alter the common-law practice of patrilineal descent through which citizenship was passed down as a birthright from fathers to children. Instead, the Virginia House of Burgesses (or freemen of the borough) decreed that enslaved women passed their lifetime bondage to their offspring (Mills and Pateman 2007). This early experiment in "democratic governance" stripped citizenship from the progeny of free white men who procreated with enslaved women. In so doing, it established a racial regime that defined slaves—including the sons and daughters of free white men—as "chattel" or personal property of their masters. It suspended the principle of *ius soli*, which established citizenship by birth within a geographical territory.

As a form of property, slaves were excluded from civil law altogether: they could not marry, own property, or testify in court. Categorized as property by law, they were excluded from citizenship. Thus, even though second and subsequent generations of slaves were born on American soil, thereby fulfilling the primary criterion for citizenship, they were denied the status of citizen by law. That the denial of citizenship had more to do with the fact of their blackness than with the condition of enslavement was made clear by laws that also denied citizenship to free blacks born on American soil, laws that were overturned only in 1868 with the passage of the Fourteenth Amendment to the US Constitution.

African Americans were not the only people of color born on "American soil" to be excluded from membership in the race-nation. Native Americans, the original inhabitants of the land, were also denied citizenship in the new republic on the grounds that they were "sovereign" peoples or independent nations, possessing the right to self-governance, including the right to enter into binding treaties with the government of the United States—treaties that were savagely violated during the continental expansion of the white race-nation.

As the United States pursued its policy of Manifest Destiny, expanding its territorial boundaries from the Atlantic to Pacific Oceans, it resorted to warfare not only to displace Native Americans, but also to acquire the northern half of Mexico. The 1848 Treaty of Guadalupe Hidalgo, which ended the Mexican-American War, gave residents of the conquered territory the option of leaving their land or becoming US citizens. More than 70,000 Mexican nationals were coerced into citizenship (McWilliams 1968, 51–52), but the terms of their citizenship were far from equal. Although the treaty promised to respect the property, language, and religion of the new citizens, none of these promises was kept as white settlements expanded across these territories. In 1930, the census enumerated Mexican Americans as a separate "race." During the Depression in the 1930s, 240,000 Mexican American citizens by native birth, along with 160,000 Mexican nationals, were deported, nearly 20 percent of the Mexican population of the United States at that time. As Mae Ngai (2004, 75) has noted, "The repatriation of Mexicans was a racial expulsion program exceeded in scale only by the Native American removals of the nineteenth century."

In her systematic examination of marriage practices in the new world, *Public Vows: A History of Marriage and the Nation,* Nancy Cott notes that the British colonies in North America were the first secular authorities to criminalize and nullify intermarriage among people of different races or colors. In 1664, Maryland enacted the first criminal law against "freeborn English women who "made shameful Matches" with African slaves (Cott 2000, 44). Six of the original colonies prohibited marriage between whites and blacks and between whites and mulattoes; three banned interracial sex outside marriage. Despite the colonists' status as a small minority in a land populated by people of color—Native Americans and enslaved and free Africans—the miscegenation laws were intended to create a white nation. Antimiscegenation laws prohibited marriage not only between people of different legal statuses, freeborn and enslaved, but also across color lines, prohibiting unions between free blacks and free whites. The number of states prohibiting interracial marriage grew throughout the nineteenth century. In the early twentieth century, thirty of the then forty-eight states enforced antimiscegenation laws prohibiting marriage not only between whites and blacks, but in many instances between whites and Asian Americans, and between whites and Mexican Americans. California, for example, passed its antimiscegenation law in 1850, prohibiting marriage between a white person and a Negro, mulatto, or Mongolian. The California legislature amended the law in 1933 to extend the prohibition to members of the Malay race (Filipinos), retroactively voiding and making illegal all previous Filipino-white marriages (Ngai 2004, 115). The California Supreme Court was the first to strike down antimiscegenation laws in 1948. The United States Supreme Court declared antimiscegenation laws unconstitutional in *Loving v. Virginia* in 1967. But the consequences of centuries of miscegenation prohibitions are systemic. As Ian Haney Lopez has noted, by constraining reproductive choices, miscegenation laws produce the physical appearance of the nation's population.

Through racialization, the United States actively created itself as a white race-nation in part by controlling marriage and sexual practices, in part by suspending birthright citizenship for people of color, and in part by controlling immigration. As a settler society in the new world, the United States proclaimed itself a nation of immigrants, but only some immigrants were deemed eligible for citizenship. Through laws governing "naturalization," the US Congress determined which immigrants could become citizens. The Nationality Act of 1790 unequivocally articulated the founding vision of a white race-nation, restricting the right of naturalized citizenship to "free white persons" of good moral character—evidenced by having lived in the country for five years without incurring any criminal record. The initial naturalization act consolidated the hierarchy of "Anglo-Saxon" over African American and Native American already embedded in the suspension of birthright and miscegenation laws and laid the foundation for intensive contestation over the legal meaning of "white person." For more than a century, changing immigration laws, court decisions, and census categories contributed to shifting definitions of who was "white" and who was "non-white," ascribing racialized meanings to physical features and ancestry in the process (Haney Lopez 1996).

The Nationality Act also introduced legal status distinctions between citizens and aliens, clearing new ground for the construction of racial hierarchies. Over the course of the nineteenth and twentieth centuries, increasingly restrictive immigration laws and naturalization policies produced new categories of racial difference by distinguishing between "assimilable" (European) aliens, deemed eligible for citizenship after fulfilling the residency requirement, and "unassimilable" aliens, deemed permanently ineligible for citizenship. As Mae Ngai (2004) has carefully documented, the legal designation "alien ineligible for citizenship" created a new subject population, resident within the borders of the nation but barred forever from the possibility of citizenship. Without rights, aliens deemed ineligible for citizenship were condemned to a "condition of racial otherness, a badge of foreignness that cannot be shed," an encompassing stigma that dramatically affected their children, born on US soil and, as such, citizens by birth (Ngai, 2004, 8).

The Chinese Exclusion Act of 1882 barred all Chinese contract laborers from entry into the United States and prohibited Chinese nationals already resident in the country from acquiring naturalized citizenship. Although the title of the 1882 legislation named only the Chinese for purposes of exclusion and ineligibility for citizenship, a series of court cases and subsequent immigration acts expanded the category of aliens ineligible for citizenship to include all "Asians." Constructing "Asian" as "a peculiarly American racial category," US immigration law homogenized all the peoples of East Asia and South Asia, creating a fictive sameness among all nations "from Afghanistan to the Pacific, except the Philippines which was an American territory" (Ngai 2004, 37). Barring half the world's population from entering the United States, this provision also codified the principle of racial exclusion into the main body of American immigration and naturalization law.

Mae Ngai (2004, 202) points out that immigration laws that altered the status of Asian nationals already living and working in the United States created the "first illegal aliens as well as the first alien citizens. Although the Supreme Court ruled in 1898 that Chinese born in the US were citizens, the premises of exclusion—the alleged racial unassimilability of Chinese—powerfully influenced Americans' perceptions of Chinese Americans as permanent foreigners. Excluded from the polity and for the most part confined to Chinatown ghettoes and an ethnic economy, Chinese Americans remained marginalized from the mainstream of society well into the twentieth century."

To be without rights as an alien ineligible for citizenship was to be at great remove from any notion of negative liberty. In the early decades of the twentieth century, immigrant farmers from Japan bought and worked farm land in California and Washington. In 1913, the California legislature passed a law banning aliens deemed ineligible for citizenship from land ownership. The State of Washington passed similar legislation in 1921. The United States Supreme Court upheld the California and Washington laws proscribing land ownership by aliens ineligible to citizenship in 1921. The Court ruled that "alien land laws did not discriminate against the Japanese because the laws applied to *all* aliens ineligible to citizenship, masking the racial foundation of the concept" (Ngai 2004, 46–47). Laws in many western states barred aliens deemed ineligible for citizenship from professional occupations, including law, medicine, teaching, and real estate. The racialization of Asians as too foreign to become American pervaded the treatment of Asian American citizens born on US soil, underwriting "formal and informal structures of racial discrimination" culminating in "major official race policies, notably the internment of 120,000 persons of Japanese ancestry during WWII (two-thirds of them citizens)" (Ngai 2004, 8).

In addition to condoning the denigration, exclusion, and total deprivation of the rights of those deemed permanently foreign and unassimilable into the American race-nation, US immigration law contributed to the "invention and codification of new racial categories . . . that put Europeans and non-Europeans on different trajectories of racial formation" (Ngai, 2004, 13). In *Impossible Subjects: Illegal Aliens and the Making of Modern America*, Mae Ngai illuminates the complex racialization involved in the concept of "national origin" deployed by the 1924 Johnson-Reed Immigration Act, legislation that was explicitly aimed at engineering the racial composition of the population. Assuming that "the American nation was, and should remain, a white nation descended from Europe," the Johnson-Reed Act established a national-origins quota system based on a "whitened" past that was sure to promote a whitened future. Put simply, "eliminating nonwhite peoples from the formula" enabled larger numbers of white Europeans to migrate to the United States (Ngai 2004, 25). The official calculation of national origins also helped erase any sense that African Americans, who comprised 9 percent of the US population in 1920, or Asian Americans "really belonged" to the American race-nation.

The official construction of the United States as a white race-nation helps to explain the pervasive racial exclusions in New Deal policies (Yanow 2003). The National Labor Relations Act of 1935, which protected workers by granting them the right to organize and to bargain collectively; the Social Security Act of 1935, which created unemployment insurance and a contributory scheme to fund pensions for the elderly; and the Fair Labor Standards Act, which established a minimum wage and maximum hours, did not apply to agricultural or domestic workers—the occupations in which the majority of workers of color were concentrated. Similarly, excluding citizens of color from the imagined community of the American nation goes some way toward explaining how hundreds of thousands of Mexican American citizens and Filipinos, who were US nationals, could have been deported during the 1930s. And the construction of Japanese Americans as inherently alien and unassimilable, helps to make intelligible the government decision to deny Japanese American citizens their constitutionally guaranteed right of habeus corpus, strip them of their possessions, and place them in internment camps for the duration of World War II, a decision subsequently upheld by the US Supreme Court in *Korematsu v. United States*. Excluded from the legally accredited conception of the nation, and constructed as inherently alien, US citizens of color had "no rights that white men had to respect" to paraphrase the infamous Dred Scott decision—despite the Fourteenth Amendment's guarantee of equal citizenship and equal protection of the laws.

RACIALIZATION AND STATE TERROR

Although racialization can operate through subtle techniques of power, it is often a far more bloody affair. As both a creation and an effect of discourse, race does not preexist the social order. As the discussion of colonization here demonstrates, the consequences of race-making can be deadly. The widespread loss of life and shortened longevity of socially despised people, whether black, brown, red, yellow, or other, are testaments to the lethal power of racialization. Loss of life can take the form of high rates of infant mortality; shooting deaths as a result of state or nonstate violence; poor health outcomes as a result of lack of access to healthcare; premature deaths from cancer, heart disease, or diabetes; or social deaths in the form of incarceration, underemployment, or debilitating mental health crises that disproportionately impact certain communities. For this reason, Ruth Wilson Gilmore (2002, 16) defines racism as the "death-dealing displacement of difference into hierarchies that organize relations within and between the planet's sovereign political territories." In the Americas, nation building has been centrally implicated in racial definitions and their management. The state itself—its consolidation, reproduction, and expression—rests upon the imposition of otherness on certain subjects as well as ongoing attempts to account for, know, and control difference. In the words of David Theo Goldberg (2002), "[R]ace marks and orders the modern racial state. It fashions, modifies, and reifies the terms of racial expression as well racist exclusion and subjugation" (112). In other words, the racial state is also the "racist" state—a state that arranges and coordinates racial hierarchy in economic, political, social, and cultural domains.

Legal scholar Michelle Alexander describes contemporary modes of racial formation as the "New Jim Crow." Characterizing the massive social and political disenfranchisement of black males as a function of US prison expansion, Alexander (2010, 2) suggests that

> [r]ather than rely on race, we use our criminal justice system to label people of color 'criminals" and then engage in all the practices we supposedly left behind. Today it is perfectly legal to discriminate against criminals in nearly all the ways that it was once legal to discriminate against African Americans. Once you're labeled a felon, the old forms of discrimination—employment discrimination, housing discrimination, denial of the right to vote, denial of public education opportunity, denial of food stamps and other public benefits, and exclusion for jury service—are suddenly legal.

Within the New Jim Crow, gender as an analytical framework retreats into the background, as the carceral state emerges as a premier site of domination and resistance for racialized subjects.

In contrast to notions of equal opportunity and equal rights, state practices of racialization deploy violence—structural violence, physical violence, and epistemic violence. Consider, for example, gratuitous violence directed against black American bodies in recent years by police officers. Although the shooting death of Michael Brown in Ferguson, Missouri, and the asphyxiation of Eric Garner in Staten Island, New York, at the hands of police caused a public outcry in 2014, widely accepted practices that target black people who live on the margins of US society for physical assault and premature death seldom make the news. Little notice was taken when Levar Edward Jones, a thirty-five-year-old African American who had been pulled over for a unspecified traffic violation, was shot four times by a South Carolina state trooper in September 2014 while trying to retrieve his driver's license from his car. The brutal beating of an African

American grandmother in Los Angeles by a California Highway Patrol trooper in July 2014 also received scant attention. Her crime appears to have been walking barefoot on Interstate-10. Although captured on film by onlookers, an air of impunity surrounds police violence; prosecutors cite the dangers of the job as justification for these actions, and juries either fail to indict or acquit police officers who perpetrate racial violence in their everyday dealings with red, black, and brown people; the poor; the homeless; and the mentally ill.

Impunity is closely linked to the criminalization of the poor as urban black and Latino youth are constructed as threats, subjected to hypersurveillance, and disproportionately arrested and incarcerated in a new regime of racial control (Cacho 2012; Alexander 2010). Criminalization justifies preemptive and abusive law-enforcement practices and court procedures, which are often celebrated in the media and public discourses as essential to law and order. In fact, racialized criminalization makes it impossible for certain bodies—usually black, brown, and/or discernably male—to be recognized as anything other than criminal. As always already criminals, poor people of color in the United States and the global South and undocumented immigrants—particularly males—are ineligible for personhood. "Ineligibility to personhood," Lisa Cacho (2012, 98) explains, "refers to the state of being legally recognized as rightless and disentitled to life."

The blackening of African American subjects like Levar Jones and the unnamed grandmother mentioned earlier is achieved through state-endorsed violence—which is fundamental rather than anterior to racialization. Alexander Weheliye (2008) explains, "The creation of the tortured as in/human might also be described as the production of both flesh (Spillers) and bare life (Agamben), since the physicality of torture and other manifestations of politicized brutality depends on the conscription of the victim as both lacking in body and full human existence." Within this framework, the process of racializing (as a verb) relies upon an active consensus by the larger political community that specifies certain lives as fundamentally less worthy of personhood and thus susceptible to political violence and terror at the hands of civil society and the state. Weheliye goes further to suggest that there are some rather obvious continuities between chattel slavery and modern biopolitical formations of postslavery: racialized subjects are subjected to "bare life." In an obvious sense, bare life could refer to living, breathing, human flesh that possesses no rights and is seen as socially and politically dead in the eyes of the state; but within today's racial landscape the polemic of "bare life" serves to direct scholarly analyses toward state-endorsed practices of racialization that effectively deprive citizens and noncitizens alike of the basic human rights they are formally guaranteed by national constitutions and international treaties.

Although crime rates in US cities have been falling steadily over the past twenty years, police have developed standard operating procedures, such as racial profiling, that result in mass incarceration. As Loïc Wacquant (2008) has documented, the US population behind bars increased fivefold between 1975 and 2000, to over two million inmates, making the United States the world leader in incarceration. Although the incidence of crime remained constant from 1973 to 1993, it fell sharply during the last decade of the twentieth century—just as imprisonment was skyrocketing. Racialization structured criminalization. As Wacquant notes, "The proportion of African Americans in each 'cohort' of criminals decreased steadily over those two decades, as their share of the carceral population increased rapidly and continually. To explain these 'mysteries,' we must move beyond the crime and punishment schema and rethink the prison as a political institution, a central component of the state" (111). As economic insecurity grows with deindustrialization and increasing urban unemployment, young men of color are warehoused in prisons as women of color are subjected to punitive "workfare" (the requirement to perform unwaged labor in order to receive minimal temporary assistance for needy families). In Wacquant's words, "Neoliberalism ushers in an era of punitive containment of the precarious sectors of the new urban proletariat by diffusing 'zero tolerance' policy" (111).

As criminalization legitimates a fear of people of color, state violence is augmented by extrajudicial violence. When Renisha McBride, a nineteen-year-old African American, knocked on the door of a white homeowner in Detroit after her car had broken down, in November 2013, he shot and killed her under the pretense that he feared she intended to harm him. When neighborhood watch volunteer George Zimmerman observed Trayvon Martin walking on the streets of Sanford, Florida, in February 2012, he targeted the black teen as a potential threat, followed him, accosted him, and shot him to death. The idea that citizens can commit violence against young black men with impunity was conveyed to Zimmerman when the Florida jury acquitted him of murder, shoring up the criminalization of "walking while black."

The irrational fear of black and Latino youth expressed by police officials and by private citizens is a product of the epistemic violence perpetrated through criminalization. Unwarranted fear structures the standard operating procedures for policing in the United States. It justifies perceptions of unidentified African American men as criminal suspects and, in turn, gives rise to various forms of police violence through interrogations, shakedowns, illegal search and seizures, handcuffings, and arrests—often accompanied by beatings or shootings to subdue unruly suspects. That "unruliness" might be associated with innocence is incompatible with the fundamental precepts of criminalization. So, too, is attentive listening to the reports and testimony of black witnesses and victims of violence in relatively poor Native American, African American, Asian American, and Latino communities. Fearing persons of color and being insulated against evidence of innocence, the police devise the abusive and too frequently fatal modus operandi manifested in the shooting deaths of Fong Lee, Allen Lock, Benjamin Whiteshield, Antonio Zambrano-Montes, Jason Harrison, and untold others.

The racist violence embedded in police standard operating procedures is sometimes supplemented with extralegal violence, as in the case of Duanna Johnson, a six foot, five inch, male-to-female transgender black woman, who was shot in the head execution style on the streets of Memphis, Tennessee, on November 9, 2008. Johnson was killed within two days of testifying in a lawsuit that she had brought against the Memphis police department for a brutal beating she survived while in police custody (which was captured on tape). Johnson was assaulted after having been subjected to police officers' pointedly transphobic taunts and insults. She was called a "faggot" and a "he/she" by two white officers, who arrested her for alleged sexual solicitation. Although the two officers were convicted of the charges documented on tape and lost their jobs, as of 2015, no charges have been filed for her murder. Memphis police officials said they had no suspects, had made no arrests, and did not have a motive for the killing. Johnson is just one of five African American transwomen murdered in Memphis in the first decades of the twenty-first century. An air of impunity surrounds these murders, too, as few produce arrests, much less convictions.

When race-gendering is accomplished through the explicit deployment of violence by police or by nonstate actors abetted by hostile or indifferent law-enforcement agencies that fail to investigate black homicides, the state establishes boundaries of permissible hate. Precisely because violent racialization has systemic effects, it is better understood under the rubric of hate crime or state terror than as aberrant practice. Noam Chomsky (2003, 188) defines terrorism as the "calculated use of violence or the threat of violence to attain goals that are political, religious and ideological in nature, through intimidation, coercion, or instilling fear." By legitimizing unwarranted fear of people of color, criminalizing young black men, brutally enforcing white privilege and traditional gender norms, neglecting murders in minority populations, and engaging in lethal violence against persons "suspected" of criminal conduct, the state positions certain communities of color outside the protection of the law, structures and normalizes relations of superiority and inferiority, and produces a form of demoralization and powerlessness that perpetuates racial domination. Violent racialization can induce a state of terror in communities of color, precisely because police impunity demonstrates that resistance can be lethal.

To invoke the language of state terrorism is to conceive violent racialization as a form of asymmetrical conflict masked by formal guarantees of equal protection of the law; to make visible structures of power that allow and condone the use of violence and intimidation against individuals who have committed no crime; and to situate these acts of violence in a political framework in which the perpetrators of violence quite literally have control of the state, using its lawmaking powers to produce laws reflecting their own interests, and using formal police powers to ensure that they could engage in violence with impunity. David Rapoport (2004, 1049) has noted that "[t]he concept of terrorism, as opposed to the activity, originated with birth of modern democracy. The French Revolution provided the vocabulary for terror. In 1795 terrorism meant 'government by intimidation' (*Oxford English Dictionary*) and 'terrorists' were the creators and implementers of that policy." Derived from the Latin *terrere*, "to frighten or deter" (Donohue 2005, 16), terrorism originally referred to a state's violence against its own citizens for purposes of social control, to produce a particular kind of subject. In organizing the "reign of terror," the Jacobins

> believed they had a new purpose and method, and when Robespierre proclaimed 'either virtue or the terror', he meant that only terror could produce true democratic dispositions—a special task of the "Revolutionary Tribunals." Ordinary courts

assessed whether defendants violated the law; but the Tribunals treated "enemies," those who would break the law if they could. Ordinary rules of evidence developed to assess behavior were scrapped as impediments because guilt or innocence in the conventional or legal sense was irrelevant. The issue was not justice, but how to treat a prisoner so that his fate would be a didactic lesson for the public by identifying appropriate and inappropriate democratic dispositions.

(Rapoport 2004, 1049)

Construing violent racialization as state terrorism underscores the strategic uses and political effects of the concept of race. Deployed by official representatives of the state, violent racialization is not an arbitrary act of violence done by one individual on another, it is a political act of oppression. As the Jacobins acknowledged, the use of state terror produces particular dispositions on the part of the dominant class and quite different dispositions on the part of those who have been terrorized. Violence and its corollary fear establish the modern equivalent of a caste system (Alexander 2010), consolidating a racial order despite formal equality. Violent racialization seeks to produce bodies of color that know their place, accept an inferior status and abandon the full possibilities of freedom.

The formal contemporary study of race and racialization has required careful thinking about and responding to these basic questions: (1) Who gets to live, and who gets to die? (2) Who gets to live well, and who gets to suffer? (3) Who has the right to hate, and thereby the right to kill? (4) Which bodies are counted as persons, and which are counted among the (living) dead? (5) How do states, governments, civil society, media, popular culture, the technologies of everyday life, and theories of political and social life either contribute to or disrupt the practices of violence that continue to make race real? These questions, while daunting, also force new generations of scholars to think carefully about the significance of small-scale movements, including common and reoccurring interpersonal and collective modes of relation that allow innovative forms of resistance and practices of freedom to flourish.

Note

1. This truncated definition of racialization is a culmination of several meditations on racialization including but not limited to the ideas of Omi and Winant (1986); Homi Bhabha (2000); Achille Mbembe (2003); and Dean Spade (2011).

References

Agamben, Giorgio. 1998. *Homo Sacer: Sovereign Power and Bare Life*. Redwood City, CA: Stanford University Press.
Alexander, Michelle. 2010. *The New Jim Crow*. New York: New Press.
Bhabha Homi K. 2000. "'Race' Time and the Revision of Modernity." In *Theories of Race and Racism: A Reader*, edited by Les Back and John Solomos, 354–372. London and New York: Routledge.

Berger, Michelle and Kathleen Guidroz. 2009. *The Intersectional Approach: Transforming the Academy through Race, Class and Gender.* Chapel Hill: University of North Carolina Press.

Cacho, Lisa Marie. 2012. *Social Death: Racialized Rightlessness and the Criminalization of the Unprotected.* New York and London: New York University Press.

Caldwell, Kia Lilly. 2007. *The Specter of Sex: Gendered Foundation of Racial Formation in the United States, Negras in Brazil: Re-envisioning Black Women, Citizenship and the Politics of Identity.* New Brunswick: Rutgers University Press.

Chomsky, Noam. 2003. "Terrorism and Justice: Some Useful Terms." In *Hegemony or Survival: America's Quest for Global Dominance,* 187–216. New York: Metropolitan Books.

Collins, Patricia Hill. 1991. *Black Feminist Thought: Knowledge, Consciousness, and the Politics of Empowerment.* New York and London: Routledge.

Collins, Patricia Hill. 2004. *Black Sexual Politics: African Americans, Gender, and the New Racism.* New York: Routledge.

Collins, Patricia Hill. 2007. *From Black Power to Hip Hop: Racism, Nationalism and Feminism.* Philadelphia, PA: Temple University Press.

Cott, Nancy. 2000. *Public Vows: A History of Marriage and the Nation.* Cambridge, MA: Harvard University Press.

Crenshaw, Kimberle. 1995. "Mapping the Margins: Intersectionality, Identity Politics, and Violence Against Women of Color" in *Critical Race Theory: The Key Writings that Formed the Movement* edited by Kimberle Crenshaw and Neil Gotanda. New York: The New Press.

Donohue, Laura. 2005. "Terrorism and the Counter-Terrorism Discourse." In *Global Anti-Terrorism Law and Policy*, edited by Victor V. Ramraj, Michael Hor, and Kent Roach, 13–36. New York: Cambridge University Press.

Gilmore, Ruth Wilson. 2002. "Fatal Couplings of Power and Difference: Notes on Racism and Geography." *Professional Geographer* 54 (1): 15–24.

Goldberg, Theo. 2002. *The Racial State.* Oxford: Blackwell Publishers.

Haney Lopez, Ian. 1996. *White by Law: The Legal Construction of Race.* New York: New York University Press.

Hartman, Saidiya. 1997. *Scenes of Subjection: Terror, Slavery and Self-Making in the Nineteenth-Century America.* New York and Oxford: Oxford University Press.

Holland, Sharon Patricia. 2012. *The Erotic Life of Racism.* Durham and London: Duke University Press.

Isoke, Zenzele. 2013. *Urban Black Women and the Politics of Resistance.* New York: Palgrave Macmillan.

Jacobson, Matthew Frye. 1998. *Whiteness of a Different Color: European Immigrants and the Alchemy of Race.* Cambridge. MA: Harvard University Press.

Kitch, Sally L. 2009. *The Specter of Sex: Gendered Foundations of Racial Formation in the United States.* Albany: State University of New York Press.

Mbembe, Achille. 2003. "Necropolitics." *Public Culture* 15 (1): 11–40.

McKittrick, Katherine. 2013. "Plantation Futures." *small axe* 42 (November): 1–16.

McKittrick, Katherine. 2014. "Mathematics Black Life." *Black Scholar* 44 (2): 17–28.

McWilliams, Carey. 1968. "North from Mexico: The Spanish-Speaking People of the United States." New York: Greenwood Press.

Mills, Charles, and Carole Pateman. 2007. *Contract and Domination.* Cambridge: Polity Press.

Morrison, Toni. 1997. *Paradise.* New York: Alfred Knopf.

Ngai, Mae. 2004. *Impossible Subjects: Illegal Aliens and the Making of Modern America.* Princeton, NJ: Princeton University Press.

Omi, Michael, and Howard Winant. 1986. *Racial Formation in the United States: From the 1960s to the 1980s*. New York: Routledge and Kegan Paul.

Omi, Michael, and Howard Winant. 2014. *Racial Formation in the United States*. 3rd ed. New York: Routledge.

Puar, Jasbir. 2007. *Terrorist Assemblages: Homonationalism in Queer Times*. Durham and London: Duke University Press.

Puar, Jasbir. 2011. "The Cost of Getting Better: Suicide, Sensations, Switchpoints." *GLQ A Journal of Gay and Lesbian Studies* 18 (1): 149–158.

Rapoport. David. 2004. "Terrorism." In *Encyclopedia of Government and Politics*, edited by Mary Hawkesworth and Maurice Kogan, 1049–1077. London: Routledge.

Rothenberg, Paula. 1992. *Race, Class and Gender in the U.S.: An Integrated Study*. New York: St. Martins.

Smith, Andrea. 2005. *Conquest: Sexual Violence and American Indian Genocide*. Cambridge, MA: South End Press.

Smith, Andrea. 2006. "Heteropatriarchy and the Three Pillars of White Supremacy." In *Color of Violence: The Incite! Anthology*, edited by Incite! Women of Color against Violence, 66–73. Cambridge, MA: South End Press.

Spade, Dean. 2011. *Normal Life: Administrative Violence, Critical Transpolitics, and the Limits of Law*. Cambridge, MA: South End Press.

Spillers, Hortense. 1987. "Mama's Baby, Papa's Maybe: An American Grammar Book." *Diacritics: A Review of Contemporary Criticism* 17 (2): 65–81.

Stevens, Jacquelyn. 1999. *Reproducing the State*. Princeton, NJ: Princeton University Press.

Stoler, Ann. 1995. *Race and the Education of Desire: Foucault's Theory of Sexuality and the Colonial Order of Things*. Durham, NC: Duke University Press.

Wacquant, Loïc. 2008. "The Body, the Ghetto, and the Penal State." *Qualitative Sociology* 32 (1): 101–129.

Weheliye, Alexander G. 2008. "Pornotropes." *Journal of Visual Culture* 7 (1): 65–81.

Weheliye, Alexander G. 2014. *Habeas Viscus: Racializing Assemblages, Biopolitics, and Black Feminist Theories of the Human*. Durham and London: Duke University Press.

Yanow, Dvora. 2003. Constructing "Race" and "Ethnicity." In *America: Category-Making in Public Policy and Administration*. Armonk, NY: M. E. Sharpe.

CHAPTER 37

RELIGION

LISBETH MIKAELSSON

Introduction

The common saying that woman is religion's best friend while religion is an enemy of the female sex signals that, in spite of religious subordination, women are more religious than men. Actually, studies of religion document that women are more committed to religion (cf. Heelas and Woodhead 2005; Trzebiatowska and Bruce 2012),[1] while a great many instances in time and space testify that male dominance and misogyny thrive in religious soil. In all the so-called world religions, male elites controlling the interpretations of sacred texts have been privileged as carriers of religious authority; whereas religious doctrine has legitimated male leadership roles, restricting women's agency in family life and society at large. Recognition of its suppressive functions made religion a target early on when modern feminism burst forth as a social movement in the middle of the nineteenth century.

This chapter presents a number of central issues in feminist scholarship about religion. An introductory overview of the relationship between religion, gender, and feminism is meant to point out the complexity of this domain and some of the effects on religion of feminist movements. The important role of myth is emphasized through a discussion of Simone de Beauvoir's *The Second Sex* and its conceptualization of women as "other." Feminist identification of the "false consciousness" involved in marginalizing women is the point of departure for entering into some of the topics theorizing from a feminist position has led to in the disciplines of theology and religious studies. The last section centers on divine gender, especially the question whether goddesses can do something good for women in one way or other. And, finally, I round off with a few thoughts on the rise of religion and the feminist critique of multiculturalism.

Religion and Feminism

Religion is truly a great challenge to feminist thinking. Altogether, religious traditions permeate both the personal and social spheres in complex and powerful ways. In the shape of symbols and mythical systems religion construes the nature of the world, humanity's place in it, how life should be lived according to divine will, and what it is to be a man or a woman. Hence, religions are rich sources of identity through their imagery and cultural expressions. In ritual activities celebrating the sacred, religion inspires awe, imparts meaning, and strengthens social belonging. The authority of religious elites generally transcends the ritual and doctrinal realms; and, as we know, especially of contemporary Islam, religion may have great formal power over family and social relations through legislation. Thus religion envelops people and their lives in intricate structures and emotional webs under the auspices of the sacred and the institutions representing it. As sociologist of religion Linda Woodhead maintains, religion is a system of sacred power interacting in different ways with secular sources of power. Since gender is a parallel power system, the relationship of gender and religion should be understood as interlacing systems of power (Woodhead 2007). The variations *between* religions and *inside* religions with respect to the relationship between religion and gender may be considerable, and there is much research to be done to grasp it more fully. Owing to its being the dominant religion in the Western world, which is the place of origin of modern feminism, Christianity has so far been the religion most studied by feminist-oriented scholars.

"Feminism" has proved to be an indispensable analytical category when studying collective efforts to address gender inequality. Because religion regularly is involved in legislation and practices organizing gender inequality, the history of feminist religion critique goes back centuries. In *European Feminisms 1700-1950: A Political History*, historian Karen Offen (2000, 20) defines feminism in the following terms: "Feminism is the name given to a comprehensive critical response to the deliberate and systematic subordination of women as a group by men as a group within a given cultural setting." Offen prefers the term *subordination* because it points to a gender regime based on institutions, laws, customs, and practices that can be investigated historically; whereas the term *oppression* connotes a subjective psychological response. Further, the concept of feminism involves a system of ideas as well as a movement for change as necessary premises (20). Affiliation with a social movement is not obligatory for categorizing someone a feminist, however: a feminist is a man or woman who challenges "male domination in culture and society in whatever geographical location or situation in historical time, or in whatever combination with other issues" (24). These definitions have several merits. They do not assume that the terms *feminism* and *feminist* are used as self-designations, a premise, for instance, of the scholarly concept "missionary feminism," which is discussed later. In religious contexts *feminism* and *feminist* are often negative terms and may therefore be evaded, as when Muslim feminists call themselves women's rights activists or Sisters in Islam (cf. Bøe 2012).

Women are the primary focus of feminism, whether in their relations with men or in the wider social matrix. The more women are dominated by men who control the systems that distribute power, the more it justifies the use of the concept of patriarchy. Patriarchy is generally understood as men's power over women and men of lower status.[2] Patriarchy is not invariant, however. There is a far cry between today's fundamentalist Christian family patriarchies and the situation in nineteenth-century colonial Bengal when the issue of women's rights was introduced. In Bengal, whether a woman had a right to life was disputed since such a right conflicted with the traditional right of family and caste to inflict death on her (Pechilis 2013, 736).

For several reasons the neutral and inclusive concept of gender is preferable to the negatively laden concept of patriarchy as the main conceptual framework for discussing women's situation. Feminist theory generally regards male and female bodies as the physical markers of gender but refuses biological determinism, regarding gender identity as basically produced by the sociocultural matrix with its gender norms, values, symbols, and roles.

In scholarship across disciplines, gender has become a descriptive, analytical, theoretical, and critical category relevant for a great variety of data (cf. Mikaelsson 2007; Warne 2000). In the world of religion, patriarchy is often an appropriate label; yet scholarship needs a general category that makes room for nuances and differences and does not predetermine a gender structure as oppressive. It is clear that male dominance may be circumvented by women precisely through religious means, such as revelations, possessions, charisma, and belief in personal callings from a deity. The Montanist movement in antiquity is a case in point. Arising in Asia Minor in the second century, it spread to many parts of the Roman Empire during the following centuries. Women had important roles in the movement as prophets and members of the clergy, holding the roles of priest and bishop along with men. The movement was condemned by the Catholic Church, apparently because of its gender equality and emphasis on continuous prophetic revelation, which challenged the male-sex monopoly of the Catholic clergy and its recourse to the Apostolic tradition as source of authority (Marjanen 2005). In her study of female possession in various cultural and geographical environments, Mary Keller (2002) agues that possessed women have authority in virtue of their receptivity to superhuman forces—in losing her own voice, the woman attains power in the social context that accredits this phenomenon.

The idea of a monolithic religious patriarchy throughout history has also been undermined by the work of feminist scholars studying women as religious practitioners in their own right.[3] The question of possible benefits and privileges for women in a patriarchal system must also be considered.

The imaginary integration of human life in divine projects and cosmological visions that become enacted ritually, morally, legally, organizationally, and personally is the most characteristic feature of gender in a religious context. The assumed connection with sacred power is the basis for the power of religions to shape or consolidate gender differences. Thus religions often exemplify the systematic nature of gender as a constitutive part of social relations, as was described by historian Joan W. Scott (1986) in her famous essay "Gender: A Useful Category of Historical Analysis." Scott identifies four elements in a gender system that systematically interact with each other: cultural symbols, normative concepts based on interpretations of myths and symbols, institutions and organizations, and, finally, subjective identity. The model sketches a dialectical interplay of levels and processes that is applicable in a variety of cases because it does not specify the contents and values at play, only the operating modes of the basic elements that produce gender difference within a social unit. Such a theoretical model is relevant for analyzing religion and gender, which can be illustrated by the major historical churches. Here, a gender system, including the central ideas of sin and salvation, operates on four levels. (1) The biblical myth of the creation of human beings as differentiated in two sexes. Even though the first human couple together is made responsible for what the church has conceptualized as human sinfulness, the divine punishment is sexually differentiated, and the heaviest burden of guilt is assigned to the woman. (2) Sinfulness is a key concept in the Christian system and its main scriptural basis is the Genesis myth. (3) The salvific cleansing of sin is ritually institutionalized in the church, while the ecclesiastical organization is defined as a community of believers in the salvific message. A powerful, mythically legitimated gender difference is established when the clergy is restricted to males leading the rituals and governing the organization. (4) Lastly, the symbols and ideas mediated by the church shape believers' personal identity in a manner that secures their identification with the organization.

The gender system does not necessarily have to be consistent or stable; rather, suppressed ideas, inconsistencies, and paradoxes will coexist with normative versions and in time cause changes. Yet the implementation of divine measures believed to be sacred makes for permanence in religious gender systems. The three Abrahamitic "book religions," Judaism, Christianity, and Islam, are all characterized by the interplay between three elements in a textual/contextual triad: belief in scriptural revelation embodied in a normative, canonical text; interpretations of the text; and the practice of applying ideas and rules that have crystallized during the history of interpretation. The gender structures of these religions therefore have similar systematic features. If pluralist and novel interpretations of the canon, as in liberal theology, are accepted in the religious community more generally, feminists may have an easier job in gaining acceptance for their claims. At the other end, fundamentalist claims that every statement in the sacred text is the word of God will oppose views perceived to go against divine directives. In the Islamic world, feminists like Amina Wadud and Asma Barlas do not direct their critiques against the Qur'an; instead, they argue that it was patriarchal exegesis and commentary throughout history that enabled a textual misogyny legitimating women's confinement and subservience in the Muslim world (Barlas 2002; Wadud 2006). Grounding their quest for equality and empowerment in Qur'anic teachings, Muslim feminists thus make the tactical move of positing themselves as advocates of Islamic authenticity and representatives of the Muslim tradition, wanting to purify it of nonessential, patriarchal elements (Saadallah 2004).[4]

The impact of the feminist critique of religion goes far beyond the circles of self-identified feminists and takes several different courses, affecting most levels, from the global to the local. Women's admittance to the clergy in Protestant denominations and the flourishing of goddess spirituality are both significant religious changes resulting from feminist influence. The immense involvement of Protestant women in foreign missions from the nineteenth century onward has to a considerable extent been motivated by ideas of women's liberation. The globalization of Christian gender regimes, the organization of millions of local women in women's associations outside the household sphere at a time when this violated common gender norms; and not least, the space provided for women's individual careers as preachers, teachers, and nurses in the mission field are all far-reaching consequences of "missionary feminism"—the concept constructed by scholars to coordinate the agendas and agencies in modern missions whose intent is to serve the welfare and humanity of women across the world (cf. Mikaelsson 2003). Missionary feminism illustrates the plurality of feminisms as well as the rootedness in space and time of a particular historical feminism. From a postcolonial perspective, missionary feminism has been critiqued for its involvement in colonialism, as well as for its promotion of Western supremacy and religious exclusivism (cf. Donaldson and Kwok 2002). Accordingly, the derogatory term "missionary-imperial-feminism" has been coined (Thorne 1999). Yet, the size, complexity, and variation in modern missions speak for different approaches and evaluations in scholarship. One could also add that it is essential that the voices of non-Western Christian women be listened to.

Equally important, feminist agendas nourish the critique of religion more generally, and thus are a contributing factor to ongoing secularization. In the opposite direction, the rise of religious fundamentalism within Christianity, Judaism, and Islam evinces a consolidation of male headship and patriarchal family structures (Hawley 1994; Jeffreys 2012, 32–56). Curiously, the influence of feminist values is perceptible even among fundamentalist critics. A study of conservative evangelicals in the United States indicates that the former household patriarchy has been refashioned into a "servant-leadership" arrangement representing a middle course between the traditional masculine leadership role and a postfeminist, egalitarian-oriented New Man ideal (Bartkowski 2007, 158).

IN THE SHADOW OF EVE: SECOND-WAVE FEMINISTS ON WOMEN

"The grand theory of religion" in modern feminism is that the major religions have been instrumental in the subordination of women and still underpin patriarchy in many societies. Addressing scriptural arguments, codified rules, and practices, feminists scrutinize official aspects of religious gender constructions. Another line of argumentation holds that religion supports gender inequality through the mystification of male power as a divine arrangement proclaimed with sublime authority by male elites. Patriarchal rule may therefore be conceived as the normal and inevitable order of things, the way of the world as God made it and therefore beyond criticism. In *The Second Sex*, "the

Bible" of second-wave feminism,[5] French philosopher Simone de Beauvoir shrewdly connects three operating modes of religion that make women accept their subordinate position: religion legitimates male superiority and thus causes women to submit to a subordinate role, and in the same breath, women are offered a compensation for their secondary status:

> Man enjoys the great advantage of having a God endorse the codes he writes; and since man exercises a sovereign authority over woman, it is especially fortunate that this authority has been vested in him by the Supreme Being. For the Jews, Mohammedans, and Christians, among others, man is master by divine right; the fear of God, therefore will repress any impulse towards revolt in the downtrodden female. One can bank on her credulity. [...] But if woman quite willingly embraces religion, it is above all because it fills a profound need.
>
> (Beauvoir 1983, 632)

According to Beauvoir, religion is as much an instrument of deception or a source of false consciousness as it is an outer constraint to women. Patriarchal religion teaches woman to be subordinate, but woman is simultaneously deceived into thinking that she is equal to the man, having the same worth in God's eyes as "his creature." Social justice is not attained through this theological panacea, however, which additionally sanctifies women's passivity. Besides, the church secures that male guardianship over women is intact (Beauvoir 1983, 633).

The central theme in Beauvoir's *The Second Sex* is that woman, since the introduction of patriarchal cultures, has been imagined as an imperfect man, forced to play a secondary role in human life. Man protrudes as the primary human subject, whose existence is not defined and restricted by his relations to woman. In contrast, woman is objectified as a sexualized "other," defined by the roles and meanings she has for men. Her position becomes marginal in the male-centered world, a creature whose sex is considered to limit her human potential. Beauvoir substantiates the thesis with a wealth of religious, philosophical, and literary material, including classical and biblical mythology. She recurrently refers to the Genesis story about the first human couple, Adam and Eve, as a paradigmatic example of the male subject–female "other" constellation, thereby assigning a central role to biblical religion. Beauvoir emphasizes Eve's secondary status, expressed in the motif of her being formed after Adam, of Adam's rib, and for his sake, her creation being explicitly motivated by Adam's need for a suitable companion. As we know, the story does not offer any reason for the creation of Adam, and before Eve arrives on the scene, Adam is given the stewardship over the world when instructed by God to look after the garden of Eden and name the animals. Adam happily greets the woman, but like Pandora in Greek myth, Eve is a morally defective figure blamed for having introduced a compound of sexuality, suffering, and sin into a world that was perfect until her arrival. Beauvoir regards the biblical story as a working myth, a mirror for both genders through its central position in Western culture. An important part of its gender message consists in the male subject position it implies:

> A myth always implies a subject who projects his hopes and his fears towards a sky of transcendence. Women do not set themselves up as Subject and hence have erected no virile myth in which their projects are reflected; they have no religion or poetry of their own: they still dream through the dreams of men.
>
> (Beauvoir 1983, 174)

The story is a male projection, but biblical religion compels women to see themselves and the world through it. Women thus live under the spell of the myth and internalize its gender scheme in their identities and agencies. In Beauvoir's interpretation the Genesis narrative becomes a main conveyor of what she conceives as the fundamental myth of woman as the "other," inexorably tied to man, considered to have little or no potential for significant achievement outside the household sphere, while the business of running the world belongs to the male sex. Woman is not fully human, so to speak.

Thus a major feat of Beauvoir's masterpiece is to ascribe influence to psychological and cultural elements, not least myth, in the subordination of women. These elements are much more slippery entities than the formal rules and established practices limiting women's agency. In the 1970s, religion in the Western world had lost much of its legal and political power, but as a major cultural tradition, it nourished gender identities and role expectations, as it still does. Without necessarily meeting institutionalized discrimination, many women have recognized their own experiences as subjects and social actors in Beauvoir's analysis of a mythical orchestration rooted in male power. The biblical Eve in *The Second Sex* steps forward as a male phantasy originating in male desire and wily projection mechanisms, but in disclosing her true origin to the philosopher, Eve becomes a feminist muse for her and successive scholars.

Beauvoir's secular, Marxist-inspired critique of religion as an oppressive nostrum reappears as an important issue among central feminist theorists during the 1970s and onward. Kate Millett's seminal book of 1970, *Sexual Politics* (published in Norwegian in 1971), emphasizes the role of religious mythology for the degradation of women in similar terms as Beauvoir. She reiterates the argument that the linking of woman, evil, and sexuality in the myths of Pandora and Eve allows the male to identify himself as primarily human, not as sexual, and the sexualized female to be seen as a less human and ambivalent creature (Millett 1971, 58–61).[6] Theologian Mary Daly (1973, 8) suggests that the story of Adam and Eve is paradigmatic for how the power of naming has been stolen from women in Western culture.

In the intellectual tradition of Beauvoir, French feminist theory has been musing on a gendered symbolic order[7] and how male power manifests itself in the subject position. Transcendent monotheism is considered a major expression of this order because, when the singular God is seen as masculine, "the other," which is not God, becomes feminine in a hierachical dichotomy (Hampson 2007). In *About Chinese Women*, Julia Kristeva explains the dichotomy as expressing men and women's different relations to God against the backdrop of Israelite patriarchal society. In her reading of the text, woman and serpent represent the polymorphic and erotic, in a polar position to "the single true and legislating principle," represented by the transcendent, monotheistic God, who is "the Guarantor of the ideal interests of the community." According to Kristeva, monotheistic unity depends on the separation of the sexes and the othering of woman as embodying pleasure and desire (quoted in Moi 1986, 141; cf. Hampson 2007, 62–63).[8]

Thus, feminist interpretations of the Genesis myth identify its central theme as a deprivation of women's full humanity. The othering of women is coupled with a hierarchical gender order in the very category of the human. A staple in patriarchal ideological power is thus uncovered, which is seen to be the myth's legacy for succeeding generations. In various guises the idea that women's equal humanity with men is denied and veiled appears as a recurrent theme in feminist discourse. When Mary Daly (1973) reflects on her former hopes for a change in the Roman Catholic refusal of female clergy, she realizes that she had missed the point about Christ as a symbol. The church argues that the maleness of Christ implies that the ministry representing him also has to be male. Daly had hoped that his humanity would be more important than his gender, but she was forced to conclude that Christ's maleness was untranscendable since it mediated a message of male supremacy. Hence the struggle for women priests would be futile (43).[9] In a study of the beheading of mythical women, religion scholar Wendy Doniger maintains that this symbolism expresses the dehumanizing of women, a transformation from being a seeing subject to a demeaned body. A consequence of this victimization is that those who see her as a blind body become blind to the woman's real nature (Doniger 1995, 15).

A significant corollary of this thinking is that women not only must fight for liberation from outward constraints; they also need to be freed from false consciousness and to overcome estrangement from their bodies and lack of self-confidence. In this perspective, the feminist movement is understood as a fundamentally empowering enterprise in which women are developing an independent subject position that enables them to act in the world as equal human beings. As will be discussed next, a Western Goddess religion develops in the wake of this thinking.

Theorizing from a Feminist Position

A notable element in the second-wave feminist movement was women's so-called consciousness raising. This concept refers to a collective awakening evolving from the communal discussions among women in grass-roots groups and women's liberation organizations about the nature of gender inequality and female subordination. In these settings, women realized that their personal experiences relating to gender disparagement and sexual harassment were shared by other women and were therefore not just an individual thing. Hence, the popular slogan about the personal being political. Beauvoir's analysis of woman as "other" could illuminate the distrust of women's abilities, unwillingness to accept women in male-dominated spheres, as well as neglect of women's achievements, in other words, the weight of prejudices and negative expectations related to their sex that women experience, even in societies well on their way to full equality, as in Scandinavia. Thus the feminist movement has had a key role in producing theoretical insights linked to agendas for making changes. In retrospect, it is evident that the vital issues raised by feminist thinkers have spurred scholarship into new trajectories of theorizing and research. Altogether, academic feminism harbors many different theoretical assumptions and approaches.[10] It can be argued, however, that the biggest changes in scholarship brought about by feminism are, on the one hand, awareness of gender blindness, male bias, and androcentrism and, on the other hand, attention to women and the workings of gender as topics of research.

Arising in the Western hemisphere, the "founding mothers" of feminist scholarship in religion were preoccupied with Christianity. In the nineteenth century the Bible was allotted a central role in consolidating female inferiority. This was highlighted in the early feminist attack *The Woman's Bible*, Parts I and II ([1885, 1889] 1985), a best-selling volume edited by Elizabeth Cady Stanton with a committee of collaborators. Here, biblical passages dealing with women were commented on and androcentric interpretations critiqued. Feminist theologians in the 1970s followed in the tradition of Stanton. The pioneering textual studies and critiques by feminist theologians Mary Daly, Rosemary Radford Ruether, and Elisabeth Schüssler Fiorenza have had a great impact across religious and disciplinary boundaries. Probably the most influential feminist theologian, still regularly referred to, has been Catholic theologian and later post-Christian philosopher Mary Daly, author of *The Church and the Second Sex* ([1968] 1975) and *Beyond God the Father. Toward a Philosophy of Women's Liberation* (1973). In strikingly gross and colorful language Daly denounces Christianity for being a woman-hating institution pervaded by patriarchal ideas and practices. Her acid critique was followed by a symbolic as well as real exodus from the Catholic Church, accompanied by her visions for a new sisterhood of women freed from the distorting slant of patriarchy and therefore capable of pioneeering intellectual achievements. Other prominent feminist scholars in religion have agreed that women's experience provides a fundamental methodological basis for their investigations (cf. Christ and Plaskow 1979, 6–7; Morgan 1999, 50; Plaskow 1991, 12). Theologian Ursula King suggests that a feminist study of religion should be marked by "participatory hermeneutics," resulting in new consciousness and attitudes. She calls for more empathic involvement and personal concern in research and is critical of the ideals of objectivity and neutrality, which she thinks collide with a feminist paradigm shift (King 1995, 26–28).

Feminist scholarship in religion is executed in different disciplinary settings and applies a number of methods and theoretical approaches. Academic theology, whether Christian or another, is generally anchored in affiliation with religion, usually one religion, and is supposed to serve it with its ongoing reflections and knowledge production. Although feminist theologians may be attacked for doctrinal and methodological reasons, scholarship aiming to make religion more egalitarian or liberal is not as such epistemologically discarded in this academic setting.

Matters are different in the other main discipline centering on religion, the history of religions, or as it is now frequently called, religious studies or religion. This discipline has a comparative approach and covers religion in all its various forms with a broad spectrum of methods. Today it is primarily legitimated by secular, epistemological claims and, secondarily, by the cultural values of tolerance and pluralism. Practitioners are especially alert to possible distortions in scholarship that seem rooted in religious adherence. At the same time, a phenomenological ideal of detached empathy with all kinds of religious traditions has been enjoined, creating a tension between gender-critical work and disciplinary principles (cf. Hawthorne 2009). Intentions to influence religion in one way or other would easily be understood as breaking with the principles of neutrality and objectivity. To *study* feminist criticism and re-envisioning of religion on a par with other religion-related phenomena, however, is perfectly legitimate. Yet, in practice it is not that simple to sharply distinguish between feminist and nonpoliticized academic studies. Feminism is more than a provider of data; it is also a provider of concepts and argumentations that work their ways into academic thinking and questioning more generally. In religious studies, gender critique helps to undermine the phenomenological paradigm that constructs religion as a sacred, separate sphere consisting of a number of universal elements. This way of conceiving religion is becoming replaced by a paradigm regarding religion as being a part of culture, shapable at any time by specific cultural conditions and geographical locations.

Strong motive powers, like feminist agendas, easily elicit suspicions of bias, in conflict with objectivity norms. This is a double challenge for feminist scholarship, first, because mainstream scholarship may have difficulty acknowledging it and, second, because ideological distortion certainly is possible. Political agendas are not the only challenges for objectivity, however. Taking one's social environment as the normal order of human life represents another variety. In the nineteenth century, Western women's subordination and exclusion from the public sphere were defended by scholars who considered such arrangements to be either the way of nature or the will of God Almighty. While academic discourse has become less parochial, a persistent target for feminist scholars has been androcentrism, or scholarly habits that allow males to represent the human and that privilege male activities as topics for research. Thus a secondary, invisible place in the world is assigned to women, illustrating that the myth of woman as "other" is compatible with academic standards and objectivity norms. Androcentrism in scholarship is encapsulated in deep-seated norms concerning what is interesting to investigate and important to preserve as knowledge, and in disciplinary lenses, traditions, and theoretical presumptions that are taught to new generations of students, male and female.[11]

In religious studies, the notion of *homo religiosus* has been targeted as an instance of androcentrism. The term has tended to function as a generic masculine, identifying the human with the male, ignoring that *vir religiosus* is not identical with *femina religiosa*, and thus leaving out women's role as coproducers of religious worlds (cf. Mikaelsson 2007, 305). As the feminist pioneer in religious studies Rita M. Gross (1996) has repeatedly insisted, androcentric bias in scholarship may not only perpetuate patriarchal norms within religions but possibly also cause misconceptions that make religions more patriarchal than they really are (66). Gross's research in Australian indigenous religion in the 1960s convinced her that earlier studies suggesting that women were deemed religiously insignificant and profane because they were denied participation in men's ceremonies had misunderstood the religious situation among the aboriginals. The truth was that women had a religious life of their own from which the men were excluded (66). Miranda Shaw accuses Western scholars of having misrepresented Tantric Buddhism in India by creating an image of Tantric women as prostitutes and witches who were sexually exploited by male seekers of spiritual liberation. Shaw (1998) constructed a gynocentric research design focusing on Tantric women's writings, scriptures, and biographical accounts, and on this basis maintains that the Tantric *yoginis* were spiritual practitioners highly respected by Tantric males. Accordingly, a gender model of complementarity and mutuality would be more adequate than the androcentric model viewing the women as insignificant and repressed (11). While an egalitarian reconstruction of a religious tradition very well may provide a more truthful version, it is also a hazard that a modern, ideological vision is imposed on a foreign context and distorts it (cf. Hawthorne 2009, 9).

More attention to women and femininity, with a critical view to possible neglect and misrepresentation in mainstream research, is a basic countermove against androcentrism. This is not always feasible in studying religious organizations or textual traditions, but a large number of studies attest that it has become a significant part of scholarship.[12] Given the hierarchical gender divides within many religious systems, focusing on women may entail attention to nonprestigious religious communities, such as women's money-collecting associations for foreign missions in Protestantism, or studying a broader range of phenomena, such as healing or self-spiritual practices in the Western cultic milieu. Its relevance is evident in *everyday religion*—a line of research investigating how religious belief and spirituality is expressed in daily life by ordinary people—an egalitarian twist in recent scholarship that is partly explicable by the impact of feminism (cf. Fedele and Knibbe 2013b). Breaking with an unreflective preconception that everyday religion is prescribed by institutionally established norms, a much more sophisticated understanding of how religion may function in people's lives is attained by this approach.[13] Additionally, singular and powerful women, such as Madame Blavatsky or Mary Baker Eddy, deserve feminist interest, not because scholars ought to do anything for their reputation or their followers, but to establish these women's contributions to the history of religions.

What Can Goddesses Do for Women?

What primarily distinguishes religion from the rest of culture is the belief in the existence of supernatural beings; communication *with* these beings through rituals, prayers, and the reading of signs; and communication *about* them in preaching, theological expositions, academic lectures, and other forms of discourse (cf. Gilhus and Mikaelsson 2012, 27). Supernatural beings, notably gods and goddesses, are frequently supposed to be both gendered and sexually active (cf. Endsjø 2009, 153–160). Even when deities are thought to transcend human gender and to be in principle unfathomable, they may be spoken of in gendered language, such as the Jewish and Christian (masculine) God.

Divine gender obviously reflects human gender when deities are personified or dressed up in male or female costumes or when they go to war or give birth. Hence, the relationship between gendered divinities and humans must be a point of great interest in feminist thinking about religion.

A main feminist proposition contends that there is a power dialectics between gendered divinity and gendered humans. The scholar who brought this argumentation to the public forefront in second-wave feminism was Mary Daly. Her much-cited phrase "If God is male, then male is God" (Daly 1973, 19; 1975, 38) sums up her idea that the linguistic and imaginary masculinity of the Jewish-Christian God makes him a divine patriarch, to be understood as a mystification of the human male in the social sex-role system. God legitimates the sex roles that give men the upper hand in society, and in turn, the sex-role system functions as a plausibility structure for theological doctrines, justifying religious and social patriarchy (Daly 1975, 13).[14]

A significant response to Western monotheism has been a turn to female divinity. If the Jewish-Christian God can do so much for men, then a Goddess must surely be beneficent for women? Musings on the empowering functions of divine gender supplement the critique of religion's negative aspects in feminist thought.

In *Womanspirit Rising* (1979), religion scholar Carol P. Christ presents a series of arguments for why goddess spirituality is good for women. Her point of departure is a theory of religious symbols, notably anthropologist Clifford Geertz's well-known definition of religion as "a system of symbols which acts to establish powerful, pervasive, and long-lasting moods and motivations" in people, and his understanding of religious symbols as representing the deepest values of society and its inhabitants (Geertz 1973, 90; Christ 1979, 274). Applying this functionalist understanding to the religious situation in Western societies, Christ argues that the worship of the Jewish-Christian God creates moods and motivations that legitimate male authority and dominance in society and simultaneously make women psychologically dependent on men and willing to submit to men's authority (Christ 1979, 275). Why not, then, just drop religion? Because, according to Christ, religious symbols play such fundamental roles in the human psyche that they cannot be rejected without creating a vacuum in the mind. Thus, there is a psychological need for other symbols. Otherwise, in times of crisis or need the mind will revert to familiar symbols (275). This theoretical diagnosis prepares the gound for recommending a Goddess religion, in other words, a mythical medicine against the marginalization of women. According to Christ, this religious panacea will empower women, encourage them to cultivate their independent will, and help them to affirm the female body and its life-giving functions as well as welcome old age as a stage of wisdom. Ancient and non-Western goddess traditions are seen as available, though not authoritative, resources for modern Goddess worshippers. Christ has no objections to an eclectic and self-opinionated tapping of non-Western traditions (276). Her article has been seminal in the development of Western Goddess religion, which allegedly replaces theology with thealogy, patriarchy with equality, dualistic religion with holistic spirituality, and intellectualistic orientation with bodily experience (cf. Fedele and Knibbe 2013, 6–7).

Perhaps just because of their sweeping topical generalizations, the works of Daly, Christ, and related feminists have for many scholars functioned as eye-openers to interesting problem areas. How likely, however, is it that the deity's gender in itself motivates social behavior and determines social structures? Are women really better off with goddess traditions? The case of Hinduism speaks against any simple, positive answer to these questions. Hinduism is the religion in today's world with the richest assortment of goddesses. Their history goes far back in time, for some, to pre-Aryan periods. Millions of men and women worship Durga, Lakshmi, Parvati, and numerous other goddesses, and in many cases both genders officiate as priests. A large branch within mainstream Hinduism, Shaktism, holds the Great Goddess, Mahadevi, as the supreme deity—the only example of a feminine supreme being among the great religious traditions of the world. *Shakti* is female power, recognized as the life-giving force in goddesses and women, but potentially dangerous if not controlled by men, or in the world of myth, by male gods. The potential threat inherent in the female principle is a central idea in the religious legitimation of Indian patriarchy. Accordingly, women's position in Indian society makes the general formula "goddess worship means social benefits for women" highly questionable.[15] In perfect justice, it can be imagined that goddess imagery compensates for women's lack of power in real life. Also, goddesses may legitimate male supremacy through being subordinated to male gods, as many of the Hindu goddesses are in their roles as wives and mothers. Evidently, the social impact of gods and goddesses must depend on more factors than gender symbolism, without excluding the possibility that symbolism in many circumstances can be decisive. The anthology *Is the Goddess a Feminist?* (Hiltebeitel and Erndl 2000) indicates that generally Hindu goddesses are no women's libbers in Indian guise. Rita M. Gross admonishes that it is not the goddesses, but the worshippers, who decide whether their goddess is or is not a feminist. To Western women, says Gross, the Hindu Goddess is a feminist because the Indian goddess symbolism promotes their humanity in powerful ways through its rich and liberating imagery (Gross 2000, 105–106).

Yet, Indian religious culture is neither monolithic nor static. Many Indian feminists are turning to Shaktism as a resource for women's empowerment and common identity in a country divided by caste, race, linguistic, and economic differences. Kathleen Erndl has studied holy women and female gurus in India and argues it is the divine model represented by the Goddess that makes it possible for women to have such spiritual status. Holy women may be allowed to not marry and to provide for themselves by performing healing and rituals. They identify with the Goddess, and are generally called *Mataji* (respected Mother), which is the most common goddess title. Yet, Matajis are exceptional women who do not influence women's roles in society (Erndl 2000, 94). Miranda Shaw maintains that Vajrayogini, the supreme goddess of the Buddhist Tantric pantheon, can be regarded as a divine feminist who is in favor of women's freedom and equality as spiritual seekers. Vajrayogini is a female Buddha iconographically represented as a naked women in graceful, dynamic poses. She identifies with women, proclaiming that "she adopts a female form so that women, upon seeing her, will recognize their own innate divinity and potential for enlightenment" (Shaw 2000, 170).

Shaw contrasts her findings with the prevailing interpretation in Western scholarship of the goddesses as primarily relevant for the psychology and religiosity of male Tantrics (167).

Hence a goddess may be but is no invariable advocate of women's interests. Historian Caroline Walker Bynum, an expert on medieval religion,[16] indicts Carol Christ for a simplistic understanding of the social impact of symbols. Referring to philosopher Paul Ricoeur, who explains symbols as multivalent, polysemic formations open to many different interpretations, Bynum (1986, 2) argues that gender-related symbols in their full complexity "may refer to gender in ways that affirm it or reverse it, support or question it; or they may, in their basic meaning, have little at all to do with male and female roles. Thus our analysis admits that gender-related symbols are sometimes "about" values other than gender."

Bynum's admonition should be kept in mind when turning to the Virgin Mary, the mother of Jesus in Christianity and thus a mythical female figure of great importance. The Virgin is the closest Christian analogy to a goddess. In theological tradition she is made a symbol of female humility; she is "the second Eve," who subjects herself to the will of God and produces a child without loosing her virginity. This makes her a model of female submission and sexual purity, apparently a patriarchal phantasy, and not the kind of figure feminists applaud. Daphne Hampson argues that the cult of Mary and Christ in the Catholic tradition has led to an absolute division of sex, and she suggests that the Protestant emphasis on the spoken word allows for greater fluidity regarding gender (cf. Hampson 2007, 68–69). Rosemary Radford Ruether, however, warns against a hasty dismissal of Mary. In Mary's maternal aspects are residues of the pre-Christian Earth Mother bestowing fecundity and renewal, which are celebrated in popular Catholic festivals. Also, her virginity may communicate a female autonomy not defined by procreation (Ruether 1979, 6–7). Add to this that alternative spirituality people are drawn to Mary as personifying the sacred energies present at pilgrimage sites, while Western Goddess worshippers may visit Maryan shrines and regard her as one of countless forms of the Goddess. The theological leadership in the Christian churches is not in control of the meanings that may develop related to figures like Christ and Mary in new religious movements or popular culture.

In conclusion, feminist thinking about the functions of divine gender has opened up exciting avenues of research. Questions asking how the deity is interpreted, by whom, in what contexts, and for what purposes, are yet obligatory. It is necessary both to have the polysemy of gendered symbols in mind and to realize that some meanings are more important with a view to their functions for social power regimes.

Final Comments

The rise in conservative and fundamentalist forms of religions means that traditional gender views have become visible elements in the existent religio-political scenario. This development has taken scholars, including feminists, by surprise. The belief that secularization would gradually drain off the power of religion has crumbled away in the face of media coverage of religious extremism and everyday meetings with Islamic women in their hijabs in Western cities. Generally skeptical toward the individualism implied in the human-rights declaration, conservative and fundamentalist groups advocate family values and traditional religious moralities, very often entailing male headship in families. How to react to this situation has become a vital and contentious issue. One feminist response has been to critique multiculturalism. This is significant because it challenges the acclamation of religious and cultural difference so central to postmodernist and postcolonial sensibilities in feminism. Multiculturalism is the ideology that for decades has guided Western immigration policies, supported by elite segments in Western democracies, including feminists. In *Is Multiculturalism Bad for Women?* (1999) political scientist Susan Moller Okin delineates the incompatibility between a commitment to gender equity and a commitment to group rights that allow oppressive practices. Thus the general question of whether there must be limitations to a multicultural politics of difference is clearly stated. The predicament gave feminist analyses of religion in the 1970s a new relevance. In her book *Man's Dominion*, Sheila Jeffreys (2012, 2) pays tribute to Daly's *Beyond God the Father* for its outspoken attack on patriarchal religion. Against believers' claims that their religion should be treated with due respect, Jeffreys declares that *disrespect* for religion is crucial for feminism: "Disrespect for it should be the natural amniotic fluid of feminist thought and activism" (5). The rise in religion will definitely create a number of different responses, one of them revitalizing the feminist critique of male religious power.

Notes

1. In their book *Why Are Women More Religious Than Men?*, Marta Trzbiatowska and Steve Bruce summarize their findings in five points: (1) Biological makeup does not explain the gendered difference in religiosity. (2) Women's reproductive role directs them more than men to the social role of carer that takes responsibility for the socialization of the young. This keeps women closer to organized religion and spirituality. (3) Since religion has a role in the control of sexuality, men are interested in pressing women to adhere to the dominant religious culture. On the other hand, religion offers women who dislike male sexual demands a reason for embracing piety. (4) More than men women are concerned with bodily purity, health, and holistic spirituality, which explains their attraction to new religious movements. (5) Secularization has affected men earlier than women for the foregoing reasons (Trzbiatoskwa and Bruce 2012, 177–178).
2. Sue Morgan (1999, 43) defines patriarchy as "an institutionalized system of male power and dominance over women, subject men and the natural world as a whole."
3. Cf. Rita M. Gross, *Feminism and Religion* (1996) and *Buddhism after Patriarchy* (1993); Miranda Shaw, *Passionate Enlightenment: Women in Tantric Buddhism* (1998).
4. Muslim feminism should be distinguished from Islamist feminism. The latter emerges from the Islamist movement, and teaches that women should not try to be equal to men, which would be unnatural and unfair, but to emphasize their integrity and dignity as

women. Muslim feminism is progressive, advocationg women's emancipation, while Islamist feminism is conservative, advocating patriarchy (Saadallah 2004, 218).
5. The book was first published in French in 1949, with the title *Le Deuxième Sex*.
6. Cognate, derogatory views on women among Christians, Jews, and Muslims are reported in Julia O'Faolain and Lauro Martines's *Not in God's Image* (1973), a compilation of textual excerpts from the early Greek period until the middle of the nineteenth century. Another overview of attitudes toward women tematizing religious misogyny is Vern L. Bullough's *The Subordinate Sex* (1973/1974), both titles associating to the feminist opinion of Eve.
7. French theorists Julia Kristeva and Luce Irigarey have both reflected on transcendent monotheism as a major element in *the male symbolic order*, a concept arising from Lacanian pychoanalytic thought comprising the realms of linguistic communication, knowledge, law systems, and so on.
8. The sexual dichotomy is deeply ingrained in biblical thought, as theologian Daphne Hampson maintains, referring to the book of Hosea. Through his prophetic speech, Hosea represents God in a male subject position, rebuking and condemning the people of Israel, who is thus positioned as female other. This becomes apparent in Hosea's metaphorical rendering of the relationship as analogous with his own marriage to the unfaithful and lewd Gomer, the wife who should have been virtuous and obeyed her husband according to Israeli law (Hampson 2007, 62).
9. Of course, many Protestant churches abandon this particular linkage between divine and human gender when allowing women entrance into the priesthood.
10. Rosemarie Tong specifies liberal theory, Marxist theory, radical theory (focus on motherhood, sexuality, and gender), psychoanalytical theory, socialist theory, existentialist theory (inspired by Simone de Beauvoir), and postmodern theory (Tong 1989).
11. Main works discussing the identification of the human with the male and the masculine bias in science are Sandra Harding and Merrill B. Hintikka (eds.), *Discovering Reality: Feminist Perspectives on Epistemology, Metaphysics, Methodology, and Philosophy of Science* (1983); and Sandra Harding, *The Science Question in Feminism* (1986).
12. Cf., for instance, Clarissa B. Atkinson, Constance H. Buchanan, and Margaret R. Miles (eds.), *Immaculate and Powerful: The Female in Sacred Image and Social Reality* (1985); Elizabeth A. Castelli (ed.), *Women, Gender and Religion: A Reader* (2001); Morny Joy, Kathleen O'Grady, and Judith L. Poxon (eds.), *Religion in French Feminist Thought* (2003); Darlene M. Juschka (ed.), *Feminism in the Study of Religion: A Reader* (2001); Ursula King and Tina Beattie (eds.), *Gender, Religion and Diversity: Cross-Cultural Perspectives* (2005); Griselda Pollock and Victoria Truvey Sauron (eds.), *The Sacred and the Feminine: Imagination and Sexual Difference* (2007).
13. Cf. Nancy T. Ammerman (ed.), *Everyday Religion: Observing Modern Religious Lives* (2007); Marion Bowman and Ülo Valk (eds.), *Vernacular Religion in Everday Life: Expressions of Belief* (2012); Meredith B. McGuire, *Lived Religion: Faith and Practice in Everyday Life* (2008).
14. Daly argues in tune with the social dialectics between objective and subjective reality outlined by Peter Berger and Thomas Luckman in their classic work *The Social Construction of Reality* (first published in 1966).
15. Several scholars have argued that the life conditions of Indian women in general speak against correlating belief in goddesses with women's social status, cf. Humes (2002); Jacobsen (2007); Pintchman (1994).

16. Cf. Bynum's well-known books *Jesus as Mother: Studies in the Spirituality of the High Middle Ages* (1982); and *Fragmentation and Redemption: Essays on Gender and the Human Body in Medieval Religion* (1992).

References

Ammerman, Nancy T., ed. 2007. *Everyday Religion: Observing Modern Religious Lives.* Oxford: Oxford University Press.

Atkinson, Clarissa W., Constance H. Buchanan, and Margaret R. Miles, eds. 1985. *Immaculate and Powerful: The Female in Sacred Image and Social Reality.* Boston: Beacon Press.

Barlas, Asma. 2002. *"Believing Women" in Islam: Unreading Patriarchal Interpreations of the Qur'an.* Austin, Texas: University of Texas Press.

Bartkowski, John P. 2007. "Connections and Contradictions: Exploring the Complex Linkages between Faith and Family." In *Everyday Religion: Observing Modern Religious Lives,* edited by Nancy T. Ammerman, 153–166. Oxford: Oxford University Press.

Beauvoir, Simone de. (1949) 1983. *The Second Sex.* Translated and edited by H. M. Parshley. Harmondsworth: Penguin Books.

Berger, Peter, and Thomas Luckmann. (1966) 1973. *The Social Construction of Reality.* Harmondsworth: Penguin Books.

Bowman, Marion, and Ülo Valk, eds. 2012. *Vernacular Religion in Everyday Life. Expressions of Belief.* Sheffield: Equinox Publishing.

Bullogh, Vern L. 1974. *The Subordinate Sex: A History of Attitudes toward Women.* New York: Penguin Books.

Bynum, Caroline Walker. 1982. *Jesus as Mother: Studies in the Spirituality of the High Middle Ages.* Berkeley: University of California Press.

Bynum, Caroline Walker. 1986. "Introduction: The Complexity of Symbols." In *On the Complexity of Symbols,* edited by Caroline Walker Bynum, Steven Harrell, and Paula Richman, 1–20. Boston: Beacon Press.

Bynum, Caroline Walker. 1992. *Fragmentation and Redemption: Essays on Gender and the Human Body in Medieval Religion.* New York: Zone Books.

Bøe, Marianne. 2012. *Debating Family Law in Contemporary Iran. Continuity and Change in Women's Rights Activists' Conceptions of Shari'a and Women's Rights.* PhD dissertation, University of Bergen.

Castelli, Elizabeth A., ed. 2001. *Women, Gender, Religion: A Reader.* New York: Palgrave.

Christ, Carol P. 1979. "Why Women Need the Goddess: Phenomenological, Psychological, and Political Reflections." In *Womanspirit Rising: A Feminist Reader in Religion,* edited by Carol P. Christ and Judith Plaskow, 273–287. San Franscisco: Harper & Row.

Christ, Carol P., and Judith Plaskow, eds. 1979. *Womanspirit Rising. A Feminist Reader in Religion.* San Francisco: Harper & Row.

Cohen, Joshua, Matthew Howard, and Martha C. Nussbaum, eds. 1999. *Is Mulitculturalism Bad for Women? Susan Moller Okin with Respondents.* Princeton, NJ: Princeton University Press.

Daly, Mary. (1968) 1975. *The Church and the Second Sex.* New York: Harper & Row.

Daly, Mary. 1973. *Beyond God the Father: Toward a Philosophy of Women's Liberation.* Boston: Beacon Press.

Donaldson, Laura E., and Kwok Pui-lan. 2002. *Postcolonialism, Feminism, and Religious Discourse.* New York and London: Routledge.

Doniger, Wendy. 1995. "'Put a Bag over Her Head': Beheading Mythological Women." In *Off with Her Head! The Denial of Women's Identity in Myth, Religion, and Culture*, edited by Howard Eilberg-Schwartz and Wendy Doniger, 15–31. Berkeley: University of California Press.

Endsjø, Dag Øistein. 2009. *Sex og religion. Fra jomfruball til hellig homosex*. Oslo: Universitetsforlaget.

Erndl, Kathleen M. 2000. "Is Shakti Empowering for Women? Reflections on Feminism and the Hindu Goddess." In *Is the Goddess a Feminist? The Politics of South Asian Goddesses*, edited by Alf Hiltebeitel and Kathleen M. Erndl, 91–103. New York: New York University Press.

Fedele, Anna, and Kim E. Knibbe. 2013. "Introduction: Gender and Power in Contemporary Spirituality." In *Gender and Power*, edited by Fedele and Knibbe, 1–27. New York and London: Routledge.

Geertz, Clifford. 1973. *The Interpretations of Cultures*. New York: Basic Books.

Gilhus, Ingvild Sælid, and Lisbeth Mikaelsson. 2012. *Nytt blikk på religion*. Oslo: Pax Forlag.

Gross, Rita M. 1993. *Buddhism after Patriarchy: A Feminist History, Analysis and Reconstruction of Buddhism*. New York: State University of New York Press.

Gross, Rita M. 1996. *Feminism and Religion: An Introduction*. Boston: Beacon Press.

Gross, Rita M. 2000. "Is the Goddess a Feminist?" In *Is the Goddess a Feminist?*, edited by Alf Hiltebeitel and Kathleen M. Erndl, 104–112. New York: New York University Press.

Hampson, Daphne. 2007. "The Sacred, the Feminine and French Feminist Theory." In *The Sacred and the Feminine. Imagination and Sexual Difference*, edited by Griselda Pollock and Victoria Turvey Sauron, 61–74. London and New York: I. B. Tauris.

Harding, Sandra. 1986. *The Science Question in Feminism*. Milton Keyes: Open University Press.

Harding, Sandra, and Merrill B. Hintikka, eds. 1983. *Discovering Reality: Feminist Perspectives on Epistemology, Metaphyscis, Methodology, and Philosophy of Science*. Dordrecht: D. Reidel Publishing.

Hawley, John Stratton, ed. 1994. *Fundamentalism and Gender*. New York and Oxford: Oxford University Press.

Hawthorne, Sian. 2009. "Religion and Gender. 'Contentious Traditions: The Study of Religions and the Gender-Theoretical Critique." In *The Oxford Handbook of the Sociology of Religion*, edited by Peter B. Clarke, 134–151. Oxford: Oxford University Press.

Heelas, Paul, and Linda Woodhead. 2005. *The Spiritual Revolution: Why Religion Is Giving Way to Spirituality*. Oxford: Blackwell.

Hiltebeitel, Alf, and Kathleen M. Erndl, eds. 2000. *Is the Goddess a Feminist? The Politics of South Asian Goddesses*. New York: New York University Press.

Humes, Cynthia Ann. 2000. "Is the Devi Mahatmya a Feminist Scripture?" In *Is the Goddess a Feminist?*, edited by Alf Hiltebeitel and Kathleen M. Erndl, 123–150. New York: New York University Press.

Jacobsen, Knut. 2007. *Hyllest til Gudinnen. Visjon og tilbedelse av hinduismens store Gudinne*. Oslo: Emilia forlag.

Jeffreys, Sheila. 2012. *Man's Dominion: The Rise of Religion and the Eclipse of Women's Rights in World Politics*. London and New York: Routledge.

Joy, Morny, Kathleen O'Grady, and Judith L. Poxon, eds. 2003. *Religion in French Feminist Thought*. London and New York: Routledge.

Juschka, Darlene M., ed. 2001. *Feminism in the Study of Religion: A Reader*. London and New York: Continuum.

Keller, Mary. 2002. *The Hammer and the Flute: Women, Power and Spirit Possession*. Baltimore and London: Johns Hopkins University Press.

King, Ursula, and Tina Beattie, eds. 2005. *Gender, Religion and Diversity: Cross-Cultural Perspectives*. London and New York: Continuum.

Marjanen, Antti. 2005. "Montanism: Egalitarian Ectstatic 'New Prophecy.'" In *A Companion to Second-Century Christian "Heretics,"* edited by Antti Marjanen and Petri Luominen, 185–212. Leiden and Boston: Brill.

McGuire, Meredith B. 2008. *Lived Religion: Faith and Practice in Everyday Life*. Oxford: Oxford University Press.

Mikaelsson, Lisbeth. 2003. "Gender Politics in Female Autobiography." In *Gender, Race and Religion: Nordic Missions 1860–1940*, edited by Inger Marie Okkenhaug, 35–51. Uppsala: Studia Missionalia Svecana XCI.

Mikaelsson, Lisbeth. 2007. "Gendering the History of Religions." In *New Approaches to the Study of Religion: Vol. 1, Regional, Critical, and Historical Approaches*, edited by Peter Antes, Armin W. Geertz, Randi R. Warne, 295–315. Berlin and New York: Walter de Gruyter.

Millett, Kate. 1971. *Sex og makt*. Oslo: Tiden Norsk Forlag. English original: *Sexual Politics* was published in 1970.

Moi, Toril, ed. 1986. *The Kristeva Reader*. Oxford: Basil Blackwell.

Morgan, Sue. 1999. "Feminist Approaches." In *Approaches to the Study of Religion*, edited by Peter Cononolly, 42–72. London and New York: Cassell.

O'Faolain, Julia, and Lauro Martines, eds. 1973. *Not in God's Image*. Glasgow: William Collins Sons.

Offen, Karen. 2000. *European Feminisms 1700–1950: A Political History*. Redwood City, CA: Stanford University Press.

Pintchman, Tracy. 1994. *The Rise of the Goddess in the Hindu Tradition*. Albany: State University of New York Press.

Plaskow, Judith. 1991. *Standing Again at Sinai: Judaism from a Feminist Perspective*. New York: HarperCollins Publishers.

Pollock, Griselda, and Victoria Turvey Sauron, eds. 2007. *The Sacred and the Feminine: Imagination and Sexual Difference*. London and New York: I. B. Tauris.

Saadallah, Serin. 2004. "Muslim Feminism in the Third Wave: A Reflective Inquiry." In *Third Wave Feminis: A Critical Exploration*, edited by Stacy Gillis, Gillian Howie, and Rebecca Munford, 216–226. Basingstoke and New York: Palgrave Macmillan.

Shaw, Miranda. 2000. "Is Vajrayogini a Feminist? A Tantric Buddhist Case Study." In *Is the Goddess a Feminist?*, edited by Alf Hiltebeitel and Kathleen M. Erndl, 166–180. New York: New York University Press.

Pechilis, Karen. 2013. "Feminism." In *Brill's Encyclopedia of Hinduism*, vol. 5, edited by Knut A. Jacobsen, et al., 734–749. Leiden and Boston: Brill.

Ruether, Rosemary Radford. 1979. *Mary—the Feminine Face of the Church*. London: SCM Press.

Shaw, Miranda. 1998. *Passionate Enlightenment: Women in Tantric Buddhism*. New Dehli: Munshiram Manoharlal Publishers Pvt. (Originally published by Princeton University Press in 1994.)

Stanton, Elizabeth Cady. (1895, 1898) 1985. *The Woman's Bible*. Introduction by Dale Spender. Edinburgh: Polygon Books. (Part I first published in 1895. Part II first published 1898.)

Thorne, Susan. 1999. "Mission-Imperial Feminism." In *Gendered Missions. Women and Men in Missionary Discourse and Practice*, edited by Mary Taylor Huber and Nancy C. Lutkehaus, 39–65. Ann Arbor: University of Michigan Press.

Tong, Rosemarie (1989) 1994. *Feminist Thought: A Comprehensive Introduction*. London: Routledge.

Trzebiatowska, Marta, and Steve Bruce. 2012. *Why Are Women More Religious Than Men?* Oxford: Oxford University Press.

Wadud, Amina. 2006. *Inside the Gender Jihad: Women's Reform in Islam*. Oxford: One World Publications.

Warne, Randi R. 2000. "Gender." In *Guide to the Study of Religion*, edited by Willi Braun and Russel T. McCutcheon, 140–154. London and New York: Cassel.

Woodhead, Linda. 2007. "Gender Differences in Religious Practice and Significance." In *The Sage Handbook of the Sociology of Religion*, edited by James Beckford and N. Jay Demerath, 550–570. Los Angeles: Sage.

CHAPTER 38

REPRESENTATION

LISA DISCH

THE concept of representation may be second only to gender in its centrality to mid-twentieth-century feminist theory and practice. Beginning in the 1970s, feminist activists mobilized to fight for increased representation of women in government and the private sector and against sexualized representations of women in popular culture. At the same time, feminist theorists developed critical approaches to the analysis of representational practices in literature, history, culture, and politics that were particularly innovative by virtue of their interdisciplinarity. Both the activism and the theory were sparked by a question peculiar to modern republican and democratic politics: What "is the relationship between aesthetic or semiotic representation (things that 'stand for' other things) and political representation (persons who 'act for' other persons)" (Mitchell 1995, 11)?

Feminist scholars have approached this overarching question in many ways. Most straightforwardly, they have explored the political necessity and advantages of "descriptive" representation, in which "representatives are in their own persons and lives in some sense typical" of those they represent (Mansbridge 1999, 629). Descriptive representation brings aesthetic and political representation together almost literally insofar as the representative typifies or pictures those for whom he or she acts. Alternatively, feminists have explored how the ways in which women are pictured, both materially and metaphorically, constrain their political action, equal exercise of rights, and general empowerment. These kinds of inquiries problematize the "politics" of aesthetic and semiotic representation, holding accustomed ways of speaking about and depicting women up to scrutiny for their political consequences.

Taking on the politics of representation was especially pressing to feminists in the 1970s, a time when woman as sex symbol was everywhere—in advertising, film, "beauty" contests—but educated and accomplished women could make few inroads into politics, the corporate world, the professions, or the arts. Yet the diverse meanings of representation and innovative feminist conceptualizations of the mechanics of representation seemed to turn theory *against* political activism. Elizabeth Cowie (1990, 113) put it especially well, "Challenging existing definitions of women, feminists confronted the problem of how to define positive or correct images as opposed to negative or oppressive images of women ... But at the same time as feminists were challenging particular images of women, new theoretical work emerged that undermined the very notion of representation on which much of the feminist critique had been based." Both epistemological and methodological issues fueled this conflict. Whereas the political project to challenge the way "women" are represented was based on the realist assumption that representations can and should be adjudicated in relation to their referents (in this case "women"), theories emerging from semiotics and psychoanalysis called these realist premises into question. They argued that representations do not stand in a mimetic or imitative relationship to reality but, rather, participate in a system of signification whose various elements derive their meaning from what they are articulated or positioned in relation to, not from what they stand for.

In short, while feminist activists worked from the commonsense premise that the objectification of women in mass culture fostered discrimination, even violence, against them on the job and in the home, some feminist theorists developed the counterintuitive argument that representations of women do not refer to or stand for real women. Instead, they signify relations of power that are articulated by means of sexual difference. This was not to deny the politics of representation but to shift its focus: feminist critique would aim, not at representation's distortion of its (real) referent, but at the relation of identity and difference that the representation presupposes to be real and at the norms those purported realities underpin. This approach recast sex difference, the presumed ground of patriarchy, from an *object* of representation, one necessarily "produced outside the system of representation," to an *effect* of that system (Cowie 1990, 118). And it redefined patriarchy from being seen as a system of domination based on sex, to being understood as "a web of psychosocial relations which *institute* a socially significant difference on the axis of sex," one "so deeply located in our very sense of lived, sexual, identity that it appears to us as natural and unalterable" (Pollock 1988, 33). Put simply, feminist theorists reconceived patriarchy from a system of sexual *domination* to one of sexual *differentiation* that makes sex "pertinent" in the first place (Delphy [1981] 1984, 144).

This chapter provides an overview of feminist explorations of the complex relations between political representation and aesthetic/semiotic/cultural representation. It analyzes three approaches, comparing feminist discussions of *vamps* (cultural representation) with *visibility* (historical representation) and *voice* (political representation). My analysis emphasizes the interdisciplinarity of feminist explorations of representation yet credits the disciplines from which some of the most pathbreaking work emerged. Film theory is especially prominent in the section "Vamps: The Politics of Mass Cultural Representation." Historiography and queer theory feature centrally in "Visibility: Women in the "Mirror of History." And history, cultural studies, and political science come together in the section "Voice: Speaking for Women as Subjects of Politics." Running through all three sections are concerns about the interplay between how representations picture women and who speaks for them, and how acts of representation work to constitute that for which they purport merely to stand.

VAMPS: THE POLITICS OF MASS CULTURAL REPRESENTATION

Feminist activists in the late 1960s and early 1970s organized direct actions to draw critical attention to mass-cultural representation of women as sex objects, most notably staging repeated protests against the Miss America Contest in the United States and seizing the stage at the 1970 Miss World Pageant at Royal Albert Hall in London. Laura Mulvey (2009, xxxiv) explains that demonstrations like these were "inspired by the belief that women's reality could be liberated from an alienating masquerade," as if real women interrupting the staging of woman as spectacle would have spell-breaking power. Such protests found their theoretical counterpart in Kate Millet's groundbreaking *Sexual Politics*, whose publication in 1969 made it "difficult for critics to ignore the wider social and political implications of sexual practice in fiction" (Kaplan 1986, 16).

Activism and theory began to part company soon thereafter as feminist scholars rediscovered Freud. Treating Freud as an apologist for patriarchy, Millet (1969) had read his notions of "penis envy" and "female castration" as simple biological reductionism. Juliet Mitchell (1975, xiii) challenged this cavalier dismissal, arguing forcefully that "a rejection of Freud's works is fatal for feminism," and pointing out that "however it may have been used, psychoanalysis is not a recommendation *for* a patriarchal society, but an analysis *of* one." In the 1970s, feminist film theory contributed significantly to a paradigm shift toward psychoanalytic approaches in feminist theory, particularly through its transformative conceptualization of representation. Feminist film theorists drew insights from and elaborated a tradition, initially defined by Raymond Bellour and Stephen Heath, which held that the "narrative and symbolic problem of establishing the difference between the sexes is the primary motivating force of the classical Hollywood film" (Penley 1988, 3). Breaking with realist assumptions, cinematic representation in the Hollywood film was recast as an "advanced representation system" that does not merely reflect or interpret sexual difference but actually produces it (Mulvey 2009, 15). As film scholar Constance Penley (1988, 3) observed, feminist analysts "discovered in film a seemingly perfect object for study. Cinema, as a sort of microcosm, provided a model for the construction of subject positions in ideology, while its highly Oedipalized narratives lent themselves to a reading of the unconscious mechanisms of sexual difference in our culture."

Mulvey's 1975 essay "Visual Pleasure and Narrative Cinema," the broadly influential and, in her words, "manifesto-like" text, was among the first feminist works to appropriate psychoanalytic theory as a feminist "political weapon" (Mulvey 2009, xvii, 14). As Penley (1988, 7) has observed, Mulvey turned that weapon against Hollywood cinema, arguing that "feminists have no choice but to reject the forms of classical cinema inasmuch as they are constructed on the basis of a male fantasy entirely detrimental to women." Mulvey's argument is frequently reduced to the claim that the "gaze" of the camera is male and its object female, but it is more complex than that: Hollywood cinema stages the patriarchal "unconscious (formed by the dominant order) [as it] structures ways of seeing and pleasure in looking" (Mulvey 2009, 15). Thus, Mulvey argues, narrative cinema affords its spectator two "contradictory" pleasures. First is the libidinal pleasure of looking at beautiful images, which have been coded feminine since the mid-nineteenth century construction of "woman *as image*" (Pollock 1988, 113). Second is the narcissistic pleasure of identifying with the film's male protagonist, which affords the "satisfying sense of omnipotence" that comes from driving the action as well as possessing the woman in it (Mulvey 2009, 21). Mulvey notes that to deliver this second pleasure, the film must "reproduce as accurately as possible the so-called natural conditions of human perception." The eye of the camera—"as exemplified by deep focus in particular"—will merge with the gaze of the protagonist and spectator, and the movements of the camera, "combined with invisible editing (demanded by realism)" will merge screen space with real space (21). While the first pleasure implies a separation between the subject and object of the gaze, the second "demands identification of the ego with the object on the screen through the spectator's fascination with and recognition of his like (19).

The spectator, then, confronts a contradiction: being asked to take up conflicting positions in relation to the images on screen—distance on the one hand, and proximity on the other. The visual economy of the film resolves this contradiction by way of what Mulvey (2009, 20) terms an "active/passive heterosexual division of labour," a division within the spectator that will necessarily define that spectator as male. Conforming to the terms of what Judith Butler (1990) would later parse as the "heterosexual matrix," the camera positions the spectator to *identify* with the male protagonist/agent of the narrative and to *desire* the female. The contradiction is resolved by a sexual differentiation of an image that positions man as the subject of the gaze and woman as both the object of the gaze and the image whose "visual presence" interrupts the narrative flow (Mulvey 2009, 19).

Up to this point, it might seem that Mulvey's argument reproduces the notion that film reiterates stereotypes of sexual difference, albeit in the rarified discourse of psychoanalysis. As Stacey (1987, 48) summarized it, "The construction of woman as spectacle is built into the apparatus of dominant cinema, and the spectator position which is produced by the film narrative is necessarily a masculine one." There is one crucial detail, however: the beautiful image is necessarily an interruption to the action, an arrest of agency that signifies ambivalently, at once conveying beauty and "implying a threat of castration" (Mulvey 2009, 22). According to Mulvey, narrative cinema, both in the story and visually, stages the two defense mechanisms by which the male unconscious wards off castration: identification with the law and separation from the object of desire. Film accomplishes identification with the law narratively as the plot unfolds as, variously, an investigation of the woman's guilt, her punishment, or her rescue. It accomplishes the second visually, neutralizing the threat by fetishizing woman as image into woman as "spectacle (woman purely *as* image)" (Rose 1986, 208).

By insisting that film stages the male unconscious both visually and narratively, Mulvey challenges the feminist critical preoccupation with film's distorted depictions of women. As Mulvey (2009, xxxiv) describes her argument thirty years later, "I argued, with the help of psychoanalytic theory, that the sexualized image of woman says little or nothing about women's reality, but is symptomatic of male fantasy and anxiety that are projected on to the female image." In other words, representations of women in film do not stand for or refer to women as subjects of sexual difference; instead, they signify or enact the psychic dynamics by which sex becomes charged as a site of difference.[1] This challenge to realist assumptions about representation opened a gap between feminist theory and practice.

It also sparked an extended debate over whether psychoanalysis was an important "political tool" for feminism, as Mulvey had claimed, or whether it was so mired in the dichotomies of psychoanalysis (e.g., male/female, active/passive, subject/object) as to lead to a political dead end. In holding out no hope for the female spectator of the Hollywood film, Mulvey's work seemed to leave feminists with no alternative but to renounce the pleasures of narrative cinema. Subsequent work in film theory, including by Mulvey herself, attempted to account for the possibility that a female or feminist or lesbian film viewer might resist the masculinized protocols of spectatorship, or, that a female or feminist or lesbian filmmaker might frustrate them (e.g., Doane 1982; Kaplan 1983; Stacey 1987).

Kaja Silverman (1996, 168) made an important intervention into these debates by shifting the emphasis from the identity of the spectator to the "cultural screen." A Lacanian concept, the "screen" is a visual repertoire: "that large, diverse, but ultimately finite range of representational coordinates, which determine what and how the members of our culture see—how they process visual detail, and what meaning they give it" (221). By mediating between the (mechanical) gaze and the (subjective) look, the screen establishes that the gaze is not, as in Mulvey, an anthropomorphic property of a male subject. It is merely the function of an "apparatus" that requires "another agency altogether"—the screen—to position subjects and solicit their identification. Looking, then, is not automatically or immediately masculine; it can be specified as such—or specified otherwise—by the protocols of the screen. To the extent that a spectator is made aware of those protocols, she may enjoy a "limited agency with respect to the representations through which he or she is apprehended" (175). This is Silverman's important advance: to derive the possibility of agency not from the attributes (e.g., gender or sexuality) of the spectator—as Doane, Kaplan, and Stacy had done—or even from those of the image-maker, but from the composition of the image itself. It may be staged to render more or less visible the cultural repertoires of representation that intervene in what we typically experience as unmediated "looking."

During this time, feminist film theory produced another essay that was equally pathbreaking, though less widely read: Elizabeth Cowie's 1978 essay "Woman as Sign." Like Mulvey, Cowie (1990, 117) decries the limitations of a feminist film criticism that is caught up with the "kinds of images of women represented in films" and, as such, treats film only as an expression of an ideology that lies outside it. Whereas Mulvey had turned to psychoanalysis for an alternative approach, Cowie deployed semiotics to theorize film as Levi-Strauss theorized kinship, as a system of communication or exchange. In film, as in kinship, woman is a "sign" whose value is given by the relations of difference and identity that materialize in and through her exchange. Cowie learns from Levi-Strauss that "woman" is not the "signified," or referent, of "'women as sign' in exchange systems"; women "as sign" rather signifies or conveys the "establishment/reestablishment of kinship structures or cultures" (130). She transposes this insight to film in order to reach a conclusion similar to Mulvey's: in film "the form of the sign—the signifier in linguistic terms—may empirically be woman, but the signified is not 'woman'" (130). Cowie (1990, 115) radicalizes Mulvey, however, by arguing that whereas the visual economy of film does produce "a binary structuring of sexual difference," it need neither assign its spectators exclusively to the division between "men and women" nor organize their relations in accordance with the oppositional logic of heterosexuality (which orients identification in opposition to desire), "for it may involve a phallic/nonphallic distinction between members of the same sex, for example mother and daughter."

The work of Cowie and Mulvey inaugurated a paradigm for feminist critical theory in disciplines other than film. Art Historian Griselda Pollock (1988, 10) emphatically sought to refocus feminist art criticism, moving it beyond "a local concern with 'the woman question'"—which, in its desire to canonize women artists and analyze the way canonical works represent women, takes sexual difference for granted—to an analysis of the production of sexual difference in art. Citing Cowie, she emphasized that it is not the stereotypes of women in art that matter, but the "construction of sexuality and its underpinning sexual difference," which are "profoundly implicated," not in representation as (mimetic) picturing, but "in looking and the 'scopic field'" (13). Also invoking Cowie, political theorist Linda Zerilli (1994, 14) urged a similar move to understand woman "as a signification" that is "constituted in and by the discourse of political theory," not as its referent.

Like Pollack, Zerilli (1994, 4) addressed her feminist colleagues, arguing that while their re-readings of canonical texts "rightly call our attention to the constructed meanings of woman," they do not forcefully challenge the "notion that theorists do little more than ascribe political significance to a sexual difference that is assumed to be produced elsewhere, that is, wholly outside the signifying structures of political theory texts themselves." Zerilli made it clear that her "quarrel" with her colleagues' ways of reading was, at base, a challenge to their "uncritical assumption of the classical model of representation, which holds both that language is a transparent vehicle for communicating (a preexisting) meaning and that the text is a reflection or mystification of social reality" (142). To hold such a conception of representation is to be taken in by political theory's rhetorical feint: it is "a signifying practice that ... passes itself off as a mode of representation, effaces the constitutive character of its own language, and thereby also occludes its own rhetorical production of woman as bearer of culture and chaos" (7). To approach texts of political theory, like works of art or like films, as a signifying system is to recognize that the feminist critic's penchant for interrogating "each theorist's attitude toward women (is Rousseau a sexist? Is Burke a paternalist? Is Mill a feminist?)" misses "the fact that these thinkers never get to *women*; they are too captivated by their struggle with *woman*."

As these examples illustrate, feminist film theory advanced a conceptual transformation in critical theories of representation that inspired feminists working in other visual fields and beyond. This work prompted a shift from a concern with media stereotypes of women to a conception of texts as signifying systems rather than mirrors, and to analyze how those systems work to constitute the identities of readers and spectators.

VISIBILITY: WOMEN IN THE "MIRROR OF HISTORY"

The field of women's history has been an equally important site from which to both challenge the politics of representation and engage in critical reflections on its practice. Simply writing about the lives of women, as feminist historians began to do in the early 1970s, was radical for both constructing women "as active agent[s] of history" and prompting "a reevaluation of established standards of historical significance" (Scott 1998, 17–18). But feminists' most far-reaching challenge to the field may have begun, not by remedying women's putative absence from the historical record, but by contesting the very the notion that history is primarily a field of stories about men and written by men. As historian Bonnie Smith (2000) so forcefully argues, women are *not* absent from history, either as its subjects or as its authors. On the contrary, since the late eighteenth century there have been "thousands of women" writing history, and telling women's stories as they do so (6). The issue is that they tend not to be counted as historians, first, because they "pursued their calling as amateurs, without the institutional affiliations of male professionals," and, second, because they left "deep reflection and weighty political topics . . . for men" (6).

For Smith, the foremost feminist challenge to history has been in exposing how history—like philosophy (Le Doeuff [1989] 2003; Lloyd 1993), science (Schiebinger 1989), music (McClary 1991), and more—has defined itself as a professional discipline in and through sexual difference. This is an epistemological problem that simple attention to women's visibility cannot remedy. Smith demonstrates this claim by way of the historian's trademark metaphor, the "mirror of history."

The mirror both figures the ideal of historical objectivity and enables the practice of "self-scrutiny" to which the historian submits so as to control for "biases and faults" (Smith 2000, 2). Yet, as Smith wryly notes, the mirror "has traditionally worked best if the observer is male . . . When the person before a mirror has been a woman, her self-regarding has appeared repetitive, even obsessive, and indicative of vanity or love of luxury—connoting the sensual rather than the rational" (3). By assigning a gender to the figure in the mirror, Smith (1992, 17) makes the reader aware of the crucial role that gender plays "in establishing the centrality of objective authorship." The mirror does more than symbolize an epistemic ideal; it actively produces history as a male preserve by "differentiating [professional historians] from a low, unworthy, and trivial 'other'" (Smith 2000, 9).

This dynamic is exemplified by the story Smith (1992) tells of the fate Michelet's wife met at the hand of Michelet's biographers and editors. An amateur historian younger than her husband by twenty-eight years, Athénaïs Michelet features in her husband's diaries as a partner in "a tender, erotic, and collaborative domestic life" (24). On his account, his was a life and a career that greatly "profited from the blurred authorship of domestic collaboration." His biographers and editors recast Michelet's narrative in terms of the "discourse of separate spheres" as a story of "sexual inversion and misrule," excising any trace of Athénaïs's authorship and depicting her presence as a distraction and torment to the Great Man (24–25). The ideal of the professional historian that they sought to advance turned on sexual difference figured as an oppositional binary. It required "sexuality and domestic detail [to be] part of the wife's character," while assigning "detachment and ennoblement" to the "authorial husban[d]" (24). In short, as Smith puts it, "[H]istorical science with its aspirations to objectivity is grounded in the rhetorical tradition of classical misogyny" (23).

Smith tells this story to reconceive sexual difference from a literal difference, understood as existing "between" two opposed sexes, to what literary critic Barbara Johnson (1980, 10, 4) terms a "critical difference," understood to be created rhetorically by positioning terms as "symmetrical opposite[s]." This rhetorical production of oppositionality is precisely what Smith demonstrates Michelet's biographers and editors to have achieved by deploying the tropes of separate spheres and unruly feminine sexuality. Whether sexual difference is conceived as a critical difference or as a literal difference gives rise to distinct ways of approaching the project of feminist history. On the one hand, there is the project of writing women into the historical record to create a more accurate representation of the past, a strategy that retains the realist metaphor of history as mirror and assumes that it works equally well for the woman observer as for the man. On the other hand, there is the recognition that historical representation does not merely reflect the past but participates in the constitution of it, producing the "categories of identity" by which subjects come to qualify or be disqualified as actors in the first place (Scott 1988, 6). This second approach resists treating historical sources as "evidence" (regardless whether they are first-order documents, such as memories or experiences, or whether they are biographies and other narratives) to recognize them instead as *texts*—rhetorical works that call for reading on the model of literary analysis (Scott 1991).

Poststructuralist techniques of reading, specifically, offered powerful tools for those feminist historians who understood sexual difference as a critical difference or rhetorical production rather than as a literal difference or simple fact (Scott 1988, 3–8). This is not to say that they imagined sexual difference to be merely linguistic but, merely, that they refused to posit or presuppose it as the "originary cause from which social organization ultimately can be derived." They conceived of sexual difference as the effect of gender rather than its origin, and they understood gender discursively, as "knowledge about sexual difference" that may produce sex as biological, oppositional, symmetrical, and so on (2).

This is gender as Scott (1988, 2) famously defined it: the "social organization of sexual difference." Scott's claim is not that sexual difference first exists in nature (e.g., as a fixed binary) and is subsequently socially organized. It is, rather, that the parsing of bodies, identities, and groups by sex is discursive, an effect of "knowledge that establishes meanings for bodily differences" whether that be biological, social scientific, psychoanalytic, or even feminist (2). Gender does not follow from sex. Rather, as Christine Delphy (1993, 3) put it so arrestingly, it is the "principle of partition" that divides the "sexes" into two in the first place, thereby making sex consequential as at once a marker of group difference and a justification for social hierarchy.

Poststructuralist techniques of literary analysis appealed to some feminist historians (notably, not to Delphy) who understood sexual difference in this way because "reading" in poststructuralist terms proceeds by the "'deconstruction'" of the binary oppositions that serve as anchors of meaning within the text. As Johnson (1980, x–xi) explains, deconstructing a text does not mean reducing it to incoherence; "it is an attempt to follow the subtle, powerful effects of differences already at work within the illusion of a binary opposition." The idea is that binarity, or the static spatialization of difference as existing "*between* entities," depends "on a repression of differences *within* entities" (x). Thus, difference is not the space between that which demarcates the identities of self and other; it is, rather, that which both consolidates identity and threatens to undo it from within (4).

Of the many possibilities, sexual (and racial) differences have been especially potent for constructing group identities because they can so readily be figured as natural and invoked to stabilize other, more precarious social distinctions. For example, Anna Clark (1995) has shown that in the early nineteenth century, the notion of "separate spheres," an ideology that purports to reflect differences of capacity and sensibility between men and women, was at once class specific and productive of class difference. It served to sharply demarcate "boundaries between plebeians and the middle class [that] were often quite blurred" until the middle classes took up the separation of "masculine work from the feminine home [as] a marker of middle-class status" (7). The Chartists, in their turn, seized on domesticity as a demand that would enable them to both contest middle-class privilege and "create a positive class identity for working people, uniting diverse elements into an 'imagined community' through political organization and rhetoric" (220). Emphasizing the indispensability of language and ideology to the formation of group agency, Clark underscores, activists "developed a *rhetoric* of class consciousness *before* the working class had been formed in sociological terms, that is, before they had become a cohesive group of people sharing common experiences and values" (8; emphasis added).

In the wake of Scott's work and the scholarship it helped inspire, it became typical to credit (or blame) her with effecting a "linguistic turn" that moved away from the "pursuit of a discernible, retrievable historical 'reality'" to the analysis of categories of identity (Canning 1994, 369). Yet those who took the "turn" would not juxtapose reality with discourse in this way. They would argue that the linguistic turn changed their orientation toward political representation, which they understood not to follow from sociological realities, but, rather, to participate in creating them by deploying "categories such as class, worker, citizen—even man and woman" to consolidate group identities (Scott

1988, 4; cf. Cabrera 2011, 32). It followed that historians, in turn, must understand these categories as being historical and bound up with the relations of power that both forge and normalize unified subjectivities, rather than as marking standpoints of resistance (Halperin 2002). Such arguments prompted a rethinking of the notion that "visibility" is the problem of women (and sexual minorities) in history and historical representation its political remedy.

As literary critic Eve Sedgwick (1990) argues in the context of queer theory, the primary mechanism of homophobic oppression (and its contestation) is not representation—cultural or political—but epistemology. Homophobia is "an *already institutionalized* ignorance" about homosexuality, which renders the "very concept of gay identity" difficult to define and, more importantly, distances "authority over its definition . . . from the gay subject her- or himself" (78–79). Coming out, then, is far from a sure-fire strategy of self-representation, let alone a straightforward step in the direction of collective political liberation. Implicitly following Foucault, Sedgwick argued that neither making visible gay people in the past nor demanding political voice and visibility in the present is adequate to disarm the epistemological tripwires that surround sexuality.

This epistemological orientation enables Sedgwick, like Scott, to analyze the discursive production of sexuality, and to do so in terms of the double binds that frame homosexuality, in particular, within two separate and contradictory discursive formations: the "minoritizing" and the "universalizing" "representational regimes." The minoritizing view takes as natural and self-evident the "opposition between gay and straight as distinct kinds of persons," and articulates a claim to legal protection based on belonging to the category of "homosexual persons as a distinct, minority population" (Sedgwick 1990, 83). Sedgwick does not dismiss this representational regime, whose political efficacy and existential "meaningfulness to those whom it defines" (not to mention its "indispensability to those who define themselves as against it") is undeniable. But she identifies a second "universalizing" regime (83–84) represented by Freud. Recognizing that sexual desire is not the foundation of identity but, rather, an "unpredictably powerful *solvent* of stable identities," this representational regime imputes bisexuality to "every human creature" in the sense that neither our identifications nor our pleasures conform to any strict masculine/feminine or homo/heterosexual definition (84–85; emphasis added). Whereas Sedgwick does not spell out the political strategy to which this universalizing move might give rise, she and others pursue it as a new critical direction that involves, as Valerie Traub (2001, 261–262) puts it, ceasing to search literary texts and historical archives for "clear antecedents or stable historical ground for contemporary lesbian identities," so as rather to explore the "implications of the radical incommensurability among erotic desires, practices, and identities." Indeed, it is the universalizing view that has motivated the aims and critical practices of queer theory as it distances itself from the identity politics associated with the minoritizing regime.

Feminist historians have made important contributions to theorizing representation both by representing women through writing "women's history" and also by historicizing the categories (such as "woman" and "lesbian") through which women have been represented. They have analyzed sexual difference not as a basis for men's and women's different roles but as a force that helps to stabilize hierarchies of class and race. Such insights, like those of feminist film theorists, were pathbreaking not only for scholars who work on women and gender but beyond.

VOICE: SPEAKING FOR WOMEN AS SUBJECTS OF POLITICS

The problem of voice is frequently posed as a question of the relationship between the subject(s) of oppression and the movements that claim or aspire to act in their names—a question that is most powerfully posed from the margins. In the history (or mythology) of feminism, Sojourner Truth is the icon of this query. "Ain't I a woman"—the "more authentically Negro" version of the purported original, "ar'n't I a woman?"—is supposed to have been asked by Truth in 1851 in an address to a women's rights convention in Akron, Ohio (Painter 1994, 464). As historian Nell Painter (1994) has painstakingly documented, Sojourner Truth spoke neither of these phrases in 1851. They were interpolated into her address roughly twelve years later by the chair of the convention, antislavery feminist activist Frances Dana Gage. The delay is significant, for it is not that Gage was so inspired by Truth that she rushed off write about her speech; rather, different versions of Truth had come to be at stake. Painter explains that Gage was "roused" to craft a portrait of Truth so long after the event by an article penned by Harriet Beecher Stowe, who had turned her hand to Truth for commercial gain (Painter 1994, 477, 476). Writing "quickly" about a subject that the Emancipation Proclamation and admission of black soldiers into the Union army had rendered "marketable," Stowe produced, for *Atlantic Monthly*, a personage who was a variation on the "black characters in *Uncle Tom's Cabin*": a "quaint, minstrel-like, nineteenth-century Negro" and authentic Christian whose "genius of spiritual inspiration [was] uncorrupted by formal education" (476, 479). Gage countered with the "account of Truth that we recognize today," producing "a tough-minded, feminist emblem by stressing Truth's strength and the clash of conventions of race and gender and by inventing the riveting refrain, 'And ar'n't I a woman?'" (478–479).

No less than Stowe's, Gage's Truth frames an oppositional racial binary that pivots on authenticity. But in Gage's rendition, unlike in Stowe's, at stake is not faith but femininity. Painter (1994), writes, "Sojourner Truth, former slave and emblematic black feminist abolitionist, works metonymically as *the* black woman in American history," the "sturdy binary opposite of the debilitated, artificial white lady" (464). Though Stowe defined Truth for the nineteenth century, Gage's portrait prevailed throughout the twentieth. It became emblematic of the demand for feminist dialogue that is "power-sensitive not pluralist 'conversation'" (Haraway 1988, 589), attuned to the fault lines of privilege that render politically suspect any claim to represent women *as* women (cf. Spelman 1988, 167). Both were at odds with the "images of herself that [Truth] wanted remembered"

(Painter 1994, 462). Late in life, when Truth sold *cartes de visite* to support herself, she did her best to stage herself for the camera as incarnating—albeit as a black woman—the ideal of bourgeois domesticity whose representative status "her" oft-cited question iconically (if apocryphally) seeks to contest.

Truth stands for a question of political representation: Who (or what) *rightly* represents? Whether she asked this question or not does not diminish its importance to feminism, which must not only contest the patriarchal arrogation of the power to speak on women's behalf but also reflect on the representativity of the movement itself. Yet it is significant that she did not speak the words, for being an icon for a question that she did not ask makes Truth emblematic of another perplexing problem: that of the relation or interplay between political and aesthetic representation. Gage's portrait of Truth can be taken up—as it was by bell hooks (1981)—as a rallying point for the black feminist critique of the "whiteness" of the 1970s feminist movement. That portrait can, in turn, be metaphorically sold to white feminists today, just as Truth quite literally sold her autobiography and images in her lifetime, to "express solidarity," not with Truth herself, but with hooks's call for an antiracist feminism (Painter 1994, 474). At stake here is not whose interests Truth may or may not represent; it is, rather, how the depiction of Truth portrays mainstream feminism, black feminism, and their relationship to one another. The concern is not to ask who speaks for a "we" but to interrogate how that "we" is pictured and to analyze the possibilities and constraints on action that such picturing produces.

Feminist theorists of political representation have taken three different approaches to exploring its relationship to aesthetic representation. Postcolonial scholar Gayatri Spivak's (1999) essay "History" offers a painstaking account of the inextricability of representation in the political sense (as speaking for) from representation in the aesthetic sense (as picturing), as well as a powerful ethical critique of the refusal to represent championed by Deleuze and other Left intellectuals in France. In contrast to Spivak's point of departure in the historical and literary criticism central to subaltern studies, political scientists and political theorists have focused on contemporary political institutions and policymaking to analyze "descriptive" representation and "constitutive" representation.

Spivak's (1999) "History" is a rethinking and repackaging of earlier two essays— "Can the Subaltern Speak?" (1988)[2] and "The Rani of Sirmur: An Essay in Reading the Archives" (1985)—which parse the problem of representation into its historical, aesthetic, and political elements. "History" is, on one level, a performance of the difficulties of historical representation, understood as a practice that is both archival and literary, when confronted with "elusive female figure[s]" whose lives cannot be narrated (Spivak 1999, 272). Spivak (1999) takes up two such cases: one, a Rani whose life was not "fully written" but only notated, insofar as she was of cost or service to the British East India company in Sirmur in 1816; and the other, a teenager who kept her life a secret to protect her comrades in the struggle for Indian independence in the 1920s (269). Spivak details her own efforts to find some evidence of how these women lived and to make sense of the "attempted speech act[s]" of their deaths: "Sati for the Rani, counter-Sati for Bhubaneswari, neither heeded as such" (201). Spivak chooses these figures because they confound the "implicit demand, made by intellectuals who choose the 'naturally articulate' subject of oppression, that such a subject come through a history that is a foreshortened mode-of-production narrative" (276). Neither the Rani nor the teen can be narrated into being as a subject of transition from one mode of production to the next. And the risk in representing them is not that the intellectual would speak for a "subaltern subject that can know and speak itself"; it is, rather, that there may be no trace of this "subject's itinerary" at all (272). Thus it is not that the representing intellectual or other elite must step aside for the subaltern to speak. Quite the opposite, for the subaltern to be heard, representation—in the sense of picturing—is required.

Indeed, the subaltern cannot speak. But neither can anyone else if speaking is conceived as direct transmission between subjects in a face-to-face encounter. Spivak subtly shifts the terms of her title question. The issue is not speaking but being heard, and hearing is more like reading than it is like listening. Spivak (1999, 309; emphasis added) writes, "All speaking, even seemingly the most immediate, entails a *distanced decipherment* by another, which is, at best, an interception. That is what speaking is." Not that speaking can be neatly transposed into being read. It involves patient perusal of archives, the retracing of steps and the emplotment of sparse facts to fashion a story.

Left intellectuals who repudiate representation conflate "by sleight of word" two distinct "senses of representation" that "are related but irreducibly discontinuous" (Spivak 1999, 260, 257). The senses are "representation as 'speaking for,' as in politics, and representation as 're-presentation,' as in art or philosophy," and they become conflated when one generalizes the critique of the subject as "representative consciousness (one re-presenting reality adequately)" from the field of philosophy to that of politics (257). Whereas Spivak herself subscribes to this critique of the subject, she insists—particularly for the sake of a Left political agenda—that it does not simply hold by analogy for politics as well. Taking Subaltern Studies as her model, Spivak maintains that historians, theorists, sociologists and other intellectuals may well be called upon to make representations not in service of accuracy but in the "active theoretical practice of the 'transformation of consciousness' " (254).

Spivak (1999) turns to German, which has a richer vocabulary for representation than English or French, to convey the crux of her argument. She maintains, first, that in the domain of politics, *vertreten* (political representation as speaking for) and *darstellen* (material or constitutive representation as picturing, depicting, portraying) are complicit. Second, she affirms that this "complicity" or "identity—in—difference is the *place of practice*" (260; emphasis added).³ The "complicity" of political and aesthetic representation is, as Spivak so elegantly demonstrates in "History," that acts of political representation follow on the more or less explicit constitution-by-picturing of the subject to be represented. This picturing might take place figuratively, by means of rhetoric; cartographically, by mapping a terrain; or symbolically, by way of identifying with a hero from the present or past. Regardless of the medium, the intersection of picturing and speaking for is the "place of practice" because it is in and through *Darstellungen* (competing representations of the represented) that *Vertreter* (would-be representatives) vie for political authority, and it is by proposing counterrepresentations (as Spivak so painstakingly does in this essay) that intellectuals and activists challenge hegemonic subject formations.

In refusing to engage in this active practice and to take responsibility for the political (speaking for) and aesthetic (picturing otherwise) acts of representation it would involve, Spivak contends that the Left intellectuals arrogate to themselves the privilege of transparency that they claim to denounce. Denial that the subaltern needs political representation is an implicit act of aesthetic representation that portrays the subaltern as "self-knowing" and "politically canny." This implicit act renders the Left intellectuals' assertion—"There is no more representation [*vertreten*]; there's nothing but action"—a performative contradiction that disavows the act of aesthetic representation (*darstellen*) that is already entailed in the very assertion that the subaltern does not need representation. The disavowal, in turn, represents the Left intellectuals "themselves as transparent": they fall back on and claim for themselves the privilege of adequately representing (*vorstellen*) that they rejected in their poststructuralist critique of the Subject. This renders them impotent in the face of a particularly pernicious contemporary mode of ideological subject-formation, namely that of the World Bank and other providers of microcredit to women in "developing" nations. The microcredit project disavows either representing women or "credit-baiting" them so as to form them all the more effectively as subjects of financialization: the "much-invoked oppressed subject (as Woman), speaking, knowing, and acting that Gender in development is best for her" (Spivak (1999, 259; cf. Keating et al. 2010).

Whereas Spivak spells out the ethical imperative to recognize the relationships among conceptual, aesthetic, and political representation while keeping them distinct, the most ardent proponents of "descriptive" representation are equally adamant about the political imperative to merge the last two. As the Anti-Federalist Brutus argued in the debates over ratifying the US Constitution, it is inherent in the very meaning of the term "representative . . . that the person or body chosen for this purpose, should resemble those who appoint them." Affirming the very premise that semiotics would later undo, he maintained that the representatives "are the sign—the people the thing signified" (Storing 1981, 379). As Brutus made so strikingly clear, "descriptive" representation is based on the literalist understanding that language "mirrors" nature, and it conveys a suspicion of political representation that it hopes to quell by what Phillips (1995, 21) has aptly termed "a politics of presence": the notion that representation will be legitimate as long as it makes present the "social characteristics" of the represented, together with its preferences and interests in the body of the representative.

Since the legislatures of Western democracies have been composed almost entirely of elite white men, the politics of "presence" has won some support among Western feminists who have advocated for forms of group representation, such as gender quotas on party lists, to raise the proportion of women in democratic legislatures (Phillips 1995, chap. 3). Yet there is a powerful feminist line of argument against such solutions, insofar as they pose what feminist legal scholar Martha Minow (1987, 12) terms the "dilemma of difference." This is an apparent no-win situation in which according differential benefits in an attempt to remedy discrimination that is already based on (naturalized) difference risks reinforcing "negative stereotypes"; but "refusing to acknowledge these differences may make them continue to matter in a world constructed with some groups, but not others, in mind" (12). Minow argues that the dilemma becomes more tractable once it is recognized that differences are not "trait[s] intrinsic to [a] person" but, rather, effects of unstated points of comparison that empower particular groups to stand for such general or universal terms as "worker" or "mother" and naturalize institutional arrangements that instantiate their privilege (14). The question of whether to notice "difference" or to ignore it becomes this imperative: to interrogate and (as much as possible) correct for the institutionalized biases that make a group or individual stand out as different in the first place.

This was the logic underlying one strand of the feminist campaign for *parité*—50 percent representation of women on party lists—in France. Rejecting gender quotas as difference-based, these feminists argued that women should be viewed as no less capable of representing "abstractly" than men (Scott 2005, 51). They took the fact that incumbent politicians were overwhelmingly male to reaffirm what Simone de Beauvoir had famously argued, that "abstract individuals were sexed" male; by contrast, women were regarded as too tightly bound to the "particularities of their sex" to qualify as individuals (Scott 2005, 52–53). French feminists campaigned for *parité*, not to grant women the right to represent women, but to "extend the possibility of abstraction to women," thereby giving "women as many possibilities as men to influence the common destiny" (54–55).

Among feminists who do support a "politics of presence," there has been a rich debate emphasizing that mere descriptive representation is not enough. Two important innovations in this literature are, first, to break with the liberal principle of individual representation and argue, rather, for the representation of marginalized groups (Young 1990; Williams 1998). This innovation has prompted a rich discussion of what it means to be a political group. Young (2000, 123) has argued that for the purposes of political representation, a group should be understood to hold together not by virtue of "common interests or opinions" but by a "social *perspective*." Social perspectives do not "contain a determinate specific content"; they consist "in a set of questions, kinds of experience, and assumptions" that provide a framework of interpretation within which interests and opinions may be defined (137). On this view, the relationship between representative and constituency is evaluated with respect to the shared perspective rather than shared "descriptive attributes," and with an emphasis on the quality of the relationship and communication between them (148; cf. Dovi 2002). A second innovation specifies precisely in what contexts and for what functions descriptive representation is useful. Mansbridge (1999, 628, 650–651) differentiates between the conditions under which it may "enhance the substantive representation of interests" and those under which it may promote goods that are detachable from interest representation, such as challenging the "social meaning" that ascribes second-class status to membership in a historically oppressed group or enhancing the legitimacy of the polity in the eyes of members of previously underrepresented groups.

Whereas the debates over descriptive representation have focused on representation by formal institutions of government, scholars of political representation have recently turned their attention to the contributions made by civil society actors, such as NGOs, advisory commissions, and even celebrities to representative democracy (Montanaro 2012; Rubenstein 2014; Saward 2010; Warren 2004). Some feminist scholars of global governance have suggested that such extraparliamentary representation may be especially advantageous in securing feminist policy goals and have singled out the European Union as a particularly "gender-friendly" governance body (Lang 2014, 266). This is due to the emergence in the EU of a collaborative or "velvet triangle" mode of governance that links "feminist bureaucrats, trusted academics and organized voices in the women's movement" together in developing policy on women and gender (Woodward 2004, 77–78).

By contrast to Theodore Lowi's (1979) "iron triangle" model of the relationships among interest groups and political decision-makers, the collaborative model of the "velvet" triangle "suggests a more fluid, less rigidly shielded exercise of power among feminist institutional and non-institutional political actors" (Lang 2014, 267). Yet, as critics have argued, it also tends to privilege the participation of "specific formalized kinds of women's movement actors: those formally organized as NGOs" who are both able and willing to compete for EU funding to pursue agendas that the EU defines (268). The consequence is that the EU has not simply presented a forum that is hospitable to the representation of women's interests; it has shaped both the organizational structure and priorities of feminist politics in ways that are strikingly at odds with the decentralization, informality, loose coordination, and spontaneity of grassroots feminist organizations.

The "constitutive" approach to representation emerged to elaborate this critique. It builds on political theorist Michael Saward's (2010, 74, 51) notion of the "representative claim," a provocative theorization of the "*aesthetic* moment in political representation" that emphasizes how both elected and nonelected representatives "construct verbal and visual images" of their constituencies, speaking of them as "'hard-working,' 'good honest folk,' 'family-oriented,' 'patriots,' and 'concerned' or 'worried' or 'angry'" (emphasis original). Saward's conceptualization does not merge the aesthetic and political as in descriptive representation; rather, it seeks to foreground the work that aesthetic representation does for political representation. Constituency images or depictions are significant in two ways. First, they form constituencies by soliciting their identification with a portrait that accords with a specific political project or initiative. Second, they put forth a bid to define what is at stake in a political contest, whether a formal election, a punctual protest, or a movement struggle. That is, claiming makes constituencies visible *as* something that is implicitly being juxtaposed against something else (think, for example, of how "we are the 99%" aimed to divide the political field against those who had profiteered on decades of upwardly distributive tax policy together with a financial collapse that wiped out middle-class assets and lower-rung employment).

Feminist theorist Judith Squires (2008, 187–188) transports Saward's concept into the field of global governance, coining the notion "constitutive representation of gender"

(CRG) to "complement the notion of the substantive representation of women" (SRW). SRW analysis, which is the focus of much of the "velvet triangle" literature, has focused on the question whether "female parliamentarians represent women's interests." By contrast, CRG aims to capture "another significant facet of representative process," that whereby "female politicians and femocrats each engage in representative claims-making, constructing the group that they claim to represent and articulating their interests in ways that are both enabling and constraining." In CRG analyses, claims about interests are understood to solicit gendered subjectivities rather than to follow from them, and the analyst focuses not on how well institutions serve women's interests but, rather, on how a particular construction of women's interests affects who is empowered and who excluded (Squires 2008, 188). By way of example, Squires cites international relations scholar Ann Towns's (2002) critique of gender equality policy in Sweden. Whereas it presents a clear victory from the SRW perspective, Towns demonstrates that Sweden's emergence "as a gender-equal state in the mid-1990s," sold gender equality at once as constituting Swedish identity and differentiating Swedes from immigrants in a new and unprecedented way: "[I]t was not until Sweden's emergence as a gender equal state that gender inequality was regularly presented as a characteristic of the 'culture' of 'immigrants'" (Towns 2002, 158). The aesthetic and constitutive moment—the portrait of Sweden as gender-egalitarian in contrast to its traditionally patriarchal immigrant populations—is intertwined with the substantive achievement of (Swedish) women's equality.

Towns's study exemplifies the production of what postcolonial feminist Chandra Mohanty (1991, 53–54) calls the "'third world difference'—that stable, ahistorical something that apparently oppresses most if not all the women in [third world] countries." This discursive move constitutes the "average third world woman [as leading] an essentially truncated life based on her feminine gender (read: sexually constrained) and her being "third world" (read: ignorant, poor, uneducated, tradition-bound, domestic, family-oriented, victimized)," implicitly juxtaposing her against "modern" Western women (56). Philosopher Uma Narayan (1997, 103) identifies a variation on "third world difference" in the ways that Western feminists represent "Third-world women's issues." She notes the tendency for Western feminists to focus on "forms of violence against women 'specific' to Third-World contexts" in their most extreme form, such as dowry murder, and to explain them "as instances of 'death by culture'" (85). Treatment of domestic violence against women in the United States, by contrast, rarely focuses on their murder by a spouse or partner, and it would be quite surprising to find such crimes linked to "Christian doctrines, myths, and practices" as dowry death is frequently linked to "'Hinduism'" (114). At stake here is not the production of Third World difference by a direct juxtaposition of the liberated Western women against her Third World other; it is, rather, its production by phenomena that *resist* juxtaposition—namely, "domestic violence in Western contexts and dowry-murders in India" (88).

There is, however, one important exception. Narayan argues that Third World difference can function *within* Western contexts when it comes to explaining social problems in communities of color. Politicians, and even academics, do not shy away from offering "'cultural explanations' for problems within communities of color," such as "female-headed households, teenage motherhood, and welfare dependency," problems for which "'white culture' is seldom indicted . . . when they occur in white communities" (Narayan 1997, 87–88). Scholars of US welfare politics have documented the political consequences of such constitutive representations, which shape the terms of the debate over welfare policy and affect the substance of welfare reform, as well as the mobilization of groups to advocate for and oppose it.

Joe Soss, Richard C. Fording, and Sanford F. Schram (2011) offer a detailed case study of the Clinton administration's welfare reform of the mid-1990s, which shifted the primary responsibility for poverty relief from the federal government to the states and added work requirements and other restrictions to benefit programs. Soss, Fording, and Schram document the tactical use of constitutive representation to create political constituencies using opinion polling data collected over time; this not only enabled them to gauge general levels of support for reform but also to analyze "which segments of the public were mobilized" (92). The data suggest two things. First, the constituency for welfare reform was an "aroused public" that existed relatively briefly during a time frame defined by an elite initiative (68). Second, the spike in concern about welfare was linked to a corresponding spike in the tendency to affirm the statement "'most blacks' [are] lazy rather than hardworking" (68). It may not be surprising that respondents who subscribed to this stereotype were more receptive to seeing welfare as an important policy priority. It is surprising, however, that the respondents most likely to shift from paying little attention to welfare to holding it as a high priority had only *begun* to affirm this stereotype starting in 1996. Soss and his coauthors read this finding as an indication that the "mobilization and racialization of mass anxieties about welfare rose and fell in tandem during the 1990s"; they blame what Saward would term "representative claims" about African American women, in particular, for deepening the "public's reliance on race as a frame for thinking about welfare" (68–69).

Political scientist and women's studies scholar Mary Hawkesworth (2003) has shown that the deployment of these stereotypes was not just an elite tactic to sway public opinion; they circulated in the legislature as well. Hawkesworth quotes Representative Barbara Collins: "The Congress unfortunately had the image of a welfare recipient as an urban black woman, who irresponsibly had children, was lazy, refused to work, was uneducated. Whereas the truth of the matter was that the majority of welfare recipients were white, white women and white families" (542). Hawkesworth documents how these "erroneous perceptions of welfare cheats and cycles of dependency" worked during the congressional debates to mobilize, on the one hand, congresswomen of color to take a costly—and futile—stand against punitive welfare policy and, on the other hand, to discredit those very congresswomen along with their white male colleagues, who regarded them as, quite literally, standing (in) for the target population (541).

Feminist scholars of politics have put the crucial question of the relationship between aesthetic or semiotic representation and political representation at the heart of their inquiries. They have approached problems of political representation from multiple perspectives, exploring the potential gains offered by "descriptive" representation and developing sophisticated methodologies for analyzing how aesthetic representations affect the formation and (dis)empowerment of political agents.

Conclusion

This chapter demonstrates the range of feminist work across the humanities and social sciences that has produced innovations in the concept "representation." One such innovation, for which feminist scholarship, by virtue of its interdisciplinarity, has been particularly generative, is the constitutive approach to representation. Constitutive representation, which emphasizes that acts of representation help to engender that for which they purport merely to stand, is an important breakthrough in linking the politics of representation (cultural, historical, and political) to the politics of knowledge and strategies for social justice. It destroys once and for all the alibi that cultural production and knowledge production in academic disciplines are innocent with respect to the creation and reproduction of racial, sexual, and gender (and other) group identities. And it sheds light on the complicity between such acts of representation and the social relations of inequality.

Acknowledgments

I thank Mary Hawkesworth for her generous comments on this chapter and my colleagues in women's studies and feminist studies at the Universities of Minnesota and Michigan, whose contributions to my thinking on these questions is evident in these pages. I am especially grateful to Dena Goodman, Susan Siegfried, and Valerie Traub for suggesting key texts; Simona Sawhney, who walked me through Spivak's "Can the Subaltern Speak?" in a Minneapolis coffee shop; Andreas Gailus for sharing his expertise on literary criticism together with his extensive library; and the students in my graduate seminars on political representation who keep me reading and learning.

Notes

1. The next line in Mulvey's (2009, xxxiv) retrospective account strikes me as a theoretical misstep insofar as it suggests that her account of film does not re-theorize the realist account of representation so much as trade one referent for another: "In this sense the image of woman that had circulated as a signifier of sexuality could be detached from reality, from referring to actual women, *and become attached to a new referent, the male unconscious*" (emphasis added).
2. Spivak first presented "Can the Subaltern Speak?" as a lecture at the University of Illinois at Urbana-Champaign in summer 1983. It was published in the journal *Wedge* in 1985 and

in 1988 was reprinted in *Marxism and the Interpretation of Culture*, edited by Cary Nelson and Lawrence Grossberg.

3. It would have made Spivak's argument easier to follow had she used all three of the German words for representation: *vertreten, darstellen,* and *vorstellen. Vorstellen* is used in philosophy to convey the conceptual representation of the world by the mind. Representation in this sense is the target of the poststructuralist critique of the subject, insofar as it pictures consciousness as at once representative and transparent to its object. Spivak's argument is, in effect, that leftist intellectuals are mistaken in assuming that if they repudiate *vorstellen* (conceptual representation), they must also refuse to engage in *vertreten* (political representation). Their refusal misunderstands the nature of political representation, which, by virtue of its "complicity" with *darstellen* (aesthetic representation), is not transparent to the world but constitutive of it.

References

Butler, Judith. 1990. *Gender Trouble*. NY: Routledge.
Cabrera, Miguel A. 2011. "Language, Experience, and Identity." In *Question of Gender: Joan W. Scott's Critical Feminism*, edited by Judith Butler and Elizabeth Weed, 368–404. Bloomington: Indiana University Press.
Canning, Kathleen. 1994. "Feminist History after the Linguistic Turn: Historicizing Discourse and Experience." *Signs* 19 (2): 368–404.
Clark, Anna. 1995. *The Struggle for the Breeches: Gender and the Making of the British Working Class*. Berkeley: University of California Press.
Cowie, Elizabeth. 1990. "Representations." In *The Woman in Question*, edited by Parveen Adams and Elizabeth Cowie, 113–116. Cambridge, MA: MIT Press.
Delphy, Christine. (1981) 1984. "Patriarchy, Feminism and Their Intellectuals." In *Close to Home*, translated by Diana Leonard, 138–153. Amherst: University of Massachusetts Press.
Delphy, Christine. 1993. "Rethinking Sex and Gender." *Women's Studies International Forum* 16 (1): 1–9.
Doane, Mary Ann. 1982. "Film and the Masquerade: Theorising the Female Spectator." *Screen* 23 (3–4): 74–87.
Dovi, Suzanne. 2002. "Preferable Descriptive Representatives: Will Just Any Woman, Black or Latino Do?" *American Political Science Review* 96 (4): 729–743.
Halperin, David. 2002. "How to Do the History of Male Homosexuality." In *How to Do the History of Homosexuality*, 104–137. Chicago: University of Chicago Press.
Haraway, Donna. 1988. "Situated Knowledges: The Science Question in Feminism and the Privilege of Partial Perspective." *Feminist Studies* 14 (3): 575–599.
Hawkesworth, Mary. 2003. "Congressional Enactments of Race-Gender: Toward a Theory of Raced-Gendered Institutions." *American Political Science Review* 97 (4): 529–550.
hooks, bell. 1981. *ain't i a woman? black women and feminism*. Boston: South End Press.
Johnson, Barbara. 1980. *The Critical Difference: Essays in the Contemporary Rhetoric of Reading*. Baltimore: Johns Hopkins University Press.
Kaplan, E. Ann. 1983. *Women and Film: Both Sides of the Camera*. New York and London: Methuen.
Kaplan, Cora. 1986. *Sea Changes: Essays on Culture and Feminism*. London: Verso.

Keating, Christine, Claire Rasmussen, and Pooja Rishi. 2010. "The Rationality of Empowerment: Microcredit, Accumulation by Dispossession, and the Gendered Economy." *Signs* 36 (1): 153–176.
Lang, Sabine. 2014. "Women's Advocacy Networks: The European Union, Women's NGOs, and the Velvet Triangle." In *Theorizing NGOs: States, Feminism, and Neoliberalism*, edited by Victoria Bernal and Inderpal Grewel, 266-284. Durham, NC: Duke University Press.
Le Doeuff, Michèle. [1989] 2003. *The Sex of Knowing*. Translated by Kathryn Hamer and Lorraine Code. New York: Routledge.
Lloyd, Genevieve. 1993. *The Man of Reason: "Male" and "Female" in Western Philosophy*. 2nd ed. Minneapolis: University of Minnesota Press.
Lowi, Theodore. 1979. *The End of Liberalism: The Second Republic of the United States*. New York: Norton.
McClary, Susan. 1991. *Feminine Endings: Music, Gender, and Sexuality*. Minneapolis: University of Minnesota Press.
Mansbridge, Jane. 1999. "Should Blacks Represent Blacks and Women Represent Women? A Contingent 'Yes.'" *Journal of Politics* 61 (3): 628–657.
Millet, Kate. 1969. *Sexual Politics*. New York: Doubleday.
Minow, Martha. 1987. "Justice Engendered." *Harvard Law Review* 101 (1): 10–95.
Mitchell, Juliet. 1975. *Psychoanalysis and Feminism*. New York: Vintage/Random House.
Mitchell, W. J. T. 1995. "Representation." In *Critical Terms for Literary Study*, 2nd ed., edited by Frank Lentricchia and Thomas McLaughlin, 11–22. Chicago: University of Chicago Press.
Montanaro, Laura. 2012. "The Democratic Legitimacy of Self-Appointed Representatives." *Journal of Politics* 74 (4): 1094–1107.
Mulvey, Laura. 2009. *Visual and Other Pleasures*. 2nd ed. London: Palgrave Macmillan.
Narayan, Uma. 1997. *Dislocating Cultures: Identities, Traditions, and Third World Feminism*. New York: Routledge.
Painter, Nell Irvin. 1994. "Representing Truth: Sojourner Truth's Knowing and Becoming Known." *Journal of American History* 81 (2): 461–492.
Penley, Constance. 1988. "The Lady Doesn't Vanish: Feminism and Film Theory." In *Feminism and Film Theory*, edited by Constance Penley, 1–24. New York: Routledge.
Phillips, Anne. 1995. *The Politics of Presence*. Oxford: Oxford University Press.
Pollock, Griselda. 1988. *Vision and Difference: Femininity, Feminism, and Histories of Art*. London and New York: Routledge.
Rose, Jacqueline. 1986. *Sexuality in the Field of Vision*. London: Verso.
Rubenstein, Jennifer. 2014. "The Misuse of Power, Not Bad Representation: Why It Is Beside the Point That No One Elected Oxfam." *Journal of Political Philosophy* 22 (2): 204–230.
Saward, Michael. 2010. *The Representative Claim*. Oxford: Oxford University Press.
Schiebinger, Londa. 1989. *The Mind Has No Sex: Women in the Origins of Modern Science*. Cambridge, MA: Harvard University Press.
Scott, Joan. 1988. *Gender and the Politics of History*. New York: Columbia University Press.
Scott, Joan. 1991. "The Evidence of Experience." *Critical Inquiry* 17 (Summer): 773–797.
Scott, Joan. 2005. *Parité! Sexual Equality and the Crisis of French Universalism*. Chicago: University of Chicago Press.
Sedgwick, Eve Kosofsky. 1990. *Epistemology of the Closet*. Berkeley: University of California Press.
Silverman, Kaja. 1996. *The Threshold of the Visible World*. New York: Routledge.

Smith, Bonnie. 1992. "Historiography, Objectivity, and the Case of the Abusive Widow." *History and Theory* 31 (4): 15–32.

Smith, Bonnie. 2000. *The Gender of History: Men, Women and Historical Practice.* Cambridge, MA: Harvard University Press.

Soss, Joe, Richard Fording, and Sanford Schram. 2011. *Disciplining the Poor: Neoliberal Paternalism and the Persistent Power of Race.* Chicago: University of Chicago Press.

Spelman, Elizabeth V. 1988. *Inessential Woman: Problems of Exclusion in Feminist Thought.* Boston: Beacon Press.

Spivak, Gayatri Chakravorty. 1985. "The Rani of Sirmur: An Essay in Reading the Archives." *History and Theory* 24 (3): 247–272.

Spivak, Gayatri Chakravorty. 1988. "Can the Subaltern Speak?" In *Marxism and the Interpretation of Culture*, edited by Cary Nelson and Lawrence Grossberg, 271–316. Champaign-Urbana: University of Illinois Press. Originally published in 1985 in *Wedge* 7/8: 120–130.

Spivak, Gayatri Chakravorty. 1999. "History." In *A Critique of Postcolonial Reason: Toward a History of the Vanishing Present*, 198–311. Cambridge, MA: Harvard University Press.

Squires, Judith. 2008. "The Constitutive Representation of Gender: Extra-Parliamentary Re-Presentations of Gender Relations." *Representation* 44 (2): 187–204.

Stacey, Jackie. 1987. "Desperately Seeking Difference: Desire between Women in Narrative Cinema." *Screen* 28 (1): 48–61.

Storing, Herbert J., ed. 1981. *The Complete Anti-Federalist.* Vol 2. Chicago: University of Chicago Press.

Towns, Ann. 2002. "Paradoxes of (In)Equality: Something Is Rotten in the Gender Equal State of Sweden." *Cooperation and Conflict* 37 (3): 157–179.

Traub, Valerie. 2001. "The Renaissance of Lesbianism in Early Modern England." *GLQ* 7 (2): 245–263.

Warren, Mark E. 2004. "Informal Representation: Who Speaks for Whom?" *Democracy and Society* 1: 8–15.

Williams, Melissa S. 1998. *Voice, Trust, and Memory: Marginalized Groups and the Failings of Liberal Representation.* Princeton, NJ: Princeton University Press.

Woodward, Alison E. 2004. "Building Velvet Triangles: Gender and Informal Governance." In *Informal Governance in the European Union*, edited by Thomas Christiansen and Simona Piattoni, 76–93. Cheltenham, UK: Edward Elgar.

Young, Iris M. 1990. *Justice and the Politics of Difference.* Princeton: Princeton University Press.

Young, Iris M. 2000. *Inclusion and Democracy.* Oxford: Oxford University Press.

Zerilli, Linda M. G. 1994. *Signifying Woman: Culture and Chaos in Rousseau, Burke, and Mill.* Ithaca, NY: Cornell University Press.

CHAPTER 39

REPRODUCTION

From Rights to Justice?

CAROLE H. BROWNER

INTRODUCTION

No woman can call herself free who does not own and control her body. No woman can call herself free until she can choose consciously whether she will or will not be a mother.

(Sanger 1919, 7)

THE social organization of human reproductive processes is political by its very nature. The concept of power is therefore omnipresent throughout this analysis because each society's norms about *which* women are entitled (or not entitled) to bear children, how many they may bear, and with whom are necessarily enforced through some means of social control. In both historical and contemporary settings, reproductive pressures on women may emanate from within and outside their own social groups. At the same time, women in every society have independently sought to influence the circumstances of their pregnancies, regardless of their society's expectations and sanctions. Certain types of sociopolitical conditions better enable women to more effectively act in their own reproductive interests, which may be codified as *reproductive rights*. Historically, this term implicitly referenced motherhood, in that men's reproduction was generally not a site for social control (although under certain conditions, men's fertility has been targeted as well).

The late twentieth-century thrust of neoliberal economic agendas[1] has opened up new possibilities for—and new threats to—women's reproductive freedom. A global trend of declining fertility has been one of the most stunning consequences of the expansion of neoliberal economic and social policies, although the full range of factors responsible for the nearly universal decline in birth rates are in fact multiple and complex. Today, population policies aimed at reducing births are in sharp decline, while pronatalistic policies are gaining momentum. This chapter provides a global analysis of contemporary struggles over women's right to reproductive freedom.

What Are Rights?

The concept of "rights" is a product of the Western cultural tradition and defined as social, legal, and or ethical rules that delineate the range of behaviors deemed appropriate by a given group. "To accept a set of rights is to approve a distribution of freedom and authority, and so to endorse a certain view of what may, must, and must not be done" (Wenar 2011). Rights are necessarily circumscribed by a specific set of social conditions as stakes claimed within a given order of things. They are, by nature, contingent and fluid—that is, subject to the will of those who hold the authority to grant or rescind them. In this regard, rights are not so much granted or endowed as fought for and claimed.

The equivalent of rights in stateless societies (e.g., bands, tribes, chiefdoms) lacking centralized sources of political power, state-backed courts, and institutionalized codes of conduct are sets of principles and restraints on action derived from customs, morals, or ethical standards that correspond to the practices on which everyday conduct is based (Malinowski 1942). They include rules delineating the society's structure of authority (e.g., parents are entitled to tell their children how to behave), and rules stipulating which individuals (e.g., midwives) and groups (e.g., male elders) are legitimately entitled to perform certain activities. The concept of "rights," would not be used in stateless societies to reference these rules and codes of conduct.

Although disagreements as to precisely what the term encompasses have persisted throughout Western history, two general types are recognized: The doctrine of *natural rights*, dating to Greek Stoics and Roman jurists, posits that humans are born with certain universal and inalienable rights that transcend the customs, laws, or beliefs of any particular government or culture. Seventeenth- and eighteenth-century Enlightenment philosophers and political theorists drew upon this doctrine to challenge the "divine right of kings" and lay the foundations for the British, French, and American revolutions (Rothbard 1998). *Legal rights*, in contrast, derive from specific sets of laws or established practices.

The doctrine of *human rights* is closely aligned with that of natural rights and rests on the same philosophical assumption of a universal moral order (Freeman 2011). Although the history of this doctrine similarly dates back hundreds of years, in 1948 it gained greater authority when the United Nations General Assembly adopted the Universal Declaration of Human Rights (United Nations 1948). Anthropologists have subsequently documented manifold ways in which human rights discourses may vary by cultural setting, are at times logically inconsistent, and can generate tensions among the constituencies that advocate for humanitarianism, human rights, and other social justice movements (Willen 2011).

What Are Reproductive Rights?

Karl Marx conceptualized biological reproduction as a social activity whose specific form of organization is determined by a society's mode of production and associated social relations. Marxist feminists subsequently expanded this profound insight, perhaps best articulated by pioneering Marxist-feminist scholar Rosalind Pollack Petchesky:

> I start from the premise that reproduction generally, and fertility control in particular, must be understood as a historically determined, socially organized activity (separate from the activity of mothering), encompassing decisions about whether, when, under what conditions, and with whom to bear or avoid bearing children; the material/technological conditions of contraception, abortion, and childbirth; and the network of social and sexual relations in which those decisions and conditions exist.... Feminist theory requires this social perspective in order to explain the great differences—of class, culture, occupation, locale, and history—in women's reproductive experience.
>
> (Petchesky 1984, ix)

Marxist feminists argue that the ways in which human reproduction is enmeshed in social relations is as much a political issue as a biological one, and, further, that the social organization of reproduction is intrinsically interlinked and in dynamic interaction with the production of culture—not a mere reflection of it. Reproductive relations often generate conflicts—or reflect preexisting ones—at every level of a society, from the cohabitating couple to the individual in relation to the state, and between societies as well (Browner 2000). Even in an imagined society characterized by gender, class, and race equality, there would nonetheless be a politics of reproduction based on tensions between the reproductive goals of individuals and those of the larger groups to which they belong.

The past two centuries have seen repeated waves of political struggle as women sought *reproductive freedom*, that is, the ability to decide for themselves whether and when to have children. Although the term *reproductive rights* is used today to characterize the objectives of these political movements, the meanings of reproductive rights and reproductive freedom are not the same.

Evolutionary anthropologists have shown that, contrary to conventional wisdom, women are "by nature" no less sexually adventurous than men (Hrdy 1981). During the approximately 200,000 years of human evolution that preceded the invention of agriculture (some 10,000 years ago), there was no concept of private property and women selected their own sexual partners. Indeed, data from the Standard Cross-Cultural Sample (SCSS) of 186 preindustrial societies shows that nearly two-thirds (61.7 percent) either permitted or only mildly disapproved of female premarital sex; in almost half (49.1 percent), it was reported to be near universal. Extramarital sex was also common, occurring at universal or moderate levels in 55 percent of the SCSS (Scelza 2013, 262, 264). The invention of agriculture, and with it, formal rights to own property, animals, and other goods of material value also gave rise to patriarchy as the dominant sociopolitical system: a woman's father, spouse, or other male kin came to control her sexuality and the rights to her children. In most societies, the birth of patriarchy signaled the loss of female reproductive freedom.

The term *reproductive rights* dates from the 1970s and was most likely coined in the United States. However, its genesis in ideas of bodily integrity and sexual self-determination has a much longer history (Forte and Judd 1998, 266). The idea that women must be free to make their own reproductive decisions had originated at least by the 1830s in the neo-Malthusian, utopian, and feminist movements in England and the United States. The earliest activists were inspired by, and sometimes aligned with, the antislavery movement and workers' struggles for freedom and equality. In the 1870s, the concept of "voluntary motherhood" became the centerpiece of a loose amalgam of "feminist" organizations (Gordon 1990, 93–113, passim). By then, "voluntary motherhood" had come to mean support for abstinence and a woman's right to unilaterally refuse even marital sex, a revolutionary demand at a time when custom and law dictated sexual submission.

Two Western conceptual frameworks inspired nineteenth- and early twentieth-century demands for reproductive rights. The individualist ("liberal" or reform) approach, emphasizing the individual dimensions of reproduction, derives from concepts of natural rights; reproductive autonomy; and principles of bodily integrity, personhood, and equality. The socialist ("social constructivist" or radical) paradigm draws on the principle of "socially determined needs": given that women are most affected by pregnancy and most responsible for childrearing and child care under the prevailing sexual division of labor, they must have final say in matters of reproduction. A few, such as the communist anarchist Emma Goldman, combined both. Inspired by Goldman, Margaret Sanger initially linked "the problem of birth control" not simply to women's struggle for social and political freedom but also, in Sanger's terms, to their need "to own and control" their bodies and "obtain sexual knowledge and satisfaction." At the turn of the twentieth century, sex radicals and bohemians also embraced birth control as part of a philosophy that valued sexuality independent of reproduction.

But by the 1920s, Sanger's activist agenda had been transformed from the sweeping goals of women's liberation and sexual freedom to a single issue: acceptance and legalization of contraception; she concluded that an alliance with the deeply conservative medical establishment was the most expedient course of action. Physicians supported birth control for eugenic reasons and because medicalizing its dissemination would be to their economic advantage. The consequences of Sanger's compromise were profound: contraception would no longer be regarded as an expression of women's rights to sexual and reproductive freedom but, rather, would be contained within the clinical desexualized rubric of "family planning" (Gordon 1990).

The 1960s antiwar and civil rights movements in the United States sparked renewed recognition among US women of their failure to have achieved parity with men in major sectors of social life and, particularly, of their continued sexual and reproductive subordination. Activists rediscovered the earlier feminist theorists who regarded reproductive and sexual freedom as fundamental preconditions for the pursuit of political, economic, and social equality (Davis 1988). As public opinion came to embrace the idea that forced pregnancy violated a woman's constitutional rights, the emerging women's movement coalesced around demands to reform or repeal laws criminalizing abortion. By 1973, the battle appeared won when the US Supreme Court in *Roe v Wade* ruled favorably on women's right to abortion. Throughout much of Europe, women were simultaneously claiming abortion rights, owing in large part to the devastating morbidity and mortality caused by soaring rates of illegal abortion.

The claim that the concept of reproductive rights was alien to women in the global South[2] because it derived from Western individualistic, secular, materialistic traditions is belied by the reality. Although Southern women's activism may not necessarily have been framed within a rubric of "rights" per se, indigenous women's reproductive health movements mobilized throughout Asia and Latin America in the early 1970s (Corrêa and Petchesky 2007, 300). Since then, Northern and Southern coalitions have worked toward common objectives, most effectively by characterizing reproductive and sexual rights as a subset of human rights, as set forth at the 1994 United Nations Conference on Population and Development:

> Reproductive rights embrace certain human rights that are already recognized in national laws, international human rights documents and other consensus documents. These rights rest on the recognition of the basic right of all couples and individuals to decide freely and responsibly on the number, spacing and timing of their children and to have the information and means to do so, and the right to attain the highest standard of sexual and reproductive health. It also includes their right to make decisions concerning reproduction free of discrimination, coercion and violence.
>
> (United Nations 1994)

At the time, however, the extent to which women throughout the world actually valued the right to reproductive autonomy was unknown. To cast light on the subject, Rosalind Petchesky and Karen Judd assembled a team to conduct field research in Brazil, Egypt, Malaysia, Mexico, Nigeria, the Philippines, and the United States on how women deal daily with their reproductive health and sexual concerns (Petchesky 1998). Their main findings, subsequently documented by a wealth of other empirical investigations, found that women want to be the ones to decide whether or not to have children and the number of children to have, although many factors may impede their ability to do so (e.g., Browner and Sargent 2011; Fordyce and Maraesa 2012; Ginsburg and Rapp 1995).

The reality of motherhood is the primary justification women draw on for what Petchesky terms a sense of "reproductive entitlement": that they themselves bear the greatest burdens and responsibilities of pregnancy, childbearing, and childrearing and should therefore have the right to make decisions regarding them. The notion of "reproductive entitlement" provided a framework for conceptualizing women's moral claims, especially on partners, kin, and other groups to which a woman may belong (a community, for instance), more than their perceptions of any sense of legal or formal entitlement. They found that women who earned money or controlled other economic resources exercised reproductive agency much more effectively than the rest. In some settings, belonging to a community group or labor union was also strongly linked to their ability to do so.

Petchesky and her colleagues further found that one of the greatest obstacles worldwide to women's ability to act on their sense of reproductive entitlement was organized religion, especially resurgent fundamentalisms. But even in societies where such religions are strong, many women reinterpret their church's doctrine to imagine a compassionate God who understands their need to, for instance, have an abortion, use contraception, or refuse sex with their husbands. Nevertheless, the reality that religious authorities wield vast power over women's ability to act on their own behalf should not be underestimated.

The Right to Abortion

> *Of all feminist demands, the right to abortion and sexual freedom appears most threatening to traditional sexual and social values.*
>
> (Petchesky 1984, 244)

Although the right to abortion may be the most contested of all reproductive rights, its existence has been documented in all known societies, although the extent of, reasons for, and attitudes associated with it vary widely (Devereux 1976). George Devereux's comprehensive survey of abortion in ancient and pre-industrial societies found a multitude of socially acceptable reasons for an abortion including political (e.g., a ruling lineage compelling women from competing lineages to abort pregnancies, women aborting pregnancies so that their children will not be born into slavery), stigmatized paternity (e.g., rape, incest, unknown father, or father of incompatible social class), family reasons (e.g., pregnant woman considered too young, youngest child still nursing, parents considered too old, or already has enough children), social pressure (e.g., premarital, extramarital pregnancies), and economic reasons. He found abortion practiced openly in some settings and secretly in others, and that social acceptance ranged from tolerance to deep disapproval from an entire society, some specific segment, or within a family group.

Throughout the course of Western history, abortion was a private matter, not a crime. Traditional European, British, and United States common law permitted abortion, as did the Catholic Church, until late in the nineteenth century. The general belief was that human life did not begin until the moment of "quickening," when fetal movement is felt for the first time. However by 1880, most of Western Europe and the United States had criminalized abortion. Movements to outlaw it were fueled by its growing use and the associated toll on women's health from unsafe procedures, the push by allopathic (mainstream) medicine to consolidate its monopoly over medical care, and fears of demographic suicide among wealthy whites. Still, the practice remained widespread and even open during most of the twentieth century. The rapid decline in birth rates between the turn of the nineteenth and twentieth centuries is attributed in large part to women's use of abortion (Potts and Campbell 2009).

In 1920, following nearly a decade of war, revolution, and economic turmoil, socialist Russia became the first European country to decriminalize the procedure, based on Leninist doctrine that no woman should be forced to bear a child, coupled with the enormous toll on women's health from unsafe abortions (Heer 1965). As Russia gained hegemony throughout Eastern Europe, its satellite socialist countries enacted similar legislation. Women's labor was desperately needed for rebuilding economies following a massively destructive war and there was a lack of effective female contraceptives. Yet despite its legality and widespread practice, the Soviet government remained strongly pronatalistic, glorifying motherhood and large families and strongly disapproving of abortion (Randall 2011), in stark illustration that contradictory population ideologies and policies may coexist and inhibit or enable women's own fertility desires and needs.

In capitalist Western Europe and the United States, a wide range of legal doctrines defined the terms of access to abortion. Ofrit Liviatan's comparative analysis shows that in some Western European countries (e.g., England), regulating abortion was delegated to the medical system, which circumvented potential moral conflicts between women's and fetal rights (Liviatan 2013). Taking a different tack, Italian legislators reached a compromise between Catholic dogma and the need to protect women's health by keeping abortion criminal—but establishing a wide range of medically, socially, and economically permitted exceptions. In Europe, then, Liviatan argues, abortion-based discourse and debate produced consensus-based regulatory regimes derived from an amalgamation of rights-based arguments and social, economic, and political agendas that effectively diffused conflict over otherwise competing ideological claims.

The United States took an entirely different approach. The Supreme Count granted women the right to abortion based on their constitutionally protected right to privacy (not their natural right to bodily self-determination). But the Court also ruled that the right to abortion was not "absolute;" that it did not entail "an unlimited right to do with one's body as one pleases," and that in so regulating it, the state had the additional duties of protecting fetal life and women's health (Petchesky 1984, 290–292). Liviatan argues that by legalizing abortion as a privacy right but limiting it through a competing fetal right to protection, the Court laid the groundwork for the volatility that ensued: US abortion politics became a perpetual struggle between activists with diametrically opposed worldviews that appeared to make compromise impossible. The ruling, moreover, allowed for legislative and judicial actions that have progressively restricted U.S. women's rights to abortion (Liviatan 2013, 397–398 *passim*).

Yet, despite the increasingly pervasive atmosphere of secrecy and shaming, more than a million abortions are performed annually in the United States: approximately one in three American women will have at least one abortion during her lifetime (Guttmacher Institute 2014). Within this corrosive setting, feminist studies scholar Carly Thomsen argues that even abortion rights activists have lost sight of their goal:

> "Pro-choice" politicians and reproductive rights activists alike often describe abortion as "one of the most difficult and complex decisions a woman will ever make." A Planned Parenthood state affiliate claims that "reducing the need for abortion is a goal we can all support." When the largest and best-known abortion rights organizations and their pro-choice political allies frame abortion in this way, abortion rights movements have a serious problem.
>
> (Thomsen 2013, 150)

Thomsen challenges reproductive rights advocates to discard this "apologist" framework that invariably characterizes abortion in negative terms: "It is certainly worth questioning the notion that reducing abortion represents progress and that abortion is always a difficult decision" (Thomsen 2013, 150). Indeed, extensive research over the past forty years shows that abortion is often a simple, easily made decision and that the vast majority of women report feelings of relief following the procedure and significantly less distress than is experienced by women denied an abortion. Strong negative responses are in fact rare (Major et al. 2000; Rocca et al. 2013).

Yet women's abortion rights are being eroded, and not just in the United States. The collapse of Communism and the sharp turn being taken throughout the continent toward neoliberalism, with the resultant "austerity" cuts to health and social services, have triggered shifts toward restrictive abortion governance (Europa 2013). Increasing immigrant flows and rapidly declining white birth rates are also contributing factors. The former Soviet republics have imposed the most draconian restrictions, in part the result of the growing power of conservative religious institutions, xenophobic activist groups, and a more generalized "remasculination" of politics (Anton, De Zordo, and Mishtal, n.d.).

Latin America's situation is fluid and complex. After Mexico City legalized first-trimester abortion in 2007, a strong backlash quickly followed, with passage of "right-to-life" laws in sixteen of Mexico's thirty-one states. Other countries (e.g., Chile, Nicaragua, El Salvador, and Haiti) continue to restrict abortion under *all* circumstances, while Latin American activists fighting to legalize abortion encounter unrelenting resistance from the Catholic Church and, increasingly, from evangelical denominations (Morán Faúndes and Peñas Defago 2013). Lynn Morgan fascinatingly shows that some of the dynamics at play throughout the continent include conservative Catholic activists appropriating the liberal language of human and civil rights to advance antiabortion agendas (Morgan 2014).

Even in the Asian Buddhist traditions, the history of the criminalization of abortion followed a trajectory similar to the West's. In Japan, for example, even though abortion was illegal for hundreds of years, it was common and rarely prosecuted—although more aggressively prosecuted in the late nineteenth century, mainly for pronatalistic reasons. It was finally legalized in 1948, amid fears of overpopulation following the end of the Second World War (Norgren 2001). Today, abortion is widely practiced and generally accepted socially. South Korea's situation is generally comparable to Japan's. Although the procedure remains illegal, it is very common, in part, because the concept of the fetus historically had little emotional or religious significance. Today, however, its social acceptance is being threatened by a small group of Catholic South Korean physicians, who are seeking to end abortion for moral reasons, and by government officials, who, because of the country's very low birth rate, are rethinking its tacit acceptance (Sang-Hun 2010).

Before European colonial expansion permanently transformed the African continent, abortion practices in Africa reflected the diversity Devereux describes in his classic cross-cultural survey of abortion (Devereux 1976). Forced Christian conversions and the imposition of European legal systems led to widespread criminalization. Today, the overwhelming majority of African women (92 percent) live in countries that outlaw the procedure (Guttmacher Institute 2012), A small number of countries (Cape Verde, South Africa, Tunisia, and Zambia) have enacted liberalized legislation, but few women can navigate the processes required to obtain a safe legal abortion, and most face additional obstacles (e.g., economic, moral views stigmatizing abortion) that further impede their access to safe procedures.

THE CONSEQUENCES OF GLOBAL POPULATION POLICIES FOR WOMEN'S REPRODUCTIVE RIGHTS

The idea of population control is at least as ancient as Plato's Republic, which described how a "Guardian" class could be bred to rule, the unfit left to die, and everyone sold the same myth that political inequality reflected the natural order.

(Connelly 2008, 7)

A defining feature of ancient and modern states is a centralized population policy administered through a hierarchical structure of concentrated power. States require that individuals filling various social positions, for example, slaves, workers, citizens, soldiers, and, above all, procreators, be assigned a value in ways never seen in kin-based societies or others based on shared resources. The principal objectives of a state's population policies are to maintain a given social order and to control population size and composition.

The impact of state population policies on women is particularly consequential because women are inextricably linked to broader societal conceptions, including of the status of women, the nature of female sexuality, the conditions of motherhood, and the structures of family organization. While state demographic policies vary markedly across historical and cultural settings, commonalities include pronatalist marriage and family laws and involuntary sterilization, infanticide, and prohibitions on contraception and abortion that are often aimed at reducing stigmatized racial and ethnic minority groups and increasing birth rates among the dominant segments (Gordon 1990; Petchesky 1984).

The rise of hierarchically organized structures of concentrated power with large populations to administer is a relatively recent phenomenon. Prior to the invention of agriculture some 10,000 years ago, the size of the human population was relatively stable. Agriculture sparked a major transformation. While necessitating more laborers than migratory foraging societies, it also allowed for the production of surpluses, which enabled societies to feed more people, which in turn made larger settlements possible. By the mid-eighteenth century, human population growth was a sustained phenomenon. The reactions of social philosophers were mixed. Utopian thinkers, such as Jean-Jacques Rousseau, William Godwin, and Marquis de Condorcet, saw population growth in a favorable light, as evidence of progress toward the perfectibility of man and society. Thomas Malthus asserted the opposite: unchecked population growth necessarily outstrips resources and would be a major obstacle to any real social progress.

As the population of Europe and the rest of the world continued to accelerate into the twentieth century, an amalgamation of Western groups, including neo-Malthusians, eugenicists, pronatalists, and nativists, united in a shared sense of alarm that the world had begun to seem smaller—while population trends appeared out of control (Connelly 2008, 9). The mid-1950s saw a convergence of views among scientists and Western politicians that the world was on the brink of a "population explosion," particularly in the global South. Biologist Paul Ehrlich captured the spirit of the times in his dystopian bestseller *The Population Bomb*. It famously began, "The battle to feed all of humanity is over. In the 1970s hundreds of millions of people will starve to death in spite of any crash programs embarked upon now. At this late date nothing can prevent a substantial increase in the world death rate" (Ehrlich 1968, xl).

Published in 1987, a mere nineteen years later, Betsy Hartmann's *Reproductive Rights and Wrongs* offered a clear-eyed response to the hysteria Ehrlich's book provoked. She demonstrated that the myth of overpopulation was one of the most pervasive in Western culture, so compelling mainly because of its simplicity: a growing population facing finite natural resources inevitably bred hunger, poverty, and political instability. Still, even without much evidence that the South even had a "population problem," governments and international agencies harkened to the idea that the widespread use of contraception would bring about a smaller, healthier, wealthier, and more politically stable world.

There were hidden agendas behind these seemingly altruistic campaigns in that the programs were, in fact, intended to mitigate the socioeconomic disruption caused by capitalist development and exploitation. And, although they were aggressively promoted at the height of a "cold" war, ostensibly between capitalism and communism, at their core lay a struggle between the demographically stable industrialized nations and a far more populous, rapidly growing global South.

Coercive practices were intrinsic to most twentieth-century population control programs. Some top policymakers even openly counseled coercion through, for example, a "stepladder" approach: "start off with soft measures such as voluntary family planning services, and proceed if necessary to harsher measures such as disincentives, sanctions, and even violence" (Hartmann 1987, 122). Yet some countries managed a transition from high to lower birth rates without resorting to overt coercion. Socialist Cuba did so by making contraceptive and abortion services freely available through its national health system, while capitalist Taiwan and South Korea launched intense propaganda campaigns that denounced as unpatriotic families with more than two children.

Yet, curiously, fertility was already declining in most of the world before family planning programs, much less coercive ones, really gained momentum. Studies showed that, despite their decades-long duration and massive bureaucracies costing hundreds of millions of dollars, population control programs explained less than 5 percent of the change in fertility levels (Connelly 2008, 338). Moreover, it remains impossible to determine whether the programs caused even the 5 percent or whether broader socioeconomic and cultural changes were responsible. According to historian Matthew Connelly,

> It turns out that about 90 percent of the difference in fertility rates worldwide derived from something very simple and very stubborn: whether women themselves wanted more or fewer children.... [This is] consistent with both historical experience and common sense. After all, French peasants did not need Napoleon to provide them with pessaries. Even then, avoiding childbirth was less expensive and troublesome than unwanted children.
>
> (Connelly 2008, 373)

Today, we appear on the verge of the opposite situation, as world population begins to decline. In most industrialized nations, roughly 2.1 births per woman are needed to sustain the population; whereas that figure ranges from 2.5 to 3.3 in less industrialized nations because of higher mortality. Globally, then, the replacement fertility rate is 2.33 children per woman.

Today, however, replacement birth rates are seldom seen. Throughout Asia, rates range from 1.7 births per woman in China to 1.2 in South Korea and Singapore. They are 1.5 in most of Europe; at or below replacement in North America (Canada, the United States, and Mexico); below replacement in some Latin American countries (e.g., Chile, Cuba, and Brazil) or close to becoming so (e.g., Colombia and Venezuela). Population is still growing in some parts of the Middle East but at much slower rates than before. Several African countries are the major exception, although there as well, birth rates have been steadily declining for years. Overall, it is now anticipated that global population growth will cease by the middle of the twenty-first century (World Bank 2014).

While this decline is a major achievement from an ecological perspective, it is, at the same time, a reflection of the structural changes undermining reproductive justice worldwide.

The story told by these globally declining birth rates is not what state governments and policymakers would have us believe: that given the means to prevent conception, women will opt for fewer children. Also at work is a neoliberal economic agenda, whose success has made childrearing less attractive and less feasible. Without strong societal commitments to policies that enable women to hold jobs while raising young children, large families become a luxury fewer and fewer can afford.

Indeed, countries with the highest birth rates (Denmark, France, Iceland, Norway, and Sweden) have social policies that encourage women to combine work and family. They share the characteristics of being universal in their coverage, not means-tested, and based on gender equality. In contrast, programs in Italy, Japan, and Singapore, which to date have failed, do not support gender equality and women's work-family balance and have not consistently devoted sufficient resources to make a difference (Kramer 2014). Accordingly, it is not necessarily the case that women want small families or no children at all. In reality, many report that they wish for larger families but already find it difficult enough to survive, let alone thrive.

Biopolitics and the Neoliberal Turn

Changes in reproductive governance must be understood within the context of neoliberalism . . . [and] political rationalities of reproduction that centre, in part, on moral regimes based on rights claims.

(Morgan and Roberts 2012, 246)

The worldwide turn toward neoliberal economic and social policies during the late twentieth century sparked major transformations in the relationship of state governments, religious institutions, and civil society groups to reproductive rights and practices. Growing interdependencies between labor, technologies, pharmaceuticals, ideologies, and state policies within the reproductive domain reflect neoliberalism's increasingly global grasp (Ginsburg and Rapp 1991, 314–315). On the one hand, many women have more choice and control through access to relatively reliable, safe, and inexpensive forms of birth control, abortion, and obstetric care. On the other hand, this access has been accompanied by increasingly repressive methods of social surveillance and regulation of reproductive practices.

The concept of *reproductive governance* introduced by anthropologists Lynn Morgan and Elizabeth Roberts provides a framework for tracing shifting political configurations enacted through *moral regimes*: the standards that govern a society's intimate behavior and ethical judgments (Morgan and Roberts 2012, 241–242). Under the pretense of advocating for universal human rights, contemporary shifts in reproductive governance give rise to new constituencies who frame their efforts to limit women's reproductive rights in a human rights rubric, pitting embryos and fetuses against women, native-born against immigrant women, heterosexual against homosexual individuals and couples, and so on (Morgan 2014). These political dynamics reinforce existing inequalities by targeting some individuals and groups with programs aimed at limiting their fertility, while giving other, possibly infertile individuals, the prospect of becoming parents (Colen 1995; Krause and De Zordo 2012). Reproductive governance in the twenty-first century has been characterized by distinctive activist groups and discourses.

Fetal Rights

The United States remains the major battlefield in the struggle over whether fetal rights necessarily supercede those of pregnant women. Fetal rights movements derive from religious and New Right/neoliberal political-social agendas that push the anti-humanist myth that women abort pregnancies chiefly for selfish reasons or to repudiate motherhood. They also invoke the concept of natural law to support the purported universal inalienable rights of embryos and fetuses. The larger issues at stake include who controls the contents of a woman's womb, the competence of adult women to exercise good judgment, and the often-overlooked issue of forced motherhood (Petchesky 1984, 329–375 passim). Further emboldening fetal rights activists are physicians who regard a fetus as their "patient," separate and independent from the woman who carries it (Casper 1998).

Men's Rights

Men's rights movements (MRMs) began in the 1960s and 1970s as part of a backlash by men who claimed feminism was undermining their interests and social status. They advocate restoring men's rights in marriage and divorce, strengthening child custody laws and fathers' rights, and legislation to establish the right of husbands and male sexual partners to block a woman from unilaterally obtaining an abortion. Men's human rights movements (MHRMs), less focused on men's family rights, reference the doctrine of universal human rights to challenge legal systems they perceive as biased toward women, for instance, in cases of rape, sexual abuse, and domestic assault (Matchar 2014).

Providers' Rights

Sharply growing numbers of physicians and ancillary clinicians are claiming a conscientious-objection right not to perform abortions or offer contraceptives. This movement is especially strong in the parts of Europe with declining white birth rates. The consequences are already extreme. At present, *no* public hospitals in Madrid offer abortions, and 69 percent of Italian gynecologists refuse as well (Zampas 2013). The fall of communist regimes, a revitalized Catholic Church, and threateningly high birth rates among immigrants from poorer, non-Christian nations further propel this movement. Providers' conscientious-objection rights are also being claimed in parts of the United States and, increasingly, in Asia and South America.

Empowerment

Although the term *empowerment*—"to give or delegate power" and "to enable or permit"—dates to the mid-seventeenth century (American Heritage Dictionary 2009), its modern-day reinvigoration is credited to Paolo Freire's renowned 1970 English-language edition of *Pedagogy of the Oppressed* (Archibald and Wilson 2011). Critics challenged Freire's radical idealistic agenda for social transformation as inherently flawed in that it "treats the symptoms but leaves the disease unnamed and untouched" (Ellsworth 1989, 306). Yet, this is also likely the reason the concept is embraced in such diverse fields as health, education, personal development, dispute resolution, management, and marketing, as helping individuals develop the capacity to act effectively within an existing system and its associated structures of power (Grace 1991). Within neoliberal global contexts, empowerment rubrics are popular in international nongovernmental organizations and agencies that work on behalf of women. For example, the recently launched UN Women "offers businesses and foundations a unique opportunity [to help achieve] gender equality and the empowerment of women," and says, "We are strongly committed to working with the private sector on common agendas leveraging collective strengths . . . [to] advance corporate social responsibility and business objectives (UN Women 2014). Whether a neoliberal global commerce agenda can actually help women achieve greater freedom to control their reproductive lives remains an open question.

FROM RIGHTS TO JUSTICE

> *The "right to have children" and the "right not to have them" are not equivalent rights.*
>
> (Petchesky 1984, 388)

Since the 1970s, some women's health activists—principally women of color—have argued that the concept of reproductive rights is class and culture-bound, relevant mainly for relatively privileged women from individualism-based Northern societies. In that light, it is well to keep in mind that reproductive *choice* assumes that a woman's body is her own, that she can and does make her own reproductive decisions, and has access to resources to obtain any needed health services. Fundamental to the concept of reproductive choice is the assumption that a woman knows she *has* reproductive rights that are recognized by her family, her community, and her nation (Chrisler 2012, 1–2).

A focus on choice also diverts attention from the fact that laws, policies, and public officials differentially reward or punish the reproductive activities of different groups of women. The 1970s rallying cry "My body, my choice!" applied mainly to white middle-class feminists, obscuring a broader, deeper set of needs by a much larger group of less privileged women: for example, freedom from sterilization abuse; access to healthcare and contraceptives; safe, accessible, and affordable child care; housing; a living wage or adequate public assistance; freedom from discrimination based on sexual orientation; and an end to toxic environments that threaten fertility.

The term *reproductive justice* was coined in the mid-1990s to conceptualize reproductive rights struggles within social justice movements (Luna and Luker 2013, 328). Loretta Ross, one of the small group that originated the term, argues that reproductive justice is a more theoretically productive way to analyze intersectionality: the ways that class, race, gender, sexual and gender orientation, culture, country of origin, and (dis)ability shape politics to produce a "complex matrix of reproductive oppression" (Ross 2011, 1). The reproductive justice framework has expanded beyond the United States to address a much broader range of issues that are not necessarily directly rooted in reproduction per se, including sexual assault, sex trafficking, prevention and control of STIs (sexually transmitted infections), female feticide and infanticide, and a woman's right to choose her own spouse (Kasai and Rooney 2012, 11; Chrisler 2012a).

Global movements for reproductive justice cast light on the interrelationships among the law, social movements, and academic scholarship. Its analytic framework of movement, praxis, and vision reveals aspects social policy previously ignored (Luna and Luker 2013, 328–330). This emphasis on multifaceted analysis and organizing differentiates the reproductive justice movement from reproductive health advocacy, which is principally concerned with unequal access to services, and reproductive rights advocacy, which focuses on legislative means to achieve social change.

Contingent Reproductive Rights

Anthropologist Shellee Colen framed the concept of *stratified reproduction* to describe the power relations that accord differential cultural, economic, and moral value to the children produced by women based on their status within social class, color, and national hierarchies. Fundamentally, this meant privileging the childbearing and childrearing of white, wealthy women over that of others (Colen 1995). As illustrated below, reproductive justice will remain an unrealized aspiration in the absence of broader social transformations in areas ranging from education, healthcare, and employment to human rights, prejudice, and discrimination.

The Right to Biological Children

The United Nations Declaration of Human Rights includes the right for women to make reproductive decisions free from coercion, including the right to the "means to do so." But what, exactly, does this right entail?

> The archeological record shows fertility to be an age-old concern; for example, the ubiquitous female figurines found throughout ancient Eurasia are commonly thought to be fertility offerings. However, no known traditional empirical remedies to treat infertility are consistently effective, and today, infertility is a global problem, and its impact is far greater in the global South. It is difficult to determine infertility's prevalence because of the involvement of both male and female factors and inconsistently applied definitions. A 2010 World Health Organization investigation of 190 countries and territories estimates that 48.5 million couples are affected, although worldwide rates vary widely (Mascarenhas et al. 2012). Overall, an estimated 8 to 12 percent of couples have difficulty conceiving a child at some point in their lives.
>
> (Daar and Merali 2002, 15)

Contrary to conventional wisdom, the 2010 study found little evidence of any change in the prevalence of infertility between 1990 and the present, with the exception of Sub-Saharan Africa, where rates fell significantly, possibly due to fewer sexually transmitted infections and improved obstetric care.

The effects of infertility can be devastating, notably in the South, as bioethicists Abdallah S. Daar and Zara Merali explain:

> The experience of infertility causes harsh, poignant and unique difficulties: economic hardship, social stigma and blame, social isolation and alienation, guilt, fear, loss of social status, helplessness and, in some cases, violence. Many families in developing countries depend on children for economic survival. Without children, men and women may starve to death, especially in old age. In some communities, infertile people are ostracized as they are perceived to be unlucky or the source of evil, or they become the object of public humiliation and shame. Some, even, choose suicide over the torturous life and mental anguish caused by infertility. In other communities infertile men and women are often denied proper death rites. For women in developing countries, infertility may occasion life-threatening physical as well as psychological violence. Childless women are generally blamed for their infertility, despite the fact that male factor causes contribute to at least half of the cases.... In developing countries, especially, motherhood is often the only way for women to enhance their status within the family and community.
>
> (Daar and Zara Merali 2002, 16; see also Nahar and van der Geest 2014; Whitehouse and Hollos 2014)

The mid-twentieth century witnessed an explosion of scientific techniques collectively known as ART (assisted reproductive technologies). They are effective to varying degrees in producing healthy children and can allow for the selection of embryos and fetuses imbued with certain traits considered desirable by prospective mothers and parents (e.g., sex, the absence of known genetic anomalies). Despite their great expense, women's desire to become biological mothers, persistent pronatalistic ideologies, and son preference have led many to extreme sacrifice in their efforts to produce a genetically related child.

Overall, the social impact of ART has been mixed. The technologies offer infertile women and couples and other individuals conventionally excluded from becoming parents (e.g., homosexuals, transgendered individuals, people living with HIV/AIDS, partnerless and postmenopausal women) the chance to reproduce. But they can also serve as a source of pressure, perpetuate gender inequalities, reinforce women's primary roles as mothers, and, perhaps most significantly, valorize biological reproduction above all other means of family formation.

The most controversial ART is surrogacy, an arrangement in which a woman gestates and gives birth to a child for a couple or another person. The practice has been decried as a commodification of reproduction, and from its beginning, feminists disagreed about its significance. Some liberal feminists defend women's right to be surrogates, using their bodies as they choose. Others are deeply troubled by surrogacy's potential to disrupt deeply held meanings of family, kinship, nature, and local moral orders. This latter has proven particularly salient in Islamic states (Clarke 2009). Moreover, relatively little is still known about the experiences and meanings of surrogacy to surrogates themselves (Bailey 2011; Berend 2010).

Unequal access to ART raises additional bioethical and social justice concerns. The technologies have been aggressively marketed in the North, typically to affluent, white, heterosexual couples. Although questions are sometimes raised about the extent of the burden these costly technologies place on society, there are far fewer opportunities for women lacking economic resources to benefit from them. National health services in Asia and Europe vary widely in infertility coverage and regulation, and in the United States, laws differ by state. Other populations facing obstacles to accessing ART include people with disabilities, prisoners, people living with HIV/AIDS, single women, and same-sex couples.

Perhaps it should not be surprising that despite their low success rate, ART marketing is also expanding in the South, raising standard bioethical concerns about its psychological and physical impact, stigma, and issues associated with identity, body commodification, kinship, and family. Additional unique considerations for Southern populations include far more insurmountable financial barriers; policies and practices set by religious and legal authorities; that the defining feature of female adulthood is biological motherhood; lack of medical resources, including trained clinicians; and a lower priority placed on treating infertility in relation to many other health concerns (Rubin and Phillips 2012, 181).

Connelly eloquently captures the nature of the social justice dilemmas inherent in ART's proliferation:

> If privileged people are permitted to pick and choose, and make themselves a breed apart, how can future generations possibly fight prejudice or promote more equal opportunities? There is therefore the prospect of a new age of population

control ... [and e]ven without top-down coercion, we may already be witnessing something less pernicious: the privatization of population control. It is governmentality without government, in which people police themselves, unconsciously reproducing and reinforcing inequality with every generation. The process is well underway in India and China because of sex-selective abortions. In the United States ... it is more subtle ... [P]eople ascribe a whole range of behaviors to good or bad genes, faithfully reciting a genetic catechism without the faintest idea of where it comes from or where it can lead. The cumulative effect of individual choices may be to make patriarchy permanent in the largest nations and endow the most privileged with genetic advantages to lord over the world.

(Connelly 2008, 382–383)

The Right to Bear Children

During the first part of the twentieth century, compulsory sterilization laws were passed in countries throughout the world (Mass 1976). While most programs were ended later in the century, some remain. There are contemporary reports of involuntary sterilization in both the North and the South, including among HIV-positive women in South Africa (Essack and Strode 2012), indigenous women in Peru (Gaebler 2011), Uzbekistan (Bukharbaeva 2005), and Native Americans and female prisoners in the United States (Gurr 2012)—all stigmatized groups who are the least able to advocate on their own behalf. Moreover, international and domestic medical and family planning establishments continue to promote "voluntary" sterilization for groups deemed "surplus" or "undesirable."

Like any technology, the meanings and uses of sterilization are embedded within specific sets of historical and cultural circumstances. For example, at the birth of the modern reproductive rights movement, activists attributed very high rates of female sterilization in Puerto Rico and among US mainland Puerto Ricans to the coercion of unwitting victims by an oppressive state. Anthropologist Iris López takes issue with this formulation to argue that "there are different degrees of agency, resistance, and reproductive freedom and these are not mutually exclusive" (López 2008, xix). Based on thirty years of historical, ethnohistorical, and ethnographic research, López characterizes Puerto Rican women as active decision-makers who choose sterilization as the best option among a set of poor alternatives. Anne Line Dalsgaard makes a similar argument about women in Northeast Brazil, finding that their motives for agreeing to and, in some cases, actively seeking sterilization derive from their desire to attain a sense of control over their lives (Dalsgaard 2004).

Among those who face nearly overwhelming obstacles to bearing children are women with physical and mental disabilities. And regrettably, reproductive rights and disability rights activists have had different agendas for many years. As Marsha Saxton writes, "The reproductive rights movement emphasizes the right to have an abortion; the disability rights movement, the right *not* to have an abortion [when the fetus is disabled]" (Saxton 2013, 88; italics in original). A reproductive justice framework can overcome this impasse by reframing the conversation more broadly than simply whether one is pro- or antichoice. Among the issues that would be considered in this larger conversation are how one's community supports or impedes particular possibilities and how stereotypes and stigmas are created and perpetuated (Rapp and Ginsburg 2001; Kato 2009).

The Right to Safe Childbirth

Childbirth is necessarily associated with the possibility of complications during pregnancy, labor and delivery, and postpartum. These risks are much higher in the South, due mainly to women's inability to access high-quality healthcare. Each year, an estimated 529,000 maternal deaths are very unevenly distributed worldwide (CRR 2006). In Sub-Saharan Africa, the lifetime risk of maternal mortality is as high as 1 in 16. In South Asia, it is 1 in 43. In contrast, the lifetime risk in Northern Europe is about 1 in 30,000.

Maternal deaths are more likely to occur during labor, delivery, and immediately postpartum, principally from preventable causes, and women in rural and poor populations are the most vulnerable (Ronsmans et al. 2006). Obstetric hemorrhage heads the list of causes; unsafe abortion and HIV/AIDS are also major risks in some settings. Other significant causes of postpartum complications are puerperal infection, preeclampsia, and obstetric fistula, the latter generally occurring as a consequence of protracted labor and in girls whose bodies are not yet ready for childbirth. Considered a disease of poverty, there are 30,000 to 130,000 new cases of obstetric fistula annually, and worldwide, more than three million women live with the condition. In addition to causing urinary and fecal incontinence and repeated vaginal and urinary tract infections, there are often major social consequences. Women who develop fistulae are usually divorced or abandoned by their husbands, often cast out by their families, rejected by their communities, and forced to live in isolation (Wall 2006). Governments must take the lead in ameliorating maternal morbidity and mortality by establishing and enforcing legal guarantees for women's right to the full complement of reproductive healthcare, including contraceptives and abortion.

By contrast, in wealthier countries, a "hypermedicalization" of childbirth has been seen through, for example, intensive monitoring of pregnant women and sharply escalating use of induced labor and cesarean section: Nearly half of babies in China and one third in the US and Australia are delivered by cesarean; in parts of Latin America, cesarean deliveries are more common than vaginal births. (The World Health Organization recommends national rates not exceed 10 to 15%.) (Gibbons et al. 2010). Marjorie Murray has demonstrated a link between rising rates of obstetrical interventions and the privatization of health care systems. She argues that under neoliberalism, maternal health care practices (e.g. scheduled childbirths) constitute new threats to women's ability to exercise authority over their own bodies and to their right to bodily integrity (Murray 2012).

The Right to Parent with Dignity

Efforts by state governments to terminate the parental rights of women deemed unfit to raise children are becoming more widespread in the United States, as deeply indebted states undertake contractual obligations to fill the occupancy quotas of a growing and lucrative private for-profit prison system: far more people in the United States are incarcerated than anywhere else in the world. The mothers in question are generally economically disadvantaged women of color (principally African American) who have been imprisoned for delivering "illegal substances" to their fetuses. The charges derive from feticide, antiabortion, and "personhood" laws (Nelson 2003).

Legal scholar Dorothy Roberts argues that obscured by the politics of fetal rights is the politics of race, which, along with a more generalized hostility toward black mothers, has made prosecuting pregnant women and punishing black women for having babies permissible, and even desirable (Roberts 2008, 369–370). Prosecuting mothers who use illegal substances also shifts public attention away from poverty, racism, and a deficient healthcare system by intimating that poor birth outcomes are due to the mother's behavior, thereby blaming women for the health problems of black communities. Astonishingly, an analysis of criminal and civil cases brought against pregnant women between 1973 and 2005 found that the husband or male partner was not mentioned in fully 77 percent of the cases, a stark reminder that gender, in concert with race and class, can reproduce increasingly complex matrices of reproductive oppression (Paltrow and Flavin 2013).

In parts of global North, the mid-twentieth century saw a woman's right to parent with dignity more subtly challenged through the adoption of a model of childrearing that shifted the locus of legitimate parental authority away from mothers' (and fathers') experiential knowledge to that of expert "authoritative knowledge," that promulgated an increasingly time consuming, supervised, and regimented form of childrearing. By the twenty-first century, these practices were being emulated beyond the global North (Faircloth, Hoffman and Layne 2013). At its core are neoliberal values that privilege individual autonomy and self-interest over collective needs. Low income, ethnic minority, and immigrant women, frequently held accountable for their children's "improper", "deviant" or anti-social behaviors, are offered or required by the state to attend "parenting workshops" that seek to inculcate mainstream middle-class Euro-American values (Jaysane-Dahr 2013). Wealthier women are extolled to engage in "intensive parenting" by investing of massive amounts of energy and economic and emotional resources in their children, who, in turn, are expected to become their mothers' principal sources of identity and self-fulfillment (Hays 1996). Unsurprisingly, perhaps, this insidious erosion of women's right to parent with dignity has coincided with the hollowing out of vital public sectors and the decline of vibrant local communities.

New, complex social, legal, medical, and ethical issues have come to the fore regarding the reproductive rights of transgendered individuals (Green 1994). Historically, medical providers required trans people to relinquish their fertility in exchange for gender reassignment treatments. This is now changing with growing awareness among clinicians that infertility is not an inevitable consequence of transsexualism. Indeed, some providers and transsexuals assert that transsexual people should be entitled to the same range of infertility treatments as those whose reproductive capability is physiologically compromised for any other reason. Still, widespread discrimination continues to challenge the ability of transgender people to receive respectful, knowledgeable reproductive health care (Cascio 2014).

The Right to a Healthy Environment

Historian Ricky Solinger has observed that governments throughout the world have generally been reluctant to consider environmental causes of pregnancy-related death and injury, despite the fact that the right to a healthy environment is essential for safe pregnancies and childbirth (Solinger 2013). This problem affects both genders, and indeed, men may be at greater risk of certain exposures. Other factors that put some individuals and groups at heightened risk include socioeconomic and racial disparities, and living or working near industrial sites emitting certain toxins, pesticides, or nuclear radiation (Fang 2014; Freinkel 2014). Exposure to lead and other heavy metals is a well-documented cause of disordered fetal development, including permanently altered gene expression and other reproductive-system abnormalities with lifelong, even intergenerational consequences (Mendola, Messer, and Rappazzo 2008; Woodruff et al. 2008).

Scientists are only beginning to understand the nature of these intergenerational processes (Dias and Ressler 2014). Recent work in behavioral epigenetics is revealing that early maternal trauma (e.g., neglect and abuse) can precipitate genetic changes in gametes that are subsequently transmitted from one generation to the next by leaving "molecular scars" that adhere to DNA (VanZomeren-Dohm et al. 2013). It is crucial to keep in mind, however, that while behavioral epigenetic mechanisms can reinforce weaknesses and deficits, they can similarly enhance strength and resiliency.

The Rights of Displaced and Refugee Women

"Refugeeization" (Allison 2013, 52), the uprooting and circulation of people without fixed homelands, has become a global phenomenon. The United Nations High Commission on Refugees reported upward of 51 million people forcibly displaced by conflict and persecution in 2014, the highest number since World War II. An additional 15.5 million were internally displaced (nearly 800,000 more than the previous year), and an estimated 10 million stateless people, worldwide (UNHCR 2015). In 2012, more than 22 million were displaced by natural disasters (e.g., earthquakes; IDMC 2014).

The complete absence of reproductive rights for displaced and refugee women is a significant, yet sorely neglected dimension of global reproductive injustices. Linda Whiteford and Aimee Eden have shown that when state authority is nebulous or entirely absent, women are excluded from basic reproductive healthcare by the humanitarian organizations ostensibly overseeing their protection. Yet displaced women's needs for such services are generally greater than beforehand because they are more vulnerable to sexual violence, rape, sexually transmitted diseases including HIV/AIDS, unwanted pregnancies, and high-risk abortion. In addition, they are typically cut off from families and other sources of social support. The most active humanitarian agencies fail to offer post-rape counseling, emergency contraception, or abortions. This is partly due to the fact that displacement and refugee camps are administered by men, their governing counsels run by men, and leadership roles held mostly by men who do not prioritize these issues. Many humanitarian aid workers minimize them as well, viewing sexual violence and rape as unfortunate but unavoidable "side effects" of complex emergencies, about which little or nothing can be done (Whiteford and Eden 2011, 227–228). Whiteford and Eden argue to the contrary that these widely held attitudes are in fact abuses of human rights and must be addressed as such.

Only broad-based reproductive justice movements will generate the political, economic, cultural, and ideological conditions for women's reproductive freedom to prevail.

Conclusions

This chapter has shown that the elements animating a society in its governance of reproduction are neither timeless and universal nor unchanging; nor are they univariate among diverse class, racial, regional, religious, and other distinct populations. Rather, as Karl Marx famously explained centuries ago, they are determined by ongoing interactions among historical, material, political, and ideological processes. Any society's reproductive concerns invariably reflect and at the same time produce profound political ramifications.

An often overlooked consequence of the expansion of neoliberal economic and social policies has been their severe impact on women's reproductive freedom: public programs guaranteeing access to reproductive health services and social policies enabling mothers to combine work with raising young children are being eliminated, significantly cut, or never initiated; women must look increasingly to the private sector—or do without.

Therefore, in reproduction—as in much else in life—in the end, individual women have to live with and by the reproductive customs, practices, and policies of the larger groups to which they belong, even though they are usually not the ones setting those reproductive agendas. Nonetheless, there is reason for optimism. Throughout the world, we see demonstrations of resourcefulness, courage, and resilience as women—and men—engineer new ways to persevere and prevail in the face of obstacles intended to deter them from exercising their rights to reproductive freedom. Global reproductive justice movements are supporting women in their fights for these rights as never before.

Acknowledgments

Heartfelt thanks to Elana Buch, Lara Braff, Anna Capitán Camañes, Silvia De Zordo, Matthew Gutmann, Ofrit Liviatan, Susan Markens, Deborah Mindry, Joanna Mishtal,

Lynn Morgan, Christine Morton, Marjorie Murray, Nahar Papreen, Loretta Ross, Brooke Scelza, Seinenu Thein, Azumi Tsgue, Muriel Vernon, Shannon Ward, Emily Wentzell, Alice Wexler, and Richard Rosenthal for resources, guidance, feedback, and support.

This chapter is dedicated to Rosalind P. Petchesky for inspiring generations of feminist scholars.

Notes

1. Neoliberalism is a set of capitalist economic policies associated with the Washington Consensus of the early 1970s, designed to foster a "free" (i.e., unregulated by state controls or oversight) economic market. Hallmarks of neoliberal policies have been decentralization of state controls; privatization of state-owned properties, enterprises, goods, and services by sale to private investors; sharp cuts in government spending on social services; replacement of the social contract and concept of the public good with policies based on market principles to maximize corporate profits; and redefinition of citizenship with reference to individual rights and responsibilities. At the heart of the expansion of neoliberal processes are economic "structural adjustment" programs and austerity policies imposed to foster economic growth, which have produced the upward redistribution of wealth and power. The sovereignty of weakened, deeply indebted states coexists with globalized international or extrastate entities, typically dominated by transnational corporations whose authority is derived from powerful financial institutions (e.g., the US Federal Reserve, the European Central Bank, the International Monetary Fund, the World Bank, and other huge international banking entities).
2. We lack satisfactory terms of reference for what used to be called preindustrial and industrial societies, developed and developing countries, or the First and Third Worlds. The global North and global South are commonly used today to distinguish affluent, privileged states from more economically marginalized ones, despite obvious conceptual limitations.

References

Allison, Anne. 2013. *Precarious Japan*. Durham, NC: Duke University Press.
American Heritage Dictionary. 2009. "Empower." Available from TheFreeDictionary.com. http://www.thefreedictionary.com/empower (accessed March 3, 2014).
Anton, Lorena, Silvia De Zordo, and Joanna Z. Mishtal, eds. n.d. "A Right That Isn't? Abortion Governance and Associated Protest Logics in Postwar Europe." Unpublished manuscript.
Archibald, Thomas, and Arthur L. Wilson. 2011. "Rethinking Empowerment: Theories of Power and the Potential for Emancipatory Praxis." 22–28. Annual Proceedings of the Adult Education Research Conference (AERC), Toronto, ON, June 10–12. http://www.adulterc.org/Proceedings/2011/papers/archibald_wilson.pdf (accessed February 12, 2014).
Bailey, Alison. 2011. "Reconceiving Surrogacy: Toward a Reproductive Justice Account of Surrogacy in India". *Hypatia* 26(4): 715–741.
Berend, Zsuzsa. 2010. "Surrogate Losses: Understandings of Pregnancy Loss and Assisted Reproduction among Surrogate Mothers". *Medical Anthropology Quarterly* 24(2): 240–262.

Browner, C. H. 2000. "Situating Women's Reproductive Activities." *American Anthropologist* 102 (4): 773–788.

Browner, Carole H., and Carolyn F. Sargent, eds. 2011. *Reproduction, Globalization, and the State: New Theoretical and Ethnographic Perspectives*. Durham, NC: Duke University Press.

Bukharbaeva, Galima. 2005. "Birth Control by Decree." Special Report. Women's Reporting & Dialogue Programme 1 (November 18, 2005). IWPR Institute for War & Peace Reporting website. http://iwpr.net/report-news/birth-control-decree-uzbekistan (accessed March 11, 2014).

Cascio, Justin. 2014. "The Reproductive Rights of Trans Men". *The Good Men Project*. http://goodmenproject.com/featured-content/reproductive-rights-trans-men/. (accessed September 3, 2014).

Casper, Monica J. 1998. *The Making of the Unborn Patient: A Social Anatomy of Fetal Surgery*. New Brunswick, NJ: Rutgers University Press.

Clarke, Morgan. 2009. *Islam and New Kinship: Reproductive Technology and the Sharia in Lebanon*. New York: Berghahn.

CRR (Center for Reproductive Rights). 2006. "Gaining Ground: A Tool for Advancing Reproductive Rights Law Reform." 26–33. http://reproductiverights.org/en/document/gaining-ground-a-tool-for-advancing-reproductive-rights-law-reform (accessed February 28, 2014).

Chrisler, Joan C., ed. 2012a. *Reproductive Justice: A Global Concern*. Santa Barbara, CA: Praeger.

Chrisler, Joan C. 2012b. "Introduction: What Is Reproductive Justice?" In *Reproductive Justice: A Global Concern*, edited by Joan C. Chrisler, 1–9. Santa Barbara, CA: Praeger.

Connelly, Matthew. 2008. *Fatal Misconception: The Struggle for Control of World Population*. Cambridge, MA: Belknap Press of Harvard University Press.

Colen, Shellee. 1995. "'Like a Mother to Them': Stratified Reproduction and West Indian Childcare Workers and Employers in New York." In *Conceiving the New World Order: The Global Politics of Reproduction*, edited by Faye D. Ginsburg and Rayna Rapp, 78–102. Berkeley: University of California Press.

Corrêa, Sonia, and Rosalind Petchesky. 2007."Reproductive and Sexual Rights: A Feminist Perspective." In *Culture, Society and Sexuality: A Reader*, 2nd ed., edited by Richard Parker and Peter Aggleton, 298–315. New York: Routledge.

Daar, Abdallah S., and Zara Merali. 2002. "Infertility and Social Suffering: The Case of ART in Developing Countries ." In *Current Practices and Controversies in Assisted Reproduction: Report of a Meeting on "Medical, Ethical and Social Aspects of Assisted Reproduction,"* Held at WHO Headquarters in Geneva, Switzerland, 17–21 September 2001, edited by Effy Vayena, Patrick J. Rowe, and David Griffin, 15–21. Geneva: World Health Organization.

Dalsgaard, Anne Line. 2004. *Matters of Life and Longing: Female Sterilisation in Northeast Brazil*. Copenhagen: Museum Tusculanum Press.

Davis, Susan E., ed. 1988. *Women under Attack: Victories, Backlash, and the Fight for Reproductive Freedom*. Committee for Abortion Rights and against Sterilization Abuse. Pamphlet #7. Boston: South End Press.

Devereux, George. 1976. *A Study of Abortion in Primitive Societies*. Rev. ed. New York: International Universities Press.

De Zordo S., Mishtal J., Anton L., (Eds.) A Right that Isn't? Abortion Governance and Associated Protest Logics in Postwar Europe. Berghahn Books: Oxford and New York. Expected publication date: 2016.

Dias, Brian G. and Ressler, Kerry J. 2014. "Parental Olfactory Experience Influences Behavior and Neural Structure in Subsequent Generations." *Nature Neuroscience* 17: 89–96. doi:10.1038/nn.3594 (accessed September 5, 2014).

Essack, Zaynab, and Ann Strode. 2012. "'I Feel Like Half a Woman All the Time': The Impacts of Coerced and Forced Sterilizations on HIV-Positive Women in South Africa." *Agenda: Empowering Women for Gender Equity* 26 (2): 24–34.

Ehrlich, Paul R. 1968. *The Population Bomb*. Cutchogue, NY: Buccaner.

Ellsworth, Elizabeth. 1989. "Why Doesn't This Feel Empowering? Working Through the Repressive Myths of Critical Pedagogy." *Harvard Educational Review* 59 (3): 297–324.

Europa. 2013. "Summaries of EU Legislation: Actions on Reproductive and Sexual Health and Rights." http://europa.eu/legislation_summaries/other/r12517_en.htm (accessed November 30, 2013).

Faircloth, Charlotte, Diane N. Hoffman, and Linda L. Layne, eds. 2013. Parenting in Global Perspective: Negotiating Ideologies of Kinship, Self and Politics. Oxon: Routledge.

Fang, Lee. 2014. "Poisoned Politics." *The Nation*, March 31.

Freinkel, Susan. 2014. "Warning Signs: Pesticides and the Young Brain." *The Nation*, March 31.

Fordyce, Lauren, and Aminata Maraesa, eds. 2012. *Risk, Reproduction, and Narratives of Experience*. Nashville, TN: Vanderbilt University Press.

Forte, Dianne, and Karen Judd. 1998. "The South within the North: Reproductive Choice in Three US Communities." In *Negotiating Reproductive Rights: Women's Perspectives across Countries and Cultures*, edited by Rosalind P. Petchesky and Karen Judd, 256–294. London: Zed Books.

Freeman, Michael. 2011. *Human Rights: An Interdisciplinary Approach*. Cambridge: Polity.

Freire, Paolo. 1970. *Pedagogy of the Oppressed*. New York: Continuum.

Gaebler, Emilee. 2011. "Thousands of Forced Sterilization Cases Reopened in Peru." *Impunity Watch*. Syracuse: Syracuse College of Law, November 14, 2011. http://impunitywatch.com/?p=21794 (accessed November 11, 2014).

Gibbons, Luz, José M. Belizán, Jeremy A. Lauer, Ana P. Betrán, Mario Merialdi, and Fernando Althabe. 2010. *The Global Numbers and Costs of Additionally Needed and Unnecessary Caesarean Sections Performed per Year: Overuse as a Barrier to Universal Coverage*. World Health Report Background Paper, 30. Geneva, CH: World Health Organization. http://www.who.int/healthsystems/topics/financing/healthreport/30C-sectioncosts.pdf.(accessed November 1, 2014).

Ginsburg, Faye D., and Rayna Rapp. 1991. "The Politics of Reproduction." *Annual Review of Anthropology* 20: 311–343.

Ginsburg, Faye D., and Rayna Rapp, eds. 1995. *Conceiving the New World Order: The Global Politics of Population*. Berkeley: University of California Press.

Gordon, Linda. 1990. *Woman's Body, Woman's Right: Birth Control in America*. Rev. ed. New York: Penguin.

Grace, Victoria M. 1991. "The Marketing of Empowerment and the Construction of the Health Consumer: A Critique of Health Promotion." *International Journal of Health Services* 21 (2): 329–343.

Green, Richard. 1994. "Transsexualism and the Law". *Journal of the American Academy of Psychiatry and the Law Online* 22 (4): 511–517. (accessed September 1, 2014).

Greenhalgh, Susan. 2008. *Just One Child: Science and Policy in Deng's China*. Berkeley: University of California Press.

Gurr, Barbara. 2012. "The Failures and Possibilities of a Human Rights Approach to Secure Native American Women's Reproductive Justice." *Societies without Borders* 7 (1): 1–28.

Guttmacher Institute. 2012. "In Brief: Facts on Abortions in Africa." Guttmacher Institute website. January. http://www.guttmacher.org/pubs/IB_AWW-Africa.pdf. (accessed April 10, 2014).

Guttmacher Institute. 2014. "Fact Sheet: Induced Abortions in the United States." Guttmacher Institute website. July. http://www.guttmacher.org/pubs/fb_induced_abortion.html (accessed November 6, 2014).

Hartmann, Betsy. 1987. *Reproductive Rights and Wrongs: The Global Politics of Population Control and Contraceptive Choice*. New York: Harper and Row.

Hays, Sharon. 1996. *The Cultural Contradictions of Motherhood*. New Haven, CT: Yale University Press.

Heer, David. 1965. "Abortion, Contraception, and Population Policy in the Soviet Union." *Demography* 2 (1): 531–539.

Hrdy, Sarah. 1981. *The Woman That Never Evolved*. Cambridge, MA: Harvard University Press.

Internal Displacement Monitoring Center. 2015. "Global Figures Displaced by Conflict and Disasters. http://www.internal-displacement.org/ (accessed September 22, 2015).

Kasai, Makiko, and S. Craig Rooney. 2012. "The Choice before the Choice: Partner Selection Is Essential to Reproductive Justice." In *Reproductive Justice: A Global Concern*, edited by Joan C. Chrisler, 1–9. Santa Barbara, CA: Praeger.

Kato, Masae. 2009. *Women's Rights? The Politics of Eugenic Abortion in Modern Japan*. Amsterdam: Amsterdam University Press.

Kramer, Steven Philip. 2014. *The Other Population Crisis: What Governments Can Do about Falling Birth Rates*. Baltimore, MD: Johns Hopkins University Press.

Krause, Elizabeth L., and Silvia De Zordo. 2012. "Introduction. Ethnography and Biopolitics: Tracing 'Rationalities' of Reproduction across the North-South Divide." *Anthropology & Medicine* 19 (2): 137–151.

Liviatan, Ofrit. 2013. "Competing Fundamental Values: Comparing Law's Role in American and Western-European Conflicts over Abortion." In *Law, Religion, Constitution: Freedom of Religion, Equal Treatment, and the Law*, edited by W. Cole Durham, Jr., Silvio Ferrari, Cristiana Cianitto, and Donlu Thayer, 385–401. Surrey, UK: Ashgate.

López, Iris. 2008. *Matters of Choice: Puerto Rican Women's Struggle for Reproductive Freedom*. New Brunswick, NJ: Rutgers University Press.

Luna, Zakiya, and Kristin Luker. 2013. "Reproductive Justice" *Annual Review of Law and Social Science* 9: 327–352.

Malinowski, Bronislaw. 1942. "A New Instrument for the Study of Law—Especially Primitive." *Yale Law Journal* 51 (8): 1237–1254.

Major, Brenda, Catherine Cozzarelli, M. Lynne Cooper, Josephine Zubek, Caroline Richards, Michael Wilhite, and Richard H. Gramzow. 2000. "Psychological Responses of Women after First-Trimester Abortion." *JAMA Psychiatry* 57 (8): 777–784.

Mascarenhas, Maya N., Seth R. Flaxman, Ties Boerma, Sheryl Vanderpoel, and Gretchen A. Stevens. 2012. "National, Regional, and Global Trends in Infertility Prevalence since 1990: A Systematic Analysis of 277 Health Surveys." *PLOS Medicine* 9 (12): e001356. doi:10.1371/journal.pmed.1001356. Also available at http://www.plosmedicine.org/article/info. (accessed March 12, 2014).

Mass, Bonnie. 1976. *Population Target: The Political Economy of Population Control in Latin America*. Brampton, Ontario: Charters.

Matchar, Emily. 2014. "'Men's Rights' Activists Are Trying to Redefine the Meaning of Rape." *New Republic*, February 26, 2014. http://www.newrepublic.com/article/116768/latest-target-mens-rights-movement-definition-rape (accessed April 12, 2014).

Mendola, Pauline, Lynne C. Messer, and Kristen Rappazzo. 2008. "Science Linking Environmental Contaminant Exposures with Fertility and Reproductive Health Impacts in the Adult Female." *Fertility and Sterility* 89 (2 supplement): e81–e94. http://www.sciencedirect.com/science/article/pii/S0015028207043154 (accessed April 13, 2014).

Morgan, Lynn M. 2014. "Claiming Rosa Parks: Conservative Catholic Bids for 'Rights' in Contemporary Latin America." *Culture, Health & Sexuality* 16(10): 1245–1259.

Morgan, Lynn M., and Elizabeth F. S. Roberts. 2012. "Reproductive Governance in Latin America." *Anthropology & Medicine* 19 (2): 241–254.

Morán Faúndes, José Manuel, and María Angélica Peñas Defago, . 2013. "¿Defensores de la vida? ¿De cuál 'vida'? Un análisis genealógico de la noción de 'vida' sostenida por la jerarquía católica contra el aborto." *Sexualidad, Salud y Sociedad: Revista Latinoamericana* 15 (10): 10–36.

Murray, Marjorie. 2012. "Childbirth in Santiago de Chile: Stratification, Intervention, and Child Centeredness." *Medical Anthropology Quarterly* 26(3): 319–337.

Nahar, Papreen, and Sjeek van der Geest. 2014. "How Women in Bangladesh Confront the Stigma of Childlessness: Agency, Resilience, and Resistance." *Medical Anthropology Quarterly* 28(3): 381–398.

Nash, Elizabeth, Rachel Benson Gold, Andrea Rowan, Gwendolyn Rathbun, and Yana Vierboom. 2014. "Laws Affecting Reproductive Health and Rights: 2013 State Policy Review." Guttmacher Institute. https://www.guttmacher.org/statecenter/updates/2013/statetrends42013.html (accessed March 16, 2014).

Nelson, Jennifer. 2003. *Women of Color and the Reproductive Rights Movement*. New York: New York University Press.

Norgren, Tiana. 2001. *Abortion before Birth Control: The Politics of Reproduction in Postwar Japan*. Princeton, NJ: Princeton University Press.

Paltrow, Lynn M., and Jeanne Flavin. 2013 "Arrests of and Forced Medical Interventions on Pregnant Women in the United States (1973-2005): The Implications for Women's Legal Status and Public Health." *Journal of Health Politics, Policy and Law* 38 (2) 299–343. http://works.bepress.com/jeanne_flavin/5/ (accessed February 18, 2014).

Petchesky, Rosalind Pollack. 1984. *Abortion and Woman's Choice: The State, Sexuality, and Reproductive Freedom*. New York: Longman.

Petchesky, Rosalind P. 1998. Introduction to *Negotiating Reproductive Rights: Women's Perspectives Across Countries and Cultures*, edited by Rosalind P. Petchesky and Karen Judd, 1–30. London: Zed Books.

Piepmeier, Alison. 2013. "The Inadequacy of 'Choice': Disability and What's Wrong with Feminist Framings of Reproduction." *Feminist Studies* 39 (1): 159–186.

Potts, Malcolm, and Martha Campbell . 2009. "History of Contraception." *Global Library of Women's Medicine*. doi:10.3843/GLOWM.10376. Also available at http://www.glowm.com/section_view/heading/HistoryofContraception/item/375 (accessed February 28, 2014).

Randall, Amy E. 2011. "'Abortion Will Deprive You of Happiness!' Soviet Reproductive Politics in the Post-Stalin Era." *Journal of Women's History* 23 (3): 13–38.

Rapp, Rayna, and Faye D. Ginsburg, 2001. "Enabling Disability: Rewriting Kinship, Reimagining Citizenship." *Public Culture* 13 (3): 533–556.

Roberts, Dorothy. 2008. "Making Reproduction a Crime." In *The Reproductive Rights Reader: Law, Medicine, and the Construction of Motherhood*, edited by Nancy Ehrenreich, 368–386. New York: New York University Press.

Rocca, Corinne H., Katrina Kimport, Heather Gould, and Diana G. Foster. 2013. "Women's Emotions One Week after Receiving or Being Denied an Abortion in the United States." *Perspectives on Sexual and Reproductive Health* 45 (3): 122–131.

Ronsmans, Carine, and Wendy J. Graham / Lancet Maternal Survival Series Steering Group. 2006. "Maternal Mortality: Who, When, Where, and Why." *The Lancet* 368: 1189–1200.

Ross, Loretta J. 2011. "Eugenics, the State, and African American Women." Unpublished manuscript.

Rothbard, Murray N. 1998. *The Ethics of Liberty*. New York: New York University Press.

Rubin, Lisa R., and Aliza Phillips. 2012. "Infertility and Assisted Reproductive Technologies." In *Reproductive Justice: A Global Concern*, edited by Joan C. Chrisler, 173–199. Santa Barbara, CA: Praeger.

Sanger, Margaret. 1919. "A Parents' Problem or Woman's?" *Birth Control Review* 3: 6–7.

Sang-Hun, Choe. 2010. "South Korea Confronts Open Secret of Abortion." *New York Times*, January 10, p. 15.

Saxton, Marsha. 2013. "Disability Rights and Selective Abortion." In *The Disability Studies Reader*, 4th ed., edited by Leonard J. Davis, 87–99. New York: Routledge.

Scelza, Brooke A. 2013. "Choosy but Not Chaste: Multiple Mating in Human Females." *Evolutionary Anthropology* 22 (5): 259–269.

Solinger, Rickie. 2013. *Reproductive Politics: What Everyone Needs to Know*. Oxford: Oxford University Press.

Thomsen, Carly. 2013. "From Refusing Stigmatization toward Celebration: New Dimensions for Reproductive Justice Activism." *Feminist Studies* 39(1): 149–158.

UNHCR (United Nations High Commission on Refugees). 2014. *Protecting Refugees and the Role of the UNHCR*. Report. UNHCR. http://www.unhcr.org/509a836e9.html (accessed September 22, 2015).

United Nations. 1948. "The Universal Declaration of Human Rights." http://www.un.org/en/documents/udhr/ (accessed February 21, 2014).

United Nations. 1994. *UN Programme of Action Adopted at the International Conference on Population and Development*, Cairo, 5–13 September 1994, para 7.3. http://www.unfpa.org/rights/rights.htm. (accessed March 15, 2014).

UN Women: United Nations Entity for Gender Equality and the Empowerment of Women. 2014. Businesses and Foundations. http://www.unwomen.org/en/partnerships/businesses-and-foundations. (accessed March 11, 2014.

VanZomeren-Dohm, Adrienne, Rowena Ng, Kamyala Howard, Molly Kenney, Lynde Ritchmeier and Jessica Gourneau. 2013 "How Trauma Gets 'Under the Skin:' Biological and Cognitive Processes of Child Maltreatment". *Children's Mental Health e-Review*, University of Minnesota Extension http://www.extension.umn.edu. (accessed September 3, 2014).

Wall, L. Lewis. 2006. "Obstetric Vesicovaginal Fistula as an International Public-Health Problem." *The Lancet* 368: 1201–1209.

Wenar, Leif. 2011. "Rights" In *The Stanford Encyclopedia of Philosophy* online. Edited by Edward N. Zalta. http://plato.stanford.edu/archives/fall2011/entries/rights/ (accessed February 19, 2014).

Whiteford, Linda M., and Aimee R. Eden. 2011. "Reproductive Rights in No-Woman's Land: Politics and Humanitarian Assistance." In *Reproduction, Globalization and the*

State: New Theoretical and Ethnographic Perspectives, edited by Carole H. Browner and Carolyn F. Sargent, 224–248. Durham, NC: Duke University Press.

Whitehouse, Bruce and Marida Hollos. 2014. "Definitions and the Experience of Fertility Problems: Infertile and Sub-fertile Women, Childless Mothers, and Honorary Mothers in Two Southern Nigerian Communities". *Medical Anthropology Quarterly* 28(1): 122-139.

Willen, Sarah S. 2011. "Do 'Illegal' Im/migrants Have a Right to Health? Engaging Ethical Theory as Social Practice at a Tel Aviv Open Clinic." *Medical Anthropology Quarterly* 25 (3): 305–330.

Woodruff, Tracey J., Alison Carlson, Jackie M. Schwartz, and Linda C. Giudice. 2008. "Proceedings of the Summit on Environmental Challenges to Reproductive Health and Fertility." *Fertility and Sterility* 89 (2): 281–300.

World Bank. 2014. "Birth Rate, Crude (per 1000 People)." The World Bank Group website. http://data.worldbank.org/indicator/SP.DYN.CBRT.IN (accessed 9, November 9, 2013).

Zampas, Christina. 2013. "Legal and Ethical Standards for Protecting Women's Human Rights and the Practice of Conscientious Objection in Reproductive Healthcare Settings." *International Journal of Gynecology & Obstetrics* 123, Suppl. 3 (December): S63–S65.

CHAPTER 40

SCIENCE STUDIES

DEBOLEENA ROY

Introduction

Over the past four centuries, science has emerged as an authoritative mode of knowledge production. Distinguishing itself from metaphysics, religion, and superstition, science has characterized its practices as rational, objective, empirical, experimental, and evidence-based. Celebrating its capacity to discover the truth through systematic observation, hypothesis formulation, rigorous hypothesis testing, and falsification, the scientific method is said to free individual knowers from the taint of idiosyncrasy, bias, prejudice, particularity, and sociocultural values. As an interdisciplinary field that draws concepts and analytic categories from anthropology, cultural studies, economics, feminist theory, history, philosophy, political science, and sociology, science studies seeks to move beyond the benign self-characterizations of science to analyze science as social practice. Investigating how science works; the historical emergence, development and dissolution of particular scientific disciplines; the dynamics of science as a social, economic, and political institution; and the epistemological foundation of scientific knowledge claims, science studies illuminate how social values permeate the practices, processes, and products of scientific research. It also illuminates the co-construction of science and society.

From early work on the history of women in science and the persistent underrepresentation of women across scientific fields to discussions of androcentrism and misogyny in scientific discourses, feminist science studies illuminates practices of devaluation, marginalization, and exclusion linked to gender, race, class, sexuality, disability, and colonialism. Rejecting the notion that these modes of exclusion are extraneous to science, feminist science studies scholars have sought to demonstrate that exclusionary practices are constitutive of particular scientific endeavors and that certain sciences have played crucial roles in consolidating constructions of women, people of color, the underclasses, the colonized, and the disabled as inferior and less worthy of respect than elite property-owning men. In marked contrast to their claims of value neutrality, various sciences have helped produce, sustain, and justify social inequalities and systems of domination.

Over the past several decades, feminist science studies have proliferated, generating rich feminist critiques of specific sciences, designing feminist practices within the sciences, and recuperating theories from the sciences for feminist ends. From the outset, feminists have pursued multiple approaches to science studies, ranging from "feminist theory of science" (Rosser 1989) and "feminist theory in science" (Roy 2004) to "feminist theory out of science" (Roosth and Schrader 2012). Entangled in various productive ways *with* science, these intersecting but divergent orientations have raised a host of epistemological and ontological issues about the nature and practices of scientific knowledge production.

In Nancy Tuana's pivotal anthology, *Feminism and Science* (1989), feminist scholars trained in philosophy, biology, and physics discussed intricate relationships between women, feminist theory, and science, albeit in not always harmonious ways. Articles in the collection highlighted discordant views on the interventions in science made possible by feminist theory, as well as the purpose and scope of feminist science studies at an early period of this burgeoning field. After providing an overview of feminist scholarship in the sciences at the time, Sue Rosser (1989, 3), for example, suggested that a major "theoretical breakthrough" presupposed a transformation in the gender of science: "More feminists in science are needed to further explore science and its relationships to women and feminism in order to change traditional science to a feminist science." Although other scholars in the collection cautioned against the idea (Tuana 1989; Longino 1989; Keller 1989; Harding 1989), Rosser's vision of the promise of a "feminist science" provides a useful point of departure for thinking about the complex issues involved in feminist analyses of sex, gender, feminism, and science. In contrast to a nonhyphenated feminist science, a more significant theoretical breakthrough in the field of feminist science studies over the past twenty-five years has been the growing openness to the complex intermingling of feminist theory with science. By tracing developments in feminist science studies including the contributions of posthumanist ethics (Haraway 2008a; Braidotti 2013; Åsberg 2013) and cosmopolitics (Stengers 2010), the chapter explores the exciting ontological, epistemological, and ethical shifts that are now shaping the field.

There are undoubtedly many ways to organize the impressive range of scholarship that falls under the scope of feminist science studies. Rosser's (1989) own catalogue included feminist influence on the pedagogical and curricular transformation in science, the history and current status of women in science, feminist critiques of science, feminist theory of science, and "feminine" science. To emphasize the evolving role of feminist theory in feminist science studies, however, this chapter will focus on the "sex/gender binary," a concept that has served as a key analytical framework in feminist theory's explication of the known world. In addition to showing how some feminist science studies scholarship has attempted to incorporate the sex/gender binary into scientific analysis, I will also explain how others have reframed the sex/gender binary and related oppositions such as nature/nurture and biology/culture to reflect ontological lessons gathered from feminist activism and involvement with scientific inquiry itself.

Different traditions of feminist knowers have contributed *theoretically* to feminist science studies. Although feminist science/health/environmental activists and feminist users and producers of scientific knowledge are typically discussed only in relation to their empirical contributions, the empirical realm itself is theoretically constituted. Indeed, everything we know is already "theory all the way down" (Roosth and Schrader 2012, 2). Feminist science studies as a field has not only responded to feminist theory's interrogations of sex, gender, and sexual difference but has drawn theoretical insights into the body, biology, and medicine from feminist, intersex, and trans activism. Long aware of the limits of feminist theory's engagement with questions of sex and gender, the field of feminist science studies has cultivated different sets of analytical tools. Rather than treat race, class, sexuality, disability, and other markers as intersectional additives to a theoretical mainframe of sex and gender analysis, questions regarding the body, matter, materiality, difference, and nature in feminist science studies have been articulated through broader frameworks attentive to transnational processes of colonialism and postcolonialism; neoliberal capitalist practices of production, consumption, and commodification; and in the US context, women's social justice movements that situated emerging reproductive and genetic technologies in relation to histories of slavery and eugenics (Murphy 2009). Through a healthy feedback mechanism, the insights and practices in feminist science studies are now informing key concepts in feminist theory.

To trace feminist science studies contributions to theorizations of raced, classed, gendered, and sexualized embodiment, this chapter is divided in three parts. The first, "From the Women Question in Science to the Question of Sex and Gender in Biology," deals with the outcomes of feminist work to advance the participation of women and marginalized groups in science. Although continued efforts to measure the presence of these groups in science, technology, engineering, and math (STEM) are often associated with "pipeline" issues, I take a different approach. I will show how the deployment of the sex/gender binary and the liberal/equal rights feminist framework in science has produced new areas of scientific research, including "gender biology." The second section, "New Materialism, Feminist Theory, and Feminist Science Studies," reviews key themes in posthumanist and new materialist arguments that have produced important insights concerning feminist theory's relation to matter. By charting feminist science studies' relation to this "material turn," I show how one strand of feminist scholarship attempts to recover from the split between sex and gender and in the process reconceptualizes the relation between nature and culture.

After several decades of theorizing a firm distinction between sex and gender, particularly in English-speaking and Western feminisms, many feminists are finding the analytical tools of scientific research and feminist science studies useful in navigating a path back to matter, and to sex (interpreted as the biological). The third section, "Ethical Practices, Social Justice Epistemologies, and the Cutting Edge of Feminist Science Studies," focuses on feminist science studies and feminist science and technology studies (STS) scholarship, which considers issues of sex, gender, and matter to reground social justice epistemologies and the development of transformative ethical practices in the sciences. Explicit in their commitments to address the politics of power, race, sex, gender, sexuality, class, ability, and more, these approaches insist that politics is not peripheral to science but constitutive of the histories, presents, and futures of scientific knowledge production and technological progress.

From the Women Question in Science to the Question of Sex and Gender in Biology

During the 1970s and 1980s in the United States, women's rights activists mobilized to raise national awareness of gender discrimination in all aspects of life, public and private. One strand of activists documented and sought to redress the systematic underrepresentation of women in academic, business, political, religious, scientific, and technological careers. Motivated by calls for inclusion from the women's movement and from women members of Congress, government agencies such as the National Science Foundation (NSF) began collecting data documenting the underrepresentation of women and minorities in STEM fields (Epstein 2007). Within a decade, the NSF moved from tracking the number of women and minorities working in STEM in 1991 to implementing a grants program, Increasing the Participation and Advancement of Women in Academic Science and Engineering Careers (ADVANCE), to "develop a more diverse science and engineering workforce" (National Science Foundation 2014). According to ADVANCE, science itself did not need to change, it simply required a more diverse workforce.

Proponents of more inclusive science noted not only the absence of women and people of color as practicing scientists but also their exclusion from clinical trials. Again in response to activist agitation and a congressional mandate, in 1994, the National Institutes of Health (NIH) issued a policy and created specific guidelines for the inclusion of women and minorities as subjects in clinical research involving humans (National Institutes of Health 2000). Although the premise was once again that science itself did not have to change, the "add women and stir" approach quickly pressed scientists to rethink their assumption that the adult male body was the norm on the basis of which all other bodies should be measured.

Consider, for example, the recent announcement by the Food and Drug Administration (FDA) that zolpidem, the active agent in many sleep aids including Ambien, is metabolized differently in women than in men, and that in women there is an increased risk of "next-morning impairment for activities that require complete mental alertness, including driving" (US Food and Drug Administration 2013). To offset that risk, the FDA recommended that the "dose of zolpidem for women should be lowered from 10 mg to 5 mg for immediate-release products (Ambien, Edluar, and Zolpimist) and from 12.5 mg to 6.25 mg for extended-release products (Ambien CR) (US Food and Drug Administration

2013). Although the biological and molecular mechanisms for this difference in zolpidem drug processing are not yet known, scientists do know that if women had been included in clinical trials from the beginning of this pharmaceutical research, years of overdosage could have prevented. As this example makes clear, the absence of women from most clinical trials is problematic, not only for the health of women, but also for the adequacy of scientific assumptions and the validity of scientific findings. Despite growing evidence of the importance of including diverse populations in scientific research, the most basic lab science involving animal research continues to use only the cells, tissues, organs and bodies of male rats and mice. To address this deficiency, in May 2014 the NIH unveiled a new policy to ensure that preclinical research was sex-balanced by including female animals and cell lines obtained from females (Clayton and Collins 2014). For some scholars, however, simply including more women or female animals in biomedical research is equally problematic. For it is often not known whether different results that appear to be related to gender (or race) might be caused by an intervening variable. In the zolpidem case, for example, the difference may have more to do with variations in height or body weight than with sex. A presumption of sex (or race) difference therefore may be as troubling for scientific investigation as the absence of diverse populations from scientific research.

In light of such vexing questions, a research team led by feminist science studies scholar Londa Schiebinger created the web-based resource Gendered Innovations in Science, Health and Medicine, Engineering and Environment. Jointly sponsored by Stanford University, the NSF, and the European Commission, this online resource seeks to transform the inclusion question from an additive model to a sophisticated deployment of sex and gender as analytical categories in research design in order to produce new discoveries. According to the website, project goals are to develop "practical methods of sex and gender analysis for scientists and engineers" and to provide "case studies as concrete illustrations of how sex and gender analysis leads to innovation" (genderedinnovations.stanford.edu/). The project explicitly seeks to move researchers beyond thinking about the category "women" as a "subgroup" of scientists who can diversify the workforce or as an additional variable to be inserted into an existing experimental protocol. The site pays particular attention to presenting feminist epistemology and methodology in science in an accessible manner for the scientific expert who is not trained as, or inclined to identify as, a feminist researcher.

In addition to providing examples of practical methods and case studies, the project defines key terms, including sex and gender, introducing feminist concepts to scientists who are unfamiliar with feminist scholarship. In keeping with the sex/gender binary, sex is defined as "a biological quality" and gender as "a sociocultural process." Although these terms are treated as analytically distinct, a section titled "Interactions between Sex and Gender" emphasizes that the terms are not independent of one another:

> Sex and gender also interact in important and complex ways. Rarely does an observed difference between men and women involve only sex and not gender, and rarely does gender operate outside the context of sex. The precise nature of their

interaction will vary depending on the research question and on other factors, such as socioeconomic status, or geographic location, interacting with sex and gender."

(Gendered Innovations n.d.)

In addition, the section titled "Analyzing How Sex and Gender Interact" explains:

"Sex" and "gender" are distinguished for analytical purposes. "Sex" refers to biological qualities, and "gender" refers to socio-cultural processes. In reality, sex and gender interact (mutually shape one another) to form individual bodies, cognitive abilities, and disease patterns, for example. Sex and gender also interact to shape the ways we engineer and design objects, buildings, cities, and infrastructures. Recognizing how gender shapes sex and how sex influences culture is critical to designing quality research. Sex and gender also intersect in important ways with a variety of other social factors, including age, socioeconomic status, ethnicity, geographical location, etc.

(Gendered Innovations, n.d.)

This project represents a committed attempt to work with basic research and industry scientists to have them seriously consider the epistemological moorings of their scientific research by rethinking research priorities, reformulating research questions, considering participatory research and design methods, rethinking language and visual representations, and more. Nonetheless, in the context of recent developments in feminist theory, efforts to have scientists consider sex and gender in a dualistic and interactionist framework creates new sets of problems.

Although women should not be excluded from biomedical and technological research that could generate interventions to improve the quality of their lives, binary and interactionist views of sex and gender may do little more than pay lip service to issues of race, class, ability, and sexuality. The inclusion of women as subjects in clinical trials may make them the target of profit-motivated pharmaceutical companies complicit in the medicalization of women's health. Feminist science studies has called attention to such unsavory consequences of uncritical deployment of the sex/gender binary, while also questioning the viability of the sex/gender binary and the nature/culture distinction.

Over the past twenty-five years, feminist theorists and feminist science studies scholars have challenged dichotomous constructions of sex/gender, reconfiguring the materiality of the body. Drawing ontological lessons from recent theories developed in biology and physics, as well from certain poststructuralist debates, feminist scholars have argued that "biological processes are not exterior to culture," and that the category of "sex cannot be definitively disentangled from gender" (Rubin 2012, 891).

In *Gender Trouble*, Judith Butler posed a series of far-reaching questions:

Can we refer to a "given" sex or a "given" gender without first inquiring into how sex and/or gender is given, through what means? And what is "sex" anyway? Is it natural, anatomical, chromosomal, or hormonal, and how is a feminist critic to assess the scientific discourses which purport to establish such "facts" for us? ... Are the ostensibly natural facts of sex discursively produced by various scientific discourses in the service of other political social interests? If the immutable character of sex is contested, perhaps this construct called "sex" is as culturally constructed as gender; indeed, perhaps it was always already gender, with the consequence that the distinction between sex and gender turns out to be no distinction at all.

(Butler 1990, 10–11)

Multiple feminist scholars have challenged the sex/gender distinction. In *Volatile Bodies*, for example, Elizabeth Grosz (1994, 14) noted that "feminists have exhibited a wide range of attitudes and reactions to conceptions of the body and attempts to position it at the center of political action and theoretical production." Differentiating "sexual difference" approaches from "egalitarian feminism," and "social constructionism," Grosz suggested that thinkers such as Luce Irigaray, Helene Cixous, Gayatri Spivak, and Judith Butler were particularly wary of the sex/gender distinction. For these feminists, the body is not accepted as a blank biological slate upon which culture or gender is projected. Indeed, many sexual difference feminists understand the body to be active. In contrast to universal notions of essences or categories, the body is a "cultural interweaving and production of nature" (Grosz 1994, 18). As such, there are irreducible differences not only between the sexes but also among members of the same sex. Turning to Gilles Deleuze to help reconceptualize the body, Grosz notes,

[A] Deleuzian framework de-massifies the entities that binary thought counterposes against each other: the subject, the social order, even the natural world are theorized in terms of the microprocesses, a myriad of intensities and flows, with unaligned or unalignable components, which refuse to conform to the requirements of order and organization . . . Identities and stabilities are not fixed.

(Grosz 1994, 181)

Emphasizing the importance of understanding bodies, biologies, and microprocesses as phenomena comprising a multiplicity of differences, feminist science studies scholars have also questioned the stable ontological moorings associated with categorical notions of sex and gender. Indeed, many feminist science studies scholars have moved from elaborating the idea of the active or "lived body" to questioning "matter" itself. Turning to biology and physics for alternatives to binary frameworks, feminist science studies scholars have advanced an important critique of "interactionist" approaches. Rather than troubling the boundaries between sex and gender, interaction presupposes the existence of two separate realms, which come into contact.

The limits of an interactionist frame can be illustrated by emerging research in so-called "gender biology." In their attempts to investigate how gender interacts with biology, typically understood in terms of a gene or group of genes, scientists often envision a Venn diagram in which biology occupies one sector, gender occupies another sector, and a small space of overlap signifies the prospect of interactions. Although this limited interactionist framework might illuminate how gender (or race or class) inequalities produce biological *effects*, scientists tend to interpret the model in a far more reductionist way. Gender biology has been interpreted by scientists in a manner reminiscent of sociobiology, which relies upon biology, whether in the form of hormones or genes, to explain the *causes* of perceived gender differences.

Feminist biologists have theorized alternative models in order to avoid the trap of biological determinism so frequently associated with the sex/gender binary system and its accompanying interactionist paradigm. Developmental systems theory (DST), for example, offers a framework for understanding biology and development in relation to several major factors including (i) joint determination by multiple causes, (ii) context sensitivity and contingency, (iii) extended inheritance, (iv) development as construction, (v) distributed control, and (vi) evolution as construction (Oyama, Griffiths, and Gray 2003). DST conceptualizes organisms beyond familiar binaries, such as nature/nurture, genes/environment, and biology/culture. Feminist science studies scholar Anne Fausto-Sterling has perhaps been the most vocal champion of this theoretical frame through her work on intersex issues (2000), bones (2005), and more recently gender development in infants (2014). Yet DST also tells a cautionary tale for those who seek to move beyond dualisms. Despite the sophistication of the parameters within DST's heuristics, many scientists slip into interactionist conclusions. As Oyama, Griffiths, and Gray have noted,

> The standard response to nature/nurture oppositions is the homily that nowadays everyone is an interactionist: All phenotypes are the joint product of genes and environment. According to one version of this conventional "interactionist" position, the real debate should not be about whether a particular trait is due to nature or nurture, but rather how much each "influences" the trait. The nature/nurture debate is thus allegedly resolved in a quantitative fashion … DST rejects the attempt to partition causal responsibility for the formation of organisms into additive components. Such maneuvers do not resolve the nature/nurture debate; they continue it.
>
> (Oyama, Griffiths and Gray 2003, 1)

To avoid this outcome, feminist physicist Karen Barad (2007) has introduced the conception of "intra-action" as a means to move beyond the binary concepts of sex/gender, nature/nurture, biology/culture. Advancing an "agential realist ontology," Barad (2007, 33) suggests that "the primary ontological unit is not independent objects with independently determinate boundaries and properties but rather what Neils Bohr terms 'phenomena.'" Inspired by feminist theory, queer theory, poststructuralism, and quantum physics, Barad advocates this ontological view of phenomena in response to questions of social constructivism, materiality, and more specifically, to feminist and queer reworkings of sex and gender. Intra-action is key to this ontological framework:

> The neologism "intra-action" signifies the mutual constitution of entangled agencies. That is, in contrast to the usual "interaction," which assumes that there are separate individual agencies that precede their interaction, the notion of intra-action

recognizes that distinct agencies do not precede, but rather emerge through, their intra-action.

(Barad 2007, 33)

Barad's theorization of intra-action reworks traditional notions of causality and challenges binary relationships. Calling the preexistence and fixedness of any entity into question, phenomena are moments of "becoming with." Whether the phenomenon under investigation is an atom, a body, an experimental apparatus, a language, a scientific knower, or a collectivity, each emerges in and through relation to other entities. Intra-action, then, illuminates a relational ontology populated by mutually constituted phenomena, whose agency vastly exceeds the notion of the liberal individual.

Working with the categories of sex and gender in science, health, medicine and engineering, feminist science studies has moved well beyond questions concerning the underrepresentation of women and minorities in science. They have identified a host of theoretical and empirical problems that emerge when sex and gender are construed as a dichotomous formation. By taking those problematics as the ground for new theorization, feminist science studies scholars work with particular sciences to envision new ontologies redolent with concepts developed in feminist theory and to press the logic of inclusion until it actually becomes inclusionary.

New Materialism, Feminist Theory, and Feminist Science Studies

In *New Materialism: Interviews and Cartographies*, Rick Dophijn and Iris van der Tuin (2012, 13) describe new materialism as a new metaphysics that reinterprets previous work and creates a "new tradition" that alters understandings of the past, present, and future. Characterizing new materialism as a "transversal" cultural theory, they suggest that it "does not privilege matter over meaning or culture over nature. It explores a monist perspective, devoid of the dualisms that have dominated the humanities (and sciences) until today, by giving special attention to matter, which has been so neglected by dualist thought" (85). Claiming to provide an "immanent answer to transcendental humanism" (110), new materialists are intent on disassembling powerful dualisms (including sex and gender) in order to "do justice to the "material-semiotic," or "material-discursive" character of all events" (90).

Multiple strands of feminist theory contribute to the new materialism. Van der Tuin (2008) situates new materialism in relation to older forms of feminist materialism that championed monism and vitalism. Positioning new materialism as "the inheritor of feminist standpoint theory" (414), she traces continuities in feminist epistemological debates and philosophical engagements with materiality including historical materialism (van der Tuin 2008, 414; 2011). The term "new materialism" or "neo-materialism" has been credited to Rosi Braidotti (Dolphijn and van der Tuin 2012), whose work on posthumanism (2013) and feminist theories of subjectivity (1994) provide a basis for new materialist thinking. New materialism also traces its origin to Donna Haraway's (1988) conceptualization of the material-semiotic. Despite these long trajectories, it could be argued that recent scholarship under the name of feminist new materialism grows out of poststructuralist feminist theory's engagement with decades of work in feminist science studies.

The material turn as conceived in relation to poststructuralism and cultural theory stems from a very specific conversation within feminist theory, one which privileged postmodern constructivism and the significance of language to such an extent that matter appeared to be discursively constituted. Criticizing preoccupation with the discursive elements of bodies and power (Alaimo and Hekman 2008), material feminists as well as feminist new materialists sought to mitigate the influence of poststructuralism's linguistic idealism on feminist theory. Judith Butler's work is often taken as emblematic of feminist theory's "flight from nature" (Alaimo 2000) or, indeed, its "failed materiality" (Dolphijn and van der Tuin 2012, 94).

In her efforts to illuminate the cultural and constructed aspects of "sex," Butler (1993, 30) suggests that the body cannot be known outside of inscription or discourse: "To posit by way of language a materiality outside of language is still to posit that materiality, and the materiality so posited will retain that positing as its constitutive condition." Critics have claimed that Butler's refusal of any distinction between sex and gender precludes the possibility of material expressions of and by the body (Kirby 2006; Hekman 2008). Indeed, many feminist new materialists have interpreted this emphasis on language as an inherent inability to think about matter—whether coded as nature, atoms, the environment, or biology.

Although Butler's work in particular has served as a fertile ground for this criticism, several European feminist scholars have suggested that Butler is emblematic of a larger problematic characteristic of a particular strand of US feminist theory. Articulating a Eurocentric approach to new materialism, Rosi Braidotti, for example, has advanced a "friendly but firm criticism of American hegemony in feminist theory, . . . attempt[ing] to develop other perspectives, drawn from historical and situated European traditions" (Dolphijn and van der Tuin 2012, 27). Braidotti and other European new materialists point specifically to misleading interpretations of Simone de Beauvoir's work on sex, gender, and sexual difference spurred by Butler's article "Sex and Gender in Simone de Beauvoir's Second Sex" (1986). In contrast to Beauvoir's complex account, critics charge Butler with installing "a strict dualism" by overemphasizing the sex/gender split, and attributing to Beauvoir "an oversimplified idea of language" (Dolphijn and van der Tuin 2012, 143). European new materialists seek to rescue Beauvoir by foregrounding the undecidability of sexual difference in her works and promoting her ideas of "sexual differing" and a "performative understanding of ontology" (Dolphijn and van der Tuin 2012, 147).

New materialist scholar Vicky Kirby has raised a number of critical challenges through her close readings of Butler's analyses of nature/culture, discursive ontology, and conceptions of materiality. Turning Butler's (1990, 11) proposition that sex is "always already gender" on its head, Kirby (2008, 214) asks the risky question, "what if culture was really nature all along?". Indeed, Kirby explores the possibility that signs are "substantively or ontologically material" (219). Drawing examples from medical research in genetics, the cognitive sciences, and immunology, Kirby suggests that "life itself" is creative encryption (Kirby 2008; 2011; 2012). Calling attention to the agency and intelligence of "biological codes," Kirby suggests that the "code-cracking and encryption capacities of bacteria as they decipher the chemistry of antibiotic data and reinvent themselves accordingly" might well be considered "language skills" (219).

In suggesting that bacteria have language skills, Kirby seeks to persuade a particular audience of feminist theorists committed to a transcendental humanistic frame that language is biological and that biology has communicative capabilities. To support this posthumanist effort to acknowledge the communicative capacities of nonhumans and to consider life itself as a text, Kirby compares two contrasting interpretations of Derrida's (1997, 2) claim that "there is no outside of text." The first interpretation reflects the view of many critics of poststructuralism that,

> we are caught in an endless slide of referral that leads from one signifier to another signifier, one meaning to yet another meaning, in a vertiginous spiral of implication that never quite arrives at its destination. As a consequence, we can never retreat or advance to some natural, prediscursive, or extratextual space in order to test the truth or adequacy of our representations because, as we have seen, intelligibility is reckoned through such systems."
>
> (Kirby 1997, 60–61)

As an alternative interpretation, Kirby appeals to "the worlding of the world" as a

> writing in the general sense [which] articulates a differential of space/time, an inseparability between representation and substance that rewrites causality. It is as if the very tissue of substance, the ground of Being, is this mutable intertext—a "writing" that both circumscribes and exceeds the conventional divisions of nature and culture. If we translate this into what is normally regarded as the matter of the body, then, following Derrida, "the most elementary processes within the living cell" are also a "writing" and one whose "system" is never closed.
>
> (Kirby 1997, 61)

Kirby (2006, 84) makes a compelling case that cells write and that "it is in 'the nature of Nature' to write, to read and to model." The ontological openness of this stance accommodates feminist theories of agency and subjectivity that have made their way into feminist science studies through Haraway's (2003) conception of *naturecultures* and Braidotti's accounts of posthumanism (2013) and nomadic subjectivities (1994). Nonetheless, Kirby's exciting ontological reorientation of feminist new materialism seems to omit critical ethical conversations ongoing in feminist science studies that raise important questions about whose interests are served by this new ontological terrain. To gain insights into the import of this omission, it is helpful to return one more time to Derrida.

Many scholars have suggested that Derrida's (1997, 158) original phrase "il n'y a pas de hors-texte" is better translated as "there is no outside-text," rather than "there is no outside of text" or "there is nothing outside of the text." Derrida (1988) later noted, "The phrase which for some has become a sort of slogan, in general so badly understood, of deconstruction (there is nothing outside the text" [*il n'y a pas de hors-texte*]), means nothing else, there is nothing outside context" (136) or that "nothing *exists* outside context" (152).

It is the lack of context in Kirby's interpretation of Derrida in relation to "writing" and "Nature" that is troubling. As critical as Kirby's ontological intervention is in extending language, reading, and writing skills to the nonhuman is, it rings hollow without context. At its best, feminist science studies scholarship is immersed in the practices and data of specific sciences. The richness and credibility of science studies depend on systematic knowledge of minute details of particular fields. Yet this specificity is not apparent in Kirby's references to the "code-cracking," "encryption capacities," and "cryptographic skills" of bacteria.

To demonstrate what is lost in the absence of specificity, the final section of this chapter turns to the question of context, examining material feminist work that is grounded in feminist science studies and in feminist STS. From its immersion in particular sciences, this tradition of scholarship offers important insights into ethical practices required to support new ontological moorings that have evolved out of the sex/gender binary in feminist theory.

Ethical Practices, Social Justice Epistemologies, and the Cutting Edge of Feminist Science Studies

New materialism takes on quite different meanings in the context of feminist science studies than it has in encounters with postmodernist philosophy and cultural theory. In contrast to traditional science's claim to value neutrality, feminist science studies suggest that materialism is enmeshed with posthumanist ethics. In the words of Cecilia Åsberg,

> [A] posthuman ethics goes to the very enactment of bodies and the material-semiotics of the world of which we are collectively a part, but also to how we relate in scholarship.... This entails also an invocation to taking posthumanist ethics seriously in

relation to how we organize ourselves scholarly (posthumanist gender studies is but one suggestion among many).

(Åsberg 2013, 11)

A long tradition in feminist science studies has been driven by social justice epistemologies, which recognize that certain bodies, such as people of color, reproductive bodies, disabled bodies, animals, plants, and bodies subjected to colonialism, racism, capitalism, patriarchy, and science, have been inextricably tied to "nature" (Philip 2004; Roy and Subramaniam, forthcoming). Not all feminists have had the opportunity or the desire to join the flight from nature or from their biologies. As an example of this tradition, consider the papers published in a recent issue of *Scholar and Feminist Online* (2013) entitled *Life Un(Ltd): Feminism, Bioscience, Race*. Focusing on topics ranging from reproductive politics, postcolonial studies, and cross-species entanglements (Lee 2013; Onaga 2013) to chemical violence, sex workers, and biomedical prevention trials (Murphy 2013; Cooper 2013), these feminist works raise complex ontological and ethical questions regarding the objects of science and the knowers in science. Like other work in this tradition of feminist science studies, this scholarship uses social justice epistemologies not to erase or escape bonds with nature, but to develop innovative ways to think about the biological body.

This strand of feminist science studies places a great deal of importance on working out the ontological and ethical implications of feminist theorizing inside specific scientific contexts. Feminist scholars who grapple with the sciences are keenly aware that there are consequences of particular conceptions of the material world, which have profound implications for species other than our own. As Stacy Alaimo and Susan Hekman poignantly state in their introduction to *Material Feminisms*,

> Redefining the human and nonhuman has ethical implications: discourses have material consequences that require ethical responses. Ethics must be centered not only on those discourses but on the material consequences as well. . . . A material ethics entails . . . that we can compare the very real material consequences of ethical positions and draw conclusions from those comparisons. We can, for example, argue that the material consequences of one ethics is more conducive to human and nonhuman flourishing than that of another. Furthermore, material ethics allows us to shift the focus from ethical principles to ethical practices. Practices are, by nature, embodied, situated actions. Ethical practices, which unfold in time and take place in particular contexts, invite the recognition of and response to expected as well as unexpected material phenomenon. Particular ethical practices, situated both temporally and physically, may also allow for an openness to the needs, the significance, and the liveliness of the more-than-human world.

(Alaimo and Heckman 2008, 7–8)

With this emphasis on ethical practices and social justice, let us return to the ontological status of bacteria that write. There are good reasons for recognizing that bacteria have special talents, of which writing may be one. However, the statement that "it is in 'the nature of Nature' to write, to read and to model" (Kirby 2006, 84), has ethical implications, precisely because it redefines the human as well as the nonhuman. Impressed with the code-cracking and encryption capacities of bacteria, Kirby advocates recognition of these talents as "language skills" (219). Yet that recognition leaves many questions unasked and unanswered. Within a framework of ethical practices and social justice epistemologies, feminist science studies and feminist STS scholars would ask, what is the context in which bacteria are granted the skill to write? What happens when a notion of language is extended to Nature? What are the specific intra-actions and material consequences of this ontological maneuvering? In the specific case of bacteria, does writing, reading, and modeling "allow for an openness to the needs, the significance, and the liveliness of the more-than-human world" (Alaimo and Hekman 2008, 8)? Or does this feminist new materialist and posthumanist gesture support, promote, and benefit only the most humanist of causes? Even if it is accepted that Nature writes, reads, and models and that signs are "substantively or ontologically material" (Kirby 2008, 219), ethical and social justice concerns raise additional questions about the specificity and context of this ontology. Saying that bacteria write is the easy part, but whose interest does that writing serve? Are all forms of bacterial writing given credence or only bacterial writing in plasmid genomes that are valued for their mechanistic appeal? Does this new ontology ultimately serve as a "reshaping" for "productionist purposes" (Haraway 2008b, 178)?

In contrast to productionist purposes that presuppose the primacy of the human, posthumanist ethics emphasize that "ethics is an integral part of the diffraction (ongoing differentiating) patterns of worlding, not a superimposing of human values onto the ontology of the world" (Barad 2010, 265). Within this posthumanist frame, ethics involves learning "to respect and meet well with, even extend care to, others while acknowledging that *we may not know* the other" (Åsberg 2013, 8). Informed by ethical practices and social justice epistemologies, feminist science studies asks whether an ontology that recognizes the writing, reading, and modeling skills of Nature actually contributes to bacterial flourishing. Recent work on bacteria and the life sciences demonstrates why this question matters.

In *Biocapital: The Constitution of Postgenomic Life*, Kaushik Sunder Rajan (2006, 3) analyzes two important domains of current global consciousness. The first includes the life sciences, which he argues are "increasingly becoming information sciences." The second is capitalism, which he suggests has "defeated alternative economic formations such as socialism or communism and is therefore considered to be the 'natural' political economic formation, not just of our time but of all times" (3). As an STS scholar, Sunder Rajan insists that the life sciences and capitalism are coproduced. Indeed, he also stresses that the "life sciences are *overdetermined* by the capitalist political economic structures within which they emerge":

> "Overdetermination" is a term used by Louis Althusser to suggest a *contextual* relationship, but not a *causal* one.... In other words, even if a particular set of political economic formations do not in any direct and simplistic way lead to particular

epistemic emergences, they could still disproportionately set the stage within which the latter take shape in particular ways (Sunder Rajan 2006, 6).

Sunder Rajan's argument suggests that to discuss the ontological status of bacteria as writers, readers, and modelers, is to discuss them in a context structured by the domains of the life sciences and capitalism. Similar to their human, animal, and plant counterparts, in the purview of the life sciences, such as genetics, recombinant DNA technologies, and, in particular, synthetic biology, bacteria not only carry information, they *are* information. The sign becomes ontologically material here only through its labor. However attractive it might be to imagine bacteria's writing and language skills within a very different onto-ethical orientation, as life sciences are practiced under contemporary capitalism, bacteria's skills conveniently serve a highly mechanistic view of life, one that not just figuratively but literally forces bacteria to write. In the realm of synthetic biology, for example, bacteria such as *Escherichia coli* are being purposely bred to write. This writing consists in transcribing DNA and translating RNA, purposes that serve human interest alone. Once they perform these tasks, the bacteria are promptly snuffed out for their valuable proteins. This is not the high-profile life of cryptographers and code-breakers. More akin to the value of "natives in the jungle" for colonial science, bacterial writing becomes bacterial labor that is "harnessed and controlled" and "its products managed and turned into profitable use through the imposition of order and predictability" (Philip 2004, 197).

Feminist science studies and feminist STS have demonstrated that the presence of antibiotic resistant genes, coupled with the skills of lateral gene transfer through transformation, transduction, and conjugation have made bacteria of utmost interest to humans—not only for the study of diseases and antibiotic resistance. The observed ability of bacterial plasmid exchange and transformations led to the advent of recombinant DNA and genetic engineering technologies in the 1970s. Synthetic biology is but the latest face of genetic engineering, which, instead of combining a single gene of interest into a bacterial genome, inserts an entirely human-designed plasmid genome into "surrogate" bacterial cells. These cells are then mass (re)produced and utilized for their writing capabilities. In the context of bacteria writing in synthetic biology, feminist scholar Melinda Cooper (2008, 4), in *Life as Surplus: Biotechnology and Capitalism in the Neoliberal Era*, asks a quite different question: "where does (re)production end and technical invention begin, when life is put to work at the microbiological or cellular level?". Discussing "biological growth" in the context of neoliberal biopolitics, Cooper suggests that "neoliberalism reworks the value of life" by "effac(ing) the boundaries between the spheres of production and reproduction, labor and life, the market and living tissues" (9). In the context of bacteria, then, it is impossible to isolate and appreciate their special talents, including writing, outside the spheres of production, reproduction, and labor.

This discussion of bacterial writing serves as an example of what a feminist science studies/STS approach that emphasizes ethical practices has to offer to feminist theory. Incorporating social-justice epistemologies informed by histories of colonialism, class politics, civil rights movements, and women's reproductive and health movements, this tradition of feminist science studies insists that ontological claims must be sustained through ethical practices. Working in labs and in the field as scientists and with scientists, feminist science studies scholars place a definite emphasis on theorizing *practice* (Haraway 1997; Barad 2007; Roy 2008, 2011, 2012). As Nancy Tuana (2008, 209) has astutely observed, "It is easier to posit an ontology than to practice it." Karen Barad's attention to practice also distinguishes her work from that of new materialists outside the sciences. Indeed, Barad calls for the cultivation of knowledge practices that recognize the mutual imbrication of ontology, epistemology, and ethics:

> Practices of knowing and being are not isolable; they are mutually implicated. We don't obtain knowledge by standing outside the world; . . . The separation of epistemology from ontology is a reverberation of a metaphysics that assumes an inherent difference between human and nonhuman, subject and object, mind and body, matter and discourse. *Onto-epistem-ology*—the study of practices of knowing in being—is probably a better way to think about the kind of understandings that we need to come to terms with how specific intra-actions matter. Or, for that matter, what we need is something like an *ethico-onto-epistem-ology*—an appreciation of the intertwining of ethics, knowing, and being—since each intra-action matters, since the possibilities for what the world may become call out in the pause that precedes each breath before a moment comes into being and the world is remade again, because the becoming of the world is a deeply ethical matter.
>
> (Barad 2007, 185)

Similarly, Stacy Alaimo's transcorporeal ethics echoes this call for the substitution of ethically informed, practice-based analysis for empty ontological stances:

> A material, transcorporeal ethics would turn from the disembodied values and ideals of bounded individuals toward an attention to situated, evolving practices that have far-reaching and often unforeseen consequences for multiple peoples, species, and ecologies.
>
> (Alaimo 2008, 253)

Feminist science studies can offer feminist theory three important insights into what might be considered a robust feedback mechanism. The first emphasizes the importance of context. As articulated by "situated feminist technoscience," feminist scholarship must engage the responsibility and challenges of context-based and ethically informed analysis (Murphy 2012, 98). The second insight involves a relentless commitment to issues of social justice, attuned to the understanding that ontologies have immediate ethical implications. The third point emphasizes that feminist theorizing benefits from sustained attention to the development of feminist practices inside the sciences. As manifested in the best work emerging in feminist science studies today, these three features work against the hubris of philosophical abstraction and scientific mastery.

Conclusion

Feminist theory in science, feminist theory of science, and feminist theory out of science might all be considered efforts to bring feminist theory and feminist science studies together, to create conditions in which each can "meet the other well." There is no question that, thanks to these encounters, feminist science studies have evolved a great deal over the last few decades. Yet like any logic of encounter, these approaches rely on the presumption of inherent separability between feminist theory and science. Within their bounded spheres, feminist theory appears mobile and changing, while science appears to remain anchored and relatively still. Attached to that stillness comes a certain weight and authority, which seem to elude the changeling—feminist theory. To gauge the power of that authority, consider how different the field might appear if it bore the label, the "science of feminist theory," "science in feminist theory," or "science out of feminist theory."

Feminist STS scholar Michelle Murphy probes the difference it might make to envision feminist knowledge as science. In her groundbreaking book *Seizing the Means of Reproduction: Entanglements of Feminism, Health, and Technoscience*, Murphy (2012, 100) reconsiders the iconic protocol of vaginal self-exams in feminist self-help movements as "the most sustained efforts to practice *science as feminism*" (emphasis added). Murphy undertakes this reformulation as a "commitment to oppositional tactics of knowledge production" (98). Thinking *science as feminism* need not entail oppositional politics rife with irony or negation; instead, it might develop oppositional politics of the cosmopolitical kind (Stengers 2010), which promotes productive, boundary-breaching work.

Feminist science studies are boundary breaching, particularly when feminist insights are culled through intensive engagement with the intricacies of particular sciences. Manifested in vastly different modes of inquiry, these innovative approaches interrogate binaries, difference, and ontologies of becoming. Imbued with rich legacies from diverse modes of feminist theory, feminist projects in science studies ask impossible questions. But it is precisely the impossibility of the questions that carves out a common space for feminist theory, feminist science studies, and science. This is the space of shared perplexity, where feminists and scientists, with their different sets of practices and expertise, come together to devise common objects of knowledge. Coming to know is an onto-ethico-epistemological process. In their labs, classrooms, and everyday research practices, feminist science scholars participate in this complex process as they seek to meet the other well, keenly aware that knowledge of the other may elude them even when they meet; and yet they bear ethical responsibility to care for the known and the unknown.

Acknowledgments

The author would like to extend thanks to the editors for their insightful suggestions in revising this chapter, and to Banu Subramaniam for commenting on an earlier draft.

References

Alaimo, S. 2000. *Undomesticated Ground: Recasting Nature as Feminist Space.* Ithaca, NY: Cornell University Press.

Alaimo, S., and S. Hekman. 2008. "Introduction: Emerging Models of Materiality in Feminist Theory." In *Material Feminisms*, 1–19. Bloomington: Indiana University Press.

Åsberg, C. 2013. "The Timely Ethics of Posthumanist Gender Studies." *feministische studien* 1: 7–12.

Barad, K. 2007. *Meeting the Universe Halfway: Quantum Physics and the Entanglement of Matter and Meaning.* Durham, NC: Duke University Press.

Barad, K. 2010. "Quantum Entanglements and Hauntological Relations of Inheritance: Dis/continuities, SpaceTime Enfoldings, and Justice-to-Come." *Derrida Today* 3.2: 240–268.

Braidotti, R. 1994. *Nomadic Subjects: Embodiment and Sexual Difference in Contemporary Feminist Theory.* New York: Columbia University Press.

Braidotti, R. 2013. *The Posthuman.* Cambridge: Polity Press.

Butler, J. 1986. "Sex and Gender in Simone de Beauvoir's Second Sex." *Yale French Studies* 72: 35–49.

Butler, J. 1990. *Gender Trouble: Feminism and the Subversion of Identity.* New York: Routledge.

Butler, J. 1993. *Bodies That Matter: On the Discursive Limits of "Sex."* New York: Routledge.

Clayton, J., and F. Collins. 2014. "Policy: NIH to balance sex in cell and animal studies." *Nature* 509: 282–283.

Cooper, M. 2008. *Life as Surplus: Biotechnology and Capitalism in the Neoliberal Era.* Seattle: University of Washington Press.

Cooper, M. 2013. "Double Exposure: Sex Workers, Biomedical Prevention Trials, and the Dual Logic of Global Public Health." *Scholar and Feminist Online* 11 (3). Available from http://sfonline.barnard.edu/life-un-ltd-feminism-bioscience-race/.

Derrida, J. 1988. *Limited Inc.* Evanston, IL: Northwestern University Press.

Derrida, J. 1997. *Of Grammatology.* Translated by Gayatri Chakravorty Spivak. Baltimore, MD: Johns Hopkins University Press.

Dolphijn, R., and I. van der Tuin. 2012. *New Materialism: Interviews and Cartographies.* Ann Arbor, MI: Open Humanities Press.

Epstein, S. 2007. *Inclusion: The Politics of Difference in Medical Research.* Chicago: University of Chicago Press.

Fausto-Sterling, A. 2000. *Sexing the Body: Gender Politics and the Construction of Sexuality.* New York: Basic Books.

Fausto-Sterling, A. 2005. "The Bare Bones of Sex: Part I—Sex and Gender." *Signs: Journal of Women in Culture and Society* 30 (2): 1491–1527.

Fausto-Sterling, A. 2014. "How Your Generic Baby Acquires Gender." Podcast available from http://www3.unil.ch/wpmu/neurogenderings3/podcasts/.

Gendered Innovations in Science, Health and Medicine, Engineering, and Environment. n.d. "Terms." Available from the Gendered Innovations website. http://genderedinnovations.stanford.edu/terms.html. Accessed July 21, 2014.

Grosz, E. 1994. *Volatile Bodies: Toward a Corporeal Feminism.* Bloomington: Indiana University Press.

Haraway, D. 1988. "Situated Knowledges: The Science Question in Feminism and the Privilege of Partial Perspective." *Feminist Studies* 14 (3): 575–599.

Haraway, D. 1997. *Modest_Witness@Second_Millenium.FemaleMan_Meets_OncoMouse: Feminism and Technoscience.* New York: Routledge.

Haraway, D. 2003. *Companion Species Manifesto: Dogs, People, and Significant Otherness.* Chicago: Prickly Paradigm Press.

Haraway, D. 2008a. *When Species Meet*. Minneapolis: University of Minnesota Press.
Haraway, D. 2008b. "Otherworldly Conversations, Terran Topics, Local Terms." In *Material Feminisms*, edited by S. Alaimo and S. Hekman, 157–187. Bloomington: Indiana University Press.
Harding, S. 1989. "Is There a Feminist Method?" In *Feminism and Science*, edited by N. Tuana, 17–32. Bloomington: Indiana University Press.
Hekman, S. 2008. "Constructing the Ballast: An Ontology for Feminism." In *Material Feminisms*, edited by S. Alaimo and S. Hekman, 85–119. Bloomington: Indiana University Press.
Keller, E. F. 1989. "The Gender/Science System; or, Is Sex to Gender as Nature is to Science?" In *Feminism and Science*, edited by N. Tuana, 33–44. Bloomington: Indiana University Press.
Kirby, V. 1997. *Telling Flesh: The Substance of the Corporeal*. New York: Routledge.
Kirby, V. 2006. *Judith Butler: Live Theory*. London: Continuum International.
Kirby, V. 2008. "Natural Convers(at)ions; or, What if Culture Was Really Nature All Along?" In *Material Feminisms*, edited by S. Alaimo and S. Hekman, 214–236. Bloomington: Indiana University Press.
Kirby, V. 2011. *Quantum Anthropologies: Life at Large*. Durham, NC: Duke University Press.
Kirby, V. 2012. "Initial Conditions." *differences: A Journal of Feminist Cultural Studies* 23 (3): 197–205.
Lee, R. 2013. "Parasexual Generativity and Chimeracological Entanglements in Amitav Ghosh's *The Calcutta Chromosome*." *Scholar and Feminist Online* 11 (3). Available from http://sfonline.barnard.edu/life-un-ltd-feminism-bioscience-race/.
Longino, H. 1989. "Can There Be a Feminist Science?" In *Feminism and Science*, edited by N. Tuana, 45–57. Bloomington: Indiana University Press.
Murphy, M. 2009. "Gender and Sex." In *The Palgrave Dictionary of Transnational History*, edited by A. Iriye and P. Saunier. London: Palgrave Macmillan.
Murphy, M. 2012. *Seizing the Means of Reproduction: Entanglements of Feminism, Health, and Technoscience*. Durham, NC: Duke University Press.
Murphy, M. 2013. "Distributed Reproduction, Chemical Violence, and Latency." *Scholar and Feminist Online* 11 (3). Available from http://sfonline.barnard.edu/life-un-ltd-feminism-bioscience-race/.
National Institutes of Health. 2000. NIH Guideline on the Inclusion of Women and Minorities as Subjects in Clinical Research. Available from http://grants.nih.gov/grants/funding/women_min/guidelines_update.htm. Accessed July 21, 2014.
National Science Foundation. 2014. ADVANCE at a Glance. Available from http://www.nsf.gov/crssprgm/advance/index.jsp.
Onaga, L. 2013. "Bombyx and Bugs in Meiji Japan: Toward a Multispecies History." *Scholar and Feminist Online* 11(3). Available fromhttp://sfonline.barnard.edu/life-un-ltd-feminism-bioscience-race/.
Oyama, S., P. E. Griffiths, and R. D. Gray. 2003. *Cycles of Contingency: Developmental Systems and Evolution*. Cambridge, MA: MIT Press.
Philip, K. 2004. *Civilizing Natures: Race, Resources, and Modernity in Colonial South India*. New Brunswick, NJ: Rutgers University Press.
Roosth, S., and Schrader, A. 2012. "Feminist Theory out of Science: Introduction." *differences: A Journal of Feminist Cultural Studies* 23 (3): 1–8.
Rosser, S. 1989. "Feminist Scholarship in the Sciences: Where Are We Now and When Can We Expect a Theoretical Breakthrough?" In *Feminism and Science*, edited by N. Tuana, 3–14. Bloomington: Indiana University Press.

Roy, D. 2004. "Feminist Theory in Science: Working Towards a Practical Transformation." *Hypatia: A Journal of Feminist Philosophy* 19 (1): 255–279.

Roy, D. 2008. "Asking Different Questions: Feminist Practices for the Natural Sciences." *Hypatia: A Journal of Feminist Philosophy* 23 (4): 134–157.

Roy, D. 2011. "Feminist Approaches to Inquiry in the Natural Sciences: Practices for the Lab." In *The Handbook of Feminist Research: Theory and Praxis*, edited by S. Hesse-Biber, 313–330. London: Sage Publications.

Roy, D. 2012. "Cosmopolitics and the Brain: The Co-Becoming of Practices in Feminism and Neuroscience." In *Neurofeminism: Issues at the Intersection of Feminist Theory and Cognitive Science*, edited by R. Bluhm, A. J. Jacobson, and H. Maibom, 175–192. New York: Palgrave Macmillan.

Roy, D., and B. Subramaniam. Forthcoming. "Matter in the Shadows: Feminist New Materialism and the Practices of Colonialism." In *Mattering: Feminism, Science and Materialism,* edited by V. Pitts-Taylor. New York: New York University Press.

Rubin, D. 2012. '"An Unnamed Blank That Craved a Name': A Genealogy of Intersex as Gender." *Signs: Journal of Women in Culture and Society* 37 (4): 883–908.

Stengers, I. 2010. *Cosmopolitics I*. Translated by Robert Bononno. Minneapolis: University of Minnesota Press.

Sunder Rajan, K. 2006. *Biocapital: The Constitution of Postgenomic Life*. Durham, NC: Duke University Press.

Tuana, N. 1989. Preface to *Feminism and Science*, vii–xi. Bloomington: Indiana University Press.

Tuana, N. 2008. "Viscous Porosity: Witnessing Katrina." In *Material Feminisms,* edited by S. Alaimo and S. Hekman, 188–213. Bloomington: Indiana University Press.

US Food and Drug Administration. 2013. "FDA Drug Safety Communication: Risk of Next-Morning Impairment after Use of Insomnia Drugs; FDA Requires Lower Recommended Doses for Certain Drugs Containing Zolpidem. Ambien, Ambien CR, Edluar and Zolpimist." Available from http://www.fda.gov/drugs/drugsafety/ucm334033.htm. Accessed July 21, 2013.

van der Tuin, I. 2008. "Deflationary Logic: Response to Sara Ahmed's Imaginary Prohibitions: Some Preliminary Remarks on the Founding Gestures of the 'New Materialism.'" *European Journal of Women's Studies* 15 (4): 411–416.

van der Tuin, I. 2011. "New Feminist Materialisms." *Women's Studies International Forum* 34: 271–277.

CHAPTER 41

SEX/GENDER

MARA VIVEROS VIGOYA

A Brief History of the Concept

The history of the modern concept of gender, which distinguishes between biological and social sex, has been sedimented over several decades, and includes contributions from different disciplines. It is important to note, as Joan Scott does (Butler et al. 2007), that the feminist use of the term *gender* is first and foremost an appropriation. Although the feminist movement of the second half of the twentieth century contributed to its widespread diffusion, the concept was not developed within the movement itself (Scott 2010).

The works of Margaret Mead and Simone de Beauvoir are often cited as antecedents of the concept. Mead's (1935) field research demonstrated that masculine and feminine roles vary socially and culturally, and do not depend on biology. She documented the arbitrariness and nonuniversal character of these cultural classifications, and defended the rights of people to freely express their individuality. Despite the importance of her work, Mead did not question the hierarchical ordering of men's and women's status (Hurtig and Pichevin 1991; Delphy 2001). This critique was advanced by Beauvoir in *The Second Sex* ([1949] 1953). Working from the existentialist view that every human being is singularly situated, Beauvoir suggested that in the case of a woman, the singularity of her situation lies in part in being positioned as Other, as an object destined to immanence, without the possibility of conceptualizing herself as a Subject through her projects. Beauvoir sought to demonstrate that women are not naturally constituted but produced as a historically variable cultural project. This is what she meant when she proposed: "One is not born but becomes a woman" (Beauvoir [1949] 1953, 267).

Several works (Fausto-Sterling 2000b; Fassin 2008; Dorlin 2008; Preciado 2009, among others) have called attention to the use of the term *gender* in medical discourses since the end of the 1940s, which in the United States, aimed to explain so-called sexual deviance. Psychologist John Money reformulated Mead's findings about the socialization of boys and girls, first introducing the concept of "gender roles" in his doctoral dissertation (Preciado 2009). Money deployed this concept in conjunction with his efforts to normalize, through hormonal and surgical treatments, the sex of "hermaphrodite" children (today labeled as intersexual), whose sexual organs were considered indeterminate by medicine (Money and Ehrhardt 1972; Preciado 2009).

Money affirmed that "sexual behavior and orientation as male or female does not have an innate, instinctive basis." Yet he did not take the additional step of claiming that the categories "feminine" and "masculine" are without biological basis. Nor did he question the assumption of the existence of only two sexes. His aim was solely to understand "normal" development (Fausto-Sterling 2000a, 73). It was psychiatrist Robert Stoller who popularized the term *gender identity* by founding the Gender Identity Research Clinic in 1954; but Stoller used the concept of gender in a descriptive rather than an analytical way. Stoller's main contribution was to differentiate sexual identity—the sense of belonging to a biological sex—from gender, which was the product of a determined socialization (Molinier in Delphy et al. 2012). Stoller developed this distinction in his book *Sex and Gender: On the Development of Masculinity and Femininity* (1968).

The transformation of a normative conceptualization of gender into a critical tool in theoretical and political terms is the result of feminism as a social movement. Indeed, in her book *Sex, Gender and Society* (1972), British sociologist and feminist Ann Oakley radicalized the use that Money and Stoller had made of the concept of gender. Interrogating the order of the sexes and sexualities from a critical perspective, Oakley suggested that a sense of belonging to the feminine or the masculine gender is not automatic but the result of learning. From Oakley on, pioneer scholars of this new field of research sought to "denaturalize" sex.

THE SEX/GENDER DYAD: FEMINIST DEBATES OF THE SECOND WAVE

In 1975, two volumes considered foundational to US feminist anthropology (Rosaldo and Lamphere 1974; Reiter 1975) advanced debates about the distinction between nature and culture, and the cultural variability of gender roles.[1] Sherry Ortner (1974) attempted to explain the origin of the subordination of women through the common association of nature with women and culture with men and the symbolic hierarchy that privileged culture over nature. Through an extensive investigation of ethnographic material, Michelle Rosaldo (1974) offered an alternative explanation of the subordination of women, grounded in the asymmetrical association of the public sphere with men and the domestic sphere with women, and the systemic privileging of the public male domain over the private.

In one of the most cited articles, "The Traffic in Women," Gayle Rubin (1975) proposed a feminist rereading of the theories of Claude Lévi-Strauss, Karl Marx and Friedrich Engels, Sigmund Freud and Jacques Lacan. Her critique provided a radical reinterpretation Lévi-Strauss's claims about the incest taboo as being not only the foundation of kinship but the norm that initiates culture. In Rubin's artful analysis, the exogamous marriage practices that Lévi-Strauss hailed as a cultural achievement were refigured as "the traffic in women." Rubin's study (1975, 158), considered today one of the most influential in gender theory, identified the existence of "a systematic social apparatus which takes up females as raw materials and fashions domesticated women as products." Referring to this transformative apparatus as the "sex/gender system," Rubin pointed out that, through marriage, kinship systems "transform males and females into 'men' and 'women,' each an incomplete half which can only find wholeness when united with the other" (179). Advancing a devastating critique of naturalist perspectives, Rubin defined gender as "a socially imposed division of the sexes" and "a product of the social relations of sexuality" (179).

Between the end of the 1970s and the mid-1980s, US feminist debates concerning "gender difference" pitted "equality feminists" against "difference feminists." Equality feminism, articulated in the early works of Betty Friedan (1963) and Shulamith Firestone (1970), dominated the US feminist scene until the end of the 1970s. Conceptualizing gender difference as an "instrument and artifact of male dominance," equality feminists sought to "throw off the shackles of 'difference' and establish equality" (Fraser 1997, 175–176). By contrast, difference feminism, which emerged at the end of the 1970s, encouraged the re-evaluation of femininity, opposing the androcentric and sexist undervaluation of feminine achievements. In her well-known work *In a Different Voice: Psychological Theory and Women's Development* (1982) Carol Gilligan, for example, argued that theories of moral development, which privileged adherence to Kantian norms of universalizability, while devaluing contextualized decision-making, reflected a masculine model of reasoning that haunted the Western philosophical canon.

By demonstrating that the biological and the social belonged to distinct domains, and that social inequalities on the grounds of sex were not "natural," feminist works sought to disrupt notions that power inequalities between men and women derived from anatomical differences. Toward that end, gender was conceptualized as the cultural elaboration of sexual difference, which opened a space for the analysis and denunciation of the social construction of inequalities between the sexes. Although Rubin had analyzed the relation between sex and gender as an interdependence, the great majority of feminist authors in this period defined gender on the basis of sex, as if sex preceded gender temporally—and therefore logically.

This widely shared presupposition was questioned by the French collectives that gathered around what is known as *materialist feminism*, a movement that conceptualized the sexes not only as "biosocial" categories but also as classes (in the Marxist sense), constituted by and through the power men have over women (Mathieu 2000). For authors such as Nicole-Claude Mathieu, Christine Delphy, Paola Tabet, Colette Guillaumin, and Danièle Kergoat, there are no natural dominations, only those that are materially constituted by dividing people into dominant and dominated groups. Delphy (2001), one of the emblematic figures of this current of thought, emphasized that power relations between men and women define gender, affording gender precedence over sex.

For Delphy, gender constructs sex by establishing a hierarchical sexual dichotomy, presenting sexual categories as antagonistic and organizing unequal norms, rights, and opportunities on the basis of sex.

One of the key concepts for this current of thought is "patriarchy," understood as a system of subordination of women based on economic relations (Delphy 2001, 141). Within this system, women are described as a "class" founded upon the production of free domestic labor, which defines women's oppression and exploitation in completely material terms (Bereni et al. 2008, 23). The sexual division of labor and the social relations of sex (*rapports sociaux de sexe*)[2] emerge as inseparable terms that form an epistemological system (Kergoat 2000, 40).

In the 1970s and 1980s, feminist theoretical reflections and political positions in France were structured around two axes—work and sexuality—which bear some resemblance to the posterior equality/difference debates in the United States. In the intense exchanges between the group Psychanalyse et Politique and the feminist materialists, sexuality[3] and work were presented as siloed and opposed domains (Molinier, 2014; Fougeyrollas-Schwebel 2005, 16). The psychoanalytic feminists accorded priority to a symbolic revolution that would redefine representations of sexual difference and open the possibility of other types of thinking and culture (Fouque 1995). Luce Irigaray ([1974] 1985) advanced a dramatic reinterpretation of fundamental categories of psychoanalysis, from the question of the feminine unconscious to the nature of the feminine body and the bond between women and their mothers. Denouncing the "hom(m)osexualité" of Freudian and Lacanian representations of female sexuality, Irigaray suggested that these phallocentric approaches radically repressed "the feminine."

The materialist feminists, by contrast, accorded primacy to the historical and social, and therefore arbitrary and reversible, character of sexual hierarchy, insisting that "women" existed as a social group as a result of their oppression and exploitation by the social class of "men." Offering contradictory diagnoses of the causes of women's oppression and opposing strategies for social change, French psychoanalytic and materialist feminists shared little ground. Those committed to critique of the dominant symbolic order and those searching to abolish "sex difference" and effective tactics to promote equality offered two irrefutable and mutually exclusive theoretical positions (Fougeyrollas-Schwebel 2005), ignoring that they are two imperative fields of feminist action and thought. Later theoretical works and political activism, however, found means to bridge the opposition that pitted work against sexuality through notions such as "sexual labor" (Molinier, 2014).

In the United States, the debates between equality and difference were based on very distinct ideological and philosophical foundations. For example, in the United States the struggle for equality between men and women is largely inspired by liberalism, as opposed to Marxism, and the criticism of androcentrism is based on object relations theory as posed by Chodorow (1999), and not on a discussion involving Freudian and Lacanian theories, as Irigaray presented. Numerous scholars criticized the "equality" versus "difference" debate in the United States for ignoring the interdependence between equality and difference and losing track of the power relations that allowed an opposition between equality and inequality to be transformed into an antagonism between equality and difference (Scott 1996; Fraser 1997; De Lauretis 1987; Fougeyrollas-Schwebel 2005; Varikas 2006; Butler et al. 2007). In subsequent analyses, "difference" emerged as a plural concept that transcended a dichotomy between the sexes and encompassed the diversity among "women," "mn" and other gender positions (De Lauretis 1987). As a consequence, the feminist agenda grew to oppose multiple social inequalities as well as cultural androcentrism and heteronormativity (Fraser 1997).

In addition, pioneering work illuminated the internal complexity and the polysemy that characterize the concept of gender (Hawkesworth 1997) and its reference to diverse levels of analysis and to diverse logics that superimpose each other and follow different historical trajectories (Connell 1987). Sandra Harding, R. W. Connell, and Joan Scott proposed multidimensional definitions of gender. Harding (1983) identified three closely related elements: gender as a category that confers meaning to social practice as a mode of organizing social relations and as a structure of personal identity. Analyzing gender as a structure, Connell (1987) distinguished relations of power, production, and *cathexis* (emotional bonds), all organized around sexual desire. In one of the most widely cited articles, Scott (1986, 1067) conceived gender as "a constitutive element of social relationships based on perceived differences between the sexes" that "involves four interrelated elements:" a symbolic aspect, a normative aspect, an institutional aspect and a subjective aspect.[4] In addition, Scott noted that "gender is a primary way of signifying relationships of power" (1069).

These theorizations of gender emphasized the complexity of the concept, the politics involved in constructions of gender, and the necessity of making more rigorous use of gender as an analytical category, "without falling into untenable claims concerning gender's explanatory force" (Hawkesworth 1997, 713). Seeking to move beyond descriptive uses of gender, Scott (1986) analyzed how gender constitutes and is constituted by the political (Varikas 2006). Connell (1987) pointed out that gender, as a structure that orders social practice, interacts with other social structures, such as race, class, nationality, or position in the world order. "To understand gender, then, we must constantly go beyond gender," since "gender relations are a major component of social structure as a whole" (Connell 1995, 76).

Despite the resistances that "gender" elicited and still elicits, this term has been incorporated into a scientific vocabulary even in languages in which it is not part of the normal lexicon.[5] The use of "gender" has given respectability to feminist studies within scientific circles, which had previously been suspicious of the partiality and militancy of feminist analysis (Scott 1986). The concept of gender and the distinction between sex and gender, which foregrounds gender as a social and cultural construction, have gained wide purchase. Nonetheless, the nature of the relation between sex and gender remains a subject of controversy (Varikas 2006), as does the place that men and masculinities can or should occupy in feminist theories and theories of gender.

Men and Masculinities in Feminist Theories and Theories of Gender

The historical relationship between feminist theories and discussions of men and masculinities is long-standing. Feminist theorists like Beauvoir ([1949] 1953) questioned the masculine appropriation of universal humanity. In the 1960s, some liberal feminists in the United States struggled for equal access of men and women to social goods and opportunities, and demanded that women and men be measured by the same standards (Gardiner 2005). Only a segment of feminism criticized the conception of rationality associated with masculinity. In the same time frame, French feminists argued that men as a group benefited from the subordination of women as a social group, despite large disparities among men or subgroups of men (Viveros Vigoya 2008).

Throughout the 1980s, feminists of color called attention to interconnections between gender inequalities and other hierarchies of difference. Black feminism and Third World feminism emphasized shared oppressions among women and men within their own communities, insisting that masculinity be organized as a historically and culturally specific construction (Combahee River [1977] 1983; Mohanty 1988). In addition, post-structuralist debates within feminism from the end of the 1990s onwards questioned binary oppositions such as men/women and heterosexual/homosexual. By contributing to an understanding that there are masculinities without men, like those expressed by lesbian subcultures, such as drag-kings, butches, *camioneras, garçonnes*, leather lesbians (Rubin 2011), this work eroded "this widespread indifference to female masculinity [. . .] [that] has sustained the complex social structures that wed masculinity to maleness and to power and domination" (Halberstam 1998, 2).

Although gender was conceived as a relational category from the outset, most feminist studies focused exclusively on women. This was due in part to feminist efforts to illuminate patriarchal oppression (Carabí and Armengol 2009), and in part, to the challenge of overcoming methodological individualism and in thinking in politico-relational terms (Stolcke 1996). In the mid-1970s, however, "women's studies" inspired a new field of "men's studies" or "masculinity studies," as Michael Kimmel (2009), one of its founders, prefers to call it.

Although there are many ways to study masculinity (Clatterbaugh 1997), Kimmel (1992) distinguishes two major orientations: those who define themselves as "allies" of feminism, ground masculinity studies in feminist theory and press men to recognize their participation in social power[6]; and those who advance an autonomous approach to studying masculinity, aimed at strengthening those men who feel devoid of power. Australian feminist R. W. Connell (1995), who has played a critical role in advancing research about masculinities, laments that the field has "failed to produce a coherent science of masculinity" because it has assumed that masculinity is "an isolated object" rather than "an aspect of a larger structure" of gender (67). Connell also notes that the field has devoted too little attention to masculinity as a structure of social practices that men and women engage through bodily experience, personality, and culture (71).

Arguing that masculinity studies are an important contribution to gender studies and to social change, Kimmel (2009, 19) has suggested that masculinity studies seek to question and transform the mechanisms that create and reproduce masculinity; while also demonstrating that most men, despite the power they have over women, do not feel powerful today. Indeed, Kimmel notes that men do not batter women when they feel powerful but when they feel powerless, or when they believe they do not possess the rights they should have. Echoing Kimmel's observation, Éric Fassin has distinguished in Fabre and Fassin (2003) between "traditional" masculine domination and "reactionary" modern domination that arises in response to a perceived loss of power.

According to Fassin, unlike traditional domination, modern masculine domination is no longer grounded on the assumed inequality between the sexes, or on the perpetuation of an immemorial and unquestionable patriarchal order. It is defined "in reaction" to challenges to the patriarchal order posed by the demands of feminist as well as gay and lesbian social movements for freedom and equality (Fabre and Fassin 2003, 42). In this sense, it constitutes an undertow or backlash phenomenon designed to curb these achievements. While traditional masculine domination presupposed masculine power, reactionary domination reflects, on the contrary, a perceived loss of power and a defensive reaction. Multiple contemporary groups in diverse nations have been created to protect the rights of men against what they have called "the excesses of feminism."

Sex and Sexuality

From the outset, feminist theory has made numerous efforts to "remove women from the category of nature and to place them in culture as constructed and self-constructing social subjects in history" (Haraway 1991, 134). For this reason, feminists have had a complicated relationship to questions concerning nature, biology, or the body, particularly as articulated in reductionist accounts that assume anatomical, hormonal, or chromosomal determinism. In early feminist works, the concept of the sexed body occupied an ahistorical and nonproblematized position. In the 1990s, however, sex was reconceptualized, not as a natural reality, but in relation to biological materiality. Feminist scholars suggested that gender precedes sex and constitutes it in a corresponding social reality, raising questions about the "evident" anatomical differences that seemed to exceed sheer social expression. As feminist theorists probed the meaning of "sex," their analyses shifted from an anatomo-physiological frame that emphasized genital organs to a discursive frame that examined rhetorical figures, such as synecdoche, in which "a part of something is used to represent the whole." When groups of people are identified by genitalia, anatomical sex becomes an exterior sign, a symbol of and principle of identification for men and women (Bereni et al. 2008, 24).

Historically, conceptualizations of sex have varied greatly. In *Making Sex* (1990), Thomas Laqueur showed that from classical Greek medical texts to the eighteenth century, feminine and masculine bodies were perceived as fundamentally similar. Within the "one-sex model," the feminine body was conceptualized not as a body of a different sex, but as a lesser version of the masculine body. The "two sex model" that defines male and female embodiment as an opposition, or as mutually exclusive categories emerged only in the seventeenth century, giving rise to the notion that sex is determined by physiopathology, the anatomy of the genital apparatus, the gonads, hormones and genetic information, etc. (Dorlin 2008). Within this determinist frame, biomedical discourse conceptualized the feminine body as alterity. The sexualization of women's bodies extended from the reproductive organs to all conceivable parts. Over the course of the nineteenth and twentieth centuries, the "essence" of femininity migrated from the uterus to the ovaries to the female sex hormones.

Feminist biologist Anne Fausto-Sterling (2000a, b) has demonstrated that the dichotomous classification of two sexes cannot withstand scrutiny. Even within a biological frame that posits anatomical, gonadal, hormonal, and chromosomal criteria to define sex, more than two sexes exist. The biological indicators for sex are continuous rather than discrete variables, and as such, they cannot differentiate all men from all women; nor can they support the claim that men and women exhaust the morphological possibilities. The naturalization of sex as a dichotomous variable, which has been enshrined in scientific discourses since the eighteenth century, is a political demarcation, not a natural designation.[7] Far from providing a neutral, objective description, biology constructs "two sexes" as a "natural" reality, ignoring that bodies are sexed through alignment with a particular gender regime—made to conform physically to the characteristics that socially define the sexes. Gender constructs sex, a process that is masked by a sex/gender opposition based on the nature/culture opposition, which sciences like biology have contributed to producing and reproducing (Harding 1986; Haraway 1991; Fausto-Sterling 2000b; Dorlin 2008).

Judith Butler (1990a, 1993a) has emphasized the persistence of the nature/culture dichotomy in the differentiation between gender and sex and explored its effects. The idea of gender as social sex is strongly imbued with a biological ideology that presumes the existence of a stable and precultural nature, altogether independent of social mediation. Butler also noted that the concept of gender adopted by a good deal of feminist theory was codified as heterosexual. Rather than being a neutral concept, it was grounded in the heteronormative regulation of sexuality. Gender and sexuality have been inextricably linked across so many historical moments that the distinction between these concepts became invisible. Only recently have scholars argued for the autonomy of sexuality as a phenomenon and a field of study. This relative independence has made it possible to pose questions about the relation between gender and sexuality, and between sexuality and feminism.

Feminist debates about sexuality initially focused on women's free disposition of their own bodies, generating the 1970s slogan "my body is mine" as a guiding principle for feminist struggles to defend the body as a privileged space of autonomy. In 1980,

Adrienne Rich built upon Rubin's analysis of marriage as an institution that produced and sustained male power over women, arguing that compulsory heterosexuality was the foundation of women's oppression. For Rich (1980), recognizing the multifaceted bonds among women, the "lesbian continuum," was one way to erode the unquestionable character of heterocentrism and build bridges between lesbians and feminists.

During the same period, Monique Wittig ([1969] 1971) condemned heterosexuality as a system that defines women only in relation to men, and facilitates men's appropriation of women. By promoting obligatory relations between men and women, heterocentric thought generated a totalizing vision of history, structured by discursive categories that only make sense within the heterosexual order (Wittig 1992). Conceptualizing lesbianism as a refusal of male domination and a strategy to abolish women as a "natural" group, Wittig (1992) sought to break the heterosexual contract according to which "woman" equals slave, and to overthrow all social sciences founded upon the category of "sex."

In 1984, Rubin revised her earlier formulations, proposing a useful way to think about sex and sexual politics in order to create a radical theory of sex. As one of the first authors to problematize the complex relationship between feminism and discourses on sex, Rubin identified two distinct perspectives: one that criticized the restrictions imposed on women's sexual conduct, reclaiming the sexual liberalization of both men and women; and another that perceived sexual liberalization as an extension of male privilege. Introducing a third alternative, Rubin mapped a stance that sought to avoid both "anti-porn fascism, on the one hand, and a supposed 'anything goes' libertarianism, on the other, [...] construing both sides as equally extremist" (Rubin 1984, 167).

Rubin characterized anti-porn feminism as antifeminist and questioned its alliance with anti-progressive political forces such as the Christian Right during the repressive years of the Reagan Administration. As envisioned by Catharine MacKinnon (1979) and Andrea Dworkin, the campaign against pornography was a struggle against gender inequality, discrimination, exploitation and gendered violence. Pointing out that feminist stances amenable to coalition with antisex forces raised powerful questions about the appropriateness of feminism as a foundation for a theory of sexuality, Rubin called for analyses that recognized gender oppression as distinct from sexual oppression. Emphasizing distinctions among gender, sexuality, and erotic desire, Rubin began to elaborate an autonomous and specific theory and politics of sexuality, attuned to the particular forms of power and oppression that characterize sexuality.

Social Movements Critical of Gender Binarism

From the 1990s onward, the generation that proclaimed itself "third-wave feminism" foregrounded the study of sexualities—plural—criticizing sex binaries that institute gender and the ideology of gender as the condition of intelligibility for human existence. Within this frame, the "trans" movement, which comprises transsexuals, transgender and intersex people, transvestites, masculine femininities, feminine masculinities, and gender nonconformists, gained great prominence. This movement challenged medical discourses that classified transsexuality as a psychiatric pathology that requires treatment (Stryker and Whittle 2006), such as sex reassignment surgery (Califia 1997), a procedure that reinforces the ideology of gender and its hierarchies. Trans activists also challenged legal systems that entrenched dichotomous sex as the condition for rights bearing and for citizenship (Bereni et al. 2008, 29-30).

Transgender people expressed, paradigmatically, not gender conformity but its disturbance (Butler 1990a), and in so doing, revealed the existence of gender norms that are usually invisible (Fassin 2008). In developing her analysis of gender, Butler (1993b) drew attention to both the normative character of the category gender,[8] and to the always open possibility of transgressing and denaturalizing these norms, and transforming heteronormative practices. Trans activism and queer critique have embraced this transgressive agenda. Unlike the identitarian model adopted by both the feminist and the gay movements in the United States, they endeavored to go beyond homonormativity—the defense of the rights of homosexuals to live their lives as heterosexuals do. Instead, they sought to transform minoritarian identities into reservoirs for political critique of majoritarian norms of life (Bourcier 2006). In summary, queer strategy consisted in developing a series of social dynamics to take advantage of "the open mesh of possibilities, gaps, overlaps, dissonances and resonances, lapses and excesses of meaning when the constituent elements of anyone's gender, of anyone's sexuality aren't made (or can't be made) to signify monolithically" (Sedgwick 1993, 8).

In contrast to the North American context, in Latin America queer studies arose in critical dialogue with Latin American feminists, striving to deepen their approaches and to make visible the forms and the people that have queered thought in, and from, Latin America (Viteri, Serrano, and Vidal Ortiz 2011, 55). This task has involved examining gender and sexualities "as fields in transit and in constant dialogue with the contexts from which they are produced and reproduced" (49). These studies have extended the use of queer theory to empirical research in the social sciences, examining different social facets of the contemporary Latin American world in all its complexity and in its connections among the local, the global, the transnational and the diasporic.

Critiques of Universalized Accounts of Gender

Since the mid-1980s, "feminists of color" have challenged the notion of a sole feminine subject, "woman," who embodies universal criteria without regard for intersecting hierarchies of power such as race, class, nationality, and sexuality. Feminists of color repeatedly criticized the arbitrariness and contingency of the binary oppositions on which the concept relied (Viveros Vigoya 2004) and challenged the validity of any attempt to subordinate all social categories to gender. Through the construction of a singular category "woman" and the "potent political myth called 'us'" (Haraway 1991, 155), theories of gender slid toward essentialism, which ignored the heterogeneity of women, and the diversity within individual women—each a nonunitary, multiple, and fragmented subject (Bonder 1999; De Lauretis 1987). To move beyond the dichotomies masculine/feminine, human/machine, and illuminate the partial, contradictory, and strategic character of contemporary identities, Donna Haraway (1991) proposed the hybrid figure of the cyborg, as a novel and powerful metaphor that allows for the exploration of complex subjectivities and innovative political projects.

Similarly, but from a different place of enunciation, postcolonial feminist Chandra Mohanty (1988) dissected the analytic and methodological ethnocentrism of many feminist theorizations of "Third World women," tracing the "orientalist," racist, and colonialist character of their representations in Western discourses. Characterized as absolute victims of patriarchal ideology embedded in their cultures, Third World women were positioned as the presumed counterpart of Western women, construed as secular and liberated, and owners of their social destinies. Postcolonial feminist scholars emphasized that caricatures of Third World women were not just wrong; they circulated an "orientalist" logic that justified the superiority of Western women and culture, legitimating Western determination of what is normal or abnormal, oppressive or liberating for particular women (Minh-ha 1989). Drawing parallels between orientalism and "discursive colonization," Trinh Minh-ha (1987) called attention to the devaluation of creative work produced by "women of color," either by disregarding their claims about race and sex or by reading their works only in relation to race and ethnicity. Within this discursive colonization, those who do not embody the norm cannot represent themselves.

Feminists of the global South noted early on the importance of producing concepts independent of European theoretical paradigms that were anchored to local realities. The central theses of Oyèrónkẹ́ Oyěwùmí's work (1997), for example, are that gender does not function in an exactly the same way in every culture and that theoretical postulates of Euro-American feminism are inadequate to analyze African cultures. Oyěwùmí based her argument on her analysis of the Yoruba language and society, suggesting that social hierarchies were grounded in seniority rather than gender. According to Oyěwùmí, Yoruba is not a gendered language, but it does organize terms in relation to seniority. Reflecting the language that organizes social relations, Yoruba social institutions and practices do not make social distinctions based on sex, nor do they determine positions or status based on anatomical differences. Bibi Bakare-Yusuf (2003) raised several questions about Oyěwùmí's arguments: interrogating her assumption that words in the Yoruba language have always had the same meaning; and challenging her claim that seniority was the only dimension of power for overlooking how seniority intersects with other power dynamics. Indeed, Bakare-Yusuf suggested that Oyěwùmí's conclusion that Yoruba women and men have the same power and opportunities because the Yoruba language does not make hierarchical gender distinctions, but only recognizes anatomical difference, confuses language and social reality. Despite these faults, Oyěwùmí made a powerful case for the necessity of generating concepts appropriate to particular African contexts, rather than relying on distorting European concepts such as the nuclear family to interpret African experience. Oyěwùmí also drew attention to other forms of recognition that can be more important than gender in structuring oppressive relations in non-Western societies (Bakare-Yusuf 2003, 4).

By analyzing gender on the basis of experiences of women racialized as "black" in North America, Hazel Carby (1987) and Hortense Spillers (1987) questioned theories such as Rubin's (1975) that linked the oppression of women to institutions of kinship and discourses of femininity defined in relation to marriage. Carby (1987) argued that black women had not been constituted as "women" in the same way that white women had, because the institution of slavery excluded them from "culture" and from the institution of marriage. As Carby noted, black women were sexually marked as femal(animals), but not as women (potential wives who could carry a last name). In that sense, while white women were exchanged in a sex/gender system that oppressed them, the institution of slavery produced distinctive groups of people (black women and men), defined as the alienable property of white men (and women). Given the specific modes of sexual oppression experienced by African American women, Spillers (1987) suggested that it was imperative that black women construct alternative discourses of femininity, reclaim the authority to represent themselves, and to constitute themselves as subjects.

In Latin America and the Caribbean, Rita Segato (2003) and Gloria Wekker (1997) have shown that African American religions do not rigidly separate the masculine from the feminine, or gender and sexuality from biology, as envisioned within dominant ideologies. Investigating the gender characteristics of the orixás, Segato emphasizes their independence from both anatomical sex and from the sexual preferences of the participants of the cult. According to Segato, relationships between orixás[9] challenge "the principles upon which Brazilian society bases the constitution of the family" and displace "marriage and blood kinship [. . .] from the central position they occupy in the framework of the dominant ideology" (190).

Wekker's research in Surinam and Segato's in Brazil question the Western vision of the sexes as discrete units and opposed binary pairs, suggesting that that the two-sex model "is not an unquestionable truth but a cultural peculiarity" (Castellanos Llanos 2006, 17). These studies also emphasize that experiences of African American women of the popular classes challenge the normative matrix of compulsory heterosexuality, which allocates reproductive, material, and symbolic resources only when congruent with heteronormativity.

Their analyses reveal the importance of the experience of slavery on African populations in America, exploring its effects on biological and social reproduction, relations of gender and kinship, and patterns of social practice and individual behavior. Within these particular conditions, religious practices emerged that erased normative boundaries of gender and sexuality and modified consciousness concerning "the behaviors of men and women in the cultural plane and the expectations about their role in the social plane" (Segato 2003, 210). This scholarship makes clear that situations of slavery (and intense poverty, as in the case described by Wekker in Surinam) must be analyzed not only as evidence of trauma but also as spaces that "make a virtue of necessity," encouraging forms of sexuality repressed by the traditional kinship systems and reformulating cognitive categories related to gender and sexuality.

Gender in Critiques of Hegemonic Feminism

Gayatri Spivak called attention to the weaknesses of positions that attempt to understand "the oppression that women of color have experienced within the global political and economic framework of First World imperialism without realizing that 'women' as a unitary category cannot hold, cannot describe, that this category must undergo crisis and expose its fractures to public discourse" (Butler 2003, 81). For Spivak, "representing" the voices of women deprived of rights involves an inherent risk; no matter how well intentioned, this "representation" reproduces the condescending attitude of the colonizer. Although Spivak (1985) opposed the pretense of constructing a unitary category "women," she also noted the political importance of making strategic use of essentialist notions like "women." As a tactic consciously used to mobilize women to press for social change, "strategic essentialism" challenges postmodern relativist positions, which are determined to dissolve identitarian categories perceived as essentialist. The risk of "essentialism" can be worth taking if it is framed from the vantage point of those who have been oppressed (Spivak 1987).

Jacqui Alexander and Chandra Mohanty have questioned seemingly inclusive feminist proposals, such as those of international feminism; and they have criticized pluralist conceptions of difference "in which women in the Third World bear the disproportionate burden of difference" (Alexander and Mohanty 1997, xviii). A "global sisterhood" cannot have as a premise "a center/periphery model where women of color or Third World women constitute the periphery" (Alexander and Mohanty 1997, xviii). Alexander and Mohanty draw attention to hierarchical strains of Western feminism to develop a comparative and relational feminist praxis that is transnational in its response to the contemporary crisis of global capitalism.

Drawing insights from Marxism, feminism, and black nationalism, Black feminism has developed numerous critiques of accounts of gender in canonical US feminism (Davis 1981; hooks 1981; Lorde 1984; Hill Collins 1990). The question posed in the mid-nineteenth century by Sojourner Truth, "Ain't I a woman?" was deployed by the Black feminist militants to reclaim and deconstruct the identity of "woman." They developed a double critique of white feminism that was not sensitive to the specificities of intersecting racial, gender, and sexual oppressions and of black movements that devalued black women's contributions (Hull et al. 1982; hooks 1981). From a critique of the patriarchal institutions from which they were excluded, black feminism redefined its own historical tradition, linking it to struggles of pioneer women in the Black movement and differentiating it from the theories of gender born of Beauvoir's thesis, "one is not born but becomes a woman" (hooks 1981).

In addition to challenging conceptualizations of gender and woman, feminists of color theorized new collective political identities. In pathbreaking works such as *This Bridge Called My Back* (Moraga and Anzadúa 1981), Asian American, African American, indigenous, and Latina feminists living in the United States reclaimed identities rooted in the borderlands, outside the founding myth of original totality or the unitary subject constructed within the binary categories of modernity (Anzaldúa 1987). Their interstitial experiences gave rise to a model of political identity that Chela Sandoval (1991) called "oppositional consciousness," cultivated by those who do not have a stable membership in the categories of race, sex, or class and who learn to read the webs of power in a trenchant way.

Parallel to the concerns of feminisms of color, Latin American feminisms strove to understand the specificities of the interrelations among gender, class, and race in the region. In Brazil, since the 1960s, "black" activists and intellectuals have addressed the specific problematics of black women and of Brazilian sexism and racism (Barroso and Costa 1983; Carneiro 2005; Werneck 2007). In the Caribbean, the works of Breny Mendoza (2001), Yuderkys Espinosa Miñoso (2007) and Ochy Curiel (2013) have centered the Latin American debate around the question of compulsory heterosexuality as a social institution, and its effects on the dependence of women as a social class, on national identity and citizenship, and on the tale of *mestizaje* as the foundation of national narratives.

In the last two decades, analyses of coloniality have illuminated the material and historical diversity of Latin American and Caribbean women while also making explicit the complicity of hegemonic feminisms in ongoing oppression (Suárez-Navaz and Hernández Castillo 2008; Bidaseca, Vázquez and Espinosa 2011).[10] Authors, such as María Lugones (2008a, 2008b), for example, have developed the concept of the coloniality of power theoretically and politically,[11] integrating it in a critical way into their feminist and gender analyses. For Lugones, this meant making visible the binary logic of modern colonial thought, which operates in categorizations of race, gender, sexuality, and class, and complicating the theory of coloniality by attending to gender and sexuality. Lugones (2008a, 2008b) analyzed forms of subordination and dispossession suffered by nonwhite colonized women, which entailed a level of dehumanization that placed them beyond colonizers' definition of the human. According to Lugones, persistent dehumanization remains the condition of possibility for colonial and neocolonial systems to the present day.

Within the framework of this colonial logic, the "colonized woman" has a sex as all nonhuman females do, but does not have a gender—the exclusive mark of the "civilized" (Lugones 2010). As constituted by the coloniality of power, indigenous and enslaved women are not women in the sense posed by Sojourner Truth's pressing question "Ain't I a woman?". From Lugones' perspective, gender is a category that emerged as part of the European epistemic matrix to account for the particular oppression suffered by Western white women, particularly those who did not belong to the working class. To decolonize gender, then, requires reconfiguring the category to include experiences of both oppression and resistance of those women who were colonized not only by the northern European empires of the nineteenth century but also by the Spanish and Portuguese *conquistadores* at the end of the fifteenth century. Lugoness' theory (2010) includes a dimension absent in Quijano's (2002) conceptualization of the coloniality of power: resistance developed by those who have been the object of oppression (on the grounds of gender, race, class, or sexuality). For Lugones, resistance is not a function of the hybrid identities of groups or individuals, but the result of multiple possibilities that grow from strategic political alliances informed by shared oppositional consciousness, as Sandoval suggested (1991).

Gender: Still a Useful Category in the Era of "Globocentrism"?

Debates sparked by dissident feminisms have made important contributions to gender theory, critiquing the implicit universal and Eurocentric character of this category; and generating suitable analytical tools to account for the coloniality of power, a dimension absent from North American and European postmodern feminist thought. Although coloniality illuminates certain continuities of global power since the fifteenth century, particularly in relation to racialization and dehumanization, global power relations have also changed, and "it is now necessary to understand gender in the era of transnational corporations, the Internet and global neoliberal politics" (Connell 2014, 12). New formations of global power link dominant centers with subordinated peripheries and metropolitan with peripheral elites, while also redefining the relation between *Occidente* and its "others." Fernando Coronil (2000) has labeled this change, a shift from Eurocentrism to "globocentrism."

The rhetoric of the "free" market masks both the inseparability of capitalism from the political project of colonialism, and how *Occidente*, deterritorialized as multinational corporations and international financial institutions, continues to depend on the subjugation of *occidental* populations and nature. Neoliberal globalization's effects on gender are multiple and contradictory. Despite positive aspects associated with discourses that promote diversity and respect for human rights, divisions have deepened between the privileged and less-favored groups in regard to gender, class, and race. Gender coordinates of the contemporary world are defined by phenomena as diverse as the masculinization of work culture in transnational and multinational corporations (Connell 2014); the gender and racial asymmetries that cyberspace produces and reproduces; the larger participation of women in *maquiladoras* and call centers, proximity services, and care work (Hochschild 2003); the reproduction of violence by "men in arms" (Falquet 2008) and the femicides in contexts marked by drug trafficking, paramilitarism, and corruption. All these phenomena deserve more systematic analysis and enhanced political interventions to address their effects.

Feminist epistemologies of the South (Mendoza 2010), anchored in diverse theorizations and experiences of women of the global South, contribute greatly both to understanding these dynamics and to resisting global gender power. To extend their reach requires wide ranging comparative studies to investigate how gender relations are made and unmade in the neoliberal globalized world, and transnational feminist praxis that makes possible coalitions and alliances to transform the spaces that global capitalism opens and closes.

Notes

1. It is important to note that the periodization of feminism into three waves has been widely questioned due to its aspiration to homogenize, in a single hegemonic narrative, the trajectories that feminism has followed in different geopolitical contexts.
2. It is worth noting the reluctance caused by the polysemy of the word *gender* in French and other Latin languages, such as Spanish (Lamas 1996).
3. In the United States, Catharine MacKinnon (1982, 515) suggested that "sexuality is to feminism what work is to Marxism," excluding work from feminist reflection, which according to her should primordially focus on how "the organized expropriation of the sexuality of some for the use of others defines the sex, woman."
4. On this point, Marta Lamas (1996) criticizes Scott, arguing that she confuses gender identity, which refers to the "social" identities of people as "women" or "men," and sexual identity, an unconscious structure that constructs the imaginary of what means to be a woman or a man.
5. In Latin America, a "gender perspective" only gains strength in the social and academic feminist world in the 1990s (Lamas, 1999).
6. In Latin America a minoritarian but active sector of masculinity researchers has positioned itself as "feminist" and has oriented its academic work towards the goal of transforming gender relations (Valdés, 2007, 62).
7. Thinkers like Fausto-Sterling (2000b), Haraway (1991) and Harding (2010) demonstrated that biological knowledge is neither neutral nor objective, but marked by the influence of gender on those who produce it as well as on how they produce it; they also showed that debates about the biology of bodies are always intensely political and ethical.
8. When the category "woman" is considered representative of an ensemble of values and dispositions, it becomes normative in character and, therefore, exclusionary in principle (Butler, 1990b: 325).
9. A spirit or deity that reflects one of the manifestations of Olodumare (God) in the Yoruba spiritual or religious system.
10. Within Latin American Indigenous women's organizations, in their vast diversity, there have been two processes: "a questioning of visions rooted in tradition and culture around models of being a woman" and a "gradual appropriation of a rights discourse" to defend themselves against social exclusions and gender violences (Sierra, 2013, 253). However, it should not be ignored that gender—as a concept and as a political category—and feminism have been received with reluctance by various organizations that prefer to talk about women, privilege the struggles waged in conjunction with the men of their community and even explicitly detach themselves from feminism (Berrío, 2008).

11. This concept, coined by Aníbal Quijano (2000), refers to a historically specific pattern of power, based on the production of a mode of classification and hierarchization in terms of what today we refer to as race, that was developed for the first time in Latin America just over five hundred years ago and has since become its inextricable foundational trait.

References

Alexander, J. M., and C. T. Mohanty, 1997. *Feminist Genealogies, Colonial Legacies, Democratic Futures.* New York: Routledge.

Anzaldúa, G. 1987. *Borderlands/La Frontera: The New Mestiza.* San Francisco: Aunt Lute Books.

Bakare-Yusuf, B. 2003. "'Yoruba's Don't Do Gender:' A Critical Review of Oyeronke Oyewumi's *The Invention of Women: Making an African Sense of Western Gener Discourses.*" *African Identities* 1 (1): 121–142. http://www.codesria.org/IMG/pdf/BAKERE_YUSUF.pdf

Barroso, C., and A. O. Costa. 1983. *Mulher. Mulheres* [Woman. women]. São Paulo: Cortez Editora, Fundação Carlos Chagas.

Bereni, L., S. Chauvin, A. Jaunait, and A. Revillard. 2008. *Introduction aux Gender Studies: manuel des études sur le genre* [Introduction to gender studies: handbook of studies about gender]. Brussels: De Boeck.

Berrío, L. R. 2008. "Sembrando sueños, creando utopías: Liderazgos femeninos indígenas en Colombia y México" [Sowing dreams, creating utopias: feminine indigenous leaderships in colombia and mexico]. In *Etnografías e historias de resistencia: Mujeres indígenas, procesos organizativos y nuevas identidades políticas* [Ethnographies and histories of resistance: indigenous women, organizational processes, and new political identities], edited by R. A. Hernández, 181–204. Castillo, Mexico: D. F.: Ciesas.

Bidaseca, K., V. Vázquez Laba, and Y. Espinosa, eds. 2011. *Feminismos y poscolonialidad. Descolonizando el feminismo desde y en América Latina* [Feminisms and postcoloniality: decolonizing feminism from and in Latin America]. Buenos Aires: Ediciones Godot.

Bonder, G. 1999. "Género y subjetividad: avatares de una relación no evidente" [Gender and subjectivity: vicissitudes of a non-evident relationship]. In *Género y epistemología. Mujeres y Disciplinas* [Gender and epistemology. women and disciplines], edited by S. Montecino and A. Obach, 29–54. Santiago de Chile: LOM Ediciones.

Bourcier, M. H. 2006. *Queer Zones: politique des identités sexuelles et des savoirs* [Queer zones: politics of sexual identities and knowledges]. Paris: Éditions Amsterdam.

Butler, J. 1990a. *Gender Trouble. Feminism and the Subversion of Identity.* New York: Routledge.

Butler, J. 1990b. "Gender Trouble, Feminist Theory, and Psychoanalytic Discourse." In *Feminism/Postmodernism,* edited by L. Nicholson, 324–340. New York: Routledge.

Butler, J. 1993a. *Bodies That Matter: On the Discursive Limits of Sex.* New York: Routledge.

Butler, J. 1993b. "Critically Queer." *GLQ: A Journal Of Lesbian and Gay Studies* 1 (2): 17–32.

Butler, J. 2003. "Transformative Encounters." In *Women and Social Transformation,* edited by E. Beck-Gernsheim, J. Butler, and L. Puigvert, 81–98. New York: Peter Lang.

Butler, J., E. Fassin, and J. W. Scott, 2007. "Pour ne pas en finir avec le 'genre'" [In order not to be done with "gender"]. *Sociétés & Représentations* 24: 285–306.

Califia, P. 1997. *Sex Changes: Transgender Politics.* San Francisco, CA: Cleis Press.

Carabí, A., and J. M. Armengol. eds. 2009. *Debating Masculinity.* Harriman, TN: Men's Studies Press.

Carby, H. 1987. *Reconstructing Womanhood: The Emergence of the African American Woman Novelist.* New York: Oxford University Press.

Carneiro, S. 2005. "Ennegrecer al feminismo" [Blackening feminism]. *Nouvelles Questions Féministes*, 24 (2): 21–26.
Castellanos Llanos, G. 2006. *Sexo, género y feminismo: tres categorías en pugna* [Sex, gender, and feminism: three categories in dispute]. Cali: Manzana de la Discordia Editores.
Chodorow, N. 1999. *The Reproduction of Mothering: Psychoanalysis and the Sociology of Gender: With a New Preface*. Berkeley and Los Angeles: University of California Press.
Clatterbaugh, K. C. 1997. *Contemporary Perspectives on Masculinity: Men, Women and Politics in Modern Society*. Boulder, CO: Westview Press.
Combahee River Collective. (1977) 1983. "The Combahee River Collective Statement." In *Home Girls: A Black Feminist Anthology*, edited by B. Smith, 272–282. New York: Kitchen Table: Women of Colors Press.
Connell, R. W. 1987. *Gender and Power: Society, the Person and Sexual Politics*. Redwood City, CA: Stanford University Press.
Connell, R. W. 1995. *Masculinities*. Cambridge: Polity Press.
Connell, Raewyn. 2014. "The Sociology of Gender in Southern Perspective." *Current Sociology* 62 (4): 550–567.
Coronil, F. 2000. "Naturaleza del poscolonialismo: Del eurocentrismo al globocentrismo" [The nature of postcolonialism: from eurocentrism to globocentrism]. In *La colonialidad del saber: Eurocentrismo y ciencias sociales. Perspectivas Latinoamericanas* [The coloniality of knowledge: eurocentrism and social sciences. Latin American perspectives], edited by Lander, E. Buenos Aires: CLACSO.
Curiel, O. 2013. *La Nación Heterosexual* [The heterosexual nation]. Bogotá and Buenos Aires: Grupo Latinoamericano de Estudios, Formación y Acción Feminista. GLEFAS), Brecha Lésbica.
Davis, A. Y. 1981. *Women, Race and Class*. New York: Random House.
de Beauvoir, S. 1953 [1949]. *The Second Sex*. New York: Knopf.
De Lauretis, T. 1987. *Technologies of Gender: Essays on Theory, Film, and Fiction*. Bloomignton: Indiana University Press.
Delphy, C., P. Molinier, I. Clair, and, S. Rui. 2012. "Genre à la française?" [French-style gender?]. *Sociologie* 3 (3). http://sociologie.revues.org/1392].
Delphy, C. 2001. *L'ennemi principal 2: Penser le genre* [The main enemy 2: thinking gender]. Paris: Syllepse.
Dorlin, E. 2008. *Sexe, genre et sexualités* [Sex, gender, and sexualities]. Paris: Presses Universitaires de France.
Dworkin, A. 1983. Right-wing Women. New York: Perigee Books.
Espinosa Miñoso, Y. 2007. *Escritos de una lesbiana oscura: Reflexiones críticas sobre feminismo y política de identidad en América Latina* [Writings of a dark lesbian: critical reflections about feminism and identity politics in Latin America]. Buenos Aires: En la Frontera.
Fabre, C., and E. Fassin. 2003. *Liberté,égalité,sexualités:actualité politique des questions sexuelles*. Paris: Belfond/*le Monde*.
Falquet, J. 2008. *De gré ou de force: les femmes dans la mondialisation* [Willingly or Not: Women in Globalization]. Paris: La Dispute.
Fassin, E. 2008. "L'empire du genre" [The empire of gender]. *L'Homme* 3-4 (187–188): 375–392. Link: www.cairn.info/revue-l-homme-2008-3-page-375.htm.
Fausto-Sterling, A. 2000a. *Sexing the Body. Gender Politics and the Construction of Sexuality*. New York: Basic Books.
Fausto-Sterling, A. 2000b. "The Five Sexes, Revisited." *Sciences* 40 (4): 18–23.

Firestone, S. 1970. *The Dialectic of Sex: The Case for Feminist Revolution*. New York: William Morrow.
Fougeyrollas-Schwebel, D. 2005. "Controverses et anathèmes au sein du féminisme français des années 1970" [Controversies and anathemas within the french feminism of the 1970s]. *Les cahiers du genre* 2 (39): 13–26.
Fouque, A. 1995. *Il y a deux sexes. Essais de féminologie, 1989-1995* [There are Two Sexes: Essays in Feminology, 1989-1995]. Paris: Gallimard.
Fraser, N. 1997. *Justice Interruptus: Critical Reflections on the "Postsocialist" Condition*. New York and London: Routledge.
Friedan, B. 1963. *The Feminine Mystique*. New York: W. W. Norton.
Gardiner, J. K. 2005. "Men, Masculinities, and Feminist Theory." In *Handbook of Studies on Men and Masculinities*, edited by M. Kimmel, J. Hearn, and R. W. Connell, 35–50. Thousand Oaks, CA, and London: Sage.
Gilligan, C. 1982. *In a Different Voice: Psychological Theory and Women's Development*. Cambridge, MA: Harvard University Press.
Guillaumin, C. 1992. *Sexe, race et pratique du pouvoir: l'idée de Nature* [Sex, race, and the practice of power: the idea of nature]. Paris: Côté Femmes.
Halberstam, J. 1998. *Female Masculinity*. Durham, NC: Duke University Press.
Haraway, D. 1991. *Simians, Cyborgs and Women: The Reinvention of Nature*. New York: Routledge.
Harding, S. 1983. "Why has the sex/gender system become visible only now?" In *Discovering Reality: Feminist Perspectives on Epistemology, Metaphysics, Methodology and Philosophy of Science*, edited by S. Harding, and M. B. Hintikka, 311–324. Dordrecht: Kluwer Academic Publishers.
Harding, S. 1986. *The Science Question in Feminism*. Ithaca, NY: Cornell University.
Hawkesworth, M. 1997. "Confounding Gender." *Signs* 22 (3): 649–685.
Hill Collins, P. 1990. *Black Feminist Thought: Knowledge, Consciousness and the Politics of Empowerment*. Boston: Unwin Hyman.
Hochschild, A. R. 2003. *The Commercialization of Intimate Life: Notes from Home and Work*. Berkeley: University of California Press.
hooks, b. 1981. *Ain't I a Woman: Black Women and Feminism*. Boston: South End.
Hull, G. T., P. Bell Scott, and B. Smith, eds. 1982. *All the Women Are White, All the Blacks Are Men, but Some of Us Are Brave*. New York: Feminist Press.
Hurtig, M.-C., and Pichevin, M.-F. 1991. "Catégorisation de sexe et perception d'autrui" [Sex categorization and the perception of the other]. In *Sexe et genre: de la hiérarchie entre les sexes* [Sex and gender: of the hierarchy between the sexes], edited by M.-C. Hurtig, M. Kail, and H. Rouch, 169–180. Paris: CNRS.
Irigaray L. (1974) 1985. *Speculum of the Other Woman*. Ithaca, NY: Cornell University Press.
Kergoat, D. 2000. "Division sexuelle du travail et rapports sociaux de sexe" [Sexual division of work and the social relations of sex]. In *Dictionnaire critique du féminisme* [Critical dictionary of feminism], edited by H. Hirata, F. Laborie, and H. Le Doaré, and D. Senotier, 35–44. Paris: Presses Universitaires de France.
Kimmel, M. 1992. "La producción teórica sobre la masculinidad: nuevos aportes" [The theoretical production of masculinity: new contributions]. In *Fin de siglo, Género y cambio civilizatorio* [Turn of the Century: Gender and Civilizational Change], edited by R. Rodríguez, 129–138. Santiago de Chile: Isis Internacional.
Kimmmel, Michael. 2008. "Los estudios de masculinidad: una introducción." In *La masculinidad a debate*, edited by En Àngels Carabí and Josep Armengol, 15–32. Barcelona: Icaría.

Kimmel, M. 2009. "Masculinity Studies: An Introduction." In *Debating Masculinity*, edited by A. Carabí and J. Armengol, 15–32. Harriman, TN: Men's Studies Press.

Lamas, M. 1996. "Usos, dificultades y posibilidades de la categoría género" [Uses, difficulties, and possibilities of the category gender]. In *El género: la construcción cultural de la diferencia sexual* [Gender: the cultural construction of sexual difference], edited by M. Lamas, 327–366. México: PUEG.

Laqueur, T. 1990. *Making Sex: Body and Gender from the Greeks to Freud*. Cambridge, MA: Harvard University Press.

Lorde, A. 1984. *Sister Outsider: Essays and Speeches*. Trumansburg, NY: Crossing Press.

Lugones, M. 2008a. "Colonialidad y género. Hacia un feminismo descolonial" [Coloniality and gender: towards a decolonial feminism]. In *Género y descolonialidad* [Gender and decoloniality], edited by Walter Mignolo, 13–55. Buenos Aires: Del Signo.

Lugones, M. 2008b. "Colonialidad y género" [Coloniality and gender]. *Tabula Rasa* 9: 73–101.

Lugones, M. 2010. "Toward a Decolonial Feminism." *Hypatia* 25 (4): 742–759.

MacKinnon, C. A. 1979. *Sexual Harassment of Working Women: A Case of Sex Discrimination*. New Haven, CT: Yale University Press.

Mathieu, N.-C. 1991. *L'anatomie politique: catégorisations et idéologies de sexe* [The political anatomy: categorizations and ideologies of sex]. Paris: Côté-Femmes.

Mathieu, N.-C. 2000. "Sexe et genre" [Sex and gender]. In *Dictionnaire critique du féminisme* [Critical dictionary of feminism], edited by H. Hirata, F. Le Laborie, H. Doaré, and, D. Senotier, 191–200. Paris: Presses Universitaires de France.

Mead, M. 1935. *Sex and Temperament in Three Primitive Societies*. New York: Harper Perennial.

Mendoza, B. 2001. "La desmitologización del mestizaje en Honduras" [The demythologization of *mestizaje* in honduras]. *Mesoamérica* 22 (42): 256–279.

Mendoza, B. 2010. "La epistemología del sur, la colonialidad del género y el feminismo latinoamericano" [Epistemology of the south, coloniality of gender and Latin American feminism]. In *Aproximaciones críticas a las prácticas teórico-políticas del feminismo latinoamericano* [Critical approaches to the theoretico-political practices of latin american feminism], edited by Y. Espinosa Miñoso, Buenos Aires: En la Frontera.

Minh-ha, T. T. 1987. "Difference: 'A Special Third World Women Issue.'" *Feminist Review* 25: 5–22.

Minh-ha, T. T. 1989. *Woman, Native, Other: Writing Postcoloniality and Feminism*. Bloomington: Indiana University Press.

Mohanty, C. 1988. "Under Western Eyes. Feminist Scholarship and Colonial Discourses." *Feminist Review* 30: 61–88.

Molinier, P. 2014. Genre, travail, sexualité" [Gender, Work, Sexuality]. In *Qu'est-ce que le genre?* [What is gender?], edited by L. Laufer and F. Rochefort, 155–170. Paris: Petite Bibliothèque Payot.

Money, J., and A. Ehrhardt. 1972. *Man and Woman, Boy and Girl*. Baltimore, MD: John Hopkins University Press.

Moraga, C., and G, Anzaldúa, eds. 1981. *This Bridge Called My Back*. Watertown, MA: Persephone Press.

Oakley, A. 1972. *Sex, Gender and Society*. London: Temple Smith.

Ortner, S. B. 1974. "Is Female to Male as Nature Is to Culture?" In *Woman, Culture and Society*, edited by M. Z. Rosaldo and L. Lamphere, 67–87. Redwood City, CA: Stanford University Press. Reprinted from *Feminist Studies* 1 (2): 5–31 (1972).

Oyěwùmí, O. 1997. *The Invention of Women: Making an African Sense of Western Gender Discourses*. Minneapolis: University of Minnesota Press.

Preciado, B. 2009. "La invención del género, o el tecnocordero que devora a los lobos" [The invention of gender, or the technolamb that devours the wolves]. In *Biopolítica del género. Conversaciones Feministas* [Biopolitics of gender. feminist conversations], edited by Beatriz Preciado et al., 13–42. Buenos Aires: Ají de Pollo.

Quijano, A. 2000. "La colonialidad del poder, eurocentrismo y América Latina" [The coloniality of power, eurocentrism, and latin america]. In *La colonialidad del saber. Eurocentrismo y ciencias sociales. Perspectivas Latinoamericanas* [The coloniality of knowledge: eurocentrism and social sciences. latin american perspectives], edited by E. Lander, 201–246. Buenos Aires: CLACSO.

Quijano, A. 2002. 'La colonialidad del poder, eurocentrismo y América Latina'. En Edgardo Lander, comp. (2002). *Colonialidad del saber. Eurocentrismo y ciencias sociales*. Quito: Clacso, UNESCO, 201-246.

Reiter, R., ed. 1975. *Toward an Anthropology of Women*. New York and London: Monthly Review Press.

Rich, A. 1980. "Compulsory Heterosexuality and Lesbian Existence." *Signs* 5 (4): 631–660.

Rosaldo, M. Z. 1974. "Women, Culture, and Society: A Theoretical Overview." In *Woman, Culture, and Society*, edited by M. Z. Rosaldo and L. Lamphere, 17–42. Redwood City, CA: Stanford University Press.

Rosaldo, M. Z., and L. Lamphere, eds. 1974. *Woman, Culture, and Society*. Redwood City, CA: Stanford University Press.

Rubin, G. 1975. "The Traffic in Women: Notes on the Political Economy of Sex." In *Toward an Anthropology of Women*, edited by R. Reiter, 157–210. New York and London: Monthly Review Press.

Rubin, G. 1984. "Thinking Sex: Notes for a Radical Theory of the Politics of Sexuality." In *Pleasure and Danger: Exploring Female Sexuality*, edited by C. S. Vance, 267–319. Boston and London: Routledge & Kegan Paul.

Rubin, G. 2011. *Deviations: A Gayle Rubin Reader*. Durham, NC: Duke University Press.

Sandoval, C. 1991. "US Third World Feminism: The Theory and Method of Oppositional Consciousness in the Postmodern World." *Genders* 10: 1–24.

Scott, J. W. 1986. "Gender: A Useful Category of Historical Analysis." *The American Historical Review* 91 (5): 1053–1075.

Scott, J. W. 1996. *Only Paradoxes to Offer: French Feminists and the Rights of Man*. Cambridge, MA: Harvard University Press.

Scott, J. W. 2010. "Gender: Still a Useful Category of Analysis?" *Diogenes*, 57 (1): 7–14.

Sedgwick, E. K. 1993. *Tendencies*. Durham, NC: Duke University Press.

Segato, R. L. 2003. "La invención de la naturaleza: familia, sexo y género en la tradición religiosa afrobrasileña" [The invention of nature: family, sex, and gender in the afro-brazilian religious tradition]. In *Las estructuras elementales de la violencia: Ensayos sobre género entre la antropología, el psicoanálisis y los derechos humanos* [The elementary structures of violence: essays about gender between anthropology, psychoanalysis, and human rights], edited by R. L. Segato, 181–224. Buenos Aires: Universidad Nacional de Quilmes Editorial.

Sierra, M. T. 2013. "Redefiniendo los espacios de género desde la diversidad cultural. Las mujeres indígenas frente a la justicia y los derechos en México y América Latina" [Redefining the spaces of gender from cultural diversity: indigenous women facing justice and rights in mexico and latin america]. In *Espacios de Género* [Spaces of gender], edited by J. Ströbele-Gregor, and D. Wollrad, 239–255. Buenos Aires: Nueva Sociedad, Fundación Friedrich Ebert, Adlaf.

Spillers, H. J. 1987. "Mama's Baby, Papa's Maybe: An American Grammar Book." *Diacritics* 17 (2): 64–81.

Spivak, G. 1985. 'Three Women's Texts and a Critique of Imperialism." *Critical Inquiry* 12 (1): 243–261

Spivak, G. 1987. *In Other Worlds: Essays in Cultural Politics*. London: Methuen.

Suárez-Navaz, L., and R. A. Hernández Castillo. 2008. *Descolonizando el feminismo: teorías y prácticas desde los márgenes* [Decolonizing feminism: theories and practices from the margins]. Madrid: Cátedra Ediciones.

Stolcke, V. 1996. "Antropología del Género" [Anthropology of gender]. In *Ensayos de antropología cultural: Homenaje a Claudio Esteva-Fabregat* [Essays of cultural anthropology: homage to claudio esteva-fabregat], edited by J. Prat and A. Martínez, 335–344. Barcelona: Editorial Ariel.

Stryker, S., and S. Whittle, eds.. 2006. *The Transgender Studies Reader*. New York: Routledge.

Tabet, P. 1998. *La construction sociale de l'inégalité des sexes: des outils et des corps* [The social construction of the inequality of the sexes: tools and bodies]. Paris: L'Harmattan.

Valdés, T. 2007. "Estudios de Género: Una mirada evaluativa desde el Cono Sur" [Gender studies: an evaluative look from the southern cone]. In *Género, mujeres y saberes en América Latina: Entre el movimiento social, la academia y el Estado* [Gender, women and knowledges in Latin America: between social movement, academia, and the state], edited by L. G. Arango and Y. Puyana, 47–63. Bogotá: Editorial Universidad Nacional de Colombia.

Varikas, E. 2006. *Penser le sexe et le genre* [Thinking sex and gender]. Paris: Presses Universitaires de France.

Viteri, M. A., J. F. Serrano, and S. Vidal-Ortiz. 2011. "¿Cómo se piensa lo 'queer' en América Latina? Presentación del dossier" [How is the queer thought of in Latin America? presentation of the dossier]. *Iconos* 39: 47–60.

Viveros Vigoya, M. 2004. "El concepto de 'género' y sus avatares: Interrogantes en torno a algunas viejas y nuevas controversias" [The concept of gender and its vicissitudes: questions around some old and new controversies]. In *Pensar. en) género. Teoría y práctica para nuevas cartografías del cuerpo* [Thinking. about) gender: theory and practice for new cartographies of the body], edited by C. Millán de Benavides and A. M. Estrada Mesa, 170–193. Bogotá: Editorial Pontificia Universidad Javeriana.

Viveros Vigoya, M. 2008. "Teorías feministas y estudios sobre varones y masculinidades. Dilemas y desafíos recientes" [Feminist theories and studies about men and masculinities: recent dilemmas and challenges]. In *Masculinidades. El juego de género de los hombres en el que participan las mujeres* [Masculinities: the gender game of men in which women take part], edited by J. C. Ramírez Rodríguez and G. Uribe Vásquez, 25–42. México: Plaza y Valdés Editores.

Wekker, G. 1997. "One Finger Does Not Drink Okra Soup." In *Feminist Genealogies, Colonial Legacies, Democratic Futures*, edited by J. M. Alexander and C. T. Mohanty, 330–352. New York: Routledge.

Werneck, J. 2007. "Of Ialodês and Feminists: Reflections on Black Women's Political Action in Latin America and the Caribbean." *Cultural Dynamics* 19 (1): 99–113.

Wittig, M. (1969) 1971. *Les guérillères*. Boston: Beacon Press.

Wittig, M. 1992. *The Straight Mind and Other Essays*. Boston: Beacon Press.

CHAPTER 42

SEXUAL DIFFERENCE

ALISON STONE

Introduction

A family of related concepts of sexual difference has become part of feminist theory, stemming from two main sources: the psychoanalytic theories of Freud and Lacan and the work of the Belgian-born philosopher Luce Irigaray, herself a practicing psychoanalyst. Ever since the 1970s, their ideas of sexual difference have been embraced by some English-speaking feminist theorists, for a cluster of overlapping reasons. These reasons will provide the framework structuring this chapter, each being considered in turn.

First (see "Psychoanalytic Roots of the Concept of Sexual Difference"), the concept of sexual difference has provided a framework within which to recognize that the psyche is not reducible to society, and that masculinity and femininity have deep and enduring roots in our psyches, being acquired together with the fundamental fantasies and mental agencies (of desire, repression, conscience, etc.) that compose our minds. Second ("Luce Irigaray's Philosophy of Sexual Difference"), the concept of sexual difference has enabled feminists to theorize the nature of the symbolic order. Not straightforwardly the same as society, a symbolic order is a set of fundamental, systematically organized meanings that structure our psyches across a diverse range of cultures and societies that all participate in the same order. Any symbolic order is embodied in language—which is not simply a neutral tool of communication but constitutes an overarching horizon of meaning and a framework for experience—and in other "discursive and signifying systems": visual art, religion, music, architecture—the whole "dimension of representations" (Grosz 1990, 22). In the West, the order of meanings embodied across all these fields has revolved around the hierarchical opposition *man/woman*, or so Irigaray and others have claimed. Third ("The Politics of Sexual Difference"), feminist analysis of the Western symbolic has generated a politics of sexual difference. Its aim is to change the symbolic order, and accompanying social practices, to create a positive feminine subject-position. Traditionally, the West has ruled this out by construing woman merely as an inferior version of man—as when Freud judges the clitoris to be a defective, shrunken penis. Fourth ("Sexed Bodies: Beyond the Sex/Gender Distinction"), the concept of sexual difference has helped feminists to rethink embodiment beyond the sex/gender distinction. Finally, there is a range of contemporary engagements with ideas of sexual difference ("Further Directions"), including the new "material feminisms" which both build on and critique sexual difference feminism's approach to embodiment.

Psychoanalytic Roots of the Concept of Sexual Difference

Psychoanalysis is the key intellectual tradition through which the concept of sexual difference has entered feminist theory. So we must re-examine Freud's account of masculinity and femininity and then Lacan's revision of this account, which has been crucial to the feminist reception of psychoanalysis.

Freud came to pay serious attention to femininity only late in his intellectual career. Until then, he approached femininity in terms of the same theory of the Oedipus complex that he had originally developed with reference to little boys. Bracketing the many problems surrounding this theory, let us review its essentials.

For Freud, every young boy, from his third to fifth years, has sexual wishes for his mother and hates his rival, the father, whom the boy wishes to kill. These sexual wishes are not for intercourse specifically but for various, vaguely imagined, kinds of bodily intimacy with the mother. To punish the boy for these wishes, he is threatened with castration, either by the father or by others invoking the father's name. This threat eventually prompts the boy to dissolve his Oedipus complex. He represses his sexual wishes for his mother, henceforward letting them become conscious only in the form of desexualized affection. He also represses his rivalrous hatred for his father, in return for the assurance that he will grow up to be a father in his own right and to "possess" his own wife—a stand-in for his beloved mother.

Initially, Freud assumed that the little girl has an inversely symmetrical Oedipus complex in which she has sexual wishes for her father and hatefully competes with her mother. Freud gradually abandoned that assumption. He set out his amended position in the 1925 essay "Some Psychical Consequences of the Anatomical Distinction between the Sexes"; 1931's "Female Sexuality" and 1933's "Femininity" (see, respectively, Freud 1977a, 1977b, 1973).

Both girls and boys first love their mothers, Freud concedes now. This is presumably due to the social convention that women and mothers be the primary child-carers, although Freud does not spell this out. Supposedly, the girl loves her mother in the same "phallic" way as the boy, wanting to perform sexual acts with her mother using her clitoris as if it were a penis. Whereas the boy relinquishes his love for his mother owing to the threat of castration, the five-year-old girl comes to reject her mother on "discovering" that she and her mother are *already* castrated, lacking the penis. In hindsight the girl blames her mother for all her other disappointments—weaning, toilet-training, displacement by younger siblings, and so forth.

Now hating her mother, the girl becomes contemptuous of other women, too, including herself. Assuming that she follows the path of "normal femininity," she takes her father as her new love, wanting through him to access a penis. From now on, she has an Oedipus complex: she loves her father and hates her mother. The girl never properly abandons this complex, for she cannot be propelled out of it by threats of castration. Rather, her castration complex pushes her *into* the Oedipus complex and leaves her there—more or less. At best, she realizes that she can never possess a penis and instead comes to wish to have a baby with, first, her father, and then a father substitute—ideally a baby boy, through whom she can access a penis.

Implied by Freud's work is a conceptual distinction between *sexual* difference and anatomical *sex* difference: sexual difference is not the same as sex difference but its psychical consequence.[1] Sexual difference is the difference between the subject-positions or sexed identities assumed by girls and boys and retained by women and men. These positions are composed of the different relationships to others that men and women adopt (e.g., loving versus hating their mothers), their different self-perceptions (as future fathers or castrated), and different sets of desires and wishes (for a mother substitute versus a penis). This psychical difference is sex*ual* for Freud because it arises from the different courses of erotic development that girls and boys undergo, the different ways that their desires become structured and the different ways that their psyches become organized around these desires.

In specifying that children acquire sexed identities only through these tortuous courses of development, Freud takes it that children begin life without any stable, sexed identities—they are originally polymorphous, or bisexual, as he variously puts it. This, too, distinguishes *sexual* from *sex* difference: the latter is given at birth; the former acquired through complex, difficult processes. By implication, sexed identity is never entirely stable or complete. Because it always emerges from an individual's pre-sexed past, everyone harbors psychical forces and desires that destabilize their acquired sexed identity. Even so, sexed identities generally endure—despite the instabilities that continually beset them. So, whereas sex is (we assume for now) fixed, sexed identities (and sexual difference) are precarious and volatile.

Since sexual difference is not anatomical but psychical (and eroticized, acquired, unstable), does sexual difference stand to sex as *gender* stands to sex? Is sexual difference just another word for gender? Let us see why not.

When the sex/gender distinction, first made by psychologists, was introduced into feminist thought, it was widely understood as follows. *Sex* is the biological difference between males and females; *gender* consists of societies' different expectations and roles for males and females (e.g., to be aggressive versus peaceful) and the differences between men's and women's personalities as they become shaped by these expectations. Biological *males* and *females* become socially *masculine* and *feminine* as they become gendered. Many feminists embraced this sex/gender distinction because it meant that men's and women's personalities and social roles are shaped by social norms rather than being direct effects of biology. And whereas biology is fixed, roles and norms vary across societies (Oakley 1972, 128); therefore, we can change these norms so that they stop steering men and women in opposed and unequal directions.

In contrast, Freud's perspective is that the psyche has its own dynamics, possibilities, and pathways, whatever gender norms prevail socially. Indeed, we only become responsive to either masculine or feminine roles on the basis of first acquiring the rudiments of a psychical identity as masculine or feminine. We do that by way of the castration and Oedipus complexes—stages that each individual must pass through psychically, regardless of their varied social situations. A core psychoanalytic insight, then, is that the psyche and its development are not reducible to, but have a level of independence of, society. As such, the *psychical* difference between the sexes is not reducible to *social* gender difference. Rather, in every society this psychical difference must exist; each society must accommodate it in some way.[2]

Further, for Freud, the psyche is not reducible to the mind as opposed to the body—whereas, under the sex/gender distinction as it was initially understood, gender obtains in the mind, sex in the body. Freud instead treats the psyche and each of its component agencies (ego, superego, etc.) as an organization of ideas *and* physical energies at once. As ideas become stabilized into fixed patterns, so our corresponding physical energies become bound into desires, drives, patterns of activity, gestures, habits, and so forth. For example, when someone suffering from hysteria represses his or her sexual thoughts, the blockage necessarily affects his or her body too: limbs may become paralyzed, speech impaired. Thus the psyche is simultaneously a bodily and mental formation.

Unfortunately, Freud compromises all these insights with his emphasis on the causal effects of anatomical sex difference, which makes it unclear how far the psyche has its own dynamics independent of biology, how unstable sexed identities are, and how far the body is something formed through and with the psyche. Moreover, Freud's emphasis on anatomy creates a litany of problems that initially impeded feminists from developing his insights. He takes it that girls love their mothers "phallically"; that the penis is the only valued sexual organ; that both sexes inevitably see the female body as "castrated" (this insight brings the castration threat home to boys); and that women's whole emotional lives revolve around "penis envy."

Feminist hostility to Freud persisted until the mid-1970s, when Juliet Mitchell's 1974 book *Psychoanalysis and Feminism* prompted a sea change. Mitchell's central point is that Freud gives us a largely accurate description of what it is to become a woman *under patriarchy* (Mitchell 1974, xiii). In a civilization that accords superior status to fathers (patriarchy means "rule of the father") and so, too, to men and symbols of paternal and masculine status, girls cannot avoid learning that, being female, they are of lesser status. Coming to measure female bodies by masculine standards, girls judge themselves defective and second-rate. Freud's mistake was to portray this process as the effect of anatomy and not culture.

Mitchell was informed by the revision of psychoanalysis developed by Jacques Lacan in France, particularly in his "structuralist" phase of the 1950s and 1960s, crystallized in his 1966 *Écrits* (Lacan 2002). Although Lacan claimed to return to Freud, in fact he shifted the focus of psychoanalysis away from biology to language and culture, rethinking the castration and Oedipus complexes as reflecting the structure of language, not the facts of anatomy. Because Lacan thus moved away from Freud's view that women's inferiority is biologically determined, Mitchell and many other feminist theorists found Lacanian psychoanalysis useful.

For Freud, the castration threat was issued by the father or in his name. From this Lacan takes the idea that there is a *paternal function*, which is to say no (he calls this the *Non/Nom-du-Père*) to prohibit the bodily union with the mother for which the child wishes (Lacan 2002: 208). Lacan equates this paternal no with the incest taboo, understood to be the universal taboo that separates culture from nature. This taboo is common to all cultures and societies—and to all the systems of kin relations by which we demarcate ourselves from animals. In all such systems, kin positions are defined in relation to one another: only *father* may have sex with *mother*, thus the position of the father is always to say no. For the child to grasp these meanings, *father, mother, child, no*, is to enter language and its system of distinctions (Lacan 2002, 66).

These points depend on Lacan's structuralist view that language is neither a neutral tool of communication nor a simple vehicle for expressing preexisting ideas that in turn mirror the external world. Rather, for Lacan, language shapes how we see the world, constituting a horizon of meaning by which all experience is mediated. Each language does this by virtue of being a complete system of differences: each term gains meaning from its differences from and relations to all the others. For example, in French, *mouton* can mean "sheep" or "mutton," conveying a different view of sheep—as always potential meat—from the English, which distinguishes the two terms. Kinship terms, then, do not simply describe preexisting positions but *establish* kin positions with particular valences. Kinship is not separate from but entwined with the whole system of linguistic meanings that, in turn, organizes all our experience.

In sum, fundamental to acquiring language is learning the meanings of the basic kinship positions that define each individual's place in the world; this requires learning that only *father* may desire *mother*, thus grasping the ban on union with the mother. Thus the father—as a symbolic figure—represents civilization and culture and is "the original representative of the Law's authority" (Lacan 2002, 299). This "father" is not the empirical, actually existing father (if indeed the child has one), who need not issue any threats. What matters is that the father have symbolic status as the one who alone may "have" the mother, and that individuals and culture at large relay this to the child—perhaps by having "church fathers," paternal heads of state, celebrating a culture's warriors and revolutionaries. Any civilization needs some arrangements to perform this paternal function of lifting the child out of his initial attachment to the mother into public, social life.

Lacan recasts the Oedipus complex as the wish to occupy the symbolic father's position and have its central emblem the phallus, *not* the anatomical penis. Lacan says many things about the phallus: it is the badge of paternal status, of the father's sexual desire for the mother, and of the complete union with the mother that only the father may enjoy. The castration complex, in turn, centers on the child's realization that he or she may not occupy the father's position, or lacks the phallus. Even the little boy undergoes this kind of castration. Henceforward, he wishes to acquire paternal status (likely by rebelling against the society's symbolic fathers—for the rebel claims authority against those in power; law and rebellion are interdependent). Yet no boy or man can ever attain paternal status psychically, for Lacan, for each man takes the father's "no" into his psyche, where it becomes the core of his superego (the prohibitive, punitive moral agency in the psyche) and of the idealized internal father figure against which each man judges himself inadequate. Because the phallus symbolizes both what we want to have and that which we lack just in wanting it, it also comes to stand for our lack of paternal status, our castration.

For Lacan, girls, too, must enter civilization by way of the Name-of-the-Father. To exit the preverbal bond with the mother and enter broader social life, mediated by language, the girl as much as the boy must relate to the paternal ideal—*not* to a maternal one, for the mother stands for the realm that must be exited. In the nature of language, then, the only possible subject-position is one arranged under the "paternal function": to become a speaking subject is to become a *masculine* subject. Structural linguistic constraints forbid women from existing as specifically feminine subjects, from speaking or desiring in any specifically female way.

In what sense, then, *do* women become feminine? The answer is that they can never fully assume the position of (masculine) subject but on entering language become, effectively, split between their subjectivity and their femininity, which locates them as objects, not subjects, of desire and speech. This happens through the role of the phallus. While the phallus is not the penis, it still constrains girls to undergo castration on different terms from boys. By (however mistakenly) equating his penis with the phallus, the boy can position himself as lacking and desiring to attain the paternal position of having the mother or woman. Unable to likewise represent and experience her desire as phallic because she has no penis, the girl is constrained to assume a different relation to the paternal phallus. The only available option here is to (strive to be) the object of the father's or man's phallic desire. Insofar as the girl takes up this feminine position, she is object; insofar as she speaks, desires, and so forth, she is (effectively) masculine.

We may take from Lacan's work several overarching points. First, that sexual difference is both the symbolic difference between the positions *father/man* and *mother/woman*—which map onto the difference *subject/object*—and the psychical difference between subjects who assume these distinct positions. Language and psyche thus interlock; Lacan calls their total complex the "symbolic order." Sexual difference as it exists within this order is reducible neither to biological sex difference nor to social gender as social norms define it; rather, sexual difference is symbolic—that is, at once linguistic and psychical. Being linguistic, sexual difference arises in the break with preverbal nature through which we which enter civilization, so that our sexed identities are always insecure, incomplete, and defined in different ways by our confrontation with lack and insufficiency, rather than giving us any sense of sexed wholeness.

Various feminist theorists in the 1970s and 1980s took forward Lacan's emphasis that sexed identity is never complete, campaigning relentlessly against any notion of being a "whole woman" or "whole man" (see, especially, Adams and Cowie 1992). Yet for Lacan, the symbolic order that regulates these incomplete identities is fixed for all time. The paternal "no" must be law; and the phallus must be the "master signifier" in every society—any society that does not meet these constraints faces collapse. Lacan holds out no prospect of changing the exclusion of women as women from civilization, then: despite their incompleteness, our sexed identities are here to stay.

This problem stems from the concept of sexual difference as it has taken shape in Lacan. Positively, the concept highlights that our psyches and systems of meaning have their own organization, not reducible to that of society; rather, there are constraints on the psyche and on possible systems of meaning that all societies must accommodate. However, negatively, Lacan puts at the center of these constraints the necessity of separating from the mother with reference to a paternal ideal. Given this constraint, any language and any system of psychical organization must leave women split between speaking subjectivity and objectified femininity, something that no change to social gender norms can overcome.

We might escape these problems by abandoning psychoanalysis or reworking it without the concept of sexual difference.[3] But then we lose the insights that the concept distils: that the psyche has its own dynamics, powered by the complex processes by which we acquire sexed identities that are always fluctuating and unstable; and that these psychical dynamics are bound up with deep-lying structures of meaning that overarch particular linguistic and social variations. We are left with an impasse between feminism and psychoanalysis (Brennan 1991), between the insights of psychoanalysis and the feminist project of effecting social change. It was chiefly Luce Irigaray whose work broke this deadlock.

Luce Irigaray's Philosophy of Sexual Difference

The foremost philosopher of sexual difference, Irigaray has massively influenced feminist thought—particularly by her earlier work of the 1970s, translated and imported into the English-speaking world from the 1980s onward.[4] Initially, Irigaray belonged to Lacan's psychoanalytic school, the Parisian École Freudienne, but she was expelled because, throughout her earlier writings, she (indirectly) criticizes Lacan for falsely raising patriarchy into the universal condition of human civilization.

Even so, Irigaray finds in Lacan the basis of a radical critique of Western civilization for its exclusion of any possibility of women speaking, thinking, or acting *as* women. The symbol of subjectivity, the phallus, is modeled on a male body part; no female body part provides an equivalent symbol inspiring women to speak and desire specifically as women. This is indicative of how woman has been cast as object, not subject, with the position of speaking, thinking subject exclusively male: "any theory of the 'subject' will have always been appropriated as 'masculine'" (Irigaray 1985a, 133). More broadly, the feminine has been construed only as the negative, inferior version or opposite of the masculine: always defined *in relation to, against*, and *beneath* the masculine, paradigmatically as object in contrast to the masculine subject. "The 'female' is always described as deficiency, atrophy, lack of the sex that has a monopoly on value: the male sex" (Irigaray 1985b, 69).

These hierarchical meanings of *male* and *female, masculine*, and *feminine*, are at the core of the Western symbolic order. They organize a whole set of binary oppositions that make up this order—that is, the underlying structure of meaning that constitutes the backbone of Western culture: contrasts of mind/body, culture/nature, reason/emotion, reality/appearance, truth/deception, good/evil, active/passive, and order/chaos. All are shot through with sexed meaning: women are closer to nature, are all liars, are at the mercy of their emotions, and so on.[5] Being female has not been the source of an independent subjective identity but merely the inverse of being male, which *has* been taken to be a positive identity. Women can escape their second-rate condition only by positioning themselves as *non*feminine: perhaps as sex-neutral reasoners or speakers (yet who, in fact, are covertly taking up a masculine position, from which their femininity always threatens to drag them down).

Irigaray concludes that no real sexual difference has ever existed at the symbolic level, in the sense that it is only as a man that one has been able to be a thinking, speaking, acting subject. Rather than genuine difference, there has only ever been hierarchy and binary opposition between 1 and 0, where 1 is male, 0 the female construed as mere lack. Irigaray nevertheless refers to this traditional refusal of genuine difference *as* sexual difference, under the hierarchical, oppositional interpretation it has had up to now.

Contrary to Lacan, Irigaray argues that this symbolic order that has ruled the West is only one of many possible symbolic orders. Our particular order originated in classical Greece. She refers here to the tragic trilogy the *Oresteia*, by Aeschylus (Irigaray 1991). The hero, Orestes, kills his mother Clytemnestra in revenge because she had murdered his father, Agamemnon. The Athenian court eventually acquits Orestes, making the "murder of the mother" a founding principle of the classical social order. For Irigaray, this exemplifies how, at this point in history, a particular "imaginary" became law (Irigaray 1988, 159)—that is, was articulated into the symbolic order that has prevailed since.

By an "imaginary," Irigaray means a structured, interrelated set of fantasies, where a fantasy consists of ideas about what we wish for, conjoined with bodily energies that charge and eroticize them. The fantasies informing the Western symbolic are, like all our most fundamental fantasies, very deep-seated and not under our conscious control; they concern the figures of the mother and father, and arise, Irigaray holds, from the peculiar difficulties that little boys face after their birth (Irigaray 1995, 107–108). All small children struggle to separate themselves from their mothers emotionally and establish a sense that they differ from their mothers in mind and body. But unlike girls, boys are born of women, who differ from them in sex. The separation from the mother that boys need to make is therefore sharper than for girls. Boys become motivated to sever all ties with their mothers at an emotional and fantasy level, and to devalue the mother and all that she stands for: the body, dependency, close relationships, passions. Effectively, boys wish to deny that they lose anything by separating from the mother by casting her entire realm as valueless and as a realm to which boys never truly belonged anyway.

To accomplish this, boys raise the father figure into the bearer of all the values that they set against the mother and the world of dependent infancy for which she stands: disembodiment; independence; separateness from others; reason as opposed to emotion. The boy aspires to embody these values, projected onto an idealized paternal position. When these fantasies are expressed as a symbolic order, culture becomes structured by binary oppositions set out along sexed lines, as illustrated by documents such as the *Oresteia*. Hence the patriarchal symbolic order described by Lacan—but Irigaray has now traced its roots in the little boy's early relation with his mother.

By seeing the symbolic order as an expression of (male) fantasies, Irigaray re-emphasizes the bodily roots of meaning, which had become somewhat lost in Lacan's work and its initial feminist reception. Ideas and bodily energies converge in fantasies, so that we have a stubborn corporeal attachment to them. The fantasies that underlie the Western symbolic order concern the mother and father as bodily figures, for this is how we experience them in infancy. The symbolic *man/woman* opposition that expresses these fantasies thus attributes hierarchical meanings to male and female bodies—as when Plato took the female womb and genitals as his model for the cave of sensory ignorance and illusion in which he believes we are all trapped.

But how does Irigaray think that the symbolic order can be changed if it expresses male fantasies to which boys are drawn because they are born male of female mothers? Irigaray's view that symbolic change is possible rests on her belief that the relation between symbolic and imaginary is reciprocal. As Margaret Whitford puts it in her exposition of Irigaray, the imaginary is a "magma" (Whitford 1991, 57) that only becomes molded into definite shape when expressed as a symbolic order. Prior to this kind of expression, fantasies are not fully definite and determinate; they are fleeting, mobile. Boys' infant situation inclines them toward certain fantasies, then, but these only settle into a fixed pattern through being expressed symbolically. So, we could channel our fantasies into different configurations if we changed our symbolic order.

Indeed, because the symbolic order structures our fantasies, which draw on drive-energies, we come to incorporate this order into our bodies. Our energies and desires become fixed into definite patterns affecting how we move, feel, act. For a woman to apprehend that being feminine is something defective, an inferior version of the masculine, is to come to live and feel this status in her body, perhaps as a visceral dislike or shame of her own body manifested, say, in eating disorders or shamefully hiding parts of her body. Irigaray understands this process of incorporation using the term "morphology" (or "imaginary morphology"), by which she refers both to collective cultural meanings surrounding our sexed bodies and to the resulting ways that we, as individuals, come to experience, feel and live our bodies. A body's morphology—from the Greek terms *morphe*, "form," and *logos*, "meaning"—is its meaning and energetic patterns.

But what motivation do we have to change the symbolic order if it structures our fantasies and bodies so that we are emotionally attached to patriarchy? Fortunately, the imaginary-symbolic fit is never total and seamless. Our psyches always contain imaginary elements that go beyond the expressive resources of the symbolic. Men have psychical remnants of their early attachments to their mothers; and women's fantasy lives, of their many kinds, find only partial outlet in the current symbolic. For example, as the little girl learns that being female is a second-class status she turns against her mother. Thus the girl's feelings of aggression and hostility toward her mother gain symbolic expression but not her earlier attachment to and love for her mother—or her love for her own body qua female. Thus, many of women's potential desires, fantasies, self-love, and bodily feelings have no morphology at present, because our symbolic order gives them no outlet.

To change the symbolic order, we need to activate and express these alternative elements in our psyches and bodies. To this end Irigaray (1985b) puts forward imagery of women's "two lips"—two sets of lips, oral and genital—touching one another, constantly communicating. A countersymbol to the phallus, the "two lips" raises women's anatomy into a sign of how women can speak specifically *as* women. The image is also intended to provide an expressive vehicle through which female self-love, self-esteem, and desire can come into culture—through which the female body can attain its own morphology.

This shows us what particular kind of symbolic change Irigaray favors. In her view, we need to create a culture of sexual difference—not a gender-neutral culture, but one that recognizes and celebrates genuine sexual difference for the first time. Being female-bodied must be completely reimagined as the basis of a positive identity in its own right. Then, being a woman would mean being a particular kind of speaking, thinking, acting subject, whose speech embodies a distinctively feminine set of fantasies and bodily processes. Reciprocally, male identity needs to be reimagined as a specific identity: one of two, not the only one.

We see why Irigaray declares that "women's exploitation is based upon sexual difference; its solution will only come about through sexual difference" (1993, 12). The problem is sexual difference as the West has understood it—as a lack of genuine difference, a binary opposition. The solution is genuine sexual difference, to come about through the creation of a symbolic order that recognizes it at last.

In sum, for Irigaray, the West has basic symbolic meanings concerning *male* and *female*, *father* and *mother*, which organize a whole series of binary oppositions reflected in all the more manifest representational schemes found in this culture. These basic meanings define *sexual difference* in the first of the complex of senses that this term has for Irigaray—namely, the symbolic difference (hierarchy) between male and female. In this first sense, sexual difference is the difference between men and women, male and female, as it is imagined, fantasized, and symbolized in Western culture. Second, sexual difference is also the psychical difference between actual men and women—their different fantasies, desires, inner lives—a difference that results from their assuming the positions *male* or *female* as the symbolic order defines them. Since the psyche is in part bodily, this difference includes the embodied difference between being male and being female as we experience it at a felt, bodily level.

Sexual difference as Irigaray understands it differs from social gender in several ways. As a symbolic and imaginary contrast, sexual difference expresses deep-seated fantasies that are not straightforwardly social in origin if by "society" we mean a set of collective arrangements into which each individual comes and by which he or she is shaped. Rather, our shared fantasies about sexual difference originate in the (male) subject in response to his earliest relationships with others, primarily his mother. These relationships are interpersonal, arising between subjects, and reflecting the inside of the subject as much as or more than the public life that frames interpersonal relationships. So, insofar as the symbolic order has roots in the psychic life of the subject, it is not directly social, for as Irigaray says, "the human subject, woman or man, is not a mere social effect" (Irigaray and Lotringer 2000, 11). Furthermore, for Irigaray, men and women assume different subject-positions by taking on these symbolic meanings, a process that establishes our basic identities as men and women (boys and girls). Only having taken on the rudiments of these identities do we then come to respond to and take on particular—socially and historically changing—gender norms. Moreover, our sexed identities are psychical and bodily, unlike gender roles, which are taken on by the mind rather than the body.

Even so, shifting our attention from gender norms to sexual difference may seem unhelpful. The shift is to a highly abstract level of analysis, away from practical problems such as unequal pay or domestic violence. Indeed, the theoretical abstraction of Irigaray's earlier work has been criticized. Perhaps in response, she made her writing of the later 1980s more practical, sketching out a politics of sexual difference. Let us turn to this.

The Politics of Sexual Difference

The politics of sexual difference is defined, above all, in opposition to a politics of pursuing equality for women. The aim of equality politics—associated with the liberal feminism of groups such as the National Organization for Women—is to enable women to participate equally in the public worlds of paid work and politics. This requires, first, securing women's formal legal equality with men (rights to equal pay, against sexual discrimination, etc.) and then real, substantial equality. The latter requires dismantling the panoply of informal barriers that hold women back, such as the unequal distribution of housework and childcare, which remain largely women's work; implicit biases against women held by appointments and promotions panels; long-hours cultures; and old boys' networks in politics and business.

Irigaray's rhetorical question to the proponents of this politics is, equal to whom? The equality sought is with *men*: the aim of equality politics is to bring women into spheres that have been historically defined as the province of men, a definition that has shaped their structure and significance. Paid work, politics, and the like, do not lose these entrenched masculine connotations just because women enter into them. Instead, women entering these fields become forced to comply with their preexisting masculine meanings and to model themselves on men—as when female politicians, such as Margaret Thatcher or Sarah Palin, adopt the same belligerent rhetoric and policies as (many) male politicians. From Irigaray's perspective, far from challenging patriarchy, equality politics reinforces it by perpetuating the age-old system that recognizes only one ideal, the masculine, to which men and women alike must aspire. Thus Irigaray (and other sexual difference feminists) complain that pursuing equality means pursuing sameness—making women the same as men.

This criticism may seem unfair to equality politics. Arguably, women cannot achieve real equality unless the institutions that they enter change, perhaps to recognize and incorporate women's difference. Treating men and women equally may require that they be treated differently in some respects. For example, perhaps women need paid maternity leave, the option of flexible work schedules, state-subsidized child care at every workplace, and facilities at work for caring for babies before they can hope to participate equally in paid work, given their "difference"—in this case the special responsibility for child care that society (and, maybe, to an extent biology) assigns to women. However, such provisions, intended to further women's inclusion in the public sphere, may reinforce the very "difference" that hinders women from achieving full inclusion.

Either way, the politics of sexual difference is not a politics of difference in this last sense. Sexual difference feminists do not aim to reshape social institutions so that they value, celebrate, recognize, or support women's difference as it already exists, because for these feminists this is not a genuine difference. Women's traditional role as mothers, for instance, is just one way in which women have been defined in relation to men, as "good women" if they love and care for men (e.g., the Virgin Mary caring for baby Jesus), "bad women" if they harm men or male interests. Motherhood has been seen not as a possible part of female subjectivity but as a mere "function," that of providing the caring background in which (infant male) subjectivity takes shape. To accommodate this or other traditional differences of women would be just another way of perpetuating patriarchy.

Still, in defense again of equality politics, we might wonder whether achieving real equality for women requires a more wholesale transformation of the institutions of paid work and politics—not so as to accommodate differences that have been heaped exclusively onto women but so as to treat *all* individuals differently than under traditional, gender-divided practice. Workplaces could be restructured to assume that all paid workers also care for family members and to value the same. Sexual difference feminists would agree that radical transformation is needed—but of what kind? For them, the goal is not to treat all individuals alike but to create social structures that recognize genuine sexual difference and, by doing so, create it for the first time. Whereas equality feminists tend ultimately to valorize a gender-neutral future, sexual difference feminists valorize a future symbolic order of two sexes. Their aim is to invent new social practices to make that order a reality.

Irigaray's proposals in this regard are mainly for new laws. She says that we must go about "redefining rights appropriate to the two sexes to replace abstract rights appropriate to non-existent neutral individuals, and enshrining these rights in the law.... civil law must be changed to give both sexes their own identities as citizens" (Irigaray 1994, xv–xvi). In particular, she proposes, women should have (1) the right to economic equality and equal representation in all civil and religious bodies; (2) the right to defend their own cultures and traditions; (3) the right to "human dignity," especially through positive representations of women in public places; and (4) rights to choose motherhood freely and to enjoy "physical and moral integrity" (Irigaray 1993, 86–89). These legal rights are intended to begin the work of creating a positive identity for women as women. Thus, Irigaray envisages the proposed equal representation of women in all civil and religious bodies in terms of women's representation there as women, who could contribute to these bodies from distinctly female perspectives (starting to create those perspectives just by articulating them). Irigaray is not opposed to women entering the professions or agencies of government—indeed, she advocates this—but she seeks ways that they can do so *as* women, without having to relinquish their femininity.

Further applications of the politics of sexual difference can be found in the history of Italian feminism. While Italy, like other countries, has always contained various feminist currents, from the late 1970s and 1980s onward several Italian groups began to raise sexual difference into one such political current. Importing psychoanalytic and philosophical ideas along with US radical feminism and Irigaray, these Italians (of whom Adriana Cavarero is best known to English speakers—see, e.g., Cavarero 1995) moved away from directly socioeconomic issues to pursue a radical transformation of the fundamental structures of subjectivity and meaning. The entire social world was to be reshaped to accommodate two different kinds of subject. This project manifested itself concretely in a range of ways.

For example, in 1986 *L'Unità* called for women to demonstrate in response to the disastrous nuclear "accident" at Chernobyl, which was, *L'Unità* declared, the predictable result of a scientific practice detached from material life and abstracted from our bodies, bodies that are necessarily sexed (Bono and Kemp 1991, 317). Since our thought, therefore, is in fact sexed—the product of the thinking activity of embodied, sexed beings—such science only masquerades as disembodied while really expressing the destructive priorities of the male sex, contrary to "a way of thinking which cares about life. . . . [that] has always been with women" (318). Such statements fed into heated debate about whether the demonstrators demonized men and falsely exalted women. Lia Melandri objected that women are complicit with modern science and its outcomes (328–329). Members of the Milan Women's Bookstore Collective—one of the main Italian groups articulating the politics of sexual difference—replied that, even so, women are still complying with institutions made by and for men. Plus, the Collective added, there are always parts of women's desire that go beyond and can turn women against the existing order (330).

The Collective developed various strategies for bringing about a culture of sexual difference. One was the controversial practice of *affidamento*—"entrustment" or "custody" (see Milan Women's Bookstore Collective 1990; Zerilli 2004). The idea is that women can only fully realize their talents and abilities if they accept and use their inequalities (of age, status, etc.), rather than stifling women's potentials in the name of a fictitious

equality. A younger or junior woman should place herself under t[he authority?]
of a woman her superior in age or professional standing, from w[hom she can?]
realize her potential as a woman, with reference to a female role m[odel?]. [Cul-?]
tural level, too, women are to recognize female authorities—"s[...]
position led to the establishment of women's bookstores and li[braries, and?]
publishing houses devoted to women's writing, and the Virgin [...]
in Rome. These institutions embody the ideal of a symbolic mou[nt of?]
authority and knowledge—whose position women can aspire to occupy as wom[en].

Having said all this about the specificity of feminism of sexual difference, its partisans may ultimately remain committed to women's equality in a fundamental moral sense. After all, they want women to be treated, at a moral level, as subjects fully equal with men—but, they add, this requires women to have a sexuate identity in their own right, so that women cease to count only as second-class men. Even so, sexual difference feminists might reply that their goal is not equality because the generally accepted meaning of gender equality is treating all individuals alike. At the least, sexual difference feminists are transforming the meaning of equality; if the language of equality masks this transformation, then it is best avoided. Anyway, what is clear is that, abstract and theoretical as it is, the concept of sexual difference has sparked a range of political interventions and strategies that have fed into feminism's diversity and vitality.

Sexed Bodies: Beyond the Sex/Gender Distinction

The concept of sexual difference has sometimes been defended on the grounds that it advances beyond perceived problems with the sex/gender distinction. So argues Moira Gatens, in particular, in her "Critique of the Sex/Gender Distinction" (Gatens [1983] 1996, chap. 1), a paper which has been very influential and remains important.

For Gatens, the sex/gender distinction has several problems. It sharply distinguishes the biological body from the mind, taking it that it is through our minds that we take on gender norms (Gatens 1996, 9). The distinction suggests that our gender is taken into our personalities without this process having any intrinsic connection with our bodies, which sit inertly by while gender acquisition takes place. Thus, for Gatens, the distinction is a legacy of Descartes's mind-body dualism. Feminists, though, should be wary of mind-body dualism, which is continuous with the long-standing symbolic hierarchy that aligns body with woman and mind with man. In addition, Gatens maintains, the sex/gender distinction comes close to suggesting that the mind is a blank slate at birth onto which "social lessons" concerning gender are written (Gatens 1996, 4).

Gatens's proposed alternative, which she couches in terms of sexual difference, has affinities with Irigaray's position. For Gatens, gender norms are actually bound up with value-laden interpretations of the meanings of male and female bodies which are held

...al, imaginary level (Gatens 1996, 9). For example, the gender norm that women should not be aggressive reflects our social imaginary that pictures the female *body* as nurturing, peaceful, and maternal. It is because the female body is so imagined that a corresponding set of gender norms arises (Gatens 1996, 13). Thus, Gatens says, it is not the case that our social institutions simply value those traits that are deemed normal (or normative) for masculinity, such as scientific and reasoning skills. In that case those traits would equally be valued in women who succeed at science or reasoning. In fact, Gatens points out (Gatens 1996, 9), society values the masculine *male*—the traits deemed normal for masculinity are only valued when men display them. If women—those with female bodies—do display those traits, excelling at science or reasoning for example, then their doing so is not valued but condemned for making them un-feminine (cold, unattractive, etc.).

Gatens further argues that, as individuals, we take on gender norms and imaginary meanings concerning the significance of sexed bodies at a *bodily* as much as a mental level. Indeed, we should not regard the mind and body as separate entities. We have already seen that Freud and Irigaray view the psyche as an organization of ideas and bodily energies both. Gatens adds insights into embodiment developed within the phenomenological tradition. Central for Gatens is the approach of Maurice Merleau-Ponty in *The Phenomenology of Perception* (Merleau-Ponty [1945] 2002). For Merleau-Ponty, I both *have* my body—as an object that I can perceive as if from without, as a third party can—and *am* my body—the one perceiving my body *is* that same body, as a living, sentient being imbued with vital awareness of itself.

On this basis Gatens suggests that it is *as* a body—the body that I am—that I apprehend, make sense of, and internalize gender norms and imaginary meanings (1996: 11). I take these collective meanings into myself-as-body, where they become the meaning that my body has for me at an ongoing everyday level. Because the two sides of my embodiment (having and being my body) coexist inseparably, these meanings come to saturate my body in its objective, perceptible aspect: they seep into my body's ingrained habits, skills, and patterns of movement, its gestures and properties. Thus women learn, for instance, to move differently from men—perhaps in a more restrained and modest way.

Gatens couches this position in terms of sexual difference in part because of its political implications. She opposes the politics of "degendering" that, she believes, flows from the sex/gender distinction (1996, 5). According to that politics, we should dismantle and eradicate gender norms so that all individuals are treated alike, their sex being seen to have no rightful bearing on how people are treated: social life should, as far as possible, be abstracted from our bodies with their sex differences. Gatens objects, first, that this politics of neutralizing the body reflects our culture's long-running *male/female* hierarchy, because this politics values what is symbolically male—mind, culture, society—over what is symbolically female—bodies. Second, she objects, this politics neglects the fact that we *are* our bodies, which as such are not merely biological objects (as the sex/gender distinction assumes) but are also the living individuals that we are. As such, no society can realistically hope to divest our bodies of significance (1994, 9).

We therefore need a different politics, one that starts by recognizing the inescapable significance of our sexed bodies but that strives to change the meanings attached to them, to render these meanings nonhierarchical. This politics championed by Gatens has clear links with the politics of sexual difference as articulated by Irigaray and others. Gatens, however, does not endorse the goal of changing the symbolic order to recognize two genuinely different sexes. For Gatens, our goal is more to change the meanings of male and female bodies so that they cease to be pitted in sharp opposition to one another and are reimagined as overlapping along a spectrum (1996, 52).

It has been objected that Gatens is unfair to the sex/gender distinction. For Val Plumwood (1989), the sex/gender distinction does not inherently involve mind-body dualism as Gatens claims. Rather, Plumwood contends, "gender" has always referred to the different norms and meanings expected of and attributed to females and males, who take on these norms at an embodied level, as specifying how they should be as female- or male-bodied individuals. For Plumwood, the sex/gender distinction already essentially accommodates all that Gatens says.

Another alternative, adopted by Judith Butler in her earlier work (e.g., Butler 1990) is to redeploy a sharp sex/gender distinction but in a newly radical way. Ordinarily, Butler maintains, it is assumed that an individual must have the gender that "fits" their sex: females must be feminine, males masculine. Effectively, gender is expected to express sex. For Butler, the sex/gender distinction allows us to question this paradigm (the "heterosexual matrix"), a harmful paradigm that marginalizes or makes "unintelligible" all those who, in various ways, are transgressively gendered or sexed—including the intersexed,[6] transsexuals, those whose gender does not "fit" their sex, and those whose sexuality does not "fit" their sex or gender. For Butler, the sex/gender distinction opens up a positive alternative: it entails that any gender can go along with any sex—a woman can be masculine, a man feminine; a woman can desire women, a man men; gender need not be polarized as when it is expected to "follow" sex, and a range of gender expressions can proliferate. From Butler's perspective there is more radical potential in the sex/gender distinction than Gatens allows—indeed, the distinction enables a politics of gender subversion that is ultimately more liberating than the politics of sexual difference.

Further Directions

Ideas of sexual difference have had a wide-ranging influence on contemporary feminist theory, and not only on those who explicitly embrace sexual difference feminism. The irreducibility of psyche to society; the embodied nature of the psyche and the inescapable significance of our sexed bodies; the symbolic disparity between men and women; language as a horizon of meaning rather than a neutral tool for communication—all these ideas are widely, although not universally, accepted.

Yet there have been major criticisms of the concept of sexual difference. Butler suggests that the construction of sexual difference as a hierarchy, while problematic in itself, may also mask a still-deeper exclusion of sexual minorities who defy or subvert the sexed binary. Another problem is that sexual difference feminists tend to regard sexual difference, not class or race, as the fundamental social-symbolic problem—Irigaray is explicit that "the problem of race" is "secondary" (1996, 47). To prioritize one form of oppression in this way unhelpfully pits the oppressed against one another and, plausibly, is misguided: gender oppression is not obviously more fundamental to the modern capitalist order than class or race.

More constructively, sexual difference feminism has enabled a host of new currents in feminist thinking to emerge, in part through the ongoing process of Anglophone theorists assimilating ideas about sexual difference. Among these currents are new directions in Irigaray's later work. She asks how to cultivate relations between women and men as subjects of irreducibly distinct kinds, and her whole view of sexual difference shifts. She now maintains that, naturally, there are two different sexes, and that our culture must be changed to express both their natures (Irigaray 1996). This shift has contributed to extensive debate, still ongoing, about how to interpret Irigaray's ideas and take them forward (see, e.g., Deutscher 2002; Stone 2011).

Beyond Irigaray, sexual difference feminism has helped to make possible the emergence of "material feminism" (see Alaimo and Hekman 2008), which takes the rejection of the sex/gender distinction further. Rather than turn away from the biological body toward social gender for fear of falling into biological determinism, "material feminists" rethink materiality as an active, dynamic, creative force—an agency of change, supporting our efforts to change society for the better. Sexual difference theorists have attended to the body but in its psychical and cultural significance, as experienced. Effectively, these theorists bring the body into the fold of culture. For material feminists, though, this neglects the biological aspects of the body and how these aspects affect what psychical and cultural significance the body takes on. Material feminists thus aim to address the body's specifically biological aspects, as they are theorized by the sciences—be they Darwinian evolutionary theory, neurobiology or quantum physics (see, respectively, Grosz 2004; Wilson 2004; Barad 2007).

Likewise building on sexual difference theory's attention to the lived body, a growing number of feminists are engaging with phenomenology to think about embodiment. This includes inquiry into natality—our existential condition as beings who are born of women; into women's lived experiences of pregnancy, birth-giving, and mothering; and renewed attention to our experience as corporeal, fleshly beings (see, e.g., Schott 2010).

A final current, deserving mention is feminist psychoanalysis. If the psyche has its own dynamics, these are not necessarily only those of the Oedipus and castration complexes—real as those complexes may be under patriarchy. There may be further fantasies, complexes, and processes that Freud and Lacan missed. Amber Jacobs (2007) identifies a law of the mother—"you shall not be in the place of the generative mother yet (girl) or ever (boy)"—which the West has repressed, yet which has covertly retained great power. Freud himself belatedly noticed the life-long importance of women's earliest "pre-Oedipal" ties to their mothers (Freud 1973). From this starting point, I have explored a psychical pattern of mothers reliving with their young children their earliest relations with their own mothers (Stone 2011).

As this overview of emerging directions illustrates, ideas about sexual difference continue to feed into the diversity and vitality of contemporary feminist thought. These ideas are unlikely to lose their influence, given that they address issues fundamental to feminist thought—the significance of the body, how far social change can change the psyche, how being female can or could perhaps become a positive identity. So, we can expect that sexual difference will be reconceived in unexpected new directions in the future.

Notes

1. Freud does not make the distinction terminologically, except insofar as he speaks of "anatomical sex difference" (in German: *anatomische Geschlechtsunterschied*) as distinct from *Geschlechtsunterschied* as such. Moreover, he speaks not of subject-positions—a later, yet still helpful term—but of "psychical maleness" and "psychical femaleness."
2. Because sexual difference is neither social nor biological, sexual difference feminists (English-speaking) tend not to use the same clear distinctions *masculine/male* and *feminine/female* that sex/gender feminists do. Instead, sexed identity as (say) a woman is sometimes described as just that, at other times as either feminine or female identity.
3. Nancy Chodorow (1978) reframes sexual difference as the *gender* difference between girls and boys that results from social conditions in which only women mother, while men are breadwinners. Because mothers unconsciously identify more with their daughters while pushing their sons away, girls develop personalities that are empathetic, caring, with a blurred sense of self, while boys become abstract, detached, independent. Thus the gender division of labor becomes reproduced in the personalities of each generation. Through shared parenting, Chodorow argues, the cycle could be broken. However, Parveen Adams (1983), a Lacanian, rightly criticizes Chodorow for reducing psychical to social processes.
4. Irigaray is reluctant to embrace the label "feminism," but has been received as contributing to it nonetheless.
5. As Hélène Cixous puts it:

    > Where is she?
    > Activity/Passivity
    > Sun/Moon
    > Culture/Nature
    > Day/Night
    > Father/Mother
    > Head/Heart
    > Intelligible/Palpable....
    > *Man*
    > Woman
    > Always the same metaphor: .... wherever discourse is organized.
    >
    > (Cixous 1986: 63)

6. Until now I have spoken as if, biologically, everyone were either male or female, but a minority of people are born intersexed. Whether sexual difference theory can adequately accommodate this or any other variation on sexual duality is debated.

References

Adams, Parveen. 1983. "Mothering." *m/f* 8: 40–52.
Adams, Parveen, and Elizabeth Cowie. 1992. *The Woman in Question*. Cambridge, MA: MIT Press.
Alaimo, Stacy, and Susan Hekman, eds. 2008. *Material Feminisms*. Bloomington: Indiana University Press.
Barad, Karen. 2007. *Meeting the Universe Halfway: Quantum Physics and the Entanglement of Matter and Meaning*. Durham, NC: Duke University Press.
Bono, Paola, and Sandra Kemp, eds. 1991. *Italian Feminist Thought: A Reader*. Oxford: Blackwell.
Brennan, Teresa. 1991. "An Impasse in Psychoanalysis and Feminism." In *A Reader in Feminist Knowledge*, edited by Sneja Gunew, 114–138. London: Routledge.
Butler, Judith. 1990. *Gender Trouble*. New York: Routledge.
Cavarero, Adriana. 1995. *In Spite of Plato: A Feminist Rewriting of Ancient Philosophy*. Translated by Serena Anderlini-d'Onofrio and Áine O'Healy. Cambridge: Polity Press.
Chodorow, Nancy. 1978. *The Reproduction of Mothering: Psychoanalysis and the Sociology of Gender*. Berkeley: University of California Press.
Cixous, Hélène, and Catherine Clément. 1986. *The Newly Born Woman*. Translated by Betsy Wing. Manchester: Manchester University Press.
Deutscher, Penelope. 2002. *A Politics of Impossible Difference: The Later Work of Luce Irigaray*. Ithaca, NY: Cornell University Press.
Freud, Sigmund. 1973. "Femininity." In *New Introductory Lectures on Psychoanalysis*, Translated by James Strachey, 145–169. Harmondsworth: Penguin.
Freud, Sigmund. 1977a. "Some Psychical Consequences of the Anatomical Distinction Between the Sexes." In *On Sexuality*, edited by Angela Richards, 323–343. Harmondsworth: Penguin.
Freud, Sigmund. 1977b. "Female Sexuality." In *On Sexuality*, edited by Angela Richards, 371–392. Harmondsworth: Penguin.
Gatens, Moira. 1996. *Imaginary Bodies: Ethics, Power and Corporeality*. London: Routledge.
Grosz, Elizabeth. 1990. *Jacques Lacan: A Feminist Introduction*. New York: Routledge.
Grosz, Elizabeth. 2004. *The Nick of Time: Politics, Evolution and the Untimely*, Durham, NC: Duke University Press.
Irigaray, Luce. 1985a. *Speculum of the Other Woman*. Translated by Gillian C. Gill. Ithaca, NY: Cornell University Press.
Irigaray, Luce. 1985b. *This Sex Which Is Not One*. Translated by Catherine Porter with Carolyn Burke. Ithaca, NY: Cornell University Press.
Irigaray, Luce. 1988. "Interview with E. H. Baruch and J. L. Serrano." In *Women Analyze Women*, edited by Baruch and Serrano, 149–164. New York: New York University Press.
Irigaray, Luce. 1991. "The Bodily Encounter with the Mother." In *The Irigaray Reader*, edited by Margaret Whitford, 34–46. Oxford: Blackwell.
Irigaray, Luce. 1993. *Je, Tu, Nous: Toward a Culture of Difference*. Translated by Alison Martin. London: Routledge.
Irigaray, Luce. 1994. *Thinking the Difference*. Translated by Karin Montin. London: Athlone.

Irigaray, Luce. 1995. "'Je—Luce Irigaray': A Meeting [with] Elizabeth Hirsh and Gary A. Olson. *Hypatia* 10 (2): 93–[114].

Irigaray, Luce. 1996. *I Love to You: Sketch for a Possible Fel[icity in History]*. [Translated by Alison] Martin. London: Routledge.

Irigaray, Luce, and Sylvère Lotringer. 2000. *Why Diffe[rent?]* Translated by Camille Collins. New York: Semiotext(e).

Jacobs, Amber. 2007. *On Matricide: Myth, Psychoanalys[is...]* New York: Columbia University Press.

Lacan, Jacques. 2002. *Écrits: A Selection*. Translated by Bruce [Fink...]

Merleau-Ponty, Maurice. (1945) 2002. *The Phenomenology of [Perception]*. [Translated] by Colin Smith. London: Routledge.

Milan Women's Bookstore Collective. 1990. *Sexual Differenc[e: A Theory of Social-Symbolic] Practice*. Translated by Patricia Cigogna and Teresa de La[uretis]. [Bloomin]gton: Indiana University Press.

Mitchell, Juliet. 1974. *Psychoanalysis and Feminism*. Harmondsworth: Penguin.

Oakley, Ann. 1972. *Sex, Gender and Society*. London: Maurice Temple Smith.

Plumwood, Val. 1989. "Do We Need a Sex/Gender Distinction?" *Radical Philosophy* 51: 2–11.

Schott, Robin May, ed. 2010. *Birth, Death and Femininity: Philosophies of Embodiment*. Bloomington: Indiana University Press.

Stone, Alison. 2011. *Feminism, Psychoanalysis and Maternal Subjectivity*. London: Routledge.

Whitford, Margaret. 1991. *Luce Irigaray: Philosophy in the Feminine*. London: Routledge.

Wilson, Elizabeth. 2004. *Psychosomatic: Feminism and the Neurological Body*. Durham, NC: Duke University Press.

Zerilli, Linda. 2004. "Refiguring Rights through the Political Practice of Sexual Difference." *differences* 15 (2): 54–90.

CHAPTER 43

SEXUALITIES

LEILA J. RUPP AND CARLY THOMSEN

Introduction

Sexuality has a lot in common with how the Supreme Court justice Potter Stewart viewed hard-core pornography: hard to define "but I know it when I see it" (quoted in Stein 2010, 313). Feminist theories of sexuality, from a host of different perspectives, confront the question of what sexuality *is*. It involves bodies (or not), has to do with desire (or not), shapes behavior (or not), connects to identities (or not), is a product of discourses (or not). In an attempt to come to grips with the slippery nature of the subject, we speak of plural "sexualities," in that manner gesturing to the ways sexuality is shaped by gender, race, class, nation, geography, ability, and other vectors of difference, as well as varying across time and cultures. Core to all kinds of feminist thinking about sexuality is that it cannot be understood simply as a fixed biological essence and that it involves power dynamics, as captured by the phrase "sexual politics."

While arguably all feminist theories of sexuality are grounded in a move beyond biological determinism and in recognition of the importance of power, that is where the agreement ends. If sexuality is not a simple product of biology, what is it? In contrast to essentialist views of sexuality, social constructionist perspectives emphasize how changes in material conditions and social organization shape sexuality in different times and places, while poststructuralist approaches complicate the relationships among sexuality, bodies, behaviors, and identities, asking how we come to exist as sexual subjects. What is the nature of women's sexuality? Are women fundamentally different than men? In pondering these questions, feminists have given a wide variety of answers. Likewise, feminist thinking on the realm of sexual politics embodies wildly divergent perspectives on the balance between victimization and agency, or danger and pleasure, in women's experiences of sexuality, and on the question of what sexual desires, practices, identities, and discourses qualify as feminist.

We begin by considering the ways that feminist theorists, from both social constructionist and poststructural perspectives, have addressed the question of what sexuality is.

We then lay out various feminist approaches to differences between women's and men's sexualities, which open the question of what role, if any, biology might play. Next we review the ways the concept of sexual politics has played out in thinking about the fierce differences on women's victimization versus agency in the realm of sexuality. We conclude by considering what the next moves might be in thinking about sexualities.

What Is Sexuality? Social Constructionist and Poststructuralist Perspectives

There is no monolithic feminist theory of sexualities, since different varieties of feminism view sexualities quite differently. The two most influential modes of thought for feminist theories of sexualities are social constructionism and poststructuralism, which answer the question of what sexuality is somewhat differently. Both engage with intersectional thinking about sexualities, examining the ways in which sexuality is transformed as it comes into contact with other modes of identification and ways of experiencing the world and as changing material conditions shape social practices. And some scholars, such as Michel Foucault, are widely acknowledged as foundational to both social constructionism and poststructuralism. Here, we tease out some of the distinctions and overlaps between these epistemologies, highlighting the capaciousness and contradictions of feminist theorizing of sexualities.

Social constructionist perspectives, emphasizing the ways that sexuality is structured by the societies in which people live, emerged in contrast to an essentialist view of sexuality as fixed across time and place. The contrast between essentialist and social constructionist views emerged most forcefully in thinking about issues of sexual identities. That is, have there always and everywhere been people with same-sex and other-sex desires, even if their societies made no such distinctions? Although he eschewed the label "essentialist," this is the position historian John Boswell (1980) took with regard to ancient Greek, Roman, and medieval European societies, as indicated by the subtitle of his provocative book, *Christianity, Social Tolerance, and Homosexuality: Gay People in Western Europe from the Beginning of the Christian Era to the Fourteenth Century*.

From a social constructionist perspective, it makes no sense to talk about "gay people" or "homosexuality" in the past; sexuality itself is a relatively modern concept, as captured by the phrase "sex before sexuality" (Halperin 1989). This is not, of course, to suggest that people in the past did not experience desire or engage in acts that we think of as sexual. Rather, it means that having particular kinds of sexual desires and being part of an interaction involving body parts and providing sexual pleasure could have entirely different meanings. Historians of same-sex sexuality have argued that elite men's privilege in ancient and early modern European cultures to penetrate their social inferiors, including women, boys, servants, and slaves, served as an expression of power rather than sexuality. Not only does this mean that a man whose penis is enclosed by another man's hand, mouth, thighs, or anus is not necessarily a particular kind of person—a homosexual—but also that the acts themselves may be something other than sexual. The very concept of sexuality in the contemporary Western world assumes that what we do with our genitals (or other body parts used in an erotic fashion) is an important aspect of who we are, but this meaning of sexuality in the Western tradition is one historians date back to the seventeenth and eighteenth centuries (McKeon 2012).

Research on sexualities in a variety of cultures makes clear that what from a contemporary Western perspective seem to be sexual acts may have different meanings. Most famously, Gilbert Herdt (1981) has shown that among the Sambia in New Guinea, boys cannot grow into adulthood without incorporating the semen of older men into their bodies, so oral sex is part of the process of growing up. All boys partake of the ritual, and once they become men, either through marriage or fathering a child, they take on the adult role with a younger male. In parts of southern Africa, slightly younger school girls take on the role of "babies" to older girls' "mummies." Mummies socialize babies into adult roles of domesticity, intimacy, and sexuality. These roles have roots in traditional cultural forms, including initiation ceremonies for girls and the practice of labia lengthening, alone or in small groups, which provides an opportunity for autoerotic or mutual stimulation. Mummies and babies kiss, embrace each other, lie in bed together, and sometimes engage in genital activity, but none of this is considered sex because a penis is not involved (Gay 1985). In these cases, what might be considered sexual acts from a contemporary Western perspective are something different in their cultural contexts.

From a social constructionist perspective, then, sexual desire may or may not be the impetus for acts involving the genitals, and sexual identities cannot be assumed on the basis of what people do with their bodies. Historians, sociologists, and anthropologists, particularly those interested in same-sex sexuality, have provided the empirical evidence of the different ways societies construct sexuality that is fundamental to feminist thinking about sexuality. Yet the question of how malleable sexuality is remains a vexed one. Is desire a biological drive that leads to a variety of sexual acts depending on cultural factors? Or is desire itself a product of social forces? As we shall see, some theorists see their work as feminist and rooted in biological understandings of the body. There is no agreement about the limits of social constructionism.

Eve Kosovsky Sedgwick's *Epistemology of the Closet* (1990), widely recognized as a key text in feminist and queer theory, intervened in the essentialist / social constructionist debate by proposing "minoritizing" and "universalizing" as alternative, and more useful, ways of viewing homosexuality. That is, a minoritizing perspective locates homosexuality within a distinct minority population of those with same-sex desires. A universalizing perspective, in contrast, sees same-sex desire as a potential in all people, however they might categorize their sexualities. Sedgwick was interested in complicating the binary of homosexuality/heterosexuality and also undermining the notion that the development of the concept of homosexuality in the late nineteenth century represented a paradigm shift away from earlier concepts of sodomy (as an act) and inversion (as a gender expression). Her emphasis on the "performative space of contradiction" (Sedgwick 1990, 48) in narratives of homosexuality is foundational to queer theory and prefigures later work on sexual fluidity.

As Sedgwick's work makes clear, poststructuralist queer theory asks a slightly different but related set of questions about sexualities than those addressed by social constructionism. Judith Butler, who radically shifted how feminist and queer studies scholars conceptualize gender and sexuality, argues, "The discourse of 'construction' that has for the most part circulated in feminist theory is perhaps not quite adequate to the task at hand" (Butler 1993, xi). For poststructuralists, the theoretical inadequacy of constructionism is rooted in its taking the (gendered, sexual, raced, classed, able-bodied) subject as a given. Poststructuralism is less concerned with how the social shapes our desires, actions, identities, and experiences, instead focusing on how we come to exist as intelligible sexual subjects in the first place. From a poststructuralist perspective, subjects do not exist prior to performances, actions, and discourses; rather, they are constituted through these iterative frames The social *produces* subjects through terms of intelligibility—subjects are not prior to power and discourse. For Butler, this enacting of the social is necessarily performative. We become gendered through repetitive corporeal acts that are naturalized to the extent that we view such performative acts as a reflection of our inherent desires or identities—gendered, sexual, or otherwise (Butler 1999). Poststructuralists view the body "not as a ready surface awaiting signification, but as a set of boundaries, individual and social, politically signified and maintained" (Butler 1990, 44). It is precisely this understanding of the body as simultaneously material and beyond the individual, as constituted through discourse and power-knowledge relations, that has drawn feminist and queer studies scholars to poststructuralism in hopes of expanding possibilities for feminist and queer analyses of sexualities.

This poststructuralist deconstruction of how one comes to be a gendered subject differs from the social constructionist tendency to see the gendered subject as axiomatic. This examination of cultural ideologies regarding gender is crucial, from a poststructuralist position, for developing feminist theories of sexuality because, as Butler argues, "'Intelligible' genders are those which in some sense institute and maintain relations of coherence and continuity among sex, gender, sexual practice, and desire" (Butler 1999, 23). Gender hierarchies and systems of compulsory heterosexuality, then, are deeply intertwined; compulsory heterosexuality is reproduced and concealed by the gendered systems that naturalize certain bodies and behaviors.

While Butler ([1988] 2003) locates the creation of the legible gendered and sexual subject in the naturalization of performative acts, Foucault defines his object of analysis as the "regime of power-knowledge-pleasure that sustains the discourse on human sexuality in our part of the world" (1990, 11). Defining this regime includes "locat[ing] the forms of power, the channels it takes and the discourses it permeates in order to reach the most tenuous and individual modes of behavior, the paths that give it access to the rare or scarcely perceivable forms of desire, how it penetrates and controls everyday pleasure" (1990, 11). While scholars have suggested that "the problem of the subject" was the most prominent theme throughout Foucault's oeuvre (Rabinow 1984, 12), the subject (along with its pleasures and desires), for Foucault and other poststructuralist scholars, is no simple, unitary, or stagnant concept. The subject cannot be understood—indeed, does not exist—outside the complicated and shifting relations among knowledge, discursive formations, and, perhaps most importantly for those with a range of feminist concerns, power.

Foucault's interrogation of the role power plays in the production of subjectivities has made his analyses particularly useful for feminist theorizing of sexualities, which have long been concerned with power. Some feminist scholars have argued that patriarchy (as an institution) remains the most discussed concept in feminist theory (Cranny-Francis et. al. 2003, 14), even though it has fallen into disfavor. The concept of patriarchy as "a social system in which structural differences in privilege, power and authority are invested in masculinity and the cultural, economic and/or social positions of men" (Cranny-Francis et. al. 2003, 15) defines power as top-down, as something possessed by men and those with other types of social privileges (and, by implication, used against women and those with ostensibly fewer social privileges).

Foucault offers a different articulation of power as multidirectional and constantly morphing. Unlike the traditional feminist definition of power, Foucault's notion does not locate power in or restrict power from particular bodies or desires. Within a Foucauldian framework, it would be impossible to say that men or heterosexuals have power and women or lesbian, gay, bisexual, and transgender people do not. For poststructuralists, power circulates in much more complicated ways; those traditionally understood as oppressed within a binary framework also possess power. Feminists who do not necessarily come out of a poststructuralist tradition have built upon these poststructuralist analyses of power to suggest that those who are oppressed in some instances by identity markers or experiences are also privileged in other moments by their other identity markers or experiences. Importantly, for poststructuralists, no one exists outside power relations and no one is without power.

This focus on power is just one of many epistemological overlaps between post-structuralism and social constructionism. While the theoretical approaches do diverge in the ways we have outlined here, they also converge in significant ways. For example, both theoretical frameworks are interested in the relation between the social and the self. The social does not exist apart from us; the social is in us and we are the social. Our subjectivities and desires are always in flux, constructed through our relationships to the social. Feminist theorists with a range of political and theoretical orientations have drawn from and expanded upon, for example, the radical rethinking of power and subjectivity (including along the lines of gender and sexuality) central to poststructural epistemologies.

This should not suggest that all feminists who are interested in analyzing sexuality or that those who see their work as emerging from poststructuralist or social constructionist traditions view themselves as in alignment with one another. For many of those critical of poststructuralism, these theorists began deconstructing what "woman" means just as women and other marginalized people came to be recognized as oppressed groups—a point that speaks to why some feminists view poststructuralism as politically immobilizing (Fraser 1995). Poststructualists counter that such critiques rest upon a homogenous understanding of feminism and presuppose that all feminist work will necessarily challenge the political and social order in prescribed ways. For poststructuralists, creating a more just world requires challenging the terms and assumptions of the debate itself: What could (and does) sexuality, gender, feminism, and social justice mean and look like? And how do normative understandings of these terms enable the very production of the oppressions feminists work against in their political engagement?

In short, the relations among various feminist theories of sexualities are as complicated as the question regarding what sexuality is. People may do things with their bodies that provide erotic pleasure but not think of such acts as sexual. People may willingly engage in what seem to be sexual acts without the erotic desire to do so. People may or may not think that what they do with their bodies has any consequence for their personal identities. People may engage in sexual interactions without being in the same physical space, as in phone and Internet sex. While social constructionist and poststructuralist perspectives on sexuality ask both similar and different questions and have both similar and different goals, both are crucial to feminist thinking about sexuality as something different than the biological aspects of arousal, orgasm, and reproduction. To paraphrase Simone de Beauvoir's famous line—"One is not born, but rather becomes, a woman"—one is not born but becomes sexual (Beauvoir 1952, 249).

Is Women's Sexuality Different From Men's?

Feminist thinking about the nature of women's sexualities has drawn from social constructionist, poststructuralist, and even essentialist approaches in different ways. In general, the role of the body has been a vexing one in feminist thinking about sexuality. As Carole Vance asked in a classic article on social constructionism, "Has social construction theory, particularly variants which see 'sexual impulse,' 'sex drive,' or 'lust' as created, made no room for the body, its functions, and physiology? As sexual subjects, how do we reconcile constructionist theory with the body's visceral reality and our own experience of it?" (Vance 1989, 23). Poststructuralist theory complicates the nature/culture and woman/man binaries by suggesting that bodies themselves are cultural constructions. Research and theorizing about transgender and intersexuality trouble the very question of whether women's and men's sexualities are more different than alike, yet there is a history of feminist thinking about sameness and difference between women and men linked to bodies as well.

If thinking about women's versus men's sexualities erases transgender, transsexual, and intersexed bodies, it also has the potential to conceptualize "woman" as a monolithic category, ignoring race, class, and all the other differences that women embody, so the deconstruction of the category "woman" that developed within feminism in the

1980s had important consequences for thinking about sexual difference. Liberal feminism and socialist feminism, the approaches most likely to conceptualize women as more similar to than different from men in general, were less interested in questions of sexuality. The critiques of feminism as centered on the concerns of white, middle-class, heterosexual women voiced by women of color, working-class women, and lesbians in the 1970s and 1980s shaped the development of thinking about sameness and difference with regard to women's sexuality. Women of color in particular have pointed to the ways that sexuality is racialized, implicitly if not explicitly foregrounding differences among women and emphasizing solidarity with men of color. The Combahee River Collective (1981), for example, stated forthrightly that "although we are feminists and lesbians, we feel solidarity with progressive Black men and do not advocate the factionalization that white women who are separatists demand" (213). Hortense Spillers, in the early 1980s, wrote powerfully about the complexities of race and sexuality for black women who have been brutalized by male power and subjected to rape, yet recognized that the men in their families have been subjected to similar violences (Spillers 1984). The hypersexualization of women of color, both within the United States and across what Joann Nagel (2003) called "ethnosexual frontiers," made clear that racial and ethnic, as well as other differences among women problematized theories that posited commonalities among women's sexualities. Work on sexuality from a transnational perspective further undermined the assumption of a universal female subject (Grewal and Kaplan 2001).

It was radical feminism, lesbian feminism, and cultural feminism, as they developed in the United States from the late 1960s into the 1980s, that emphasized fundamental differences between women's and men's sexuality, although in a variety of ways. The distinctions among these theoretical approaches are somewhat murky. Radical feminism developed a critique of male domination of women's sexuality (sometimes advocating sexual freedom for women, sometimes celibacy, and early on focused on heterosexuality); lesbian feminism, including lesbian separatism, critiqued or ignored heterosexuality; and cultural feminism celebrated women's sexuality as fundamentally different from, and better than, men's. Alice Echols, in her history of radical feminism, painted cultural feminism as the depoliticization of radical feminism focused on women's difference from men and valorization of "female values" (1989). Her critique has had lasting power in vilifying cultural feminism, which is often conflated with lesbian feminism (Taylor and Rupp 1993).

Shulamith Firestone, an early radical feminist, rooted her analysis of women's inequality in biology but took the radical step of arguing that it was possible to overcome nature through freeing women from reproduction and the nuclear family. Firestone used feminism to link Marx and Freud, arguing that unlike economic class, "sex class sprang directly from a biological reality: men and women were created different, and not equally privileged" (1970, 8). The division of labor based on sex for Firestone was the basis of class and all other divisions, including racism. But even though what she called the "sex class system" was natural, it could be overturned through artificial means of reproduction and freeing women from childcare. The feminist revolution would restore what Freud called polymorphous perverse sexuality, encouraging *"women and children to do whatever they wish to do sexually* [emphasis in the original]" (236).

In a different way, Adrienne Rich, in her pioneering work on both motherhood and what she termed "compulsory heterosexuality," also linked women's reproductive capacity to the oppression of women. Rich analyzed motherhood as both institution and experience, and although she offered a scathing critique of motherhood under patriarchy, the fact that women give birth mattered: "The one unifying, incontrovertible experience shared by all women and men is that months-long period we spent unfolding inside a woman's body" (1976, 11). Rich made clear her belief that "female biology— the diffuse, intense sensuality radiating out from clitoris, breasts, uterus, vagina; the lunar cycles of menstruation; the gestation and fruition of life which can take place in the female body—has far more radical implications than we have yet come to appreciate" (39). Motherhood was core to sexuality in Rich's thinking because, although both women and men are "of woman born," institutionalized motherhood and institutionalized heterosexuality insist that girls alone shift their earliest erotic feelings away from women. This is an insight, also articulated by Firestone, that Rich developed in her now-classic article, "Compulsory Heterosexuality and Lesbian Existence" (1980). Here she analyzed the societal forces that tear women away from love for other women. As in *Of Woman Born*, Rich pointed to mothering, both the physical act of giving birth and the social role of caretaking, as deeply implicated in women's sexuality.

Other radical and lesbian feminist theorists concentrated on women's genitalia rather than their reproductive capacities in articulating differences between women's and men's sexuality, emphasizing female sexual pleasure (Gerhard 2001). Anne Koedt's famous essay "The Myth of the Vaginal Orgasm" (1973) celebrated the clitoris as the source of sexual pleasure and blamed the Freudian emphasis on the need to achieve vaginal orgasm for what was deemed women's frigidity. Like other radical and lesbian feminists, Koedt emphasized that recognizing the centrality of the clitoris in orgasm undermined the need for men's participation in women's sexual lives. In contrast to Koedt's celebration of clitoral orgasm, Australian feminist theorist Germaine Greer echoed Firestone's call for a polymorphous sexuality rooted in the entire body, including the vagina (1970). Whether focused on the clitoris or on women's bodies as a whole, such radical feminist theories of women's sexuality celebrated women's capacity for extraordinary pleasure, including multiple orgasms, in contrast to men's more limited capabilities.

In response to such paeans to women's sexual pleasure rooted in the body, some radical feminists, foreshadowing cultural feminism, rejected the drive for orgasm and named what was ostensibly a distinctively female desire for intimacy. Dana Densmore (1973) from the radical feminist group Cell 16 in Boston, for example, called for independence from the male-defined sexual revolution. While not denying that sex could be pleasurable, she suggested that "the real thing we seek is closeness, merging, perhaps a kind of oblivion of self that dissolves the terrible isolation of individualism" (114). The move from sexual pleasure to the politics of woman-bonding emerged clearly in "The Woman Identified Woman," issued by Radicalesbians (1973). "What is a lesbian? A lesbian is the rage of all women condensed to the point of explosion.... It is the primacy of women relating to women, of women creating a new consciousness of and with each other, which is at the heart of women's liberation" (240, 245). The themes of a unique female sexuality and the centrality of bonds between women—core to Rich's work on motherhood and her concept of lesbian existence—became the hallmark of cultural feminism.

A focus on sexual difference, genitalia, and the uniqueness of women's sexuality is also evident in what has come to be known as French feminism, despite the fact that there is no homogeneous French feminist theory (Descarries 2014). Produced primarily in the 1970s and 1980s, this variety of feminism started from the premise that the masculinist ideologies—what the French feminists dubbed *phallogocentric*—that undergird Western ways of thinking systematically suppress and devalue women's bodies and experiences. In a review of the most well-known French feminist theorists—who include Hélène Cixous, Luce Irigaray, and Monique Wittig—Ann Rosalind Jones suggests that core to French feminist theory is the belief that "if women are to discover and express who they are, to bring to the surface what masculine history has repressed in them, they must begin with their sexuality. And their sexuality begins with their bodies, with their genital and libidinal difference from men" (Jones 1981, 374).

This discovery and expression that begins with one's sexuality happens, according to these French feminists, through the development of feminine writing and feminine language, what they called *l'écriture féminine*. Deploying sensual erotic language, these theorists called for alternative non-phallogocentric ways of talking about women's sexuality. They encouraged women to write *through* their bodies (Cixous 1975), to resist their oppression through creating closeness with other women (Irigaray 1977), and to think about how their bodies might begin to work differently (Wittig 1969). They argued that women's liberation is only possible through radically altering how we understand the relationships of women's bodies to their language use. Liberation might be enabled by recognizing one's autoeroticism, described by Irigaray as specific to women, who necessarily and constantly touch themselves through their "two lips in continuous contact" (1977, 363). This touching itself is not enough to restructure or resist the dominant social order, but thinking through one's oppression and socialization might be required for the achievement of one's sexual pleasure

The position articulated here—that by virtue of the physicality of their bodies, women might come to deconstruct how the world has created and devalued their bodies in the first place—epitomizes why some scholars have described these French "difference" feminist theorists' articulations of the relations among gender, sexuality, bodies, knowledge, and power as essentialist and others have characterized them as poststructuralist. Although reclaiming woman's body and sexuality is, for these feminists, crucial, it cannot be done without engaging in processes that examine the social world. As such, they collectively approach with suspicion "efforts to change the position of women that fail to address the forces in the body, in the unconscious, in the basic structures of culture that are invisible to the empirical eye" (Jones 1981 370).

Despite their focus on sexual difference (what we would now describe as difference in terms of both gender and sexuality), these French feminists, along with radical, lesbian, and cultural feminists, are often critiqued for failing to acknowledge other forms of marginalization women may face, an omission that led to charges of essentialism. For these theorists, women's sexualities are fundamentally different from men's, a difference both socially produced and rooted in the physical differences between men's and women's bodies. While such a position does not necessarily deny differences among women, it does decenter difference in favor of a unitary female subject.

Yet women of color theorists have also theorized women's sexualities as fundamentally different than men's while also recognizing the centrality of race, ethnicity, and other factors. Black feminist theorist and poet Audre Lorde, for example, developed the theme of women's difference from men into a complex account of the erotic as power. Lorde viewed the erotic as a "resource within each of us that lies in a deeply female and spiritual plane" (1984b, 53), "an assertion of the lifeforce of women" (55). It was the "european-american male tradition" that equated the erotic with the pornographic or merely sexual, and it was "women-identified women brave enough to risk sharing the erotic's electrical charge without having to look away, and without distorting the enormously powerful and creative nature of that exchange" (59) who had the potential to use the erotic to change the world. In pointing to both the oppression and power of women's sexuality, her concept of the erotic recalled the French feminist analysis of women's sexualities as both repressed and having the power to create a point of view through which women could deconstruct social controls. Lorde combined a radical/lesbian/cultural feminist analysis of the special qualities of women with an acute recognition of differences among women. In an open letter to Mary Daly after the publication of *Gyn/Ecology* (Daly 1978), for example, Lorde critiqued Daly's Eurocentric perspective, pointing out that "the oppression of women knows no ethnic nor racial boundaries, true, but that does not mean it is identical within those differences" (Lorde 1984a, 70).

Gloria Anzaldúa, too, in her pioneering work on the types of boundary crossings that are inherent to living in a constant state of difference, conceptualized women's sexuality as unique (Anzaldúa [1987] 2003). She coined the phrase "mestiza consciousness" to refer to a politicized and healing consciousness that transcends borders, in particular the "Borderlands" of the southwestern United States and Mexico. The mestiza consciousness is, for Anzaldúa, rooted in the bodies of those who live in this region; it is a "consciousness of the Borderlands" and a gendered consciousness, "*una conciencia de mujer*" (179). Although Anzaldúa is "not sure exactly how" one develops the acceptance of ambivalence, ambiguity, and contradiction that is central to mestiza consciousness (181), she suggests that this new consciousness is created through "racial, ideological, cultural, and biological cross-pollenization" (179).

In advocating this cross-pollenization via a transgressing of (racial, gendered, sexual) borders, Anzaldúa furthers the feminist project of articulating the differences among women—differences that are rooted in race, class, and sexuality. For her, "the struggle of the mestiza is above all a feminist one" (184). Anzaldúa's mestiza consciousness, like Lorde's concept of the erotic, recognizes women's oppression and also locates power, hope, and possibility in women and in lesbian sexuality. "As a mestiza I have no country, my homeland cast me out; yet all countries are mine because I am every woman's sister or potential lover. (As a lesbian I have no race, my own people disclaim me; but I am all races because there is the queer of me in all races.)" (182).

While Anzaldúa examined the differences between women, she also focused on the relations between gender and sexuality and viewed women as distinct from men. "Men, even more than women, are fettered to gender roles. Women at least have had the guts to break out of bondage. Only gay men have had the courage to expose themselves to the woman inside them and to challenge the current masculinity" (184). The sorts of slippages among race and sexuality and gender and sexuality evident in Anzaldúa's work might be seen as the type of (figurative and material) border crossings to which the mestiza consciousness refers—crossings that both reproduce and obscure the lines between and among the social and biological, race and ethnicities, and genders and sexualities.

The question of women's sexuality in relation to men's has faded away in the face of poststructuralist and queer theoretical approaches that challenge the binary upon which seeing women as distinct from men relies. This is not to suggest that contemporary queer theorists have not considered the relationships between and among masculinity and femininity and gender and sexuality. Quite the contrary. Judith Halberstam, for example, argues that an examination of "female masculinity," even termed at one point "lesbian genders" (1998, xii), helps us to grapple with the complex ways that masculinity itself is constructed. Lauren Berlant tracks the emergence of and engagement in what she calls the first "intimate public" culture: a "women's culture" that is defined by the assumption that women necessarily "have something in common and are in need of a conversation that feels intimate, revelatory, and a relief even when it is mediated by commodities, even when it is written by strangers who might not be women, and even when its particular stories are about women who seem, on the face of it, vastly different from each other" (2008, ix). The work of Halberstam and Berlant epitomizes queer theoretical examinations of gender and points to the ways that such theories assist in interrogating the relations between gender and sexuality.

The queer theoretical commitment to examining as fluid and contextual those things that have been produced as fixed is also evident in Lisa Diamond's *Sexual Fluidity* (2008), which traced the sexual attractions, behaviors, and identities of US "sexual minority women" across time, showing how much movement there is across the lines of heterosexuality, bisexuality, and lesbianism. Building on the work of sociologists and other psychologists, Diamond argued for both social and physiological causes for women's capacity to shift desires, behaviors, and identities. Recalling earlier work in the radical, lesbian, and cultural feminist traditions, Diamond attributed unique qualities to women's sexuality, in this case based in part on the role of oxytocin, a hormone associated with motherhood, attachment, and bonding. While not discounting the influence of culture and socialization, Diamond speculated that "the fact that women tend to place more emphasis than men on the relationship aspect of sexuality, and the fact that women often fall in love with one specific person and develop novel sexual desires for that person, are both connected to oxytocin's joint, gender-specific role in sexual arousability and attachment" (Diamond 2008, 233). That sexual fluidity in women can be found across time and place might, instead, be a consequence of a regime of compulsory heterosexuality that does not consider what women do with their bodies in the absence of a penis as sex, or does not care what women do with their bodies as long as they marry men and bear children, or finds that sex between women might be accommodated, even useful, in a heterosexually organized society (Rupp 2012). And perhaps sexual fluidity is not just a characteristic of women. More recently, Diamond has titled a talk, scheduled for the Sexuality Preconference of the Society for Personality and Social Psychology, "I was wrong! Men are pretty darn sexually fluid, too" (http://www.sexatspsp.com/schedule).

Feminist theory, then, has taken a variety of approaches to differences between women's and men's sexuality. This is the area of thought about sexuality that has incorporated the most essentialist explanations, from Firestone's biologically based inequality to Rich's emphasis on the physical bond between mother and daughter to French feminists' focus on women's genital and libidinal differences from men. Yet all feminist thinkers—even Firestone, who after all asserted that what was "natural" could be transformed—have argued that there is more than biology at work in shaping women's sexuality. That is the case for contemporary theorists who incorporate biology into their thinking (Garcia 2012; Grosz 1994). Recognition of the roles of social forces, discourse, and power is fundamental to both poststructuralist and social constructionist feminist theories of sexualities.

Sexual Politics: Danger and Pleasure

A second core theme in feminist thinking about sexuality is that sexuality is political. The term "sexual politics," coined in Kate Millett's (1969) pioneering book by the same name, made clear that sexual interactions are shaped by power dynamics and are not merely personal intimate relations. Millett analyzed examples of sexual interactions in literature to argue that patriarchy is a political institution, and that sex, too, is political. "Coitus can scarcely be said to take place in a vacuum; although of itself it appears a biological and physical activity, it is set so deeply within the larger context of human affairs that it serves as a charged microcosm of the variety of attitudes and values to which culture subscribes. Among other things, it may serve as a model of sexual politics" (43). Millett defined politics in this context as "power-structured relationships, arrangements whereby one group of persons is controlled by another" (43). Her theory of patriarchy pointed to all the ways—ideological, biological, sociological, economic, educational, cultural, and psychological—in which men's domination of women is "the most pervasive ideology of our culture and provides its most fundamental concept of power" (45). The analysis of sexual politics made Millett an instant celebrity.

The idea that sexuality is political has become foundational in feminist theory, but with no agreement about the nature of power dynamics within sexual relations. The Foucauldian concept of power as multidirectional complicates a theory of patriarchy that locates all power in men. In addition, the portrayal of women as victims of patriarchy foregrounds the dangers of sexuality over its pleasures. Feminist thinking about sexual politics encompasses both victimization and agency, danger and pleasure. The danger perspective emphasizes victimization and focuses on men's power over women, while the pleasure perspective centers women's sexual agency. Of course, sexuality has the potential to involve both victimization and agency. The tension between danger and pleasure emerged most publicly in what have come to be known as the "feminist sex wars" of the 1980s, pitting opponents of pornography, sadomasochism, butch-fem sexual arrangements, and other phenomena against those advocating openness to a range of sexual representations and practices. Although in the sex wars the lines between danger and pleasure, victimization and agency, and what came to be called anti-sex and pro-sex hardened, they were never absolute. In her introduction to *Pleasure and Danger*, the anthology that came out of the Barnard Conference that is generally considered to have launched the sex wars, Carole Vance made that clear: "Sexuality is simultaneously a domain of restriction, repression, and danger as well as a domain of exploration, pleasure, and agency" (Vance 1984, 1). All feminists opposed rape, domestic violence, sexual harassment, and other forms of violence against women, so the question was the balance of attention to the dangers versus the pleasures of sexuality. The conflict among feminists came to focus on pornography, since there was no agreement about whether pornography incited violence against women or could be a source of pleasure. Nor was there agreement about what were acceptable forms of sexuality.

The sexual politics of danger and pleasure have been central to feminist thinking about women of color, both in the United States and across the globe. Harking back to Millett's work, Patricia Hill Collins analyzed the intersections of race, gender, and sexuality, emphasizing the impact of racism on the sexualities of both women and men but, through focusing on the shifting nature of power, attended to love and romance as well (2004). The hypersexualization of women of color, the history of rape of black enslaved women, and the global forces that shape the demand for and supply of women sex workers make clear the victimization of women of color. In the nineteenth century, elite African American women adopted a "politics of respectability" (Higginbotham 1993) as a means of opposing the stereotyping and rape of black women, and that emphasis on respectability has had lasting power not just for black women but for other women of color as well (Garcia 2012). At the same time, women of color theorists have insisted on the importance of moving beyond understanding sexuality primarily in terms of danger, as Lorde did in advocating the erotic as power. Scholarship on global sex work has complicated the assumption that First World white women choose sex work and Third World women of color are trafficked into sexual slavery (Kempadoo and Doezema 1998). And feminist theorists and writers have resisted the politics of respectability to celebrate the sexuality of women of color at the same time that they call out racist depictions (Davis 1998; Hollibaugh and Moraga 2003; Miller-Young, 2014). The poem by hattie gossett "is it true what they say about colored pussy?" does this by beginning with stereotypical stories of how "black and latina pussies are hot and uncontrollable," moving on to sexual violence against women of color, and ending with the assertion that "colored pussies are yet un-named energies whose power for lighting up the world is beyond all known measure" (gossett 1984, 411–412).

Radical feminists, as we have seen, began with a critique of heterosexuality, and lesbian feminists and cultural feminists continued to take aim at men and male values as responsible for women's oppression, including in the realm of sexuality. As a result, analyses of women's sexual victimization at the hands of men dominated the discourse in the 1970s and 1980s, as they do today in discourses about sex trafficking. Adrienne Rich denounced men's denial of women's sexuality through clitoridectomy and infibulation, chastity belts, death for adultery and lesbian sexuality, and psychoanalytic denial of the clitoris; and men's forcing of sexuality on women through rape, incest, prostitution, and pornographic depictions of women responding pleasurably to sexual violence (1980). Mary Daly dubbed male torture of women "the Sado-Ritual syndrome," detailing Indian widow burning, Chinese footbinding, African genital mutilation, European witch burnings, American gynecology, and Nazi medicine (1978). Such analyses led to a focus on sexual violence as central to the maintenance of patriarchy, overwhelming any discussion of sexual agency and pleasure. Although Susan Brownmiller called rape violence rather than sexuality, a flood of feminist literature on rape and pornography cemented the association of sexuality with danger for women (1975). Catharine MacKinnon, equating heterosexual sex with rape, pointed to "the extent to which the institution of heterosexuality has defined force as a normal part of 'the preliminaries'" (1979, 219). This position, and some feminists' insistence that sexual domination of women by men is the root of women's oppression (MacKinnon 1989), aroused fierce criticism on the grounds of essentialism, universalizing "woman," and denying agency and resistance on the part of women.

MacKinnon, along with Andrea Dworkin, another prominent player in what came to be known as the anti-sex side of the feminist sex wars, became (in)famous for their work on legislation to make pornography a violation of women's rights. But even Dworkin (1974, 1979), with her relentless focus on men's sexual abuse of women, did not rule out sexual pleasure. She claimed that while "unambiguous conventional heterosexual behavior is the worst betrayal of our common humanity," this did not mean that "'men' and 'women' should not fuck. Any sexual coming together which is genuinely pansexual and role-free, even if between men and women as we generally think of them. . ., is authentic and androgynous" (1974, 184). In the utopian community she envisaged, "human and other-animal relationships would become more explicitly erotic, and that eroticism would not degenerate into abuse" (188) and children would "have every right to live out their own erotic impulses" (191–192). Dworkin's call for a reimagined pansexuality, despite its limitations, harks back in some ways to Firestone's vision of a world freed from "natural" male dominance and reproduction.

Ironically, Dworkin's openness to human/other-animal and child eroticism in a world free of male domination, despite her insistence on androgyny and denunciation of roles, is reminiscent of Gayle Rubin's critique of what she called the "charmed circle" of sexuality. Rubin, a pro-sex theorist and key player in the sex wars, contrasted what society viewed as "Good, Normal, Natural, Blessed Sexuality" (i.e., heterosexual, married, monogamous, noncommercial, in pairs, in a relationship, same generation, in private, no pornography, bodies only, vanilla) to "Bad, Abnormal, Unnatural, Damned Sexuality" (i.e., homosexual, unmarried, promiscuous, nonprocreative, commercial, alone or in groups, casual, cross-generational, in public, pornography, with manufactured objects, sadomasochistic) (1984, 281). What was at stake between the opposing sides in the sex wars was the nature of power within sexual interactions and relationships. Pro-sex feminists such as Joan Nestle, in her celebration of butch-fem relationships (1981), and Pat (now Patrick) Califia, in defense of sadomasochism (Samois 1981), embraced rather than denounced power dynamics within consensual sexuality, emphasizing the complexity of power between masculine and feminine women and tops and bottoms.

Rubin's call for a "radical theory of sex" that did not conflate gender and erotic desire and her position that feminism offers theories of gender oppression but is not "the privileged site of a theory of sexuality" (Rubin 1984, 307) was in retrospect a call for queer theory. In a 1994 interview by Judith Butler, Rubin explained that feminism "dealt inadequately with sexual practice, particularly diverse sexual conduct" (2011, 280), and that her "Thinking Sex" was a move away from "an early structuralist focus on the binary aspects of language . . . toward the more discursive models of later poststructuralism or postmodernism" (283). Rubin troubled the too-simplistic tethering of sexuality to gender so that we might be able to examine the contours of sexuality differently, a disruption considered by some to be one of the founding moments of what came to be called queer theory.

Queer theory's commitments to non-binaristic epistemologies and utilizations of poststructural theories that deconstruct subjectivities and identities have meant that gender—or the relation of gender to sexuality—is not necessarily the primary concern of many recent queer theoretical texts. Instead, queer theorists have centered sexuality in order to examine a dizzying array of topics that, on the surface, might even appear to have little to do with sexuality or sexual politics. Queer theorists have interrogated how, for example, optimism might impede one's ability to flourish (Berlant 2011); Muslims have come to occupy an abject subject position as "terrorists" (just as lesbian, gay, bisexual, transgender, and queer people are being folded into the national citizenry (Puar 2007); a focus on futurity might counter the normalizing tendencies of gay rights groups (Muñoz 2009); the affective dimensions of labor and organizing on the United States/Mexico border meet crucial needs that propel social action (Hennessy 2013); rurality can be a "premier site of queer critique" (Herring 2010, 6; see also Gray 2009; Thomsen, forthcoming); compulsory able-bodiedness is profoundly linked to compulsory heterosexuality (McRuer 2006; Kafer 2013); and binaristic divisions between human and animal, life and death, animate our very sociality (Chen 2012). For queer theorists, these myriad issues are rooted in complex sexual politics that require examining sexuality as it relates to and is expressed through power relations and political institutions.

This quick referencing of queer theoretical texts highlights the field's capaciousness, a gesture toward recent directions in the scholarship on theories of sexuality. It is not meant to suggest that feminist and queer theories are somehow distinct. In dominant narratives of feminist theory and women's studies, queer theory is often framed as "coming after" feminist theory. Because queer theory has become almost synonymous with poststructuralism, such narratives also implicitly position poststructuralism as coming after (the ostensibly more simplistic) social constructionism (of feminist theory). These narratives also ignore that much early feminist work was quite "queer" in that it refused binaries and advocated anti-assimilationist positions, and also that some recent scholarship on sexuality might not be widely understood as queer. As such, these distinctions, which frame queer theorizations of sexuality as if they are more advanced and less essentialist than feminist theorizations, are intellectually unhelpful. Just as a neat division does not exist between social constructionism and poststructuralism, neither does one exist between feminist and queer studies, and attempting to create such distinctions can lead to the flattening of both intellectual trajectories (Weed and Schor 1997).

Feminist thinking about sexual politics, then, is grounded in agreement that sexual interactions are shaped by power. Whether that power is the "power over" of men dominating women or the "power to" exercise sexual agency is where the line between danger and pleasure has been drawn. But, of course, both victimization and agency are part of the story of women's sexuality. Despite the bitter disputes of the sex wars over what are acceptable forms of sexual representations and interactions, there is no disagreement over the fact that sexuality is political.

Rethinking Our Narratives: Toward a More Capacious Account of Feminist Theories of Sexuality

We have provided here an overview of feminist theoretical analyses of what sexuality is and how we have come to see sexuality in these ways. We have discussed the relations between and among feminist social constructionist and poststructuralist theories of sexuality, feminist scholars' positions on sexual difference, and feminist debates over women's sexual agency and victimization. We have not attempted comprehensive coverage but have focused on central themes that have emerged since the mid-twentieth century. We have not told a story in chronological order in an attempt to avoid reproducing the kind of simplistic progress narrative that has plagued feminist scholars' and activists' renditions of the history of feminism. And yet, in telling one story of the history, politics, and epistemologies of feminist theories of sexuality, we have reproduced other types of feminist narratives, particularly regarding who and what count as feminist and who and what are crucial to this field. In crafting an overview of feminist theories of sexuality, we have necessarily cited those players who are widely considered key to the development of feminist thinking about sexuality. Contestations over how theorists and their theories are positioned as feminist or as central to feminist theories of sexuality are deeply political.

It is precisely the political nature of narratives that Clare Hemmings (2011) analyzes in her deconstruction of dominant feminist stories about feminist theory's past. Hemmings suggests that feminist stories are often told through the familiar registers of progress, loss, and return. Progress narratives suggest that feminism has moved from a problematic focus on the unitary (white, middle-class, woman) subject to examine the varying experiences of diverse women. Narratives of loss often locate the demise of feminism in those poststructuralist feminist academics who have deconstructed the category of woman, rather than participating in feminist activism. Return narratives claim that we can enliven earlier forms of feminism that focus on connections among women through the lessons of poststructuralist feminism, in that way moving "on from the current theoretical and political impasse" plaguing feminism (2011, 5). Hemmings suggests that each of these types of sweeping claims regarding feminism's history must be rethought in order to create more ethical, accountable, and politically valuable histories.

Hemmings' cautions and interventions are particularly apropos here. We recognize that we have reproduced aspects of these dominant feminist narratives in our retelling of how feminists have talked about sexualities. We have done so because, as Hemmings suggests, these narratives are themselves a part of the history of feminist theories of sexuality. But as feminist theorists of sexuality have rightly argued, dominant narratives—within feminism or more broadly—both emerge and are sustained via political commitments. As such, we have attempted to complicate these dominant narratives even as we have gestured toward and reproduced them. We work here to avoid the pitfalls of viewing, for example, the radical feminist and French feminist focus on differences between women's and men's sexualities as irreconcilable with the call of women of color theorists to attend to the racialization of sexuality. Both French feminists and women of color theorists argued for the need to reclaim that which has been subject to abjection and shame. French feminists argued that women's resistance requires breaking through a language not created for them, while Anzaldúa described the Chicano and mestizo discomfort associated with language inadequacy as the result of racial hierarchy. Women of color feminists argued for the need to expand the category of woman to account for (racial) difference while French feminists, using the framework of multiplicity and abundance, called for a recognition of (sexual) difference. These provocative points of connection go unexamined when we view these bodies of scholarship as oppositional.

We draw from Hemmings to suggest that feminist theorizing of sexualities would be strengthened by both critically considering the existing epistemological assemblages among various fields and approaches that have been produced as distinct and also examining the ways in which ideologies are obscured by the teleology of feminist narratives about theories of sexuality. For example, Hemmings argues that, despite a temporality that situates French "difference" feminists as occurring first, the response of women of color feminism as second, and the poststructuralist turn as occurring third, each of these feminist epistemologies existed in the 1980s. The framing of each of these bodies of thought as coming "before" or "after" allows feminist narratives of progress, loss, and return to continue.

Likewise, we have seen that feminist theorists from all perspectives have recognized the centrality of power in sexual interactions, although they have viewed the nature of that power very differently. Despite the fierceness of the feminist sex wars, some on both sides acknowledged that women's sexualities always have the potential for both victimization and agency. At the same time, a linear teleology, in addition to producing various bodies of thought as contained, also functions to suggest that these debates are settled, that we have moved beyond them. Yet debates over victimization and agency live on in contemporary struggles between those feminists who see all women engaged in sex work as trafficked or otherwise victimized (Dines 2010) and those who focus primarily on sex work as a form of labor similar to other forms under late capitalism (Berg 2014).

While we suggest that future feminist theoretical analyses of sexuality will benefit from critically interrogating the feminist narratives in which our arguments are grounded, our overview of this field also points to the sweeping range of feminist theories of sexuality already in circulation. As we have suggested here, feminists have understood sexualities in a plethora of ways: as the material site of victimization, oppression and hardship; as individual and collective, literal and figurative, produced and experienced; as containing possibilities for theorizing the relationships among institutions, power, knowledge, discourses, and ideologies; as a site for reconfiguring subjectivities through performativity and play; as a canvass from which we can celebrate, transform, resist and reclaim that which has been made abject. We have gestured toward these understandings to highlight the ways in which feminist theoretical analyses of sexualities contain possibilities for actualizing those alternative epistemologies and social orders for which feminists have long fought.

References

Anzaldúa, G. (1987) 2003. "La Conciencia de la Mestiza: Towards a New Consciousness." In *Feminist Theory Reader: Local and Global Perspectives*, edited by Carole McCann and Seung Kyung Kim, 179–187. New York: Routledge.
Beauvoir, Simone de. 1952. *The Second Sex*. Translated and edited by H. M. Parshley. New York: Bantam Books.
Berg, H. 2014. "Laboring Porn Studies." *Porn Studies* 1 (1–2): 75–79.
Berlant, L. 2008. *The Female Complaint: The Unfinished Business of Sentimentality in American Culture*. Durham, NC: Duke University Press.
Berlant, L. 2011. *Cruel Optimism*. Durham, NC: Duke University Press.
Boswell, J. 1980. *Christianity, Social Tolerance, and Homosexuality: Gay People in Western Europe from the Beginning of the Christian Era to the Fourteenth Century*. Chicago: University of Chicago Press.
Brownmiller, S. 1975. *Against Our Will: Men, Women and Rape*. New York: Simon and Schuster.
Butler, J. (1988) 2003. "Performative Acts and Gender Constitution: An Essay in Phenomenology and Feminist Theory." In *Feminist Theory Reader: Local and Global Perspectives*, edited by Carole McCann and Seung-Kyung Kim, 415–427. New York: Routledge.

Butler, J. (1990) 1999. *Gender Trouble: Feminism and the Subversion of Identity*. New York: Routledge.
Butler, J. 1993. *Bodies That Matter: On the Discursive Limits of Sex*. New York: Routledge.
Chen, M. 2012. *Animacies: Biopolitics, Racial Mattering, and Queer Affect*. Durham, NC: Duke University Press.
Cixous, H. (1975) 1997. "The Laugh of the Medusa." In *Feminism: An Anthology of Literary Theory and Criticism*, edited by Robin Warhol and Diane Price Herndl, 347–362. New Brunswick, NJ: Rutgers University Press.
Collins, P. H. 2004. *Black Sexual Politics: African Americans, Gender, and the New Racism*. New York: Routledge.
Combahee River Collective. 1981. "A Black Feminist Statement." In *This Bridge Called My Back: Writings by Radical Women of Color*, edited by C. Moraga and G. Anzaldúa, 210–218. Watertown, MA: Persephone Press.
Cranny-Francis, A., Waring, W., Stavropoulos, P., and Kirby, J., eds. 2003. *Gender Studies: Terms and Debates*. New York: Palgrave Macmillan.
Daly, M. 1978. *Gyn/Ecology: The Metaethics of Radical Feminism*. Boston: Beacon Press.
Davis, A. 1998. *Blues Legacies and Black Feminism: Gertrude "Ma" Rainey, Bessie Smsith and Billie Holiday*. New York: Vintage.
Densmore, D. 1973. "Independence from the Sexual Revolution." In *Radical Feminism*, edited by Anne Koedt, Ellen Levine, and Anita Rapone, 107–118. New York: Quadrangle / New York Times Book Company.
Descarries, F. 2014. "Language Is Not Neutral: The Construction of Knowledge in the Social Sciences and Humanities." *Signs: Journal of Women in Culture and Society* 39: 564–569.
Diamond, L. 2008. *Sexual Fluidity: Understanding Women's Love and Desire*, Cambridge, MA: Harvard University Press.
Dines, G. 2010. *Pornland: How Porn Has Hijacked Our Sexuality*. Boston: Beacon Press.
Dworkin, A. 1974. *Woman Hating*. New York: E. P. Dutton
Dworkin, A. 1979. *Pornography: Men Possessing Women*. New York: Perigee Books.
Echols, A. 1989. *Daring to Be Bad: Radical Feminism in America 1967–1975*. Minneapolis: University of Minnesota Press.
Firestone, S. 1970. *The Dialectic of Sex: The Case for Feminist Revolution*. New York: William Morrow and Company.
Foucault, M. 1990. *The History of Sexuality. Vol. I, An Introduction*. Translated by Robert Hurley. New York: Vintage.
Fraser, N. 1995. "False Antithesis." In *Feminist Contentions: A Philosophical Exchange*, edited by S. Benhabib, J. Butler, D. Cornell, and N. Fraser. New York: Routledge.
Garcia, J., C. Reiber, S. G. Massey, and A. M. Merriwether. 2012. "Sexual Hookup Culture: A Review." *Review of General Psychology* 16 (2), 161–176.
Garcia, L. 2012. *Respect Yourself, Protect Yourself: Latina Girls and Sexual Identity*. New York: New York University Press.
Gay, J. 1985. "'Mummies and Babies' and Friends and Lovers in Lesotho." *Journal of Homosexuality* 11 (3–4): 97–116.
Gerhard, J. 2001. *Desiring Revolution: Second-Wave Feminism and the Rewriting of American Sexual Thought 1920 to 1982*. New York: Columbia University Press.
gossett, h. 1984. "Is it true what they say about colored pussy?" In *Pleasure and Danger: Exploring Female Sexuality*, edited by Carole S. Vance, 411–412. Boston: Routledge and Kegan Paul.

Gray, Mary. 2009. *Out in the Country: Youth Media and Queer Visibility in Rural America.* New York: New York University Press.

Greer, G. 1970. *The Female Eunuch.* London: MacGibbon and Kee.

Grewal, I., and C. Kaplan. 2001. "Global Identities: Theorizing Transnational Studies of Sexuality." *GLQ* 7 (4): 663–679.

Grosz, E. A. 1994. *Volatile Bodies: Toward a Corporeal Feminism.* Bloomington: Indiana University Press.

Halberstam, J. 1998. *Female Masculinity.* Durham, NC: Duke University Press.

Halperin, D. 1989. "Sex before Sexuality: Pederasty, Politics, and Power in Classical Athens." In *Hidden from History: Reclaiming the Gay and Lesbian Past*, edited by Martin Bauml Duberman, Martha Vicinus, and George Chauncey, Jr., 37–53. New York: New American Library.

Hemmings, C. 2011. *Why Stories Matter: The Political Grammar of Feminist Theory.* Durham, NC: Duke University Press.

Hennessy, R. 2013. *Fires on the Border: The Passionate Politics of Labor Organizing on the Mexican Frontera.* Minneapolis: University of Minnesota Press.

Herdt, G. 1981. *Guardians of the Flutes.* Vol. 1, *Idioms of Masculinity.* Chicago: University of Chicago Press.

Herring, S. 2010. *Another Country: Queer Anti-Urbanism.* New York: New York University Press.

Higginbotham, E. B. 1993. *Righteous Discontent: The Women's Movement in the Black Baptist Church, 1880-1920.* Cambridge, MA: Harvard University Press.

Hollibaugh, A., and C. Moraga. 2003. "What We're Rollin' Around in Bed With." In *Sexual Revolution*, edited by Jeffrey Escoffier, 538–552. New York: Thunder's Mouth Press.

Irigaray, L. (1977) 1997. "This Sex Which Is Not One." In *Feminism: An Anthology of Literary Theory and Criticism*, edited by Robin Warhol and Diane Price Herndl, 363–369. New Brunswick, NJ: Rutgers University Press.

Jones, A. R. (1981) 1997. "Writing the Body: Toward an Understanding of *l'écriture féminine.*" In *Feminism: An Anthology of Literary Theory and Criticism*, edited by Robin Warhol and Diane Price Herndl, 370–383. New Brunswick, NJ: Rutgers University Press.

Kafer, A. 2013. *Feminist, Queer, Crip.* Bloomington: Indiana University Press.

Kempadoo, K., and J. Doezema. 1998. *Global Sex Workers: Rights, Resistance and Redefinition.* New York: Routledge.

Koedt, A. 1973. "The Myth of the Vaginal Orgasm." In *Radical Feminism*, edited by Anne Koedt, Ellen Levine, and Anita Rapone, 198–207. New York: Quadrangle/New York Times Book Company.

Lorde, A. 1984a. "An Open Letter to Mary Daly." In *Sister Outsider: Essays and Speeches by Audre Lorde*, 66–71. Trumansburg, NY: Crossing Press.

Lorde, A. 1984b. "Uses of the Erotic: The Erotic as Power." In *Sister Outsider: Essays and Speeches by Audre Lorde*, 53–59. Trumansburg, NY: Crossing Press.

MacKinnon, C. A. 1979. *Sexual Harassment of Working Women: A Case of Sex Discrimination.* New Haven, CT: Yale University Press.

MacKinnon, C. A. 1989. *Toward a Feminist Theory of the State.* Cambridge, MA: Harvard University Press.

McKeon, M. 2012. "Symposium: Before Sex." *Signs: Journal of Women in Culture and Society* 37 (4): 791–848.

McRuer, Robert. 2006. *Crip Theory: Cultural Signs of Queerness and Disability.* New York: New York University Press.
Miller-Young, M. 2014. *A Taste for Brown Sugar: Black Women, Sex Work and Pornography.* Durham, NC: Duke University Press.
Millett, K. 1969. *Sexual Politics.* New York: Avon Books.
Muñoz, J. 2009. *Cruising Utopia: The Then and There of Queer Futurity.* New York: New York University Press.
Nagel, J. 2003. *Race, Ethnicity, and Sexuality: Intimate Intersections, Forbidden Frontiers.* New York: Oxford University Press.
Nestle, J. 1984. "The Fem Question." In *Pleasure and Danger: Exploring Female Sexuality*, edited by Carole S. Vance, 232–241. Boston: Routledge and Kegan Paul.
Puar, J. 2007. *Terrorist Assemblages: Homonationalisms in Queer Times.* Durham, NC: Duke University Press.
Rabinow, P., ed. 1984. *The Foucault Reader.* New York: Pantheon.
Radicalesbians. 1973. "The Woman Identified Woman." In *Radical Feminism*, edited by Anne Koedt, Ellen Levine, and Anita Rapone, 240–245. New York: Quadrangle/New York Times Book Company.
Rich, A. 1976. *Of Woman Born.* New York: W. W. Norton.
Rich, A. 1980. "Compulsory Heterosexuality and Lesbian Existence." *Signs: Journal of Women in Culture and Society* 5 (4): 631–660.
Rubin, G. S. 1984. "Thinking Sex: Notes for a Radical Theory of the Politics of Sexuality." In *Pleasure and Danger: Exploring Female Sexuality*, edited by Carole S. Vance, 267–319. Boston: Routledge and Kegan Paul.
Rubin, G. S. 2011. *Deviations: A Gayle Rubin Reader.* Durham, NC: Duke University Press.
Rupp, L. J. 2012. "Sexual Fluidity 'Before Sex.'" *Signs: Journal of Women in Culture and Society* 37: 849–856.
Samois. 1981. *Coming to Power: Writings and Graphics on Lesbian S/M.* San Francisco: Samois.
Sedgwick, E. K. 1990. *Epistemology of the Closet.* Berkeley: University of California Press.
Spillers, H. J. 1984. "Interstices: A Small Drama of Words." In *Pleasure and Danger: Exploring Female Sexuality*, edited by Carole S. Vance, 73–100. Boston: Routledge and Kegan Paul.
Stein, M. 2010. *Sexual Injustice: Supreme Court Decisions from Griswold to Roe.* Chapel Hill: University of North Carolina Press.
Taylor, V., and L. J. Rupp. 1993. "Women's Culture and Lesbian Feminist Activism: A Reconsideration of Cultural Feminism." *Signs: Journal of Women in Culture and Society* 19 (1): 32–61.
Thomsen, C. Forthcoming. "In Plain(s) Sight: Rural LGBTQ Women and the Politics of Visibility." In *Queering the Countryside: New Directions in Rural Queer Studies*, edited by M. Gray, C. Johnson, and B. Gilley. New York: New York University Press.
Vance, C. S., ed. 1984. *Pleasure and Danger: Exploring Female Sexuality.* Boston: Routledge and Kegan Paul.
Vance, C. S. 1989. "Social Construction Theory: Problems in the History of Sexuality." In *Homosexuality, Which Homosexuality? International Conference on Gay and Lesbian Studies*, edited by D. Altman, C. Vance, M. Vicinus, et al., 13–34. Amsterdam: Dekker/Schorer.
Weed, E., and N. Schor. 1997. *Feminism Meets Queer Theory.* Bloomington: Indiana University Press.
Wittig, M. 1969. *Les Guerilleres.* Translated by David Le Vay. Boston: Beacon Press.

CHAPTER 44

STATE/NATION

JOHANNA KANTOLA

Introduction

The state and nation are closely intertwined in everyday language and usage. Yet theoretically and conceptually, distinct literatures have developed around the two concepts, also in feminist theory, and are covered in this chapter as *feminist theories of the state* and *gender and nation* debates. What unites feminist debates on these two concepts is a deep uneasiness about them. Feminists often quote Virginia Woolf, who wrote, "As a woman I have no country, as a woman I want no country," which reflects the suspicions toward the state as a patriarchal institution that co-opts women's movement demands, and toward nationalism as a patriarchal ideology that often fails the equality claims of women who have joined nationalist struggles. At the same time, feminist scholars have been quick to point out women's active roles in these institutions and ideologies, as well as women's resistance to their traditional roles and appropriations of them.

Despite the distinct nature and profile of the feminist debates on the state and the nation, they share some key concerns that reflect the shifts in feminist theory. Traditionally, the key feminist questions in relation to the state and nation have included analyses of the paradoxes and dichotomies, such as the public-private, in and out of the state and relationships of the state and nation to feminist politics and struggles. Feminist debates on these two concepts have, first, moved away from *essentialist* notions about women and men and the state and nation. Black feminist theorizing about gender, race, ethnicity, sexism, and racism (hooks 1984; Hill Collins 1991; Lorde 1997) has become more mainstream with the popularity of the notion of intersectionality (Crenshaw 1991), which highlights how gender intersects with race and ethnicity, sexuality, disability, class, and other inequality categories (e.g., Yuval-Davis 2011). Second, instead of the state and nation being real essentialized objects, feminist theories tend to explore them as relational entities that need to be perpetually *reproduced* through discourses, practices, or material circuits. Feminist scholars explore the power relations behind these constructions, the femininities and masculinities they rely on and reproduce, and their differentiated gender impacts. State processes, policies, institutions, discourses, practices, and norms are shown to be gendered and gendering and constitutive of gender orders. States and nations are also racialized and sexualized in that they use norms around heterosexuality to reproduce the state and nation. Feminist scholars have coined the terms *homonationalism* and *homoprotectionism* to illustrate how the states and nations draw new boundaries between "us" and "them," the Others (Lind and Keating 2013; Puar 2007). In these approaches, state interests are constructed in the very processes whereby they are represented or articulated (Kantola 2007).

Third, these concepts are now theorized as highly *context specific* rather than universal. Context-specific states are termed abusive, women-friendly, developmental, fragile, coercive, postmodern, central, or postcolonial in feminist debates to reflect the differences both between and within states and state institutions (Bumiller 2008; Prügl 2010; Kantola and Dahl 2005). Nationalism and nations mean very different things in different contexts too. Despite general trends toward using women as symbols of nations (as in Mother India or Mother Russia) or as biological and cultural reproducers of nations (Yuval Davis 1997), nations appropriate women and men, femininities and masculinities, and sexualities and race and ethnicity in different ways. The "affective turn" in feminist theory, in turn, points to the role of emotions in holding nations and states together (Ahmed 2004). Finally, the *changing political and societal context* is reflected in the feminist debates about the state and nation. What was first discussed as "globalization" has now been specified as neoliberalization that takes different forms in different parts of the world. Neoliberal governmentality reflects the infiltration of market-driven truths and calculations into the domain of politics (Ong 2007, 4). A cross-cutting theme in current feminist research is the manifold impacts of neoliberalism in states and nations and the feminist engagements with them to the extent that we can talk about a move toward "market feminism" (Kantola and Squires 2012). Feminist scholars explore, in particular, the ways in which neoliberalism is often combined with other ideologies, such as conservatism, radical-right populism, or homonationalism, and the gendered outcomes of this.

Feminist Theories about the State

Feminist theories were long dominated by a deep uneasiness about the state, which was seen as patriarchal and therefore beyond feminist politics. This discomfort culminated in arguments that feminists did not have a theory of the state (Mackinnon 1989) and that it was not a feminist concern to theorize the state (Allen 1990). Judith Butler (1997), too, whose gender theory has been so influential among poststructural feminists and beyond, has conceptualized the state in a strongly anti-statist way—in contradiction with her other anti-essentialist thinking (Lloyd 2007). Despite these tendencies, a variety of feminist perspectives on the state exists. The "canon" includes liberal, radical, Marxist/socialist, Nordic, and poststructural feminist perspectives (see e.g., Chappell

2013; Kantola 2006; Waylen 1998) and, most recently, new materialist and postcolonial feminist perspectives on the state. Feminist stories and the citing practices that go with them often inflate differences between approaches, for example, between poststructural and new materialist feminisms, and rejecting what comes before relates to a need "to authorize a new terrain" (Ahmed 2008, 33; Hemmings 2011). In this chapter, I take this critique seriously, and rather than present a coherent narrative, discuss different feminist answers to some key questions. These include feminist theories' answers to such questions as, what is the state? how is it gendered, racialized, classed, and sexualized? what do the states do and with what effects? and what roles do states play in advancing equalities/perpetuating inequalities?

For some feminist scholars, the state represents a neutral institution that can be targeted and lobbied to achieve progressive gender-equality legislation. The state is an institution that is a source of potentially women-friendly legislation and policies. For example, in the liberal feminist classic *The Feminine Mystique* (Friedan 1962), equality of opportunity for women is to be achieved by changing the legislation on equal pay, working hours and outlawing discrimination in the workplace. Women's access to the state in terms of political institutions (parliaments, governments, bureaucracies) becomes an important political question and goal.

While liberal feminists recognize that state institutions are dominated by men and that policies reflect masculine interests, they argue that the state is to be "captured back" from the interest group of men. In other words, the state is a reflection of the interest groups that control its institutions, a notion that resembles pluralist state theories in political science (Dahl 1961). The notion of the state put forward by liberal feminists is symptomatic of liberal feminist appropriation of key concepts in general: they take the existing ideas and apply them to the case of women (cf. about power, Lloyd 2013, 113). More women in the state would entail more women's policy, a presumption that has since been challenged in the debate about women's substantive representation (Celis et al. 2008, 2014).

The benign notion of the liberal state also informs the work of Susan Moller Okin (1989), who argues that the liberal models of justice are to be extended from the sphere of the benign state to the sphere of family, and criticizes the state's indirect role in the reproduction of inequalities in families. For Okin, the solution to these problems lies within the liberal state: in its public policies and reforms of family law. The arguments about the benign liberal state surface in recent debates about feminism and multiculturalism. Okin (1999) argues that the liberal state should set boundaries to multicultural group rights when these rights harm women.

A similar benign notion of the state can be discerned from a different feminist tradition—namely, Nordic theorizing of the women-friendly welfare states. Helga Maria Hernes (1987) defines Nordic states as potentially women-friendly societies, which signifies that women's political and social empowerment happens through the state and with the support of state social policy. The social democratic citizenship tradition results in an optimistic acceptance of the state as an instrument of social change. For Hernes (1988, 210), Nordic women act in accordance with their own culture in turning to the state, even in those instances when they wish to build alternative institutions. Studies of the Nordic women-friendly welfare states argue that women become empowered as political subjects through the institutionalization of gender equality. This draws attention to women's contributions and roles in both maintaining and changing gender relations (Siim 1988).

Nordic feminism is more pessimistic than liberal feminism is in its analysis of gender and the state. The private dependency of women on individual men is transformed into public dependency on the state in the women-friendly welfare states (Dahlerup 1987). The expansion of the public sector, even if it benefits women, is planned and executed by a male-dominated establishment. The parameters for distribution and redistribution policies are still determined within the framework of the corporate system, where women have an even more marginal role to play than in the parliamentary system. Thus, women are the objects of policies. The tendency is exacerbated by the observation that women's lives are more dependent and determined by state policies than men's (Hernes 1987, 77) and that the Nordic welfare states are based on a gendered system of power and hierarchies.

A number of theoretical traditions in feminist theory indeed view the state less optimistically or positively. In these, the state is theorized as patriarchal, abusive, or capitalist. These critiques come from very different theoretical traditions, ranging from Catharine MacKinnon's radical feminism to Marxist and socialist feminism to Judith Butler. The state is theorized to work together with ideologies or modes of governance such as neoliberalism or capitalism to appropriate feminist movement goals, for example, in relation to sexual violence (Bumiller 2008).

Radical feminists stress the patriarchal nature of the state, which requires analyzing its role in perpetuating gender inequalities. The state is not an isolated, neutral, and narrow institution but rather is embedded in broader gendered societal structures that in turn shape women's engagement with the state and the policies that emanate from it (Eisenstein 1986, 181). With Kate Millett, the concept of patriarchy acquired a new meaning (1970). Until her *Sexual Politics*, patriarchy had signified the rule of the father or the rule of the head of the household. Millett argues that patriarchy is actually about the rule of men—male supremacy—the most fundamental form of oppression. The concept of patriarchy captures the insight that the oppression of women is not haphazard or piecemeal; rather, the diverse forms of oppression are interconnected and mutually sustained. The radical nature of this feminist analysis stems from the claim that the state is not contingently patriarchal, but essentially so. Furthermore, patriarchy is global and universal. The particular forms that states take matter less than the fact that all are patriarchal states.

Catharine MacKinnon (1987, 1989) articulates a radical feminist stance on the state:

> The state is male in the feminist sense: the law sees and treats women the way men see and treat women. The liberal state coercively and authoritatively constitutes the social order in the interest of men as a gender—through its legitimating norms, forms, relations to society, and substantive policies.
>
> (MacKinnon 1989, 161–162)

Feminists cannot expect the state to liberate women because it is impossible to separate state power from male power. MacKinnon directs her critique at the liberal state in particular and criticizes its laws and policies. Even if the laws on rape, abortion, and pornography are formally there, they are never fully enforced. At the same time, states enforce the equation of women with sexuality, which adds to their oppression. For Carole Pateman (1988), the origins of patriarchy lie in the social-sexual contract that gives men the political right over women and access to their bodies. An exclusive focus on integrating women into state institutions produces a situation that perpetuates dominant patriarchal discourses and norms rather than challenge them. Important questions are not asked, critical arguments are not formulated, and alternatives are not envisioned (Ferguson 1984, 29, 193).

While liberal feminists understand the state in terms of its political institutions, radical feminists extend their focus to the wider structures of the state and society. Radical feminist work shows the patriarchal nature of the formal and informal practices of politics and connects this to the "personal"—families, sexuality, intimate relations, violence—which significantly expands the scope of what is studied as politics and the political. The concept of patriarchy informs feminist strategies and political goals: the entire structure of male domination must be dismantled if women's liberation is to be achieved (Acker 1989, 235). Civil society, rather than the state, is the sphere in which women should concentrate their energies in order to challenge patriarchy. Via consciousness raising it becomes possible to rediscover what is truly female and to struggle to speak with women's own voice.

Whereas for radical feminists, the state is patriarchal, for Marxist feminists, the state is essentially capitalist (McIntosh 1978, 259). The state is not just an institution but also a form of social relations. Women's subordination plays a role in sustaining capitalism through the reproduction of the labor force within the family. Women are oppressed in work and excluded from it, and Marxist feminists argue that the familial ideology is to blame. When criticizing welfare states, Marxist feminists argue that the state helps to reproduce and maintain the familial ideology primarily through welfare state policies. In contrast to radical feminism, Marxist feminists argue that women are important in the struggle against capitalism as workers, not as women (McIntosh 1978) and the category of women is employed in reproductive terms (Sargent 1981, xxi).

Socialist feminists attempt to combine the insights of both Marxist and radical feminism. From radical feminists socialist feminists derive the understanding of the system of oppression called patriarchy; and from Marxist feminists, the importance of the class oppression defining the situation of all workers. The two approaches are combined in analyses of this "dual system" of capitalism and patriarchy. For Zillah Eisenstein (1979, 17), the notion of capitalist patriarchy captures the "mutually reinforcing dialectical relationship between capitalist class structure and hierarchal sexual structuring." Michele Barrett, in turn, identifies a number of ways in which the state promotes women's oppression: women are excluded from certain sorts of work by protective legislation, the state exercises control over the ways sexuality is represented through pornography laws, and the state's housing policy is resistant to the needs of nonnuclear families

(1980, 231–237). The socialist feminist debates revolve around the relative autonomy of the two systems. Some theorists argue that patriarchy has causal priority over capitalism (Hartmann 1981; Harding 1981); and others, that capitalism is more autonomous (Young 1981). For Eisenstein (1984), the capitalist class does not rule the state or government directly but instead exercises hegemony. A large part of the mystificatory role of the state is in this seeming identification of male interests and bourgeois interests.

More recently, the work of Judith Butler (1997) evidences a strong anti-state account that is critical of deflection of political battles into the courts and is based on the belief that democratization works best through civil society. In *Excitable Speech*, Butler (1997, 23) is critical of feminists who want to criminalize hate speech and argues instead that other forms of politics are more effective: "Nonjuridical forms of opposition, ways of restaging and resignifying speech in contexts that exceed those determined by the courts." Butler is suspicious about the arbitrary nature of the state power, and for her, the regulation of hate speech is an example of a means by which the state can extend its power (Lloyd 2007, 127). As Moya Lloyd (2007) explains in her interpretation of Butler, constructs such as hate speech become legal mechanisms for the state to "extend its own racial and sexualized discourses," which in turn result in inclusions and exclusions (129). These forms of state regulation curtail the opportunities of resignification in civil society. In sum, Butler's position stresses the productivity of state discourse and calls for understanding the ways in which laws can be misappropriated and used in anti-progressive ways (129).

Critical commentators have suggested that Butler assumes that legal protection is necessarily reactionary and hence dismisses the ways in which states may promote progressive equality politics (Jenkins 2001; Mills 2003; Lloyd 2007; Passavant and Dean 2001). Butler's notion of the state is also contradictory, signifying at times a very narrow judicial institution and, at other times, a broader set of conflicting institutions, practices and discourses. In her later work, Butler offers a qualified definition of the state and suggests that the state "is not reducible to law," and that it comprises plural institutions whose interests do not always coincide and where there are, consequently, multiple sites for political resistance (see Lloyd 2007, 131). However, Lloyd suggests that Butler's skepticism toward the state remains. Lloyd (2007, 132) argues that there is indeed a fundamental paradox in Butler's account of the state: she implies that "hate-speech and pornography can be radically recited but denies this possibility to state speech, or rather she allows that it can be recited but only in anti-progressive directions."

The above theorizing often comes from specific contexts that are not always made explicit. There is a strong body of feminist work on the state that stresses the importance of different contexts where states are theorized and the linkages between theory and this practice. Development scholars point to the fundamentally different meaning of the state in non-Western countries (Afshar 1996; Alvarez 1990; Dore and Molyneux 2000; Rai and Lievesley 1996; Visvanathan et al. 1997). Like Western debates, these literatures are concerned to examine the processes of state institutions in exercises of power in various areas of public and private lives of women and women's resistance to these intrusions (Rai and Lievesley 1996, 1). However, there are important differences.

Postcolonialism, nationalism, economic modernization, and state capacity emerge as key issues in the Third World literature; whereas Western feminists often take these issues for granted, focusing instead on how best to engage with the state (Chappell 2000, 246). For example, in Indonesia, the colonial state introduced the emphasis on motherhood and the domesticity of women that was characteristic of Victorian European societies (Wieringa 2002, 47). During the process of decolonization, women were first urged to join the battle against the colonizers but later their rights were forgotten or put aside, leading even to more conservative construction of women's roles in the state (Wieringa 2002, 47).

When exploring women's activism, for example, in Africa, the ways in which patriarchy is combined with the (neo)patrimonialism in the state becomes central (Tripp 2001; Njagi 2013). In neopatrimonial states, "claims to authority are based on personal relations of loyalty and dependence that stand above the law" (Tripp 2001, 106). When combined with patriarchy, they can exacerbate women's positions and chances in the states (Njagi 2013). Hence, questions of women's autonomy acquire a different significance from those of Western states. For example, the Ugandan women's movement has been able to claim a greater degree of autonomy from the state, which has been critical to its success (Tripp 2001, 105). Again, these practices vary greatly between the states and need to be studied contextually.

Poststructural feminists have sought to deconstruct the internal unity of the state and to theorize the differentiated state as a diverse set of institutions. Rosemary Pringle and Sophie Watson (1990, 1992) challenge the unity of the state and argue that the state consists of a set of arenas that lacked coherence and Elisabeth Prügl (2010, 448) defines the postmodern state as "a decentered state in which authority is shared by multiple levels of government." In poststructural analyses then, the state is a differentiated set of institutions, practices, agencies, and discourses. The state is depicted as a discursive process, and politics and the state are conceptualized in broad terms. The state unity is reproduced discursively (see e.g., Kantola 2007; Kantola, Norocel, and Repo 2011). The state is not inherently patriarchal but was historically constructed as patriarchal in a political process whose outcome is open. The patriarchal state can be seen, then, not as the manifestation of patriarchal essence, but as the center of a reverberating set of power relations and political processes in which patriarchy is both constructed and contested (Connell 1987, 1994). Particular discourses and histories construct state boundaries, identities and agency (Kantola 2006, 2007). Masculinity is central for understanding "the multiple modes of power circulating through the domain called the state" (Brown 1995, 177). German feminists, such as Birgit Sauer (2001) and Marion Löffler (2001), use the Weberian notion "rule" (*Herrschaft*) to describe attempts to create order that operate in state institutions and society (Prügl 2010). The state emerges from this work as a set of legal rules that reinforce social practices of masculine domination (Prügl 2010).

Wendy Brown's poststructuralist approach attends to the constitutive character of state's gender orders, the contradictions inherent in them, and the ways in which state processes occur across very different sites (Brown 1995, 167). Elisabeth Prügl (2010), although inspired by Brown's work, critiques her for giving insufficient attention to feminist struggles and to the ways in which these have been institutionalized in state based laws and policies. A number of other poststructural feminists have asked what the most effective strategies are for empowering women in their engagements with the state (Randall 1998, 200). In other words, feminists aim to make sense not only of the state's impact on gender, but also of the ways in which the state can be made use of and changed through feminist struggles (Kantola 2006). The analyses allow the complex, multidimensional and differentiated relations between the state and gender to be taken into account. They recognize that the state can be a positive as well as a negative resource for feminists, thus deconstructing the dichotomy between "in" and "out" of the state. Within a framework of diverse discourses and power relations, gender diversity and differences in women's experiences come to the fore (Kantola and Dahl 2005).

"Renewed materialist feminism" conceptualizes the state as differentiated too. However, the state and its effects cannot be understood merely in terms of discourses but are embedded in the material phenomena and processes (Coole and Frost 2010, 2–3). The renewed material feminism accepts social constructionism but conceptualizes the material realm as irreducible to culture and discourse (Coole and Frost 2010, 27; for debates about feminist new materialism, see Ahmed 2008; Davis 2009; Irni 2013). In terms of the state, this signifies combining the "Weberian insights of critical theory regarding the bureaucratic state, whose tentacles reach increasingly deeply to control ordinary lives through governance and governmentality, and aspects of Foucauldian genealogy that describe how the minutiae of power develop and practically manage embodied subjectivities" (Coole and Frost 2010, 27).

When explaining the renewed scholarly interest in materialism, Diana Coole and Samantha Frost (2010) single out not only the advances in natural sciences and biopolitical and bioethical issues but also the global political economy and understanding its structural conditions such as neoliberalism (6–7). From the point of view of theorizing the state, what becomes important is the biopolitical interest of the modern state: the state's role in managing the life, health, and death of its populations through management of "fertility rates, marriage and funeral rites, epidemics, food hygiene, and the nation's health" (23). Seemingly technical questions about biological life processes enter the political order because the state must make decisions about the worthiness of different lives (23). In this way, states exert powers in shaping, constraining, and constituting life chances and existential opportunities. The exercise of these powers take place in complex circuits "whereby discursive and material forms are inextricable yet irreducible and material structures are simultaneously over- and undermined" (27). While economic factors and capitalism become central, the capitalist system is not understood in a narrowly economistic way but, rather, "as a detotalized totality that includes a multitude of interconnected phenomena and processes" (29). This view encourages scholars to take Foucauldian analysis of governmentality, biopolitics, and the role of discourse in maintaining social order seriously, and to incorporate the state's role in maintaining the conditions of capital accumulation into the analyses (30).

Empirical research on gender and the state has used these feminist theories in different ways. For example, the so-called comparative state feminist literature has studied the ways in which women's movements engage with one branch of the state—women's policy agencies—and evaluated the factors that effect the successes and failures of these engagements for overall gender policy in the state (see Stetson McBride, and Mazur 1995; McBride and Mazur 2010). Lee Ann Banaszak (2010) conceptualizes the state in terms of its organization and bureaucracy and explores the favorable locations for gender activists and the impact of changes in these for feminist struggles. An important shift in Europe has been states' engagements with political intersectionality that have expanded state policies on different inequality categories, from gender and race to, for example, sexual orientation, age, disability, religion, and belief, in a contested political process that has been termed by feminist scholars "institutionalizing intersectionality" (Kantola 2010; Krizsan, Skjeie, and Squires 2012). Feminist new institutionalists, in turn, study the state as a variety of separate institutions that include both formal and informal institutions, such as norms and rules (Chappell 2013, 607; 2003; see also Krook and Mackay 2011). The body of work draws attention to the importance of institutional legacies, path dependencies, and possibilities for change (Chappell 2013, 608).

Neoliberalism has become an important theme for feminists seeking to understand contemporary states. Neoliberal logics of governance have resulted in changes in state powers that have been described as state power evaporating upward, downward, sideways, and laterally to international organizations, substate organizations, nonelected state bodies, private enterprises, public-private partnerships, and civil societies, with manifold consequences for feminist politics and engagements with the state (Banaszak, Beckwith, and Rucht 2003, 4–7; Kantola and Outshoorn 2007, 8–14). The European Union (EU) is an example of a suprastate actor whose powers result in fundamental changes in member states through processes of Europeanization, challenging conventional notions of state sovereignty (Kantola 2010; Lombardo and Forest 2012). For Elisabeth Prügl, the EU "epitomizes the decentered postmodern state and the loss of nation-state autonomy in the context of globalisation," which engages actors beyond and below the nation-state (Prügl 2010, 448). Neoliberalism has also been conceptualized as a new relationship between government and knowledge through which governing activities are recast as nonpolitical and nonideological problems that need technical solutions (Ong 2007, 3). These changes in states are also transforming state-based feminist strategies and practices from previous "state feminism" to "market feminism" (Kantola and Squires 2012) or governance feminism (Prügl 2011; Woehl 2008), where feminist knowledge is appropriated and transformed to the service of neoliberal states.

Gender and Nation

While the state is conceptualized in a wide variety of ways, its connotations point to institutions and bureaucracy, their processes and legitimacy. The nation, in contrast, relates to the people. Inclusion and exclusion, the politics of belonging and of drawing boundaries are some of the key questions that the relation to people gives rise to.

For feminist scholars, the gendered, racialized, classed, and sexualized constructions of people in relation to nations are of central interest.

Nira Yuval-Davis (2011, 82) calls answers to the "what is a nation" question "shopping lists." They are political lists of required characteristics for certain purposes of inclusion and exclusion. Theoretically, understandings of the nation have evolved from primordial "natural nations"—that is, extensions of family and kinship units—to modernist notions in which nations are constructed in specific historic times, yet have a "concrete objective reality" (as explained by Yuval-Davis 2011, 84) to imagined communities (Anderson 1983) and nations as narrations (Bhabba 1994). Billig (1995) coined the influential term "banal nationalism" to describe the need of nations to be reproduced all the time, not just at times of crises and conflict. Nationalism, in turn, can be seen variously as (i) as a discourse that produces the idea of the nation, (ii) a project pursued by specific social movements, or (iii) an evaluation where political and cultural ideologies claim superiority of particular nations (Calhoun 1997, 6). The role of the state is oftentimes central in reproducing nations. The "nation-state" is an example of a powerful political construct as the boundaries of nations rarely coincide with those of the states (Yuval-Davis 1997, 11). Rather, the political world is characterized by stateless nations, such as the Roma or Sami in Europe, or multination states.

Nations are constructed on different lines which effects their inclusiveness and exclusiveness. Nira Yuval-Davis (1997; 2011, 20) differentiates between lines of *Volknation* (based on the myth of common descent), the *Kulturnation* (based on common culture, religion, or language), and *Staatnation* (based on loyalty and solidarity based on common values). Nations based on the myth of common descent tend to be most racialized and least permeable to those coming from outside or deemed as the nation's Others. Nations based on common identities and common culture, religion, or language result in national identities that are more open to voluntary, often assimilatory, identification. Finally, those nations based on loyalty and solidarity based on common political values have the most permeable boundaries (Yuval-Davis 2011, 20–21). Yuval-Davis (2011, 10) now speaks of "the politics of belonging" to analyze the specific political projects aimed at "constructing belonging to particular collectivity/ies which are themselves being constructed in these projects in very specific ways and in very specific boundaries." Importantly, the politics of belonging involves both a hegemonic project of the maintenance and reproduction of the boundaries of the community of belonging and also "their contestation, challenge and resistance by other political agents" (20).

Feminist scholarship has explored the different gendered relations that underpin the constructions of nations and nationalisms: the roles of the women as reproducers of the nation *biologically, culturally,* and *symbolically* (Yuval-Davis and Anthias 1989; Yuval-Davis 1997, 2). The gendered constructions have been closely intertwined with race and ethnicity, and class. Lately, feminist scholarship has paid increasing attention to masculinities (Norocel 2013) and sexualities (Puar 2007; Nagel 2000; Peterson 1999) in the constructions of nations. Constructing and upholding nations requires constant doing by the nation: nations constitute their subjects, and their existence requires the subjects' repetitive acts and performances in which different parts of their identities play a central role.

Women's roles as the biological reproducers of the nation bring clearly to the fore the gendered roles attributed to women and men in relation to the nation and nationalism (Yuval-Davis 1997, 22). This makes a number of biopolitical questions directly relevant to debates on gender and nation: women's reproductive roles and struggles for reproductive rights, forced sterilization, abortion, contraception, population growth, population control, eugenicist discourse, and the regulation of who should have children (22). Racism has always been a strong theme because, for example, the forced sterilization of Roma women still happens in Europe today (Anthias and Yuval-Davis 1992; Kantola 2010).

Constructions of nations have tended to rely on essentialized gendered roles: women act as the mothers and biological reproducers of the nation; men as the soldiers, leaders, and protectors of the nation. The public-private distinction relegates women to the private sphere and reserves the public for property-owning men. Normative motherhood represents an ideal type of femininity, combined with normative heterosexuality (Norocel 2013, 64–66), proper gender roles, and sexual behaviors (Nagel 2000, 113), and the institutionalization of heterosexuality (Peterson 1999, 39). These roles take on different manifestations in different contexts. For example, in Serbia, from the 1980s onward with the growth of nationalism, the "reproductive potential of women" was stressed and women were to reproduce not just new citizens but also soldiers for the nation. Women's heroism, then, was determined by her willingness to sacrifice her children for the nation (Bracewell 1996, 29). The heightened role of Serbian women as biological reproducers of the nation can be compared to that of women in in India, where the nationalist movement privileged the symbolic category of women as mothers of the nation whose role was to maintain a specific national identity (Thapar-Björkert 2013, 814). In Indonesia, in contrast, during the anticolonial struggle, women had combined the roles of actors in the political arena and "good" mothers and wives but were disappointed after the national liberation was won and their roles were reduced to the domestic sphere (Wieringa 2002, 97–99).

Women have also used this maternal role for political activism, as in the case of Argentina's Las Madres de Plaza de Mayo, who claimed justice from the repressive government and demanded the return of their disappeared children. In this process, the women politicized their roles as mothers and reclaimed public spaces through demonstrations (Alvarez 1990). Women's resistance to these roles of biological and cultural reproducers of the nation and the expectations that nationalism places on them is captured by Athena Athanasiou's (2005) analysis of the Women in Black. Standing silently in black these women resist the constructions of "Others" that cannot be mourned: "performing an alternative feminist politics which involves being radically disloyal, instead of unconditionally supportive, to 'their' men in time of war" and "non-exclusionary notion of who counts as a 'woman': people of all genders and sexualities are welcomed to participate as women in their actions of ritual mourning" (41). Women's active support for nationalist struggles was a key contribution of feminist scholarship outside the West (Jayawardena 1986). Women were shown to take up arms, to refuse the role of the protected in violent conflicts in national struggles as for example in Peru (Romero Delgado). Yet, the role of the mother still haunts the descriptions of women's roles in violent conflicts, and "the mother narrative" is used a key explanation to women resorting to violence and arms (Sjoberg and Gentry 2007).

Gender is central to the cultural and symbolic reproduction of nations, too. The cultural production of the nation signifies the "cultural codes of style of dress and behavior as well as more elaborate bodies of customs, religion, literary and artistic modes of production, and, of course, language" (Yuval-Davis 1997, 23). Here, nations and nationalism are based on gender symbols and constructions of femininity and masculinity and women act as "symbolic border guards of the nation and as embodiments of the collectivity" (23). This entails strict norms about how women behave or dress (Chatterjee 1990). It also entails forms of normative masculinity based on fatherhood, honor, patriotism, bravery, duty, and heterosexism (Nagel 2000, 252; Norocel 2013, 70–71).

The norms constitute hierarchies between nations, as in the case of colonialism and postcolonialism and the role of oriental women and men in this process (Enloe 1989). "Native women" and their oppression were used to justify European civilizing missions. Colonialism, gender, and power hierarchies are tied together in a number of ways historically. Colonized nations are feminized, which entails the subordination of whole nations (Thapar-Björkert 2013, 810). Colonized men are feminized too to stress their inferiority to colonial men. In a highly sexualized process, sexuality and nation intersect to produce notions about other nationalities' sexual character and potential threats related to this (Thapar-Björkert 2013, 811). Women's bodies have also become concrete battle grounds through rape as a weapon of war and militarized prostitution and entertainment businesses. Freeing oppressed women is an imaginary still in use as in the case of US-led wars in Afghanistan and Iraq in the 2000s.

These gendered nationalist hierarchies are also highly pertinent within countries. For example, in the Nordic countries in Europe, gender inequality is increasingly identified with the culture of the "Others"—namely, the immigrant populations or other national minorities. Their harmful gendered practices, such as female circumcision, forced marriage, and honor killings, are contrasted with the presumably gender-equal majority culture (Keskinen et al. 2009). The political consequences of this process include both homogenized and essentialized notions of gender inequalities in minority cultures and avoiding tackling gender equality problems in the majority culture.

The populism of the radical right draws on these gender hierarchies and binaries in contemporary Europe. A central feature of these ideologies is to equate nations with families based on very traditional heterosexual gender roles for women and men (Norocel 2013). Exploring the cases of Romania and Sweden, Norocel shows how radical-right populist parties construct their respective national families as vulnerable, in the hands of a remote and detached elite, and where the constructed *people* represents the most vulnerable classed part of the society, at mercy of globalization. Men are constructed as idealized working-class breadwinners, and the constructions of women draw on normative motherhood or are "reduced to merely decorative positions of sexual objects for the masculine heterosexual competition and reward for the people's men and their (male) Others" (Norocel 2013, 173). Unsurprisingly, radical-right populist parties in these countries have had problems with women's political participation, which is interesting considering Sweden's long history as a women-friendly welfare state and high numbers in politics. Norocel argues that being a woman and a politician went against the radical right's populist ideology, indicating that their constructions of nation as a family rely on constructing women's emancipation as a threat to the dominance of men in the public sphere and to women's motherly instincts, which, in turn, sets the very survival of the people under threat (Norocel 2013, 174).

The conservative politics of radical-right populism can take different forms too. Jasbir Puar (2008) has famously studied the "reintensification of racialization through queerness." The rise of the global gay right wing in Europe divides the world into "gay-friendly and not gay-friendly nations" (Puar 2007, xiv) to draw distinctions between certain European and Muslim countries and nations.

Puar's notion of homonationalism is based on Lisa Duggan's notion of homonormativity, the new neoliberal sexual politics in which "the possibility of a demobilized gay constituency and a privatized depoliticized gay culture are anchored in domesticity and consumption" (quoted in Puar 2007, 38).

This has signified a transition in the relations of queer subjects and nation-states "from being figures of death (i.e., the AIDS epidemic) to becoming tied to ideas of life and productivity (i.e., gay marriage and families)" (Puar 2007, xii). The ways in which homonationalism appropriates homosexuality and queer subjects challenges dichotomous portrayals of nations as only "supportive and productive of heteronormativity and always repressive and disallowing of homosexuality" (39). Homoprotectionist policies can serve to consolidate national identity and legitimate the centralization of state authority. State officials seek to create a more positive image of their government, nation, human rights record, economic policy framework, or foreign policy agenda by promoting or speaking about LGBT rights (Lind and Keating 2013, 519). Lind and Keating (2013) illustrate how homoprotectionist policies were combined with a very ambivalent stance toward gender and women's rights, including reproductive rights in the case of Ecuador.

When seeking to understand the complex relations between gender and the nation, the "affective turn" has signified a shift away from text and discourse to understanding emotions, affects, and the body. In other words, the emotional politics of contemporary constructions of nation are based on power circulating not just through discourses but also through feelings, emotions, bodies, and affects (Ahmed 2004; Pedwell and Whitehead 2012, 116). As Carolyn Pedwell (2012) argues, "Emotions are conceptualized most productively 'not as affective lenses on 'truth' or 'reality' but, rather, as one important (embodied) circuit through which power is felt, imagined, mediated, negotiated, and/or contested." Power works through affect to shape individual and social bodies in a gendered process whereby subjects learn emotional rules that help to maintain the hierarchies of gender, race, and class that exist in nations (Boler 1999). One of Sara Ahmed's (2004, 12) central insights is that "emotions can attach us to the very conditions of our subordination." This "affective attachment to social norms" explains the difficulties in achieving change in unequal power relations (11–12).

Conclusion

The state and nation continue to play key roles in challenging gendered, racialized, and sexualized hierarchies in contemporary societies. Feminist scholarship theorizes them as powerful constructs in which gender, race, class, and sexuality occupy a central position. Feminist answers to the "where are the women" question (Enloe 1989) exposed the power of the public-private distinction that had traditionally kept women outside the state in the private sphere and in the role of the biological reproducers of the nation. At the same time, this research showed women's active roles in the states and nations. A fundamental shift in feminist theory from the study women to the study of gender transformed the feminist study of states and nations too. Theoretically, it required focusing on both femininities and masculinities, on the broader power relationships in the societies, and on structural and institutionalized hierarchies in states and nations. The power relations between gender and the state and nation were no longer theorized as either top-down or bottom-up but as co-constitutive and complex. The relations that shape gendered nations and states also go beyond traditional state boundaries, to the supranational, international, and local levels and spheres. Later Judith Butler's (1990) influential work on the performativity of gender impacted on feminist theories about the state and the nation too. Gender, the state, and nation were now theorized in terms of doing rather than being: they need constant repetitive acts by subjects to uphold them. The states and nations are discursively produced in processes where gender, race and ethnicity, and sexuality and class play a central role. The new materialist turn in feminist theorizing suggests that these processes are not just discursive but are material and bodily as well, and affects and emotions strengthen the ties between them and make change harder.

References

Acker, Joan. 1989. "The Problem with Patriarchy." *Sociology* 23(2): 235–240.
Afshar, Haleh, ed. 1996. *Women and Politics in the Third World*. London: Routledge.
Ahmed, Sara. 2004. *The Cultural Politics of Emotion*. New York and London: Routledge.
Ahmed, Sara. 2008. 'Open Forum: Imaginary Prohibitions; Some Preliminary Remarks on the Founding Gesture of the "New Materialism."' *European Journal of Women's Studies* 15(1): 23–39.
Allen, Judith. 1990. "Does Feminism Need a Theory of 'The State'?" In *Playing the State*, edited by Sophie Watson, 21–37. London: Verso.
Alvarez, Sonia E. 1990. *Engendering Democracy in Brazil: Women's Movements in Transition Politics*. Princeton, NJ: Princeton University Press.

Anderson, Benedict. 1983. *Imagined Communities: Reflections on the Origins and Spread of Nationalism*. London: Verso.

Anthias, Flora, and Nira Yuval-Davis. 1992. *Racialized Boundaries: Race, Nation, Gender, Colour and Class and the Anti-Racist Struggle*. London: Routledge.

Athanasiou, Athena. 2005. "Reflections on the Politics of Mourning: Feminist Ethics and Politics in the Age of Empire." *Historein* 5.

Banaszak, Lee Ann. 2010. *The Women's Movement: Inside and Outside the State*. Cambrdige: Cambridge University Press.

Banaszak, Lee Ann, Karen Beckwith, and Dieter Rucht. 2003. "When Power Relocates: Interactive Changes in Women's Movements and States." In *Women's Movements Facing the Reconfigured State*, edited by Lee Ann Banaszak, Karen Beckwith, and Dieter Rucht, 1–29. Cambridge: Cambridge University Press.

Barrett, Michèle. 1980. *Women's Oppression Today: Problems in Marxist Feminist Analysis*. London: Verso.

Bhabba, H. 1994. "Dissemination: Time, Narrative and the Marginso of the Mdoern Nation." In *The Location of Culture*, edited by H. Bhabba, 139–170. London: Routledge.

Billig, M. 1995. *Banal Nationalism*. London: Sage.

Boler, Megan. 1999. *Feeling Power: Emotions and Education*. London: Routledge.

Bracewell, Wendy. 1996. "Women, Motherhood and Contemporary Serbian Nationalism." *Women's Studies International Forum* 19(1–2): 25–33.

Brown, Wendy. 1995. *States of Injury: Power and Freedom in the Late Modernity*. Princeton, NJ: Princeton University Press.

Bumiller, Kristin. 2008. *In an Abusive State: How Neoliberalism Appropriated the Feminist Movement against Sexual Violence*. Durham and London: Duke University Press.

Butler, Judith. 1990. *Gender Trouble: Feminism and the Subversion of Identity*. London: Routledge.

Butler, Judith. 1997. *The Psychic Life of Power*. Redwood City, CA: Stanford University Press.

Calhoun, C. 1997. *Nationalism*. Buckingham: Open University Press.

Celis, Karen, Sarah Childs, Johanna Kantola, and Mona Lena Krook. 2008. "Rethinking Women's Substantive Representation." *Representation: The Journal of Representative Democracy* 44(2): 99–110.

Celis, Karen, Sarah Childs, Johanna Kantola, and Mona Lena Krook. 2014. "Constituting Women's Interests through Representative Claims." *Politics & Gender* 10(2): 149–170.

Chappell, Louise. 2000. "Interacting with the State." *International Feminist Journal of Politics* 2(2): 244–275.

Chappell, Louise. 2003. *Gendering Government: Feminist Engagement with the State in Australia and Canada*. Vancouver: University of British Columbia Press.

Chappell, Louise. 2013. "State and Governance." In *The Oxford Handbook on Gender and Politics*, edited by Georgina Waylen, Karen Celis, Johanna Kantola, and Laurel Weldon, 603–626. New York: Oxford University Press.

Chatterjee, P. 1990. "The Nationalist Resolution of the Women's Question." In *Recasting Women: Essays in Colonial History*, edited by K. Sangari and S. Vaid, 233–252. New Brunswick, NJ: Rutgers University Press.

Connell, Robert W. 1987. *Gender and Power*. Cambridge: Polity Press.

Connell, Robert W. 1994. "The State, Gender and Sexual Politics: Theory and Appraisal." In *Power/Gender*, edited by H. Radtke and H. Stam, 136–173. London: Sage.

Coole, Diana, and Samantha Frost. 2010. "Introducing New Materialisms." In *New Materialisms: Ontology, Agency and Politics*, edited by Diana Coole and Samantha Frost, 1–43. Durham and London: Duke University Press.

Crenshaw, Kimberle. 1991. "Demarginalizing the Intersection of Race and Sex: A Black Feminist Critique of Antidiscrimination Doctrine, Feminist Theory and Antiracist Politics." In *Feminist Legal Theory: Readings in Law and Gender*, edited by K. Bartlett and R. Kennedy, 57–80. San Francisco: Westview Press.

Dahl, R. 1961. *Who Governs?* New Haven, CT: Yale University Press.

Dahlerup, Drude. 1987. "Confusing Concepts—Confusing Reality: A Theoretical Discussion of the Patriarchal State." In *Women and the State*, edited by Anne Showstack Sassoon, 93–127. London: Routledge.

Davis, Noela. 2009. "New Materialism and Feminism's Anti-Biologism: A Response to Sara Ahmed." *European Journal of Women's Studies* 16(1): 67–80.

Dore, Elizabeth, and Maxine Molyneux, eds. 2000. *Hidden Stories of Gender and the State in Latin America*. Durham and London: Duke University Press.

Eisenstein, Zillah. 1979. "Developing a Theory of Capitalist Patriarchy and Socialist Feminism." In *Capitalist Patriarchy and the Case for Socialist Feminism*, edited by Zillah Eisenstein, 5–40. New York and London: Monthly Review Press.

Eisenstein, Zillah. 1984. *Feminism and Sexual Equality: Crisis in Liberal America*. New York: Monthly Review Press.

Eisenstein, Zillah. 1986. *The Radical Future of Liberal Feminism*. Boston: Northeastern University Press.

Enloe, Cynthia. 1989. *Bananas, Beaches and Bases: Making Feminist Sense of International Politics*. Berkeley: University of California Press.

Ferguson, Kathy. 1984. *The Feminist Case against Bureaucracy*. Philadelphia, PA: Temple University Press.

Friedan, Betty. 1962. *The Feminine Mystique*. New York: Dell.

Harding, Sandra. 1981. "What Is the Real Material Base of Patriarchy and Capital?" In *Women and Revolution: The Unhappy Marriage of Marxism and Feminism*, edited by Lydia Sargent, 190–233. London: Pluto Press.

Hartmann, Heidi. 1981. "The Unhappy Marriage of Marxism and Feminism: Towards a More Progressive Union." In *Women and Revolution: The Unhappy Marriage of Marxism and Feminism*, edited by Lydia Sargent, 1–42. London: Pluto Press.

Hemmings, Clare. 2011. *Why Stories Matter: The Political Grammar of Feminist Theory*. Durham and London: Duke University Press.

Hernes, Helga Maria. 1987. *Welfare State and Woman Power*. Oslo: Norwegian University Press.

Hernes, Helga Maria. 1988. "Scandinavian Citizenship." *Acta Sociologica* 31(3): 199–215.

Hill Collins, Patricia. 1991. *Black Feminist Thought: Knowledge, Consciousness and the Politics of Empowerment*. New York: Routledge.

hooks, bell. 1984. *Feminist Theory: From Margin to Center*. Boston: South End Press.

Irni, Sari. 2013. "The Politics of Materiality: Affective Encounters in a Transdisciplinary Debate." *European Journal of Women's Studies* 20(4): 347–360.

Jayawardena, Kumari. 1986. *Feminism and Nationalism in the Third World*. London: Zed.

Jenkins, Fiona. 2001. "The Heeding of Differences: On Foreclosure and Openness in a Politics of the Performative." *Constellations: An International Journal of Critical and Democratic Theory* 8(3): 364–375.

Kantola, Johanna. 2006. *Feminists Theorize the State*. New York and London: Palgrave Macmillan.
Kantola, Johanna. 2007. "The Gendered Reproduction of the State in International Relations." *British Journal of Politics and International Relations* 9(4): 270–283.
Kantola, Johanna. 2010. *Gender and the European Union*. New York and London: Palgrave Macmillan.
Kantola, Johanna, and Hanne Marlene Dahl. 2005. "Gender and the State: From Differences between to Differences Within." *International Feminist Journal of Politics* 7(1): 49–70.
Kantola, Johanna, Cristian Norocel, and Jemima Repo. 2011. "Gendering School Shootings in Finland." *European Journal of Women's Studies* 18(2): 183–198.
Kantola, Johanna, and Joyce Outshoorn. 2007. "Changing State Feminism." In *Changing State Feminism*, edited by Joyce Outshoorn and Johanna Kantola, 1–20. Basingstoke and New York: Palgrave Macmillan.
Kantola, Johanna, and Judith Squires. 2012. "From State Feminism to Market Feminism." *International Political Science Review* 13(3): 382–400.
Keskinen Suvi, Sari Irni, Salla Tuori, and Diana Mulinari, eds. 2009. *Complying with Colonialism: Gender, Race and Ethnicity in the Nordic Region*. Aldershot: Ashgate.
Krizsan, Andrea, Hege Skjeie, and Judith Squires, eds. 2012. *Institutionalizing Intersectionality? Comparative Analyses*. Basingstoke: Palgrave Macmillan.
Krook, Mona-Lena, and Fiona Mackay. 2011. *Gender, Politics and Institutions: Towards a Feminist Institutionalism*. New York and Basingstoke: Palgrave Macmillan.
Lind, Amy, and Christine Keating. 2013. "Navigating the Left Turn. Sexual Justice and the Citizen Revolution in Ecuador." *International Feminist Journal of Politics* 15(4): 515–533.
Lloyd, Moya. 2007. *Judith Butler: From Norms to Politics*. Cambridge: Polity Press.
Lloyd, Moya. 2013. "Power, Politics, Domination and Oppression." In *The Oxford Handbook on Gender and Politics*, edited by Georgina Waylen, Karen Celis, Johanna Kantola, and Laurel Weldon, 111–134. New York: Oxford University Press.
Lombardo, Emanuela, and Maxime Forest. 2012. *The Europeanization of Gender Equality Politics*. New York and London: Palgrave Macmillan.
Lorde, Audre. 1997. "Age, Class, Race and Sex. Women Defining Difference." In *Dangerous Liasons: Gender, Nation and Postcolonial Perspectives*, edited by Anne McClintock, Aamir Mufti, and Ella Shohat, 374–380. Minneapolis: University of Minnesota Press.
Löffler, Marion. 2001. "Herrschaft als zentrales Konzept zur Entschlüsselung der Geschlectlichkeit des Staates." In *EU, Geschlect, Staat*, edited by Eva Kreisky, Sabine Lang, and Birgit Suer, 15–31. Vienna: WUV Universitätsverlag.
Mackinnon, Catharine. 1987. "Feminism, Marxism, Method and the State." In *Feminism and Methodology*, edited by Sandra Harding, 135–156. Milton Keynes: Open University Press.
Mackinnon, Catharine. 1989. *Towards a Feminist Theory of the State*. Cambridge, MA, and London: Harvard University Press.
McBride Stetson, Dorothy, and Amy Mazur. 1995. *Comparative State Feminism*. London: Sage.
McBride, Dorothy, and Amy Mazur. 2010. *The Politics of State Feminism: Innovation in Comparative Research*. Philadelphia, PA: Temple University Press.
McIntosh, Mary. 1978. "The State and the Oppression of Women." In *Feminism and Materialism: Women and Modes of Production*, edited by A. Kuhn and A. Wolpe, 254–289. London: Routledge and Kegan Paul.
Millett, Kate. 1970. *Sexual Politics*. Garden City, NY: Doubleday.

Mills, Catherine. 2003. "Contesting the Political: Butler and Foucault on Power and Resistance." *Journal of Political Philosophy* 11(3): 253–272.
Nagel, Joanna. 2000. "Ethnicity and Sexuality." *Annual Review of Sociology* 26(1): 242–269.
Njagi, Jane Wambui. 2013. *The State and Sexual Politics: An Analysis of Abortion Discourses in Kenya*. PhD thesis. University of Waikato.
Norocel, Cristian. 2013. *Our People—a Tight-Knit Family under the Same Protective Roof: A Critical Study of Gendered Conceptual Metpahors at Work in Radical Right Populism*. Helsinki: University of Helsinki.
Okin, Susan Moller. 1989. *Justice, Gender, and the Family*. New York: Basic Books.
Okin, Susan Moller. 1999. "Is Multiculturalism Bad for Women?." In *Is Multiculturalism Bad for Women?*, edited by Susan Moller Okin, et al., 7–24. Princeton, NJ: Princeton University Press.
Ong, Aihwa. 2007. *Neoliberalism as Exception. Mutations in Citizenship and Sovereignty*. Durham and London: Duke University Press.
Passavant, Paul, and Jodi Dean. 2001. "Laws and Societies." In *Constellations: An International Journal of Critical and Democratic Theory* 8(3): 376–389.
Pateman, Carole. 1988. "The Patriarchal Welfare State." In *Democracy and the Welfare State*, edited by Amy Gutman, 231–260. Princeton, NJ: Princeton University Press.
Pedwell, Carolyn. 2012. "Affective (self-)transformations: Empathy, neoliberalism and international development." *Feminist Theory* 13(2): 163–179.
Pedwell, Carolyn, and Anne Whitehead. 2012. "Affecting Feminism: Questions of Feeling in Feminist Theory." *Feminist Theory* 13(2): 115–129.
Peterson, V. Spike. 1999. "Sexual Political Identities/Nationalism as Heterosexism." *International Feminist Journal of Politics* 1(1): 34–65.
Pringle, Rosemary, and Sophie Watson. 1990. "Fathers, Brothers, Mates: The Fraternal State in Australia." In *Playing the State*, edited by Sophie Watson, 229–243. London: Verso.
Pringle, Rosemary, and Sophie Watson. 1992. "'Women's Interests' and the Post-Structuralist State." In *Destabilizing Theory*, edited by Michele Barrett and Anne Phillips, 53–73. Cambridge: Polity Press.
Prügl, Elisabeth. 2010. "Feminism and the Postmodern State: Gender Mainstreaming in European Rural Development." *Signs* 35(2): 447–475.
Prügl, Elisabeth. 2011. "Diversity Management and Gender Mainstreaming as Technologies of Government." *Politics and Gender* 7(1): 71–89.
Puar, Jasbir. 2007. *Terrorist Assemblages: Homonationalism in Queer Times*. Durham and London: Duke University Press.
Rai, Shirin, and Geraldine Lievesley, eds. 1996. *Women and the State: International Perspectives*. London: Taylor and Francis.
Randall, Vicky. 1998. "Gender and Power: Women Engage the State." In *Gender, Politics and the State*, edited by Vicky Randall and Georgina Waylen, 185–205. London: Routledge.
Sargent, Lydia. 1981. "New Left Women and Men: The Honeymoon Is Over." In *Women and Revolution: The Unhappy Marriage of Marxism and Feminism*, edited by Lydia Sargent, xi–xxxii. London: Pluto Press.
Sauer, Birgit. 2001. *Die Asche des Souveräns: Staat und Demokratie in der Geschlechterdebatte*. Frankfurt: Campus.
Siim, Birte. 1988. "Towards a Feminist Rethinking of the Welfare State." In *The Political Interests of Gender*, edited by Kathleen Jones and Anna Jónasdóttir, 160–186. Oxford: Sage Publications.

Sjoberg, Laura, and Caron E. Gentry. 2007. *Mothers, Monsters and Whores: Women's Violence in Global Politics*. London and New York: Zed.

Thapar-Björkert, Suruchi. 2013. "Gender, Nations and Nationalisms." In *The Oxford Handbook on Gender and Politics*, edited by Georgina Waylen, Karen Celis, Johanna Kantola, and Laurel Weldon, 803–828. Oxford: Oxford University Press.

Tripp, Aili Mari. 2001. "The Politics of Autonomy and Cooptation in Africa: The Case of the Ugandan Women's Movement." *Journal of Modern African Studies* 39(1): 101–128.

Visvanathan, Nalini, Lynn Duggan, Laurie Nisonoff, and Nan Wiegersma, eds. 1997. *The Women, Gender and Development Reader*. London: Zed.

Waylen, Georgina. 1998. "Gender, Feminism and the State: An Overview." In *Gender, Politics and the State*, edited by Vicky Randall and Georgina Waylen, 1–17. London: Routledge.

Wieringa, Saskia. 2002. *Sexual Politics in Indonesia*. London and New York: Palgrave Macmillan.

Woehl, Stephanie. 2008. "Global Governance as Neo-liberal Governmentality: Gender Mainstreaming in the European Employment Strategy." In *Global Governance: Feminist Perspectives*, edited by Shirin Rai and Georgina Waylen, 64–83. Basingstoke: Palgrave. Macmillan.

Young, Iris Marion. 1981. "Beyond the Unhappy Marriage: A Critique of the Dual-Systems Theory." In *Women and Revolution: The Unhappy Marriage of Marxism and Feminism*, edited by Lydia Sargent, 43–70. London: Pluto Press.

Yuval-Davis, Nira. 1997. *Gender and Nation*. London: Sage.

Yuval-Davis, Nira. 2011. *The Politics of Belonging. Intersectional Analysis*. London: Sage.

Yuval-Davis, Niram, and Flora Anthias, eds. 1989. *Woman-Nation-State*. London: Macmillan.

CHAPTER 45

STORYTELLING/NARRATIVE

SHARI STONE-MEDIATORE

SINCE the 1980s, feminist theorists across the disciplines have challenged the norms of scholarly and public debate by embracing experience-based storytelling as a distinctly rigorous and democratic mode of engaging the world. By promoting stories of personal struggle, testimony of the everyday effects of public policy, and other creative narrations of personal and historical experience, feminist thinkers have pushed the boundaries of academic and political debate to make room for voices and styles long denied a public audience or intellectual credibility. Such appeals to experience-oriented stories, however, have not only unsettled mainstream discourses but have raised vexing questions within feminist theory itself, including questions about the extent to which storytelling really is more critical and democratic than the discourses to which it has been contrasted.

Turns to experience-based storytelling have troubled feminist theory because, on the one hand, storytelling has presented feminist thinkers with an appealing alternative to the rigid and exclusionary discourses that have dominated academic and public life. Inspired by feminist consciousness-raising groups of the 1970s and spurred on over the next several decades by critical inquiry into the classist, racist, and sexist biases of ostensibly neutral academic and public forums, many feminist thinkers have turned to storytelling to engage "the experience of the world that is not admitted into dominant knowledge paradigms" (Razack 1998, 36) and to "br[ing] into the open" the "power dynamic" behind such exclusions (MacKinnon 1989, 92). On the other hand, however, especially since the 1990s, feminist critics have warned that storytelling can be just as mired in power and ideology as any ruling discourse. Not only have sexist and racist communities used storytelling as enthusiastically as feminist ones, as critics have argued, but even women's stories and stories from the margins can follow identity categories, plot types, and conventions of telling and listening that reflect received ideologies and social hierarchies. Far from challenging power dynamics, some have charged, women's experience-based stories "inadvertently redraw the very configurations and effects of power that they seek to vanquish" (Brown 1995, ix).

The mixed feminist reactions to storytelling tempt one to conclude that storytelling has no unique affinities to feminist goals and, moreover, that feminist enthusiasm for storytelling risks providing a guise of liberatory speech to practices that reproduce structures of exclusion and domination. And yet, feminist engagements with storytelling have reached no neat conclusion. Even after the critiques, feminist thinkers and activists have continued to tell stories of experience in efforts to "break open political space" for "under-told and unauthorized experiences and knowledge" (Carbine 2010, 384; Pitter 2010, 185). Such tenacious turns to experience-based storytelling challenge us to ask, what compels feminist and progressive thinkers to veer from the norms of rational discourse and to invoke more explicitly engaged and literary forms, notwithstanding their risks and contradictions? And what might the persistent appeal of storytelling tell us about the politics of our knowledge practices?

Storytelling in Practice

Feminist scholarly interest in storytelling has been catalyzed, in large part, by women's turning to storytelling to grapple with everyday struggles. In the United States, storytelling came to the forefront of the women's movement with the consciousness-raising groups of the late 1960s and 1970s, which provided a forum for (mainly white, middle-class women) to exchange stories of their frustrations. In supportive communities, women shared stories of discontent with their daily lives as housewives, anger at degrading treatment by men, and confusion about their uneasiness with their ostensibly natural roles. By sharing their stories, advocates of consciousness-raising argue, the women not only supported one another emotionally but came to trace their seemingly personal anguish to their roles as women in a patriarchal society (MacKinnon 1989). During the same time, many women in the global South and women of color in the United States generated new perspectives on their identities and histories by pursuing testimonies, creative memoirs, and other experience-based texts. These stories ventured further than white, middle-class women's stories insofar as they mixed languages and genres to explore simultaneous oppression and "the politics of multiple identities" (Torres 1991, 272); however, analogously to white women's story sharing, these stories also used "the politics of everyday life" to cultivate new historical knowledge and political consciousness (Mohanty 1991a, 39).

The consciousness-raising movement in the United States has met with criticism from within feminism. Too often, critics have argued, the emphasis on personal stories has led women to focus on their individual problems without concern for the struggles of differently located people or the broader sociohistorical mechanisms of oppression. According to this argument, women of all social and cultural backgrounds face such risks, but the risks are greatest for privileged-class white women, whose examination of their own difficulties offers little insight into racial and socioeconomic systems of oppression. Finally, critics have warned that when women turn to storytelling as a means to reclaim their essential selves or to "authenticate 'their own oppression'" (Mohanty 1991a, 34), they merely claim for themselves the kind of authority that elite men have held and fail to question models of subjectivity and knowledge that have allowed some people to make confident claims by silencing others (Code 1991, 252–259; Brown 1995, 41–42; hooks 1989, 105–110; Mohanty 1991a, 34).

Such critiques raise important questions (some of which are pursued later in this chapter) about the dangers of myopia and the potential lack of self-critical awareness in experience-based narration; however, the transformative effects of story sharing on at least some groups of women have encouraged numerous feminist scholars to pursue the value of storytelling for feminist projects. Thus, before turning to the criticism, the following sections present several of the most fully theorized achievements that feminist scholars have attributed to storytelling: the turning of everyday experiences of discontent into critical insight, the disruption of practices of domination, the promotion of more inclusive democracies, and the encouragement of more rigorous and community-accountable knowledge practices.

Storytelling as Link between Experience and Critical Insight

In the wake of popular turns to storytelling, many feminist scholars of the 1980s and 1990s sought to theorize how women's everyday lives could provide the starting point for critical insight. Some transnational and Latina feminists specifically addressed "the importance of *writing* in the production of self- and collective consciousness"; that is, they stressed that "simply being a woman, or being poor or black or Latino, is not sufficient ground to assume a politicized oppositional identity," but that "the practice of storytelling," including the collective and reflective work of "remembering and rewriting," is vital to transforming daily suffering into collective political consciousness (Mohanty 1991a, 33, 34, 35; italics in the original). In contrast to the focus on writing in transnational feminism, feminist standpoint theorists have focused specifically on the epistemic resources contained in women's daily experiences. Nonetheless, not unlike their transnational colleagues, feminist standpoint theorists have stressed the importance of "finding ways of speaking [about women's experience] and ways of speaking it politically" (Smith 1987, 58). They also have recognized the complicated character of experience and the "struggle to articulate the forbidden, 'incoherent' experience that makes possible new politics and subsequent analysis" (Harding 1991, 282). Such remarks indicate the need for creative, interpretive work—in effect, storytelling—to transform women's everyday experiences of discontent into feminist knowledge.

Creative, community-situated, and historically attuned storytelling plays an essential (although undertheorized) role in the work of standpoint theorists, such as Dorothy Smith and Sandra Harding. Storytelling is essential to their accounts of the feminist standpoint because the epistemic resources that they find implicit in our everyday lives are not directly accessible or easily representable. On the contrary, such experiences are "forbidden, 'incoherent,'" and have a double-edged relationship to systems of domination; double-edged in the sense that our experiences are both formed by and formed in reaction to ruling institutions. Thus, on the one hand, standpoint theorists argue that a web of social, political, and cultural systems of domination organize our everyday lives. In the modern world, such "relations of ruling" operate, in part, with the aid of academic and professional discourses, for the latter provide the categories by which state bureaucracies and other ruling institutions subsume the particularities of our lives under standardized labels and rules (Smith 1987). For instance, the category *housewife* allows state bureaucracies to treat many women as "nonworkers," which, in turn, allows their husbands and many women themselves to conceive of women who maintain their family's homes as unproductive, dependent beings. In this way, an ensemble of social, cultural, and political institutions govern our daily lives as well as "keep us in our places by invading our own consciousness" (Smith 1987, 50).

On the other hand, however, standpoint theorists also identify elements of experience that resist established institutions. Such resistant experiences often lack "rightful means of expression," given that the public and professional vocabularies available to describe our lives tend to reflect the standpoint of professional-class men, who are comfortable within established institutions (Smith 1987, 51). Nonetheless, a pre-articulate discontent with the social order can agitate us on multiple levels, destabilizing our socially formed consciousness and potentially spurring us to share stories of our discontent with others. In the case of women's consciousness-raising groups, for instance, a "barely submerged discontent" that the women related to being female "in some inchoate way" prompted them to gather together to share stories and reflect on the source of their frustrations (MacKinnon 1989, 85).

In this account, experienced tensions provide the initial impulse for critique. But a critical standpoint is achieved only with collective interpretive work. Collective and historically oriented interpretive work is needed in order to explore patterns of oppression that "are occluded by the individual and untheorized experience" and "are only fully revealed in discoveries that go beyond what direct experience will teach us" (Harding 1991, 282; Smith 1987, 107). Going beyond direct experience, people can gain experience-based critical insight by tracing links between experienced tensions and the broader socio-historical world so as to foreground the obscured power dynamics that have organized their lives. Such work often probes painful experience and often demands community-supported, genre- and discipline-defying speech and writing, as people explore how to sort out their lives, not in ways that suit others' theories, but in ways that are illuminating for themselves (Harding 1991, 272–276; MacKinnon 1989, 85–90; Smith 1987, 58–60, 78–97). Neither detached analysis nor the mere reporting of data is adequate to this task. Neither is conventional autobiography adequate for tracing forces that affect an individual's daily life but whose mechanisms are invisible in the everyday world. Rather, the work that standpoint theorists describe as crucial to transforming an oppressed person's experience into critical insight is a specific kind of discursive practice: emotionally engaged, community-situated, socio-historically aware, and innovative storytelling.

STORYTELLING AS STRATEGY OF RESISTANCE

Like feminist standpoint theorists, transnational and multicultural feminists have stressed the value of "utiliz[ing] our lived relations as a basis of knowledge" about the social world (Mohanty 1991a, 34, 35) and, likewise, the importance of "drawing the *connections* between the experiences of the women and the powers exerted upon them" (Panjabi 1997, 155–156, italics in the original). However, while standpoint theorists have only gestured toward the discursive work that turns marginalized experience into feminist knowledge, transnational and multicultural feminist theorists have foregrounded this discursive work. They have examined the specific stylistic and narrative innovations that women who have been reduced to victims or have felt torn between identities have employed to "theoriz[e] their experience in radical and innovative terms" (Torres 1991, 274). And they have affirmed that experience-oriented writing itself is "at the heart of the struggle" insofar as it creates a space for people to speak about "multilayered facets of their histories and concerns" that have been shamed into silence or dismissed as "'feminine' experience" (Million 2009, 54). "[T]he very practice of remembering and rewriting" by Third World women, says Chandra Mohanty, "is significant not merely as a corrective to the gaps . . . of hegemonic masculinist history," but also because writing is "a space for struggle and contestation about reality itself" (1991, 34a). Narrative representations of our lives, these theorists stress, affect not only how we record and remember history, but also how ruling institutions exercise power over us and how we resist such domination.

In her analysis of the prison narratives of Third World women, Kavita Panjabi demonstrates how narration can use everyday experience to gain critical political insight and, too, how narration itself serves as a strategy of resistance against authoritarian states. Panjabi examines two prison testimonials from the 1970s: Jaya Mitra's memoir of her imprisonment in West Bengal, India, and Alicia Partnoy's testimony of her concentration camp internment during Argentina's "dirty war." Each author makes clear that she seeks not merely to document torture but to use her experiences "as a springboard for probing systems of domination" (Panjabi 1997, 155). In the vein of feminist standpoint theory, each woman uses her experiential reflections as "a focused prismatic index of the functioning of patriarchy and state power" (Panjabi 1997, 153). For instance, both narratives describe the gender-specific torture of imprisoned women—including special "exercises" for one pregnant woman and the coerced in-prison prostitution of women who had been arrested for their (forced) participation in prostitution—alongside accounts of prison officials' exhorting the women to fulfill their proper roles as mothers. Such strategic narrations of prison life expose the hypocrisy of state discourses of morality as well as indicate how those discourses facilitate authoritarian rule by legitimizing control over women's minds and bodies. At the same time, both narratives highlight "not victimization but resistance" (Panjabi 1997, 155). As context-specific narratives, each presents a diversity of women, as well as tensions among women, but each also tells of women's solidarity in the face of daily struggles for survival—for instance, by sharing food and caring for each other. The women's supportive modes of personal interaction thus "drive a wedge" in the state's coercive and technical modes of rule, which at times even threatens the confidence of the guards (Panjabi 1997, 168). Panjabi argues that by narrating everyday cooperative and communicative forms of resistance and artfully juxtaposing them to the state's coercive forms of rule, the authors link women's daily interpersonal activities to "strategies of collective resistance in the public sphere" (1997, 169). The narratives thereby intervene in discourses of political agency and help to promote an oppositional feminist political consciousness. In effect, they constitute "form[s] of mobilization through writing" (Alexander and Mohanty 1997, xxxviii).

Storytelling also can "mobilize through writing" insofar as strategically constructed stories can subvert and reclaim the identity categories that have regulated our lives. Gloria Anzaldúa's now classic "Toward a Mestiza Consciousness" has gained wide recognition for the way it uses creative, historically sensitive, and theoretically informed narration of experience to subvert binary-structured identity categories and recast the mestiza as essential to our planet's future. For instance, by reflecting on her memories of cultural confusion—memories of being American yet having her traditions and language devalued as "un-American," watching her father and those who grow the nation's food being worked to death, facing sexism from the men who shared her language—Anzaldúa sorts through the pressures she has faced as a biracial, bilingual, "queer" American, and thereby begins to take control over the significance of her borderlands existence. Moreover, by thematizing her labor of remembering and rewriting painful experiences, including her temptation "to block with a counterstance" and her decision to pursue instead a path beyond "the split," Anzaldúa also highlights the creative, engaged, experientially and theoretically informed discursive work by which she not only documents but transforms her "mixed breed" identity (1990, 377, 378). Through creative discursive work, she "turns the ambivalence into something else": *una mestiza* who embraces her border-defying, joining-together existence, and whose multiplicity, akin to crossbred corn, "will survive the crossroads" (Anzaldúa 1990, 379, 380). Far from merely authenticating individual oppression or empowering an autonomous individual, such a narrative helps those of us with whom it resonates to "see ourselves as part of history" (hooks 1989, 110): a history that shapes our everyday difficulties but that also can be shaped by our own creative reckoning with conflict and our narration of new "images and symbols that connect us to teach other and to the planet" (Anzaldúa 1990, 380).

Storytelling as Essential to Democracy

Other feminist theorists also have recognized storytelling as a vehicle "for those excluded from the [ruling] discourse" to gain "public voice" (Young 2000), but they have addressed such capacities of storytelling to limitations in current theories of democracy. Scholars, including Iris Young (1993, 2000), Lisa Disch (1994), and Rosemary Carbine (2010), have argued that greater integration of experience-based storytelling in civic forums can contribute to maintaining a democratic public sphere in ways that both mainstream political theorists and current political institutions have overlooked. Many of their claims dovetail with those of critical race theorists, who have advocated for storytelling by marginalized groups as a way to "shatter complacency" with entrenched social narratives and create public space for historically marginalized voices (Delgado 1995, 65).

Of central concern to these theorists is that free and pluralistic public debate has been hailed as a cornerstone of Western democracy, and yet such ostensibly democratic conversation often has excluded people from more marginalized social groups. "U.S. public life," says Carbine, "is still largely limited by longstanding marginalizing norms and practices" that "prevent marginalized peoples, especially African American citizens, from meaningful civic participation" (2010, 377, 378). Such limitations arise not only from blatant economic inequities, these theorists argue, but also from subtle exclusionary effects of discursive norms, which undermine democracy in ways that leading theorists of deliberative democracy have overlooked. The latter have based the legitimacy of democracy on a public realm in which people participate freely in rational debate; however, they have failed to consider how, in practice, what has passed as "rational debate" has been constrained by discursive norms that have favored some social and cultural groups over others (Carbine 2010; Disch 1994; Young 1993; Million 2009).

Young has identified specific ways that discursive norms in industrial democracies have obstructed the civic participation of the more marginalized members of the polity. So-called rational public debate, she argues, has been identified with linear, dispassionate, and seemingly neutral, universalistic speech. At the same time, such universalistic speech has been associated with professional-class, white, heterosexual males, such that what has passed as rational argument has been colored by a "*culture* of deliberation": a culture that has cast the rational deliberator as a neutral, detached, professional-class, white man, who speaks in terms familiar to his fellow male professionals (Young 1993, 127; italics in original). People whose race, gender, or demeanor veer from this image of rationality, or who present their views in more creative, engaged, or personalized forms, "will not be respected as equal citizens in the deliberative public" (Young 1993, 127). For instance, the stories by First Nation women who narrate their "felt knowledge" of gendered colonialist violence have fit neither the discourses of Euro-American feminism,

Native men, or the Canadian courts, and thus have been dismissed as unscientific and not essential to the public record, despite their insights into the aftermath of colonialist policies that continue to haunt the Canadian state (Million 2009). Moreover, when elected officials present policy decisions as if they are the result of free public discussion, or as if they represent a general public good, they gloss such differences of discursive power and suppress any demands for further discussion or a broadening of the debate (Disch 1994, 25–26, 218–219; Young 1993; 2000, 55–71).

Young and more recent feminist narrative theorists have proposed public storytelling as one response to the biased structure of political debate. They have argued for greater respect for experience-oriented storytelling, in a variety of media and styles, as a legitimate form of civic engagement, as well as for a more regular inclusion of stories from marginalized groups in official political and legal forums. According to these theorists, a greater role for storytelling in civic life would enhance democratic community and political judgment, first, because the "felt knowledge" conveyed by stories is an integral though often unrecognized dimension of our historical reality. Native American narrative theorists, in particular, have emphasized that "our bodies... participate in our 'knowing'" and that such whole-person knowing is essential to understanding and transforming historical conflicts, which "live on as long as their descendants live on" (Martinez 2005, 305, 307). In this account, the wounds of historical violence linger in people's bodies and psyches, and only when the broader public engages with the stories of those who carry the pain can the community begin to consider the profound human implications of historical policies, recognize past and present wounds, and respond meaningfully to historical crimes (Million 2009, 54).

Others have emphasized that stories are a crucial means by which members of marginalized groups can edge their way into forums dominated by more privileged social groups. Whereas argumentative claims often provoke defensiveness, stories work indirectly, inviting listeners to "visit" others' worlds; that is, rather than command that listeners follow a peremptory logic to a definite conclusion, stories ask for imagination, exploration, and consideration of "what life is like for others" (Delgado and Stefancic 2001, 41). Such story-facilitated imagination is especially important when people have experienced wrongs that seem to them abusive but that do not fit current legal categories of wrongdoing. In such situations, those suffering "may have no language for expressing the suffering as an injustice, but nevertheless they can tell stories that relate a sense of wrong" (Young 2000, 72).

In a similar vein, feminist narrative scholars have attributed to storytelling the potential to disrupt entrenched ways of seeing and provoke consideration of phenomena that defy familiar narratives. Stories that achieve such effects contribute to responsible political judgment, not by imposing abstract principles, but by enhancing our attention to unregistered and unexpected aspects of specific political phenomena (Disch 1994, 106–121; Stone-Mediatore 2003, 25–45). For instance, Carbine describes the importance of unique congressional hearings on FEMA (the US Federal Emergency Management Agency) in which African American (mainly female) survivors of Katrina were able to present their stories. When testifiers recounted military police who "caged us, laughed at us, took pictures of us with their camera phones" and who left them interned without food and water, congresspersons were challenged to consider gender, class, and racially-stratified effects and obligations related to Katrina that defied their "assumption of the United States as a color-blind society" (Carbine 2010, 377, 378). Such stories can be strengthened with empirical data and historical context, which can indicate the broader significance of the problems narrated; however, when entrenched beliefs have constrained public debate, important data are often ignored. For instance, data on police abuse are often explained away in terms of "black criminality" or are simply not recorded (Butterfield 2001). In such contexts, "narrative functions in an irruptive way, precisely to break open political space for hearing and empathizing with excluded peoples" whose stories can "shed a new critical light on our public life" (Carbine 2010, 384).

Finally, feminist theorists have embraced experience-oriented storytelling for its potential to help those who have been excluded from public life to regain dignity and recognition as important members of the polity. This was especially valuable for the Katrina survivors, who were stereotyped and misunderstood by the dominant culture and who enjoyed little previous access to public forums. More local and federal hearings such as those devoted to the Katrina survivors, feminist theorists have suggested, are valuable not only for holding Congress accountable for the effects of public policies on a diverse public but also for removing some of the barriers that have prevented marginalized members of the polity from becoming active political subjects (Carbine 2010, 378–384; Young 1993, 133–137).

Interestingly, many marginalized groups have not waited for invitations from lawmakers to avail themselves of public storytelling. Increasingly since the 1960s, a range of social movements "from immigration rights to marriage equality to climate justice—[have been] making narrative a core part of their strategy" (Moe 2014, 47). For instance, "using their own stories as political tools," undocumented youth have shared them—at Coming Out Day events, during congressional testimony, and via social media videos—so as to transform themselves "from stereotypes or projections into fleshed out characters" (Moe 2014, 47). Against stock stories that have opposed "Americans" to "aliens" and cast undocumented people as criminals, story-centered immigration rights projects have challenged people to recognize immigrants as complex, socially situated, and often hardworking human beings who are integral to the country, thereby "encourage[ing] a more in-depth and human conversation about immigration" (Benigno 2011). Through public story sharing, undocumented people also have moved from living partially clandestine and isolated lives to exposing their vulnerabilities but forming networks of support and resistance (Moe 2014, 49). In this account, even if we refrain from "romanticizing [immigrants' stories] as the expressions of authentic experience" (Apostolidis 2010, 4), we can still recognize the stories as political tools that have empowered immigrants as participants in public life, thus invigorating democratic debate about the meaning of "American" and the aims of immigration policy.

Storytelling as Rigorous Knowing

The popularity of public storytelling has been accompanied by feminist turns to storytelling in academia. In fields ranging from ethics to geography, legal studies to biology, and history to epistemology, feminist scholars have brought experience-based storytelling into disciplines that, ironically, have distinguished themselves as serious endeavors by separating themselves from seemingly amateur, subjective discourses like storytelling. In this context, ventures in academic storytelling have appeared as threats to rigorous knowing (Abrams 1991, 979; Brison 2002, 24–35; Code 1995, 154–176; 2006, 57; Million 2009, 65–68; Stone-Mediatore 2000, 91–92).

Some feminist scholar-storytellers have avoided trying to defend storytelling out of concern that doing so would subordinate storytelling to academic conventions that are at odds with storytelling's aims; however, others have argued that a formal defense of storytelling's intellectual value could encourage wider professional recognition of it and help feminist and marginal-voice thinkers to approach storytelling more reflectively. Lorraine Code, Katherine Abrams, and Dian Million, in particular, have presented epistemic justifications for storytelling. Their work bridges the insights of feminist standpoint theory, transnational feminists, and feminist political theorists with more conventional epistemic standards. At the same time, they recast the latter in ways that affirm the historical situatedness and community accountability of all knowledge making.

Critiques of Orthodox Knowledge

Code and other defenders of scholarly storytelling often have presented it as an antidote to the overly rigid, remote-from-historical-life, and un-self-critical modes of knowing that have dominated academia. As Code explains, the mystification in industrial societies of modern science has generated "an exaggerated ideal of scientific knowledge making" (2006, 9). In this idealized model, knowledge making is regarded as a matter of logical analysis of observational claims, where the latter have a clear-cut truth-value that is independent of the knower and historical context. Feminist critics stress that this model originated in industrial colonial Europe and represents only one way that human beings have effectively interacted with their world; however, the model presents itself as if it were a universal model of knowledge, the only one whose projects "are entitled to be called sciences" (Harding 2008, 4). Insofar as this model of knowing has come to dominate popular and academic conceptions of rigorous inquiry, its standards of objectivity, certainty, and universality have come to define any knowledge "worthy of the name" (Code 1991, 2).

Post-Enlightenment critiques of this knowledge paradigm are wide-ranging, but feminist epistemologists have addressed the model's excessive abstraction, rigidity, and lack of critical self-awareness in ways that are particularly relevant to the turn to storytelling. For instance, feminist critics have pointed out that the model's universalistic pretensions "choke out ways of knowing that depart from the stringent dictates of an exaggerated ideal of scientific knowledge making" (Code 2006, 8–9). In particular, the model denies epistemic value to inquiry that is socially and emotionally close to its subject matter; that listens to ordinary citizens; or that exhibits humility, wonder, and openness to mystery. And yet, according to some feminist and critical theorists as well as some human rights and environmental justice activists, such undervalued epistemic approaches are essential to knowing the living world. They are especially crucial to detecting social wrongs and imagining social possibilities that ruling discourses have ignored (Carson 1987, 296; Code 2006, 36–62, 207–236; Farmer 2003, 1–17, 25–28; Pitter 2010; Million 2009; Sandberg and Sandberg 2010; Stone-Mediatore 2010)

Feminist scholars also have criticized the model of scientific rationality for its failure to examine the interpretive underpinnings of our knowledge practices. This model of knowing, they explain, ignores the way that all knowledge practices are conditioned by socio-historical factors, including available technologies, politically situated negotiations over the selection and reading of evidence, and culturally given ways of interpreting phenomena (Code 1995, 24–30; 2006, 99–133; Harding 1991, 79–99). Feminist and critical race theorists have been particularly concerned with the interpretive frames that inform knowledge making and have described them in various ways. For instance, Code has explained how "a web of assumptions" about "humans" and "nature" make up "entrenched *social imaginaries* [that] work to hold certain conceptual frames in place" (2006, 22, 29). Smith has traced how the perspective of dominant social groups has informed the basic "questions, solutions, themes, styles, standards, [and] ways of looking at the world" that govern academic discourses, and how scholarship must participate in such "institutionalized discourses" to be recognized as credible work in the field (1987, 18). Critical race theorists have described how "key players in the legal system have tended to share a conceptual scheme" that is informed by "norms and values that derive directly from their social location" but that are effaced by the "fiction of objectivity," which casts legal authorities as if they were "simply interpreting what is before them" (Razack 1998, 38). These conceptual schemes often take the form of "stock stories," such as the story that the United States has made continual progress toward racial equality and that any remaining incidents of racial discrimination are anomalies that civil rights law adequately redresses (Delgado 1995). When the model of scientific rationality denies such cultural influences on knowledge making, knowers tend to overlook and unwittingly repeat received cultural frameworks, especially when the latter are shared by all the "key players."

Finally, feminist critics have warned that standards of universality, objectivity, certainty, and detachment represent only one historically specific and, ultimately, skewed way of meeting concerns for epistemic rigor. These standards, critics claim, reserve knowledge making for "highly credentialed experts" who present themselves as infallible knowers but who tend to view the world through rigid, "[d]iscipline-specific" lenses (Pitter 2010, 186). Likewise, these standards encourage theorists to prioritize "ready-made universals," which are amenable to neat and certain knowledge claims but which suppress the nuance and ambiguity that characterize any particular state of affairs; in effect, they encourage theorists to seek certainty and universality by "superimposing a grid upon events, experiences, and situations, tucking in the bits that spill over the edges, letting putative aberrations drop through the cracks" (Code 2006, 227, 280). Such disregard for living complexity is facilitated by divisions of labor in which staff such as nurses and research assistants (often women) work directly with particulars and process them for the scholars and scientists, who remain at a "professional distance" from the living world (Smith 1987). At the same time, professionals who work under guises of certainty, universality, and detachment tend to disappear behind masks of generic minds, thus denying any human ties to their subject matter or responsibility for the effects of their knowledge practices (Code 2006, 228; Stone-Mediatore 2010, 27–28, 34–36). Moreover, when they present their claims as "objective" and "certain," they place them above the public realm of discussion and debate, thereby further insulating themselves from community accountability (Code 2006, 228; Disch 1994, 68, 95; Stone-Mediatore 2003, 61).

Turns to Scholarly Storytelling

In light of these criticisms, scholarly turns to storytelling can be understood as responses to the lack of rigor and responsibility in conventional knowledge practices. If conventional knowledge practices "tend to filter out experiential details too difficult to accommodate" in their conceptual grids (Code 2006, 227), experience-based story-telling is presented as a way of returning to phenomena their nuances and specificity especially "the knotty details of life," the emotionally rich "deeper meaning," the unexpected, "messy and ambiguous," and "hard to grasp" aspects of phenomena and their context-dependent relations with other phenomena (Abrams 1991, 1004; Code 1991, 169; Million 2009, 54; Pitter 2010; Stewart 1996, 5). In this respect, feminist theorists have argued, storytelling can promote the empiricist virtues of careful and patient attention to the living world better than can conventional empiricist and theoretical approaches that deny epistemic value to emotional experience and narrow their view to discrete and fungible entities that are abstracted from their context (Code 1995, 159–168; Disch 1993, 668–669; Million 2009). In legal realms, for instance, experience-based storytelling can return particulars to a legal process whose focus on universal rules often overlooks important details of specific situations (Razack 1998, 37). By focusing on the messy details of specific affairs, legal storytellers also can expose the biases and limitations of seemingly neutral legal discourses. For instance, when scholar-storytellers Susan Estrich and Martha Mahoney interweave tales of their own and others' rape and battering experiences into their legal analyses, they belie the male bias of received categories of "force" and "victimhood," which have obscured the complex power relations and the subtle forms of "strength and resourcefulness in the midst of struggle" that often characterize crimes like rape and battering (Abrams 1991, 994).

At the same time that defenders of scholarly storytelling have emphasized its careful attention to particular phenomena, they also have stressed that storytelling's greatest value lies not in providing more detailed or accurate information, or in replacing dominant narratives with an alternative "smooth story" (Stewart 1996, 7), but in unsettling the frameworks through which we have interpreted the world. The claim is not that storytellers escape received conceptual frames, but that effective storytellers allow for more "interplay" between received frames and particular phenomena (Code 2006, 44). In other words, when storytellers reckon with "knotty details," confusing memories, and overlooked traces of complex experiences, they do not present "uncontested sites of fact-finding" or "'pure,' innocent telling[s] of how reality has imprinted itself upon a receptive consciousness" (Code 1995, 160, 169). They can, however, "fashion a gap in the order of things" (Stewart 1996 3), opening a discursive and imaginative space for us to explore phenomena that push the limits of entrenched disciplinary divisions and conceptual frames.

For instance, when survivors of colonialist sexual violence narrate somatic and emotional resonances of the abuse, they address phenomena that "can never be proper history" within "objective history" but that challenge us to exceed the latter in order to achieve "present healing in a past properly understood" (Million 2009, 73). Patricia Williams (1989) also leads us beyond discusrive conventions when she probes complicated aspects of her own encounters with racism. For instance, when Williams grapples with her uncharacteristic silence when she overheard salespeople sharing anti-Semitic remarks, and when she relates how her urge to protest the remarks was stifled by her desire to be an "insider," she does not offer a universal or definitive account of events; however, she does confound ready-made categories of self and other, of good guy and bad guy, and prompts us to consider subtle ways that our own societies or we, ourselves, might perpetuate the racism that dominant narratives proclaim we have overcome (1989, 2148–2150).

Stories of environmental problems, especially those that have traced the effects of environmental ills on specific communities, have also disrupted familiar conceptual schemes. For instance, while the ruling narratives of climate change have presented it as a global problem that is managed through nation-states, market economies, and scientific experts, the stories told by social movements, citizen-activists, and the scholars who have listened to them have put the problem in a different light: these stories have highlighted connections between environmental crises and social inequities, stressed the uneven costs and benefits of fossil fuel use, and pointed toward systemic causes of the problem, such as the corporatization of the economy, thereby reframing the problem as one of *climate justice* (Pitter 2010; Sandberg and Sandberg 2010). Even the Katrina testimonials served less as uncontested sites of fact-finding than as disrupters of received narratives, reopening the story of a "natural disaster" and prompting listeners to link such environmental problems to racially stratified power relations.

Importantly, defenders of scholarly storytelling argue that its power to unsettle received conceptual frames lies in its embrace of undervalued epistemic traits. It is precisely by engaging with their subject matter on deeply felt levels, by practicing humble and attentive listening to unexpected occurrences and muted voices (including the muffled and shamed voices within themselves), and by grappling creatively with phenomena that are not entirely knowable that scholar-storytellers such as Williams, climate-change critics, and First Nation narrators of colonialist sexual violence have compelled rethinking of dominant narratives. In effect, their closely engaged and creative stories have "help[ed] us unlearn what we have presumed to know" (Jennifer Geddes, quoted in Code 2006, 234) and changed "what *could* be said" in academic and public discourses (Million 2009, 54; italics in original).

Likewise, when stories convey the impressionistic but often deeply provocative insights of the people directly affected by events, they suggest the limitations of "relying exclusively on experts" and the value of engaging "a wide variety of sources" (Abrams 1991, 995). In her path breaking *Silent Spring*, Rachel Carson exemplified the kind of critical insight that is possible when storytellers combine scientific evidence collection with humble listening to ordinary people, who, Carson claimed, often "show a keener understanding of the dangers and inconsistencies of [pesticide] spraying than do the officials who order it done" (Carson, quoted in Code 2006, 45). It was because she combined empirical rigor with humble listening to local families and rangers talking about their experiences with illness and dead animals, and then combined both with creative reflection on the significance of her findings, that Carson not only collected startling evidence of pesticide dangers but also changed what counts as evidence and recast the framing of pesticide use from that of "eradicating pests" to a "war against nature" (Carson 1987, 7).

According to supporters, scholarly storytelling also has epistemic advantages over more conventional knowledge practices insofar as it stimulates discussion from a plurality of standpoints. Whereas peremptory and self-certain claims close off discussion, storytelling—especially when it presents itself as situated and perspective-laden—serves to provoke more storytelling from other perspectives. Scholarly storytelling thereby situates knowledge making in a community of activists, citizens, and scholar-storytellers, which helps to keep knowledge claims accountable to the broader community (Carbine 2010, 385; Code 1995, 159–169; Disch 1993, 668, 681; 1994, 85–105; Stone-Mediatore 2003, 60–64)

Finally, feminist theorists have argued that we can include storytelling in academic inquiry without uncritically accepting all stories, for stories can be held to standards suited to their character and aims. We can evaluate stories, for instance, in terms of the degree to which they turn our attention to socially important but overlooked phenomena, the degree to which they help us to imagine experiences different from our own while also reminding us of our inability ever to know those experiences with certainty, and the degree to which they acknowledge their partial and constructed character and thereby generate discussion and the rethinking of a problem from a plurality of standpoints (Abrams 1991, 1027–1029; Code 1991, 3; 2006, 228–234; Stone-Mediatore 2003, 67–94). In this account, storytelling is compatible with other forms of inquiry, including scientific evidence collection and social analysis. When added to the mix, however, storytelling reopens the discussion of what counts as evidence and as adequate analytic categories, while it resituates such discussions in the broader community.

Feminist Critiques of Storytelling

Even as storytelling has gained wide appeal as an alternative to rigid and exclusionary mainstream discourses, many feminist scholars (including many who are sympathetic to storytelling) have warned that too great a confidence in storytelling risks reproducing the hierarchies, exclusions, and dogmatisms that feminist storytellers have sought to redress. Such critiques gained momentum in the 1990s; however, rather than supersede feminist interest in storytelling, they have continued alongside the latter in a braid of unresolved plots. The story includes feminist scholars who have completely rejected the value of storytelling as a critical discourse as well as feminist thinkers who have identified the dangers in simplistic appeals to stories but who reserve a place for more self-critical and nuanced narration. Although critiques of storytelling have never yielded a neat conclusion, they nonetheless have pushed feminist advocates of storytelling to explore how we might tell and invoke experience-based stories in ways that more clearly distinguish such practices from a naïve embrace of all stories.

Storytelling as Naive Realism

For some feminist theorists, storytelling risks lapsing into a naive realism that takes experience at face value and insulates from criticism the social and cultural processes that have structured experience. For instance, these critics points out that simplistic appeals to experience forget that "experience lies to us" insofar as it often presents the socially organized world as if it were a naturally existing reality (Harding 1991, 287). Simplistic appeals to personal experience also risk merely substituting "experience" for the empiricist's sense data without examining the interpretive dimensions of knowledge-making (Code 1995, 63). Likewise, when we turn to oppressed people as "transmitters of authentic 'human experience,'" we leave "little room for questioning those voices or texts" or confronting them as socially conditioned, fallible, and interpretive constructions (Razack 1998, 45).

Other feminist critics have focused on the ideological dimensions of narration. Even women's stories and stories from the margins, these critics argue, work within the context of received narrative patterns, which they often reproduce uncritically (Cameron 2012, 574). For instance, white feminist scholars who have presented narratives of Third World women often have presupposed Eurocentric historical paradigms that cast the Third World as a cultural and historical backwater, and thus reduce Third World women to passive victims of history and their own cultures (Mohanty 1991b). Others have argued that stories of the oppressed tend to follow the typical good-guy-versus-bad-guy trope, thus allowing those of us who identify with "the good side" to overlook the multiple relations of domination in which we are all entangled (Razack 1998, 44–45).

While the theorists cited above have warned of ideological tendencies present in some experience-based writing, Joan Scott (1991) and Wendy Brown (1995) have rejected any attempt to engage experience as a resource for social critique. Like the other feminist theorists, Scott and Brown have criticized appeals to experience that treat the experience as if it were an internal truth, "the hidden truth of women's existence" that must only be expressed to provide "the foundations of feminist knowledge" (Brown 1995, 41, 42); however, Scott and Brown specifically depart from feminist standpoint theorists insofar as standpoint theorists embrace the possibility of more subtle and creative engagements with experience, whereas Scott and Brown regard all experience-based texts as naive "feminist foundationalism" (Brown 1995, 41). The disagreement lies, in part, in their different views of experience. Whereas feminist standpoint theorists recognize fissures and tensions within experience that exceed the dominant ways of ordering experience, Scott and Brown consider experience to be "thoroughly constructed" (Brown 1995, 41); nothing more than "a linguistic event" that is produced by discourses on the subject that differentiate and regulate desires, interests, identities, and spheres of existence (Scott 1991, 793). In this account, any narration of women's experiences and feelings only reifies the discursive processes that have "produced and inscribed" women's subordination precisely by the "positioning of us as private—sexual, familial, emotional," and by carving such logics into "domestic and psychic interiors" (Brown 1995, 42). Insofar as our psychic interiors are thoroughly structured by such logics, the narration of experience "precludes critical examination of the workings of the ideological system" (Scott 1991, 778).

Such critiques have provoked lively discussions about the danger of appealing uncritically to stories of the oppressed; however, insofar as the critiques have denied entirely the critical potential of experience-based texts, they have seemed to some to risk "throwing out the baby with the bathwater" (Varikas 1995, 99). Such concerns arise because, when critics like Scott and Brown characterize all feminist engagements with experience as "feminist foundationalism," they overlook the many experience-oriented texts that, even in the late 1980s and 1990s, had already emphasized the culturally mediated, ambiguous character of experience as well as the creative, community-situated, strategic character of narration. Such stories have not sought a "hidden truth" of experience as much as they have explored the "multiple forces weighing on [people's] choices and actions" and the creative tensions that arise from "bringing together the individual story and legitimated histories" (Varikas 1995, 99; Knaller 1999, 111). Put another way, the more sophisticated stories have not assumed that experience is a prediscursive truth but only that experience includes pre-articulate resistances and unpredictable reactions to dominant orderings of experience; storytellers can work creatively within the web of dominant discourses and reactions to them, so as to sketch perspectives on experience that help us respond more effectively to the factors organizing our lives (Knaller 1999; Stone-Mediatore 1998, 120–131; 2003, 97–122).

Unless we allow for some experience that reacts to and exceeds determination by dominant discourses and some way of gleaning from that experience a critical perspective on dominant ideologies, it is not clear how anyone—including critics like Scott and Brown—can step outside of dominant discourses to analyze them. Insofar as Scott and

Brown reserve for themselves a place outside the discourses that they claim entrap storytellers and experiencing subjects, they replicate the hierarchy between experts and others that many feminist scholars, including Code (1995, 58–82), Judith Grant (1993), and Linda Alcoff and Laura Gray (1993), have found to be disempowering to women and marginalized social groups.

Storytelling as a Power-Laden Relationship

Scholars including Razack, Alcoff, and Gray have been sympathetic to women's storytelling but have warned that such storytelling risks being absorbed into established social hierarchies unless we pay greater attention to the power relations that have structured storytelling practices. In particular, they argue, we need to address the dangers of co-optation by those who collect, interpret, and distribute others' stories. "There are land mines strewn across the path wherever stories are used," warns Razack, and any responsible call for storytelling must "pay attention to the interpretive [and institutional] structures that underpin how we hear and how we take up the stories of oppressed groups" (1998, 37).

These critics explain that, in a society with socially stratified institutions of expertise, telling and listening relationships often form rigid hierarchies, in which "some participants are accorded the authoritative status of interpreters and others are constructed as 'naïve transmitters of raw experience'" (Alcoff and Gray 1993, 264). As a result, storytelling can sometimes further marginalize the storytellers, especially when the storytellers are from marginalized social or cultural groups, which are not represented among the expert interpreters. For instance, when African Americans have told stories in court about abuse from racist speech, which they understood as legally actionable harm, the white, middle-class judges often have interpreted their tales in terms of freedom of speech (Razack 1998, 41). Similar hierarchies of discursive power have faced women who tell their stories of sexual assault. Although the women have challenged taboos against speaking out, they also have risked having the stories exploited by a sensationalist media or co-opted by psychiatric establishments, which tend to construct the storytellers as victims dependent on psychiatric experts (Alcoff and Gray 1993, 262–275). Even in the feminist academic community, storytelling can be dangerous when women from oppressed groups are expected to provide their stories to women from more privileged groups, for such demands often recreate hierarchies between those who are expected to provide the stories and those who theorize about them (Kadi 1996, 40; Razack 1998, 46–48).

For these critics, the solution is not to halt experience-based storytelling but to examine critically the forums in which stories are told and distributed. Those of us who tell our stories, they argue, should refuse the problematic division between storytellers and expert interpreters and should "become the theorists of our own experience," "teaching each other," with particular attention to how we construct our identities through telling our stories and how we might gain collective discursive power through such tellings

(Kadi 1996, 55; Alcoff and Gray 1993, 284). Likewise, those of us who seek others' stories should examine our own listening and reading strategies and the political effects of how we use others' stories (Razack 1998, 55).

Storytelling as the Inverse of Patriarchal Knowledge

Finally, feminist critics have scrutinized the dichotomy that is often presupposed between storytelling and conventional knowledge. When feminists define storytelling as "everything patriarchal knowledge is not," these critics warn, we merely reverse the hierarchies of scientific rationality while leaving intact its binary structure (Razack 1998, 45). In other words, when we associate storytelling with "the good side" of emotions, creativity, and particulars as opposed to "the bad side" of detached and abstract theory, we fail to examine critically the division of epistemic modes into two supposedly opposite camps (Razack 1998, 45). Such an approach not only reinscribes received binaries but confines storytelling to the personal and emotional side of the binary, which tends to discredit storytelling in the broader culture (Apostolidis 2010, 4). Moreover, when feminist theorists uncritically embrace the storytelling side of the hierarchy, we place our own storytelling practices outside of critical scrutiny.

Disch and Razack have suggested that we might approach storytelling more productively if we were not so stuck in the "oppositional approach," that is, not so set on "choos[ing] *between* narrative and theory," and instead questioned the opposition itself (Razack 1998, 45; Disch 2003, 260, italics in original). Disch pursues a way beyond the opposition between story and theory by tracing the deceits that maintain it. The pretense that theoretical reasoning transcends figurative language, she argues, is a fiction that is based on a rhetorical ploy: Theoretical reasoning "figures the world" *as if* it were a world of discrete objects that can be analyzed through strictly linear, abstract analysis; however, it "disavows the as" by means of a realist style that conflates its figurative construction with reality (Disch 2003, 262). At the same time, she says, storytelling is not as opposed to abstraction (and to its own rhetorical ploys) as it may seem. Experience-based storytelling may seem to be anchored more directly in lived reality and thereby to provide a counterforce to excessively abstract theoretical discourses; however, insofar as storytelling presents us with a coherent story, it, too, abstracts from the chaos of life and "weaves an ontological fantasy," in this case, the fantasy of life as a coherent narrative (Disch 2003, 264). In effect, insofar as storytelling assumes a realist style, it commits a deception not unlike that of scientific and theoretical texts: It disavows the cultural codes and literary tropes that subtend its textual coherence and "encourages us to mistake the figurative for the ontological" (Disch 2003, 264). If we recognize the ways that both storytelling and theory construct worlds through rhetorical maneuvers, says Disch, then we can no longer draw such a stark line between the two. We can, however, be more attentive to the ways that both stories and theoretical discourses use language to order and encode experience, and we can evaluate particular stories for their effects on how we organize our lives.

Other feminist scholars have examined how stories themselves can facilitate the kind of critical awareness about narration that Disch and Razack encourage. When stories thematize their own creative work, defy expectations for closure, or strategically juxtapose fragments of different narratives, they underscore the plurality of ways that we can envision "reality," define our communities, and arrange our projects (Knaller 1999; Stewart 1996, 20–40; Stone-Mediatore 2003, 81–92). In effect, such stories compel us to "meet our own gaze as creators of images" (Knaller 1999, 112), as people who—through theories, histories, and personal narratives—construct the conceptual frames that orient our lives, and who are responsible for how we do so.

Conclusions

If storytelling has no unique or guaranteed link to feminist aims, the persistent turns to storytelling by feminist and progressive thinkers nonetheless indicate the importance to feminist projects of constantly unsettling the intellectual styles and habits that we (even feminists) have taken for granted. In effect, if many scholars and activists have continued to invoke experience-based stories, notwithstanding their dangers and contradictions, it is because standard academic and political forums have proven inadequate to many voices and concerns. Through storytelling, many scholars and activists have sought to encourage communication among people of different backgrounds; to open intellectual forums to people directly immersed in social problems, who often have been more attuned than experts to deeply felt, unexpected, and uncategorized aspects of those problems; and to reconfigure images, categories, and discursive logics that have suppressed the complex subjectivities and aspirations of many members of our community. Critics of storytelling warn us that each such instance of storytelling must be scrutinized for how it affects our image making and our power relations. In turn, storytellers show us that such evaluations of our narratives cannot be determined by universal standards or "experts," but can be continually questioned and refigured by a plurality of readers and storytellers.

References

Abrams, Kathryn. 1991. "Hearing the Call of Stories." *California Law Review* 79 (4): 971–1052.
Alcoff, Linda, and Laura Gray. 1993. "Survivor Discourse: Transgression or Recuperation?" *Signs: Journal of Women in Culture and Society* 18 (2): 260–290.
Alexander, Jacqui and Chandra Talpade Mohanty. 1997. "Introduction: Genealogies, Legacies, Movements." In *Feminist Genealogies, Colonial Legacies, Democratic Futures*, edited by Jacqui Alexander and Chandra Talpade Mohanty New York: Routledge.
Anzaldúa, Gloria. 1990. "La consciencia de la mestiza: Toward a New Consciousness." In *Making Face, Making Soul Haciendo Caras*, edited by Gloria Anzaldúa. San Francisco: Aunt Lute Books.

Apostolidis, Paul. 2010. *Breaks in the Chain: What Immigrant Workers Can Teach America about Democracy*. Minneapolis: University of Minnesota Press.

Benigno, Andrés. 2011. "Undocumented for 16 Years." http://www.defineamerican.com/story/post/326/undocumented-for-16-years/ (accessed July 31, 2014).

Brison, Susan. 2002. *Aftermath: Violence and the Remaking of a Self*. Princeton, NJ: Princeton University Press.

Brown, Wendy. 1995. *States of Injury*. Princeton, NJ: Princeton University Press.

Butterfield, Fox. 2001. "When the Police Shoot, Who's Counting?" *New York Times*, April 29, 5.

Carbine, Rosemary. 2010. "Turning to Narrative: Toward a Feminist Theological Interpretation of Political Participation and Personhood." *Journal of the American Academy of Religion* 78 (2): 375–412.

Carson, Rachel. 1987. *Silent Spring*. 25th anniversary edition. Boston: Houghton Mifflin.

Cameron, Emilie. 2012. "New Geographies of Story and Storytelling." *Progress in Human Geography* 36 (5): 573–592.

Code, Lorraine. 1991. *What Can She Know? Feminist Theory and the Construction of Knowledge*. Ithaca, NY: Cornell University Press.

Code, Lorraine. 1995. *Rhetorical Spaces: Essays on Gendered Locations*. New York: Routledge.

Code, Lorraine. 2006. *Ecological Thinking. The Politics of Epistemic Location*. Oxford: Oxford University Press.

Delgado, Richard. 1995. "Storytelling for Oppositionists and Others: A Plea for Narrative." In *Critical Race Theory: The Cutting Edge*, edited by Richard Delgado. Philadelphia, PA: Temple University Press.

Delgado, Richard, and Jean Stefancic. 2001. *Critical Race Theory: An Introduction*. New York: New York University Press.

Disch, Lisa. 1993. "More Truth Than Fact: Storytelling as Critical Understanding in the Political Writings of Hannah Arendt." *Political Theory* 21 (4): 665–694.

Disch, Lisa. 1994. *Hannah Arendt and the Limits of Philosophy*. Ithaca, NY: Cornell University Press.

Disch, Lisa. 2003. "Impartiality, Storytelling, and the Seductions of Narrative: An Essay at an Impasse." *Alternatives* 28: 253–266.

Farmer, Paul. 2003. *Pathologies of Power: Health, Human Rights, and the New War on the Poor*. Berkeley: University of California Press.

Grant, Judith. 1993. *Fundamental Feminism*. New York: Routledge.

Harding, Sandra. 1991. *Whose Science? Whose Knowledge? Thinking from Women's Lives*. Ithaca, NY: Cornell University Press.

Harding, Sandra. 2008. *Sciences from Below: Feminisms, Postcolonialities, and Modernities*. Durham, NC: Duke University Press.

hooks, bell. 1989. *Talking Back: Thinking Feminist and Thinking Black*. Boston: South End Press.

Martinez, Inez. 2005. "Imagining Our Way Together." In *Women's Studies for the Future*, edited by Elizabeth Lapovsky Kennedy and Agatha Beins. Piscataway, NJ: Rutgers University Press.

Kadi, Joanna. 1996. *Thinking Class: Sketches from a Cultural Worker*. Boston: South End Press.

Knaller, Susanne. 1999. "Scattered Voices. Some Ranks on a Narrative Theory of Postcolonial Storytelling." Translated by Joe Compton. *Germanic Review* 74 (2): 99–115.

Mackinnon, Catherine. 1989. *Toward a Feminist Theory of the State*. Cambridge, MA: Harvard University Press.

Moe, Kristin. 2014. "Change Starts with Your Own Story." *Yes Magazine* 70: 47–50.

Million, Dian. 2009. "Felt Theory: An Indigenous Feminist Approach to Affect and History." *Wicazo Sa Review* 24 (2): 53–76.

Mohanty, Chandra Talpade. 1991a. "Cartographies of Struggle." In *Third World Women and the Politics of Feminism*, edited by Chandra Mohanty, Ann Russo, and Lourdes Torres. Bloomington: Indiana University Press.

Mohanty, Chandra Talpade. 1991b. "Under Western Eyes: Feminist Scholarship and Colonial Discourse." In *Third World Women and the Politics of Feminism*, edited by Chandra Mohanty, Ann Russo, and Lourdes Torres. Bloomington: Indiana University Press.

Panjabi, Kavita. 1997. "Probing 'Morality' and State Violence: Feminist Values and Communicative Interaction in Prison Testimonios in India and Argentina." In *Feminist Geneologies, Colonial Legacies, Democratic Futures*, edited by M. Jacqui Alexander and Chandra Talpade Mohanty. New York: Routledge.

Pitter, Jay. 2010. "Unearthing Silence: Subjugated Narratives for Environmental Engagement." In *Climate Change: Whose Carrying the Burden?* edited by L. Anders Sandberg and Tor Sandberg. Ottawa: Canadian Centre for Policy Alternatives.

Razack, Sharene. 1998. *Looking White People in the Eye: Gender, Race, and Culture in Courtrooms and Classrooms*. Toronto: University of Toronto Press.

Sandberg, L. Anders, and Tor Sandberg. 2010. "From Climate Change to Climate Justice in Copenhagen." In *Climate Change: Whose Carrying the Burden?* edited by L. Anders Sandberg and Tor Sandberg. Ottawa: Canadian Centre for Policy Alternatives.

Scott, Joan. 1991. "The Evidence of Experience." *Critical Inquiry* 17: 773–797.

Smith, Dorothy. 1987. *The Everyday World as Problematic*. Boston: Northeastern University Press.

Stewart, Kathleen. 1996. *A Space on the Side of the Road: Cultural Poetics in an "Other" America*. Princeton, NJ: Princeton University Press.

Stone-Mediatore, Shari. 1998. "Chandra Mohanty and the Revaluing of 'Experience.'" *Hypatia* 11 (2): 116–133.

Stone-Mediatore, Shari. 2000. "Hannah Arendt and Susan Griffin: Toward a Feminist Metahistory." In *Presenting Women Philosophers*, edited by Cecile Tougas and Sara Ebenreck. Philadelphia, PA: Temple University Press.

Stone-Mediatore, Shari. 2003. *Reading across Borders: Storytelling and Knowledges of Resistance*. New York: Palgrave Macmillan.

Stone-Mediatore, Shari. 2010. "Epistemologies of Discomfort: What Military-Family Anti-War Activists Can Teach Us about Knowledge of Violence." *Studies in Social Justice* 4 (1): 25–45.

Torres, Lourdes. 1991. "The Construction of the Self in U.S. Latina Autobiographies." In *Third World Women and the Politics of Feminism*, edited by Chandra Mohanty, Ann Russo, and Lourdes Torres. Bloomington: Indiana University Press.

Varikas, Eleni. 1995. "Gender, Experience, and Subjectivity: The Tilly-Scott Disagreement." *New Left Review* 211: 89–101.

William, Patricia. 1989. "The Obliging Shell: An Informal Essay on Formal Equal Opportunity." *Michigan Law Review* 87: 2128–2151.

Young, Iris Marion. 1993. "Justice and Communicative Democracy." In *Radical Philosophy: Tradition, Counter-tradition, and Politics*, edited by Roger Gottlieb. Philadelphia, PA: Temple University Press.

Young, Iris Marion. 2000. *Inclusion and Democracy*. Oxford: Oxford University Press.

CHAPTER 46

SUBJECTIVITY AND SUBJECTIVATION

ANNA MARIE SMITH

Introduction

Beauvoir's (2010, 267) famous aphorism "one is not born, but rather becomes, a woman" interrupts our assumptions about the givenness of biological sex and gender, just as Du Bois's classic meditation on the double consciousness of the African American (Du Bois 1999) challenges naturalized racial domination discourse. To raise the question of gender justice is to challenge the status quo in which it is taken for granted that boys and men constitute the normal subject, and girls, women, and transgender persons represent the marked "other," the subject who is structurally relegated to a subordinate role and whose consciousness and practices are shaped in advance with respect to hegemonic narratives. The cross-cutting effects of capitalism, structural racism, and sexuality, and nationality immediately complicate gendered subject formation, as captured by intersectionality theory (Crenshaw 1989; Davis 1981; McCall 2005).

Feminist theory accomplishes several important strategic objectives when it attends to subjectivity and subjectivation. It underlines the fact that becoming a subject is a historical process that is tightly mediated by the established social structures (for example, heterosexism; racism, and ethnic chauvinism; patriarchal domination; "law and order" and the modern carceral system; global capitalism; xenophobia, jingoism, imperialism and militarism, and so on) that make up a given society but that that process is animated by the agent's always protean and unruly desire for recognition. As Foucault or Althusser would put it, the sense that we are subjects who were fully formed prior to sociopolitical relations—each with our own natural interests and each with a simple and immediate relationship to our natural bodies—is a profoundly ideological misrecognition. Under this ideological view, it is only later, after the subject is fully formed, that subjects encounter structures and find themselves asymmetrically relegated into their respective structural positions, as dominators or the subjugated. Further, it appears, from this ideological perspective, that power is simply a tool wielded by the dominant to undermine or to attack the subordinate, as the former seek to regulate, exploit, punish, denigrate, contain, and expel the latter. Viewed as such, we get the impression that feminist politics is simply a problem of a pluralist political game in which subjects dealing with their variegated allotments of power work within entrenched institutions to pursue their natural interests.

There is no need, from this ideological perspective, to raise questions about the possibility that naturalized interests and desires, and their material expression in the body itself, might be produced at least in part by the very structures that are supposed to come later, after the subject has been fully formed. There is also no question, when we succumb to this viewpoint, that the subjugated might be able to exercise even a quasi-autonomous form of agency; on the contrary, it is taken for granted that to be the target of domination is to be nothing more than a passive victim.

This account, however, conceals more than it reveals. With the critical concept of subjectivation, we denaturalize the entire process of becoming a subject who is endowed with given set of interests, preferences, and choice matrices, and we question what it means to say that a structure merely "represents," "empowers," or "disempowers" the subject. Adopting a Foucauldian-Althusserian perspective, we ask whether the formation of the subject is not itself a strategic and always incomplete historical achievement, and whether the subject is not a being who is conceived in the force field of power relations. To the extent that we accept the paradigm shift that subjectivity theory demands, it becomes clear that the relationship between subjects and structures is much more complex and insidious than the ideological perspective would predict.

At one end of the subjectivation spectrum, domination seems to be so overwhelming that the subject "answers the hail" of the structure almost perfectly; she seems to be "interpellated" or called to act out her victim script without any protest or deviation. For example, biopower and law appear to "produce" the abject deviant who engages in recidivism such that "law and order" forces can easily organize consent in the public sphere for the expansion of the modern carceral system. For "law and order," the Madonna/whore dualism produces two ideal types—either the prisoner is the "good inmate" who is deeply ashamed about her crime and wants to show the parole board that she is eager to make amends to society or she is the "bad inmate" who turns even more hardened in her posture "against the system" as she seeks approval from the worst criminals inside. Either way, for "law and order," it is supposed to be a win-win proposition: incarceration either produces model rehabilitants or the recidivists whose continuing crime careers support the voracious demand of "law and order" for ever greater prison expenditures. Looking deeper into the lives of incarcerated men and women, however, we find much richer stories of individual expression and complex motivations, rather than a seamless fit with the "law and order" narrative. Even in extreme conditions, such as the prison, domination loses its complete grip on its target populations, as the scripted narratives of recognition fail to reach their objectives.

A feminist theory of subjectivity predicts and demonstrates that the subject's desire always contains a degree of resilient alterity; there are always moments of structural weaknesses and moments in which domination remains incomplete. Indeed, in times of full-blown historical crises, there are fertile opportunities for the kinds of agonistic deviations that introduce nonassimilable forms of dissidence and the rising up of democratic social movements. Despite severe discrimination, extreme resource deficits, and stigmatization, low-income people with AIDS across the globe have often enjoyed some political success as they have organized collectively to identify as deserving citizens entitled to dignified treatment, adequate healthcare services, and culturally sensitive forms of state-subsidized care work.

This chapter will probe these themes with reference to three paradigms of feminist theory; with each paradigm, I will discuss in some detail the work of one exemplary practitioner. My paired samples are as follows: liberal feminism: Nancy Hirschmann; antiracist socialist feminism: Angela Davis; and Foucauldian-Derridean feminism: Judith Butler.

Liberal Feminism and the Primacy of Relational Freedom: Nancy J. Hirschmann

At first glance, the question of subject formation in liberal democratic theory appears to be an oxymoron. According to a caricatured account of the paradigm, the individual self is an atomistic and acquisitive being who is utterly prior to institutions and relationships. From this perspective, the major problem of liberal democratic theory is to generate a theory of obligation that explains why and to what extent the naturally free individual has an obligation to consent to being governed by a sovereign. This caricature, however, cannot withstand examination. In Locke's (1980) own state of nature, the individual is oriented toward social cooperation. The Rawlsian individual subject is so thoroughly influenced by her surrounding institutions that justice in the ideal society is defined as the character of those institutions, which Rawls (1999) refers to as the basic structure.

For Nancy J. Hirschmann (2003), however, even the interpretations of the liberal democratic tradition offered by Locke and Rawls are inadequate. From her feminist perspective, they fail to grasp the extent to which liberal democratic theory is shot through with masculinist assumptions. She contends that one helpful entryway into the problem is to review, through a feminist lens, Isaiah Berlin's (1958) famous distinction between "negative" and "positive" liberty. If we take the "negative liberty" perspective, we understand liberty as a condition in which the individual is not subject to the interference of others. The self is understood here as a naturally autonomous self-constituted subject who is fully endowed with her own personal set of preferences and interests before she enters into social relations. On this view, the individual is free to the extent that she is liberated from arbitrary outside interference.

The "negative liberty" liberals assume that the individual works up her own preferences and interests in a primordial space in which external forces are entirely absent. This is not to say that the subject would have an impoverished range of preferences and interests. The subject's desires and her corresponding drive for their realization may be pressing or subtle in nature. Further, the self is not necessarily overwhelmed by his or her interests; she might choose to postpone the gratification of desire in a prudential manner, and she might succeed in doing so. The key point for understanding subject formation in "negative liberty" theory is that the self who is prior to the social is the primary locus in which her own preferences and interests are constituted. This autonomous self is entirely capable of becoming conscious of her desires and of becoming her own master. She can become aware that she is a being who wants A rather than anti-A, B rather than anti-B, C rather than anti-C, and so on. Because she is a rational actor who maximizes her interests and minimizes her losses; and, because she has this particular preference matrix, she will utilize her resources to pursue goods A, B, and C. To the extent that she is free, she will in fact acquire them in due course.

Having established this starting point, "negative liberty" liberalism then debates which barriers to the pursuit of individual desires are necessary for ordered liberty, given scarce resources and the no-harm and fairness principles. Ideally, the individual is subject only to nonarbitrary limits—that is to say, the rules that withstand the scrutiny of public reason. For a "negative liberty" liberal, there is a world of difference between basic traffic regulations (legitimate) and the state censorship of controversial academic literature (illegitimate). Some barriers will illegitimately encroach upon the individual's liberty rights, and the power of the state to impose those barriers must be firmly curtailed in order to safeguard the "negative liberty" of the individual (cf. Nozick 1974).

The masculinist dimension of the "negative liberty" viewpoint, replies Hirschmann, stems from the fact that it negates the essential connectedness and dependency of the individual. With relational feminists (Chodorow 1989; Hartsock 1998; Nedelsky 2012; West 1999) and the ethics of care feminists (Fineman 2004; Tronto 1993; Sevenhuijsen 1998), Hirschmann foregrounds the fact that each individual is inevitably thrown into relations of caregiving, both as a dependent (in infancy, for example) and as a caregiver (as a parent or as a friend of a person with temporary disabilities). However, Hirschmann also argues that feminist theory should bear in mind "negative liberty's" definition of freedom as the absence of external impediments. Hirschmann adapts this principle to argue that the individual only has the capacity to exercise and fulfill her rights insofar as she has access to a threshold amount of necessary resources. Poverty, for example, is a serious external impediment that makes it impossible for the self to flourish. Here, Hirschmann makes contact with the important work of liberal thinkers, such as Sen (2009) and Nussbaum (2000), for whom the provision of the resources corresponding to the minimum capacity to exercise basic rights and entitlements—the right to life, food, respect for intimate relationships, decent employment at living wages, educational opportunity, leisure, freedom of expression, political rights, and so on—establishes a threshold standard of justice.

Hirschmann also takes Berlin's "positive liberty" theory into account; she is especially attentive to its internal psychological dimension. For "positive liberty" liberals, we cannot take for granted that the individual always develops her preferences and interests in an autonomous space. Indeed, the condition of "heteronomy" in which the subject encounters distorting pressures such that she becomes an inauthentic or divided self is a serious problem for "positive liberty" liberals. Hirschmann argues that feminist theory should abandon the search for the "authentic self"; while it is true that patriarchal institutions have an insidious effect on the constitution of the preferences and very identity of women and girls, we are all "socially constructed" all the way down. Hirschmann produces a novel theory by borrowing specific elements from both of Berlin's liberties. Freedom must be achieved both at the internal level—that is, the self must be emancipated from the patriarchal forces that misrepresent reality in ways that are detrimental to a woman's interests, such that she can become a more autonomous self, and at the external level—namely, each woman must have access to the threshold material resources necessary for the genuine exercise of her rights and entitlements.

For Hirschmann, then, the female subject is never simply an autonomous freely choosing agent; in our nonideal world, she typically lacks access to the threshold level of the resources that she needs to realize her abstract rights, and she is subject to profoundly distorting forces that operate on the psychological, emotional, and epistemological registers. Hirschmann presses us to bring in, for example, the truly formidable empirical evidence pertaining to domestic violence in this regard. How should feminists respond, for example, when a woman who is the victim of domestic violence enters a shelter and quite plainly reports that she intends to leave her abusive husband, but then, on the very next day, repudiates her earlier position, leaves the shelter, and returns to the home that she shares with her abuser (Hirschmann 2003, 103–137)? To make things even more complicated, we could consider the dilemma from the legal prosecutor's perspective. At her arrival at the shelter, the victim brings a minor child with her, and makes it clear that the child has witnessed the abuser's violent attacks upon her. As long as the prosecutor and trial court judge are competent, the woman is cooperating with the prosecutor in her dual role as concerned custodial mother and complainant wife, and the shelter is providing sensitive and well-funded "wrap around" services, the situation is relatively straightforward.

However, what should feminists ask the state to do when the wife-mother withdraws her complaint, leaves the shelter, and brings her child back into the home of the abusive husband-father? Hirschmann cannot, of course, solve this dilemma for us, but she nevertheless demonstrates that her feminist version of subjectivity in which both internal and external factors play a role in shaping the woman's agency permits us to grapple with the problem in a more productive manner. The wife-mother is not a self-generating autonomous subject for whom liberty is merely a question of removing external sources of interference; given her own contradictory statements and behavior, and the serious implications for the child, it would be grossly inadequate to argue that the best response on the part of the state and the community as a whole would be to guarantee state non-interference across the board. There is a possibility that the wife-mother is too poor to strike out on her own and has a well-founded skepticism about the availability of poverty assistance benefits. Alternatively, she may have been drawn into a harmful psychological dependency complex in which she feels safest when she keeps the abusive husband-father at close range. Even worse, her psychological condition may be causing her to neglect the needs of her child and the harm that is caused when the child is exposed to domestic violence at close range. At the very least, Hirschmann would argue, the prosecutor, the court, and the social services department ought to work together to ensure that the wife-mother is relieved of external interference as she makes her decisions about responding to her abusive relationship. She should have access to basic income supports, safe housing, and meaningful employment opportunities. In a better-world scenario, she should not be subject to such socioeconomic deprivation that remaining in an abusive home with her dependent child presents itself as her best option. In a better world, this wife and mother would also be given supports to help her to address the distorting psychological pressures associated with patriarchal ideology that inevitably cloud her judgment. She would have access to sensitively constructed social services and well-run self-help groups consisting of similarly situated peers so that she could begin to speak about her experiences and work out for herself what she really needs for herself and what she really wants for her child (cf. Schneider 2000; Corrigan 2013).

For Hirschmann, then, the choosing subject of liberal democratic theory is always already "socially constructed" in the sense that her values and desires—the way that she sees and experiences the world, or her very being—are thoroughly shaped by relationships with others and historically specific institutions. As such, attention must be paid to the whole range of gendered forms of domination.

> If we are socially constructed, feminists have argued, male domination has played an important part in that construction; its laws, customs, rules, and norms have been imposed by men on women to restrict their opportunities, choices, actions, and behaviors . . . This construction of social behaviors and rules comes to constitute not only what women are allowed to do, however, but also what they are allowed to *be*.
>
> (Hirschmann 2003, 11; emphasis in original)

In many respects, Hirschmann's argument overlaps with rational choice theory and its conception of "adaptive preferences" (Elster 1983; Nussbaum 2000; Khader 2011) wherein the subject who faces constraints unconsciously internalizes that constraint, and develops a very limited view of her capacities and preferences. If a whole cohort of young female primary-school pupils live in a relatively closed world in which college admission places are strictly reserved for males, then their own preferences will probably be shaped as a result; it may be the case, for example, that while their brothers routinely look forward to college, few of the school girls will openly express a desire to pursue higher education. However, Hirschmann's "social construction" of the self is a more complicated and deeply layered theory of subject formation. With "adaptive preferences," it is assumed that there is a natural subject already lying underneath domination and that the more we remove domination from the scene, the more the true subject will be directly revealed. Hirschmann argues instead that the "social construction" of the subject is primary, and that this process at one and the same time empowers and constrains the subject. For Hirschmann (2003, 199), the emancipation of the female subject requires attentiveness to "the interaction and mutual constitution of the external structures of patriarchy and the inner selves of women." By cultivating this attentiveness, feminist theory gains a better purchase on the ways in which patriarchal social structures operate in both obvious and very subtle manners, such that we can draw up best practices in key sites, such as domestic-violence shelters. Women and girls are often obliged to make choices in much more constrained conditions than are similarly situated men and boys; public policies that take the male subject as the norm will therefore fail to meet social justice objectives. Hirschmann also values consciousness raising, radical democratic participation, and feminist collective action that, taken together, can change oppressive contexts. She concludes, for example, that girls and women are not trapped within their "social construction" or subjectivity since they can put their observations about the systematic character of gender subjugation into language and enter into critical and self-reflexive dialogues with one another about their experiences and the possibilities for progressive reforms. Under felicitous conditions, this would be much more than a conversation; it would be, instead, a process of becoming a more liberated subject (2003, 207, 221, 237).

SOCIALIST FEMINIST THEORY AND THE CRITIQUE OF THE CARCERAL: ANGELA DAVIS

Subjectivation theory has often been misunderstood in feminist studies as a critique that cannot accommodate women of color feminist theory. One of the central claims of antiracist socialist thinkers like Angela Davis is that black women have been relegated to a minimal role in the feminist literature or even excluded altogether. The project of recovering the agency of women of color may seem to be entirely at odds with subjectivation theory's denaturalizing and anti-foundationalist orientation. It may seem, at first glance, that women of color feminist theory has no place for a theory that decenters the subject and foregrounds the contingency of subject formation; it might appear that subjectivity theory risks the erasure of the subject altogether and therefore contradicts the project of foregrounding the experience and the theoretical contributions of women of color. In actual fact, the two approaches share a theory of ideological legitimation—the proferring, on the part of hegemonic institutions and discourses of misleading but seductive and reassuring appearances—and both rightly insist upon the importance of unmasking domination's ideological work through critique. Both women of color feminism and subjectivation theory admire the dissident democratic spirit of Rosa Luxemburg (2006, 214): "Freedom is always and exclusively freedom for the one who thinks differently." They both bear in mind the warning against nihilist pessimism on the question of the possibility of resistance that is issued by Marcuse. He states that critical social theory ought to be concerned with

> the historical alternatives which haunt the established society as subversive tendencies and forces. The values attached to the alternatives do become facts when they are translated into reality by historical practice. The theoretical concepts terminate with social change.
>
> (Marcuse 1964, xi-ii)

For Angela Davis, a student of Marcuse, socialist theory correctly locates the problem of subjectivation with respect to the embodied subject engaged in labor—both for subsistence and as a result of the subject's class/gender/race relationship to private property. In virtually every society, becoming a subject revolves around the corporeal-intellectual practice of labor as the core human activity. Labor is regarded by socialist theory as an indispensable practice that yields, in the simplest terms, the means of subsistence. It is also a process in which the individual is brought into a purposive relationship with the natural world and her fellow producers. However, in the nonideal historical formations, these relationships are never shaped according to one's will; in the capitalist context, the private-property foundation of the global economy forms the economic base, which determines in turn, one's structural position, either as a worker or as an owner-manager of private property. To legitimate the massive inequality that inevitably follows from unregulated capitalism, the worker's relations with her fellow producers are tremendously distorted and obscured, and all sorts of sociocultural myths about the accumulation of wealth are deployed to conceal inequality or to explain it away.

For socialist theory, subjectivity in nonideal societies also revolves around the crucial element of alienation. "Alienation" is a complicated term that has several meanings. There is the obvious alienation or "exploitation" involved with the capture of the worker's surplus product by the employer, thanks to the way in which private property relations are rigged from the start to favor the owners. Then there is the much more profound intellectual-political problem of alienation—namely, the promotion of responsibility myths such as the "work ethic," "responsible parenting," and the "American Dream," that instruct the worker to hold herself accountable for her structural position and that of her children, despite the fact that domination has imposed enormous constraints upon her life chances (see Mink 2002; Hancock 2004; Smith 2007). With alienation, the worker is psychologically entrapped by capitalism's misrecognition of her humanity—capitalism reduces her to nothing but an instrument for making a profit. Finally, the worker is alienated in the sense that the very workings of the global economy are determined by the management/owner class; she stands in a relationship of virtual disempowerment before the very structure that establishes the background conditions that profoundly shape her life chances. She is alienated, then, in the sense that she is stripped of sociopolitical power. The worker as subject is dependent upon an entire global economy that operates largely behind her back; she cannot grasp its complicated workings and capital blocks the workers at every turn when they attempt to make the global economy the object of collective democratic determination.

Davis would largely agree with these socialist critical diagnoses, but she would argue that their account of structural conditions, subject formation, and alienation is incomplete. Davis grants the foundational socialist premise—namely, that the labor process is central to subjectivity—but she would further argue that the exploitation of labor is much more deeply racialized and gendered than most socialists would grant. By extension, the theory of alienation that is implicit throughout Davis's work—one that can be traced back to her Marcusian intellectual formation (1964, 1966)—is highly attentive to the "divide and rule" strategies employed by capital, as white women and men of all colors are set up by their employers and by mass consumerism to wield power over women of color and to enjoy a symbolic sense of superiority over them.

For example, Davis rejects overly sweeping arguments by liberal feminists about the historical entrapment of women within the tradition of couverture and the simultaneously respected and constraining role of the "lady." Liberal feminists have often argued that women can gain power by joining the wage labor force and seeking success in professional career tracks. To be sure, white married women of modern societies rarely worked outside the home for wages until very recently. In this sense, they were relatively sheltered from the whole process of crushing exploitation and alienation that is integral to the experience of the disempowered in labor relations. Davis observes that since the colonial period black women from virtually every class background typically worked outside the home as slaves, domestic servants, sharecroppers, farm laborers, cleaners and nurses' aides; in the case of the elite, freeborn African American families, black women often worked as teachers in traditionally black schools. Today, with the collapse of the real value of men's earnings and the high cost of living generally, working outside the home in return for a wage is much more common for white women. Symbolically, however, difficult, filthy, and disrespected labor remains profoundly associated with black women and Latinas.

For Davis, this ideological association of black femininity with compulsory and derogatory labor is but one dimension of subjectivity in a society deeply marked by unfinished business, namely, the vestiges of slavery. The slave system defined Africans as chattel belonging to the slavers; the slave woman was first and foremost a full-time worker and a breeder of children, rather than a wife, mother, and homemaker. Slavers would beat black women slaves like beasts of burden and then subject them to gender specific forms of torture and rape by turns. In other words, Davis is underlining the superexploitation and hyperalienation of women of color through coercive labor relations; the combination of racial domination, patriarchal power, and coerced labor produce extreme patterns of violent dehumanization among slave women.

Vestigial racist discourse from the slavery era continues to construct black women as subhuman and irrational beings incapable of adequate parenting and naturally prone to criminality and promiscuity (Davis 1981, 5–29). In this dimension of her work, subjectivity emerges as a theme in its negation: the enormous barriers that black women face in becoming autonomous and self-determining beings emancipated from exploitation, ideological misrepresentation, and alienation, and subjects who are recognized by others as normal human beings and deserving citizens. Davis features profoundly engrained tropes of race, gender, and sexuality in her interpretation of United States society, drawing, as she does, deep continuities between the figures of the rebellious slave and the black male superpredator, or the "Jezebel" seducer and the sexually irresponsible single mother on welfare. In this regard, she has much in common with the psychoanalytic feminist thinker, Hortense Spillers (1987), for whom the traces of slavery make up a national unconscious and a "grammar book" that determines the very conditions of the possibility of discourse in the contemporary United States (see also hooks 2000; Collins 2008). Going further than Spillers, however, Davis (1981) demonstrates the historicity of racialized gender formations and probes the historical record for extraordinary moments of resistance, ranging from black women's participation in the abolition movement, Reconstruction, progressivism, and the civil rights anti-lynching campaign to socialist and communist organizing in the first half of the twentieth century. In this sense, she shares with Marcuse and Foucault an acute sense of the incomplete nature of domination, exploitation, and alienation and the genuine possibility of resistance on the part of women of color that has not been assimilated by dominant institutions in advance.

With her attention to the complex and contradictory positioning of black women within the racialized and gendered capitalist formation, Davis is well positioned to launch devastating critiques of insufficiently critical thinking on the part of white liberal feminists. She takes Susan Brownmiller to task, for example, for her "resuscitation of the old racist myth of the Black rapist"(Davis 1981, 178). Like all women, black women have to contend with sexual harassment and sexual assault, and the offenders may be white men or men of color. In Brownmiller's writing, however, there is a troubling tendency to endow all black males with an urgent desire to possess, through sexual conquest, each and every white woman whom they encounter. Davis (1981, 179–201) argues persuasively that white women in the anti-rape movement have all too often trusted the police, the courts, and the prison system; in reality, these institutions are only too pleased to use the anti-rape movement as a legitimation for the expansion, through arbitrary means, of their punitive grip upon the liberties of black men and women. In many instances, white working-class men and women will actually make decisions that are detrimental to their collective well-being in order to shore up race differences and white privilege; with this sort of extreme alienation, they are blinded by racist ideology to the potential for powerful democratic coalition building. Again, these numerous facets of alienation underline the barriers to democratic alliances and collective organizing among white and black women together, highlighting in turn the negation of black women's subjectivity.

Whereas some white and white ethnic social groups have historically overcome stigmatization and exclusion by engaging effectively in minority politics (the example of wealthy white gay men in the pro-same-sex marriage movement is appropriate here), thereby seizing upon statist opportunities for the realization of democratic subjectivity, black women are typically much less successful in this regard. Concerned simultaneously about the abrogation of black men's rights, mass incarceration, and the problem of violence against women in all communities, black women are understandably skeptical that police officers and judges will respond appropriately to their demands for safe homes, safe streets, and a democratically accountable criminal justice system (Davis 1981, 173). Moreover, black women, from sex workers to civil rights activists, have themselves been singled out for rape—in many cases, gang rape—on the part of police officers (Davis 1981, 173). White liberal feminists active in the anti-rape movement often speak from the position of the confident and entitled citizen as they demand a more interventionist state in response to violence against women. Because of their historical experiences, black women, by contrast, typically value anti-statist solutions that are rooted in autonomous community organizations (Davis 1981).

Ultimately, the intertwining of the "prison industrial complex," late capitalism, structural racism, and misogyny is profound and enduring. Slavery and the modern carceral system are the "others" of United States democracy; now the surplus "underclass" population that cannot be made into the laboring instrument of the capitalist owners is "managed" by the criminal justice system. "Labor" and alienation remain the key problems for Davis with respect to subjectivity, but she now locates them firmly within our contemporary conditions in which long-term unemployment is widespread among low-educated blacks and Latinos, and these specific minority fractions are highly overrepresented within the prison population. Today, it is the prison that absorbs and manages this otherwise socially disruptive, nonworking mass. In this sense, the space for nonassimilated resistance has in fact been so reduced that the preservation of genuine agency in these populations becomes an extremely precarious project. The hypersegregated "ghetto" conditions of low-income black families provide very little opportunities for individual flourishing and collective organizing. Even the spontaneous "play" of the local rap artist or basketball player in the ghetto is always already commodified in advance and prepared for assimilation within hugely powerful media and sports corporations (Rose 2008; Kelley 1998). Democratic societies genuinely committed to social justice and the restoration of emancipated subject formation and recognition on fair terms of equality would ideally come to terms with their histories of violence and exclusion. The punishments associated with premodern barbarism—compulsory labor, torture, and the death penalty—are, in the United States' case, retained and practiced disproportionately upon African Americans, Latinos, and Native Americans. Because race/ethnic otherness tends to define the target population of the carceral, these eternally returning barbarisms continue to define our racial identities. Whiteness becomes a condition of forgetting; whites rarely question, for example, the way that the incarcerated are deprived of the right to vote (Davis 2005, 37–38). Alienation in this moment takes the form of a division of humanity that is becoming increasingly difficult to overcome; middle-class and wealthy whites rarely consider the ties of common humanity that bind them together with their incarcerated counterparts. Davis calls for the consolidation of a feminist analysis that is equal to the task of critiquing the gendered dimensions of neoliberal retrenchment, structural racism, and the rise of the late-capitalist carceral system; tackling the substantial barriers to feminist solidarity and collective action; and unearthing the fugitive forms of resistance that continue to haunt the dominant structures.

Derridean-Foucaultian Feminist Theory and Constitutive Exclusions: Judith Butler

Working in the Derridean and Foucaultian tradition, Judith Butler offers a feminist theory of subject formation that is at one and the same time attentive to hegemonic power relations and to the mobile, context-sensitive, and decentered character of subjugated identities. Butler would endorse the antiracist socialist feminist's argument that the subject is constituted by the social structure. It is not simply that the subject encounters barriers to the realization of her desires, but that, more fundamentally, she is constructed as a desiring subject in discourse. In Marx's terms,

> Men make their own history, but they do not make it just as they please; they do not make it under circumstances chosen by themselves, but under circumstances directly found, given, and transmitted from the past.
>
> (Marx 1978, 595)

Like Marx, Butler locates the subject's formation within powerful structures of domination; she certainly concedes the relevance of class and race formations (see Butler 1997; Smith 2001) but in several of her texts, she takes gender and sexuality rather than labor, capital accumulation, and structural racism as her primary focal points. At the same time, she further concedes that we never find a social formation in which there is nothing but gendering and sexualization at work; like Hirschmann and Davis, she is deeply committed to an intersectional approach to subjectivity.

Borrowing from Derrida's deconstructive intervention in speech act theory (1988) and from Foucault's disciplinary theory of subject formation (1977), Butler begins with the argument that the subject is never prior to discourse, but is worked up as an effect of, and a vehicle for, discourse. At the same time, however, there is a certain incompletion or openness to the discursive structure, such as heterosexism or structural racism, such that there is always the possibility of scandalous reversal. Beauvoir's "woman" is made, not born, and she is subjected by misogyny, in the sense that she is an object for the masculine existential perspective. Further, the masculine perspective is misrepresented as the universal—the abstract reason that transcends embodiment—while the feminine is associated with the particular and that which is trapped within the corporeal. For all that subjection, however, "woman" is a person of mystery to masculinist culture; indeed, she constitutes the very limit of knowability. For the masculine subject of desire, the feminine is his "constitutive other": he defines himself as the not-woman, he gains his abstract universalism by disavowing and denigrating the feminine embodied particular, and, on that basis, proclaims his masculine autonomy. However, at the same time, the woman is the subject who must be known and mastered by him, and, scandalously enough, she ultimately escapes his epistemological grip. In the end, the masculine subject realizes that he is not so autonomous after all, because he depends on the feminine "other" for his very sense of selfhood; and he himself is vulnerable to the dialectical reversal of power (Butler 1990).

For Butler, however, this account is itself incomplete, since it leaves intact several ideological myths, such as the "natural" female/male binary, and compulsory heterosexuality. Traditionally, feminist theory has been more willing to regard gendered signifiers, such as femininity and masculinity, as cultural expressions that vary according to historical formations and the differences related to class, race, ethnicity, and nationality. By contrast, traditional feminist theory asserts that we are born and objectively classified in the biological register as either male or female in an unproblematic manner. It is only then that each of us is "socialized" by the reigning sociocultural norms to take up the gender costume and script that corresponds to our given biological sex: masculinity and heterosexual desire for all males; femininity and heterosexual desire for all females. Butler argues that feminist theory has been less likely to interrogate the givenness of the biological sexed body that is said to serve as the natural substratum for gendering and its allegedly natural relationship to heterosexual desire. In addition, she rejects the one-dimensional concept of "socialization" in favor of the much more complex theory identification in Freudian and Lacanian terms, a process that is much more complex and vulnerable to failure. Butler questions the internal stability of the very terms *biological male* and *biological female*, and argues that they, too, are the product of power-laden historical formations. Borrowing from Nietzsche and Foucault, Butler calls for the genealogical interrogation of biological sex as well as the categories of gender and sexuality. The point of the exercise, Butler reminds us, is to ask which types of power are promoted when this particular interpretive grid is installed, affirmed by official discourse, and reiterated at the level of informal practices over and over again? Who tends to gain by receiving symbolic recognition as the "normal," and who tends to lose out as the excluded "other" as a result? In other words, what are the costs associated with this type of domination—both subtle and brutal in nature—over time?

Butler's response is devastating for feminists who are unwilling to interrogate the biological sex binary. She demonstrates persuasively that although gender regimes are complex, shifting, and multiple in origin, phallocentrism and compulsory heterosexuality gain enormous ground with each and every reassertion of this massively powerful corporeal interpretive scheme. To be sure, there is some room for parodic gender impersonations that destabilize the allegedly natural fusions of sex, gender, and sexual desire. Butler argues that the dualisms that are supposed to secure the garrisons of phallocentrism and compulsory heterosexuality and their corresponding sex/gender structure—the natural versus artificial pretense, depth versus surface, original versus imitative copy, and so on—are constantly collapsing and consistently require shoring up. However, we can view their instability most readily at the cultural margins, where already excluded subjects have little to lose, and every pleasure to gain, from mocking the gender police. It is for this reason that Butler values the Bakhtinian carnival of gay male drag shows; they colorfully and stylishly dramatize the fact that the iteration of hegemonic sex-gender-sexuality formations can go ridiculously awry such that the comic arbitrariness of compulsory heterosexuality is brought to the fore. Indeed, the prohibition of deviance—homosexuality, cross-dressing, transgender transitions, hermaphroditism, and so on—risks the eroticization of the outlaw, and the corresponding incitement of radical identifications (Butler 1990).

Butler's theory of subject formation and subjectivation has important implications for several different types of hegemonic configurations of power. For example, Butler points out the illegibility of the transgender person; because the latter refuses to conform to the hegemonic gender regime, s/he is often regarded as a subhuman, targeted for discrimination by employers and landlords, singled out by thugs for violent assault, denied crucial social services, exposed to abusive policing, and treated roughly at border crossings. In many states, the government patronizingly interprets their body and identity on their behalf in a coercive form of pastoral "care": although s/he may want to change their official identity documents to reflect their gender transition on her own terms, the state insists on speaking on their behalf, according to its own rules. Similarly, Gayatri Spivak argues that the subaltern woman is virtually silenced by discourses ostensibly developed to offer her protection. Both the British colonizers and the Hindu nationalists speak in her name on the issue of sati, or widow self-immolation, but their purportedly caring statements are framed in such a way that there is no possibility of a third position from which the subaltern woman could speak for herself (Spivak 1988; see also Mohanty 2003; Eisenstein 2004).

Since gender is a practice that is performed, over and over again, in the context of constraining yet incomplete structures, and because this incessant activity is at least partly unconscious and unguided by a purposive rationality, then gender cannot be automatic or mechanical; it is, instead, "a practice of improvisation [conducted] within a scene of constraint"(Butler 2004, 1). It is inescapably social since "one is always 'doing' [gender] with or for another, even if the other is only imaginary" (Butler 2004, 1). With the prior existence of this disciplinary field of constraint, and the dialectical exchange between the self and other that is inherent in any gender performance, the subject never owns the terms of her own gender; those terms are "outside oneself, beyond oneself in a sociality that has no single author" (Butler 2004, 1). Being coherently gendered for others is the condition of possibility of recognition, which every subject desires. But recognition is a site of power and contestation, since the terms of legibility are mutable and bear the traces of past practices, including both domination and radical resistance (Butler 2004, 2). The dilemmas that are confronted by those persons who defy established gender norms to such an extent that they are routinely denied recognition—such as the transgendered—are extraordinarily difficult. One could choose to betray one's deviant sense of self in order to become legible for official institutions, but conformity comes at an extreme cost: I risk becoming unrecognizable to myself, and, ultimately, I risk knuckling under and living an unbearable life in which I become abject to myself. At the other end of the spectrum, I could avoid the loathsome task of conformity and choose survival, that is, the achievement of maximum estrangement from the social norm. This would involve, however, the difficult work of developing a profoundly critical relationship to social norms and consistently deferring the need for official recognition; those tasks can only be performed insofar as I identify closely with a radical social movement that collectively articulates an alternative world vision (Butler 2004, 3). The point is not to celebrate difference for its own sake but "to establish more inclusive conditions for sheltering and maintaining life that resists models of assimilation" (Butler 2004, 4).

The anti-assimilationist politics that Butler embraces cannot be easily transcribed into the standard social science terms and concepts, such as pluralism and interest-group politics, generally used for the study of democratic social movements. Cristina Beltrán's (2010) recent work on Latino identities that draws upon Deleuzian theory is a much more promising source of inspiration in this respect. Referring to the immigrant-rights demonstrations of 2006, Beltrán comments,

> Subjects marked "Latino" do *not* represent a preexisting community just waiting to emerge from the shadows. Instead, "Latino politics" is best understood as a form of enactment, a democratic moment in which subjects create new patterns of commonality and contest unequal forms of power.
>
> (Beltrán 2010, 157; emphasis in the original)

Like Butler, Beltrán contends that subjectivity is never simply given, such that we can easily identify the attitudes and interests that are supposed to be collectively shared by the persons who are officially recognized as belonging to a given socioeconomic or cultural category. She argues that Latino politics "has often been generated by transgressive and evanescent moments of collective identification" (2010, 157). The ideological diversity among Latinos is such that it is deeply misleading to attribute to each and every member of the Latino community a set of common experiences and a shared sense of linked fate. To assert the existence of a stable and authentic Latino identity is to engage in a loaded game of naturalization in which the nonconformists are made to pay the price—namely, of being excluded (159–160). Beltrán is neither saying that Latino subjectivities are groundless nor ignoring the fact that Latino politics necessarily take place on a terrain always already marked by deeply institutionalized and widely practiced forms of racism and xenophobia. She is, instead, acknowledging the multiplicity, provisionality, and always shifting character of the Latino/pro-immigrant rights movement, and welcoming renewed debate and contestation about the movement's meaning and purpose.

Beltrán argues persuasively that *Latinidad* resembles Deleuze and Guattari's rhizomatic forms of life, in that it has no fixed center and expresses itself in multiplicities, unexpected assemblages, and plural directions in motion. Instead of the teleological and rigid segmentarity that are the properties of the arboreal, the rhizomatic approach encourages us to grasp the ways in which social movements can engage in unpredictable "lines of flight" as well as developments that can be traced back to a strong central core of established commitments (Beltrán 2010, 157–170). It may very well be the case that the most promising forms of anti-assimilationist and critical feminist activism that Butler identifies and anticipates will feature similar forms of dynamic becoming, decenteredness, the sprouting of unpredictable connections and assemblages, and the creation of surprising deviations from established routines of practice and expression.

Once we adopt this critical Foucauldian-Althusserian-Deleuzian posture toward agency and structure, it becomes clear that subject formation is a radically contingent process, even in conditions of extreme asymmetrical social structures. The gendered subject emerges, consciously and unconsciously, within and as the product of, a complex force field made up by discourses of domination and resistance. The forces of disciplining and incitement of performativity, the invitations to iteration and the imposition of constraint generate the subject—this particular constellation of identifications—but the outcome could have gone the other way. In felicitous conditions, even a deeply entrenched tradition such as the biological sex-gender binary can be undermined through sustained, radical collective action (cf. Fausto-Sterling 2000). This feminist interrogation underlines the historical specificity and the diversity of the discursively shaped experiences of persons who are regarded by official sources as "belonging to" the same sex-gender category, and it brings the irreducible intersectionality of our consciousness and social structures to the fore. Subjectivity theory tackles the problem of conceptualizing the relationship between agency and social structures without falling into the trap of a strict determinism in which resistance has been always already been anticipated and wholly contained in advance.

References

Beauvoir, Simone de. 2010. *The Second Sex*. New York: Knopf.
Beltrán, Cristina. 2010. *The Trouble with Unity: Latino Politics and the Creation of Identity*. New York: Oxford University Press.
Berlin, Isaiah. 1958. *Two Concepts of Liberty*. Oxford: Clarendon Press.
Butler, Judith. 1990. *Gender Trouble: Feminism and the Subversion of Identity*. New York: Routledge.
Butler, Judith. 1997. "Merely Cultural." *Social Text* 52/53 (Fall/Winter): 265–277.
Butler, Judith. 2004. *Undoing Gender*. New York: Routledge.
Chodorow, Nancy. 1989. *Feminism and Psychoanalytic Theory*. New Haven, CT: Yale University Press.
Collins, Patricia Hill. 2008. *Black Feminist Thought: Knowledge, Consciousness, and the Politics of Empowerment*. New York: Routledge.
Corrigan, Rose. 2013. *Up against a Wall: Rape Reform and the Failure of Success*. New York: New York University Press.
Crenshaw, Kimberlé. 1989. "Demarginalizing the Intersection of Race and Sex: A Black Feminist Critique of Antidiscrimination Doctrine, Feminist Theory and Antiracist Politics." *University of Chicago Legal Forum*: 139–167.

Davis, Angela Y. 1981. *Women, Race, and Class*. New York: Random House.
Davis, Angela Y. 2003. *Are Prisons Obsolete?* New York: Seven Stories Press.
Davis, Angela Y. 2005. *Abolition Democracy: Beyond Empire, Prisons, and Torture*. New York: Seven Stories Press.
Derrida, Jacques. 1988. *Limited Inc*. Evanston, IL: Northwestern University Press.
Du Bois, W. E. B. 1999. *The Souls of Black Folk*. New York: W. W. Norton.
Eisenstein, Zillah. 2004. *Against Empire: Feminisms, Racism and the West*. London: Zed Books.
Elster, Jon. 1983. *Sour Grapes: Studies in the Subversion of Rationality*. New York: Cambridge University Press.
Fausto-Sterling, Anne. 2000. *Sexing the Body: Gender Politics and the Construction of Sexuality*. New York: Basic Books.
Fineman, Martha. 2004. *The Autonomy Myth: A Theory of Dependency*. New York: New Press.
Foucault, Michel. 1977. *Discipline and Punish: The Birth of the Prison*. New York: Pantheon.
Hancock, Ange-Marie. 2004. *The Politics of Disgust: The Public Identity of the Welfare Queen*. New York: New York University Press.
Hartsock, Nancy C. M. 1998. *The Feminist Standpoint Revisited and Other Essays*. Boulder, CO: Westview Press.
Hirschmann, Nancy J. 2003. *The Subject of Liberty: Toward a Feminist Theory of Freedom*. Princeton, NJ: Princeton University Press.
hooks, bell. 2000. *Feminist Theory: From Margin to Center*. Boston: South End Press.
Kelley, Robin. 1998. *Yo' Mama's Disfunktional! Fighting the Culture Wars in Urban America*. Boston: Beacon Press.
Khader, Serene J. 2011. *Adaptive Preferences and Women's Empowerment*. New York: Oxford University Press.
Locke, John. 1980. *Second Treatise of Government*. Indianapolis, IN: Hackett.
Luxemburg, Rosa. 2006. "The Russian Revolution," In *Reform or Revolution and Other Writings*, 183–222. Mineola, NY: Dover Publications.
Marcuse, Herbert. 1964. *One-Dimensional Man: Studies in the Ideology of Advanced Industrial Society*. Boston: Beacon Press.
Marcuse, Herbert. 1966. *Eros and Civilization*. Boston: Beacon Press.
Marx, Karl. 1978. "The Eighteenth Brumaire of Louis Bonaparte." In *The Marx-Engels Reader*, Karl Marx and Friedrich Engels, edited by Robert Tucker, 594–617. New York: W. W. Norton.
McCall, Leslie. 2005. "The Complexity of Intersectionality." *Signs* 30(3): 1771–1800.
Mink, Wendy. 2002. *Welfare's End*. Ithaca, NY: Cornell University Press.
Mohanty, Chandra Talpade. 2003. *Feminism without Borders: Decolonizing Theory, Practicing Solidarity*. Durham, NC: Duke University Press.
Nedelsky, Jennifer. 2012. *Law's Relations: A Relational Theory of Self, Autonomy, and Law*. New York: Oxford University Press.
Nozick, Robert. 1974. *Anarchy, State, and Utopia*. New York: Basic Books.
Nussbaum, Martha. 2000. *Women and Human Development: The Capabilities Approach*. New York: Cambridge University Press.
Rawls, John. 1999. *A Theory of Justice*. Cambridge, MA: Harvard University Press.
Rose, Tricia. 2008. *The Hip-Hop Wars: What We Talk about When We Talk about Hip-Hop and Why It Matters*. New York: Basic Civitas.
Schneider, Elizabeth M. 2000. *Battered Women and Feminist Lawmaking*. New Haven, CT: Yale University Press.
Sen, Amartya. 2009. *The Idea of Justice*. Cambridge, MA: Harvard University Press.

Sevenhuijsen, Selma. 1998. *Citizenship and the Ethics of Care: Feminist Considerations on Justice, Morality, and Politics.* New York: Routledge.
Spillers, Hortense. 1987. "Mama's Baby, Papa's Maybe: An American Grammar Book." *Diacritics* 17(2): 64–81.
Spivak, Gayatri. 1988. "Can the Subaltern Speak?" In *Marxism and the Interpretation of Culture*, edited by Cary Nelson and Lawrence Grossberg, 271–313. Urbana, IL: University of Illinois Press.
Smith, Anna Marie. 2001. "Missing Poststructuralism, Missing Foucault: Butler and Fraser on Capitalism and the Regulation of Sexuality." *Social Text* 67 (Summer): 103–125.
Smith, Anna Marie. 2007. *Welfare Reform and Sexual Regulation.* New York: Cambridge University Press.
Tronto, Joan. 1993. *Moral Boundaries: A Political Argument for An Ethic of Care.* New York: Routledge.
West, Robin. 1999. *Caring for Justice.* New York: New York University Press.

CHAPTER 47

TEMPORALITY

BONNIE G. SMITH

TIME or temporality is a concept by which humans confront the experience of duration—past, present, or future. Time and temporality are commonplace in our lives, as witnessed in the ubiquity of instruments for indicating time, such as watches, time clocks in businesses, portable phones, computers, and large public clocks or scrapbooks, photo albums, baby books, and other means of remembering it. Simultaneously, time and temporality seem to be obviously associated with women, who are said to have biological clocks, whose bodies experience periodicity, and whose aging is constantly noted, not just in physical changes, but also in public discussions. Still, temporality is a multivalent and uncertain topic, one that sparks a range of debate and is perhaps less straightforward than it appears. Feminism itself looks to a better future for women and hopes to achieve it by solving problems in the present. As with most aspects of life, temporality is also experienced and produced through language, narratives, myth, and many other ingredients of human traditions that pertain to feminism.

Societies do not share a uniform sense of temporality. As an idea and organizing part of everyday life, it has a variety of meanings, which themselves have evolved over the centuries. South Asian concepts hold time to be infinite; so-called human, animal, and vegetable life is a fleeting incarnation within the cosmic infinitude of time. This larger sense of time is eternal and transcendent, virtually a timelessness. Early on in the Western tradition, human time was somewhat similarly posed against the time of God's eternity, or timelessness. Philosophers such as Plato posited time as "a moving image of eternity," while Aristotle held time to be a regular series of markings without meaning in and of itself. This sense of time, as the idea developed over the centuries, was an abstract, mathematical concept susceptible to increasingly precise measurement: a "number" or "measure" of motion and rest, as Aristotle put it. Isaac Newton systematized temporality or time as mathematical—now commonly accepted as especially important in science and productivity.

These varied concepts of an abstract nonhuman time stand in contrast to the everyday time of human existence on earth, often associated with the concept of temporality. For the Roman author Virgil, truth was "the daughter of time," or, alternatively, time was "the devourer of things"—statements that begin to capture the complex, even paradoxical meanings of time. In ancient Indian thought, especially as expressed in Hindu and Buddhist ideas, human time is defective, chaotic, and tending toward deterioration. As a human ages, life is increasingly composed of pain and suffering and characterized by growing weakness or entropy—all of these signaling the defectiveness of life. In this explanation, time itself is at the root of such corrosive tendencies as greed and the oppression of others. Once, the *Vayu Purana* (1:8:77) relates, "people lived in perfect happiness. . . . Then, because of the great power of time and the changes it wrought upon them, they were overcome by passion and greed." Thus, in this vision of time, the stages of life call optimally for a gradual withdrawal from everyday occupations once responsibilities to family and community have been fulfilled. At that point, one retreats, for example, to the forest and ultimately renounces all things of this world. These ideas prefigured the Christian idea of using life seriously and ascetically as a preparation for eternity or an infinite, unknowable world beyond the human.

In the Western tradition, temporality (chronos, tempus) was expressed grammatically in the form of tenses—past, present, and future. Theorists today maintain that our entire understanding of time is expressed through language and that there is no time beyond those expressions, however varied or stereotypical they might be. Intellectual historian Hayden White writes about narrative as it structures temporality especially by stringing together events in meaningful ways. Ordinarily, White claims, events—that is, moments in present time—are chosen by authors and made into stories with a "message." All such messages grow out of the specific structuring of the chaos of events into a beginning, middle, and end. The end carries weight for the reader, giving the entire tale or history or sociology a morality. We see that the weight of gender is closely connected to the narratives of time, including such notions as tradition, modernity, and future outcomes. Feminists have created such narratives, selecting past events and welding them into an ordered story of injustices or triumphs over adversity. Narratives or representations of temporality have thus helped define the power inherent in the relations between male and female.

Feminist and Women's History

Multiple senses of time and temporality have long operated in women's history and feminist activism, having been used in describing and analyzing the situation of women. In the South Asian tradition, the entropic notion of time by which there is a tendency toward chaos and decay demands constant reparation in the form of healing and recuperative rituals. Women have served as participants in these rituals (Pintchman 2007). Christian women have for centuries enmeshed their devotions and the practices of everyday life in the belief that reaching a heavenly eternity is eventually their goal. In world religions, the faithful make pilgrimages in observance of certain times of the year or special religious occasions, to atone for faults or give thanks for blessings, or to mark certain events in one's life in cyclical patterns of time. Women have been especially active in pilgrimages across the centuries, operating in several senses of time.

For many women adherence to the time of eternity has led them to occupy their lives entirely with prayer and devotion by choosing a religious vocation. Declining to participate in family and a secularly oriented life, they become nuns of Buddhist, Catholic, or other sects. Additionally, women have shown devotion and obedience to religious or quasi-religious principles through the commemoration of meaningful events or people in the human past. Chinese women have participated in commemoration of ancestors, and in the past, many have wanted to reach a level of virtue and accomplishment so that they themselves will be commemorated long into the future—that is, throughout time. Jewish women regularly prepare celebrations of the history of their faith and relate to their children the stories of those in the past who were courageous or dutiful heroines of the faith. Religious women thus mark multiple levels of time in their daily lives; but these activities connected to time are an expression of women's importance. These actions in time give weight to present concerns.

Feminist thinkers have taken the past as a point of departure, using the present as a constant backdrop. In the fifteenth century, Christine de Pisan's *Book of the City of Ladies* charted women's acts of heroism in ancient times in the face of male abuse—sexual, political, and social. She showed her readers women's valor in the past in order to counter her contemporaries' charges of women's inferiority and passivity (Pizan 1999). Several centuries later, Wanyan Yun Zhu collected women's poetry from family archives to demonstrate women's accomplishments and to use them as markers for present women so that they not forget this past excellence. Today, women's studies and women's history classes essentially do the same thing, consolidating information and analysis about women in the past to make judgments about the present. More than that, the situation of women in the past has been used for over a century and a half of activism as motivation, building determination that over time things must change.

The writing of women's history over the centuries has made two conflicting judgments about the experience of women over the centuries. The first judgment of past experiences considers the events of centuries ago to have been a golden age. Evidence backing this judgment consists of such elements as the supposed existence of equality among women and men, the hypothetical instances of matriarchy, the power of women as rulers and consorts, and the more "natural" experience of their bodies in childbirth, and other life-course changes—to name a few points of evidence. This last example of bodily autonomy is often posed against the alienating medicalization of procedures such as caesarian sections in hospitals, and even the present-day prevalence of hospital births. Additionally, the past is judged as offering women more access to a wider variety of expertise in crafts, midwifery, and amateur science and, in some societies, to more egalitarian care for children. The fact that women and children today constitute 80 percent of the world's poor and that violence against women appears to be accelerating is taken to suggest that past societies were far more equitable.

In other instances, the past is envisioned as the bad old days compared to the present. Historians draw a stark picture of women's denigration in the past, including their status as "polluted," especially during menses and childbirth. They point to women's general status as impure beings and note the horrific conditions they endured during childbirth. The bad old days saw arms and legs ripped from infants during delivery and permanent gynecological damage inflicted. Although some societies might have valued women for their reproductive capacity and honored the status of motherhood, in the main, women were treated more harshly than men, for instance, in the case of adultery. The general devaluation of women disqualified them from social and political responsibility and made their lives far more difficult than those of men. The fact that women held positions of power is seen as anomalous. Generally, the judgment is that men were able to take up the best livelihoods, while women's work was the most demeaning and lowest paid. Conditions in today's world are posed against this harsh picture of the historical past: women now live longer; their fate in childbirth is much improved; their fertility is falling; many of the superstitions about women's bodies have lifted in the face of science; and women are applauded as rulers, innovators, and leaders.

Some scholars hold that the treatment of women in the past was more deeply and enduringly consequential than ever before suspected. Skeletons from tens of thousands of years ago show that men and women were once equal in size. Over time, there appeared a dimorphism, and women's skeletons became dramatically smaller than men's—a physical inequality that exists to this day. The hypothesis is that at some more recent point in the past, women were seen to merit an inferior standard of living and thus given less food. As a result, men could overpower women and hold them under their sway. Physical prowess, whether on the battlefield or in domestic relations, became a measure of value and general human worth. Far back in the past, women's imputed inferiority today was born of so basic a disparity as the unequal distribution of food. All evidence suggests that this basic inequality of tens of thousands of years ago continues to have physical manifestations and, as importantly, political, social, economic, and cultural ones. This inequity lives on today in women's bodies.

Alongside the so-called facts of women's and feminist history is a less certain and at times questioned tradition. One is history as orality and testimonial, especially as recounted by women or dealing with women's lives. Oral traditions, still prevalent in many regions of the world, were important in recalling the accomplishments of individual men and families, giving them temporal weightiness just as written history has done. The *griot* in West Africa is a teller of stories and histories, among them the histories of great deeds and men. The Queen Mother, a powerful co-ruler and adviser to the king, is chosen for a variety of qualities. One of them is her ability to recount the familial histories and alliances from the distant past through to the present. Knowing the development over time of alliances, foibles, and character constitutes a powerful resource for political rule.

The oral tradition and oral history have also been important in recording the history of "voiceless" people who were not considered worthy of inclusion in the written history or whose history, as in the case of slaves in the United States, is underdeveloped because very few were ever given the opportunity to learn to write. Some women slaves had their life histories written by abolitionists. In the nineteenth century, Lydia Maria Child took down and had published the harrowing tale of Linda Brent/Harriet Jacob, for example. The history of the Quiche people of Central America was transcribed late in the twentieth century by a woman anthropologist for the Nobel Peace Prize–winner Rigoberta Menchu, and these words served in Menchu's mind as a living testimonial to her people. In both cases, researchers and detractors worked to find flaws and errors in the accounts in order to discredit both the cause and the oral historian. Fatima Amrouche's oral history of living under colonialism in Algeria was transcribed by her son, a well-respected author. Interestingly, this work did not receive the harsh scrutiny that Brent's and Menchu's did. There is no doubt that oral history captures past time and offers a precious record for those without literary voice.

Because it is not written down, oral history becomes suspect. Even then, however, the factual veracity of oral history as an account of people in a past time has been questioned. In particular, Joan Scott argues that histories of feminism are endowed with fantasies, especially those of women as pioneering mothers and orators. While not denying the existence of feminist activists in history, Scott suggests that the production of such history has the quality of an echo shaped by psychic structures as well as by written factual evidence. In making this argument, Scott urges consideration of our psychic investment in writing feminist history—or indeed in constructing accounts of the past.

Temporality and Feminist Politics

Temporality has been a ground for women's political movements. In a simple example, we note the acronym for the National Organization of Women: NOW. It signals a present in which injustice reigns and immediate action is needed. A temporal urgency has often characterized demands for the vote; legislative reform in matters of bodily autonomy, including divorce, abortion, and contraception; alleviation of poverty; access to jobs; and equal wages—again, to name just a few measures where equality could not wait for time to pass. Violence against women also was seen in a temporal spectrum of an ongoing evil of immediate concern. The present resonated and resonates with injustice and danger for women. The future must be different. Feminist politics was embedded in temporality.

A second aspect of feminist temporality is the calculation that feminism has existed and exists as successive "waves" of activism. These waves consist of a first wave centered around the suffrage movement of the late nineteenth and early twentieth centuries, a second wave in the 1960s and 1970s, and a third wave beginning at some point in the 1980s. Each wave is distinct in time, subject matter, and tactics, and each follows the liberal time of progress. Additionally, there is sometimes the invocation of a break in time: for example, when some of those in the second wave refused to acknowledge the existence of the first or were utterly ignorant of it. "Women's history," one women's liberation participant claimed, "we invented it," indicating a rupture or break with the many feminist histories written in the past. This break with a linear past marks an element of presentism whereby feminists take a parthenogenetic approach, in which the past of women's movements is denied.

Those in the third wave have often worked to distance themselves, not just in time but also in tactics and doctrine from those in the second wave, calling them strident and full of hatred for men, in contrast to their own attitudes. Additionally, second-wave feminists were antique, not to mention evil, in their racism, homophobia, and classism, according to the third wavers. Having grown more enlightened, kinder, and frankly better, those in the third wave had supposedly reached a higher level of consciousness over time. Within the so-called first wave, time similarly made a difference or was seen to make a difference. Some young women in the 1920s hoped to distance themselves from the elder stateswomen who had lobbied for suffrage. They viewed the older generation as loud, outmoded, aged, and ugly following the liberal idea of progress combined with a Darwinian notion of fitness and superiority in succeeding generations.

A subsequent submovement called postfeminism has been molded in a similar temporal vein, although this is often equated with aspects of a third wave or even a fourth wave. The prefix *post* implies something following a terminal moment, but many postfeminists deny the accusation that they are reveling in a supposed death of feminism. Some see themselves as part of a feminist evolution, and some disavow that cohort of postfeminists who judge feminism to be dead. Each stance puts its adherents together in a linear, progressive temporality. Yet, to contrast their own laid back stance with the urgency of NOW in the mid-1960s, postfeminists announce themselves as a breed distant in time from the "old" feminist movement. Enjoying the accomplishments of those earlier activists, postfeminists feel themselves to be empowered rather than victims, friends to the media, not its enemies, and far more intellectually sophisticated—all of this implying progress and thus further iteration of liberal, progressive time (Genz and Brabon 2009).

Grrrll culture was part of postfeminism or of a third or fourth wave, with a decidedly temporal flair. Grrrllll culture declared an appreciation for the fearless young instead of the older, sometimes too ladylike generations embedded in outmoded ideas, causes, and a disguised but nonetheless vicious racism. Adolescent vigor, freshness, and fierceness characterized their stance. More obviously, Riot Grrlll, as articulated by Kathleen Hanna in the Riot Grrll Manifesto, the polymorphously perverse child who could and would do any kind of act is revived in the twerks of pop star Miley Cyrus. To be free was to regress in biological time to a moment of utter freedom from civilization's constraints, including its gender norms. In the United States, a milder form of this regressive freedom appears on the blog/news consolidator *Jezebel.com*, which employs naughty words (among other things) to make fourth-wave feminist judgments. Such a use of generational difference to construct a robust feminism contrasts with the amalgamation of life spans in the Beijing Conference (1995) platform that fused women and the girl-child in its concerns and policy agenda. Nonetheless, there is among one segment of liberal feminists a disavowal of liberalism and its progressive forward-looking ethos. For example, postfeminism (as interpreted through the academic constructs of postmodernism, postcolonialism, and posthumanism) takes a stance against the progressive individual of liberal theory. That individual exists as a reformer who will use time to bring about change. In contrast, that branch of postfeminism, residing in universities, rejects the liberal depiction of the individual as autonomous and rational, moving progressively through time on a trajectory of improvement. Instead, time is plastic, flowing, and subject to one's own open and fluid volition. Thus, Chicana lesbian poet Gloria Anzaldua refuses to imagine a better future or to have any aspirations for one—the touchstone of racist and homophobic feminist politics in the past.

In many of these iterations, temporality is assigned mostly to the years from 1800 to the present, with narratives of women's lives and activism having virtually no importance. Historian of medieval Europe Judith Bennett has pointed to the presentist contours of programs such as the Berkshire Conference of Women Historians and the American Historical Association. She reveals the astonishing numbers of presentations at the annual meetings of both organizations that are largely focused on twentieth-century topics. We will see some qualifications of this judgment later in the chapter, but a "presentist" and "modernist" bias informs feminism in part because of an urgent focus on current issues. Another hindrance to the appreciation of women's past ideas and experiences is the existence of enduring myths of long standing, with deep roots in the past. Some mythical heroines and goddesses such as Radha, Indian partner of Krishna, and the dutiful daughter and Chinese warrior Melun have long offered models to emulate, as have the mothers of both the ancient Chinese philosopher Mencius and Jesus, son of the Christian God. More generally, however, mythical and religious cultures have focused on women's sinfulness as embodied in the temptress Eve. Buddha explained that he would allow women into the religious life despite their evil nature. The list of mythical evils attributed to women is endless.

Antifeminists have also invoked temporality to block political agendas calling for greater justice for women. In some instances their arguments invoke mythical and religious figures who led domestic lives or lives devoted to the well-being of children and the wider family. Women's selfless devotion, not their rights, have anchored the world, antifeminists often claim, whereas changes in the status of women have only brought disaster. Moreover, women rulers have been suspect if not outright disastrous: the dowager empress Cixi or Bloody Mary of England, to name just two. Power corrupts women more than men goes another argument for returning to healthier times. Tradition in many forms has thus long been the watchword for antifeminists.

TIME AND EVERYDAY LIFE

Twentieth-century German philosopher Martin Heidegger proposed an idea of temporality that has been taken up by many theorists. He rejected the abstract and absolute notions of time proposed by Aristotle, Isaac Newton, and Immanuel Kant and endorsed by others since. For Heidegger, temporality was human and not mathematical. Rather, it was entirely intertwined with being, especially being as it existed at the moment or in the present. Others have combined their scrutiny of everyday life tasks, including the performance of industrial work, with mathematical time, while still others talk about time in the most human of everyday terms, as a kind of immediate and unmediated experience.

In the West, sociologists, government officials, and feminist activists have since the nineteenth century concerned themselves with the time women spend in their everyday tasks. Clocking women's working day has a long and controversial heritage. Early reformers during the industrial revolution believed that women's work was overly long. They targeted the activities of women both in and outside the home. Reformers felt that women's work outside the home in mines and factories was far too long and wearing. Sweated workers, such as seamstresses, could work twenty hours a day, and even longer when the work demanded it. The schedules of many women workers were erratic, however, because of seasonality and the ups and downs of the economic cycles. Reformers believed that the time women worked was excessive, dangerously unpredictable, or threatening to women's reproductive capacity. Often, the aim of reform efforts was to curtail the amount of time women and children worked with little regard for the resulting economic hardship.

Whatever the industrial setting in the early days, time weighed heavily. Women and girls at work during Japanese industrialization in the late nineteenth century experienced their jobs as excessively long and fatiguing. They wrote "Song of the Living Corpses" (c. 1890s) in which several verses mentioned the early hours at which they were forced to rise:

> We friends are wretched,
> Separated from our homes in a strange place,
> Put in a miserable dormitory
> Woken up at four-thirty in the morning,
> Eating when five o'clock sounds,
> Dressing at the third bell,
> Glared at by the manager and section head,
> Used by the inspector.
> How wretched we are!

Even in the 1920s, when factory hours had generally been reduced, workers talked about lived time, both on the job and at home. In 1929, a group of German women produced an account of their time, titled *My Workday, My Weekend* (*Mein Arbeitstag, Mein Wochenende*), that featured an astonishing array of activities. In the 1970s, sociologists charted the life of an office worker in Budapest, Hungary; in the Soviet Union, Natalya Baranskaya's *A Week Like Any Other* (1968) chronicled the incredibly long days of a woman engineer, who held her job, stood in long lines, did hours of housework, and was chastised for not being a good enough Communist. The short story spoke volumes to those who read it and became an important testimonial to the need for reform in women's lives simply in terms of time. Although these women talked about time in measurement, they were in fact calling forth the human aspects of lives set within time. These testimonials were able to capture the immediacy of the moment.

In the West, middle-class feminists were from the nineteenth century on also aware of the organization of everyday temporality as it shaped women's daily lives. Believing in liberal principles of harmony and balance, they found the amount of time devoted to individual tasks dangerously unbalanced. The average woman of their class, they believed, spent too much time in household work and reproduction, including sexual labor. This imbalance accounted for nervous conditions and also for problems within marriage. Women's days needed a reorganization of time so that there was greater equilibrium among household activities, hobbies, exercise, education, rest, and service to the public. Men's lives were also out of balance because of an inordinate amount of time spent at work and in the public, and little time devoted to the household. Time was a major component of feminist theory in the nineteenth century and remains so today.

In recent years, many debates surround the time men and women spend in household activities. It is a trope for many, no matter what the agenda, in public discourse. The discussion revolves, on the one hand, on the miniscule amount of time men contribute to the common life of the family and household. On the other hand, because of the time women spend nurturing children, tending the home, and provisioning the family with food, they are exhausted, especially if they have jobs. Women are said not to have "time to themselves" or "time for themselves." Feminists around the world have been acutely aware of this discrepancy and the costs to women in terms of financial security. If 80 percent of the world's impoverished people are women and children, it is because of the time constraints on earning imposed by this double burden. Employers talk of women's potential in terms of the amount of time they will be able to give to a responsible job; women are said to want time off to begin or expand a family and "flexible" hours, which does not correspond to a managerial position, and so on. Because women have so little consistent or quality or focused time for work, the idea of economic leaders is that they should fill lower paying and less important jobs. Time looms large when public figures and working men and women themselves construct gender.

Some commentators embrace women's connection to household time. American Studies scholar Mary Trigg engages insights drawn from the literature on temporality. *Of Mothers and Time* situates ideas about motherhood in relation to competing temporal frames, which are themselves embedded in racialized, classed, and ethnic experiences. She conceptualizes mothering in relation to varying practices concerning keeping, marking, transcending, and memorializing time. She theorizes mother love, spending time with children, teaching children to use and measure time, and memory work in the context of diverse modes of American mothering. Some women have more time for motherhood's temporality, and the classed and racialized aspects can include the memory capacities that mothers in "voiceless groups" might develop in their daughters, among others.

Time, Embodiment, and Sexuality

One of the long-standing aspects of time in women's lives that has been noted is that associated with the temporarility of the female body. Its reproductive rhythms have been emphasized in prehistoric statuary depicting women's fertility and in creation and other myths. Down to the present, taboos have surrounded reproductive temporality. These include the ostracism of menstruating women through seclusion in special dwellings or in separate parts of the house. Women's periodicity could prevent them from participating in household functions, such as canning and other food preparation, and even from being in proximity to family members. Menstruation in particular captured attention because of its cyclical as opposed to linear qualities. Women were thus associated with the phases of the moon or with instability and insanity because of their menses.

The temporality of the female body generated a range of confounding, discriminatory, and disenabling observations. Until recently even so-called scientists had difficulty using neutral terms to describe cyclical periodicity; one US medical textbook in the 1970s explained women's periodicity as "the uterus crying for a baby." In the West, "that time of the month" was supposed to make women irrational and thus unfit for holding public office, serving on juries, or acting as lawyers and stock brokers. Research into the temporality of fertility determined the periodicity of the spontaneous release of the female egg known as ovulation. Reaction in the West to the discovery of this involuntary regularity varied, with one school of thought judging that this involuntary release meant that women were in general passive and passionless when it came to sexual relations. Others found the discovery liberating because of the possibility for limiting conception by avoiding intercourse around the time of ovulation. For a long time, however, spontaneous ovulation equated women more firmly with those devalued animals whose estrus cycles seemed similar to menstrual ones.

Pregnancy and childbirth were also said to be especially important modes of temporality over a woman's life course. At childbirth or during its aftermath, seclusion might occur again. Alternatively, pregnancy could be considered unremarkable and pass virtually unmarked in the course of one's work life. Peasant women around the world were said to return to the fields immediately after delivery with no time release for recuperation. Alternatively, in contemporary societies, governments and employers often award parturient women varying amounts of time in "maternal leave," prolonging the temporality of reproduction.

The cessation of fertility's temporal characteristics in women's bodies likewise garnered attention and often needed special markings. Clothing sometimes changed, as did habitation. Today, medication is available to mediate the physical manifestations of this temporal trajectory. The gendered temporalities of a woman's life course have also involved charges that menopause is a time when women become older looking in years than their male counterparts. They age badly, it is said, and, once again, become shrewish and possibly crazy. Alternatively, aging women are sometimes seen as sweet and adorable, rarely possessed of the gravitas or wisdom of senior men. This is often the case in Western society; however, the Nazis murdered old men and women alike deeming them unfit to live because of their years.

Some societies in the past have respected and even obeyed mature and aging women. The Queen Mothers of West Africa offer an example of women empowered by their long and practiced memories, from which they culled good advice for the ruler. Among the Iroquois in North America, women were clan mothers because the societies were matrilineal. Leading women chose chiefs and distributed food, showing a closeness to power that few Western women enjoyed. In parts of West Africa and Southeast Asia older women controlled local and interregional trade networks because of the skill and connections they had developed over time.

In contrast to Western ideas of embodiment and sexuality, Hindu ideas of temporality suggested a core self (or *atman* in the case of early Indian thought) that existed in cosmic time. This core self was also reincarnated in various forms both human and animal, even as the core continued on in time. Some thinkers took these beliefs to include changes in the gender of the outward manifestations of this core. For example, theosophists formed an influential and numerous international group of believers in the hidden wisdom of the cosmos, and they developed from a range of non-Western thought a series of practices to uncover that wisdom as it had existed in Egypt, South Asia, China, and other regions. One of their beliefs involved the outward change of gender identity over the course of reincarnations. Just as the single core self could reincarnate in animal and human forms, the outward manifestation of a self could change from masculine to feminine across rebirths.

Such a belief influenced ideas of sexuality and gender identity among Western feminists and other reformers from the late nineteenth century on. British feminist Annie Besant was a confirmed theosophist practitioner who moved to India to help the theosophist movement thrive there, even as she was part of a growing theosophist contingent among Western feminists. The plasticity of gender identity appealed to many of her cohort and allowed activists, such as Eva Gore-Booth, and writers, such as Radclyffe Hall, to affirm their homosexuality and transgendering as a higher form of reincarnation. Sex reformer Edward Carpenter turned to the Chinese Daoist thinker Lao-tse for confirmation of the idea that those who had known both the male and female forms of existence were more distinguished, thus proposing that from this series of revolving gendered reincarnations there emerged a "third sex" of a superior order.

Writers of fiction were enchanted by such beliefs in the intertwined movement of gender and cosmic time. Virginia Woolf's novel *Orlando* (1928) describes the life of a young man striding across the centuries. He does great deeds and encounters grand people, all the while aiming to be a recognized poet. A few centuries after the story opens, Orlando awakens to sense that incremental changes are taking place in his body and temperament. Soon Orlando has become a fully modern woman in the present, still full of poetic aspirations. Woolf wrote this story of reincarnation over time as a tribute to her friend Vita Sackville-West. Woolf had, however, long been interested in the thought of philosophers and theorists such as Henri Bergson, who himself had developed some of his ideas sabout the flow of time from the non-Western influences that were shaping European sensibility in those days.

Woolf's writing also portrayed psychic time, contrasting with a more public temporality. In *To the Lighthouse* (1927), the thoughts and speculations of the characters are punctuated by the rumblings of war so that public time and private time intersect. *Mrs. Dalloway* (1925) showed the intersection of psychic time with family time, and of family time with social time. Woolf validated those inner wanderings, driving her narratives with their progress, rather than with the sequence of events of World War I. She also showed how family time and social time interrupted those seemingly fragmented musings, suggesting that these conventionally more important temporalities can undermine an autonomous self.

Although women had written history over the centuries, late in the 1960s the feminist movement influenced greater numbers of women to get professional degrees—many of them in history. The aim of these historians was to bring scholarship on women into scholarship on the past. One result, they believed, would be a drastic change in history's temporal dimensions, most notably, periodization. Feminist historians claimed to alter the conventional temporal divisions of historical narrative into distinct chunks of time, such as the Renaissance. "Did Women Have a Renaissance?" author Joan Kelly asked. The answer of many historians echoed Kelly's view that many of the canonical aspects of the Renaissance did not apply to women. The world of art and music was not open to them, nor did they become "Renaissance women" who ruled city-states and simultaneously cultivated a deeply cultured humanistic self.

Ultimately, historical periodization did not change much in the hands of women historians, nor even at the hands of world historians or practitioners of deep history. Nonetheless, the events and large trends concerning women seemed significant enough to call for a rethinking of historical time. For example, the history of the world since circa 1850 has been punctuated in large part by terrifying warfare and massive casualties suffered during those wars. Simultaneously, however, an equally significant numerical change has occurred in the even more dramatic reduction in women's fertility. Rates first began to decline in France and the United States at the beginning of the nineteenth century. From the 1880s to 1930 the fertility rate of women had been cut by half in most of Europe; after 1945, rates continued to drop there, and then the curtailment occurred across much of the world. The potential births that did not occur because of this phenomenon would number in the hundreds of millions, if not billions. Is a re-periodization in history needed that might be calculated along the lines of fertility, rather than mortality in wartime?

Temporality, the State, and Modernity

Modern narratives of time focus on the nation-state and its predecessors, such as colonies, cities, and empires. This narrative of the nation-state as anchored in deep time carefully constructed by scholars legitimizes that particular political entity. It has been important to feminists that the deep time of the nation-state is composed almost exclusively of the deeds of men. Historical existence over long stretches of time has thus produced believable and gendered societies, constructing men as its actors and women as its invisible supporting cast, or simply as invisible. The gendering of historical time provides temporal depth to this very young political institution, making it look inevitable and part of a liberal history of progressive improvement. The richness of masculinity, generation after generation, has appeared in the trajectory for the West that begins in Rome and ends with the excitement of World Wars I and II. Or it can be anchored in the mythical era of the sun goddess of Japan and then proceed to the beautiful prince Genji through the shoguns and the Meiji emperor. The vigor of masculine time is the backbone of nation-state politics.

In the masculine time out of which history is constructed, the movement is toward political modernity. The movement from tradition to political modernity can lead to the comparison of repetitive household time with the forward thrust of national and industrial time. Modern time, however, was always open to dispute. Special occasions throughout the calendar have led to gender inversions in such events as charivari, Mardi Gras, and other moments when "the world is turned upside down." During these events, the poor mock the rich and men dress as women, calling the social order into question for a brief, specifically marked time. This kind of exuberant time was also associated with traditional societies and traditional ways of doing things, most notably for our purposes, with the tasks of the household. The task-oriented time of the household and peasant order was increasingly seen as laden with feeling and experiential richness, which was contrasted to the impoverished, mechanical, if ultimately more consequential time of the nation-state and industrial society. Women and students were cited by such scholars as E. P. Thompson as still existing in a task-oriented, richly experiential time. Whereas clock time was efficient and money-making, household time was less efficient and concerned with feelings, not capital. Increasingly the household's time was seen as taken up with psychological nurturing and maintaining tradition, while the outside world created forward-looking progress. In some instances, aspects of feminism could be said to associate themselves with the forward march of time, while others featured the domestic and experiential.

The association of women with all that was backward, temporally retarded, and tradition-bound expanded across the disciplines and theories of Western thought to interpret other societies. Societies distant from the West were interpreted as similarly backward and thus feminine. Taking time backward summoned the feminine and developmentally retarded, while futurity and intellectual promise were masculine. Simultaneously, imperial ideology held that regions under colonialism were not ready for independence because their women were treated in such backwards ways and not modernized, for example, by learning to read, wearing modern clothing, or becoming generally secularized.

Some nationalist liberation movements picked up this theme of the temporality of the female, citing it to establish the cultural and social richness that distinguished their nation because it complemented the futurity of the men in these movements. Women's encapsulation in traditional time served as a kernel of essential ethnic or national purity alongside the broader contamination of time under colonial or Western domination. In contrast to the West, where women had moved into the cold, emancipated world of men, women in colonized countries had maintained culture and sex roles. In China, however, modernizers sought to update women by liberating them from rigid patriarchal control, foot-binding, and child marriage, and by providing them with an education that was current.

Still, some modernizing nations saw the need to modify sex roles, especially those associated with sexual identity. Heterosexuality was seen as modern and informed; whereas homosexuality represented all that was backward. Moreover, the heterosexuality of modernity was one in which men dominated the economy, legal system, and the nation. In nineteenth-century Persia, as one example, the drive to become modern entailed producing gender that was more dimorphic in terms of power and sex roles. Clothing changed, as did the flag, from which female symbols virtually disappeared. Homosexuality, which had played a role in everyday life, was now condemned as backward, signaling unenlightened values.

Feminist Futurities

Feminists have a long tradition of considering the present in regard to the past and present—usually a baleful, treacherous present. They then work in the present to create mental and policy springboards to a hoped-for better future. Additionally, writers have created visions of women's condition out of time—"The Sultana's Dream," for example, by the Bengali author Rokeya Sakhawat Hossain. In 1905, Hossain published the tale of a place called Ladyland, in which women ruled, having banished men to the *zenana*, or "harem." Ladyland was a beautiful place where there was perfect order because women used advanced technology to maintain peace and well-being. Hossain juxtaposed her out-of-real-time vision against a past and present in which men ruled and misruled almost exclusively through the military and the seclusion of women.

In the West, Christine de Pisan created her "City of Ladies" as an escape challenge to the misogyny of her contemporaries. US author and feminist activist Charlotte Perkins Gilman also imagined an escape into a world run lovingly by women, in her futuristic novel *Herland* (1915). Of interest to women since the nineteenth century, Marxian time presents temporality as the medium for the ups and downs of women's condition, showing an egalitarian society deep in the human past and a deterioration of that society with the advent of private property. Like feminist authors, Marx saw a bright future with the coming of socialism, and urged immediate organizing to overthrow the lethal socioeconomic order. The Communist Revolution saw the appearance of several women writers and artists, especially after 1917 and through 1930, whose work contributed to the hoped-for liberation of women at some point in the near future.

Simultaneously, there have been dystopian writers whose fiction depicts a deterioration of women's condition and sometimes of human society in general as the present continues its evil ways into the future. Ecofeminism is based on the vision of an apocalyptic future time if the present is not corrected. Indeed, feminist scholars write urgently today about the condition of the world—distracted, violent, warlike. The constant global warfare and even genocide make the present unbearable, while the preoccupation with technology keeps people off-balance and unable to think clearly. A corrosive capitalist order, the idea goes, undermines human relationships among individuals, across societies, and around the globe. In this situation, attention to the future is desperately needed so that people stop drowning in a soupy nostalgia for a past harmony that never was. For the moment, this critique explains, a relentless consumerism can likewise entrap individuals and even society as a whole, preventing resistance to the present and action in the future.

Postmodernist Rethinking of Temporality

University-based philosophers and other intellectuals loosely clustered together as postmodernists provide additional insights on temporality and on futurity. Their theories once again connect to the work of Martin Heidegger and his pupil Hans-Georg Gadamer, whose thinking facilitates this critical approach to time. Gadamer posited the "fore-structures" of knowledge in which thinking was situated—that is, something that predates thinking now. French philosopher, Michel Foucault, drawing heavily on a range of German theorists, including Nietzsche, Heidegger, and Gadamer, derived from these a "critical theory" of the present that should be the outcome of thinking. According to Foucault, one worked to uncover the structures of history's present in one's thinking about the past. In other words, he asked what the intellectual surround of any present moment was that allowed ideas or schools of thought—even competing ones—to emerge. Foucault rejected chronological, linear time that saw one idea emerging from another that emerged from an earlier one, and so forth. Thus, in examining the past, one looked for the a priori or archive through which an event or intellectual structure or train of thought came into being (Roth 1981).

Writing in the tradition of Foucault's critical theory and other theories relevant to the poststructuralism of the past three or four decades, feminists thinkers, including those calling themselves queer theorists, have revised concepts of temporality. One direction consists of confronting time head-on, as do those who analyze the stages and waves of feminism. Concentrating intently on the meaning of stages or waves can yield insights, such as those of Julia Kristeva in her article "Women's Time," written in the 1970s during the so-called second wave. Kristeva, unlike the fourth-wave or postfeminists, celebrates the second wave for blasting away at the linear time of male hegemony. In this regard,

Kristeva's work points to time as rupture, but her ideas are also full of concern. Women's time, she stresses, is either monumental and cyclical or familial, having to do either with myth and the enduring cycles of the female body or with the reproductive and familial. Against this, and constituting the separation of the sexes into male and female, is linear time—the time of making money and war. Although Kristeva celebrates the second wave for determining that women, too, will participate in the male time of the market and politics, she also worries about the decline and even disappearance of the familial and the sense of sexual difference that comes from the female body and the family.

Celebrated, Julia Kristeva is part of an older, less ethereal group of feminist theorists of time because she talks of entities that she takes as constituting the "real," such as the self, the family, money, and politics. Judith's Butler's theory of gender as performativity, dismissing the conception of an authentic and autonomous self, holds that gender is a citation of roles that are always already existent in time. However, one's enactment of those rules occurs in the present, or now-time. Gender is an effect of this enactment, not the expression of some biological "reality." The time of performativity can be categorized as repetitive time, thus breaking with linearity. Although some criticize Butler's theory as allowing little room for radical change, other commentators envision this emphasis on now-time as carrying the potential for transformative political action. It could lead to changing the future by acting outside of historical time with its constraints and rules and, instead, always acting in now-time (Dinshaw 2007; Honkanen 2007).

Philosophers such as Elizabeth Grosz hold still another view of time, discussing its "untimeliness." For Grosz, time is neither the abstraction of science and clock time nor the now-time of being, consciousness, or an event. Instead, her sense of time seems to meld the two into a temporality of becoming. There is some connection with French feminist theorist Luce Iragaray, who talks of moments of wonder and surprise at appearance of difference or of other moments that prick us to attention. Additionally, Darwin features in Grosz's discussions, referencing the becoming of evolution. Grosz compounds this consciousness of time as signaling the potential both to notice time and to envision time as becoming, the combination allowing for the kind of transformation that the feminist concern for futurity has called for. In arguing for becoming/thinking/time, she sees swirls of force that flow through minds and thought/practice—thus moving into a queer space of infinite possibility. Deliberate policies and organized activism, one might suggest, are the stuff of linear time and for Grosz, more or less a dead end. Endless becoming is a break with adherence to masculine and feminist time alike as outlined by Kristeva. For Grosz, to recast temporality is to open a way to more effective and active politics.

Other thinkers devise similar sorts of poetic (in Jean Baudrillard's sense of the resonant as opposed to the scientifically demonstrable), imaginative work with time, arriving at a range of queer understandings and extraordinary leaps out of now-time and out of ordinary notions of past, present, and future. The unfolding of queer time came about in several ways. First, the AIDS crisis truncated the future for the victims, and there was little in the future that one could count on with certainty. Moreover, for queer theorists, the gay and lesbian way of life had little to do with the heterosexual time of family, reproduction, and children. The result was a range of queer temporalities (Halberstam 2005). Some queer scholars have jettisoned linear time, with its emphasis a forward progression and historicist sense of not reversing time, while others similarly refuse the dynastic and genealogical tendencies in recounting the past. For them, queer temporality permits closer contact and identity with historical subjects. Queer theorists in literature note, for example, the presence of situations with queer temporal implications in works such as Virginia Woolf's *Mrs. Dalloway,* in which the time of youthful same-sex love gives way to heterosexual time, opening opportunities that Woolf herself took for a queering of past and futurity or an interruption of family time. Woolf would elaborate this potential most fully in *Orlando*. Queer time has engendered a rethinking of the normative temporal path to adulthood and the ultimate accomplishment of heterosexuality in all its manifestations as a template, and queer scholars can disrupt this normative (hetero)temporal past by finding characters in the past whose lives are outside standard linear, biological, and psychic trajectories. Others celebrate writers or fictional figures whose lives involve temporalities shaped by drugs, hallucinations, visions, and madness. Queer temporality has offered an imaginative field for a wide range of thinkers and artists.

Conclusion

This survey of feminist temporalities briefly covers a sweep of the immense literature on time as it relates to feminism, broadly and imprecisely conceived. Time itself appears in all literature, whether that of biology, astronomy, literature, philosophy, history or psychology. Temporality appears as cosmic in the thought, for example, of Karl Jung, who in the twentieth century envisioned our residence in a timeless matrix of cosmic ideas. It also appears in theories of individual lives and social development as well as in the history of states and social movements, among them, feminism. The conventions of grammar—past, present, and future—are the house in which notions of temporality reside; in the gendering temporality of grammar feminist articulations take shape. Linguistic temporality carries feminist histories and analyses of feminist oppressions, victories, and policies, as well as the fantastical imaginings of feminist futures. Alongside what some might see as elitist notions of time as becoming and flow are working women, whose repetitive work on an assembly line, intertwined with consuming tasks at home, places their lives in a time of necessity and exhaustion. The work of temporality as feminist concept, practice, measurement, life cycle, fiction, tool, bodily sensibility, and dream of the future calls for our consideration.

Suggestions for Further Reading

Gaard, Greta, Simon C. Estok, and Serpil Oppermann. *International Perspectives in Feminist Ecocriticism.* New York: Routledge and Taylor and Francis, 2013.

Hesford, Victoria, and Lisa Diedrich. *Feminist Time against Nation Time: Gender, Politics, and the Nation-State in an Age of Permanent War*. Lanham, MD: Lexington Books, 2009.

References

Dinshaw, Carolyn, et al. 2007. "Theorizing Queer Temporalities: A Roundtable Discussion." *GLQ: A Journal of Lesbian and Gay Studies* 13(2–3): 177–195.

Foucault, Michel. 1970. *The Order of Things: An Archeology of the Human Sciences*. New York: Vintage Books.

Genz, Stephanie, and Benjamin A. Brabon. 2009. *Postfeminism: Cultural Texts and Theories*. Edinburgh: Edinburgh University Press.

Grosz, Elizabeth. 2004. *The Nick of Time: Politics, Evolution and the Untimely*. Sydney: Allen and Unwin.

Halberstam, Judith. 2005. *In a Queer Time and Place: Transgender Bodies, Subcultural Lives*. New York: New York University Press.

Heidegger, Martin. (1927) 1962. *Being and Time*. Translated by John Macquarrie and Edward Robinson. New York: Harper Collins.

Honkanen, Kattis. 2007. "Aion, Kronos and Kairos: On Judith Butler's Temporality." *Journal of Queer Studies in Finland*.

Pintchman, Tracy. 2007. *Women's Lives, Women's Rituals in the Hindu Tradition*. New York: Oxford University Press.

Pizan, Christine. (c. 1405) 1999. *Book of the City of Ladies*. London: Penguin.

Roth, Michael. 1981. "Michel Foucault's 'History of the Present.'" *History and Theory* 20(1) (February).

Scott, Joan. 2012. *The Fantasy of Feminist History*. Durham, NC: Duke University Press.

White, Hayden. 1973. *The Content of the Form. Narrative Discourse and Historical Representation*. Baltimore, MD: Johns Hopkins University Press.

CHAPTER 48

TRANSNATIONAL

LAURA BRIGGS

The scholarship of transnational feminisms is organized by arguments about even its most basic terms and ethical orientation. Some scholars write that it is an exciting, positive intervention that replaces a hackneyed and unsustainable notion of international female sameness as "global sisterhood" (i.e., Morgan 1984), restores socialist feminism to its rightful place in feminist thought, re-centers US Third World feminism and internationalist solidarity for decolonization, and draws attention to the often brilliant activism of feminists in the global South focused on issues like food justice and water (Mohanty 1984; Grewal and Kaplan 1994; Kaplan and Grewal 1994; Basu 1995; Das Gupta 2006; Swarr and Nagar 2010; Blackwell 2014). Others mistrust it on opposite grounds: it is liberal, Western, white, and through nongovernmental organization (NGOs), private foundations, and even explicit alliance, linked to international organizations (IGOs) such as the World Bank, to globalizing capital, and imperial militaries (Spivak 1996; Alvarez 2000; Fernandes 2013). These two positions, although sometimes opposed to each other, might also both be true: global capitalism and imperial ambition could be the conditions of possibility for transnational feminisms, from below or even alongside (Naples 2002).

Genealogies

Transnational feminism has had this dual character from the first, simultaneously a pessimistic account of the state of gender and globalization, especially in the wake of intensifying forms of gendered disenfranchisement associated with World Bank and International Monetary Fund's (IMF) neoliberal state austerity plans—structural adjustment programs (SAPs)—in the 1980s and 1990s, and a hopeful account of new possibilities for thought and action in their aftermath. Massive state disinvestment in food subsidies, healthcare, and education spread through the Third World as a result of SAPs in the eighties, resulting in the intensification of both resistance and (gendered) migration patterns. Inderpal Grewal and Caren Kaplan introduced the term "transnational feminism" in 1994 as an alternative to "global" feminism in the introduction to their edited collection, *Scattered Hegemonies: Postmodernity and Transnational Feminist Practices* (1994). They argued for attention to the heterogeneity of what globalization produces, not just a hegemonic West versus the rest or a Disneyfication of the world. They noted the ways that both "global sisterhood" and much of feminist theory preclude engagement with those outside "the West," either because its imagination ended at the borders of the United States, Australia, and Western Europe, or because it homogenized what it found there. They argued for attention to new activisms, ideas, and forms of cultural production throughout the Third World, particularly but not exclusively in relation to gender and capitalism.

Others took up the term, which was traveling with *globalization* through international business circles, and seemed to resonate, too, with feminists' desire for something that took the experiences of migration seriously—the political possibilities and forms of repression resident in the places migrants left and how that interacted with what they found in new homes. In *Feminist Genealogies, Colonial Legacies, Democratic Futures* (1997), Jacqui Alexander and Chandra Mohanty wrote that they found themselves situated awkwardly as immigrant feminists constructed as "women of color" in the integral yet vexed relation of the Black freedom movement to US feminism. Finding themselves only partially hailed by this US-based feminist conversation about race, gender, and class, they turned to activism related to gender and sexuality in India and the Caribbean, drawing on rich traditions for thinking about political economy and the state and turning their attention to heterosexualization and women's work.

Other early optimistic accounts of the possibilities of transnational feminisms followed quickly, include the launching of the journal *Meridians: Feminism, Race, Transnationalism* in 2000 (see Basu 2000). Key articles by Sonia Alvarez (2000) marked the rapid growth of transnational feminist organizing in Latin America in the 1980s and 1990s in international feminist *encuentros* (encounters) organized around identities (such as the Black identity movement) or issues (e.g., the Latin American and Caribbean Network against Violence against Women). Yet Alvarez also sounded some alarms about the increasing bureaucratization of the feminist movement through its relationships with IGOs and NGOs and the United Nations (UN), particularly through the process of regional meetings designed to influence policy, the UN's 1995 Fourth World Conference on Women. Amrita Basu wrote in the same issue about the rapid growth of transnational feminist organizing in other regions. Other work through the nineties kept the focus on the "transnational" as encompassing not just questions of self-conscious political organizing, but also issues of representation and desire (especially via ways of thinking poststructuralism and cultural studies), the accelerating rhythms of migration and globalizing labor and consumer markets (Grewal, Gupta, and Ong 1999; Moallem 1999; Puri 1999). In feminist theory, echoing the ambivalent tone on the relationship of capital and feminist activism, Gayatri Spivak (1996) conceptualized the "transnational" as a world in which states cannot escape the effects of neoliberalism, while Suzanne Bergeron (2001) argued against a "globalocentric" vision of the effects of globalizing capital as too totalizing and obscuring cleavages, resistances, and activism.

Despite the growing momentum around the transnational, however, postcolonial feminist thought was far more influential in this period. Although questions of gender and feminism came late to postcolonial studies, and largely through the question of women and nationalism (Chatterjee 1990, 1993), the work of postcolonial and subaltern studies entered the consciousness of most US scholars through feminist intervention: in particular, the edited collection by Ranajit Guha and Gayatri Spivak and, *Selected Subaltern Studies* (1988). Arising as a critique initially of the Marxist-nationalist scholarship in Indian history, postcolonial studies resonated with the skepticism toward Marxist accounts in the United States and specifically among the feminist left in the aftermath of the fall of the Berlin Wall (Chakrabarty 2002; Prakash 1994). At the same time, postcolonial studies always understood its object of study as the *subaltern*, and provided a compelling way of reworking its Marxist inheritance. Postcolonial studies provided a fascinating method and toolbox for investigations of the imperial past of the globalizing present in its effort to re-center processes of colonialism and law, its understanding of the archive as always a record of the "prose of counterinsurgency," and its concern with the construction of the modernity/tradition divide (Guha 1999). Gayatri Spivak's arresting interventions in US feminist thought owed a great deal to her engagements with subaltern and postcolonial studies, from her influential argument that "the subaltern cannot speak," to her attention to the productive power of text to a critical distance from Marxism that still expressed itself as an analysis of culture and activisms that never strayed far from an investigation of transnational capitalism and neoliberalism (Spivak 1985, 1988a, 1988b, 1998, 1999).

Deeply indebted to postcolonial studies, "transnational feminisms" did not solidify as the name of an intellectual field in gender and sexuality studies right away—with lines to hire on and its own conferences—and perhaps never would have except for the utility of allying with corporate globalization. In 2001, when four scholars whom we would inescapably link with the field—Amrita Basu, Inderpal Grewal, Caren Kaplan, and Liisa Malkki—edited a special issue of *Signs* containing many articles about the resurgent importance of internationalist socialist feminism, they called the field "gender and globalization." In the 1990s, women's historians and other gender studies scholars toiled in a field called gender and empire, with roots in the Third World decolonization activism of the 1940s, 1950s, and 1960s (e.g., Guy 1988; Findlay 1999; McClintock 1995; Hunt 1999; Burton 2003; Levine 2003). The words *transnational feminism* did not appear in books like *Reproducing Empire* (Briggs 2002) or *The Revolutionary Imagination in the Americas and the Age of Development* (Saldaña-Portillo 2003); rather, these texts marked the processes they considered in the United States, Latin America, and the Caribbean with a lexicon that situated development, modernization, and globalization as part of a broader process of colonialism and its relationship to the postcolonial. Influential feminist critics such as Ann Stoler and Amy Kaplan understood their work in relation to empire and its aftermath (Stoler 1992; Cooper and Stoler 1997; Kaplan 1993). When Chandra Mohanty published *Feminism without Borders* (2003), she did not use the term *transnational*, either. That book includes a crucial set of meditations on the failures of the intellectual and activist project of "global sisterhood," whereby a homogenous group called Third World women are just like US women only more so, oppressed by things called "religion" or a universal patriarchy.

Whatever might have happened in feminist scholarship with these cross-cutting trends—to say nothing of the not-quite-acknowledged desire to ignore altogether what happens outside the United States, something that has been resident in feminism and other US social movements since the rise of McCarthyism and the death of Popular Front internationalism—funding changed it all. *Transnational* and *global* became the names of fundable positions at universities. In the 1990s, the Social Science Research Council and others urged universities to produce more global knowledge and faculties, and less bounded area studies (Cumings 2002; Briggs, Way, McCormick 2008). Business schools and general education curricula alike responded to the demands of global corporations for a workforce educated in the transnational. Resourceful and entrepreneurial, Women's studies departments asked for new lines in transnational feminism. For better or for worse, that cemented it: the transnational was here to stay. The claim that transnational feminism is global capitalism's fellow traveler was proven correct, again, as women's studies took up the university's implicit and explicit alliances with globalizing corporations and their labor force. It is significant to note that transnational feminism was incorporated in the work of feminist studies as a marginal subject, however. In the United States, as the Women's Studies programs of the nineties moved toward adding gender and sexuality to their names, questions of race and the transnational were perhaps even more explicitly *not* named as the field's objects of study.

Capitalism, State Feminism, and Protest

Is transnational feminism, then, primarily the handmaiden of global capitalism, displacing "empire" and the (post)colonial in feminism? It is certainly a more anodyne term, one without the political force of the other two. In a set of provocations that deserved more response than it got, Hester Eisenstein (2005) argued that feminism is dangerously useful to global capital; feminism provides the crucial set of terms without which microcredit loans, the feminization of labor in export-processing zones, or even, ending welfare "as we know it" in the United States, could not take place. By providing a language for gender-based liberation, she suggests, it is quite useful to those who want to produce women as a cheap labor force or a market for credit products, which is to say, the project of creating more debtors for finance capital out of impoverished women in the global South (Joseph 2002). Likewise, the United States or Western Europe could not go to war to save women or protect victimized gay folks without feminism (Puar 2007). Feminists, particularly in the United States, *have* articulated the idea that women's autonomy is enhanced by waged labor, and thereby have also played a role in the destruction of the notion of a family wage, which makes employers responsible for social reproduction. It seems persuasive to suggest that this line of argument has played a role in what Patricia Fernández-Kelly has called the global assembly line—the feminized work force responsible for manufacturing globally—however much this was not an outcome that feminists imagined or sought (Nash and Fernández-Kelly 1983; Fernández-Kelly 1984). Following Eisenstein, we could also note the indirect implication of the transnational migration of feminism in what Rhacel Parreñas and others have tirelessly chronicled as the globalization of child care, housework, and even sexual intimacy. They describe how some women in an archipelago of places across the formerly colonizing nations have entered the formal labor force, as others, from the formerly colonized world, have become responsible for their caring labor—creating a care-work gap in their home countries and families that leaves children to some degree to fend for themselves (Parreñas 2001, 2005, 2011). As Anna Sampaio notes, the effects of globalization have been very uneven, producing poverty as well as wealth, leaving half the world's population living on less than US$2 a day, with the effects of neoliberalism being particularly disproportionately felt by women (Sampaio 2004; World Bank 2000).

At the same time, we could point to the ways feminism has been a real force of critique of the effects of globalizing capital on women's and poor folks' lives, from the scholars just noted who have articulated these very problems to the transnational linkages produced through international encounters. Manisha Desai (2002) argues that we can see the ways transnational feminist activism around child care, domestic violence, food sovereignty, ecological devastation, and reproductive and sexual autonomy has been born in a matrix of analysis concerned with colonialism, racism, and neoliberalism. She locates its emergence in the grassroots activist organizations from diverse parts of the globe that met at the Mexico City conference of 1975. Or better, perhaps, we might situate those 1970s encounters, as Maylei Blackwell and Judy Wu suggest, in the 1971 meeting in Vancouver at which Third World women activists met to discuss the United States war in Indochina (Blackwell 2014; Wu 2013). The UN-sponsored international women's decade of 1975–1985 provided one intensifying set of meetings for these encounters, as did the other autonomous spaces activists pioneered—tribunals, caucuses, and *encuentros* (Alvarez 2003). It's no accident that the *internacionales*, indigenous, and other groups who have supported *Zapatismo*, the anti-World Trade Organization (WTO) movement, Occupy, and the World Social Forum have brimmed with feminists. Feminist networks were one of several capillaries through which a very Latin American, indigenous, and socialist analysis of neoliberalism and global capital, and more importantly, a set of techniques for leaderless organizing and the production of free, autonomous spaces spread through Europe and the United States (Conway 2007; Alvarez 1998, 2000, 2003; Briggs 2008).

At the same time, something more insidious was afoot in feminist activism in the aftermath of the UN world conferences on women's process—symbolized by the appearance of US first lady Hillary Clinton and secretary of state Madeleine Albright at the 1995 Beijing conference. State feminism, historically linked to the former Soviet states, at least for a moment took center stage in the IGO world and never really left, as the subsequent imperial wars to "save Afghan women" from the Taliban (see Abu-Lughod 2002)—and, more confusingly, later saving Iraqi women from a secular dictatorship installed by the United States. Meanwhile, although the NGO delegates in 1995 were located twenty miles away, outside the choking smog of Beijing, their role, too, was rapidly being institutionalized and bureaucratized as a form of transnational governance. Feminists have articulated a powerful critique of NGOs and IGOs as sites of oppressive transnational governmentality, what some came to refer to as the troubling "NGO-ification of feminism" (Lang 1997; McLaughlin 2004; Squires 2008).

The Nation as Analytic: Securitization, Borders, Surveillance, Incarceration

Some feminist scholars have suggested that the "transnational" obscures the work of the nation, that it is a bit of naiveté that needs to be destroyed about how the hard-edged work of security and imperial war machines work. They are responding to formulations that emerged particularly in anthropology in the 1990s, such as that of Nina Glick Schiller and colleagues, in which transnationalism was defined "as the process by which immigrants build social fields that link together their country of origin and their country of settlement" (Schiller et al. 1992). There was also Arjun Appadurai's account of "flows," "ethnoscapes," "ideoscapes," and "mediascapes," which sought to account for diasporic imaginaries and the cultural work of migration and media in deterritorialized ways that made it seem as if borders did not matter, thereby, some argued, flattening out the inequalities of globalization (Appadurai 1991, 1996). By extension, for some theorists it has come to mean something like the receding importance of the nation as a social and even political form. The trouble is that while this relativizing account of the transnational may characterize the situation of global elites, capital, and multinational corporations, it is very inadequate to describe the context in which working-class, impoverished, and racially minoritized people find themselves constrained by national borders and the violence of imperialism and political economic forces. Indeed, Aihwa Ong (1999), with characteristic brilliance, took seriously the invitation within the question of transnationality to engage in a riveting ethnography of Chinese elites' globalized lives that vividly demonstrated the class specificity of who could easily cross borders.

Transnationalism, however, need not require a turning away from feminists' historical concern with subalternization. In fact, with a slight turn of the paradigm's kaleidoscope, we could say that attending to the transnational offers an analytic, an optic on the nation with a great deal of explanatory power about the articulation of the imperial and the national. For example, the tightening of citizenship requirements and the militarization of borders that took place after September 11, 2001 in response to attacks by al Qaeda against the World Trade Center towers and US Pentagon represented (1) the acceptance by large numbers of nations that this was a military and not a criminal matter; (2) the widespread assumption that increasing harassment of noncitizens and the use of militaries to patrol borders would prevent similar such incidents in the future; and (3) the replication of US securitization measures across an extraordinary variety of landscapes. The tightening of borders that ensued, from Afghanistan to Zimbabwe, Germany to Turkey, Mexico to Argentina, was partly mimetic and partly coerced, as border securitization became both a condition of continued US foreign aid and a set of technologies sold by global contractors. It is, in other words, a technology that produces the nation for the benefit of transnational security companies, among other things.

Furthermore, other crucial technologies of the nation at this political conjuncture—surveillance, policing, prisons, biometric technologies at customs, torture—are equally transnational, circulating at the conferences of those that produce the technologies, carried from one country to another by the transnational corporations that install and sometimes implement these techniques, passed deliberately or accidentally from one nation's intelligence agency to the next. Feminist scholars such as Gina Dent, Angela Davis (2001), and Julia Sudbury (2004) have explored the globalization of prisons for women, examining the transnationalization of techniques like super max; others have written about the transnational circulation of sexualized torture (Briggs 2014; Lazreg 2008); scholars such as Zoe Hammer (2004) have also explored how the militarization of the United States–Mexico border has been rendering it profitable for transnational private prison corporations. It is not that the "transnational" is some soft and fuzzy version of the nation; it is a site of theorizing how violence is done in the name of the nation.

Numerous substantive areas of feminist scholarship have broadened and deepened our understanding of the transnational. In these next sections, I explore some of these, albeit more briefly than they deserve.

Queer and Sexuality Studies

From the outset, transnational feminist scholarship has engaged queer and sexuality studies, particularly through Jacqui Alexander's work on the ways the economic and legal relations of the Caribbean rely on enforced heterosexuality at the same time that they incorporate gay tourist dollars (1994, 2005; see also Kaplan and Grewal 2001; Kempadoo 1999). Echoing the ambivalent voice of transnational feminism, the "transnational" is simultaneously characterized as a space within which to consider exploitative relations of economic inequality, racial formation, and imperial wars, and to explore the production of new terrains of resistance and desire. To the extent that sexuality and queer studies were and are subfields of feminism, this scholarship was already part of the transnational turn in feminism, and began explicitly to engage it. To the extent that feminism and sexuality studies have had separate careers, queer studies has responded to the consolidation of transnational feminism as a distinct subfield (alongside subfields in other disciplines like transnational history, sociology, and so forth), with engagement, although in the United States and Canada, not a great deal. Likewise, work on globalization has productively engaged queer theory (Gibson-Graham 1999).

Some of the most exciting work in queer studies has been migration scholarship, where feminist scholars like Eithne Luibhéid (2002), Chandan Reddy (2011), Nayan Shah (2011), and Martin Manalansan (2003) have engaged the violence of states in their regulation and exclusion of homosexuals and the complexities of migration in the context of the imperial role of a United States that proclaims itself liberatory (see also Luibhéid 2008). Others have pointed out how the regulation of homosexuality and sex panics produce the space of neoliberal contraction of the state (Duggan 2004), or, conversely, how regimes of state support for homosexuality have underwritten neoliberal governance (Hoad 2007; Patton 2002). Jasbir Puar's (2007) intervention, asking us to think about "homonationalism" and how the (gay, married, normalized) homosexual subject has been deployed as part of a claim about the Middle East's (backward, terrorist, homophobic) difference, echoes the insight about the uses of "saving Muslim women" for US wars (and, before that, for British imperialism). Indeed, the theorization of "homonationalism" (and, in relation to Israel and the proclamation of a singular "safe" space for GLBT people in the Middle East, the related notion of "pinkwashing"—the call for progressives in Europe and the United States to see Israel in terms of gay freedom rather than military occupation of Palestinian territories) seems to have opened up extensive new horizons for queer activism and theorizing.

Feminist Disability Studies

Feminist disability studies has likewise expanded how we see the transnational. It has found these same moves to be productive: looking at transnational organizing and activism as producing useful solidarities and outcomes, such as the UN Convention on the Rights of People with Disabilities, and also a space of injury, a geopolitics and political economy that produces impairment. Taking up questions of rape, castration, and torture in war, for example, or the pesticide gas leak from the Union Carbide plant that killed an estimated 8,000 people and injured hundreds of thousands, or the estimated one million people in Vietnam disabled by dioxin exposure by the US military's use of Agent Orange in the United States' war in Indochina, scholars of transnational feminist disability studies have asked whether it is possible to bring together a progressive politics of disability (as simply part of the range of what it is to be human) with a politics of reparations for the bodily harms of colonialism, war, and transnational capitalism that does consider disability as loss or even tragedy (Soldatic and Grech 2014). Others have considered disability in a postcolonial frame, thinking through the relations of postcolonial states to their colonial legacies in terms of politics of heredity, health, and disability (Parekh 2007). Still others have raised the inclusion question: What are the inclusions and exclusions with respect to the politics of, and people with disability in UN and other intergovernmental and NGO spaces, transnational feminists organizing, or intercountry treaties? (Arenas Conejo 2011).

WOMEN OF COLOR FEMINISM

The relation of women of color feminism to the transnational is more complex. On the one hand, it has been so integral to the development of transnational feminism that it is hard to separate them sufficiently to put them in conversation. Aihwa Ong (2006) locates the distinction between the two as one of emphasis and history; for her, "transnational" names an emergent, post-1965-immigration-reform axis of difference, a narrative that is not the civil rights one within which US academic protest has long articulated itself but one which centers "new immigrants" and the new forms of globalization and its resistance. Yet others have suggested that US ethnic studies (and hence women of color feminism) are concerned with the "domestic" to the exclusion of the rest of the world, aligning ethnic studies with multiculturalism (Shohat 2001; Kaplan and Grewal 2002). As Sandy Soto (2005) points out, this locates women of color feminisms as part of what is subsumed and overcome by a celebratory "transnational" feminism, which hardly seems fair, given the powerful engagements with decolonization and related politics by women of color feminism.

Maylei Blackwell offers a compelling genealogy that locates women of color feminism at the center of transnational feminism. She argues that intellectually and in activist terms, it was Third World feminism—expressed as solidarity with Third World decolonization movements—and then women of color feminism that gave rise to transnational feminism. Before, outside, and alongside the UN and associated meetings, there were those self-consciously articulating a feminist politics in relation to Third World decolonization, who jumped scales when pathways forward were blocked at the regional and national levels (Blackwell 2006, 2014). There are traces of this specific genealogy in Chicana feminisms, for example, beginning with Gloria Anzaldua's *borderlands/nepantla* epistemology, which argues for the literal Southwest and the metaphorical in-betweenness of both border violence and Chican@ identity as neither here nor there, United States nor Mexico, akin to what later Chicana feminist theorists call the liminal "Third Space" of politics, spirituality, and nationality (Pérez 1999; Blackwell 2010; Guidotti-Hernández 2011; Lugones 2010; Licona 2012). Likewise, we could point to the critical importance of Toni Cade Bambara's writing about Vietnam in her short stories (1977), or Caribbean feminist Audre Lorde (1984) and her work on, for example, Cuba and the Africa-Soviet Union nexus, or the central concerns of influential Puerto Rican feminists, such as Helen Rodriguez Trias, with birth control and sterilization politics, echoing moves from the island (Morales 1996; Nelson 2001; Rodríguez-Trias 1978), or—while not really a women of color feminism—the centrality of decolonization and sovereignty to Native feminism (e.g., Shanley 1984), which we turn to next.

Native Feminism and Settler Colonialism

Some of the most interesting work coming out in feminist scholarship today is by Native feminists, and questions of the transnational are no exception. For Native and indigenous feminist scholars, *transnational* at once articulates the current state of the question—think how many Native nations cross current national borders, with people on both sides—but also poses a problem: if decolonizing politics grounded in resistance to settler colonialism frees us from thinking of the nation as a given, why should we care about nations at all, "trans" or otherwise (Smith 2008; Byrd 2011; Goeman 2009; Hall 2008, 2009; Arvin, Tuck, and Morill 2013)? Doesn't any "transnational" feminism reify the nation all over again and reiterate the unspoken and hence ungrievable legacy of settler colonialism? At the same time, analysis of a gendered politics of settler colonialism has precisely led to an analysis that links Britain, Canada, Australia, New Zealand, the United States, as well as Spain and France in the Americas, Asia and the Pacific Islands more broadly—a cartography of American Indians or Native Americans in the United States, Aboriginals in Australia and New Zealand, First Nations in Canada, and indigenous peoples in Latin America, that is certainly "trans"-something (Kauanui 2008; Simpson 2008; Jacobs 2014; Aikau and Spencer 2007; Ouellette 2002). Conversations between Native feminisms and women of color feminism continue to complicate and deepen the strand of transnational feminism born in conversation between Third World and Fourth World feminisms (Ramírez 2008; Oullette 2002). On a different note, too, feminists and others have called attention to the way Indian wars and the frontier continue to haunt and populate other imperial ventures—calling enemy territory in Vietnam "Indian Country" during the US war in Indochina, for example, or conversely, considering the disproportionate representation of Native people in the US military (Erdrich 1993; Silko 1977; Denetdale 2008). Thinking through tribal nations has led others to think of relations among diverse indigenous peoples as intrinsically transnational.

Furthermore, while the UN has sometimes been a useful location from which to raise issues related to indigenous peoples (as for example the Permanent Forum on Indigenous Issues, the Declaration on the Rights of Indigenous Peoples, or the International Decades of the World's Indigenous Peoples), through its "women" decades and conferences, it routed the concerns of indigenous peoples through their national delegations—which is to say, it made the relations of settler colonialism central to its formulation of "women's" concerns. Blackwell (2006) has argued that indigenous women in Latin America responded to this demand that they incorporate themselves with mestiza or Ladina women by generating the current massive wave of trans–Latin America indigenous feminist organizing.

Who Can Do the Work of Transnational Feminism?

One of the ways scholars and activists have tried to resolve the issue of whether transnational feminism too much aligned with the interests of global capital or imperial states to have any critical power is by asking the question: Who can do transnational feminism? Can local grassroots activists outside metropolitan centers be transnational feminists, strengthening their local organizations and their fights through international alliance, or do these alliances primarily benefit international funding agencies, NGOs, and the World Bank? Is it a framework that can serve scholars from outside the United States, Western Europe, and similar places, producing more international publics for their intellectual production, or is it just another career-builder for global academic elites with research budgets in euros or dollars that allow travel to multiple research sites and a strong passport that gives them freedom of movement?

Michelle Murphy's (2012) brilliant analysis of a feminist problem space in reproductive justice politics—cervical cancer—provides an appropriately ambivalent reply that seems worth exploring at length for the ways it is paradigmatic of how transnational feminism is currently configured. Scholarship and activism on reproductive politics has arguably been more transnational than in most substantive areas in feminism, as the political fight for birth control was twinned with population control in the post–World War II period. Even before that, Margaret Sanger's activism was supremely international. More recently, Shellee Colen's 1995 paper on "stratified reproduction"—on the relationship of structural adjustment in the West Indies to childrearing in New York (by West Indian women whose own children stay in the islands)—has proven an enduring paradigm for how we understand transnational relations of reproduction. Feminist anthropology has also persistently grappled with reproduction and kinship in a transnational frame (Gordon 1976; Ramírez de Arellano and Seipp 1983; Colen 1995; Inhorn 1994; Press and Browner 1997; Strathern 1992; Browner and Sargent 2011).

Murphy begins with the Pap smear, a laboratory technology for examining vaginal and cervical cells under the microscope, usually collected by a gynecologist or physician at an annual pelvic exam, to allow the early detection of cancerous cells. Self-administered Pap smears and cervical awareness were a centerpiece of the US and Canadian women's health movements in the 1970s, as feminists taught each other how to use a speculum to look at their cervices. Across Western Europe and the United States in the seventy years since the development of the laboratory test, the Pap smear has reduced mortality from cervical cancer by 90 percent, while having very little effect on cancer rates among medically underserved populations in Latin America, Africa, and Asia. Even in the United States, Canada, and Western Europe, however, the test largely reaches a whiter and wealthier population of women, and cervical cancer has become a disease of poor people and people of color in the North and South. This fact has entwined cervical cancer both in technologies of control and in progressive efforts at empowerment. On the one hand, the Black Women's Health Project went from door to door, spreading information in Black communities in and around Atlanta about cervical cancer and the Pap smear. On the other, the call for more Paps in communities of color turned into mandatory gynecological exams and Pap smears in prisons, often at admission, a practice we know sometimes amounts to little more than medicalized rape. It was essentially a strategy for reintroducing the mandatory vaginal cavity search.

With the development of the HPV (human papillomavirus) vaccine and the reformulation of our understanding of cervical cancer as a vaccine-preventable sexually transmitted disease, the demand for coercive Pap smears did not recede, but the pharmaceutical company Merck lobbied hard to make the HPV vaccine mandatory for nine- to thirteen-year-old girls. That effort briefly succeeded in Texas, then failed in the face of organized pushback from the conservative Right. Merck ultimately succeeded only in requiring it for new immigrants seeking permanent status in the United States, aged eleven to twenty-six years. Both efforts—mandatory Pap smears in prison and required Gardasil for immigrant women and girls—have been the subject of organized resistance that has ultimately been (mostly) successful. But they offer a powerful picture of what happens when a gynecological condition is constructed as a disease of women of color.

This twinned legacy of progressive grassroots politics and corporate and state control followed cervical cancer into its career as a transnational feminist issue. The International Women's Health Coalition (IWHC), an NGO out of New York, with annual galas featuring Hollywood stars and politicians like Hillary Clinton and Kofi Anan and no links to grassroots women's health activism, became the funders and champions of a transnational feminist agenda around cervical cancer. At their international policy meeting in Bellagio, Italy, full of funders and UN folk, they decided to roll cervical cancer into a category of "reproductive tract infections," which linked HPV to other things, such as putting leaves in the vagina as a method of birth control and genital cutting. To give the organizers their due: this was essentially the campaign that they brought to the IGO Cairo Conference on Population and Development in 1994, in which they sponsored the "war room" that successfully organized to replace the neo-Malthusian language on population control in the proposed resolution with "reproductive health." The result has been a remarkable sea change in international development efforts and funding, with family-planning money flowing more generously and less coercively to nations around the globe. On the other hand, it's still development money—linked to the IMF and World Bank SAPs that have robbed local hospitals of the means to do their work and drastically impoverished many communities in the name of fiscal responsibility. The organized transnational feminist campaign was again allied with the forces of global capital and coercion.

At the same time, the IWHC also organized an autonomous meeting with the Women and Development Unit at the University of West Indies (WAND) that produced a much more interesting grassroots campaign. WAND, working together with the Latin American and Caribbean Women's Health Network, described cervical cancer as a problem of inequality. Neoliberalism and development, they argued, had produced the inability of women in the Caribbean to get access to appropriate cancer screening. The group's pamphlets also stressed inequality between women and men and sexual coercion as part of the problem, and called for research on vaginal microbicides against HPV that could be used without male partners' knowledge or consent, and without preventing wanted pregnancies. The campaign, called "Demystifying and Fighting Cervical Cancer," was led by the activist Andaiye, a Guyanese Marxist feminist, friend of Audre Lorde's, and the cofounder in the 1980s of Red Thread, which organized to value women's unwaged labor. Her group linked the high rates of cervical cancer among impoverished women in the Caribbean to state and corporate devaluing of human life, to pollution, and the continued absence of legislation to protect workers. This campaign, funded by IWHC through foundations, is also a face of transnational feminism—not only in its funding, but also in its literal copying of images of Pap smears from a Vancouver women's health pamphlet and the language of reproductive tract infections from IWHC. It is a fascinating and genuinely progressive campaign reassembled out of intellectual pieces from the US and Canadian women's health movements, from the international NGO sector, and Third World feminist and Marxist traditions.

So this, then, is the fundamentally ambivalent state of transnational feminism—whether as activism or analytic: it lives in a space produced by global capitalism and NGO-ification, while simultaneously producing real and profound resistances.

Acknowledgments

Briggs wishes to thank her conversation partners Maylei Blackwell and Minnie Chiu, as well as the audience at the Thinking Transnationalism Summer Institute at Ohio State in 2014, for assistance with this piece. That conversation was published as a roundtable in Frontiers 36:3 (Spring 2016).

References

Abu-Lughod, Lila. 2002. "Do Muslim Women Really Need Saving? Anthropological Reflections on Cultural Relativism and Its Others." *American Anthropologist* 104 (3): 783–790.

Aikau, Hokulani. K., and James H. Spencer. 2007. "Introduction: Local Reaction to Global Integration: The Political Economy of Development in Indigenous Communities." *Alternatives: Global, Local, Political* 32 (1): 1–7.

Alexander, M. Jacqui. 1994. "Not Just (Any) Body Can Be a Citizen: The Politics of Law, Sexuality and Postcoloniality in Trinidad and Tobago and the Bahamas." *Feminist Review* 48 (1): 5–23.

Alexander, M. Jacqui. 2005. *Pedagogies of Crossing: Meditations on Feminism, Sexual Politics, Memory and the Sacred*. Durham, NC: Duke University Press.

Alexander, M. Jacqui, and Chandra Talpade Mohanty, eds. 1997. *Feminist Genealogies, Colonial Legacies, Democratic Futures*. New York: Routledge.

Alvarez, Sonia E. 1998. "Latin American Feminisms 'Go Global': Trends of the 1990s and Challenges for the New Millennium." In *Cultures of Politics/Politics of Cultures: Re-visioning Latin American Social Movements*, edited by Sonia E. Alvarez, Evelyn Dagnino, and Arturo Escobar, 293–324. Boulder, CO: Westview Press.

Alvarez, Sonia E. 2000. "Translating the Global: Effects of Transnational Organizing on Local Feminist Discourses and Practices in Latin America." *Meridians: Feminism, Race, Transnationalism* 1 (1): 29–67.

Alvarez, Sonia E., Elisabeth Jay Friedman, Ericka Beckman, Maylei Blackwell, Norma Stoltz Chinchilla, Nathalie Lebon, Marysa Navarro, and Marcela Ríos Tobar. 2003. "Encountering Latin American and Caribbean Feminisms." *Signs* 28 (2): 537–579.

Appadurai, Arjun. 1991. "Global Ethnoscapes: Notes and Queries for a Transnational Anthropology." In *Recapturing Anthropology: Working in the Present*, edited by Richard G. Fox, 191–210. Santa Fe, NM: School of American Research Press.

Appadurai, Arjun. 1996. *Modernity at Large: Cultural Dimensions of Globalization*. Minneapolis: University of Minnesota Press.

Arenas Conejo, Míriam. 2011. "Disabled Women and Transnational Feminisms: Shifting Boundaries and Frontiers." *Disability & Society* 26 (5): 597–609.

Arvin, Maile, Eve Tuck, and Angie Morril. 2013. "Decolonizing Feminism: Challenging Connections between Settler Colonialism and Heteropatriarchy." *Feminist Formations* 25 (1): 8–34.

Bambara, Toni Cade. 1977. *The Sea Birds Are Still Alive: Stories*. New York: Random House.

Basu, Amrita. 1995. *The Challenge of Local Feminisms*. Boulder, CO: Westview.

Basu, Amrita. 2000. "Globalization of the Local/Localization of the Global: Mapping Transnational Women's Movements." *Meridians* 1 (1): 68–84.

Bergeron, Suzanne. 2001. "Political Economy Discourses of Globalization and Feminist Politics." *Signs* 26 (4): 983–1005.

Blackwell, Maylei. 2006. "Weaving in the Spaces: Indigenous Women's Organizing and the Politics of Scale in Mexico." In *Dissident Women. Gender and Cultural Politics in Chiapas*, edited by Shannon Speed, Rosalva Aída Hernández Castillo, and Lynn Stephen, 240–318. Austin: University of Texas Press.

Blackwell, Maylei. 2010. "Líderes Campesinas: Nepantla Strategies and Grassroots Organizing at the Intersection of Gender and Globalization." *Aztlán: A Journal of Chicano Studies* 35 (1): 13–47.

Blackwell, M. 2014. "Translenguas: Mapping the Possibilities and Challenges of Transnational Women's Organizing across Geographies of Difference." In *Translocalities/Translocalidades: Feminist Politics of Translation in the Latin/a Américas*, edited by Sonia E. Alvarez, Claudia de Lima Costa, Verónica Feliu, Rebecca J. Hester, Norma Klahn, Millie Thayer, and Cruz Caridad Bueno, 299–320. Durham: Duke University Press.

Briggs, Laura. 2002. *Reproducing Empire: Race, Sex, Science, and U.S. Imperialism in Puerto Rico*. Berkeley: University of California Press.

Briggs, Laura. 2008. "Activisms and Epistemologies: Problems for Transnationalisms." *Social Text* 26 (4): 79–95.

Briggs, Laura. 2014. "Making Race, Making Sex: Perspectives on Torture." *International Feminist Journal of Politics* 16 (4): 1–20.

Briggs, Laura, J. T. Way, and Gladys McCormick. 2008. "Transnationalism: A Category of Analysis." *American Quarterly* 60 (3): 625–648.

Browner, Carol H., and C. F. Sargent, eds. 2011. *Reproduction, Globalization, and the State: New Theoretical and Ethnographic Perspectives*. Durham, NC: Duke University Press.

Burton, Antoinette M. 2003. *After the Imperial Turn: Thinking with and through the Nation*. Durham, NC: Duke University Press.

Byrd, Jodi A. 2011. *The Transit of Empire: Indigenous Critiques of Colonialism*. Minneapolis: University of Minnesota Press.

Chakrabarty, Dipesh. 2002. *Habitations of Modernity: Essays in the Wake of Subaltern Studies*. Chicago: University of Chicago Press.

Chatterjee, Partha. 1990. "The Nationalist Resolution of the Women's Question." In *Recasting Women: Essays in Indian Colonial History*, edited by Kumkum Sangari, and Sudesh Vaid, 233–253. New Brunswick, NJ: Rutgers University Press.

Chatterjee, Partha. 1993. *The Nation and Its Fragments: Colonial and Postcolonial Histories*. Princeton, NJ: Princeton University Press.

Colen, Shellee. 1995. "'Like a Mother to Them': Stratified Reproduction and West Indian Childcare Workers and Employers in New York." In *Conceiving the New World Order: The Global Politics of Reproduction*, edited by Faye Ginsburg and Rayna Rapp, 78–82. Berkeley: University of California Press.

Conway, Janet. 2007. "Transnational Feminisms and the World Social Forum: Encounters and Transformations in Anti-Globalization Spaces." *Journal of International Women's Studies* 8 (3): 49–70.

Cooper, Frederick, and Ann Laura Stoler, eds. 1997. *Tensions of Empire: Colonial Cultures in a Bourgeois World*. Berkeley: University of California Press.

Cumings, Bruce. 2002. "Boundary Displacement: The State, the Foundations, and Area Studies during and after the Cold War." In *Learning Places: The Afterlives of Area Studies*, edited by Masao Miyoshi and Harry D. Harootunian, 261–302. Durham, NC: Duke University Press.

Das Gupta, Monisha. 2006. *Unruly Immigrants: Rights, Activism and Transnational South Asian Politics in the United States*. Durham, NC: Duke University Press.

Davis, Angela, and Gina Dent. 2001. "Prison as a Border: A Conversation on Gender, Globalization, and Punishment." *Signs* 26 (4): 1235–1241.

Denetdale, Jennifer. 2008. "Carving Navajo National Boundaries: Patriotism, Tradition, and the Diné Marriage Act of 2005." *American Quarterly* 60 (2): 289–294.

Desai, Manisha. 2002. "Transnational Solidarity: Women's Agency, Structural Adjustment, and Globalization." In *Women's Activism and Globalization: Linking Local Struggles and Global Politics*, edited by Nancy A Naples and Manisha Desai, 15–33. New York: Routledge.

Duggan, Lisa. 2004. *The Twilight of Equality: Neoliberalism, Cultural Politics, and the Attack on Democracy*. Boston: Beacon Press.

Eisenstein, Hester. 2005. "A Dangerous Liaison? Feminism and Corporate Globalization." *Science & Society* 69 (3): 487–518.

Erdrich, Louise. 1993. *Love Medicine*. New York: Holt.

Fernandes, Leela. 2013. *Transnational Feminism in the United States: Knowledge, Ethics, Power*. New York: New York University Press.

Fernández-Kelly, Patricia. 1984. *For We Are Sold, I and My People: Women and Industry in Mexico's Frontier*. Albany: State University of New York Press.

Findlay, Eileen. 1999. *Imposing Decency: The Politics of Sexuality and Race in Puerto Rico, 1870-1920*. Durham, NC: Duke University Press.

Gibson-Graham J. K. 1999. Queer(y)ing Capitalism in and out of the Classroom. *Journal of Geography in Higher Education* 23 (1): 80–85.

Goeman, M. R. 2009. Notes toward a Native Feminism's Spatial Practice. *Wicazo Sa Review* 24 (2): 169–187.

Gordon, Linda. 1976. *Woman's Body, Woman's Right: A Social History of Birth Control in America*. New York: Grossman.

Grewal, Inderpal, Akhil Gupta, and Aihwa Ong. 1999. "Asian Transnationalities: Media, Markets and Migration." *Positions: East Asia Cultures Critique* 7 (3): 653–666.

Grewal, Inderpal, and Caren Kaplan. 1994. *Scattered Hegemonies: Postmodernity and Transnational Feminist Practices*. Minneapolis: University of Minnesota Press.

Guha, Ranajit. 1999. *Elementary Aspects of Peasant Insurgency in Colonial India*. Durham, NC: Duke University Press.

Guha, Ranajit, and Gayatri Chakravorty Spivak, eds. 1988. *Selected Subaltern Studies*. Oxford University Press.

Guidotti-Hernández, Nicole M. 2011. *Unspeakable Violence: Remapping U.S. and Mexican National imaginaries*. Durham, NC: Duke University Press.

Guy, Donna J. 1988. "White Slavery, Public Health, and the Socialist Position on Legalized Prostitution in Argentina, 1913-1936." *Latin America Research Review* 23 (3): 60–80.

Hall, Lisa Kahaleole. 2008. "Strategies of Erasure: U.S. Colonialism and Native Hawaiian Feminism." *American Quarterly* 60 (2): 273–280.

Hall, Lisa Kahaleole. 2009. "Navigating Our Own 'Sea of Islands': Remapping a Theoretical Space for Hawaiian Women and Indigenous Feminism." *Wicazo Sa Review* 24 (2): 15–38.

Hammer-Tomizuka, Zoe. 2004. "Criminal Alienation: Arizona Prison Expansion, 1993-2003." Diss. University of Arizona.

Hoad, Neville. 2007. *African Intimacies: Race, Homosexuality, and Globalization*. Minneapolis: University of Minnesota Press.

Hunt, Nancy Rose. 1999. *A Colonial Lexicon of Birth Ritual, Medicalization, and Mobility in the Congo*. Durham, NC: Duke University Press.

Inhorn, Marcia C. 1994. *Quest for Conception: Gender, Infertility, and Egyptian Medical Traditions*. College Park: University of Pennsylvania Press.

Jacobs, Margaret. 2014. *A Generation Removed: The Fostering and Adoption of Indigenous Children in the Postwar World*. Lincoln: University of Nebraska.

Joseph, Miranda. 2002. *Against the Romance of Community*. Minneapolis: University of Minnesota Press.

Kaplan, Amy. 1993. "'Left Alone with America': The Absence of Empire in the Study of American Culture." In *Cultures of United States Imperialism*, edited by Amy Kaplan and Donald Pease. 3–21. Durham, NC: Duke University Press.

Kaplan, Caren, and Inderpal Grewal. 1994. "Transnational Feminist Cultural Studies: Beyond the Marxism/Poststructuralism/Feminism Divides." *positions* 2 (2): 430–445.

Kaplan, Caren, and Inderpal Grewal. 2001. "Global Identities: Theorizing Transnational Studies of Sexuality." *GLQ: A Journal of Lesbian and Gay Studies* 7 (4): 663–679.

Kaplan, Caren, and Inderpal Grewal. 2002. "Transnational Practices and Interdisciplinary Feminist Scholarship: Refiguring Women's and Gender Studies." *Women's Studies on Its Own: A Next Wave Reader in Institutional Change*, 66–81. Durham, NC: Duke University Press.

Kauanui, J. Kehaulani. 2008. "Native Hawaiian Decolonization and the Politics of Gender." *American Quarterly* 60 (2): 281–287.

Kempadoo, Kamala. ed. 1999. *Sun, Sex, and Gold: Tourism and Sex Work in the Caribbean*. Lanham, MD: Rowman and Littlefield.

Lang, Sabine. 1997. "The NGOization of Feminism." In *Transitions, Translations, Environments: Feminisms in International Politics*, edited by Joan W. Scott, Cora Kaplan, and Debra Keates, 101–120. New York: Routledge.

Lazreg, Marnia. 2008. *Torture and the Twilight of Empire: From Algiers to Baghdad*. Princeton, NJ: Princeton University Press.

Levine, Philippa. 2003. *Prostitution, Race, and Politics: Policing Venereal Disease in the British Empire*. New York: Routledge.

Licona, Adela C. 2012. *Zines in Third Space: Radical Cooperation and Borderlands Rhetoric*. Albany: State University of New York Press.

Lorde, Audre. 1984. *Sister Outsider: Essays and Speeches by Audre Lorde*. Berkeley, CA: Crossing Press.

Lugones, Maria. 2010. "Toward a Decolonial Feminism." *Hypatia* 25: 4.

Luibhéid, Eithne. 2002. *Entry Denied: Controlling Sexuality at the Border*. Minneapolis: University of Minnesota Press.

Luibhéid, Eithne. 2008. "Queer/Migration: An Unruly Body of Scholarship." *GLQ: A Journal of Lesbian and Gay Studies* 14 (2): 169–190.

Manalansan, Martin F. 2003. *Global Divas: Filipino Gay Men in the Diaspora*. Durham, NC: Duke University Press.

McClintock, Anne. 1995. *Imperial Leather: Race, Gender, and Sexuality in the Colonial Conquest*. New York: Routledge.

McLaughlin, Lisa. 2004. "Feminism and the Political Economy of Transnational Public Space." *Sociological Review* 52 (1): 156–175.

Moallem, Minoo. 1999. "Transnationalism, Feminism, and Fundamentalism." In *Between Woman and Nation*, edited by Caren Kaplan, Norma Alarcon, and Minoo Moallem, 320–348. Durham, NC: Duke University Press.

Mohanty, Chandra Talpade. 1984. "Under Western Eyes: Feminist Scholarship and Colonial Discourses." *Boundary 2* 12/13 (3/1): 333–358.

Mohanty, Chandra Talpade. 2003. *Feminism without Borders: Decolonizing Theory, Practicing Solidarity*. Durham, NC: Duke University Press, 2003.

Morales, Iris. 1996. *Pa'lante, Siempre Pa'lante: The Young Lords*. New York: Third World Newsreel.

Morgan, Robin, ed. 1984. *Sisterhood Is Global: The International Women's Movement Anthology*. New York: Feminist Press.

Murphy, Michelle. 2012. *Seizing the Means of Reproduction: Entanglements of Feminism, Health, and Technoscience*. Durham, NC: Duke University Press.

Naples, Nancy. 2002. "Changing the Terms: Community Activism, Globalization, and the Dilemmas of Transnational Feminist Praxis." In *Women's Activism and Globalization: Linking Local Struggles and Transnational Politics*, edited by Nancy A. Naples and Manisha Desai, 3–14. New York: Routledge.

Nash, June, and Patricia Fernández-Kelly. 1983. *Women, Men, and the International Division of Labor*. Albany: State University of New York Press.

Nelson, Jennifer. 2001. "Abortions under Community Control": Feminism, Nationalism, and the Politics of Reproduction among New York City's Young Lords. *Journal of Women's History* 13 (1): 157–180.

Ong, Aihwa. 1999. *Flexible Citizenship: The Cultural Logics of Transnationality*. Durham, NC: Duke University Press.

Ong, Aihwa. 2006. *Neoliberalism as Exception: Mutations in Citizenship and Sovereignty*. Durham, NC: Duke University Press.

Ouellette, Grace Josephine Mildred Wuttunee. 2002. *The Fourth World: An Indigenous Perspective on Feminism and Aboriginal Women's Activism*. Halifax, NS: Fernwood.
Parekh, Pushpa. 2007. "Gender, Disability and the Postcolonial Nexus." *Wagadu* 4: 142–161.
Parreñas, Rhacel Salazar. 2001. *Servants of Globalization: Women, Migration and Domestic Work*. Redwood City, CA: Stanford University Press.
Parreñas, Rhacel Salazar. 2005. *Children of Global Migration: Transnational Families and Gendered Woes*. Redwood City, CA: Stanford University Press.
Parreñas, Rhacel Salazar. 2011. *Illicit Flirtations: Labor, Migration, and Sex Trafficking in Tokyo*. Redwood City, CA: Stanford University Press.
Patton, Cindy. 2002. "Stealth Bombers of Desire: The Globalization of 'Alterity' in Emerging Democracies." In *Queer Globalization: Citizenship and the Afterlife of Colonialism*, edited by Arnaldo Cruz Malavé and Martin F. Manalansan, 195–218. New York: New York University Press.
Pérez, Emma. 1999. *The Decolonial Imaginary: Writing Chicanas into History*. Bloomington: Indiana University Press.
Prakash, Gayan. 1994. "Subaltern Studies as Postcolonial Criticism." *American Historical Review* 99 (5): 1475–1490.
Press, Nancy, and Carole H. Browner. 1997. "Why Women Say Yes to Prenatal Diagnosis." *Social Science & Medicine* 45 (7): 979–989.
Puar, Jasbir K. 2007. *Terrorist Assemblages: Homonationalism in Queer Times*. Durham, NC: Duke University Press.
Puri, J. 1999. *Woman, Body, Desire in Post-Colonial India: Narratives of Gender and Sexuality*. New York: Routledge.
Ramírez de Arellano, Annette B., and Conrad Seipp. 1983. *Colonialism, Catholicism, and Contraception: A History of Birth Control in Puerto Rico*. Chapel Hill: University of North Carolina Press.
Ramírez, Renya K. 2008. "Learning across Differences: Native and Ethnic Studies Feminisms." *American Quarterly* 60 (2): 303–307.
Reddy, Chandan. 2011. *Freedom with Violence: Race, Sexuality, and the U.S. State*. Durham, NC: Duke University Press.
Rodríguez-Trias, Helen. 1978. "Sterilization Abuse." *Women and Health* 3 (3): 10–15.
Saldaña-Portillo, María Josefina. 2003. *The Revolutionary Imagination in the Americas and the Age of Development*. Durham, NC: Duke University Press.
Sampaio, Anna. 2004. "Transnational Feminisms in a New Global Matrix." *International Feminist Journal of Politics* 6 (2): 181–206.
Schiller, Nina Glick, Linda Basch, and Cristina Blanc-Szanton. 1992. "Towards a Definition of Transnationalism." *Annals of the New York Academy of Sciences* 645 (1): ix–xiv.
Shah, Nayan. 2011. *Stranger Intimacy: Contesting Race, Sexuality, and the Law in the North American West*. Berkeley: University of California Press.
Shanley, Kate. 1984. "Thoughts on Indian Feminism." In *A Gathering of Spirit: Writing and Art by North American Indian Women*, edited by Beth Brant, 213–215. Rockland, ME: Sinister Wisdom Books.
Shohat, Ella, ed. 2001. *Talking Visions: Multicultural Feminism in a Transnational Age*. Cambridge, MA: MIT Press.
Silko, Leslie Marmon. 1977. *Ceremony*. New York: Penguin.
Simpson, Audra. 2008. "From White into Red: Captivity Narratives as Alchemies of Race and Citizenship." *American Quarterly* 60 (2): 251–257.

Smith, Andrea. 2008. "American Studies without America: Native Feminisms and the Nation State." *American Quarterly* 60 (2): 309–315.

Soldatic, Karen, and Shaun Grech. 2014. "Transnationalising Disability Studies: Rights, Justice and Impairment." *Disability Studies Quarterly* 34 (2).

Soto, Sandra K. 2005. "Where in the Transnational World are U.S. Women of Color?" In *Women's Studies for the Future: Foundations, Interrogations, Politics*, edited by Elizabeth Lapovsky Kennedy and Agatha Beins, 111–124. New Brunswick, NJ: Rutgers University Press.

Spivak, Gayatri Chakravorty. 1985. "Three Women's Texts and a Critique of Imperialism." *Critical Inquiry* 12 (1): 243–261.

Spivak, Gayatri Chakravorty. 1988a. "Can the Subaltern Speak?" *Marxism and the Interpretation of Culture*, edited by Cary Nelson and Lawrence Grossberg, 271–313. Urbana: University of Illinois Press.

Spivak, Gayatri Chakravorty. 1988b. "Subaltern Studies: Deconstructing Historiography." *Selected Subaltern Studies*, edited by Ranajit Guha and Gaytri Spivak, 3–34. New York: Oxford University Press.

Spivak, Gayatri Chakravorty. 1996. "Diasporas Old and New: Women in the Transnational World." *Textual Practice* 10 (2): 245–269.

Spivak, Gayatri Chakravorty. 1998. "Cultural Talks in the Hot Peace: Revisiting the 'Global Village.'" *Cosmopolitics: Thinking and Feeling beyond the Nation*, edited by Pheng Cheah and Bruce Robbins, 329–448. Minneapolis: University of Minnesota Press.

Spivak, Gayatri Chakravorty. 1999. *A Critique of Postcolonial Reason: Toward a History of the Vanishing Present*. Cambridge, MA: Harvard University Press.

Squires, Judith. 2008. "The Constitutive Representation of Gender: Extraparliamentary Representations of Gender Relations." *Representation* 44 (2): 187–204.

Stoler, Ann L. 1992. "Sexual Affronts and Racial Frontiers: European Identities and the Cultural Politics of Exclusion." *Comparative Studies in Society & History* 34 (3): 514–551.

Strathern, Marilyn. 1992. *Reproducing the Future: Essays on Anthropology, Kinship and the New Reproductive Technologies*. Manchester, UK: Manchester University Press.

Sudbury, Julia, 2004. ed. *Global Lockdown: Race, Gender, and the Prison-Industrial Complex*. Routledge.

Swarr, Amanda Lock, and Richa Nagar. 2010. *Critical Transnational Feminist Praxis*. Albany: State University of New York Press.

World Bank 2000. *The World Bank Group Annual Report*. The International Bank for Reconstruction and Development. http://www.worldbank.org/html/extpb/annrep2000/.

Wu, Judy. 2013. *Radicals on the Road: Internationalism, Orientalism, and Feminism during the Vietnam Era*. Ithaca, NY: Cornell University Press.

CHAPTER 49

VIOLENCE

JINEE LOKANEETA

The World Health Organization (WHO 2002, 4) defines violence as "the intentional use of physical force or power, threatened or actual, against oneself, another person, or against a group or community, which either results in or has a high likelihood of resulting in injury, death, psychological harm, maldevelopment, or deprivation." Although the WHO definition captures the scope of harm associated with violence, it does not draw attention to the victims, the perpetrators, or the reasons for inflicting such harm. In their explorations of violence, feminist scholars have sought to distinguish between manifold forms of violence, sometimes pointing to how these forms of violence exist on a continuum while also contextualizing these diverse phenomena, analyzing their discursive and material origins and effects, and situating them in relation to processes of racialization and gendering. In contrast to legitimizing constructions of the state as representing the "monopoly of violence" linked to maintaining order, feminist scholars have pointed to the sexual and racial violence that ground the state and imperial orders. From theoretical discussions of the "sexual contract" that precedes and informs the "social contract" (Pateman 1988) to historical studies of slavery, colonial violence, ethnic conflicts, and genocide, feminist analyses have shattered states' claims concerning their "rational, controlled, and purposive" deployment of violence for the public good. Instead, they have drawn attention to group-based patterns of violence enacted by some to the detriment of others within and beyond national communities in both everyday and extraordinary contexts. Feminist scholars have also provided nuanced accounts of structural violence (suffering induced by economic and political forces, such as extreme poverty, unjust healthcare policy, slum demolition); representational and symbolic violence (discursive constructions that dehumanize and objectify some humans, while celebrating the "natural superiority" of others), and epistemic violence (forms of knowledge production that deny or undermine the agency and subjectivity of particular populations). They have also conceptualized and documented forms of racialized and gendered violence ignored in mainstream approaches, developing pathbreaking works that address racialized violence (e.g., Middle Passage, branding, slave plantation, lynching, prison industrial complex) and gendered violence (e.g., rape, kidnapping, domestic violence, sexual harassment, feminization, forced sterilization). In these studies, feminist theorists have examined the complex roles of states, non state actors from dominant classes and communities and individual perpetrators in the enactment of violence with impunity and they have also traced intricate modes of resistance in response to violence. This chapter provides an introduction to this scholarship.

State and Legal Violence

Within political and legal theory, one of the primary arenas of studying violence has been in relation to state and law. Broadly, one can consider three subthemes in this context—namely, the origin and nature of violence, limits on violence, and negotiation of violence.

Origin and Nature of Violence. The most vexed debates on the nature of violence have taken place in the context of liberalism and liberal democratic states. Classical liberals or proto liberals, such as Thomas Hobbes (1997), famously identified the basis for centralized power, premised on terror or brute force of the *Leviathan*, as avoidance of a "state of war" and for the sake of self-preservation. A range of scholars such as Austin Sarat, Thomas Kearns (1991), and K. G. Kannabiran (2003) also locate "fear" as a founding moment for law. As Kannibiran (2004, 3795) puts it, "None of us seem to feel free without constraint." The liberal state, premised on a social contract, is of course constituted of several forms of exclusions. As Carole Pateman (1988) has famously pointed out, the social contract is primarily a story of a contract between men and prefaced by a sexual contract between them. Consequently, women are excluded from this original act and thereby deprived of the rights of equality and liberty in the newly formed state and society. The role of the state in creating race and racialized exclusions is also visible in the fixed racial classifications adopted in state activities, such as the census (Stevens 1998). In addition, as Stevens has pointed out, the intentional nature of the state's acts in recreating material racial hierarchies are visible in the fact that historically the state did not just passively allow for wealth to be passed by whites to their own children but deliberately helped this process by excluding interracial marriages. Thus, exclusions and violence are foundational to the formation of the liberal state.

Limits on Violence. In liberal legal theory, the fact that law emerged ostensibly in the wake of an imagined state of war meant that it could not rely entirely on violence and that it leads to certain limits on violence. Limits on violence can best be explained in relation to the methods of execution in the United States. Austin Sarat (2001) and Timothy Kaufman-Osborn (2002) have written extensively on the shift in the methods of execution, from hanging to the gas chamber to the electric chair and, finally, to lethal injection. This shift is often explained in terms of a liberal state's desire to be humane, in contrast with an "inhumane" non-state actor. Thus, the argument is that while a liberal state does use violence, what characterizes the violence is that it is "rational, controlled and purposive" as opposed to violence of a non-state actor (Sarat 2001, 6). As Upendra

Baxi explains, "The legal system, always and everywhere, seeks to delegitimize and criminalize violence by actors other than those authorized to use violence . . . and provides a normative language which camouflages the core coercion underlying the law" (Baxi 1993 19). Consequently, each of the newer methods of execution is proclaimed to be less painful than the previous one, even though botched executions in all these methods have constantly (often visibly) belied this claim. The latest in a series of botched executions, this time in a lethal injection, was observed in the case of Clayton Locket in 2014 when he was found writhing in pain soon after the drug was administered and he died later from a heart attack linked to the faulty procedure. In this context, it is important to remember that one of the arguments for upholding the three-drug protocol (especially the paralytic drug after the anesthetic) in the 2008 US Supreme Court case *Baze v. Rees* was precisely to make the pain less visible rather than to ensure its absence.

As Austin Sarat (2001) has argued more generally, developing humane methods is not for the sake of the person being executed because there is often a desire for visible pain, especially by victim rights groups. Instead, it is so that the liberal state's violence will appear more humane, on the one hand, and witnesses will be spared watching the pain and gore of executions, on the other. Even in other contexts, it is common for theorists to comment on the limits liberal states place on their own violence. According to Michael Ignatieff (2004, 2), the liberal state is actually defined as "a constitutional order that sets limits to any government's use of force." Thus, a large part of the claim that sustains a liberal discourse on state and legal violence concerns the limits and controlled nature of the violence.

This debate on the controlled nature of violence within the law assumes a different meaning when considered in the context of racialized and sexualized exclusions that were foundational to state and law. As Saidiya Hartman (1999) pointed out in her powerful work on slave law, rape in the context of slavery was unimaginable. The enslaved women, being the property of the master, could not be protected under the law since that would require accepting her as a person who could exercise her will and consent. Thus, a discourse of seduction sets in to explain the nature of the violence. As Hartman explains, "As the enslaved female is legally unable to give consent or to offer resistance, she is presumed to be always willing" (113), further noting that "the extremity of power and the absolute submission required of the slave not only renders suspect, or meaningless, concepts of consent and will, but the sheer lack of limitations regarding the violence 'necessary' to the maintenance of slave relations, that is, black submission, unmoors the notion of 'force'" (113–114).

Forgetting of Violence and Negotiation of Violence

Emphasis on limits of violence often has the impact of what Sarat and Kearns (1991) have called the "forgetting of violence" in legal and political theory. In other words, law and judicial decision-making appear to be based on norms, principles, and abstract rules as opposed to the use of violence. This denies the important observation made by Robert

Cover (1992, 203), and other theorists, that "legal interpretation takes place in a field of pain and death." As Timothy Kaufman-Osborn (2002) explains in the context of death penalty, violence is not seen in the "words" of the judge but, rather, only in the "deeds" of the executioner, thereby distancing legal interpretation from legal enforcement as opposed to recognizing the integral relationship between the two.

The impact of such a theorization is most apparent in the post-9/11 United States in that when torture techniques do become the subject of news and debate, scholars and practitioners consider them as exceptions, aberrations, and as returned in times of crises (Agamben 1998, 2005). In turn, the presence of racialized and sexualized violent acts in different sites, such as prisons, detention centers, and police stations, get recognized as aberrations by deviant actors, thereby denying the continuities between violence in routine and in so-called exceptional contexts. Another kind of forgetting of violence occurs in the context of colonial histories (of liberalism) that occurred within an explicitly racialized logic of holding on to power for "civilizational" and material purposes with violence at their core.

In addition, a certain kind of forgetting occurs in postcolonial contexts, such as in Egypt, where the logic of the security state translates itself into an "Islamophobic, gendered and working class phobic" discourse of "Arab street" where peaceful people challenging that state violence become "unrecognizable mobs" as happened in the Tahrir square protests (Amar 2011, 308). Here, the efforts of Egyptian feminists to see sexual harassment on the street as an aspect of the repressive power of the state similar to torture in custody is denied and subverted to be limited to the function of the unruly "Arab street."

Despite this attempt at the forgetting of violence at various levels, one result of the emphasis on limiting violence in liberal states is a paradoxical relationship of law to violence. Liberal states cannot deny the use of violence, but they have to make it appear humane, and this becomes the basis of a constant negotiation that liberal law and states undertake with violence. Indeed, as I have argued, torture has to be understood not as an exception or aberration but as a manifestation of the liberal state's tension with violence, its negotiation with violence, and its inability to contain excess violence (Lokaneeta 2011). I define excess violence "as a constantly negotiated category that exists on a continuum of acts ranging from coercion to torture" (32).

Just as the visibility of the brutality in executions leads to the search for more humane methods, similarly in the context of torture, there is a need felt for more "sanitized" and "less painful" methods. The problem, of course, is that the result is a less scarring form of violence as opposed to a less painful one (Rejali 2007). The imagery of torture, as well as attempts to define torture in a narrowly brutal way, despite the more expansive definition of torture and "cruel, inhuman and degrading treatment" in international law, is precisely meant to deny the very presence of torture and excess violence in liberal states.

Theorizing excess violence makes two interventions. First, it avoids the consideration of torture on a different plane from violence, pointing to torture as a routine problem of violence in liberal states as well as illiberal ones. Second, it considers the distinct possibility of the emergence of moments of crisis when acts of violence reach such a threshold of severity that their policy justification cannot be sustained by the liberal state without a challenge to its legitimacy. In the Indian context, for example, extraordinary laws on terrorism were allowed to lapse or be repealed, despite the most exceptional national and international rhetoric against terrorism in their favor, and despite the fact that the Indian Supreme Court had upheld them as constitutional (Lokaneeta 2013). Thus, even in the most favorable circumstances for exceptional policies, these withdrawals become important to recognize the law's tension with violence. Ironically of course, it is not the severity of the impact of the violence on the bodies of subjects that is a determining factor prompting crisis, but rather the failure of conditions of the possibility of sustaining an exceptional policy that leads to its rejection. For instance, in the context of the post-9/11 United States, it was only when the Bybee torture memo (2002) emerged alongside the Abu Ghraib pictures of abuse that the crisis of legitimacy became apparent and led to the memo being withdrawn, not the gendered and racialized narratives of pain and suffering that were emerging from Guantánamo Bay, Cuba, and Abu Ghraib prison, Iraq. Similarly, the continually racialized and sexualized narratives in everyday encounters with the state do not lead to the acknowledgment of the centrality of violence in law. Regardless of whether liberal states negotiate and sometimes even withdraw exceptional acts because of their desire to appear humane, such a shift is important even if it is inadequate in understanding and addressing violence.

Political and legal theorists have often focused on the state and legal aspect of violence. But that has meant that the impact of violence on particular racialized and gendered bodies and subjectivities is not a central part of the story, and indeed, the state and legal discourses are framed in ways that deny these particularities. In turn, postcolonial theorists, anthropologists, and feminists have pointed to the impact of violence and initiated the consequent theorization of other institutions and processes integral to understanding violence. A substantial literature has thus focused attention on the bodily impact of violence and the fact that the effects of violence are exacerbated on certain bodies. As Alfred Arteaga (2003, vii) writes, "The violent act, the violent event, is a bodily occurrence." The bodily impact—interior and exterior—of sexual, racial and colonialist violence has gained centrality in studies on violence (Aldama 2003).

Colonial Violence and Postcolonial Implications

The different aspects of colonial violence have only gradually become foundational for any study of violence. Anthropologists Nancy Scheper-Hughes and Philippe Bourgois, for instance, have pointed to the "historic centrality of these [colonial] processes in shaping contemporary patterns of violence across the world" (Scheper-Hughes and Bourgois 2004, 5). They point to the lacuna in anthropology for its failure to acknowledge the role of colonial violence and genocide in the discipline's quest for understanding other aspects of communities such as kinship practices. One could extend that critique of silence with respect to certain facets of colonialism to the study of violence in other contexts including Western political and legal theory.

Classic articles such as Michael Taussig's (1984) "Culture of Terror-Space of Death" articulate the role that brute violence alongside representational violence played in the context of colonialism. Taussig's piece, though written in the context of Roger Casement's Putomayo Report on British colonial enterprises in Africa and South America in 1910, characterizes the nature of colonial interventions in general. The Putomayo Report noted the flogging, scalping, lashing, and deliberate starvation of the colonized people, often by Indian guards, in the rubber plantations, which Tausig (1984, 43) terms the "banality of cruelty." The deep bodily and psychological impact of French colonialism on Algerians (and other colonized peoples) led both Jean Paul Sartre and Frantz Fanon to theorize the long-term impact of colonial violence and to locate within that violence the origins of revolutionary violence discussed later (Sartre 1963; Fanon 1963).

Taussig's "Culture of Terror" also explains why the excessive violence on these plantations was not just for disciplining labor. Instead, there was a construction of "wild Indians" as "evil savages," both to preempt any Indian rebellions and to feed into colonial fantasies about Indians such that "rebellion was perceived in a mythic and colonially paranoid vision in which the image of dismemberment and cannibalism glowed vividly" (Taussig 1984, 48). Here, storytelling, rumor, and gossip become the primary ways in which colonial ideology takes hold and leads to the use of brute violence.

The centrality of coercion in British colonial rule in India is also well captured in Ranajit Guha's concept of "dominance without hegemony" (Guha 1997). Guha explains that there were attempts toward dominance *with* hegemony through the use of persuasion. The latter was apparent in a policy of improvement through education and reforms, but coercion became the primary method of colonial rule in India. As he puts it, "There can be no colonialism without coercion, no subjugation of an entire people in its own homeland by foreigners without the explicit use of force" (Guha 1997, 24). The need for order in the colonial state required the use of the coercive state apparatus (army, penal system, and police, etc.), which was much more directly involved than in Western states in extracting the labor power of the people. Guha further notes that the emphasis on coercion was combined with the *danda* (stick): an expression of violence on the part of the precolonial upper-caste and higher-class Indian elites against the subordinated.

Colonial ideology was by definition contradictory, which made the relationship between the empire and the colonial subjects fraught. As Ann Stoler (1992, 515) has powerfully argued, for example, *metissage* (interracial unions) were frequent occurrences in both French Indochina and Netherland Indies; yet these unions were considered "subversive," a "threat to white prestige," and "an embodiment of European degeneration and moral decay." To protect and preserve the "superiority" of the colonizers, bans on *metissage* were enacted. Yet in both contexts, the language of these exclusionary policies made it difficult to discern whether the source of the "threat" was based on gender, class, race, or other cultural markers, working in conjunction with each other. As Stoler notes, in the attempt to exclude the *metissage*, if blood or race could no longer be the criterion of exclusion, the category of "native culture" could be invoked.

Even the colonial government had to struggle with its relationship with violence, however. For instance, in 1919, a British general, Reginald Dyer, ordered his troops to open fire on a peacefully protesting crowd in Jallianwalla Bag, Punjab, India. The 1,650 rounds that were fired with no warning killed at least 379 people and injured thousands according to official records. While describing the horrific nature of the Jallianwalla massacre, Nasser Hussain (2003) notes that although the attack was committed for the political imperative of continuing colonial rule, the British were not able to completely defend the "excessive force" committed by the General. Similarly, in her discussion of the torture and death of a native Indian named Gunnoo (accused of robbing and drowning his five-year-old niece), Anupama Rao (2006) notes that it was important for the British colonial government to ensure an inquiry and initiate the punishment of the *foujdar* (official). This act was essential for the colonial state because of its need to differentiate its own rule from the (Indian) natives who were known to be "associated with practices of physical mutilation and disfigurement understood to have been prevalent in Old Regime politics" (Rao 2006, 157). As Rao and Pierce (2006, 4) explain, the problem of violence was the "paradox of colonial discipline."

Here again, the colonial government created commissions on torture, and even explained away torture as inherent to the "violent nature" of the native Indians, in order to preserve its claim to be more "civilized" and to ground its governance in the "rule of law." Yet it forced colonial regimes to negotiate their own use of violence. Scholars investigating colonial violence also focused attention on the racialized and gendered nature of violence experienced by the colonized. But the category of the "colonized" was not restricted to those living in "formal" colonies. The concept of "internal colonization" refers to historical systems of oppression developed to subjugate diasporic subjects (and their descendants), who migrated either voluntarily or involuntarily to the lands of the colonizers.

Dennis Childs, for example, analyzes the embodied violence experienced by African-Americans in the Angola prison (called "the farm") in Louisiana. The "farm" at one point was a slave plantation, and was later converted to a farm worked by convicts, and then to a prison, becoming a "living monument" to the timelessness of racial subjugation in the United States (Childs 2003, 189). Supplementing concern for the high rates of incarceration of African Americans in US prisons with a focus on the conditions of their confinement, Childs draws attention to the striking similarity between the slave plantation and the prison—from the erasure of the name of the person in detention to the "architectural violence" created by a similarity between a slave ship and a prison cell (Childs 2003, 193). From physical to metaphorical branding, the criminal is stigmatized as one who could never be reformed. Treated more like animals than humans, enslaved and imprisoned blacks experience "social death" across space and time (Childs 2003). Internal colonization can be deployed to explain conditions of otherness faced in various contexts, ranging from formal colonies to immigration detention centers and public and secret prisons.

IMPACT OF VIOLENCE

Violence and Subjectivity. The impact of violence on everyday life and subjectivity is a significant aspect of the study of violence, particularly in the works of anthropologists, postcolonial theorists, and feminist scholars. In their introduction to an important collection titled *Violence and Subjectivity*, Veena Das and Arthur Kleinman (2000, 2) focus on how "violence is actualized—in the sense that it is both produced and consumed." Das and Kleinman define subjectivity as "the felt interior experience of the person that includes his or her position in a field of relational power" (1).

The impact of violence has been considered both during times of extraordinary violence, such as war and organized conflict, and in the context of violent actions that permeate everyday lives. Violence against women during partition of India in 1947, for example, has been widely documented (Butalia 1998). Massive violence on both sides of the newly constructed border between India and Pakistan took the form of abductions, rapes, and sexual violence (close to 100,000 women were abducted). Treating the violated women as a symbol of the "nation's honor" that needed to be "restored," both India and Pakistan subsequently attempted to forcibly return the women to their original communities, without much concern for the subjectivities of the women who had been victimized or the communities to which they returned. Women's bodies literally inscribed nationalist aspirations, territorial battles, national victory, and defeat. But the restoration of "national honor" operated quite differently from the fate of the raped women returned to their natal homes. Some women were killed by men in their own community who sought to preserve both family and national honor (Das 1997). In other national contexts, such as El Mozote in El Salvador in 1981, women and children have been killed by state security forces on the suspicion of disloyalty, as counterinsurgency operations routinely eradicated "potential guerillas" (Danner 1993).

These experiences have had a formative impact on the everyday lives and subjectivities of women. Although states and individuals themselves often sought to establish a zone of silence around these issues (Das 1997), women often drew connections between the extraordinary violence of civil war and the everyday violence of rape and domestic violence, blurring the boundaries between war and peace and between ordinary and extraordinary contexts. In addition, as Das has noted in the context of partition, the impact of the violence had long-term effects: kinship relationships were transformed in the post-partition period by "conditions of scarcity" and "memories of brutality;" women and men became living witnesses to the everyday betrayal in familial relationships (Das 2000).

One can observe here the tremendous impact of feminist theory and practice. Broader theoretical interventions that challenge the public-private divide central to liberal theory point to the patriarchal basis of law, state, and nationhood. By investigating the intersections among different forms of oppression and the raced and gendered nature of violence, feminist scholarship illuminated the interdependence of the local and the global, the individual and the national, the symbolic and the physical, and subjectivation and objectification. In the last several decades, a remarkable number of detailed studies document particular forms of gendered violence such as rape, sexual harassment, gun violence, dowry deaths, sati, and acid burning and their relation to larger structural and historical processes. By demonstrating the connections between specific experiences of violence and nation-building, feminist theory and practice has made major contributions to the conceptualization of violence and to the methods by which it is investigated. In the following sections, I discuss two illustrations of these feminist interventions. The first example shows how feminist scholars challenged the state's denial and trivialization of violence against women in organized conflict and fought for the recognition of rape as a weapon in war and a crime against humanity. In the second, I focus on how another important arena of violence—namely, war and militarism—was radically reconceptualized based on feminist understandings of gender and sexuality, on the one hand, and critiques of racialized imperial encounters, on the other.

Rape as Torture

Over the past twenty-five years, feminist scholars and activists have transformed international law's treatment of rape and sexual violence. Despite evidence of massive rape during World War II and its aftermath, rape had primarily been considered to be an issue under *humanitarian* law in the international context (Blatt 1992). As Catharine MacKinnon (1994) has noted, the violation of women's human rights was often ignored. Whenever women suffered alongside men or were tortured or killed, it was recorded as a violation of the human rights of people in particular communities, and not as violation of women's rights. Further, the everyday violence faced by women was not considered to be a violation of human rights because it was seen as specific to women and linked to sex. "What is done to women is either too specific to women to be seen as human or too generic to human beings to be seen as specific to women" (MacKinnon 1994, 6).

One of the classic ways in which the trivialization of sexual violence was observed was in the characterization of rape as ill treatment (not torture), implying that it involved less pain and suffering than torture, and also that it was not political. In *Cyprus v. Turkey* (1982), for instance, the European Commission termed the rapes of women in Cyprus by Turkish soldiers during the invasion as constituting inhuman and degrading treatment rather than torture, despite state complicity and the high level of suffering women experienced in these assaults. Torture was considered a political act, whereas rape was considered a private sexual act, even when the facts demonstrated that the rapes were "systematic and group based." States were not considered responsible for preventing rape or for holding other nations accountable for systematic rape in war. Domestic laws and courts were seen as adequate to deal with the issue of rape. The hierarchical distinction between the public—construed as a male terrain—and the private, where women were invariably situated, contributed to the trivialization of rape in organized conflict. Whether construed as everyday private crimes or as a byproduct of other extraordinary events, rapes were not given that much importance (Mackinnon 1993).

In response to the trivialization of rape, feminists argued that rape survivors undergo all the symptoms of torture victims, most notably post-traumatic stress disorder (PTSD), and face isolation and guilt long after the event. For this reason, women raped in war ought to be considered torture victims as well (Aswad 1996). In addition, rape by government officials (for a political purpose) meet the requirements of the UN definition of torture: severe pain and suffering for a political purpose by government officials.

Using intersectional analysis, feminists conceptualized rape as an instrument of war and genocide, challenging mainstream tendencies to treat rapes either as attacks on one community by another, or as attacks by men against women. Mackinnon points out that the latter argument seems like a feminist position because it frames rape as a gender crime; but in civil war conflicts, this generic approach obscures the fact that certain women were being raped because of their community status:

> Attacks on women, it seems, cannot define attacks on a people. If they are gendered attacks, they are not ethnic; if they are ethnic attacks, they are not gendered . . . But when rape is a genocidal act, as it is here, it is an act to destroy a people. What is done to women defined that destruction. Also, aren't women a people?
>
> (MacKinnon 1994, 10)

Beyond the category of everyday rapes, genocidal rapes are specific to particular forms of conflict. These rapes are not just everyday occurrences perpetrated by men but rape as policy, "rape under orders" for the purpose of destroying a community (MacKinnon 1994, 11). In the aftermath of the systemic use of rape as an instrument of ethnic cleansing and genocide in the former Yugoslavia and Rwanda, feminist human rights activists pressed for changes in international law to recognize rape as a crime against humanity and as a mode of torture. This characterization made a crucial link between the ordinary and the extraordinary contexts of power assertions.

Yet, despite such powerful legal campaigns that have foregrounded the issue of sexual violence and rape in international and national contexts, Pratiksha Baxi, in her fascinating book *Public Secrets of Law: Rape Trials in India*, writes about the "widespread tolerance of intolerable sexual harm," and how legal trials themselves play a major role in denying justice to the survivors of sexual violence (Baxi 2013, 344). As she explains, "It remains a public secret that rape trials inscribe extreme indignity and humiliation on womens' bodies . . . by imposing a disciplinary discourse on shame and stigma" (341–343). The legal system within the nation-state utilizes medico-legal processes to disqualify a woman's testimony and, additionally, denies the intricate ways in which different categories of oppression based on caste, gender, and ethnic and religious identity determine the nature of sexual violence. Despite decades of feminist activism, legal amendments, feminist theorization of sexual violence, the law and state fail to provide justice to rape survivors, reinforcing rather than overturning phallocentric notions of justice (Baxi 2013; Das 2006). Although Baxi focuses on the case of India, some of the critiques echo the experiences of feminists nationally and internationally, and sexual violence continues to be a site of struggle.

Feminist Critiques of Militarism

Feminist interventions have also radically transformed understandings of violence in relation to militarism and war. Applying feminist critiques of fixed notions of sex and gender and dominant models of masculinity and femininity, and recognizing the intersectional nature of sexual violence, Cynthia Enloe (1990, 2007a) advanced a paradigmatic critique of war and militarism. Deploying a concept of "feminist curiosity" about the absence of women from mainstream discourses, Enloe (2007b) developed a feminist methodology to investigate militarism and war as masculinist projects, focusing attention on institutional and sexual violence within the military, as well as violence committed by military women. One of the most fascinating feminist discussions of the multifaceted dimensions of racialization and gendering in organized conflict takes as its point of departure the pictures of women in the US military's torturing of Iraqi men in Abu Ghraib prison in Iraq in the early 2000s.

In a speech that circulated widely on the Internet, noted feminist author Barbara Ehrenreich (2004) asserted that women's participation in acts of abuse in a detention center run by the US military must be construed as an (sad) example of gender equality. Noting her own shock at seeing the images, Ehrenreich gave voice to her secret "hope" that military women would behave differently in war contexts than men. When confronted with evidence of military women's equal depravity, Ehrenreich acknowledged the extinction of that hope, stating that "a lot of things died with those photos." Ehrenreich's argument was effectively criticized by several feminist scholars for assuming an essentialist notion of femininity that presupposed women's moral superiority, and failing to theorize the manifestations of power. Yet Cynthia Enloe (2007a, 95) called attention to a different kind of gendered effect at Abu Ghraib, noting a process of "feminization" through which "allegedly feminine characteristics"—fear, sexual vulnerability, docility, subservience—were imposed on Iraqi men. The goal of feminizing someone (or something), according to Enloe, is to lower their status. Within Enloe's framework, gender is detached from individual bodies and encapsulated in subordinating practices. These acts of feminization could be conducted by men or women on men or women, respectively, an argument echoed by other feminists. Angela Davis noted that the expression of shock signifies an assumption that women are primarily considered as victims, rather than as perpetrators of sexual and sexualized violence:

> Seeing images of a woman engaged in behavior that we associate with male dominance was startling. But it should not have been, especially if we take seriously what we know about the social construction of gender. Especially within institutions that rely on ideologies of male dominance, women can be easily mobilized to commit the same acts of violence expected of men.
>
> (Davis 2007, 25)

These feminist critiques simultaneously challenge essentialist notions of sex and gender and point toward gendered institutions, drawing attention to the masculinized culture of the military, which had long excluded women and which remained intact even after women became a part of the institution.

Bringing these strands of argument together, Timothy Kaufman-Osborn (2005) argued that the events at Abu Ghraib were not related to feminist goals of equality in any way. On the contrary, Abu Ghraib involves a set of gendered disciplinary practices associated with US military power that are "performed" by individuals. Whether men or women play out the "logic of emasculation," these tactics are rooted in military history and culture. Gendered practices of emasculation are detached from the particular "male" and "female" bodies that exercise power over the male detainees and "strip prisoners of their masculine gender identity and turn them into caricatures of terrified and often infantilized femininity" (Kaufman-Osborn 2005, 606). The violence embodied in Iraqi men at the hands of US military women and men manifests masculinist, imperial modes of domination that cannot be explained without a feminist curiosity.

Just as militarism per se is masculinized, discourses pertaining to nuclear weapons are both masculinized and sexualized, routinely exhibiting phallic imagery and metaphors of sexual domination. In her classic article, "Sex and Death in the Rational World of Defense Intellectuals," Carol Cohn documented how the rhetoric of male military officers and think-tank consultants appropriates gendered symbolism. For example, defense intellectuals typically claimed that any notion of limited nuclear power was ridiculous because "it's a pissing contest," characterizing nuclear confrontations as a "competition for manhood" and also minimizing the destructive power of nuclear weaponry by classifying it as "boyish mischief" (Cohn 1987, 356). Male nuclear scientists characterized their work as giving "birth" to nuclear bombs, and freely articulated their preference that their offspring be boys, not girls (duds), thus simultaneous expressing misogyny and aligning themselves with the modern notion that the function of science is to dominate Mother Nature (Cohn 1987, 357). Ensconced within a closed community of users, the language of these defense intellectuals shows no serious concern for those whose lives are destroyed by militarism, although it works admirably to distance lay people from questioning the dominant framework and challenging this mode of violence.

By contextualizing institutions, ideologies, and actors that enable, trivialize or deny violence, feminist scholars have suggested radical ways to rethink the nature, scope, and causes of violence.

Resisting Violence: State, Social, and Symbolic

One of the most important aspects of feminist studies of violence is resistance, which may take the form of political violence, the creation of forums to articulate alternatives to violence, or the development of mechanisms to negotiate everyday life in a way that mediates the effects of such violence. In the context of partition violence in India and Pakistan, for example, resistance included strategies of mourning, as well as renegotiating familial relationships by transgressing long-established norms (Das 2000). In the context of the Indian Emergency (1975–1977), one of the darkest periods of postcolonial Indian politics, during which there was large-scale suspension of rights; increasing incidences of torture and disappearances; and implementation of violent state policies, such as slum demolitions and forced sterilizations, Emma Tarlo (2000) investigated resistance in the form of new subjectivities emerging through complex processes of solidarity and tensions among victims. At a moment when the oppressive power of the state was enacted on the bodies of the working poor by requiring them to undergo sterilization to qualify for a new housing plot, even as their previous homes were being demolished for the sake of urban renewal, Tarlo shows how victims were forced to victimize other community members in order to participate in and resist the state's violent policies.

Much of the discussion of resistance revolves around the emergence of political violence or revolutionary violence in response to the brutal oppression of the colonial or national state. In "Colonial War and Mental Disorders" (an excerpt from his classic book *Wretched of the Earth*), Frantz Fanon (1963) details the pernicious effects of colonial violence on both the tortured Algerians and the French perpetrators. But Fanon argues that brutal colonial oppression gives rise to resistance in the form of revolutionary violence as the colonized seek to reassert their humanity, a view wholeheartedly supported by Jean Paul Sartre. By conceptualizing revolutionary violence as a legitimate means to counter abusive state violence, Fanon and Sartre challenge the Weberian notion that the state and the state alone can legitimately use force.

In the context of Sri Lanka, where the minority Tamil population has been subjected to violence at the hands of the dominant Sinhalese as part of the postcolonial experience, several scholars have investigated resisting subjectivities that have emerged in face of systematic state violence and given rise to political violence. A very distinct model of resistance is represented by women who joined the armed militant groups as a way to challenge state violence. In contrast to the cultivation of "militarized masculinity" as theorized by Cynthia Enloe and other feminist scholars, women who joined the militant movements such as the LTTE (Liberation Tigers of Tamil Eelam) developed a very different mode of subjectivity. Yamuna Sangarasivam (2003) suggests that women cadres in the LTTE developed a strong sense of agency and empowerment. Even when they suffered death in combat, the women cadres were memorialized for their sacrifice and hailed as martyrs for a moral cause. Receiving such public recognition for their revolutionary role, women cadres not only transformed their traditional gender roles but became symbols of "regenerative" violence. Although Sangarasivam's research suggests that women in certain radical armed groups may experience the liberatory effects of revolutionary violence predicted by Fanon, she does not address other challenges faced by women in conflict areas when they are part of patriarchal armed groups or when they are captured and subjected to violence from the state for their revolutionary action (as in the North East of India). Nor does Sangarasivam discuss the effects of revolutionary violence on noncombatant women in conflict areas who suffer at the hands of both militant groups and state forces due to an increased militarization of life (Banerjee 2009).

Scholarship that focuses on armed militancy often investigates collectivities and individuals who identify with those collectivities, whether they be state-aligned forces or revolutionaries. Jonathan Spencer (2000) has suggested that these approaches fail to explain or attend to individual agency on the part of those individuals who manifest "avoidance," a refusal to identify with or engage in military forces. Spencer examines the life experience of Piyasena, a radical Sinhala youth in Sri Lanka, who was detained under an extraordinary law (the Prevention of Terrorism Act), yet refused to join the People's Liberation Front (*Janata Vimukti Peramuna* [JVP]), a radical Sinhalese militant group. Spencer suggests that neither the accounts of Das nor Bajwa can make sense of Piyasena's decisions. In theorizing the link between violence and community, one model claims that experiences of oppression lead to sacrifice and martyrdom, while the second leads the oppressed to exchange of violence for vengeance. Piyasena, however, chose neither course. Instead Piyasena's actions manifested an "intentional refusal to comprehend" violence, and consequently, a "refusal to act" (Spencer 2000, 136). Thus Spencer suggests that an adequate account of resistance must also encompass individuals whose identity is not completely explained by or subsumed within a collective desire to engage in political violence.

For other scholars, revolutionary violence does not emerge only in the context of colonialism or postcolonial conflicts. Instead, resistance often is articulated against structural violence that emerges across different contexts. For instance, Randhir Singh suggests that in postcolonial India resistance arises to stark inequalities:

> In a society like ours which is "structurally" saturated with violence, with exploitation, and oppression and inequality, there is always room for revolutionary violence. To reject such violence and uphold nonviolence on principle has no justification, rational or moral, in the light of the historical experience of the struggles of the oppressed the world over.
>
> (Singh 2009, 245)

Of course, this structural violence may not remain restricted to traditionally defined marginalized sectors such as races, genders, classes, or castes. Kleinman, for example, conceptualizes social violence as suffering that "social orders ... bring to bear on people," which includes diseases and poverty that affect the poor but also others in society (Kleinman 2000, 226). It even includes media appropriation of that suffering and the policies that are meant to address them, but which end up increasing the violence. Although similar to the concept of structural violence that Paul Farmer (1997) and Randhir Singh articulate, Kleinman makes an additional intervention about "the violences of everyday life," which affect "people throughout the social order" (Kleinman 2000, 228). These violences range from the everyday stress of coping with the demands of a middle-class woman's existence, to the ways in which hemophilia patients in the

United States were never warned of the dangers of using blood that had been infected with HIV and causing AIDs. Kleinman advances a theory that captures the everyday violences that "occur in collective experience and in the subjectivity of personal experience" (Kleinman 2000, 238). Some critics suggest that Kleinman's concept of social violence is so broad that it may take away focus from particularity of experiences of violence. In contrast, social violence helps illuminate a continuum of violence that exists in society. Violence lies not just in cataclysmic events, but also in the way society is structured, represented, experienced, and responded to. Conceptualizing violence as a continuum, then, brings together all the different elements of violence and resistance.

Pierre Bourdieu's (2001) essay on "Gender and Symbolic Violence" calls attention to an additional aspect of violence. Bourdieu emphasizes the role that structures of domination play in reinforcing passive and submissive consciousness among the dominated within a particular *habitus*. In particular, he challenged the idea that mere consciousness raising at the level of the individual or a collective is adequate to do away with symbolic violence, which requires an actual dismantling of the weapons that enable the domination by certain agents (including men) and institutions. Sometimes the dominated may continue to exhibit submissive consciousness long after the actual conditions of production change. Transformation of consciousness may be possible only if the social conditions of the production of those dispositions change.

Each of these broader theorizations of violence are linked to different models of resistance. While a good deal of the focus is on revolutionary or armed models of resistance, there are other equally powerful militant initiatives. The emergence of maternal citizenship is an excellent example. Cynthia Bejarano (2003), for example, writes about the mothers and grandmothers of young adults who have organized themselves in response to the thousands of killings and disappearances that have taken place in Argentina (1976–1983), El Salvador (1979–1992), and Mexico (1993 onward). In Latin America, groups such as Las Madres de la Plaza de Mayo in Argentina, CoMadres in El Salvador, and the Voices sin echo and CICH in Juarez, Mexico, eschew all recourse to violence while organizing global protests against murder with impunity, state complicity, and the failure of the state to protect its citizens.

Challenging the public/private divide in all these contexts, women stepped out on the streets to protest with pictures, scarves with names of victims, home memoirs, and living altars to the missing and the killed. Various states tried to represent these women as bad mothers for raising subversive or immoral children to try and deflect the state's role in creating oppressive conditions. By skillfully using international networks, the mothers deftly countered those narratives. As Bejarano explains, the mother's role was traditionally assumed to be limited to a few public spaces, such as playgrounds and schools. But their concern with state violence made their actions unacceptable to the state. The example of mothers organizing to demand justice against state violence is also prominent in Kashmir in the form of the Association of Parents of Disappeared Persons (APDP). Furthermore, 2014 marked the tenth anniversary of the protest by the Manipuri women who used naked bodies to shame the Indian state for the murders, rapes, and disappearances enabled by extraordinary laws such as the Armed Forces

Special Powers Act in the North East of India (Banerjee 2009). The good woman/bad woman divide is struck down by these acts of resistance against the structural, social, and symbolic violence.

Conclusion

Feminist theorizations of violence have greatly expanded public understandings of the scope of violence, developing a continuum that spans genocide, war, civil conflict, and state-sponsored terror as well as everyday forms of violence that are often rendered invisible or indeed legitimate (Coronil and Skurski 2006). Rather than accepting a teleological understanding that positions modern nations as a "civilizing force" that constrains "premodern" violence, feminist scholars insist that violence is constitutive of modern states and nations (Coronil and Skurski 2006, 2). Focusing both on individual and collective experiences of violence and resistance, feminist theory and practice have significantly expanded understanding of complex and multilayered forms of violence, as well as their physical and discursive effects, while also creating a methodology attuned to racialization and gendering in the study of violence and resistance.

Acknowledgments

I thank the wonderful editors Mary Hawkesworth and Lisa Disch for their painstaking efforts and invaluable comments, and Ruchi Chaturvedi for useful readings.

References

Agamben, Giorgio. 1998. *Homo Sacer: Sovereign Power and Bare Life*. Translated by Daniel Heller-Roazen. Redwood City, CA: Stanford University Press.
Agamben, Giorgio. 2005. *State of Exception*. Translated by Kevin Attell. Chicago and London: University of Chicago Press.
Aldama, Arturo J. 2003. "Violence, Bodies, and the Color of Fear: An Introduction." In *Violence and the Body: Race, Gender, and the State*, edited by Arturo J. Aldama, 1–16. Bloomington: Indiana University Press.
Arteaga, Alfred. 2003. "Foreword: The Red and the Black." In *Violence and the Body: Race, Gender, and the State*, edited by Arturo J. Aldama, vii–viii. Bloomington: Indiana University Press.
Amar, Paul. 2011. "Turning the Gendered Politics of the Security State Inside Out? Charging the Police with Sexual Harassment in Egypt." *International Feminist Journal of Politics* 13 (3) (September): 299–328.

Aswad, Eveleyn Mary. 1996. "Torture by Means of Rape." *Georgetown Law Journal* 84 (May): 1913–1943.

Banerjee, Paula. 2009. "Gendered Face of Extraordinary Powers in North-East India." In *Human Rights and Peace: Ideas, Laws, Institutions and Movements*, edited by Ujjwal Kumar Singh, 130–146. Delhi: Sage.

Baxi, Upendra. 1993. *Marx, Law, and Justice*. Bombay: N.M. Tripathi.

Baxi, Pratiksha. 2013. *Public Secrets of Law: Rape Trials in India*. New Delhi: Oxford University Press.

Bejarano, Cynthia. 2003. "Las Super Madres de Latino America: Transforming Motherhood and Houseskirts by Challenging Violence in Juarez, Mexico, Argentina and El Salvador." In *Violence and the Body: Race, Gender, and the State*, edited by Arturo J. Aldama, 404–428. Bloomington: Indiana University Press.

Blatt, Deborah. 1992. "Recognizing Rape as a Method of Torture." *Review of Law and Social Change* 19 (4): 821–865.

Bourdieu, Pierre. 2001. "Gendered and Symbolic Violence." In *Violence in War and Peace: An Anthology*, edited by Nancy Scheper-Hughes and Philippe Bourgois, 339–342. Malden, MA: Blackwell Publishing.

Butalia, Urvashi. 1998. *The Other Side of Silence: Voices from the Partition of India*. Delhi: Penguin Books.

Childs, Dennis. 2003. "Angola, Convict Lease, and the Annulment of Freedom: The Vectors of Architectural and Discursive Violence in the U.S. 'Slavery of Prison.'" In *Violence and the Body: Race, Gender, and the State*, edited by Arturo J. Aldama, 189–208. Bloomington: Indiana University Press.

Cohn, Carol. (1987) 2004. "Sex and Death in the Rational World of Defense Intellectuals." In *Violence in War and Peace: An Anthology*, edited by Nancy Scheper-Hughes and Philippe Bourgois, 354–362. Malden, MA: Blackwell Publishing.

Cover, Robert. 1992. "Violence and the Word." In *Narrative, Violence and the Law: The Essays of Robert Cover*, edited by Austin Sarat, Michael Ryan, and Martha Minow, 203–238. Ann Arbor: University of Michigan Press.

Danner, Mark. 1993. "From *The Massacre of El Mozote: A Parable of the Cold War*." In *Violence in War and Peace: An Anthology*, edited by Nancy Scheper-Hughes and Philippe Bourgois, 334–338. Malden, MA: Blackwell Publishing.

Das, Veena. 1997. "Language and Body: Transactions in the Construction of Pain." In *Violence in War and Peace: An Anthology*, edited by Nancy Scheper-Hughes and Philippe Bourgois, 327–333. Malden, MA: Blackwell Publishing.

Das, Veena. 2000. "The Act of Witnessing: Violence, Poisonous Knowledge, and Subjectivity." In *Violence and Subjectivity*, edited by Veena Das, Arthur Kleinman, Mamphela Ramphele, and Pamela Reynolds, 205–225. Berkeley: University of California Press.

Das, Veena. 2006. "Sexual Violence, Discursive Formations, and the State." In *States of Violence*, edited by Fernando Coronil and Julie Skurski, 393–424. Ann Arbor: University of Michigan Press.

Das, Veena, and Arthur Kleinman. 2000. Introduction to *Violence and Subjectivity*, edited by Veena Das, Arthur Kleinman, Mamphela Ramphele and Pamela Reynolds, 1–18. Berkeley: University of California Press.

Davis, Angela Y. 2007."Sexual Coercion, Prisons, and Female Responses." In *One of the Guys: Women as Aggressors and Torturers*, edited by Tara McKelvey, 23–28. Emeryville, CA: Seal Press.

Ehrenreich, Barbara. 2004. Commencement Address at Barnard College. New York, NY. Available at http://www.longviewinstitute.org/research/ehrenreich/becommencement

Enloe, Cynthia H. 1990. *Bananas, Beaches and Bases: Making Feminist Sense of International Politics*. Berkeley: University of California Press.

Enloe, Cynthia H. 2007a. "Wielding Masculinity inside Abu Ghraib and Guantanamo: The Globalized Dynamics." In *Globalization and Militarism: Feminist Make the Link*, edited by Cynthia Enloe, 93–114. New York: Rowman & Littlefield.

Enloe, Cynthia H. 2007b. "Crafting a Global 'Feminist Curiosity' to Make Sense of Globalized Militarism: Tallying Impacts, Exposing Causes." In *Globalization and Militarism: Feminists Make the Link*, edited by Cynthia Enloe, 1–18. New York: Rowman & Littlefield.

Farmer, Paul. 1997. "On Suffering and Structural Violence: A View from Below." In *Violence in War and Peace: An Anthology*, edited by Nancy Scheper-Hughes and Philippe Bourgois, 281–290. Malden, MA: Blackwell Publishing.

Fanon, Frantz. 1963. "Colonial War and Mental Disorders." In *Violence in War and Peace: An Anthology*, edited by Nancy Scheper-Hughes and Philippe Bourgois, 443–452. Malden, MA: Blackwell Publishing.

Guha, Ranajit. 1997. *Dominance without Hegemony: History and Power in Colonial India*. Cambridge, MA: Harvard University Press.

Hartman, Saidiya. 1999. "Seduction and the Ruses of Power." In *Between Woman and Nation: Nationalisms, Transnational Feminisms, and the State* edited by Caren Kaplan, Norma Alarcon, and Minoo Moallem, 111–141. Durham, NC: Duke University Press.

Hobbes, Thomas. 1997. *Leviathan*. Edited by Richard E. Flathman and David Johnston. New York: W. W. Norton.

Hussain, Nasser. 2003. *The Jurisprudence of Emergency*. Ann Arbor: University of Michigan Press.

Ignatieff, Michael. 2004. *The Lesser Evil: Political Ethics in an Age of Terror*. Princeton, NJ: Princeton University Press.

Kaufman-Osborn, Timothy V. 2002. *From Noose to Needle: Capital Punishment and the Late Liberal State*. Ann Arbor: Michigan University Press.

Kaufman-Osborn, Timothy V. 2005. "Gender Trouble at Abu Ghraib?" *Politics and Gender* 1 (4): 597–619.

Kannabiran, K. G. 2003. *The Wages of Impunity: Power, Justice and Human Rights*. New Delhi: Orient Longman.

Kannabiran, K. G. 2004. "Repealing POTA: Some Issues." *Economic and Political Weekly* 39: 3794–3795.

Kleinman, Arthur. 2000. "The Violences of Everyday Life: The Multiple Forms and Dynamics of Social Violence." In *Violence and Subjectivity*, edited by Veena Das, Arthur Kleinman, Mamphela Ramphele, and Pamela Reynolds, 226–241. Berkeley: University of California Press.

Lokaneeta, Jinee. 2011. *Transnational Torture: Law, Violence, and State Power in the United States and India*. New York: New York University Press.

Lokaneeta, Jinee. 2013. "Extraordinary Law and Torture in India in an Era of Globalization." In *The Politics of the Globalization of Law: Getting from Rights to Justice*, edited by Alison Brysk, 199–218. New York: Routledge.

MacKinnon, Catherine. 1993. "On Torture: A Feminist Perspective on Human Rights." In *Human Rights in the Twenty-First Century Global Challenge*, edited by Kathleen H. Mahoney and Paul Mahoney, 21–31. Dordrecht / Boston: Martinus Nijhoff.

MacKinnon, Catherine. 1994. "Rape, Genocide, and Women's Human Rights." *Harvard Women's Law Journal* 17: 5–16.
Pateman, Carole. 1988. *The Sexual Contract*. Redwood City, CA: Stanford University Press.
Rao, Anupama. 2006. "Problems of Violence, States of Terror: Torture in Colonial India." In *Discipline and the Other Body: Correction, Corporeality, Colonialism*, edited by Steven Pierce and Anupama Rao, 151–185. Durham and London: Duke University Press.
Rao, Anupama, and Steven Pierce. 2006. "Discipline and the Other Body: Humanitarianism, Violence, and the Colonial Exception." In *Discipline and the Other Body: Correction, Corporeality, Colonialism*, edited by Steven Pierce and Anupama Rao, 1–35. Durham and London: Duke University Press.
Rejali, Darius. 2007. *Torture and Democracy*. Princeton, NJ: Princeton University Press.
Sangarasivam, Yamuna. 2003. "Militarization of the Feminine Body: Women's Participation in the Tamil Nationalist Struggle Violence, Bodies, and the Color of Fear: An Introduction." In *Violence and the Body: Race, Gender, and the State*, edited by Arturo J. Aldama, 59–76. Bloomington: Indiana University Press.
Sarat, Austin. 2001. *When the State Kills: Capital Punishment and the American Condition*. Princeton, NJ: Princeton University Press.
Sarat, Austin. 2001. "Situating Law between the Realities of Violence and the Claims of Justice: An Introduction." In *Law, Violence and the Possibility of Justice*, edited by Austin Sarat, 3–16. Princeton, NJ: Princeton University Press.
Sarat, Austin, and Thomas R. Kearns. 1991. "A Journey through Forgetting: Towards a Jurisprudence of Violence." In *Fate of Law*, edited by Austin Sarat and Thomas Kearns, 219–273. Ann Arbor: University of Michigan Press.
Sartre, Jean-Paul. 1963. Preface to Frantz Fanon's *Wretched of the Earth*." In *Violence in War and Peace: An Anthology*, edited by Nancy Scheper-Hughes and Philippe Bourgois, 229–235. Malden, MA: Blackwell Publishing.
Scheper-Hughes, Nancy, and Philippe Bourgois, eds. 2004. *Violence in War and Peace: An Anthology*. Malden, MA: Blackwell Publishing.
Singh, Randhir. 2009. "Terrorism, State Terrorism and Democratic Rights." In *Human Rights and Peace: Ideas, Laws, Institutions and Movements*, edited by Ujjwal Kumar Singh, 220–251. Delhi: Sage.
Skurski, Julie, and Fernando Coronil. 2006. "Introduction: States of Violence and the Violence of States." In *States of Violence*, edited by Fernando Coronil and Julie Skurski, 1–32. Ann Arbor: University of Michigan Press.
Spencer, Jonathan. 2000. "On Not Becoming a 'Terrorist': Problems of Memory, Agency, and Community in the Sri Lankan Conflict." In *Violence and Subjectivity*, edited by Veena Das, Arthur Kleinman, Mamphela Ramphelem, and Pamela Reynolds, 120–140. Berkeley: University of California Press.
Stevens Jacqueline. 1998. "Race and the State: Male-Order Brides and the Geographies of Race." *Theory and Event* 2 (3).
Stoler, Ann. 1992. "Sexual Affronts and Racial Frontiers: European Identities and the Cultural Politics of Exclusion in Colonial Southeast Asia." *Comparative Studies in Society and History* 34 (3): 514–551.
Tarlo, Emma. 2000. "Body and Space in a Time of Crisis: Sterilization and Resettlement during the Emergency in Delhi." In *Violence and Subjectivity*, edited by Veena Das, Arthur

Kleinman, Mamphela Ramphele and Pamela Reynolds, 242–270. Berkeley: University of California Press.

Taussig, Michael. 1984. "Culture of Terror—Space of Death: Roger Casement's Putumayo Report and the Explanation of Torture." In *Violence in War and Peace: An Anthology*, edited by Nancy Scheper-Hughes and Philippe Bourgois, 39–53. Malden, MA: Blackwell Publishing.

World Health Organization. 2002. *World Report on Violence and Health*. Geneva: World Health Organization.

Index

Note: Page numbers followed by the italicized letter *n* indicates material found in notes.

abortion. *See also* fetal politics;
    fetus/fetal emblems;
    reproduction, politics of
  attitudes towards, 81
  availability of, 517
  body politic and, 209
  concept of power and, 620
  gendering effects in policy, 617
  in health activism, 334–336
  international conservatism and, 319
  Marxist-feminist perspective on, 805
  neoliberalism and, 311
  politics and, 643, 701, 809
  right to, 807–811
  speak-outs on, 598, 608*n*6
  for women of color, 338
About Chinese Women (Kristeva), 767
Abrams, K., 254, 943
Abrego, Leisy, 496, 502
Abu-Lughod, Lila, 47, 660
Achieving Our Country: Leftist Thought in Twentieth Century America (Rorty), 647*n*4
Acker, Joan, 370
activism. *See also*
    consciousness-raising groups
  academic practices and, 2
  civil rights activism, 388, 593–596, 598
  cultural representation and, 783
  feminist health activism, 330, 332–335, 337, 341, 1002
  feminist standpoint theory and, 268
  in fetal politics, 701
  for gender justice, 201
  identity politics and, 52, 346–347, 349
  inspiration for, 601
  labor, 283
  on militarization, 509, 521–524
  narratives and, 909–910
  in new media, 668
  norms/normalization and, 551–552, 555, 557, 565
  political, 403, 636, 781, 855, 925
  prison, 721, 729
  queer, 998
  for reproductive rights, 807, 1001
  sexual exhibition and, 666
  on sexual violence, 1019
  temporality and, 974–975, 977, 979, 988
  trans/intersex feminisms and, 409, 412, 861
  transnational, 314, 317–318, 321, 509, 921, 991–993, 995, 998, 1003
  on welfare policy, 556
  women's identity and, 240
Adams, Carol J., 536
Addams, Jane, 508
"add women and stir" approach, 372, 509–510, 835
Adorno, Theodor, 57, 241, 653–654
Aesara of Lucania, 1, 12*n*1
aesthetic representation, 782, 792–794, 796–799. *See also* representation
affective turn
  in critical theory/research, 16
  description of, 19–23
  politics of, 683
The Affective Turn: Theorizing the Social (Clough and Halley), 19
affect studies
  affective labor, 444–446
  autonomy in, 26–27
  contextualization in, 33–35
  definitions/definitional debates, 23–24, 27–29

affect studies (*Cont.*)
  emotion in, 23–24
  feminist research on, 16–19
  inside-out/outside-in model critique, 24–26
  main orientations of, 22–23
  methodology in, 31–33
  on militarization, 519
  ontology/epistemology in, 29–31
  psychoanalysis and, 30
  on race/racialization, 745
The Affect Theory Reader (Gregg and Seigworth), 22
African American studies, 102, 166–168, 651
"Afrocentric feminist epistemology," 233
Against Our Will: Men, Women and Rape (Brownmiller), 234
Agamben, Giorgio, 63–66, 68–70, 76–77
agency
  cross-cultural analysis, 46–50
  of cultural producers, 662
  descriptive/prescriptive aspects of, 40–44
  feminist theories of, 39–40
  in neoliberal era, 57–58
  posthuman theories of, 53–56
  post-identity perspective, 50–52
  resistance as, 43–46
"agential realism," 54–55, 544, 683
agriculture
  feminization of, 435, 438
  global food production, 437
  hierarchical structures and, 812
  industrialization of, 143–144, 151, 434
  neoliberal globalization and, 314
Ahmed, Leila, 84–86
Ahmed, Sara, 20, 24–29, 31, 34, 927–928
Alaimo, Stacey, 686, 844, 847
Alam, S. M. Shamsul, 156
Alarcón, Norma, 353
Albright Madeleine, 995
Alcoff, Linda Martin, 7, 52, 950
Alexander, Jacqui, 864, 992, 997
Alexander, Michelle, 754
Alexander-Floyd, Nikol, 398, 403–404
alienation, 962–963
All China Women's Federation (ACWF), 321n1
Allen, Amy, 52, 478, 485

All the Women Are White, All the Blacks Are Men, But Some of Us Are Brave (Hull, Bell Scott and Smith), 353
Althusser, Louis, 239, 350, 586, 845, 955–956
Alvarex, Sonia, 992
"ambition gap," 373
American Medical Association, 337
anarchist feminism, 4
Anderson, E., 271
Anderson, Lorraine, 534
androcentrism, 84, 224, 769–771, 832, 855–856
Ang, Ien, 655
Anglo-American feminist theory, 227–230, 238–240, 243
anorexia, 219–220
Anthony, Susan B., 283
anthropocene feminism, 546–548, 683–684
anticolonial feminist theory
  antecedents to, 100–101
  decolonial feminism, 114–119
  decolonial theory, 111–114
  emergence/submergence of, 101–104
  intersectionality and, 104–107
  postcolonialism and, 107–111
antidepressants, 341
anti-discrimination
  blind-spots in, 603
  in institutions, 372–373
antipornography movement, 235–237, 584
antipoverty programs, 148, 198, 293
Anzaldúa, Gloria
  border thinking/borderland subjects, 101, 161, 353, 999
  identity politics and, 102
  influence of, 410
  mestiza consciousness, 114, 413, 903–904, 910, 939
  temporality and, 979
Appadurai, Arjun, 996
Aptheker, Bettina, 233
The Arab Woman (*La Femme Arabe*) (Daumas), 91
Arendt, Hannah
  on agency, 41
  on birth, 708–709, 716–717
  "common world" concept, 648n6
  ideas of agency, 54

on identity, 50, 640, 642, 648n5
notion of enlarged thought, 49
"Arendt Question in Feminism" (Honig), 51
Aristotle, 77, 209, 708, 973, 979
armed resistance movements, 513. *See also* militarization and war
Armillary Sphere Diagram (Su), 1, 12n1
Arms and the Enlisted Woman (Steihm), 511
Armstrong, J., 623
Arteaga, Alfred, 1014
Åsberg, Cecilia, 542–543, 546, 843–844
Asian American culture, 168–169
Asian Communities for Reproductive Justice (ACRJ), 338
assemblage/assemblage theory, 394, 396–397, 401, 462, 465–466, 744–745
assisted reproductive technologies (ART), 818–820
Astell, Mary, 348, 472
asylum, immigration practices and, 171–173
Athanasiou, Athena, 57, 925
Atkinson, Ti-Grace, 229
Austin, J. L., 572–577, 580–581, 583–587
Austin, Mary, 534
autonomous affects, 26–27. *See also* affect studies
autonomy, relational, 43
Avery, Byllye, 338
Avila, Ernestive, 495

Bacchi, C. L., 617, 621, 624
Baer, Judith, 249
Bagemihl, Bruce, 539
Baird, Karen L., 335
Bakare-Yusuf, Bibi, 862
Baker, Josephine, 215
Balsamo, Anne, 126, 130–131, 134, 139, 705
Banaszak, Lee Ann, 312–313, 377–378, 923
Bangladesh Rural Development Committee (BRAC), 156, 158–160, 447
Barad, Karen
  agential realism of, 54–56, 544, 683
  "intra-action" concept of, 136–137, 462–463, 545, 839
  new materialism of, 346, 360
  on practices of knowing, 847
Baranskaya, Natalya, 980
Barbie aesthetic, 666

"bare life," 64, 67, 69–70, 77, 741, 755
Barker, Drucilla, 185–186, 432
Barklow, Tanner King, 510
Barlas, Asma, 764
Barrett, Michelle, 460, 919
Barrientos, Stephanie, 435
Barthes, Roland, 27, 662
Bartky, Sandra, 218–220, 477–478, 485
Bartlett, Kathleen, 255
Bartman, Sarah, 215
Basu, Amrita, 992, 993
Basu, Soumita, 520
Baxi, Pratiksha, 1019
Baxi, Upendra, 1011–1012
Baze v. Rees, 1012
Beale, Frances, 388
beauty industry, 554
Beauvoir, Simone de
  on abstract individuals, 795
  on becoming sexual, 899
  on concept of experience, 228
  feminist opinion formation and, 634
  on gender as set of "acts," 574–575
  humanistic universalism and, 674, 857
  on identity, 241–243, 640
  misleading interpretations of, 841
  on religion, 766–768
  role of myth, 761
  on sexual assault, 215
  on social forces, 532–533
  theories of gender, 852, 865
  on the vagina, 224n3
  on women as "other," 348–349, 552
  on women's embodiment, 210–213
Bebel, August, 90
Bechdel, Alison, 556
Becker, Gary, 181
Beckwith, Karen, 312–313
Bedford, Kate, 196
Beijing Platform for Action, 319–320
Bejarano, Cynthia, 1024
Belkin, Aaron, 524
Bellour, Raymond, 783
Bell Scott, Patricia, 353
"beloved community," 593, 595
Beltrán, Cristina, 969
Benedict, Helen, 510

Beneria, Lourdes, 146
Benhabib, Seyla, 49, 610
Benjamin, Harry, 409
Benjamin, Jessica, 352
Benjamin, Walter, 653–654
Bennett, Jane, 468
Bennett, Judith, 979
Bentham, Jeremy, 724
Berger, John, 657
Bergeron, Suzanne, 992
Bergson, Henri, 54, 983
Berlant, Lauren, 17–18, 29, 34, 904
Berlin, Isaiah, 957, 959
Berry, Chris, 593
Bertelsen, Lone, 23, 26
Bevir, Mark, 306, 309
Beyoncé, 215
Beyond Economic Man: Feminist Theory and Economics (Ferber and Nelson), 430
Beyond God the Father, Toward a Philosophy of Women's Liberation (Daly), 769, 775
Bhabha, Homi, 101
Bickford, Susan, 641
The Big Feminist Porn Book (Taorimo et al), 661
Bilge, Sirma, 387, 404
Billig, M., 924
Biocapital: The Constitution of Postgenomic Life (Rajan), 845
bioethics, feminist, 327–329
biological determinism, 10, 116, 351, 462, 573, 763, 839, 890, 894
Biological Exuberance: Animal Homosexuality and Natural Diversity (Bagemihl), 539
biomediated body, 28
biophilia, 210, 216. *See also* embodiment
"Biophilia, Creative Involution and the Ecological Future of Queer Desire" (Chisholm), 541
bio-philosophy, 20–21
biopolitics
  affirmative theory of, 69–70
  biomediated body in, 28
  control as extension of, 21
  death-oriented interpretation of, 63–65, 76–77
  environmental qualities of, 69–70
  feminist critiques of, 67–75
  neoliberalism and, 32
  neoliberal turn and, 814–815
  reach of scholarship on, 63–67
  as scholarly term, 61–62
  sexual/reproductive regulation as, 65–67
biopower, governmentality and, 478–482. *See also* governmentality, Foucault's concept of
Birmingham School, 653–654, 667, 682
birth, as revelation/beginning, 708–709. *See also* fetal politics
"The Birth of Biopolitics" (Foucault), 480–481
Bitter Fruit: African-American Women in World War II (Honey), 511
Bjarnegård, Elin, 320–321
black Americans
  criminalization of, 728
  profiling of, 725
The Black Atlantic: Modernity and Double Consciousness (Gilroy), 166–168
black body. *See also* embodiment
  hair styles, 216
  in intersectional theorizing, 394
  racialized embodiment, 214–215
black cultural studies, 166. *See also* African American studies
black feminism, 8, 102, 104–106, 208, 214–216, 224, 230, 352–354, 380, 385, 387, 389–391, 397, 399–404, 416, 556, 564, 599–600, 641, 659, 736, 743, 791–792, 857, 864, 903, 915, 963
"A Black Feminist Statement" (Combahee River Collective), 230, 353. *See also* Combahee River Collective (CRC)
Blackman, Lisa, 21
black masculinity, 664, 733
Blackwell, Antoinette Brown, 533
Blackwell, Maylei, 995, 999, 1000
Blankenhorn, David, 254
Blavatsky, Madam, 771
"boat people," 167, 172
Bobo, Jacqueline, 659
Boderlands/La Frontera (Anzaldúa), 114, 353
"bodice-rippers," 655–656
Bodies That Matter: On the Discursive Limits of Sex (Butler), 126, 358, 542, 576

Bodily Natures: Science, Environment, and the Material Self (Alaimo), 545
body
  disciplining the female, 476–478
  health activism and, 335–337
Body & Society (journal), 21
body politic, politics of the body and, 207, 217–224
Bohr, Neils, 544, 839
Boillat, Sebastian, 537
border thinking, 101–102
Bordo, Susan, 209, 216–220
Bornstein, Kate, 408, 410, 413, 422
Boserup, Ester, 150, 181, 371
Boston Women's Health Care Collective, 334, 335–336, 643–644
Boswell, John, 895
Bosworth, Mary, 728
Bourdieu, Pierre, 52, 1024
Bourgois, Philippe, 1014
BRAC (Bangladesh Rural Development Committee), 156, 158–160, 447
Bradby, Hannah, 331
Bradwell v. Illinois, 249
Braidotti, Rosi, 28, 68–71, 75, 76–77, 135–137, 139, 346, 466, 537, 545, 615, 841–842
Braziel, Jana Evans, 177
"breadwinner," male as, 189, 194–195, 431–432, 616, 726
Brennan, Denise, 185
Brennan, Teresa, 23–25, 34
"bride trafficking," 498–499
Briggs, Laura, 148–149
British black feminism, 354
Brown, Wendy, 46, 247, 641, 949–950
Brownmiller, Susan, 234–235, 721, 907, 964
Brown v. Board of Education, 563
Brown Wendy, 921
Bruce, Steve, 775n1
Buddhism, 771. *See also* religion
bureaucratic politics model, 307, 613. *See also* policy/policy studies
Burkholder, Nancy Jean, 410
Bush, George W., 319, 563
Buszek, Mary Ann, 665
Butler, Judith. *See also* gender performativity
  on activism, 524
  on agency, 57
  cross-cultural analysis and, 49
  on existence of bodies, 542
  gender analysis/description of, 236, 552, 837–838, 861, 897
  on gender performativity, 44–46, 53–54, 218, 375
  "heterosexual matrix," 784
  on identity, 346, 347, 356, 357–358
  on identity politics, 641
  on militarization of affect, 519
  on nature/culture dichotomy, 859
  on *Paris is Burning*, 417
  on productive power, 475–476
  on resistance, 220, 483
  on sex/gender distinction, 841–842, 889
  on subject formation, 966–970
  on subversion of norms, 621
  trans and intersex feminisms and, 410
  view of the state, 918, 920
Butler, Octavia, 125
Bynum, Caroline Walker, 774

Cacho, Lisa, 741, 755
Cairo Conference on Population and Development, 319
CAIS (complete androgen insensitivity syndrome), 412
Califia, Pat, 908
Camacho, K. L., 513
Camera Obscura (journal), 2
Cameron, Jenny, 186
Campioni, Mia, 350
Canning, Kathleen, 460
Canovan, Margaret, 642
"Can the Subaltern Speak?" (Spivak), 109, 792
capitalism
  colonialism and, 112
  destructiveness of, 110
  economy of the household under, 432
  gendered markets and, 429–430
  posthumanism and, 135
  race as central to, 101
  social reproduction and, 179, 185, 187, 189–192, 200, 286, 290–293, 433, 440
  women's emancipation and, 156
Captive Genders: Trans Embodiment and the Prison Industrial Complex (Stanley), 223

Carbado, Devon, 393, 396, 398–399
Carbine, Rosemary, 940–941
Carby, Hazel, 400–401, 863
care, ethics of, 42–43
care work. *See also* social reproduction
   affective component of, 182–183
   capitalist spheres and, 186–192, 201
   commodification of, 184–186
   in formal labor markets, 192–197
   global care economy, 441–443
   visibility as economic activity, 179–182, 200
   work/life balance, 179, 195, 201
Caribbean studies, 166
Carreiras, Helen, 511
Carson, Rachel, 947
Cartwright, Lisa, 657
Case, Mary Ann, 253–254
Casement, Roger, 1015
Castillo, Ana, 353
Castoriadis, Cornelius, 634
Casualties of Care: Immigration and the Politics of Humanitarianism in France (Ticktin), 331
Catholic Church, 113, 709, 763, 768–769, 774, 809–811, 816, 975. *See also* religion
Centers for Disease Control and Prevention (CDC), 331
Centre for Contemporary Cultural Studies. *See* Birmingham School
Certeau, Michel de, 656
Césaire, Aimée, 100, 675
Chamallas, Martha, 247
Chappell, Louise, 319–320, 375
Charkiewicz, Ewa, 537
"charmed circle" of sexual behaviors, 560, 561*f*
Charrad, Mounira, 81–82
Chase, Cheryl, 408, 410, 412–413, 424
Chatterjee, Partha, 93, 101
Chavez, Cesar, 639
Cheah, Pheng, 57
Chibber, Vivek, 101, 108
Chicago, Judy, 224n3
Childs, Dennis, 1016
child-welfare system, 555
China, 1, 149, 314, 317–318, 321n1, 813, 820–821, 983, 986
Chinese Americans, 639, 752

Chinese Exclusion Act (1882), 752
Chisholm, Dianne, 541
Cho, Grace, 518
Chodorow, Nancy, 352, 855, 891n3
"choice," language of, 338
"choice feminism," 606
Chomsky, Noam, 757
Chow, Rey, 554, 558
Christ, Carol P., 772–774
Christensen, Kimberly, 335
Christianity, 555, 762, 764, 765, 769, 774. *See also* religion
Christianity, Social Tolerance, and Homosexuality: Gay People in Western Europe from the Beginning of the Christian Era to the Fourteenth Century (Boswell), 895
The Church and the Second Sex (Daly), 769
citizenship
   alien ineligibility, 752
   biopolitical/juridical, 68
   denial of, 750
civilization/civilizations
   concept of, 79–80
   contemporary context, 94
   as contextually unfolding, 86–87
   in 18th-century Enlightenment thought, 87–90
   "internal" debates on, 95
   as sociocultural entities, 80–82
   women in history of Islam, 81–82, 84–86, 92–93
   women in western civilization, 82–84
"civilizing missions," 91–94
civil rights activism, 388, 593–596, 598
civil society, 314–315
Cixous, Hélène, 357, 838, 891n5, 902
Clancy-Smith, Julia, 91
Clark, Anna, 789
Clarke, Averil, 402
Clark-Mane, Rebecca, 394
The Clash of Civilizations (Huntington), 80
classification/taxonomic systems, 2–4
Cleage, Pearl, 353
clientelism, 320
climate change, marginalized groups and, 270
Clinton, Bill, 563
Clinton, Hillary, 995, 1002

Clough, Patricia Tiniceto
    on affective turn, 19–21
    on affect studies methodology, 31–33
    on biomediated body, 28
    on temporality of affect, 27
Clover, Carol, 658
Clynes, Manfred, 123
Code, Lorraine, 943–944, 950
Cohen, Cathy, 416
Cohn, Carol, 508, 512, 517, 518, 521, 523, 1021
Colebrook, Claire, 546–548
Coleman, Rebecca, 18
Colen, Shellee, 817, 1001
"collaborative governance," 310
Collingwood, R. G., 241
Collins, Patricia Hill, 232–233, 353, 368, 380, 394, 556, 743, 906
colonialism, 91–94. *See also* anticolonial feminist theory
coloniality of gender, 116–119
"Colonial War and Mental Disorders" (Fanon), 1022
A Colored Woman in a White World (Terrell), 387
Combahee River Collective (CRC), 388, 389, 600–601, 603, 641, 900
Comics Code, 656
commercial surrogacy, 444–445
"Commercial Surrogacy in India: Manufacturing a Perfect Mother-Worker" (Pande), 445
Committee to End Sterilization Abuse, 337
"the commons," concept of, 457
Communist Party, 232
companion species theory, 137–138, 538, 545, 680
complete androgen insensitivity syndrome (CAIS), 412
compost, as figure/metaphor, 128
"Compulsory Heterosexuality and Lesbian Existence" (Rich), 351, 901
Connell, R. W., 368, 376, 857
Connelly, Matthew, 811, 813, 819
consciousness-raising groups, 231, 265, 484, 556, 597–599, 601, 603, 633, 637, 641, 645, 647n3, 768, 919, 934–935, 937, 961, 1024
conservative networks, in international forums, 319–321

Consortium on the Management of Disorders of Sex Development, 409
Constable, Nicole, 499
"Constitutional Law and Black Women" (Murray), 388
constitutive representation, 796–799. *See also* representation
constructivist materialism, 460
contextualization, in affect studies, 33–35
Coole, Diana, 922
Cooper, Anna Julia, 105, 387, 389
Cooper, Christine, 606
Cooper, Melinda, 686, 846
Coronil, Fernando, 866
Cott, Nancy, 750
Coulter, C., 513–514
Council on Ethical and Judicial Affairs (AMA), 337
counterhegemonic groups/publics, 46, 621, 624
Cover, Robert, 1012–1013
Cowie, Elizabeth, 781, 785–786
Crasnow, S., 271
"Creating Disturbance: Feminism, Happiness and Affective Differences" (Ahmed), 27
Crenshaw, Kimberlé, 105, 251–252, 353, 380, 385–387, 389–391, 395, 397, 601, 603–604, 730, 736, 743
CRG (constitutive representation of gender), 796–799
criminal punishment. *See also* prison/prisons
    class/identity and, 723–726
    norms and, 555
    power relations in, 722
critical theory, feminism and, 237–242
"Critique of the Sex/Gender Distinction" (Gatens), 887
cross-cultural analysis, role of resistance in, 46–50
cultural feminism, 351
The Cultural Politics of Emotions (Ahmed), 24
cultural representation, 235, 352, 360, 486, 652, 782–787. *See also* popular/visual culture
cultural vs. moral genitalia, 422–423
"The Culture Industry: Enlightenment as Mass Deception" (Adorno and Horkheimer), 653

"Culture of Terror-Space of Death" (Taussig), 1015
Curiel, Ochy, 865
Curtis, Edward S., 531
Cusicanqui, Silvia Rivera, 100, 115, 118
cybertypes/cybertyping, 131–132
Cybertypes: Race, Ethnicity, and Identity on the Internet (Nakamura), 131
cyborgs. *See also* "A Manifesto for Cyborgs: Science, Technology, and Socialist Feminism in the 1980s" (Haraway)
   as "companion species," 137–138, 545, 680
   in cultural theory, 129
   as figure for feminist theory/politics, 122–123, 133–134, 139–140
   gender technologies and, 129–131
   hybridity, notion of, 133–134, 136, 161, 168
   material-discursive domains of, 126–128
   metaphoric resonance of, 134–135
   racial inscriptions and, 131–133
Cyprus v. Turkey, 1018
Cyrus, Miley, 978

Daar, Abdallah S., 818
Dahl, Robert, 231
Dalsgaard Anne Line, 820
Daly, Mary, 351, 767–769, 772–773, 907
The Darker Side of the Renaissance (Mignolo), 101
Darwin, Charles, 54, 72, 464, 533, 539, 540, 683, 890, 978, 988
Darwinian feminism, 539
Das, Veena, 58, 1017
Daughters of Bilitis, 410
Daumas, Eugène, 91
Davis, Angela, 169, 214–215, 222, 335–336, 338, 645, 727, 729, 957, 961–966, 997, 1020
Davis, Dana-Ain, 335
Davis, Kathy, 336, 636
Dawkins, Richard, 126
Dayan, Colin, 167
death, as biopolitical, 63–65, 76–77
The Death of Nature: Women, Ecology, and the Scientific Revolution (Merchant), 535–536
Decade for Women, 316
Declaration of Sentiments and Resolutions (Seneca Falls conference), 249
decolonial feminism, 114–119
The Decolonial Imaginary (Perez), 114
decolonial theory, 111–114. *See also* colonialism
De Goede, Marieke, 446
Delaney, Samuel, 125
DeLargy, Pamela, 517
Deleuze, Gilles, 18, 20–21, 26–27, 29, 33, 394, 681, 838
Delphy, Christine, 456–458, 633, 789, 854–855
"Demarginalizing the Intersection of Race and Sex: A Black Feminist Critique of Antidiscrimination Doctrine, Feminist Theory and Antiracist Politics" (Crenshaw), 251, 385
denaturalization
   of difference, 4–6
   in feminist new materialism, 462–463, 467
   of feminized labor, 457–458, 460
   of gender/gendered body, 131, 380, 861
   of global political economy, 190
   in household labor, 181
   of identities, 356
   in norms/normalization, 556, 562, 565
   in queer studies/diasporas, 173
   of sex, 853
   of structures, 369
   subjectivity/subjectivation and, 956, 961
Densmore, Dana, 901
Dent, Gina, 997
"dependent," women's identity as, 189, 212, 351, 379, 432, 500, 728, 772, 882, 918, 937, 958, 960, 963
Der Derian, James, 518
Derrida, Jacques
   deconstruction theory of, 63
   on identity, 355
   on performativity, 573–577, 580, 585–586
   postcolonial theorists and, 107
   "there is no outside of text," 842–843
Desai, Manisha, 995
Descent of Man (Darwin), 533
descriptive representation, 781, 792, 794–796. *See also* representation
determinism, as agency concept, 40–41, 970. *See also* biological determinism
developmental systems theory (DST), 839

development/development policies
  experts role, 144–146
  gender/gendering in, 146–147, 152–155, 183
  NGO activities, 156–160
  reproduction and "welfare," 148–150
  structural adjustment programs (SAPs), 155–156
  theory/practice of, 143–144
  waged labor in, 150–152
  "women's standpoint," 160–161
Devereux, George, 808
The Dialectic of Sex (Firestone), 676
Diamond, Lisa, 904–905
Diamond, Milton, 412
diaspora
  in black cultural studies, 166–170
  queer, 173–176
  in racialized settings, 170–173
  term/concept of, 164–166
Diaspora: A Journal of Transnational Studies, 164
Di Chiro, Giovanna, 540
Dick, Kirby, 510
difference debates/dilemma, 4–6, 248, 250, 255, 465, 603–604, 792. *See also* sexual differences
difference feminism, 3–4, 5, 233, 838, 854, 874–875, 885, 887, 889–890, 902, 910
"The Dinner Party" (Chicago), 224n3
Dinnerstein, Dorothy, 330, 352
disability theory, 329–330
Disch, Lisa, 459–460, 940, 951–952
disciplinary power
  appropriations of, 476–478
  and the norm, 552–557
  violence and, 554–555
Discipline and Punish (Foucault), 477, 724–725
"Disembodying Women" (Duden), 701
Doane, Mary Ann, 658, 785
The Doctor's Case against the Pill (Seaman), 334
Does Khaki Become You? (Enloe), 508
"Doing Gender" (West and Zimmerman), 579, 587
Dolphijn, Rick, 466, 840
domestic work. *See* care work; labor/labor markets; migration

domination
  vs. power relations, 483
  system of, 232
Doniger, Wendy, 768
Don't Ask, Don't Tell policy, 510. *See also* militarization and war
"double-handicap," 387–388
Douglas, Susan J., 666–667
Dowd, Nancy, 255–256
Downer, Carol, 334
downloading (of responsibilities), 312–313
drag, Butler's analysis of, 44–46
Dreby, Joanna, 496, 502
Dred Scott decision, 753
Dreger, Alice. D., 408–410, 412
DuBois, W. E. B., 100, 392, 659
Dubriwny, Tasha, 341, 342
duCille, Ann, 400
Duden, Barbara, 702, 703, 705, 706, 707, 709, 711–712, 713
Duggan, Lisa, 927
Dussel, Enrique, 101, 115
Dworkin, Andrea, 235–236, 582, 584, 660, 860, 907
Dworkin, Ronald, 584
Dye, T. R., 612

Echols, Alice, 599, 900
Ecofeminism: Women, Animals, Nature (Gaard), 536
Ecofeminist Natures (Sturgeon), 536
ecological feminism/ecofeminism, 4, 682–683
Écrits (Lacan), 878
Eddy, Mary Baker, 771
Edelman, Lee, 541
Edwards, Brent Hayes, 164
Edwards, Penny, 91, 92
Egypt, mosque movement in, 47–48
Ehrenreich, Barbara, 184, 1020
Ehrlich, Paul, 812
Einhorn, Barbara, 315
Eisenstein, Hester, 994
Eisenstein, Zillah, 919
Elliott, Beth, 410
Elshtain, Jean Bethke, 509, 512
Elson, Diane, 190

"Eluding Capture: The Science, Culture, and Pleasure of 'Queer' Animals" (Alaimo), 540
embodiment
  biophilia, 210, 216
  body politic and, 216–217, 222
  female body practices, 218–219
  in feminist theory, 207–208
  male, 209
  philosophical traditions (Western), 208–210
  politics of, 8–9
  racialized, 214–217
  somatophobia, 207–208, 210, 214, 216, 224
emotion
  in affect studies, 23–24
  distinction from affect, 27–28
"emotional labor," 184, 193, 292, 444. *See also* care work; gendered divisions of labor
empirical adequacy thesis, 264, 266–268
employment, gender segregation in, 193–194
empowerment strategies, 2, 45, 49, 58, 81, 83, 92–93, 153–155, 198, 293, 315, 335, 447, 559, 603, 620–622, 624–625, 636, 746, 764, 773, 781, 799, 816, 917, 1002, 1022
Encountering Development: The Making and Unmaking of the Third World (Escobar), 145
"The Enemy of the Species" (McWhorter), 540
"The Enfranchisement of Women" (Mill), 348
Eng, David L., 173
Engels, Friedrich, 90, 350
England, Paula, 432
Enlightenment
  concept of civilization in, 87–90
  universal rights of, 5
Enloe, Cynthia, 508–512, 519, 1020, 1022
environmental feminisms, 534–537
environmental qualities
  of biopolitics, 69–70
  human-nonhuman entities and, 136
epistemic advantage thesis, 264, 272–275
Epistemology of the Closet (Sedgwick), 896
"The Equality Crisis: Some Reflections on Culture, Courts and Feminism" (Williams), 247
"equality-difference" debate. *See* difference debates/dilemma; sexual differences

equality feminism, 3–4, 854
Equal Protection Amendment (14th), 388
Erickson, Bruce, 540
Erndl, Kathleen, 773
Escobar, Arturo, 144–146, 160
essentialism
  nature as type of, 530
  strategic, 355, 864
Estrich, Susan, 945
estrogen, 543–544
ethical practices, in feminist science studies, 843–847
"ethics of care," 42, 233, 535, 958
ethnic cleansing, 172, 559, 563, 1019
eugenics/eugenics movement, 74, 480, 559, 834
Eurocentrism, 100, 102–103, 108–111, 113–116
European Feminisms 1700-1950: A Political History (Offen), 762
European Society for Pediatric Endocrinology, 409
Evans, Sara, 594–595, 599, 607*n*1
"The Evidence of Experience" (Scott), 241, 476
Evolution's Rainbow: Diversity, Gender, and Sexuality in Nature and People (Roughgarden), 539
Excitable Speech: A Politics of the Performative (Butler), 585, 587, 920
existentialism, 241
experience. *See also* consciousness-raising groups; feminist standpoint theory
  concept of, 227–228
  critical theory and, 237–242
  moral development theories, 12*n*1, 233, 854
  origins/development of, 228–234
  of sexual intercourse, 235
  sexuality debates and, 235–237
  of socialization, 233
  standpoint theory and, 231–232
experts, dependency on, 703–704

Fabre, C., 858
"false consciousness," 43, 350, 761, 766, 768
family formation, 106, 402, 445, 562–564, 819
"family wage," 431
Fannin, Maria, 704
Fanon, Frantz, 100, 659, 675, 678, 1015, 1022
Farmer, Paul, 1023

Farquar, Mary, 593
Fassin, Eric, 858
Fasteau, Marc, 508
Fausto-Sterling, Anne, 410, 412, 417, 461, 859
Featherstone, Lisa, 702
Featherstone, Mike, 32
Federici, Silvia, 457
Feinberg, Leslie, 408, 410
Feiner, Susan, 185–186, 432
Feldman, Shelley, 158
"Female Sexuality" (Freud), 875
femicide, 222, 866
The Feminine Mystique (Friedan), 349, 473, 917
"Femininity" (Freud), 875
Feminism and Science (Tuana), 833
Feminism Confronts Technology (Wajcman), 130–131
"Feminism's Apocalyptic Futures" (Wiegman), 346
Feminism Unmodified (MacKinnon), 581
Feminism Without Borders (Mohanty), 993–994
feminist bioethics, 327–329
Feminist Bioethics: At the Center, on the Margins (Scully et al.), 328
Feminist Bioethics: Beyond Reproduction (Wolf), 328
feminist civil society, 314–315
feminist disability theory, 329–330
feminist empiricism, 261, 263, 268, 275, 278. See also feminist standpoint theory
Feminist Genealogies, Colonial Legacies, Democratic Futures (Alexander and Mohanty), 992
feminist jurisprudence
  development of, 247–249
  gender and sexuality in, 252–253
  intersectionality theory in, 251–252
  masculinity studies and, 254–257
  from women's rights to, 249–251
feminist peace politics, 509
Feminist Politics and Human Nature (Jaggar), 349
feminist porn, 661–662
feminist psychoanalysis, 890–891
Feminist Review (journal), 2
feminist science studies, 537–539, 840–847. See also science/science studies

Feminist security studies (FSS), 520–521
feminist standpoint theory
  bias correction/minimization, 273
  empirical adequacy thesis, 264, 266–268
  epistemic advantage thesis, 264, 272–275
  as essentialist, 275–276
  female experience and, 231–232
  historical development of, 261–263
  interpretation/defense of, 264
  logical inconsistency claims, 278
  materialism in, 458–459
  methodological thesis, 264, 269–272
  normative commitment thesis, 264, 268–269
  objections to, 275–278
  participation of marginalized groups, 273
  risk of moral relativism, 277–278
  situated knowledge thesis, 264–266
  socially responsive science, 275, 276–277
Feminist Studies (journal), 2
feminist theory
  academic institutionalization of, 2
  classification/taxonomic systems, 2–4
  core themes, 3
  defining features, 2
  denaturalizing difference in, 4–6
  intersectionality in, 8
  origins, 1
  politics of embodiment in, 8–9
  situated knowledge in, 6–8
"feminization." See also care work
  of agriculture, 435, 438
  in international hierarchies, 89
  of migration, 439–441
  militarism and, 1020
  racialization parallels, 211
  of workforce/labor, 124, 179, 192–194, 197–200, 287–290, 294, 435–441, 994
La Femme Arabe (The Arab Woman) (Daumas), 91
Ferber, Marianne, 430
Ferguson, Kathy, 468
Fernández-Kelly, Patricia, 995
Ferree, Myra Marx, 622
fetal politics
  dependency on experts, 703–704
  feminist analysis of, 701

fetal politics (*Cont.*)
  from a feminist standpoint, 700
  fetal rights, 815
  governance and, 704–705
  pregnancy and, 702
  responsibility/reasonableness/rationality and, 704–705
  technologies and, 702–703
fetus/fetal emblems
  biological facts, 712–713
  birth, as revelation/beginning, 708–709
  historical depictions, 707
  as modern construct, 705–706
  in non-Western cultures, 709–710
  in visual culture, 710–712
Field, Connie, 511
Fifty Shades of Grey (James), 669
film/film theory, 783–787
financialization, concept of, 446–447
Fineman, Martha, 248
Fiorenza, Elisabeth Schüssler, 769
Firestone, Shulamith, 210, 212–213, 229, 351, 647*n*2, 676, 854, 900–901, 905, 907
Firth, Simon, 667
"The Five Sexes" (Fausto-Sterling), 412, 417
Flax, Jane, 352
Floyd, Nikol Alexander, 102
Folbre, Nancy, 181
"The Force of Fantasy: Feminism, Mapplethorpe, and Discursive Excess" (Butler), 346
Ford Foundation, 315, 318
Fording, Richard C., 798
formal sector, waged labor in, 150–152
"Foucault, Femininity and the Modernization of Patriarchal Power" (Bartky), 477
Foucault, Michel
  on autonomy/self-responsibility, 705
  biopolitical framework of, 21, 62–63, 557–559
  body/power relationship of, 207, 217–218
  on cultural production, 662
  "death of man," 678
  on desire, 237
  on disciplinary power, 552–554, 557
  on discipline/normalization, 221
  gender conceptualization, 573
  governmentality concept of, 304–305, 375
  on health, 326
  ideas of agency, 54
  on identity, 355
  postcolonial theorists and, 107
  on practices of the self, 47
  on prisons/punishment, 724–728
  productive power, 473–476
  "regimes of truth," 659
  on resistance, 482–486
  on role of power, 898
  on sexuality, as regulated, 553
  silence on gender, 67–68, 75
  on subjectivity, 955–956
  on subversion of norms, 621
Fox, Richard, 373
Fraad, H., 189
Frank, Adam, 25
Franke, Katherine, 253, 257*n*2
Frankfurt School, 653, 723
Franklin, Sarah, 682, 702, 705, 713
Fraser, Nancy, 57, 297, 482, 610, 621
freedom, politics as practice of, 644–645
Freeman, Carla, 194
Freeman, Jo, 597
Freire, Paolo, 816
French feminist theory, 227–228, 241, 242–243*n*1
Freud, Sigmund, 24, 351–352, 783, 874–878, 888, 890–891
Friedan, Betty, 349, 473, 854
Friedberg, Anne, 659
Friedman, Susan Sanford, 637
"From Private Violence to Mass Incarceration: Thinking Intersectionally about Women, Race, and Social Control" (Crenshaw), 389
"From State Feminism to Market Feminism" (Kantola and Squires), 313
Frontiers (journal), 2
Frost, Samantha, 346, 464, 922
Frye, Marilyn, 419
Fugitive Flesh: Gender Self-Determination, Queer Abolition, and TransResistance" (Stanley), 223
Fujimura, Joan, 465
Futures of Reproduction: Bioethics and Biopolitics (Mills), 73

Gaard, Greta, 536
GAD (gender and development), 144, 152–155. *See also* development/development policies
Gadamer, Hans-Georg, 987
Gage, Frances Dana, 791–792
Gamble, Elizabeth Burt, 533
Gammeltoft, Tine, 710
Gamson, W. A., 622
Gandhi, Leela, 109
Garcilaso de la Vega, Inca, 101, 112
Gardner, Paula, 340, 341
Garfinkel, Harold, 422, 579–580
Garland-Thomson, Rosemarie, 330, 660
Gatens, Moira, 34, 209, 887–889
gay drag, Butler's analysis of, 44–46
gay identity. *See also* trans and intersex feminisms
    diaspora studies, 173–176
    homophobia and, 790
    politics of, 54
Geertz, Clifford, 772
Geiger, Susan, 6
gender. *See also* gender performativity
    as citational practice, 218, 577
    coloniality of, 116–119
    concept of, 532, 852–853
    cyborgs and, 124
    in definitions of crime, 726–727
    in development policies, 146–147
    as distinct from sex, 573
    as "doing," 578–581, 587
    in era of globocentrism, 866–867
    in formal labor market participation, 192–197
    in informal economy, 197–200
    institutions and, 370–371
    in medical discourses, 852–853
    men/masculinities in theories of, 857–858
    "New Jim Crow" and, 754
    racial hierarchy and, 89
    in racialization process, 743
    second-wave feminist on, 853–856
    sex/sexuality distinction, 858–860
    sexuality studies distinction, 252–253
    technologies of, 129–131

gender and development (GAD), 144, 152–155. *See also* development/development policies
"Gender and Symbolic Violence" (Bourdieu), 1024
Gender and the Military: Women in the Armed Forces of Western Democracies (Carreiras), 511
"Gender: A Useful Category of Historical Analysis" (Scott), 764
"gender confirmation" surgery, 418
gendered divisions of labor
    concept of, 284–286
    feminist theory and, 283–284
    feminization of labor, 287–290
    global care chains, 290–292
    neoliberalism and, 292–295
    research/alternatives, 295–297
Gendered Innovations in Science, Health and Medicine, Engineering and Environment, 836
gendered norms
    as decontextualized, 578
    as racialized, 551, 554–556, 565–566
"Gender for a Marxist Dictionary" (Haraway), 467
gender/gender binarism
    in hegemonic feminism critiques, 864–866
    social movement critiques of, 860–861
    universalized account critiques, 861–864
gendering
    abortion policy and, 617
    colonialism and, 114, 119
    in development policies, 146–147, 152–155, 183
    dynamics of, 9
    in global finance, 446–447
    of labor markets, 436
    in militarization and war, 510–512
    as political construct/process, 4
gender mainstreaming, 154, 321, 372, 623–624
gender norms/normativity
    in affect studies, 19
    in care work, 185
    challenging hegemonic norms, 666
    in Christian gender regimes, 765
    communication technology and, 496

gender norms/normativity (*Cont.*)
  in fourth wave feminism, 978
  identity and, 352, 644, 884
  in intersectional theorizing, 8, 252
  in labor, 295
  marriage migration and, 497–500, 502
  patriarchal power and, 484–485
  in penal discipline, 727
  political critiques of, 474
  posthumanism and, 687
  psychical differences, 877, 880
  in queer studies/diasporas, 174, 414, 541, 861
  racialization in, 551, 554–557, 565–566, 757
  sex/gender distinction and, 887–888
  sexuality and, 254
  subjectivity/subjectivation and, 968
  trans and intersex oppression, 419
Gender Outlaw (Bornstein), 410
gender performativity
  as accountable, 580
  Butler on, 44–46, 54, 128, 218, 358–359, 576, 988
  as citationality, 577
  concept of, 572–578, 586–588
  "doing gender," 578–581, 587
  "happy" performatives, 577, 585
  hate speech and, 584–586
  language and, 581
  pornography and, 581–584
  in queer theory/studies, 586–587
Gender Politics and MTV: Voicing the Difference (Lewis), 664
gender segregation, in employment, 193–194
gender self-determination, 223
gender socialization, 180, 262, 371
"gender trespassing," 223
Gender Trouble: Feminism and the Subversion of Identity (Butler), 236, 358, 475–476, 572–576, 586, 837
gender variance. *See* trans and intersex feminisms
Generalized Other, 41
genitalia, cultural vs. moral, 422–423
Georges, Eugenia, 703
Gershik, Zsa Zsa, 510
Giffney, Noreen, 540
Giles, W., 517

Gilligan, Carol, 42, 233, 854
Gilman, Charlotte, 283
Gilman Sander, 215
Gilmore, Ruth Wilson, 754
Gilroy, Paul, 164, 166–168, 675, 679
Ginsburg, Ruth Bader, 255, 257n4
"girl power," 666–667
Gitlin, Todd, 639, 642, 647n4
Glenn, Evelyn Nakano, 190
global care chains, 290–292
Global Divas: Filipino Gay Men in the Diaspora (Manalansan), 174
global feminism, 638
global finance, gendering and, 446–447
globalization. *See also* transnational feminism
  vs gendered global restructuring, 433
  neoliberal, 305, 311, 314–315, 321, 441, 518, 866
  neoliberal policies and, 434–436
Gluck, Sherna B., 511
goddess religions, 771–774
Goetz, Anne Marie, 159
Goffman, Erving, 578–580
Goldberg, David Theo, 558, 754
Goldman, Emma, 283, 508
Goldstein, Joshua, 517, 519
Göle, Nilüfer, 93
González, Jennifer A., 133
Goodbye Gauley Mountain: An Ecosexual Love Story (Stephens), 541
The Good-Natured Feminist: Ecofeminism and the Quest for Democracy (Sandilands), 536
"good theory," 21, 236
Gopinath, Gayatri, 170, 173–176
Gorton, Kristyn, 17
gossett, hattie, 906
Gossip, Markets, and Gender (Pietilä), 430
Gouges, Olympe de, 1
governance
  bureaucratic politics model, 307, 613
  civil society, 314–315
  concept of, 304, 321
  conservative networks and, 319–321
  feminist critiques of, 311–314
  gendered effects of, 310–311
  gendered networks in, 318–321

"good governance" problem, 309–310
governing levels, 308–309
governing mechanisms, 307–308
multiple actors in, 306–307
neoliberal roots of, 309–310
NGO activities, 315–318
organizational process model, 307
as praxis, 305–306
rational actor model, 307, 613
"governance feminism," 248
Governance without Government (Rosenau), 308
governmentality, Foucault's concept of, 304–305, 478–482, 486n7
Graham, Allison, 614
Graham, J., 191
Graham-Gibson, J. K., 191
Grameen Bank, 156, 158, 160, 447
Gramsci, Antonio, 107, 111, 239
Grant, Judith, 3, 950
Gray, Linda, 950
Gray, R. D., 839
Greer, Germaine, 412, 901
Gregg, Melissa, 22, 25
Gregory, John, 89
Grewal, Inderpal, 992, 993
Griffin, Susan, 534, 536
Griffiths, P. E., 839
Grimshaw, Jean, 675
Gross, Rita M., 770, 773
Grossberg, Lawrence, 24, 33, 363n18
Grosz, Elizabeth, 28, 53–54, 56, 346–347, 350, 464–465, 539, 689, 838, 988
Grove, Jairus, 519
Grrrll culture, 978
Guamán Poma de Ayala, Felipe, 101, 112
Guattari, Felix, 18, 20, 26–27, 29, 33, 394, 681
Guha, Ranajit, 101, 993, 1015
Gunderson, Gregory, 513
Gun-Free Kitchen Tables, 523
Gunn, Sakia, 222
Gunn Allen, Paul, 114–115
Gunnarsson, Lena, 468
Gyn/Ecology (Daly), 902
"gynesis," 12
"gynocriticism," 11–12

Ha, Trinh T. Minh, 169
hair styles, of black women, 216
Halberstam, Judith/Jack, 904
Hall, Stuart, 401, 662, 664
Halley, Janet, 248, 254
Hambly, Gavin R. G., 84
Hames-García, Richard, 466
Hammer, Zoe, 997
Hampson, Daphne, 774
Hancock, Ange-Marie, 401–402, 660
Haney Lopez, Ian, 615, 749, 751
Hanisch, Carole, 633
Hanna, Kathleen, 978
"happy" performatives, 577, 585
Haraway, Donna
    companion species theory, 129, 137–139, 545
    cyborg analogy of, 133–135
    "A Cyborg Manifesto," 122–125, 135
    feminist science studies, 537–539
    on gendered subjects, 615
    influence of, 410
    on informal economy, 199
    on late capitalism, 131
    material agency model of, 544
    on materialism, 467
    material-semiotic concept of, 462, 841
    naturecultures, conception of, 842
    as posthuman thinker, 679–680
Harding, Sandra, 232, 675, 856, 937
Hardt, Michael, 184, 444
Harlequin Romances, 655
harmonia, 12n1
Harper, Frances E. W., 353
Harris, Angela, 732, 736
Harry Benjamin International Gender Dysphoria Association (HBIGDA), 409
Harry Benjamin Standards of Care, 409
Hartman, Saidiya, 169–170, 1012
Hartmann, Betsy, 812
Hartmann, Heidi, 187–188
Hartouni, Valerie, 716
Hartsock, Nancy, 188, 231–233, 391, 458, 636–637
Hashemi, Syed M., 156
Hashmi, Taj I., 159
Häsler, Sabine, 537
hate speech, 584–586

Hawkesworth, Mary, 643, 798
Hayden, Casey, 596–597
Hayden, Tom, 593
Hayles, N. Katherine, 126–128, 135–136
The Hays Code, 656
Hayward, Eva, 546, 686
"head of household," 379, 432
health, in feminist theory
    achievement era, 333, 340–341
    bioethics, 327–329
    disability theory, 329–330
    health activism, 332–333
    healthism, 341
    inclusion era, 333, 335
    neoliberalism and, 339
    Our Bodies, Our Selves, 335–337, 636–637
    resistance era, 333, 335
    self-regulation in, 340–341
    shifting concepts of, 333–335
    social science approaches, 330–332
    structures, prioritization of, 337–339
healthcare, right to, 326–328
Healy, Stephen, 186
Healy, Bernadine, 337
Heath, Stephen, 783
Hegel, Georg Wilhelm Friedrich, 112, 652
hegemonic norms, challenging, 665–668
Hegemony and Socialist Strategy (Mouffe and Laclau), 635
Heidegger, Martin, 979, 987
Hekman, Susan, 347, 349, 355, 544, 844
Held, Virginia, 42
Hemmings, Clare, 3, 30–32, 34, 347, 360, 910
Hennessy, Rosemary, 460
Herdt, Gilbert, 896
Herland (Perkins), 986
hermaphrodite. *See* trans and intersex feminisms
Herndon, April M., 408–409, 414
Hernes, Helga Maria, 917
"Heterogeneity, Hybridity, Multiplicity: Making Asian American Differences" (Lowe), 168
heteronormativity, 45, 116, 160, 173–175, 183, 185–186, 196, 201, 254, 340, 409, 413–414, 451, 516, 535, 539, 573, 575, 577, 587, 615–617, 621, 624–625, 656, 661, 664, 668, 856, 859, 861, 863, 927

heteropatriarchy, 382, 551, 557, 559–560, 564. *See also* patriarchy
heterosexism, 262, 264, 388, 459, 535, 566, 926, 955, 966
"Heterosexualism and the Colonial Modern Gender System" (Lugones), 116
Heyes, Cressida, 419, 484–485
Heyzer, Noeleen, 436
Highmore, Ben, 31
Hill, Anita, 582
Hill Collins, Patricia, 106, 730–733, 736
Himmelweit, Susan, 184
Hinduism, 773, 797. *See also* religion
Hinton, Peta, 463
Hird, Myra J., 539, 540
Hirschman, Linda, 606
Hirschmann, Nancy J., 957–961
"History" (Spivak), 792
history, women's representation in, 787–791
The History of Sexuality (Foucault), 62, 473, 479, 482, 483
History of the Women's Health Movement (Ruzek), 333
Hitchcock, Alfred, 657
Hobbes, Thomas, 208–209, 217, 1011
Hochschild, Arlie, 184–185, 444, 494
Holland, Sharon Patricia, 745
Hollywood film, 657–658, 662, 783, 785
Holmes, Morgan, 414
The Holy Family (Marx and Engels), 90
Home, Henry, 88
homo economicus conception, 431
homonationalism, 916, 927, 998
homoprotectionism, 916
homosociality, 320–321
Hondagneu-Sotelo, Pierrette, 491, 495
Honey, Maureen, 511
Honig, Bonnie, 50–51
hooks, bell, 193, 215, 222, 353, 641, 659, 792
Hoque, Serajul, 159
Horkheimer, Max, 238, 241, 653–654
Hoshino, Lina, 519
household labor. *See also* care work
    migrating women and, 439–441
    theories of, 180–181
    unpaid, 180
households, economy of, 432–433

How to Do Things with Words (Austin), 576, 585
Huggins, Jackie, 354
Hull, Gloria T., 352, 389
human-nonhuman relation, 134–139. *See also* cyborgs
human papilloma virus (HPV) vaccines, 270, 1002
human rights, 804
Huntington, Samuel, 80–81
Hutchings, Kimberly, 43
hybridity, notion of, 133–134, 136, 161, 168
hypermasculinity, culture of, 732
hyphenation model, 2–3

Icons of Life (Morgan), 711
identity/identities
    black feminism on, 352–354
    Chicana/Latina feminists on, 353–354
    domination/subordination and, 349, 352
    essentialism and, 355
    as gendered, 358
    gendered/racial oppression and, 348
    as intersectional, 353
    language/linguistics in, 357
    lesbianism, 351
    liberal feminism on, 349–350
    as multifaceted, 353
    new materialism on, 346–347, 360
    ontological focus, 360
    postcolonial feminism on, 354–355
    in poststructuralist feminism, 355–357, 359
    psychoanalysis on, 351–352
    radical feminism on, 350–351
    for socialist feminists, 350
    term usage, 347
    as universalized, 350
    as Western humanist supposition, 348
    women of color feminism on, 354
"identity-invalidation," 420
identity politics. *See also* personal is political
    Arendt on, 640
    crisis/criticism of, 639–640
    Gitlin on, 639
    Hekman on, 355
    Kruks on, 362n9
    literature on, 638–642
    in multicultural societies, 646, 647n4
    politically constituted character and, 640
    postidentity agency, 50–52
"Identity: Skin, Blood, Heart" (Pratt), 603
identity tourism, 131–132
"I'd Rather Be a Cyborg Than a Goddess: Becoming Intersectional in Assemblage Theory" (Puar), 396
Ignatieff, Michael, 1012
Illinois, Bradwell v., 249
illocutionary speech/acts, 581, 583, 585, 588n11
immigration, diaspora and, 164, 169
immigration law, 172, 500, 563–564, 751–753
Imperial Leather (McClintock), 105
Impossible Desires: Queer Diasporas and South Asian Public Cultures (Gopinath), 173
In a Different Voice: Psychological Theory and Women's Development (Gilligan), 233, 854
inclusion, politics of, 106, 335
"Incorporating Gender in Research on Indigenous Environmental Knowledge in the Tunari National Park in the Bolivian Andes" (Serrano et al), 537
Increasing the Participation and Advancement of Women in Academic Science and Engineering Careers (ADVANCE), 835
incrementalist models, 613. *See also* policy/policy studies
indeterminacy, 26–27
indigenous feminism, 4, 117, 536, 566, 1000–1001
industrial production, 438
informal economy, 197–200. *See also* care work
information sciences/theory, in biopolitics, 71–73
information systems, virtual bodies and, 126–128
Inglehart, Ronald, 81
Inhorn, Marcia, 330–332
Inman, Mary, 534
inside-out/outside-in model critique, 24–26
institutions
    anti-discrimination policies in, 372–373
    biological sex and, 371–373
    conceptualization of, 367
    dynamism in, 376–377

institutions (Cont.)
    formal vs. informal, 377–378
    gender and, 370–371
    gendered, 373–374
    intersectional analysis and, 372–373, 380–382
    pay inequity in, 372–373
    power/patriarchy in, 374–376
    as producers of gender, 378–380
    structural analysis of, 368–370
    term usage, 367
"Integrating Gender into the World Bank's Work: A Strategy for Action" (World Bank), 154
interactive service labor, 291–292
Intercourse (Dworkin), 235
interculturality, 115
International Labor Organization (ILO), 153, 197
International Monetary Fund (IMF), 154, 183, 309, 434, 440, 991
International Women's Health Coalition (IWHC), 1002–1003
International Women's Year, 316
intersectionality
    anticolonial theory and, 104–107
    assemblage concept in, 394
    central problems of, 391
    diaspora and, 164
    emergence of, 385
    equivalent oppressions and, 394
    feminist jurisprudence and, 251–252
    identity theories in, 353, 380–382, 386, 390, 392
    intellectual genealogies of, 387–389
    as methodology, 400–405
    paradigmatic black female subject, 397–400
    political intersectionality, 386
    politics of embodiment and, 8–9
    postintersectional discourses, 400
    on prisons/punishment, 729–733
    in public policy, 623–624
    race/racialization approaches, 742–745
    state-based recognition and, 395–396
    systems of power and, 389
    term usage, 385
    term usage/definition of, 385, 391
    trans/intersex feminisms and, 415–417
    universalizing tendency, 403–404
    in war and militarization, 516–517
Intersex Society of North America (ISNA), 408, 410–412, 414
intersexuality, medical intervention and, 408–409. *See also* trans and intersex feminisms
intimate labor, 184. *See also* care work
Into Our Own Hands (Morgen), 333
The Invisible War (Dick), 510
in-vitro reproduction, 213, 543
Irigaray, Luce
    on abstract ideal of Man, 678
    on identity, 213–214, 356–357
    psychoanalysis categories and, 855
    on sex/gender distinction, 838
    on sexual difference, 539, 874, 880–886, 888–890, 891n4, 902
Irni, Sara, 467
Iskra, Darlene, 511
Islam. *See also* religion
    approach to women's rights/gender equality, 81–82
    Huntington's representation of, 80–81
    media coverage of, 775
    Qur'anic teachings, 764
    Sisters in Islam, 762
    women in history of, 84–86, 92–93
Islamaphobia, 47
Is the Goddess a Feminist? (Hiltebeitel and Erndl), 773
It Ain't Me Babe (comic), 665

Jackson, John, 664
Jackson, Patrick Thaddeus, 86
Jacobs, Amber, 890
Jacobson, R., 517
Jaggar, Alison, 349, 676
James, E. L., 669
"Jane Crow," 388
Japanese Americans, 753
Jayawardena, Kumari, 1
Jeffreys, Sheila, 775
Jenkins, Henry, 656
Jessop, Bob, 428
Jezebel.com, 978

Jim Crow, 754
Johnson, Barbara, 788–789
Johnson, Ericka, 546
Johnson, Lyndon B., 594
Jones, Ann Rosalind, 902
Joseph, Gloria, 188
Judd, Karen, 807
Jung, Karl, 989
juridical power, 396
juridical illegibility, 392
jurisprudence. *See* feminist jurisprudence

Kabeer, Naila, 154
Kannabiran, K. G., 1011
Kant, Immanuel, 979
Kantola, Johanna, 313–314
Kaplan, Amy, 993
Kaplan, Caren, 992, 993
Kaplan, E., 785
Karim, Lamia, 157
Kaufman-Osborn, Timothy, 1011, 1013, 1021
Kearns, Thomas, 1011, 1012
Keating, Christine, 927
Keller, Helen, 508
Keller, Mary, 763
Kelly, Joan, 675, 984
Kenney, Sally, 370, 377
Kenny, Meryl, 377
Kessler, Suzanne, 6, 410, 422, 580
Khanna, Ranjana, 29–30
Kim, Minjeong, 499
Kimmel, Michael, 255, 857–858
King, Deborah, 388
King, Martin Luther, 593, 595, 639
King, Mary, 596–597
Kinsella, Helen, 95
Kirby, Vicky, 346, 842–843
Kirk, Gwen, 513
Kitch, Sally, 743
Kitchen Table Press, 389
Klein, Nathan, 123
Kleinbaum, Abby, 84
Kleinman, Arthur, 1017, 1023–1024
knowledge, situation of, 6–8, 264–266
Koedt, Anne, 229, 901
Kohlberg, Lawrence, 233
Koivunen, Anu, 19, 30

Kolko, B. E., 131–132
Kolodny, Annette, 536
Kontopoulos, Kyriakos, 102
Koobak, Redi, 546
Korematsu v. United States, 753
Koyama, Emi, 415, 417, 418, 419
Kristeva, Julia, 357, 767–768, 987–988
Krizsan, Andrea, 622–623
Kronsell, Annica, 523
Kruger, Barbara, 531–532
Kruks, Sonia, 241, 362n9, 454
Kurzweil, Ray, 126
Kwan, Peter, 390–391, 396

labor/labor markets. *See also* care work; gendered divisions of labor; markets/marketization
  affective labor, 444–446
  family vs. industrial modes, 456–457
  feminization of, 179, 194, 197–200, 287–290, 438, 994
  gendered operations and, 192–197
  sexual division of, 130
Lacan, Jacques, 355, 658, 874–875, 877–882, 890
Lacanian psychoanalysis/theory, 11, 776n7, 785, 855, 878, 967
Laclau, Ernesto, 635, 637
Lairap, Josephine, 447
Lamble, Sarah, 733–735
Lander, Edgardo, 114
Langton, Rae, 582–584, 587
language
  gender performativity and, 581
  hate speech and, 584–586
  pornography and, 581–584
  role in identity, 357
Laqueur, Thomas, 5, 859
Lasswell, Harold, 231
lateral loading (of responsibilities), 312–313
Latour, Bruno, 11, 542
Lauretis, Teresa de, 356
law enforcement, hypermasculinity in, 732. *See also* prison/prisons
Lawless, Jennifer, 373
Lawson Wilkins Pediatric Endocrine Society, 409
The Lay of the Land (Kolodny), 536

Lean In (Sandburg), 373
legal rights, 804
Leithauser, Marcia, 511
lesbians/lesbianism
　identity/identities, 351
　in military, 510
　self-definition in, 410–411
　women's sexuality and, 900
Leviathan (Hobbes), 1011
Levi-Strauss, C, 239, 785, 786, 853–854
Levit, Nancy, 256
Lewis, Lisa A., 664
liberal feminism, 2, 4, 192, 349–350, 551, 884, 900, 918, 957
The Life and Times of Rosie the Riveter (Field), 511
Life as Surplus: Biotechnology and Capitalism in the Neoliberal Era (Cooper), 846
Life Un(Ltd): Feminism, Bioscience, Race, 844
Lind, Amy, 927
Lindsay, Beverly, 388
Lioness (film), 510
Liviatan, Ofrit, 809
Living Along the Fenceline (film), 519–520
Lloyd, Genevieve, 675
Lloyd, Moya, 920
locational feminism, 636–637
Locke, John, 957
locutionary speech, 581
Löffler, Marion, 921
Lombardo, E., 617, 622–623
The Lonely Soldier: The Private War of Women Serving in Iraq (Benedict), 510
Longino, H., 267
"loosers/choosers" paradigm, 43
López, Iris, 820
Lorde, Audre, 103, 125, 230, 602–604, 641, 745, 903, 906, 999
Lose Your Mother: A Journey along the Atlantic Slave Routes (Hartman), 169
Lott, Eric, 664
Louverture, Toussaint, 675
Love, Heather, 34
Love and Theft (Lott), 664
Loving v. Virginia, 751
Loving with a Vengeance (Modleski), 655
Lowe, Lisa, 168–169, 170, 172

Lowi, Theodore, 796
Lu, Melanie, 500
Lucashenko, Melissa, 354
Lugones, Maria, 100, 102, 115–118, 865–866
Luibhéid, Eithne, 998
Lukacs, Georg, 232
Lukes, S., 618
Lury, Celia, 682
Luxemburg, Rosa, 508, 962

MacKinnon, Catherine, 231, 235–237, 253, 376, 582, 584–585, 587, 660–661, 860, 907, 918, 1018–1019
Madianou, M., 495–496
Mahmood, Saba, 47–49, 220–221
Mahoney Martha, 945
"mail-order bride," 498
mainstreaming. *See* gender mainstreaming
The Making of the English Working Class (Thompson), 241
Making Sex (Laqueur), 859
Maldonado-Torres, Nelson, 101, 114
male breadwinner model, 189, 194–195, 431–432, 616, 726
male gaze, 18, 207, 210, 478, 657–658, 660, 665
male networking, 320
Malkki, Liisa, 993
Malraux, Andre, 675
Malthus, Thomas Robert, 148, 812
The Managed Heart (Hochschild), 444
Manalansan, Martin, 173–174, 185, 998
Mandela, Nelson, 675
Mander, Jenny, 88
Maneuvers (Enloe), 511
"A Manifesto for Cyborgs: Science, Technology, and Socialist Feminism in the 1980s" (Haraway), 122–125, 135, 467, 538, 680
Mansbridge, Jane, 795
Man's Dominion (Jeffreys), 775
Man's Fate (Malraus), 675
"Mapping the Margins: Intersectionality, Identity Politics and Violence against Women of Color" (Crenshaw), 251, 381, 386
Marchand, M., 433, 435

Marcuse, H., 962
margins, studying from the, 264, 269–271
Margulis, Lynn, 689
Mariátegui, José Carlos, 101
market feminism, 313, 916, 923
markets/marketization
    affective labor, 444–446
    agriculture production, 437
    financialization and, 446
    gendered global restructuring, 433
    gendered nature of, 430, 448
    global care economy, 441–444
    homo economicus conception, 431
    industrial production, 438
    "male breadwinner," invention of, 431
    market sociology, 433
    migrating women, 439–441
    neoclassical economic theory, 429
    re-gendering of labor markets, 436
    service sector, 439
    sex tourism, 443–444
    in social relations, 429
    in vocabulary/speech, 428
marriage laws, 379, 431
marriage migration, 497–501, 502–503
marriage practices, 750, 854
marriage rights/advocacy, 559–564
Martin, Biddy, 603
Martin, Emily, 331
Marx, Karl, 41, 90, 805, 824
Marxist theories
    on human reproduction, 805
    ideology critique in, 652
    materiality in, 456
    on unpaid household labor, 180–181, 187
masculinity/masculinity studies
    feminist jurisprudence and, 254–257
    law enforcement and, 732–733
Massumi, Brian, 25–26, 27, 29, 30, 31–32, 34, 744
"The Master's Tools Will Never Dismantle the Master's House" (Lorde), 602
material feminisms
    emergence of, 890
    nature and, 542–548
Material Feminisms (Alaimo and Hekman), 844

materialisms
    the commons, concept of, 457
    constructivist materialism, 460
    difference, valuation of, 465–467
    feminist new materialism (FNM), 461–467
    feminist poststructuralist approaches and, 459–460
    feminist standpoint theory and, 459
    in feminist theory, 454–455
    historical materialist feminisms (HMF), 455–461
    materiality of women's labor, 456–457
    metaphysical intervention in, 462, 464
    networked agency in, 463
    oppression and, 458–459
    power/responsibility relations in, 463–464
    race/racism and, 466–467
    signification and, 461
material-semiotics, 124, 126, 132, 135, 462–463, 538, 840–841, 843
maternalism, culture of, 494
Maternal Thinking: Toward a Politics of Peace (Ruddick), 509
Matsuda, Mari, 585
Mayeri, Serena, 249
Mazur, Amy, 313
Mbembe, Achille, 137, 221–223, 224
McBride, Dorothy, 313
McBride, Renisha, 222, 756
McCall, Leslie, 251, 401–402
McClintock, Anne, 92, 105
McDonagh, Eileen, 714
McDonald, Cameron, 492, 494
McDowell, Linda, 195, 291–292
McKenna, Wendy, 6, 410, 422, 580
McKittrick, Katherine, 747
McLagan, Meg, 510
McLaren, Margaret, 484
McLeod, Laura, 521
McNay, Lois, 482
McPherson, Tara, 132
McRobbie, Angela, 57, 666–668
McWhorter, Ladelle, 356, 480, 540
Mead, Margaret, 852
"The Meaning of Freedom" (Davis), 645
media/media worlds
    cyborgs in, 129–133, 135

media/media worlds (*Cont.*)
  Eurocentric bias in, 110
  feminist scholarship and, 16, 17
  framing by, 341
  hegemonic gaze and, 659–660
  Islamic culture and, 82, 775
  male domination of, 599
  on militarization, 523
  new media representations, 668–670, 682
  promotion of norms, 554
  racialized criminalization, 755, 758
  representations of women, 556, 665
  seduction of the public, 653–654, 656
  stereotypes in, 663, 787
  storytelling and, 941–942, 950
  on structural violence, 1023
  on women's migration, 497–498
medicalization, of women's bodies, 644. *See also Our Bodies, Our Selves* (Boston Women's Health Collective)
Mehta, Brinda, 170
Meier, P., 617
Meloy, Ellen, 541
Mendoza, Breny, 114, 865
men's rights movements (MRMs), 815
menstruation, 210, 212–213, 331, 336, 340, 351, 411, 901
Merali, Zara, 818
Merchant, Carolyn, 535
Meridians: Feminism, Race, Transnationalism (journal), 992
Merleau-Ponty, Maurice, 888
mestiza consciousness, 413, 903–904, 910, 939
methodological thesis, 264, 269–272
methodology
  in affect studies, 31–33
  contextualization as, 35
Methodology of the Oppressed (Sandoval), 134, 140n5
Mexican Americans, 750–751, 753
MHRMs (men's human rights movements), 815
Michaels, Meredith W., 716
Michelet, Athénaïs, 788
Michigan Womyn's Music Festival, 410–411
microcredit, 154–160, 198–200, 293, 794, 994
microfinance, 155–156, 293, 318, 447

microphysics of power
  biopower/governmentality in, 478–482
  concept of, 472–474
  disciplining the female body, 476–478
  productive power, 474–476
  resistance, 482–486
Middle East, gender equality and, 82. *See also* Islam
Mignolo, Walter, 101–102, 114, 115
migration
  capitalism and, 490
  for domestic work, 492–494
  feminization of, 439–441
  gendered nature of, 490–491, 501
  marriage migration, 497–501, 502–503
  transnational mothering, 495–497
Milan Women's Bookstore Collective, 886
militarization and war
  "add women and stir" approach, 509–510
  feminist critiques of, 1020–1021
  "feminist curiosity" in, 512
  feminist explorations of, 517–519
  feminist literature on, 508–509
  gender, approach to, 514–515, 524
  gendering of, 510–512
  intersectional theory in, 516–517
  "let us in" approach, 512–514
  as overtly political, 512–513
  research/activism on, 521–524
  scholarship dilemmas, 509–510
  securitization theory, 519–521
  symbolic associations in, 516
Militarized Currents (Shigematsu and Camacho), 513
Mill, Harriet Taylor, 348
Millar, John, 88
Miller, D., 495–496
Miller-Young, Mireille, 665
Millett, Kate, 229, 633–634, 637, 767, 783, 905–906, 918
Million, Dian, 943
Mills, Catherine, 73–75, 77
Mills, C. Wright, 639
Minh-ha, Trinh, 862
Miñoso, Yuderkys Espinosa, 865
Minow, Martha, 792–793
Minsky, Marvin, 126

mirror of history, 787–791. *See also* representation
Mirza, Heidi Safia, 354
miscegenation laws, 596, 615, 751
Mitchell, Juliet, 230, 352, 533, 783, 877
Mitchell, Koritha, 392
Mitchell, Lisa, 703, 710
Mitra, Jaya, 938
Moallem, Minoo, 354
modernity, colonialism and, 112–113
Modernity/Coloniality Group, 101–102, 107, 112
Modleski, Tania, 655
Mohanty, Chandra Talpade, 109–110, 144, 160, 354, 603, 797, 862, 864, 938, 992, 993
Money, John, 408, 409–411, 424, 852–853
Mookherjee, N., 516
Moraga, Cherrie, 125, 353
moral development theories, 12n1, 233, 854
Morales, Evo, 118
moral vs. cultural genitalia, 422–423
Moravec, Hans, 126
"More Lessons from a Starfish: Prefixial Flesh and Transpeciated Selves" (Hayward), 546
Morgan, Lewis, 90
Morgan, Lynn, 709, 711, 716, 810, 814
Morgan, Robin, 410, 638
Morgen, Sandra, 333
Morrison, Toni, 741
Mortimer-Sandilands, Catriona, 540. *See also* Sandilands, Catriona
Morton-Robinson, Aileen, 354
Moser, Carolyn, 148, 440
mosque movement, 47–48, 220–221
Mother Camp: Female Impersonators in America (Newton), 576
motherhood
 development policies and, 148
 experience of, 233
 Safe Motherhood initiative (World Bank), 156
 transnational mothering, 495–497
motherhood environmentalism, 535
Mother Nature trope, 534, 535
Mouffe, Chantal, 635, 637
Moving Beyond G.I. Jane: Women and the US Military (Ziegler and Gunderson), 513

Moya, Paul, 415
Moynihan, Daniel Patrick, 600
Moynihan Report ("The Negro Family: the Case for National Action"), 563, 600, 660
MRMs (men's rights movements), 815
Mrs. Dalloway (Woolf), 984, 989
multiculturalism, 115, 395, 499, 639, 647n4, 775, 917, 999. *See also* identity politics
Is Multiculturalism Bad for Women? (Okin), 775
multiple jeopardy, 388
Mulvey, Laura, 657–658, 783–786
Murphie, Andrew, 23, 26
Murphy, Michelle, 333, 848, 1001
Murray, Marjorie, 821
Murray, Pauli, 388
Muslim women, 47–48, 220–221, 775–776n4, 998
"The Myth of the Vaginal Orgasm" (Koedt), 229, 901

Nagel, Joann, 900
Nakamura, L., 131–132, 139
Nakano Glenn, Evelyn, 190
Namaste, Viviane, 413, 417
Narayan, Uma, 84, 354, 797
narrative. *See* storytelling/narrative
Nash, Jennifer, 252, 385, 391–393
National Black Feminist Organization (NBFO), 599
National Black Women's Health Project, 338
National Center for Transgender Equality, 734
National Coalition of Anti-Violence Programs (NCAVP), 734
National Conference for New Politics (NCNP), 597, 607n5
National Institutes of Health Office of Research in Women's Health, 334
Nationality Act, 751
National Organization for Women (NOW), 884, 977–978
National Science Foundation (NSF), 835
National Security Entry-Exit Registration System (NSEERS), 172
Native Americans
 characterization of, 89
 incarceration of, 731–732

naturalization
  care work and, 180
  development and, 153
  of differences, 684
  embodiment and, 9
  of heteronormativity, 516
  of identity, 484
  of men and machines, 130
  in migration process, 500–501, 751–752, 969
  of patriarchal gender practices, 508
  of performative acts, 897
  in posthuman subjectivity, 137
  of sex, 859
  of social roles, 210
  of web interface design, 132
  of women's work, 458
"Naturally Queer" (Hird), 540
natural rights, 804
nature
  anthropocene epoch, 546–548
  concept of, 531
  environmental feminisms, 534–537
  estrogen and, 543–544
  ethics of the Real, 536
  feminist flight from, 531–534
  feminist science studies, 537–539
  in feminist theory, 530–531
  in indigenous feminisms, 536–537
  material feminisms and, 542–548
  natural woman, 535
  nature/culture dualism, 533
  in postcolonial feminisms, 536–537
  queer natures, 539–541
  traditional ecological knowledges (TEK), 537
  trans-corporeality, 545
  as type of essentialism, 530
  women's nature, 532
Nazis/Nazism, 64, 65, 480, 487n8, 983
necropower/necropolitics, 137, 221–224, 735
negative liberty, 957–958
Negri, Antonio, 444
"Negroes," characterization of, 89
"The Negro Family: the Case for National Action" (Moynihan), 563, 600, 660
Nelson, Julie A., 430

neoliberal globalization, 305, 311, 314–315, 321, 441, 518, 866
neoliberalism, 155. *See also* governmentality, Foucault's concept of
  abortion rights and, 810
  agency and, 57–58
  ascendance of, 304
  biopolitics and, 32, 814–816, 821, 922
  Cooper on, 846
  cybertechnologies and, 136
  defined, 825n1
  development and, 1003
  divisions of labor and, 292–295
  feminist research and, 916, 918
  as form of governmentality, 481, 923
  globalization and, 995
  marketization and, 441
  personal responsibility and, 339
  political critiques of, 474, 485
  privatization imperatives and, 155
  RPV framing in, 190–191
  transnational feminism and, 992–993
  Wacquant on, 756
neo-materialism, 466
New Jim Crow, 754
Newman, Karen, 711
new materialism
  feminist affect studies and, 18–19
  feminist science studies and, 840–843
  identity theories, 346–347, 360
New Materialism: Interviews and Cartographies (Dophijn and van der Tuin), 840
new media representations, 668–670
new social movements, 594, 596, 607, 607n3, 635, 676
Newton, Esther, 576
Newton, Isaac, 973, 979
Ngai, Mae, 751, 752
Ngai, Sianne, 27
Nietzsche, Friedrich, 54, 575, 580, 967, 987
Nike Foundation, 193
Nilsson, Lennart, 711
Nkrumah, Kwame, 100
Nochlin, Linda, 654
No-Conscription League, 508, 523
No Future (Edelman), 541

No Longer Patient (Sherwin), 328
nonconsensual surgical alteration, 418
non-governmental organizations (NGOs), 157–160, 195, 293, 295, 306–307, 314–320, 796, 991–992, 996, 999, 1001–1003
nonhuman-human relations, 134–139. *See also* cyborgs
normative commitment thesis, 264, 268–269
norms/normalization. *See also* gender norms/normativity
    biopolitics and, 557–559
    concepts/processes of, 551–552
    disciplinary power, 552–557
    feminist interventions and, 551–552, 558
    feminist resistance formations, 555–557, 564–567
    heteropatriarchal conditions, 551, 557, 559–560, 564
    same-sex marriage (case study on), 559–564
Norris, Pippa, 81
North, Douglass, 370
Not Just Race, Not Just Gender: Black Feminist Readings (Smith), 400
"Not Symbiosis, Not Now: Why Anthropogenic Climate Change Is Not Really Human" (Colebrook), 547
Nussbaum, Martha, 708, 958
Nyman, Joanna, 520

Oakley, Ann, 853
Obama, Barack, 403, 563
objectivity, conceptions of, 7
object relations, 11, 352, 458, 855
occupational segregation, 179, 194, 200, 436
Oedipus complex, 875–878
offloading (of responsibilities), 312–313
Of Mothers and Time (Trigg), 981
Of Woman Born (Rich), 901
Ogden, Stormy, 732
oil/oil production, gender equality and, 82
Okin, Susan Moller, 81, 610, 775, 917
Oksala, Johanna, 444, 481
Olivia (music collective), 410
Omi, Michael, 742–743
"One is Not Born a Woman" (Wittig), 532
one sex model, 5
Ong, Aihwa, 996, 999

"On Ideology and Ideological State Apparatuses: Notes Towards and Investigation" (Althusser), 350
Only Words (MacKinnon), 581, 661
On the Genealogy of Morals (Nietzsche), 575
ontology, in affect studies, 29–31
oppositional consciousness, 125, 133–134, 675, 865
"ordinariness," 135, 140n6
organizational process model, 307
Orientalism (Said), 100
Origin of the Family, Private Property and the State (Engels), 90
Orlando (Woolf), 983, 989
Ortner, Sherry, 853
Our Bodies, Our Selves (Boston Women's Health Collective), 327, 335–336, 636–637
outside-in model critique, 24–26
overkill (interpersonal violence), 223–224
overpopulation, 148–150, 811–812
Oyama, S., 839
Oyewumi, Oyeronke, 115, 116, 117, 160, 862–863

Page Act (1875), 563–564
paid/unpaid work, 146, 179, 181–182, 190, 193–195, 198, 219, 283, 286, 296, 492, 494, 535, 726, 884–885
Painter, Nell, 791
Palmer, Ingrid, 152
Pande, Amrita, 445
Panjabi, Kavita, 938–939
panoptical gaze, 219
Paradise (Morrison), 741
Parashar, S., 521
Paredes, Julieta, 116
parental leave, 380, 616
Parisi, Luciana, 70–73, 75, 77, 689
Paris is Burning (film), 417
Parkin, Michael, 428
Parreñas, Rhacel, 491, 495–496, 995
Parsons, Talcott, 231
Partnoy, Alicia, 938
Pateman, Carole, 379, 431, 610, 919, 1011
patriarchy. *See also* heteropatriarchy
    consciousness-raising about, 231
    as constructed system, 229–230
    cross-cultural critiques of, 47–48
    in institutions, 374–376

"Paul Gilroy's Slaves, Ships and Routes" (Dayan), 167
pay inequity, in institutions, 372–373
Payne, Carol Williams, 597
peace politics, 509
Pedagogy of the Oppressed (Archibald and Wilson), 816
Pedersen, Jean Elisabeth, 68
Pedwell, Carolyn, 927
Penley, Constance, 656, 783
Perez, Emma, 114
performativity. *See* gender performativity
Perkins, Charlotte, 986
perlocutionary speech/acts, 581, 585, 588n11
personal is political. *See also* identity politics
    consciousness-raising groups, 597–598
    in contemporary context, 606–607
    historical emergence, 594–596
    phrase origins/meaning, 593–594, 632–634
    private/public distinction in, 604–605
    "sex wars" and, 599
    speak-outs, 598–599
    Vagina Monologues, 605–606
personal politics, 227, 229, 240, 607n1
personhood
    agency and, 40–41
    in Andean society, 118
    biological facts, 712–713
    in biopolitical framework, 73
    of black women, 601
    credos about, 701
    feminist theory of, 715–716
    fetal individuals and, 699
    fetal status/representations, 709, 711, 714
    of married women, 249
    of mothers, 446
    in new social movements, 607
    of the oppressed, 601
    physical autonomy and, 708
    politicization of, 604
    politicized notions of, 604, 607
    relational theory of, 715
    social, 118
    in surrogacy contracts, 446
    trans identity and, 416
    of trans/intersex women, 416
    universal feature of, 40–41
Petchesky, Rosalind, 315, 711, 805, 807, 816
Peterson, V. Spike, 190–191, 433, 517, 518
Phelan, Shane, 602
The Phenomenology of Perception (Merleau-Ponty), 888
Phillips, Anne, 792
philosophical traditions (Western), 2–3
Pierce, Steven, 1016
Pietilä, Tuulikki, 430
piety practices, 221
pink-collar workers, 193–194, 287, 289. *See also* gendered divisions of labor
Pinto, Samantha, 168
Pitts, Rebecca, 534
Planned Parenthood, 810
Plato, 208, 210, 224n1, 304, 811, 973
Pleasure and Danger: Exploring Female Sexuality (Vance), 237, 906
Plumbwood, Val, 535, 536, 889
policy/policy studies
    components/models of, 613
    concept of, 610–614
    constructivism turn, 614–618
    development of, 612–613
    domination/empowerment and, 620–622
    feminist contributions to, 612, 625–626
    feminist criteria for, 622–625
    framing policies, 616–618
    future research recommendations, 626
    gendered policies, 614–616
    gender mainstreaming, 154, 372, 623–624
    governments/institutions in, 613–614
    intersectionality in, 623–625
    transforming gendered power, 618–619
political intersectionality, 386. *See also* intersectionality
political representation, 781–782, 789, 792–796, 798
politics. *See also* personal is political
    feminist theory and, 632–634
    of location, 636–638
    as means to an end, 643–644
    in multicultural societies, 639, 646, 647n4
    as power, 634–635
    as practice of freedom, 644–645

of representation, 781–782, 787, 799
of sexual difference, 884–887
The Politics of Ourselves (Allen), 485
Politics of Piety (Mahmood), 47
politics of the body, in body politic, 207, 217–224
Pollock, Griselda, 786
"Polluted Politics? Confronting Toxic Discourse, Sex Panic and Eco-Normativity" (Di Chiro), 540
Polsby, Nelson, 231
popular/visual culture. *See also* pornography; representation
　challenging hegemonic norms, 665–668
　concepts/analytical strategies in, 651–654
　feminist ways of seeing, 657–660
　fetal emblems in, 710–712
　in new media, 668–670
　porn wars, 660–661
　representation and reality in, 662–665
　representations, analysis of, 652
　women writers/artists, 654–657
The Population Bomb (Ehrlich), 812
population control, 149–150, 499, 558–559, 562–563, 686, 748, 811, 813, 820, 925, 1001–1002
population growth, 148, 702, 812–813, 925
pornography
　male domination and, 235–236
　performativity and, 581–584
　representation and injury in, 660–662
positive liberty, 957–959
postanthropocene feminism, 680–684
postcolonial feminism, 108–111
postcolonialism, 107–108
postcolonial theorists, on identity, 354–355
The Posthuman (Braidotti), 545
posthuman feminism
　affective turn in, 683
　agency and, 53–56
　anti-humanist roots of, 676–677
　cultural studies and, 682
　ecofeminism and, 682–683
　Haraway's vision of, 679–680
　humanist legacy, 673–676
　new media and, 682
　politics and, 685–688

postanthropocentric turn, 680–684
postcolonial theory and, 677–678
poststructuralism and, 678–679
queer science studies and, 686–687
relational ontology in, 690
sexuality beyond gender in, 688–689
term usage, 674
posthumanist materiality, 543, 545–547
postidentity agency, 50–52. *See also* agency
postmodern feminism, 3–4, 38, 123, 374, 516, 531, 615, 866
poststructuralist feminism, 3–4, 355–357, 459–460, 539, 678–679, 897–899
"Posttranssexual Manifesto" (Stone), 410
post-traumatic stress disorder (PTSD), 1019
Poulain de la Barre, François, 348
poverty
　assumptions about, 147
　eradication of, 153–155
　overpopulation and, 148–150
　as test of economic development, 145
"The Poverty of Theory and Other Essays" (Thompson), 241
power. *See also* microphysics of power
　biopower/governmentality, 478–482
　concept of, 472–474
　disciplining the female body, 476–478
　in institutions, 374–376
　market-based theories of, 232
　productive, 474–476
　resistance, 482–486
The Power Elite (Mills), 639
The Practice of Everyday Life (Certeau), 656
Pratt, Geraldine, 495
Pratt, Minnie Bruce, 603
pregnancy. *See also* fetal politics; reproduction, politics of
　cultural images of, 699
　feminist perspectives on, 713–717
　as somatic stance, 706–707
The Presentation of Self in Everyday Life (Goffman), 578–579
Preves, Sharon, 414
Primate Visions: Gender: Race, and Nature in the World of Modern Science (Haraway), 538, 680
Pringle, Rosemary, 921

prison-abolition movement, 565–566
prison/prisons
    abolition of, 223, 565–567, 729, 735
    class/identity and, 723–726
    feminist theories of, 721–722
    in histories of punishment, 726–729
    intersectional theories of, 729–733
    private prison companies, 729, 997
    scholarship directions on, 736–737
    trans prison scholarship, 733–735
    women's prisons, 554, 727–728
Probyn, Elspeth
    on affect studies methodology, 32
    on genders as drag, 576
pro-choice/pro-life frameworks. *See*
    fetal politics; fetus/fetal emblems;
    reproduction, politics of
productive power, 474–476. *See also*
    microphysics of power
"pro family" stances, 319
The Promise of Happiness (Ahmed), 34
"The Promise of Monsters" (Haraway), 538
Prosser Jay, 417
Prügl, Elisabeth, 921, 923
psychoanalysis
    feminist engagement with, 30
    in identity theory, 351–352
    representations and, 782–785
Psychoanalysis and Feminism (Mitchell), 230, 352, 877
Puar, Jasbir, 385, 394–398, 401, 404, 744, 927, 998
public policy. *See* policy/policy studies
Public Secrets of Law: Rape Trials in India (Baxi), 1019
Public Vows: A History of Marriage and the Nation (Cott), 750
public women, 222
Punishment and Social Structure (Rusche), 736
Purdy, Laura, 702
Putin, Vladimir, 318, 322n3
Putomayo Report, 1015

Queer Ecologies: Sex, Nature, Politics, Desire (Erickson and Mortimer-Sandilands), 540, 541
Queering the Nonhuman (Giffney), 540

queer science studies, 686–687
"Queer Theory and Native Studies: The Heteronormativity of Settler Colonialism" (Smith), 175
queer theory/studies
    diasporic, 173–176
    on gender and sexuality, 908–909
    gender performativity and, 586–587
    queer natures, 539–541
    representation in, 790
Quijano, Anibal, 101–102, 113–116, 866

race and racialization
    affect theory and, 745
    assemblage theory and, 744–745
    biological notions of, 748–753
    citizenship denial, 750
    colonialism and, 110, 113–114, 117, 119
    conceptualizations of, 741–742
    cyborg identity and, 131–133
    diaspora and, 170–173
    Europeaness, 747
    feminist post slave studies, 745–748
    in hierarchical social systems, 113–114
    materiality of, 466–467
    as political construct/process, 4
    racial formation theory, 742–745
    state terrorism and, 753–758
race-gendered institutions, theory of, 9
Race in Cyberspace (Kolko, Nakamura and Rodman), 131
"race problem," 387
racing-gendering, dynamics of, 9
Racism and Sexual Oppression in Anglo-America (McWhorter), 480
radical feminism
    on identity, 350–351
    trans/intersex feminism and, 410–415
Radway, Janice, 655–656
Rahman, Aminur, 158
Rai, Shirin, 314
Ramamurthy, Priti, 435
Ramirez, Renya, 175
Rana, Junaid, 172
"The Rani of Sirmur: An Essay in Reading the Archives" (Spivak), 792
Rao, Anupama, 1016

rape
    Brownmiller's analysis of, 234–235
    slavery and, 214–215
    as torture, 1018–1019
    in US military, 510
Rapoport, David, 757–758
Rapp, Rayna, 331
rational actor model, 307, 613. *See also* policy/
    policy studies
Raven-Roberts, Angela, 516
Rawls, John, 41, 957
Raymond, Janice, 407, 410–415, 419, 422–423
Razack, Sharene, 950–952
Reading the Romance (Radway), 655–656
Reagan, Ronald, 309, 334, 434, 556, 660, 860
Reagon, Bernice Johnson, 601, 602, 603,
    642, 646
reality reinforcement, 420–424
reciprocal care relations, 500
recognition, in law, 395–396
Reddy, Chandan, 998
Redstockings/Redstockings Manifesto, 230,
    602–603
Reed v. Reed, 249
Rees, Baze v., 1012
refugees, racialization and, 171–173. *See also*
    migration
*The Rejected Body: Feminist Philosophical
    Reflections on Disability* (Wendell), 329
relational autonomy, 43
religion
    androcentric bias in, 770
    feminist scholarship on, 761–765
    goddess religions, 771–774
    multiculturalism and, 775
    patriarchal nature of, 763–770, 774–775
    reproductive entitlement and, 808
    rise in fundamentalism, 774–775
    "in the shadow of Eve," 765–768
    theorizing on, 768–771
representation. *See also* popular/visual culture
    aesthetic, 782, 792–794, 796–799
    concept of, 781–782
    constitutive, 796, 798, 799
    cultural, 235, 352, 360, 486, 652, 782–787
    descriptive, 781, 792, 794–796, 798
    political, 781–782, 789, 792–796, 798
    politics of, 781–782, 787, 799
    problem of voice, 791, 796
    queer theory and, 790
    semiotic, 782, 785, 794, 798
    of women's history, 787–791
Reproducing Empire (Briggs), 993
reproduction, politics of
    abortion rights, 808–811
    compulsory sterilization, 820
    concept of rights, 804–805
    contingent reproductive rights, 817–824
    empowerment, 816
    fetal rights, 815
    men's rights, 815
    neoliberal turn in, 814–815
    population policies, 811–814
    providers' rights, 815–816
    religious authorities and, 808
    reproductive governance, 814–815, 824
    reproductive justice, 816–817
    reproductive rights, 805–808
    rights of displaced/refugee women, 823–824
    right to bear children, 820–821
    right to biological children, 818–820
    right to healthy environment, 823
    right to parent with dignity, 821–823
    right to safe childbirth, 821
    welfare and, 148–150
*The Reproduction of Mothering: Psychoanalysis
    and the Sociology of Gender*
    (Chodorow), 352
reproductive, productive, and virtual (RPV)
    sectors, 190, 433
reproductive justice, 338
reproductive labor, commodification of, 290–292
Reproductive Rights and Wrongs
    (Hartmann), 812
reproductive rights movement, 338, 701, 820
reproductive technologies, 11, 73–74, 676, 682,
    701–702, 818–820
resistance
    agency as, 43–46
    feminist resistance formations, 564–567
    Foucault's understanding of, 482–486
    storytelling as resistance strategy, 938–940
    of violence, 1021–1025
    in women's healthcare movement, 333, 335

resistance groups (armed), 514. *See also* militarization and war
Resnick, S., 189
"Rethinking Intersectionality" (Nash), 391
return (diasporic), 169. *See also* diaspora
The Revolutionary Imagination in the Americas and the Age of Development (Saldaña-Portillo), 993
Rhodes, Rod, 306, 308
Rich, Adrienne, 213, 233, 351, 573, 636, 860, 901–902, 905, 906, 907
Ricoeur, Paul, 774
Riefenstahl, Leni, 653
rights, concept of, 804–805. *See also* reproduction, politics of
Riley, Ann P., 156
Ringrose, Jessica, 18
Rios Tobar, Marcela, 317
Risman, Barbara, 369
Rist, Stephan, 537
Rizzo, Helen, 81
Roberts, Dorothy, 328–329, 339, 342, 822
Roberts, Elizabeth, 814
Robertson, William, 88
Robinson, Cedric, 558, 748
"Rock and Sexuality" (McRobbie and Firth), 667
rock music, 667
Rodman, G. B., 131–132
Rodríguez-Trias, Helen, 337, 999
Roe v. Wade, 710, 807
romance novels, 655–656
romantic individualism, 667
Rönnblom, M., 621
Rorty, Richard, 647n4
Rosaldo, Michelle, 853
Rosenau, James, 308
Rosie the Riveter Revisited: Women, the War, and Social Change (Gluck), 511
Ross, Loretta, 817
Ross, Luana, 732
Ross, Michael, 82
Rosser, Sue, 833
Rothman, Barbara Katz, 703–704
Roughgarden, Joan, 539
Rubin, Gayle, 236–237, 253, 454, 532, 560, 853–854, 907–908

Rubin, Henry, 414
Rucht, Dieter, 312–313
Ruddick, Sara, 233, 509
Ruether, Rosemary Radford, 769, 774
Runyan, Anne Sisson, 433, 435
Rusche, George, 723–729, 734, 736
Ruzek, Sheryl Burt, 333

Sackville-West, Vita, 983
sadomasochism (SM), 236
Safe Motherhood initiative (World Bank), 156
Saffin, Lori, 223
Safran, William, 165, 166, 169
Safri, Maliha, 191
Said, Edward, 100, 660, 675, 677, 679
Salafism, 48
Salamon, Gayle, 416
Saldanha, Arun, 466
Saltwater Slavery: A Middle Passage from Africa to American Diaspora (Smallwood), 169
Salzinger, Leslie, 195, 288
same-sex marriage advocacy, 559–564
Sampaio, Anna, 995
Sandburg, Cheryl, 373
Sandilands, Catriona, 535, 536. *See also* Mortimer-Sandilands, Catriona
Sandoval, Chela, 102, 125, 134, 140n5, 169, 865–866
Sangarasivam, Yamuna, 1022
Sanger, Margaret, 558, 803, 806, 1001
Santa Cruz Feminist of Color Collective, 105
Sarat, Austin, 1011–1012
Sartre, Jean-Paul, 241, 678, 1015, 1022
Sassen, Saskia, 438
Sauer, Birgit, 921
Saussure, Ferdinand de, 652–653
Savage, Mike, 379
Saward, Michael, 796
Saxton, Marsha, 820
Scattered Hegemonies: Postmodernity and Transnational Feminist Practices (Grewal and Kaplan), 992
Schaeffer, Felicity, 499, 500
Scheper-Hughes, Nancy, 1014
Schiebinger, Londa, 836
Schiller, Nina Glick, 996

Schilt, Kristin, 253
Schiwy, Freya, 115
Scholar and Feminist Online, 844
Schram, Sanford F., 798
Schueller, Malini Johar, 133
Schuler, Sidney Ruth, 156
Schwartzman, Lisa, 585
science/science studies
    ethical practices, 843–847
    feminist theory in, 537–539, 832–835
    new materialism and, 840–843
    overdetermination and, 845
    sex/gender binary, 835–840
    social justice epistemologies in, 834, 844–846
    as socially responsive, 275
Scott, Catherine, 155
Scott, Joan, 241–242, 250–251, 368, 379, 476, 763–764, 788, 789, 852, 856, 949–950
Seaman, Barbara, 334
Sebastini, Silvia, 87, 89
The Second Sex (Beauvoir), 212, 228, 348–349
second-wave feminist theory. *See* personal is political
Secret Service: Untold Stories of Lesbians in the Military (Gershik), 510
"Securitization" (Nyman), 520
"Security, Territory and Population" (Foucault), 480
Sedgwick, Eve, 25–26, 320
    adaptations of, 29
    affect usage/definitions, 29
    Hemmings' critique of, 30
    on homophobia, 790
    on identity, 356
    on sexuality, 896–897
Seduction of the Innocent (Wertham), 656
Segal, Lynne, 523
Segal, Mady, 508, 511, 512
Segato, Rita, 100, 115, 117, 863
Seigworth, Gregory J., 22, 25
Seizing the Means of Reproduction: Entanglements of Feminism, Health, and Technoscience (Murphy), 333, 848
Selected Subaltern Studies (Guha and Spivak), 993

Self-Employed Women's Association (SEWA), 447
Self-Transformations: Foucault, Ethics, and Normalized Bodies (Heyes), 484
semiotic representation, 782, 785, 794, 798. *See also* representation
Sen, Lipi Biswan, 112
Seneca Falls, 249
"sensuous activities," 455–460, 464, 468
Serano, Julia, 415
A Serious Proposal to the Ladies (Astell), 348
Serrano, Elvira, 537
service sector, restructuring of, 439
Sever, Charlotte, 315
sex, as political construct/process, 4
Sex, Gender and Society (Oakley), 853
"Sex and Death in the Rational World of Defense Intellectuals" (Cohn), 508–509, 1021
Sex and Gender: On the Development of Masculinity and Femininity (Stoller), 853
"sex-change" surgery, 418
sex discrimination, 211, 249, 251–254, 256, 257n2, 318, 373, 385, 388. *See also* feminist jurisprudence
"Sex Diversity in Nonhuman Animals" (Hird and Giffney), 540
sex tourism/trafficking, 443–444
sexual assault, slavery and, 214–215
sexual behaviors, ranking of, 560, 561f
sexual differences. *See also* difference debates/dilemma
    concepts of, 874–875
    feminist psychoanalysis and, 890–891
    Irigaray's philosophy of, 880–884
    politics of, 884–887
    psychoanalytic roots of, 875–880
    sex/gender distinction critique, 887–890
sexual dimorphism, 5–6, 116, 465
Sexual Fluidity (Diamond), 904
sexual harassment
    in feminist jurisprudence, 252–254
    in workplace, 265
sexual intercourse, political nature of, 235
sexuality
    feminist theories of, 909–911
    as modern concept, 895–896

sexuality (*Cont.*)
　　poststructuralist perspective, 897–899
　　regulation of, 63, 68, 376, 553
　　sexual politics and, 905–909
　　social constructivist perspective, 895–896
　　women's vs. men's, 899–905
sexuality debates, as turning points, 235–237
sexuality studies, gender distinction in, 252–253
sexual-orientation harassment, in feminist jurisprudence, 252–254
Sexual Politics (Millett), 633–634, 767, 783, 918
sexual politics, sexuality and, 905–909
A Sexual Politics of Meat: A Feminist Vegetarian Critical Theory (Adams), 536
sexual/reproductive regulation, 67. *See also* reproduction, politics of
Shah, Nayan, 998
Shakur, Assata, 731
Shaw, Miranda, 771, 773–774
Shephard, Laura, 520
Sherry, Michael, 519
Sherwin, Susan, 328, 708, 714–715
Shigematsu, S., 513
Shimizu, Celine Parrenas, 665
Shiva, Vandana, 537, 675
Shrader-Frechette, Kristin, 271
"Signature Event Content" (Derrida), 576
Signs (journal), 2
Silent Spring (Carson), 947
Silverman, Kaja, 785
Sims, J. Marion, 333
Singh, Randhir, 1023
Sisterhood is Global (Morgan), 638
Sisters in Islam, 762
Sisters of the Earth (Anderson), 534
situated knowledge, 6–8, 264–266
Sjoberg, Laura, 518
slavery
　　Dred Scott decision, 753
　　feminist post slave studies, 745–748
　　marriage prohibition, 562–563, 600
　　plantation system, 106, 112
　　sexual violence in, 214–215
　　US prison system as successor to, 725–726
Smallwood Stephanie, 169

Smelik, Anneke, 682
Smith, Andie, 175
Smith, Andrea, 338, 731, 745, 748
Smith, Anna Marie, 311
Smith, Barbara, 353, 389
Smith, Bonnie, 787–788
Smith, Dorothy, 937
Smith, Greg, 578
Smith, Valerie, 397, 400–401
Snitow, Ann, 533, 655
Social Darwinism, 531
social hygiene, 149
socialist feminism, 4, 125, 350, 900, 918, 957, 991, 993
social justice epistemologies, 834, 844–846
social movements, new, 594, 596, 607, 607n3, 635, 676
social reproduction, 179, 185, 187, 189–192, 200, 286, 290–293, 433, 440, 863, 995
"Society Must Be Defended" (Foucault), 62, 480
soldiers. *See* militarization and war
Solomon, Robert C., 24
somatic experiences, of pregnancy, 706–707
somatophobia, tradition of, 207–208, 210, 214, 216, 224. *See also* embodiment
"Some Psychical Consequences of the Anatomical Distinction between the Sexes" (Freud), 875
Sommers, Daria, 510
Soros Open Society Institute, 315
Soss, Joe, 798
Soto, Sandy, 999
The Souls of Black Folk (Du Bois), 659
South Asian Subaltern Studies Group, 101, 105, 107–109, 111–112
Southern Student's Organizing Committee (SSOC), 594–595, 607n4
sovereign agency, 41, 54
Spade, Dean, 382, 733–735
Spanish Inquisition, 113
speak-outs, 598–599
"Speech Acts and Unspeakable Acts" (Langton), 582
Spencer, Jonathan, 1023
Spillers, Hortense, 744–746, 863, 900, 964
Spinoza, Baruch, 23, 26, 28, 137

Spivak, Gayatri Chakravorty, 101, 108–109, 111, 114, 347, 355, 362n7, 554, 729–730, 792–794, 838, 864, 992, 993
Split Decisions: How and Why to Take a Break from Feminism (Halley), 248
Sprinkle, Annie, 541
Squires, Judith, 313–314, 357, 796–797
SRW (substantive representation of women), 797
Stacey, Jackie, 682, 784, 785
standpoint feminism. *See* feminist standpoint theory
standpoint theory. *See* feminist standpoint theory
Stanko, Elizabeth, 271
Stanley, Eric A., 223
Stanton, Elizabeth Cady, 348, 769
state feminism, 313–314, 922–923, 994–996
state/nation
    feminist theories on, 915–923
    gender and, 923–928
    gender hierarchies in, 926–927
    gender orders in, 921–922
    homonormativity/homoprotectionism in, 927
    inclusion/exclusion, 923–924
    legal protections, 920
    materialism in, 922
    neoliberalism and, 923
    as neutral institution, 917
    patriarchal nature of, 918–920
    political activism in, 925–926
    women as reproducers in, 924–925
    women-friendly welfare states, 917–918
    women's activism in, 921
state terrorism, racialization and, 753–758
Staudt, Kathleen, 149, 154
Staying Alive: Women, Ecology, and Development (Shiva), 537
Steihm, Judith, 511
Stephens, Beth, 541
Stephenson, Carolyn, 316
sterilization campaigns/abuse, 149, 222, 227, 338–339, 559, 812, 817, 820, 925, 999, 1022
Stevens, Jacqueline, 1011
Stewart, Kathleen, 27, 31
Stewart, Maria, 105
Stiehm, Judith, 508

Stoler, Ann, 65–66, 68, 554, 745, 747, 993, 1015–1016
Stoljar, Natalie, 43
Stoller, Robert, 853
Stone, Sandy, 408, 410, 412–413, 421, 424
storytelling/narrative
    as essential to democracy, 940–942
    experience-based, 934
    experience/insight link, 936–938
    feminist reactions to, 935
    as naive realism, 948–950
    orthodox knowledge critiques, 943–945
    patriarchal knowledge and, 951–952
    as power-laden relationship, 950–951
    in practice, 935–936
    as resistance strategy, 938–939
    as rigorous knowing, 943
    scholarly storytelling, 945–947
Stowe, Harriet Beecher, 791
"strategic essentialism," 355, 864
Strathern, Marilyn, 712, 715
stratified reproduction, 817
Strid, S., 623
structural adjustment programs (SAPs), 155–156, 309, 434, 991
structural intersectionality, 386. *See also* intersectionality
structures of feeling, 34
Stryker, Susan, 410
Student Non-Violent Coordinating Committee (SNCC), 593–596, 607–608n5, 607n4
Students for a Democratic Society (SDS), 595, 597
Studlar, Gaylyn, 658
Sturgeon, Noel, 536
Sturken, Marita, 657
"subalternists," on decolonization, 107
"Subaltern Studies: Deconstructing Historiography" (Chibber), 101
subjectivity/subjectivation
    concept of, 955–957
    Derridean-Foucaultian feminism on, 966–970
    liberal feminism on, 957–961
    socialist feminism on, 961–966
    violence and, 1017

subordination to men, theorization of, 348–349
substantive representation of women (SRW), 797
A Subtlety (Walker), 224n3
Sudbury, Julia, 997
Sunder Rajan, Kaushik, 845–846
surrogacy, 444–445, 819
Su Ruolan, 1, 12n1
Sykes, Roberta, 354
Sykke, Nina, 682
Sylvester, Christine, 515
synthetic hermaphrodites, 412–413. *See also* trans and intersex feminisms

"Take Back the Night," 598–599
Taller de Historia Oral Andina (Cusicanqui), 115
Tantic Buddhism, 771. *See also* religion
Tapper, Marion, 641
Tarlo, Emma, 1022
Taussig, Michael, 1015
taxonomic/classification systems, 2–4
Taylor, Janelle, 704
Teaiwa, Teresia, 521, 524
technologies. *See* reproductive technologies
Technologies of the Gendered Body (Balsamo), 130
technology, biopolitics and, 71–73
technoscientific worlds. *See* cyborgs
TEK (traditional ecological knowledges), 537
temporality
    as concept, 973–974
    everyday life and, 979–981
    of female body, 982
    feminist futurities and, 986–987
    feminist politics and, 977–979
    mature/aging women, 983
    nation/state narrative of, 984–985
    postmodernist rethinking of, 987–989
    pregnancy/childbirth and, 982
    queer time, 989
    sexuality and, 983–984
    women's history and, 974–977
Temporary Assistance to Needy Families, 311
Terada, Rei, 23
Terrell, Mary Church, 353, 387–388

Testing the Woman, Testing the Fetus (Rapp), 331
Textual Poachers (Jenkins), 656
Thatcher, Margaret, 309, 434, 885
"Thinking Sex: Notes for a Radical Theory of the Politics of Sexuality" (Rubin), 237, 253, 560
third world woman
    depiction of, 160–161
    term usage, 361–362n6
"Third World Women" (Mohanty), 144
This Bridge Called My Back (Moraga and Anzaldúa), 865
Thompson, Elizabeth, 92
Thompson, E. P., 241, 985
Thomsen, Carly, 810
"thug life," 733
Ticktin, Mariam, 331, 342
Tinker, Irene, 146–147
Tlostanova, Madina, 115
Toews, John, 241
Tomkins, Silvan, 25–26
Tomlinson, Barbara, 392–393, 399
Tompkins, Jane, 654–655
To the Lighthouse (Woolf), 984
"Toward a Feminist Theory of Disability" (Wendell), 329
"Toward a Mestiza Consciousness" (Anzaldúa), 939
"Toward Decolonial Feminism" (Lugones), 116
Towns, Ann, 5, 797
traditional ecological knowledges (TEK), 537
"The Traffic in Women" (Rubin), 532
trafficking in women, 498
Trainor, Stephen, 511
trans and intersex feminisms. *See also* gender performativity
    emergence of, 408–409
    ethics of transformation in, 419
    gender variant terms, 408
    identity-invalidation, 420
    intersectionality and, 415–417
    intersex activism, 409–410
    moral vs. cultural genitalia, 422–423
    posthumanism and, 546
    radical feminism and, 410–415
    reality reinforcement, 420–424

sex/gender based oppression in, 407
trans oppression, 419
trans prison scholarship, 733–735
wrong-body model, 418
transcendence, 41, 54, 58, 122, 127, 129, 132, 135, 139, 207, 210, 211–212, 214, 216, 224, 253, 412, 545, 767
trans-corporeality, 545
transgender. *See* trans and intersex feminisms
Transgender Nation, 410
"The Transgender Question," 417
transnational feminism
    capitalism and, 994–996
    disability studies in, 998–999
    doing the work of, 1001–1003
    genealogies, 991–994
    native feminism and, 1000–1001
    queer/sexuality studies in, 997–998
    securitization and, 996–997
    women of color feminism and, 999–1000
transphobia, 407, 412, 415
Transpositions: On Nomadic Ethics (Braidotti), 28
Transsexual Empire (Raymond), 410
The Transsexual Phenomenon (Benjamin), 409
transsexual/transsexuals. *See also* trans and intersex feminisms
    deception and, 414–415, 420–422
    rape and, 414
    term usage, 408
transversal subjectivity, 137
Traub, Valerie, 790
trickle-down development, 153
Trigg, Mary, 981
Tripp, Aili, 315
Triumph of the Will (film), 653
"The True Clash of Civilizations" (Inglehart and Norris), 81
Truth, Sojourner, 348, 353, 791–792, 864, 865
Trzebiatowska, Marta, 775n1
Tuana, Nancy, 463, 544, 833, 847
Tubman, Harriet, 353
Tuck, Eve, 103
Turkey, Cyprus v., 1018
Turner, Tina, 216
Turner, Victor, 575
"Turning the Century" (Reagon), 602

Twine, Richard, 328
two sex model (Laqueur), 5

Unborn Victims of Violence Act (2004), 700
UN Decade for Women, 160
underdevelopment, as policy problem, 144–145. *See also* development/development policies
"Under Western Eyes" (Mohanty), 109–110
UN Development Program (UNDP), 152, 154, 193
Undomesticated Ground: Recasting Nature as Feminist Space (Alaimo), 533
United Nations Conference on Population and Development, 807
United Nations Development Fund for Women (UNIFEM), 154, 436
United States, Korematsu v., 753
"universal caregiver," 297. *See also* gendered divisions of labor
Universal Declaration of Human Rights, 804
universal rights, of Enlightenment, 5
uploading (of responsibilities), 312–313
urination, 212
US Agency for International Development (USAID), 151, 315
US Foreign Assistance Act, 151
Utas, M., 513

Vagina Monologues (Ensler), 605–606
Valladolid debates, 112
Valverde, Mariana, 484
Vance, Carole, 237, 899, 906
van der Tuin, Iris, 463, 466, 840
Venn, Couze, 21
Verloo, M., 617, 623–624
Vertigo (film), 657
Vienna Conference on Human Rights, 319
A Vindication of the Rights of Women (Wollstonecraft), 348, 472, 635
Vinver, Jacob, 145
violence
    colonial/postcolonial implications, 1014–1016
    defined, 1010
    disciplinary power and, 554–555
    feminist critiques of, 1020–1021

violence (*Cont.*)
    feminist theories of, 1010–1011, 1025
    forgetting/negotiation of, 1012–1014
    impact of, 1017–1018
    limits on, 1011–1012
    marginalized groups and, 381
    origins/nature of, 1011
    rape as torture, 1018–1019
    resistance of, 1021–1025
    state and legal, 1011–1012
Violence and Subjectivity (Das and Kleinman), 1017
Violent Crime Control and Law Enforcement Act (1994), 738n4
Virgil, 973–974
Virginia Woolf Cultural Centre, 887
virtual bodies. *See* cyborgs
virtuality, condition of, 127–128
visual culture. *See* popular/visual culture
"Visual Pleasure and Narrative Cinema" (Mulvey), 657, 658
"Visual Pleasure and Narrative Cinema" (Mulvey), 783
vitalist materialisms, 53, 684, 689, 690
Volatile Bodies (Grosz), 838
voluntarism
    as agency concept, 40–41, 44
    gender and, 418, 478
voluntary motherhood, 806

Wacquant, Loïc, 725, 736, 755–756
WAD (women and development), 143, 148–150. *See also* development/development policies
Wade, Roe v., 710
Wadud, Amina, 764
wage gap, 194, 296, 439, 557
Wages for Housework Campaign, 457
Waithe, Mary Ellen, 12n1
Wajcman, Judy, 130–131, 139
Walby, S., 623
Walker, Kara, 224n3
"The Walking Woman" (Austin), 534
Walsh, Catherine, 115
Walsh, Elizabeth Miller, 83
war. *See* militarization and war
war on drugs, 733

Warren, Mary Anne, 708
Watching Dallas (Ang), 655
Watson, Sophie, 921
wave metaphor, 12n2
Waylen, Georina, 314
Ways of Seeing (Berger), 657
Weasel, Lisa, 417
We Became Posthuman (Hayles), 127
Weber, Max, 41, 369, 721, 921, 922, 1022
A Week Like Any Other (Baranskaya), 980
Weeks, Kathi, 457
We Have Never Been Modern (Latour), 542
Weheliye, Alexander, 744, 755
Weir, Lorna, 703, 705
Wekker, Gloria, 863
Weldon, Laurel, 377–378
welfare
    reforms, 310–311
    reproduction and, 148–150
welfare queen myth, 554, 556, 660
Wells, Ida B., 222, 353, 387
Wells-Barnett, Ida B., 353
Wendell, Susan, 329–330
Wertham, Frederic, 656
West, Candace, 579–580, 587, 588n6
Westbrook, Laurel, 253
West Cost Lesbian Conference, 410
Western civilization
    Huntington's representation of, 80–81
    women in history of, 82–84
Western philosophical traditions, 2–3
When Species Meet (Haraway), 135, 137
Whitbeck, Caroline, 714–715
White, Hayden, 974
White by Law (Haney Lopez), 749
whitestream feminism, 102
white supremacy, 222, 565, 600, 679, 736
The Whole Woman (Greer), 412
Why Are Women More Religious Than Men? (Trzebiatowska and Bruce), 775n1
"Why Have There Been No Great Women Artists?" (Nochlin), 654
WID (women in development), 143, 150–152. *See also* development/development policies
Wiegman, Robyn, 346, 347, 385, 393, 395, 398–399, 404

Wieringa, Saskia, 537
Wilkinson, Claire, 521
Williams, Linda, 662
Williams, Patricia, 946
Williams, Raymond, 34
Williams, Wendy W., 247, 250
Wilson, Elizabeth, 360, 463
Winant, Howard, 742–743
Wittig, Monique, 125, 532, 573, 860, 902
Witz, Anne, 379
Wolf, Susan, 328
Wolff, R., 189
Wollstonecraft, Mary, 1, 217, 283, 348, 472, 486n1, 533, 635
Wolmark, J., 134
Woman and Nature: The Roaring Inside Her (Griffin), 534, 536
"Woman as Sign" (Cowie), 785
The Woman Beneath the Skin (Duden), 706
"The Woman Identified Woman" (Radicalesbians), 901
The Woman in the Body (Martin), 331
woman question, 51, 147, 255, 387, 786
"Woman Question in Arendt" (Honig), 51
The Woman's Bible (Stanton), 769
Womanspirit Rising (Christ), 772
Women, the Environment, and Sustainable Development: Towards a Theoretical Synthesis (Braidotti), 537
women and development (WAD), 143, 148–150. *See also* development/development policies
Women and Development Unit at the University of West Indies (WAND), 1002–1003
Women and Gender in Islam: Historical Roots of a Modern Debate (Ahmed), 85–86
Women and War (Elshtain), 509
women in development (WID), 143, 150–152. *See also* development/development policies
Women in Development Office (USAID), 151
Women in Western Civilization (Walsh), 83
women of color scholarship/feminisms, 100, 102–105, 110, 354
Women's Comix (comic), 665

women's empowerment, 2, 154–155, 193, 196, 198, 447, 773
Women's Health Conference, 334
Women's International League for Peace and Freedom, 508, 523
Women's Movements Facing the Reconfigured State (Banaszak, Beckwith and Rucht), 312
Women's Music Festival, 601
"Women's Participation in Armed Forces Cross-Nationally: Expanding Segal's Model" (Iskra), 511
Women's Peace Party, 508
women's prisons, 554, 727–728. *See also* prison/prisons
women's rights. *See* feminist jurisprudence
Women's Role in Economic Development (Boserup), 150
"Women's Time" (Kristeva), 987
"Women: The Longest Revolution" (Mitchell), 533
Woodhead, Linda, 762
Woolf, Virginia, 915, 983–984, 989
Working with Affect in Feminist Readings: Disturbing Differences (Liljeström and Paasonen), 33
work/life balance, 179, 195, 201
"The Work of Art in the Age of Mechanical Reproduction" (Benjamin), 653
workplace, sexual harassment in, 265
World Bank, 154, 156, 181, 183, 193, 196, 198, 434, 440
World Conferences on Women, 315, 316, 436
The World Health Organization (WHO), 1010
World Professional Association of Transgender Health, 409
World Trade Organization, 434
World Values Survey, 81
Wretched of the Earth (Fanon), 678
Wright, Melissa, 222–223, 287
wrong-body model, 418
Wu, Judy, 995

Xtravaganza, Venus, 417
Xuangi Diagram (Su), 1, 12n1

Yang, K. Wayne, 103
Young, Iris Marion, 212, 368, 379, 676, 795, 940–941
Yours in Struggle (Pratt), 603
Yuval-Davis, Nira, 924

Zerilli, Linda, 49, 51–52, 786
Ziegler, Sarah, 513
Ziering, Amy, 510
Zimmerman, Don, 579–580, 587, 588n6
Zizek, Slavoj, 54, 56

Lightning Source UK Ltd.
Milton Keynes UK
UKHW052125201020
371892UK00013B/339